Twentieth-Century
Literary Criticism

Guide to Gale Literary Criticism Series

For criticism on	Consult these Gale series
Authors now living or who died after December 31, 1959	*CONTEMPORARY LITERARY CRITICISM (CLC)*
Authors who died between 1900 and 1959	*TWENTIETH-CENTURY LITERARY CRITICISM (TCLC)*
Authors who died between 1800 and 1899	*NINETEENTH-CENTURY LITERATURE CRITICISM (NCLC)*
Authors who died between 1400 and 1799	*LITERATURE CRITICISM FROM 1400 TO 1800 (LC)* *SHAKESPEAREAN CRITICISM (SC)*
Authors who died before 1400	*CLASSICAL AND MEDIEVAL LITERATURE CRITICISM (CMLC)*
Authors of books for children and young adults	*CHILDREN'S LITERATURE REVIEW (CLR)*
Black writers of the past two hundred years	*BLACK LITERATURE CRITICISM (BLC)*
Short story writers	*SHORT STORY CRITICISM (SSC)*
Poets	*POETRY CRITICISM (PC)*
Dramatists	*DRAMA CRITICISM (DC)*
Major authors from the Renaissance to the present	*WORLD LITERATURE CRITICISM, 1500 TO THE PRESENT (WLC)*

For criticism on visual artists since 1850, see

MODERN ARTS CRITICISM (MAC)

ISSN 0276-8178

R

Volume 51

Twentieth-Century Literary Criticism

**Excerpts from Criticism of the
Works of Novelists, Poets, Playwrights,
Short Story Writers, and Other Creative Writers
Who Lived between 1900 and 1960,
from the First Published Critical
Appraisals to Current Evaluations**

Laurie Di Mauro
Editor

**Jennifer Brostrom
Jeffery Chapman
Jennifer Gariepy
Alan Hedblad
Drew Kalasky
Thomas Ligotti
David Segal**
Associate Editors

 Gale Research Inc. • *DETROIT* • *WASHINGTON, D.C.* • *LONDON*

STAFF

Laurie Di Mauro, *Editor*

Jennifer Brostrom, Jeffery Chapman, Jennifer Gariepy, Alan Hedblad, Drew Kalasky, Thomas Ligotti, David Segal,
Associate Editors

Pamela Willwerth Aue, Christine Bichler, Joseph Cislo, Nancy Dziedzic, Ian Goodhall, Margaret Haerens, Kelly Hill,
Sean McCready, Matthew McDonough, Lynn M. Spampinato, *Assistant Editors*

Jeanne A. Gough, *Permissions & Production Manager*
Linda M. Pugliese, *Production Supervisor*
Donna Craft, Paul Lewon, Maureen A. Puhl, Camille P. Robinson, Sheila Walencewicz, *Editorial Associates*
Jill H. Johnson, Elizabeth Anne Valliere, *Editorial Assistants*

Sandra C. Davis, *Permissions Supervisor (Text)*
Maria L. Franklin, Josephine M. Keene, Michele Lonoconus, Shalice Shah, Kimberly F. Smilay, *Permissions Associates*
Jennifer A. Arnold, Paula M. Labbe (co-op), Brandy C. Merritt, *Permissions Assistants*

Margaret A. Chamberlain, *Permissions Supervisor (Pictures)*
Pamela A. Hayes, Keith Reed, *Permissions Associates*
Susan Brohman, Arlene Johnson, Barbara A. Wallace, *Permissions Assistants*

Victoria B. Cariappa, *Research Manager*
Maureen Richards, *Research Supervisor*
Robert S. Lazich, Mary Beth McElmeel, Donna Melnychenko, Tamara C. Nott, Jaema Paradowski, *Editorial Associates*
Karen Farrelly, Julie Leonard, Stefanie Scarlett, *Editorial Assistants*

Mary Beth Trimper, *Production Director*
Catherine Kemp, *Production Assistant*

Cynthia Baldwin, *Art Director*
Barbara J. Yarrow, *Graphic Services Supervisor*
Sherrell Hobbs, *Desktop Publisher*
Willie F. Mathis, *Camera Operator*

Library of Congress Catalog Card Number 76-46132
ISBN 0-8103-8914-2 (set)
ISBN 0-8103-2429-6 (main volume)
ISBN 0-8103-8913-4 (index)
ISSN 0276-8178

Printed in the United States of America
Published simultaneously in the United Kingdom
by Gale Research International Limited
(An affiliated company of Gale Research Inc.)
10 9 8 7 6 5 4 3 2 1

The trademark **ITP** is used under license.

Contents

Preface vii

Acknowledgments xi

Preface

S ince its inception more than ten years ago, *Twentieth-Century Literary Criticism* has been purchased and used by nearly 10,000 school, public, and college or university libraries. *TCLC* has covered more than 500 authors, representing 58 nationalities, and over 25,000 titles. No other reference source has surveyed the critical response to twentieth-century authors and literature as thoroughly as *TCLC*. In the words of one reviewer, "there is nothing comparable available." *TCLC* "is a gold mine of information—dates, pseudonyms, biographical information, and criticism from books and periodicals—which many libraries would have difficulty assembling on their own."

Scope of the Series

TCLC is designed to serve as an introduction to authors who died between 1900 and 1960 and to the most significant interpretations of these author's works. The great poets, novelists, short story writers, playwrights, and philosophers of this period are frequently studied in high school and college literature courses. In organizing and excerpting the vast amount of critical material written on these authors, *TCLC* helps students develop valuable insight into literary history, promotes a better understanding of the texts, and sparks ideas for papers and assignments. Each entry in *TCLC* presents a comprehensive survey of an author's career or an individual work of literature and provides the user with a multiplicity of interpretations and assessments. Such variety allows students to pursue their own interests; furthermore, it fosters an awareness that literature is dynamic and responsive to many different opinions.

Every fourth volume of *TCLC* is devoted to literary topics that cannot be covered under the author approach used in the rest of the series. Such topics include literary movements, prominent themes in twentieth-century literature, literary reaction to political and historical events, significant eras in literary history, prominent literary anniversaries, and the literatures of cultures that are often overlooked by English-speaking readers.

TCLC is designed as a companion series to Gale's *Contemporary Literary Criticism,* which reprints commentary on authors now living or who have died since 1960. Because of the different periods under consideration, there is no duplication of material between *CLC* and *TCLC*. For additional information about *CLC* and Gale's other criticism titles, users should consult the Guide to Gale Literary Criticism Series preceding the title page in this volume.

Coverage

Each volume of *TCLC* is carefully compiled to present:

- criticism of authors, or literary topics, representing a variety of genres and nationalities

- both major and lesser-known writers and literary works of the period

- 10-15 authors or 4-6 topics per volume

- individual entries that survey critical response to each author's work or each topic in literary history, including early criticism to reflect initial reactions; later criticism to represent any rise or decline in reputation; and current retrospective analyses.

Organization of This Book

An author entry consists of the following elements: author heading, biographical and critical introduction, list of principal works, excerpts of criticism (each preceded by an annotation and followed by a bibliographic citation), and a bibliography of further reading.

- The **Author Heading** consists of the name under which the author most commonly wrote, followed by birth and death dates. If an author wrote consistently under a pseudonym, the pseudonym will be listed in the author heading and the real name given in parentheses on the first line of the biographical and critical introduction. Also located at the beginning of the introduction to the author entry are any name variations under which an author wrote, including transliterated forms for authors whose languages use nonroman alphabets.

- The **Biographical and Critical Introduction** outlines the author's life and career, as well as the critical issues surrounding his or her work. References to past volumes of *TCLC* are provided at the beginning of the introduction. Additional sources of information in other biographical and critical reference series published by Gale, including *Short Story Criticism, Children's Literature Review, Contemporary Authors, Dictionary of Literary Biography,* and *Something about the Author,* are listed in a box at the end of the entry.

- Most *TCLC* entries include **Portraits** of the author. Many entries also contain reproductions of materials pertinent to an author's career, including manuscript pages, title pages, dust jackets, letters, and drawings, as well as photographs of important people, places, and events in an author's life.

- The **List of Principal Works** is chronological by date of first book publication and identifies the genre of each work. In the case of foreign authors with both foreign-language publications and English translations, the title and date of the first English-language edition are given in brackets. Unless otherwise indicated, dramas are dated by first performance, not first publication.

- Critical excerpts are prefaced by **Annotations** providing the reader with information about both the critic and the criticism that follows. Included are the critic's reputation, individual approach to literary criticism, and particular expertise in an author's works. Also noted are the relative importance of a work of criticism, the scope of the excerpt, and the growth of critical controversy or changes in critical trends regarding an author. In some cases, these annotations cross-reference excerpts by critics who discuss each other's commentary.

- **Criticism** is arranged chronologically in each author entry to provide a perspective on changes in critical evaluation over the years. All titles of works by the author featured in the entry are printed in boldface type to enable the user to easily locate discussion of particular works. Also for purposes of easier identification, the critic's name and the publication date of the essay are given at the beginning of each piece of criticism. Unsigned criticism is preceded by the title of the journal in which it appeared. Some of the excerpts in *TCLC* also contain translated material. Unless otherwise noted, translations in brackets are by the editors; translations in parentheses or continuous with the text are by the critic. Publication information (such as footnotes or page and line references to specific editions of works) have been deleted at the editor's discretion to provide smoother reading of the text.

- A complete **Bibliographic Citation** designed to facilitate location of the original essay or book follows each piece of criticism.

- An annotated list of **Further Reading** appearing at the end of each author entry suggests secondary sources on the author. In some cases it includes essays for which the editors could not obtain reprint rights.

Cumulative Indexes

- Each volume of *TCLC* contains a cumulative **Author Index** listing all authors who have appeared in Gale's Literary Criticism Series, along with cross references to such biographical series as *Contemporary Authors* and *Dictionary of Literary Biography*. For readers' convenience, a complete list of Gale titles included appears on the first page of the author index. Useful for locating authors within the various series, this index is particularly valuable for those authors who are identified by a certain period but who, because of their death dates, are placed in another, or for those authors whose careers span two periods. For example, F. Scott Fitzgerald is found in *TCLC,* yet a writer often associated with him, Ernest Hemingway, is found in *CLC.*

- Each *TCLC* volume includes a cumulative **Nationality Index** which lists all authors who have appeared in *TCLC* volumes, arranged alphabetically under their respective nationalities, as well as Topics volume entries devoted to particular national literatures.

- Each new volume in Gale's Literary Criticism Series includes a cumulative **Topic Index,** which lists all literary topics treated in *NCLC, TCLC, LC 1400-1800,* and the *CLC* yearbook.

- Each new volume of *TCLC,* with the exception of the Topics volumes, includes a **Title Index** listing the titles of all literary works discussed in the volume. In response to numerous suggestions from librarians, Gale has also produced a **Special Paperbound Edition** of the *TCLC* title index. This annual cumulation lists all titles discussed in the series since its inception and is issued with the first volume of *TCLC* published each year. Additional copies of the index are available on request. Librarians and patrons will welcome this separate index; it saves shelf space, is easy to use, and is recyclable upon receipt of the following year's cumulation. Titles discussed in the Topics volume entries are not included *TCLC* cumulative index.

Citing *Twentieth-Century Literary Criticism*

When writing papers, students who quote directly from any volume in Gale's literary Criticism Series may use the following general forms to footnote reprinted criticism. The first example pertains to materials drawn from periodicals, the second to material reprinted from books.

[1]T. S. Eliot, "John Donne," *The Nation and the Athenaeum,* 33 (9 June 1923), 321-32; excerpted and reprinted in *Literature Criticism from 1400 to 1800,* Vol. 10, ed. James E. Person, Jr. (Detroit: Gale Research, 1989), pp. 28-9.

[2]Clara G. Stillman, *Samuel Butler: A Mid-Victorian Modern* (Viking Press, 1932); excerpted and reprinted in *Twentieth-Century Literary Criticism,* Vol. 33, ed. Paula Kepos (Detroit: Gale Research, 1989), pp. 43-5.

Suggestions Are Welcome

In response to suggestions, several features have been added to *TCLC* since the series began, including annotations to excerpted criticism, a cumulative index to authors in all Gale literary criticism series, entries devoted to criticism on a single work by a major author, more extensive illustrations, and a title index listing all literary works discussed in the series since its inception.

Readers who wish to suggest authors or topics to appear in future volumes, or who have other suggestions, are cordially invited to write the editors.

Acknowledgments

The editors wish to thank the copyright holders of the excerpted criticism included in this volume, the permissions managers of many book and magazine publishing companies for assisting us in securing reprint rights, and Anthony Bogucki for assistance with copyright research. We are also grateful to the staffs of the Detroit Public Library, the Library of Congress, the University of Detroit-Mercy Library, Wayne State University Purdy/Kresge Library Complex, and the University of Michigan Libraries for making their resources available to us. Following is a list of the copyright holders who have granted us permission to reprint material in this volume of *TCLC*. Every effort has been made to trace copyright, but if omissions have been made, please let us know.

COPYRIGHTED EXCERPTS IN *TCLC*, VOLUME 51 , WERE REPRINTED FROM THE FOLLOWING PERIODICALS:

American Speech, v. XXXV, February, 1960. Copyright © 1960, renewed 1988 by the University of Alabama Press. Reprinted by permission of the publisher.—*Ariel: A Review of International English Literature,* v. 1, July, 1970 for "The Twilight of the Big House" by F.S.L. Lyons. Copyright © 1970 The Board of Governors, The University of Calgary. Reprinted by permission of the publisher and Peters, Fraser & Dunlop Group Ltd.—*Book World,* October 27, 1968. © 1968, *The Washington Post.* Reprinted by permission of the publisher.—*Canadian Literature,* n. 63, Winter, 1975. Reprinted by permission of the author.—*Canadian Children's Literature,* n. 3, 1975; n. 30, 1983; n. 37, 1985; n. 42, 1986; n. 52, 1988; n. 55, 1989. Copyright © 1975, 1983, 1985, 1986, 1988, 1989 Canadian Children's Press. All reprinted by permission of the publisher.—*The Dublin Magazine,* v. 3, Spring, 1964. —*Éire-Ireland,* v. III, 1968 for "John Bull's Other Ireland: A Consideration of 'The Real Charlotte' by Somerville and Ross" by Sean McMahon. Copyright © 1968 Irish American Cultural Institute, 2115 Summit Ave., No. 5026, St. Paul, MN 55105. Reprinted by permission of the publisher and the author.—*Encounter,* v. XLVII, July, 1976 for "Hole and Corners: Sade and the Structuralists" by Ronald Hayman. © 1976 by the author. Reprinted by permission of Peters, Fraser & Dunlop Group Ltd.—*English Literature in Transition: 1880-1920,* v. 30, 1987. Copyright © 1987 *English Literature in Transition: 1880-1920.* Reprinted by permission of the publisher.—*Journal of European Studies,* v. 21, September, 1991 for "Creating a Literature: Mistral and Modern Provençal" by Thomas R. Hart. Copyright © 1991 Seminar Press Limited. Reprinted by permission of the author.—*Journal of Popular Culture,* v. VII, Spring, 1974. Copyright © 1974 by Ray B. Browne. Reprinted by permission of the publisher.—*Journal of the Association of Teachers of Japanese,* v. 22, November, 1988 for "What's So Strange about 'A Strange Tale?' Kafu's Narrative Persona in 'Bokutô Kidan' " by Steven D. Carter. Reprinted by permission of the publisher and the author.—*The Kenyon Review,* v. XVI, Winter, 1954 for "Orwell the Edwardian" by Henry Popkin. Copyright 1954, renewed 1982 by Kenyon College. All rights reserved. Reprinted by permission of the author./v. XXVIII, January, 1966 for "The Big House of Ross-Drishane" by Thomas Flanagan. Copyright 1966 by Kenyon College. All rights reserved. Reprinted by permission of the author.—*The Literary Criterion,* v. XX, 1985. Reprinted by permission of the publisher.—*The Old Northwest,* v. 4, June, 1978. Copyright © Miami University 1978. Reprinted by permission of the publisher.—*Partisan Review,* v. LIX, Winter, 1992 for "Bruno Schulz Redux" by Susan Miron. Copyright © 1992 by *Partisan Review.* Reprinted by permission of the author.—*Poetry,* v. LXXVII, December, 1950 for "Apollinaire" by Wallace Fowlie. Copyright 1950, renewed 1978 by the Modern Poetry Association. Reprinted by permission of the Editor of *Poetry* and the author.—*Polish Perspectives,* v. XXX, March, 1987 for "Bruno Schulz's Sanatorium Story: Myth and Confession" by Russell E. Brown.—*The Polish Review,* v. XXX, 1985. © copyright 1985 by the Polish Institute of Arts and Sciences in America, Inc. Reprinted by permission of the publisher.—*The Sewanee Review,* v. LXXXVII, Summer, 1979. © 1979 by The University of the South. Reprinted by permission of the editor of *The Sewanee Review.*—*Slavic and East-European Journal,* v. XIII, Winter, 1969. © 1969 by AATSEEL of the U.S., Inc. Reprinted by permission of the publisher.—*The Southern Humanities Review,* v. II, Fall, 1968. Copyright 1968 by Auburn University. Reprinted by permission of the publisher.—*Theatre Quarterly,* v. VII, Autumn, 1977. Copyright © 1977 TQ Publications Ltd.—*The Times Literary Supplement,* n. 3863, March 26, 1976; n. 3942,

October 14, 1977. © The Times Supplements Limited 1976, 1977. Both reproduced from *The Times Literary Supplement* by permission.

COPYRIGHTED EXCERPTS IN *TCLC*, VOLUME 51 , WERE REPRINTED FROM THE FOLLOWING BOOKS:

Bal, Sant Singh. From *George Orwell: The Ethical Imagination.* Arnold-Heinemann, 1981. © Sant Singh Bal.—Buckley, Harry E. From *Guillaume Apollinaire as an Art Critic.* UMI Research Press, 1981. Copyright © 1981, 1969 Harold Buckley. All rights reserved. Reprinted by permission of the author.—Cronin, Anthony. From *Heritage Now: Irish Literature in the English Language.* Brandon Books, 1983, St. Martin's Press, 1983. © Anthony Cronin 1982. All rights reserved. Reprinted by permission of Brandon Book Publishers. In North America by St. Martin's Press, Incorporated.—Cronin, John. From "Dominant Themes in the Novels of Somerville and Ross," in *Somerville and Ross: A Symposium.* The Queen's University, 1969. Reprinted by permission of the author.—Cronin, John. From *Somerville and Ross.* Bucknell University Press, 1972. © 1972 by Associated University Presses, Inc. Reprinted by permission of the publisher.—Eagle, Solomon. From *Books in General, second series.* Alfred A. Knopf, 1920. Copyright 1920. Renewed 1947 by J.C. Squire.—Farrell, James T. From "The Frontier and James Whitcomb Riley," in *Poet of the People: An Evaluation of James Whitcomb Riley.* By Jeannette Covert Nolan, Horace Gregory, and James T. Farrell. Indiana University Press, 1951. Copyright 1951 by Indiana University Press. Renewed 1979 by Alan T. Nolan. Reprinted by permission of the publisher.—Fowlie, Wallace. From *Climate of Violence: The French Literary Tradition from Baudelaire to the Present.* The Macmillan Company, 1967. Copyright © 1967 by Wallace Fowlie. All rights reserved. Reprinted with the permission of Macmillan Publishing Company.—Fussell, Paul. From *Thank God for the Atom Bomb and Other Essays.* Summit Books, 1988. Copyright © 1988 by Paul Fussell. All rights reserved. Reprinted by permission of Paul Fussell. In North America by Summit Books, a division of Simon & Schuster, Inc.—Gregory, Horace and Marya Zaturenska. From *A History of American Poetry, 1900-1940.* Harcourt Brace Jovanovich, 1946. Copyright, 1942, 1944, 1946, by Harcourt Brace Jovanovich, Inc. Copyright renewed © 1974 by Horace Gregory and Marya Zaturenska. Reprinted by permission of the Estate of Horace Gregory and Marya Zaturenska.—Hall, Wayne E. From *Shadowy Heroes: Irish Literature of the 1890s.* Syracuse University Press, 1980. Copyright © 1980 by Syracuse University Press. All rights reserved. Reprinted by permission of the publisher.—Kalechofsky, Roberta. From *George Orwell.* Frederick Ungar Publishing Co., 1973. Copyright © 1973 by The Ungar Publishing Company. Reprinted by permission of the publisher.—Keene, Donald. From *Dawn to the West, Japanese Literature of the Modern Era: Fiction, Vol. 1.* Holt, Rinehart and Winston, 1984. Copyright © 1984 by Donald Keene. All rights reserved. Reprinted by permission of Henry Holt and Company, Inc. In the British Commonwealth by Georges Borchardt, Inc. on behalf of the Author.—Kelley, David. From "Defeat and Rebirth: The City Poetry of Apollonaire," in *Unreal City: Urban Experience in Modern European Literature and Art.* Edited by Edward Timms and David Kelley. Manchester University Press, 1985, St. Martin's Press, 1985. Copyright © Manchester University Press. All rights reserved. Reprinted by permission of Manchester University Press. In North America by St. Martin's Press, Incorporated.—Lief, Ruth Ann. From *Homage to Oceania: The Prophetic Vision of George Orwell.* Ohio State University Press, 1969. © 1969 by the Ohio State University Press. All rights reserved.—Little, Roger. From *Guillaume Apollinaire.* The Athlone Press, 1976. © Roger Little 1976. Reprinted by permission of the publisher.—Lockerbie, S.I. From an introduction to *Calligrammes: Poems of Peace and War (1913-1916).* By Guillaume Apollinaire, translated by Anne Hyde Greet. University of California Press, 1980. Copyright © 1980 by The Regents of the University of California. Reprinted by permission of the publisher.—Lodge, David. From *The Modes of Modern Writing: Metaphor, Metonymy, and the Typology of Modern Literature.* Edward Arnold, 1977. © David Lodge 1977. All rights reserved. Reprinted by permission of the publisher.—Masters, Brian. From *Now Barabbas Was a Rotter: The Extraordinary Life of Marie Corelli.* Hamish Hamilton, 1978. Copyright © 1978 by Brian Masters. Reprinted by permission of the author.—Montgomery, L.M. From *The Alpine Path: The Story of My Career.* Fitzhenry & Whiteside, 1974. © 1974 Fitzhenry & Whiteside Limited, 195 Allstate Pkwy., Markam, Ontario L3R 4T8. All rights reserved. Reprinted by permission of the publisher.—Nagai Kafū. From *Geisha in Rivalry.* Translated by Kurt Meissner and Ralph Friedrich. Charles E. Tuttle Company, 1963.—Nash, Suzanne. From "Apollinaire's 'Alcools' and the Disorder of Modernity," in *The Ladder of High Designs: Structure and*

Guillaume Apollinaire

1880-1918

(Pseudonym of Wilhelm Apollinaris de Kostrowitzki; also transliterated as Kostrowitski and Kostrowitzky) French poet, playwright, critic, short story writer, and novelist.

For further information on Apollinaire's career, see *TCLC,* Volumes 3 and 8.

INTRODUCTION

Apollinaire is considered one of the most important literary figures of the early twentieth century. His brief career influenced the development of such artistic movements as Futurism, Cubism, Dadaism, and Surrealism, and the legend of his personality—bohemian artist, raconteur, gourmand, soldier—became the model for avant-garde deportment. Although some critics hesitate to rank him with the greatest poets of the century, Apollinaire's legacy is claimed by such important literary innovators as Philippe Soupault, Louis Aragon, Jean Cocteau, and Gertrude Stein. Just before Apollinaire died, the writer Jacques Vaché wrote to André Breton, the leader of the Surrealist movement, and stated: "He marks an epoch. The beautiful things we can do now!"

According to most sources, Apollinaire was born in Rome, the illegitimate son of a Polish woman and an unidentified man—there is speculation that his father may have been an Italian military officer, a prelate, or even a cardinal in the Church; his friends, Pablo Picasso in particular, liked to joke that Apollinaire was the son of the Pope himself. He spent most of his youth traveling in Europe and as a result developed a cosmopolitan outlook and a fascination with a variety of cultures and fields of study. By the age of eighteen Apollinaire had finished school and settled in Paris. After securing work as a bank clerk he became friends with and an avid supporter of avant-garde artists including Picasso, Georges Braque, Henri Rousseau, and Marcel Duchamp. Never affiliated solely with one group or school but, seemingly, a partisan of all modern artists, Apollinaire was intrigued by, and tended to associate with, those who appeared challenging or antagonistic toward bourgeois society; this inclination probably led to his six-day imprisonment in 1911 when he was wrongly suspected of being connected with the theft of the *Mona Lisa.* In 1914 he joined the French army, volunteering to defend his adopted country in World War I. Although initially a member of an artillery division that was relatively safe from active combat, he soon volunteered to fight at the front with the infantry. He suffered a head wound in 1916 and was sent back to Paris, where he saw the staging of his drama *Les mamelles de Tirésias: Drame surréaliste* (*The Breasts of Tiresias*). This play, the subtitle of which was later adopted by a group of artists and writers known as the Surrealists, established a model for advanced avant-garde theater and influenced such authors as Tristan Tzara, the titular leader of the Dada movement, and André Breton. In 1917 Apollinaire delivered the lecture "L'esprit nouveau et les poètes," a modern art manifesto in which he called for pure invention and a total surrender to inspiration. Apollinaire, weakened by the wound from which he never fully recovered, died of influenza two days before Armistice Day.

Apollinaire's earliest publications, the short story collections *L'enchanteur pourrissant* and *L'hérésiarque et cie* (*The Heresiarch and Co.*), prefigure his subsequent work in their extravagant use of the imagination. The fantastic characters and situations depicted in these stories signal Apollinaire's repudiation of the realistic and naturalistic approaches to writing, which he felt, like the symbolist writers before him, imposed arbitrary limitations on the writer's vision. Unlike the symbolists, however, whose work intentionally ignored everyday reality, Apollinaire's writing demonstrates a serious attempt to confront and transform worldly experience in its diversity, from the crises and joys of personal emotional life, to the advancements of technology and the tragedies of war. As Anna Balakian has observed, Apollinaire's ambition was "to change the world through language." Among his other works of fiction, the novel *Le poète assassiné* (*The Poet Assassinated*) introduces the theme of the poet as a creator of new worlds—a role that Apollinaire himself assumed in his major works, the poetry collections *Alcools* and *Calligrammes* (*Calligrams*).

Both *Alcools* and *Calligrams* are notable for their stylistic experimentation and the novelty of their themes and subjects. Many of these motifs—particularly those taken from contemporary life, such as technology and the alienation of modern existence—had never been treated before in serious poetry. Moreover, in his treatment of such traditional poetic themes as war and romance, Apollinaire revealed his astonishing willingness to contemplate the severest emotions from new points of view. For example, his unique and liberating sense of humor serves to clarify—rather than diminish—the poignancy of his often tragic themes. He frequently achieved this somewhat paradoxical effect through stylistic innovations—such as the avoidance of punctuation in *Alcools* and the shaping of verse text into various objects in *Calligrams*—which a number of critics view as his most significant contributions to modern poetry. In addition to its technical innovations, *Alcools* contains what many critics regard as his most successful individual poems, "Zone" and "La chanson du mal-aimé" ("Song of the Ill-Beloved"), which, with their hope and excitement in modernity, their erudite literary references, and poignant expressions of disappointed love, embody the full range and complexity of his poetic vision. Apollinaire's works, from his visual poems to pornographic novels like *Les onze mille verges* (*The Debauched Hospodar*), as well as his flamboyant personality, present numerous illustrations of those artistic traits which led the Surrealists and other literary experimentalists to claim him as one of their predecessors. Critics agree that Apollinaire's most striking qualities were his vitality and his constant readiness to take both personal and artistic risks.

PRINCIPAL WORKS

L'enchanteur pourrissant   (short stories)   1909
L'hérésiarque et cie   (short stories)   1910
   [*The Heresiarch and Co.*, 1965; also published as *The Wandering Jew, and Other Stories*, 1967]
Le bestiaire; ou, Cortège d'Orphée   (poetry)   1911
Alcools   (poetry)   1913
   [*Alcools*, 1964]
Méditations esthétiques: Les peintres cubistes   (criticism)   1913
   [*The Cubist Painters: Aesthetic Meditations*, 1913]
Case d'armons   (poetry)   1915
Le poète assassiné   (novel)   1916
   [*The Poet Assassinated*, 1923]
Calligrammes   (poetry)   1918
   [*Calligrams*, 1970]
"L'esprit nouveau et les poètes"   (lecture)   1918
Les mamelles de Tirésias: Drame surrealiste   (drama)   1918

[*The Breasts of Tiresias*, published in journal *Odyssey*, 1961]
La femme assise   (novel)   1920
Il y a   (poetry)   1925
Ombre mon amour   (poetry)   1947; also published as *Poèmes à Lou*   [revised edition], 1955
Les onze mille verges   (novel)   1948
   [*The Debauched Hospodar*, 1953]
Couleur de temps   (drama)   1949

CRITICISM

Gabrielle Buffet   (essay date 1922)

[*In the following essay, Buffet lauds Apollinaire's spirit of artistic innovation.*]

Guillaume Apollinaire has had a profound influence on the literature and perhaps still more on the arts and the spirit of this modern period. His influence emanated from his personality rather than from his work—of which he did little, in spite of the wonderful activity of his sensitive intelligence. No doubt it was just this lively activity which made the idea of a long, sustained piece of writing intolerable to him; such a continuous and absorbing effort would have locked him up in himself and kept him from the new contacts which were the food of his spirit. It is therefore impossible to consider the writing separately from the man, whose force and originality are not by any means adequately mirrored therein. Apollinaire spent the best of his creative powers in living, in the search for new joys and new forms, in pushing back existing boundaries. He was possessed of different and almost contradictory forces; a poetic and lyric tendency so powerful as to make his thought come in rhythms automatically when he wrote—at times to change the most banal letter into a poem; and a spirit of research which seized him and carried him towards those experiments in writing which, though cut short by his premature death, form the point of departure for the whole modern evolution. His work comprises several volumes of poetry and prose, which I shall cite in order of their appearance:

L'Enchanteur Pourrissant, published in 1903 in a journal called *Le Festin d'Ésope.* A sort of prose poem which gave free rein to all his lyrical verve; it made him famous.

Le Bestiaire, a collection of short poems full of wit and delicacy.

Hérésiarque & Cie., 1912, said to be his prose masterpiece; a collection of strange tales in which he gets an intensity at once mysterious and fantastic; he never attempted the *genre* again.

Alcools, 1913, his most important work in verse. I find here the palpable conflict between the mind and the muse, the search for the new word, the attempt to let flow unimpeded the clear spring of poetry.

Le Poète Assassiné, written early in the war, complex, a sort of obscure, lyrical autobiography, mirror of the author's vision of life and of himself.

Calligrammes, which contains many verses composed at the front together with examples of his new discovery—calligrammatic poetry.

La Femme Assise, posthumous prose.

He collaborated in no end of journals and reviews, the *Mercure de France* among others, where his *chroniques* displayed an intelligence and a style of exceptional subtlety. He translated and annotated many erotic authors, Aretino, the Marquis de Sade, and so forth; founded and edited several reviews, *Le Festin d'Ésope,* already mentioned, 1903-1904, *Les Soirées de Paris,* 1913-1918, which he consecrated mainly to the defence of modern painting.

Apollinaire was undoubtedly the first to discuss the ideas of a whole generation, ideas which later, having been clearly defined, became the slogan of Dadaism: "Aesthetic value is no more than suggestion, the grip of a strong mind on a weaker, the skill of a juggler doing a trick before spectators."

—*Gabrielle Buffet*

The influence of Guillaume Apollinaire on painting is one of the most curious manifestations of his personality. The abstract investigations of the cubists fitted in with his own innovative needs and he found a starting point for his experiments among the pure inventions of his friends, the younger generation of painters. An important exchange took place between them. Apollinaire's sympathy, the ardour with which he defended and encouraged them publicly, the constant effort on his part to facilitate the public's comprehension of these often incomplete and arid works, were an important factor in the vitality of modern painting. He lived on intimate terms with innovators like Picabia, Picasso, Derain, Vlaminck—it was he who hit on the name Orphism for Picabia's painting and differentiated the two schools. He wrote a book on Les Peintres Cubistes. In return the new spirit set upon him its indelible mark, and his work from that time on was impregnated with the tendency towards abstraction and negation—negation of the spirit of lyricism within him—negation of traditional literary and poetic procedures. From that time on he tried to separate poetry from all romantic sentiment, from all convention of art and good taste. He wanted to make use of every element that life affords without restriction. Speaking of poets he said:

> In the field of inspiration their liberty cannot be less than that of the daily paper which deals on one page with the most divers matters, covers the most widely separated countries. One would like to know why the poet should not have at

least an equal liberty and why he should have to be circumspect about spatial relationships, in an age of telephones, wireless telegraphs, and airplanes.

For him words are to be used without literary artifice, free and direct as in conversation. Hence the *"poèmes conversations"* of Calligrammes. André Billy tells of their invention in a subtle article on Guillaume Apollinaire.

> He, Dupuy, and I are sitting at Crucifixe with three glasses of vermouth. Suddenly Guillaume bursts out laughing—he has completely forgotten to write the preface to Robert Delaunay's catalogue, which he promised to put in the last mail that evening. 'Quick waiter, paper, pen, ink. Three of us will get through with this in no time.' Guillaume's pen runs already:
>
> *'Du rouge au vert tout le jaune se meurt.'*
>
> The pen stops.
>
> But Dupuy dictates:
>
> *'Quand chantent les aras dans les forêts natales.'*
>
> The pen starts off again, transcribing faithfully.
>
> It is my turn:
>
> *'Il y a un poème à faire sur l'oiseau qui n'a qu'une aile.'*
>
> Reminiscence from *Alcools*—the pen writes without hesitation.
>
> 'A good thing to do, if there is any hurry,' I said, 'would be to send your preface over the telephone.'
>
> And so the next line became:
>
> *'Nous l'enverrons en message telephonique.'*
>
> I no longer remember all the details of this peculiar collaboration, but I can state that the preface to the catalogue of Robert Delaunay came out entire.

He was undoubtedly the first to discuss the ideas of a whole generation, ideas which later, having been clearly defined, became the slogan of Dadaism: "Aesthetic value is no more than suggestion, the grip of a strong mind on a weaker, the skill of a juggler doing a trick before spectators." But at that time, and in Apollinaire's mind, the formula was not so crudely explicit; he foresaw the trend of the modern spirit and worried at the same time about its consequences. He did his best, however, to explain it and to relate it to a logical tradition, and give it a foundation. He wrote in the *Mercure de France:*

> The new spirit announces its direct inheritance from the classics of solid good sense, a sure critical judgement, well integrated views upon the universe and the soul, and a sense of duty that strips the feelings bare and limits or rather governs their expression. It claims to inherit from the romanticists a curiosity which explores every field capable of furnishing a literary material that could possibly exalt life. It searches for truth quite as readily in the domain of ethnolo-

gy, for example, as in that of the imagination. These are the principal traits of this new spirit.

Let us add that in spite of, and perhaps precisely because of, this will to veracity which dominates all the investigations, endeavours, and reachings out of the new spirit, we should not be surprised to see a good number of its efforts turn out barren and even ridiculous. The new spirit is full of snares and dangers.

But that is all part of the spirit of the day, and to condemn these endeavours wholesale would be an error comparable to the one attributed rightly or wrongly to M Thiers, who is said to have declared that railroads were nothing but scientific toys and that the world could never produce enough iron for a track from Paris to Marseilles.

The new spirit then encourages literary experiments which are often hazardous and sometimes far from lyrical. And it is for this reason that lyricism plays only a small part in modern poetry, which is often content to experiment without bothering to give its experiments a lyrical significance. The poet, the new spirit, are gathering material, and this material is to furnish a foundation of truth, the simplicity and modesty of which ought to repel no one who realizes what great, what very great things may result therefrom. In years to come, students of the literary history of our time will be astonished to learn of poets and dreamers who, like the alchemists, and without even a philosopher's stone for pretext, gave themselves to experiment which made them a butt for journalists and snobs.

But their inquiries will be useful, will constitute the foundation of a new realism, which will be perhaps not inferior to the wise and poetical realism of Ancient Greece.

From 1914 Guillaume Apollinaire was haunted by the notion of the possibility of a union of poetry and painting. He had printed a subscription announcement of a work entitled Et Moi Aussi Je Suis Peintre. His *Calligrammes* are a good sample of the "new trick" which he was to attempt before the public. The following letter to André Billy will illustrate better than any explanation his state of mind:

Paris, July 29, 1918.

Mon cher André:

I have been a long time writing to thank you for the fine and sensitive article which you wrote about *Calligrammes.* It was by a lover of poetry and a true friend. I hope I may repay you for it! Observe that I find you rather hard on *clichés.* They are a modern method of which one would be wrong to deprive oneself. This book was the first one of its kind, and nothing stands in the way of somebody else's going farther towards perfection in this manner than its originator; some day there may be very fine calligrammatic books. War book as it is, it has life in it and will go farther than *Alcools,* I think, provided fortune smiles on my poet's reputation. That's what

I think. As for the reproach that I am a destroyer, I reject it formally, for I have never destroyed, but on the contrary have tried to build. The classic form of verse was knocked in the head before my time, yet I have often used it, so often in fact that I gave new life to the verse of eight feet, for example. In the arts, too, I have destroyed nothing; I tried to give a chance to new schools, but not at the expense of the old. I attacked neither symbolism nor impressionism. I applauded publicly poets like Moréas. I never put myself forward as a wrecker, but always as a builder. The *Merde* in music from my manifesto-synthesis published by the Futurists did not apply to the work of the ancients but to their name raised as a barrier to new generations. As for *Calligrammes,* they are an idealization of vers-libre poetry, a precise use of typography at the moment when typography is closing brilliantly its carrier in the dawn of the new methods of reproduction, cinema and phonograph.

If ever I stop my investigations it will be because I am tired of being treated as a fool simply because experiments seem silly to people who are satisfied with following the beaten track.

But God is my witness that I have wanted no more than to add new domains to art and letters in general, without at all ignoring the value of the true masterpieces of past and present. . . .

Guillaume Apollinaire.

Apollinaire was not destined however to carry farther his literary experiments and his struggle to free the new spirit. He had been wounded in the head in 1917, and had never completely recovered. In November 1918 he died of influenza two days, I think, before the armistice. He was thirty-eight years old. (pp. 267-72)

Gabrielle Buffet, "Guillaume Apollinaire," in The Dial, *Chicago, Vol. LXXII, March, 1922, pp. 267-72.*

H. L. Mencken   (essay date 1924)

[*From the era of World War I until the early years of the Great Depression, Mencken was one of the most influential figures in American letters. His strongly individualistic, irreverent viewpoint and writing style helped establish the iconoclastic spirit of the Jazz Age and significantly shaped American literature of the time. As a social and literary critic, Mencken excoriated numerous facets of American life that he perceived as humbug, and his literary criticism encouraged American authors to shun the anglophilic, moralistic bent of nineteenth-century literature and to practice realism. In the following excerpt from an essay that originally appeared in the* American Mercury, *March 1924, he attributes Apollinaire's fame to his popularity with the trendy and impressionable younger literary generation; further, Mencken decries the short story collection* The Poet Assassinated.]

Whatever may be said against the young literary lions of the Foetal School, whether by such hoary iconoclasts as

Ernest Boyd or by such virginal presbyters as John S. Sumner, the saving fact remains that the boys and girls have, beneath their false faces, a sense of humor, and are not shy about playing it upon one another. (p. 169)

In [*The Poet Assassinated*] there is jocosity in the grand manner. For a long while past, as time goes among such neologomaniacs, the youths of the movement have been whooping up one Guillaume Apollinaire. When this Apollinaire died in 1918, so they lamented, there passed out the greatest creative mind that France had seen since the Middle Ages. He was to Jean Cocteau, even, as Cocteau was to Eugène Sue. His books were uncompromising and revolutionary; had he lived he would have done to the banal prose of the Babbitts of letters what Eric Satie has done to the art of the fugue. Such news was not only printed in the *Tendenz* magazines that come and go; it was transmitted by word of mouth from end to end of Greenwich Village. More, it percolated to graver quarters. The estimable *Dial* let it be known that Apollinaire was a profound influence on the literature and perhaps still more on the art and spirit of this modern period. Once, when Dr. Canby was off lecturing in Lancaster, Pa., his name even got into the *Literary Review*.

This electric rumor of him was helped to prosperity by the fact that specific data about him were extremely hard to come by. His books seemed to be rare—some of them, indeed, unprocurable—, and even when one of them was obtained and examined it turned out to be largely unintelligible. He wrote, it appeared, in an occult dialect, partly made up of fantastic slang from the French army. He gave to old words new and mysterious meanings. He kept wholly outside the vocabulary at the back of "Collège French." Even returning exiles from La Rotonde were baffled by some of his phrases; all that they could venture was that they were unprecedented and probably obscene. But the Village, as everyone knows, does not spurn the cabalistic; on the contrary, it embraces and venerates the cabalistic. Apollinaire grew in fame as he became unscrutable. Displacing Cocteau, Paul Morand, Harry Kemp, T. S. Eliot, André Salmon, Paul Valéry, Maxwell Bodenheim, Jean Giraudoux and all the other gods of that checkered dynasty, he was lifted to the first place in the Valhalla of the Advanced Thinkers. It was Apollinaire's year. . . . (pp. 170-71)

[*The Poet Assassinated*] is the pricking of the bladder—a jest highly effective, but somewhat barbarous. . . . For what does *The Poet Assassinated* turn out to be? It turns out to be a dull pasquinade in the manner of a rather atheistic sophomore, with a few dirty words thrown in to shock the *booboisie*. From end to end there is not as much wit in it as you will hear in a genealogical exchange between two taxicab drivers. It is flat, flabby and idiotic. It is as profound as an editorial in the Washington *Star* and as revolutionary as Ayer's Almanac. It is the best joke pulled off on the Young Forward-Lookers since Eliot floored them with the notes to *The Waste Land*.

M. Josephson rather spoils its effect, I believe, by rubbing it in—that is, by hinting that Apollinaire was of romantic and mysterious origin—that his mother was a Polish lady of noble name and his father a high prelate of the Catholic Church—that he himself was born at Monte Carlo and baptized in Santa Maria Maggiore at Rome. This is too much. Apollinaire was, like all Frenchmen of humor, a German Jew. His father was a respectable waiter at Appenrodt's, by name Max Spritzwasser: hence the *nom de plume*. His mother was a Mlle. Kunigunda Luise Schmidt, of Holzkirchen, Oberbayern. (pp. 171-72)

> H. L. Mencken, "A Modern Masterpiece," in his Prejudices, fifth series, *Alfred A. Knopf, 1926, pp. 169-72.*

Apollinaire on his poetry:

Unfortunately there is nothing of Anatole France in me and I am by no means a Voltairian poet. Yet my poetry is not like that of [Lautreamont]. It is something quite different. Will you permit me to believe that it is much more profound? This is only an egoistical opinion, but go into it. . . . I am only trying to find a lyricism which is at once new and humanist. My masters are far in the past, from the authors of the Breton cycle to Villon. That is all and the remainder of literature is nothing but a sieve for my taste. Do you see what I mean?

> *Guillaume Apollinaire, in a letter to Toussaint-Luca, May 11, 1908.*

Wallace Fowlie   (essay date 1950)

[*Fowlie is among the most respected and comprehensive scholars of French literature. His work includes translations of major poets and dramatists of France (Molière, Charles Baudelaire, Arthur Rimbaud, Paul Claudel, Saint-John Perse) and critical studies of the major figures and movements of modern French letters (Stéphane Mallarmé, Marcel Proust, André Gide, the Surrealists, among many others). Broad intellectual and artistic sympathies, along with an acute sensitivity for French writing and a first-hand understanding of literary creativity (he is the author of a novel and poetry collections in both French and English), are among the qualities that make Fowlie an indispensible guide for the student of French literature. In the following excerpt, he perceives in Apollinaire's poetry the attempt to represent the multiplicity of life.*]

One of the signs of greatness in a man is the capacity to harmonize forces which would disrupt and mutilate another kind of man. Apollinaire illustrates this principle in a particularly brilliant way. His culture was eclectic, fashionable for the '90's. He preferred the Latin of the mystics to that of Virgil, heretical theologians to St. Thomas, Italian story tellers of the Renaissance to Dante, the Kabbala to the Bible. By contrast to his learning, his heart was simple and limpid. At the publication of *Alcools* in 1913, Georges Duhamel called Apollinaire a peddler with the mingled characteristics of a Levantine Jew, a South American, a Polish gentleman and an Italian porter. To these roles might be added that of the innocent hero, part braggart, part simpleton, who discovered in war the brotherhood of man, and revealed to his many friends one of the truly noble, truly good souls of our age. His poetry is composed with influences, readings, memories, with echoes of many poets, from Villon to Nerval and Jarry. But his voice is also bare and personal, and increasingly so as we grow willing to listen to its deepest resonance.

The story of his life was the effort he made to guard secrets and mysteries, and to create for his friends and his public a character whom they would love and yet not know too intimately. The buffoonery of his character, his endless anecdotes and pranks, permitted him to conceal or disguise the nostalgia and sadness and even perhaps the tragedy of his life. But the poetry of Guillaume Apollinaire is not mask and deceit. It is fantasy in the deepest sense of the word. It is lawful fantasy: its images rightfully conceal and communicate at the same time the emotions he had experienced.

His poetic fantasy was, first, that of revolt, by which he always remained precious and close to the surrealists. He broke with the familiar patterns of thought, with the poetic clichés and literariness of the Parnassians and Symbolists, and with the familiar units and rules of syntax. His poetry comes together in a great freedom of composition, as if he allowed the images and emotions to compose themselves. In his poetry, phantoms, wanderers, mythic characters bearing sonorous names, appear and disappear as the laws of syntax and prosody do. His verse is not literary in any strict sense, and in that he marks a revolt against the poetic research and endeavor of the entire preceding period. He didn't read the obvious books that were being read in his time: Stendhal, Zola, Whitman, Rimbaud (although he was decidedly influenced by Rimbaud). But he read avidly the stories of *Fantômas,* which were a series of popular detective-mystery stories.

It was quite appropriate that Apollinaire, coming after the highly self-conscious and studied literary school of Symbolism, would, in rebellion against such artifice, seek to return to the most primitive sources of lyricism. I have a feeling that only because such a fully developed literary tradition was in him, as a part of his background, was he able to allow in his verse the seemingly spontaneous mixture of emotion and irony, of nostalgia and cynicism. Both by the form and content of his poetry, he seems to be making a kind of plea or defence for moral disorder, or moral relaxation. The adventure of Apollinaire, if we were to extract such a subject from his work, would closely resemble the adventure of Gide: the lessons on freedom and gratuitousness and individual morality, which were being formulated at the same time. Apollinaire thus prolongs the lesson of Rimbaud and Mallarmé, in considering poetic activity as a secret means of knowledge, self-knowledge and world-knowledge.

All the opposites are joined and harmonized in his poetry: fire and water, day and night, the bookish and the popular, the libertine and the sorrowing lover. Apollinaire was not born in France, and until his fifth year he spoke Italian and Polish. He has written about his astonishment at French when he began to read it. This gift for astonishment never left him. Poets are always, to some extent, foreigners to their language. His very birth helped Apollinaire to separate himself somewhat from words in order to dominate them and use them more skillfully.

His friends have all written about his qualities of a child which he never lost. These traits are visible also in his poetry: in his almost cruel assurance of a performer, in the inevitability with which he pierced to the heart of a problem, in his mania for asking only the most important questions, in his willful persistence to be always vulnerable. His native gifts of a poet have made weepers out of other poets who didn't possess his particular kind of genius. He was, for example, more in love with love than with women. His love was a pretext for his exaltation. Mme. Faure-Février tells how he sent the same love poem, with very few changes, to three women. And yet, in such a poem as **"L'Amour, le Dédain et l'Espérance"** there are some of the saddest and most poignant accents that may be found in any love poetry of the world.

His lyricism is discontinuous and disjointed. It reflects a seeming ambiguity, but its deepest mystery is precisely in the rare success he creates out of his use of the discontinuous. All great poetry has at least a fundamental subterranean continuity. In his surface discontinuity, Apollinaire has gone very far in avoiding all the temptations of eloquence, and in attaining to a unity which is not purely verbal. The miracle of his poetry is the number of word surprises it contains, the abrupt appearances and disappearances of emotions and images. The unity of the poem is the never-broken but infinitely fragile and subtle thread of poetic pleasure felt by the poet in all the varied manifestations of his experience. All the myths are in his verses, in close company with pure inventions. He calls upon his immediate knowledge of cities and ports, of unscrupulous voyous and popular songs, in order to speak in his tone of prophet and discoverer. His universe is one of chance and naiveté, of a certain childlike candor which the surrealists will later try to reconstruct. He is the first to use a facile exoticism which today is found in American films and jazz music. But in the most facile of his songs, as in **"Le Musicien de Saint-Merry,"** he is able to generate a delicate irony from the shifts in tone.

> **Apollinaire's lyricism is discontinuous and disjointed. It reflects a seeming ambiguity, but its deepest mystery is precisely in the rare success he creates out of his use of the discontinuous.**
>
> **—Wallace Fowlie**

The familiar type of poem of the 19th century aimed always toward its conclusion which it prepared so carefully that the final effect was quite predictable. The fluidity of Apollinaire's poems and their intermittent surprises, usually including a surprise ending, place them in another domain of aesthetics. **"Adieu,"** a poem of only five lines has the total simplicity of Apollinaire's most ingenuous manner, the rhythm of a folk song and the surprise ending of abrupt poignancy.

> J'ai cueilli ce brin de bruyère
> L'automne est mort souviens-t'en
> Nous ne verrons plus sur terre
> Odeur du temps brin de bruyère
> Et souviens-toi que je t'attends.
>
> [I picked this bit of heather
> Autumn is dead remember
> We'll see no more on the earth
> Odor of time bit of heather
> And remember I'm waiting for you.]

There is a record of Apollinaire's voice reciting **"Le Pont Mirabeau,"** which contains his most persistent theme, the passing and change of sentiments and the poet's own stability.

> Vienne la nuit sonne l'heure
> Les jours s'en vont je demeure

The chance meetings in the world and their dissolutions bear relationship with the chance meetings of words in a poem. Apollinaire is first a poet of regret, of delicate nostalgia, and then, in a very mysterious way, he is the poet of resurrection and exaltation. His memory of the dead makes them into constant presences. **"Vendémiaire,"** the long poem which ends **Alcools,** is a striking evocation of Paris and of all the myths of poetic preservation, of Orpheus and of Icarus who tried to possess the world. The wine of the universe brought contentment to "oceans animals plants cities destinies and singing stars." The poem does contain accents of sorrow and Apollinaire's familiar reference to the sadness of children with their salt tears that taste of the ocean, but it is at the same time a poem on hope and one of the most stirring of the century.

The contrast between Apollinaire's extraordinary erudition, nourished on pornography, magic, popular literature, encyclopedias, and his total simplicity of a song writer, explains to some degree the profound irony pervading almost all of his poetry. It is the irony of curiosity always seeking to harmonize the multiple manifestations of life and the mysteries of the past. Apollinaire's appearance, at the beginning of the 20th century, coincided with many new aesthetic preoccupations to which he brought his own inventiveness and speculative inquiry. His work joined with that of Max Jacob, Picasso, Braque, Derain, Matisse in a series of fantasies and works of art which have gone far in shaping modern sensitivity. A farcical festive air presided over many of the modes of art which were given the names of cubism, fauvism, Negro art, cosmopolitanism, erotology. Apollinaire himself was responsible for the term surrealism. He literally became a prophet in his support of aesthetic innovations which were to become the accepted forms of the future. His articles on painting place him second only to Baudelaire among the aestheticians of modern France.

With the recent rediscovery and republication of Sade, the erotic aspect of Apollinaire's writings reveals greater depth and proportion than has heretofore been suspected. René Guy Cadou's small book of 1948, *Guillaume Apollinaire ou l'Artilleur de Metz,* indicates the importance of this study but doesn't develop it. The influence of Walt Whitman as well as that of the more frankly licentious writers such as Sade, whom Apollinaire read at the Bibliothèque Nationale, will be studied one day as the sources of Apollinaire's freedom of expression and thought. The first edition of **L'Hérésiarque,** his boldest book of erotology (not including his deliberately pornographic writings) was of 1910. The previous year, he wrote an introduction to an edition of selected writings of Sade which must have necessitated a detailed study and documentation. The erotic is almost always for Apollinaire a way of expressing his joy. He seems never to doubt his human power, his potentiality of a man who affirms this power in order to affirm himself. As for Rabelais, salaciousness was a fervent expression for Apollinaire, a way of taking possession of the world, of making to life a total gift of himself. Both Rabelais and Apollinaire were intoxicated by life and erudition. A love of gastronomy would join them if nothing else did. Apollinaire is less a sensualist than an epicurean, a deliberate gourmandizer who enjoyed good cooking and varied cuisines. His menu was often a means of mystification, such as the dinner reported by Vlaminck (in *Portraits avant décès*) when Apollinaire served pears with mustard and dandelions with Eau de Cologne.

Most men have some memory of a barracks life and comradeship in arms. The war was an essential experience for Apollinaire. He realized that a man in uniform is not one but many, and that he changes his character, or deepens it, in the extraordinary frankness of a barracks existence. He was interested in the lives of all his fellow soldiers as, in civil life, he had shown interest in all types: countesses, jockeys, artists. He had a tender predilection for the obscene songs of soldiers and students, songs whose rhythms were natural to him and whose language was not as coarse as it was mysteriously simple.

The lesson about poetry which Apollinaire teaches is the most profound in France since Rimbaud's. (**"La Chanson du Mal-Aimé"** has become for our age what *Le Lac* and *Tristesse d'Olympio* were for the 19th century.) In many ways Apollinaire's lesson comes from Rimbaud's which it completes. Poetry is the act whereby that which is essentially foreign to formal language passes into formal language. Surrealism, with the examples of Rimbaud and Apollinaire, was to recognize that the real domain of the poet is just outside what is called the world of reason. The great resources of a poet are in the night where he cohabits with his phantoms. Apollinaire taught, by the example of his work, that the poetic act is the creative act in its fullest purity. Whatever is named by the poet has something ineffable about it, and his function is precisely to explain that, to study what refuses to be cast into explicit language. In this way, poetry is able to restore to language something of its primitive mystery and origins. Poetry like Apollinaire's doesn't try to fathom the supernatural or the miraculous, but simply to state the incomprehensibleness of the ordinary and the commonplace. Every human expression Apollinaire saw became sphinx-like for him, and every word he overheard resembled a sibyl's utterance. His language has a baptismal gravity about it. Nascent language it would seem to be, rediscovering its virginity, as the poet, performing his earliest role of demiurge, calls the world to be born again by naming it. (pp. 162-67)

Wallace Fowlie, "Apollinaire," in Poetry, *Vol. LXXVII, No. 3, December, 1950, pp. 162-67.*

James R. Lawler (essay date 1956)

[*Lawler is an Australian-born critic whose writings on French literature include many studies of the poet Paul Valery. In the following essay, he provides an overview of Apollinaire's life and career as a poet.*]

Few poets have enjoyed so soon after their death a vogue comparable to that of Apollinaire. He died at the age of thirty-eight in 1918, but his name was not allowed to be forgotten. From 1920 on, his literary reputation was enriched by the tributes of painters he helped make famous—Picasso, Braque, Chagall, and also by the younger generation of poets. There is hardly one of them, from Eluard to Cocteau, who has not testified to his fertile influence and example. It seems therefore not without some justification that the first half of this century has been called the 'âge apollinarien' of French art.

Over the last ten years several important texts have come to light which have allowed of a more complete knowledge of his life and work. The poems written to Lou from the war-front (**Ombre de mon amour,** 1947) revealed the amazing lyrical facility, the violent emotions of this soldier for whom the phenomena of war become so many images that evoke his memories of love. We may also mention the letters published in 1952 (**Tendre comme le souvenir**). These were written to a young schoolteacher of Oran whom Apollinaire met for a few hours in the train between Nice and Marseilles. From the trenches he wrote to her, sent her poems, imagined her as some idyllic beauty. He even became engaged to her—by post; but when the two finally met, it would appear that, naturally enough, the reality could not measure up to the dream.

These works have renewed interest in Apollinaire. In 1951 a street near St. Germain-des-Prés was named after him (Baudelaire and Rimbaud do not have theirs yet) and in 1954 a special quarterly review was founded in Paris, to be devoted entirely to the study of his life and work. It is called *Le Flâneur des deux rives,* after one of Apollinaire's books. Now the first full-length biography of the poet to appear in English has reached Australia: *Apollinaire,* by Marcel Adéma.

M. Adéma's book was subtitled in the original French version: *le mal-aimé* by which the author suggested that the key to the poet's personality lay in a nostalgia for some impossible Eve. That is certainly part, but not the whole, of the answer. In any case it would be futile to read M. Adéma's book in search of psychological subtlety. The author presents the facts, and these are indeed interesting enough in themselves.

One major discovery that M. Adéma has made is related in the first chapter. It had long been known that Apollinaire was born out of wedlock to a young Polish aristocrat of twenty, who had kicked over the traces of her convent. The identity of the father remained a close secret. The poet

allowed it to be rumoured that it was some personage of high esteem in the Church; and Picasso went so far as to draw his friend with a papal tiara on his head. But M. Adéma shows, with legal documents to support him, that the father was a Francesco Flugi, aged forty-five, officer in the Italian army, of the noble family of d'Aspremont, and that the child's birth took place on August 26, 1880.

The unusual mixture of Polish and Italian blood goes some way toward explaining the temperament of the poet. Alongside the nostalgia and emotional violence he may well derive from his mother, he inherits from his father a Latin eroticism and gaiety.

Until the age of five years he lived in Rome; his later work will contain echoes of the carnavals, the familiar scenes of the Italian capital. In 1881, Mme. de Kostrowitzky, abandoned by her lover, goes to live in Monaco. Together with his brother, Albert, Guillaume grows up in the free atmosphere of the Côte d'Azur, with a minimum of parental guidance. Rather unexpectedly he is a good pupil. At the College Saint-Charles the honour-roll is studded with his name. He experiences the mystical fervours of adolescence, prays all night in the school chapel. But soon we find him reading all the current Symbolist reviews and writing verse, now in the style of Hugo, now imitating Henri de Régnier or Maeterlinck.

In 1899, having failed to obtain his *baccalauréat,* he accompanied his mother to Paris. Then, while she was trying her luck in the Belgian Casinos, he stayed for three months at Stavelot near the Belgian border. Here it was that he wrote his first love-poems for Maria, an engaging maid-servant: anagrams, sonnets, free verse. The object of his outpourings may have been humble but Maria did confirm Apollinaire in his resolution to be a poet. Throughout his career we find constant allusions to his stay at Stavelot, to the flat grey heath, where his love was awakened for the first time.

> J'ai cueilli ce brin de bruyère
> L'automne est morte souviens-t'en
> Nous ne nous verrons plus sur terre
> Odeur du temps brin de bruyère
> Et souviens-toi que je t'attends
>
> I have picked a twig of heather
> Autumn days are dead, remember
> We shall never meet again
> Time's perfume this twig of heather
> And for you I wait and remain

His full originality will not be evident however until 1901 when he spends a year near Honnef on the Rhine, as tutor in the employ of the wealthy Viscountess Milhau. He is immediately attracted by the German countryside, sings the autumn and winter of the Rhine forests. The German poets serve as inspiration, especially Heine and Brentano, of whose 'Loreley' he has given us a remarkable French adaptation. The folksongs also please him and he has translated their rhythms in a ballad concerning Schinderhannes, the famous Rhineland Robin Hood.

But the main event of this year is the acquaintance with Annie Playden, a young English governess who is also employed by Mme. Milhau. She captivates Apollinaire by her fresh beauty, her reserve. One day he takes her to the top of a nearby mountain and threatens to kill her if she will not marry him. Out of fear she accepts, but later adamantly refuses him, in spite of two visits to London that the poet undertakes to ask for her hand. Finally, to escape his importunity, Annie decides to go to America, where she is still alive today.

The unusual wildness of this passion produces several love lyrics, a few of which have rarely been equalled among modern poets in their accents of melancholy and despair. There is a constant mastery of sound, worthy of Verlaine. Some of the images, also are startlingly new: as that of the saffron which evokes both the beauty and poison of his love:

> Le pré est vénéneux mais joli en automne . . .

An account of Apollinaire's passion for Annie is found in the long poem, **"La Chanson du mal-aimé."** The fifty-nine stanzas composed of octosyllabic quintains are divided into seven sections, in which the emotions vary and clash, from sudden tenderness to scorn and hate. The total impression, however, is not fragmentary but one of fidelity to the complex nature of the poet's love. And throughout the poem, from the intimate passages where the expression is veiled by a personal symbolism to the moments of lucid despair, the echo of inevitability resounds, 'Destins destins impénétrables.'

About 1903 Apollinaire settled in Paris and tried to resign himself to the loss of Annie. He completed a strange mythical evocation in prose, *L'Enchanteur pourrissant,* in which he identified himself with the sorcerer Merlin, betrayed in love by Viviane.

It was then that he met Picasso, who had not long arrived from Barcelona. Together they began exploring new avenues of art. One day they discovered a negro statuette: the *époque nègre* of Picasso was born and so also was a whole new era of modern painting. Between 1905 and 1908 Apollinaire devoted himself to art criticism, introducing the younger generation of painters to the public. In 1905 he wrote the first critical consideration of Picasso. Later followed articles on Matisse, Marie Laurencin and many others. Among these was the Douanier Rousseau whom Apollinaire discovered and revealed to the public, launching the taste for his primitivism.

For Apollinaire himself these years were a time of research into his own art. He also seems to have undergone an artistic and moral crisis. The poetic fruit of this appears in 1908: **"Les Fiançailles,"** another lengthy poem in ten parts dedicated to Picasso. The 'engagement' (fiançailles) that the poet announces is to some Heraclitean fire of artistic vision. The themes of fire and of flame recur with the insistence of a mystic's testament.

> Je ne sais plus rien et j'aime uniquement
> Les fleurs à mes eux redeviennent des flammes
>   . . .

After 1908 Apollinaire experienced a period of calm. He was becoming well-known as the champion of Cubism, and his views were quoted in the respectable monthlies. Hard pressed for money as usual, he spent a good part of his time turning out very conscientious editions of pornographic literature, such as the works of de Sade, Aretino and Delicado. At the same time a liaison with the painter, Marie Laurencin, brought him a certain emotional stability.

But in 1911, when the Mona Lisa disappeared from the Louvre, Apollinaire was to be implicated in an unfortunate manner. The poet had as secretary a Belgian youth who spent his spare time borrowing objects of interest from museums. A few negro figurines were of special interest to Apollinaire and his friends, and the secretary procured them. But when the Mona Lisa was stolen (not, as it turned out, by the Belgian), Apollinaire became afraid and decided to send back anonymously the objects he had been holding. Unluckily his name was divulged, he was arrested and put in gaol on a charge of being an accomplice and in possession of stolen goods. Meanwhile the secretary had fled. In spite of the protests of a number of his friends Apollinaire was detained for a week at the Santé, during which he wrote a series of six poems that stand comparison, in their anguish and sober expression, with those of Poor Lelian, Paul Verlaine, in the prison of Mons.

> Avant d'entrer dans ma cellule
> Il a fallu me mettre nu
> Et quelle voix sinistre ulule
> Guillaume qu'es-tu devenu
>
> Le Lazare entrant dans la tombe
> Au lieu d'en sortir comme il fit
> Adieu adieu chantante ronde
> O mes années ô jeunes filles
>
> Before I stepped into my cell
> They made me strip to the skin
> And some voice cried like a voice from Hell
> Guillaume what a plight you are in
>
> Lazarus entering the earth
> Instead of coming towards the light
> Farewell farewell round of mirth
> Oh my years past oh girl-fresh sight

A few months after his release from prison, Marie Laurencin broke off their relationship. The friendship had lasted for five years, and the shock was a hard one for Apollinaire. We hear again in **"Marie"** and the beautiful **"Pont Mirabeau,"** both composed during this period, similar accents of nostalgia and regret to those which Annie had inspired.

His first collection of verse *Alcools* (1913) contains these two poems as well as forty-eight of his other compositions dating from as far back as 1898. Deliberately he avoided a chronological order and arranged his poems to a symphonic pattern. The appearance of the book was hardly noticed. Georges Duhamel, a poet from the rival Unanimist school, branded its author bookish, unoriginal, 'a cheap antique-dealer.' He has since been able to revise his opinion.

In this same year Apollinaire gathered together his main articles on Cubism and the Cubist painters under the title *Méditations esthétiques.* His pages contain one of the most perceptive interpretations of Cubism as well as affording a glimpse into the aesthetic of the poet. The main ideas which are put forward concern the 'falseness' of the work of art, that is to say its antinatural, gratuitous character. The poet rejects all artistic canons. The distinction he draws here between artists is not between classicist and romanticist, nor ancient and modern, but between personal and impersonal: the spontaneous lyricist and the Rimbaldian creator. In the career of Picasso he traces a movement from one form of expression to the other, from the 'époque bleue' to the Cubist period when, says Apollinaire, 'the world became his own formulation.'

The influence of painting is strongly present in the poetic compositions of 1913 and 1914. Apollinaire sought to transpose verbally what Delaunay was doing with his 'simultaneous' canvases. Disconnected phrases of bar-room conversations are written down, juxtaposed, arranged: subject fires subject in a multicolour of impressions. These are the 'poèmes-conversations.' We may also mention another technical development of this same period, the calligrams. In the line of a number of poets from Simmias on, Apollinaire wants to render by the typography of his poem the very form of the object described. Mallarmé wrote a letter to Gide concerning this same ambition toward the end of his life: 'The rhythm of a phrase concerning an act or even an object, has no sense except in so far as it imitates them, traced on the paper, reproducing by the letters on the page the cast of the original die . . . ' A lyricism whose lay-out is its own image. The houses Apollinaire describes, the starry nights, the inhabitants of Montparnasse, the Eiffel Tower, come to us in a precise and formal simplicity—and not without a large injection of humour. One is tempted to compare them with Eric Satie's contemporary *Morceaux en forme de poire*.

In 1914, still deeply affected by the break with Marie Laurencin, he finds himself in Nice a few months after the beginning of the war. He falls in love with a young lady of high birth, Louise de Coligny, who rejects his pleas. Disappointed, he joins the army. He had already made up his mind to fight for his adopted country, but Lou's coldness causes him to take the final step sooner than intended. Lou then proceeds to follow him to Nîmes where the garrison is stationed, and together they enjoy a week or so of ardent love. But Lou tires quickly. Apollinaire leaves for the front but continues to write for her poem after poem of unrequited passion (*Ombre de mon amour*).

When he is not busy carrying out his duties as a gunner, he spends his time writing hundreds of letters; in eighteen months it has been estimated that he sent off 3,000 of them. The most important constitute the correspondence with Madeleine (*Tendre comme le souvenir*). Writing to a young lady whom he had met for a mere two or three hours, we see him gradually become the victim of his autoeroticism. The poems he sends are imbued with a breathless movement, a desire to make incarnate forcibly, as it were, the idyllic figure of his imagination.

As regards his reaction to the war, Apollinaire rejoices at the sight of his uniform, his horse, his spurs, marvels at the ardour of the battles. 'Joy is everything in life,' he writes from the front, 'joy is the great soldier of victory.'

His boyish attitude changes the war into a fantasy. He thinks of two teams of children playing larks: 'Yonder they're playing hide-and-seek, we're playing blind-man's buff.' And when the artillery opens fire, the scene is like some immense circus:

> . . . fusées détonateurs
> Funambules qui attendent leur tour
> de passer sur les trajectoires

The battle is a game; it is also a terrible act of love from which the soldier must hope a better world will be born.

> Les canons membres génitaux
> Engrossent l'amoureuse terre . . .

Few poets since Rimbaud and Hopkins have given proof of such profound animism, and joy in the workings of analogy. That does not mean that Apollinaire is ignorant of the tragedy of war. **"Exercise"** for example recounts a brutal fact: four soldiers killed by one blast. The anecdote is heightened by what seems a moral, almost mythical, sobriety.

This war-poetry was destined to come to an abrupt end. On March 17, 1916, while he was reading a copy of a French review, he noticed blood running over the page. He had been seriously wounded in the head by a piece of shrapnel. Taken to Paris, he began to show signs of paralysis. He was trepanned at the Valde-Grâce military hospital, and the operation seemed a success. But his robust health was alarmingly weakened, he had only two years left to live. During these two years he prepared his war-poems for publication (*Calligrammes*), as well as a collection of short stories. He also wrote two plays: one, in a burlesque style, concerning the problem of depopulation (*Les Mamelles de Tiresias*); the other (*Couleur du temps*) an allegorical indictment of the lack of commitment of present-day intellectuals.

Two poems dating from this period are worthy of mention. **"Tristesse d'une étoile"** is written with almost Parnassian restraint. The poet speaks of his trepanned head: 'From within my head has sprung a fair Minerva.' His suffering, the stitches on his head which resemble 'a star of blood,' have brought him, he says, new maturity. But there is another kind of suffering, a moral one, which he feels now more acutely than ever and which is the prelude to each new generation of ideas and images: a flame of suffering whose very pain is a promise 'like the sweet-smelling pollen in the heart of the lily.'

The other poem is entitled **"La Jolie Rousse."** It takes its name from Jacqueline, whom Apollinaire married in May 1918, six months and seven days before his death. He formulates here a kind of poetic credo in which he sees in the person of his wife, or more exactly in the sunlight on her red hair, the symbol of ideal beauty. All poets, he says, strive toward an ideal, but some do so on the side of tradition and order, others on the side of adventure and discovery. Apollinaire pleads for those who, like himself, 'fight on the frontiers of the future and the limitless.'

> Nous ne sommes pas vos ennemis
> Nous voulons vous donner de vastes et
>   d'étranges domaines
> Où le mystère en fleurs s'offre à qui veut le cueil-
>   lir

The poetic testament of Apollinaire is thus a plea in favour of revolutions and not of anarchy. For him the existence of an order gives a meaning and direction to artistic novelty.

In early November 1918 Apollinaire was stricken with influenza. On the 9th of the same month he died in his flat on the Boulevard St. Germain. His funeral two days later had to make its way through crowds celebrating the Armistice and shouting 'Conspuez Guillaume'—the cry was directed at Kaiser Bill. His grave in the Père-Lachaise cemetery is sober. On the granite menhir may be read these lines from *Calligrammes*:

> Je me suis enfin détaché
> De toutes choses naturelles
> Je peux mourir mais non pécher
> Et ce qu'on n'a jamais touché
> Je l'ai touché je l'ai palpé
> Je peux mourir en souriant

Apollinaire's most outstanding trait in his poetic vitality. 'We do not love enough the joy of seeing new and beautiful things.' Here was the answer to the *fin de siècle* ethic. Apollinaire rejects Symbolist hermeticism, as well as the 'I am the Empire at its decadent end' of Verlaine.

His lifelong ambition was not merely to express himself. Like Rimbaud he also wanted to 'change life,' to give to the familiar a new name and face. His vocabulary refuses to restrict itself to any French poet. In addition he rejects the codes of versification so as to proclaim the right of every poet to find his own form. 'There can be today no authentic lyricism without complete freedom for the poet, and even if he writes in regular verse, it is his freedom which tells him to do so.'

His images, like his vocabulary, are rich in colour and emotional content. No object is static, everything is in continual change. The verbs become the focal point of each notation, constantly shift the lighting of an electric universe. There is no merging of one term into another but rather a juxtaposition. Each contact lights a new combination, the two objects must play against each other in an 'étonnant contraste' which, however, reveals a common law and destiny. Fire and music, we find, are the most frequent themes, referring now to a nostalgic past, now to an empyrean future.

This creation is highly conscious. Study of the poet's manuscripts shows that he makes a practice of taking a line or a stanza from a previous jotting and weaving it into an entirely new framework. His poetry is, very much in the Cubist sense, a 'construction,' a 'composition.' But underlying this succession of impressionist images is the dictate of song. Like ballad-writers and folk poets in general, Apollinaire wrote his words to fit the melody he was humming. Sometimes it was a folksong, more often a chant modelled on the Vespers which he had heard regularly as a child at Monaco. One important consequence of this was the suppression of punctuation in order to communicate more amply the flow of the poem. 'Punctuation could not be applied to my songs,' he once wrote.

The dynamic force behind his poetry resides in this internal continuity of music and its urge to reach a new synthesis, where the totality of the outside world will be embraced in the song of one poet. What however separates him from the Whitmanian tradition and gives his work its particularly modern accent is the note of exile which most often is heard in the last lines of his poems. The music then appears to us as broken; subject and object remain irrevocably disjoined: 'Les jours s'en vont je demeure.' Language refuses to be resolved into an egocentric dream. Yet, in spite of this evident failure, we may feel justified in believing that salvation for post-symbolist literature could lie only in some new and tragic confrontation with outer reality, such as we find in Apollinaire.

His life is almost equally divided between the nineteenth and twentieth centuries. Born into the Symbolist period, he was later to invent the term 'surrealism' which André Breton finally adopted in 1923 to describe the new movement in art. But Apollinaire's poetry escapes definition as either symbolist or surrealist. Perhaps it owes its sense of urgency partly to this isolation. In any case he was conscious of an artistic tension: 'cette longue querelle de la tradition et de l'invention.' His energy enabled him to live out this tension to the full and to create from it an original and exciting harmony of French poetry. (pp. 364-73)

> *James R. Lawler, "Guillaume Apollinaire," in* Meanjin, *Vol. XV, No. 4, December, 1956, pp. 364-73.*

Wallace Fowlie (essay date 1967)

[*In the following excerpt, Fowlie maintains that Apollinaire's* Alcools *explores conflict between the poet's inner life and the outside world.*]

The vast amount of documentation available on Apollinaire is largely due to his colorful enigmatic personality. Many of those who knew him in Paris have tried to explain his character and have left in their memoirs or monographs portraits and anecdotes and interpretations of the anecdotes. Placed side by side, these documents would offer the portrait of a monstrous, complex, and unpredictable personage. The truth is probably more simple.

This very pure French poet had a Polish mother, of Slavic ancestry, and an Italian father. After a Mediterranean childhood (he was born in Rome), when he studied in Monaco and Nice, he came to Paris where, after a brief Rhineland voyage of great importance to his personal life and poetry, he gradually assumed the role of impresario of the arts, especially of poetry and painting. But Apollinaire was far more cosmopolitan than most of the Paris poets. The persistent curiosity that stimulated his mind led him to cultivate his taste for the unusual book in literature and the exceptional kind of human being whom he chose as friend and companion. He espoused and then helped direct the intellectual and artistic bohemianism of Montmartre and Montparnasse. His knowledge, a curious kind of erudition, and the exuberance of his character, made him quickly into the leader of his group of friends. In an extreme sense, he was a performer for whatever circle of friends he was with. But in a private and personal sense, he was an attentive friend, generous and sympathetic to a wide variety of friends. It is obvious today that no

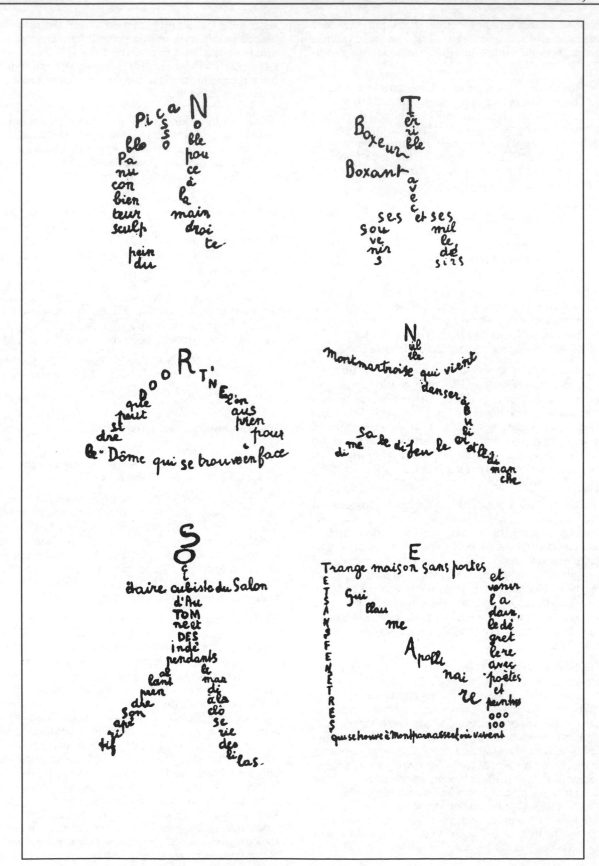

Visual poems by Apollinaire.

one friend was acquainted with all of Apollinaire's life. There were many compartments in this man's nature, many friendships and interests that were maintained concurrently. He was strongly attracted to women, both erotically and sentimentally. Apollinaire probably demanded too much from his relationships with women: both carnal excitement and deep tenderness. He forged for himself and the future of his name: *le mal aimé,* the one who was badly loved. But he himself corrected this and said he was probably *le mal aimant,* the man who did not know how to love well.

More than anyone else, Apollinaire dominated and illustrated the new art of his age—the first decade and a half of the twentieth century—not in reality by inventing the new art forms, but by adopting them instantly, by using them in his own work, and by interpreting them to others. He was both assimilator and stimulator. Every conversation, every encounter, every aesthetic experience became for him an intellectual adventure. His mind and his heart were always open to what was new and unpredictable. André Breton, some time after Apollinaire's death, in attempting to assess the place of the poet and his contribution, said that to the highest degree, Apollinaire incarnated the "intellectual adventure." This judgment, on the whole, was accepted by the other surrealists who were the first to understand and acknowledge the importance of Apollinaire. The religious problem did not exist for him. In late childhood he seems to have lost his Catholic faith. Without metaphysical worries, he was a far different poet from Baudelaire, for example, in his indifference to religious faith and the philosophical anguish of many of the European writers.

During the First World War and the years that immediately followed it, Baudelaire's influence was strong on two generations of writers: on Proust and Valéry, and on the Catholic writers, Claudel, Bernanos, Mauriac, and Maritain. Not until World War II and the years following it, did Apollinaire reach a comparable position in his effect upon writers and the life of literature. Since those years, all of his work has been examined and is being examined by scholars in France (Durry and Décaudin), in Australia (Lawler) and America (Shattuck, Breunig, Greet)—his two major collections of poems, **Alcools** and **Calligrammes,** and three briefer posthumous volumes, **Ombre de mon amour** (for Louise de Coligny), **Tendre comme le souvenir** (for Madeleine Pagès) and **Le Guetteur mélancolique.** His critical writings are also the object of considerable study.

Today Apollinaire speaks directly to the young poet and the young student of literature. They see in him the authentically modern poet. They approve of the importance he gave to the word modern. They are fascinated by the relationship they sense between his poems and the art of Braque, Picasso, Derain, Matisse. They are struck by the efforts Apollinaire and the painters made to reach beyond the *real* to the *surreal.* It is true that much of the serious poetry being written today in the 1960's in France, such as that of Yves Bonnefoy, owes more to Mallarmé than to Apollinaire. But the example of Apollinaire for poets of the 1930's and 1940's, for Eluard, Aragon, Cocteau, is obvious. The recent Sorbonne course on Apollinaire by Mme Durry, which has now been published in three volumes, significantly marks a new era when the once seemingly rebellious poet becomes the object of scholarly investigation. Mme Durry's own accomplishments as poet, in addition to her scholarly competence, has made her one of the ideal interpreters of Apollinaire. American scholars have made significant contributions. Professor Breunig, of Barnard College, has studied the sources and structure of **"La Chanson du Mal-Aimé."** Roger Shattuck, of the University of Texas, and Anne Greet, of the University of California, further illustrate the attraction that Apollinaire still exerts on the new kind of teacher who is both practicing poet and scholar.

Apollinaire came midway between the two great generations of the symbolists and the surrealists. But he does not appear overshadowed by either one: he inherited many of the traits of symbolism and announced the new traits to come, of surrealism. The case of Rimbaud had somewhat fixed the portrait of the youthful poet as a vindictive, sullen, and even persecuted adolescent, hostile to family and state and religion. The case of Apollinaire changed this portrait to that of a young man without family and country, and without a sentiment of vindictiveness. His attitude was one of gratitude to France for receiving him (an attitude similar to that of many artists—Picasso, Picabia, Chagall, Giacometti), of constant gratitude to his family of friends. Breton called him a *jobard* ("easy mark") by temperament. And yet the major poems of Apollinaire (which are among some of the most mysterious and beautiful poems in the French language) were the result of a secret solitary life. The poems perfectly preserve the ambiguity of his character and the secrecy of his inner life.

The famous lecture, given by Apollinaire shortly before his death, and published a month after his death, in December, 1918, in *Le Mercure de France,* is the synthesis of his major theories on poetry and the modern spirit in art. It helps to explain even his earliest poems, written at a time when he was trying to formulate his theories and experiment with them.

A sense of exuberance or exaltation must preside over the source of the new spirit: a desire to explore everything, to explore regions of the world and regions of the mind; to bring to every experience that critical sense and that common sense which the Frenchman believes he inherits at birth. An artistic form can never be static. The artist is the searcher of new forms, of new combinations. He must never neglect the new popular form of art (Apollinaire would say "pop art" today): the movies, for example, for which Apollinaire was a prophet. With his mind open, with an indefatigable curiosity, the modern artist will acquire an encyclopedic knowledge, information on everything, so easily found in newspapers and on the radio. The machine age, with its telephones, aviation, magazines, records, art collections, puts the world within every man's grasp. The age of vague sentimental dreaming and isolation for the artist is over. Apollinaire uses the word *wagnérisme* to designate the artist's romantic revery and he uses it in a deprecatory sense. A new sense of order and duty demands that we pay attention to everything that is happening in the world. As the world itself is constantly reordering itself, recomposing itself, so the poet has to follow the same principle of searching for new combinations of words and images. There is no end to possible new combinations. And each combination, if it is struck off with genius, will be a surprise. The new spirit, according to Apollinaire, is in the power of surprise. The era of the airplane has invalidated the flight of Icarus. His story is no longer a fable. It is the poet's duty to imagine and create new fables. The art of poetry and the creativeness of man are identical. It is therefore possible to be a poet in every domain of human activity. What is indispensable for the new poet is the spirit of adventure, the spirit of rediscovery. The point of departure for this kind of adventure may well be a trivial circumstance, a thoroughly innocuous event. Apollinaire imagines the example of a handkerchief falling: this could be, he insists, the genesis of a new universe, the beginning of a vast synthesis. As other examples, he gives the striking of a match, the cry of an animal, the odors of a garden after rainfall. These examples of trivia may bring about the element of surprise, which he calls the mechanics of the new poetry. (*La surprise, l'inattendu est un des principaux ressorts de la poésie d'aujourd'hui.*)

The passage on dreams, in "L'Esprit Nouveau," on the closed night world of dreams, will be a valuable guide for the surrealists. The life of dreams exemplifies for Apollinaire man's perpetual renewal of himself, the endless creation of himself, so comparable to poetry, a force that is always being reborn and by which man lives. Apollinaire looks upon France as a seminary of poets and artists, a land where the modern poets are creators and inventors and prophets, and in that sense, they are opposed to aestheticism, to formulas in art, to cultism and snobbishness. The new poet will thus work differently from poets in other periods, in his struggle to understand clearly his own age, to open up a new understanding of the exterior world around him and the inner world of his spirit and his dreams. He will be, in fact, the first to understand his age, because he will be the poet of the truth of his age. Truth is constantly being renewed and reassessed with the change of time and customs.

In *L'esprit nouveau* Apollinaire looks upon France as a seminary of poets and artists, a land where the modern poets are creators and inventors and prophets, and in that sense, they are opposed to aestheticism, to formulas in art, to cultism and snobbishness.

—*Wallace Fowlie*

Alcools of 1913 was the first collection of poems published by Guillaume Apollinaire, but almost all the poems (written between 1898 and 1913) had previously appeared in magazines. They are not arranged chronologically in the collection. "**Zone**," for example, opens the series and was

one of the last to be written. Slight changes had been made in several since their first appearance in magazines, and all punctuation had been suppressed.

The year 1913-14 was a remarkable one in the annals of French poetry and art, the *annus mirabilis*. Apollinaire published both *Alcools* and his book on the new painters, *Les Peintres Cubistes*; Proust, *Du côté de chez Swann;* Alain-Fournier, *Le Grand Meaulnes;* Gide, *Les Caves du Vatican.* Jacques Copeau opened his theatre of *Le Vieux Colombier.* Stravinsky directed the first performance of *Le Sacre du Printemps.* Cubism, as a new school in painting, had been founded in 1908, with the first cubist paintings of Braque and Picasso. By 1913, it was a fully established school, sometimes called "orphic cubism," when the paintings would be made up of elements created by the artist and not necessarily copied from reality, but elements endowed by the artist with a surprising sense of reality.

These visions of the painters, which Apollinaire had contemplated during the period when he was composing his poems of *Alcools,* reflected for the poet a universe of phantoms juxtaposed with the real universe of humanity. The diversity of cubism is in the diversity of *Alcools,* with its symbolism (as in "**Ermite**"), its elegiac tones (as in "**Le Pont Mirabeau**"), its program of modernism (as in "**Zone**"), its theme of nostalgia, reminiscent of Verlaine (as in "**A la Santé**"), its obscure poetry (as in "**Le Brasier**").

Apollinaire avoids all rhetorical bombast, all pointed melodramatic effects. There is no overt perversion in his eroticism, no maudlin quality in his tenderness. There is no direct imitation of nature when he speaks of a river, of a city landscape, of the memory of a distant country, of the stars, of a woman's body. When he evokes a theme close to the occult and the mysterious, he avoids any direct mysticism. As he avoids, at the other extreme, any rationalistic approach to a theme. There is no concept of sin in the poems, but Apollinaire is a moving poet when he speaks of the heart's distress. He is able to describe simultaneously the tenderness of a love experience and its ruin. He is a magician when he uses a commonplace, a worn-out poetic theme and transfigures it. There is no such thing as poetic language for Apollinaire, and with this belief and practice he did institute an important change in poetry, almost as significant a change as that brought about first by Baudelaire, and then by Rimbaud. In deflating the traditional concepts concerning poetic language, he established his new code of shock and surprise. Somewhat in the tradition of Rimbaud, but especially in that of Alfred Jarry, Apollinaire at times used coarseness or comic or absurd traits in his effort to hold his reader by an effect of surprise.

Two poems in particular from *Alcools* will hold our attention in an attempt to analyze Apollinaire's reaction to experiences of violence. He has said that each of his poems is a commemoration of an event in his life. This is luminously clear in the first of these poems, "**La Chanson du Mal-Aimé**", his most famous and one of his longest. The second poem, "**Le Brasier**," is perhaps less clearly autobiographical. The two poems amply illustrate the degree of seriousness with which Apollinaire considered existence. In his role of jovial companion that has been so often related in books, he refused to take himself seriously. But in his art of poet, in the most profound instances of this art, he underscored the tragedy of man's solitude. **"La Chanson du Mal-Aimé"** and **"Le Brasier"** are two exercises, two experiments on this solitude, seen not from a purely personal egotistical viewpoint, but in a wider context of mythological man, and man in his specific dilemmas of today's history.

In the epigraph preceding **"La Chanson du Mal-Aimé"**, Apollinaire tells us that this love poem, *cette romance,* was written in 1903, when he knew his love affair with Annie Pleyden was over, when he was still suffering from her rejection, or at least her refusal to marry him, and before he realized that his love, like the phoenix of mythology, would rise up again. This is doubtless an allusion to his love for Marie Laurencin, which began in 1908. The long poem of 295 lines is in six fairly distinct parts. Professor Leroy L. Breunig has convincingly demonstrated that the various parts were written at different times, and then placed together, in a fairly flexible sequence (cf. *La Table Ronde,* September, 1952). There are moments in the poem of tenderness, moments of recall when the poet's heart had been full of hope for the realization of his love. But **"La Chanson du Mal-Aimé"** is primarily a poem on the violence of suffering, of that special kind of suffering that comes from unreciprocated love. Everything that occurs to the lover, every encounter, every memory, brings back his love to him, and the knowledge that his life is, at least momentarily, emptied of every reason for living. This agony is extreme because the lover is alone and humiliated.

In a literal sense, the action begins in a London street, in the fall of 1903 (lines 1-25), just after Annie has told Apollinaire she will not marry him and is going to America; and it ends in Paris, in June, 1904 (lines 271-295), when the failure of his love is definitive and when his *romance du mal-aimé* takes its place beside other tragic love songs of the past.

The opening line resembles the beginning of a tale,

> Un soir de demi-brune à Londres,

but the rest of the stanza (lines 2-5) is a picture of startling violence in the street scene of London fog. A boy coming up to him and looking at him suggestively embarrasses the poet, but such is the power of his love that the boy (*voyou*) personifies Annie, and the poet follows him. The boy, his hands in his pockets, whistles and leads the way to what he obviously believes a facile conquest. But the boy disappears immediately from the poem as the violence of the poet's torment grows. The image that describes this torment is as sudden and spectacular as the unpredictable identification of Annie with a youthful male prostitute. The sinister walk in the London street suddenly becomes the flight of the Hebrews in Egypt. The space between the two rows of houses becomes the Red Sea. The waves have parted as in the Bible story. The poet's love, in the guise of a boy, is the Hebrews, and the poet himself is Pharaoh. The red bricks of the houses and the evening gas light in the fog permitted the tortured mind of the poet to make

this transformation. The reality of a street scene in 1903 is converted into the *Exodus* story of a flight from slavery.

> So the Israelites went through the midst of the sea dry-shod, with its waters towering up like a wall to right and left. (*Exodus* 14:22)

And we know the end of the story. We know that the Hebrews (the boy) escaped and the pursuer (Pharaoh) was destroyed when the waves crashed over him. This ending is not given in the poem, because it is not necessary. Only the violence and degradation are related.

The poet first gives an intimation of his fate by the analogy he establishes with Pharaoh: complete annihilation. And then, he wants, in one sustained cry (stanza 3), to declare the power of his love. The story of *Exodus* will still serve him. The reality of his feelings (of his suffering) is such that he calls upon the brick waves on either side of him to collapse if his love for Annie is not true. If she is not his one love, then he is the sovereign lord of Egypt,

> Je suis le souverain d'Egypte,

and moreover, to make the comparison more hyperbolic, he is his own sister-bride, his own army. He needs to utter an oath to testify to the truth of his love. An event in biblical history, the crossing of the Red Sea, is used to describe the face of reality.

In contrast with the examples of two faithful wives—Penelope waiting for the return of Ulysses and Sakontala waiting for the return of Dushmanta—the modern poet denounces the infidelity and cruelty of his love. In the eighth stanza, which terminates the initial scene in the London street, he thinks of those kings who had been happy in love,

> J'ai pensé à ces rois heureux,

and contrasts that happiness with the falseness of his own love: *le faux amour*. He has confused his love with the shadowy figures, first of a boy and then of a woman coming out of a pub. These strange encounters and the inevitable identification with Annie had distressed him, because his love is still strong.

The struggle is now clear. It is the effort of the poet to get beyond his suffering, to move beyond the memory of his life, and the persistence of this memory, the tenacity of his love. Sadness and anger alternate, because he calls Annie's infidelity a betrayal.

As this initial passage reaches its conclusion, the poet says farewell to this betrayal:

> Adieu, faux amour . . .

He has lost the woman he loved, and he knows he will not see her again. He raises his eyes from the street scene, and he forces his thoughts to move beyond the cases of history he has just evoked. He looks up at the sky in order to question the stars, as men have done since the earliest times when they are curious to know what their fate is to be.

In one of the most beautiful stanzas, which Apollinaire will repeat as a refrain near the end of the poem, he speaks to the Milky Way: *Voie lactée.* From the minuteness of the

London street scene, he looks up at the vast accumulation of stars and sees it as a whitish wave over the night sky. The stanza is both an intense meditation on how the suffering poet can move beyond his suffering and transcend it and an example of an extraordinary mingling of images. The Milky Way is called the luminous sister of the white rivers of Chanaan.

> Voie lactée ô soeur lumineuse
> Des blancs ruisseaux de Chanaan.

The whiteness of milk in *lactée* must have suggested to the poet the description of the Promised Land that God had given his people: "a land flowing with milk and honey." It is another allusion to the book of *Exodus* (chapter 3). In Greek mythology, the whiteness of the Milky Way was accounted for by the drops of milk that had fallen from the breast of Juno as she nursed Hercules.

The third line of the stanza is more surprising still. The Milky Way is also the sister of the white bodies of women in love:

> Et des corps blancs des amoureuses.

The poet is imagining his love as belonging, in time, to all other lovers, elevated to the heavens. He wonders whether he and other men, with great effort, swimming in death, will continue to follow the ones loved, like a river, rising toward other accumulations of stars in the heavens.

> Nageurs morts suivrons-nous d'ahan
> Ton cours vers d'autres nébuleuses.

The entire stanza is based upon the first word *Voie*, "way." Here, this word designates the ultimate way to be taken by lovers, in order to transcend momentary betrayals and disappointments. In France, the Milky Way (*voie lactée*) was once called *le chemin de Saint Jacques*, in honor of the famous medieval pilgrimage to Saint James of Compostella, in Spain. The stanza is a question, with its key verb: *suivrons-nous*—"shall we follow?" Will the poet's fate change after the failure of his love? With the word *ahan*, one senses the great effort necessary to bring about the change of fate, and once the change is made, the continuing effort afterward to reach some mysterious redemption. An answer is not given to the question.

Midway in the poem (vss. 166-170), a poignant stanza speaks of the double suffering of the poet in his spirit and in his flesh. The spirit is evoked by the unicorn (*la licorne*), associated with virginity, and the flesh, by the goat (*le capricorne*) or capricorn, associated with carnal desire.

> Douleur qui doubles les destins
> La licorne et le capricorne.

In the first line, the poet addresses his suffering and uses the unusual verb *doubler*. Suffering is so close to destiny, that it resembles a lining. It accompanies destiny as closely as a lining accompanies a coat. The body and its suffering, like a coat and its lining, like the duality of unicorn and capricorn, are called, in the third line, spirit and flesh:

> Mon âme et mon corps incertain
> Te fuient ô bûcher divin qu'ornent
> Des astres des fleurs du matin.

The adjective *incertain* is used to modify the body (*mon corps*) because of the body's double vocation of sanctification and sensuality. Suffering is here conceived of as a part of destiny, willed by the gods. And the poet's impulse is to avoid this sacrifice, this sacrificial fire. Suffering is designated as a strange ornamentation for the body, and the poet here is in revolt against it, and against the romantic cult of self-sacrifice.

The final stanza of the poem, used once previously in lines 91-95, is an important motif for the entire piece and a solution to the harassing problem of the suffering from love. It is not a conclusion, in a literal sense, but it is a statement about poetry and man's need to write poetry. It is perhaps the best answer that Apollinaire offers to the kind of violence from which he is suffering. The art of poetry is a science that has accompanied the entire history of man. Lyricism is a remedy, a magical incantation, a charm that permits man to live and to understand or at least to accept his fate.

In this refrain stanza, which is the last one heard in **"La Chanson du Mal-Aimé,"** nothing is concluded and everything begins again. This, after all, is the characteristic of a "song," and indeed of all of poetry, because the poet's ego, his particular dramas and sufferings and aspirations, are repeated in each reader. Already, in the *Voie lactée* stanza, Apollinaire had identified himself with his reader, and with all lovers living and dead: *Nageurs morts suivrons-nous*.

Auspiciously the stanza opens with the personal pronoun *moi*, but immediately the poet's personality is submerged in a series of names designating forms of poetry. Each of the five lines has one form of the poetic art: *lais, complaintes, hymnes, romance, chansons*. And each genre is succinctly defined:

1. *Moi qui sais des lais pour les reines.* The medieval *lays* were narrative poems of tragic love. The queen Marie de France herself wrote some of the most celebrated.

2. *Les complaintes de mes années.* A *complaint* is a personal poem, a chronicle of the poet's own life and usually of his own self-pity. The term today is often associated with Jules Laforgue.

3. *Des hymnes d'esclave aux murènes.* For the term *hymn*, Apollinaire makes a learned allusion to the Roman gastronome Vadius Pollion who, to punish a slave, had him thrown into a pool where he kept carnivorous fish called *murènes* (muraena or moray). A hymn is traditionally an entreaty, and in this verse doubtless stands for the prayer of the slave as he is being thrown to the sea monsters. It is a line of extreme violence in an otherwise subdued stanza.

4. *La romance du mal-aimé* is Apollinaire's own poem by means of which he places himself in the center of a long tradition and calls himself the man badly loved. This role he ascribes to himself is in each of the terms used to designate the poem—lay, complaint, hymn, romance, and, of course the word in the last line:

5. *Et des chansons pour le sirènes.* The fable of the Greek mythology and the Lorelei, of the seductresses leading the

mariners to their death, has its significance in Apollinaire's poem. The stanza is composed of all degrees of suffering from love, from the lover's complaint to the slave's useless exhortation for pardon before his violent death. In each case, the male is the sufferer, and the woman who is loved is reported as cruel and oblivious to her lover's torment.

The poet's fate is unjust, but it is a reduplication of a recognized fate. Lyricism has a soverign power to alleviate suffering, not only for the composer himself, for the poet who writes, but for the reader of the poem, who listens and assimilates his own with the poet's fate.

Before its appearance in *Alcools,* the poem **"Le Brasier,"** initially entitled *Le Pyrée,* had been published twice. Apollinaire had a predilection for this poem which he considered one of his most successful. It is a difficult piece, one of the richest in metaphor, one in which lines of regular versification are followed by free verse, and in which visions of fire and destruction are allied with theories of poetry. **"Le Brasier"** is a poem of violence and an *ars poetica* at the same time. It is an experiment in lyricism and also a commentary on a new type of humanism. Reality often seems to us discontinuous, an upsetting series of contrasts and contradictions, without an even motivation, without a unified functioning and a visible goal. Poetry, according to Apollinaire, may reproduce this effect of discontinuity, of violent contrasts, of experiences so different one from the other, that any meaning of experience seems impossible to ascertain. **"Le Brasier,"** of 1908, written at a time when Apollinaire was in love with the painter Marie Laurencin, is an example of the poet's art that tries to reproduce the convulsions of living, the destructions and the rebirths that figure in the reality of living.

The title itself, **"Le Brasier,"** evokes a funeral pyre, a burning brand, a sacrificial or purificatory ceremony. All the allusions are in the poem: the sorcerer's death and the heretic's, the phoenix rising up from its ashes, the concept of hell and eternal suffering, the heroism of suffering, the fire of love, both mystical love and passionate love. This poem, more directly than any other of Apollinaire, brings to mind *Les Illuminations* of Rimbaud, in the difficult intense passages of fire imagery where a human experience is metamorphosed into the experience of language.

The first part of the poem (vss. 1-25) is written in five-line stanzas, of octosyllabic lines. They are strong vigorous lines, a deliberately bold beginning, where the poet tells us he is casting into the fire the Past (a word he capitalizes and personifies.) The Past is a being, and the poet is obeying the will of the flame, the will of the "noble fire," in hurling into it the skulls representing what is dead in his past. Thus the poem opens with the destruction of the past, and the fire, the means of destruction, is worshiped by the poet. He dedicates the past to the power of the flames.

And immediately the entire cosmos is involved in this act. The stars are heard galloping across the skies, and this sound is mingled with the neighing of the male centaurs in their breeding grounds. All growing things, plants and trees, utter plaintive sounds. The fire ceremony of the first

stanza is accompanied by a vision of cosmic sexuality, in the second, where the forces of copulation are audible.

> Le galop soudain des étoiles
> . . . . .
> Se mêle au hennissement mâle
> Des centaures dans leurs haras
> Et des grandes plaintes végétales.

And then just as suddenly as the gallop of the astral bodies was heard, the poet turns inwardly, in the third stanza, in lines obviously reminiscent of Villon (with whom Apollinaire has so much in common) and the personal lament replaces the cosmic act of reproduction. He asks: Where are the lives he once lived?

> Où sont ces têtes que j'avais?

Where is the god of his youth?

> Où est le Dieu de ma jeunesse?

This god referred to is love, and he is named in the third line:

> L'amour est donc mauvais.

Love is no longer that force celebrated in **"La Chanson du Mal-Aimé."** It is bad. It has become a force of evil that has kept him from self-realization. The word *brasier* is now used, when the poet hopes to see flames reborn, as his soul is stripped and bared before the sun. The fire is indeed purificatory.

> Qu'au brasier les flammes renaissent
> Mon âme au soleil se dévêt.

The fourth stanza seems to justify this harsh interpretation of the third. The heads of the dead, which had designated the poet's past in the opening stanza,

> Ce passé ces têtes de morts,

are now called heads of women, or heads of his former loves, and they are the stars that have bled. The image of heads and stars is transported to the land (*Dans la plaine*) where the poet's heart, in its various incarnations, hangs like fruit on lemon trees. The entire stanza is startlingly similar to a surrealist picture by Tanguy or Magritte.

In the final stanza of this opening section, the poet seems at a great distance from the earth. He sees the river as if it were a ribbon pinned on the city:

> Le fleuve épinglé sur la ville.

The fire brings about this visual effect. The fire is comparable to a creator, to Orpheus who made the animals obey him, and to Amphion who, by playing on the lyre, made the stones of Thebes take their place on the ramparts.

> Partant à l'amphion docile.

This is a difficult line which means "at your departure, you obeyed Amphion." This peacefulness, this docility, where the flames take on all colors and invest the very stones with agility, is the creation of the poem.

> Tu subis tous les tons charmants
> Qui rendent les pierres agiles.

The fire (*le brasier*) is the force of rejuvenation, which begins by destruction. The poet has to be stripped and burned, as in a holocaust. He is, first, victim of the flames, and then he is his own metamorphosis, a new being, alone and separated. Everything seems, at first, in the poem, hermetic. But that is because the poet, in his propitiatory act, described in the five opening stanzas, is renewed and revived, and is facing the unknown. His death in the flames is cosmic. He is not alone there because he dies with and to the universe. But he is alone, afterward, in the rebirth, in the aesthetic rebirth of the poem. (pp. 173-87)

> *Wallace Fowlie, "Apollinaire: Violence of the Surreal," in his* Climate of Violence: The French Literary Tradition from Baudelaire to the Present, *The Macmillan Company, 1967, pp. 173-87.*

Gabriele Annan   (essay date 1976)

[*In the following excerpt, Annan suggests that* The Debauched Hospodar *is a surrealist farce.*]

Guillaume Apollinaire was famous for his jokes, an *enfant terrible* at a time of heavy competition in the field. The illegitimate child of an Italian-Swiss aristocrat and a Polish lady, he pretended to be her son by a prince of the Church: an anticlerical jest which makes it possible to identify him (up to a point) with the Romanian hero of *Les onze mille verges* who calls himself a prince although he is only a hospodar. Virginia Woolf and her friends sent up the establishment with the Dreadnought hoax: Apollinaire sent up the French literary world and himself with it by giving them bit parts in this pornographic novel. He wrote it and another in 1907 because he needed the money; he might have worked in a café, perhaps, or read proofs, but he had a friendly interest in erotic literature: in 1900 he had already written *Mirely ou le petit trou pas cher,* and he was shortly to edit and write the introductions for two collections of licentious writings by authors ranging from Pietro Aretino through John Cleland to Sade.

Les onze mille verges was edited and moved up on to the counter in 1973 by Michel Décaudin who had brought out the collected official works in 1966. . . . [The novel offers] every conceivable combination of buggery, pederasty, coprophily, necrophily, incest and sexual murder. Perversions and bodies, dead and alive, pile up like a huge gâteau St Honoré. The book seems to inspire culinary metaphors. Richard N. Coe, in his introduction [to Nina Rootes' English translation of the novel], talks about "indigestible erotic hunks [dissolving] in the pungent broth of their own inherent absurdity". . . . [The] lashings (literally) of sex crammed into the [short book mean] . . . that the tempo has to be lightning picaresque: but then so it is in most pornographic novels. . . .

"Fucking is always much the same", Steven Marcus glumly observed in his book on Victorian pornography. But . . . this is fucking with a difference—a cheerful sadistic romp. Pornographic romps are common, with or without flagellation, but serious sadism has to be taken seriously and most sadistic novels are joke-free *romans noirs*. This was a new genre: a surrealist farce. (Apollinaire after

all invented the term "surrealist"; could he also be the inventor of the bad taste joke?)

Another new genre emerging at the time was social realist pornography: in the famous Austrian novel *Josephine Mutzenbacher* you can smell the sauerkraut on the staircase of the tenement where the heroine lives. Apollinaire's novel has no elements of social or psychological realism whatsoever, but it has links with real history: the murder of the Yugoslav Obrenovic dynasty comes into it, and the hero fights and dies in the Russo-Japanese War. But these events serve only to undermine the reality of the fantasy world where the streets are peopled with girls called Culculine. Apollinaire is playing with reality-unreality and using a collage technique to do it. He pastes in historical events as Braque pastes in newspaper cuttings. He also pastes in the names of real though obscure people, bestowing them on his fictional characters. Professor Coe has traced some of these "intermediate characters", as he calls them, with the help of the librarian of the School of Slavonic Studies and by consulting old Russian army staff lists. "A quand *Les onze mille verges* dans les programmes universitaires?" asks M Décaudin. Any time now.

The "intermediates" from remote pockets of the Slav world are a very recondite and therefore safe joke. Apollinaire went further and used the attributes, with barely disguised names, of people from his own milieu: two Symbolist poets keep a brothel in Port Arthur and an actress from the Comédie Française joins in a sleeping-car orgy. In addition to these *Private Eye* antics the book is riddled with private jokes and joking allusions to gossip and literature (a line from Corneille, for instance, is embedded in a sexy sonnet by the Romanian prince). The very title of the book is a pun: *verge* means rod as well as prick, and the 11,000 refers to St Ursula and her virgins (or *vierges*).

> *Gabriele Annan, "The Surreal Thing," in* The Times Literary Supplement, *No. 3863, March 26, 1976, p. 339.*

Ronald Hayman   (essay date 1976)

[*A prolific English biographer and drama scholar, Hayman has written about the lives of such noted literary figures as Bertolt Brecht, Franz Kafka, Friedrich Nietzsche, Jean-Paul Sartre, and the Marquis de Sade. His writings on theater include* Techniques of Acting *(1969) and* How to Read a Play *(1977) as well as many works on contemporary playwrights such as Eugene Ionesco, Samuel Beckett, Harold Pinter, Arthur Miller, and Edward Albee. In the following excerpt, Hayman finds that Apollinaire blurs the distinction between reality and unreality in* The Debauched Hospodar.]

Apollinaire, who predicted in 1909 that Sade might come to dominate the 20th century, also made the point that he was still being read in the wrong way: no one seemed capable of looking beneath the disgusting surface. Apollinaire's own novel *Les onze mille verges,* which was written in 1907 when he was 27, is more disgusting, more shocking, more economical and more poetically inspired. It contains a charming description of a small Japanese prostitute who draws her knees up towards her stomach and opens her legs as if they were pages in a book. The early chapters are written with an engaging lightness of touch which depends partly on the comic intrusions of everyday reality. Horses fart. Birds sing. A cab-driver interrupts an orgy of flagellation to reclaim his whip. A trio of fellatio and coprophilia becomes a quintet after two burglars have broken in.

At first Apollinaire's narrative is, like Sade's, finely balanced between relish and disgust. Both dwell lovingly on the holes and corners of human experience which are conventionally relegated to distasteful silence, but Apollinaire deliberately upsets the balance which Sade holds. The Sadean progression is accumulative and, [as Roland Barthes argues in *The Pleasure of the Text*], the irony depends on the fastidious combination of rawness and rhetoric to scorch away the patina left by centuries of literary politeness. Apollinaire's strategy is to let the disgust gradually come to outweigh the relish as he pours in more and more elements of contemporary reality, using Balkan politics to curdle the pornographic fantasy. There is a high-spirited, highly fictional account of a perverted orgy which involves members of the secret society that factually organised the assassination of the King and Queen of Serbia in 1903. The Russo-Japanese war looms large in the novel's final sequences, creating an uncomfortable confusion between the casual slaughter that had become normal in contemporary history and the casual slaughter that has become normal in the fiction after abnormal sexual appetites have been sated. [In *Violence in the Arts,* John Fraser] compares Sade's fantastication of violence with the modern newspaper's desiccation of the real thing; Apollinaire was exploiting the real thing to make his fantasies all the more vicious. (pp. 73-4)

> *Ronald Hayman, "Holes and Corners," in* Encounter, *Vol. XLVII, No. 1, July, 1976, pp. 71-6.*

Roger Little   (essay date 1976)

[*In the following excerpt, Little examines Apollinaire's originality as evidenced in his fiction and the drama* The Breasts of Tiresias.]

Reverting to the *Œuvres complètes* as our basic source of reference, we turn . . . to Apollinaire as prose writer and dramatist. In both fields he nonetheless remained very much the poet in so far as he continued to show an active interest in the obscurer byways of language and continued to attitudinise, as if anything goes once the label 'Poète: appellation contrôlée' has been stuck on. Beyond a certain amount of posturing, however, we find not only an agreeable companion but an accomplished raconteur. The easygoing charm suggested by a title such as *Le Flâneur des deux rives,* a collection of relaxed anecdotal tales of odd corners of the Paris Apollinaire loved, sets the tone. Yet in another way the straining always remains, and is perhaps a function of the poet's ambiguous attitude towards originality: on the one hand he is happy to adopt and adapt the time-honoured themes of myth and folklore while on the other he is at visible pains to make his mark. As in the poems, he proves himself most at ease and most successful in an albeit limited way when he allows his sense of tradition to absorb his self-consciousness.

I propose in this [essay] to look first at *L'Enchanteur pourrissant,* 'ce testament de [sa] première esthétique', then at aspects of the short stories collected in *L'Hérésiarque et Cie, Le Poète assassiné* and *Contes retrouvés.* To close, I shall consider the only one of Apollinaire's plays which seems to warrant attention in the context of the present [discussion]: *Les Mamelles de Tirésias.*

L'Enchanteur pourrissant first appeared in serial form in *Le Festin d'Esope* in 1904 and in a limited de luxe edition illustrated by André Derain in 1909, but probably dates back to 1898 in conception and partial composition. 'Onirocritique' was added as a tailpiece for the book version. Based on the thirteenth-century prose *Merlin,* an embroidered development of the Arthurian wizard with certain direct or symbolic links with Apollinaire— illegitimate birth, magical powers, captivation (metaphorical or literal) by a woman—the tale is a loosely-knit sequence of visits paid to the magician's tomb. Buried there by a woman's treachery, he is both dead and alive, being immortal. The effect of the visitations is episodic and chaotic, but the central message of the tortuous rigmarole is clear: man and woman are doomed to a separation which no love can bridge. The closing dialogue between Merlin and the Lady of the Lake underlines the possessive urge on either side, an urge which turns equality into rivalry and love into a kind of death. 'L'homme est au centre de notre éloignement; nous l'entourons comme un cercle. . . . Au lieu de cette bonne vie au centre de notre éloignement, il préfère chercher à nous saisir afin que l'on s'entr'aime'. The circle is indeed a vicious one. Each sees the other as 'décevant et déloyal'. The array of witnesses that Apollinaire brings trooping on—animals, druids, Morgan Le Fay, sphinxes, three fake Wise Men, Medea, Helen, heavenly choirs, the archangel Michael, monsters, Empedocles and some of the characters mentioned in **'Zone'** such as 'Enoch Elie Apollonius de Tyane' and Simon Magus ('ai-je beaucoup de noms compris?')—serve mostly to emphasise the inevitability of the pessimistic conclusion. But they, and many more I have not listed, also create the chaos which corresponds to the writer's magical powers of evocation from his eclectic reading. The principle of selection yields here to the principle of unrestrained syncretism validated by the choice of so universal a theme that creative selectivity is made almost irrelevant. It leads of course to a lack of focus but also shows an imagination brimming over with ideas, even if these are usually borrowed.

'Onirocritique' takes up the major theme—'j'avais la conscience des éternités différentes de l'homme et de la femme'—in a condensed dream sequence not without its echoes of traditional legend but not overtly parading this in the manner of the body of the work. Surrealists and psychoanalysts find much to interest them and exegetes of **'La Chanson du mal-aimé'** note the name Sainte-Fabeau related here to the tongues of chestnut-coloured snakes and in **'Les Sept Epées'** to the fifth sword, 'un cyprès sur un tombeau', 'un flambeau'. All these images merge life and death, and all may be interpreted as phallic. All of them too are set in an unreal context with elements of fairy-tale and little evident relationship to material reality. Magic, dreaming, wishful thinking, psychosis? Eeny, meeny, miney, mo . . .

Isaac Laquedem (the Wandering Jew) and Simon Magus reappear in stories collected in *L'Hérésiarque et Cie,* 'Le Passant de Prague' and 'Simon Mage' respectively. The three kings figure indirectly in 'La Rose de Hildesheim ou les trésors des Rois Mages' and direct echoes of *L'Enchanteur pourrissant* might still be heard in a story in *Le Poète assassiné,* 'Arthur roi passé roi futur'. Such continuity of reference and preoccupation, while perfectly acceptable and understandable in itself, suggests that some failure in imaginative renewal may have contributed more importantly than any physical injury to the relative dullness and unoriginality in Apollinaire's writing, thinking and, according to his friends, personality after 1916.

Rather than attempt to survey the fifty or so short stories collected in the *Œuvres complètes,* I propose to illustrate three major elements in them, namely Apollinaire's use of myth and legend, his unashamed eroticism, and his interest in language. His frequent recourse to traditional mythology, legend and folklore as the narrative basis for his tales is not necessarily the mark of a lack of imagination. Rather does it suggest that Apollinaire wished to reserve his imaginative effort for other aspects of his writing. Yet it does indicate his familiarity with and respect for traditional narrative patterns, and indeed the structures of his short stories rarely depart from those analysed in folktales by Vladimir Propp [in his *Morphology of the Folktale*]. Repentance (in 'Le Juif latin') and virtue ('L'Infailibilité') are rewarded; lovers are reunited ('Le Cigare romanesque') or spited ('La Rose de Hildesheim'); poets die ('La Serviette des poètes') and priests procure to maintain a tradition ('L'Otmika') or beget a hermaphrodite monster ('D'un monstre à Lyon ou l'envie'); paradoxes (of the criminal's 'sanctity' in 'Le Juif latin', of Orfei's gluttony and mortification in 'L'Hérésiarque') and coincidences (e.g. in 'Histoire d'une famille vertueuse, d'une hotte et d'un calcul') abound; gruesome interest is shown in the impaling of a lovely boy ('Le Giton'), in gratuitous violence ('Un beau film') and in the eating of human flesh ('Cox-City'); the Holy Trinity appears (in 'L'Hérésiarque') as does the eternal triangle (e.g. in 'La Disparition d'Honoré Subrac' and 'Le Matelot d'Amsterdam'); and the supernatural which so appealed to nineteenth-century writers frequently figures. These examples taken from *L'Hérésiarque et Cie* could not only be multiplied by reference to later stories but their development and pursuit traced in them.

One less traditional and rather revealing subject which occurs in the later collections is pseudo-science or scientific experiment that is monstrously abused. Just as the evangelising obsession of the botanist Horace Tograth in 'Le Poète assassiné' leads to totalitarian intolerance and Croniamental's death, so in 'Train de guerre' people are wired up to produce energy, in 'Le Toucher à distance' a discovery is abused and brings about a false second coming, in 'L'Orangeade' a doctor kills his patient to discover how he has managed to cure him, and in 'Chirurgie esthé-

tique' the monsters of mythology are brought to life by the liberal addition of eyes, noses and teeth presented in a dead-pan manner that distances the monstrosity only by setting the tale in Alaska. Such reference to science, along with tales where men become invisible (e.g. 'La Disparition d'Honoré Subrac') and others where a 'time machine' is brought into play (e.g., 'Traitsment thyroïdien'), seem to reflect familiarity with the work of H. G. Wells whom Apollinaire asks in November 1915 to 'indiquer un moyen pratique de réaliser la machine à explorer le temps et l'homme invisible, procédés qui rendraient les plus grands services dans cette guerre'. It is a war in which, as we remember from 'Il y a' in *Calligrammes,* 'l'art de l'invisibilité' plays an important role. Just so there is much artlessness concealing art in Apollinaire's stories, and the art might go unnoticed were it not that in a relatively undemanding and usually entertaining way it proves a good companion to our leisure. If we are looking for variety of tone and topic—the pathetic interspersed with the outrageous, the erotic with the exotic, the quest with the discovery—in a language always alert and sometimes very self-aware, we are likely to find Apollinaire's prose pleasant reading.

If, in addition, we are titillated by licentious tales where men are men and women are horizontal, Apollinaire will also prove stimulating if again unoriginal. Yet he clearly enjoys his literary eroticism: it is not simply for him a means of earning necessary extra cash. In the short stories there is already some variety of intercourse and the occasional homosexual ('La Rencontre au cercle mixte') or pederastic ('Le Giton') implication. There is the same breezy gusto about sexuality as one finds in such medieval or Renaissance tales as *Les Cent Nouvelles Nouvelles* or those of Chaucer, Boccaccio or Rabelais. Aretino and Sade, for whose works Apollinaire wrote introductions of no mean interest, are part of the tradition continued here. The lusty relish should not be taken, in a cold climate, to be the over-compensation for puritanical repressions: it is the frank enjoyment of an Italo-Slav. Yet, as Apollinaire reminds us, 'Il serait injuste d'attribuer à un auteur tout ce qu'il lui plaît de prêter aux personnages de son imagination'. At least we may say that all the written evidence suggests a sustained interest in sexual matters and in a wide range of sexual practices. Repetition would be even more tedious were it not often accompanied by humour, sexual intercourse generally being treated not as an end in itself (as is the tendency in pornography) but as a narrative means. In this respect, the uncollected *Les Onze Mille Verges* is exemplary, being a sheer escapist romp. *La Fin de Babylone* (of disputed attribution and again not collected in the *Œuvres complètes*) relies less on fantasy and humour and more on the exotic lure of an escapist 'mystic orient'. *Les Trois Don Juan* is a re-telling of the well-known tale as handled by Tirso de Molina, Mérimée and Byron. A dash of Molière adds flavour, but the mixture smacks essentially of Apollinaire's particular sense of humour and eroticism. No apology is made for borrowing from *El Burlador de Sevilla, Les Ames du purgatoire, Don Juan* and *Dom Juan,* and clearly Apollinaire considered none necessary. Such archetypes belonged to the public domain and could be re-used and re-fashioned at will.

What gives such work its interest is the particular tone and style created by the language, and it is here that we detect the poet behind the *prosateur*. Not only is there precision and elegance, there is also a conscious display of language. This shows in the rare words Apollinaire is so fond of, in verbal play, and in the use of dialects for particular effect. Several rare words featuring in the poems also occur in the prose. 'Egypans' and 'pyraustes' will be recalled from **'La Chanson du mal-aimé'**; in **'Que vlo-ve?'** one finds both 'la maclotte' (cf. **'Marie'**) and 'les pouhons' (cf. **'La Petite Auto'**). Apollinaire is clearly no more afraid than Jules Verne of stepping outside the average reader's lexical range to heighten the effect of strangeness and wonder while still hoping to win popularity. Yet there is often a gratuitous element in Apollinaire's choice, even if this is governed by euphonic considerations, and opacity increases the more he departs from a recognisably French word: consider the sequence 'feuilloler', 'foleur', 'înel', 'pihis'. Apollinaire's delight in language is anecdotal rather than profound: he uses his disparate knowledge to surprise and impress. Yet that delight is real enough. In **'Simon Mage'** palindromes are accorded magical significance beyond the simple play of letters. In **'La Lèpre'** the coincidence of the words for 'leprosy' and 'hare' in Italian provides the basis of the tale. Puns abound, 'le calembour créateur' of Apollinaire's poetry, suggesting once again a poet's interest in the texture of words as well as their primary sense. Certainly this is also the case, though in an essentially serious way, where Apollinaire's ear for particular modes of speech, and notably of dialects, gives rise to writing of enormous brio as he transcribes such speech to give a special flavour as well as local colour to his work. Here, his international background and sojourns in various parts of Europe play an important part. But most of all he reveals an extraordinary capacity to listen and transcribe carefully. Like a thieving jackdaw he seizes jewels and gewgaws alike, but the power of such tales as **'Que vlo-ve?'** and **'Les Pèlerins piémontais'** is undoubtedly heightened by Apollinaire's appropriation of language to his subject.

A more ambitious tale like **'Le Poète assassiné'** mixes these ingredients as before, but its extra length taxes Apollinaire's narrative inventiveness. It becomes episodic and shows more clearly its dependence on earlier models. Rabelais is much in evidence, not only in the biographical presentation of the Gargantuan hero, Croniamental, but also in many a point of detail. (pp. 73-8)

It is scarcely surprising that Apollinaire should have proved good company to his friends nor indeed that they should have served as models for some of his characters. In Tristouse Balerinette and l'oiseau du Bénin of **'Le Poète assassiné'** we have evocations of Marie Laurencin and Pablo Picasso. Picasso figures too as Pablo Canouris with Moïse Deléchelle (Max Jacob—'de l'échelle'!) in *La Femme assise,* an even less thinly-veiled autobiographical narrative recalling Apollinaire's *belle époque*. While it is of some interest to have Apollinaire's reminiscences of Picasso and others, it may be taken that the tale in itself is of only passing concern: as prose it is remembered mostly by the cultural historian of the period.

Only specialists too seem to resuscitate *Les Mamelles de Tirésias* and I am bound to say I think it a shame, for it has a boisterous roistering quality about it which makes it no less a romp in performance than its illustrious predecessor, Jarry's *Ubu roi.* Both plays are episodic, both borrow from medieval sources and both offer the slapstick fun of the circus ring and belly-laughs galore. Many an Artaud theory is there anticipated, and likewise many a *nouveau théâtre* play. The story is slight and vulgar, the repopulation of France after the depredations of war. If it has its serious side, Apollinaire reserves it for the prefatory remarks; in the play itself, the proliferation (in the Ionesco manner) of balloons symbolic of breasts bears the message of the farce to an appropriately festive conclusion. The interest of the play, it must be confessed, lies not so much in the body of it, written in 1903, as in the prologue, added in late 1916. In it, the 'directeur de la troupe' presents certain ideas about the theatre which, while borrowing something from the recent production of *Parade* (which had its première on 8 May 1917 and for which Apollinaire wrote a programme note using the word 'surréalisme' for the first time,) suggests the main lines of a theatrical programme which have been fruitfully pursued and as yet by no means exhausted. In *Parade,* the result of collaboration between Picasso, Erik Satie, Leonid Massine and Jean Cocteau, Apollinaire saw an expression of his own theories about 'l'Esprit nouveau' and looked forward to 'l'allégresse universelle'. In his prologue to *Les Mamelles de Tirésias,* he clearly hopes to persuade his readers and spectators that the following pantomime partakes of the new spirit, and while in the event we are hardly persuaded, some passages from the prologue . . . show not only how proficient an exponent of the latest ideas Apollinaire can be but also how seminal may prove even apparently outrageous experiments and attitudes. . . . (pp. 80-1)

The stage Apollinaire imagines, a theatre in the round with a central stage and a second circular one around the outside of the audience, may not have been constructed but in effect has been used in many a production still considered experimental. The collaboration of different arts with a view to 'total theatre' is equally familiar now, owing more to the circus and music hall than to the traditional proscenium-arch theatre, and developed in their different areas by such innovators, theorists and practitioners as Claudel, Artaud and Jean-Louis Barrault. Part of Apollinaire's programme is a specific reversal of the time-honoured neo-classical norms of the French theatre: he calls for variety of tone (such as many a neo-classical French critic condemned in Shakespeare), 'l'usage raisonnable des invraisemblances', and rejection of the unities of time, place and action. Such an overthrow of established conventions is a healthy and necessary step which we should not condemn just because it might lead to a different but equally limiting orthodoxy. For it in turn would be overthrown either by the swing of the pendulum of fashion or by the creative iconoclasm of a new Apollinaire. (pp. 82-3)

Roger Little, in his Guillaume Apollinaire, *The Athlone Press, 1976, 145 p.*

Apollinaire on the modern art of his native France:

The art of today invests its creations in a grandiose, monumental appearance, which in this regard goes beyond all that which has been conceived by the artists of the preceding epochs. Moreover, there is no trace of exoticism in this art. Certainly our young artists are acquainted with the works of Chinese art, the images of the Negroes and Australians, the trifles of Islamic art, but one finds no trace of any of these influences in their works, nor of primitive Italian or German painters. Contemporary French art was born spontaneously on French soil. And this proves the vitality of the French nation, that it is far from decadence. One could easily establish a parallel between this contemporary French art and Gothic art, which has scattered admirable monuments upon the soil of France and throughout all Europe. The Greek and Italian influences are finished. Here is the renaissance of French art, that is to say, the renaissance of Gothic art, and spontaneously, without the appearance of a pastiche. Today's art is attached to Gothic art through all which the intermediate schools have had of the genuinely French quality, from Poussin to Ingres, from Delacroix to Manet, from Cézanne to Seurat, from Renoir to the *Douanier* Rousseau, that humble but so expressive and poetic expression of French art.

The vitality of this energetic and infinite art which has issued from the soil of France offers us a marvelous spectacle. But no one is a prophet in his own country and this is why it encounters here more resistance than everywhere else.

Guillaume Apollinaire, in "The New Painting," Les Soirées de Paris, May 1912.

Annabelle Henkin Melzer   (essay date 1977)

[*In the following essay, Melzer recounts the premiere of Apollinaire's* The Breasts of Tiresias; *declaring the play a pioneering work in surrealism, she describes the immediate impact of the June 24, 1917 performance.*]

By 1917, the year of the premiere of his first full-length play, **Les Mamelles de Tirésias,** Guillaume Apollinaire was the main French impresario of the avant-garde. It was thanks to him that Picasso and Braque met in 1907. As early as 1909, he had written the first major article to be published on the eccentric Alfred Jarry, and it was he who helped organize the cubist Room 41 at the 'Salon des Indépendents' of 1911. In 1912 he vacationed with the Spanish painter Picabia who, for his work at the 'Salon d'Automne', had received the dubious plaudit, 'The prize for idiocy this year is retained by M. Picabia' [*The Paris Journal*, 30 September 1912], and met with the Italian painter de Chirico who had written, 'to become truly immortal, a work of art must escape all human limits, logic and common sense will only interfere'.

Apollinaire had baptized orphism, moved in the centre of the simultaneist movement, and was a staunch supporter of futurism—his own futurist manifesto, **'L'anti-tradition futuriste',** proclaiming 'suppression of poetic grief in syntax, punctuation, lines and verses, houses, boredom'. He had launched and directed the journal *Soirées de Paris,*

one of the principal organs of the avant-garde before the war, had promoted the dada poems of Tristan Tzara in the review *Nord-Sud,* and in 1917, barely a month before the opening of **Les Mamelles,** was attending rehearsals of the Diaghilev-Picasso-Satie-Cocteau ballet *Parade,* for which he wrote the programme's **'Introduction'.** He was, in *plein pouvoir,* a dean of the 'esprit nouveau'.

Naturally, Apollinaire had a coterie of followers, and when, on Sunday 24 June 1917, the small theatre of the Conservatoire Renée Maubel on the rue de l'Orient in Montmartre opened its doors for the premiere of his first play—'drame surréaliste en deux actes et un prologue, choeurs, musiques et costumes selon l'esprit nouveau'—an audience of nearly fire hundred artists, poets, critics, and bizarre types seized on the opportunity to revel amidst the grim sobreity of wartime Paris.

Among the crowd that late afternoon were Paul Fort, Gallimard and Mme. Rachilde (who had promoted Jarry's *Ubu*), André Breton and Louis Aragon (twenty-one and twenty-two years old, and just introduced to Tzara's dada poems *chez* Apollinaire), the actors Pierre Bertin and Louise Lara (who arrived by bicycle), and the critics of all the major newspapers—all the 'opinion parisienne'. While a number of the guests finished their aperitifs at the nearby cafés, Apollinaire moved among the crowd. Eye-catching dress was *de rigueur.* Mme. Maubel, mistress of the conservatory, wore a dress of 'violent emerald', and two young ladies, 'conspicuously cubists', painted their faces a raw yellow while smearing their eyelids with blue. The critic of *La Rampe* afterwards lamented:

> How I regretted not having sported a suit the colour of unripe lemon and a red paper gendarme's hat. One can't think of everything. [12 July 1917]

Jean Cocteau was there as well, but rather sombre—barely having recovered from the excitement generated by his ballet *Parade,* produced a month earlier.

It is not surprising that Apollinaire's 'drame surréaliste' was compared to the Cocteau-Picasso-Satie work. Here again was that new word 'surréaliste' which Apollinaire had first employed in his **'Introduction'** to the programme of *Parade,* though many people saw the text of **Les Mamelles** as a rather conventional *pièce a thèse:*

> Essentially Guillaume Apollinaire is a traditionalist, and beneath the apparent disorder of ideas, beneath his raucous clowning, fantasy, and guignol, he demands a return to order. [Guillot de Szis, *Le Théâtre,* 29 June 1917]

There was, however, no doubt that the production was directly in line with such scandal-evoking 'cubist' events as were produced by the Diaghilev ballet.

> The novelty of this play, so violently drafted, is less in the subject matter, which wants to be merely an interesting fantasy, than in the synthetic decor which envelopes it. [Jean Gourmont, *Mercure de France,* 25 June 1917]

The masks, the patchwork houses of the backdrop, the gendarme's horse, were all reminiscent of Picasso's designs for *Parade,* which Apollinaire, in his **'Introduction'**, had signalled as having for the first time achieved an alliance with theatre that heralded a more comprehensive art to come:

> This new alliance—I say new, because until now scenery and costumes were linked only by factitious bonds—has given rise, in *Parade,* to a kind of sur-realism which I consider to be the point of departure for a whole series of manifestations of the New Spirit that is making itself felt today, and that will certainly appeal to our best minds.

Parade was, for Apollinaire, a work in which the traditional limits of art had fallen by the wayside. Collage had already brought nails and newsprint to the canvas, and 'extraplastic phenomena' such as noise were considered a new part of painting as well. Now painting was beginning to change the movement of performers on the stage. In 1913, a conservative critic stated that in Debussy's *Jeux,* Nijinsky had forced himself and his two female partners into cubist distortions: that he had 'twisted Karsavina's precious limbs in the name of Matisse, Metzinger, and Picasso'.

Although the static architecture of cubism was fundamentally opposed to the representation of movement in the action of a play, this school of art had succeeded in proposing a new relationship to space. Volumes now unfolded themselves on a flat surface and several views of the same object became common. Apollinaire's sympathies lay with both the analytic and the synthetic tendencies of cubism— the first reconstructing the world of nature according to the rigid rules of geometry, and best represented by the French Braque, Gleizes, and Metzinger, the second stressing creation, surprise, and spontaneity as in the works of the Spanish Picasso, Gris, and Picabia. But it was finally Picasso, with his concept for the Managers in *Parade*— carrying sets and costumes as one on their backs, blurring the line between actor and object—who found the way to advance beyond collage and step over into movement and performance.

With such models of experimentation in mind, the expectations of the spectators at the *Les Mamelles* premiere were high, and inside the hall the audience, primed with anticipation, was restless. Stamping feet demanded that the play begin, while outside the theatre an angry crowd who could not get in banged on the locked doors. Pierre Albert-Birot, editor of the avant-garde journal *SIC,* which had sponsored the performance, later published an apology:

> We sincerely apologize to the people who could not get in, for it was only with the greatest regret that we shut the doors—but the additional number of spectators in the hall was such, that we were compelled to make this radical decision so as to avoid riots or accidents. [*SIC,* 18 June 1917]

Aragon, speaking for those who did get in, later wrote, 'one expected anything—it was something else' ['Le 24 juin 1917', *SIC,* 27 May 1918].

Admission was free, but the public was required to pay one franc for a programme which bore a suggestive drawing by Picasso, and a Matisse woodcut. A classic blue curtain hid the stage and amidst the tumult, Mme. Rachilde called out, 'The curtain is too blue . . . remove the blue'. Finally a somberly dressed Edmond Valée, in the role of the 'director', emerged from the prompter's box to vaunt in the medieval tradition—'So here I am once more among you'—and to deliver the prologue. Apollinaire's invitation in this prologue to his French comrades to recall the tragedies of war was later unanimously commended:

> remarkable—an ardent poem in which is inscribed the tragic mirage of a night of war. . . . [*L'heure,* 26 June 1917]

But no one seems to have noticed the author's use of the prologue to propose a new kind of theatre as well: 'a theatre in the round with two stages, one at the centre, the other surrounding the spectators.' No one, that is, but the management of *SIC,* whose invitations for that afternoon proposed that the public also attend a lecture entitled 'The spirit of the avant-garde (a propos cubism, futurism, and nunism.)'

'Nunism', derived from the Greek word *nun* (now), was the name Pierre Albert-Birot had given to his own study of a new type of theatre, 'le théâtre nunique.' In a number of brief articles which he published in *SIC,* Albert-Birot described this theatre: having left the three unities behind, it would now focus on acrobatics, sounds, projections, pantomimes, and cinematographic elements. It would be a 'grand simultaneity', encompassing all the methods and all the emotions capable of communicating life in its vitality and intensity to the spectator. In order to convey this intensity, multiple actions would take place simultaneously on stage as well as in the auditorium.

Being bound to no unity of time or place, these scenes could take place, 'in Paris, in New York, in Tokyo, in a house, beneath the sea, underground, in the air, in prehistoric times, in the middle-ages, in 1916, in the year 2,000.' The scenes would therefore be set by light alone using a wide palette of colours to create the appropriate atmosphere. The theatre area itself would be a vast circus-like expanse with the audience placed at the centre, while on a rotating platform on the periphery, the actors would play their various scenes. It is quite likely that Apollinaire was influenced by Albert-Birot's concept of the Nunique stage when he described his new theatre as:

> A circular theatre with two stages
> One in the middle and the other like a ring
> Around the spectators permitting
> The free unfolding of our modern art
> Often connecting in unseen ways as in life
> Sounds gestures colours cries tumults
> Music dancing acrobatics poetry painting
> Choruses actions and multiple sets
>   [Prologue to ***The Breasts of Tiresias***]

and a year previous, in an interview in *SIC,* he had already advocated a type of circus theatre which would have a more widespread appeal because of its new simplicity and broad effects.

Albert-Birot relates that it was he, in 1916, who asked Apollinaire to write, for production and publication by

SIC, a play that would illustrate some of Apollinaire's own theatrical ideas, including the wish he had one day expressed that the theatre of the future be free of 'odious realism'. He claims as well to have been influential in Apollinaire's choosing the phrase 'surréaliste' for his first play:

> When Apollinire and I, in 1917, searched for a term to describe **Les Mamelles de Tirésias,** Apollinaire suggested 'surnaturaliste', and I cried out, No! No!, 'surnaturalisme' is something entirely different. In principle, the 'surnaturel' is a miracle. Immediately Apollinaire replied, 'That's right—let's put in then "drame surréaliste".'

It was only at the last minute that the word was rushed to the printer.

Whatever the source of the inspiration, Apollinaire, in his own defence of the term, wrote: 'Surrealism is not yet in the dictionary and it will be more convenient than "Surnaturalisme", which is already used by the philosophers'. As for the meaning of the word, he wrote:

> In order to attempt, if not a renovation of the theatre, at least an original effort, I thought it necessary to come back to nature itself, but without copying it photographically. When man wanted to imitate walking he created the wheel which does not resemble a leg. In the same way he has created surrealisme. . . . ['Preface', *The Breasts of Tiresias*]

Albert-Birot's strong involvement in the project, however, is undeniable. Even his wife, Germaine, wrote the music for the piece. As for the directing of the play, it seems to have been a joint effort, with Albert-Birot largely responsible but with Apollinaire himself taking an active part. In an article written on the production of the poet's following play *Coleur de Temps,* Albert-Birot expresses regret that, because of his illness, Apollinaire, unlike in his work on *Tirésias,* could not take part 'in the vital process of creation inspired by the rehearsals themselves'. ['*Couleur du temps:* drame de Guillaume Apollinaire', *SIC,* 36 December 1918]

The overture to Apollinaire's play about Thérèse, who rejects her female functions in order to do as she pleases ('Just because you made love to me in Connecticut / Doesn't mean I have to cook for you in Zanzibar'), was begun on a piano (the full score for orchestra was not executed because of the difficulty of obtaining musicians during the war), and the curtain rose on the market place in Zanzibar. Long stripes of coloured paper, patched with rectangles of contrasting colours, 'à la Gaugin cubiste', covered the wings. When asked to explain the small, irregularly pasted squares, Serge Férat, the painter and designer, answered:

> Those, why they're windows, and look, that piece of blue paper there on the white rectangle—it's a curtain behind the window. It's all to indicate the intimacy of a family setting. [*La Rampe,* 12 July 1917]

At stage left stood an actor-cum-newstand, covered with newspapers of the day: *Le Journal, L'Action Française,*

Paris-Midi. At the back were scrawled illegible inscriptions in red, green, yellow and blue. When asked how he had put the set together, Férat ingenuously replied, 'Lord—I bought seven francs worth of paper which I cut up—that's all'.

The costumed characters and their activities were no less startling. Thérèse-Tirésias entered in black face with a long dress on which the painter Irène Lagut had splashed highly-coloured tropical fruits. With her she carried all those 'instruments' relating to her role as housewife, and as a climax to her opening tirade against the making of children, she removed the two huge celluloid balloons—her breasts—and threw them to a startled audience as a beard suddenly shot up about her face. The crowd went wild. A baby started to cry and someone shouted, 'Pass him your breasts, Tiresias . . . the baby wants some milk.' 'If it's ugliness he wants', a nearby scoffer replied, 'why, that's already been served up!'

Meanwhile, upstage, [an actor], in red-face, playing the role of 'the people of Zanzibar', occupied himself with all manner of musical sound effects, using a toy flute, cymbals, an accordion, wood blocks, and broken dishes to punctuate the speeches of the actors. Niny Guyard backed him up with eccentric and dissonant music on a piano which stood on stage throughout the entire performance.

Having thrown all her household utensils at the audience, Thérèse achieved the final transformation into Tirésias by forcibly dressing her husband in her own clothes. Simultaneously, in the auditorium, Messrs. Presto and Lacouf, two bourgeois, started a quarrel as to whether they were in Paris or in Zanzibar. The audience soon joined in shouting invectives. The two mounted the stage to fight a duel which finished them both off, while Tirésias, frightened by the noise, ran off. A gendarme (Juliette Norville), astride a cardboard horse, entered to restore order and wound up seducing the husband in drag, while the latter, still raging at his wife's refusal to bear more children, cried out: 'If woman won't make more, why then man will do it.' The husband promised to produce a huge progeny within nine days. On this battle cry the first act ended.

Even for Apollinaire, who in his *Calligrams* had already tested the physical restraints of the printed page, the release from the restrictions of flat black on white was an exhilarating experience. The first act was marked by a sensuous assault of shapes and sounds. Cries from the audience mingled with the text—itself accompanied by music and sound effects. Visually, splashes of colour, clusters of flying props, and a great deal of traffic between the stage and the hall, made for a fast-paced spectacle, vaudevillian in tempo. Just as in all his poetry beginning with *Alcools* (1913), Apollinaire admitted no punctuation, so in *Les Mamelles* the action rants on, admitting no stops, delighting in the new grammar of a liberated imagination.

The use of a single actor to represent the entire 'people of Zanzibar' recalled Jarry's instructions for *Ubu,* that a single soldier represent the entire Polish army, and the press itself continually recalled *Ubu:*

> It's Jarry Montmartre-ized, modernized, and martyrized. [*La Griffe,* 6 July 1917]

Group of Artists, 1908 by Marie Laurencin. Left to right: Pablo Picasso, Marie Laurencin, Guillaume Apollinaire, and Fernande Olivier.

It's an art which makes one think of Jarry, Jarry to the twentieth power. [*L'heure,* 25 June 1917]

One thought oneself at *Ubu Roi.* . . . [no source]

Most interesting however, was the use of simultaneous action—such as Tirésias 'raped' into his wife's clothes on stage as Presto and Lacouf begin their quarrel in the auditorium. The Presto-Lacouf episode is unrelated to the main action of the text, but, in performance, receives equal focus with the Thérèse-Tirésias combat. The inclusion of such an experiment in simultaneity is not a chance occurrence, for simultaneity was well in the forefront of Apollinaire's interests, and, as he wrote in his preface to the play, 'it is legitimate, in my opinion to bring to the theatre new and striking aesthetic principles which accentuate the roles of the actors and increase the effect of the production'.

Writing on the 'Salon des Indépendents' in March 1913, Apollinaire had referred to 'L'Orphisme, peinture pure Simultaneité', and the two terms became largely synonymous. It is out of orphisme—that ancient term which

Apollinaire revived to describe the art of Robert Delaunay—that simultaneism grew.

The importance of simultaneism is in its new grasp of structure—a structure which is the 'opposite of narration', and which represents 'an effort to retain a moment of experience without sacrificing its logically unrelated variety' [Roger Shattuck, *The Banquet Years,* 1968]. Simultaneism wanted to present a plurality of actions at the same time. In poetry, abridged syntax and unpunctuated abruptness tended to merge disparate moments into an 'instantané'. Passages were set, one next to another, to encourage a feeling of conflict between them rather than a link. From this setting of one thing beside another without a connective it is but a short jump to obscurity, illogicality, and abruptness—to surprise, shock and 'chance'.

In the production of **Les Mamelles,** instances of simultaneism abound. From the opening scene, sensual assaults on the audience overlapped, issuing from several areas on stage simultaneously. 'The people of Zanzibar', feather sticking out of his head and occupied with the making of his noise-music, shared the focus with Thérèse who, herself, 'attempt[ed] to dominate the sound of the orchestra'.

The human kiosk (who, with its proprietress, was 'one' and simultaneously 'two'), could be expected to enter the activity at any moment; the at-one-with-his-horse-gendarme (again the many faceted actor / object), pranced off and on; and, if all the onstage happenings proved insufficient, there were also voices of women 'in the wings'. The characters of Thérèse-Tirésias themselves played out a rondelay of a multiplicity of masks—they changed roles before they changed clothes, but even in drag each of them was never quite identical with himself.

The performance was full of 'doing'. The extent of commotion and activity which reigned on stage recalls the well-made-play (then still enjoying a huge success at the boulevard theatres), but with the intrigue-machinery gone awry. The narrative dimension had been critically attenuated, and the 'events' or 'activities' which remained were difficult to keep in focus serially, for they had almost no causal relationship. Time, besides, was no longer a matter of chronology, but of will. No sooner did Thérèse *will* to become a man, than the change took place. Later, she rose in rank as fast as the titles could be pronounced: 'long live Tiresias, long live General Tiresias, long live deputy Tiresias'. Finally, at the end of the play she is 'head of the army in Room A at City Hall', as well as being a fortune teller and the lover of three influential ladies. The husband is equally prodigious in his accomplishments: he wills and in one day creates 40,050 children who, while still crying in their cradles, have already taken their places in the world: the novelist, the poet, the divorcee, the journalist.

It is difficult to try and recapitulate the plot of the play, for the impact is in the overlay and crowding of events. The collision impact of simultaneism and the activity-mutation are the dominating forces. Without the audience's being able to register its exact meaning, a new structure and topography of psychological space-time was in the making.

Apollinaire was certainly not the first artist to use simultaneity on stage. The dadaists—as much poets rooted in painting as he—had already begun to take simultaneism to its fullest extensions in the area of performance. Hugo Ball, who with Tristan Tzara had founded the Cabaret Voltaire in Zurich in February 1916, had defined simultaneism in its performance qualities as pushing the experience beyond canvas and paper to a stage of three dimensional space and actual time. Simultaneous poetry, when recited, he wrote, is

> a contrapuntal recitative in which three or more voices speak, sing, whistle, etc., simultaneously in such a way that the resulting combinations account for the total effect of the work—elegiac, funny, or bizarre. [Hugo Ball, in *Dada: Art and Anti-Art* by Hans Richter]

Richard Huelsenbeck, another Zurich dada, describes it as an abstraction referring to the *occurrence* of different events at the same time:

> It presupposes heightened sensitivity to the passage of things in time . . . and attempts to transform the problem of the ear into a problem of the face. Simultaneity is against what has become

and for what is becoming. [*The Dada Painters and Poets,* edited by Robert Motherwell]

The futurists had been as enthusiastic as the dadaists in their use of the techniques of simultaneity. In Marinetti's play *I Vasi Communicanti,* the action on stage goes on in three different unrelated locations at the same time. Linear and homogenous time was out; in its place stood a new dynamism to be achieved by the simultaneous reduction and overlapping of time and space.

Apollinaire was far from unaware of the futurists' activities or the dada experiments which had been carried out at the Cabaret Voltaire in the year which preceded the premiere of *Les Mamelles.* Apollinaire was friendly with Marinetti, and had written a number of articles on futurism starting in 1913. We know that Apollinaire was in correspondence with Tzara by 1916, for the first issue of *Le Cabaret Voltaire* features his work as well as that of Tzara, Picasso, and Marinetti. Tzara, in 1917, contributed to Pierre Albert-Birot's *SIC,* and Albert-Birot contributed to Tzara's *Dada.* Albert-Birot's studio was in the same building as that of Gino Severini, a friend of Marinetti, and an artist whose wedding in 1913 had been attended by Apollinaire. *SIC,* in 1917, featured a description of the futurist movement written by Luciano Folgore, a futurist himself. By 1917, then, Apollinaire stood at the vortex of a network for the receiving of information from futurists and dadaists alike.

As a further connection with dada, the intermission of *Les Mamelles* provided its own excitement. Jacques Vaché, a follower of the tradition of Jarry-Ubu who lived in his own world of 'umour', had entered the theatre with a revolver. Master of the provocative gesture and the openly destructive act, and excited by the scandal of the performance, he had brandished the gun at the intermission audience, threatening to fire into the crowd. André Breton was filled with admiration for this contemporary of dada and later recalled Vaché's act in his Second Surrealist Manifesto, where he wrote that 'the simple surrealist act consists of going out into the street revolver in hand, and firing at random into the crowd as often as possible.'

Simultaneous activity was continued as the second act opened with a chorus in the form of a simultaneous song, not printed in the text:

> You who cry watching the play
> Wishing the children to be the winners
> See the imponderable ardour
> Born of sex-change.
> [From the sheet music of the play, reproduced in *SIC*]

Max Jacob and Paul Morisse sang the verses plus a number of encores while the post-natal husband rocked his many children in their cradles (designed by M. Sternberg). Throughout this act as well, the audience continued to interrupt the performance.

> The public was at a feverish pitch. Seeing that the play was a farce, they participated fully, including themselves in the proceedings. The performance played itself out in the hall as well as

on stage. [Paul Sonday, 'Une Pièce cubiste', *Paris-Midi,* 26 June 1917]

'One must create life', I heard one enthusiast cry. But what was created was tumult. [Bernard Lecastre, 'La Vache entragée']

Animal noises were among the sounds voiced, and Mme. Rachilde cried out, 'Go call the police, there are some crackpots in the house'.

Only for a moment did an attentive hush fall on the audience, as the husband began to enumerate the qualities of a good journalist and loudspeakers on stage proceeded to answer questions about specific 'colleagues' in the profession. But riot was soon restored as a fortune-teller in a luminous head-dress quarreled with the gendarme and strangled him. It was a repentant Thérèse in disguise, and she revealed herself as the gendarme (who had merely fainted) to join the now happy couple for an upbeat end to the play.

In the days which followed, the critics were hard put to it as to what to call the performance. They tried 'futurist', 'simultaneist', and 'cubist', but when Gaston Picard, editor of *Le Pays,* asked Apollinaire himself, 'Which -ism seems most appropriate to you?' Apollinaire answered:

> How little the epithet matters. Time will decide. We carry through history labels which usage has consecrated. As for myself, I do have my preferences—Orphisme or surnaturalism—that is, an art which is not merely photographic naturalism but which nonetheless reflects nature—that interior of unsuspected marvels: imponderable, pityless, and joyous.

For his part, Picard concluded:

> . . . let people say cubist or futurist according to their preference, or surnaturalist with Monsieur Apollinaire. We will say 'appolinairien!' ['M. Guillaume Apollinaire et la nouvelle école littéraire', *Le Pays,* 29 June 1917]

The interview drew a host of angry responses—most violent among them from a group of cubist painters, who were outraged at the word 'cubist' being so bandied around. In a letter to Picard, they wrote:

> As cubist painters and sculptors, we protest against the unfortunate link which people are straining to establish between our work and certain theatrical or literary fantasies which are none of our business to judge.
>
> Those among us who were present at the *SIC* and *Art et Liberté* manifestations formally declare that they have nothing in common with our plastic experiments. ['Lettres', *Le Pays,* 29 June 1917]

The letter was signed: Metzinger, Juan Gris, Diego Rivera, Lipschitz, Henri Hayden, Andre Lhote, Kissling, Gino Severini. The painters, however, had merely leaped into the fray. The press had declared, 'Allah is cubist and M. Birot is his prophet', and nothing was going to stop the battle over nomenclature. The critic Victor Basch decided that what Apollinaire really meant by the word 'surrealist'

was 'symbolic', while other critics connected the new term with what was eccentric and dissonant. The only thing that seemed clear was that no one had been left indifferent. André Breton later said:

> Never again, as at that evening, did I plumb the depths of the gap which would separate the new generation from that preceding it. [*Entretiens 1913-1952,* edited by André Parinaud]

And Aragon wrote:

> I will always cherish, from that afternoon of the 24th of June, 1917, the souvenir of a unique freedom which permits one to forsee a theatre liberated from the philosopher's cares. [*SIC,* 27 May 1918]

Not everyone was so impressed. The critic of *L'heure* angrily wrote:

> This prank might be amusing, recounted by a bantering and unctuous Apollinaire one Tuesday, or acted by Max Jacob in a left-bank studio, but to baptise it 'drame surréaliste' and to present it seriously to an audience, is to say the least, indecent. . . . The play was acted by people whose profession was obviously not acting. The sets . . . stolen! [26 June 1917]

Léo Poldes in *La Grimace* could not contain himself and burst out:

> Let the artists pardon me, let the reader excuse me, three words spill from my pen in summation—'Ah, the swine'.

In *Le Petit Bleu,* Davin de Champclos ranted:

> The 'new spirit'? . . . I must be awfully regressed, backward, conventional, traditionalist, sodden, and reactionary, because this new spirit seemed to me the most tremendous hoax and practical joke.

and for the critic of *Le Cri France,* a single sentence sufficed:

> **Les Mamelles de Tirésias** has alienated from Guillaume Apollinaire many of his admirers.

As for Apollinaire, he did not take the criticism lightly. Four days after the premiere, he wrote to his friend Pierre Reverdy:

> I have just experienced the greatest joy, and with it the greatest pain in my life. I've given the most personal, the most lyric, the most joyous thing in **Les Mamelles de Tirésias,** which has had the greatest success except for Metzinger, Gris, and other asses of that kind.

The following November, in a lecture at the Théâtre du Vieux Colombier, Apollinaire himself turned to answer his detractors, and specifically championed the element of surprise as the most exacting defining characteristic of the new movement:

> Surprise is the greatest source of what is new. It is by surprise, by the important position that has been given to surprise that the new spirit distinguishes itself from all the literary and artistic

movements which have preceded it. [**'L'Esprit nouveau et les poètes'**]

Apollinaire's mark on performance had, however, been indelibly made. For the likes of Breton and Aragon, young 'littérateurs' who would later participate in the experiments of Paris-dada performance, the 1917 production of **Les Mamelles de Tirésias** served to embody the basic elements of a tradition of radical theatre. Surprise and shock were paramount, preferably raised to the level of scandal. The text emerged as peripheral and the performance elements, as conceived and executed by director, actors and designer, became the crucial elements of the production. Sets and costumes often merged, with the actor carrying both as one on his back. Wearing a huge mask, or painting his face, walking within a box, or padding himself beyond recognition, the performer often moved in the grey zone between actor and object. Shock and surprise had forged a bridge in the gap that traditionally separated the audience from the stage and a new oneness was felt between public and performers, even as they taunted one another. (pp. 3-13)

> *Annabelle Henkin Melzer, "The Premiere of Apollinaire's 'The Breasts of Tiresias' in Paris," in* Theatre Quarterly, *Vol. VII, No. 27, Autumn, 1977, pp. 3-14.*

Margaret Davies   (essay date 1977)

[*Davies is an English critic whose numerous essays and full-length studies on French authors include* Apollinaire *(1964). In the following excerpt, she notes merits of Apollinaire's fiction.*]

The burgeoning interest in Apollinaire during the past twenty years has been devoted mainly to his poetry and art criticism rather than his other works in prose. And yet contemporaries thought highly of his short stories. *L'Hérésiarque et Cie* nearly won the Prix Goncourt in 1910, André Breton considered **"Que vlo-vé"** to be the source of "surnaturalisme", and Apollinaire himself . . . believed that he had a "grand talent de conteur" as well as a "grand talent de poète". (I was once shown by Tristan Tzara an unpublished letter from Apollinaire, in which he said that the short story was his great speciality.)

[Michel Décaudin, an editor of Apollinaire's works, has attributed] this critical lop-sidedness to the unavailability of the texts, to faulty editions and the lack of necessary background material, a large part of which has now seen the light of day since the death of the poet's widow Jacqueline. It is certainly true that much recent French criticism, with its stress on themes and the "structures de l'imaginaire", has concerned itself with Apollinaire's work as a whole, underlining the obsessive themes and images that criss-cross through stories and poems, articles and letters. In this way many of the most cryptic references in the poems themselves have come into focus, and new interpretations have been made possible.

It is also true that, more than most writers, Apollinaire seems to make no conscious division between prose and poetry. The particular poetic quality of his prose meant that he could transcribe word for word an earlier short story and print it as the poem **"La Maison des morts"**. Stories are poems, poems are letters and letters pour out in verse—even his occasional journalism takes flight into lyricism. From the thematic point of view prose and poetry are one. Sometimes, however, one wishes more emphasis could be placed on pinpointing the variables rather than the constants, on discovering what makes the poem different from the story, what gives a particular confrontation of images its unique spark, what endows the individual work with its specificity.

[What do Apollinaire's prose works offer?] One remembers, for instance, the comparative lack of success of the Brussels company which four years ago put on a stage version here of **L'Enchanteur pourrissant,** and the adverse criticism in the English press, which was directed more against the work itself, a strange hybrid with its mixture of legend, fairy tale and abstruse symbolism, than against its ingenious staging. It is certainly quite out of fashion today, attractive perhaps only to the collector of curiosities or to the scholar tracking down an early appearance of major themes. Again, **La Femme assise,** an ungainly work patched together, as Apollinaire admitted, in haste, is not likely to produce more than a fleeting interest in its highly-coloured episodes of Mormon history. Even the two erotic works [**La Fin de Babylone** and **Les trois Don Juan**] will be disappointing to anyone who has had his appetite whetted by the cruder and more overtly pornographic **Les onze mille vierges** and **Les Exploits d'un jeune Don Juan.**

The fact is that Apollinaire was no novelist, at least in the traditional sense, nor did he think that the traditional novel-form had much life left in it. He lacked any talent for putting himself inside the skin of a character, or for playing out its psychological tensions. It is as if, in doing so, he can discover only himself and his own obsessions, and, moved though he is to explore and exorcize his interior dramas, he is also, like many poets, equally shy of baring his heart to public gaze. Most of [his manuscript] corrections of both poems and stories move in the direction of covering up over-revealing admissions. What he is attracted by in other people is the external detail, the bizarre oddity, whatever will set his imagination wandering through the maze of memory, anecdote, and snatches from old books. In the unfinished but gripping story **"La Dame blanche des Hohenzollern"** of 1917-18, he sees in a train a mysterious lady with violet eyes and a scar on her neck: "Et aussitôt mon imagination d'entrer en jeu et de battre la campagne à propos de cette cicatrice."

It is clear that this random movement of the imagination does not lend itself easily to the rigours of sustaining over a period all the threads of a long intrigue. Within the confines of the short story, however, where he is obliged to concentrate on a single anecdote Apollinaire can, at his best, work wonders of condensation and economy, following the story-line with speed and verve, maintaining suspense, as well as suggesting a wealth of local colour and setting the *fait divers* in a mythical framework. **"Que vlo-vé"** with its highly original mixture of lyricism and the local lore of the Ardennes, of sadism and eroticism, **"Les**

Pélerins piémontais" with the tense atmosphere of the pilgrim church, the dying girl and the blasphemous imprecation of her monk-lover, **"Le Passant de Prague"** which mixes the real atmosphere of Prague with the legendary appearance of the Wandering Jew, are all masterpieces of the genre. Critics are right to talk of Hoffmann and Poe, of Villiers de l'Isle Adam and Barbey d'Aurevilly.

M Décaudin underlines most appropriately in these stories—as indeed in Apollinaire's writing generally—the basic "ligne de force", which consists of the play between the false and the true, between dream and reality. To this opposition I would add other terms: love and death (most of the stories end with a death), flesh and spirit (nothing human is to be alien to this inquiring mind), idealism and blasphemy, and the corresponding registers of lyricism and irony.

For the modern reader perhaps the most interesting story is **"Le Poète assassiné."** This unaccountable work combines the real and the false, lyricism and satire, autobiography and myth. New or old? Successor to Rabelais, precursor of surrealism, or something even newer, situated in the future? In it one sees Apollinaire at his familiar tricks of composition, what M Décaudin calls "le patchwork". Indeed the manuscripts present a curious appearance, being cobbled together from handwritten fragments of different periods with different names for the hero scored over, passages pasted on or cut out, printed articles which have already appeared; in short a real collage. What emerges from this distillation of high spirits and ironical melancholy is the myth of the poet, redolent with archetypal symbols and prophecies of persecution by scientist, mob, and woman; and, most modern feature of all, the storyline is actually generated by a sheer joy in punning and word play.

Although there is no question of Apollinaire's "talent de conteur" suddenly taking over from his reputation as a poet, anyone who is fascinated by the poetry will find much to delight and astonish him in [Apollinaire's fiction].

Margaret Davies, "The Patchwork Principle," in The Times Literary Supplement, *No. 3942, October 14, 1977, p. 1206.*

S. I. Lockerbie   (essay date 1978)

[*In the following excerpt, Lockerbie offers an overview of* Calligrammes.]

Calligrammes is, with *Alcools,* the second major volume of poetry on which rests Guillaume Apollinaire's reputation as one of the great modern poets in French literature. Linking the two volumes are deep and persistent continuities, rooted in Apollinaire's vision of the world and the fundamental nature of his lyric gift. There is also a marked proximity in time, for the first poems of *Calligrammes* were written in December 1912 and early 1913, immediately after the completion of *Alcools* in November 1912. Yet these affinities do not prevent most readers being struck—and rightly so—by considerable differences in tone, style, and theme between the two volumes. *Calli-grammes,* particularly the first section entitled "Ondes," reveals a novelty of accent and composition which clearly rests on aesthetic assumptions different from those underlying the main poems of *Alcools,* assumptions that can conveniently be drawn together under the concept of modernism.

Although a modern note is frequently struck in *Alcools,* and increasingly so as we move from the earlier to the later poems, Apollinaire's conception of poetry in that volume is one that essentially derives from Symbolism. It is an introspective poetry in which the poet is concerned with the troubled depths of the psyche, the transitoriness of experience, and the quest for identity and permanence. The shadowy and obsessive nature of the poet's states of mind is reflected in elliptical, elusive, and sometimes hermetic expression. Like the great Symbolist poets, Apollinaire finds deep aesthetic satisfaction in the beauties of obscurity and allusiveness of utterance. Even the supremely musical short poems on which his fame as a popular lyric poet rests—**"Le Pont Mirabeau"** and others—acquire their melodic ease through a process of distillation and condensation which makes them more appealing than immediately intelligible.

The force with which an urgent form of consciousness is increasingly deployed in this poetry, tempering the melancholy, widening the imaginative span, and revitalizing the language, is Apollinaire's major creative achievement in *Alcools.* But, with some exceptions, it is an achievement that does not seek to renew the poet's vision of the world. This is so even in **"Zone,"** the opening poem but the last to be written, which in its early lines makes the first forceful statement of the new enthusiasm for the modern world which was to burst out in *Calligrammes.* The initial optimism, however, is not sustained. The final mood that is established is one of anguish and suffering, and the poem ends with the poet assuming what is his most characteristic role throughout the volume, that of the lonely wanderer in the hostile and ominous environment of the modern city.

In *Calligrammes,* on the other hand, the mood reflects much greater confidence and enthusiasm for life. In the first part of **"Liens"** and **"Les Fenêtres"** the poet is no longer posited as a lonely wanderer in a harsh cityscape but as a "new man" whose vision radiates across frontiers and continents and unites the modern world in a network of concordances. The shadowy, claustrophobic atmosphere of earlier poems now gives way to urgent, syncopated rhythms and to the play of sensuous color and light. The final lines of **"Les Fenêtres,"**

> La fenêtre s'ouvre comme une orange
> Le beau fruit de la lumière
>
> [The window opens like an orange
> The lovely fruit of light]

symbolize a new openness to experience in the poet and a sense of communion with the world, even in its farther-flung reaches.

It is not only in Apollinaire that this remarkable change in outlook is encountered. The whole prewar generation of artists in Paris was caught up in a similar wave of extrovert enthusiasm. It was a change of mood that stemmed ultimately from the rapid technological advances of the early years of the twentieth century and the general widening of horizons brought about by such inventions as the motorcar, the airplane, radiography, cinematography, and radio communications. Suddenly modern man seemed to be living in a totally different context from the older, slower world of the nineteenth century. His ability to manipulate his environment, and his capacity for experience, had been infinitely increased. Now he seemed the triumphant master of his own destiny.

It is not surprising that this new sensibility should produce a new tempo in the arts and a general desire for artistic change. All the prewar movements, from the Futurists to the most ephemeral and obscure, declared that the artistic forms of the past were no longer adequate to express the new spirit and had to be radically renewed. Apollinaire stands out as the most masterly innovator in an avant-garde hectically devoted to experiment, not because his ideas were the most original, but because he had the creative genius to transform aesthetic concepts that were in general circulation into powerful and appealing poetry.

Central among these aesthetic ideas was the notion that the modern work of art must adequately reflect the global nature of contemporary consciousness. In the conditions of modern life man has achieved totality of awareness: through worldwide communications he is as aware of what is happening in New York as in Paris; through newspapers, radio, and the cinema his imagination is stimulated by a constantly changing stream of information and ideas; in the streets and cafés his senses are assailed by a kaleidoscopic multiplicity of sights, sounds, and sensations. To be able to mirror such a multiple form of consciousness the work of art had to abandon linear and discursive structures, in which events are arranged successively, in favor of what Apollinaire called *simultaneity*: a type of structure that would give the impression of a full and instant awareness within one moment of space-time.

Essentially this conception led Apollinaire to a radical dislocation of poetic structure. To create an impression of multiple and simultaneous consciousness, perceptions and ideas are abruptly juxtaposed in the poems in an arrangement that, at first reading, seems to be one of considerable disorder. Many poems of *Alcools* had already been characterized by elliptical syntax and collocations of disparate images, but the novelty in *Calligrammes* is that the discontinuities are much more radical, forcing the reader into a greater effort of synthesis to discover the underlying unity. It was this effort of synthesis that, for Apollinaire, produced the "simultanist" vision, insofar as it short-circuits the normal discursive process of reading and requires the reader to reassemble the apparently random fragments in a new order that is independent of the flow of time and is experienced in one global act of consciousness.

Undeniably Apollinaire was encouraged in his thinking by the similar fragmentation of structure he observed in Cubist painting, particularly in the work of Picasso, which he also considered to stem from the simultaneous depiction of the same object from several viewpoints. What he admired above all in Picasso was the sheer imaginative boldness with which the painter had broken with all previous conceptions in Western painting. He describes Picasso in *Les Peintres Cubistes* as a heroic figure who had dared to disrupt the established order of the universe and to rearrange it as he thought fit:

> La grande révolution des arts qu'il a accomplie presque seul, c'est que le monde est sa nouvelle représentation. . . . C'est un nouveau-né qui met de l'ordre dans l'univers pour son usage personnel, et aussi afin de faciliter ses relations avec ses semblables. Ce dénombrement a la grandeur de l'épopée.

> [The great revolution in the arts which he almost alone has accomplished is that the world is now in his image. . . . He is a newborn babe who rearranges the universe for his personal convenience and to facilitate understanding with his fellowmen. His cataloguing has an epic grandeur.]

The important thing here is that the elaborating of a new structure is identified with personal creativity of the highest order. The process of reordering the world according to the artist's own vision testifies not only to his global, all-embracing consciousness but also to his unique powers as an inventor. The distinguishing feature of the modern artist is that he produces a new art object, profoundly original in conception and form and freed from servile imitation of nature, which becomes the projection of his own creative personality onto the world.

Apollinaire stands out as the most masterly innovator in an avant-garde hectically devoted to experiment, not because his ideas were the most original, but because he had the creative genius to transform aesthetic concepts that were in general circulation into powerful and appealing poetry.

—*S. I. Lockerbie*

The different emphases in Apollinaire's own experiments in poetic form which emerge implicitly from his account of Picasso can be traced, in greater or lesser degree, in most of the poems of "Ondes," the section of *Calligrammes* which contains his prewar innovative work, but are particularly evident in the two poems that Apollinaire himself dubbed "conversation poems": **"Les Fenêtres"** and **"Lundi Rue Christine."** The descriptive label refers to the fact that frequent use is made of snippets of spoken language, assembled from what seem to be unrelated and disconnected conversations being held in some public place. The intention seems to be to face the reader with a mass of unintegrated details, not unlike the profusion of planes that, at first sight, obscure the overall design and organization of a cubist painting. The difference between the poems is that when a synthesis begins to emerge from the jigsaw, it is achieved in a high key in **"Les Fenêtres"** and in a lower and subtler key in **"Lundi Rue Christine."** In **"Les Fenêtres"** the mixing into the jumble of conversation of sensuous evocations of light and color, and flashing impressions of a worldwide scene, quickly suggests that there is a powerful controlling consciousness at the heart of the poem, unifying it through the force of its own aspiration. In this poem, therefore, simultanist form is directly expressive of the creator's personality and power of vision. In **"Lundi Rue Christine,"** on the other hand, the poet is virtually absent, or is reduced to the role of an eavesdropper, and the reader has to build up the picture of a café scene from quizzical hints that arise in the disorderly buzz of conversation. Here the emphasis falls on the autonomy of the work of art that has been created: it stands out as an arbitrary but fascinating construction whose existence is justified by its status as a deliberately fabricated object. The distinction, however, is not absolute. In both poems, and in its many other uses in the poems of "Ondes," the terse, fragmented structure operates on two levels at once, suggesting both the multiple consciousness of the poet at the center of the modern world and the formal intricacy of an innovatory approach to poetic form.

A similar judgment can be made of the use of language in the conversation poems. The question of language is as central to modernism as the notion of simultaneity. One of Apollinaire's principal convictions was that a poetry that seeks to express the quintessence of the modern world must also use the direct and forceful speech of contemporary life. Already in **"Zone"** there is the statement that the stylistic models for the modern poet should be those that he can find in the public uses of language all around him:

> Tu lis les prospectus les catalogues les affiches
>   qui chantent tout haut
> Voilà la poésie ce matin et pour la prose il y a
>   les journaux
>
> [You read handbills catalogues advertisements
>   that
>   sing out loud and clear
> There is where poetry is this morning and for
>   prose
>   there are the newspapers]

And in many other contexts the poet who had once argued for the necessary obscurity of poetry now condemns the convoluted nature of Symbolist verse and declares his faith in an art that has broad popular appeal.

The use of fragments of ordinary speech in the conversation poems is a striking example of the extension of poetic language to include popular usage. Phrases that have none of the characteristics of conventional poetic diction are shown to acquire meaning and expressiveness when manipulated in a certain way. This amounts to the destruction of any notion of hierarchy in language and to the removal of artificial barriers between the kinds of speech that can be used by poets. In this sense Apollinaire can be said to have stripped the remaining ornaments of rhetoric from the language of poetry. But here also there are implications that are formal and internal. It is because he is defeated in his attempt to find an immediate discursive meaning linking the various fragments that the reader is

thrown back onto the text and interrogates the linguistic network more closely, discovering unexpected resonances and connections in apparently banal phrases. The poem thus becomes a self-reflexive object, in which it is the internal echoes and the relationships of the snippets of language among themselves which provide the aesthetic pleasure, as much as any externally directed act of communication.

The interaction of style and structure throughout the modernist poems makes it clear that they are creatively original and independent of the painters. However much Apollinaire may have been stimulated by the example of Picasso, and for a shorter period by that of Robert Delaunay, he could draw no more than general inspiration from them. It is only through particular combinations of words and images that the poems achieve their success, and in this respect they are as innovatory at the level of poetic style as they are at the level of structure.

The range of Apollinaire's modernism can be gauged from the fact that it is expressed not only in the simultanist experiments, but also in poems that, in technique and conception, are at the opposite extreme. Where the experimental pieces abandon linear and discursive structures and turn their back on narration and description, two major poems of "Ondes"—**"Un Fantôme de Nuées"** and **"Le Musicien de Saint-Merry"**—adopt a linear form and discursive narration as their fundamental modes of expression. Moreover, in these poems and others (**"Sur les Prophéties"** and many later pieces) coherence and continuity are restored to language. The language remains the casual speech of everyday life, but, as against the elliptical juxtapositions of the conversation poems, the registers of the spoken language are used in a fluent, relaxed way, producing an impression of spontaneity and naturalness of utterance.

Narration, description, unforced naturalness of style— these conventions imply a respect for empirical reality and an acceptance of its intrinsic value. Rather than manipulate the real world in order to impose his highly structured vision upon it, the poet, in this approach, sees it as a continuum and tries to preserve its homogeneity. This is, to an extent, a rehabilitation of mimesis as a literary mode, a confidence in the power of literature to render the essence of unadorned reality through attentive observation. It testifies to the pull of the real world on Apollinaire's imagination, counterbalancing the powerful attraction of artistic innovation, and demonstrates the strength of his ambition to make his poetry a truly popular art, accessible to an undifferentiated public. Few French poets in the twentieth century have gone so far in capturing what Zola called the everyday "sense of the real," or written poems so immediately readable and appealing as **"Un Fantôme de Nuées"** and **"Le Musicien de Saint-Merry."**

In this approach the personal vision of the poet is not absent but is allowed to grow out of the common area of experience that the poem renders. Apollinaire's delight in the ordinary world stemmed not only from its colorful diversity but also from its multilayered ambiguity, which he saw as the task of the poet to explore and exploit. It was at this time that he began to formulate the concept of surprise as a key element in a modernist aesthetic and to suggest, in **"Sur les Prophéties,"** that magical and superstitious interpretations of reality have their own validity. It is symptomatic that he was also drawn to the works of such eminently surprising and enigmatic painters as Chirico and Chagall, whose disconcerting canvases undoubtedly stimulated his interest in the dimension of the irrational. (There does seem to be some influence of Chagall behind Apollinaire's first attempts in **"A Travers l'Europe"** to use the kind of apparently unmotivated imagery that points in the direction of surrealism.) These strands in his view of reality come together in the concept of *surnaturalisme,* which may be described as a blend of realism and fantasy in the poet's approach to the world, allowing him to move easily between both poles and to suggest, as in **"Sur les Prophéties,"** that the marvelous is an integral part of our everyday experience. The successful application of this aesthetic is to be seen in **"Un Fantôme de Nuées"** and **"Le Musicien de Saint-Merry."** The first is remarkable in bringing about an untroubled epiphany with minimal departures from a casual narrative tone. The second is no less so in encompassing the whole range of Apollinaire's conflicting emotions within the framework of a narrative fable, set in the heart of modern Paris. The past and the present, fatalistic obsession with the loss of love and delight in the multiplicity of the modern world, are all brought together, in perfect balance, in what is indeed a new form of twentieth-century *merveilleux:* a sense of the real suffused with personal vision.

It is not only in **"Le Musicien de Saint-Merry"** but throughout "Ondes" that a state of inner anxiety, reminiscent of the mood of *Alcools,* makes itself felt. For all the novelty of accent and outlook of *Calligrammes,* Apollinaire's sensibility remains one haunted by uncertainty and doubt. This is what distinguishes his modernism from the more aggressive and strident version of his contemporaries. Where they were condemning subjectivity as outmoded and self-indulgent, he declares only partial loyalty to the bright new world of extrovert energy and admits to an enduring attachment to the poetry of personal emotion and elegiac sadness. Far from seeking to minimize his inner contradictions, he articulates them clearly in the prefatory poem **"Liens,"** raising self-division to the rank of the major theme around which the whole modernist section of the volume is constructed. His instinctive gravitation toward images of sadness and pain, and the melodious incantatory phrases in which they naturally seek expression, are not to be explained solely in terms of the unhappiness that followed his separation from Marie Laurencin in 1913—although echoes of the suffering that produced the late lyric masterpieces of *Alcools* are certainly among the most plangent notes of *Calligrammes.* Beyond that, there is a more general anxiety in the face of experience which seeks refuge in the comfort of the past and fears, rather than welcomes, confrontation with the new. This explains why, on occasion, even the modern world, and the future itself, can lose their dynamic associations for the poet and become equivocal and ominous. In **"Arbre"** it is a barren and comfortless world that is about to be born. The new beings who will usher it in bear the mark of divinity in the mystic number three, but nevertheless hark back to the *acteurs inhumains claires bêtes nouvelles* of **"Le Brasier"** [inhuman actors bright new beasts], symbolizing a soulless new race, insensitive to the old world of emotion and memory.

Every dynamic theme in "Ondes," therefore, has its antithesis which reverses the mood and the associations. Despite the apparent assertion of **"Liens,"** this represents not so much a conflict within the poet—although for vividness of expression images of conflict are often used—as a creative tension between two states of sensibility that are felt to be indivisible parts of the self. Melancholy and confidence are each so instinctive in Apollinaire that only when they have been resolved and brought into balance can he feel that he has fully expressed the wholeness of his personality. His lyricism derives all its power and rich ambiguities precisely from this resolution of inner contradictions into a complex but profoundly unified state of sensibility.

It was no doubt to ensure that the depth of personal experience which characterizes Apollinaire's modernism was adequately represented that he included **"Les Collines"** in "Ondes," out of chronological order. Not written until 1917, after the poet had gone through the maturing turmoil of war, this poem presents, more powerfully than any other in the section, the commitment to modernism as a testing spiritual adventure. The picture it gives of the modern poet as an innovator and a prophet radically enlarges that notion as it was expressed in **"Sur les Prophéties."** Rather than the gift of everyday observation within the power of any man, prophecy now becomes the prerogative of the poet as a seer who acquires his privileged insights into the mysteries of the universe through struggle, trial, and suffering. The poet again takes on the persona of the martyr-hero of *Alcools,* mourning the loss of youth, wracked by the exceptional experiences he undergoes, but gaining as his prize a multiplication of his powers and an oneiric understanding of life and death. In its exalted tone, denseness of allusion, and complexity of expression, **"Les Collines"** thus achieves the higher resolution of all Apollinaire's complexities and colors the whole context of "Ondes." Inevitably the reader is induced to see the poet's modernism, even in its more apparently fanciful experiments, as a poetic undertaking of the highest seriousness of purpose.

The calligrams may have seemed fanciful experiments to many contemporary and later commentators, but they were not so in Apollinaire's eyes. By giving to the whole volume the title he invented for these exercises in what he called "visual lyricism"—even though only a small minority of poems are composed in that style—he made plain the importance he attached to them. His famous lecture in 1917, **"L'Esprit Nouveau et les Poètes"** [The New Spirit and the Poets], leaves no doubt that he saw visual or spatial poetry as an important new development, and had he lived he would probably have pursued it much further.

In conception the calligram derives directly from the techniques of fragmentation and recombination employed in the conversation poems. It stems from the conviction that the simultaneous nature of consciousness can be even more powerfully rendered by abandoning not only discursive expression but also the traditional linear layout of the poem as well. In a phrase that has had a famous history, a friendly critic described this typographical revolution as inevitable "because it is necessary that our intelligence become accustomed to understanding synthetico-ideographically instead of analytico-discursively" [G. Arbouin, in an article on **"Lettre-Océan"** in *Les Soirées de Paris,* July-August 1914]. That is to say that in a spatial layout, where the poem is displayed in a multiplicity of patterns on the page rather than being arranged in one linear sequence, the reader is forced to grasp the complex interrelationship of the whole in a global perception which is (apparently) more instantaneous than his recombination of the fragmented structure of the conversation poem and leads to a more powerful illumination. The fact that some of his understanding comes to him through a visual, as well as a verbal, communication of ideas further reinforces the direct sensory awareness that is characteristic of a modern consciousness.

While Apollinaire was certainly encouraged in his thinking about this concept by a desire to emulate his painter friends, as is demonstrated by his original intention to publish the poems separately under the title "Et Moi Aussi Je Suis Peintre" [I, too, am a painter], the calligram remains indisputably a form of poetry that, in its combination of spatial and linguistic factors, points toward the concrete poetry movement of recent years. Yet, intriguingly, his implementation of his bold plan has served to obscure the originality of his thought and has led to some misunderstanding of the poems. The confusion arises from what seems like a dramatic change of heart between the publication of the first calligram, **"Lettre-Océan,"** and those that followed.

In [the] article about **"Lettre-Océan"** published in Apollinaire's own review, *Les Soirées de Paris,* G. Arbouin welcomed the poem as a revolutionary innovation but expressed the important reservation that the new technique could destroy the rhythmic basis of poetry, on which the communication of emotion depended, and thus create an arcane art reserved for the initiated. One must assume that these views reflected Apollinaire's own uncertainties about the proper mode of application of spatial poetry and his own constant desire to combine innovation with broad popular appeal. He must, therefore, have been susceptible to Arbouin's argument that the calligram would perforce evolve toward a pictorial shape directly related to its subject matter. Inwardly he must have felt that to give the spatial poem a pictorial shape was to restore it to a more immediately intelligible form and one that was more compatible with the rhythmic expression of feeling.

That is indeed what happened. After **"Lettre-Océan,"** in which a global view of the modern world is imprinted on the page in an exploded structure of radiating lines and pulverized language, the calligrams that immediately follow it are composed of coherent phrases fashioned into extremely simple and instantly recognizable shapes. Any intention of expressing a simultaneous consciousness seems to have disappeared, so that some readers have fallen into the trap of thinking that the shape is simply a tautological repetition of what the referential or discursive meaning of the words already clearly conveys.

But to do so is to misunderstand the different nature of the reading operations involved in even the simplest association of word and picture. Tautology is impossible between a linguistic statement and the instant impression conveyed by a shape. Inevitably, and in poetic use deliberately, the words refine and add connotations and overtones that extend and complicate the initial response. The eye and the mind of the reader describe a circle that leads from recognition of the object to the exploration of the poet's reflections on it, and back again to the picture overlaid with a new significance. This significance must be considerable when, as in most of Apollinaire's poems, the language is richly lyrical. Whether in compact or languorous form—in **"Paysage"** or in **"Il Pleut"**—the calligrams encapsulate much of his most incantatory writing. It is, in fact, the nature of their lyricism, more than their mode of operation, which distinguishes the pictorial calligrams from **"Lettre-Océan."** Rather than expressing the poet's delight in the pulsating modern world, they are concerned with the realm of private feeling; however, the process by which an instantaneous graphic perception is enriched by the accumulated associations of extended reading is common to both. In a nonfigurative poem like **"Lettre-Océan,"** the eye can take a larger number of paths through the shape, and the mind may have to hold together a larger number of different associations, but the delayed-reaction effect, before the experience is complete, is the same. Provided that one understands that "simultaneity" is really the eventual end result of a process of reading rather than the instant perception that Apollinaire sometimes implied, it can be seen that **"Lettre-Océan"** and the pictorial poems share one kind of simultaneity that distinguishes them from noncalligrammatic poems like the conversation pieces: the fusing together of two different modes of apprehension of the same idea or feeling, one mode working through visual association and the other through verbal.

Such a manner of operation gives particular satisfaction when the picture itself carries immediately as much impact as the words. If in some of the calligrams the picture is emblematic and acquires its richness of significance from the words in an initially one-way process, as is possibly true of the watch, the house, or the crown, other shapes instantly impress themselves on the eye with their own suggestive power before being enriched by the words. The vivid outline of the lovers in **"Paysage,"** the oval of the mirror, the graceful lines of the fountain, the falling rain, the shell, the smoking cigar, the harmonious balance of forms in **"La Mandoline l'Œillet et le Bambou"**—all these and others demonstrate that Apollinaire immensely increased the capacity of figured verse to assume a wide variety of flexible and striking forms. Since antiquity pictorial poetry had confined itself to a relatively small number of elementary shapes, which were solidly filled with unbroken lines of type. Departing from this static tradition, Apollinaire's calligrams use single lines of type to trace bold or delicate outlines on the printed page with all the spontaneity of handwriting, producing a much wider range of plastic images. The fluid nature of his composition has always posed problems for printers, but by the same token, when the calligrams are successfully realized in type, they have a freshness of effect that gives them im-

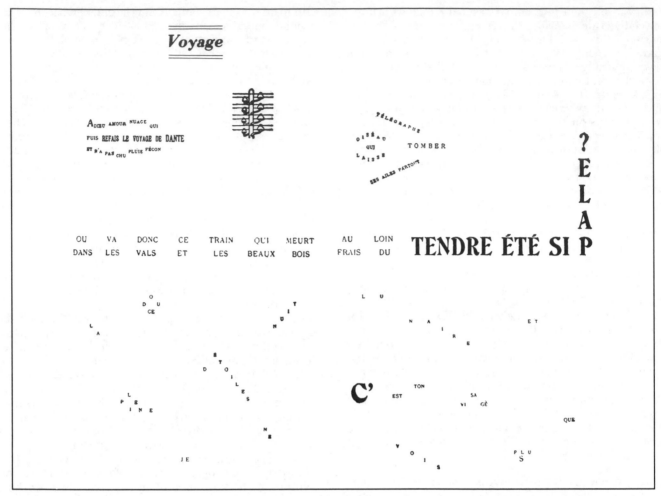

Apollinaire's calligram "Voyage."

mediate expressiveness and explains why they have been so often reproduced and imitated, even by advertisers.

In a significant number of examples the inherent expressiveness of the graphic form adds a dimension of meaning to the poem which is inseparable from its appearance on the printed page and cannot emerge from the words alone. The shape of the lovers in **"Paysage"** can be interpreted pictorially in different ways, with considerable consequences for the overall meaning of the poem, and, whatever the interpretation, the shape says something that the words do not. The same is true in many other poems. Nor are the visual implications necessarily restricted to those associated with the object that is pictured. In calligrammatic compositions, no less than in visual art generally, graphic form itself can be directly expressive. It is instructive, from this point of view, to compare the three different typographical representations of rain in Apollinaire's work (. . . **"Il Pleut"** and **"Du Coton dans les Oreilles"**) where the different nature of type, line, and spacing on each occasion produces three quite different statements. It can even happen that certain graphic forms—notably the sinuous line—are so imprinted with associations that they contradict the verbal statement that the poem is making

and create a much more complex mood than is immediately apparent (see . . . **"Du Coton"**).

It is observable that Apollinaire becomes increasingly sensitive to the possibilities of spatial expression. While the earlier poems, with the exception of **"Lettre-Océan,"** are pictorial, later sections of the volume show his interest in less figurative uses of the medium. In the section "Case d'Armons" there are examples of handwritten script and bold layout which make their effect in purely plastic terms. In the calligrams proper, in the same section, abstract graphic values can be seen to assume equal importance with the representational. Even a simple emblematic likeness of a gun in **"S P"** has formal qualities that transcend the shape, whereas in **"Loin du Pigeonnier"** and **"Visée"** the graphic form is sophisticated and suggestive on several levels. Again, if a figurative intention is present in the later works, such as **"Aussi Bien Que les Cigales"** and **"Éventail des Saveurs,"** these poems also make an impact as a pleasing pattern of lines and as an exercise in the formal grouping of shapes on the page. A freer approach to layout is to be found even in conventionally printed poems, as in the marginal additions or offset lines of **"Saillant," "Echelon,"** and **"Oracles."** These have less an explicit significance than the general function of calling attention to the poem as a deliberate composition in both structural and plastic terms, and thus of raising the reader's consciousness of the spatial dimension.

Within these freer designs, language is used in a freer way also, sometimes in marked contrast with the coherent, well-formed phrases of most of the picture poems. Apollinaire realized that one of the most potent features of the calligram is the heightening effect it has on the words from which it is made, and that it thus lent itself to his constant endeavors to restore high expressiveness to language. One of the ways in which the form serves this purpose is to act as a vehicle for the dense allusive utterances that he had favored since his Symbolist beginnings. The one-line poem **"Chantre,"** which he added at the last moment to the proofs of *Alcools,* is a formulation of this kind, and it could be read as the first tentative calligram. Poems such as **"Visée"** and **"Éventail des Saveurs,"** however, not only multiply the power of **"Chantre"** tenfold, by accumulating a succession of such "autonomous" lines, but confer visual as well as auditory eloquence on the statements by the beauty of their graphic composition. More boldly, the expressions that are encapsulated in other calligrams are in a much lower poetic register. These can be prosaic, repetitive slogans (**"Aussi Bien Que les Cigales"**), fragmentary phrases (**"Loin du Pigeonnier"**), or simple declarative sentences and exclamations (**"1915," "Carte Postale à Jean Royère"**), but here also the intention is clearly to elevate the statement through its isolation in a striking graphic structure and thus give it the self-sufficiency of a complete poetic thought.

However few in number, therefore, the calligrams are a significant poetic achievement. Nothing could be more mistaken than to think of their shape, whether pictorial or more abstract, as incidental or merely decorative. On the contrary, their graphic form interacts with the verbal text to create a new form of poetry in which Apollinaire has had many successors. They also play their part, like the conversation poems before them, in extending the range of poetic expression and increasing the number of uses of language in which we can find aesthetic satisfaction.

The war poetry, although the product of circumstance, is far from circumstantial in the pejorative sense. The vast poetic output (only part of which found its way into *Calligrammes*) of the fifteen months between December 1914, when Apollinaire enlisted in the artillery, and March 1916, when he was wounded in the head, testifies to the stimulating effect of events on his imagination. The drama of a creative personality faced with a phenomenon on an unprecedented scale unfolds through the five sections of the volume which chronicle his changing reactions to the different aspects of war.

Throughout its evolution the commanding feature of Apollinaire's attitude is his desire to respond to these events as a new dimension of experience. The general social climate at the outbreak of hostilities—which was, curiously, one of eager anticipation—together with the more specific optimism and energy of his own modernist outlook led him to welcome the coming conflict as the opening of a new era of infinite promise. It takes only a reading

of **"La Petite Auto,"** the poem that is virtually the overture for everything that follows, to see that his vision of the war was an epic one. The almost apocalyptic images that swell the tone of this poem represent the simultanist vision of the 1913-1914 period carried to a new pitch of intensity. Embracing within himself the dimensions of earth, sky, and ocean as well as the armies spreading across the face of Europe, the poet feels that coming events can only multiply his powers further. The pattern that can be traced throughout the succeeding work is that of Apollinaire's attempt to maintain this larger vision in face of the realities of war. Aragon's belief that "ce serait un crime de montrer les beaux côtés de la guerre . . . même si elle en avait" [it would be a crime to show the attractive face of war . . . even if it had one] is the very antithesis of what Apollinaire was trying to achieve ["Beautés de la guerre et leurs reflets dans la littérature," *Europe,* December 1935]. The division of the effects of war into horrors and beauties is one that he sought to transcend in order to grasp it as a total experience that could multiply his imaginative powers and his capacity for living.

The synthesis was perhaps easiest to achieve in the period covered by **"Étendards"** and **"Case d'Armons."** Novelty enhanced the enthusiasm with which Apollinaire entered upon his training as a soldier and underwent his first engagements in artillery combat at the front. He was proud that, as an intellectual and a poet, he could prove the equal of the other recruits (mostly much younger than himself) in becoming a man of action, and he derived immense satisfaction from mastering the pragmatic skills of soldiering. The sense of being part of a vast collective effort, and the experience of comradeship, brought the kind of fulfillment that was sought in more imaginative terms in the prewar period. Echoing the proud statement of a liberated personality in **"Le Musicien de Saint-Merry"**—"J'ai enfin le droit de saluer des êtres que je ne connais pas"—the enlisted poet can say with equal force but more literal truth, "Me voici libre et fier parmi mes compagnons." That is not to say that Apollinaire felt none of the alienating effects of his situation. The loneliness and the apprehension that could afflict him are strongly expressed in **"La Colombe Poignardée et le Jet d'Eau,"** while the reinforcement of the basic polarities of his nature, under pressure of the war situation, is densely formulated in one line of **"Visée"**: "Guerre paisible ascèse solitude métaphysique." But at this early stage inner doubts are conquered by an effort of the will and the imagination. The sense of purpose felt in his life spills over into his creative activity. As in the prewar period, his self-confidence is expressed equally in vigorous simplicity of expression and lively formal innovations, represented on the one hand by the easy discursive verse of **"2ᵉ Canonnier Conducteur," "A Nîmes,"** and **"Veille,"** and on the other by the typographical experiments and bold plastic values of many poems of "Case d'Armons."

The recurring image in "Case d'Armons" which crystallizes the freedom of spirit of the early months at the front is that of *le bois* or *la forêt,* suggesting a private enclave, a time out of war, which the poet has created for himself. It is a fact that Apollinaire's battery was stationed during this period (April-June 1915) in a small wood at some distance from the front line. His letters are full of delighted accounts of its plant and animal life and the hours of leisure he enjoyed within it, in relative safety, writing and making rings out of shell cases. But the poems—"Échelon" especially, with the white wound of the trenches seen beyond the wood and Death dangling at the perimeter—heighten this real-life situation by a process of fabulation in which the wood takes on the associations of a privileged, almost magic, sanctuary. A sense of security, therefore, spreads throughout the poems, exorcising danger. An artillery bombardment becomes an exciting and enchanting event: "La forêt merveilleuse où je vis donne un bal." Death-dealing shells are transformed into swift and beautiful birds of prey, pastoral harbingers of love, or tightrope dancers full of the grace of spring. Because he is sheltered by the wood, the soldier of **"Les Saisons"** can see his life as an ordered succession of happy moments, the time of war being indistinguishable from the time of peace. This is not escapism, or obliviousness of death and danger, whose presence is acknowledged in the background and occasionally filters into the poems. It is rather that the ominous associations of war are sublimated in a release of energy, prompted by a situation with an unusual appeal to the poet's imagination and stimulating him to a unique appreciation of life, given greater force by its context.

At this and all subsequent stages love is, of course, one of the major ways in which Apollinaire tried to sustain his vision. The significant group of poems here are those written for Madeleine Pagès. The dying loves for Marie Laurencin and Louise de Coligny add to the singular richness of love themes in the volume, generating elegiac poems in that vein of condensed and evocative lyricism of which he was a consummate master. The sequence of quatrains in **"Lueurs des Tirs"** which he wrote for Marie conceal ambivalent depths of meaning beneath a limpid surface with a skill that he rarely surpassed. What is special about the poems to Madeleine, however, is the way in which they are deliberately made to fulfill a vital need for spiritual replenishment and creative stimulation. Particularly in the autumn and winter of 1915, when the first euphoria of war had subsided and his battery had moved forward into front-line combat in one of the major battle zones of the war, Madeleine is made the focal point of his determination to be equal to events as a poet no less than as a man. In a real sense, as **"Dans l'Abri-Caverne"** lucidly recognizes, his love is as much a creation of his imagination as actual feeling for another person. Although such poems as **"Simultanéités," "Chevaux de Frise," "Désir,"** and **"Un Oiseau Chante"** often have the enraptured tone and ecstatic imagery of highly self-conscious love poetry, literary *préciosité* does not arise, because the aim is clearly to invest a grim reality with human significance. The metaphoric connections that are woven so persistently between the battlefield and the distant object of the poet's dreams draw together two widely different realities and, by enlarging the poet's awareness of both, allow him to transcend his immediate situation.

Remarkably, the escalating eroticism of the poems is made to fulfill a similar function. The whole violence of war is colored by the poet's sexual longing and becomes the ex-

Undoubtedly the greatest challenge to Apollinaire's powers as a poet was that of finding a convincing form and style in which to convey his epic vision of the war, without insensitivity to the real horror and suffering that were involved.

—S. I. Lockerbie

pression, not of a destructive aim, but of a fierce celebration of passion. Ultimately the erotic drive extends beyond the poet himself and is projected in many poems as a fundamental life-force which is larger than hate and unites the combating nations in "le terrible amour des peuples" [the terrible love of the (warring) peoples] (**"Le Chant d'Amour"**). This is not a Freudian hypothesis about the link between sex and aggression, but rather an attitude of quasi-religious awe at the convulsion which shakes humanity. It is an attempt to humanize and make sense of violence by seeing it as an expression of a vital urge which ultimately transcends its death-dealing function.

The dangers of celebrating violence at so high-flown a level are only too obvious, and Apollinaire has more than once been accused—but short-sightedly—of turning a horrific situation into a private egotistical "fête" and thus of revealing serious emotional inadequacy. Undoubtedly the greatest challenge to his powers as a poet was that of finding a convincing form and style in which to convey his epic vision of the war, without insensitivity to the real horror and suffering that were involved. The solution is found in a constant striving to elevate events to a mythic dimension, beyond the notions of death and destruction. In some instances (**"La Petite Auto," "Merveille de la Guerre"**) it is the poet's own self that is mythologized so that he takes on a larger identity, capable of seeing beyond the cataclysm to the transfigured future that will be born from it. In other poems (**"Chant de l'Horizon en Champagne," "Le Vigneron Champenois"**) there is a suggestion that events are seen from the viewpoint of larger-than-life deities and thus take on, in their broader vision, a significance that escapes the merely human eye. A wider imaginative perspective is also created by uses of the simultanist technique of the modernist period (**"Il y a"**), by the involvement of extrahuman, as well as human, forces (**"Chant de l'Honneur"**), and by the visionary qualities of much of the imagery (the long night of labor of **"Désir,"** for example). By these means there is a successful heightening of the traumatic events of war, which does not imply blindness to death and suffering but rather an optimistic conviction that humanity can survive the holocaust and emerge magnified by the experience.

There is ample evidence in the poems from the last months of Apollinaire's service that he was aware of the real horrors of war. The poems written after his transfer to the infantry at the end of November 1915 are increasingly grave. In the artillery the dugout had been, like the wood, a symbol of security, but now that it is a front-line infantry dugout it is given, in the hallucinatory images of **"Océan de Terre,"** new associations of dread and fear. **"L'Avenir"** and **"Exercice,"** in their sobriety of form and statement, are overshadowed by an awareness of death; they speak of the need for a stoic retreat within the self as the only safeguard against the dehumanizing effect of war. Yet, even in this period of great gravity, Apollinaire is still impelled to prove himself equal as a poet to the scale of the conflict in which he is enmeshed. **"Du Coton dans les Oreilles,"** one of the last poems written at the front, is also one of his major compositions in its successful attempt to match, in the span and controlled confusion of its parts, the cacophony and frenzy of war. It is at once a definitive expression of the anarchy of war and yet, in the way the wild sweep of events is artistically channeled, a demonstration of the poet's control over disorder.

It is, therefore, by the overall breadth of his vision and the quality of his artistic achievement that Apollinaire is to be judged as a war poet, and not—as has too often been done—by the single criterion of the degree of pathos that he achieves in selected poems. War for him was a total and complex experience whose contradictions can be reconciled only within a heightened poetic vision. His achievement is that his war poetry as a whole successfully embodies that vision.

The final creative period of Apollinaire's life is the short span of two years between the autumn of 1916, following his (partial) recovery from a head wound received in March 1916, to his death in November 1918. The dominating aesthetic ideas of this period are a more mature and more pronounced form of his prewar modernism. They are most fully elaborated in his famous lecture **"L'Esprit Nouveau et les Poètes"** in November 1917, whose central theme is the need for constant experiment and innovation if poetry is to maintain its place in the modern world. The miracles achieved by contemporary science and technology are so staggering, according to Apollinaire, that poetry risks being left behind in the ability to express the creative spirit of man. To rival the achievements of the scientists, poets have to rid themselves of outmoded forms and conventions and seek to renew their art by every means possible. The new spirit in poetry will be distinguished by its power of absolute invention and its capacity to surprise and astonish. As in the prewar period, but in a much stronger sense, prophecy and surprise are proclaimed to be the two cardinal virtues of a modern poetics. Through prophecy the artist will constantly be able to look into the unknown and anticipate the mysteries of the future; through surprise the new will constantly be created and recreated.

This radical commitment to innovation is qualified by the statement that a modernist aesthetic should nevertheless seek to retain the finest elements of the past. If the new spirit inherits from Romanticism its restless quest for novelty, it must draw from classicism certain traditional qualities. Limits are set to innovation, dictated by common sense and an awareness of the need for discipline and order: by these standards some of the more hectic of recent experiments are suggested to be puerile. These concessions to tradition, however, strengthen rather than weaken a paean of praise which performs the considerable rhetorical feat of bestowing on the avant-garde spirit both a cloak of heroic glamour and a mantle of authority.

The ideas of **"L'Esprit Nouveau"** form the very stuff of the last great poems of *Calligrammes*—**"La Victoire," "La Jolie Rousse,"** and, of course, **"Les Collines,"** which truly belongs to this period—but are developed there with a significant difference of tone and mood. Whereas the lecture was enthusiastic and confident, anxiety and uncertainty again invade the poems. **"La Victoire"** may seem to be calling for an uninhibited assault on traditional poetic language which is consistent with the lecture and Apollinaire's previous practice, but the constant faltering of the tone points to underlying inhibitions and self-doubt. More strikingly still, where the alliance between the old and the new seems easy and unproblematic in the lecture, there is a sharper polarization in **"La Jolie Rousse"** which speaks of a "long quarrel" between tradition and invention, which the poet will have to struggle to surmount, knowing that there will be many compromises and failures on the way.

It is sometimes said that this note of self-doubt is attributable to personal difficulties and changing circumstances in the last two years of Apollinaire's life. His head wound had left him debilitated and frequently depressed; as **"Tristesse d'une Étoile"** seems to hint, he may even have feared permanent impairment of his poetic powers. He also suddenly found himself elevated to the status of a recognized master for a whole new generation of poets, but he was uneasily aware that some of his disciples were prepared to be more radically iconoclastic than himself (hence some veiled criticisms in the lecture). There is no doubt some substance in these explanations, but, looking deeper, the most profound reason for the tone of the poems is less a failure of purpose than a positive choice of conflict and tension as a preferred creative state of mind. As in the 1913-1914 period, Apollinaire is intuitively aware of the inspiration he can find in doubt and uncertainty, and he values the dramatic heightening of mood that results from a clash between optimism and anxiety. He needs, even more strongly than in **"Liens"** and the prewar work, to bring all his conflicting emotions to bear on a theme that is of central importance to him and to make a definitive statement that embraces all aspects of his creative personality.

This theme is the heroic anguish of the poet as the explorer of the future. Whereas in **"Liens"** the conflict was experienced in the private area of Apollinaire's own sensibility and attitude to the world, the emphasis in **"La Victoire," "Les Collines,"** and **"La Jolie Rousse"** is thrown entirely onto the poet's public persona as an artist undertaking an arduous responsibility on behalf of humanity. It is this sense of a mission, requiring all the vision and courage of a man who had lived through the tumult of war and suffered personally, which provides the resolution between anguish and optimism and makes the final poems, particularly **"Les Collines"** and **"La Jolie Rousse,"** the definitive statement of Apollinaire's credo. The moving quality of **"La Jolie Rousse"** comes partly from our knowledge that it was virtually Apollinaire's last word before his untimely death. But, even without this extraneous knowledge, it stands as a remarkably complete summation of his achievement and genius as they now appear before history. He can rightly claim to be the one poet above all others who unites the virtues of a long poetic tradition and those of a new phase of bold experiment and change. In the depth of his vision and his consummate mastery of poetic language he is in complete continuity with the great poetry of the past. In his determination to make poetry assume an adventurous and pioneering role in creating a new sensibility for a new and rapidly changing world, he is a man of the future. It is fitting that his poetic testament should be so lucid and poignant a recognition of his unique position. (pp. 1-20)

> *S. I. Lockerbie, in an introduction to* Calligrammes: Poems of Peace and War (1913-1916) *by Guillaume Apollinaire, translated by Anne Hyde Greet, University of California Press, 1980, pp. 1-20.*

Paul Zweig on the greatness of Apollinaire the poet:

Like Eliot and Pound in America, Apollinaire worked to extend the appetite of his poetry, including in his bestiary of images such unpoetic marvels as the airplane, the Eiffel Tower, the executive secretary, and the farting automobile. But he never relinquished that delicate lyricism which is the genius of the French language. Like Verlaine before him, he dealt in unexpected harmonies, expressing, with his array of modernisms, an infinitely tender sensibility. Poems like **"Zône," "La Ballade du Mal Aimé,"** and **"Cortèges"** are among the greatest of our century. For the first time in France a poet was able to combine the new language of the cities with a taste for the esoteric—Apollinaire was a scholar of the occult—and a truly lyric imagination. But what has made Apollinaire a hero for recent New York poets like Frank O'Hara and John Ashbery, is the bizarre freedom of association, the disconcerting leaps from image to image which characterize so many of his poems. . . .

If we are to learn from Apollinaire, however, we must remember that his imaginative freedom belonged above all to a poetry of love. There is a tenderness in his rhythms which seems to have escaped men like Ashbery or O'Hara. Apollinaire was a poet in revolt, but it was a revolt of love, an attempt to free the emotions from the tired rails they had been confined to for so long.

> *Paul Zweig in "French Chronicle," Poetry, November 1967.*

Harry E. Buckley (essay date 1981)

[*In the following excerpt, Buckley assesses Apollinaire's art criticism.*]

Guillaume Apollinaire apparently needs little praise in the present decade. His personality and creativity have received in recent years more than adequate attention. As a colorful figure he has most recently been celebrated by Roger Shattuck in *The Banquet Years,* by Cecily Mack-

worth in *Guillaume Apollinaire and the Cubist Life,* and by Francis Steegmuller in *Apollinaire: Poet Among the Painters.* His poetry has always been recognized as of primary significance for the twentieth century; there is, for instance, this statement in the last study mentioned:

> **Alcools,** this selection by Apollinaire of fifty-five of the many poems written between his eighteenth year and his thirty-third, called by Albert Camus one of the most 'astonishing' works, along with Rimbaud's *Les Illuminations,* that French poetry has produced, has become for the modern world one of the best known and most appealing volumes of verse of any century.

For decades Apollinaire has lived in art history in a rather shadowy fashion. Speak of Picasso and the *Bateau-Lavoir* at the birthday of Cubism and Apollinaire was there. When critics describe the avant-garde's high regard for Henri Rousseau in the last years of his life, they usually mention his apotheosis at a famous banquet in 1908—a banquet at which Apollinaire served as a leading spokesman. In fact, Apollinaire introduced the *Bateau-Lavoir* circle to Rousseau. Who led the Futurists about Paris in their mismatched stockings in 1911 but Apollinaire? When Robert Delaunay moved from abstract to nonobjective painting, the poet was by his side. Who was the first to comment favorably upon the miraculous color of Marc Chagall, the first to remark upon the compelling mystery of Giorgio de Chirico, the first to use the term "surrealistic"? Very probably the ubiquitous Apollinaire. He seemed to be involved in everything that eventually emerged as fundamental to the course of modern art.

In addition to this involvement in the creative and social lives of the avant-garde in Paris between 1905 and 1918, it was generally known that Apollinaire had served as a spokesman for the new ideas developing at this time. His function as a critic appeared to be of immediate value because of his presence on the scene at those momentous occasions in modern art. In 1913 he produced a book on Cubism, **Les Peintres cubistes: Méditations Esthétiques,** his only book on art. After the powerful impression generated by his attractive personality and exciting poetry, **Les Peintres cubistes** was a severe shock. A haphazard jumble of confused ideas and remarks, it lacked the critical insight of Daniel-Henry Kahnweiler's *Der Weg zum Kubismus* (1920). It could not claim to have been the first document of Cubism; that place had already been taken by Albert Gleizes' and Jean Metzinger's *Du Cubisme* (1912), a serious theoretical study of the movement. The adverse reaction to the book put Apollinaire into a limbo as an art critic and art historian; it was decided that one might find useful material in his biography or in his poetry, but he was best ignored as a critic. However, this book contained only some of the poet's criticism. Few realize that the book is composed in large degree of articles written for and published in periodicals in previous years (1905-1913).

The general condemnation of Apollinaire as a critic following publication of his one book on art blinded scholars to another realm of Apollinaire's critical expression: the articles in reviews, journals and newspapers. Only recently have the greater part of these articles been brought together from their scattered sources by LeRoy C. Breunig in a collection entitled *Chroniques d'Art.* And the only scholarship focused upon them in this country has been the work of literary scholars, such as LeRoy C. Breunig, Anna Balakian, Francis J. Carmody, and Roger Shattuck.

The genuine calibre of Apollinaire as a critic can only be discovered after a study of his principal criticism, consisting of the many notes, notices, comments, essays and studies he wrote for journalistic sources between 1905 and 1918. These, his most representative writings on art, emerge most directly and spontaneously from the years in which he was involved in the artistic adventures of the avant-garde.

Not a little of their value derives from their immediacy. Apollinaire drew his ideas from the concepts being bandied about the studios of the avant-garde in Paris. The very nature of his criticism is determined by the context in which the articles were written. And, despite the years that have intervened, his critical articles still very often convey more clearly than any other source—later historical studies, or even the remarks of the artists themselves—the situation of the avant-garde in the early twentieth century. (pp. 1-2)

When viewing the whole of Apollinaire's criticism, it appears to fall into four periods: Period I (1905-1907), essentially his initiatory period as a critic, in which only a few, widely varying articles appear; Period II (1907-1911), productive years in which Apollinaire reveals himself as a more mature, effective writer upon the art and artists of the avant-garde; Period III (1912-1914), a brief but very active period for Apollinaire as a writer on art, in which he expands his interest beyond his earlier allegiance; and Period IV (1914-1918), coinciding with the First World War, when, for several reasons, Apollinaire's criticism is sharply curtailed. (p. 3)

Roger Shattuck contended in his [introduction to] *Selected Writings of Guillaume Apollinaire* that the three distinguishable aspects of his being—the legend, the biography and the poetry—should not be separated. This attitude is as valid now as it was in 1948. To those three areas should be added the criticism which cannot be studied in isolation from the other aspects of his being without losing its essential significance and power. For there is an organic nature to the life of Guillaume Apollinaire that causes such a fragmentation to overlook the heart of the contribution he made in the multiple roles he played. (p. 4)

The periodic examination of his writings on art is essential to a fuller understanding of them. Within the chronological context, it is possible to develop the details which are so necessary to such an examination. It is a particular quality of Guillaume Apollinaire as a critic that he should seem less discerning, less significant when he is read apart from the historical context. Apollinaire produced a body of critical works intrinsically tied to their times; to remove them is to dilute them. But this has also been the effect of separation of his literature or his biography. This makes it extremely difficult to do what is now necessary: to remark generally upon aspects of Apollinaire's criticism.

The key point in defining the broad basis of his criticism is recognition of the manner in which Apollinaire was a critic of the avant-garde. At least three implications of note occur in this initial characterization of him as a critic. It correctly suggests that Apollinaire as a critic expresses ideas and attitudes of currency within the most advanced artistic circles. Secondly, it implies that the critic is favorably inclined toward those ideas and attitudes. And finally, the assertion indicates that his critical attention is almost exclusively focused upon the most recent manifestations in art.

A significant element of this critical position is to be found in Apollinaire's rejection of the past. As part of his working philosophy it explains the indifference or antagonism which he displayed toward the preceding generations. In the visual arts the rejection is directed toward Impressionism and Symbolism. Impressionism was considered by the avant-garde of the early twentieth century to have been a movement in which the artist subjugated himself to nature. The explicit expression of this view has been seen in the condemnation from **"The Three Plastic Virtues"** of 1908: "Nevertheless, too many artists, particularly painters, still adore plants, stones, water, or man," and in the direct remarks of the catalog preface for the Braque exhibition of 1909.

But the artists we know as the Post-Impressionists—Seurat, Cézanne, Van Gogh and Gauguin—arrived at artistic stances that in effect undermined the Impressionist solution. The impetus which these painters gave to the generation of Apollinaire's day has since been delineated; but the influence in the crucial period between 1902 and 1908 upon artists such as Matisse, Derain, Vlaminck, Picasso and Braque was not so obvious nor so concerted in nature as later history has presented it. Of these four artists, Seurat was overshadowed by his successors, active pointillists such as Signac and Luce; Van Gogh, without a following of this sort, influenced Derain and Vlaminck but received no significant critical recognition at the time; Cézanne exerted a considerable influence after 1904 on many of the younger generation, and obtained the clearest signs of recognition; and Gauguin was in a somewhat similar eclipse as Seurat through the active presence of the Symbolists, Denis and Sérusier notably. All in all, these Post-Impressionists through their individualism did not assume either the status of significant forebears or enemies to the new directions taken by the generation of the first quarter of the twentieth century.

Symbolism was the most visible recent artistic movement at the time. Knowing the manner in which the Symbolist painters themselves sought a reformation of art that would avoid the deficiencies of Impressionism, one would expect them to be applauded by Apollinaire's circle. The important role assigned to subjectivity, the liberation of the artist from a subjugation to a mechanical rendering of a material universe, and hence the formal freedom gained by the artist were factors which the avant-garde of the first two decades of the century could appreciate. And recognition of the Symbolist effort occurred in Apollinaire's criticism. . . . (pp. 123-24)

But it is essential to establish at this point that Symbolism in painting had taken on an appearance which discounted its contributions to the youthful artists of his acquaintance. The earlier signs of liberality had tended to diminish in Denis and Sérusier, the spokesmen for Symbolism. As the movement became older, it developed a more inflexible, programmatic attitude. Three serious flaws were prominent: the supression of individualism (or, more mildly, the direction of individuality toward common goals), the circumscription of the artist, and a divorce of art from life (or more simply, a failure to provide any meaningful or profound statement on life in their art). There is a certain justification for this view of later Symbolism, but it cannot be developed here; it is sufficient to the purpose to recognize that Symbolism had become in the main discredited for the newer generation of painters and poets, and that the discreditation left a vacuum within which the artists were faced with the problem of constructing a system which would possess validity and inspiration.

This last statement may read like a truism, for is it not in the character of every generation to create such a scheme? Perhaps so, but it is the particular feature of the generation of Apollinaire that their proposals should bear a stamp that distinguishes them as belonging to the modern period.

If Apollinaire was of signal importance for detaching the new age from the old in his literature, one expects to find evidence of this action in his criticism. Although there is not a precise coincidence between his own work as an artist and the observations on art made in his critical writings, there are ample signs of such evidence. In company with his friends among the visual artists, Apollinaire set out to define the new attitude, which he would term the "New Spirit" in the last year of his life (in the lecture of November, 1917, published posthumously).

From the beginning this was an attitude proclaiming the freedom of the artist. Although the artist of the earlier twentieth century living in Paris may seem to have enjoyed a more liberal environment than his counterpart in any previous period, the spirit of revolt remained. There were still restraints to be thrown off. Perhaps the most constraining was the unwarranted prestige assigned to tradition. Conservative artists and critics, who maintained themselves through an identification with tradition designed to disguise the lack of abilities other than a vacant eclecticism and technical skill, could expect to find support in official quarters, an approval which still carried weight to an uninformed public. The pretense involved in this alliance could not be tolerated by the avant-garde of the Fauves and the *Bateau-Lavoir* circle; the impatience of youth was at work in the formation of their intolerance.

The anarchy in art for which they seemed to stand is more apparent than real. Admittedly, there were episodes in which the anarchistic spirit is strong; several humorous incidents (the Lolo-Boronali escapade, and Apollinaire's own satirical review of the Salon d'Automne of 1907) could be cited as evidence of this impulse. Ridicule was a vehicle of antagonism toward the official powers in art who were attempting to stifle the avant-garde (to follow up the latter example, the rejection of Fauvist work by the Salon jury, which was of Symbolist persuasion). Such humorous antagonism is only a negative facet of the "New Spirit," though one worthy of recognition.

More positive aspects of the anarchistic spirit may be discovered in the manner in which Apollinaire expressed sympathy for experimental tendencies. Here there was a complete alliance between poets and painters; together they made common cause against Symbolism. Even the most excessive actions in art must be sanctioned; to do otherwise would be to hedge on the freedom allowed the artist. This may invite chaos, as Apollinaire admitted; but it will be chaos which will neither damage nor deter the artist.

The youthful rebelliousness of the avant-garde of which Apollinaire was a member was moderated in time; the signs of moderation can be seen in the second period of his criticism, that is, after late 1907. The tone of Matisse's remarks included by Apollinaire in his article on the painter at that time, the nature of his critical writings thereafter, and what we know of the development of Cubism after 1907, all coincide to present an image of the younger generation's seriousness. But the demand for artistic freedom was never relinquished by Apollinaire, as evidenced by his statement in his article when he notes that the experiments of the Italian and Russian Futurists are "excesses" this may be read as a negative criticism by Apollinaire, but it is not a condemnation of the right to experimentation. Artistic failure through excess is preferable to artistic bondage, however slight.

And it was Apollinaire's sensitivity to the matter of esthetic freedom that ultimately determined the breadth of his criticism and its predominantly affirmative character. He sought to recognize novelty—not to approve it, but at least to recognize it. He will therefore report on such manifestations, although he will not necessarily evaluate them. No doubt he welcomed such experimental novelties, not because he lacked discrimination, but because he desired to enlarge the domain of art . . . in short, to increase the artist's freedom.

The anarchy of the avant-garde was not as extreme as it was sometimes pictured during the lifetime of Apollinaire. The serious tone recognized within Matisse, Picasso and the Cubists and within the avant-garde generally (a point frequently made by Apollinaire), implies a responsibility about their actions. At times this responsibility may seem to be defined in narrow, selfish terms; this is particularly true when Apollinaire writes critically of an autonomy in art. In this view the artist is removed from consideration in terms of practicality or morality; he is the master, alert only to the artistic possibilities within himself.

Yet almost as often as he presents this view of the artist, Apollinaire has remarked on the contribution which the artist has made or can make to society. The two views are not irreconcilable, for it is possible that the painter or poet who is most fully absorbed in himself in his art may well make the most meaningful contribution to our experience. When in 1914 Apollinaire speaks of the artist desiring "to renew our vision of the world and finally to know the universe," this renewal and knowledge are possible effects of the artist's subjectivity.

> It was Apollinaire's sensitivity to the matter of esthetic freedom that ultimately determined the breadth of his criticism and its predominantly affirmative character. He sought to recognize novelty—not to approve it, but at least to recognize it.
>
> —*Harry E. Buckley*

The artists of his generation were thrown back upon themselves to provide the resources to fill the vacuum left by the dismissal of the pertinency of Impressionism and Symbolism. Initially those resources were only vaguely sensed, and more than a little bravado marks the gestures of the younger generation of the first decade of the century. The courage and audacity which Apollinaire displayed in his own poetry and so frequently applauded in his painter friends was made possible by a certainty which they felt about themselves.

Apollinaire thought of these artists (and it should be added that he included himself among them) as heroic. . . . In his mind the heroism consisted of the courage to construct a new framework within the chaos of the artistic arena bearing the ruins of Impressionism and Symbolism.

The structure that arose, whether in Apollinaire's poetry, his criticism, or the painting, is not a single, simple thing. And it is not entirely pristine; for, to follow the image, there are signs of the past in the construction of the "New Spirit." The creation of order from chaos (which can be recognized as the definition of art given by Apollinaire in 1907) could hardly take place in a true vacuum, although vacuum has been used in this [essay] to describe the situation in which the avant-garde artist found himself. The retention of Symbolist as well as other traditional elements in the poetry of Apollinaire beyond 1908 (which has been considered the year in which his distinctly new approach to poetics is visible), the stylistic dependencies of Matisse and the Cubists: both of these indicate that the past was not entirely abandoned.

In this regard it can be remarked that Apollinaire the critic is not always in concert with Apollinaire the poet. After the burst of innovation that occurred in his poetry of 1908, he does not therefore avoid all the devices and elements of tradition. The statements made in 1912 and 1913 in articles on art (such as **"The New Painting"** and **"Modern Painting"**) are much more advanced than his own poetic compositions of the same period. This disparity was possible when he wrote on a creative field other than his own. He encouraged a boldness for the visual artist that forecasts the period of poetic invention which he entered in 1913.

The examination of Apollinaire as a critic of the avant-garde has been pursued at some length because in a very direct fashion it determines various major characteristics of his criticism. For example, the impartiality of which he has been accused is a sign of his identification with the avant-garde. The degree of indiscriminate approval which some recognize in his criticism may be understood to result from his acceptance of the role of spokesman for the artistic vanguard. In tandem with this is his tendency upon occasion to be over-emphatic in his approval. In particular this characteristic is generated by his impulse to attain acceptance for that art of which he approved. It is not characteristic of the whole of Apollinaire's writings, however, but is chiefly present in those of Period III when . . . those artists and movements which he felt deserving of attention were receiving a heavy critical attack from the more conservative elements in art.

The infrequent use of art historical reference in his criticism indicates a pronounced ignorance of the past; his attention was absorbed in the present. In addition, Apollinaire's position as spokesman for the avant-garde explains his willingness to attend to almost everything that was available in the visual arts of his lifetime; he admitted to a weakness of speaking favorably about the many artistic manifestations between 1905 and 1918. What may be considered indiscriminate approval on the one hand can, on the other, be considered a generosity of intellect and spirit that is not without value. In particular, it led Apollinaire to give attention to ideas that were all too often dismissed as worthless or minor by critics who held a position which led them to a more consistent body of criticism through their bigotry.

Now, to return to Apollinaire's expression of ideas and attitudes of contemporary currency. This is of notable value historically, inasmuch as his criticism becomes useful in recreating the milieu in which modern art was born. It is pertinent to note again some of the current concerns of art which are identifiable within the writings of Apollinaire here, apart from the chronological context, in order to emphasize the important service which Apollinaire performed in articulating these ideas and attitudes at the moments when they were effective.

A most revealing attitude can be briefly dealt with, since it has been introduced already in considering the character of his criticism. This is the general disdain in which the avant-garde held their predecessors in art; in particular, their antagonism to Impressionism, expressed in the catalog preface for the Braque exhibition of 1909, is extremely helpful in sensing their impatience with the past, felt as a dead weight by the younger generation of painters. Favorable mention is made in scattered references to those artists we now know as Post-Impressionists: it is especially Cézanne, the most often mentioned, who had a pertinency to the contemporary problems and concerns of the avant-garde. Yet because such favorable references are few, we are able to feel the sense of need for a continued struggle to find a suitable means of expressing a truly contemporary reality.

Another attitude is clearly revealed in Apollinaire's remarks on abstraction, [which should be noted] as one instance of his prophetic ability. Here one can discover the way in which his friends among the painters of Paris reacted toward the problem of realism in art. Insofar as the history of art is an exercise in the recreation of what is real as demonstrated through the art of a given period, Apollinaire's statements become helpful documents to supplement the visual evidence of the paintings and sculptures. In Apollinaire's comments upon abstraction between 1908 and 1918, we are given an impressive insight into the progressively more abstract art of his own time. Apollinaire appears unique in his critical recognition of this particularly crucial aspect of modern art.

Of near equal significance to the manner in which Apollinaire reveals the avant-garde attitude toward abstraction is the manner in which his writings illuminate these artists' formalistic concerns. The persistence with which the consideration of the formal business of the artist appears as a theme in his articles demonstrates that it is a dominant idea within the studios during the period between 1907 and 1918.

Apollinaire's statements as indications of contemporary ideas and attitudes are still not exhausted. One of his characteristics may at first glance be considered a defect rather than a value: his tendency to avoid precise distinctions between schools of art. It results not merely from an inability to discover differences, but from a conviction that artists' common features needed to be stressed as much as the characteristics that separated them. In certain instances this is particularly salutary; for examples, his recognition of an intuitive aspect within early Cubism—an aspect that is often attributed only to Fauvism—is an extremely valuable insight, and his constant tendency to blur distinctions between movements is, to a limited extent, a sign of their underlying common quality or purpose. The latter attitude is especially notable in Apollinaire's criticism; it should be mentioned that it was maintained without doubt in the face of fierce partisan claims to artistic independence made by members of the various groups. Because of the validity of the position, and because of the manner in which Apollinaire avoided being a captive of the claims of any one group, it appears to be the most valuable of all the factors that define his contribution as a spokesman on artistic matters.

The manner in which his journalistic writings represent current thought within the avant-garde has been stressed in this study. He spoke from a base of authority enjoyed by no other critic active at that time. There were a few who maintained an association with one or another of the smaller coteries. But there was no one else who was so closely involved with these artistic groups—Fauvism, Cubism, Section d'Or and Orphism—at the moment of their formation and the initial formulation of their ideas. This direct involvement, while it did not insure the production of critical documents of supreme significance, at least demands that the writings of Apollinaire be given special attention.

Besides explaining ideas and attitudes displayed by the poet-critic, his identification with the avant-garde determines the flexibility which marks his criticism. Visible in the form of changes of mind about artists, this may be considered a flaw (the sign of a vacillating critic who displays an inconsistency of thought) or a virtue. Considering that his criticism falls within a span of thirteen years, it is not unexpected that changes should occur (as in his attitude toward Henri Rousseau, or his switch in allegiance from Cubism in the narrow sense to the Section d'Or and Orphism in 1912). Flexibility was a factor throughout Apollinaire's life; critically it meant that he was always open to the possibility of revised opinion or acceptance of a new idea in art. No doubt the primary reason for seeing his flexibility as a virtue is that it resulted in writings on the whole spectrum of the arts in Paris between 1905 and 1918. Few critics had any inclination or capacity for appreciation of other than a narrow range within the visual arts.

Apollinaire sought to encourage the artists of his generation in their ventures; he supported them wholeheartedly, lending his prestige as a poet as well as his technique in this action. He was not a connoisseur in the arts, if we accept the definition of a connoisseur as one who achieves a critical accuracy in his discriminations within a comprehensive, coherent scheme of esthetic appreciation. Apollinaire had an appreciation for the artists whom he knew, eliciting informal evaluative judgments not ordinarily supported by closely reasoned argument.

The informal evaluative judgments, marked by lyrical language upon occasion, by enthusiasm and partiality, make it difficult to classify all the periodical articles of Apollinaire as "criticism" in the strictest sense of the term. "Writings on art" might be a more accurate designation for them in this sense. If they were to be called criticism some qualification is necessary; the most applicable one is subjectivist. This qualification contains the effort to define the critic who assigns a value to works of art upon the basis of their impact upon his taste, without feeling the need to achieve exact consistency or to provide a carefully defined explanation of how he arrived at his evaluation.

The poetic quality of some of Apollinaire's criticism in certain instances caused two defects in his articles: a weakness in descriptive or analytical efforts, and the creation of dense or uncertain meanings in his comments. Yet this quality in his approach was also to result in passages and articles of critical value. The effectiveness of this approach is twofold: it gives evidence of Apollinaire's sympathetic intuition, and it keeps alive through its lyricism the creative environment of that art upon which he remarks. The best example of this is **"The Three Plastic Virtues"** of 1909. The fervor of his lyric statements could hardly be surpassed as a means of conveying the spirit that moved the avant-garde of Paris at that time.

Apollinaire's rhetoric can be displayed forcefully and effectively; when this occurs, it remains as convincing now some fifty years later as it was when it was published. The hortatory value of Apollinaire's criticism is less tangible than other characteristics of his writings, but it is by no means the least effective. The conviction that rings through his rhetoric accounts for much of the impact that Apollinaire has had on the generation of artists after the second World War. And it is also accountable in part for the enthusiastic approval of the most fervent admirers of Apollinaire as a critic.

To a great extent, this quality in Apollinaire is a retention of the older impressionistic criticism; and it is indispensable to note once again that in those articles in Period II when he gives signs of moving toward an analytical criticism, Apollinaire is establishing a foundation for a more acceptable critical expression in the later twentieth century.

The subjectivist critic is by no means lacking in our time. The rhetorical exercises of their writings on art approach the poetic nature of instances with Apollinaire's writings. All too often, perhaps, they cloak their pronouncements in such an obscure manner that their desire for a better criticism in the form of a poetic equivalent, justified in their opinion by Baudelaire and Apollinaire, succeeds only in creating impenetrable sibylline statements. Apollinaire would have disapproved of this, for his obscurity is never deliberate; at the bottom of all his subjectivist criticism was a hope of illuminating the experiences of his audience, not darkening them under a shadowy veil.

Ultimately Apollinaire may be considered a paradigm of the critic with a modern attitude. And it is of utmost importance to distinguish wherein this attitude may be defined. It goes beyond the fact that his writings on art represent the current concerns of his friends among the avant-garde. The modern attitude is a creative position which belongs to the twentieth century, setting it apart from the preceding period. This attitude was specifically called by Apollinaire the "New Spirit" in the last year of his life, in that lecture-article entitled **"The New Spirit and the Poets."** Apollinaire attempted to define the qualities and aspects of the modern creative mentality. Although he did not specifically distinguish between an attitude of the nineteenth century and that of his own time, his remarks upon the "New Spirit" taken in conjunction with his own biography and creativity define a new attitude which distinctly belongs to our own time.

The critical shift begins with the rejection of this former view: the conception of art as organic in the sense that it consisted of a progression or development through a series of stages incipient from an initial point. Within this conception it is apparent that art, or at least each movement in art, has a point of resolution. The latter might be represented as a plateau attained after a more or less regular inclination.

Apollinaire does not present a view of art that agrees with this conception. He has no idea of a progressive or developmental scheme to replace the old; if he had, he would not represent a "New Spirit." He seeks no resolution. Rather, spontaneity, instability and mobility seem to characterize his view of creativity. These characteristics may be seen in his poetry. For example, his poetic production cannot be fitted into a coherent progressive scheme, but can be described as a number of oscillations between periods of experimentation and intervals of expression more traditional in tone. And as another example, there are the abrupt dislocations he employed within single poetic compositions; what is most revealing about this practice is that it succeeds in ridding the work of transitions—the very necessary factor for progressive development.

In his writings on art, such a conception of art is never explicitly stated. But does it not provide reason for various

ideas he did express, and for certain characteristics of his criticism? Thus his elevation of surprise to such prominence in art; his most common phrase of praise is to salute the novel, which generates surprise. Surprise is created by the unpredictable, by something for which one is not prepared, as would be the case in a progressive development. It also works to explain the relativism that marks his opinions on the matters of truth and reality with regard to art: "But reality will never be discovered once and for all. Truth will always be new." There is no goal in art in the sense of a point of conclusion.

This conception helps to clarify several of the characteristics of his criticism: his indifference to the history of art which appeared to be a discipline concerned with establishing progressive schemes; the contradictions that may be found, for it would be strange to expect a coherent progression of commentaries in one who has no use for such an expectation; Apollinaire's flexibility with regard to various artists or groups as he shifts his allegiance; and the underlying spontaneous effort which his criticism conveys.

To discover this conception of art among the painters of his company, one need go no further than Picasso, whom Apollinaire considered to be one of the greatest artists among the avant-garde. The stylistic oscillations of this artist during their friendship, the continued shifts from 1918 until this day, do not form a pattern of progression. So very often Apollinaire's pronouncements in his writings on art seem to coincide closely with the creativity of Picasso; it would be reasonable to believe that this is the result of a consanguinity of conceptions about the nature of creativity.

Sharing in the anti-intellectual atmosphere of the *Bateau-Lavoir* period, the environment was of considerable significance in fixing both their attitudes. The unsystematic nature of their milieu between 1905 and 1914 was both their product and in turn a factor of influence upon them. Both Apollinaire and Picasso displayed a similar dislike for the partitioning and labelling of their work, that is, an antagonism toward the establishment of fixed schemes. Both tended to cultivate the eccentric and the ambiguous primarily as a means of fending off such attempts. For example, the manner in which Apollinaire denied knowledge of works that had been proposed as sources for his poetic work was a deliberate effort at mystification, a lie to escape a discovery of this sort. Picasso's denial that he knew anything about African sculpture (*Action,* April 1920) is a falsehood provoked by those who wished to simplify one problem about the origin of Cubism, an explanation which would doubtlessly have been viewed by Picasso as a distortion.

To summarize the elements identified thus far within the working philosophy of Apollinaire, we have: (1) a rejection of the immediate past; (2) a desire to compose a new basis for creativity; (3) an insistence upon absolute freedom for the artist; (4) a belief in the efficacy of art; (5) an emphasis upon the subjectivity of creation; and (6) a rejection of the organic conception of art. Of these points, the last one is by far the most important, and requires consid-

> **Both Apollinaire and Picasso displayed a similar dislike for the partitioning and labelling of their work, that is, an antagonism toward the establishment of fixed schemes. Both tended to cultivate the eccentric and the ambiguous primarily as a means of fending off such attempts.**
>
> —*Harry E. Buckley*

eration in other perspectives to establish how crucial a distinction it is.

To deny the validity of the organic conception of art involves numerous results, some of which—spontaneity, instability, mobility, abandonment of transitions, relativism, lack of coherent development, flexibility—have been briefly mentioned. Rejection of the primarily logical system of the past, however, is still only a negative stance, and such a negativism appears insufficient to explain the enthusiasm and conviction that can be found in Apollinaire the poet and critic of art. It must be realized that the new conception of creativity that stands behind Apollinaire's poetry and which is mirrored in his critical writings is finally a positive philosophy.

This philosophy is not so susceptible to precise definition and clear presentation as those philosophies that proceed logically from their assumptions. Yet it is nonetheless as functional as a way of life. Apollinaire proposed his "New Spirit" as a framework for action in his own day, and desired that it, like any philosophy, should encompass most fully the features of human existence in its time. It embraced intuition, memory, sentiment, reason, humor, play, provocation and ethical purpose, and it did so in a manner that sought to avoid a compartmentalization of the motives and sensations that compose a being. In short, the philosophical position of Apollinaire is an effort at unification. The new unification cannot be expected to have a sequential arrangement, because the reality which it seeks to describe is only partially susceptible to such schematization. The unification is composed of all the disparate, even contradictory aspects and impulses of man; it is not a fusion of those aspects and impulses (they remain disparate and contradictory), but rather is in the nature of an equilibrium maintained among them. Sometimes spontaneously, sometimes by plan, one motive or sensation is in the ascendancy; the reality of life is a constant balancing act, without a firm platform of conclusion.

Simultaneity is a term that can be applied to the sense of unity sought by Apollinaire. The very attraction exerted by this concept is illustrated by his enthusiasm in 1912-1913 for dramatism in literature and Orphism in painting. Conceptually, it expressed the nature of creativity as defined by the "New Spirit," and caught as well the essential basis of human experience. Simultaneity has its technique: plasticity. In poetry this refers to those dislocations, the abrupt shifts that appear in Apollinaire's composition.

Apollinaire was not alone in forming this philosophy. Indeed, he could not have formed it had it not been for his extreme sensitivity to the currents of his own time. Thus, although there seems to be no direct influence, one cannot help but realize that concepts of Henri Bergson bear a resemblance to those identified in Apollinaire; the role of intuition as defined by Bergson had its impact upon the poet-critic; the concept of *élan vital* invites consideration with respect to Apollinaire's "New Spirit." In his rejection of any progressive scheme of creativity, Apollinaire struggled against the effect of the doctrine of mechanistic materialism; at almost precisely the same time, the writings of Henri Poincaré reveal an acceptance of relativism in science that succeeds in performing a similar severance from the nineteenth century in the scientific field, thereby proclaiming a plasticity for science that Apollinaire was asserting as the true nature of artistic creativity. Even the new technology acted to encourage Apollinaire in the formation of the "New Spirit"; the community of thought which he saw within art, science and technology led him, near the end of his life, to call for the artist to attend to the latter areas of experience; this represented a desire for something beyond a unification of the aspects and features of individual experience, entailing a broad, sweeping unification of nature, art, science and technology.

Here it might be useful to return to the background of Apollinaire's actions. The Symbolist attitude, which in the early twentieth century stood as a survival of the old age, appeared to encourage fragmentation inasmuch as it promoted the pursuit of style. This is a generalization of dangerous simplicity, but probably represents fairly well Apollinaire's opinion of the movement; in his eyes the Symbolists sought to narrow the concerns of art in order to promote fulfillment of narrow goals, whereas Apollinaire wished to do the opposite—to open up the range of art until it would be all-encompassing, until art would be synonymous with life as it was known then.

It is the grandiose nature of Apollinaire's dream that generates a new consideration of his attitude. Isn't it possible to consider him a representative of romanticism? Accepting this term in the generic sense as defined by Jacques Barzun [in his *Romanticism and the Modern Ego,* 1944], there is often a close resemblance between the elements associated with Apollinaire in this [essay] and the factors which Barzun establishes as defining the romantic artist. The latter is a revolutionary, and an individualist, an apostle of freedom, a realist, and a subjectivist; the romantic life (in the historic sense) was marked by productivity, energy and robustness, and a faith that society could be changed. And most strikingly, romantic individuals are termed "theorists of equilibrium in motion."

Does anything remain which would make it possible to say that the romanticism of Apollinaire is distinctly modern? To say that the environment of the early twentieth century differed from that of historical romanticism begs the question. The modern attitude must be delineated in the individual's response. And it is indeed possible to distinguish between the romantic attitude and that of Apollinaire. However much romanticism overlaps with the "New Spirit," there are two elements that belong to our own time particularly: humor and simultaneity.

Humor as it appears in the "New Spirit" is not just an aspect of human experience that receives emphasis; it also becomes a device of creativity. Consider the phenomenon of historical romanticism; humor is hardly a characteristic of the period. However, with Apollinaire, humor achieves a status of significant degree. His gestures may evolve from it. His literature frequently displays it. His critical writings, though removed from the creative category of his poetry and prose, are not wholly free of it; and at one point (in his **"The New Spirit and the Poets"**) he espouses the cause of humor as a means of creativity. Apollinaire's elevation of humor would influence the later twentieth century; Apollinaire's example encouraged Dada and Surrealism to exploit humor in their art; and, though no influence is implied, the extension of humor into absurdity, which occurred in the avant-garde of the early twentieth century, has a philosophical counterpart in the philosophy of Existentialism.

Simultaneity is not so readily established as a modern element. The romantics of the nineteenth century presented oppositions in their production; the dynamism of romanticism often operated from the tension of such a juxtaposition. What seems to distinguish the romantic of the last century from Apollinaire is that the juxtapositions of the former are usually oppositions, that is, contrasts, dualities or polarities, while the simultaneity of the twentieth century becomes multiple in nature. The effect of the two is

more than a respective distinction between simplicity and complexity; it may also be a difference between clarity and obscurity, and is certainly a difference between the possibility of resolution or synthesis and the impossibility of such a clear-cut result. Surrealism would make use of this principle in its own dislocations and juxtapositions, though this perspective is not exclusively derived from Apollinaire. The cinema since 1918 seems to express more obviously the idea of simultaneity. But the principle is not absent in the arts of recent times: the approach of the "Beat" poets is clearly an expression of simultaneity, and there is the "Happening" in the visual arts. The concept must remain valid as long as it possesses any meaningful impact; the loss of that meaning will occur when it is demonstrated that simultaneity is not a tenable view of human existence.

The prominent place assigned to humor and the concept of simultaneity among the aspects of Apollinaire's "New Spirit" is determined by the manner in which they illustrate that his attitude is more than a resurrection of a previous mode of creativity. The feature of repetition is present, insofar as he represents romanticism in his revolutionary intent, his insistence upon freedom, his subjectivity, his realism, and the dynamic nature of his life. With humor and simultaneity we have a romanticism particularized to meet the early twentieth century. It was the genius of Apollinaire to be in the vanguard in devising the new attitude. (pp. 124-36)

As a critic of art, Guillaume Apollinaire leaves a multiple impression. No doubt this accounts for the varied estimations of his critical ability. But the evaluation of his criticism can be more certain now that his writings on art have been collected; too many of the earlier estimations were based upon a limited knowledge of his criticism, focusing primarily upon his book of 1913, *Les Peintres cubistes.* The wider range of his journalistic criticism presents a picture frequently confused, yet demonstrating an underlying consistency representing the period we call modern.

Heretofore Apollinaire's biography and literature have been considered illustrations of the modern age. But his criticism has been considered only in an incomplete or subsidiary fashion.

The functions of any criticism seem to be multiple and often indistinguishable. Journalistic criticism, written frequently under the pressure of a deadline about an immediate event, is all the more likely to vary in quality and purpose.

Apollinaire directed his attention toward what was occurring at the moment he wrote. His interest seldom strayed to other periods. . . . The very nature of their immediacy may account for certain flaws in his critical articles, but it also explains their value as statements on the contemporary scene. For Apollinaire's criticism stands at the beginning of the formation of a criticism of the twentieth century art.

Over the thirteen year span of his criticism, much of it appears tentative and hasty. We may be annoyed at the looseness with which he sometimes characterizes the art he was observing. We may complain about his failure to

A 1914 sketch of Apollinaire by noted Russian painter and stage designer Mikhail Larionov.

employ effective language. We may be impatient when his writings reveal changes in allegiance, contradictions and uncertainties. But is it entirely just to condemn Apollinaire in retrospect for failing to possess the critical vocabulary of the present day? The development of an adequate vocabulary requires a collaboration between criticism and art history, and almost of necessity this collaboration involves a method of trial and error over a number of years. Apollinaire was writing within days or weeks of the appearance of the art which was his subject.

And the tentative aspects of his periodical criticism are nothing more than a trifling annoyance considered in a balance against the usefulness they possess historically as records of their time: they were produced within an atmosphere of creativity itself characterized by the remarkable speed of development of certain movements in art, and a tentative subscription almost always on the part of artists attached to those movements. The urgency and vitality of that age come to life again in the writings of Apollinaire, and afford an antidote to one possible failure of art history: a tendency to remove or overlook contradictions in a desire to see regular progressions with clear-cut antecedents, well-defined components at each stage, and obvious, measurable influences beyond the point of their dissolution.

No amount of recollection some thirty or forty years later by artists who lived through those years could supersede the writings. This is not to condemn the artists who have produced such commentaries; rather, it is to recognize that in their artistic concerns they have moved out of that time, and it would be remarkable for them to recreate with precision the reasons, the impulses, the environment in all its subtle factors. Apollinaire's writings would seem more reliable documents than memories removed by great lengths of time.

Because this kind of subjectivist criticism has been continued, one must look elsewhere to find the most outdated quality of his writings on art. Anna Balakian has discovered it in the optimism which Apollinaire displays there—an optimism visible as well in his poetry ["Apollinaire and the Modern Mind," *Yale French Studies,* 1949]. The optimism is compounded from several factors. In the creative area of which he wrote in his articles it is generated by his firm idealism. The humanism which stands behind his broader view of art also contributed to his positive faith. Apollinaire felt himself capable of influencing, from his position of creative freedom, the formation of a new and better world for man.

Isn't this the more convincing explanation of his wariness regarding Dada? To conjecture on "what might have been" if Apollinaire had lived beyond 1918 is for the most part idle exercise, but he did witness the emergence of this movement in art, yet never gave it any attention in his journalistic criticism. [In "Guillaume Apollinaire," *L'Esprit Nouveau,* July 1924] Francis Picabia has contended that in time Apollinaire would have been a Dadaist. This would seem to be a misreading of the man's character. Although he undoubtedly took a delight in the company of Marcel Duchamp and Picabia—an association which possessed to an incredible degree the atmosphere of the *Bateau-Lavoir* circle of some five years earlier—and

would have found encouragement in the movement to sustain his experimentation and fresh outlook on life, it seems certain that Apollinaire's idealism, humanism and optimism would always have kept him removed from Dada. As much as he appreciated a good joke, as much as he laughed at himself and others, it would have been impossible for him to accept the dominating air of futility that runs through the gestures of Dada.

If Apollinaire's critical writings seem dated—or outdated—in their optimism, we can nevertheless be grateful for that optimism. Is it not an essential ingredient of the interest, enthusiasm and appreciation which characterize his writings on art, if not a major factor in his decision to become a critic of art?

That decision has left us an incomparable body of critical writings upon the art of the period between 1905 and 1918. No other critic produced the quantity of material that is now available in the book and collected journalism of Apollinaire. No other critic displays for the avant-garde the interest which Apollinaire possessed; and inasmuch as the avant-garde exerted a determining influence upon the later course of art, the record of that interest should be a concern to us. In isolation Apollinaire's writings on art may be secondary in their own time, or they may be superseded. Considered together as a record of their time, Apollinaire's critical articles are a unique collection illuminating the formation of modern creativity.

It is with some nostalgia that one looks back toward Apollinaire, and the period in which he lived. In that time his actions and those of the avant-garde take on the appearance of heroic gestures. The nostalgia is present, one feels, because the first World War acted as a damper on the enthusiasm and conviction of that period; the "innocence" of that era could not be regained thereafter. What we have lost of Apollinaire may be only his optimism. There is no intention here of tracing the extent of Apollinaire's contribution after 1918. Nevertheless, his literature remains greatly significant; his critical writings, of lesser value, are a vital record of that time; and the attitude which can be reconstructed from both areas and his biography is of continued interest as its originality belongs to our century. (pp. 137-39)

> *Harry E. Buckley, in his* Guillaume Apollinaire as an Art Critic, *UMI Research Press, 1981, 341 p.*

John Updike   (essay date 1984)

[*Considered a perceptive observer of the human condition and an extraordinary stylist, Updike is one of America's most distinguished men of letters. Best known for such novels as* Rabbit Run *(1960),* Rabbit Redux *(1971),* Rabbit Is Rich *(1981), and* Rabbit at Rest *(1990), he is a chronicler of life in Protestant, middle-class America. Against this setting and in concurrence with his interpretation of the thought of Søren Kierkegaard and of Karl Barth, Updike presents people searching for meaning in their lives while facing the painful awareness of their mortality and basic powerlessness. A contributor of literary reviews to various periodicals, he has frequently written the "Books" column in the* New Yorker *since 1955. In the following excerpt, Updike discusses the stories in* The Poet Assassinated, *which he describes as a "halfhearted and ragged collection."*]

The volume entitled *The Poet Assassinated* was assembled by Apollinaire while recuperating in a Paris hospital from a head wound suffered in battle on March 17, 1916; it included stories and sketches composed since the publication of his previous collection of short fiction, *L'Hérésiarque et Cie.* A number of the pieces had previously appeared in such magazines as *Le Matin* and his own *Soirées de Paris.* . . . (p. 89)

[In] eighteen titled episodes, or chapters, [the story **"The Poet Assassinated"**] presents a highly distorted autobiography in the guise of the frenzied rise and fall of Croniamantal, "the greatest living poet." Apollinaire was born in 1880, the illegitimate son of Angelica Alexandrine de Kostrowitzky, a twenty-two-year-old renegade daughter of a minor Polish nobleman; Apollinaire's father, it is probable if not certain, was her lover of many years, the aristocratic Italian officer Francesco Flugi d'Aspermont, who disappeared not only from Angelica's life but from the world at large after 1885. These muddled beginnings are outrageously parodied in the casual roadside mating of Viersélin Tigoboth, an itinerant Walloon musician, and the voluptuous and impulsive Marcarée, "a dark young woman, shaped with pretty globes," who bares her breasts at the musician, copulates "under love's power, behind the blackthorns," and gets back on her bicycle and pedals away. She finds herself pregnant, debates abortion with herself, and ends, after rapturously apostrophizing her own "stretchy, bearded, smooth, bombed, dolorous, round, silky, ennobling belly," by having the child. Unlike Angelica de Kostrowitzky, Macarée gets rich at gambling, marries a baron, and dies in childbirth. The child is christened Gaétan-François-Étienne-Jack-Amélie-Alonso Desygrées, scarcely more fantastic than the string of names with which Apollinaire's mother, at the Roman Municipal Records Office, saddled her fatherless infant—Guillaume Albert Wladimir Alexandre Apollinaire de Kostrowitzky. She always called him Wilhelm. He spent his early years in Rome with a foster family; when Guillaume was six, his mother, he, and a younger, also illegitimate brother, Alberto, moved to Monaco. There, in several schools along the Côte d'Azur, he became a good and enthusiastic student; his language became French, and his poetic vocation was well developed by the time, in 1899, that the Kostrowitzkys left Monaco and made their way, with many a detour, to Paris.

Croniamantal, when his foster father the Baron des Ygrées commits suicide as a consequence of gambling debts, is adopted by an erudite Dutchman, Janssen, and is educated by him. When Janssen dies, Croniamantal takes his inheritance and goes to Paris "so he could peacefully indulge his taste for literature, because for some time now, and secretly, he was writing poems which he kept in an old cigar box." The young poet is described running up the Rue Houdon: "His eyes devoured everything they saw and when his eyelids came together rapidly like jaws, they engulfed the universe which was endlessly renovated by him as he ran along imagining the smallest details of the enormous worlds he was feasting his eyes on." He visits the atelier of a painter called the Bird of Benin, and experiences the bliss of paint: "In the atelier there were joys of all colors. A big window took up the northern side and all you could see was sky-blue, like a woman singing." The Bird of Benin announces that he has laid eyes on the perfect girl for Croniamantal: "She has the somber, childlike face of those who are destined to cause suffering. I'm telling you, I saw your woman. She is ugliness and beauty; she is like everything we love today. And she must have the taste of bay leaf." This closely parallels a real incident: in 1907, Picasso, having just met Marie Laurencin in an art gallery, told Apollinaire, "I have a fiancée for you." He introduced them, and shortly thereafter the poet moved out of his mother's apartment to pursue the affair, which lasted until 1912. Revising **"The Poet Assassinated"** after the breakup with his mistress, Apollinaire substituted the phrase "destined to cause suffering" for the original "made for eternal loves," and inserted a passage including the sentences

> Six months passed. For the last five of them Tristouse Ballerinette had been Croniamantal's mistress, and she loved him passionately for a week. In exchange for this love, the lyrical boy had made her immortal and glorious forever by celebrating her in marvellous poems.
>
> "I was unknown," she thought, "and now he's made me illustrious among all living women."
>
> "They used to think I was generally ugly with my thinness, my oversized mouth, my horrible teeth, my asymmetrical face, my crooked nose. But now I'm beautiful and all the men tell me so."

Though Picasso and Marie Laurencin have been firmly related to these fanciful incidents, no one has unambiguously identified Paponat, the rich "fonipoit" (in the French, *"fopoîte;"* that is, *"faux poète"*) who becomes Tristouse's new lover, or Horace Tograth, the German who, from the unlikely launching pad of a French-language newspaper in Adelaide, Australia, inaugurates a worldwide antipoet crusade to which Croniamantal falls victim. The poet's assassination is a savage, though farcical, business:

> And raising his cane, [a man whom the charismatic Tograth has cured of baldness] thrust it so adroitly that it burst Croniamantal's right eye. He fell backwards. Some women fell upon him and beat him. Tristouse was prancing around with joy, as Paponat tried to calm her down. But with the point of her umbrella she went up and poked out Croniamantal's other eye, which saw her doing it. He cried out:
>
> "I confess my love for Tristouse Ballerinette, the divine poetry that consoles my soul." . . .
>
> The ladies stepped quickly aside and a man wielding a butcherknife laid in his palm threw it so that it stuck right in Croniamantal's open mouth. Other men did the same. The knives stuck in his belly and chest, and pretty soon there was nothing left on the ground but a corpse spiked like a big sea urchin.

The literary analogy is with the death of Orpheus, torn to pieces by the Thracian women in a Dionysian orgy. The Bird of Benin, announcing that he is a sculptor as well as a painter, executes a memorial for the poet (a hole in the ground), and in fact forty years after Apollinaire's death a memorial statue by Picasso (the head of a woman) was placed in the garden beside Saint-Germain-des-Prés.

The primary interest of **"The Poet Assassinated"** lies in its masked revelations of Apollinaire's life. As a narrative, in its cold violence and clattering burlesque, it functions under the malign influence of Alfred Jarry, a self-destructive visionary whose extravagances fascinated bohemian Paris and who, toward the end of his short life, generously partook of absinthe and talk with the young Italian, seven years his junior. Certain rhapsodies and stretches of cultural satire show Apollinaire's softer, irrepressibly fluent touch. A fantasy on female fashion, for instance, is put into the mouth of Tristouse:

> "This year," said Tristouse, "fashions are bizarre and common, simple and full of fantasy. Any material from nature's domain can now be introduced into the composition of women's clothes. I saw a charming dress made of corks. . . . A big designer is thinking about launching tailor-made outfits made of old book-bindings done in calf. It's charming. All the ladies of letters would want to wear them, and one could approach them and whisper in their ear under the pretext of reading the titles. Fish bones are being worn a lot on hats. . . . Dresses embellished with coffee beans, cloves, cloves of garlic, onions, and bunches of raisins, these will be perfect for social calls. Fashion is becoming practical and no longer looks down on anything. It ennobles everything. It does for materials what the Romantics did for words."

A reader at all acquainted with Apollinaire's biography will be struck by what is suppressed, in this fantasy version, of his formative years. Angelica (or Olga, as she called herself in Monaco) de Kostrowitzky was a mother more outrageous and tenacious than the obligingly doomed Macarée; aristocratic in bearing, with nothing of the demimondaine about her appearance, and with no sympathy for her elder son's career in the arts, she had been a rebel against conventions since the age of sixteen, when she was expelled from an exclusive convent academy run by French nuns for the children of the Roman nobility. She took up with the dashing Francesco, then in his forties, and after his defection became a virtual courtesan, who paraded a succession of "uncles" before her two boys and who—as revealed by documents published for the first time in Steegmuller's biography in 1963—was ordered expelled from the principality of Monaco shortly after she arrived in 1887. She was named in this official order (which she somehow evaded, staying in Monaco for twelve years) as a "*femme galante*" and mentioned in a memoir of the time as an "*entraîneuse*"—one who "leads men on" at the gambling tables and is financed partly by the proprietors thereof. One of her admirers, a Lyonnais silk manufacturer with bookish tastes, perhaps contributed to the shadowy persona of Janssen, Croniamantal's protector. Her most sustained liaison, contracted in Mo-

naco but continued in Paris until her death, was with an Alsatian gambler named Jules Weil. She herself was a devoted gambler. The insecurities the sons of such a mother endured, the deceits and pretenses forced upon them, must be mostly imagined, though in 1899 the young "Russians," as the Kostrowitzkys were called, made the newspapers and the court records. In a case of considerable local interest in the Ardennes town of Stavelot, the two teen-aged boys (their mother and Weil having returned to Paris) were hauled into court for sneaking out of a *pension* without paying the bill, causing the proprietors to postpone their daughter's wedding. Something evasive and too volatile remained part of Apollinaire; his handwriting, for instance, was so changeable his bank required him to file five or six specimens of his signature. His mother, in the months after his birth, recorded him under three different sets of names, and he ended by naming himself. Yet Olga never relinquished the role of mother, nor Apollinaire that of son. He lived with her off and on well into adulthood, and they stayed in close touch. His shabby and unsettled upbringing left scarcely a shadow on his sunny, energetic personality, and almost the only complaint he committed to print is the line (from a poem, **"Le Larron,"** written when he was about nineteen) *"Ton père fut un sphinx et ta mère une nuit"* ("Your father was a sphinx and your mother a night"). "A night," the poem goes on to say, "which charmed with its glow Zacinth and the Cyclades." The fictive Macarée's sexy glow is the most vivid thing about her, and she dies in a mixture of laughter and tears convenient moments after "giving the world a healthy, masculine child."

Apollinaire emerged from childhood with the imaginative writer's basic tool—a need to lie.

—John Updike

Apollinaire emerged from childhood with the imaginative writer's basic tool—a need to lie. His fancy served to transmute and dismiss his past. Of the fifteen shorter stories in *The Poet Assassinated,* a few give refracted glimpses of this past. **"Giovanni Moroni"** presents, as the memories of an Italian-born Parisian bank employee "of no great culture," a sumptuous child's Italy: "I had all kinds of toys: horses, Punches, swords, bowling pins, puppets, soldiers, wagons. . . . These feast days for the Three Kings, when I ate so many candied orange peels, so many anise drops, have left me with a delicious aftertaste!" Nothing is known of the Roman foster family with which the two little "Russians" were left in the pre-Monaco days, but Giovanni Moroni's recalled household of Beppo the toymaker and his superstitious wife, Attilia, with its delicious foods, its cockroaches exterminated with boiling water ("the unfortunate bugs, whose final agitation, running, and chaotic jumping enchanted me"), its murky encounters with a young monk who is naked beneath his dirty habit and with a gang of masked carnival celebrants who leave behind a corpse, has a resonance, an unliterary richness of feeling rather rare in Apollinaire's inventions. His first set of stories, *The Heresiarch and Co.,* had more of his earthiness, more anecdotal force and Mediterranean color, including an obsessive interest in Catholicism and blasphemy; it was published before *Alcools* and *Les Peintres Cubistes,* and it may be that, with his roles as poet and as chief propagandist for modern painting relatively undefined, the young Apollinaire tried harder as a short-story writer.

Not that some of these later pieces, tossed off though they feel, are not accomplished; the poet—who wrote many of his letters in perfect verse, it came to him so easily—was also a prolific journalist and an editor. He could do a literary job. **"The Favorite,"** though it ends on the note of slightly crazed misogyny that lurks like a sinister clown in Apollinaire's imagination, begins with the sunstruck bluntness of Hemingway or Unamuno, with a symbolist touch:

> It was in Beausoleil, near the Monacan border, in that part of Carnier called Tonkin and inhabited almost exclusively by Piedmontese.
>
> An invisible executioner bloodied the afternoon. Two men were bearing a stretcher, sweating and breathing hard. From time to time they turned toward the sun's slit throat and cursed it, their eyes almost closed.

The stories, generally no longer than three or four pages, are smoothly built about a single idea, and slide quickly toward their shrug of catastrophe. Some—**"The Departure of the Shadow," "The Deified Invalid"**—are so Borgesian in tone and form that one wonders if Borges, in his Continental sojourn of 1914-21, ran across them. The Borgesian theme of mental simultancity—of all phenomena concentrating to a single point—occurs several times, and the word "atrocious" in this sentence has the Argentine's ring: "We were walking along without talking, and, after a while, when I felt the desire to see our shadows again, I saw with a singularly atrocious pleasure [*un plaisir singulièrement atroce*] that Louise's had left her." Sometimes Apollinaire can think of little to do with his characters but kill them (**"The Meeting at the Mixed Club," "The Eagle Hunt"**). His cruel fables have a double face, of Gothic relish and Latin stoicism. Unlike some poets launched into prose, he seems in firm control of his effects. **"The Talking Memories,"** as a story, is almost slick, with a satisfying "twist" at the end, like a Saki or a Roald Dahl, and **"Little Recipes from Modern Magic"** could appear in a contemporary humor magazine:

> *Incantation for beating the stock market*
>
> Every morning you will eat a red herring while uttering forty times before and after: "Bucks and plug, clink and drink." And after ten days your dead stock will become live stock.
>
> *Recipe for glory*
>
> Carry with you four fountain pens, drink clear water, have a great man's mirror, and often look at yourself in it without smiling.

One small story, originally dedicated to his mother and believed to be based upon her reminiscences of the girlhood years she spent in the Roman convent, is a gem of psychologically authentic hallucination: a group of twelve-year-old convent girls hear beyond the walls the sound of a hunter's horn, and in the following days they all encounter in the corridors a disembodied blue eye, "making a beautiful azure splash in the darkness." Gradually, they cease to be frightened of it, and coquettishly seek to be seen: "None of us would have wanted to be seen by the blue eye with our hands spotted with ink. Each did her best to look her best when going down the halls." The convent holds no mirrors, but some of the doors have panes of glass, and "a section of black apron flattened behind the pane formed an improvised mirror, where quick, quick you'd look at yourself, arrange your hair, and wonder if you were pretty." The blue eye slowly disappears from the halls, having been conjured up by a group need and having served to objectify the first intense flash of budding vanity and sexuality in cloistered females: "You have never seen the blue eye go by, O little girls of today!"

The last story, written in 1916, caps a halfhearted and ragged collection with a startling burst of terrible beauty; only a poet could have written it. **"The Case of the Masked Corporal, That Is, the Poet Resuscitated"** contains some pictographic verbal arrangements like the shaped poems in *Calligrammes* and also an attempt to round up the characters of the preceding stories, a hurried grab at unity. Like Borges's Funes the Memorious, the resuscitated Croniamantal, now a soldier, sees everything at once: "He saw the battlefields of eastern Prussia, of Poland, the quiet of a little Siberian town, fighting in Africa, Anzac, and Sedul-Bar, Salonika, the stripped and terrible oceanic elegance of the trenches in Barren Champagne, the wounded second-lieutenant carried to the ambulance, baseball players in Connecticut, and battles, battles." The battlefield is evoked with a passion beyond protest: "And the Front lit up, the hexahedrons were rolling, the steel flowers were blossoming out, the barbed wire was growing thinner with bloody desires, the trenches were opening like females before males." Apollinaire had eagerly enlisted; as a foreigner—one, furthermore, in his mid-thirties—he could have sat the war out in Paris, as did Picasso. His first application to the Army, in August, 1914, was ignored; he successfully enlisted in Nice, and jubilantly punned, "I so love art that I have joined the artillery . . . " Later, he was to leave the relative safety of his artillery unit to become an infantry officer in the front-line trenches. Thus he demonstrated his courage and his loyalty to France, as if these had been in question. His mother, the daughter of a Polish-Russian colonel, approved of his soldiering as of no other aspect of his career. "How beautiful are the rockets that light up the night," he was to proclaim, in faint echo of "*ta mère une nuit.*" The Italian Futurists, to whom Apollinaire the critic was attracted after Cubism, had a theoretical thirst for violence; though he once wrote, "*Ah Dieu que la guerre est jolie,*" the letters he poured out as a "*soldat de la douce France*" show him shedding whatever naïve illusions he held concerning "the simple horror of the trenches." Yet Apollinaire's wound, in its fictional rendering, is ennobled by a myth: "The corporal in the blind mask was smiling amorously at the future, when a fragment of a high caliber shell hit him in the head, from which sprang, like pure blood, a triumphant Minerva. Stand up, everybody, to give a courteous welcome to victory!" Croniamantal has gone from being torn Orpheus to fruitful Jupiter; Apollinaire, who was never quite himself after his head wound, and who weakly succumbed to disease a few years later, has among his laurels a claim to being the last poet to write of war as a theatre of glory. (pp. 89-93)

> *John Updike, "Art and Artillery," in* The New Yorker, *Vol. LX, No. 21, July 9, 1984, pp. 89-93.*

LeRoy C. Breunig on Apollinaire's role as a champion of modern art:

It was thanks to Apollinaire that Braque and Picasso had met in 1907. It was he who had helped organize the cubist Room 41 at the Salon des Indépendants of 1911; established liaison between the Montmartre and the Puteaux cubists; lectured at the important Section d'Or exhibit in 1912; selected Derain and Dufy as his illustrators; posed for portraits by Vlaminck, Rousseau, Metzinger, Picasso, De Chirico, Modigliani, Larionov, and Marie Laurencin; baptized orphism and become its champion at a Delaunay show in Berlin; launched and directed the *Soirées de Paris,* one of the principal organs of the avant-garde before the war; issued a manifesto for futurism; and coined the term surrealism apropos of the Cocteau-Satie-Picasso-Massine production of the ballet *Parade.* His magnetism, his all-embracing enthusiasms, his very ubiquity in prewar Paris made him beyond a doubt the main impresario of the avant-garde.

> *LeRoy C. Breunig, in his introduction to* Apollinaire on Art *by Guillaume Apollinaire, edited by Breunig, translated by Susan Suleiman, 1972.*

David Kelley   (essay date 1985)

[*In the following essay, Kelley asserts that in many poems Apollinaire attempts to uncritically represent the modern urban experience.*]

Both the importance of the city in Apollinaire's work and the complex ambivalence of his attitude towards it are suggested by the two long poems which open and close the collection **Alcools** (1913), that is, **'Zone'** and **'Vendémiaire'**. For, however exaggerated it might be to talk of an 'architecture secrète' of the kind which underlies Baudelaire's *Fleurs du Mal,* Apollinaire clearly took some care in the ordering of the pieces contained within his first major collection, and the reader is certainly led to compare and contrast the two poems I have referred to, if only by the different moods evoked by the walk back along the Seine embankment to Auteuil:

> Tu marches vers Auteuil tu veux aller chez toi
> à pied
> Dormir parmi tes fétiches d'Océanie et de Guinée
> Ils sont des Christ d'une autre forme et d'une
> autre croyance

Ce sont les Christ inférieurs des obscures espérances.

> (You walk back to Auteuil you want to walk home
> To sleep in the midst of your fetishes from Guinea and the South Sea Isles
> They are the Christs of another form and another faith
> These are the lesser Christs of obscure aspirations)

and:

> Un soir passant le long des quais déserts et sombres
> En rentrant à Auteuil j'entendis une voix
> Qui chantait gravement se taisant quelquefois
> Pour que parvînt aussi sur les bords de la Seine
> La plainte d'autres voix limpides et lointaines

> (One evening wandering along the deserted darkened embankment
> Walking back towards Auteuil I heard a voice
> Singing with solemnity now and then falling silent
> To allow to be heard on the banks of the Seine
> The lament of other limpid and far-flung voices)

To make the walk through Paris the central theme of both poems is clearly to emphasise the significance of the city in **Alcools,** even if the poems within the collection dealing with specifically urban themes are probably in the minority. But it is also interesting that the dominant experience of the city in the opening poem, **'Zone'** should be one of fragmentation and desolation, and that of **'Vendémiaire'** one of cosmic intoxication, whereas in formal and stylistic terms **'Zone'**—which was probably the last poem in **Alcools** to be written—is extremely 'modern', and the concluding poem seems often to remain anchored in the aesthetic and the rhetoric of a Victor Hugo.

In some ways this paradox should not surprise us. As Peter Collier has shown in ["Nineteenth-Century Paris: Vision and Nightmare," in *Unreal City,* edited by Edward Timms and David Kelley], both of these responses to the city are part of an existing tradition in French poetry. Baudelaire in particular, was able to perceive life in Paris both as an image of human exile in the imperfect—as in 'Le Cygne' ('The Swan')—and as the potential source of a kind of imaginative intoxication—as in the prose poem 'Les Foules' ('Crowds'). It is nevertheless interesting that many of the poems which derive from the kind of aesthetic outlined in 'Les Foules'—notably 'Les Petites Vieilles'—tend also to present images of human desolation and alienation. Indeed, for the French Romantics and Symbolists, the city, however fascinating as an accumulation of cultures and individuals, tended to be used as an image of the world-weariness of an old civilisation, one which was felt to have lost its faith, and one in which an excess of knowledge had alienated men from themselves and from the natural world. And technical progress, of which the urban metropolis was the high temple, was associated with that sense of alienation.

But the uneasy sense of self and its relationship with actuality and relativity of an experience in which God might no longer be in his heaven that defines so much French Romantic writing did not inevitably lead poets to seek escape from the realities of their experience in nostalgia or exoticism. For some—notably Gautier, Nerval and Baudelaire—it led instead to the attempt both to confront and transcend urban experience with and through language. And this involved them in a radical redefinition of the process of writing and reading which is central to the emergence of what is termed Modernism.

For Baudelaire's theory of 'correspondances' and his practice of writing, both of which are seminal to Symbolist poetry, are intimately related to the problem which confronted most nineteenth-century poets and painters in one way or another, that of creating an 'absolute' beauty out of a finite experience which appeared almost unutterably trivial or ugly. Whereas the 'naïve' poet of Antiquity was considered to have been able to arrive at 'beauty' by the direct expression of his harmonious relationship with the natural world, the modern poet, faced with an incoherent and fragmented experience of the 'real', manifested most acutely in the modern city, was obliged to construct a harmonious pattern of *verbal* relationships and meanings. And precisely because Baudelaire sought to create, on the level of language, a state of absolute intensity, the poem became important, not so much for its capacity to evoke specific relationships or to state specific meanings, as for its ability to create patterns of dense and complex meaning. With Mallarmé, of course, this process is carried much further, and these lines from his famous 'Sonnet en x':

> Sur les crédences, au salon vide; nul ptyx,
> Aboli bibelot d'inanité sonore,
>
> (On the shelves, in the empty drawing room, no
>   ptyxia,
> Negated knick-knack of sonorous stupidity.)

exploit to the full the capacity of language both to negate the real and to create a mental reality, and at the same time to discover meaning in the assertion of its own meaninglessness.

Around the turn of the century a rather more positive perception of modern experience began to be more current in poetic writing. Those aspects of urban and industrial life, the sense of physical and intellectual relativity engendered by technological advance and by modifications in scientific and philosophical ideas which poets had seen as negative, began to be much more currently a source of enthusiasm for poets. This is of course most evident in the case of the Italian Futurists who, largely thanks to the publicising zeal of their leader Marinetti, had considerable influence in France. Their violent attack on all forms of 'passéiste' culture singled out for particular attention the moonlight which epitomised for them the nostalgic and sentimental attitudes of Romanticism and Symbolism. To the moonlight of the Romantics they oppose the dynamism of the sun and the brilliance of modern electric lighting. For central to their preoccupations was the notion that the whole sensibility of man was being changed by scientific and technological discoveries—life was at once more multiple and dynamic than it had been before. A new, heroic, Nietzschean man was being born, participating of the

strength and violent beauty of the machines he had created. And the similarity between such ideas and those current in France is suggested by the very nature of some of the contemporary poetic 'movements'—Dynamisme, Machinisme, Paroxysme, Impulsionnisme. . . .

The relationship between the Futurists and their French equivalents and the poetry of the previous century is, however, a more complex one than their own more aggressive remarks might suggest. I have already hinted at an important sense in which the central question which preoccupied Romantic writers and artists was precisely that of modernity—that is, the feeling that conditions of life in the nineteenth century are different to those of preceding ages, and that traditional notions of beauty and modes of representation are no longer adequate. Their nostalgia and their exoticism, derided by the Futurists, were more often than not the manifestation of an aspiration towards vitality, dynamism, and a naïve and total engagement with the present, which they felt to be impossible in the post-Christian urban culture in which they lived. In this sense, the aggressive endorsement of the immediacy, dynamism and energy of the machine culture on the part of the Futurists can be perceived as a displacement of Romantic values on to the present, and their formal experiments as an attempt to forge a language capable of recreating a naïve and direct relationship—that of traditional lyric poetry—between experience, language and poetic form, of a kind which a Baudelaire or a Mallarmé had felt to be impossible.

The Futurists therefore proposed a whole series of apparently extremely radical linguistic and formal experiments—but with interesting exceptions, those experiments are to do with expression. They do not perceive language itself as being problematic in the ways in which it can refer to the outside world. And this is perhaps one of the reasons why so much of their writing appears dated to our generation, which is no longer filled with a sense of wonder at the sensation of speed and the consciousness of spatial and temporal relativity. The ambition to sweep away the past implies an attempt to wish away the cultural conflicts engendered by new modes of perception and a new technology, which is perhaps what remains interesting to us today. The phenomena they are writing about now seem quaint rather than exciting, the experience they evoke everyday, and to be taken for granted, and the words have little ambition beyond the representation of those phenomena and the expression of that experience. The texts therefore have little more than archeological interest.

And many of the attempts on the part of their French contemporaries to create a lyricism adequate to the new age derive from what seems to be a rather forced desire to perceive in the new technology the means to a heroic totalisation of the fragmentation of the world. In formal terms, they often consist of tacking onomatopoeic effects of the kind recommended by Marinetti and his followers onto a very dated poetic rhetoric. As in the case of this experiment with polyphonic voices by Henri-Martin Barzun, in which the Modernism is fundamentally superficial, the feelings conventional, the personification banal:

Le Chef pilote:	Que les moteurs *vrombissent* et rugissent
Les moteurs:	—Vrom vromb, vreu, vron, ron ou, or ou, or meu
Les Chef pilote:	Que les hélices *tournent* follement
Les moteurs:	—Ronvronronvron dron, vreu—oo, ouaarr
Le Chef pilote:	Que le sillage d'air *baigne* les faces qui se lèvent
Les helices le vent:	—wirl, wou, wirl, wou-ll, woua, wirl—weu ll
Les pavillons:	—clac, *clac*—fro *ou* clac—rrou sss
Le Chef pilote:	En avant! au-dessus des cités! et saluons l'oeuvre des hommes . . .
La Sirene du bord:	—Ho! huu—uu—ho! hohu! huohuohuoho-hu
First pilot:	Let the engines *throb* and roar
Engines:	—Throb throb throarr ouarrr orr
First pilot:	Let the propellors *rotate* frenetically
Engines:	—Robthrobthrobthrob from, throarr, oo, ouarr
First pilot:	Let the wake of air *bathe* the upturned faces
Propellors wind:	—whirl, wow, wheerl, wow-ll wowah, wheerl—whir
Flags:	—flap, *flap*—fro *ow* flap—rroo sss
First pilot:	Forward! over the cities! and let us salute the works of men.
Airship siren:	—ho! huu—uu—ho! hohu! huohuohuoho—hu

The initial impression **'Zone'** creates is one of aggressive modernity of a rather dated kind, with its references to the trappings of early twentieth-century technology, deliberately used in incongruous metaphorical relationships: 'Bergère ô tour Eiffel le troupeau des ponts bêle ce matin' (Shepherdess O Eiffel Tower the flock of bridges baas this morning'); telescoped images reminiscent of the Futurist attempts to renew syntax: 'Soleil cou coupé' ('Sun severed neck'); the construction of the poem as a whole in terms of fragmentary, disconnected images, apparently suggesting temporal and spatial ubiquity or interpenetration between inner and outer worlds.

In fact **'Zone'** reveals a very complex engagement with the experience of time, past and present, in both cultural and personal terms, and with that of poetic language and form. The deliberately incongruous associations of the Eiffel Tower with pastoral shepherdesses, of religion with aircraft hangars, of Christ with the first aeroplane, of childhood piety and innocence with the brash brightness of an industrial street in the morning sunlight, all occurring in the opening sequences of the poem, are part of a subtle play with the private and cultural associations of youth and age, innocence and world-weariness, modern and ancient. Within the history of Western culture, what might appear to be the freshest and most vital manifestations of the present can also be perceived as the all too predictable

effects of decadence: 'Ice même les automobiles ont l'air anciennes' ('Here even the motor-cars seem old-fashioned'), and what might appear to be oldest and most irrelevant—Christianity—as a lost innocence and freshness of civilisation.

Towards the end of the first part of the poem, however, there is an attempt to reconcile the terms of the opening paradox, and arrive at a synthesis. The new century, like Christ, the first aeroplane, rises in a glorious ascension, accompanied by the high-flyers of mythology—Icarus, Enoch, Elijah, Apollonius of Thyana—and a whole host of real and mythical birds. It is, perhaps, the search to find in a synthesis of Christian culture and technological innovation the basis for an artistic rebirth parallel to the synthesis of Christian and pagan cultures which had marked the Renaissance. But the interpenetration of memories of the past and perception of the Parisian present which constitute the remainder of the poem reverse this positive movement, offering an overwhelming sense of nostalgic sexual and religious guilt which culminates in the horrifying image of the rising sun—traditionally an image of hope and rebirth—as an image of death: 'Soleil cou coupé'.

The poem thus resumes the ambiguity of the urban present as it was experienced by poets of the late nineteenth and early twentieth-centuries: on the one hand as fragmentation and absence, on the other as a source of exhilaration—or, perhaps most authentically, as both. And this ambiguity is also present in the formal structure and language of the poem, as is clearly revealed by the final line which I have just quoted. The initial impression which it creates is one of striking modernity—the simple and jarring juxtaposition of two visual images, the disk of the sun against the skyline and a neck from which the head has been severed—the alliterative and onomatopoeic effects of 'cou coupé' contributing to the impression of shock which the image produces. But the line is probably the deliberate inversion of a metaphor deriving from the Romantic and Symbolist tradition. Its direct origin, via a series of reworkings by Apollinaire himself, would appear to be found in the famous line from Baudelaire's 'Harmonie du soir': 'Le soleil s'est noyé dans son sang qui se fige' ('The sun is drowned in its setting blood'). And the Baudelaire poem can be seen as a kind of model for the Symbolist practice of exploiting linguistic ambiguity to create, by a play on the associative memory, an impression in the reader of total harmony of spirit and senses, and to recreate, in the poem, a transcendent unity, a more perfect world.

The quite opposite effect of disruption and surprise which the line 'Soleil cou coupé' has on the reader derives at least in part from that inversion, from the fact that both formally and significantly it is working both against and within the tradition from which it derives. For it also acts on many levels to draw together the divergent strands of the poem. It focuses the references to blood scattered throughout—the blood of the Sacred Heart, the blood of women. And by its contrast with the sunrise in the 'industrial street' of the beginning of the poem—a sunrise full of hope, prefiguring the glorious ascension of the new century—it helps to define the narrative and symbolic structure of the text as a walk through Paris, beginning one morning and continuing through a whole day and night until the next morning, the image of an Orphic journey to the Underworld from which there is no triumphant return, the image of the traditional cycle of birth, death and renaissance figured by the cyclic rising and setting of the sun, but with the conventional image of rebirth transformed into an image of death.

So the line plays an important part in a narrative and symbolic structure which makes the poem legible in traditional terms, and contributes to the transcendence of the sense of fragmentation which it powerfully expresses. Nevertheless its powerful ellipsis also corresponds to the positive aesthetic of the city which it appears to be denying—I noted earlier its resemblance to the Futurist telegraphic techniques. Indeed the primitive sculptures, 'lesser Christs of obscure aspirations', which in the context of the poem appear to suggest the nadir of metaphysical confidence, are of course one of the models that Derain, Picasso and Braque were, to Apollinaire's knowledge, using as the basis for an artistic rebirth. The final image of **'Zone',** like the poem as whole, demonstrates in its functioning the problematic sense of the relationship between language and an experience of the actual which is, perhaps, the principal subject of the text. Both work within limits and tend to extend those limits.

In this sense **'Zone'** is a paradigm of the volume *Alcools*. The superficially heterogeneous appearance of the collection led it to be seen on publication as an assembly of literary bric-à-brac. The traditions of the German folk-lyric, Graeco-Roman mythology, Romantic and Symbolist preoccupations with medieval allegory and legend, are all to be found in conjunction with contemporary urban or machinist images, whose register varies from that of Baudelairian/Laforguian kitsch to the Expressionism *avant la lettre* of:

> Soirs de Paris ivres du gin
> Flambant de l'electricité
> Les tramways feux verts sur l'échine
> Musiquent au long des portées
> De rails leurs folies de machine
>
> (Paris evenings drunk on gin
> Blazing with electricity
> Trams green lights along the spine
> Scream to the score of their lines
> The music of the madness of machines)

And indeed, in the poem from which these lines are taken, **'La Chanson du Mal-Aimé',** all these occur within the same text.

Nevertheless, even where Apollinaire seems to be working within a tradition which would seem to be at the opposite extreme from a poetry of the city—that of the German *Volkslied* for example—he tends also to be doing something with that tradition which can only be read within the context of a modern, urban, experience. In **'Nuit rhénane'** (**'Rhineland Night'**), elements of German myth and legend, the picturesque enchantment of the decor as perceived by a city-dwelling tourist, combine to create magic intoxication:

> Le Rhin le Rhin est ivre où les vignes se mirent
> Tout l'or des nuits tombe en tremblant s'y re-
> 　fléter
> La voix chante toujours à en râle-mourir
>
> (The Rhine the Rhine is drunk where the vines
> 　are mirrored
> All the gold of the nights falls in flickering re-
> 　flections
> The voice still sings to its dying fall)

an intoxication which is broken by the jarringly elliptical image of the glass breaking: 'Mon verre s'est brisé comme un éclat de rire' ('My glass shattered like a burst of laughter'). The disjunctive narrative structure of the *Volkslied* is exploited to the ironic ends of a post-symbolist neurosis.

'Marizibill' appears to be an ironically sentimental evocation of the alienation of city life, playing on the cliché of the golden-hearted whore. But in the concluding lines of the poem the terms of the problem are thrown into question:

> Je connais gens de toutes sortes
> Ils n'égalent pas leurs destins
> Indécis comme feuilles mortes
> Leurs yeux sont des feux mal éteints
> Leurs coeurs bougent comme leurs portes
>
> (I know people of every kind
> They are not equal to their destiny
> Indecisive as dead leaves
> Their eyes are ill extinguished fires
> Their hearts flutter like their doors)

The apprent drift of the poem would seem to imply that the haphazardness of Marizibill's sexual encounters is an image of emotional fragmentation, of the inadequacy of destiny to the personal qualities of the individual. But the word 'ègalent' subverts such a reading, suggesting on the contrary, that the multiplicity and indeterminacy of existence are precisely what people cannot face up to. So that Marizibill's problem is the absurd nostalgia for emotional security which makes her faithful to her grotesque pimp, her inability to espouse the relativity of urban experience.

If the problematic attitude towards modern urban experience and the formal and linguistic ambivalence which characterise **'Zone'** make it an excellent introduction to *Alcools*, **'Vendémiaire'** would seem to be a no less apt conclusion. The modern city is perceived positively, as a source of dionysiac intoxication for the poet. But the experience of Paris as presented in the poem is in no way a simple affirmation of the present or a rejection of the cultural traditions of the past like that of the Futurists. Certainly it contains aggressively modern images—like the factory chimneys of the north of France:

> Les viriles cités où dégoisent et chantent
> Les métalliques saints de nos saintes usines
> Nos cheminées à cie! ouvert engrossent les uées
> Comme fit autrefois l'Ixion mécanique
>
> (The virile cities where belch forth and sing
> The metallic saints of our holy factories
> Our chimneys open to the sky impregnate the
> 　clouds
> As did in days gone by the mechanical Ixion)

But the association of the phallic chimneys with the Ixion of Classical mythology places this reference in a similar context to that of the opening passages of **'Zone'**. The intoxication offered by Paris and its variety and multiplicity derives not from its opposition to past cultures, but, on the contrary, from its position as the vat in which multiple and various cultural traditions are pressed and fermented to produce a uniquely heady poetic wine.

The blending and fermenting of cultural traditions within the vast human agglomeration which is Paris corresponds to the blending and fermenting of poetic themes, traditions, and techniques which is the collection *Alcools.* It is matched by the interplay of codes within the poem. The title, **'Vendémiaire'**, situates it as an autumnal poem, with the ambivalent significations of the season, period of nostalgia and regret, but also season of fruition, and more particularly, the making of wine. But *vendémiaire* is of course also a month in the revolutionary calendar, and the 13 *vendémiaire* the date of an unsuccessful Royalist revolt. And this helps to give sense to the opening lines of the poem:

> Hommes de l'avenir souvenez-vous de moi
> Je vivais à l'époque où finissaient les rois
> Tour à tour ils mouraient silencieux et tristes
> Et trois fois courageux devenaient trismégistes

> (Men of the future remember me
> I lived at the time when kings were coming to
>   an end
> In turn they died silent and sad
> And three times courageous became trismegistic)

particularly if they are read in conjunction with the text of the crown motif from **'Coeur couronne et miroir'**: 'Les rois qui meurent tour à tour renaissent au coeur des poètes' ('The kings who die in turn are reborn in the hearts of the poets'). The revolution which marked the end of kings and the old ordered universe can be seen in relation to the poetic revolution which is also a poetic rebirth or Renaissance. And, like the culture of the Renaissance, the fusion of diverse strands of civilisation, the new poetic culture of which Paris is the centre represents the bringing together, not only of Pagan and Christian traditions—and the poem plays heavily on the role of wine and the notion of rebirth or recuscitation in both—but also of the new technological civilisation manifested by the factory chimneys to which I have just referred.

If, however, the poem offers a positive resolution of some of the tensions and problems introduced by **'Zone'**, and worked out in the course of the volume, it is nevertheless a more dated and less satisfactory poem than **'Zone'**. It endorses the cultural relativity of the metropolis, but only by totalising it. It reaches back to the Baudelairian sense of intoxication to be derived from experience of the city. And if it avoids the narrowness of the Futurist refusal of tradition and culture in its accumulation of the past which is the present, it nevertheless does so in terms of the kind of vitalism which I suggested to be, in the case of the Futurists, a retarded Romantic trait. Indeed, if its difficulty as a poem derives from the density and intricacy of reference that characterises the 1907-8 poems by Apollinaire, **'Le Brasier'** and **'Les Fiançailles'**, it reaches back, formally, even further than Baudelaire. For its basic metaphorical structure, founded on the multiple voices that the poet hears on his way home to Auteuil in the lines quoted at the beginning of this essay, voices whose songs and cries then constitute the body of the poem, has something of the literal-mindedness of Victor Hugo's 'Ce qu'on entend sur la montagne' ('What is heard on the mountain') of 1829 and, as I noted at the beginning of this [essay], something of its rhetorical pomposity.

A flyer announcing the 1917 gathering at which Apollinaire delivered the lecture "L'esprit nouveau," a call for pure invention and a total surrender to inspiration in the arts.

It marks, however, the transition between *Alcools* and the first section of *Calligrammes*, 'Ondes' ('Waves'). For if it expresses an affirmative attitude to the city, what it fails to register is the acceptance of the variability and indeterminacy of urban experience which is hinted at in **'Marizibill'**. And in the small group of poems collected in *Calligrammes* under the title 'Ondes', mostly written between the publication of *Alcools* and the outbreak of war, Apollinaire seems to be striving, in a number of ways, to discover a lyricism of modern urban experience which is neither transcendence through language in the sense in which I have described it in Baudelaire, nor vitalistic totalisation, nor simply celebratory in the innocently expressive sense, but one which is founded on the creation of an affirmative poetic unreality out of the transient and fragmentary nature of twentieth-century city life.

The kind of reading which Philippe Renaud proposes of **'Lundi rue Christine'** [in *Lecture d'Apollinaire*, 1969] goes in this sense. Apollinaire referred to this kind of poem as a 'poème conversation', defined in the following terms: 'The poet at the centre of life records so to speak the ambient lyricism.' Looked at in conjunction with the lyrical ideogram **'Lettre-Océan'** in which the Eiffel Tower radio transmitter sends out simultaneous 'poetic' messages to all parts of the world, this suggests a relationship with the Futurist notion of 'simultaneity' and the technological means of its production. But the Apollinaire poem does not itself reveal this. It is—or could be thought to be—the simple and direct notation of a specific place—rue Christine—at a specific time—Monday. What is interesting is the ambiguity of these notations. They fall into several different categories—notations of décor, or of fragments of conversations picked up in the room, or magisterial pronouncements on the part of the poet, or comments on its development. But it is often extremely difficult to ascribe any particular line to any specific category—'Ça a l'air de rimer' ('That seems to rhyme / make sense'), for example, could be either a piece of conversation or a wry comment on the text itself.

> **What is excitingly new about the Apollinairian poem is that it neither laments the fragmentation of self and world, nor attempts to totalise or transcend it.**
>
> **—David Kelley**

In this way, the solidity of the real, apparently simply transcribed with the utmost immediacy, is dissolved. Its hard edges, the contours by which we can situate ourselves in it according to any fixed perspective, are blurred, and a strange dreamlike world is created in which everything is also *un*real. In a sense it recalls the Mallarmé sonnet quoted earlier. But Mallarmé's text literally negates the contingency of the world in order to create an absolute reality of the text in metaphysical terms. What is excitingly

new about the Apollinairian poem is that it neither laments the fragmentation of self and world, nor attempts to totalise or transcend it. It is a lyrical affirmation of the incidental and arbitrary nature of experience within time, and within the specific time of the present which does not negate the conditions of that experience. Without direct reference to the trappings of modern city life, and working almost uniquely in terms of a play with the ways in which language conventionally refers to the outside world—since the poetic unreality I have alluded to derives principally from the multiple and unstable possibilities of reading which the poem offers—he arrives at a poetic articulation of an experience of city life.

In certain ways **'Lundi rue Christine'** might be compared to certain contemporary works by Picasso and Braque, particularly the *papiers collés*, which offer a similar play of ambiguities deriving from a use of the actual and the everyday. The materials used, scraps of newspaper or pieces of *trompe-l'oeil*, like the false panelling in the Braque *Bottle, Glass and Pipe*, are there in their materiality and at the same time made to represent an accidental reality of the moment. But they relate in an ambiguous and unstable way to other elements in the work—to the clearly representational drawing of the bottle and the glass, or to the pipe, which exists like the Mallarméan 'ptyx' as an absence, since its form is cut out of a piece of newspaper. And a similar ambiguity and instability define the spatial relationships of the picture. The dark brown piece of real false panelling is foregrounded to appear to be in front of the bottle, but the drawing of the bottle is continued over it to contradict this indication of depth. Elements of the real and representations of the real are ambiguously combined to create an autonomous reality which refers to the real in its most everyday manifestations and which nevertheless refuses any simply realistic interpretation.

Another poem from 'Ondes', **'Un Fantôme de nuées'** (**'A Phantom of Clouds'**), confirms, by a discreet homage to Picasso, this connection between Apollinaire's poetic experiments of 1913-14 and the contemporary development of Cubism. Like **'Lundi rue Christine'**, **'Fantôme de nueés'** is firmly fixed in the actuality of a Paris experience. The subject of the poem is a chance encounter with a group of street acrobats. The time and place are firmly foregrounded—four o'clock on 13th July between Saint-German-des-Prés and the statue of Danton. But that time and place—near the statue of Danton on the day before the anniversary of the taking of the Bastille—recall the references to the revolution in **'Vendémiaire'**, and imply the desire to lend some kind of legendary or mythical significance to the chance everyday occurrence. And, since the 'fantôme de nuées' of the title, associated in the last line with the art of the new century, 'Siècle ô siècle des nuages' ('Century O century of clouds') is an allusion to the apparition of Juno constructed out of clouds to deceive Ixion, the poem is also centred on a reference to the myths of classical antiquity which play such a large part in *Alcools*. Indeed, if the poem is perhaps above all an 'art poétique' defining the kind of poetic revolution that Apollinaire is attempting to conduct in 'Ondes', it also suggests the continuity of the intellectual preoccupations of both poet and painters' in spite of the apparent stylistic voltes-face in which they had been engaged over the preceding decade.

For there is a resemblance which seems to be too close to be accidental between the acrobats of Apollinaire's poem and those of Picasso's paintings of 1905. The first of Apollinaire's acrobats carries the ashes of his forefathers on his face in the form of a grey beard, and is grinding out on his barrel organ a music of ironic lament, while looking towards the future. He is followed by another, who is faceless, and dressed only in his shadow, and finally by a young acrobat described in the following terms:

> Une jambe en arrière prête à la génuflexion
> Il salua ainsi aux quatre points cardinaux
> Et quand il marcha sur une boule
> Son corps mince devint une musique si délicate
>   que nul parmi les
> spectateurs n'y fut insensible
>
> Un petit esprit sans aucune humanité
> Pensa chacun
> Et cette musique des formes
> Détruisit celle de l'orgue mécanique
> Que moulait l'homme au visage couvert
>   d'ancêtres
>
> (One leg behind ready to kneel
> He made his bow thus to the four cardinal points
> And when he walked upon a sphere
> His slim body became a music so delicate that
>   no-one amongst the specta-
> tors could be insensitive to it
>
> A tiny spirit completely bereft of humanity
> Thought everyone
> And that music of forms
> Destroyed that of the barrel organ
> Ground out by the man whose face was covered
>   by his ancestors)

And one of the 1905 Picassos shows a child acrobat balanced on a sphere with an older male figure in the foreground seated with his back to the spectator on a cube, while another contemporary painting depicts an ancient hurdy-gurdy player. What is even more interesting, is that the first of these two paintings shows a resemblance that is also too close to be accidental to an image from a sixteenth-century emblem book by Alciati of the kind on which Apollinaire's 'Bestiaire' is clearly based. The Alciati emblem shows Hermes, god the arts, sitting on a cube, together with Fortune, balancing on a sphere, the image is accompanied by the following text:

> Sur un boulet Fortune a tous hasards:
> Sur un quadragle, Hermes preside aulx ars
> Contre Fortune est faict art pour remede
> Car mauvais sort au bon art requiert ayde
> Appren bon ars (O jeunesse opportune)
> Qui hont en soy redresse de Fortune.
>
> (On a ball Fortune open to chance:
> On a quadrangle, Hermes presides over the arts
> Art is made as remedy for fortune.
> For the misfortunes of fate require help from
>   skilful art
> Learn skilful arts (O likely lads)
> Who have it in them to redress Fortune.)

The text from the Alciati emblem book corresponds very closely to the preoccupations of the Apollinaire of *Alcools* as I defined them in my comments on 'Marizibill'. But in 'Un Fantôme de nuées' he is voluntarily misreading it, or inverting its implications. The lines from the Alciati text encourage the pursuit of art—in the sense of useful and lucrative skills—as a way of redressing fate and dominating the vagaries of chance. Whereas in Apollinaire's poem the infant acrobat is not Fortune as such, but the representative of an alternative form of art—an art which espouses the apparently haphazard relativity of urban experience, and whose precarious balancing act produces a formal music—literally a music of the spheres?—capable of destroying and replacing the traditional plaintive music of the barrel-organ played by the Harlequin/Hermes, which, within the Symbolist tradition had precisely the function of transcending the chance contingencies of finite experience. And when, at the end of the poem, the child acrobat disappears, the reaction of the spectators is one of almost religious awe:

> Mais chaque spectateur cherchait en soi l'enfant
>   miraculeux
> Siècle ô siècle des nuages
>
> (But each spectator sought within himself the
>   miraculous child
> Century O century of clouds)

in which hints of the Christian Nativity and Ascension are associated both with the Classical myth of Ixion and the new century.

The positive note on which the poem ends suggests that the aesthetic adumbrated and practiced in the poem is perceived as a resolution of some of the problems posed in 'Zone'—and particularly in the opening sequences. That is, how to find a poetic language capable of affirming without contradicting by the nature of that affirmation, the conditions of modern urban experience, one which can accommodate the sense of cultural fragmentation which is an important element in that experience—the 'heap of broken images' of which Eliot speaks in *The Waste Land*—without attempting to totalise it in a way which belies its nature, one which can replace the perspectives of European civilisation since the Renaissance without denying the significance of its cultural inheritance or residue, which can make out of what had been perceived as an artistic decadence, artistic rebirth. (pp. 80-96)

> *David Kelley, "Defeat and Rebirth: The City Poetry of Apollinaire," in* Unreal City: Urban Experience in Modern European Literature and Art, *edited by Edward Timms and David Kelley, St. Martin's Press, 1985, pp. 80-96.*

Suzanne Nash   (essay date 1991)

[*In the following excerpt, Nash analyzes the feeling of discontinuity and disunity that many critics have argued characterizes the collection of poems in* Alcools.]

Alcools, as a collection of poems written between 1901 and 1912, is on the threshold of the new age, and it derives its lyrical and dramatic force from the erratic shifts in tone and attitude in which the sequence of poems reveals the poet as protagonist of contemporary life. The collection does not tell a coherent story about the birth and coming of age of the new poet, but registers with great affective intensity and range the poet's effort to identify and control what appear as fundamentally irreconcilable forces, both seductive and threatening, in his experience of this new age. Feelings of loss and obsolescence vie with curiosity about the future; self-awareness and solitude, with the impulse to connect with a still impersonal collectivity. Occasionally, as in the case of the **"A La Santé"** or the Rhineland texts, poetic sequences constitute islands of emotional coherence, but they float detached, as part of the debris of a past in the process of breaking up, rather than as cohering elements.

Alcools thus provides us with a moving testimony to the sacrifices involved in Apollinaire's advocacy of the "new spirit" precisely because most of it was written during the years when the young poet was still trying to find contemporary meaning in outdated nineteenth-century forms. Reverence for a past that he is not yet willing to relinquish is cut through by irony, humor, and a sense of frustration, which surround the effort to conserve old ideals. It was, perhaps, the gathering together of his poems for *Alcools* in 1913 that provided him with the insight for the sentence . . . from "L'Esprit nouveau et les poètes": "C'est aux poètes à décider s'ils ne veulent point entrer résolument dans l'esprit nouveau, hors duquel il ne reste d'ouvertes que trois portes: celle des pastiches, celle de la satire et celle de la lamentation, si sublime soit-elle" ("It is up to the poets to decide if they will not resolutely embrace the new spirit, outside of which only three doors remain open: that of pastiche, that of satire, and that of lamentation, however sublime it be"). A comparison of *Calligrammes* and *Alcools*—strikingly different in form and tone, yet each containing poems written in 1912—would suggest that Apollinaire saw himself undergoing a distinct shift in his attitude toward the uses of the lyric at the time of the publication of *Alcools.* Whereas *Calligrammes* follows a fairly straightforward chronological ordering and for the most part is an enthusiastic yea-saying to the poet's role as inventor of new forms, *Alcools,* which contains poems from Apollinaire's very earliest, antisymbolist phase (1901-05) as well as poems written later in response to his discovery of the new art of cubism, thoroughly obscures chronology as an ordering principle. The poems taken as a whole seem to constitute a complex, poeticized story of the postromantic crisis that necessitated a new lyric mode and that required of the poet a painful detachment from certain cherished moral and aesthetic certainties.

The Orpheus myth, clearly alluded to at key moments throughout the collection ("Une épouse me suit c'est mon ombre fatale"—**"Signe"**; "A wife pursues me my fatal shadow"—**"Sign"**; "J'ai eu le courage de regarder en arrière"—**"Les Fiançailles"**; "I have had the courage to look backward"—**"The Betrothal"**;) organizes Apollinaire's peculiar backward-glancing and sacrificial view of his role as poet of the modern age. But a living Orpheus, tied to the memory of his living bride—

Au soleil parce que tu l'aimes
Je t'ai menée souviens-t'en bien
Ténébreuse épouse que j'aime
Tu es à moi en n'étant rien
O mon ombre en deuil de moi-même
        (**"La Chanson du mal aimé"**)

Shadow-wife I led you where
You like to walk in sun and air
In being nothing you were mine
O my dear shadow wearing black
You mourn for me behind my back
        [**"Song of the Poorly Loved"**]

—contrasts with the dismembered Orpheus floating down the river of time to sing with the depersonalized and collective voice of contemporary humanity ("Il vit décapité sa tête est le soleil / Et la lune son cou tranché"—**"Les Fiançailles"**; "It lives headless its head is the sun / And the moon cut off at the neck"—**"The Betrothal"**). Thematic repetitions specifically evocative of the alienated modern condition and reminiscent of the fin de siècle lyric (exile, disappointed love, *faux semblant,* prostitution), as well as certain characteristic formal procedures (refrain, use of negation, intratextual and intertextual echoings) suggest, nevertheless, the collections' obscured integrity. One feels, somehow, that these poems belong together, between the same covers and within the frame of the two poems written in 1912, **"Zone"** and **"Vendémiaire."** On the other hand, one is hard put to describe what constitutes the unity of *Alcools* in any convincing way. There is a disorderly aspect to the collection—what Georges Duhamel described correctly, but without any insight into its aesthetic or philosophical significance, as reminiscent of a *boutique de brocanteur* ("secondhand shop"). It is worth quoting Duhamel's cruel, even racist review of 1913 because it reveals how unprepared the pre-war reading public still was for this subversion of an aesthetics of wholeness, continuity, and originality rooted in romantic and symbolist theory.

> Je dis: boutique de brocanteur parce qu'il est venu échouer dans ce taudis une foule d'objets hétéroclites dont certains ont de la valeur, mais dont aucun n'est le produit de l'industrie du marchand même. C'est bien là une des caractéristiques de la brocante: elle revend; elle ne fabrique pas. Elle revend d'ailleurs parfois de curieuses choses; il se peut qu'on trouve, dans ses étalages crasseux, une pierre de prix montée sur un clou. Tout cela vient de loin; mais la pierre est agréable à voir. Pour le reste, c'est un assemblage de faux tableaux, de vêtements exotiques et rapiécés, d'accessoires pour bicyclettes et d'instruments d'hygiène privée. Une truculente et étourdissante variété tient lieu d'art, dans l'assemblage des objets. C'est à peine si, par les trous d'une chasuble miteuse, on aperçoit le regard ironique et candide du marchand, qui tient à la fois du juif levantin, de l'Américain du Sud, du gentilhomme polonais et du facchino.

> I say: secondhand shop because in this shack there is a collection of discarded, anomalous objects, some of value, but none of which is the product of the merchant's own effort. That is one of the characteristics of the secondhand

trade: it does not make anything, it resells; occasionally it even resells some surprising things; one may actually find on the grimy display shelves a precious stone mounted on a nail. All the stuff comes from far away; but the stone is a pleasure to see. As for the rest, it is an assortment of phony pictures, exotic, patched clothes, accessories for bicycles, and implements for personal hygiene. A truculent and dizzying variety replaces art, in the amassing of things. Through the moth holes of an old chasuble one can just see the ironic and bold glance of the merchant, who has something of the Levantine Jew, the Latin American, the Polish gentleman, and the Italian railway porter.

Rather than a secondhand shop, one might have called this collection the atelier of modern art, a term more relevant for the kinds of experimentation that Apollinaire was practicing and that link him eventually to later, more obviously political writers like the surrealists, Brecht, or Francis Ponge. If in *Alcools* a melancholy tone and the psychological alienation of the lonely city dweller seem to dominate, potential sentimentality or despair are undercut by iconoclastic humor ("Mon verre s'est brisé comme un éclat de rire"; "My glass has shattered like a peal of laughter"). Baudelairean spleen, moreover, gives way to a sacrifice of the remembering self for a collective dynamics that promises new forms of social and spiritual communion. I say promises because the collectivity with which the lyric voice allies itself in the more self-consciously revolutionary **"Vendémiaire"** is one that sums up in hymnlike tones rather than one that challenges the achievements of its age. Nevertheless, it is the move from personal to collective that disrupts what, in Apollinaire's view, had become a fetishistic attachment to a romantic vocabulary by the turn of the century. The shift in attitude that in part, at least, accounts for the drama of *Alcools* when read as a whole is reflected in the difference between the two poems that Apollinaire chose to frame his collection. The speaker of **"Zone"** stresses the already worn-out nature of the modern city and the exhaustion of the sacred, finding freshness only in the religion of his childhood and coded personal references to private experiences. The speaker of **"Vendémiaire,"** on the other hand, while still consigning himself to the past for his future readers—

Hommes de l'avenir souvenez-vous de moi
Je vivais à l'époque où finissaient les rois

Men of the time to come remember
Me I lived when the kings were finishing

—nevertheless proclaims himself the distilled voice of his time ("le gosier de Paris"; "the throat of Paris") drunk with the factory-made saints and barbarian monarchs who have replaced the sacred pope of Rome as spiritual leaders of an industrialized Europe. The divided, alienated self of **"Zone"**—

Tu n'oses plus regarder tes mains et à tous moments je voudrais sangloter
Sur toi sur celle que j'aime sur tout ce qui t'a épouvanté

You don't dare look at your hands any more and I am forever wanting to cry

About you about her I love about all that has scared you

—becomes the voice of *universelle ivrogueric* ("universal drunkenness") in **"Vendémiaire."** One might say that *Alcools* represents what Renato Poggioli has identified as the agonistic moment in the avant-garde experience, whereby "catastrophe is transformed into miracle and the self-immolation of the creative personality into an art of the future." The present is understood in **"Vendémiaire"** and in the ordering of the entire collection, as a "forge of history in continual metamorphosis." Poggioli's distinction between reverence for the past that ends in conservatism and appreciation of the uses of the past for future reconstruction seems appropriate for a reading of *Alcools:* "Tradition itself ought to be conceived not as a museum but as an atelier, as a continuous process of formation, a constant creation of new values, a crucible of new experiences."

It cannot be denied, however, that *Alcools* has certain museum or antique shop characteristics—through its revival of old forms: *chanson de toile,* aubade, *complainte;* through the use of symbolist parody: **"Clair de lune," "Palais," "Rosemonde,"** for example; and through the recurrence of fin-de-siècle themes and motifs: *saltimbanques, tziganes* (gypsies), *Salomé, voyage, naufrage* (drowning). This faded, nostalgic quality gives one the feeling of reliving something—not as truth, however, in the way a latter-day symbolist poet like Henri de Regnier might, but self-consciously and with a touch of cynicism, as reproduction, in the way a professional forger of antiquities would see it.

J'ai vu travailler un faussaire à Honnef, au bord du Rhin. . . . Il m'avait pris en amitié et je le vis une fois agenouillé dans son jardinet et salissant avec de la terre humide des poteries neuves qu'il vendit quelques mois après à un pasteur protestant amateur d'antiquités rhénanes. Ce faussaire n'était parfaitement heureux que les jours où il avait maquillé quelque fausseté. Il l'admirait ensuite en souriant et disant: "J'ai fabriqué un dieu, un faux dieux, un vrai joli faux dieu." Puis il prenait sa guitare et chantait, en tordant sa bouche édentée, de vieilles chansons allemandes qui célébraient Kaëtchen de Heilbronn ou Schinderhannes. (**"Des Faux"**)

I once saw a counterfeiter at work in Honnef, on the Rhine. . . . He had taken a liking to me, and I once saw him kneeling in his little garden, smudging some pieces of brand-new pottery with moist earth. A few months later, he sold those pieces to a Protestant minister who was a collector of Rhenish antiques. That old counterfeiter was completely happy only on the days he had disguised some forgery. He would then admire his work with a smile and say, "I have created a god, a false god, a real, pretty, false god." Then he would take his guitar, and screwing up his toothless mouth, he would sing some old German lieder celebrating Katchen of Heilbronn or Schinderhannes.

(**"Fakes"**)

It is Apollinaire's use of pastiche as a form of self-criticism that Duhamel did not grasp and that constitutes the off-key tone of *Alcools.*

The celebratory voice of **"Vendémiaire,"** which concludes *Alcools* and announces the collective reader of *Calligrammes,* is not arrived at easily. The analogy of the poet to a new Orpheus is complemented and offset by another analogy—that of Lazarus pulled haggard out of his tomb ("Tu ressembles au Lazare affolé par le jour"—**"Zone"**; "Looking like Lazarus unwitted by the daylight")—and the promise of a new Coming is, more often than not, disappointed, as in the persistence of the theme of betrayal in **"L'Ermite"** (The hermit), **"Un Soir"** (One evening), **"Les Fiançailles,"** or **"A La Santé,"** for example. Loss of the sacred and loss of a true love are analogous and suggest the loss of those aestheticist values of "unity," "purity," and "truth" that Apollinaire wanted to believe were embodied in the cubist painting of the "fourth dimension." The theme of *faux semblant* is not only a romantic lament of betrayed love in **"La Chanson du mal aimé,"** but a recognition that poetic language can never coincide with experience through symbolic figuration. Renaissance does not mean birth of the same, but the beginning of something else. The opening stanzas of **"La Chanson du mal aimé,"** which suggest a hellish scene—Orpheus in search of his dead bride—stress, through the repetition of various forms of the word *sembler* ("to seem"), the impossibility of all adequate connection or coming to rest in fixed values. The speaker, his *voyou*-shadow self, his unfaithful lover, and all of her avatars in history from the sirens to the Danaides to Annie Pleyden at once resemble each other and seem to be forms of mutual betrayal.

> Un soir de demi-brume à Londres
> Un voyou qui ressemblait à
> Mon amour vint à ma rencontre
> Et le regard qu'il me jeta
> Me fait baisser les yeux de honte

> In London on a dismal night
> I met a hoodlum in the street
> Who might have been my love
> He looked so much like her his gaze
> Made me blush and drop my eyes

The knowledge of this certain deception is the legacy of the modern poet and the source of his tormented humor. One can hear it in the furious rejection of the elaborate metaphor of the Red Sea (which cunningly turns him into the persecutor of his shadow self) for a return to the literal, concrete (brick) origins of his experience, and an exasperated declaration of eternal love, even as he tries to write that love out of existence:

> Je suivis ce mauvais garçon
> Qui sifflotait mains dans les poches
> Nous semblions entre les maisons
> Onde ouverte de la mer Rouge
> Lui les Hébreux moi Pharaon

> Que tombent ces vagues de briques
> Si tu ne fus pas bien aimée

> I trailed him as he slouched along
> Hands in pockets whistling
> The street became a trough
> Two billows of the Red Sea rose

> And I was Pharoah he the Jews

> Oh if I have not loved you well
> Let that brick ocean comb and fall

It is there again in **"Les Sept Epées"** (**"The Seven Swords"**), where he resorts to coded language for the expression of his most private desires and hopes. One can see it as well in the dramatic development of certain poems such as **"Palais"** (**"Palace"**), **"Clair de lune"** (**"Moonlight"**), or **"Les Fiançailles,"** which in allegorizing the poet's mission, begin optimistically and end in betrayal or uncertainty. In **"Clair de lune"** the poet perversely chooses the meretricious language of symbolic self-mystification to express his skepticism regarding the instrument of his vocation:

> Lune mellifluente aux lèvres des déments
>   . . . . .
> J'ai peur du dard de feu de cette abeille Arcture
> Qui posa dans mes mains des rayons décevants
> Et prit son miel lunaire à la rose des vents

> The honeyflowing moon is on every madman's
>   tongue
>   . . . . .
> But I fear the bee Arcturus and his fiery sting
> Who having put these slippery beams in my
>   hands
> Took his lunar honey from the rose of the winds

Like the pretty woman of **"1909,"** the language is all too seductive, all too easily assimilated by the sentimental reader of his period. In **"Palais,"** where the poet ends up dining on his own dead thoughts in the palace of the king's concubine, Apollinaire puns, through the word *palais* (meaning "palace" and "palate") on the relationship of corrupt language to corrupt values.

But even more depressing than the bland taste of his own thoughts and tongue is the sight of the other guests eating them with relish:

> Or ces pensées mortes depuis des millénaires
> Avaient le fade goût des grands mammouths
>   gelés
> Les os ou songe-creux venaient des ossuaires
> En danse macabre aux plis de mon cervelet

> Et tous ces mets criaient des choses nonpareilles
>   Mais nom de Dieu!
>   Ventre affamé n'a pas d'oreilles
> Et les convives mastiquaient à qui mieux mieux

> But these thoughts dead for thousands of years
> Had the stale taste of huge frozen mammoths
> Bones and dreams were coming from the char-
>   nel-houses
> In a *danse macabre* in the folds of my cerebellum

> And all those meats shouted unheard-of things
>   But god almighty
>   A famished belly has no ears
> And the guests went on munching one outdoing
>   the other

To cling to this illusionary "rose world" (**"Rosemonde"**) is a form of sickness: "L'amour dont je souffre est une maladie honteuse," (**"Zone"**; "The love I suffer from is a shameful sickness") or even worse, necrophilia, as when the corpses in **"La Maison des morts"** (The house of the dead) declare eternal fidelity to one another in the clichéd language of old love lyrics. At rare moments, as in **"Le Brasier"** or at the beginning of **"Les Fiançailles,"** a genuine hope for renewal is expressed, and the poet imagines himself a new Prometheus, a modern version of Rimbaud, fueling himself on the sacrifice of his former beliefs for a kind of cosmic rebirth in a world of radically altered forms. At these moments he can say:

> Il n'y a plus rien de commun entre moi
> Et ceux qui craignent les brûlures
>
> ("Les Brasier")

> There is no longer anything in common between
> me
> And those who fear burning
>
> ("The Brasier")

But more often the lyric speaker presents himself behind the smile of the toothless forger, singing old folk songs to the tourists to give them the impression that they are getting the real thing. The modern poet of **"L'Emigrant de Landor Road,"** who sets out ahead of everyone else to found a new country, experiences his vocation as that of a leave-taking and a departure for an unknown future, dressed in the used clothes of a dead past:

> Mon bateau partira demain pour l'Amérique
>   Et je ne reviendrai jamais
> Avec l'argent gagné dans les prairies lyriques
> Guider mon ombre aveugle en ces rues que
>   j'aimais

> My boat will leave for America tomorrow
>   And I'll never come back
> With the money I've earned on the lyric prairies
> To lead my blind shade through these streets
>   that I have
>   loved.

He is something of a clown rather than a Christ figure (**"L'Ermite"**—the betrayed prisoner of **"A La Santé"** poems, who turns like a bear in his cage and sees rays of light dance in the form of *pitres* ("buffoons") on his verses. The muse of the modern world is neither corrupt nor beautiful and is not especially seductive. She is a tired working woman, marked by time and disappointed hopes.

> Ces femmes ne sont pas méchantes elles ont des
>   soucis cependant
> Toutes même la plus laide a fait souffrir son
>   amant
> Elle est la fille d'un servent de ville de Jersey
> Ses mains que je n'avais pas vues sont dures et
>   gercées
> J'ai une pitié immense pour les coutures de son
>   ventre
>
> ("Zone")

> These are not bad women but they have their
>   troubles
> And even the ugliest one has made her lover suf-
>   fer
> She is the daughter of a policeman from the Isle
>   of Jersey
> Her hands which I hadn't seen are hard and raw

> I feel an immense pity for the scars on her stom-
>   ach
>
> ("Zone")

> J'aimais les femmes atroces dans les quartiers
>   énormes
> Où naissaient chaque jour quelques êtres nou-
>   veaux
> Le fer était leur sang la flamme leur cerveau
> J'aimais j'aimais le peuple habile des machines
> Le luxe et la beauté ne sont que son écume
>
> ("1909")

> I have loved atrocious women in monstrous
>   places
> Where new creatures came to birth daily
> Iron was their blood and flame their brain
> I loved I loved the people expert with machines
> Luxury and beauty are only their dross
>
> ("1909")

The new music that will accompany her appearance in the mechanized urban world is a strident one that grates on the spine as it voices the death cry of the old lyric:

> Les dimanches s'y éternisent
> Et les orgues de Barbarie
> Y sanglotent dans les cours grises
>   . . . . .
> Soirs de Paris ivres du gin,
> Flambant de l'éléctricité
> Les tramways feux verts sur l'échine
> Musiquent au long des portées
> De rails leur folie de machines
>
> ("La Chanson du mal aimé")

> A barrel-organ sobs below
> Eternity instead of hours
> Is Sundays like this in a row
>
> The nights in Paris all drink gin
> And fall asleep with their streetlights on
> Trolley-cars are mad machines
> To make green sparks and scream like queens
>
> ("Song of the poorly loved")

The basic tension of *Alcool,* one that is supported by the ordering of the individual works within a single collection, is expressed by two of the most lyrically powerful and haunting stanzas of **"La Chanson du mal aimé."** The first voices the struggle to preserve a sacred but naive memory of the past against oblivion, in words that, like flowers pressed under glass, maintain their antique beauty.

> Je ne veux jamais l'oublier
> Ma colombe ma blanche rade
> O marguerite exfoliée
> Mon ile au loin ma Désirade
> Ma rose mon giroflier.

> Oh let me not be cured of her
> My pretty dove my calm harbor
> Still let memory see
> That argosy that isle of spice
> The petalled flower of her face

The second stanza expresses a recognition that loyalty to the past can end in a thralldom that may kill the lyric voice altogether, poisoned by the tears of its salty lament:

> Mon beau navire ô ma mémoire

Avons-nous assez navigué
Dans une onde mauvaise à boire
Avons-nous assez divagué
De la belle aube au triste soir

O pretty ship my memory
Isn't this far enough to sea
And the sea not fit to drink
Haven't we drifted far and lost
From fair dawn to dreary dusk

But if this tension over the past ends in a deadlock, the ironic and skewed versions of familiar nineteenth-century forms inaugurate the spirit that will inform Apollinaire's work after 1914. Discontinuity is used as a conscious strategy for the (dis)ordering of this collection that means to break with an aesthetics of autonomy. Just as there is no clear-cut chronological progression from early to late poems or autobiographical development from young to old poet, there is no clear-cut evolution from old to new forms. Orpheus is both yearning for union with his bride and alternatively ready to scatter notions of unity to the four winds—"la rose des vents." When in one fell swoop Apollinaire removed all of the punctuation from the poems on the proofs of *Alcools,* he dislodged individual words and lines from their fixed positions, making the elements of his poems free-floating entities. This gesture was his leave-taking of the aestheticist principles of his symbolist heritage.

Adieu faux amour confondu
Avec la femme qui s'éloigne
Avec celle que j'ai perdue
L'année dernière en Allemagne
Et que je ne reverrai plus

Farewell false love I took you for
The woman that I lost last year
Forever as I think
I loved her but I will not see
Her any more in Germany

Significance is no longer preordained; there is no longer any neat subordination of part to whole. The collection becomes a workshop rather than a finished form as one poem borrows parts from another to make up new configurations that may even bring the original poem's meaning into question. What Duhamel saw as tricky imitation, Apollinaire presents as contemporary recovery of the debris of the past. He is purposely disrespectful of his own work, imitating himself as pastiche in **"Rosemonde"** (Rosamond), **"Signe,"** or **"Palais"** (Palace) for example, presenting a kitsch version of **"Zone"** or **"La Chanson du mal aimé"** in **"Hôtel,"** or using lines from rejected poems to patch up new ones in **"Le Voyageur," "L'Adieu,"** or **"Les Fiançailles"** Apollinaire's own offhand accounts of the genesis of many of his poems (**"Le Voyageur"** improvised while humming to himself in the street or **"Le Marriage d'André Salmon"** written on the top of the bus on his way to his friend's civil ceremony) bear out his impulse to desacralize the image of the creator as demigod and replace it with tinkerer, mechanic, or inventor, thus anticipating the rhetorical question of "L'Esprit nouveau et les poètes" of 1918: "Peut-on forcer la poésie à se cantonner hors de ce qui l'entoure, à méconnaître la magnifique exubérance de vie que les hommes par leur activité ajoutent à la nature et qui permet de machiner le monde de la façon la plus incroyable?" ("Can poetry be forced to establish itself outside of what surrounds it, to ignore the magnificent exuberance of life which the activities of men are adding to nature and which allow the world to be mechanized in an incredible fashion?").

Apollinaire's well-known preference within individual poems for the isolated and shocking image, for the free-floating line (**"Chantre"** [singer]), or the word or even letter for its own sake (**"Pâline," "Noubousse," "Malourène," "Podolie," "Salonique," "Zaporogue,"** or the illuminated letters of *Les Bestiaires*) is reflected in the discontinuous, often disorienting arrangement of the poems in the collection as a whole. They do not tell a coherent story, but give unexpected meaning to fickle moments of creative activity by their surprising juxtapositions. Nevertheless, it is only by reading the poems of *Alcools* together rather than separately that the reader can begin to understand that this is a poetry that takes itself seriously in a new way—as a "continuous process of formation." *Calligrammes,* many of which were written in the trenches, would be Apollinaire's most heroic acceptance of such a view, because there each poem-experiment offers itself to the reader as such—ready to be thrown away, impossible to collect or recite or remember except as a visual image—a sky rocket that requires a temporary but intense collaboration between reader and writer. These are inventions that will not carry over into a tradition and that are never in danger of becoming a style—pure "coonskinism" or "potshots taken at the Redcoats," as Harold Rosenberg puts it in "Parable of American Painting." In fact Rosenberg's comments on the American Action painters are entirely appropriate for Apollinaire's most experimental work: "In this gesturing with materials the aesthetic, too, has been subordinated." These are moments "when the modern artist feels himself released from value"; "acts of risk and will." But what Apollinaire learned about the uses of the past in the "agonistic" phase of *Alcools* is not lost in the "activistic" stage of his understanding of the present in *Calligrammes.* He does not mistake this revolutionary art for an ultimate act either. There is no dream of permanence in revolt here, as seems to be the case for the futurists and the surrealists. Intratextual echoings and repetitions are as present in *Calligrammes* as they are in *Alcools,* and a more traditional narrative poetry dialogues with the explosive visual shapes in a way reminiscent of **"La Chanson du mal aimé,"** written in 1903. The frame poems—**"Liens"** and **"La Jolie rousse"**—insist on connections of a new sort that do not bind or strangle, although the exaltation of these modern forms of communication is always accompanied by a yearning for what is being let go:

D'autres liens plus ténus
Blancs rayons de lumière
Cordes et Concorde

J'écris seulement pour vous exalter
O sens ô sens chéris
Ennemis du souvenir
Ennemis du désir

Ennemis du regret
Ennemis des larmes
Ennemis de tout ce que j'aime encore

("Liens")

Other more tenuous chains
White rays of light
Cords and Concord

I write only to exalt you
Oh senses oh cherished senses
Enemies of memory
Enemies of desire

Enemies of regret
Enemies of tears
Enemies of all I still love

("Chains")

Ayez pitié de moi

("La Jolie Rousse")

Have pity on me

("The Pretty Redhead")

Apollinaire's poetry continues to move us because it does not throw away the past easily—it enters the deconstructive phase of modernism in full awareness that the force of the new art will be in the strength of its sacrifices. (pp. 157-70)

> *Suzanne Nash, "Apollinaire's 'Alcools' and the Disorder of Modernity," in* The Ladder of High Designs: Structure and Interpretation of the French Lyric Sequence, *edited by Doranne Fenoaltea and David Lee Rubin, University Press of Virginia, 1991, pp. 150-71.*

FURTHER READING

Biography

Adéma, Marcel. *Apollinaire.* London: William Heinemann Ltd., 1954, 298 p.
   The first full-length biography of Apollinaire to appear in English. Noted Apollinaire scholar LeRoy C. Breunig has described Adéma's study as "the first solid, factual biography of Apollinaire."

Bates, Scott. *Guillaume Apollinaire.* Rev. ed. Twayne's World Authors Series: French Literature, edited by David O'Connell. Boston: Twayne Publishers, 1989, 204 p.
   Biographical and critical study.

Davies, Margaret. *Apollinaire.* London: Oliver & Boyd, 1964, 312 p.
   Includes critical examinations of Apollinaire's works.

Mackworth, Cecily. *Guillaume Apollinaire and the Cubist Life.* New York: Horizon Press, 1964, 244 p.
   Focuses on Apollinaire's social and professional relationships with the leading figures of the Cubist movement.

Steegmuller, Francis. *Apollinaire: Poet among Painters.* New York: Farrar, Straus & Co., 1963, 305 p.
   Illuminates the many autobiographical references in Apollinaire's works.

Criticism

Amelinckx, Frans. "Apollinaire's *Les onze mille verges:* Humor and pornography." *Philological Papers* 29 (1983): 8-14.
   Contends that in *Les onze mille verges* Apollinaire "uses the pornographic genre to explore the grotesque aspects of mankind and to create almost a comedy of black humor."

———. "Apollinaire's *Les trois don Juan:* The Seduction of Language." *Philological Papers* 30 (1984): 27-30.
   Asserts that in *Les trois don Juan* Apollinaire conflates existing myths about Don Juan, creating "a playful collage not only of the multi-faceted Don Juan, but even more of the infinite diversity of language."

Balakian, Anna. "Apollinaire and the Modern Mind." *Yale French Studies* 2, No. 2 (1949): 79-90.
   Maintains that Apollinaire rejected the pessimism that characterized early twentieth-century artists who were disheartened by the ostensible suppression of human creativity and expressiveness by science, industry, and mechanization.

Bohn, Willard. "A New Play by Apollinaire." *Comparative Drama* 11, No. 1 (Spring 1977): 73-87.
   Assesses Apollinaire's contribution to the little-known collaborative pantomime *What Time Does a Train Leave for Paris?*, which Bohn states is based on Apollinaire's poem "The Musician of Saint Merry." Bohn suggests that *What Time Does a Train Leave for Paris?* might justifiably be called " 'The First Surrealist Play.' "

Breunig, LeRoy C. Introduction to *Apollinaire on Art: Essays and Reviews, 1902-1918,* by Guillaume Apollinaire, edited by Breunig, pp. xvii-xxx. Translated by Susan Suleiman. New York: The Viking Press, 1972.
   Provides an overview of Apollinaire's career as an art critic, proclaiming him "the main impresario of the avant-garde."

Coe, Richard N. Introduction to *Les onze mille verges; or, The Amorous Adventures of Prince Mony Vibescu,* by Guillaume Apollinaire, pp. 7-21. Translated by Nina Rootes. London: Peter Owen, 1976.
   Contends that even in Apollinaire's pornographic novel *Les onze mille verges*—acknowledged by Coe as hack writing and "a Dream peopled with glossy plastic marionettes"—the author's poetic nature is evident.

Hamburger, Michael. "Apollinaire." *Poetry Quarterly* 12, No. 3 (Autumn 1950): 171-75.
   Stating that Apollinaire may have been the first of the modern poets, Hamburger attributes his modern quality to the "naïvete" manifested in both Apollinaire's innocent enjoyment of life and the "simple," surprising character of his verse.

Mathews, Timothy. *Reading Apollinaire: Theories of Poetic Language.* Manchester, England: Manchester University Press, 1987, 251 p.
   Focuses on individual poems by Apollinaire, treating each "as a provisional fragment of his self-reflection." Mathews states that Apollinaire attempts through poetry "to dismantle the perimeters of the self, to be absent within them, to take apart the censorship of the invasion incessantly dramatised by word and sensation."

Read, Peter. *"Apollinaire Libertaire:* Anarchy, Symbolism, and Poetry." *Forum for Modern Language Studies* XXI, No. 3 (July 1985): 239-56.

Suggests that the theme of libertarianism and the figure of the anarchist pervade Apollinaire's poetry throughout his career. The critic quotes extensively in French.

Rees, Garnet. Introduction to *Alcools,* by Guillaume Apollinaire, edited by Rees, pp. 1-35. London: The Athlone Press, 1975.

Examines the biographical context, facts related to publication, and order in which the poems of *Alcools* were composed; Rees further discusses Apollinaire's philosophy of poetry, as well as the style and form of his verse. The critic quotes extensively in French.

Rieder, Dolly S. "Time and Emptiness in Apollinaire's Poetry." *L'Esprit Createur* X, No. 4 (Winter 1970): 308-18.

Finds Apollinaire to be preoccupied in his poetry with the isolation and discontentment of present experience as well as uncertainty about the future. The critic quotes extensively in French.

Rinsler, Norma. "The War Poems of Apollinaire." *French Studies* XXV, No. 2 (April 1971): 169-86.

Chronologically discussing Apollinaire's war poems in *Calligrammes,* Rinsler defends his verse against the charge that it beautifies war and expresses excessive passion. The critic quotes extensively in French.

Stamelman, Richard Howard. *The Drama of Self in Guillaume Apollinaire's "Alcools".* North Carolina Studies in the Romance Languages and Literatures, No. 178. Chapel Hill: University of North Carolina Press, 1976, 229 p.

Studies the search for self-knowledge in Apollinaire's *Alcools,* which contains, according to Stamelman, representations of the "diverse and often contradictory selves" that comprised the poet's identity.

Steegmuller, Francis. Notes to *Alcools: Poems, 1898-1913,* by Guillaume Apollinaire, pp. 223-42. Translated by William Meredith. Garden City, N.Y.: Doubleday & Company, 1964.

Offers poem-by-poem commentary on the verses in *Alcools.*

Sullivan, Dennis G. "On Time and Poetry: A Reading of Apollinaire." *MLN* 88, No. 4 (May 1973): 811-37.

Explores Apollinaire's poetry and prose in order to discern his understanding of the nature of poetry. Sullivan contends that poetry, according to Apollinaire, stands above all other forms of representation as the sole mode of defining reality. The critic quotes extensively in French.

Themerson, Stefan. *Apollinaire's Lyrical Ideograms.* London: Gaberbocchus Press Ltd., 1968, 40 p.

A stylized, heavily illustrated appreciation of Apollinaire's visual poetry.

"The New Spirit." *Times Literary Supplement,* No. 3450 (11 April 1968): 361-62.

Argues that Apollinaire's modernity is superficial, alleging that he incorporated many stylistic and linguistic innovations in his poetry but provided no new insight into human experience.

Williman, Joseph P. "The Title of Apollinaire's *Alcools."* *Symposium* XXIII, No. 1 (Spring 1969): 80-92.

Proposes that the title of *Alcools* has various levels of meaning which support the perception of the work as a "coherent and meaningful whole." The critic quotes extensively in French.

Marie Corelli

1855-1924

(Born Mary Mackay) English novelist, essayist, short story writer, and poet.

INTRODUCTION

Best known for her highly imaginative novels of fantasy, romance, and the supernatural, Corelli enjoyed widespread popularity around the turn of the century. Drawing elements from Christian iconography as well as various occult and pseudo-scientific sources, she attempted to evoke what she called "the underlying spiritual quality of life." While critics during her lifetime often dismissed her works as didactic and sensationalistic, present-day assessments emphasize Corelli's importance as an icon of popular culture.

Born in London, Corelli was the illegitimate daughter of Charles Mackay, a journalist and musician. Wishing to avoid the stigma of her birth, she maintained that she was of Italian ancestry and had been adopted by Mackay, who she claimed was a doctor. Although Corelli studied music in preparation for a career as a concert pianist, she turned to writing in 1885 following a "psychical experience." Her first novel, *A Romance of Two Worlds,* depicts a young musician involved in a mystical love affair, undertaken by means of out-of-body travel. The work was well received, as were several books that followed it, especially her biblical epic *Barabbas,* which was published in 1893. Two years later, following the release of *The Sorrows of Satan,* Corelli had become Britain's most popular novelist. However, commercial success was not matched by critical acclaim; commentators denigrated Corelli's writings, and she responded by refusing review copies of her books. In 1901 Corelli moved to Stratford-on-Avon, believing that her presence there would confer dignity on the town of Shakespeare's birth. She continued to write prolifically throughout the remainder of her life, publishing a total of twenty-eight novels, numerous essays, and poetry. She died in 1924.

In her works Corelli employed moral didacticism in an attempt to combat the corruptive powers she saw preying on individuals and society. Such vices as greed, self-indulgence, status-seeking, and the vain quest for scientific knowledge and worldly power are eschewed or overcome by her idealized heroes and heroines, whose actions express Corelli's belief in the power of divine love to redeem humankind. Critics have largely disapproved of Corelli's moralizing, many also having cited a number of technical and aesthetic flaws in her works. The scientific views she expounded in her novels, for instance, are thought to rely more on mysticism and personal intuition than on empirical evidence. Similarly, critics have noted that her social commentary lacks humor and irony, rarely rising above

the level of personal invective. Louis James has observed that the author's "writing has the fascination of an intense, emotive imagination almost totally uninhibited by considerations of style, taste, or factual reality." Despite such strident objections, a number of critics have admired the passionate manner in which Corelli expressed lofty ideals of love, hope, and spirituality in an age of skepticism and disbelief. Summarizing her accomplishment in this regard, Henry Miller has written that Corelli "had tremendous courage and imagination, and dealt with questions of the highest order."

PRINCIPAL WORKS

A Romance of Two Worlds (novel) 1886
Vendetta! or, The Story of One Forgotten (novel) 1886
Thelma: A Society Novel (novel) 1887
Ardath: The Story of a Dead Self (novel) 1889
Wormwood: A Drama of Paris (novel) 1890

The Silver Domino; or, Side Whispers, Social and Literary (novel) 1892

The Soul of Lilith (novel) 1892

Barabbas: A Dream of the World's Tragedy (novel) 1893

The Sorrows of Satan; or, The Strange Experience of One Geoffrey Tempest, Millionaire (novel) 1895

Cameos (short stories) 1896

The Mighty Atom (novel) 1896

The Murder of Delicia (novel) 1896

Jane (novel) 1897

Ziska: The Problem of a Wicked Soul (novel) 1897

Boy: A Sketch (novel) 1900

The Greatest Queen in the World: A Tribute to the Majesty of England, 1837-1900 (essay) 1900

The Master-Christian: A Question of the Time (novel) 1900

"Temporal Power": A Study in Supremacy (novel) 1902

God's Good Man (novel) 1904

Free Opinions Freely Expressed on Certain Phases of Modern Social Life and Conduct (essays) 1905

The Treasure of Heaven: A Romance of Riches (novel) 1906

Woman, or—Suffragette? A Question of National Choice (essay) 1907

Holy Orders: The Tragedy of a Quiet Life (novel) 1908

The Devil's Motor (novel) 1910

The Life Everlasting: A Reality of Romance (novel) 1911

*The Strange Visitation of Josiah McNason (novel) 1912

Innocent: Her Fancy and His Fact (novel) 1914

The Young Diana: An Experiment of the Future (novel) 1918

My 'Little Bit' (essays) 1919

The Love of Long Ago, and Other Stories (novel and short stories) 1920

The Secret Power: A Romance of the Time (novel) 1921

Love—and the Philosopher: A Study in Sentiment (novel) 1923

Open Confession to a Man from a Woman (nonfiction) 1924

Poems (poetry) 1925

*This work was originally published in the journal *The Strand* in 1904.

CRITICISM

H. T. Peck   (essay date 1896)

[*Peck was an American editor, educator, and critic specializing in the study of classical literature. Known for his erudition and wit, he was widely influential in the decades between 1890 and 1910, an era in which he served as editor of the* Bookman. *In the following review*

of The Sorrows of Satan, *Peck asserts that the novel will delight readers with its sensational style and satirical condemnation of privileged society.*]

Whenever we finish the perusal of one of Marie Corelli's novels, we feel an intense desire to stamp fiercely on the floor and cry "Ha!" and mutter in our beard, and address the first person who happens along as a "vampire." This is an unconscious tribute to Marie Corelli's power, and incidentally an indication of what sort of book it is that Marie Corelli writes. She is, in fact, in her general literary style, the natural successor of Ouida, and we imagine that her public is identical with that upon which Ouida in her best days used to let loose her exuberant vocabulary and her pyrotechnic imagination. But Marie Corelli's morality is not that of Ouida—far from it. In the present volume she is very severe upon the prurient literature of the day; she impales Mr. Swinburne with many adjectives, she fleers at the hypocrisy of society, she denounces the shams of modern Christianity, and she even mocks at the alleged strictness of Her Majesty's court. Altogether she undertakes a large contract of denunciation, and carries it out with satisfactory and even exuberant completeness. It is said in London that Mr. Andrew Lang has had the honour of serving as one of her studies for this volume; and the good and virtuous heroine, Mavis Clare who writes such successful books, is evidently Marie Corelli herself, as the initials of the name also help to show.

The book is delightfully diabolic, and furnishes at least one thrill to every three pages, which is all that any one can reasonably ask for at the price. Satan, it appears, comes to London in the disguise of a handsome, mysterious, and immensely wealthy prince, whose name, Lucio Ramânas, learnedly suggests both Lucifer and Ahriman. He is very popular, though his eyes often have a "strange glitter," and he not infrequently laughs a "mocking laugh." He is especially loved by a certain Lady Sibyl, whose morality has been seriously impaired by reading Mr. Swinburne's poems; and she finally, "with a sudden, swift movement, flung herself upon his breast," while "the moonbeams showed her eyes alit with rapture." Lucio, strange to say, thrust her from him and politely called her "false and accursed" and "a fair fiend" and other names. Thereupon she resolved to kill herself, and after providing a liberal supply of stationery and a bottle of poison, sat down before a large mirror in order that she might "see her face radiate in the glass," remembering, as she cheerfully says, that "in a few days the worms will twine where the smile is now." Having done this she writes what would make, we should estimate, some sixty pages of manuscript about Mr. Swinburne, literature, the scientific heresies of the day, and other matters, and then takes the poison. Although, as she says herself, "torture indescribable" makes her "a writhing, moaning, helpless creature," she keeps on writing for some fifteen pages more, and at the last, it being revealed to her just who Lucio really is, she ends with this:

> Serve me, dear hand, once more ere I depart;
> . . . my tortured spirit must seize and compel
> you to write down this thing unnamable, that
> earthly eyes may read and earthly souls take
> timely warning! . . . I know at last WHOM I

have loved!—whom I have chosen, whom I have worshipped! . . . I know WHO claims my worship and drags me into yonder rolling world of flame!

Besides such exciting things as this, there are any number of epigrams and skits, and an unusual collection of adjectives, besides one or two new adverbs that we do not recollect to have seen anywhere before.

Altogether it is a great book and one to be recommended to all who like this sort of thing. When they have finished it, they, too, will feel an intense desire to stamp fiercely on the floor and cry "Ha!" and mutter in their beards, and address the first person who happens along as a "vampire." (pp. 424-25)

> *H. T. Peck, in a review of "The Sorrows of Satan," in* The Bookman, *London, Vol. II, No. 5, January, 1896, pp. 424-25.*

A. St. John Adcock   (essay date 1909)

[*Adcock was an English novelist and radio dramatist. In the following excerpt, she presents an appreciative overview of Corelli's most popular works, focusing on the author's style and subject matter and denouncing her detractors while affirming her deeply Christian worldview.*]

[Among the highest of Corelli's novels] I rank **Ardath, Barabbas, Thelma,** and **The Sorrows of Satan.** The conception of Satan, in the latter, is as magnificent as it is strikingly original; I know of nothing to compare with it, for its forcefulness and shadowed majesty, in modern fiction. The story satirises fiercely, sometimes bitterly, the follies and sins of latter-day society, and over it all broods that sinister, wistful, tragic figure of "Lucifer, Son of the Morning," forced to fulfil his self-appointed task of luring humanity to its destruction, sinking farther from bliss himself with every victim who yields to his tempting, and rising rapturously a little nearer to his lost estate when his wiles are resisted and his burden of doom so lightened. Where is the other living novelist who could grasp so great a theme and handle it with such easy mastery? Or where the other living novelist who could take that even more tremendous subject, that "dream of the world's tragedy," the trial and crucifixion and resurrection of Christ, and fashion it so resourcefully, with such a daring and masculine imagination, and yet with such infinite reverence, into so noble a piece of work as **Barabbas**?

The Master-Christian, "Temporal Power," Vendetta, Wormwood, The Mighty Atom, Cameos—that charming collection of picturesque sketches and stories; **Delicia, The Treasure of Heaven**—no names of recent novels are more familiar in our ears, for no novels of our time have been awaited more eagerly, discussed with more gusto, more warmly admired, or, in a word, proved more universally acceptable. When Miss Corelli was once asked by a *persona grata* at court whether, if it were offered, she would accept a title, she replied that she valued above all possible titles the goodwill and love of her readers, and these, as her correspondence and her unrivalled popularity testify, she has in far larger measure than any novelist among her contemporaries.

Cold and unemotional natures invariably despise those that are more alive than themselves and so more sensitive to the pleasures and pains, the laughter and pathos, the hopes and the despairs of humanity; they complacently miscall their own dead indifference culture and dignity, and the finer sensitiveness of those others illiterate emotionalism; and so it comes that certain critics, failing to understand the intense spiritual vitality of Marie Corelli's style, because they have nothing in themselves with which to compare it, denounce it as "verbose" and "hysterical." Nevertheless, there are some among them, men that really live as well as write, who unhesitatingly endorse the opinion that Mr. John Bygott has frankly expressed. Mr. Bygott, a Double Medallist and First Prizeman of the Society of Arts in English (and so entitled to the respect of even the academic), is the author of *The King's English, and How to Write It,* and in presenting a copy of this book to Miss Corelli, he wrote: "The work aims at inciting students to attain a good literary style by studying our great masterpieces, and though I have scrupulously avoided commenting upon living writers, I have long regarded you as being without an equal as a 'stylist.'"

The style of Miss Corelli's novels varies fittingly with their varying themes, but it is everywhere vivid, lucid, glowingly imaginative, burningly alive; through all of them runs the same deep undercurrent of earnestness and strong sincerity; whether they go back, as in **Barabbas,** to a sacred story of long ago, or, as with **The Treasure of Heaven** and **Holy Orders,** deal with the problems and the complex life of our own day, they are inspired by the same profound sense of spirituality, the same wide knowledge of the world and of human nature, the same vision of and reverence for the divine essence that is the soul of all things seen; the same pity for the weak and intolerance of wrong that find frankest expression in the pages of her **Free Opinions.** She is an absolute and devout believer in the Christian faith, and has embodied her religious theories more especially in **A Romance of Two Worlds, Ardath,** and **The Soul of Lilith.** She attends the Church of England, but is wisely tolerant of all creeds.

> "In every form of religion there is some attempt made to reach the divine—we should therefore respect all creeds, even if we regret a mistaken or ignorant conception of Eternal Truth. For myself," she remarks, "I believe solely and entirely in the message brought to human souls by the Gospel of Christ. If we followed Him truly we should be happy—it is because we do *not* follow Him that we miss the way to peace. In this day all the things that Christ prophesied are coming true so quickly that I wonder more people do not realise it; and I especially wonder at the laxity and apathy of the Churches, except for the fact that this also was prophesied. Some of us will live to see a time of terror, and that before very long. The blasphemous things which are being done in the world today cannot go on much longer without punishment. We know by history that deliberate scorn of God and divine things has always been met by retribution of a sudden and terrible nature and it will be so again."

(pp. 76-8)

A. St. John Adcock, "Marie Corelli: A Record and an Appreciation," in The Bookman, *London, Vol. XXXVI, No. 212, May, 1909, pp. 59-78.*

George Bullock   (essay date 1944)

[*In the following essay, Bullock denigrates Corelli's works, attributing her ephemeral celebrity to the deluded tastes of her contemporaries.*]

In 1885 the July edition of *Temple Bar* had an article, "One of the World's Wonders," describing an oyster-built grotto at Margate. Like today's film trailers, the title was pretentiously misleading, but the author, a lady from Kensington, did not doubt she had written something wonderful. Fair-haired, pretty, actually looking younger, she was thirty and tubby. Her scribbling was no sudden seaside inspiration, but a serious anxiety for fame. She was determined to be "someone". She had already given a concert, undertaking in the presence of the audience to compose a "forest" symphony and fourteen other "pieces". Even with Swinburne in the audience, the improvisation had raised no *réclame*. Now, paid ten guineas for describing a grotto, she wondered what a novel might not bring. In three volumes surely she could cause a *furore?* It would have to be a special novel—one of the world's wonders, in fact—for a "mere" person could produce one that was ordinary. Having begun to write, she was positive of a God-given inspiration. Her book would be a spiritual restorative to people less perfect than herself. Scorning "mere" life again, her imagination would soar celestially. The heroine (if she could be called by such a conventional name) would possess extraordinary gifts, but retain a perfect womanliness. The romance would be the purest to be had. As for "copy" (a word not mentioned in connection with divine revelations) there was herself, perfect and unique. She felt certain it could be done. In six months the spiritualistic concoction, filled with accounts of psychic experiences, healing baths, and supernal romance, was ready for the spiritually ailing. The publisher's readers (among them Hall Caine) argued its merits, but *A Romance of Two Worlds,* with an advertising preface, received attention from the public. It was a respectable success. The author, Marie Corelli, had established herself as a doctor of literary patent medicine. Grateful letters poured in. One man had been saved from suicide, a lady had felt ennobled after reading it twice. There was a demand for more, which the copyright owner had every intention of supplying. She had a large store of the tonic which only needed bottling. Encouraged by Mr. Bentley, her publisher, who advised a love story *pur et simple,* she lost no time. In a few months another supply was available, and for more than twenty years new consignments rolled in. *Vendetta, Thelma, Ardath, Wormwood* (what did the title matter so long as the properties remained effective?) were bought by an ever-increasing public. The appearance of a new Corelli novel became an event. An edition was sold in a few hours. On the day of publication queues waited outside the literary pharmaceutists, anxious for their half-yearly dose. Each time the mixture grew stronger, *Barabbas* almost took their breath away. By the time *The Sorrows of Satan* appeared the testifying letters were overwhelming. The Corelli tonic was famous, and some who swore by it were the highest in the land. Queen Victoria after reading the first novel asked for Miss Corelli's other books to be sent to Balmoral. Tennyson wrote: "You do well to care nothing for fame." Gladstone called on the authoress and stayed two hours. "*Ardath* is a magnificent conception," he is reported to have said. Meredith closed one book tearfully. The Dean of Westminster quoted *Barabbas* from the pulpit. Only the reviewers, "the literary cliques" as Marie Corelli called them, withheld praise. They did worse—they ridiculed. They sneered at the authoress's self-proclaimed divinity. As literary analysts they exposed her as a fraud. They maintained her tonic to be pretty coloured water. Her publisher's advice restrained her from taking action, but even he had no consolation to give that could stop her feeling outraged. The critics, she raved, were leagued against her, and she intended returning that hatred. The publishers were ordered to send out no review copies of *The Sorrows of Satan.* Members of the press, she stated on the front page, could obtain it "in the usual way".

She competed with people like Ellen Terry for publicity. Self-advertisement, she declared, was abhorrent to her, and proceeded to campaign for it. The public naturally wanted to know everything concerning their benefactress, and their benefactress was very willing for them to be told, but certain difficulties existed. There were facts about her life that must be veiled. There was even a skeleton that needed draping. To give Marie Corelli to her public—perfect with wisdom, virtue, and purity—a little juggling had to be done. When necessary, however, the authoress could do more than juggle. She could be acrobatic, especially with facts. In the first permitted biography she gave details of her "mixed Scottish and Italian parentage". She was, she said, the *adopted* daughter of Dr. Charles Mackay, LL.D. There was no information regarding her mother. For herself she hinted at a Contessa's title. Nothing, it was obvious, was too good for Marie Corelli. But until 1885 there had been no Marie Corelli: in her place had existed for thirty years a girl called Minnie Mackay. What then of her?

She was the illegitimate daughter of Charles Mackay, an able but unsteady journalist and writer, who had been editor of the *Illustrated London News* and a colleague of Dickens. When her mother became Mackay's second wife Minnie (or Mary) was six years old. They went to live at Box Hill, where Meredith was a neighbour. For Minnie there followed some years of loneliness, without teaching or discipline, during which she formed her determination to be different—to be "someone". Many hours were spent in the "Dream Hole", a mossy retreat in the garden, where day-dreams fertilized a luxuriant imagination. She decided not only to be different but superior as well. ("I *will* do something!—I *will*!") Knowledge of her illegitimacy came to re-enforce this purpose. She would prove herself wonderful, better than everyone else, and a predisposition to narcissism helped to convince her that she had a good start on the way. When she was twenty-one her mother died, and shortly afterwards a move to Longridge Road, Kensington, made Ellen Terry a neighbour. At this house

Minnie and her father were joined by Bertha Vyver, destined to become the lifelong friend—"better than gold." Here household expenses were a powerful drive to Minnie's ambition. It was becoming financially necessary for her to be "someone". Even more agitating were those dreams of "Society", her longing to drive in a carriage and to be known as a lady. She was growing daily more dissatisfied with Minnie Mackay. She was ashamed of her birth, her mother (who had been of inferior rank), of her ragged education, of her poverty. She was determined to forget them—indeed, they were already forgotten. Dreams as powerful as hers were astonishingly effective. She became another person. She became Signorina Marie Corelli. And in this lady there was no flaw. She excelled in everything in beauty, in birth, in wisdom, in purity, in intellect. Minnie Mackay had been short and plump, Marie Corelli should be stately and tall. Minnie Mackay had been illegitimate and poor, Marie Corelli should be aristocratic and rich. So she dreamed. Draped in white satin, adorned with pure lilies, soon the dream was ready for the public, disguised as Thelma or Mavis Clare, as the heroine of *The Life Everlasting,* or as Marie Corelli herself.

For the next fifteen years her novels satisfied a public ranging from the Queen at Balmoral to the front row of the Gaiety chorus. *The Sorrows of Satan* had a sale greater than that of any previous English novel. *The Master*

Corelli dressed as "Pansy" at a Shakespeare fancy-dress ball.

Christian sold a quarter of a million copies. All her dreams came true. She attacked "Society" for its sins, but no fashionable dinner-party was complete without her. She posed as a recluse and her publicity was enormous. She preached the evils of riches and earned £20,000 yearly. She criticized the Church, and its Deans quoted her appraisingly from the pulpit. The Prince of Wales held her hand in his, and invited her to his coronation. Oscar Wilde printed her stories in the magazine he was editing. "You tell of marvellous things in a marvellous way," he said. She was asked to write the life of Christ, the life of Queen Alexandra. Once, sometimes twice, a year a new novel appeared. *The Mighty Atom, God's Good Man, "Temporal Power"* were bought like a new edition of an evening paper. Her preaching grew more frenzied, her rhapsodizing more luxuriant, her attacking more virulent. With each success she became more righteously indignant at criticism. In declining health she retired to Stratford-on-Avon, meaning to establish herself Shakespeare's co-equal in English literature (so the spiteful people remarked). She interfered in local affairs and the Press resounded with her lawsuits, her angry letters. She floated down the Avon in an Italian gondola. On Mayday she drove through the town behind ponies wreathed in flowers. Her figure was so tightly laced she dare not risk a stoop. She quarrelled with the Governors of the Memorial Theatre, and pilloried them in her next novel. The Press omitted her name from a Royal gathering, then printed her letter of complaint. The townspeople at Stratford were irretrievably estranged by the so-called "Stratford-on-Avon Controversy" in 1903. At last, if not beaten, she was wearied. "County" folk, she declared, were her abhorrence. She was rich. She was famous. She was lonely. She was still dissatisfied. She ignored the Summer Time Act and kept her clocks an hour slow. "God's time," she said, "is good enough for me." She derided matrimony; at fifty, stout and podgy, she had what she believed was a passion for a second-rate painter. "Pendennis," she called him, and he made fun of her accent. To be revenged she wrote *Open Confession,* a book with some moments of true pathos. She continued castigating women of fashion for trying to appear younger than they were, though at sixty her own tresses were still bright gold. But she was not trying to look young; perpetual youth, she believed, was one of the natural results of living on a spiritual plane. About 1910 her sales began to decline. The public had digested all it could take of her particular kind of phantasy. As a personality her antics continued for a time to be of interest. By the end of the Great War she ceased being a best-seller. A new literary druggist had appeared with a novel called *The Way of an Eagle.*

At her death in 1924 the name of Marie Corelli aroused only an echo among the contemporary generation. Her reputation as an eccentric among older people was great enough to constitute front-page news. She died worth £20,000, and directed her home, Mason Croft, to be preserved for ever. Books, furniture, curios, all were to be kept intact. But her dream of immortality was one that did not come true. In 1942 her friend, Bertha Vyver, died almost penniless, and the estate was sold. The pony-cart in which Marie had exhibited herself was bought by a theatrical producer for a London pantomime. The gondola—to everyone's surprise—fetched 57 guineas.

Her unimportance as a writer cannot be doubted. In another twelve years her centenary will be at hand, but it is unlikely that anyone will wish it celebrated. Her books are already unreadable, by then we presume they will be unread. A best-seller, in the novelette sense, once his or her vogue is over, cannot be read seriously, if at all; in the same way as some present-day audiences get only satirical amusement from watching a film made fifteen or twenty years ago. As a novelist Marie Corelli was inferior to Ouida, with whom she has been compared. She had one pure heroine—it was herself she thought she was portraying—her other characters were ridiculous either from extremes of virtue or unmitigated wickedness. Even with her faults unmentioned she cannot be considered a novelist. Her books were an expression of her own day-dreaming, and primarily a compensation to herself for the exaggerated demands she was driven to make upon life. A reviewer—obviously a Corelli "taker"—has suggested the admiration of Queen Victoria and Gladstone as proof of her literary merit. Oscar Wilde and Tennyson were also reported admirers. But Tennyson received a presentation copy of *Ardath,* to which his short note was a reply. Wilde's compliments were ambiguous, and a later judgment was that because of the way she wrote Marie Corelli should have been with him in Reading Jail. No doubt we should see kings and statesmen through a haze of reverence, but are we commanded to believe them never windy or commonplace? The taste of the highly exalted is not unquestionable. Would we not consider it absurd if asked to believe that a great man's weakness for detective yarns proved Edgar Wallace a genius? In the nineties there were worthy people (Mr. Gladstone no doubt among them) nervous of the "clever" new writers who made "sin" so attractive. To them Marie Corelli's missionary zeal and moral uplift were comforting and reassuring.

She must be judged as a supplier of daydreams, to people whose imaginations could not produce phantasies quickly enough, or splendidly enough, for themselves. The reason why she had an enormous public was not because she was "different": it was her longing to be as like everybody else in general (and the British aristocracy in particular) that brought Marie Corelli phenomenal fame. The Victorian Age, great in many directions, was not great in the apprehension of reality. It was an age that liked to consider its own solemnity. Religion was a sort of æsthetic fog, enjoyable if one watched it grow dense from the fireside. Sadness, of the kind evoked by reading *In Memoriam,* was a mournful pleasure. There was small liking for humour, none for criticism. In everything the highest moral tone was successful. Marie Corelli's writings satisfied a large number of people because they satisfied herself. In many ways she was a typical Victorian. Her "beautiful" descriptions, her use of scientific jargon, her incapacity to mention "sex stuff", and her fervent religiousness put all qualms to rest. Like the patent medicines, she could be given without fear to children of all ages. "The Million," as she called them, were able not only to forget the day's drudgery in her tales of spiritualistic trances and Italian Counts; they were left feeling improved. Of humanity in the characters, of humour, or of any connection with reality there was no sign. She wrote with characteristic energy, and a passionate self-belief gave her books their power.

Her popularity declined when the public no longer reacted vigorously to her particular kind of phantasy. She was replaced then by a writer who gave the same kind of satisfaction with a different flavour, and in a more modern scene. To-day "the million" that might have rushed to buy *The Treasure of Heaven* go instead to the luxury cinemas. Or they buy one of the many weekly magazines, and get excitement from reading the *Daily Mirror* and the Sunday newspapers. The man who is saved from suicide now sends his testimonial to the manufactures of tonic pills and pain soothers. It is a smaller public, and a more worldly one, that Marie Corelli's successors have inherited. (pp. 140-47)

George Bullock, "The Corelli Wonder," in Life and Letters To-Day, *London, Vol. 41, No. 82, June, 1944, pp. 140-47.*

D. L. Hobman   (essay date 1947)

[*In the following essay, Hobman examines the ways in which Corelli's eccentric persona dominates her works.*]

Why, at the turn of the century, did Marie Corelli achieve a popularity seldom gained by any novelist before or since? Not only did she make a fortune by her sales, but she drew her readers from all classes of the population, rich and poor, intelligent and otherwise. If Ella Wheeler Wilcox literally knelt at her feet, Meredith also was deeply moved; Tennyson encouraged her; Mr. Gladstone visited her in order to express his admiration and discuss her power to sway the masses; Mr. Asquith demanded an autographed copy of one of her books. She was on friendly terms with Royalty in this and other countries, and was said to be the only writer whom Edward VII invited to be present at his coronation. Strangers wrote to her from all over the world, Indian princes, officers, nurses, miners; in my schooldays we had an appeal from the Mission to Seamen for her novels as the favourite books of sailors at sea. They were translated into most European and some Asiatic languages; at home they supplied texts for Father Vaughan and Mr. Spurgeon, and extracts were read aloud from the pulpit at Westminster Abbey. She was invited to lecture to gatherings such as the Philosophical Society of Edinburgh. She met many famous people, Burne-Jones and Labouchere, who became her friends, Rider Haggard, Mark Twain, Robert Browning ("a charming old gentleman, so cheery and kind"), Oscar Wilde. She was a vain and angry woman, feverishly imaginative, sincere, undisciplined, thwarted in spite of all her success. What was the way of escape which she offered to her contemporaries, and which they were so eager to tread?

Her stories are melodramatic romances, fairytales having little connection with the world. Films, even at their worst, keep some link with reality through a background of street scenes and the like; Marie Corelli's characters move in a realm created by fantasy rather than observation. Her heroines have eyes which flash with mingled tenderness and scorn, and hearts which flutter wildly like snared birds. Their delicate hands, white as rose-petals, sparkle with diamond rings adorning the taper fingers; when they are happy they utter blithe peals of musical laughter like the ripple of a lark's song, and when they grieve their tears are a sparkling dew. A husband refers to an unfaithful wife as a fallen rose of womanhood, but usually they prefer death to dishonour. Fortunately, the hero can always be relied upon to behave with the gallant grace of a soldier and a gentleman, unless he happens to be some unscrupulous baronet, a notable figure in swagger society. In *Boy* an old maid (aged forty-five) thinks "Such sweet and holy thoughts! . . . a mind which was as white and pure as the Taj Mahal." Indeed, one feels that, as with a well-known brand of soap-flakes, one never knew before how white the souls of women could be. Considering the effect which these ladies have upon a man "it is more to his honour than his shame if his senses swoon at the ravishing vision, and he, despite his rough masculinity and brute strength, becomes nothing but the merest slave to passion." When one adds that the pages are richly strewn with exclamation marks, inverted commas and capital letters, the resemblance to the novelette is obvious enough; the difference is more difficult to analyse.

There is, to begin with, an immense preoccupation with religion and morality, and whole chapters are frequently no more than tracts or sermons. The novels are padded with lengthy dissertations on immortality, transmigration of souls, the need for religious education, the nature of the First Cause—emphatically not the Mighty Atom. (But since her day it has been split and so is mightier yet.) The Christ-Child is rejected in Rome, the Devil is a handsome and popular figure in English society; at the end of *The Sorrows of Satan* he disappears, arm-in-arm with a Cabinet Minister, within "the House of England's Imperial Government." Secondly, she dabbled in science, then rapidly unfolding its mysterious potentialities. She was fascinated by electric power, by radio-active vibrations, by all the current scientific jargon, and occasionally, among her most fantastic speculations, she had a queer kind of Wellsian intuition: "The wildest fairy-tales might come true, and earth be transformed into a paradise! And as for motive power, in a thimbleful of concentrated fuel we might take the largest ships across the widest ocean." (*The Life Everlasting.*) Thirdly, she had violent prejudices which must have aroused sympathetic echoes in some readers and amusement in others. Society was a mob of sycophants, liars and hypocrites; Paris, a witches' cauldron: "Her men are dissolute—her women shameless—her youth of both sexes depraved—her laws are corrupt—her arts decadent—her religion dead." Prurient modern novels were denounced:

> To judge from the commendation which is bestowed upon these sort of books by the press, it is very evident that the wave of opinion is setting in the direction of letting girls know all about marriage before they enter upon it, in order that they may do so with their eyes open—*very* wide open!

She detested machines and newspapers; hated actors; above all, she abused reviewers. She carried on a perpetual feud with literary critics, gibing at their ignorance in her novels, pointing out how often genius had been misjudged in the past, and how Dante's enemies were in the end immortalised by him in Hell.

She was easy prey, being incapable of hiding her emotions. It is interesting to note, for instance, that the theme of illegitimacy, of the unwanted child who finally makes good, recurs often:

> There's many a piece of wicked injustice in the world, but nothing more wicked than to set shame or blame on a child that's born without permit of law, or blessing of priest. For it's not the child's fault—it's brought into the world without its own consent—and yet the world fastens a slur upon it!

This is said about Innocent, the heroine of the book of that name. Marie Corelli herself, born in 1855, was the daughter of Charles Mackay, a brilliant if erratic journalist, who married her mother two years after the death of his first wife, in 1861. She was an uneducated woman, and it is supposed that the child spent her first years among her mother's very poor relations; although in later life she allowed romantic legends to be spread about her origin (that her mother was an Italian Countess, and so on), it is clear that her early dreary memories and the unjust stigma of her birth made a deep wound, and that she was unable to hide the scar. Her heroines are frequently women of outstanding genius, who force their male rivals reluctantly to acknowledge their gifts. There is, for instance, Mavis Clare in *The Sorrows of Satan,* a writer like Marie Corelli, and by a curious coincidence with the same initials; as well as being pretty and well-dressed, she had "clearness of thought, brilliancy of style, beauty of diction . . . united to consummate ease of expression and artistic skill . . . The potent, resistless, unpurchaseable quality of genius." One cannot wonder that when her name was uttered, "a sort of hush fell on our party as though an 'Angelus' had rung." After all, why should not women write? "Would you have them all the slaves of man's lust or convenience?" Marie Corelli was always very bitter about the alleged inferiority of her sex, and chose a woman surgeon rather than a man to perform a serious operation upon herself, yet for all that she would have nothing to do with feminism. On one occasion, replying to the toast of the ladies by the American Ambassador, she claimed her right as a woman to tie loveknots between nations although she was no suffragette. She attacked Ibsen for his advanced views on the subject, and idealised the humble and submissive wife. It is here—in this contradiction, this making the best of both worlds—that we may find the answer to the riddle of her immense popularity; this was something which found a deeper echo in the minds of her readers than her religious philosophising, her pseudo-science or her explosive fits of rage. As with feminism, so with all else: she managed to let her readers both have their cake and eat it.

There was, for instance, the matter of the social conscience, uneasily awakening, like the Sleeping Beauty, behind a sheltering hedge of many centuries. Writers were still able to ignore it if they pleased; if they would not, or could not, the alternative seemed to be a fierce Dickensian championship of the poor. Marie Corelli was not even aware of the dilemma, quite content to take now one side, and then the other, according to the mood of the moment.

In *"Temporal Power"* the revolutionary cries out to the king:

> Have you ever seen young children crying for bread? I have! Have you ever seen strong men reduced to the shame of stealing bread, to feed their wives and infants? I have! I think of it as I stand here, surrounded by the luxury which is your daily-lot—knowing what I know, I would strip those satin-draped walls, and sell everything of value around me if I possessed it, rather than know that one woman or child starved within the city's precincts!

She might deplore the poverty of the masses, or assert that all the greatest men came from the toilers, but that did not prevent her from referring to "the unwashed, beer-drinking, gin-swilling classes who clamour for shortened hours of labour, and want work to be expressly invented for their benefit." Inconsistency never troubled her. She, whose friends included Beerbohm Tree, George Robey and especially Ellen Terry, invariably wrote of actors as mountebanks and unprincipled rogues. She could outdo Kipling in patriotic sentiment, yet could be as sensitive as her contemporary Olive Schreiner to a new kind of Pacifist feeling.

> War—especially nowadays—is a mere slaughterhouse—and the soldiers are the poor sheep led to the shambles. The real nature of the thing is covered up under flags and the shout of patriotism, but, as a stern fact, it is a horrible piece of cowardice for one nation to try murdering another just to see which one gets its way first. *(Boy)*

So, too, with religion. She made violent attacks upon its institutions, especially upon Roman Catholicism ("the theatrical jugglery of Rome"), yet upheld a nebulous Christianity all mixed up with semi-theosophical ideas, and only her villains expressed atheism. She once wrote to the vicar of Stratford-on-Avon that she herself belonged to a fraternity which did not accept any of the Church forms. In her novels one was able to wallow in a pool of mystic emotion and, as it were simultaneously, to sprawl on the dry sands of rationalist criticism. This ambivalent attitude towards religious and social questions must have been comforting to a generation uneasily conscious that the deep-rooted prejudices of the nineteenth century were being exposed to the cold winds of the twentieth.

Marie Corelli's aggressiveness led to frequent quarrels in Stratford, where she spent the later part of her life. The townspeople disliked her and were frequently unjust, for, in her own way, with a genuine love for Shakespeare and for the past, she did them some service. She saved from destruction the old cottages which were supposed to have belonged to the poet's grand-daughter, and she secured Harvard House, the home of John Harvard's mother and made it a link between England and America. Her own house, Mason Croft, she left to the nation for the benefit of distinguished visitors to the town. The clause "absolutely excluding actors and actresses and all persons connected with the stage" has been declared void, so that today, under the British Council, it has become the accepted meeting-place between foreign guests and members of the cast of the Memorial Theatre. In her personal relations she was most kind. Her servants loved her; she was a good friend, and a helpful and devoted daughter—adopted daughter, as she called herself—to Charles Mackay. She died in 1924 when her fame had long declined. Her symbolism of doves and flowers—violets, roses, even orchids in florists' windows—had faded years before; yet perhaps it gave more pleasure and did less harm than no orchids for anyone at all.

> *D. L. Hobman, "Books in General," in* The New Statesman & Nation, *Vol. XXXIV, No. 856, August 2, 1947, p. 93.*

Richard L. Kowalczyk   (essay date 1974)

[*In the following essay, Kowalczyk surveys Corelli's works, discussing her romantic vision and its confrontation with the social, aesthetic, and epistemological paradigms of her age.*]

Popular writers reorganize the facts of human experience in order to suspend the reader's critical judgment temporarily, allowing the emotions to sweep him into accepting the possibility of an untainted, perfect world. Popular fiction is an imaginative return to the garden of Eden and no writers were better adept at creating this journey than the early twentieth-century romanticists Hall Caine, Anthony Hope, Arthur Conan Doyle, and Rudyard Kipling. Standing apart from this select group, in terms of sheer popular appeal, was Marie Corelli, a literary phenomenon and darling of the publishing world from 1886 until her star was obliterated by the First World War.

Her three collections of short stories and twenty-five romances do not outnumber the output of Anthony Hope or E. F. Benson, but during the Edwardian period, her works outsold the combined sales of her associates. But her popularity died after the war. On April 21, 1924 the *London Times* appropriately asked in her obituary, "Who Was Marie Corelli?" and thus noted what drastic cultural changes had occurred. The moral voice in her novels relied upon the pieties of both Puritan and Evangelical in America and England. She always rewarded virtue and punished vice, sanctioned higher learning as a preparation for understanding divine providence—extolled the virtuous hero in terms which implied that the divinely elected stood highest on the scale of evolutionary development.

No one questions the judgment literary history places upon Corelli's works; nevertheless one should not overlook the impact of her ideas, her immense popularity, and sudden demise in the public's esteem. Because Marie Corelli sustained an international reputation with a readership whose tastes were rapidly changing, her career allows us to understand popular culture at the turn of the century, its common feelings, moral preferences, and psychological needs.

William Stuart Scott, in *Marie Corelli: The Story of a Friendship,* accurately pinpoints her claim to immortality, one which most contemporary novelists would wish to avoid. He said that the novelist knew her public and gave it precisely what it wanted and deserved. She carved her niche in fiction as a moralist, enhanced it with the myth of the romantic artist of mysterious origins, and excited her audience with hermetic lore and pseudoscientific formulae which became emblems implying that divine providence was no longer patient with a culture dying because of its formalism and hypocrisy. Marie Corelli chose a dangerous arena for success, and part of her claim to remembrance lies in her attempts to persuade a general readership to revivify the Old World values which had survived late Victorian cynicism.

Her fiction was based on one belief, that the artist's powers shaped and sustained the existence of ideals which could not endure in modern life. This theme is central to all of Corelli's works, the key to her biography, and the reason behind her popularity. From the milieu of aestheticism, which she abhorred, Corelli learned that art permits one to cover darker urges with a mask of harmony and beauty. She created a perfect mystique in the face of almost universal condemnation by her reviewers. The nucleus of this mystique was found in material that derives from the non-intellectual, common-sense impulses which Carlyle, Kingsley, and Maurice made fashionable in their reaction to eighteenth-century rationalism. For example, Corelli's first romance, *A Romance of Two Worlds* (1886), preached a gospel of spiritual righteousness in a mysterious, fifth-dimensional world called the Electric Ring. Its dimensions were "perpetually creative and perpetually absorbent," uniting the electric spirits of God and man. As in her later works, Corelli made the best of three worlds, appealing to the sentimental Christian who was attentive to the moral tonics of fiction, the enthusiastic student of science or of psychic forces who attempted to expand the boundaries of the mind, and the sober members of the working class who would benefit from a steady fare of exotically forbidden stories promising material rewards for virtue. *A Romance of Two Worlds* was Corelli's first offering in a series of imaginative adventures into psychic kingdoms bordering on the spiritual world. Its social overtones were distracting but sufficiently muted to prevent radical feelings against established structures in society:

> The power of performing miracles, the gifts of healing and prophesy, and the ability to see beyond the things of this world, are all obtainable, but only through absolute faith in Christ. The smallest hesitation, the least grain of that insolent and foolish pride which dares to deny the existence of the Creator, the faintest shadow of self-seeking or self-love, and the inner spiritual force is instantly paralyzed.

Ardath (1889) continued the line of instinctive piety suggested in *Romance*. It was preceded by *Vendetta* (1886) and *Thelma: A Norwegian Princess* (1887), two melodramatic romances aimed at pleasing the public with the palpable subject of marriage. *Vendetta* depicts a husband's gory scheme of revenge when he overhears his unfaithful wife's love-talk with his best friend. *Thelma* tests the artificialities of English society against the natural inclinations of Corelli's nature child. But *Ardath* found the novelist within her own element once more. The plot centers around Theos Alwyn (God-All-Wise), an agnostic poet, who transports himself through the powerful energy of his

will to a strange, decaying civilization 5000 years B.C. After a confrontation with his other self in this prior state of existence, the poet learns of God's active presence in Nature, denounces immorality, and extols feminine sensibilities. As in her other best selling novels, a mystical form of science strengthens the hero's faith in a creator whose presence is found scientifically in the world. This faith reveals love's energy, much like an electrical force, to be at the center of the universe and the doorway into undiscovered worlds. The Electric Ring (often referred to as the extended personality of God) is an intermingling of male and female attributes. The fictional embodiment of Corelli's ideal scientist, Helobias, is also her spokesman in the early stories. He is a mystic, poet, and scientist, who has discovered scientific sanctions for traditional religious beliefs. A mortal, he becomes godlike, impervious to old age and death, and directly attuned to the "spiritual telegraphy" expressed by Nature in its processes. By implication, Marie Corelli promises more than orthodox theology can, the transformation of mere mortals into the God-head while they do not lose natural feelings for pleasure.

Pseudo-science and mystic theories form the speculative center of *The Soul of Lilith* (1892) in which Corelli suggests the frustration of man's potential union with God. The novel studies the vanity of a scientist unprepared for the task of demonstrating how "the whole majestic Universe swings round in its appointed course . . . in fulfillment of its laws, carrying out the Divine command with faithful exactitude." Helobias warns El-Rami, the novel's protagonist, against damaging nature's balance for selfish purposes. El-Rami's experiments with the dead Lilith frustrate the union existing between the masculine and feminine agencies in creation, Corelli's notion of Love behind all existence:

> There are two governing forces of the Universe . . . one, the masculine, is Love; the other, feminine, is Beauty. These Two, reigning together, are God—just as man and wife are One. From Love and Beauty proceed Law and Order. You cannot away with it—it is so. Love and Beauty produce and reproduce a million forms with more than a million variations, and when God made Man in His Own image it was as Male and Female.

The novel offers Corelli's standard trademark—shocking lines of action with salacious overtones. Her gothic theme concerns how the overbalanced will of a scientist turns against the natural course of Love. The central pattern of action involves the practice of necrophilism. El-Rami conducts experiments on a young girl, Lilith, who has been dead for four years. Lilith passively receives marvelous powers which transport her into unimagined universes and states of existence far beyond man's present stage of evolution. She is ultimately transformed into Nature itself, "In the flowers, in the trees, in the winds, in the sound of the sea, in the silence of the night, in the slow breaking of the dawn" and identified with "the essence of God in the transient shape of an angel." El-Rami fails to discover the meaning of Lilith's experiences. When she momentarily returns to him, his mind becomes seared with the knowledge she brings and he lives out the remainder of his days with the vacant mind of an idiot.

Corelli's scientific novels are attempts to revive older fictional structures and with them traditional attitudes. In practice, Corelli favored the romance genre. She attacked in theory the school of naturalism, an "exclusive set . . . sworn to put down virtue and extol vice." Corelli called such writers the members of the "Ishbosheth cult" of which Zola was the chief spokesman:

> Capable of fine artistic work he prostituted his powers to the lowest grade of thought. From the dust-hole of the frail world's ignorance and crime he selected his olla-podrida of dirty scrapings, potato-peelings, candle-ends, rank fat, and cabbage water, and set all to see them in the fire of his brain, till they emitted noxious poison, and suffocating vapours calculated to choke the channels of every aspiring and idealistic soul.

The naturalists lacked second sight of imaginative scope and failed to produce dramatic surroundings or circumstances which reflected the writer's eye-witness reports on the spiritual world. Modern journalists, her "sons of the inkpot," belonged to the school of naturalism because they greatly contributed to the cynical temper of the times by exploiting both an apathetic readership and the parasites of the Old World. *The Silver Domino* (1892), the novelist's most concentrated attack upon contemporary literature and only piece of satirical wit, indicts both manners of society and the literary taste bred of this "languid, listless indifference to God and man."

Corelli's fiction was based on one belief, that the artist's powers shaped and sustained the existence of ideals which could not endure in modern life. This theme is central to all of her works, the key to her biography, and the reason behind her popularity.

—*Richard L. Kowalczyk*

Marie Corelli's indiscriminate critiques point generally to a type of fiction which "metaphorically kissed the cowboots of Buffalo Bill." According to Corelli, its exemplars failed as artists because they focused on life's pettiness and disappointments. Art supposedly uplifted man by moving him to experience something beyond the ordinary. For this reason, Corelli felt that Hardy's *Tess* contained no art. Hall Caine had a "bow-wow" style which was utterly incapable of change. Kipling's intellect and wit worked like a hydraulic pump; his men characters were coarse bears, and women mere trifles. Bret Harte found a new groove for popularity but filled his audience to satiety with it. Corelli called her own works "one of our newest inflictions" because they treated heaven and hell as though she had seen and enjoyed both experiences. But Corelli's whimsicality appears only in *The Silver Domino,* because it did

not fit public image. Marie Corelli hoped her public would accept the voice in her novels to be the direct result of personal experiences revealing the Truth behind the veil of phenomena. Only William Shakespeare, who joking newsmen said was the only man perfect enough for Corelli to marry, fulfilled the romance writer's notion of high art.

Marie Corelli's theory of romance is a refraction of the Romantic vision. Byron dramatized for her the individual daring of the artist, Keats was admirable for his ability to focus the senses upon one state of revery piled upon another, but Ruskin provided the moral-aesthetic principles for her art. Though not systematized, Corelli's theory of fiction contains a certain boldness for insisting upon Romantic values long after the wave of this movement had reached its crest. In the main, her romantic theory of fiction centers in the belief that the artist's consciousness is unique. His imaginative perception of reality and his sense of love and beauty coerce the writer's poetic instincts for prophecy. The primary obligation of art, as well as the basis by which it is to be judged, questions how successfully the artist stimulates his readers into experiencing his perception of higher truths. The obligation of art was clear.

In a lecture delivered to the Edinburgh Philosophical Society [1901; reprinted as **"The Vanishing Gift,"** in her *Free Opinions Freely Expressed*] the novelist argued for the revival of imaginative works of art. She claimed that the death of the imagination was a symptom of a corrupt agnostic culture. Invitations to lecture before the Philosophical Society were considered a rare honor and this suggests the extensive influence Marie Corelli possessed as a moralist. A time-honored tradition inspired her. Aware that Macaulay, Emerson, Thackeray, Dickens, and Kingsley preceded her, Corelli associated writers of romance (herself by implication) with poets of high seriousness. She borrowed more from John Ruskin than from Arnold in assuming that a revitalization of imaginative art brings about the rebirth of a culture's spiritual energy:

> No king—no statesman, can do for a country what its romancists and poets can—for the sovereignty of the truly inspired and imaginative soul is supreme, and as far above the conquests of Alexander. And when the last touch of idealistic fancy and poetic sentiment has been crushed out of us, and only the dry husks of realism are left to feed swine withal, then may we look for the end of everything that is worth cherishing and fighting for in our much boasted civilization.

The possession of creative skills is a "magic talisman" making life beautiful, intensifying and transfiguring incidents into history and philosophy.

Marie Corelli was a long time popularizer of evolutionary theories and believed that without proper leadership, men tended to return to the stage of a savage. Though his violent qualities were necessary for survival as he evolved from a state of animalism to higher stages of development, man became semi-apathetic to these higher roads of progress and "to the steady unfolding of that endless perspective of order and beauty intended for the individual happiness of every individual soul. . . . " The romance genre engages the reader's willing suspension of disbelief to a high degree. Since this act is a form of release from the Self, the reader's mental and psychological activities, while he is engrossed in a story, instigate higher experiences:

> They cannot realize the unspeakable delight and charm of giving one's self up to one's author, *sans* prejudice, *sans* criticism, *sans* everything that could possibly break or mar the spell, and being carried on the wings of gentle romance away from Self, away from the everyday cares and petty personalities of social convention, and observance, and living 'with' the characters which have been created by the man or woman whose fertile brain and toiling pen have unitedly done their best to give this little respite and holiday to those who will take it and rejoice in it with gratitude.

For Corelli, one escapes through art and returns to reality with a keener perception of its higher truths. The subject matter which most successfully soothes man's savagery is love. Love was the "keynote of Art" and the cohesive force of a healthy culture: "With all its [Love's] folly, sweetness, piteousness and pathos . . . its fool musings take shape in exquisite verse, in tales of romance and adventure, in pictures that bring nations together to stand and marvel, in music that makes strong men weep." While "imaginary love" can be considered an exciting premise for popular writers, Corelli's use of its various themes strongly argue that her publishing successes were attributed primarily to the moral sanction her writing gave to this "most supersensual of all delicate sensations." In the scheme of her art, love provided the basis of Corelli's carefully constructed allegories which highlighted universal moral truths and feelings.

The ingenious allegorical system in her fiction uses as its point of reference contemporary data and scientific theories found in English magazines and journals appealing to the *Daily Illustrated* mentality. Hermetic and scientific images within the stories supported the author's values. Instead of appealing to an ordered body of ideas to make her allegories work successfully, Corelli referred to the vague and amorphous feelings surrounding Christian myths as an area of consensus between author and reader. Basically, Spirit is a radiant force emanating from God's mind, giving birth to the eternal energies of creation. One universe links with another and at its center we find Love directing the process, as electrical charges control electrons. Altogether the universe is composed of an Electric Ring or extensions of God's personality. This Ring is ever expanding and evolving. But instead of evolving without interruption into higher forms, the cycle can be aborted by man's will. The will, itself, is a faculty which receives the atomistic impulses of Love's electricity. However, the natural inclination of the will toward the Good and the Beautiful may be overbalanced by the impulse of evil stemming from one's selfish behavior. Evil also causes man's afflictions, sickness, old age, and death. The central force in creation, then, is love. It guides man's destiny as long as self-love does not negate its influences. Man is governed by psychic impressions from pre-existent states and

these indelible qualities influence the will in its moral decisions. Corelli compares these psychic impressions to the superior characteristics of an organism which evolves into a higher stage of life. In the case of man's development, growth is circuitous until he becomes one with the will of nature's Creative Force and is identified with it. At this stage, the spirit of man may move freely through the barriers of time and space in numerous forms of existence.

To use Corelli's imagery, the power of God is a masculine agency, ever active and yet incomplete. Mankind, the "female" element in creation, can potentially develop an infinite number of psychic and spiritual identities and so may be considered an essence, either complementary or essential, to God's eternal nature. Man's receptivity to this eternal power or "grace" depends entirely upon the total identity of his will with God's, as for example a musical chord must harmonize with an entire symphonic arrangement. Most importantly, this relationship between God and man is never more clearly possible than in dream-like revery or highly emotional states. Art is a culture's way of producing this intense state of feeling.

While art for Corelli produces this intense feeling, at the same time it could morally instruct. Her fiction, when judged as social criticism, emphasizes a panorama of ethical misfits, creatures who failed in Corelli's system, because they represented conventional values of society. Just as Corelli opposed naturalism in her statements on art, she reinterpreted the theory of evolution for her popular readers and adopted its language to condemn the behavior of men whom the Electric Ring of Nature (God's personality) would destroy because of their inferiority. Few areas of social behavior and manners escaped her pious vengeance.

Wormwood (1890) anticipated by fifteen years the European controversy to abolish the Swiss production of absinthe. The main protagonist, Gaston Beauvais, narrates the tragedy of his own addiction and the decline of his character until he cannot accept life except on its primary level:

> Oh, if there is one thing I rate at in the Universe more than another, it is the uncertainty of Creation's meaning. Nature is a great mathematician, so the scientists declare—then why is the chief number in the calculation always missing? Why is it that no matter how we count and weigh and plan, we can never make up the sum total? There is surely a fault somewhere in the design—and perchance the great unseen, silent, indifferent Force we call God, has, in a dull moment, propounded a vast Problem, to, which He Himself may have forgotten the Answer!

The burden of the plot shows that the design is indeed perfect, but man has distorted its meaning. Thus, Beauvais' philosophy is erroneous and he finally confesses that absinthe had "killed the last vestige of my flickering conscience in me with a final blow—and I became—*what I am!*" As a moral outcast, the *absintheur* descends the scale of creation to a lower form of evolution: "I am a slinking, shuffling beast, half-monkey, half-man, whose aspect is vile. . . ."

Wormwood drew the attention of prohibition groups and it was in response to their requests that Marie Corelli wrote *Holy Orders* (1908). The romance's subtitle, **"The Tragedy of a Quiet Life,"** suggests the "extent of the evil wrought on these rural populations by the tyranny of the Drink-Traffic." The author attempts to draw open sympathy with the arduous task of "some of the best and most hard-working clergy," demonstrated in this case by the Rev. Richard Everton who struggles to improve working conditions and move the common workers of Shadbrook to daily Christian behavior. The town's economy is controlled by a local distiller whose angry orders are misinterpreted by an intoxicated guard. The result is the murder of Everton's wife. Deprived of this underlying strength to his ministry, Everton eventually learns to experience a new kind of love in Christian dedication to his duties. The process of Everton's re-entry into the life of simple piety continues after evil has been dealt with. The distillery is destroyed by fire and its monstrous owner with it. The heroic minister continues his crusade, but he rejects honors and titles in his own church, believing that it is infected by "the high-criticism of pigmy scholars." Like Corelli's other social novels, *Holy Orders* fails to question the novelist's own implied overview. The narrator continually interrupts the action; his comments are often repeated in the Everton speeches. This one-to-one reference from narrator to hero, and back again to author, makes for grim dogmatizing. The overview is a calcified version of earlier themes, demonstrating the lack of moral cohesion in the culture. Everton's rapid ascent on the imaginary scale of spiritual evolution implicitly highlights his antagonists' descent to primitive stages of savagery.

In contrast to the simple goodness of an Everton, and remarkable in their own right for Corelli's ability to give spatial density to abstract evil, stand Lucifer and Josiah McNason. Lucifer appears first in the guise of Lucio Rimanez, a being who consciously seeks to be defeated by man's goodness. God has decreed that in this way he may learn the meaning of salvation. Lucio's will to be destroyed is paralleled by Lady Sibyl Elton's desire for damnation. Lucifer's hope of being conquered is frustrated by Lady Elton who represents the indifference, selfishness, and viciousness of modern society. In *The Devil's Motor,* Lucifer comes to claim the twentieth-century as his own, when "The forests dripped like broken reeds, the mountains crumbled into pits and quarries, the seas and rivers, the lakes and waterfalls dried up into black and muddy waters, and all the land was bereft of beauty." Lucifer's judgment of modern man, "All Creation shall rejoice to be cleansed from the pollution of your presence," fittingly condemns men, like Josiah McNason, who participate in a money morality which infects their will with a "cancer of selfishness."

Corelli's social criticism is strongest when she submerges her rigid base of judgment to permit the reader a glimpse into the struggle of a burdened humanity utterly deprived of the promises it feels life owes to it. This more sophisticated vantage point appears frequently in her short stories and in romances which were published after the war, when, perhaps, she was retreating more deeply into her own fictional world to escape values formed under a differ-

ent manner of perception. At her best as a reformer of English culture, Corelli used characters who were doomed to the bitterest phases of human experience. Because they could not feel the touch of divine love in their own lives, their diplomatic gestures to society, their brittle philosophical insights and conventional platitudes indict a culture which incorporated these values. Humor and half-serious ambivalence had no place in the characterization of Corelli's moral outcasts, because the novelist was in earnest when she wished her readers to accept them as "the biggest Fraud nature and art ever perpetuated." Society suffers because the religious attitudes and scientific concerns of figures, like Claude Ferrers in *Holy Orders* and Diana May in *The Young Diana,* or the fervent artistic visions of young Jocelyn in *Innocent: Her Fancy and His Fact,* mask a degeneracy which Corelli believed threatened English and American culture.

The composition of Corelli's allegories depends upon a tableau of actions involving two types. On the positive side, we find heroes and heroines who mirror the author's notion of the Divine Will. They have, in brief, mastered the complex issues of life. Cast into various degrees of villainy are those characters whose source of action is "contradiction, negation, or defiance." If life was, as Corelli claimed, "a bogle tale," its tragedies were not necessary. Heroes, like Barrabas, Cardinal Bonpré in *The Master Christian,* Morgana Royal in *The Secret Power,* or Mary Deane in *The Treasure of Heaven,* possessed inner serenity, because their independent minds and strong wills pursued the vast knowledge which Corelli intimated existed in the universe. The cosmos was composed of dimensions of reality which went far beyond the illusions of time and space. In gaining this knowledge, the heroes discovered an unending peace. Their search for Love in the cosmos promised perpetual development along higher stages of existences. They were heroic in so far as they were receptive to the personality of God surrounding them in the objects of nature. Coincidentally, the Corelli hero and heroine were rich and successful enough not to be affected by materialistic goals. As the novelist's spokesmen, these figures confronted the realities of the Spiritual World in face of society's effete snobbery, foolish dissensions, and universal pettiness. The Corelli hero survived all tests of established convention because he could match his inferiors' dissipation with astonishing insights into life's problems. He had experience totally under control, but his behavior disrupted established norms of conduct. Like the operation of higher organisms in evolution, the hero's actions necessarily destroyed corrupt social values in order to prepare the way for something higher and nobler. The outcome of the conflict between hero and society was readily predictable and when the fiber of Corelli's plots stretched too much, she resorted to an emphasis on character portrayals which borrowed from evolutionary theories. In her character depiction, Marie Corelli contrasted her hero with a large fictional population of moral misfits. She thus implied the range of potential development in man by giving the reader illustrations from her stratified scale of moral conduct, from its lowest forms to the highest ideals found in the hero. The misfit was to Corelli an unnatural creature who could never survive in her psychic, suprasensual world. Since Corelli's first intention was to move her

Mason Croft, Corelli's home at Stratford-on-Avon.

readers' attitudes in line with her own rigid overview, her fictional misfits showed, in a negative way, dramatic evidence of men who failed the ideals of Christianity. The romanticist could reaffirm her own values by creating an imaginative world where one viewed an evolutionary system of ethics in which were placed Christian hybrids as well as nature's immoral freaks. A survey of a few romances, which Corelli considered central to her role as social and theological reformer, demonstrates how the mixture of Christian tradition and nineteenth-century evolutionary theories appealed to the popular mind.

God's Good Man (1904) attacks the upper classes for hypocrisy, "the lowest type of modern decadence," by placing in opposition to it, the simple values of a country parson. John Walden dedicates his life to serving ignorant farmers who reside in the community of St. Rest. He turns this parish into a community where the ideals of Christianity organically develop from the villagers' simple and harmonious lives. The philosophical commentary of Corelli's narrator argues, as he frequently interrupts the flow of action, that St. Rest is a microcosm of modern society about to be invaded by the alien forces of materialism. John Walden is successful because his world-view has been inspired by the past. He spends his fortune in restoring his fifteenth-century church, improving its gardens, and redistributing his land to the country folk. Walden's special world allows him "To use the innermost eyes of his soul in . . . looking backward down the stream of Time, as well as in looking forward to that 'crystal sea' of the un-

known future." Walden finds it possible to move across time and space because he is a member of a highly selected group, a man whose potential growth ultimately leads him to a state which approximates total will for the Good. Yet, Walden's vision is incomplete. He and his parishioners must face the invasion of London's upper classes as well as the threat of a greedy tourism which had already infected a neighboring city. Walden finds an ally in Maryllia Vancourt, who has forsaken international society to return to her childhood home. Their mutual attraction and admiration develop into intense love after Maryllia barely escapes death and the couple become aware of a higher existence. In this case, the thinking of the clergyman and of his decorous, agnostic lover has moved their consciousness to a point where sectarian divisions disappear, because the lovers experience the Love behind the cosmos. At the end, Walden's act of faith, "I accept Him as the true manifestation of the possible Divine in Man," and Maryllia's desire for love, "only found in poems and story books," provide a marriage of spirits actuating the felt presence of God. Like Richard Everton in *Holy Orders* (1908), they were "cramped by conventions" and sought higher responsibilities which benefited the common good of society.

The hero's responsibility to a larger unit in society raises the question of how one can find a vigorous spiritual climate when the structures of modern society encourage artificiality and corruption. Corelli never probes deeply enough to suggest a resolution, but *The Treasure of Heav-*

en: A Romance of Riches (1906) optimistically illustrates how the Corelli hero and heroine survive the dilemma. This novel focuses upon David Hemsley's "first process of . . . evolution . . . the awakening of conscience, and the struggle to rise from his mere Self to a higher ideal in life—from material needs to intellectual development." Hemsley, a divorced millionaire, discovers on the remote highlands of Scotland an innocent way of life taught by Mary Dean, a child of instinct. Hemsley decides to rid himself of all his wealth, the cause of his former distress and spiritual distemper. Though he mistakenly believes that someone else might be able to use the money well, Hemsley's decision is the first important step in the growth of his character. Hemsley's development is analogous to stages of evolutionary progress. He feels, while in London controlling his business empire, like an inhuman mechanism. While fleeing from society, he lives with the wild elements of nature among the animals. His last act of self-denial prepares him for a final ascent into heaven after death. However, Hemsley's denial of self, ironically tests the love which his new friend, Mary Dean, has for Angus Reay, a poet. She inherits the Hemsley fortune and with it a taint that threatens her coming marriage. Reay cannot accept an inferior role, since, besides his male vanity, such a relationship would stifle the poet's creative powers. Fortunately, Mary never has to make the choice between fortune and love, because the poet returns to his beloved in time to prevent her suicide. Nothing is, nor need be, said about Hemsley's millions or the artist's creativity, because the lovers have found a greater treasure.

The atrocities of the First World War did not abate Corelli's intense idealism, though she no longer would insist upon the possibility of returning her public to the Old World. This significant shift in attitude gave her romances a tone of cynicism. In technique, Corelli altered her practice of polarizing conventional systems against the values of her heroes. *The Young Diana* (1918) and *The Secret Power* (1921) indicate that these less clear distinctions between hero and moral outcast implied the impossibility of reviving Old World virtues. These last novels show an abandonment of her former ideas and a deeper retreat into art.

In *The Young Diana,* Corelli's most pessimistic statement of art, the heroine is "an awkward numeral in a sum," not knowing "why she came in and how she was to be got out" of existence. Diana May forsakes her well-to-do life in England and searches with a Doctor Dimitri for the way to master the secrets governing chemical atoms in man. This discovery promises eternal life and, unlike Tithonus, great beauty and youth. However, Diana May's willingness to be Dimitri's subject is traced back to her hatred of life. Dimitri's experiments shame and humiliate his protegé. She feels as dehumanized as when she faked suicide to escape the boredom and neglect of her parents. Diana receives the gift of beauty and eternal life, but Corelli clearly signifies that her protagonist has not benefited from hermetic science. Diana is a being warped by both convention and psychic studies alike. The novelist describes her as an "ice queen," a goddess of the moon hunting her prey. The story also adapts Corelli's principle of psychic impressions from the past influencing the will of the protagonist, but

here Diana is the reincarnation of Queen Rajuna, who disapproves of her lover, slowly hacks him to pieces, and keeps him alive as long as possible in her terrifying presence. Diana's rebirth is a triumph of psychic science, but she is not the familiar Corelli heroine who embodies the glories of womanhood. Diana May returns to England and uses that beauty, which transformed her into a "maiden goddess moulded from a dream," to humiliate and destroy all persons who violated her individuality. The first victim is her former fiance, but Diana's sexual triumph over him is only a prelude to more horrible vengeance. She sets out next to destroy her father, Captain Cleve, by arousing his passions so that he may each day be more aware of his age and approaching death. As the impersonal object of psychic investigation, Diana will live forever to be an instrument of vengeance upon modern man. In the early works of Marie Corelli, beauty was identified with God's feminine attributes and it complemented the virtue of wisdom, thus affording man the means of raising himself in Corelli's scale of spiritual evolution. Here, knowledge and beauty are instruments of terror. They are inflicted upon a society which fully deserves punishment. Corelli's apocalyptic vision recedes without a saving view of order:

> She [Diana] lives as the light lives—fair and emotionless—as all may live who master the secret of living, a secret which . . . shall yield itself to those, who before very long, will grasp the Flaming Sword and 'take and eat of the fruit of the Tree of Life.' The Sword turns every way—but the blossom is behind the blade. And in this Great Effort neither the love of man nor the love of woman have any part, nor any propagation of an imperfect race, for those who would reach the goal must relinquish all save the realization of that 'new heaven and new earth,' of splendid and lasting youth and vitality when 'old things are passed away.'

Interestingly enough, when Corelli's fictional methods changed, her simplistic opposition of crass materialism to a noble, romantic idealism became more ambiguous and her writing came closer to acceptable art. *The Secret Power* dramatically uses the broad background of American and English life as an atmosphere to render practical science and hermetic lore in their most dangerous aspects. Roger Seaton conducts experiments with radium in the desert of California to discover the source of all power. He feels that by harnessing this source he will be able to dictate peaceful policies to the major nations of the world. Seaton's noble plan is motivated by a deep cynicism. In pursuing the "Great Secret" he totally isolates himself from any feelings of community. His plan to end all wars forever almost destroys the world. Also implicit in the novel's design is Corelli's attack upon politicians who had vowed that World War I was a necessary risk in order to end war forever. At the same time Seaton revels in his bitter, self-imposed exile, Morgana Royal, "a fey, magic person," conducts experiments on a flying machine (whose energy source is more mystical than mechanical) and searches for a legendary place called the "Golden City." This mystic abode is inhabited by psychic spirits which have reached the highest stage of evolution. Morgana receives telepathic messages from these beings, inviting her to enter into this form of existence. However, she is warned that no one may ever return to twentieth-century society after entering the city's gates. After rescuing Seaton from an earthquake which his experiments caused, Morgana journeys to the fabled city and passes through its walls. Morgana's journey symbolically represents the perspective of hermeticism and its power to convey one to a higher state of consciousness, one that surpasses the "dreams of philosophy and science." The promising conclusion of the novel is questionable. Morgana dwells with "the secret Maker of the New Race . . . the Gods of the Future" but can never return to the modern world. For his part, Seaton endures a vegetable existence, one in which he vacantly cries with no comprehension, "There shall be no more wars. There can be none! I say it! It is my Great Secret! I am master of the world." Both characters possess the secret to society's ills but are powerless. Morgana leaves her own friendly group of followers with a sense of failure and may indicate Corelli's own awareness of her failure to alter the direction of her reader's values. Morgana, like the artist, departs alone, conscious of the fact that her union with and love for Seaton will be unfulfilled.

Just as *The Young Diana* indicts psychic investigations and finds them as misleading as conventional beliefs, *The Secret Power* reveals Corelli's final retreat into the magical garden of her writing, a necessarily lonely exile because modern life cruelly contradicted her system with more valid scientific facts. By this time in Corelli's career, she was a forgotten artist, living among the curios and prizes given to her by an appreciative public, and perhaps an embarrassment to a nation which once placed her name next to Shakespeare and Dickens. Her early works, which were personal efforts to halt the direction of English attitudes at the turn of the century, would find their way from the clergyman's pulpit and the parlors of the elite to used bookstore shelves containing naughty literature. If Corelli's works were simplistic, their charm is contained in an intense idealism, because the light in her universe was centered in the efficacy of divine love. As the possibility of re-establishing the firm values of an older order waned, the heat of her romanticism dissipated and its light extinguished. (pp. 850-62)

Richard L. Kowalczyk, "In Vanished Summertime: Marie Corelli and Popular Culture," in Journal of Popular Culture, *Vol. VII, No. 4, Spring, 1974, pp. 850-63.*

Brian Masters (essay date 1978)

[*Masters is an English biographer and critic whose works include numerous studies of notable British personalities, especially members of society and the aristocracy. In the following excerpt, he describes Corelli as a moralist, whose writings propound a romanticized and popularly compelling view of religion and science.*]

If 50,000 people buy a novel whose shortcomings render it tenth-rate, we may be sure that they have not conspired to do so, and also that their strange unanimity is not due to chance. There must be another explanation of the phenomenon.

Arnold Bennett

Never disregard a book because the author of it is a foolish fellow.

Lord Melbourne

The unprecedented success of Marie Corelli is more than a comment on popular taste in the late Victorian period. It was thought by some to be an indictment against universal education which had been rightly lauded as a boon but which had [according to G. M. Trevelyan in his *Illustrated History of England*] 'produced a vast population able to read but unable to distinguish what is worth reading, an easy prey to sensations and cheap appeals'. Whereas before about 1870 the educated reader had set the standards by which literature was to be judged, he was now swamped by the tide of suburban intelligence whose demands were pitched much lower. England was entering upon the age when the majority would decide what was best and its decisions would be unassailable. Marie was one of the products of this evolution, and her critics were the rearguard force of a less 'educated' but more literate age. The battles they fought were destined to be stalemated, because they were as foreign to each other as, in our day, Barbara Cartland would be to Lord David Cecil.

Marie held her audience spellbound, hypnotised, because she shared their prejudices, and could be relied upon to be second-rate even at her best. The older generation held her in awe as some sort of inspired goddess and would have considered it a privilege to touch the hem of her frock. While one may deplore such a trite appeal from the point of view of literature, one cannot afford to disregard it as the barometer of popular culture; one B.B.C. critic in a programme devoted to discussing Marie's significance was bold enough to point out that 'she said and did things we would all like to say and do, for we are all of us Marie Corellis under the skin'. If this be so, then it is beholden on us to find out why, and not simply to sweep her books aside as George Sampson [in *The Cambridge History of English Literature*] did with the comment that they were 'the pretentious treatment of lofty themes by the illiterate for the illiterate'. Rebecca West was more tolerant, and more perceptive, when she wrote in an article for the *New Statesman* called 'The Tosh Horse' (reprinted in her *Strange Necessity*, 1928),

Marie Corelli had a mind like any milliner's apprentice; but she was something much more than a milliner's apprentice . . . her incurably commonplace mind was incapable of accurately surveying life, but some wild lust for beauty in her made her take a wild inventory of the world's contents and try to do what it could with them . . . she rode the Tosh-horse at full gallop.

Her simplistic view of the world, of God and of love, of motive and accident, her vitality, her sentiment, all this made her the perfect romantic novelist. No matter how often she tried to make her books differ, following a melodrama by a romance by a spiritual prophecy by a moral allegory by another melodrama and so on, her books were all peopled with the same dummies, there was always the confrontation of a hero (or more likely a heroine) by a moral outcast, and the *dénouement* was almost always the trouncing of the latter by the former. Thus she had the supreme value of predictability, demanding no great effort of thought from her readers, and certainly not the enervating task of summoning up a fresh response to a new situation. The kind of person who will not listen to Wagner because he or she has never listened to Wagner, and can only feel happy in the recognition of what is familiar, he and millions like him constituted Marie's public, unable to distinguish between literature and trash and unwilling to try. All that they asked of her was that she should stabilise attitudes they already cherished, by provoking stock mechanical responses which obviated the need for genuine thought or feeling. Marie obliged, thinking to do the opposite. She was the mistress of cliché.

Marie did not achieve all this in cold blood. She was no cynic in this respect, believing quite firmly that she was engaged on the creation of literature. She was able to sustain this illusion by the almost impenetrable armour of self-defence which . . . [she built] during her life, and by her fundamental immaturity of emotion. She saw the adult world through a child's eyes, and had a child's reaction to the imperfection she perceived. She retreated into a facile optimism which maintained that Life could be beautiful if only we would reject the evil (represented by the grown-ups), and embrace the good (represented by Marie and the various childlike personifications of her in her books). Claire Ritchie, in *Writing the Romantic Novel* (1962), offered a blueprint which bears a close resemblance to the substance of Marie Corelli's art:

> You must yourself believe that good ultimately triumphs over evil, that happiness comes when we try to make others happy, and that Love, or 'sweet charity' as someone has described it, is the greatest power in the world—stronger than trouble, disaster, separation and death.

To this Marie added the element of Hope, the promise that the mysteries of God's world would be dispelled at the appropriate time; she appealed to discontented souls and gave them a powerful injection of self-confidence by her example and by her robust style. R. A. Gregory wrote to her in 1918,

> You would not expect me to subscribe literally to all the views embodied in your romance, but I can with a whole heart say that I appreciate the uplifting character and intention of the book. It is good to be carried even in imagination into realms above earth-level; and your book suggests to people that they may reach out and touch the stars if they wish.

It is precisely because there was identity of mental development and ethical preoccupations between author and reader that Marie was able to speak with unparalleled directness to her public and to enjoy a power which none other has ever been able to equal. She seemed to know this strength within her even before she knew success; it impelled her forward with the faith of a fanatic. In 1890 she had written of this feeling to George Bentley:

> My dear friend, the public heart is so full of multitudinous aches and pains that I ache and burn

with it, and out of that close and intense sympathy, I write. It was this, I believe, that made the success of the **Romance** and **Ardath**, because I know instinctively how in this period of rush and infinite weariness and cynicism, the multitude crave for something higher and more lasting, and ask to have their feelings set into words.

Seventeen years later, after much punishment at the hands of the literary establishment, she wrote to Peter Keary, editor of the *Rapid Review:*

> I can feel the pulse of the people ringing and beating through me as if I were a mere glass bell for it to sound against. . . . Do not be weary of trying to instruct the people. It often seems hard. Ruskin broke his heart over it.

Her approach was anti-intellectual. To those who sneered, she replied that she wrote from the heart, not, like a dry professor, from the brain alone, and it was thus she was able to enter into a communion with her admirers and carry out her good work. 'I have always tried to write straight from my own heart to the hearts of others, regardless of opinions and indifferent to results,' she said, and paid due tribute to the influence of Carlyle upon her attitude. 'I owe much to his brave teaching,' she told Annie Davis. The *Pall Mall Gazette* commented, 'Education, knowledge of life, knowledge of English, these are nothing. What is wanted for a "literary" success is a heart; nothing pays like it. *Magna est impudentia et proevalebit.*'

Like other romantic writers who scoff at the 'novel of the brain', Marie had the power to arouse enthusiasm in people whose lives were devoid of any colour, to 'excite in the ordinary person an emotional activity for which there is no scope in his life.' According to Q. D. Leavis [in her *Fiction and the Reading Public,* 1968], the instrument of this appeal was a standard emotional vocabulary which provokes warm surges of feeling associated with religion and religious substitutes, and she gives as examples words like life, death, love, good, evil, sin, noble, gallant, purity, honour, words which induce involuntary responses even from the self-aware, who have learned to guard against them. Marie's audience revelled in these feelings. Mrs. Leavis goes on to say,

> This vocabulary as used by bestsellers is not quite the everyday one; it is analogous to a suit of Sunday clothes, carrying with it a sense of larger issues; it gives the reader a feeling of being helped, of being in touch with ideals.

Conscious of what she considered to be her responsibility to instruct, Marie Corelli used her dangerous power to mingle vague poetic sensibility with lofty philosophising and sturdy religiosity in an attempt to mould public opinion against the incursions of Darwinism and scientific scepticism. Undoubtedly she saw her rôle as that of an evangelist, whose function was to comfort a population assailed by the insidious attractions of rationalism. Hence her sermonising, and her books being used as sermons by responsible prelates. The fact that she was pilloried for her teaching merely added to her prestige. With great intuitive wisdom she knew that her message would carry more weight if she herself bore misfortune bravely, if she could conform to the ancient archetype which required the healer at the same time to be a man of suffering, a wounded creature. Hence her frequent allusion to being a voice in the wilderness, to whom little heed would be paid. Her martyrdom added a sacred dimension to her mission.

The reading of fiction, i.e. 'light' reading, had been regarded earlier in the nineteenth century as a form of dissipation, discouraging independent thought and producing atrophy of the intellect. Coleridge had condemned it as 'such an utter loss to the reader, that it is not so much to be called pass-time as kill-time'. When Marie Corelli rose to her exalted position, this was no longer the case. The popularity of the circulating libraries and the demise of the 'three-decker' in favour of a single-volume novel (bringing romantic fiction within the financial grasp of a vast public), had swept all opposition before them and made redundant the warnings of intellectuals. The *Westminster Review* and the *Daily Mail* articles on Marie attempted to show how harmful was an addiction to her work, but to no avail. The public wanted to read what she wrote, and the public was fast becoming, for the first time in literary history, the supreme arbiter.

To this day, those who remember Marie claim that her books were read only in the servants' hall, and were forbidden 'above stairs'. This is simply not true. The middle classes were just as addicted, though for different reasons. They longed to ape the manners of the aristocracy, whose activities they followed avidly in the weekly magazines, and mistakenly supposed that, because Corelli books were packed with aristocratic ladies, the author's knowledge was authentic. Even society ladies enjoyed being flogged in print at the hands of Miss Corelli. It has been said that society loved to hear its vices abused, whether in church or in fiction, and that such abuse was the precursor of the moral stripping now undertaken by psychoanalysts.

Marie's technique consisted of a relentless vitality and virile imagination in the service of higher aims.

Imagination was paramount among her literary equipment. She was infuriated by the charge that she could not know what she was writing about because she lacked experience. 'It is not necessary for the poet to personally experience the emotions whereof he writes,' she said (*Ardath*). Her address in Edinburgh on 19 November, 1901, was on the subject of imagination, which she called **'The Vanishing Gift'**. 'Most of the great imaginative works of the world are beyond experience,' she said. 'To the poet and romanticist "Imagination" is Experience. It is the Eye of the Soul, which sees all Earth and all Heaven.'

Photograph of Corelli, taken about 1906.   *Authorized (retouched) version of photo at left.*

Not only did she claim for the imaginative faculty the powers of perception normally reserved for understanding, which is at least an arguable point of view, but she maintained that it made geographical knowledge and scientific training equally unnecessary. When writing about places she had never visited, she said, 'I *imagine* it must be so, and I find it generally *is* so', and if this was not disarming enough, she explained further,

> for accuracy of detail, we can consult a guidebook—but for a complete picture which shall impress us all our lives long, we must go to the inspired author whose prescience or second-sight of brain enables him to be something more than a mere Baedeker (**'The Power of the Pen'**, in *The Writer*, August, 1901).

George Bernard Shaw said that she 'represented the victory of a powerful imagination over an inadequate array of facts.'

Marie entirely missed the point of what it was the realists and naturalists, whom she detested, were trying to do. They only paint the appearance, she said, and miss the *inner* reality of a man's soul; she could not understand that they were not interested in souls and would happily leave her to devote her attention to them while they concerned themselves with actual living. When she could not convince, she lost her temper and resorted to abuse . . . heaping vilification upon Zola whom she thought must be the devil incarnate. She never realised that being an idealist was not of itself a virtue, but a description.

To the realists' contention that morality had no place in an artistic production, Marie responded with scorn. It was 'one of the most unintelligent and fallacious theories ever propounded,' she said. 'The head and front of English literature, Shakespeare, never wrote a play without a moral' (**'The Comfort of Criticism'**, in *Rapid Review*, September 1906). The realists, as opposed to the idealists, were guilty, in her view, of degrading and debasing human thought, and, what is more, of using vulgar language with which to do so. It comes as some surprise to find her castigating other writers for 'careless and ignorant brutality of style which makes havoc with the finest capabilities of language' (**'A Little Talk about Literature'**).

As early as 1893, she was telling Mr. Bentley that her purpose was to idealise a given subject like a sculptor or a painter, by means of words, to something higher than a story of mere lovemaking, murder, and money-trouble. Yet that is precisely the level at which she remained.

Marie maintained that Zola and his disciples subordinated their concern for the truth of character to their determination to carry their socialist message to conviction, not noticing that she offended in the same way in the service of the contrary propaganda. 'Look at the curious phases of people's *minds,*' she wrote, 'their humours, their fantastic whims, their oddities, their ambitions.' This was advice that she herself never accepted. Her own work was just as 'committed', and therefore interfered with the development of character to the same degree; her people are mere ciphers, subservient to her purpose. They exist to express her views, and are manipulated by her to this end. Virginia

Woolf's strictures on the art of Marie's friend George Meredith would apply equally well to Marie herself. There is nothing that characters in fiction resent more, says Mrs. Woolf, than being puppets of their creator's will. 'If, they seem to argue, we have been called into existence merely to express Mr. Meredith's views upon the universe, we would rather not exist at all.' More recently, Jean-Paul Sartre has attacked François Mauriac for a similar failing. Characters must be allowed to fulfil their own destiny, says Sartre, independently of whatever ideas their creator may have as to how they *should* fulfil it. Marie Corelli never once released her grip on her characters; she was as possessive towards them as she was towards everything else which threatened to escape her. Consequently, the characters have no life at all.

Propaganda was Marie Corelli's principal aim in writing. She had been chosen as a little girl to carry a message, and nothing would deflect her from this purpose. When asked to define literature, the heroine of ***The Murder of Delicia*** replies:

> The power to make men and women think, hope and achieve; the power to draw tears from the eyes, smiles from the lips of thousands; the power to make tyrants tremble, and unseat false judges in authority; the power to strip hypocrisy of its seeming fair disguise, and to brand liars with their name writ large for all the world to see.

Marie might have achieved some lasting monument in this direction had she not fatally lacked the ingredient of humour. She could not look upon the world and smile. She had to attack, abuse, denounce, excoriate. She could not see that mankind was irredeemably imperfect. She could not settle for some small improvement. Thus she was destined always to be disappointed, and eventually forgotten. 'The man who threatens the world is always ridiculous', said Dr. Johnson, 'for the world can easily go on without him, and in a short time will cease to miss him.'

. . . . .

Marie's evangelism was opportune. Darwinism had raised some awkward questions and had postulated an altered perspective on man's place in the universe. The evolutionary idea blurred any distinction of value between men and apes and created several real problems for believers to grapple with. When did men get souls? Did prehistoric man go to Heaven? The time was ripe for an unhesitating reaffirmation of theological doctrines, such as were provided in America by Moody and Sankey, and in England by Marie Corelli.

She was predisposed by nature to be a successful preacher. The three necessary presumptions of a God-orientated person were accepted by her with never the shadow of a question—that there was a purpose to the universe, that Man was a unique creation in that universe, and that moral standards were absolute. To these attitudes the new scepticism opposed some rational views. In the first place, it said, 'purpose' is a concept which is scientifically useless, and therefore not worth arguing about; the universe had no truck with such abstractions. Secondly, it was difficult to maintain a view that Man was unique and uniquely important when you took into account that he was the newest and youngest among thousands of species on a planet which was one of millions revolving around a sun which itself was a part of a huge galaxy; further, that that galaxy containing countless billions of other planets and stars was only one of millions of such galaxies, all as big and as crammed as the one of which we form such an infinitesimal part. Thirdly, the post-Darwin sceptics promulgated a return to pragmatism in moral matters. There was no longer any absolute authority. As Bertrand Russell [in his *Impact of Science on Society*] has written, 'Pragmatism appeals to the temper of mind . . . which desires religion, as it desires railways and electric light, as a comfort and a help in the affairs of this world, not as providing non-human objects to satisfy the hunger for perfection.' This was a temper of mind totally foreign to Marie.

From the very beginning, Marie had tackled the enemy with headlong audacity, confidently stating her case in the introduction and prologue to her first book, *The Romance of Two Worlds*:

> In spite of the doctrines of agnostics and materialists, there is a perpetual, passionate craving in the souls of many for that inward peace and absolute content which can only be obtained by a perfect faith in God and the coming Life Eternal.

She showed that she understood the arguments of her opponents, but she simply rejected them out of hand because they did not confirm her illusions. Assertion took the place of argument:

> There are no proofs as to why such things should be; but that they are, is indubitable. The miracles enacted now are silent ones, and are worked in the heart and mind of man alone. Unbelief is nearly supreme in the world today. Were an angel to descend from Heaven in the middle of a great square, the crowd would think he had got himself up on pulleys and wires, and would try to discover his apparatus.

Human reason, Marie said, is inadequate to the task of understanding the cosmos. 'Mistrust that volatile thing called Human Reason, which is merely a name for whatever opinion we happen to adopt for the time—it is a thing which totters on its throne in a fit of rage or despair—there is nothing infinite about it.'

She returned to the theme in *Ardath,* arguing more cogently but in the framework of a book which is self-consciously philosophical and 'heavy' and therefore unreadable to all but the Gladstones of this world:

> The poor and trifling comprehension of things that we, after a lifetime of study, succeed in attaining, is only just sufficient to add to our already burdened existence, the undesirable clogs of discontent and disappointed endeavour. We die—in almost as much ignorance as we were born—and when we come face to face with the Last Dark Mystery, what shall our little wisdom profit us?

Ardath ambitiously examines philosophical viewpoints one by one, and declares them all preposterous. Marie Co-

relli finds hedonism and epicureanism revolting (she envelops them both under the name 'sensualism'), empiricism silly (because if we cannot trust the evidence of our senses, then what can we trust?), the arguments relating to first causes illogical (because the material is the 'effect' which has a spiritual 'cause'). Philosophy, she maintains, can prove anything, and all its conclusions are therefore thrown into doubt:

> Education is advancing at a very rapid rate, and the art of close analysis is reaching such a pitch of perfection that I believe we shall soon be able logically to prove, not only that we do not actually exist, but moreover that we never have existed!

The Mighty Atom, a far more banal affair, written down to be comprehensible to the masses, restated another mode of attack adumbrated in *The Romance of Two Worlds,* namely that if education is to be henceforth restricted to that information accessible to human reason at the expense of faith in spiritual things, then the 'purblind philosophers, miscalled wise men, are bringing down upon the generations to come an unlooked-for and most terrific curse'. Marie presaged the end of England as we know it if we refused to take note of her warnings, and saw a parallel between England in 1900 and the last years of the Roman Empire, likewise poisoned by scepticism. When all else failed, she pointed with a sneer to scientists and atheists who 'strut forth like bantams on a dung-hill, crowing their little opinions about the sun-rise' (*Free Opinions*).

Marie never for a second doubted her most essential belief in the immortality of the soul, the one last great Hope which compensates for all earthly disappointments. She thought of life on earth as an 'exile', a link in the chain of intended experience. Death could not therefore be an end. 'Life means to me not only the blessing of Itself,' she wrote, 'but the promise of a Higher Life,—and I live it joyously, devoutly, hopefully and lovingly—accepting it, not as a mere "chance" arrangement, doomed to disperse in a purposeless Nothingness,—but as a divinely appointed schooling, which when it shall arrive at what is called the "End", will have placed me happily at a new Beginning.'

In her address to the Theosophical Lodge of Leeds, she spelt out her beliefs quite precisely:

> There is nothing in all this universe more real than the Spiritual Creature within each one of you—the Personality which is actually you, and will always be You—and which will *never die* . . . that Spiritual Self is an Emanation of the Spirit of God. From the first radiant cell, it has evolved in past phases of experience a complex network of cells, composing a delicate and ethereal organisation which *is still in the process of development.*

This is fairly orthodox stuff, but the point to note is the skilful merging of conventional religion with the new Darwinism. Marie is no longer rejecting evolution, she has adopted and absorbed it, making the modifications necessary to ease its adaptation to her views. Darwin was clever, she implies, but not clever enough to understand the meaning of his own discovery. Thus she offered her public the best of both worlds, religion *and* science, neatly packaged to her own specifications, and guaranteed to give comfort and pleasure. No need to despair, to turn agnostic, to commit suicide, to reject the angels and the life eternal. Spiritualism is part of evolution too!

Yet she had frequently to defend what she meant by 'spiritualism', a term she was accused of misusing. She insisted that her first book had been written by the bedside of her dying father (it wasn't—he died six years later) and was true in substance because it grew out of the stress of a personal spiritual experience. With its undercurrent of reincarnation and its bold theories of electric soul-migration, **The Romance of Two Worlds** naturally appealed to those readers inclined towards the occult (and is still sold most widely in occult bookshops). Alarmed at a misreading of her intention, Marie explained in the Introduction to the second edition that she had no time for table-turners. The present 'craze', she said, is mere charlatanism. 'The so-called "signs and wonders" of modern self-styled "spiritualists" are always contemptibly trivial in character, and vulgar, when not absolutely ridiculous, in display . . . disembodied spirits never become so undignified as to upset furniture or rap on tables. Neither do they write letters in pen and ink and put them under doors.'

Nevertheless, some of Marie's popularity must be attributed to her cult with the 'spiritualists', which survived even her death (or especially her death). At least five books were written by other hands purporting to be guided by the spirit of Marie Corelli. In 1931 there was *'Paulus Antonius: A Tale of Ancient Rome,* being a true story of some second-century incarnation, by Marie Corelli (in spirit) through the hand of Marie Elfram'. Two years later a rival publication appeared, *The Voice of Marie Corelli,* by Dorothy Agnes, being fragments dictated by the posthumous Marie from a novel called *The Immortal Garden.* The most extraordinary of all was *The Great Awakening* by E. G. Pinnegar, published in 1948. Fifteen years earlier, Marie had appeared in the dream of a Welsh lady, Mrs. Eira Pinnegar, urging her to write a book on the reality of spiritualism. Marie made it a condition that the book should be written on her own octagonal oak table, which would inspire Mrs. Pinnegar, since that very table had seen the creation of all Marie's books. In 1933 this presented a problem, for Bertha Vyver was still alive, and the house and contents were managed by a trust. Mrs. Pinnegar bided her time. When the auction came up ten years later, she sent in a bid for the table, and secured it without any trouble for thirty-six guineas, having first described it accurately as Marie had instructed her. (Marie also said in the dream that though her books were currently out of fashion, they would one day be prominent again.) So Mrs. Pinnegar got to work and wrote her book, dedicated to 'the late famous Edwardian authoress Marie Corelli'. The latest in this *genre* are *Judith,* by Blanche A. Webb, dictated by the spirit of Marie Corelli (Boston 1950), and *No Matter* by C. A. Wild, guided by Lalasal and Marie Corelli, which appeared in 1969.

Her religion was in fact simplistic. 'I am of no formula,' she wrote to Cuming Walters. 'I have based my life on the New Testament alone, and from that I evoke my spiritual life.' To which one ought to add a certain naïve deism. Marie had only to look at the flowers and listen to a lamb's bleat to know that God existed, which was handy in view of her detestation of churchmen and reluctance to be seen among a congregation.

Nor did her creed allow for any Lutheran predestination to be affixed to the human condition. 'Men make their own choice and form their own futures, and never let them dare say they are not *free* to choose' (*The Sorrows of Satan*). She much admired a book called *In Tune With the Infinite* by R. W. Trine (1899) wherein it is stated 'We are told that God hardened Pharaoh's heart. I don't believe it. Pharaoh hardened his own heart and God was blamed for it.'

It cannot be emphasised too strongly that the element of calculation in Marie Corelli's words is minimal. She wrote with the earnestness of passionate conviction and the excitement of a novice who has just learned how to construct a sentence. There is no sophistication, no selection, no device, no trick wherewith to hoodwink her audience, an audience which would have seen through such cynicism before long and discarded its idol. No, Marie endured because she was transparently sincere, she believed every word she wrote. That was ultimately her secret, and it swept thousands along with it into the vortex of her enthusiasm. 'If I were given such a choice as this,' she wrote in her article **'The Power of the Pen'**, 'to write something entirely opposed to my own feeling and conscience for a thousand pounds, or to write my honest thought for nothing, I would write my honest thought, and let the thousand pounds go.'

It is easy to lay examples of hypocrisy at Marie Corelli's door ('if we hate or envy or slander any person, THEN WE ARE NOT CHRISTIANS'—*Free Opinions*), but they miss the point. When she was writing, she believed ardently, fervently in the rightness of what she was saying *at that time* and in the invincibility of her principles. This was no ordinary honesty, which could be placed in the dock, but a demoniac sincerity. Michael Sadleir, who heard her speak, testified that she 'impressed upon her audience a sense of it *mattering* what she said. This was the real merit of the business. I think she really believes in herself. I'm sure she believed what she said.'

Marie gushed forth her unrestrained prose as if not a word could be spared in the effort to make herself understood. When the purity of her intentions went unappreciated, she was deeply hurt. Marie had, then, an emotional bond with her audience which carried her to triumph. As Rebecca West pointed out:

> One cannot reach the goal of best-selling by earnest pedestrianism, but must ride thither on the Tosh-horse. No one can write a best-seller by taking thought. The slightest touch of insincerity blurs its appeal.

Leonard Woolf, reviewing the **Open Confession,** came to a similar conclusion:

> if one can forget the ordinary standards of literature, one sees that it [the book] has a distinct quality which is not possessed by the hundred best-sellers which do not sell and of 'popular'

novels which are never really popular. The ordinary popular novel has something mechanical about it; the expert who examines its surface sees at once that it is machine-made; it is written because the author wants to write a popular novel, no real belief in what the typewriter is tapping out. But you have only to read five sentences of Marie Corelli to recognise the passionate conviction with which they are written. . . . Instead of an ancient plot dipped into a thin mixture of sentimentality and bathos, you have a fierce orgy of both. And that goes straight to the heart of the great public.

Marie's admirers confused this 'portentous sincerity' (to use H. B. Samuel's phrase) with art. There was no art in Marie Corelli's work; it was all ingenuousness, and the very antithesis of literature. It is all very well to give the public what it wants and to mean every syllable you write, but to make a literary creation you have on the contrary to surprise, produce the unexpected, risk, dare, be unreliable, experiment and wonder. J. P. Stern, writing in the *Times Literary Supplement* about a modern novelist, said:

> One might almost define literature as that mode of experience whose most appropriate value judgements depend not, alas, on the goodness, or honesty, or even the integrity of the mind at work, but on the freshness and the articulated energy of the prospect presented.

It is a sad paradox that Marie Corelli's greatest quality should thus relegate her to the postscripts of literary history instead of placing her among the great moralists. The pedestal to which she aspired can never be erected. (pp. 291-305)

> *Brian Masters, in his* Now Barabbas Was a Rotter: The Extraordinary Life of Marie Corelli, *Hamish Hamilton, 1978, 326 p.*

FURTHER READING

Bigland, Eileen. *Marie Corelli: The Woman and the Legend.* London: Jarrolds Publishers Ltd., 1953, 274 p.

   Investigates the lonely private life of this very public figure.

Elwin, Malcolm. "Best Sellers: Hall Caine and Others." In his *Old Gods Falling,* pp. 290-328. New York: The Macmillan Co., 1939.

   Briefly characterizes the peculiarities of Corelli's personality and writings, comparing the author with other popular writers of her day.

Kersher, R. B., Jr. "Joyce and Popular Literature: The Case of Corelli." In *James Joyce and His Contemporaries,* edited by Diana A. Ben-Merre and Maureen Murphy, pp. 51-8. New York: Greenwood Press, 1989.

   Discusses Joyce's reference to *Sorrows of Satan* in his *Ulysses,* outlining similarities between the two works and their authors.

Sadleir, Michael. "The Camel's Back; or, The Last Tribulation of a Victorian Publisher." In *Essays Mainly on the Nineteenth Century: Presented to Sir Humphrey Milford,* edited by Geoffrey Cumberlege, pp. 127-49. London: Oxford University Press, 1948.

   Recounts the portion of Corelli's literary career prior to the publication of her first widely popular novel *Barabbas.*

Nagai Kafū

1879-1959

(Pseudonym of Nagai Sōkichi) Japanese short story writer, novelist, playwright, translator, and essayist.

INTRODUCTION

One of the most popular and prolific Japanese writers of the early twentieth century, Kafū is best known for works which depict the world of the geisha and women of the backstreets and pleasure quarters of pre-westernized Tokyo. His recollections of life in Japan immediately prior to 1868—the beginning of the Meiji era and the year of Tokyo's designation as Imperial capital—have been critically acclaimed for their vivid realism and unromanticized rendering of this milieu. As Donald Keene has written, Kafū's "mastery of Japanese prose style won him fame in his own day and a following he retained even after the world he described had become remote."

Kafū was born in the Koishikawa district of Tokyo, near the Shimbashi pleasure quarter, which is frequently depicted in his writings. Kafū's interest in this area was apparent at an early age, as can be seen in his decision, when in middle school, to defy his parents and take flute lessons in the geisha district. Kafū wrote in his diary that "later regrets would be bad compensation for a youth not properly savored" and became a regular patron in his late teens of pleasure quarters in Tokyo. At this time Kafū also attempted to begin a literary career by serving apprenticeships at various times to a popular author, a burlesque storyteller of the geisha district, and the chief playwright of the Kabuki Theater. In 1903 Kafū was sent to the United States by his father, who believed that an American education would better prepare his son for a prosperous career. After attending universities in Seattle and Tacoma, Washington, and Kalamazoo, Michigan, Kafū worked for the Japanese Legation in Washington, D.C., and later the New York branch of a Japanese bank. In 1907, Kafū was transferred to Lyon, France, where he resided for one year before returning to Japan. Drawing from these travel experiences, Kafū wrote the short story collections *Amerika monogatari* (*American Stories*), published in 1908, and *Furansu monogatari* (*French Stories*), which was banned by the government censor for its perceived erotic subject matter but reached the public surreptitiously. One of Kafū's best known works, the novella *Sumidagawa* (*The River Sumida*), was published in 1909 and established his position among the most prominent of Japan's young literary figures of the early twentieth century.

In 1913 Kafū published *Sangoshū* (*Coral Anthology*), a collection of his own translations of poems by the French poets Henri Régnier, Paul Verlaine, Charles Baudelaire, as well as several others who, according to Edward Seidensticker, "thanks to Kafū, are probably better remem-

bered today in Japan than in their own land." His next major work was the novel *Udekurabe* (*Geisha in Rivalry*), which tells of the antagonism between the geisha Komayo and her competitors, who conspire to steal her generous patrons. Kafū wrote less frequently in the 1920s and 1930s, composing mainly short stories and burlesque plays. His best-known works from this period are the novel *Tsuyu no atosaki* (*During the Rains*), a depiction of the life of a prostitute, and the novella *Bokutō kidan* (*A Strange Tale from East of the River*), which tells the story of an aging writer who spends his evenings with a young prostitute. During the increased Japanese militarization of the 1930s and the Second World War, Kafū's works were withheld from publication because the government perceived them as frivolous. At the end of 1945 he released a collection of his pre-war essays, as well as the novels he had written during the war. His fame increased considerably in the postwar period and in 1952 Kafū received the Imperial Cultural Decoration, the highest honor awarded to Japanese writers and artists. He primarily wrote burlesque theater skits late in his career and died in 1959.

Commentators have observed Kafū's depiction of the world of the geisha to be of a documentary rather than judgmental nature. This approach accords with the tenets of literary naturalism as outlined by Emile Zola, whose novels Kafū admired. Critics have also noted Kafū's tendency to portray these denizens of Tokyo's pleasure districts as representatives of the traditional Japanese way of life which was disappearing in the early twentieth century. Kafū's vivid descriptions of the pre-westernized Tokyo of his youth are frequently acclaimed by critics, who admire his delineation of urban life and architecture, Tokyo's parks and rivers, seasonal change, and the atmosphere and setting of the pleasure quarters.

PRINCIPAL WORKS

Jigoku no hana (novel) 1902
Yashin (novel) 1902
Yume no onna (novel) 1903
Amerika monogatari (short stories) 1908
Furansu monogatari (short stories) 1909
Sumidagawa (novella) 1909
  [*The River Sumida,* 1965]
Kōcha no ato (essays) 1911
Shinkyō yawa (short stories) 1912
Sangoshū [translator] (poetry) 1913
Udekurabe (novel) 1918
  [*Geisha in Rivalry,* 1963; *Rivalry* (partial translation)
  1965]
Okamezasa (novel) 1920
Azabu zakki (short stories) 1924
Tsuyu no atosaki (novel) 1931
Bokutō kidan (novella) 1937
  [*A Strange Tale from East of the River,* 1965]
Odoriko (novel) 1946
Kunshō (short stories) 1947
Kafū the Scribbler (novellas and short stories) 1965
A Strange Tale from East of the River and Other Stories
  (short stories) 1972

CRITICISM

Ryôhei Shioda (essay date 1939)

[*In the following excerpt from the Japanese government-sponsored* Introduction to Contemporary Japanese Literature 1902-1935, *Shioda asserts that Kafū's novel* Tsuyu no atosaki *contains social criticism distinctly colored by sensuality and dilettantism.*]

The author who depicted the *geisha* in **Udé Kurabé (Trial of Strength)** and **Sumida-gawa (The Sumida River)**, and who drew the portrait of the unlicensed prostitute in **Okamé Zasa** and **Hikagé no Hana (A Flower in the Shade)**, has [in **Tsuyu no atosaki (During the Rains)**], and in **Yukigé (Melting Snow)**, written about the café waitress.

Describing as it does the double life of the café waitress, [*Tsuyu no atosaki*] is a novel which raised a storm of criticism at the time of publication. Its delineation of sensual feelings in a ferment against the gloomy, depressing prospects before and after the *tsuyu,* or rainy season in June, exhibits the shrewd seasonal effects peculiar to the writings of this author. In his centralizing the theme of his about the Ginza and the café waitress, one can, we believe, observe the lineaments of the author's social criticism—an attempt to reproduce a sort of pathos arising from the scenes of a city patterned after the West as well as the changing atmosphere of the times. This is the kind of observation, tinged with cynicism and exhortation, that the author discloses through the point of view of such characters as old Matsuzaki and Kiyoöka, the doctor of literature. Yet it is not a thorough-going one in the coldly objective sense. His vision is in large part clouded by a sense of his own inhibition, and the result is that his depiction of the sensual, dissipating life of the café waitress is rather of the nature of a curiosity-seeking dilettantism, giving the impression of a tepid sort of lewdness. This provides, in addition, just the right touch of sexuality in keeping with the subject-matter and undoubtedly constitutes one of the fascinating features of the work.

Some time after its publication, Jun'ichirô Tanizaki, a leading figure among the first-rank writers of the age, criticized it with the statement that the author of this story has handled its characters like a puppet-player manipulating his dolls, so that his subjectivism is not clearly brought out. The critic Hideo Kobayashi next cited this critical comment and stated that that is precisely the sort of work which may be called a "pure novel." (pp. 362-63)

Ryôhei Shioda, "Tsuyu No Ato-Saki (Before and After the Rainy Season) 1931 by Kafū Nagai," in Introduction to Contemporary Japanese Literature: 1902-1935, *edited by*

Kafū on the aims of his fiction:

There is a purely animalistic quality in man. Probably this is due to the physiological temptation of flesh which composes the human body. Or it may be the ancestral inheritance which developed from an animal. Be it as it may, human beings formed religions and ethics by their customs and circumstances which brought the highly cultivated civilization of to-day. They termed this phase of animality crime and sin. Now then, how does this dark animality of mankind go on in such an established social life? If we expect to form perfect and ideal human life, I am of the firm conviction that we must make a special investigation of this dark side. This must be done in the exactly the same manner as criminal cases, which must be thoroughly studied before the light of justice is sought in the court. Therefore I want to describe most vividly without any modification the numerous cases of passions or violence accompanying our inheritance from ancestors and environmental circumstances.

Tadao Kunitomo, in his Japanese Literature since 1868, *1938.*

Kokusai Bunka Shinkokai, Kokusai Bunka Shinkokai, 1939, pp. 360-64.

Okazaki Yoshie   (essay date 1955)

[*In the following excerpt, Okazaki examines naturalist and nostalgic currents in Kafū's fiction.*]

Like Tengai, who, in copying the mode of Zola, had tried to give an artistic expression of the force of heredity but who, because of his lack of power to express it in concrete form, ended by depicting puppets of heredity, Kafū also attempted to deal in his novels with heredity and the animal nature of man. However, in the case of Kafū, too, the original design was not fulfilled and remained merely inchoate.

Nagai Kafū (Sōkichi) first studied Edo *gesaku* writing. After entering the school of Ryūrō, his style approached that of the pathos novel (*Hisan shōsetsu*). However, when he started to read French novels, he became a devout follower of Zola. This was illustrated in *Yashin (Ambition)* (1902). This novel deals with the young head of an old established firm who attempts to copy the successful methods of French merchants, and, fired with ambition, tries to renovate his shop into an elaborate department store in opposition to his mother and relatives. Finally, one of his employees who hates him and is engaged to wed his younger sister and take over the store, sets fire to and destroys the new shop which was almost completed. The author has depicted an immature but passionate youth who is swayed by the superficial spirit of reform, but, when faced with harsh reality, sees his ambitious dreams crumble to the ground. The collapse of romantic dreams seems to be the principal theme, and the author apparently borrowed this theme from Zola's *Au Bonheur des Dames.* The actual story, however, is completely different. Zola's novel deals with a man who starts his life penniless, but finally succeeds in establishing a large department store in the center of Paris. In his counterpart, Kafū has the hero's friend express the idea that such ambition as that displayed by the hero is merely a "fever" or "demoniac design."

Jigoku no Hana (The Flower of Hell) (1902) is known to the world for its preface which is the author's declaration of the Naturalistic creed. In this declaration, the author states that there is a bestial side to human nature. This is an inevitable aspect, and if we are to aspire for idealistic life, we must conduct special research in this bestial aspect. "From this standpoint, I am planning to make a daring exposure of the naked desires, brutality, violence, and other dark passions which result from heredity and environment." Actually, heredity is almost neglected in the work itself, which makes only a slight mention of naked desires and violence. The heroine, Tsunehama Sonoko, an English teacher, falls in love with a magazine reporter who is a Christian. However, she discovers that he is on intimate terms with the mistress of the family where she is serving as an English instructor. At the same time, the heroine is violated by her schoolmaster and driven to despair. However, she decides to free herself from conventional ideas, such as respect and honor, and lead a new and unrestricted life. In making this decision, the heroine is influenced by the fact that Tomiko, the daughter of the family where she is serving as an English instructor, has plunged into a new and free life, in order to strike back at the world which made unfair criticism of her family. Thus, Tomiko enjoys a carefree life as a means of resisting the world, but the heroine Sonoko exploits her free situation to return to nature, and attempts to reconstruct her life on the basis of her animal nature, which in the case of Tomiko is despised by the world as a hell of filth. Furthermore, the heroine believes that only by attaining a beautiful moral life in the midst of such defiling life, can one become a person deserving eternal praise. This conclusion is moral, but the point that the heroine returns to nature and to bestial life as a means of challenging the society filled with pretense and vanity displays the strong influence of Naturalism.

Yume no Onna (The Woman of Dreams) (1903) deals with a woman of a samurai family, whose life is ruined by a series of inevitable circumstances. The heroine resembles Saikaku's Ichidai Onna or Zola's Nana. However, the author has shown no effort to shed light on heredity and has merely exaggerated the inevitable power of environment. Furthermore, the heroine Shisō is a normal human being, and the bestiality of human nature can be found only in the erotic desires of the males surrounding her. As a result, the significance of this work, as in his later novels, lay in his beautiful description of the erotic sentiments of the world of prostitutes, with the heroine serving as the pillar of the whole story. In this work, too, we can point to evidence of the influence of Zola, but it was not a display of genuine Zolaism.

It appears that at the time he was writing these works, Kafū was reading Zola's works. Immediately after publication of *Yume no Onna* he compiled "Joyū Nana Kōgai" ("An Outline of the Actress Nana"), "Kōzui" ("The Flood"), and "Emīru Zora to Sono Shōsetsu" ("Emile Zola and his Novels"), and published a book entitled *Joyū Nana (The Actress Nana)*. This work tells us of his achievements in his research on Zola but does not contain any remarks advocating Zolaism. It appears to be a serious book of research; however, we can observe that Kafū at this period was studying Zola in order to cultivate a field in Naturalism. (pp. 225-28)

In 1908, Kafū returned from his travels through America and France, and, compiling a number of stories, some of which he had published during his trip overseas, published them under the title of *Amerika Monogatari (Tales of America)* immediately prior to his return to Japan. He then made public a series of stories which were later published under the title *Furansu Monogatari (Tales of France)* (1909). The fresh expressions imbued with rich sentiment, his sympathy for and his penetrating observations on the maturity of the Western civilized countries, were all astonishingly new to his contemporaries. It seemed as if the literary world was witnessing the birth of a new literature.

1909 was the year which saw the Naturalist movement rise to its zenith. . . . New literary magazines advocating a new Romantic movement, such as *Subaru* and *Okujō Teien,* were published, and made way for the aesthetic and epicurean atmosphere. In this situation, Kafū, who was rather the poet type, and who, though leaning towards Naturalism, also showed a disposition toward Decadent poetry, wrote numerous short stories as a poet-novelist. The stories **"Kitsune"** (**"The Fox"**), **"Fukagawa no Uta"** (**"The Song of Fukagawa"**), **"Donten"** (**"Clouded Skies"**), **"Kangokusho no Ura")** (**"Behind the Prison"**), **"Shukuhai"** (**"Toasts"**), **"Kanraku"** (**"Bacchanals"**), **"Botan no Kyaku"** (**"The Guest of the Peonies"**), and **"Shinkichōsha no Nikki"** (**"The Diary of a Newly-Returned Traveler"**) were all written in this year. Also written in this year through the next were the medium-length novel *Sumidagawa* (*The Sumida River*) and the lengthy work *Reishō* (*The Sneer*).

As shown by the fact that all of the short stories mentioned above were compiled in a volume entitled **Kanraku,** the short story by this name was his representative work of this period. The hero shows interest only in romance and literature. From the age of sixteen he has been involved with numerous women, but each affair merely ends as short-lived sensual pleasure. But with the approach of forty, the hero bids farewell to his past pleasures, and lamenting his departing youth, is overcome by a deep loneliness. The contrast of the sweet pleasures of youth with the resulting decadent and lonesome feelings is expressed in a lyrical style. This contrast, pervaded by a poetical mood, forms the pillar of the story. In the concluding part, Kafū refers to a poem by the hero's favorite poet, Jean Moréas, and advocates a life in which pleasure and bitterness must be thoroughly experienced and one in which one should be satisfied, after that, by reminiscing over the past dreams. This vision of life is appropriate to an epicurean author.

However, it must be noted that at the beginning of the story the author states that he is against old-fashioned romanticism, and that a human being does not necessarily need to devote himself to a single romance. From this standpoint, the author depicts numerous love-affairs. Furthermore, the author cannot resist depicting the ugliness as well as the beauty of women. There is something common here with Naturalism. In addition, from the standpoint of a poet, Kafū expresses vehement resistance against the vulgar society which oppresses and destroys the aesthetic world. The novel, in this sense, marked the beginning of a series of works which were to be imbued with a spirit of criticism of the contemporary civilization. **"Shukuhai"** deals with a hero who, in his younger days, learns the taste of sensual pleasure. He violates an innocent girl, but because he is fortunate enough to escape from the situation, decides that he must give a toast to his success. (Hence the title.) In this study, the author was expressing his resistance against the religious men and educators who were intimidating students with commandments which did not fit the actual world. This resistance, however, inevitably led toward a feeling of resignation, as exemplified in **"Shinkichōsha no Nikki"** and **Reishō.**

Kafū, charmed by the beauty of Western civilization, returned home to find that the native culture lay in ruins. Unable to control his anger over the desolate situation, he resisted the militarism which was the principal destructor

of culture. However, discovering that his resistance was a puny thing, Kafū sank into a passive, nostalgic mood, gazing back at the culture of the past. At first, Kafū

An excerpt from *Geisha in Rivalry*

It was still intermission. Everywhere in the corridors of the Imperial Theater there was a jostling confusion of strolling people. A geisha who was about to ascend the main staircase almost collided with a gentleman coming down, and as they exchanged glances, both appeared to be overcome with surprise.

"Oh! Yoshioka-san!"
"Ah! So it's you!"
"Well! . . . And how are you?"
"I say, are you working as a geisha again?"
"Since the end of last year. . . . I came out again."
"Oh, really. Anyway, it's been a long time."
"Since then . . . it's exactly seven years ago that I quit."
"Really? Seven years?"

The bell announced the end of intermission. For a while the confusion in the corridors became still worse as everyone engaged in the struggle to be first to his seat. The geisha, taking advantage of this moment when no one would be noticing her, stepped a bit closer to the gentleman. Looking up at his face, she said: "You haven't changed a bit, have you?"
"Really? You seem to have grown much younger yourself."
"Shame on you! You're joking. At my age . . ."
"Don't say that. You really haven't changed at all."

Yoshioka stared at the woman's face in honest surprise. Thinking back to the time when she had been a geisha before, he figured that she must have been seventeen or eighteen. If seven years had passed since then, she must already be twenty-five or twenty-six. But as she stood there before him, she didn't look a bit older than on the day when she had been promoted from apprentice to full-fledged geisha. Medium in figure, bright-eyed, and still with the deep dimples in her round cheeks. And the look of her mouth when she laughed and showed her right eyetooth. After all, she had somehow not lost her childish face.

"Won't you meet me sometime for a little talk?"
"What do you call yourself now? Still the same name?"
"No. I call myself Komayo now."
"Oh, do you? I'll call you one of these days."
"Please do."

From the stage came the sound of the wooden clappers announcing the opening of the curtain. With quick little steps Komayo hurried down the corridor to the right to find her seat. Yoshioka started off just as quickly in the opposite direction, but for some reason he suddenly stopped and looked back. In the lobby only the girl ushers and the refreshment-stand salesgirls were left. Komayo had disappeared. Yoshioka sat down on a nearby sofa in the corridor and lit a cigarette. Before he quite realized it, he was recalling what had happened seven or eight years ago.

Nagai Kafū, in his Geisha in Rivalry, *Charles E. Tuttle Company, 1963.*

seemed to be a poet glorifying the beauty of Western civilization and turning his back on that of the Orient; however, since he came to understand that it was foolish to seek Western civilization in this country, he turned his attention to the mature culture of the Edo Period. Thus, he complacently sought the remnants of the past in various corners of modern Tōkyō. In the story **"Fukagawa no Uta,"** he reminisces over the Edo days, while standing in the desolate Fukagawa district. In **"Botan no Kyaku,"** he relates his pleasure in visiting a peony garden in the Kōtō district with a geisha as his companion. In **"Sumidagawa,"** the author attempts to find the shadows of the past in the lives of such people as a female instructor of *tokiwazu,* a *haikai* master, the geisha, and stage actors. And, in depicting this complex world, he attempted to evoke the essence of pure Japanese-style romance, with a strong note of loneliness and submission to fate.

When he came to **Reishō,** he drew a conclusion from his philosophical position. In this story, Kafū gives a picture of five eccentric characters such as often appeared in Edo-style *gesaku* stories. They come together, and, in resistance to the vulgar world, make free criticism of the tastelessness of the society, constructing an epicurean life among themselves. Although this work is regarded as representative of the Epicurean school, the author himself thought of it differently. In his article **"About My Story Reishō,"** included in **Kōcha no Ato (After the Tea),** he says, "I attempted to depict the epicurean heroes, their motives, the melancholy caused by the stifling atmosphere of the society, and their efforts to enter into a world of resignation symbolized by the *senryū* (comic *haiku*) mood, and into a world of detachment." This vision of life is indicated by the title **Reishō,** which means a sneer, or a sarcastic smile. After writing this work, Kafū became more deeply concerned with expressing "a mood of resignation and detachment" than in making a serious study of "agony and melancholy." In other words, in a mood of resignation and detachment, he sought to unearth the dreams of the past, inevitably moving in a direction of finding beauty in flowers in the shade. All the stories written in 1912, including **"Shōtaku"** (**"The Mistress' Home"**) and the tales contained in **Shimbashi Yawa** (**"Night Tales of Shimbashi"**), are attempts to find vestiges of the beauty left by the old indigenous culture. (pp. 286-90)

> *Okazaki Yoshie, "The Development of Realism" and "The Rise of Neo-Idealism," in Japanese Literature in the Meiji Era, edited by Okazaki Yoshie, translated by V. H. Vigielmo, Ōbunsha, 1955, pp. 192-237, 268-316.*

Edward Seidensticker   (essay date 1965)

[*Seidensticker is an American educator and translator of Japanese literature. In the following excerpt from his full-length study* Kafū the Scribbler, *he discusses early influences on Kafū's literary career and cites* Yume no onna *as an exemplar of his fiction.*]

[Kafū wrote] his first short stories while still in middle school. They seem to have been in the manner of Tamena-

ga Shunsui, stronger on incident than character, and they do not survive. The very first was about a nurse who attended him during [a] long illness, and who, it is said, was his first love. She, too, was responsible for his "elegant sobriquet" or pen name, Kafū (his legal name was Sōkichi). She was called O'hasu, "Miss Lotus," and Kafū means "Lotus Breeze." His literary efforts were concealed from his family. The art of fiction had been frowned upon by the Tokugawa Shogunate and was still not admired in conservative families. (p. 9)

Japanese practice required that he enroll himself as the disciple of some literary elder, and so, armed with four or five stories, he went knocking at the gate of Hirotsu Ryūrō, and was admitted. This was in 1898.

Ryūrō was not precisely an elder, being at the time in his late thirties, but he was one of the more distinguished writers of the day. It was a rather tentative day, when a flirtation with European realism had led to little but a warming-over of Tokugawa romanticism and a debate on literary language. The literary language of Edo, full of sinicisms and antiquated verbs, did not seem up to the demands of modern realism, and something very close to colloquial speech was coming into its own for literary uses. Ryūrō was among the experimenters with the vernacular, but his matter was familiar, merchant and courtesan torn by the contradictory pulls of duty and feeling. When Kafū came asking to be admitted to the profession, Ryūrō was fresh from his greatest success, *Double Suicide at Imado.* About the drowning of a Yoshiwara courtesan and a merchant who was her customer, this work belongs to the genre in which Ryūrō specialized, the "distressing novel." Distressing novels deal with sordid and sensational events, frequently of the demimonde, and do not, on the whole, fear being accused of a certain improbability in plot and characterization. They derive from the amorous literature of late Tokugawa, as does Ryūrō's favorite technique, a reliance on dialogue at the expense of description.

Kafū's earliest published stories could have been written by Ryūrō. Indeed some of them appeared either as joint works of the two or as Ryūrō's alone, and it has been suggested that when, as shortly happened, Kafū began edging away from Ryūrō to place himself under the tutelage of Iwaya Sazanami, a writer known chiefly for juvenile fiction, his reason had to do with Ryūrō's habit of pocketing manuscript money.

"Misty Night" (**"Oboroyo"**), written in late 1898 or early 1899, almost completely in dialogue, is Kafū's first surviving story, although others were published earlier. It tells of a courtesan and her mother, the latter a contrite woman who admits early mistakes and now hopes only that her daughter may be prevailed upon to pursue a more seemly calling. It is touching in a slight way, but the issue is never really in doubt, for daughter and calling seem beautifully matched. **"Flower Basket"** (**"Hanakago"**), which Kafū called his "virgin work," apparently with reference to date of publication and not date of composition, won a prize in 1899 in a contest sponsored by a newspaper. It tells of a young lady who through no fault of her own fails to maintain her purity for her bridegroom; and, with didactic intent, it shakes a finger at well-to-do rapists in such loaded lines as this: "Ah, poor Shizue, who had awaited this day to be decorated with beautiful roses and violets—ah, her name was a sad one, in all the papers, a raped woman, and her father, who was in the service of the evil count, could do nothing!"

The year of his first published fiction, 1899, was the year of another enterprise that had to be kept from his family. He apprenticed himself to a professional monologuist, a teller of *rakugo* comic stories. *Rakugo* men were, if anything, in worse repute with proper Confucian families than novelists. For more than a year Kafū frequented the variety theaters, going first to the master's house in Shitaya; then, in late afternoon, proceeding to the theater with the master's paraphernalia on his back; and, finally, crossing the city once more to sneak in the back door of his father's house. It was a strenuous life, but it had its little idylls, as when, one winter night, he and a pretty girl, a fellow disciple, saw with a simultaneous insight that they could not make it back across the city in the snow, and put up together at an inn. The episode, said Kafū, who was to recount it more than once, was like something out of a *ninjōbon,* a romantic novel of the Tokugawa Period. It was from Fukagawa that the two set out on their interrupted journey, and Fukagawa, on the left bank of the Sumida River, was one of the places in which Culture and Enlightenment had not yet awakened the unlettered masses from their Edo slumber. So one may assume that Kafū enjoyed himself; but not for long. A family retainer chanced one night to see a performance at which Kafū was in attendance, and he was led home by the ear.

The next year he had another try at giving himself to Edo. He entered the Kabuki Theater (Kabukiza) as apprentice to Fukuchi Ochi, the chief playwright. This episode, too, had to be kept secret. Although it was no longer improper for the better sort of people to see Kabuki, it was very improper indeed for them to be associated with it. And even in Kabuki circles, the playwright was not an honored figure. Traditionally he was a sort of craftsman, rather like a property man or stagehand, and it was his function, like that of the cameraman today, to show off the great actor to best advantage.

Ochi himself was representative of a new sort of playwright. A distinguished journalist and once a fairly distinguished politician, he was close to the management of the new Kabuki Theater, which opened in 1889. He was also close to the ninth Danjūrō, the greatest of Meiji actors, and therefore in a stronger position than most playwrights.

Kafū's own position was more conventional.

> My duty as an apprentice playwright was to clap twice with wooden clappers at the opening of each act (the process was described as practice in using the clappers), and to clap again each time the revolving stage came into position or drums signaled the end of an act. I also kept the theater records, noting down curtain times and the like; and when there was an urgent notice to be passed around backstage, I was charged with making sure that no one missed it. I went from dressing room to dressing room, I saw the prop-

erty men and stagehands and custodians of wardrobes and wigs, and I saw the flutists and drummers. From the first welcoming drum to the end of the day's performance I sat stiffly at attention in the playwrights' room, cloakless even in the dead of winter, forbidden to smoke; and if the head of the company appeared, or any notable guest, I was charged with making tea for him and disposing of the sandals he had stepped out of. When the chief playwright came in, I had to help him out of his cloak and fold it for him and see to all his needs and follow him around until he left again.

Ochi made it clear that Kafū need expect no modern informality. He did not once look at the younger man in the course of their first meeting.

Kafū's career as a playwright lasted not quite a year. It is not recorded that he wrote any plays. In the spring of 1901 he left the Kabukiza to become a reporter for the *Yamato Shimbun,* an important daily. He specialized in the miscellaneous pieces, vaguely gossipy and scandalous, that in Japan go by the name "social reports," and he serialized a romance about the Yoshiwara, for which he also wrote the advance notices. "Kafū's subtle and delicate pen," these notices said, "will call up for the reader all the voluptuous treasures of Utamaro's lovely women." The title of the work was borrowed from Tamenaga Shunsui, as was the plot, and the technique came largely from Ryūrō. Despite its distinguished parentage, it was never finished. Early in 1902, Kafū was selected out, as the management of the newspaper described the process.

Brief though it was, the experience had its rewards. While working on the *Yamato,* Kafū came to know Jōno Saigiku, one of the last true Edo dilettantes, in the last months of the old man's life—he died in 1901 at the age of seventy. Saigiku was an Edo-style *gesakusha,* a "frivolous writer" of fiction and fugitive essays. A true townsman, he had been the chief clerk at an Edo dry-goods store, and had descended from there into the disreputable world of fiction, his particular genre being rather like Ryūrō's "distressing novels." For Kafū, he was a man who had had the fortune to be part of a balanced, harmonious Edo composition. "After the death of Kanagaki Robun," wrote Kafū later, "there was but one man in Meiji to make us see what the plebeian writer had been in Edo. That man was Saigiku. I feel tears coming when I think how we sat there at our desks day after day and listened to him talk." Kanagaki Robun was a *gesakusha* who died in 1894.

If Kafū was looking back to Edo, he was also aware of new winds. As early as 1901 he was reading Zola in English, and the following year he entered night school to learn French.

Zola's position in the development of modern Japanese letters is a curious, contradictory one. With Ibsen, he was early in this century proclaimed the leader of a band of Japanese writers who called themselves naturalists, and from whom the "main current" of modern Japanese literature is generally said to flow. Whether or not he would have recognized his followers is another matter, for banners and standards have a way of getting turned upside down when they are imported into Japan. It is enough here to say that efforts to throw off the didacticism, the eroticism, and the excessive decoration of late Tokugawa fiction became a concerted literary movement at about the time of the Russo-Japanese War; that its more active participants, self-appointed disciples of Zola, turned in their quest for unadorned, impersonal truth to their own experience; and that virtually undisguised autobiography thereupon became the orthodox medium for Japanese prose naturalism.

Meanwhile certain other writers and scholars were doing what the naturalists proper never quite got around to, studying Zola in the original. At least one of them, Kafū, emerged from the study to produce fiction that would probably have been more acceptable to Zola than that which called itself naturalist. Yet when Kafū presently came into his own as a power in the literary world, he was called antinaturalist—for he never admitted that flat, shapeless household reports were the ultimate in fiction. The categories of Japanese literary history are sometimes very curious.

In 1902 and 1903, at the height of his Zola fever, Kafū published three medium-length novels: *Ambition* (*Yashin*), *Hell Flowers* (*Jigoku no Hana*), and *The Woman of the Dream* (*Yume no Onna*). His most famous statement of what he thought himself up to is in the epilogue to the second: "There can be no doubt that a part of man is beast. . . . He has built up religious and moral concepts from customary practices and from the circumstances in which he has found himself, and now, at the end of long discipline, he has come to give the darker side of his nature the name sin. . . . I wish to set down quite without reserve the whole of this darker side—the lust, the violence, the naked force that we have from our surroundings and from our ancestors." The first edition of *The Woman of the Dream* carries on its cover a picture of a naked lady with much in it suggesting "the darker side."

It is easy to make fun of these early exercises in Darwinism that shake tremulous, irritable fingers at Meiji hypocrisy and threaten to end up didactic after all. The male beasts are rather bloodless bourgeois sorts, unenthusiastic polygamists; and the women, despite the lure on that cover, are seldom caught in compromising positions except when they are victims not of heredity but of circumstance. All done up in white, they remind one more of Emily Dickinson than of Nana. In the first two of the three novels, Kafū simply does not go where the reader has been given every reason to expect him to go. The contrived plots—Kafū was not one to be apologetic about coincidence—and the wan characters are likely to call Ryūrō to mind before Zola.

But the third novel, given the age of the author and the time of writing, is a commendable work. Published in 1903, four years before the date at which literary historians generally place the beginning of the "naturalist" movement, *The Woman of the Dream* is an impersonal narrative with an illusion of independent life such as the naturalists were seldom able to manage. The impulse to preach sometimes comes very near the surface, but on the whole the work is a quiet, straightforward, and touching chronicle of a woman's life, a remarkable exercise for its

day in setting forth without decoration or comment the essential facts about a fictitious person in real difficulties at a real moment in history. The fact that the person should be fictitious is important, for the writers who called themselves naturalists assumed that the only reality within their grasp was about real persons, themselves.

O-nami, the heroine, is the daughter of a provincial samurai lost in the new world of Meiji. To keep the family going, she indentures herself, first as a kept woman in Nagoya, and then, when her father has permitted himself to be swindled out of the money thus earned, as a prostitute in the Suzaki section of Tokyo. Despite bloodshed and scandal, she is eventually able to open an establishment of her own, and so to bring her family to Tokyo; but in the end her sacrifices come to nothing. Her sister runs away, and her father spends all his time asking why he ever left the provinces. As they bury him on a snowy afternoon, O-nami wonders what the point of it all has been:

> She heard her mother weeping, and she heard her daughter call "Grandfather." But O-nami herself was numb to sorrow. Sad things, painful things, they all had gone beyond a limit. She stood there blankly, as if wandering through some cold, aimless dream. Then, when she climbed into the carriage that was to take her home, and the temple gate was behind them, she was overcome by a sudden, indescribable wave of hopelessness and exhaustion. . . .
>
> Her dead heart, her hollow body, how would they get through the months and years stretching ahead? Behind her, in another carriage, were her mother and her fatherless little daughter. With dull, listless eyes O-nami looked out through the curtain. A wind had come up, and snow, swirling and twisting, was in process of burying everything, groves, houses, road, telegraph poles.
>
> Tonight the city, its countless lives, would lie silent under a blanket of white, like the cemetery. By the time the carriages had made their perilous way back to the house in Tsukiji, nothing was visible between snow and snow but lights like blood.

So the book ends. It begins in November, and the mood is autumnal throughout: O-nami sitting alone in the gathering darkness, watching the charcoal embers glow, and trying to summon up courage for a visit to the widow of her keeper; O-nami on an autumn day passing the house where she was born and hearing a girl inside at a music lesson; O-nami arriving in Tokyo in a drizzling autumn rain; O-nami looking out over a wasted autumn garden in Suzaki, listening to the autumn insects, and getting drunk out of terror at the prospect of another night without customers—for her career has entered a slump.

The mood of the book is elegiac, a lament for a wasted life. Sometimes scene and emotion fuse in a manner far more Japanese than Zolaesque:

> There were already lights on the railing of the long steel bridge, and there were a few stars dim in the ashen sky. The buildings on the islands that blocked the wide mouth of the river, the

houses that lined the banks, were sinking into the shadow of night, and new lights were numberless upon the water. The sailboats anchored in the river sent up a forest of lights, some high and some low near the water, red and green in a disordered show of fireworks. Coming to the middle of the stream, O-nami leaned absently against the railing. She thought of how, years before, she had come the long road from the provinces, and had crossed this same long bridge to give herself to the Quarter. The sounds she had heard then were still in her ears: the waves, studded then and now with a confusion of lights, churned up in the sea wind and lapping at the stone piers; the whistles of the steamboats; and the rickshaw that had carried her across, its wheels grinding against the planks of the bridge. . . . Each new crisis had brought her across the same long bridge. She looked over the railing, at the dark waters that would be flooding out to sea, and on to the far shores, and she wondered what strange power deep under the waters might be controlling her destiny, a destiny that had become so much a part of the view from this bridge.

Against a background of autumnal landscapes, chilly houses, and feckless men incapable of love, sometimes incapable even of conversation, the life of a woman unfolds. She is alone in a world that eludes and defeats her, but the illusion that she has life is complete, as perhaps in no other novel of the period. The student of Kafū's career may suspect that he pulled back in astonishment and uncertainty at having accomplished so much, for it was rather a long time before he gathered himself for another such sustained effort at fiction, the art of creating memorable life.

If *The Woman of the Dream* as a work of fiction stands in somewhat frightened isolation, it is yet in comfortable company as the first of Kafū's elegies, and O-nami stands at the head of the parade of women upon whose shadowed lives the elegies were to center. She dominates the scene as few of the rest of them are able to, but the scene is always present, as if waiting to flood forward and absorb actor and emotion into a single lyrical solution. (pp. 9-17)

> *Edward Seidensticker, in his* Kafū the Scribbler: The Life and Writings of Nagai Kafū, 1879-1959, *Stanford University Press, 1965, 360 p.*

Donald Keene   (essay date 1984)

[*An American educator and translator, Keene has published works on Japanese art, literature, and theater, and has rendered into English the works of many Japanese authors. In the following excerpt from his two-volume history of modern Japanese literature* Dawn to the West, *he assesses Kafū's most significant works, noting common thematic and stylistic traits of his oeuvre.*]

The beauty of Kafū's style, at once clear and evocative, is a glory of modern Japanese literature, and his choice of details is unerring. Even when he temporarily forgets his story and lets an alter ego expatiate on the unfortunate changes that have occurred since the [Meiji Restoration in 1868], he is never less than interesting. But Kafū is seldom ranked among the four or five outstanding Japanese writers of the twentieth century if only because his works do not require elaborate commentary and seem rarely to take themselves seriously. His best achievements were scattered over some thirty or forty years, notably *Sumidagawa* (*The River Sumida*, 1909), *Udekurabe* (*Rivalry*, 1917), *Okamezasa* (*Dwarf Bamboo*, 1920), *Tsuyu no Atosaki* (*Before and After the Rains*, 1931), and *Bokutō Kitan* (*A Strange Tale from East of the River*, 1937). A half-dozen short stories, though sometimes hardly more than sketches, confirmed his unique gifts. Essays, diaries, and translations also formed an important part of his oeuvre.

The River Sumida is probably Kafū's most affecting work. It tells of a boy named Chōkichi whose mother teaches *tokiwazu* music and whose uncle is a professional haiku master. Oito, the girl he loves, becomes a geisha. Chōkichi is naturally drawn to playing the samisen and to the theater, a world he feels he knew even before he was born, but his mother is determined that he follow the Meiji pattern of success and become an official. She sacrifices herself to send him to school, but Chōkichi detests his studies, for which he has no aptitude. At the end, despairing of ever finding happiness, he exposes himself to the rain while suffering from a cold in the hopes of contracting pneumonia. His uncle, imagining the boy lying in his sickbed, cries out in his heart that he will stand by Chōkichi. He will see to it that the boy becomes an actor and marries Oito.

Nothing in Kafū's later writing is superior to *The River Sumida*, though the story itself is hardly typical of Kafū. . . .

—*Donald Keene*

The curiously sentimental ending of *The River Sumida* is less characteristic of Kafū than of early nineteenth-century examples of gesaku fiction, and the characters lend themselves to being portrayed by ukiyo-e artists. Chōkichi is the pathetic victim of his mother's ambitions, but she in turn is a victim of the changes in society. Her brother, the haiku master Ragetsu, also belongs to the past. The tone of *The River Sumida* is elegiac, for Kafū was describing a disappearing way of life. Even the dingy little room where Chōkichi's mother gives music lessons— the wick of the lamp trimmed to save on oil, the wallpaper stained, and a scurrying of mice heard from the ceiling—is somehow appealing because of its associations with the past. Kafū stated that he had been stirred into writing *The River Sumida* by *Les vacances d'un jeune homme sage* (1903), the novel by Henri de Régnier, but the resemblances are slight. Régnier said of his book that it was created around little happenings of childhood, which, recalled in later years, "make one smile, as one smiles over the past, with regret and melancholy." This may have been Kafū's point of departure, but the past goes back much further than Chōkichi's or Kafū's childhood. At one point in the story Chōkichi is dejectedly wandering the streets of the old part of Tokyo, just after his uncle has urged him to be more diligent at school.

> Chōkichi noticed by chance on one of the houses of the neighborhood a sign with the name of the street, Nakanogō Take-chō. He recalled at once that this was the very street mentioned in Shunsui's *Plum Calendar,* which he had avidly read not long before. Ah, he sighed, did those unhappy lovers live in such a dank, sinister street? Some of the houses had bamboo fences exactly like the ones in the illustrations to the book. The bamboo had completely dried out, and the stalks were worm-eaten at the base. Chōkichi thought they would probably disintegrate if he poked them. An emaciated willow tree drooped its branches, barely touched with green shoots, over the shingled roof of a gate. Yonehachi must have passed through just such a gate to the lonely house inside when she secretly visited the ailing Tanjirō of a winter's afternoon. And it must have been in a room of such a house that Hanjirō, telling ghost stories one rainy night, dared to take Oito's hand for the first time. Chōkichi experienced a strange mixture of fascination and sadness.

Even more than such evocations of the past, Kafū's extraordinarily affecting descriptions of the changes brought by the seasons are likely to linger in the reader's memory. The Japanese language, as employed in such passages in *The River Sumida,* is almost indescribably beautiful, and even in translation something of its quality survives:

> For a while the late afternoon sun beat down even more fiercely than at the height of summer. The broad band of the river's surface was aflame, and the light reflected dazzlingly from the white-painted boards of the university boathouse. Suddenly, as if a lamp had gone out, everything turned a dull grey, and only the sails of the cargo boats gliding over the swelling evening tide still glowed a pure white. Quickly, so quickly there was not time to see, the early autumn twilight had become night, as though with the dropping of a curtain. In the harsh glare from the water the figures of people aboard the ferryboat were dyed an inky black, with the bold relief of a monochrome. The long row of cherry trees on the opposite bank seemed of an almost terrifying blackness. The cargo boats, which for a while had been plying to and fro in long chains, as if deliberately to create a charming effect, had disappeared all at once in the direction of the upper reaches of the river, and now there were only little fishing boats, back perhaps from the open sea, which floated here and there like leaves on the water. The River Sumida, as far as one could see, was again calm and lonely through all its expanse. Far off, in a corner of the sky upriver, a bank of cloud that still showed traces of summer was rising, and again and again lightning flashed in thin streaks.

The constant attention Kafū gave to each aspect of the transformation brought about by the seasons may puzzle a non-Japanese reader—who may even consider that such

passages interrupt the flow of the narrative—but the story as such is of less importance than the atmosphere Kafū is evoking. The river, the little houses on the embankment, the bridges, the groves of trees visible in the temple grounds across the river are as much "persons" in the story as Chōkichi, Oito, and the rest. Without such descriptions the story would be much less successful. The characters are hardly more than sketched, and remain two-dimensional, but the composition, as in a beautifully executed ukiyo-e, is flawless, and the coloring exquisite.

Nothing in Kafū's later writing is superior to *The River Sumida,* though the story itself is hardly typical of Kafū, the hedonist. *Rivalry,* perhaps his most widely read novel, has an ingenious plot, and it describes geishas and their world more effectively than any other modern Japanese work, but it is memorable less for its plot or characters than for the digressions, notably the description of the house and garden in the old part of Tokyo owned by Kurayama Nansō, a would-be bunjin and another alter ego of Kafū.

The story of *Rivalry* concerns a geisha named Komayo who has returned to the profession after her marriage ended with the death of her husband. By accident she meets an old patron, Yoshioka, and they soon resume their relationship, to the dismay of Rikiji, the geisha he has been keeping in the meantime. Unfortunately for both Yoshioka and Komayo, she falls in love with an actor and is unfaithful to her patron. Yoshioka shifts his affections

Self-Portrait, 1932.

to another geisha at the same house as Komayo, an unattractive young woman who Komayo has never even considered as a possible rival. Komayo is too absorbed with her affair with the actor to realize what has happened, and she suffers further misfortune when Rikiji takes revenge by promoting an affair between the actor and an ex-geisha who has inherited a fortune. Komayo, deprived of both patron and lover, is desperate, but cheers up at the end when she learns that the owner of the house where she lives has decided to turn over the business to her.

The plot of *Rivalry* is mechanical, and none of the characters comes alive, but Kafū conveys such a vivid picture of how geishas live that some critics have interpreted the novel as a work of social commentary, though this does not seem to have been Kafū's intent. Perhaps as a sign of his indebtedness to the French Naturalists, Kafū is exceptionally open in the sexual descriptions (two sections of the book, originally available in a private edition, were published only after the war), and he is almost coldly objective in his descriptions of professional women and their wiles. But there is no suggestion of disapproval of the institution of the geisha; Kafū never forgets that these women, despite their faults, give men pleasure. Komayo and her colleagues are foolish, unscrupulous, shallow women, and Kafū in no way idealizes them, but he made it absolutely clear why men were ready to lose their fortunes and, occasionally, even their lives for such women. To ask for more would be like craving intellectual distinction from a face by Utamaro.

Kafū's most skillfully constructed novel is *Okamezasa* (*Dwarf Bamboo,* 1920). The title, as he explained in a prefatory note, bore no relation to the content of the work. He had been experiencing unusual difficulty in giving the novel a title, even after completing ten installments for serialization. One day, just after he had been discussing with a gardener an order for dwarf bamboo to be planted along the hedge, an editor appeared to claim the manuscript. Without further thought, Kafū gave it the title *Dwarf Bamboo.* As a matter of fact, the title is a suitable image for the central character of the work, a man of no distinction who survives and even flourishes, rather like the dwarf bamboo, a hardy though insignificant perennial.

Dwarf Bamboo is the story of Uzaki Kyoseki, an unsuccessful painter. As a boy he became the servant of the famous artist Uchiyama Kaiseki, and eventually drifted into his master's profession, though he himself had no talent. His devotion extends even to the master's worthless son, Kan, who depends on Kyoseki to clean up the mess left in the wake of escapades with geishas and other women, to all of whom he promises marriage. By the end of *Dwarf Bamboo* we have learned that every character in the novel is corrupt, each in his chosen or predestined manner. Kyoseki accidentally discovers that his own inept paintings are being sold as original works by Kaiseki, apparently with Kaiseki's collusion. The girl whom Kan eventually marries, though she comes from a distinguished family, breaks down one night and reveals she is illegitimate. This disclosure precipitates a bout of hysterics, to which she is congenitally susceptible. Kan's unstable character stems not only from having been spoiled as an only son, but from

the traits he has inherited from his father. Kimiyū, a geisha who seemed to be genuinely in love with Kan, is interested in him only professionally, and the letter she sends describing her misery at having been abandoned was composed solely for business motives; two months later she has even forgotten that she sent it. Kan's father-in-law, for all his pompous airs as a former governor, sells fake antiques that he mixes with genuine ones and passes off on unwary buyers who assume that anything purchased from so distinguished a man must be authentic. Kyoseki is rewarded with bribes and a position of art consultant. At the end everybody is happy except Kan's wife, who dies of the venereal disease he transmitted to her. Kan is sent to America to get him out of the way for a while; Kyoseki, prospering as a connoisseur, visits every day a geisha whom he has set up in business.

Dwarf Bamboo is an exceptionally successful Japanese example of Naturalism in the French style. Not only are the familiar themes of heredity and environment prominent, but the corruption within each person is unsparingly revealed. But there is a difference too. *Dwarf Bamboo* is marked throughout by an irony rare in the novels of the Naturalist tradition. Kafū shows no respect for any of his characters, but he does not hate them either. The venal Kyoseki is even rather appealing, and it would be hard to imagine any reader begrudging him his ill-gotten fortune. Kohana, the geisha whom Kyoseki set up in business, is described in a tone typical of the entire work:

> Over the long years Kohana had become completely inured to her profession, and now did not think of it as being especially unpleasant but, on the other hand, it was not particularly interesting either. The nature of the business was such that as long as she had customers it did not make much difference who they were. She had lost all feelings of preference with respect to old or young, handsome or ugly, but she did seem to feel apprehension as a woman when she thought of her future, and she wanted a man she could call her own, no matter how ugly he might be, a man with whom she could relax a little and have her own way with once in a while. Never having been clever enough to trick a man out of his money, she preferred a quiet, kindly man to the dangerous kind of customer who cuts a great swathe and everybody makes a fuss over. She entertained the extremely modest hope that it would be wonderful if, when she was really in desperate need, she could obtain from that man a little pocket money.

Kohana might have been portrayed by another kind of novelist as a victim, both of her family's poverty and of her inherited stupidity, but Kafū does not think of her as especially to be pitied. She has slid into a way of life that is now the only possible one for her and, considering her temperament, perhaps that is just as well. Chikamatsu would have treated such a woman quite differently. Certainly he would not have dwelled on her least attractive traits, and he might have found a meaning for Kohana's unimportant life in the love she had at last discovered for a customer, even one so unprepossessing as Kyoseki. Kafū would not make such concessions: Kohana admired

Kyoseki more than her other customers because he kept his promise to visit her again, but she was definitely not in love with him. For that matter, Kyoseki's decision to give Kohana the money she needed to open her own geisha house was less an indiction of love than of embarrassment over having earlier accepted a bribe.

Hardly a single action described by Kafū in *Dwarf Bamboo* would stand up to conventional moral examination, but he was not trying, in the manner of a true Naturalist, to expose the sordid motives of the people whose lives he treated; with the cynical humor of a man who has never had any illusions, he revealed that all the factors that are commonly said to make life worthwhile are deceptions. The world Kafū depicts contains no love, no honesty, no religion, no respect for family, no sense of social obligation, no deference toward art. Decency is never rewarded, but sometimes there are rewards for complicity or even for out-and-out corruption. In the hands of another writer *Dwarf Bamboo* could easily have developed into a bitter exposé, but Kafū writes so engagingly, with so many wry touches, that for most readers this novel is a comic masterpiece.

"Ame Shōshō" ("Quiet Rain," 1921), Kafū's next important work, has been acclaimed by some critics as the summit of his entire body of works. It is treated as a work of fiction, though it contains hardly a single novelistic element. The narrator is a man of means and education who brings to mind Kafū in his fondness for the literature and music of the Edo period and sometimes also in biographical details. Kimpu, as he is called, exchanges views with an old crony of similar tastes on the decline of the traditional music, the problems of setting up a separate household for a mistress, the ignorance young people display of the old traditions, and other subjects in this vein. For all the reader can tell, it may well be a factually accurate description of a period of Kafū's life, but this is not the point of "Quiet Rain"; the title suggests the general atmosphere not only of this story, which takes place during the rainy month of September, but of Japan itself. For Kafū, whose sensitivity to the weather is attested by almost everything he ever wrote, rain was the prevailing weather of Japan, the most characteristic setting for Japanese life. Rain, as the narrator tells us, is disagreeable when encountered outdoors, but even for a bachelor in a lonely house there is a special pleasure in reading old books to the sound of the rain outside.

During the decade after "Quiet Rain" Kafū wrote little that is recognizable as fiction. His writings suggest instead the antiquarian or the bibliographer, seemingly as the result of the influence of Mori Ōgai, whose *Shibue Chūsai* inspired Kafū to delve into the lives of similar figures of the Tokugawa period. Kimpu in "Quiet Rain" writes his friend, "I have quite given up my main work, writing novels. In order to discourage publishers, I ask the ridiculous price of a yen a word." No doubt it suited Kimpu (and Kafū) to cultivate his bunjin tastes, rather than bother himself with creating works of fiction.

Kafū's antiquarian tastes were nothing new, of course. *Hiyori Geta (Fair-Weather Geta,* 1915), which bears the

> Kafū rarely let his mind dwell on the darker aspects of traditional life. Instead, he described with compelling charm the wayside shrines, ancient trees, temples, rivers and canals, hills and cliffs, and even the sunsets that had remained unchanged in the modern city of Tokyo.
>
> *—Donald Keene*

subtitle "Promenades in Tokyo," is a record of his walks in the city in search of the lingering remains of the past. He states that his readings in the "light literature" of the Edo period induced him to begin these walks, and finds parallels between what he is doing and the dilettantism of certain French authors, though he, unlike the conscientious Frenchmen who recorded their observations of the Paris streets, totally lacks social concerns. Kafū was only thirty-six when he wrote *Fair-Weather Geta,* but he already thought of himself as a recluse with neither obligations nor responsibilities to society. His strolls were an expression of his independence: they required neither money nor companionship, and had no objective other than his own pleasure. He explained the reasons for his wandering in these terms:

> I do not take my strolls in order to admire the magnificent spectacle of the new city called Tokyo so as to discuss its aesthetic values, nor, for that matter, am I eagerly searching for remains of the old city that was called Edo in order to advocate its preservation. When people attempt today to preserve old art they only succeed in destroying its charm. It does not bother me if all they do is to surround the old shrines and temples with iron chains and put up the usual signboards warning, "It is forbidden to. . . ." But repairs carried out in the name of the preservation of old shrines and temples are tantamount to ruthless acts of destruction. I need not give examples here. That is why I feel quite satisfied if I can wander the streets aimlessly and scribble down whatever comes into my head. As long as one has the time, nothing is better than walking. It is certainly better than staying at home and despairing of the world at the sight of a wife's hysterical face, or of being assaulted by visits from newspaper and magazine reporters who leave the hibachi, which one has just cleaned, littered with the butts of their Shikishima cigarettes.

Kafū searched for buildings in the back streets that had been spared by modern city planners (and not yet destroyed by the earthquake of 1923). The kind of street he liked best was one that twisted for no reason, was lined with little, low houses and was not defaced by painted signboards or imitation Western architecture. He felt uneasy at every sign of new industries, the product of the age, but when he saw old people living on some poverty-stricken street in the manner they had always lived, he could not refrain from feeling not only sympathy but respect. And when it occurred to him that the daughters of such old people might be working as geishas somewhere, he was moved to reflections on the Japanese traditions of filial piety and the custom of women selling their bodies. However, Kafū rarely let his mind dwell on the darker aspects of traditional life. Instead, he described with compelling charm the wayside shrines, ancient trees, temples, rivers and canals, hills and cliffs, and even the sunsets that had remained unchanged in the modern city of Tokyo.

During the 1920s Kafū published a few stories, some volumes of researches into the careers of figures of the late Edo and early Meiji periods such as Narushima Ryūhoku and Ōnuma Chinzan, and various essays (*zuihitsu*). The earthquake of 1923, which so profoundly affected many writers, inspired Kafū to write one story, **"Kashima no Onna" ("The Woman in the Rented Room,"** 1926), an effective description of the city soon after the earthquake, though the story itself is unconvincing. The end of the decade was a particularly bleak period for Kafū, who wrote only one short story each in 1929 and 1930.

In 1931 Kafū returned to active literary composition. His sudden reemergence as an author is sometimes attributed to internal factors, but other scholars have associated it with the changed climate in the literary world that had resulted from governmental pressure directed at left-wing writers. Whatever the reasons for Kafū's reawakened interest in fiction, it did not last long; after the cluster of works that appeared in 1931, he again lapsed into a silence that was broken only by occasional essays and a story published in 1934. The second period of silence has been attributed to Kafū's dismay over the outbreak of war in Manchuria, the suppression of the Communist party, the May 15 Incident, and so on, but probably was occasioned mainly by a loss of interest in writing. In any case, the works of 1931, the single story of 1934, and the one major work that appeared in 1937 represented almost all of Kafū's published output of fiction between 1930 and 1945.

"Ajisai" ("Hydrangea"), the first of the 1931 stories, enjoys a high reputation among Japanese critics, probably because of the effortless manner of narration. The story is hardly compelling, and the ending so melodramatic as to recall Ken'yūsha fiction. Perhaps the great admiration for **"Hydrangea"** was an expression of pleasure at hearing again so distinctive a voice as Kafū's. The story, related in the objective manner of French Naturalism, describes a man's infatuation with a low-class geisha for whom he feels mingled contempt and longing. At the end, just at the point where he has decided to kill her and has even bought a knife for the purpose, another man anticipates him. It is hard to imagine what attracted Kafū to this theme.

Tsuyu no Atosaki (Before and After the Rains), published later in 1931, is a far superior work; indeed, it ranks as one of Kafū's finest achievements. The central character, Kimie, is a familiar Kafū figure: she has become a waitress (a euphemism at the time for an unlicensed prostitute) not because of desperate poverty or because she grew up in an environment that led her to take up such employment, but because she enjoys the profession. Kimie left her home in the country in order to avoid marrying a boring man, and

ran away to Tokyo. For a while she went through the motions of working for an insurance company, but before long she found more congenial employment at the Don Juan, a smart café where men of wealth made assignations with the waitresses. Her happiness in her chosen calling is marred by a series of untoward events. First, someone slit the sleeve of her kimono. Next, a dead kitten was discovered in her wardrobe. Finally, an anonymous article in a scandal sheet mentioned that the two moles on her inner thigh have now become three, a development known only to Kimie herself and two male admirers. Worried, she consults a fortune-teller, who is unable to calm her fears. Later we discover that the culprit responsible for these incidents was the novelist Kiyooka, a successful though not a good writer. Kiyooka is Kimie's lover, despite his being married and also keeping an actress on the side. He had supposed Kimie was faithful to him, but one night he followed her to a house of assignation (*machiai*) and, in the manner familiar from other Kafū stories, he peeped in on Kimie to discover that she and another woman were helping to divert an elderly man. This sight comes as such a shock that Kiyooka determines to take revenge on Kimie.

Kiyooka seems to be a cruel self-portrait by Kafū; in other respects Kafū's alter ego is Kiyooka's father, a retired professor of Chinese literature who lives to the west of Tokyo. The other characters include Kiyooka's wife, a rarity among Kafū's female characters in that she comes from a good family and resents her husband's philandering, and various men who are current or past lovers of Kimie. The exceptional praise that *Before and After the Rains* won from discriminating critics was occasioned chiefly by the novelistic interest. The detached analysis of a group of people makes the story read like a work of French Naturalism, though a few passages, mainly those relating to Kiyooka's father, evoke the beauty of place and season in the typical Kafū manner. Kimie is neither lovable nor pitiful, but the reader does not despise her either, and her last gesture, giving herself to an old man out of compassion, recalls the courtesan's generosity, as described in a work of Edo fiction.

Soon after *Before and After the Rains* appeared [the novelist Tanizaki Jun'ichirō] wrote a review in which he pointed out the similarities between this novel and those of the Ken'yūsha in the use of coincidences, the insistence on plot, and the shallowness of the psychological insights. Tanizaki thought it ironic too that, a dozen or more years after the official demise of Japanese Naturalism, Kafū had written a work that proved that Naturalism—at least in the manner of Maupassant—was still a valid approach to the world. He was impressed especially by what he termed the "local color"—the minor characters who make brief appearances but lend an indisputably authentic tone to the work. Tanizaki concluded by expressing surprise that a writer like Kafū, who constantly turned to the past for inspiration, never went back further than the early nineteenth century. Why, he wondered, could Kafū not discover something of interest in the Genroku or even in the Muromachi periods? No doubt this criticism reflected Tanizaki's own interests at this stage, when he was writing such works as *The Blind Man's Tale,* but the point was well taken, and served to define the limitations of what

Kafū derived from the Japanese past; he was the last of the gesaku writers.

Before and After the Rains is absorbing throughout, even though it lacks the beauty of Kafū's early work, and even though it reveals little of what twentieth-century writers had been striving to achieve in new forms of expression. Kafū's exceptional ability to summon up place and atmosphere—in this case, the world of Kimie during the rainy season—is nowhere more effectively displayed, but it is difficult to feel empathy with the characters, who are portrayed with what might be termed excessive fidelity. Kafū may have been impelled to write *Before and After the Rains* in his capacity as the chronicler of disappearing Tokyo because he feared that cafés and waitresses might not survive the rigors of a national emergency such as the war in China, but readers of a later generation are likely to decide that this would have been no great loss: Kimie and her friends arouse little nostalgia.

Kafū's next important work, *Hikage no Hana (Flowers in the Shade,* 1934), was based on the account he had heard a few years later from a man who, by his own testimony, had lived off women his entire life. This short novel describes various people who are "flowers in the shade"—women and men whose lives are spent in the obscurity of the world of unlicensed prostitutes, café waitresses, and the like. The story is related largely in flashbacks, a device Kafū often employed. The reader sometimes gets the impression that the incidents related in these flashbacks are there not because of what they contribute to the story so much as because they had actually occurred. For example, when Jūkichi, the kept man, recalls how he first slid into this way of life, he describes in quite unnecessary detail the backgrounds of two relatives who appeared to claim their share of an estate, though these persons never again figure in the story. No doubt Jūkichi or anyone else might recall with mysterious clarity such extraneous information, but it is hardly essential to the narration. In the end, however, we may feel that such details, by contributing verisimilitude, have helped to make us forget the creaky mechanism of coincidence that otherwise carries along the plot.

Flowers in the Shade is another example of Kafū's special variety of Naturalism. He makes us see and all but smell the dingy rooms he describes, without ever allowing us to pass judgment on them or their inhabitants. Kafū neither approves nor disapproves of his characters, and if he tells us in detail about their past it is not in order to demonstrate how environment and heredity have determined their lives, though this was probably true, but to assuage our curiosity as to how Jūkichi came to live off women, how a particular woman happened to become a prostitute or a procuress, and so on. Despite the flaws of narration, *Flowers in the Shade* is unquestionably the work of an exceptional writer.

Kafū's next work of fiction, *Bokutō Kitan (A Strange Tale from East of the River),* published in 1937, has often been praised as Kafū's finest work. It was closely based on personal experiences, as we can surmise from the care with which he corrected minor errors of fact when the work was reprinted. Kafū seems to have been guided equally by Mori Ōgai's passion for historical accuracy and by Zola's inveterate habit of carrying out endless observations before putting pen to paper. *A Strange Tale* is a surpassingly beautiful example of Kafū's style and the most affecting expression of his longing for the vanishing past. This longing now embraced the Meiji period, which he had hated in his youth; the passage of time and the rapid deterioration of manners had enabled him at last to understand what was unique and genuine in that period.

The narrator, once again an alter ego of Kafū, is a collector of old magazines, old kimonos, old lore about the past. One day he wanders into the Tamanoi Quarter, a section of dilapidated houses from which unlicensed prostitutes call to passing men. It starts to rain, and a woman asks to shelter under his umbrella. By way of thanks she invites him into her house and they chat for a time together. Oyuki, as she is called, is reluctant to discuss her past, but he is intrigued by the little clues she gives. He returns often to Tamanoi, finding in this street forgotten by time a refuge from the noisy radios blaring from open windows in his own neighborhood:

> It was not the humble quarter of the twentieth century; it rather brought the far-off sadness of the past, the sadness one feels in the Kabuki plays of Tsuruya Namboku, for instance.
>
> The figure of Oyuki, her hair always in one of the old styles, and the foulness of the canal, and the humming of the mosquitoes—all of these stirred me deeply, and called up visions of a past now dead some thirty or forty years.

There is also a subplot to *A Strange Tale,* in the manner of Gide's *Les faux-monnayeurs:* the narrator is writing a novel, of which one chapter and several other excerpts are given in the course of *A Strange Tale.* It was partly in order to perfect his knowledge of the setting for this story that the narrator visited Tamanoi so often. The novel is never completed, and *A Strange Tale* itself ends inconclusively, but on exactly the right note, with a poem in free verse that tells of the end of summer, the last of the mosquitoes, and the coming of the first frost. Oyuki disappears from the narrator's life without either ever learning the other's identity. It was an unforgettable interlude for the narrator, if only because Oyuki has temporarily served as his muse, a muse "who had accidentally called back into a dulled heart shadows of the past. If she had not been drawn to me, or if I had not thought she was, I would without doubt have torn up the manuscript that had long been waiting on my desk."

A Strange Tale deserves its reputation as one of Kafū's best works, though it defies most of the prescriptions for effective writing. Its success depended on Kafū's ability to evoke the derelict Tamanoi Quarter, where the past lingered in the battered old houses. Oyuki is not drawn in the round, but that was not Kafū's intent. Her beauty, reminiscent of the illustrations found in books of the Edo period, and her conversations, trivial but curiously affecting, are just right for the story; and the season, the hot Tokyo summer, lends a heavy, indolent atmosphere. *A Strange Tale* enjoyed great popularity while it was being serialized in a newspaper, and the critics acclaimed the completed book when it appeared in August 1937, though this was on the heels of the outbreak of the China Incident.

The times were not propitious for Kafū to continue writing in the vein of his recent triumph. The government became less and less tolerant of frivolous writing, as it deemed Kafū's works to be, and even editors who normally would have been delighted to publish anything that Kafū wrote refrained from asking for manuscripts. As a consequence, Kafū published extremely few works of fiction from this time until after the war had ended in 1945. Although he in no way opposed the war in China or in the Pacific, his devotion to the past, rather than to Japan's glorious present, and his fondness for describing women of the demimonde, rather than heroic women who inspire their sons and husbands to do battle, led the authorities to judge that he was their enemy, and they were right. Kafū wrote absolutely nothing in support of the war or even in mourning for its victims. His diary is filled with expressions of contempt for the militarists and their policies. Even during the war years, however, he went on writing, though with no prospect of publication as long as the war lasted.

In 1946, when literary activity resumed after the hiatus of the war years, Kafū at once moved into the limelight, thanks to his backlog of manuscripts. He published in that year *Kunshō* (*The Decoration*), written in 1942; *Ukishizumi* (*Sinking and Swimming*), written in 1942; *Odoriko* (*The Dancing Girl*), written in 1944; and *Towazugatari* (*A Tale No One Asked For*), written in 1944-1945. These works are all of interest, and Kafū's audience became larger than ever before, but they added little to his lasting reputation.

One other work of importance was published after the war, his diary *Danchōtei Nichijō,* kept from 1917 to 1959. During the worst of the bombings Kafū's first concern—after his own life—was with saving the manuscript of the diaries, which he kept constantly by his side. Of all his works Kafū thought most highly of these diaries, and some critics concur in this judgment, whether because they are impressed by Kafū's observations or because they admire the severely concise style. Even if one is reluctant to rate the diaries above the three or four works of fiction for which Kafū will surely be remembered, they are an important literary achievement and occupy a distinguished place in the development of a peculiarly Japanese genre. Kafū's diaries were clearly meant for publication, and he was careful to reveal of himself only what he wanted readers to know. In his wartime diaries, for example, he omitted all mention of the terror that the bombings inspired in him. Some critics believe that he tampered with the diaries before they were published, adjusting his opinions to the climate of a later day. Certain overtly antimilitaristic sentiments, which a man as prudent as Kafū might have hesitated to put down on paper during the war, are among the most intriguing parts of the diaries, but whether the diaries are taken at face value or read as works of fiction, rather in the manner of *A Strange Tale from East of the River,* they are of exceptional interest.

Kafū continued writing stories almost to the end of his life. Most of the late works are without literary importance, though they contain occasional flashes of the old Kafū. In his advanced years he became celebrated for his eccentricities, which tended to overshadow his literary activity. He died alone, as he had lived for many years, unmourned but not forgotten by his many admirers. . . . (pp. 420-36)

Donald Keene, "Nagai Kafū," in his Dawn to the West, Japanese Literature of the Modern Era: Fiction, Vol. 1, *Holt, Rinehart and Winston, 1984, pp. 386-440.*

Jay Rubin (essay date 1984)

[*Rubin is a translator and professor of Japanese literature. In the excerpt below, he examines the reasons for and effects of state censorship on Kafū's writings.*]

It came as a shock . . . to Nagai Kafū and the publisher of his **French Stories** (**Furansu monogatari**) when that large volume, containing over five hundred fifty pages of fiction, drama, impressionistic sketches, and essays, much of which had been published in periodicals, was banned on the very day it was submitted to the censors. This was probably on March 22, 1909, since the colophon of the few copies in "temporary binding" that survived shows a publication date of March 25. In any event, the police confiscated the newly printed volumes so quickly that not a single copy could be distributed to the bookstores. "From *their* point of view, it was a great success," remarked Kafū dryly. The publishing company lost its entire investment and made the "outrageous" demand that Kafū repay his royalty on the first edition.

Since most of the other pieces in the volume had been published in periodicals without incident, Kafū assumed that the story **"Dissipation"** (**"Hōtō"**) and the play **"Love in a Foreign Land"** (**"Ikyō no koi"**), both previously unpublished and given special prominence as the first two works in the book, were at fault. Of course, the mere fact that the police had overlooked something in a magazine was no guarantee that it would measure up to their standards the second time around. . . . An examination of some of the other stories and their subsequent publishing history suggests that these two pieces were not alone in catching the censor's eye.

The dissipation in the story of that title was doubtless considered objectionable because it involved no ordinary citizen but a government official, a young Japanese diplomat stationed in Paris. So disillusioned has he become with his country, his work, and even with the prostitutes whose aid he has sought in attempting to drown his sorrows, that he would like to commit suicide. "His is not the bravura manner, however, and we leave him hoping to be run down by a streetcar," notes Edward Seidensticker [in his *Kafū the Scribbler*]. "The story is a very wordy one, and it must have been still wordier when the industrious censor pushed his way through it."

But Seidensticker was reading the story in the 1948 complete works version, by which time it had been restored to something approximating its original form. It had been excluded from both the 1915 revised (i.e., expurgated) version of *French Stories* and the 1919 complete works, but Kafū published it in a 1923 collection with the new title "Clouds" ("Kumo") and containing ten suppressed passages with *fuseji* [symbols indicating a censor's deletion] totaling 510 characters—or about a page's worth. The second edition of the complete works was published in 1926 at the height of the "Taishō democracy" years, when censorship policy was generally more liberal, and "Clouds" was included among the *French Stories* for the first time. Even more remarkable, seven of its suppressed passages were restored. That text has since remained standard, but the editors of the Iwanami complete works (1962-1965) have supplied the three missing passages in their notes. Of the three, only one is erotic, briefly describing the heat of a nearby fire against naked flesh. The other two passages question the value of serving the country and assert that the only reports of the Russo-Japanese War that ever made it through censorship were reports of victory.

Seidensticker describes "Love in a Foreign Land" as "the sort of play one can scarcely imagine seeing performed. It has to do with a young Japanese who commits suicide with a young American lady, and another young Japanese who goes over the whole problem very articulately and finally returns to Japan, 'where human emotions are killed.'" Kafū himself assumed that the following speech mocking the glories of Meiji civilization had something to do with the censors' decision:

> Ladies and gentlemen. I am grateful to be allowed the honor of introducing the up-to-date Japanese Empire to my dear American friends. . . . It is so peaceful a country that drunken gentlemen sleep happily in gutters. The state and the police and the people are as close as parents and children. Wherever the people gather, therefore, at political meetings, at performances of various sorts, at athletic contests, there the police are in their grand uniforms, a source of boundless popular pride. . . . Wishing to make the earth in which their ancestors sleep as rich as possible, the Japanese decline to build sewers, but rather see to it that the last drop of sewage sinks into the earth and is not lost in the maws of fishes.

Kafū also suggests that the police censor may have been disturbed by an exchange in which America is blamed for the vulgarization of Japan. Another unflattering view of Japan was contained in the story "Revulsion" ("Akkan"), which had been printed earlier in 1909 but which did not resurface until its postwar inclusion in the complete works—with a new title: "A Few Hours in Singapore" ("Shingapōru no sūjikan").

At this rate, there seem to have been more diplomatic and political than moral elements involved in the banning of *French Stories,* despite the official rationale. "Love in a Foreign Land" and "Revulsion" were not even reprinted in the daring 1926 complete works, and in fact the play had to wait until the publication of the drama volume of the postwar complete works in 1953 before it could join a definitive edition of Kafū. Readers in 1909 were not entirely deprived of these works, however: an article in the May *Waseda Bungaku* protesting the banning of *French Stories* gave detailed summaries of both.

"Dissipation" and "Love in a Foreign Land" were probably not the only pieces that the censors objected to in March 1909. "Dance" ("Butō", later "Yowa no butō" or "Midnight Dance") and "The Dancer" ("Maihime"; originally "Opera no maihime" or "Opera Dancer") had appeared together in a magazine in December 1908. They would not be included uncut in *French Stories* until the 1926 complete works, probably owing to the glimpses of bare thigh in "Dance" and the narrator's still more physical longing for a dancer on the Lyon opera stage: "This yearning can only be assuaged on that night when you allow my hands and lips to caress your tender flesh." The vignette "Past Noon" ("Hirusugi") had not been published before and was never seen in print until 1948, in the postwar complete works. This short piece evokes the narrator's dreamlike mood when he awakens in the late afternoon to find the ravishing Paulette sleeping naked on his arm (presumably after a night of passionate lovemaking): "Your opulent breast rests against my cheek like a ripe fruit about to fall." Japan needed forty years to prepare itself for such unbridled eroticism. (Or perhaps the censors had better literary judgment than they were given credit for. The volume, full of "young artists . . . bent on parodying themselves," [according to Seidensticker] might have been banned for offensive silliness. What else but good sense could explain the elimination of "Worshipping the Statue of Maupassant" ["Mōpasan no sekizō o hai-su"] from all but the postwar editions? Kafū's abject prostration of himself before the image of Maupassant is almost embarrassing.)

Having spent his anger on the previous year's bannings of Molière and Zola, Kafū told a newspaper reporter, the suppression of his own work did not come as such a dreadful shock. He did not see how either "Dissipation" or "Love in a Foreign Land" could disrupt the public morality, but he concluded that "my thoughts on the matter are irrelevant." He was, he said, just a weak poet facing a strong government. No Japanese has ever fought for his rights in court as Flaubert, Baudelaire and others did to bring French art to its present state of freedom. I know, he continued, that the proper thing to do now is fight, but when I consider my chances of winning, I recall the general tone of freedom-loving French society, where art is highly prized: "If an author is going to struggle with the authorities for his rights, he must have sympathy derived from the general drift of society." Contemporary Japanese society has no great need for either freedom or art. The only ones who demand these are the few stepchildren of society who may have read Western books. The majority are pleased to have Japan's glory rest on military accomplishments.

Kafū had two more occasions to express himself on censorship that year, and each time he stressed his identification with the stepchildren of society, the sensitive young artists in a hostile land. "As a writer, I have no particular thoughts regarding the suppression of a literary work in Japan," Kafū told an interviewer in the July 1909 *Chūō Kōron* after the June issue had been banned for Oguri

Fūyō's story "Big Sister's Little Sister" ("Ane no imōto"). "The authorities don't read our stories and novels as literature or art: they treat them strictly as 'printed matter.'" He went on to say that writers neither knew nor needed to know the standards employed by the authorities. "We who publish fiction and the authorities who suppress it live in different worlds." Rather cynically, Kafū noted that they had banned Fūyō's story because "they wanted to, that is all. Of course, this sort of incident is deplorable for Japanese literature, but that is true only for those few of us who comprise the society of writers; for the state, which declines to recognize the existence of fiction and the other arts, it is simply a matter of course. . . . For them, fiction is nothing but a filthy abscess. . . . In order for the state to recognize the existence of art, the people must first come to respect art." In another interview, Kafū added, "If we simply write what we believe and the authorities act on their perceptions, I see no objection to that. But as the age progresses, this problem will become increasingly difficult and will eventually have to be brought to some sort of conclusion."

Kafū himself was not prepared to force the issue, and while he implied that writers ought to take the censors to court, he knew very well that there existed no judicial apparatus by which this could be done. In the end, faced with an impossible situation, Kafū could only conclude that writers and policemen lived in two separate worlds, that art was an irrelevancy, a means of escape. He concluded this and concluded this and concluded this over and over and over again in fiction, poetry, essays, and interviews until he had fashioned for himself and the public a unique persona embodying his bitter rejection of all that was respectable and thus acceptable to the state. There may well have been useless outsiders in Japan who dabbled in Edo art and erotica because they felt there was no place for them in the authoritarian state, but we do not know about them. They did not make a public career of it as Kafū did. "Look at me," his works say, "I am useless in your ugly, materialistic, hypocritical police state." Call it a pose; call it a rationalization for cowardice (although the fact is that most of his countrymen would have supported the censors all the way); the one thing that Kafū's stance did *not* represent was smug self-satisfaction. He tells us what he is escaping from and why. Nor is he afraid to admit that the escape is not completely satisfactory.

A story Kafū published in July 1909 is of interest both as an early example of the persona that Kafū spent his life creating and as a concrete demonstration of the kinds of steps taken by writers and editors to deal with the censors. While it does tend to be "wordy" and "diffuse," as Seidensticker says, **"Pleasure" ("Kanraku")** is a simple narrative of three love affairs in the life of a writer in his forties as told to a younger associate. The theme is the collision between passion and reality, and in the course of spelling out the decline of passion in his life, the writer provides—at the cost of narrative cohesion, to be sure—something of a theory of art as practiced by Nagai Kafū.

It should be kept in mind that we have the story in four forms: (1) the magazine galley proofs with editorial markings; (2) the text as published in the magazine, which (to confuse matters) *was* banned, but not for **"Pleasure"**; (3) the text as it appeared in the book **Pleasure,** published on September 20, 1909, which was also quickly banned, apparently owing to the title piece and one or two other stories; and (4) the modern text.

As presented in **"Pleasure,"** the writer (or "poet") lives for emotion, for recreating the profound, selfless ecstasy aroused by the sensual experience of life in all its varied forms:

> For me, there is nothing else but this passion, this desire to sing—without purpose or plan—of the whole of life and nature as my eyes have seen it and my heart has felt it. . . . To write good poetry, one must prize solitude. One must insulate oneself from family encumbrances, from the sanctions of society. . . . Now, I am utterly indifferent to what my family thinks of me. I am a poet; they are ordinary human beings. We belong to different lands, different races. Neither do I feel anger toward the state for its treatment of art. It was my choice and mine alone to rebel against parents and teachers and become a poet, a man unneeded—indeed, violently suppressed—by the state. . . . The state may try, with the sickle of the law, to cut poets down to nothing, but they can never succeed: we are like weeds that shoot up after the rain. . . . We are non-citizens, . . . and so I have lived alone in rooms and chosen not to mix with people of good family. My only park has been the streets of shame and degradation, my only gospel Baudelaire's *Flowers of Evil.* . . . Not even the birds could match my freedom, for I was not merely indifferent to the welfare of my parents and to whether my brothers were alive or dead: I truly paid no heed to my own tomorrow.

The magazine editor took most of this in stride, but he apparently felt that in the last sentence Kafū had gone too far, for the original manuscript read, "I was not merely indifferent to whether my parents might die or *the country might perish (kuni no sonbō)*." Kafū wrote a note in the margin of the galley proofs saying he saw no objection to the italicized phrase, but that the editor could suppress it with *fuseji* if he wished—which he did. The modern text quoted above follows the phraseology as Kafū rewrote it shortly afterward for the book—which, of course, was banned anyway.

In this story about the pleasures of love for a writer determined to live life fully and sensually, several passages had to be composed with an eye to the censor. Kafū claimed in one interview that he never wrote with such questions in mind but left those decisions to the editor or publisher. This was not entirely true in practice, as the following passages demonstrate: "At dawn, the weather suddenly turned cold, *and in our sleep we tightened our embrace, pressing our bodies together ever more closely,* until at length we awoke from the sheer discomfort." The italicized section was crossed out in the galley proof, becoming *fuseji* in the magazine. The book and the modern text read: "At dawn, the weather suddenly turned cold, and feeling this we awoke." Another passage originally read as follows: "I would sit by a window or a pillar of the veranda, *arms folded as I felt her leaning against me, the warmth of her skin seeping through the soft silk of my sleeping robe.* And I would gaze at the shapes of the trees." The proof page containing this and the sentence previously quoted has a marginal note from the editor asking Kafū to revise the marked passages. Here again, the magazine substituted *fuseji* for the italicized section, and Kafū later rewrote the sentence as follows: "Folding my arms across the soft silk of my sleeping robe, I would sit by a pillar of the veranda or a window, and gaze at the shapes of the trees." This revision appeared in the banned book and appears in the modern text of the complete works.

Having been angered by the publisher's demand for repayment of his first edition royalty on **French Stories,** Kafū was doubly gratified—and obligated—when the publisher of **Pleasure** (a different company) made no mention of his returning their advance of one hundred yen. He had submitted his manuscript in good faith, assuming that the previous untroubled publication of all nine stories meant no risk was involved. He immediately submitted a safer manuscript when the book was suppressed, and in late October of 1909 (just one month after the publication date of **Pleasure**) *A Kafū Anthology* (*Kafū shū*)) was published with six of the nine stories and one additional piece. Missing were **"Pleasure,"** plus a moving prose-poem on another Kafū-style social misfit entitled **"Behind the Prison"** (**"Kangokusho no ura"**) and a story with a checkered past entitled **"A Toast"** (**"Shukuhai"**).

Like Masamune Hakuchō's 1908 story "Where?," **"Behind the Prison"** might be seen as another predecessor to Sōseki's *And Then,* the ultimate portrait of a young Meiji intellectual too aware of his society's hypocrisy to become its willing participant. *And Then* would begin serialization in June 1909. Sōseki's protagonist, like the narrator of **"Behind the Prison"** (March 1909), would also be a thirty-year-old supported by a wealthy, sternly moralistic father and unable even to conceive of a suitable profession. In both works the change of the seasons plays a major role, but the seasons are primarily a backdrop to Sōseki's Westernized love melodrama. In Kafū's more traditional, contemplative short story the delicate, sensual perception of seasonal change becomes the central concern. Kafū has neither the space nor the intellectual apparatus for the extended development of ideas seen in the Sōseki novel, but **"Behind the Prison"** is not lacking in sharp social commentary. Here is one passage that may have excluded the story from the safer anthology:

> I thought of becoming an artist. But no, Japan is Japan, not the West. Japanese society does not need artists; indeed, it finds them a nuisance. The state has established education-by-intimidation and forces us to learn grotesque languages made up of sounds that no member of the Yamato Race ever pronounced—T, V, D, F. And if you can't say them, you have no right to exist in Meiji society. They have done this in the hopes that someday we will be able to invent some new-style torpedo or gun, certainly not to have us read the poems of Verlaine or Mallarmé—and still less to have us sing the "Marseillaise" or the "Internationale," with their messages of revolution and pacifism.

Such observations were not arbitrarily inserted into the protagonist's mouth but were to be understood as the rationale both for his subdued lifestyle and for the somber tone of the whole. [In "Konnen no tokuchō mittsu," *Bunshō sekai*, December, 1909] Uchida Roan was only reaffirming his antipathy toward escapist literature when he enthusiastically endorsed **"Behind the Prison,"** hailing Kafū as Japan's "first authentic artist in the European sense": not an irrelevant entertainer, but "a man who draws the pure air of creativity from the foul stench of real life."

The other story excluded from *A Kafū Anthology*, **"A Toast,"** tells us less about the author than about the uses of *fuseji*. If moralistic critics needed any proof that the young could be corrupted by what they read, **"A Toast"** was it. The protagonist of this ugly little piece learns most of what he needs to know about sex from Edo erotica, modern novels, medical textbooks, and newspapers—plus variety theater performances and advice from his barber. Then he goes on to the whorehouses and searches for other ways to fulfill his "low, shameful, selfish desire" to fool around with women while he is still a student and unprepared to commit himself to anything permanent. His most despicable act is to help his similarly cultivated friend, Iwasa, hide out from the waitress whom Iwasa has made pregnant. Ten years go by, and Iwasa, now a respectable bank employee with a family of his own, hears that the waitress had a miscarriage and has become a prosperous madame. He cries out in joy to his friend, "We

Kafū in 1950 beside a poster advertising the movie version of one of his burlesque skits.

must have a toast! . . . My old sins are obliterated! . . . If only I had known, my conscience wouldn't have bothered me all these years!" It is unclear at the end whether we are meant to join in the two men's laughter or condemn them for their hypocrisy.

With its ambiguous moral stance, **"A Toast"** leaves a bad aftertaste, and it received mixed reviews when it appeared in the May 1909 *Chūō Kōron*. Several reviewers mentioned the unusually large number of suppressed passages. Apparently there were suggestions that many of these *fuseji* had been inserted in obviously innocuous places merely for the sake of arousing the reader's curiosity, and that because **"A Toast"** had been such a big hit for *Chūō Kōron,* the magazine was planning to print an even bolder piece in June with even more *fuseji*. "We were shocked at such slanderous notions," said the editors, "but even more shocking are the rumors that the police believed such articles and waited, ready to pounce on the next issue the very day it appeared." The editors related this in a special appendix to the July issue devoted to the banning of the previous month's issue for Fūyō's "Big Sister's Little Sister." "We are worshippers of literature and we are law-abiding citizens," they continued. "Thus we took the step of inserting a few *fuseji* in 'A Toast,' a fine piece of fiction, in order to make it harmonize with the law of the land. We agonized over each phrase, discussing it among ourselves for half a day."

But **"A Toast"** had more than just "a few" *fuseji,* and some of them may well have been inserted gratuitously. *Chūō Kōron* is justly admired as a last bastion of liberal thought in the 1940s, but at this stage in its career—and especially in comparison with *Taiyō*—it was not an entirely serious magazine. Much of the hoopla it raised over literary censorship, beginning with the Fūyō appendix, seems to have been more in the interest of commercial gain than intellectual freedom.

A few examples of *fuseji* in the *Chūō Kōron* version of **"A Toast"** will serve to suggest the editors' approach. The narrator's nocturnal restlessness frequently brings him to bookstores, where, after some hesitation, he becomes "bolder and increasingly shameless, ardently poring over ******* books of fiction, art, or ********** medicine and such, not only for the momentary relief they provided, but in a calculated attempt to gain knowledge for future experimentation." In the modern complete works, the first omission has been filled in with "all sorts of," and the second—into which it would be grammatically impossible to fit anything much worse than nouns such as "anatomy" or "physiology"—has simply been eliminated. In the modern text, the description of the narrator's first encounter with a prostitute moves directly from his awkward attempts at sophistication beforehand to his leaving the pleasure quarters the next morning, describing nothing in between. The magazine version is equally reticent, but it underscores the silence with a full column of dots. A little later in the text, the word "experienced" has been turned into *fuseji*.

The censors could not have been ignorant of all the controversy surrounding **"A Toast"** and almost certainly banned *Pleasure* in part to make up for having missed the story the first time around. Apparently they took a bit more time to ban *Pleasure* than they had with *French Stories,* however. Enough copies were distributed for the book to be not only widely reviewed but eventually praised by *Waseda Bungaku* as the outstanding work of fiction for 1909.

Since *Waseda Bungaku* was supposed to be a naturalist journal, and since Kafū was supposed to be a decadent antinaturalist, this event gave rise to one of the most heated (if typically pointless) literary debates of the late Meiji years. The naturalists were accused of not knowing their own minds, and apologists for the magazine tried to prove that Kafū's writing was perfectly acceptable as naturalism (after all, he had started out as a Zolaist, hadn't he?). In other words, this theoretical war, which raged on for months during 1910, had as its object a book that could not legally be sold but which everyone seemed to have read. The fact that it had been banned was never made an issue, even by the *Waseda Bungaku* editors who honored Kafū. As with *French Stories,* the individual works eventually found their way into print, but the collection *Pleasure* was not reassembled in its original form until 1964, when the Iwanami publishers brought out volume 4 of the current complete works. (pp. 117-25)

[A contemporary reaction to repressive government policies, Nagai Kafū's *Death of a Scribbler (Gesakusha no shi)*] was begun late in 1912 and serialized in *Mita Bungaku* through April 1913, then extensively revised and republished the following year as *Willows Shedding Their Leaves at an Evening Window (Chiru yanagi mado no yūbae).*

Edward Seidensticker has noted that *Death of a Scribbler* was part of "an excursion, the only extended one of [Kafū's] career, into historical fiction," and he tends to minimize its contemporary relevance. But Kafū makes it clear that he intends this story of events set in 1842 to be read as a critique of his own day. At several points, characters mention the traditional technique of disguising a commentary on current events as historical fiction or drama—even painting, as if to remind the reader that that is exactly what Kafū is doing. And Kafū's protagonist, the Edo novelist Ryūtei Tanehiko (1783-1842), is in trouble with the authorities for having rewritten the eleventh-century classic, *The Tale of Genji,* as an indirect exposé of the contemporary ruler's decadence.

> Kafū's *Death of a Scribbler* was written by a man who had been doing a lot of thinking about his function as a writer living under an oppressive regime.
>
> —*Jay Rubin*

[According to Donald Keene in his *World Within Walls,*] the absurd aspect of the Tokugawa authorities' sudden interest in Tanehiko's *The False Murasaki and the Rustic*

Genji (*Nise-Murasaki inaka-Genji*) was that it was "a work that had begun to appear twelve years earlier, a book which was moreover not in objectionable taste." The change had occurred not in Tanehiko's writing, nor in any of the other artistic and social practices that the government was now finding objectionable (objectionable primarily because conspicuous consumption only demonstrated that the money was no longer in samurai hands): Kafū's point is that the sumptuary edicts of the Tenpō Reforms, which were robbing daily life of all color and enjoyment, were simply arbitrary changes inaugurated by an oppressive government.

Kafū portrays the authorities as devoid of sympathy for the suffering of the ordinary townspeople, caused in the hopes of restoring a puritanical atmosphere more appropriate to periods of war or natural disaster than to the peaceful Tokugawa period. The legendary phoenix has at last appeared to signal peace and prosperity, says one of Tanehiko's young disciples, and all the authorities want to do is wring its neck. The most a writer can do at times like this, he says, is subtly ridicule the authorities in comic poetry. But while waiting for restrictions to ease, an aging writer like Tanehiko might go blind, and—what is worse—the new crisis has aroused in him an anguish that cannot be joked away.

Tanehiko does not tell his disciples this, but he has just learned more than he bargained for from an inquiry to a friendly official concerning the likelihood of his being punished. Until recently, the official has been a comrade in dissipation, but he has suddenly become grave and duty-minded on learning that foreign "black ships" have been making alarming appearances at several ports. Tanehiko is shocked to see the change in his friend, and even more shocked to find that his own childhood samurai training still has a grip on his heart. For Tanehiko *is* a samurai. When the official asks Tanehiko to exploit his intimate knowledge of popular sentiment to help the ruling class explain the intent of the sumptuary regulations to the masses, he begins to regret that his frivolous life has rendered him useless in this threatening situation. Still, having long ago decided to throw in his lot with the people, unfettered as they are by official duties, he resents the government's sudden intrusions into their lives.

Everywhere he walks through Edo, Tanehiko sees the new regulations bearing down on the lives of the people, but he can do nothing to help. Years of cowardly artistic compromise have convinced him that protest would be useless. He turns from the present, where there is "only terror," and gives himself over to "profitless memories of the past." As if to emphasize the self-accusation of cowardice, Kafū has Tanehiko die of a stroke brought on by the arrival of a summons. (The exact circumstances of Tanehiko's death are not known.)

Death of a Scribbler was written by a man who had been doing a lot of thinking about his function as a writer living under an oppressive regime. More particularly, this was a writer from a respectable family who had consciously turned his back on establishmentarian hypocrisy to embrace a romantic conception of the demimonde as the only locus of true feeling. Kafū's conversion from "samurai"

to "townsman" was far from complete, however: there was still the nagging awareness that he ought to be "useful" in a manner that could be recognized by respectable society. This tension can probably be cited as the vital force behind all of Kafū's writing.

It is important to emphasize that Kafū's works do exhibit this tension. They are not the writings of an author who has settled comfortably in a groove. Kafū himself is wrong about his own works in the famous paragraph he penned in the 1919 essay **"Fireworks" ("Hanabi")** which seems so neatly to summarize the effect of the High Treason case [in which radicals were executed for allegedly plotting against the emperor] on his attitude toward his profession:

> In [1910], when I was teaching in Keiō University, I often chanced on my way to class to see five or six police wagons go past Yotsuya [carrying Kōtoku and the other defendants] to the Hibiya courthouse. Of all the public incidents I had witnessed or heard of, none had filled me with such loathing. I could not, as a man of letters, remain silent in this matter of principle. Had not the novelist Zola, pleading the truth in the Dreyfus Case, had to flee his country? But I, along with the other writers of my land, said nothing. The pangs of conscience that resulted were scarcely endurable. I felt intensely ashamed of myself as a writer. I concluded that I could do no better than drag myself down to the level of the Tokugawa writer of frivolous and amatory fiction. Arming myself with the tobacco pouch that was the mark of the old-style dandy, I set out to collect Ukiyoe prints, and I began to learn the samisen. It was a matter of no interest to such inferior persons as the writer of light Edo fiction or the maker of color prints that Perry's Black Ships had arrived at Uraga, or that Ii Kamon no Kami, Great Minister of the Shogunate, was assassinated at the castle gate. They thought it better to know their place and remain silent. Quite as if nothing had happened, they went on writing their indecent books and making their indecent prints.

But Kafū was no more successful at shutting out the real world than his Tanehiko had been, as demonstrated not only by his fiction (witness the omnipresent policemen in *A Strange Tale from East of the River* [*Bokutō kidan*, 1936-1937]) but by the essay **Fireworks** itself. It poses as an elegant little divertissement, but it is in fact a unified essay with a clearly stated theme.

It opens when the "pop" of distant fireworks reminds Kafū that most of Tokyo is off celebrating Armistice Day, while he is engaged in the elegant pastime of reading old letters and discarded manuscript sheets that he is using to patch a crumbling section of wall. He is moved to realize how withdrawn he has become from what interests most other people, and he goes on to make some astute observations. Celebrations such as today's are a modern phenomenon imported from the West and are quite distinct from traditional Shintō festivals. They are marked by pompous headlines, displays of the national flag, and huge crowds that invariably trample to death some child or old woman. And "beneath the surface of these modern festivals there usually lurks some ulterior political motive." Kafū describes his minimal relationship to several other examples of orchestrated nationalism and to various major public events, . . . remarking that official holidays bear a marked similarity to riots. One of the great successes of bureaucratically inspired nationalism, he says, was to bring out to the Taishō emperor's enthronement ceremony a large contingent of painted prostitutes—who were, unfortunately, set upon by the savage crowd and, in several instances, raped in broad daylight.

Seidensticker is surely correct when he says that Kafū "had never shown much sign of being a Zola," and "the common notion that the Kōtoku case was somehow crucial to Kafū's writings . . . has about it an ex-post-facto look." Granted, Kafū was no Zola—and no Sōseki, for that matter—but he was a modern writer, too conscious of his inner life and its relation to society ever to become a mere Edo scribbler (if, in fact, Edo writers were "mere" scribblers). It was this that Uchida Roan had in mind when he called Kafū Japan's first genuine artist in the European sense. (pp. 190-93)

> Jay Rubin, "Working Under the Mature System" and "Other Writers React," in his Injurious to Public Morals: Writers and the Meiji State, *University of Washington Press, 1984, pp. 115-42, 169-94.*

Steven D. Carter (essay date 1988)

[In the following essay, Carter studies Kafū's narrative style as evinced in Bokutō kidan.]

From beginning to end, Nagai Kafū (1879-1959) was a Tokyo man. He was born and raised there, and it was in that city, at around the turn of the century, that he began his career as a writer. Upon his return to Japan in the late summer of 1908 from a five-year sojourn in the West, it was in Tokyo that he set up house; and it was in Tokyo, five full decades later, that he died—leaving his tribute to the streets he loved in novels, stories, essays, poems, and a diary that tells as much, perhaps more, about his place of residence as about himself. Not surprisingly, his bibliography reads like a gazetteer of the city he loves, with titles like **"A Song of Fukagawa"** ("Fukagawa no uta," 1908), *The River Sumida* (*Sumidagawa,* 1911), **Night Tales from Shimbashi** (**Shimbashi yawa,** 1912), *Tidings from Ôkubo* (*Ôkubo dayori,* 1913-14), **Azabu Miscellany** (**Azabu zakki,** 1924), and the novella that will likely keep his name longest in memory, *A Strange Tale from East of the River* (*Bokutô kidan,* 1936).

But the title Kafū chose for this last story is not as straightforward as most others of his "Tokyo stories." In an essay written just after the tale, Kafū revealed that he had borrowed the word *boku,* a neologism meaning "ink black water" that refers to the River Sumida, from the Edo period Confucianist Hayashi Jussai (1768-1841), who had himself created the word for use in the title of a collection of his Chinese poetry. Thus even the word that begins Kafū's book is somewhat obscure—a strange beginning to a strange tale.

About *kidan,* the other word in his title, Kafū said noth-

ing. But it too is a rare word, if one whose meaning is more clear: it refers to an "extraordinary story," meaning usually a story with an elaborate design and structure. In modern writings the word is encountered very seldom, indicating again that from the beginning Kafū wants to signal his readers that his story is something out of the ordinary. One can also assume that by using it he meant to allude to the homophonous *kidan,* a truely "strange" or "mysterious" story.

But just what is so strange about Kafū's **Strange Tale**? Certainly not its plot, which, if reduced to its essence, is so simple that it can be summarized in one sentence: One Ôe Tadasu, a writer who seems to spend more time out walking than at his desk, meets a young prostitute named O-yuki one summer evening, visits her in her Tamanoi rooms several times, and then decides to end the brief affair in early autumn. Nothing out of the ordinary happens between the two people, nor is there anything unusual about their surroundings, especially for those already familiar with Kafū's preoccupations. The affectionate references to flowers and insects, costumes and coiffeurs, the concern for the plight of unfortunate women, the impatience with modern things and people, the nostalgia for the lost world of the old city that can still be seen here and there on the writer's strolls—all of these are familiar to anyone who has read Kafū.

So if there is something truly strange about **Bokutô kidan,** it has nothing to do with plot, setting, or atmosphere. When it comes to narrative approach, however, more than one critic has registered his fascination with Kafū's methods. As Donald Keene puts it [in *Dawn to the West: Japanese Literature in the Modern Era*], the book "defies most of the prescriptions for effective writing." And, indeed—although one may argue that it is precisely this feature of Kafū's writing that makes it so charming—Kafū's tale is told in a rambling style not generally encountered in fiction. The characters are faintly drawn, and there is more time devoted to descriptions of the Tamanoi streets than to psychological analysis or even dialogue. Add to this the fact that Kafū chose to include a number of other kinds of writing in his work besides the story of Tadasu and O-yuki—a letter from an old geisha friend, quotations from *Dream of the Red Chamber* and Yoda Gakkai's *Twenty-four Views of the Sumida,* an essay on the recent history of the Tamanoi district, a few haiku by Kafū himself, and even a chapter from another unfinished fiction the narrator is supposedly working on at the moment—and one begins to see why Edward Seidensticker concludes [in *Kafū the Scribbler: The Life and Times of Nagai Kafū*] that the work is less fiction than "discursive essay."

And there is more that can be said about the unusual narrative scheme of the book. For not only is the method of storytelling oblique, so is the source of the narration—the narrator, whom some have called an "alter-ego" of Kafū himself but may be more correctly described as a persona the author has adopted for several related purposes. Seen in this way, the narrator and his tale can tell us much about Kafū's approach to the art of writing in this and other stories of his later period.

The first thing obvious to anyone with a knowledge of

Kafū's life is that the narrator is in some ways identifiable with the author himself, a writer born, as the story tells us, in 1879, who is obviously a native of Edo and whose interests, career, and acquaintances turn out to correspond almost exactly to Kafū's own. Thus we have mention of several of Kafū's real-life friends—Satô Haruo (1892-1964), Sôyô Kôjirô (d. 1935), and Inoue Aa (d. 1923)—and references to some of his own works, including **"Early Afternoon" ("Hirusugi,"** 1912), **"House for a Mistress" ("Mekake taku,"** 1912), and **"Unfinished Dream" ("Mihatenu yume,"** 1910), all of which make us accept the work as at least partly autobiographical. Even Ôe Tadasu is a name with a connection to Kafū's family. Finally, as if to leave no doubt about the matter, the narrator even mentions an attack against Kafū from the pages of *Bungei shunjû,* giving the actual year and month (April, 1929) and includes a quotation from the author of the attack, the popular novelist Kikuchi Kan (1888-1948), who was then serving as that magazine's editor.

Yet the way Kafū uses the *Bungei shunjû* episode in his story is enough to tell us that his narrator should not be taken to represent the author in a direct way: he is Kafū, yes, but not *simply* Kafū. For the most wicked accusation in the attack as reported in **Bokutô kidan**—that he is "corrupter of young women" (shojo yûkai)—is nowhere to be found in the actual article. This part of Kikuchi's attack Kafū has quite simply made up—along with many of the other details of his account—reminding us in the process that what we are dealing with in his story is something less, or more, than unadorned fact. His narrator is not Nagai Kafū *per se* but a version of Nagai Kafū that, along with the other dimensions of his tale, exists to be put to artistic use.

And just what sort of a person is the narrator as he is presented in the story? First of all, he establishes early on, and with some insistence, that he is a wanderer, indeed almost a self-avowed "vagrant" (yûmin) who takes on new identities as occasion demands. At the very beginning of the story, for instance, he replies to a policeman interrogating him that he is an unemployed man with a wife and mother at home, only to lead O-yuki to believe later on that he is unmarried and a writer of "secret" books. Throughout his tale he describes himself as playing parts and telling lies as they come to him. In one passage he even interrupts a dialogue with O-yuki to talk about his protean habits—or might they be better termed "strategies"?—openly.

> As the woman's speech became rougher, I made mine rougher, too. Wherever I go and whomever I am with, I take on the speech of my companion as my own, much as one takes on the speech of a foreign country. When he chooses a rude, rustic manner of address, I find myself doing the same thing.

This strategy does not stop with his speech. Later in the story, when he feels a necessity to justify himself to his readers for his deceitful conduct towards O-yuki, he admits that whenever he goes into the Quarter, he goes incognito:

> I have neglected to say that since I had taken to spending my nights in the Quarter, since I had

come to feel at home there, I had made it a practice to remodel myself before I left home, and follow the fashions of the people I saw strolling among the night stalls. The change required no great effort. A striped shirt, collar open, no necktie; a coat carried in one hand; no hat; hair so matted that one wondered if it had ever seen a comb; trousers as thin at the seat and knees as possible. No shoes, in their place sandals with the rear clog worn away. Only the cheapest cigarettes. And so on and so on. It was no trouble at all. I have only to change from the clothes I wore when I was in my study or when I received guests to the clothes I wore when I raked the garden or cleaned away soot, and borrow a pair of old sandals from the maid.

> Put on a pair of old sandals and a pair of old trousers, find an old towel and tie it carelessly around your head, and you can walk through the eastern flats of Sunamachi on the south to Senjû on the north and Kanamachi on the northeast, and never have to worry that passersby will turn to stare.

What Kafū's narrator seems to be hinting at here is that, above all, he wants to remain free from inquiring eyes on his strolls, to be as inconspicuous as possible, just a rambler out for a stroll. A writer he may be, and even a "man of property," as another policeman refers to him in an attempt to warn him away from the Quarter, but for the duration of the summer that is the setting for **Bokutô kidan,** he wants only to be a wanderer whose identity is produced by his surroundings at the moment.

Another way of putting this is to say that Kafū's narrator wants to create an impression that many writers would not: that he acts—and writes, as we shall see—not out of choice, but quite by chance. This is one of the reasons that he continually refers to his trips to Tamanoi not as excursions with any special purpose but occasions of "escape" or "flight"—from his neighbor's radio, an obnoxious pimp, the danger of reckless cabbies, the crowds at Marunouchi and Ginza, and the police. In this way Kafū defines his narrator as one who *reacts* rather than acts. At one crucial point, he specifically enunciates his position by making it clear from the beginning that even his meeting with O-yuki—the central "event" of the story, if there is one—is purely a product of coincidence, symbolized quite appropriately by a flash of lightning, a clap of thunder, and a sudden summer rain shower:

> After walking about for a time, I bought a package of cigarettes at a corner shop with a postbox before it. I was pocketing my change when someone shouted: "It's going to rain!" A man in a white smock scurried by, and took shelter in a shop across the way. Next came a woman in an apron, and after her several flustered strollers. An air of expectancy fell over the street. In a sudden gust of wind a reed blind fell clattering to the ground. Paper and rubbish skated down the street like ghosts. A sharp flash of lightning. Then, to a somewhat sluggish clap of thunder, great drops of rain. The sky, so beautiful in the evening, had not prepared us for this.

> I had for some years been in the habit of carrying

an umbrella whenever I left home; and, however beautiful a day it might be, this was the rainy season. I was therefore not unprepared. I had calmly opened my umbrella and was setting off to inspect the streets and the sky when someone called me from behind. "Let me walk with you. You won't mind—just over to there." A white neck darted under the umbrella. The high Japanese-style chignon—one knew from the smell of oil that it was freshly dressed—was tied up in long silver threads. I remembered that I had passed a hairdresser's shop with its glass doors open.

It would be a pity to have the silver threads disarranged in the storm. I held out my umbrella to her. "I don't matter myself." My own foreign clothes hardly seemed worth worrying about.

As a matter of fact, the lights from the rows of shops were bright, and even I was a bit bashful about sharing a cozy umbrella with her.

"You don't mind? Just over to there." She took the umbrella, and with the other hand hitched up the skirt of her kimono.

It bears noting here that it is O-yuki who initiates first contact, not the narrator, who in fact says that he "doesn't matter"—an innocent enough comment in the dramatic context, but one that has important implications nonetheless. Throughout the narrative, Kafū's persona insists time and time again that the true details of his life don't matter in O-yuki's world, that he is a man of no promise, no security, a kind of tramp in whom his prostitute friend should place no trust. He knows from the beginning, and takes care to tell his readers so, that theirs is a chance meeting that must lead to an aimless and casual relationship with no future. It is for this reason he can sum up his tale with a nonchalant comment that reads more like truth than what it is—rationalization.

In the end, neither O-yuki nor I knew the other's name or home. We became friends in a house by a canal east of the river, amid the roar of mosquitoes. We were such that once we parted, there would be neither chance nor means to bring us together again. One might say that we played frivolously at love. Still, there was a particular warmth in knowing from the outset that we would part and not meet again. If I try to describe it, I will only exaggerate, and if on the other hand I toss it off lightly, I will know the distress of having been unworthy of the occasion. The power with which just such feelings are described at the end of Pierre Loti's *Madame Chrysanthemum* is enough to bring tears to one's eyes. If I were to attempt that particular shading of fiction for my strange tale, I would bring ridicule upon myself as an imitator of Loti who has not imitated well enough.

If the reader has any doubts that Kafū is a skilled rhetorician and not just a "forgotten old author," this passage must put them to rest: for he succeeds here in creating the melodramatic scene he says he must deny himself, all through a simple allusion to one of the most romantic of western tales about Japan, the ending of which—

describing the feelings of the narrator on the boat as it makes its way away from Japan, after he has left his *musume* behind—is indeed as wistful and melancholy as Kafū claims. One short passage makes the tonal similarities between Kafū and Loti clear.

In my cabin, one evening, in the midst of the Yellow Sea, my eyes chance to fall upon the lotus brought from Diou-djen-dji;—they had lasted for two or three days; but now they are faded, and pitifully strew my carpet with their pale pink petals.

I, who have carefully preserved so many faded flowers, fallen, alas! into dust, stolen here and there, at moments of parting in different parts of the world; I who have kept so many, that the collection is now almost a herbarium ridiculous and incoherent—I try hard, but without success, to get up a sentiment for these lotus—and they are the last living souvenirs of my summer at Nagasaki.

I pick them up, however, with a certain amount of consideration, and I open my porthole.

From the grey misty sky a livid light falls upon the waters; a wan and gloomy kind of twilight creeps down, yellowish upon this Yellow Sea. We feel that we are moving northwards, that autumn is approaching.

I throw the poor lotus into the boundless waste of waters, making them my best excuses for giving to them, natives of Japan, a grave so solemn and so vast.

Thus Kafū evokes a romantic scene through the power of Loti's suggestion. Moreover, in his appeal to Loti, Kafū also manages to work in a final reference to his own "unworthiness"—as a writer, this time—in words that attempt to absolve him of any responsibility for his acts. Once again, he claims not the agency of will but of chance, or fate, which is the same thing without the implications of a justifying power, for his actions. O-yuki has now become part of the summer landscape for him, like a street to be passed through on his evening peregrinations. No one need take responsibility for the fleeting results of an evening shower.

This of course leads us to the question of why Kafū would want to create such an impression of passivity in a tale where impressions play so great a part. Why does he want to deny himself—on the surface, at least—what most authors assume to be at the heart of their project, namely, the idea of intent? For the narrator of *Bokutô kidan* is not just an ironic device of the sort one finds in some other novelists; he is in most ways the central figure in the story—not a bystander, despite his attempts to dismiss himself as such, but an important character as well as a narrator who is responsible for the shape, tone, and design of his story. Why then does he claim not to act but to be acted upon?

The first and most obvious answer to this question is that Kafū may not have been creating an impression at all but writing from direct experience—a view of the work that may not be artistically pleasing, but which finds a great deal of support not only in his diaries but in comments like the following from the story itself:

> In Tokyo, and even in the Occident, I have known almost no society except that of courtesans . . .
>
> So that I might become friends with them, so that they would not draw back in awe of me, I thought it best to hide my identity. It would have been most cruel to have the women think that I was one who had no reason to come, and might better stay away. I wanted at all costs to avoid being taken for one who looked down upon them and their wretched lives, as if watching them act a play. There was no help for it but to hide my identity.

However unpleasant the notion may be to those not fond of autobiographical fiction, this passage sounds like Kafū talking—the Kafū who can be shown by other sources to have walked the streets of the Tamanoi with his narrator at the very time that he was engaged in writing his strange tale. It may well be that in his strolls through the seedier sections of Tokyo, Kafū adopted just such a strategy for the reasons he describes, as well as to avoid being recognized by those he derisively refers to in his story as "the austere and upright of the world." Thus the simplest explanation for why the narrator of *Bokutô kidan* seems so to lack volition or a sense of engagement may be that the same was true of the author himself.

Having said this, however, one must hasten to add that the reality of his own strategies for dealing with the pleasure quarters need not have been the only reason Kafū had for creating so passive a narrator. He was an artist, after all, and to the artist "reality" is just another kind of raw material. No writer as well read or as self-conscious as Kafū—witness his many intrusions into his own text for the purposes of apology, commentary and reflection—could be unaware that his narrator is as much a feature of his text as are details of scenery. In other words, the narrator of Kafū's strange tale, whatever his relationship to Kafū the man, deserves more attention than a strictly autobiographical reading can give. He is one part of a particular tale that has significance for readers over and above its origins.

What kinds of significance? No doubt many, several of which are of great importance for what they say about Kafū as a writer. The first of these has to do with the public image of himself Kafū attempted to put forward in this and other writings, for Kafū is one writer who admitted openly that he cultivated an image. As early as 1919, for instance, he described himself as a modern day *gesakusha,* or writer of frivolous tales:

> . . . I concluded that I could do no better than drag myself down to the level of the Tokugawa writer of frivolous and amatory fiction [gesakusha]. Arming myself with the tobacco pouch that was the mark of the old-style dandy, I set out to collect Ukiyoe prints, and I began to learn the samisen. It was a matter of no interest to such inferior persons as the writer of light Edo fiction or the maker of color prints that Perry's Black Ships had arrived at Uraga, or that Ii

> Kamon no Kami, Great Minister of the Shogunate, was assassinated at the castle gate. They thought it better to know their place and remain silent. Quite as if nothing had happened, they went on writing their indecent books and making their indecent prints.

Before anything else, one must say that there is a good deal of self-censure in this passage, arising mostly from the author's feelings of political impotence in the face of events such as the Kôtoku Shûsui case of 1910-1911. But even before that time Kafū seems to have begun portraying himself as a kind of modern gesakusha, and for reasons that were as much artistic as political. In a word, one may say that in such passages Kafū is invoking a *tradition,* almost a genealogy, that connects him with the writers of Edo he had come to admire most—men such as Tamenaga Shunsui (1790–1843) and Tamenaga Shunkô (d. 1889), both of whom are mentioned, not coincidentally, in the story of Ôe Tadasu and O-yuki. Dismissed by most scholars and writers of Kafū's time as representatives of tired native genres and affections, Shunsui and Shunkô—both writers of *ninjô-bon* ("books of feeling") for which the story of Tadasu and O-yuki, spare as it is, is a direct descendant—seem improbable models for a writer as well educated in European literature as Kafū, who had begun his career as a student of French naturalism and an advocate of the clinical realism of Emile Zola. Yet it is clear from numerous comments in his diaries and miscellaneous writings from the thirties especially that it was not to Zola but to late Edo writers that he looked for inspiration in his later work. And what appealed to him in such men was, as the passage above and others like it make clear, precisely the same sort of pose one finds in the narrator of *Bokutô kidan*: the playful pose of the passive "man of letters," wandering about the streets of the city, jotting down whatever he comes upon with little care for design or structure but a fine sense of style. It is not by chance that in his 1920 essay **"Shôsetsu sakuhô" ("How to write a novel")** Kafū placed more emphasis on atmosphere and description than on careful plotting and characterization: already some years before *Bokutô kidan* he was moving away from western models of narrative toward his own country's past, as exemplified by the Edo gesakusha and their Chinese forebears. [In *Nagai Kafū to Edo Bun'en,* Takahashi Toshie] has even shown that the famous rainstorm meeting between Tadasu and O-yuki may owe much to a similar scene in a Shunsui romance—a not unlikely explanation when one learns that Kafū referred to that very scene in his study of Shunsui some years later. For all these reasons, one must conclude that Kafū's mentors at the time he was writing his strange tale were not the great European novelists, or even the *shôsetsuka* ("novelists"?) of the Meiji era, but the gesakusha of the early and mid-1800s whom most other writers of his time believed beneath contempt.

It was among such "scribblers," then—idlers and vagabonds, to return to the vocabulary of the "strange tale"—that Kafū wished to be perceived, which means that the nonchalance of the narrator of *Bokutô kidan* may be little more than an extension of the studied pose Kafū presented to the world both in his life and in his work. One must remember that it is a pose, of course, a literary front made up of allusions and patterns borrowed largely from the past; again, however, its significance appears to be found largely outside of the tale itself, in Kafū's personality and psychology.

But this image has importance within *Bokutô kidan* as well. For one can see immediately that the pose of the gesakusha, whatever Kafū's ultimate reasons for adopting it, is above all artistically *useful*: because just as such a pose allows Kafū's narrator freedom to move in the demi-monde without inhibition, it also allows Kafū the writer a kind of *artistic* freedom that those affiliated with the main trends of novelistic discourse in his time could not hope to attain. The narrator of the tale is therefore more than a character based on Kafū the man; he is in addition Kafū the writer, announcing in ironic terms his freedom from not only social but also literary norms. Seen in this way, the gesakusha pose is not limiting, but liberating, a means by which Kafū can afford himself the luxury of mixing genres and introducing materials into his text that would be out of place in the orthodox novel. This, I believe, is in fact the main artistic reason for Kafū's creation of so passive a narrator: for by denying himself conscious intent, the narrator is in effect allowing his materials the illusion of shaping themselves, which is an ironic way of saying that, despite appearances to the contrary, in Kafū's text the author is in complete control of his resources. What Kafū has created in *Bokutô kidan* is a free form, a novel-cum-essay that refuses to follow consistently either the conventions of fictional or expository discourse.

There are of course many indications of this ironic strategy in the story itself, the chief one being, as stated before, its strange mix of "fiction" and "fact," of poetry and prose and correspondence and essay. Perhaps the most open avowal comes when the narrator interrupts his story with apologies, as in the following scene, included just after Tadasu's first encounter with O-yuki in the midst of the summer shower noted above:

> After the manner of Shunsui, I should like to make a remark or two here. The reader may feel that the woman was just a little too familiar when she met me there by the road. I merely record the facts of our meeting, however, and add no coloring, no shaping or contriving. Inasmuch as the affair had its beginning in a sudden shower, moreover, certain readers may be smiling at me for having used a well-worn device. Precisely because I am mindful of the possibility, I have refrained from giving the incident another setting. Put in motion by an evening shower, it seemed to me interesting for the very reason that it was so much in the old tradition. Indeed I began this book because I wanted to tell of it.

What is the function of such intrusions? For one thing, they make us aware of Kafū's strong affinity for Shunsui and his style of writing, which does indeed rely on coincidence as one of its chief conventions. And it also must be said that apologies of this sort are presented, on the surface at least, as one way to establish the authenticity of Kafū's account—confronting "fact" with "fiction" in the most obvious way. But this is only true on the surface, since, rhetorically speaking, such disclaimers produce

more questions than they answer. In the end, one may simply say that through his asides Kafū signals to his readers the dubiousness of his position. For the elegiac tone of Kafū's words here and throughout the story makes it impossible to accept the notion that he has in truth added "no coloring" to his account—which is, one must remember, an account embroidered throughout with digressions into history and commentary. Indeed, one might say that *Bokutô kidan* is almost all color, and a good part "shaping and contrivance"—the very tools of the narrator's craft. No writer, not even one who claims to base his descriptions on real experience, can escape the import of his own choices in the arrangement and articulation of material. That Kafū claims to do so is thus more than anything else a reflection of his ironic stance: throughout his text, he claims bondage to "fact" only to escape into the freedom of the gesakusha tradition of digression. The idea that the story has constructed itself is the ultimate ironical avowal of freedom from convention.

Kafū plays along the line between fiction and fact until the very end of *Bokutô kidan,* but always only to obscure that line by tracing an ironic zigzag along its edges.

—*Steven D. Carter*

Finally, then, what the passive narrator of *Bokutô kidan* may signify is Kafū's rejection of the mainstream of novelistic discourse in his time, that is, of conventional plotting and narrative approaches that leave little room for the details he wants to include in his story. Ôe Tadasu thus becomes a modern gesakusha, free to indulge in long and seemingly superfluous descriptions of Edo scenery or essays on the history of the Tamanoi quarter, and unafraid to use whatever device may suit his artistic fancy—all under the guise of representing the "facts." In an essay on Shunsui written by Kafū much later, he quotes his mentor in words that do much to explain his own avowed motives in writing works like *Bokutô kidan*: "It may appear that I am recording trivialities here," says Shunsui, "but I put them down most innocently, thinking only to show the customs of my age to gentlemen a hundred years ahead." Such an ambition may in itself seem silly to a more "serious" novelist. That Kafū shared it with Shunsui, however, cannot be denied when one reads in a later work that his main motive in writing *Geisha in Rivalry* (*Udekurabe,* 1916)—one of his more conventionally "fictional" stories—was to record for posterity the customs of the late Meiji geisha world. Like Kurayama Nansô, the newspaper novelist of the latter story, Kafū too seems to have "considered it a writer's duty" to preserve for the future "the eyewitness reports of an age now past."

This does not mean that Kafū the man may not have met a woman like O-yuki in a sudden shower while out on a walk on a summer eve, of course; but would even the most naive reader be satisfied to take Kafū's apology at face value? Despite his protestations, it is clear that Kafû has chosen his digressions, with the intent of creating a story that he felt could not be properly told in another way. In the end, that story is not strange because it is true, as Ôe Tadasu says he wants us to believe, but true—meaning powerful, and endearing—because it is strange: a modern frivolous essay (story?) by a twentieth-century gesakusha.

Needless to say, such an approach has philosophical implications that are only marginally related to the gesakusha pose, which can be seen in the end as merely another dimension of the story that Kafû as a writer is putting to artistic use. Thus Kafû is again more self-conscious than his manner would have us suppose. For one of the reasons he may use the playful, ironic pose of the gesakusha is to show that distinctions between fact and fiction—for this modern gesakusha, at least—are not as easy to make as some "serious" novelists may think. Not only does Kafû reject the methods of more conventional novelistic discourse in his strange tale, then, but also one of its underlying assumptions: that "fact" or "essay" and "fiction" can be separated in any truly meaningful way. Is Ôe Tadasu really Kafû? Well, yes, the story seems to say, and no: he shares some statistics with Kafû, but finally admits himself that the identity he adopts for his duration as narrator is an acquired one that suits his purposes at the moment. Is O-yuki an actual woman Kafû met in Tamanoi? Again, yes and no: she may well be based upon a person Kafû met in 1935, but when it comes to actual details we have only Tadasu's own imagination, in which she becomes a "courtesan of thirty years before," or an actor in a Namboku play, or "a woman from a not-too-cheap house in the Yoshiwara or Suzaki." In the final analysis, Kafû's treatment of O-yuki makes her a product of the story—she is a player with an identity as tentative as Kafû's own, what the narrator calls "the muse who had accidentally called back into a dulled heart shadows of the past." The by now familiar word "accidentally" is again not accidental itself, but ironic: there is nothing haphazard about O-yuki's appearance in the story. She is a part of the atmosphere Kafû has created with great care, no more or less real than the supposedly "real" mosquitoes Kafû memorializes in his haiku.

Kafû plays along the line between fiction and fact until the very end of his story, but always only to obscure that line by tracing an ironic zigzag along its edges. Indeed, this may even be identified as one of the overt themes of Kafû's story, although one that has received little attention from the critics: that the distinctions between fiction and fact or appearance and reality are not real ones in the first place—something gesaku writers, those players and dabblers of an earlier age, seemed to know all along. Can it be without significance, for instance, that Kafû's fiction within a fiction, a story with the ironic title "Whereabouts Unknown" (*shissô*) should remain unwritten—despite the narrator's insistence that it was to collect material for the story that he went to Tamanoi in the first place—while the "real" story of Ôe Tadasu and O-yuki, also a creation of Kafû's ironic intents, gets told? Many critics have noted that "Whereabouts Unknown" is uninteresting, and some have pointed out that it is a "story within a story," but few have noted its obvious thematic purpose. Here again Kafû

seems to be toying with his readers, declaring that life is more interesting than art. But then one must remember that throughout his tale the narrator has shown both Tadasu and O-yuki creating imaginary identities for each other, and that Kafû has excused himself continually for using literary formulas and allusions that make his experience seem more imagined than real. Thus art loses to life, but only for life again to lose to art. Finally, to confuse the scheme even more, Kafû let it be known after his story was written that he had in mind a specific model for the hero of his uncompleted story within a story, Taneda Jumpei—a bookseller and tutor who in fact was later to become one of the writer's friends. So if Kafû's "facts" cannot be trusted as facts, neither can his fictions be trusted as fictions. Kafû wants it, and has it, both ways: art is life, life is art, art is life again. In the end, the distinctions he seems to make are all straw men erected only to be cut down.

A final example of this ironic strategy is available in the last pages of the book, where Kafû chooses to include two endings for his story, one presented as a fictional possibility and the other presented as "fact" but equally full of color and contrivance.

> I must now lay down my brush, my strange tale from east of the river finished. To give it an ending in the old style, I should perhaps add a chapter describing how, quite by accident, six months or a year later, I met O-yuki in a wholly unexpected place. She had changed her profession. And if I wished to make the scene yet more effective, I could have the two of us see each other from the windows of passing automobiles or trains, unable to speak, however intense the longing. My scene would have a very special power if we were to pass on ferries, on, say, the murmuring River Tone, in the time of the autumn leaves and flowers.
>
> In the end, neither O-yuki nor I knew the other's name or home. We became friends in a house by a canal east of the river, amid the roar of mosquitoes . . .
>
> The roofs of the dirty, jammed-in houses, on and on. O-yuki and I, in the black upstairs window, looking up at lights reflected in a sky heavy before a storm, one damp hand in the other. Suddenly, as we sat talking in conundrums, a flash of lightning, and her profile. The picture is here before my eyes, and will not leave.

Here once again Kafû is playing rhetorical tricks, denying himself an ending that he manages to include all the same. And is his actual ending less imaginative and literary than the fictional one? The flash of lightning, harking back as it does to the first meeting of the lovers, can hardly be fortuitous. If not creating them altogether, Kafû has at least *re-created* his materials—although playing the unknowing, innocent gesakusha to the end.

But by this time the reader should be aware that when Kafû says at the end of his story that he is writing not with any clear intent but simply letting "his brush go where it will," he is stating not a truth but an attitude, not fact but an approach to writing. In a final ironic touch, Kafû fills up the remaining space on his paper with that most self-conscious of literary forms, a poem, in which his talent for lyrical statement is displayed in one last symbolic form:

> . . . the corner a stricken butterfly
> Wavers on broken wings
> In the shade of a dying stem of amaranth
> Which it takes to be a flower, a return of spring.

Whom does the butterfly represent—O-yuki or Tadasu? The references remain uncertain. But by ending with such an avowedly literary statement, Kafū clearly puts the lie to his pretense of passivity: here is an artist working in an openly contrived form. As Yamamoto Kenkichi has said,

Kafū had too much education in both Chinese and European literatures to be, like Shunsui—a man of meager education indeed—a true gesakusha of the late Edo period. For him, the gesakusha image was little more than a pose adopted for his literary peregrinations. And as much as the pose itself, it is those literary peregrinations, with their carefully constructed sense of ironic play, that give his tale its strange power. (pp. 151-65)

Steven D. Carter, "What's So Strange about 'A Strange Tale?' Kafu's Narrative Persona in 'Bokutô Kidan'," in Journal of the Association of Teachers of Japanese, *Vol. 22, No. 2, November, 1988, pp. 151-68.*

Additional coverage of Nagai Kafū's life and career is contained in the following sources published by Gale Research: *Contemporary Authors,* Vol. 117.

Frédéric Mistral

1830-1914

Provençal poet, lexicographer, philologist, autobiographer, and playwright.

INTRODUCTION

Awarded a Nobel Prize in literature in 1904, Mistral is best known for epic poems depicting the landscape, people, history, and legends of his native Provence. In an attempt to preserve the Provençal culture, which flourished in France from the twelfth to the fourteenth century, he composed his works in the Provençal language and endeavored to revive the tradition of poetry that was identified with the medieval troubadours. Critics have praised Mistral's combination of local color with traditional poetic forms.

Mistral was born in Maillane, a village in the Rhone Valley of southern France, and grew up speaking Provençal, also known as the *langue d'oc.* As a child he was sent to boarding school in Avignon, where he was inspired by his teacher Joseph Roumanille, a poet who wrote in Provençal and sought to reestablish it as a literary language. Under Roumanille's supervision, Mistral translated Virgil's first eclogue into Provençal. Mistral studied law at the University of Aix and, upon graduating in 1851, returned to Maillane. With Roumanille and several other writers, he formed a literary group, the Félibrige, dedicated to reviving the tradition of Provençal language and literature. Mistral established his reputation with *Mirèio,* an epic poem that remains his most highly acclaimed work. Like *Mirèio,* the epic poems *Calendau, Nerto,* and *Lou pouèmo dóu Rose (Anglore: The Song of the Rhone)* were composed in Provençal and translated by Mistral into French. He also compiled *Lou tresor dóu Felibrige,* a dictionary of Provençal language, legends, and proverbs. Mistral declined a place in the French Academy in order to remain in Provence and in 1904 jointly received the Nobel Prize with Spanish playwright José Echegaray y Eizaguirre. Mistral used his prize money to create the Museon Arlaten, a museum of Provençal artifacts and culture. At the age of eighty-two he published his last work, a collection of short poems entitled *Lis oulivado.* Mistral died in 1914.

In his epic poems, Mistral depicted in vivid detail various aspects of Provence. Set in the farmlands of the Rhone region, *Mirèio* is about a young woman whose parents will not allow her to marry the man she loves. Mistral's second epic, *Calendau,* is a patriotic poem glorifying the history of Provence. Set in the eighteenth century before the French Revolution, the story relates a simple fisherman's chivalrous attempts to win the love of a beautiful princess. The narrative contains descriptive renderings of the Provençal seacoast and mountains and historical accounts of the days of courtly love and the troubadours. In *Nerto,*

Mistral explores medieval Provençal legends and superstitions concerning the devil, relating the story of a thirteen-year-old girl who attempts to save herself when she learns that her father sold her soul to Satan. *Lou pouèmo dóu Rose* describes the journey of a fleet of boats down the Rhone River, incorporating Provençal folklore and stories associated with the towns and castles that line the river's banks.

Much critical commentary on Mistral has discussed the classical orientation of his writing, emphasizing a concern with idyllic beauty, use of the epic form and elevated language, and a pervading theme of human nobility. Jean Carrère has stated: "No poet in the whole history of letters was more completely, more purely, more naturally saturated with the Hellenic spirit—more *classical,* in a word—than Mistral. He belongs to the same great, luminous family as Homer, Plato, Vergil, Dante, Petrarch, and Racine." Some critics, however, criticize his works as provincial and therefore lacking the universal appeal of great classical literature. Nevertheless, commentators consistently note Mistral's genuine devotion to Provence and the value of his contribution to the preservation of Provençal culture. Charles Alfred Downer asserted: "All the charm and beauty of that sunny land, all that is enchanting in its past, all the best, in the ideal sense, that may be hoped for in its future, is expressed in [Mistral's] musical, limpid, lovely verse. Such a poet and such a leader of men is rare in the annals of literature. Such complete oneness of purpose and achievement is rare among men."

PRINCIPAL WORKS

Mirèio (poetry) 1859
  [*Mistral's Mirèio: A Provençal Poem*, 1872]
†*Calendau: pouémo nouveu* (poetry) 1867
‡*Lis isclo d'or* (poetry) 1875
Lou tresor dóu Felibrige (dictionary) 1879-1886
Nerto (poetry) 1884
§*La rèino Jano* (drama) 1890
¶*Lou pouèmo dóu Rose* (poetry) 1897
  [*Anglore: The Song of the Rhone*, 1937]
Moun espelido (autobiography) 1906
  [*Memoirs of Mistral*, 1907; also published as *The Memoirs of Frederic Mistral*, 1986]
Lis oulivado (poetry) 1912

*This work, translated by Mistral into French as *Mireille,* was adapted as the opera *Mireille* by Charles Gounod in 1864.

†Translated by Mistral into French as *Calendal.*

‡Translated by Mistral into French as *Les isles d'or.*

§Translated by Mistral into French as *La reine Jeanne.*

¶Translated by Mistral into French as *La poème du Rhône.*

CRITICISM

The North British Review (essay date 1868)

[*In the excerpt below, the critic describes the progression of events in* Mirèio, *praising Mistral's artful depiction of rural life and his use of Provençal language.*]

Avignon, the old city of the Popes, a place full of historical associations, is the centre of the Provençal movement, and from the press and the book-stalls of Avignon have already gone forth some remarkable literary efforts in the revived *patois.* These authors and their works were noticed in a late number of the *North British Review,* and the attention of the reading public was called in particular to the *Mirèio* of M. F. Mistral, to which we propose to dedicate this [essay]. Mistral is the greatest of the new Troubadours, and *Mirèio,* his own favourite, is the most successful and popular of his works. The poem is now in its third edition.

It would seem that the pastoral or idyl thrives best in *patois.* Without going back to the Doric of the Greek shep-

herds, and eschewing the vile affectation of rusticity in some of our English pastorals, we have the best example among ourselves. [Robert] Burns was far greater when singing the simple language of the Kyle ploughman, in his shepherd plaid, by the banks of the Doon, than when living the conventional life, and using the book-language of his patrons and patronesses in Edinburgh. He felt himself more a man, more a true poet, when, like his own immortal "Tam-o'-Shanter," buffeting the rough weather, and—

> Now crooning o'er some auld Scots sonnet,
> Now haudin' fast his gude blue bonnet.

It is true that Burns had an advantage over those Provençal poets, and indeed over other writers in a provincial dialect. Burns's song, in the broadest Scots, was something else than vulgar then. In his day, not a high-born dame of Scotland but had heard that language in her nursery, and learnt to love the sweet sentiment as well as the melody of our old ballads from her nurse, long before she was called to weep over the tender verses of—

> Ye banks and braes o' bonny Doon,
> How can ye bloom sae fresh and fair?

The educated classes had not to look back to Barbour, or even to Dunbar and Lindsay, for the Ayrshire ploughman's dialect. The rhythm was familiar. Was it not the ring of the Border ballad of love and war, as it was still sung by the blythe milkmaid and the crone at her wheel! Even the broad musical Saxon tongue was still the common language of the nursery, and of the never-forgotten companions of nursery days. Feeling that our own partiality should put us out of court, we call in the authority of Longfellow, who, speaking of his own version of Jasmin's pretty pastoral, the "Blind Girl," says—

> Only the tongue of Lowland Scotland might,
> Rehearse this little tragedy aright.

We accept the testimony of the pure English poet, though it may have an unconscious bias from associating the language with the genius of Burns.

Now, something of Burns's advantages the knot of Provençal enthusiasts claim to have. They pretend to resuscitate an ancient poetical language—the *langue d'oc,*—the speech, a thousand years ago, of the Princess and Counts of the court of Toulouse, where the constitution was not merely, as was said later of France, "a despotism tempered by songs," but where songs were paramount to politics and the constitution. It is not a mere romance. For several centuries, in all that country, kings and queens, knights and soldiers thought it their highest honour to make verses, and to sing them. Love and song were the business of life; and lords and ladies held debates about the tender passion, the philosophy of love, with as much gravity as serious people now throw into a dispute about church music. But that language, cultivated by the old Troubadours, and fixed by them, was gone; either quite forgotten, or preserved only in the mouth of the uneducated peasant, who has handled it roughly and degraded it to vile uses. It was gone as thoroughly as the Latin of the Roman *Provincia,* as the Greek in which St. Cesaire preached to the people of Marseilles in the sixth century.

Has the character of the people as much changed? It is hard to say. The people are still peculiar; very different from the Gauls of midland France. Tradition, or belief of ancestry, does not go for much in national character. But the shepherd of the Gardon, who has never heard of the Greek colonists who settled Massilia, for whom Theocritus may have invoked the Sicilian Muse two thousand years ago, does not look without emotion on the marvellous aqueduct that spans his native valley, on the remains of Roman art scattered round Arles and Nîmes, telling the tale of imperial power and colonial civilisation. He does believe that his forefathers had something to do with those stupendous monuments. Tradition is something real when vouched by such evidence.

Actual "race" and blood descent will have more influence than the traditionary belief and pride of ancestry. Why should we doubt that it will affect the character as it is known to affect the physical constitution of animals and mankind! We Britons are ready enough to fancy the stout Anglo-Saxon strain cropping out in the uttermost parts of the earth. Those Greeks, be they Dorian or Ionian, capable of such early civilisation, of so poetical a temperament—those middle-age Troubadours, living in an atmosphere of church and chivalry and song, may perhaps have influenced the character of the present people who inhabit their seats—a people addicted to music, of a very poetical temperament, religious to extreme superstition,—sober, gentle, slow, almost dull—yet so easily excited to dangerous excesses.

It is possible, then, that the peculiar character of the people, like their language, may be traced to their historical ancestry. That may be one element. Another is more certain. About their climate there can be no mistake. It is still the sunny land of love and of song, where the blood bounds with a wilder throb of passion, where the rudest music has the effect of the tarantula, and the common air breathes sweet and wooingly through the mulberry leaf and the almond blossom.

The French critic, like the French policeman, is all for centralization and submission to "the authority" in all things. He sees no advantage in reviving a language dead or doomed to die. He has not much sympathy with the wish to speak to that fine impulsive people in the only tongue they understand, to save them from the polluted ribaldry of their familiar songs, and to give them the use and the delight of a homely literature of pure thoughts, not unmixed with humour and gaiety. If the people are capable of appreciating something above their coarse *virelays,* let them learn French! If their authors feel the power of the true artist, let them write to intelligent men in French! We poor insulars may be pardoned for cherishing a different opinion. Without fighting the battle of suppressed nationalities, we submit that the Avignon revivalists have done well in writing pastorals and tales and songs in the language of their countrymen, simple *patois* though it may be. We are prepared to maintain that there are good reasons for writing popular poetry in the language of the people, and there are special reasons against writing it in French.

Of modern languages, perhaps French is the least suited for pastoral or idyllic composition. Its very perfections, which none but a Parisian can hope to master, are against such a use. Its sharp precision, the unyielding accuracy of its grammar, its intolerance of colloquial "vulgarisms," of incomplete sentences, of childish prattle, all join to make the polished language unfit for the talk of ideal shepherds and ploughmen. May we say further, there is a want of frank, natural, kindly, old-world expressions in its vocabulary, and of full rich tones in its speech. French is best adapted for the life of cities. It is the special language of science. It is admirable in the witness-box, more excellent and admirable in comedy, and in familiar letters,—especially ladies' letters—and indeed generally in the conversation and intercourse of educated people. But it is not a poetical language, as compared with English or German, nor a musical speech, when compared with Italian or Spanish or Lowland Scotch.

But this is not a question of comparison of languages. The simplicity which unfits the Provençal *patois* for expressing the loftier or more subtle thoughts of educated men, recommends it to the ear of the peasantry of southern France; and any language is worth cultivating that is spoken by millions—any language that is the sole speech of a people. It is hardly possible to confer a greater boon on a people situated like these *patois*-speakers of the South, destitute of anything worthy of the name of literature, than by opening to them, in their own tongue, a wholesome literature, full of innocent, generous, tender charities, sympathizing with their rude but well realized feelings of religion, and brought home to their common occupations and daily use.

Perhaps it would have been better if the adventurous champions of the new or restored language had banished French readers entirely from their thoughts, and French translation from their pages. When Burns, under the full *afflatus* of the Muse, sang to his peasant-love, his bonnie Jean, or told a tale to his neighbours that was destined to immortality, he despised for the nonce Edinburgh critics, and took no thought of Homer and Virgil. What would have been his answer, had Creech proposed to print "Tam-o'-Shanter" with an English version *en regard!* Undoubtedly those Provençal enthusiasts at first meant their songs for the shepherds and peasants of the Rhone valley; but, bolder grown, they strike for the honour of Provence and its literature as worthy to rank with French. In other words the poet who prints at Avignon, though he loves his beautiful province and its people, has an *arrière pensée*—"what will they think of me at Paris?" Perhaps no Frenchman can overcome that feeling. Moreover, M. Mistral is a scholar and a classic. In the first lines of his pastoral he professes himself *"umble escoulan dou grand Oumero;"* and he shows in some places too plainly that he is imitating his great master. His pastoral poem would have been more successful if he had written for the Provençals rather than the Parisians, and banished Homer quite from his thoughts for the time.

But the convenience of the Paris public demands a translation; and it is only part of the evil that M. Mistral encumbers his racy Provençal poem with a literal French prose version, like a school Horace with "Smart" *vis à-vis,* if, as the French critics tell us, the work bears marks of the original Provençal being cut and carved to suit the French translation.

But now we have done of our critical growl. In truth the faults we have found are not so much the author's, as arising out of the circumstances which he has to contend with; and shall now endeavour to make our English readers in some degree acquainted with his very singular and very charming poem. In one particular, M. Mistral has had rare good fortune. He has found among his own countrymen, even in the great trading city of Marseille, a gentleman well versed in Provençal, perhaps to the manner born, in every respect worthy to render into English this remarkable poem. Mr. Grant evidently appreciates the beauties of the original, yet with infinite taste forbears from any embellishment of his own. His natural unaffected English, following the order of the original where possible, becomes really musical, and contrasts, to our mind, favourably with the French prose which M. Mistral has joined to his Provençal poetry. For the most part we propose to use Mr. Grant's translation in the specimens we shall require for making the poem known to our readers. We say, for the most part, but having said so, we shall not consider ourselves bound to follow Mr. Grant in every instance, nor to break our narrative by stating when we leave his translation for one we prefer.

The scene of M. Mistral's pastoral is not in the most beautiful spot of the Provençal Arcadia. At the mouth of the Rhone, on the left bank, is a district some twenty or thirty miles broad, of wild, rugged land, that seems in some remote prehistoric age to have been overspread with the *débris* brought down by the two great rivers from their Alpine valleys. The natives called it the *Crau,* and M. Minstral, willing to keep up the connexion with the Greek colonists, derives the name from the Greek κραυροσ—*arid.* The books tell us that it is part of the old *campi lampidei.* It is pastured by wild, shaggy cattle and sheep, and only in a few spots is capable of tillage. One of these oases is cultivated from the *Mas de Falabrego,* that is, the farm-steading of the lotus or nettle-tree. You can tell it at a good distance by the fine old olives, and hedges and alleys of almonds and vines. It is one of the best properties in the Crau. Master Ramon, its possessor, has six ploughs at work, and the plough marks but a small part of the produce of a farm in that land of the silk-worm, of the olive and almond, not to speak of the grape, and all manner of fruits. The farmer is as proud of the land he has reclaimed with the sweat of his brow as Tennyson's northern farmer was of stubbing Thornaby Waäste. His daughter, Mirèio, is the heroine of the tale. The author translates her name into French, Mireille, and we beg leave for the present to call her Muriel. She is the prettiest girl, and promises to have the best dower in the Crau.

For such a girl there is no lack of suitors.

> Vengue lou tems que li viouleto
> Dins li pradello frescouleto
> Espelisson a flo—

Come the season when the violets in the meadows so fresh blow in bunches; when the sea calms down her angry

bosom, and her billows gently heave! in that sweet season come three suitors for fair Muriel's hand. First is Alári:—

> Vengué proumié lou pastre Alári
> Dison qu'avié milo bestiári . . .

They say he had a thousand sheep that grazed the rich sea pastures all the winter through. In summer he went with his flocks to the Alps, but when the snow came on the hills, you should have seen the rich flocks passing down from the glens of Dauphine to pasture on the broad plain of the Crau!

> You should have seen this multitude
> Defile into the stony road;
> The early lambkins heading the whole band,
> Come on in merry throngs,
> The lamb-herd guiding them: then come
> The asses with their bells, in pairs, their foals beside,
> Or in disorder trotting after them.
>
> . . . . .
>
> Captains of the Brigade
> With horns turned back;
> Next come on abreast, jingling their bells,
> And with looks askance,
> Five proud buck-goats with threatening heads.
> Behind come the mothers
> With their little mad-cap kids.

After march the rams, the sires and leaders of the flock, with muzzles in the air. You know them by their great horns thrice twisted round their ears. At the head of the flock goes the head-shepherd, his plaid about his shoulders; and then in a cloud of dust, hurrying and hustling, come the ewes answering with their bleating to their bleating lambs; the woolly wedders slowly follow.

From break to break the shepherd boys are heard to their dogs shouting—*a la vouto!*—(*far yaud!*) Then comes the flock immense, all pitch-marked on the sides. Apart the yearling ewes, the two-year-olds, and ewes from whom they have taken their lambs, and the twin-breeders that wearily their heavy burdens bear along.

And all these sheep and goats are Alári's—all young and old and fair and foul. And when before him they defile, and march past in hundreds, his eyes sparkle, and as a sceptre he grasps his maple cudgel. When to pasture going, followed by his large white sheep-dogs, his knees in leather leggins buttoned, with looks so calm and brow so wise, you would take him for the beautiful King David, as at even to the wells of his fathers he went in his youth to water his flocks.

Alári, with his flock and his noble presence, is too Homeric a figure to suffer any degradation. He should not imitate Virgil's shepherd boys, and offer Muriel a boxwood bowl of his own carving, all cut with his own shepherd knife! He should not occupy his leisure in carving castanets and sheep-bells and collars. It savours too much of the drawing-room shepherds of Watteau. The bowl might be a masterpiece worthy of Aleimedon, but that was not the way for the noble shepherd Alári to woo his love. Perhaps Muriel thought so. She examined the bowl and admired the figures carved upon it—three nymphs wakening a sleeping shepherd by putting a bunch of grapes on his mouth—and then she tells Alári to take back his bowl, and she goes off with a bound, crying, "Shepherd, your offering is very pretty, but my lover has one more beautiful."

> Moun bon-ami n'a 'no plus bello!
> Soun amour, pastre! E quand me bélo,
> O fau que baisse li parpello,
> O dins iéu sènte courre un bonur que me
>   poun. . . .

> . . . My lover hath one more beautiful!
> It is his love, shepherd! And when on me he
>   looks
> Needs must I close my eyelids,
> Or else a bliss runs through me that destroys
>   me. . . .

> Then like a sprite the maiden vanished.
> Alári the shepherd wrapped up
> His goblet carefully again, and slowly, in the twi-
>   light,
> Departed from the farm, disturbed to think
> A maid so fair so much in love should be
> With any one but him.

The next of Muriel's suitors is Veran, from Sambue, in the great salt marshes, where he has a hundred mares, all white, cropping the reeds of the marsh—a hundred white mares, with manes uncut and wildly floating. Doubtless they are the horses of the sea, broke away from the car of Neptune:

> For when the sea moans and scowls,
> When ships part their cables,
> The stallions of Camargue neigh for joy,
> And smack like whipcord
> Their long hanging tails,
> And paw the ground,
> And feel within their flesh
> The trident of the terrible god
> Who raises the tempest and the flood,
>   And stirs from top to bottom the depths of the
>   sea.

This Veran, the master of the fiery steeds, comes proudly, with long white frock, of the fashion of Arles, thrown over his shoulder, with belt chequered like a lizard's back, and hat of wax-cloth, shining in the sun. Of old his grandsire had lent his wild teams to tread out the corn on the threshing-floor of the Falabrego Mas, and now he approaches, not the maid herself, but Muriel's father, Master Ramon, and claims acquaintance. He tells of his great stud and ever-increasing store, and offers himself as the old man's son-in-law. Master Ramon hears, well pleased. He soon tells Muriel. The poor girl hears him, pale, and trembling with emotion, prays her father not to think so young to send her from him. She reminds him how he has told her, that before one marries one should know and be known. Her mother comes to her aid, and the lord of the wild horses retires with a smile,—"For I tell you," says Veran, "a Camargan stud-master knows the bite of a mosquito!"

In the course of the same summer comes a third suitor, Ourrias, *"lou toucadou,"* "the brander"—the cattle-brander of the *Souvage,* the desert beyond the river. Black and fierce are the famous cattle of the Souvage; and there, in midst of his herd, born there, brought up with his oxen,

Ourrias was like them in shape, in the savage eye, and in blackness. Between his eyes he has a scar, got in a famous bull-fight, a single combat, hand to horn, with a savage bull, at a great branding, still remembered in Camargue.

The mighty "brander" finds Muriel at the well alone, with sleeves and skirt tucked up, washing her cheese-forms. Saints of Heaven! how beautiful she was! (*Sainto de Diéu! coume era bello!*) her little feet in the clear water dabbling!

"Good day, fair maid," said Ourrias, "if you don't forbid me, I will give my white beast a drink at this clear well." "Oh!" said the girl, "the water never fails here. You may let her drink as much as you please at the dam-head." Then follows a dialogue of sharp repartee, which ends with Muriel sending the black brander about his business. And now—

> The shadows of the white poplars are lengthen-
>   ing,
> The Ventourese breeze is freshening;
> Still has the sun two hours of height;
> The weary ploughmen are turning their eyes
> To him from time to time, and wishing
> That eve would come, that they might meet their
>   wives
> On the threshold.

That was the time that Ourrias the brander left the spring, revolving in his mind the insult he had received from Muriel. His head was in a whirl, and from time to time the rush of gathered rage sent the blood of shame to his brow. Across the fields he gallops, furious, muttering his wrath. He could have fought with the pebbles of the fields. He could have charged the sun with his spear!

In this mood "the brander" meets with a foe to vent his rage upon; but for this new and chief person of our simple drama we must turn back some leaves.

The hero of our tale, Muriel's love, is no lord of mighty flocks and herds, no prince in disguise; M. Mistral is incapable of that vulgarity. Vincent is the son of a poor cottager of Valabrego, on the left bank of the Rhone, and he and his father earn their bread by making baskets,—the large crates used in the husbandry of olives and almonds, of mulberry-picking and vintaging. We introduce them in a musical stanza:—

> De long dóu Rose, entre li pibo
> E la sauseto de la ribo
> En un paure oustaloun pér l'aigo rousiga
>   Un panieraire demouravo
>   Qu' emé soun drole piéi passavo
>   De mas en mas e pedassavo
> Li canestello e li panié trauca.

> Among the willows by the river side,
> The Rhone with poplars bordered,
> In a poor damp mouldy hut,
>   A basket-weaver dwelt,
>   Who, with his son,
> At times went round from *mas* to *mas,*
> And patched old cribs and baskets full of holes.

One evening—it is the opening of our pastoral—the basket-makers, father and son, seek shelter at the Mas of Falabrego, where wanderers are not rejected. They have their supper with the household, servants and family, all at one stone table. Muriel, active and graceful, seasoned a dish of beans with olive oil, and, running, brought it to them.

Muriel is not quite fifteen—a true Provençal! Her brown cheek shows the ripening of the sun, and her bright, honest face and sparkling black eyes would banish sorrow. About her head her glossy black tresses fall in wavy curls. Twin peaches not fully ripe her rounded bosom seems. Somewhat shy she is, yet merry, laughter-loving.

Much pressed by all, chiefly by Muriel, and cheered by a goblet of Crau wine, the old basket-maker sings a song of the sea. Old Master Ambroi had sailed and fought with Suffren, and he fights his battles and beats the English o'er again, in song, like a true tar. Then the labourers, delighted with the old sailor's song, from table rose, and went to lead their six yoke to the stream; and while their mules are drinking they beneath the branches pendent from the trellis still keep humming the old Valabregan's song. Meanwhile Muriel sits and talks with Vincent, the young basket-maker.

Vincent is sixteen, with cheeks as swarthy as you please,—but darkish land is known to yield the finest wheat, and black grapes make the wine that sets all dancing:

> Certo, acó 'ro un beu drole e di miéu estamps.

> He was, I assure you, a handsome boy in face and figure.

Muriel and he talk of their lives and daily labours. She envies him for travelling about and seeing so much. "Oh! what ancient castles and wild places you must see! What places of pilgrimage and holy saints! While we, we never leave our dovecot!" So encouraged, he tells of his wanderings—of the path through the olives all draped with flowers, when the whitened orchard loads the air with their perfume—of hunting the *cantharis*—of picking the gallnuts from the oak—of getting leeches in the good old way, by wading till the wader's leg is covered with the bloodsuckers—and other gipsy-boy trades. But above all, he tells her of the wonders of *i Santo*, the shrine of the "Three Maries" of Carmague, where there is such divine music, where all the people bring their sick to be cured, where the blind receive their sight. "Ah! young lady, should ever misfortune overtake you,

> *Courrés, courrés, i Santo! aures leu de soulas,*

Run, run to *i Santo*. There you will have solace!" Then he changed the strain, and described with vivid words and gesture a foot-race at Nîmes, in which he had himself run and been defeated. Muriel and Vincent sat close together. She was never tired of listening. "Oh, mother! sleep is for winter! Now the nights are light, too light to sleep: let's listen, listen to him! I could pass my evenings and my life in hearing him!"

Another day of spring, when the mulberry was in leaf, and all the girls of Provence were picking its leaves in baskets and sacks for their silk-worms, Muriel, as she climbed a mulberry-tree, saw Vincent passing, and called him. He asks leave to help her in stripping the branches, and the

pair of children are soon busy picking leaves, taking a bird's-nest, and making love in simple, innocent, charming prattle. In the midst of their talk the branch on which they were sitting broke, and both fell to the ground in each other's arms. Vincent eagerly asks if Muriel was hurt. No, the fall had not hurt her; but something was the matter, something tormented her—took away sight and hearing, and sent her blood bounding through her body. Poor Vincent makes guesses at the cause of her disturbance. Was it fear of her mother chiding for idleness? Was it a stroke of the sun? "No, no! it is none of these that ails me. My breast can hold it no longer. Vincent! Vincent! must you know it?—I love you, Vincent"—*"De tu neu amouroso."* Vincent is at first incredulous—that the princess of the Mas should love the poor basket-maker! But the Provençal girl scorns the difference of fortune. "What matters it to me whether my lover be a baron or a basket-maker!" and her lover answers to her passion in a fine rhapsody. There is nothing he would not do for her—nothing she could desire that he would not get for her. If she wished the bright star above them, he would rush through seas, woods, torrents, nor fire nor sword should stop him; to the tops of the peaks touching the heaven he would go, to seize it, and, on Sunday, he would hang it on her neck. The passionate girl heard him, nothing loath, and no doubt the eloquence came bettered from his lips—for he was a beautiful young fellow, full of life and vigour and confidence in himself, though estimating his love so far above him. It is the passion of the South, with the innocence of childhood and of simple manners. In the whole scene there is nothing to raise a blush, nothing to require even the thin veil of the uncouth *patois* to gain admittance to modest ears. The youth had ventured once to clasp the maiden to his breast—had ventured one kiss,—when a shrill voice, the voice of an old woman, is heard in the alley,—"Muriel, the silk-worms will have nothing to eat at mid-day!" Like a covey of sparrows when a stone is thrown among them, the lovers separate—she to the *Mas*, without a word, with her gathering of leaves on her head; he stands immovable, and watches her from a distance, as she ran swiftly across the fallow.

Such was the person whom the savage Ourrias encountered as he rode from the well at the Mas, galloped over the fields, raging, ready to fight with man, or bull, or devil, with the stones on the fallow, or the moon in the sky. He had no reason to suspect that Vincent was his favoured rival, but he was going in the direction of the Mas, he was at least acquainted with its inhabitants. At any rate he was a victim to vent his rage upon. "I suppose it is you, you ragged barefoot," he cried, "who have bewitched that foolish girl of the Mas?" and then he spoke insultingly of Muriel, and sent contemptuous messages to her. Vincent was roused to madness, and both men were ready for battle, but they spent some time in the preliminary war of words, after the fashion of the old world, when men about to fight loved to whet the appetite for the feast of battle with threats and boasts, which we moderns—perhaps more correctly, we English—have banished even from the most plebeian encounters. Ourrias screams and howls with rage, and our hero is not silent. The war of words over, they rush together like two bulls. The ground shakes, the pebbles fly from under them. Vincent is light and quick, and plants the first effective blow, but when he was following it up, Ourrias catches him with his huge fist, and fells Vincent to the earth. Then more boasting. Then Vincent is up, and they rush together and grapple—like Scotsmen—like Lancashire men,—it is a fierce wrestle more than a boxing-match. In their fury they scratch and bite:—

> Diéu! quenti cop Vincen i'ajounglo!
> Diéu! quenti bacelas mando lou bouvatiè!

> Heavens! how Vincent peppers him with blows!
> Heavens! what awful hits the herdsman deals!
> His club-like fists crushing, smashing!

It is the battle of two of Homer's heroes. And again it is the fight of Dares and Entellus.

Tired of storming round and round him, Vincent puts down his head and makes a rush full at his stomach. Then as he bent—

> The puissant herdsman seized him by the small, and in Provençal fashion tossed him o'er his shoulder like a shovel of wheat, into a field a far way off.

But the youth rises, claims a third round, and—

> At the risk of perishing, on the Camargan savage rushes, and a blow delivers him, a straight-out-from-the-shoulder blow, fair in the stomach. The Camargan staggers, feels for something to support him, to his misty optics all seemed turning. Icy cold sweat broke out on his forehead. Then upon the stony plain, and with a falling tower's crash, great Ourrias falls! Into deep silence all La Crau was hushed.

Vincent places his foot on his breast, but, after a time, dismisses him with a jeer, vanquished. The savage brander skulks away and mounts his horse, which he had tied to a tree, and then—

> Chafing, storming, cursing all around! What is he seeking? Aie! Aie! he stoops. Now he has found it! Now he brandishes his trident savagely, and rushes right upon Vincent.

"Say your prayers," thundered the traitor. Vincent fell under his huge spear as he looked a last look at the white dwelling of his love. The brander gallops off, scattering the pebbles as he flies. "To-night," he says, "the Crau wolves will have a feast!"

Yet, not without compunctious visitings the traitor rides away from the scene of his murder, and coming to the river bank, hails a boat to take him over. Three fishers in the boat take him on board, and his mare swims at the stern. "Ho! master pilot. have a care! your boat is shaky!" "I have noticed it just now."

> Pourtan un marrit pes, vous dise,
> Responde lou pilot, et piéi digué plus ren.

> "We have a wicked freight, I tell you," the pilot
> said, and no word then said more.

But when the boat pitched and staggered, and took in water till she was like to sink, said the pilot again—

> "As tua quaucun miserable!"

> "Villain, you've murdered some one!"

At last the pilot gets communicative. The Rhone is full of phantoms to-night, and ghosts and spiritual appearances; for it is St. Medard's night, when the souls of the drowned revisit the earth, taper in hand, searching, searching, seeking for any good deed of their past life, any act of faith that may open the gate of Paradise to them. There are ghosts of fishers—

> Fishers who caught the lamprey and the perch, and now have food become for perch and lamprey. Now behold another troop defiling. All disconsolate on the shingle, they are maidens fair and loving, who, abandoned by their lovers, in despair besought the Rhone for hospitality, and in the river drowned their grief immense.

> Desesperado
> An demanda la retirado
> Au Rose, pér nega soun immenso doulour.

> There is a band of atheists, traitors, murderers. These also seek some saving deed, but in the gravel of the river find but heavy sins and crimes, in shape of stones, 'gainst which they stumble with their naked feet. . . . Beneath the roaring wave, Heaven's pardon these shall seek in vain, for ever.

Here Ourrias clutched the pilot's shoulder. "The boat is filling!"

"The bucket's there," replies the pilot quietly. And Ourrias sets to bale with all his might. And he toils bravely: *but that night the spirits of the river danced on Trincataio bridge.*

Courage! bale, Ourrias, bale! The mare tries to break her halter. "What is it, Blanco? Art afraid of the dead"? said her master, his own face white as chalk, and his hair on end. And silently the water rises, rises to the gunwale, plashes over!

"Captain, I cannot swim! Can you save her?—save the boat!"

"No! In the twinkle of an eye she'll sink; but, from the river's bank a cable will be heaved us by the dead—that procession of ghosts that frighten you so." And as he spoke down went the boat in the Rhone.

In the dark distance, the pale lamps trembling in the hands of the drowned send a long ray as bright as lightning from bank to bank, and as you have observed a spider spinning her thread in the sun, and then gliding along it, those fishers, who were spirits, caught the brilliant beam and slid along it. From the middle of the gurgling water, Ourrias, too, stretched his hands to seize that cable; *but the spirits of the river that night danced on Trincataio bridge,*—and down went the assassin to the bottom!

A passage like this suffers from the condensation necessary here. But even in our bald rendering, relieved here and there by Mr. Grant's version, the whole episode of Ourrias seems to us highly vigorous and picturesque. In the closing scene, the supernatural is not employed till the mind of the assassin, equally with the mind of the reader, is worked up to the pitch necessary for receiving such impressions. None of Scott's ghostly scenes are so fine or so natural. The *diablerie* of "Tam-o'-Shanter," though perfect in its kind, is pitched on a lower key.

But, after all, Vincent is not killed outright. He is found in a miserable state by some swineherds returning from the fair of St. Chamas the Rich, and borne by them to the nearest dwelling,—the Mas of Falabrego. The bliss of the wounded knight, tended by his lady love, the ecstasy of recovering health in her company, are not for him, however, or they must be supplied by the reader's imagination. M. Mistral prefers an unmeaning visit of the lovers to a witch's cavern,—a very foil to the scene we have just described. Vincent recovers and returns to his father's hut, from whence the presumptuous youth sends his father on an embassy to the Mas of Falabrego.

The old basket-maker arrived on St. John's Eve, along with a gang of reapers, who were to begin cutting next day; but first they had their feast at Master Ramon's board, and then they went, as befitted, to heap and trim the balefires proper on that night. Ramon the farmer, and Master Ambroi, are left together at table. The ambassador tells his tale cunningly in the third person, and asks advice. Ramon has plenty, and all for stern coercion. "If a father is a father, he should make himself obeyed. When we were young, had any son opposed his father's will, it's more than like his father would have killed him."

> Mais afebrido e blavinello
> L'enamourado pichounello
> Ven alor a soun paire. Adone me tuarés
> O paire! Es iéu que Vencén amo
> E, davans Diéu et Nostro Damo,
> Res autre qu'én n'aura mon amo!
> Un silenci mourtau li prengué touti tres.

Fevered and pale, the impassioned girl interrupts her father, "You will kill me then, my father. It is me that Vincent loves, and, before God and Our Lady, none but he shall have my heart!" A dead silence held all three.

Her mother first gives Muriel a good scold. "You have refused Alári with his thousand sheep, and Veran the great stud master, and Ourrias so rich in cattle! Well—be off! Tramp with your beggar-love from door to door. Go! join the gipsy troop, and boil your porridge-pot upon three stones under a bridge."

But her father was even more furious. She should not go though he should chain her, or put a hook in her nose like a wild animal! "Though I should see your cheeks grow pale and wear away with sorrow—fade like snow upon the hill-sides under the hot sun, yet you shall stay. You shall never see your beggar more!" And he struck the table a blow with his fist that made it tremble. As a vine its overripe grapes sheds to the wind, pearl by pearl Muriel sheds her tears.

The old farmer then turned upon Master Ambroi. "And who knows, you old traitor, but you and your young beggar have woven this plot together in your hut?"

But now Ambroi is roused.

> Malan de Diéu! cridé tout d'uno
> Se l'avén basso la fourtouno,
> Vuei aprenes que pourtan lou cor aut!

"God's mischief!" cried he all at once;

> if our fortune is low, you shall know this day that we carry our hearts high. I am yet to learn that poverty is vice or stain. Forty years I have served my country. Scarce could I a boat-hook handle when I went as a ship-boy in a man-of-war. I have seen the empire of Melinda, and heard the cannon roar with Suffren in the Indian war. As a soldier too I have traversed the globe, done my duty in the mighty wars of the great Captain who rose from the South and scattered destruction from his hand over Spain and to the steppes of Russia, till the world, at the sound of his drum, shook like a tree of wild pears; and in the horrors of boarding, in the agony of shipwreck, the rich have never done what I have. But I, child of poverty—I, who have not in my native land a corner to put a plough in—for my native land I have bled and suffered for forty years, but no one remembers it!

"What would the old grumbler have?" said Master Ramon;

> I too have heard the bombs rattle, filling with thunder the valley of the Toulon folk. I have seen the bridge of Arcola fall, and the sands of Egypt soaked in blood! What then! When we returned from those wars we set ourselves to work like men, to dig and scarify the ground. We were at it tooth and nail. Our day began before the sun was up, and the moon has caught us hanging over the hoe. They say the earth is generous, but it is like the walnut-tree, it must be well beaten first! Ah! if one could count the knocks and drops of sweat each morsel of this ground has cost me to reclaim! By Saint Anne of Apt! and am I to hold my peace? or, like a satyr, toil and moil always; eat my siftings, that the homestead might grow rich—that I might with honour stand before the world! and then I am to give my daughter to a beggar haunting the hay-lofts! Go, in the name of thunder!—keep your dog; I will keep my swan!

Such was the rough talk of the farmer. The other old man, rising from the table, took his cloak and his stick, and said but two words:—"Adieu! may you never have cause to rue this day!"

And as he left the Mas, his path was lighted by the fires of St. John's Eve, round which the reapers were dancing the farandole, and shouting, "St. John! St. John! St. John!"

And what of Muriel? In her sombre little room, dimly lighted by the stars, she on her bed is lying weeping, with her brow between her hands: "Oh! tell me, our Lady of Love, tell me what to do!" (*Nostro Damo d'Amour, digas me que farai!*) Oh! cruel fate! Oh! father hard who treads me under foot! If you saw my heartbreak and trouble, you would have pity on your child—me whom you called your darling!"

While thus upon her bed the lovely child laments, her heart consumed with love, with fever throbbing, while she recalls the springtime of her love—bright moments, happy hours,—she remembers too Vincent's counsel: if mischief or misfortune come, run, run to "the Saints" for solace! Now has misfortune come. "Let me go! I shall return content." Then from her little white crib sliding she descends the wooden staircase stealthily, carrying her shoes in her hand, removes the heavy door-bar, recommends herself to the good Saints, and rushes out into the dark night. She makes her way through servants and shepherds unperceived; the dogs know her, and are quiet. She had to travel right across the rugged plain of Crau; to cross the Rhone, and through Camargue to the chapel and shrine of her patrons (*i Santi*) the Three Maries.

> Ni d' aubré, ni d'oumbro, ni d'amo!

> No tree, no shade, no living soul.

> Under a sun of June Muriel flies.
> (*Lampo, e lampo, e lampo*) runs, and runs, and
>   runs.

As the sun rose high the heat was dreadful. Sinking with thirst she called on good St. Gént:

> Lou bon Sant Gént, de l'empirèio
> Entemdegne prega Miréio.

The good Saint Gént, from the empyrean, heard her prayer, and suddenly she beheld a well, an old well with a stone cover, shrouded in ivy. And then there is a charming episode of a little boy sitting and playing by the well, and singing to the basket of snails which he had gathered; but we have not room for this pure and graceful idyl. The child is good to Muriel, and takes her to his father's hut, a fisherman on the Rhone, and tells her, by the way, of the marvels and grandeur of Arles, and of the sea, which the maid of the Crau had never seen. At length, said the boy,

> see, yonder! there is the canvas of our hut moving in the wind. Look! on the white poplar which shades it my little brother is climbing. He is hunting grasshoppers, or maybe looking out for me. Ah! now he has seen us. My little sister, Zeto, who lent her shoulder to help him up, turns; and you see her running to my mother, to tell her to prepare the *bouillabaise;*

—and then the hearty playful welcome of the honest fisher! It is a bit of pure Arcadian, unspoilt by affectation.

But Muriel has half her journey still before her. Next morning the little boy rows her across the broad Rhone, and saw her jump ashore. Then, handling his sculls, "he backed with one, and with the other pulled his boat's head round." Over the desert of Camargue, through the treeless, burning desert, through the marshes crusted with salt, through the rank fen herbs, the home of gnats, through the delusion of the mirage, under a fiery cloudless sky, poor Muriel flies, with Vincent in her thoughts. At length the relentless sun pierces her brow as with arrows, and she falls death-stricken on the sands. A friendly swarm of gnats find her prostrate, and sting her poor hot hands, and all her neck and brow, till she is forced to crawl forward, and arrives at the chapel of the Saints of the Sea. There she casts herself down on the pavement, and has strength to pray:

> Oh! Holy Maries, who can into smiles change bitterest tears, I am a maiden young, and love a youth. Handsome Vincent!—him, dear Saints, I love! I love with all my heart! I love him! I love him as the brook loves to run! as the bird loves to fly! And they would have me extinguish this cherished fire, which will not die; and they would have me tear up the almond-tree! Oh! Holy Maries, who can change our tears into flowers, quick incline your ear to my grief!

The poor child, gasping on the flags, her head bent backward, her eyes wide open, seems to see heaven open, and three women, divinely lovely, in white shining robes, descending down a path strewed with stars. "Poor Muriel!" they say,

> take comfort. We are the three Judæan Maries. We are the patron saints of Baux. Your complaint ascended to us ardently as flames of fire. Your faith is great, but your prayer distresses us. You would drink at the fountains of pure love foolishly before death! Where have you seen happiness in this world below? . . . This is the great saying that man forgets—Death is life! (*La mort es la vido.*)

> The meek, the simple, and the good are blessed. With favouring gales they wing their way to heaven quietly, and, white as lilies, leave a world where the saints are stoned.

> Oh Muriel! could you but see how full of suffering is your nether world, how poor and foolish your passion after matter and your fears of the grave, unhappy lamb! you would bleat for death and forgiveness. But the seed-corn must decay before it shoots. It is the law (*Es la lei*). We too, before we had our beams of glory, had drunk of the bitter cup.

And then the three Saints of the Sea tell their earthly history, of their leaving Jerusalem after the ascension of our Lord; while the people of Judea were still lamenting—

> Ah lou plagnien dins la Judéo
> L'ou beu fustié de Galileio
> Lou fustie de peu blound!

> Ah they mourned in Judea the handsome carpenter of Galilee, the carpenter of the fair hair!

They tell of their miraculous voyage—a crowd of men and women, without sail or oar. Martial and Saturnin, and Trophimus and Maximin; Lazarus and his sister Martha, and the Magdalen; Eutropius and Sidoneus, and Joseph of Arimathea, and Marcellus and Cleon; and of their being cast ashore in the marshes of the Rhone. At Arles they were struck with horror at the Pagan rites in honour of Venus. The people singing—

> Canten Venus la segnouresso,
> La maire de la terro e dou pople Arlaten.

> Venus they sing, the lady, mother of the earth and of the people of Arles.

Then Trophimus, with the mere name of Christ, tumbles the statue of the goddess from her pedestal. The enraged crowd is appeased by the serene face of Trophimus, as if already encircled with a glory; and by the beauty of the Magdalen, more lovely than their Venus. The Provençal poet, writing to his countrymen, speaks to their senses. It is the beautiful Jesus with the fair locks!—the Magdalen more lovely than the Pagan Venus!—Magdalen, whom angels peeped through the chink of her cot to look out, and when she let fall a tear, gathered it and placed it in a golden chalice. But we do not care to criticise such painting with Protesting coldness. When all Provence and Languedoc had been brought to the true faith by that shipful of Saints, the three Maries found their rest on the wild shore of Camargue. Their tomb was long forgotten, till they revealed its situation to the last king of gay Provence. King René handed down the reverence of the Saints of the Sea to France.

The Saints bid adieu to Muriel, and ascend to prepare, against her death, the roses of the snow-white robe for the virgin, the martyr of love (*vierginenco e martiro d'amour*). Their words fade in the distance—

> As when at eve, harmonious, the sounds of bleating goats, of shepherd's pipe, of songs of love, along the serpentining Argen's banks, over the hills and fields, along the lanes, grow faint and die among the mountains brown, and night and melancholy come (*e vén l' oumbro emé la languissoun*), so their words fainter grew and fainter, from cloud to cloud of gold—seemed the last note of some church hymn, or like a far-off strain of music floating o'er the ancient church, swept by the breeze—and Muriel seemed to sleep.

There her parents find her. The hard old father is quite broken.

> Mirèio ma bello mignoto
> Es iéu que sarre ta manoto
> Jéu toun paire.

> Muriel, my pretty darling! it is I that press your hand, it is I, your father. . . . . Oh Saints, let her live, she is so pretty, so innocent, such an infant! Take my life instead. Send my old bones to dung the mallows!

They move her to the upper chapel to catch the sea-breeze, and there her quick sense tells her her lover is come. He too had hurried madly over the fatal plain, so fatal to his love, and finds her dying. He raves wildly. "What have I done to be so punished? Have I cut the throat of her who suckled me? Has any one seen me light my pipe at a lamp in a church, or drag the cross through thistles like the Jews? It wasn't enough to refuse her to me, but they must make a martyr of her!" Then he embraced his love. *"E'mbrassé soun amigo."*

The Saints breathed over the dying girl a little strength, and her face flushed with a sweet joy, for the sight of Vincent was to her pleasure unspeakable. *"Car de véire Vincèn i agradé que nounsai."*

"Tell me, love," said she,

> do you remember that time when we were sitting together talking under the trellis, you said to me, if any misfortune come, run quick to the Sainted

Maries, and soon will you have solace. Oh, dear Vincent, that you could see into my heart as in a glass. Of solace! of solace my heart is running over! (*De soulas, de soulas, n'en regounflo moun cor!*)

> My heart is a spring running over of delights of all sorts—graces, pleasures—of all I have abundance. I see, I see the choirs of God's angels!

Then again she is rapt in ecstatic vision, and passes into a sweet delirium. "Would," said Vincent, "I had seen the Saints who cheered her. Oh! I would have said, Queens of heaven, our only help remaining, take my eyes from my head, my teeth from my mouth, the fingers from my hands. But her, my little fairy! oh, give her back to me in health!"

> Mai elo, ma bello fadeto
> Oh! rendés-me-la gaiardeto!

It is evening; they give her the last rites of the dying. All is still. In the chapel nothing is heard but the *Oremus* of the priest.

> Against the wall the setting sun his horizontal last beams casts, and slowly come the sea's long waves, and dully break upon the beach—her parents and her lover knelt sobbing around her.

Muriel speaks again—"The time of parting is at hand—quick! shake hands! Lo, the glory waxes on the Maries' brows. Already, along the Rhone the rosy-hued flamingoes are assembling, and the tamarisks in bloom beginning to adore. Oh blessed souls! they beckon me to go with them. They whisper I have nought to fear, their bark to Paradise will take me straight, and they the constellations know." Then the old father broke out in a piteous wail,—"What boots it to have grubbed up all that wild wood, my darling! What use is it if you leave the house? All my courage came from you. The heat struck down, the fire of the turfs parched me, but the sight of you carried off both heat and thirst."

She said to him, "Good father, when you see a moth fluttering round your lamp, that will be me. The Saints are on the prow waiting me. Yes, dear Saints! wait but a single instant. I cannot go fast, I am so ill."

Then breaks out the mother:—

> "It is too much! you shall not die! Stay with me! you must! Then, when you're well again, my Muriel, we will go together and carry a basket of pomegranates to your aunt Aurane. It isn't far!"

> "No, it isn't far, good mother, but you will go alone. My mother, give me my white dress! See you the white and splendid mantles the Maries wear! the snow on the mountains is not so bright."

Then it was the swarthy basket-weaver that spoke;—

> "My all! my beautiful! thou who hadst opened for me your fresh palaces of love! thy love! my flowering almond. Thou, thou, by whom my poor clay brightened as a mirror,—thou, the pearl, of Provence,—thou, the sun of my young

life!—shall it be said that you, great Saints! have seen her in her agony, and embracing your sacred lintels in vain!"

The maid replied, all softly (*plan-planeto*):—

> "O my poor Vincent! what is it you see? Death,—that deceitful word! what is it? A cloud which vanishes with the knell of the bell! a dream that wakes us at the end of night. No! I do not die! with ready step on the bark I mount! Adieu! Adieu! Now we are at sea. The sea—the beautiful rippling plain is the avenue to Paradise. The blue sky meets the sea all round. Aie! how the water rocks us! Among so many stars hung up there, I shall soon find one where two loving hearts can love at freedom. Saints! Is that an organ playing in the distance?"

And the dying girl sighed and turned her brow as if to sleep.

A smile was on her face as while she spoke; but she was dead.

We know nothing more. Vincent proposes to die, and be buried with his love. He asked to have one grave for both in the sand, where, beneath the trembling water, she at his ear may still speak to him of her Maries:—

> Aqui ma bello a moun auriho
> Tant-e-piéi mai de ti Mario
> Me parlar.

Whether his wishes were fulfilled our author saith not.

Such is the simple story of rustic love, round which M. Mistral has thrown the graces of genuine poetry. Like a true artist, he has dashed in some pictures of the rural life and occupations of his dear countrymen, not less poetical that they are absolutely true—the labours of the field, relieved with the pleasure which in that happy climate the mere cessation of labour gives; the song, the dance, the rustic feast, are there not ideal—not like the deluding festivities of English cottagers, admitted one day of the year to the Squire's park in holiday suits to make their obeisance. Some of our extracts show with what taste M. Mistral has discarded the scenic dresses and adornments that disfigure our English and some Scotch pastorals. He has painted his countrymen as they are—in the simplicity of nature—an uncultivated but impressible and poetic nature, not readily passing into vulgarity or falling into childishness. His shepherd of the Alps is a real shepherd; his Veran, the master of the wild white horses, dressed up to the dandy standard of Arles in blouse and glazed hat, is not thereby spoilt for the purposes of Art. How true to nature is the sweet heroine herself, with her airs of spoilt daughter, rural beauty, heiress, village queen! Her impertinences to her suitors, even her burst of rebellion against her parents, we forgive them all for such sweetness of charity, such a fulness of passionate love, such a present sense and feeling of religion, as are to be found nowhere else in literature except in some of Shakespeare's characters, where, as here, we find the truth of real passion—the passion of the South—sudden, absorbing, consuming, freed by its very intensity from any taint of coarseness. (pp. 181-92)

"Mistral Mirèio," in The North British Review, *Vol. XLVIII, June, 1868, pp. 180-94.*

Harriet W. Preston　(essay date 1874)

[*Preston translated many of Mistral's works into English. Below, she offers a detailed overview of* Calendau.]

Nine years after the appearance of **Mirèio**, Frédéric Mistral published simultaneously at Avignon and at Paris, and in parallel Provençal and French, a second poem of heroic proportions, entitled **Calendau.** The critics, who had been quite thrown off their guard by the strangeness and the sweetness, the innocent ardor and frank garrulity of the earlier poem, were far more wary in their reception of its successor. Their verdict was unanimously and even emphatically favorable, but it was still a verdict, not a startled cry of admiration. **Calendau** won priceless praise, but it created comparatively no excitement, was not long talked about, and never, we believe, translated.

It is proposed to give some account of this riper and more formal production of M. Mistral's genius, which, if it have not quite the wayward and fascinating audacity of its elder, does yet give evidence of immense vigor in its author, and of a wealth of imagination sufficiently rare; while it seems to include almost all of legendary and picturesque Provence not portrayed, or at least touched with light, in the previous work.

The reader of **Calendau** must begin by disabusing himself of the idea that the sensations which he received from **Mirèio** are to be precisely repeated. Nothing, indeed, is in the nature of things more unlikely than that we shall be twice surprised by the same person, in the same way. The curious *naïveté* of the former tale is abandoned, perhaps deliberately, along with the rather transparent pretense of singing for "shepherds and farmer-folk alone." The usual reading public is addressed in **Calendau,** and means not wholly unusual are employed to excite and detain our interest.

In the first place the lovers in **Calendau** are not children. They are young, indeed, to judge by our slow northern standards, but they are, to all intents, man and woman, and the lady at least has lived and suffered much when we see her first. Then, it is not a story of to-day; and there can be no doubt that the romantic charm of **Mirèio** is perpetually enhanced by the wonder that so artless and idyllic a life as the one there described can be lived anywhere at the present time. The date of **Calendau**'s adventures is placed a hundred years back, and very skillfully. In the dark and desperate times which preceded the outbreak of the first great revolution in France, rapine and bloodshed, flight, treachery, and siege were matters of frequent occurrence, and the wildest incidents were unhappily probable. Moreover, the shadows of even one century are sufficient to confuse the wavering line between nature and the supernatural, and thus to afford all needful latitude to an imagination which, although capable, as we know, of a most winning playfulness, does yet appear to be essentially sombre. And this introduction of a semi-supernatural element, together with the stress continually laid on the ancient literature and mediæval honors of Provence, impart to **Calen-**

dau a kind of transitional character, which is far from impairing its interest. The work seems, whether the author intended it or no, almost to bridge the strange chasm between the old Provençal poetry and the new, and to give an effect of continuity to the unique and brilliant literature of Southern France. And if the fresh realism of **Mirèio** be not here, and we deem this a little more like ordinary books than the other, that very likeness is also of use sometimes, as affording us a distinct and accurate measure of the poet's own undeniable originality.

He opens his poem conventionally with an allusion to his earlier effort, and in the same metre.

> I, who once sang the love and sorrows sore
> Of a young maiden, now essay once more—
> God helping me—to tell a tale of love;
> How a poor fisherman of Cassis strove
> And suffered, till he won a shining crown,
> Stainless delights, and honor, and renown.

There follows an invocation to the spirit of Provence, as illustrated in the famous past, and then the opening scene of the story, which is characterized by a suppressed fervor, a kind of silent intensity of light and color and emotion, hardly to be paralleled in English verse.

> One summer day, from a high mountain-seat,
> Rock-built and with the blossoming heather
>   sweet,
> Two lovers watched the white caps come and go
> Like lambs upon the shining sea below,
> While the note only of the woodpecker
> Startled the silence of the noontide clear.
>
> Cornice-like hung in air the narrow ledge,
> The dark pines thronged beneath; but, from the
>   edge,
> One saw the sun-touched faces of the trees
> Laugh to the laughter of the southern seas.
> White on the beach gleamed Cassis: far away
> Sparkled Toulon, and the blue Gardiole lay
>
> Cloud-like along the deep. So spake the youth
> Unto the maiden: "Never, in good sooth,
> Did hare or pigeon eager huntsman tire
> Like thee! Have I not won at thy desire
> Fortune and fame, and wrought all prodigies?
> Poor dreamer whom my dream forever flies!"

And he goes on to describe, in ardent fashion, the impossibilities he would yet undertake for the sure hope of winning her. The lady answers with tears in her divine eyes, owning for the first time, seemingly, that she loves him, and him alone, but hinting at some insurmountable obstacle to their union. Her lover interrupts her with a burst of impetuous gratitude for her confession:—

> "Why should not then our joy be perfected?
> We love, we are young, we are free as birds!" he
>   said.
> "Look! how the glowing Nature all around
> Lies in the soft arms of the Summer bound,
> Courts the endearments of the tawny queen,
> And drinks the breath of her dark beauty in!
>
> "The azure peaks, the faint, far hills, lay bare
> Their beating bosoms to the radiant air.
> The changeful sea below us, clear as glass,

> Hinders the ardent sun-rays not to pass
> Into its deepest depth; and joys no less
> Of Rhone and Var, to feel the mute caress.
>
> "Nay, do not speak! But hark how earth and sea
> Have both one language, how exultantly
> They tell the passionate need they have of love!
> Dost tremble, sweet? I bid thy fear remove.
> Come, let me lead thee to the altar straight,
> Life at its longest is too brief." "Oh, Fate!
>
> Oh, cruel star!" brake forth the woman's wail.
> "Thou must not! Cease, in God's name, lest I fail
> To keep my truth."

And after murmuring something of dishonor to an ancient and unstained name, she breaks off with a passionate prayer that the sombre woods and mountain solitudes about her may continue to shelter her, as they have hitherto, from the wrath of her enemies, and the seductions of her own heart. There follows a picture of the two lovers, without which the reader can hardly form a clear idea of their personality.

> She sprang upon her feet, inspired, erect.
> Oh, beauteous was her head! and well-bedecked
> By its dense coronal of shining hair,
> Whereof the twin-coils were as broom-boughs
>   fair
> With yellow flower, and from her eye sincere
> Storms might have fled, and left the heavens
>   clear.
>
> White were her teeth, as the fine salt of Berre,
> And shy, at times, the lofty glances were
> Of the proud orbs, whose wondrous hue recalled
> The steadfast splendors of the emerald.
> And desert sunshine faint reflected shone
> In the warm tint her peach-like cheeks upon.
>
> So towered the lithe, tall shape divinely molded
> By the white linen robe her limbs that folded.
> While, at her knees, her rapt love listening,
> As in the blue he heard an angel sing,
> Leaned on his elbow with up-gazing eyes,
> And he,—he too was made in splendid wise:
>
> With supple limbs, yet strong as sail-yards be
> (A score of years or barely more, had he),
> And large eyes sad with love, and black as night;
> The down upon his lip was soft and light
> As on vine branches—

He renews his suit in the most fervid and persuasive terms, and, when he is again tenderly repulsed, grows keenly reproachful and hints at toils and sufferings undergone for her sake, which he scorns to dwell upon in detail. Is she a woman, he demands at length, or is she Esterello, the fairy who is said to haunt that mountain region, teasing men with her loveliness, luring them to her pursuit, but always eluding them in the end? And she replies, in sad jest, that she is Esterello, and can never reward, however she may return, any mortal love. Then she invites him to a grotto hard by, where the stalactites weep perpetual pearls.

> "And this, my friend," she in her dreamy way,
> "Is Esterello's palace! Look, I pray,
> At these fair hangings! God himself," said she,
> "Wrought all this foliage of white jewelry

The rainfall feeds. Wilt try my leaf couch here?
My only seat,—but heights are ever drear.

Is it not sweet here? This most quiet spot
The raging heats of summer enter not,
But all is cool." He took the leafy seat,
She dropped upon her knees beside his feet,
And the strange light that flooded all the place
Clothed them, as in one garment, with its rays.

In this becoming attitude the lady tells her true story. She
was, by birth, a princess of Baux, the last representative
of one of the most ancient and illustrious houses in Provence. In her impoverished orphanhood, for only the Castle of Aiglun had descended to her out of all the vast pos-
sessions of her family, she had had many suitors, and had
fixed her choice upon the least worthy. He was a stranger
of brilliant and commanding, but always sinister, appearance, whom, when benighted in a great storm, she had received into her castle, who had described himself to her
as Count Severan, an adventurer of high birth with a large
secret following, by the help of which he intended one day
to avenge upon a corrupt government the wrongs of their
beautiful province, and who had completely subjugated
the fancy of the young girl. Their banns were hastily published, and the night of their wedding-feast arrived, but,
as the bridegroom presented the guests, one after another,
by high-sounding but wholly unfamiliar names, the bride
noted with terror that they had more the air of *come* (that
is, the overseers of gangs of galley slaves) than of gentlemen. A scene of furious revelry ensued, but while the
bridegroom was in the midst of a pompous oration, there
forced his way into the brilliant hall an unbidden guest.

He stopped midway of his insensate boast,
For in the open doorway rose a ghost.
An old, most miserable, coarse-clad man,
Down whose gaunt cheeks the grimy sweat-
    drops ran,
The threshold crossed of that high banquet-hall,
And stood, a loathly shape, before us all.

White turned the bridegroom, and a deadly ray
Leaped from his eyes as he the steps would stay
Of the strange comer, but it might not be.
Forward he came silently, solemnly,
As when God takes a beggar's shape sometimes
The rich man to confound amid his crimes.

With slowly-trailing steps he neared the host,
And scanned him long with lean arms tightly
    crossed.
Till on the breast of each expectant one,
Great terror fell as with a weight of stone.
An icy wind blew from the night, and flared
The festal lamps, and at last some one dared

To break the silence with a brutal sneer—
"Ho for a famine, this curst land to clear
Of beggar vermin! or in four more days
We are devoured!" "What dost thou in this
    place,
And with this bridal pair, old fool?" they cried.
The insulted stranger not a word replied.

Then some began to jeer his hairless pate,
His bloodshot eyes, and heavy, shambling gait:
"Were it not better, thou ill-omened bird,

To hide thy glum face in thy hole?" He heard
And still unmurmuring each affront he took,
Yet on the host bent one beseeching look.

But others—"Come, old fellow, these fine folk
Are not worth minding! They must have their
    joke
But do thou glean about the board! Make haste,
And snatch a joint or carcass where thou mayst;
Look! Are thy jaws not equal to a chine
Of pork? Or wilt toss off a cup of wine?"

"Nay, masters," answered wearily and slow
The wan intruder; "you'll not tempt me so,
For I want no man's leavings. I am here
To seek my son." "His son! 'Tis mighty queer!
Why, pray, should this old snakeskin vender's
    son
Be haunting the fine lady of Aiglun?"

There was a base doubt in the mocking look
Of them which stung, and I could illy brook.
But still they plied him: "Tell us which he is,
This son of thine, and tell the truth in this,
Or from the gargoyle of the highest tower
Of old Aiglun thou 'lt dangle in an hour!"

Then the old man: "Behold, I am denied!
Spurned like the sweeping of the floor aside!
Now shall ye hear the raven croak!" quoth he,
And rose up in his rags right awfully.
"Hold!" cried the Count, "out with him from
    the hall!"
Stony his face, and pallid as the wall.

"Fall on him, valets! Hunt the spectral thing!"
Two tears that I can yet see glistening,
Hot, bitter tears in aged eyes and weak,
Rose and rolled down the beggar's furrowed
    cheek.
Heart-rending memory! Pale as death we grew,
While he took up his broken tale anew.

"I am like Death," he moaned, "of all forgot!
Yet comes he to the feast, though bidden not.
Oh, ay, and woe is me! I fain once more
Would see my son—he drives me from his door.
'Fall on him! Hunt him!' says he in his ire;
Thou haughty bridegroom, I am still thy sire."

The beggar then turns upon the horrified bride, and denounces his unnatural child to her as a base-born churl,
a common robber, a murderer. None dares dispute, or
seeks to detain him as he turns to leave the hall, save the
lady herself, who, in her first revulsion of feeling, springs
forward, calling the old man *father*, and praying him to
stay. He puts her aside with a pitying prophecy, and she
swoons away. Awaking late in the night, she finds herself
in her own chamber with only her old nurse mourning
over her. The castle is still. She collects her thoughts, realizes the ruin that has befallen her life, thanks God that she
is, at least, the wife of Severan only in name, and resolves
to fly, leaving her ancestral home in the possession of the
banditti below. After long wanderings and many priva-
tions, she had made herself a kind of hermitage on this
Mount Gibal, at the southern extremity of Provence,
where she had ever since lived a mysterious and ascetic
life, accounted a supernatural being by the peasantry who
caught occasional glimpses of her. Here Calendau, the

brave young fisherman from Cassis on the beach below, had long since found, and loved, and sought to woo her, although himself regarding her with a kind of superstitious awe. Hence, after the fantastic fashion of the ladies of old, she had sent him forth to deeds of high emprise, which he had achieved one after another, returning to lay his trophies at her feet, and only now, after many such adventures, to learn that his lady returned his love and to hear her tragic story.

> She ceased. As one who from an evil dream
> Awakes, Calendau rose, fist clenched, a gleam
> Of fury in his eyes. "No longer fear
> Thy bandit lord, but think that I am here,
> Adore, and will release thee! He or I,
> I swear it by the fires of hell, shall die."
>
> But she: "Ah no! Thine eyes affright me more
> Than ever he. Go not! Stain not with gore
> Our sinless love!" "Nay, but his life must end!"
> "Am I not then thy sister, thy sweet friend?
> Oh, leave me not!" He answered sullenly,
> "I have one only word: *The wretch shall die,*—
>
> "Being a robber and accurst. And oh,
> Thou knowest full well whether I love or no."
> "I will no murderer's love! All undefiled
> The hand I take must be." He said, and smiled.
> "Princess, fear not! This hand hath ne'er a stain,
> And white for thy dear sake it shall remain.
>
> "Not as a felon will I seek his death,
> But as one brave another challengeth,
> I will appease my wrath! Alone, breast bare
> I will go down into the tiger's lair,—
> God grant my foot slip not!—and once within
> Will smite amid his band this new Mandarin.
>
> "Farewell, my queen!" He said, and made one dash,
> Swift as the swamp-fire's gleam, the lightning's flash,
> Forth of the grot, then paused. She, at his side,
> "Thou goest to thy death!" in anguish cried,
> "Cannot love stay thee? Art thou mad to brave
> Twenty fierce outlaws in their highland cave?"
>
> "Yea, were there twenty thousand in their stead,
> I would not strike my sail! Behold," he said,
> "Love is my strength,—what better following?"
> Adown the mount he plunged with valiant spring,
> Flung back his vest as the bold Gascons do,
> And turned him to far lands and conflicts new.

The third canto opens with a rapid account of Calendau's journey across Provence. It is a series of pictures, each brilliant, distinct, and harmonious in coloring, a lovely panoramic view. M. Mistral had shown himself a master of this kind of painting in those cantos of **Mirèio** which describe the muster of the farm laborers, and the flight of the heroine across La Crau and Camargue. We cull a stanza here and there.

> Afar over the sage-fields hummed the bees,
> Fluttered the birds about the sumac-trees.
> How lucid was the air of that sweet day!
> How fair upon the slopes the shadows lay!
> The ranged and pillared rocks seemed to upbear

> Levels of green land, like some altar-stair.
>
> O'er the sheer verge the golden pumpkin hung
> His heavy head, the rock-born aloes flung
> Its flowery rays abroad like God's own lustre.
> Deep in the dells, full many a coral cluster
> The barberry ripened. The pomegranate red
> Reared like an Indian cock its crested head.

As Calendau drew near his lady's ancestral home, he asked of all he met the way to the Castle of Aiglun.

> "O, cheery plowman, in thy furrow toiling,
> O, merry pitch-man, thy sweet resin boiling,
> How far from this to old Aiglun?" he cried,
> "Climb, gallant, climb!" the laborers replied;
> "Then down the deepest chasm, if so be
> The horrid heights no terror have for thee."
>
> So he went down the deep, chill, darksome vale.
> The frowning precipice well-nigh made fail
> Even his high heart. There the unwilling day
> On snake and lizard flings one noontide ray,
> Then hides behind the cliff. The gorge along
> Tumbles in foam the angry Esteron.

Presently, however, the defile widened, giving to view an open space where Calendau came suddenly upon the self-styled count himself, surrounded by some thirty or forty of his followers, both men and women. The outlaws were reposing after the fatigues of the chase, and taking their noonday lunch upon the sunlit turf. The intruder is of course ordered to stand and deliver, but his beauty attracts the women, and his boldness the men. The count himself sees in the audacious stranger a possible recruit, and the end of it all is that he is invited to share their repast on condition that he will tell his story, and declare his business there. Calendau asked no better. His tale, he says, is one of love, and of many labors wrought in the hope of rendering himself worthy of his lady's distinguished favor. Some say that lady is a fairy, Esterello by name, and it is certain that she lives alone in a wild solitude, that her beauty is more than human, and her thoughts and visions too high for earth. At all events he will call her Esterello.

The next six cantos are occupied chiefly with Calendau's recital of his own exploits. After each feat performed he seeks his lady in her retreat, but finds her for a time ever harder and harder to win. The strenuous and often rude action of the hero's narrative is beautifully broken and relieved by the moonlight quiet and mystery of these scenes upon the mountain. Other themes are also introduced, which both lighten the monotony of grotesque or stern adventure, and assist in preserving the continuity of the main story: the irrepressible comments of Calendau's listeners; the wonder, and sometimes incredulity of the men; the sentimental admiration of the women; and, on the part of Severan himself, the secret suspicion, early aroused and constantly strengthened, that Calendau's austere and angelic lady-love is none other than his own fugitive bride, of whom he had never been able to obtain a trace. He chooses, however, to allow the young enthusiast to finish his tale, both that he may become possessed of the fullest possible information, and also that he may have time to mature some perfectly effectual plan of vengeance on the two.

Calendau begins by telling them that his own birth was humble. He came of honest and thrifty fisherfolk from Cassis, on the Mediterranean coast, and he cannot help lingering lovingly over some of the details of his simple early life.

> "I would you once had seen the goodly sight,
> The Cassis men under the evening light!
> And in the cool, when they put out to sea,
> Hundreds of fishing craft go silently
> And lightly forth, like a great flock of plover,
> And spread abroad the heaving billows over.
>
> And the wives linger in the lone doorways,
> Watching, with what a long and serious gaze,
> For the last glimmer of the swelling sail.
> And if the sea but freshen, they turn pale,
> For well they know how treacherous he is,
> That cruel deep—for all his flatteries.

>   . . . . .

> But when the salt sea thunders with the shocks
> Of rude assault from the great equinox,
> And bits of foundered craft bestrew the shores,
> Then can we naught but close our cottage doors,
> And young and old about the warm fireside
> Wait the returning of the summer-tide.
>
> Ah! those were evenings—when the autumn
>   gales
> Blew loud, and mother mended the rent sails
> With homespun thread; ay, and we youngsters
>   too
> Were set to drive the needle through and
>   through
> The gaping nets, and tie the meshes all
> There where they hung suspended on the wall.
>
> And in his tall chair by the ingle nook
> My father sat, with aye some antique book
> Laid reverently open on his knee,
> And "Listen, and forget the rain," quoth he,
> Blew back his mark, and read some tale divine
> Of old Provençal days, by the fire-shine.

But Calendau asks pardon for dwelling on these scenes of childhood. Manhood had begun for him when he met his lady in the forest. He had first thought to win her with gold, and had undertaken to make himself rich by the difficult and dangerous tunny-fishing of the Mediterranean coast, in which immense fortunes are sometimes made. The fifth canto of the poem "La Madrago" describes this exciting sport. The sketch is one of great power, and has a kind of restless brilliancy. Many local legends and wild superstitions of the coast are introduced, yet it is intensely real. We give the passage which describes Calendau's crowning success:—

> But when with dawn the pallid moon had set,
> The whole unnumbered shoal into the net
> Came pouring. Ah, but then I was elate!
> Drunk with my joy, thought I had conquered
>   fate;
> "Now, love," I said, "thou shalt have gems and
>   gems;
> I'll spoil the goldsmiths for thy diadems"
>
> Love is the sun, the king of all this earth—
> He fires, unites, fulfills with joy, gives birth,

> Calls from the dead the living by the score,
> And kindles war, and doth sweet peace restore.
> Lord of the land, lord of the deep is he,
> Piercing the very monsters of the sea
>
> With fire-tipped arrows. Lo the tunny yon'
> Now in one silver phalanx press they on;
> Anon they petulantly part and spring
> And plunge and toss, their armor glittering
> Steel-blue upon their crystal field of flight,
> Or rosy underneath the growing light.
>
> 'T was nuptial bliss they sought. What haste!
>   What fire!
> With the strong rush of amorous desire
> Spots of intense vermillion went and came
> On some, like sparkles of a restless flame,
> A royal scarf, a livery of gold,
> A wedding robe, fading as love grew cold.

>   . . . . .

> So at the last came one prodigious swell,
> And the last line, that seemed invincible,
> Brake with the pressure, and our boats leaped
>   high.
> "Huzza! the prey is caged!" we wildly cry;
> "Courage, my lads, and don't forget the oil!
> The fish we have,—let not the dressing spoil!"
>
> "Bout ship!" We bent our shoulders with a will,
> Our oars we planted sturdily but still,
> And the gay cohort, late alive with light,
> Owned, with a swift despair, its prisoned plight,
> And where it leaped with amorous content,
> Quivered and plunged in fury impotent.
>
> "Now then, draw in! But easy, comrades bold,
> We are not gathering figs!" And all laid hold
> With tug and strain to land the living prize,
> Fruit of the treacherous sea. In ecstasies
> Of rage our victims on each other flew,
> Dashing the fishers o'er with bitter dew.
>
> Too like, too like our own unhappy people,
> Who, when the tocsin clangs from tower and
>   steeple
> Peril to freedom and the land we cherish,
> Insensate turn like those foredoomed to perish,
> Brother on brother laying reckless hand,
> Till comes a foreign lord to still the land.
>
> Yet had we brave and splendid sport, I ween,
> For some with tridents, some with lances keen
> Fell on the prey. And some were skilled to fling
> A wingèd dart held by a slender string.
> The wounded wretches 'neath the wave with-
>   drew,
> Trailing red lines along the mirror blue.
>
> Slowly the net brimful of treasure mounted;
> Silver was there, turquoise and gold uncounted,
> Rubies and emeralds million-rayed. The men
> Flung them thereon like eager children when
> They stay their mother's footsteps to explore
> Her apron bursting with its summer store
>
> Of apricots and cherries.

The wealth thus suddenly acquired Calendau spends with ostentatious profusion. He appoints a *fête* at Cassis, to be celebrated with public games, boat-racing, and trials of strength, and promises largess to the crowd. He then buys the costliest trinkets, fit only for a queen's casket, and proceeds to offer them to his Esterello, by whom they are refused with a sort of gentle disdain. She reminds him that she has no further use for jewelry, and that the field-flowers are, for her, a far more appropriate garniture, and she reproves his shallow confidence and youthful vanity. Still further mortification awaits him at the Cassis fête, to which the next canto is devoted, and where he had anticipated a public ovation; but where certain comrades, who are jealous of his prosperity, overcome him by treachery in the games, and poison the minds of his townsfolk against him. Wounded and sore, both in body and mind, he repairs again to his fair recluse, and this time she is kinder.

> I came once more unto my lady's eyrie,
> Heart hot with sense of wrong and limbs a-
>   weary,
> And oh, the rest I found there, and the balm!
> Coolness as of clear water, and a calm
> Celestial. "Oh entreat me pityingly,
> My strange white Fay," I said; "no gems have
>   I
>
> For thee to-day. One only laurel-bough
> Thick set with thorns is all I offer now;"
> And so I dropped under the shady trees,
> And told her of my hard-won victories,—
> All barren,—and my shame; and she, grave-
>   eyed,
> Looked up and listened from the grass beside.

Then she tells him a thrilling story, or rather chants him a ballad, out of that legendary lore of Provence with which her memory is stored, and on which, in her solitude, her imagination is ever brooding. We give it entire:—

> At Arles in the Carlovingian days,
> By the swift Rhône water,
> A hundred thousand on either side,
> Christian and Saracen fought till the tide
> Ran red with the slaughter.
>
> May God forefend such another flood
> Of direful war!
> The Count of Orange on that black morn
> By seven great kings was overborne,
> And fled afar,
>
> Whenas he would avenge the death
> Of his nephew slain.
> Now are the kings upon his trail;
> He slays as he flies; like fiery hail
> His sword-strokes rain.
>
> He hies him into the Aliscamp,—
> No shelter there!
> A Moorish hive is the home of the dead,
> And hard he spurs his goodly steed
> In his despair.
>
> Over the mountain and over the moor
> Flies Count Guillaume;
> By sun and by moon he ever sees
> The coming cloud of his enemies;
> Thus gains his home,
>
> Halts, and lifts at the castle gate
> A mighty cry,

> Calling his haughty wife by name,
> "Guibour, Guibour, my gentle dame,
> Open! 'T is I!
>
> Open the gate to thy Guillaume
> Ta'en is the city
> By thirty thousand Saracen,
> Lo, they are hunting me to my den;
> Guibour, have pity!"
>
> But the countess from the rampart cried,
> "Nay, chevalier,
> I will not open my gates to thee;
> For, save the women and babes," said she,
> "Whom I shelter here,
>
> And the priest who keeps the lamps alight,
> Alone am I.
> My brave Guillaume and his barons all
> Are fighting the Moor by the Aliscamp wall,
> And scorn to fly!"
>
> "Guibour, Guibour, it is I myself!
> And those men of mine
> (God rest their souls!), they are dead," he cried,
> "Or rowing with slaves on the salt sea-tide.
> I have seen the shine.
>
> Of Arles on fire in the dying day;
> I have heard one shriek
> Go up from all the arenas where.
> The nuns disfigure their bodies fair
> Lest the Marran wreak
>
> His brutal will. Avignon's self
> Will fall to-day!
> Sweetheart, I faint; oh let me in
> Before the savage Mograbin
> Fall on his prey!"
>
> "I swear thou liest," cried Guibour,
> "Thou base deceiver!
> Thou art perchance thyself a Moor.
> Who whinest thus outside my door,
> My Guillaume, never!
>
> Guillaume to look on burning towns
> And fired by—*thee!*
> Guillaume to see his comrades die,
> Or borne to sore captivity,
> And then to *flee!*
>
> He knows not flight! He is a tower
> Where others fly!
> The heathen spoiler's doom is sure,
> The virgin's honor aye secure,
> When he is by!"
>
> Guillaume leapt up, his bridle set
> Between his teeth,
> While tears of love and tears of shame
> Under his burning eyelids came,
> And hard drew breath
>
> And seized his sword and plunged his spurs
> Right deep, and so
> A storm, a demon, did descend
> To roar and smile, to rout and rend
> The Moorish foe.
>
> As when one shakes an almond-tree,
> The heathen slain

Upon the tender grass fall thick
Until the flying remnant seek
Their ships again.

Four kings with his own hand he slew,
And when once more
He turned him homeward from the fight,
Upon the drawbridge long in sight
Stood brave Guibour.

"By the great gateway enter in,
My Lord!" she cried,
And might no further welcome speak,
But loosed his helm, and kissed his cheek,
With tears of pride.

The docile Calendau goes on his way inspired and heartened. His next feat is to scale Ventour, the most precipitous peak in Provence, hitherto considered inaccessible, and he signalizes his achievement by felling a grove of larches on the very crest of the mountain. The difficult ascent is very graphically described:—

"Savage at once and sheer, yon tower of rocks;
To tufts of lavender and roots of box
I needs must cling, and as my feet I ground
In the thin soil, the little stones would bound
With ringing cry from off the precipice,

And plunge in horror down the long abyss.

Sometimes my path along the mountain face
Would narrow to a thread; I must retrace
My steps and seek some longer, wearier way.
And if I had turned dizzy in that day,
Or storm had overtaken me, then sure
I had lain mangled at thy feet, Ventour.

But God preserved me. Barely as I strove
With only death in view, I heard above
Some solitary sky-lark wing her flight
Afar, then all was still. Only by night
God visits these drear places: Cheery hum
Of insect rings there never. All is dumb.

Oft as the skeleton of some old yew,
In a deep chasm, caught my downward view,
"Thou art there!" I cried; and straightway did
　discover
New realms of wood towering the others over,
A deeper depth of shadows. Ah, methought
Those were enchanted solitudes I sought!

From sun to sun I clambered, clinging fast
Till all my nails were broken. At the last,
The utter last,—oh palms of God—I caught
The soft larch-murmur near me, and distraught,
Embraced the foremost trunk, and forward fell,

Mistral reading his poem Calendau *to a group of Félibres in 1866.*

How broken, drenched, and dead, no words can
  tell!

But sleep renews. I slept, and with the dawn
A fresh wind blew, and all the pain was gone,
And I rose up both stout of limb and glad;
Bread in my sack for nine full days I had,
A drinking flask, a hatchet, and a knife
Wherewith to carve the story of my strife

Upon the trunks. Ah! fine that early breeze
On old Ventour, rushing through all the trees!
A symphony sublime I seemed to hear,
Where all the hills and vales gave answer clear,
Harmonious. In a stately melancholy
From the sun's cheerful glances hidden wholly

By the black raiment of their foliage
The larches rose. No tempest's utmost rage
Could shake them, but with huge limbs close en-
  twined,
Mutely they turned their faces to the wind;
Some hoar with mold and moss, while some lay
  prone
Shrouded in the dead leaves of years agone.

A sudden fear assailed my spirit bold.
"O kingly trees!" I cried; "O hermits old!
All hail, and pardon! And thou too, Ventour,
Long steeled the tempest's torment to endure,
Wilt thou not howl in all thy caves to-day,
Because thy stately crown is rent away?"

But now the deed is done, the battle dared.
Mightily swings the ax, and rent and scared
Are the millennial slumbers of the place.
Mightily cleaves the iron relentless ways
Along the wood, and every resinous scale
Weeps drops of gold, but these shall not avail

To stay the slaughter. A heart-rending shriek
Springs as the great trunk parts, from root to
  peak;
From bough to bough quivers a dying groan,
As falls the monarch headlong from his throne,
And thunders down the vale, spreading about
Tumult and din as of a water-spout.

Not content with the havoc thus wrought in the forest solitudes, and the consternation excited in the valley below,
and heedless even of the blandishments of a certain lady
of Maltbrun, who desires to regale and refresh him in her
highland castle after his exploit, Calendau next assails
what is called the Honey-comb Rock, a series of clefts and
fissures where the mountain bees have been for ages depos-
iting their honey undisturbed; and barely escapes with his
life from the consequences of this last piece of bravado.
But when he approaches Esterello once more, bearing a
larch bough and a slice of honey-comb as his trophies, he
finds her rather amused, than overawed, by his latest
achievement. She cannot help praising his prowess, and
half relenting to his fantastic fidelity, but she declares her
fervent and somewhat mystical belief, that the solitudes of
nature are sacred, and that he who wantonly invades and
violates them deserves a severe punishment. She reminds
him once more that her beloved heroes of old fought to
redress human wrong, and mitigate human suffering, and
tries to awaken him to a higher ideal of life and love.

Count Severan can hardly restrain himself at this stage of
the story.

"Go then in peace," she said, "and if one day
A man and knight indeed thou comest my way,
Then,"—with a sudden smile,—"then I will tell
Whether I found thy honey sweet!" Ah well,
Bright seemed the word, and kind, and the day
  bright,
And the birds sang, and the stream leapt in light.

"So, at the last, thou hadst her?" Severan
Burst forth. "Thy tale is growing tedious, man."
"Pardon, my gracious lord!" Calendau cried,
"And deign a little longer to abide;
'T were base to cheat your honor of the rest,
Seeing my story's end will be its best!"

In the eighth canto, Calendau signalizes his devotion to
a loftier ambition, by interposing between two hostile
bands of freemasons, whom he finds one day engaged in
a fierce and sanguinary fight, and finally, by common consent of the parties, arbitrating and restoring peace among
them. The theme hardly seems a very poetic one, but it is
treated with the dignity which never forsakes Mistral,—a
deal of strange and sombre history, or rather mythology,
is introduced, and the rival claims and bizarre pretensions
of the children of Hiram and Solomon are detailed with
a certain weird pomp. Again Severan interrupts Calendau's narrative fiercely and scornfully, and with a wrathful side-glance at the listeners who hang upon his lips.

"At least they named thee their Grand-Chief, I
  hope,
Their master, king,—whate'er they call it,—
  pope,"
Hissed Severan. "Nay," was the tranquil word,
"Nor pope, nor king, nor general; but, my lord,
Provence and Aquitaine, do not forget,
Will one day give me a name nobler yet,—

He who won Esterello." "Oh, have done!"
The huntresses 'gan clamor, all as one;
"Nor look that look that freezes all our blood!"
For now, with lifted eyes the hero stood,
And sweet and misty was their gaze afar,
Like his who sees a vision or a star.

And now Calendau goes on to relate how he addressed
himself to the most perilous and unselfish of all his under-
takings,—the achievement of which brings the reader to
the commencement of the story. There was a certain brig-
and named Marco Mau, the pest and terror of all southern
Provence, much as Severan himself was of the north. No
hearth or home or sanctuary, or life of man or chastity of
woman, was safe from the violent assaults of this ruffian
and his armed band; and him Calendau, at the head of a
small picked company, tracked, defied, besieged in his
stronghold, and finally slew. Of course he won the enthusiastic gratitude of his townspeople and countrymen in general, and they became eager to make amends for all the
petty jealousies of the past, and whatever injustice they
had previously done him. In the great city of Aix he was
received like a prince, and rare civic honors were bestowed
upon him. And when he enters the lists at the Fête-Dieu
and is proclaimed victor in one after another of the
strange, antique games which characterize that festival,

the enthusiasm of the people mounts to the highest pitch, and Calendau himself is filled with a sacred joy and gratitude, as unlike as possible to the vain exultation of his earlier days. He knows that his present honors and popularity have been well won by hard and beneficent service, and he thinks his Esterello must approve him at the last. We are now at the crisis of the story, and the interest deepens rapidly.

"What maudlin tales these foreigners do spin!
Is it not supper-time?" once more brake in
Count Severan. "Come, hurry to the end!
For whither, boaster, does thy prowess tend?
Thou hast not won her yet! So much I know,—
And others will yet reap where thou didst sow!"

"Will reap! What mean you, scoundrel? storm
    and war!"
Cried the young fisher in tones louder far
Than e'en the bandit's, and more awesome still;
"But I *have* won her! Laugh or weep, who will!
My plume is flying free, and I can guide
Full well the stormy clouds whereon I ride!

I would that you had seen my lady bright,
As once again I climbed her balmy height.
'To-day they named me Chief of Youth,' I said.
Flamed in her cheeks two roses of deep red,
And her throat swelled, and in her glorious eyes
I saw the lucent, loving tears arise.

Ay, and I drank those tears! And from that
    hour,—
Whether it be yon nectar's wondrous power,
I know not,—but my doubts, my fears are dead.
The flowers bloom, look you, wheresoe'er I
    tread,
And wheresoe'er I turn my blessed vision,
The land is all one scene of peace Elysian,—

The sky seems vaster than it did of old;
And I can hear the concords manifold
In Nature's varying voices. And I know
Why the winds cry aloud or whisper low,
Why strives the angry sea, and by what token,
Weary and sad, retires with pride all broken.

For hearken what she said, this queen of mine:
'Now is my soul, Calendau, wholly thine,
Only my body must I keep mine own;
But thee I love, my knight, and thee alone!
'T were sweet,—and why stay I my steps like
    this,
Nor rush with open arms to utmost bliss?

Now shalt thou know! A treacherous bond,'
    cried she,
'And yet invincible, constraineth me,—
I am an outlaw's wife.' " "Ho! not so fast!"
The huntsmen jeered. "The rocket bursts at
    last!"
But the poor women trembled where they sate
Yearning o'er him who thus had sealed his fate.

While he—Calendau—cast his cap aside,
Leapt up, "And that same impious bond," he
    cried,
"By the good grace of God, I break to-day!
Yet if I fail let not my slayer say
I am abased; for what I have, I ween

Is bliss enough—an ocean deep, serene,

As heaven itself! E'en death shall powerless
    prove,
And break his horns against our mighty love.
Fair as the day my lady's body is,
And yet the whitest pearl of rich Ganges
A boar may swallow. She I dare call mine
Is but the angel whom that pearl doth shrine.

The low, the evanescent love of sense
Is but a madness. It is long gone hence.
I love my sister's soul, and enter there,
And come and go, and all I see is fair.
Oh, never painter lived who could retrace
Even in symbol that angelic grace!

O ye unspeakable joys of the spirit,
Ye are the paradise true souls inherit!
Ye are indeed the purifying fires
Wherein love loseth all its low desires.
O oneness wonderful! Accord complete,
Tender and piercing, sad because so sweet!

Death shall erelong to marble turn our frames,
But the twin thought of us, the inseparate flames
Of divine essence, by the self-same road
Shall journey to the Infinite of God!
The one adored, the one who doth adore,
Giving and taking blessing evermore."

Thus the enraptured youth, like the brave sower
Who goes forth full of hope the rude fields o'er,
And sows broadcast, on all the stony plain
And hard, his sacred and life-giving grain.
Large drops his forehead beaded, but his smile
With faith was radiant and content the while.

And they who heard him dumbly felt a thrill,
Born of that zeal divine, unwonted steal
Through all their frames, and hearkened eagerly
As the mule pricks his ears when he sees fly
The sparks from off the anvil. But the view
Of that clear river of love, forever new,

Incapable of stain, marriage of soul
Made but for heaven, that smiles at Death's con-
    trol,
Stirred to its utmost spite one felon heart;
And scowling Severan, where he sat apart,
While hate burned like a blister at his breast,
Brooded revenge with feverish unrest,

Yet held as with a leash his passions in,
Muzzled like ravening dogs, until his spleen
Took shape. "Calendau hath won all things
    now,
The aureole is growing round his brow;"
So his thought ran. "Of heaven he is sure,
And there of honor bright and favor pure.

He hath her soul! He is become as God!
Now, though the lightning lay its fiery rod
Upon him, and his frame be ground to dust,
He is not dispossessed of that fair trust.
He hath her soul, and what to him is death?
Ha! ha! I'll break the sword and leave the sheath!

By the insidious poison of a bliss
More deadly than all pain, that soul of his
I will make one corruption! Ay, the germ
Of yonder tree of life shall feed the worm!

And were thy baser passions tighter reined
Than now, proud youth, thy doom were still or-
　dained."

With this infernal thought the count arose,
Blandly a signal gave, and all of those
About set forth together for Aiglun,
Climbing the tortuous torrent-side. The sun
Set suddenly behind the mountain-wall,
And swift and sombre 'gan the night to fall.

Till from the east the early moon did peep,
As a maid, risen from her couch of sleep,
Her lattice opes, the coolness to inhale.
The crickets chirred incessant in the vale,
And where the onion-fields lay black in shade,
The courtil-mole trilled forth her long roulade.

Rarely from far above the piercing cry
Of some belated quail fell mournfully,
Or a young partridge in the vale astray
Whimpered afar. And cooler grew alway
The air, until the deepened shades of night
Were cloven by the bat's precipitous flight.

The eleventh canto, "The Orgie," is devoted to the fulfillment of Severan's sinister design, and it reveals a wholly
new aspect of M. Mistral's versatile genius. The inconceivable luxury of the bandit's castle, the costly profusion of
the garden feast, the music, the tempered light, the heavy
odors, and the artfully intensified beauty of the women,
whom Calendau seemed hardly to have heeded before, are
all described in diction infinitely voluptuous, and with an
effect of sensuous splendor and enchantment hardly at-
tainable in a northern tongue. The revelry, restrained at
first to a certain languorous measure, grows faster, while
from time to time the lurid scene is relieved by glimpses
of the summer night scenery, with what effect those will
readily understand who remember the peaceful light of
sunset sky and sea around the fierce duel of the rivals in
Mirèio.

There were swift clouds abroad that night, and
　dark,
Hiding the moon at times. The restless spark
Of myriad fire-flies, like an emerald shower,
Quivered in all the air. And hour by hour
Warmer the night turned, and heat lightnings
　parted
From the far heights, and through the ether
　darted.

And if the mad mirth failed, at intervals
Sounded distinctly all the waterfalls
And tinkling fountains; and anon there came
Dashes of cooling spray to cheeks aflame.
For a cascade that plunged adown the hill,
By art compelled, with many a silver rill

Threaded the pleasance,—seeming now asleep,
Then hurrying to a verge with one gay leap,
Dispersed in diamond rain, it passed from view.
Only the grass below right verdant grew,
And loveliest flowers, jasmine and the tuberose,
Freighted the dark with sweets,—how sweet to
　those

Hot revelers! And the cantharides
Shook their keen odors from the great ash-trees.
At last the host: "And are ye satisfied

With feasting? Ho then for a dance!" he cried.
"Young, rosy limbs in play I hold a sight
Aye worth the rapture of a gallant knight."

There followed one of those intoxicating and lascivious
dances, indigenous in the neighborhood of Marseilles, and
parent of the Carmagnole and more modern abomina-
tions. In the midst of it Calendau finally shakes off his
gathering stupor and challenges Severan to instant and
mortal combat. A scene of frightful confusion ensues, but
the struggle is, of course, a brief one; Calendau is overpowered by numbers, bound and flung into a dungeon, and his
torture exquisitely enhanced by the assurance that Severan and his troop, following the clue furnished by Calendau's story, will set forth that very night to capture and
bring back, alive or dead, the lost lady of Aiglun. From
this dungeon he is released at early daybreak, by Fortune-
to, the youngest, fairest, and tenderest of the unhappy
slaves whose allurements he had resisted the night before,
and he flies to the defense of his lady. He is only just in
season. The "cornice-like ledge" where we saw them first
forms a kind of natural fortress, and there the young lover,
informed with the valor of ten, holds the troop at bay for
one long twenty-four hours, and at last disables so many
that they retreat, but only to set fire to the woods that gir-
dle the mountain. A terrible night ensues, during which
the two can do no more than wait for death together; but
when the first rays of dawn are struggling with the lurid
flames and stifling smoke, the bells are suddenly heard to
ring in Cassis and all along the shore. The rumor has
spread that Calendau, the darling and benefactor of the
coast, is in uttermost peril, and the whole population turns
out to fight the flames. The strange battle is made sufficiently thrilling and dubious, although the reader fore-
knows its end. Severan is killed by the fall of a burning
trunk, and—

Two thousand souls, a people in its might,
Engage the roaring fires in sturdy fight,
Felling a pathway to the mountain-crest,
Just as the sun leaps up to flood the east
With radiance; and the child of yonder wave
And the white fairy of the highland cave,

He with his nostrils wide to the pure morn,
She with the torrent of her bright hair borne
Downward, like jujube flowers, stand forth to-
　gether,
The glory of the blue bejeweled weather
Flung like an arch triumphal o'er the twain.
Hand in hand on the height they hear again

And yet again exultant shouts ascending,
Two thousand voices in one pæan blending
"Hail to Calendau! who hath brought renown
And praise of men to our poor fishing-town!
Who hath won Esterello! Plant the may
For him who is our consul from to-day!"

The happy crowd therewith in triumph bear
Forth of their citadel the rescued pair,
The tried, the true, the blest beyond desire;
While the sun, which is God's own realm of fire,
Goes up his dazzling way with blessing rife,
Calling new lovers and new loves to life.

So happily ends the poem. The brief abstract here given

conveys a very inadequate idea of the abundance of incident, the range of tone, and the immense variety of action by which it is characterized. Where nearly every page is strikingly picturesque, selection becomes a difficult task. (pp. 406-16)

Harriet W. Preston, "Mistral's 'Calendau'," in The Atlantic Monthly, Vol. XXXIII, No. CXCVIII, April, 1874, pp. 406-16.

The Catholic World   (essay date 1885)

[*In the following essay, the critic summarizes the events presented in* Nerto *and praises Mistral's use of epic form.*]

A new poem by Frédéric Mistral is a great literary event. Though he is not of the Academy, the author of **Mireille** is probably the truest, if not also the greatest, poet now living in France. Born, dwelling, writing in Provence and in Provence's own enchanting language, he is a very lily of all that was best in the spirit of the Romance ages, flowering with a great strength in this rude century of iron and steam. He is a type of that lofty and abiding Faith that won once for France the title of Eldest Daughter of the Church, and of that knightly grace and principle that set her on the throne as the Queen of Chivalry.

Mistral has just produced another poem, of which we shall try to give a brief summary.

Although he modestly calls his new volume, **Nerto,** a Provençal novel, it is divided into seven cantos, preceded by a prologue and followed by an epilogue. It has also the qualities and proportions, the tone and the elevation, of an epic work.

Nerto is a young girl whose father sold her to the devil, and who, after moving vicissitudes and terrible trials, escapes from the power of the infernal spirit. The scene is laid in the middle ages, in the country of the author, near the gates of Avignon, the papal city. The poem is written in verses of eight feet, and the volume has on the left page the Provençal text facing on the opposite page, for the benefit of readers not familiar with the beauties of the *langue d'Oc,* a French translation made by M. Mistral himself.

It is a considerable risk to speak of an epic poem in our age, especially one in French. The poets of the present century, even the greatest—Lamartine, for example, or Alfred de Musset—have given to their poetic works a character purely personal and, if we may so express ourselves, egotistic. They sing throughout their doubts, their uncertainties, their despairs, their revolts. The world with all its splendors figures as secondary scenery and as a sort of setting or background to their personalities. What they have to tell about is—themselves. This is what the Germans call subjective poetry.

Without depreciating the value of that conception of the merit of their works, it is allowable to say that their idea of poesy, from the standpoint of the highest art, degrades it to the level of a philosophical monologue.

Recent French poets, nay, the French poets of this century, have nearly all failed to grasp the true relations of the exterior world to their art. The painter, the sculptor, the architect, the musician, the poet—it is their mission to widen our views of life and to spread before us the existence of forms, of colors, of personages, of heroes which will be sought vainly in the natural order. Graced by their touch, the real world will be elevated to the altitude of their vision of the ideal. It is not with the poet a mere question of perspective or of grand surprises: he gives a body and a soul to the representations of his thought; he dresses them so with graces and ennobles with such qualities that the names alone of his heroes and heroines suffice to move our minds and make our hearts beat.

It is strange that the poets of our day have relinquished the mighty gift of lively invention and allowed it to fall into the hands of a lower grade of literature. Poets are the men who should naturally create personages destined to pursue a certain course and accomplish high achievements. Romancers have now the monopoly of this gift.

It must not, however, be believed for a moment that the romance can under any circumstances become the equivalent of the epic poem, unless we desire to repeat the absurd saying of M. Philarète Chasles that the *Odyssey* of Homer is a romance in which the principal personage is the captain of a ship. The romance of our days has nothing of poetic spontaneity. It is not that powerful synthesis which, with one living and concentrated stroke, pictures the man speaking and acting, but it is a long, detailed, minute analysis, or less than an analysis—an inventory. It has neither the love of seeking knowledge nor the enthusiasm of inflaming one; documents are its weapons; it is an inquest in which it desires to interest you.

The epic poem has nothing to do with this method of information and exposition. Its method consists, not in saying a great deal, but, on the contrary, in saying little. It suffices a poet to mark merely the essential traits of the soul and body in order that the character live and move and the imagination of the reader take it in; our spirit is moved by his thoughts and our attention roused by a glance.

Epic poetry has a superiority which places it high over all other kinds. The discourses of Homer's heroes have always been cited as incomparable models of eloquence. The retorts that the warriors exchange from chariot to chariot as they rush to battle breathe of the liveliest passion and realize the ideal of dramatic dialogue. The invocations of the poet are full of lyrical inspiration, and all the resources of descriptive art are brought to bear in order that the reader may view the scene and behold the aspects of the characters.

This is why epic works are so rare in the history of the world: this is why the poets of our times dare not risk themselves in too high a strain. In order to accomplish anything it requires qualities of mind very powerful and unfortunately not often found combined: fecundity, variety of invention, the sobriety which knows how to say everything in a few words and to pass with ease from one subject to another without abridging by omission or drawing out too long. Failure of fecundity, and consequently of variety, is perhaps one of the most marked characteristics of our times. Ours is a worn-out and discouraged epoch. The painter who one day happens on a fine inspiration passes his life reproducing the same picture with imperceptible variations: always the same models, the same effects of perspectives and of colors. It is the same in literature: each author follows out an idea, a hobby; and if you wish to arrive at the quintessence of him, eliminate his trifling variations and you will find the same naked theme from the first page to the last. All is sameness.

Let us pass now to the poem of *Nerto.* It would be difficult to find in all French literature a more pliable, varied, and fecund talent than is displayed here. The author unconsciously calls our attention to the diversity of ideal types which he proposes to place before our eyes. He gives a different title to each of the seven cantos comprised in his poem: "Le Baron," "Le Pape," "Le Roi," "Le Lion," "La Nonne," "L'Ange," "Le Diable."

The introduction of the poem is singularly dramatic. After a strophe which paints *en silhouette* the castle of Château-Renard we are taken into the presence of the Seigneur Pons. The noble châtelain is about to quit life. He is stretched upon his bed of agony, having just been brought in from his war-horse wounded unto death. Arrived at this terrible pass, he avows to his daughter, Nerto, who is praying at the foot of his bed, the most terrible of all his secrets. Once, when he had played and lost, he sold her to the demon. Nerto was to have sixteen years. It was the delay fixed by the compact. Nerto, on hearing this terrible news, wrings her hands in despair; she invokes the help of all the saints. Her father again speaks:

Château-Renard is situated near Avignon, where was the see of Pope Benedict XIII. The Sovereign Pontiff has been besieged for four years and is on the point of falling into the hands of his enemies. There was for him, however, a means of escape. During the first years of the papal sojourn at Avignon a subterranean passage had been created by prudent hands. This passage, unknown to all, opened in the centre of the papal fortress. It was through it that Nerto alone could seek the Sovereign Pontiff; it was through it that she alone could save him; and as the price of this service she would be protected by his power from falling into the flames of hell.

The Seigneur Pons expires, and Nerto obeys him.

Here in the first canto must we mark the art and the exquisite delicacy with which the poet averts us from thinking this wicked father too odious, and at the same time shocks us by this execrable abuse of paternal power.

In the second canto the scene is shifted to Avignon at the moment when the great Schism of the West was ending. Benedict XIII, who occupies the pontifical see there, is an anti-pope; but the author does not touch upon this question—he ignores it. He treats Benedict XIII as the true successor of St. Peter and the representative of Jesus Christ. He shows Benedict to us a stranger in the midst of this city of the middle ages. The picture of Avignon, traced with the hand of a master by M. Mistral, will recall to many the features of that celebrated chapter in the romance of *Notre Dame de l'aris,* "Paris à vol d'oiseau." Aside from the qualities which are found in the

archæological erudition of the academicians of Inscriptions and Belles-Lettres, M. Mistral's description has the quality of being alive as well as exact. Some one has remarked that a reader can get a better idea of Grecian mythology from reading the poems of John Keats than from perusing all the works of all the profound scholars who have ever written on the subject. M. Mistral is the John Keats of the middle ages. He pictures Benedict XIII, in his sacerdotal majesty and with the tiara on his head, defying the attacks of man. It is impossible, while reading these lines, not to compare the situation with that of Pope Pius IX besieged in Rome.

Nerto, issuing from the subterranean passage, finds herself face to face with the Chevalier Rodrigue, nephew of the pope and commander of the troops which defend him. Rodrigue is the type of the elegant and debauched young seigneur. He murmurs in the ear of Nerto the first words of love she ever heard. Meanwhile the enemy is upon the point of making an assault. Nerto, introduced into the presence of the pope, makes known to him the means of safety of which her father had given her the secret, on condition that His Holiness should protect her. After giving a last benediction to the two armies and to the whole world the pope disappears and seeks refuge in the castle of Château-Renard.

The third canto, entitled the "King," shows us the pope, Benedict XIII, a refugee in the subterranean parts of the fortress of Château-Renard. He finds there the Comte de Provence, who, following the custom of the house of Anjou, had taken the title of "Roi de Forcalquier, de Naples et de Jérusalem." This king is on the point of espousing his fiancée, Yolande of Aragon, recently arrived from Spain. The ceremony is to take place in the church of St. Trophime at Arles, several leagues distant from Château-Renard.

Nerto, in the terror of the siege and the precipitation of the flight, had not had time to reveal to the pope the terrible secret which concerned her. She now tells him of it and demands of him a release from the chains of the demon. The Sovereign Pontiff replies that his power is without virtue against hell. He exhorts the young girl to become the bride of Jesus Christ and to take the veil in the convent of St. Césaire of Arles.

Then comes the triumphal procession of the pope and the queen and the king. Rodrigue, on the route, approaches Nerto and makes proposals in order to prevent her from becoming a religious.

Upon the road which leads from Tarason to Arles an antique column marks the limits which divide the abbey lands of St. Césaire and of Montmajour. Here the bourgeois of the city of Arles meet the king of Provence. Arles has preserved from the Roman epoch the pretension of being free and of recognizing no other king than the lion which guards the entrances to the city. Before passing the shadow of this column, called in popular language "le Baton de Saint-Trophime," the king speaks respectfully of franchises and municipal liberties, after which the noble cortége receives a grand ovation in this old Roman city.

The next canto, entitled the "Lion," opens as the nuptials

of the king of Provence and the beautiful Yolande close. The poet, in order to give a new and lively feature to his verses, has recourse here to an ingenious artifice. Instead of giving the description as from himself, he introduces a man of the people, who, notwithstanding his humble position, has an office which allowed him to view the scene. It is Master Boisset, the archivist. Surrounded by the different citizens of Arles, he is questioned not a little; and he, nothing loath, in lively and picturesque language gives full career to his naïve erudition and enthusiastic inspiration. He describes the beautiful spectacle of those women who were equal to those who, in the first scene of "Œdipus at Colonus," of Sophocles, Antigone presents to the monarch's view as the chosen flowers of Attica. This Master Bertrand Boisset was not an imaginary personage; he was that very bourgeois of Arles who has left us his memoirs covering the years from 1376 to 1404. These memoirs, still unpublished, are written in the Provençal language, and in them are mentioned the combat of the lion of Arles with a bull on the 18th of May, 1402. On the 4th of April, 1553, the council of the city suppressed the practice of keeping up the traditional lion.

The whole court proceeds in solemn procession to assist at the combat between the lion of Arles and four bulls. This episode of cruel sport recalls the epic poems of old. The recital has a tragic ending. Three bulls, one after the other, are slain by the noble animal, which, wounded by the fourth, clears by an enormous leap the obstacles that surround him and rushes furiously on the king, queen, and Nerto. Just in time to save them, Rodrigue kills the lion with his sword, and the bourgeois, who see in this event a decree of Heaven, salute the Comte de Provence as the new king of the city of Arles.

The fifth canto is called the "Nun," and is a faithful picture of life in the great cloisters of the middle ages. All is in movement at the convent; Pope Benedict, followed by his whole court, comes to assist at the profession of Nerto. Sitting on his throne, the Sovereign Pontiff solemnly accords her the necessary dispensations to pronounce her vows. Nerto utters a cry of regret as Prioress Banale gives the signal for the ceremony. The remembrance of Rodrigue is more lively than ever in her distracted heart. The genius displayed here can only be compared to that found at the end of *René,* where Chateaubriand describes the taking of the veil by Amélie. But, to the honor of M. Mistral be it said, we do not find here the evil and despairing tone of the author of the memoirs of *Outre Tombe.* The sorrow of Nerto is a sorrow chastened, resigned, Christian; it recognizes itself and does not despair.

Rodrigue, however, is not resigned. He assembles a band of Catalans and roving free lances. He storms the convent and carries off Nerto in a fainting state. The combat rages. Rodrigue places the fainting Nerto in the tomb of Roland—for the struggle occurs in a cemetery. Nerto revives, finding herself alone, and she flies at hazard out into the open country.

The next canto is entitled the "Angel." The author adopts an ascending succession in his poem. First we find described the morals and the warlike habits of the people; then we assist at the grand spectacles of religious and mili-

tary pomps. We enter now into the domain of the soul and the higher region of the supernatural. The grandeurs of nature, which have been painted with an incomparable inspiration, fade now in the presence of God, and the contrast reanimates in us the knowledge of eternal truths.

Nerto, with broken heart and bruised body, flies until the sun is about to set. At last she sees a refuge of peace and hope. The chapel of St. Gabriel appears high up on the side of a mountain; a hermit descends from it, gives her nourishment, and speaks to her in thrilling tones of the benevolence and providence of God. Certainly these beautiful verses approach the fine pages of Fénelon where he treats of the "Existence of God," just as they surpass the most admired tirades of the poem on "Religion" by Louis Racine.

The hermit learns of the compact which chains the young girl. He promises her the intercession of the Angel Gabriel. Each day the celestial messenger appears to him on the last stroke of the Angelus and brings him food.

It is now midday. The hermit presents his request to the Angel Gabriel; he has promised to save Nerto from the demon:

> "Pareil à l'onde cristalline
> Sur laquelle passe un nuage,
> L'ange Gabriel se rembrunit,
> —'Pincée de poussière! dit-il,
> Dans ton désert, contre les forces
> De celui qui chemine par les voies tortueuses,
> Le sais-tu bien si tu as combattu?
> Tu as grand' peine à te sauver toi-même,
> Et tu prétends sauver les autres?
> Oh! pauvre jonc! Ah! pauvres que vous êtes?'
> Et le bel ange, cela dit,
> Avait pris l'essor vers les astres."

At these words the hermit is seized with a holy terror. He believes that the presence of Nerto is evil; and, repenting anew, he returns to the retreat which he should not have left.

The seventh and last canto is entitled the "Devil." In order to prepare the perhaps incredulous mind of the reader for this episode the poet has affixed a prologue to his work. With the fervor of good Christian sense and a power of philosophical logic, the poet openly argues that if the name alone of the malign being suffices often to provoke one to sorrow and repentance, it is one of the ruses of hell to persuade men to incredulity, after which they will not be guarded against the inspirations and attacks of the enemy of humankind.

Rodrigue after the combat remains in the cemetery of Alyscamps, vainly seeking Nerto in the tomb where he had placed her in a fainting condition. Despairing, he invokes Lucifer. Although a Christian and the nephew of the pope, the chevalier, during the long siege of Avignon, has had the curiosity and leisure to search among the secret archives where the church, with maternal vigilance, had entombed the cabalistic books of sorcerers and necromancers.

At the first invocation of Rodrigue the demon responds in a deep voice and without showing himself; for the poet, with a great deal of art, retards the apparition in order to render it more solemn. The infernal spirit promises the chevalier to construct for him, at the foot of the mountain of St. Gabriel, a magnificent château, in which Nerto will be delivered to him without defence. A word suffices to raise this palace of fantastical architecture. Nerto comes from out the shadows of the night into this flaming illumination. Rodrigue receives her at the door. He walks with her through splendid halls with golden pillars and capitals. He wishes to renew his proposals of love. Nerto, full of Christian fervor, exhorts him to repent and to seek her in heaven.

Here Satan intervenes. He strikes three resounding blows upon the door and appears under the form of a gentleman clothed in black and red. He passes his arm within that of Rodrigue and felicitates him on the good fortune which has fallen to him.

The dénouement of the poem presents a moral crisis. The love of Rodrigue takes a more elevated and tender form. He demands of the demon the relinquishment of this soul. Satan's response is inspired by triumphant rage, hatred, and revolt:

> Tu voudrais, toi, me souffler l'âme
> Que j'ai achetée toute neuve
> Et payée, moi, au poids de l'or?
> Tu me prends donc pour quelqu'un autre!
> Des âmes noires, fi! j'eu ai à verse . . .
> Mais depuis que je règne sur les régions d'en bas,
> Je n'avais pas encore réussi une proie
> Immaculée comme cette âme!
> M'angélique et blanche Nerto
> Sera la perle précieuse d'enfer!
> Elle sera mon triomphe et ma gloire!
> Car sa capture dément la rédemption,
> Elle dément la grâce baptismale,
> Elle dément le mystère entier . . .
> Attends un peu que minuit frappe,
> Et Nerto va tomber dans l'abîme.

At these words Rodrigue, full of a holy indignation, draws his sword to strike the devil. Peals of thunder vibrate; everything crumbles; the magical illusion disappears, and before his eyes looms on a single isolated column, like Memnon in the desert of Egypt, the form of a gigantic nun with her white veil falling on both sides and her hands clasped in supplication. They say that there is still to be seen in this country at the moment of the midday Angelus this immense statue exposed to the ardent rays of the sun. Listen, and the soft Latin words of the "Ave Maria" flow gently from its lips.

As in the prologue the poet took care to guard us against a proper incredulity, so in the epilogue he succeeds in impressing upon us somehow that the whole is simply an historical document. In default of other testimony relative to this antique legend he conducts us over the spots where took place the events he has recounted.

In conclusion he carries us to the solitude of the old hermit, and we find him abandoned by the Angel Gabriel for three days. On the fourth day the celestial messenger appears once more. His absence has been occasioned by the fêtes which have just taken place in paradise, where the nuptials of Nerto and Rodrigue have been celebrated with divine rites.

Then the poet speaks in his own person and laments the melancholy condition of these latter days, given over to scepticism as they are:

> Si quelque jour, bénévole lecteur,
> Tu voyageais par la contrée
> De Laurade ou de Saint-Gabriel,
> Tu peux, au cas où tu le croirais nécessaire
> T'assurer de ce récit.
> Dans la campagne, au milieu des moissons,
> Tu venas la Nonne de pierre,
> Portant au front la marque
> De l'Infernal et des foudres:
>
>   . . . . .
>
> La petite église romane
> De Saint-Gabriel, non loin de là,
> Semble, pauvrette, s'ennuyer,
> Abandonnée par les chrétiens,
> Depuis nombre et nombre d'années.
> Entre les touffes d'oliviers,
> À sa façade, Saint-Gabriel,
> Sous une arcade creuse,
> Y salue la sainte Vierge
> En disant: Ave, Maria!
> Et le serpent entortillé
> Autour de l'Arbre de la science,
> Y tente le cœur innocent,
> D'Adam et d'Eve. . . . Puis plus rien.
> L'homme laboure, indifferent.
> Celui qui salua la Vierge
> N'a plus un cierge à son aute!
> Mais les plantes du bon Dieu;
> Dans le préau de son parvis,
> Aux trous des murs massifs,
> Entre les pierres de son tout de dalles,
> Ont pris racine et fleurissent:
> Encens agreste que la chaleur du jour
> Épanche seul au sanctuaire.

M. Mistral's friends are speculating as to whether he will present himself to the French Academy; and if he does, whether he will be admitted. Only one objection is urged against his admirable poems—viz., that they are written in the Provençal tongue. But Provençal is an older language than French—in fact, the mother-tongue of French to some extent—and capable of poetry in a larger degree than its too polished offspring. But whether or not M. Mistral obtains a seat among the Forty Immortals, certain it is that he is the king of "Félibres" and the favorite of all French poets with foreigners. (pp. 684-93)

> *"A New Provençal Poem,"* in The Catholic World, *Vol. XL, No. 239, February, 1885, pp. 684-93.*

Arthur Symons (essay date 1886)

[*Symons was a prominent late nineteenth-century English critic, poet, dramatist, short story writer, and editor who influenced modern poetic theory through his emphasis on the importance of symbolism. In the following essay, he provides an overview of Mistral's provincial background and discusses aspects of Provence depicted in several of his major works.*]

Mistral—last of the veritable
Troubadours—was truly gifted in that he
was an erudite philologist who possessed a
rare creative sense of poetic form.

*—Stuart Henry, in his "The Last of the
Troubadours,"* The Bookman, *May, 1914.*

The name of Frederi Mistral is familiar to most as that of
the leader of the Provençal movement known as the Felibrige; a movement which, during the last thirty years, has
restored to Provence a language and a literature. His name
is familiar, but I question whether his works have received
in England that consideration which they emphatically
deserve. The fact that Mistral's poetry is written in Provençal must necessarily exclude most English readers
from reading him in the original; but even those who know
no language but their own have the opportunity of reading
a translation of *Mirèio,* while for those who are acquainted with French it is possible to enjoy a good deal of the
Provençal poet's charm in the French version which accompanies every work. And Mistral is a poet decidedly
worth knowing. In his quaint simplicity, his perilous
closeness to nature, his fresh emotion and early largeness
and clearness of song; as an epic poet in the nineteenth
century, a pastoral poet in the age of steam-ploughs; as a
rustic painter of the most scrupulous realism, a historical
painter of brilliant picturesqueness: he is often unique, and
always charming. If only as a daring and successful innovator, a linguistic ghost-raiser who has restored and reclaimed the beautiful language of the Troubadours, Mistral is a notable figure; and he is something more than that.
I think it may be worth our while to look a little closely
into the character of his work, all the more worth our
while since it lies somewhat out of the way of ordinary
travellers along the high-road, and might easily be overlooked.

Frederi Mistral was born on the 8th of September, 1830,
at Maiano (*Fr.* Maillane), a village of 1,500 inhabitants,
in the arrondissement of Arles; a small, out-of-the-way,
quiet place, set in the midst of a singular country, full of
beautiful and exceptional charm, and among places that
have memories still about them of a wonderful past. His
father lived on his own farm, which he managed till his
death in 1865. He was a man of the old school, simple,
pious, unworldly, stern and romantic, of few words, with
a heart and hand always open to a worker. By the side of
the old man, whose scarcely idealized portrait meets us
again and again in his son's works, the boy passed his
childhood and early youth, familiar from his first years
with those "majestic acts of the rustic life" which he was
afterwards to chronicle in his verse. This environment, so
rare in our days, and suggesting the pastoral simplicity of
the early ages, had naturally a strong influence over him.
He lived in a world apart, a romantic world; not of the
imagination, but in reality. The life of the fields and farm,
that life which seems to us the closest to Nature, the most
poetical in its handicraft, was his real existence, the only

one he knew; and in Provence the rustic life is exceptionally poetical and dignified. Nothing of the sordidness of
town-dwellers could come near him; none of the mean
conditions of town-life, so utterly destructive of poetry, so
entirely without dignity or picturesqueness. He passed his
days in the open air, among the proud peasant labourers
of the fields and vineyards, and in addition to this, as if still
further to educate him for his special task in poetry, he
could retreat, when he liked, into the other, dimmer world
which lies about childhood, a world to which Perrault is
chamberlain, and of which most mothers hold the keys.
For, beyond most countries, Provence has a special wealth
of songs and legends. Mistral tells us how his mother used
to sing to him, as she sat at her spinning-wheel, old songs,
and nursery rhymes, and popular ballads. It was she who
taught him the very name of *Mirèio.* All this sank deep
into the child's heart—part for the song's sake, and part
because of the singer's; and we may assign, I think, to this
cause the commencement of that passionate affection for
the old language and literature of Provence which was afterwards to bear such good fruit.

At the age of nine or ten Frederi went to school at Avignon, to be cooped up, he tells us, still with a whimsical
impatience at the recollection, "more straitly than the
lambs in my father's sheepfolds." All children feel a soli-
tariness and strangeness on the first leaving home for
school; but the change for him was not a mere change of
residence. Not only was he taken from friends to strangers, and from the fields to the town, but at Avignon he
found himself in a world speaking a new language. At
home he spoke Provençal; here he had to speak French.
The lessons were hateful to him; his heart was still at the
farm; and he cherished the recollection of his mother's
Provençal songs as the one delightful, and at the same
time sad, recollection. Gradually this feeling of distaste
wore off. He began to find in Virgil and Homer the manners and ideas of his own land, and a strong bond of sympathy drew him to them. Then, in his words, "the sublime
beauty of the ancient writers penetrated his heart"; and it
was not long before he essayed, in secret, to translate into
Provençal the first Eclogue of Virgil. About this time, in
the year 1845, an event occurred which still further influenced him in the direction of poetry and Provence. This
was the entrance into the *pensionnat,* as teacher, of a
young man named Roumaniho (*Fr.* Roumanille), an old
neighbour and soon a close friend. Roumaniho, "already
stung by the Provençal bee," had written a series of poems,
afterwards published as *Margarideto—*"Daisies," in the
old language of his land. He showed them to Mistral. It
was enough. "When he showed me, in their spring freshness, these pretty meadow-flowers, a great trembling took
hold of my being, and I cried: 'Behold the dawn that my
soul awaited to awaken!' " From that time the two friends
had but one aim—to restore the beautiful language spoken
by their mothers, the beautiful dead speech of the Troubadours, and to make it once more a living language of song.
We may date from this moment the Provençal Renaissance.

In 1848, after nearly a year spent on his father's farm—a
fruitful year, which witnessed the birth of a poem four
cantos long on **"The Harvests,"** probably a foretaste of

Mirèio, and which gave his parents to see that their son was too poetically fond of the farm to be ever a good farmer,—Mistral went to Aix to study law. He must have pursued his legal studies with tolerable vigour, for in 1851 he took his degree; but it is very evident that even then there was another study more engrossing to him than law, and that was poetry. At Aix he met his old schoolfellow and fellow-poet Ansèume (Anselme) Mathièu. The two legal students delighted, as he tells us, to refresh with poetry the dryness of the Pandects and the Civil Code; and when Roumaniho, about this time, issued at Avignon his book of *Prouvençalo* (*Les Provençales*), some of Mistral's verses were published in it. On returning home in 1851, Mistral's father was wise enough to allow him to follow his bent. He threw his lawyer's gown on a hedge, and gave himself up to Provence and poetry.

Under the leadership of Roumaniho, a band of young poets, Mistral, Aubanèu (Aubanel), Mathièu, Crousihat (Crousillat) and others, began frequently to meet together, now here, now there, but most often at Avignon, for the purpose of encouraging one another in their work, reading their new poems, and holding fête. At one of these reunions, held at Font-Segugno, May 21st, 1854, the name of Felibrige was adopted for the league, and the members of it assumed the title of Felibre. The exact meaning of the word is hard to say, and the story sometimes told of its origin may be true or not. This is the account given in a curious book, entitled *Miejour, or the Land of the Felibre,* by J. Duncan Craig, D.D.—a work in which some valuable information is given respecting the Felibrige, but so inextricably embedded in a mass of Provençal legends, missionary talk, guide-book information, and philological disquisition, as to be practically useless.

> Frederi Mistral, Anselme Matthieu, Joseph Roumanille, and some four others were assembled one evening in a garden of roses, 'neath the shade of a trellised vine, to form an association of poets using the Provençal language. Suddenly an old wrinkled woman appeared, and as she looked upon the band, exclaimed thrice, 'Felibre—Felibre—Felibre—' and then this aged sibyl vanished from the garden. 'Let us call ourselves Felibre,' cried Frederi Mistral—and so the name began.

Such, at least, (in his own English,) is Mr. Craig's account.

At some of these meetings Mistral read aloud, not without applause, portions of a poem on which he was engaged for seven years—*Mirèio,* the first and perhaps the greatest of his works. It was published at Avignon in the beginning of 1859, and the reception accorded to it, not only in Provence, but throughout France, was very remarkable. Although the poem was written in a language which had fallen into discredit, a language which had become a patois, it was received by the French critics with enthusiastic recognition; Lamartine, then at the height of his fame, welcomed the new poet with generous praise; the book was crowned by the Académie; and, finally, Gounod took from it the subject of an opera, which has recently been performed, I believe, in London. From an obscure local poet, Mistral became a Parisian celebrity. More than that, he was permitted to take his place among the most eminent poets of his time. This place he has since maintained by the publication of two other notable works: *Calendau,* in 1867, *Nerto,* in 1884; besides a volume of miscellaneous poems, *Lis Isclo d'Or,* issued in 1875.

Mistral's position at the head of an important philologico-poetical movement is apt to dim our eyes to his great merit—that of being, in the pure sense, a poet. But he is this, and he has been called a great poet, and compared quite seriously, by serious and critical persons, with Homer, Theocritus, Dante. For myself, while I cannot quite say that I consider M. Mistral either a Homer or a Dante, I am assured that as an epic poet, pastoral and romantic, the author of *Mirèio* fills a vacant place in contemporary literature, and that his work has the property of exciting in us that "peculiar quality of pleasure which we cannot get elsewhere," to which the most exquisite critic of our day refers the charm of all original work. I shall, therefore, attempt in [this essay] not so much a description of Mistral the Felibre as an analysis of Mistral the poet. That Mistral has assisted in reviving the language of Provence, and that he writes in Provençal, is an accident—an accident of supreme importance, indeed, and of which I have tried in the foregoing pages to explain the cause; but still an accident. For the tone which it has contributed to his verse we must consider it with attention; but it is necessary to remember that it is a quite secondary matter, after all. The first question, in this case as in every case, is, Of what value is this body of poetry? what is its individual charm?

It seems to me that the special charm of Mistral's poetry lies in a certain way of looking at nature and life, and of depicting them, which I might, perhaps, express by calling the poet a sort of epical Theocritus. His works are not exactly epics; they are not precisely idyls. They unite some of the characteristics of a Theocritan idyl with an approach to the general manner of a Homeric epic—the *Odyssey,* not the *Iliad.* The epic is the special growth of primitive ages, and it has been lost from amongst us because we have lost, in our life and in our thought, the simplicity and the straightforward objectiveness of the early world. But Mistral succeeds in producing epical narratives, without the least affectation or antiquarianism, because his Provence is still primitive, still simple, pastoral, and romantic, and because he himself is absorbed in the life he paints. Instead of saying that each of his three chief poems is a little epic, it would, perhaps, be preferable to say that the three combine in one, and that together they make a single Epic of Provence. *Mirèio* deals chiefly with the pastoral aspect, with the life of the field and the farm. It is a rustic tale, full of a large leisure and serenity; the apotheosis of the country life. *Calendau* gives us the life of the mountains and the sea-coast; it is a story of adventure, of romance; it shows us something of the towns, of the towns *en fête,* and of the picturesque robber-chivalry of the past. *Nerto* takes us back to the fifteenth century, the age of the Avignonese popes, and paints, in a tableau of surprising largeness and brilliance, the whole Provençal life of the Middle Ages. Always Provence. It is Mistral's distinction that he has devoted all his genius, without any exception or reservation, to the exposition of his country. For him, it is probably as much a matter of patriotism, education, natural sympathy and tendency, as of deliberate artistic selection; perhaps more so; but it is certain that nothing more fortunate for his art could have happened. The presence of this figure of Provence, everywhere Provence, contributes a certain special "note" to his poetry, like the inevitable Scotland of Burns, whom Mistral resembles in this, that by writing exclusively in the idiom of his native country, and on topics relating to his country only, he becomes, for the general world, that country's representative; so that when we say Mistral we say Provence, as when we say Burns we say Scotland. This is to be a specialist, but a specialist of a very noble kind; for in poetry intensity is everything.

Mirèio, I have said, represents the pastoral side of Provence, and it is as a pastoral poet that Mistral is most unique and most satisfying. In England our great pastoral poet is Wordsworth; but Wordsworth approaches nature and the country life in a very different spirit from Mistral, and has an entirely different material to work upon. Wordsworth regards nature with awe, with admiration, with an intense but lofty affection; he has a preference for sublimity, the mountains, the clouds, or in turn "the meanest flower that blows"; but for these individually, as parts of nature and of God's creation, not from their connection with either humanity or the English soil. But Mistral looks at nature from a Provençal stand-point, his descriptions are of distinct places, and are faithful to every detail; and they are always employed, elaborate as they are, as a background to the story. Then the story, instead of being (as in Wordsworth) a simple annal of the poor, is a romantic tale, a narrative with the interest of a novel, or like that of a poem of Walter Scott. The rustic novels of Thomas Hardy occur to me as, perhaps, after all, the nearest parallel in our language with Mistral's *Mirèio.* The parallel, of course, only holds good to a certain extent; even if *Mirèio* were written in prose it would possess a romantic poetry, an imaginative splendour of which we can find no trace in the quiet novels of Mr. Hardy. But, for all that, there is a certain resemblance, not to be overlooked, between the matter and manner of *Mirèio* and, let us say, *Far from the Madding Crowd,* or *Under the Greenwood Tree.* Mistral's pictures of the farmer's daughter, of her father, of her suitors, of the basket-making hero, the old labourers, the harvest, cattle-tending, and the like, have all the precision and completeness, if little of the humour, with which we are familiar in Mr. Hardy's novels; while in the poem these are elevated, by sheer simplicity of imaginative realism, to really exquisite poetry.

The chief charm of *Mirèio* lies, no doubt, in the vivid truth and the realistic beauty of its rustic scenes; but I doubt whether these would be in themselves quite so charming were it not for the romantic interest which, all through the poem, is thrown over the fortunes of the lovers. The central story of Vincen and Mirèio is genuinely romantic; and this romance receives its most appropriate setting in the contrasted circumstances of the pastoral life. Like a clear ripple of sun-smitten water through a meadow of grazing kine, the love-story of these two, at once simple and passionate, threads the course of this rustic tale. Not romance merely, but supernaturalism, enters into Mistral's picture; but of this I shall speak more fully when we come to

Nerto. Nerto is pre-eminently the supernatural, as *Calendau* is specially the romantic, section of the grand Epic of Provence; *Mirèio,* containing in considerable measure both qualities, is by comparison chiefly of a homely naturalism—a picture of Provence in its rural aspect, exact, minute; a description, not a vision, yet in every detail poetical, trivial in none.

When Mistral wrote *Mirèio* he tried to render it completely representative of Provence. He filled it with Provençal lore, he crowded it with tales and legends of the past, as well as with pictures and stories of the present; but with all his pains, and notwithstanding the wealth of material which he lavished upon it, there remained unrecognized and unrecorded much which found a place among his impressions, and which he desired to chronicle in his epical verse. After seven years of patient labour a new poem, *Calendau,* written in the same measure as *Mirèio,* appeared. The poem has not become so popular as its predecessor; and in this case I think that the popular verdict, the verdict of seven editions against one, is substantially a just one. Naturally, Mistral will not allow that *Calendau* contains less poetry than *Mirèio.* In the latter, he says, nature predominates; in the former, imagination; and that is why people prefer the earlier work. There is some truth in the distinction, but it is not the whole truth. *Calendau* is on the whole a less admirable work, because, though more elaborate in its scheme, it is less perfect and unique, less fresh and charming in tone and workmanship, a little more modern and artificial. But no doubt it manifests a certain strength and breadth which are scarcely to be found in its predecessor.

Mirèio, by the very perfection of its plan, is limited within a somewhat narrow range of pasture-land and lowland; but in *Calendau* the author follows the fortunes of his hero from town to town, from height to height, painting the life of the fisher and the hunter with a brilliant and shifting scenic background. Now we see the tumult and brisk action of the tunny-fishing—a scene treated with epical fulness of detail; now the water-tournament, the popular fête, the pine-clad summits of the Esterels, a combat with bandits, a *fête-dieu,* an orgy, and a mountain-wood on fire. Every scene is described with Mistral's customary fulness and graphic force, now broadly touched, now minutely indicated, but always with the same reverent veracity, always with the same imaginative realism. Mistral is a painter who can paint either frescoes or miniatures; in this book, for instance, there are passages which for painstaking minuteness would do credit to the compiler of a guidebook, while elsewhere a scene or a landscape will be flashed on us with a touch or a phrase. Here are a couple of stanzas, which I have rendered into prose in order to retain the exact quality of the original—its quaintness, its simplicity, its curious truthfulness.

> And over the abrupt tiers hangs the huge-headed pompion; and from amongst the stone-heaps the vigorous aloe shoots up towards God its candelabrum; and the fruit of the barberry grows black in the ravines; and like a turkey-cock the red pomegranate crests the thickets.

> The olive-trees, intermingling their lines with the vine-rows, cover the terraces with silvery

forests; chestnuts and oaks overshadow the mountain-slope; and the old pines, making melody, darken the hill-tops.

These details are literal, if you will, but the picture is touched with fancy as well, just so little transformed in the process, however, as to leave some resemblance to the scene described, a merit not always to be found in poetry.

Unlike Mistral's other works, *Calendau* has a leading purpose, a sort of Pilgrim's Progress air, which is so much commoner in literature that it is hardly an equivalent for *naiveté*. Running through the whole strange series of sights and adventures, and linking them together into a certain sort of unity, is one aim, never lost quite out of sight; an attempt, namely, to represent the gradual elevation, through the ennobling and refining influence of true love, of a soul buffeted by temptation, and in danger, by its very strength and force, of resting content in some great material achievement. It may be that there is something superior in having a purpose of this sort; no doubt there often is; but I for one cannot help thinking that Mistral might better have left it alone. His *genre* is of another kind, his method of treatment essentially different, and the *genre* which he professes receives no accession of dignity, I imagine, by the introduction of a leading motive apart from the ever-present Provençal passion, which, even in this book, dominates really, thrusting into actual secondariness the apparently ruling quality. *Calendau* is the second part of the Provençal epic, and with it Mistral closes the chronicle of the present, I should say, rather, of the recent past. *Mirèio* and *Calendau* are in no sense historical; they are, if not absolutely of the present, yet comparatively so. Moreover, they are devoted to the outdoor life, the peasant existence, the fields, villages, mountains; together they present a panorama of all Provence. *Nerto,* on the other hand, to complete the picture, deals with the remote past, and is a historical romance enacted in the throng of cities and in the thick of notable events.

The poem was published in 1884. It is in a different measure from *Mirèio* and *Calendau*; short, light couplets, in alternate single and double rhymes, in place of the modulated sweep of the seven-lined stanza. Perhaps even more than that, it conveys the idea of improvisation; which with Mistral, as with the original troubadours, is literally the case. We are told that he sings his verses as he makes them, often in the open air. *Nerto* reminds one a little of Scott; but the compliment of the comparison is to Scott, and not to Mistral. There is a richness, a colour, in the work of the Provençal which the English poet had no conception of; while Scott, with all his worship of the past, has never compressed into verse so much of the real spirit of the Middle Ages as Mistral has done in this astonishingly brilliant romance. In a series of tableaux, arranged with the most consummate skill, the poet has revived for us one typical period of mediæval Provençal history, the period when Avignon still held, soon to hold no longer, the last of her popes, Benedict XIII. Mistral has raised the dead, and set the ghosts of history to move before us, arranging and ordering them in our sight, so that they may play their parts as if they lived. And although the part of the historic ghost-raiser is a difficult one, he has played it with singular success. Something of the hue and heat of life is about his men and women of the past; they crowd the sunlight of his pages, not as if they were ghosts, but as if they really lived. It is a genuine mediæval picture, painted with full knowledge and power, and with a perfection of sympathy which avoids the least shock of an intruding nineteenth-century touch. There is an old-world simplicity in it, a mode of presentment which cunningly simulates that love of colours, of textures, of distinct and definite traits, which characterizes the old romances, and withal a combined broadness and minuteness in the treatment which seems exactly to catch the mediæval spirit and precisely to represent it.

Nerto is purely romantic, but its romance is derived from love, from history, and from superstition—if so gross a title may be used to express so delicate an essence as the angelic and demonic legends of early Catholicism. The mere names of the cantos are enough to show how finely representative is the poem: the Baron, the Pope, the King, the Lion, the Nun, the Angel, the Devil. In the earlier cantos we have more especially the history. Baron, Pope, and King pass before us, and the air is full of bustle and shouting; throngs, holiday-dressed, press and sway in the dust; and all that is most picturesque, all that is most significant in the life of the time, is presented to us, in lines that are full of sunlight and bright colour. Passing onwards, we behold the sad serenity of the convent, "where the nuns walk quietly, like shadows, wearing their veils so great and long"; and again the wonderful forest-scenes, beautiful as the forest poetry and music in the *Siegfried* of Wagner, scenes of a more exquisite charm than Mistral has perhaps ever elsewhere conceived. This, too, is in the Middle Ages, when devil and angel still visibly walked the world; so we have, towards the end, the very apotheosis of the Catholic spirit. The description, in the last canto, of the palace of the Seven Deadly Sins, the enchanted castle with its "zigzag ways and labyrinthine gardens, where whoever enters is lost, with evil words heard and with sighs behind the clusters, and twisted trees and sombre plants, with strange flowers and perfumes that daze you like a smoke": this description, full of weird and fantastic beauty, is to my mind one of the finest pieces of imaginative writing to be found in the works of any living poet. Singularly enough in a French poet, Mistral has an exceptional mastery over the supernatural. In *Mirèio* he showed in two places—the description of the death-voyage of Ourrias, in the 5th canto, and the whole canto of *The Sorceress*—a true Teutonic feeling for the grotesque and unearthly, to which I can recollect no parallel in French literature except in that prose-poem of Michelet, *La Sorcière*. In *Nerto* the supernatural is more constantly employed, and in a somewhat different way. It is that note of other-worldliness which so completely fascinated the brains of the Middle Ages, and which translated itself into a thousand bizarre and beautiful and grotesque forms, into the gargoyles of their sacred edifices, the illuminated dragons of their missals, and the legends, so simple that they seem almost intentionally humorous, of their poets and romancists *manqué*. Here we see faith and humour hand-in-hand, laughing but reverencing—a combination which we have lost, and which only an art such as Mistral's, fed from a country which belongs even now to the past, can recall and represent.

It is by his three great poems that Mistral's name will live, but these do not represent the whole of his work. During the last twenty years he has been engaged in the stupendous task of compiling a Provençal Dictionary, one might almost say of creating it—a task now well-nigh finished, it is said. Besides this, he has written a large number of miscellaneous pieces—popular songs and ballads, occasional poems, wedding songs, toasts, &c. Many of these are published in the volume entitled *Lis Isclo d'Or,* or *The Isles of Gold.* Even in this varied collection there is scarcely anything not relating, directly or indirectly, to Provence. Mistral has indeed composed many of them for the express purpose of awakening a taste for their native language among the peasants; a purpose in which he has been so signally successful that there is now scarcely a village in Provence where his songs are not sung. To give some idea of these poems, I have attempted in English, in the measure of the original, a version of the **"Song of the Sun"** (**"Lou Cant dou Soulèu"**), one of the finest things in Mistral, and, we are told, already the popular song of the South of France,

> Mighty sun of our Provence,
> Gay the Mistral's boonfellow,
> Thou that drainest the Durance
> Like a draught of wine of Crau,
> Light thy shining lamp on high,
> Let the shade and sorrow fly,
> Soon, soon, soon,
> Rise, fair sun, into the sky!
>
> Though thou scorchest like a flame,
> Yet, ere quite the summer pale,
> Like a god's these shout thy name,
> Arles, Avignon, and Marseille!
> Light thy shining lamp on high, etc.
>
> Poplars, for a sight of thee,
> Higher and ever higher shoot,
> And the very mushroom, see,
> Comes up at the thistle's foot.
> Light thy shining lamp on high, etc.
>
> 'Tis the sun, friends, brought to birth
> Work and song, twin boons to bless,
> And the love of mother earth,
> And the tender homesickness.
> 'Light thy shining lamp on high, etc.
>
> 'Tis the sun brings heat and light,
> God forbid it e'er befall
> That he hide his face from sight—
> That would be the end of all!
> Light thy shining lamp on high
> Let the shade and sorrow fly,
> Soon, soon, soon,
> Rise, fair sun, into the sky!

As a sample of the lighter pieces, take this pretty fancy **"Li Grihet," "The Crickets"**:—

> "How comes it, little cricket, pray,
> Shining and black as jet, all day
> You do not sing a single tune,
> And yet, at even, with the moon,
> You chant the labourer's vesper-lay?"
>
> "Ah! such a gabbling makes the throng
> Of drones and bees the whole day long,

> That if we sang you could not hear,
> And if it rose into the air
> The birds would eat us for our song!"
>
> "Poor crickets!" "But when, prudently,
> Dame Bustle gathers homeward, we,
> All very silent, waiting till
> Each sound subsides and all is still,
> Upon the turf watch patiently.
>
> And then all softly we unite
> Our little voices with delight
> That a sweet strain they may upraise;
> And the moon hears, spinning her rays,
> Our little song upon the night."

But these minor poems are, after all, only the diversions of an epoist. Beautiful as they are, it is conceivable that other pens might possibly have written them; while it is absolutely inconceivable that any other poet of our day, save Mistral only, could have written the Provençal triad, *Mirèio, Calendau,* and *Nerto.* Mistral has shown, in an age when the prevailing tone of poetry is a tone of doubt, unrest, and uneasy self-consciousness, that it is possible still to be simple, still to retain the clear sanity of the early singers, finding life joyous, and a beloved fatherland an unfailing inspiration. He has shown that it is still possible to strike the true pastoral note, still possible, in these late days, to write an epic and to write it without falseness or incongruity. And in this lies his distinction, and his importance for us. (pp. 659-70)

Arthur Symons, "Frederi Mistral," in The National Review, *London, Vol. VI, No. 35, January, 1886, pp. 659-70.*

Charles Alfred Downer   (essay date 1901)

[*In the following essay, Downer addresses the limitations of Mistral's verse but praises his originality and his attempt to preserve Provençal culture and language.*]

It would be idle to endeavor to determine whether Mistral is to be classed as a great poet, or whether the Félibres have produced a great literature, and nothing is defined when the statement is made that Mistral is or is not a great poet. His genius may be said to be limited geographically, for if from it were eliminated all that pertains directly to Provence, the remainder would be almost nothing. The only human nature known to the poet is the human nature of Provence, and while it is perfectly true that a human being in Provence could be typical of human nature in general, and arouse interest in all men through his humanity common to all, the fact is, that Mistral has not sought to express what is of universal interest, but has invariably chosen to present human life in its Provençal aspects and from one point of view only. A second limitation is found in the unvarying exteriority of his method of presenting human nature. Never does he probe deeply into the souls of his Provençals. Very vividly indeed does he reproduce their words and gestures; but of the deeper undercurrents, the inner conflicts, the agonies of doubt and indecision, the bitterness of disappointments, the lofty aspirations toward a higher inner life or a closer communion with the universe, the moral problems that shake a human soul, not a syllable. Nor is he a poet who pours out his own soul into verse.

External nature is for him, again, nature as seen in Provence. The rocks and trees, the fields and the streams, do not awaken in him a stir of emotions because of their power to compel a mood in any responsive poetic soul, but they excite him primarily as the rocks and trees, the fields and streams of his native region. He is no mere word-painter. Rarely do his descriptions appear to exist for their own sake. They furnish a necessary, fitting, and delightful background to the action of his poems. They are too often indications of what a Provençal ought to consider admirable or wonderful, they are sometimes spoiled by the poet's excessive partiality for his own little land. His work is ever the work of a man with a mission.

There is no profound treatment of the theme of love. Each of the long poems and his play have a love story as the centre of interest, but the lovers are usually children, and their love utterly without complications. There is everywhere a lovely purity, a delightful simplicity, a straightforward naturalness that is very charming, but in this theme as in the others, Mistral is incapable of tragic depths and heights. So it is as regards the religious side of man's nature. The poet's work is filled with allusions to religion; there are countless legends concerning saints and hermits, descriptions of churches and the papal palace, there is the detailed history of the conversion of Provence to Christianity, but the deepest religious spirit is not his. Only twice in all his work do we come upon a profounder religious sense, in the second half of **"Lou Prègo-Diéu"** and in **"Lou Saume de la Penitènci."** There is no doubt that Mistral is a believer, but religious feeling has not a large place in his work; there are no other meditations upon death and destiny.

And this *âme du Midi, spirit of Provence,* the genius of his race that he has striven to express, what is it? How shall it be defined or formulated? Alphonse Daudet, who knew it, and loved it, whose Parisian life and world-wide success did not destroy in him the love of his native Provence, who loved the very food of the Midi above all others, and jumped up in joy when a southern intonation struck his ear, and who was continually beset with longings to return to the beloved region, has well defined it. He was the friend of Mistral and followed the poet's efforts and achievements with deep and affectionate interest. It is not difficult to see that the satire in the "Tartarin" series is not unkind, nor is it untrue. Daudet approved of the Félibrige movement, though what he himself wrote in Provençal is insignificant. He believed that the national literature could be best vivified by those who most loved their homes, that the best originality could thus be attained. He has said [in *Revue de Paris,* 15 avril, 1898]:

> The imagination of the southerners differs from that of the northerners in that it does not mingle the different elements and forms in literature, and remains lucid in its outbreaks. In our most complex natures you never encounter the entanglement of directions, relations, and figures that characterizes a Carlyle, a Browning, or a Poe. For this reason the man of the north always finds fault with the man of the south for his lack of depth and darkness.

> If we consider the most violent of human passions, love, we see that the southerner makes it the great affair of his life, but does not allow himself to become disorganized. He likes the talk that goes with it, its lightness, its change. He hates the slavery of it. It furnishes a pretext for serenades, fine speeches, light scoffing, caresses. He finds it difficult to comprehend the joining together of love and death, which lies in the northern nature, and casts a shade of melancholy upon these brief delights.

Daudet notes the ease with which the southerner is carried away and duped by the mirage of his own fancy, his semi-sincerity in excitement and enthusiasm. He admired the natural eloquence of his Provençals. He found a justification for their exaggerations.

> Is it right to accuse a man of lying, who is intoxicated with his own eloquence, who, without evil intent, or love of deceit, or any instinct of scheming or false trading, seeks to embellish his own life, and other people's, with stories he knows to be illusions, but which he wishes were true? Is Don Quixote a liar? Are all the poets deceivers who aim to free us from realities, to go soaring off into space? After all, among southerners, there is no deception. Each one, within himself, restores things to their proper proportions.

Daudet had Mistral's love of the sunshine. He needed it to inspire him. He believed it explained the southern nature.

Concerning the absence of metaphysics in the race he says:—

> These reasonings may culminate in a state of mind such as we see extolled in Buddhism, a colorless state, joyless and painless, across which the fleeting splendors of thought pass like stars. Well, the man of the south cares naught for that sort of paradise. The vein of real sensation is freely, perpetually open, open to life. The side that pertains to abstraction, to logic, is lost in mist.

(pp. 237-42)

Daudet mentions the contrast [between the Provençals' ability as storytellers and responsiveness as listeners] to be observed between an audience of southerners and the stolid, self-contained attitude of a crowd in the north.

The evil side of the southern temperament, the faults that accompany these traits, are plainly stated by the great novelist. Enthusiasm turns to hypocrisy, or brag; the love of what glitters, to a passion for luxury at any cost; sociability, the desire to please, become weakness and fulsome flattery. The orator beats his breast, his voice is hoarse, choked with emotion, his tears flow conveniently, he appeals to patriotism and the noblest sentiments. There is a legend, according to Daudet, which says that when Mirabeau cried out, "We will not leave unless driven out at the point of the bayonet," a voice off at one side corrected the utterance, murmuring sarcastically, "And if the bayonets come, we make tracks!"

> **No poet, it would seem, was ever so in love with his own language as Mistral; no artist ever so loved the mere material he was using. . . . Mistral's love is for the speech itself aside from any meaning it conveys.**
>
> **—*Charles Alfred Downer***

The southerner, when he converses, is roused to animation readily. His eye flashes, his words are uttered with strong intonations, the impressiveness of a quiet, earnest, self-contained manner is unknown to him.

Daudet is a novelist and a humorist. Mistral is a poet; hence, although he professes to aim at a full expression of the "soul of his Provence," there are many aspects of the Provençal nature that he has not touched upon. He has omitted all the traits that lend themselves to satirical treatment, and, although he is in many ways a remarkable realist, he has very little dramatic power, and seems to lack the gift of searching analysis of individual character. It is hardly fair to reckon it as a shortcoming in the poet and apostle of Provence that he presents only what is most beautiful in the life about him. The novelist offers us a faithful and vivid image of the men of his own day. The poet glorifies the past, clings to tradition, and exhorts his countrymen to return to it.

Essentially and above all else a conservative, Mistral has the gravest doubts about so-called modern progress. Undoubtedly honest in desiring the well-being of his fellow Provençals, he believes that this can be preserved or attained only by a following of tradition. There must be no breaking with the past. Daudet, late in life, adhered to this doctrine. His son quotes him as saying:—

> I am following, with gladness, the results of the impulse Mistral has given. Return to tradition! that is our salvation in the present going to pieces. I have always felt this instinctively. It came to me clearly only a few years ago. It is a bad thing to become wholly loosened from the soil, to forget the village church spire. Curiously enough poetry attaches only to objects that have come down to us, that have had long use. What is called *progress,* a vague and very doubtful term, rouses the lower parts of our intelligence. The higher parts vibrate the better for what has moved and inspired a long series of imaginative minds, inheriting each from a predecessor, strengthened by the sight of the same landscapes, by the same perfumes, by the touch of the same furniture, polished by wear. Very ancient impressions sink into the depth of that obscure memory which we may call the *race-memory,* out of which is woven the mass of individual memories.

Mistral is truly the poet of the Midi. One can best see how superior he is as an artist in words by comparing him with the foremost of his fellow-poets. He is a master of language. He has the eloquence, the enthusiasm, the optimism of his race. His poetic earnestness saves his tendency to exaggerate. His style, in all its superiority, is a southern style, full of interjections, full of long, sonorous words. His thought, his expressions, are ever lucid. His art is almost wholly objective. His work has extraordinary unity, and therefore does not escape the monotony that was unavoidable when the poet voluntarily limited himself to a single purpose in life, and to treatment of the themes thereunto pertaining. Believers in material progress, those who look for great changes in political and social conditions, will turn from Mistral with indifference. His contentment with present things, and his love of the past, are likely to irritate them. Those who seek in a poet consolation in the personal trials of life, a new message concerning human destiny, a new note in the everlasting themes that the great poets have sung, will be disappointed.

A word must be said of him as a writer of French. In the earlier years he felt the weight of the Academy. He did not feel that French would allow full freedom. He was scrupulous and timid. He soon shook off this timidity and became a really remarkable wielder of the French tongue. His translations of his own works have doubtless reached a far wider public than the works themselves, and are certainly characterized by great boldness, clearness, and an astonishingly large vocabulary.

His earlier work is clearly inspired by his love of Greek literature, and those qualities in Latin literature wherein the Greek genius shines through, possibly also by some mysterious affinity with the Greek spirit resulting from climate or atavism. This never entirely left him. When later he writes of Provence in the Middle Age, of the days of the Troubadours, his manner does not change; his work offers no analogies here with the French Romantic school.

No poet, it would seem, was ever so in love with his own language; no artist ever so loved the mere material he was using. Mistral loves the words he uses, he loves their sound, he loves to hear them from the lips of those about him; he loves the intonations and the cadences of his verse; his love is for the speech itself aside from any meaning it conveys. A beautiful instrument it is indeed. Possibly nothing is more peculiarly striking about him than this extreme enthusiasm for his golden speech, his *lengo d'or*.

To him must be conceded the merit of originality, great originality. In seeking the source of many of his conceptions, one is led to the conclusion, and his own testimony bears it out, that they are the creations of his own fancy. If there is much prosaic realism in the ***Poem of the Rhone,*** the Prince and the Anglore are purely the children of Mistral's almost naïve imagination, and Calendau and Esterello are attached to the real world of history by the slenderest bonds. When we seek for resemblances between his conceptions and those of other poets, we can undoubtedly find them. Mireille now and then reminds of Daphnis and Chloe, of Hermann and Dorothea, of Evangeline, but the differences are far more in evidence than the resemblances. Esterello is in an attitude toward Calendau not without analogy to that of Beatrice toward Dante, but it would be impossible to find at any point the slightest imitation of Dante. Some readers have been reminded of Faust in reading *Nerto,* but beyond the scheme of the Devil to secure a woman's soul, there is little similarity. Nothing could be more utterly without philosophy than *Nerto.* Mistral has drawn his inspirations from within himself; he has not worked over the poems and legends of former poets, or sought much of his subject-matter in the productions of former ages. He has not suffered from the deep reflection, the pondering, and the doubt that destroy originality.

If Mistral had written his poems in French, he would certainly have stood apart from the general line of French poets. It would have been impossible to attach him to any of the so-called "schools" of poetry that have followed one another during this century in France. He is as unlike the Romantics as he is unlike the Parnassians. M. Brunetière would find no difficulty in applying to his work the general epithet of "social" that so well characterizes French literature considered in its main current, for Mistral always sings to his fellow-men to move them, to persuade them, to stir their hearts. Almost all of his poems in the lyrical form show him as the spokesman of his fellows or as the leader urging them to action. He is therefore not of the school of "Art for Art's sake," but his art is consecrated to the cause he represents.

His thought is ever pure and high; his lessons are lessons of love, of noble aims, of energy and enthusiasm. He is full of love for the best in the past, love of his native soil, love of his native landscapes, love of the men about him, love of his country. He is a poet of the "Gai Saber," joyous and healthy, he has never felt a trace of the bitterness, the disenchantment, the gloom and the pain of a Byron or a Leopardi. He is eminently representative of the race he seeks to glorify in its own eyes and in the world's, himself a type of that race at its very best, with all its exuberance and energy, with its need of outward manifestation, life and movement. An important place must be assigned to him among those who have bodied forth their poetic conceptions in the various euphonious forms of speech descended from the ancient speech of Rome.

In Provence, and far beyond its borders, he is known and loved. His activity has not ceased. His voice is still heard, clear, strong, hopeful, inspiring. *Mireille* is sung in the ruined Roman theatre at Arles, museums are founded to preserve Provençal art and antiquities, the Felibrean feasts continue with unabated enthusiasm. Mistral's life is a successful life; he has revived a language, created a literature, inspired a people. So potent is art to-day in the old land of the Troubadours. All the charm and beauty of that sunny land, all that is enchanting in its past, all the best, in the ideal sense, that may be hoped for in its future, is expressed in his musical, limpid, lovely verse. Such a poet and such a leader of men is rare in the annals of literature. Such complete oneness of purpose and of achievement is rare among men. (pp. 242-51)

Charles Alfred Downer, in his Frédéric Mistral, *The Columbia University Press, 1901, 267 p.*

The New York Times Book Review   (essay date 1908)

[*In the following review of Mistral's* Memoirs, *the critic discusses the development of the Félibre movement and Mistral's efforts to revive Provençal literature.*]

Although the literature of Provence, in those days when it had a literature all its own, is not distinguished by any isolated mountain peaks of achievement, through which it might claim an equality of rank with those creative movements that have given such names as Dante, Homer, Shakespeare, and Goethe to humanity, it has ever had a flavor of genuine poetry, of gentle idealism that has made it for centuries an important and recognized factor in the intellectual life of Southern Europe. But the actual poets whose musical verse shed a romantic lustre on the court of King Rene—the troubadours whose metrical passion for some queen of beauty took the place of politics in the affairs of the realm—who were they? Pierre Vidal, Jaufre Rudel; are scarcely known to-day for their lyrical triumphs outside their own country, although their personal adventures as professors of the "Gay Science" still furnish themes for the poets of less sunny climes.

> There lived a singer in France of old,
> By the tideless, dolorous, midland sea,
> In a land of sand and ruin and gold.
> There shone one woman, and none but she.
> And finding life for her love's sake fall,
> Being fain to see her, he bade set sail,
> Touched land, and saw her as life grew cold,
> And praised God, seeing; and so died he.

In these twentieth-century days such an experience would hardly be credited as anything more than fantastic imagining of some lover of romance; and yet, Swinburne's muse merely puts into a stanza what tradition tells us actually befell that typical troubadour of Provence, Jaufre Rudel, Prince of Blaza, who died in a poetic rhapsody at the feet of his mistress on the shores of North Africa.

The literature of Provence, however, was doomed to suffer practical extinction for several centuries following the period of its glory. Provencal writers of a later generation ignored the language of the troubadours, and chose instead the language of France or of Italy. The primitive themes, the romantic idyls, lost their appeal, and Provence as the native home of poetry was forgotten, until, within the present generation, a brotherhood of literary patriots— "Les Felibres," they called themselves—was instituted for the avowed purpose of reviving the distinctive Provencal literature. The leader in this movement, Frederic Mistral, became the recipient two years ago of the Nobel prize for patriotic literature, at the same time that he refused the honor of an election to a seat among the famous Forty of the French Academy. Mistral is an old man today, and the unique campaign which he has waged in the interest of a native literature has occupied him for the best part of a lifetime. In a delightful volume of his *Memoirs,* the English translation of which has just been published, he tells of his youthful experiences and aspirations, and above all furnishes a picture of the real life of Provence today that suggests a fitting environment for this first and greatest of modern troubadours.

In Mistral's consecration to one great artistic purpose, the

revival of a bygone literary era, there is a reminiscent flavor of the vows taken by his great English contemporaries
in the formation of the "Pre-Raphaelite Brotherhood."
The idea of dedicating himself to this purpose came to him
when he was a small boy on his father's farm. "When occasionally a townsman visited our farm, one of those who
affected to speak only in French," he writes in his **Memoirs,**

> it puzzled me sorely, and even disconcerted me,
> to see my parents all at once take on a respectful
> manner to the stranger, as though they felt him
> to be their superior. I was perplexed, too, at
> hearing another tongue.
>
> "Why is it," I asked, "that man does not speak
> like we do?"
>
> "Because he is a gentleman," I was told.
>
> "Then I will never be a gentleman," I replied re-
> sentfully.

When Mistral was 21 he made a vow to become a "Felibre":

> Then and there, with my foot on the threshold
> of the paternal home, and my eyes looking to-
> ward the Alpilles, I formed the resolution, first,
> to raise and revivify in Provence the sentiment
> of race that I saw being annihilated by the false
> and unnatural education of all the schools; sec-
> ondly, to promote that resurrection by the resto-
> ration of the native and historic language of the
> country, against which the schools waged war to
> the death; and, lastly, to make that language
> popular by illuminating it with the divine flame
> of poetry.

Mistral was educated for the law, his entrance into college,
a mere farmer's lad dressed in the rough garb of the peasantry, forming one of the most delightful chapters in his
Memoirs, but, in view of his oath, he "abandoned, once
and for all, inflammatory politics, even as one casts off a
burden on the road in order to walk more lightly, and
from henceforth I gave myself up entirely to my country
and my art—my Provence, from whom I had never received aught but pure joy."

In fulfillment of his patriotic purpose he joined hands with
four of his countrymen who cherished a similar ambition
to bring back the days of the troubadours and to expel the
literature of France from Provence. These men were Roumanille, Aubanel, Felix Gras, and Anselme Mathieu. To
Roumanille Mistral gives the credit for having originated
the "Felibres" movement, and he describes how he met
this poet, who was his elder by a dozen years, at school
in Avignon, and vowed to him that he would "write verse
in Provencal."

This effort to restore the language of Provence to its literary supremacy, now that it has been accomplished, seems,
in a way, a not difficult undertaking. But Mistral points
out that the native tongue had come under the ban of cultivated people, and was considered suitable for only "common or droll subjects," at the time when he and Roumanille, sixty years ago, made up their minds that it was
capable of the best literary expression. There was thus a

national prejudice to be overcome before these five devoted poets could hope to win their countrymen to an appreciation of the beauties of Provencal—something of the
same prejudice that existed immediately prior to the days
of Chaucer, when the Anglo-Saxon tongue was considered
fit for nothing but the commonest usage, while French, or
Latin, was alone deemed worthy the pen of the scholar or
the poet.

As a practical method for conducting their educational
campaign these Felibres, or Brotherhood of Provencalists,
again like Pre-Raphaelites of England with their periodical publication of *The Germ,* issued a magazine which
they called the *Provencal Almanac,* devoted to the propa-
gation of their literary faith and filled with their poetical
effusions, interspersed with a number of charming stories
of primitive life in Provence, some of which are given in
the present volume of **Memoirs.** So striking was the literary quality of these contributions that they attracted the
attention of such men as Daudet, Arene, Blavat in Paris,
and were speedily translated into French. Mistral's epic
poem, **Mireille,** also won the enthusiastic approval of Lamartine, who hailed this modern troubadour as a "second
Homer"; and thus, instead of singing "only for the shepherds and people of the soil," Mistral, in the effort to revive a native literature, became the recipient of a personal
fame that far transcended the bounds of his own country.
Still faithful to his original purpose, however, Mistral has
devoted his latter years to the compilation of a dictionary
of the Provencal language, the publication of which and
its general acceptance by his countrymen seem to give the
final crown of success to his patriotic endeavors.

The memoirs of Mistral not only recount the steps which
were taken by him and his confrères in the Felibres movement, but they are filled also with charming details of Provencal farm life, the legends and primitive customs of the
Provencal peasantry; there are many little personal anecdotes that give a picturesque view of some of the poet's experiences at school and on the paternal farm, his amusing
contact with some of his peasant neighbors and the whole
leaves the reader with the belief that there may still be
room for the romantic troubadour, the follower of the
"Gay Science" in our modern civilization.

> *"Mistral, Last of the Troubadours," in* The
> New York Times Book Review, *January 11,
> 1908, p. 18.*

Percy F. Bicknell (essay date 1908)

[*In the following essay, Bicknell comments on Mistral's*
Memoirs, *noting the account of the Félibre movement's
origin and praising Mistral's descriptions of rural life.*]

On the appearance of Frédéric Mistral's **Mirèio** in 1859,
Lamartine hailed its author, then only twenty-eight years
old, as the Homer of his native land, and Adolphe Dumas
styled him the Virgil of Provence. Honors and titles have
ever since been offered him—some accepted, but perhaps
more refused—and it was not long before his great epic enjoyed the distinction of translation into other and more
widely known tongues. Miss Harriet Waters Preston's English version, published in Boston in 1872, has long been

familiar to American and British readers. Of the poet himself, his fair land of Provence, its folk-lore and its dialect, much has been written, in periodicals and in books, by Miss Preston herself as well as by Mr. Janvier, Mr. Arthur Symons, the Pennells (collaborating with pen and pencil), Mr. C. T. Brooks, Alphonse Daudet, and others. Of the movement known as *Félibrige,* started by Joseph Roumanille, but more properly and more closely associated with the name of Mistral, it may be well to give here a little account before taking up the early life of him who has made the word *Félibre* familiar to the reading world. In the **Memoirs of Mistral,** as translated by Miss Maud from the poet's **Mes Origines,** it is told how seven poets of Provence had assembled on the 21st of May, 1854, in the full tide of spring and youth, at the château of Font-Ségugne, when it was proposed, in view of the failure thus far of the young school of Avignon patriots to rehabilitate the Provençal tongue, that these seven should "band together and take the enterprise in hand."

> "And now," said Glaup, "as we are forming a new body we must have a new name. The old one of 'minstrel' will not do, as every rhymer, even he who has nothing to rhyme about, adopts it. That of troubadour is no better, for, appropriated to designate the poets of a certain period, it has been tarnished by abuse. We must find something new."
>
> Then I took up the speech. "My friends," said I, "in an old country legend I believe we shall find the predestined name." And I proceeded: "His Reverence Saint-Anselme, reading and writing one day from the Holy Scriptures, was lifted up into the highest heaven. Seated near the Infant Christ he beheld the Holy Virgin. Having saluted the aged saint, the Blessed Virgin continued her discourse to her Infant Son, relating how she came to suffer for His sake seven bitter wounds." Here I omitted the recital of the wounds until I came to the following passage: "The fourth wound that I suffered for Thee, O my precious Son, it was when I lost Thee, and seeking three days and three nights found Thee not until I entered the Temple, where Thou wast disputing with the scribes of the Law, with the seven 'Félibres' of the Law."

At this phrase, "the seven 'Félibres' of the Law," the seven young men cried out in chorus: "Félibre is the name!" Then followed, from one after another, the suggestion of various derivative terms, as "félibrerie," to denote a branch of Félibres numbering not fewer than seven members; "félibriser," meaning to meet together as the seven at Font-Ségugne were then doing; "félibrée," a festival of Provençal poets; "félibréen," an adjective descriptive of the new association and its aims, and so on. The conjectural derivation of *Félibre,* from *faire* and *livre,* may be referred to in passing. The task of compiling a dictionary of the *Langue d'Oc* was assumed by Mistral himself, and completed after twenty years of devoted labor. Of this "Treasury of the Félibres" it has been said, by a competent judge:

> The history of a people is contained in this book. No one can ever know what devotion, knowledge, discrimination and intuition such a work represents, undertaken and concluded as it was during the twenty best years of a poet's life. All the words of the Oc language in its seven different dialects, each one compared with its equivalent in the Latin tongue, all the proverbs and idioms of the South, together with every characteristic expression either in use or long since out of vogue, make up this incomparable Thesaurus of a tenacious language, which is no more dead today than it was three hundred years ago, and which is now reconquering the hearts of all the faithful.

But it is not for the completing of his dictionary that the world has of late had occasion to admire and applaud this poet-lexicographer; but for his quiet refusal of a seat among the Immortals of the French Academy, when, contrary to all precedent, the vacant chair was pressed upon him without previous solicitation on his part. Last year, too, he received the Nobel prize for patriotic literature—a prize that has been devoted by him to the cause dearest to his heart as a citizen of Provence. The gift from Sweden has gone toward the purchase of an ancient palace in Arles, to be known hereafter as the Félibréan Museum, and to take the place of the small and inadequate building now occupied by the collection of Provençal antiquities and curiosities.

The little village of Maillane, situated in the midst of a wide and fertile plain, is the scene of M. Mistral's childhood and youth. His early life here, and in the near vicinity at school, is delightfully pictured in the volume of memoirs now first offered to English and American readers two years after their translation into French from the still earlier Provençal original. They cover only the years from 1830 to 1859,—that is, from the poet's birth up to the publication of his best-known work. He was the only child of his father's second marriage, a marriage pleasingly pastoral and romantic as described in the **Memoirs.**

> One summer's day on the Feast of St. John, Master François Mistral stood in the midst of his cornfields watching the harvesters as they mowed down the crop with their sickles. A troop of women followed the labourers, gleaning the ears of corn which escaped the rake. Among them my father noticed one, a handsome girl, who lingered shyly behind as though afraid to glean like the rest. Going up to her he inquired: "Who are you, pretty one? What is your name?"
>
> "I am the daughter of Etienne Poulinet," the young girl replied, "the Mayor of Maillane. My name is Delaïde."
>
> "Does the daughter of Master Poulinet, Mayor of Maillane, come, then, to glean?" asked my father in surprise.
>
> "Sir, we are a large family," she answered, "six daughters and two sons; and our father, though he is fairly well off, when we ask him for pocket-money to buy pretty clothes, tells us we must go and earn it. That is why I have come here to glean."
>
> Six months after this meeting, which recalls the

old biblical scene between Ruth and Boaz, the brave yeoman asked the Mayor of Maillane for his daughter's hand in marriage; and I was born of their union.

The scenes of country life and domestic happiness depicted in the *Memoirs* have all the fresh beauty and simplicity that might have been expected from the pen that drew them. The lack of any word for "home" in the French language, and the common but hasty inference that home-life also, at its best, is unknown to the people of France, seem strange enough to one reading again and again in French memoirs the homely and touching accounts of family life and family joys and sorrows. Taine's early years at Vouziers and the tender relations existing between him and his mother have recently been described; and now we have a still more charming picture of happy and affectionate domestic life in a Provençal farming community. Equally effective is the writer's presentation of the primitive agricultural methods of those unsophisticated peasant farmers of a day that is fled. Before introducing the scene of peace and innocence that he associates with his boyhood, he refers with sorrow to the invasion of American methods and American machinery.

> Now at harvest time the plains are covered with a kind of monster spider and gigantic crab, which scratch up the ground with their claws, and cut down the grain with cutlasses, and bind the sheaves with wire; then follow other monsters snorting steam, a sort of Tarascon dragon who seizes on the fallen wheat, cuts the straw, sifts the grain, and shakes out the ears of corn. All this is done in latest American style, a dull matter of business, with never a song to make toil a gladness, amid a whirl of noise, dust, and hideous smoke, and the constant dread, if you are not constantly on the watch, that the monster will snap off one of your limbs. This is Progress, the fatal Reaper, against whom it is useless to contend, bitter result of science, that tree of knowledge whose fruit is both good and evil.

Contrast with this the simple ways of those earlier tillers of the soil of whom the poet's father was one. The word "corn" is of course to be taken in the generic, not the specific or American, sense.

> As in the days of Cincinnatus, Cato, and Virgil, we reaped with the sickle, the fingers of the right hand protected by a shield of twisted reeds or rushes. . . . Every day at dawn the reapers ranged themselves in line, and so soon as the chief had opened out a pathway through the cornfield all glistening with morning dew, they swung their blades, and as they slowly advanced down fell the golden corn. The sheaf-binders, most of whom were young girls in the freshness of their youthful bloom, followed after, bending low over the fallen grain, laughing and jesting with a gaiety it rejoiced one's heart to see. Then as the sun appeared bathing the sky all rosy red and sending forth a glory of golden rays, the chief, raising high in the air his scythe, would cry, "Hail to the new day," and all the scythes would follow suit. Having thus saluted the newly risen sun, again they fell to work, the cornfield bowing down as they advanced with rhythmic

harmonious movement of their bare arms. . . . It was in this company, the grand sun of Provence streaming down on me as I lay full length beneath a willow-tree, that I learnt to pipe such songs as **"Les Moissons"** and others in *Les Iles d' Or.*

Although the son of Master François Mistral was sent away to learn his Latin and afterward to study law, he seems never for a moment to have proposed for himself the practice of the profession for which he had made these preliminary studies. But rather, when he reached the age of one-and-twenty, it was his resolve

> first, to raise and revivify in Provence the sentiment of race that I saw being annihilated by the false and unnatural education of all the schools, secondly, to promote that resurrection by the restoration of the native and historic language of the country, against which the schools waged war to the death; and lastly, to make that language popular by illuminating it with the divine flame of poetry.

And on a later page he says: "So it came to pass that I abandoned, once and for all, inflammatory politics, even as one casts off a burden on the road in order to walk more lightly, and from henceforth I gave myself up entirely to my country and my art—my Provence, from whom I had never received aught but pure joy." A high resolve, and nobly fulfilled. (pp. 36-8)

> *Percy F. Bicknell, "The Romance and Poetry of Provence," in* The Dial, *Chicago, Vol. XLIV, No. 518, January 16, 1908, pp. 36-8.*

The Count de Soissons   (essay date 1914)

[*In the following excerpt, written upon the occasion of Mistral's death, Soissons surveys Mistral's career and major works, praising his exploration of human nature and his celebration of beauty and transcendence.*]

At all times the pedagogical problem which seems to be the most important in human science has prepossessed the men who loved their country and were interested in its welfare. Consequently, every regime sought to direct education according to its conceptions concerning man's general nature and the special destiny of a nation. The Middle Ages saw in man, before all, the Christian, and strove to guide his soul towards eternal aspirations. The seventeenth century cultivated universal qualities, which constitute an honest man and *l'homme comme il faut.* After Cartesius the mind was developed before everything. From about 1792 politics became the almost exclusive preoccupation, and centralisation waged a cruel war with provincial life. In France the centralising regimes were Richelieu, Louis XIV, the Convention, Napoleon, and finally the Republic. We lived under that fallacious doctrine until well into the nineteenth century, when an important poetical movement, started at first in Provence by *literati* fond of the language of their countries, appeared in the ancient provinces of Southern France. This movement was a sudden blossoming of dialect literature, the consequence of which is an ardent desire for individual provincial life, for the preservation of ancient customs and manners, language and traditions, that were disappearing under the grey billows of uniform, monotonous modern tendencies erroneously called civilisation. Provence, the land that first gave the world a literature after the decay of the classic, had provided such an impulse to *belles lettres,* especially through Count Béranger and Raymond Count de Tholose (Toulouse), that the Italians were obliged to acknowledge in all honesty—as did Bembo in his prose, and Spero Sperone in his dialogue of languages, as well as Aequicola in his books of love, and as one can see in the work of Dante, *lequel embelist une partie de ses écrits de plusieurs traits mi partis du Provençal que François*—that they held their poetry from ours. But Provence was entirely eclipsed after the gory Albigensian war. This obscuration, however, does not mean that the Provençal language was not used by men of talent, for Saboly composed in it his quaint *Noëls* sung all over the region of the Rhône, and Jasmin's poetry was known among those who love culture through Sainte-Beuve's appreciation and Longfellow's rendering of his work into English, but certainly it had not its former importance and splendour. The particularist spirit of the musical *langue d'oc*—comprising the Provençal, the Languedoc, the Gascon, the Limousin, the Bearnais, and the Catalan dialects or *langues romanes*—resisted all the influences and assaults of the *langue d'oil* so well that to-day it is more beautiful than it was in the time of the Troubadours and of the *Jochs florals* of King René, of Bertrand de Born, of Adelaïde de Toulouse, and of Clémence Isaure. Joseph Roumanille, son of a gardener, occupying the modest post of a *surveillant* in a country college, was an unconscious precursor of this very important literary, linguistic, and especially ethnic and patriotic movement, whilst Frederi Mistral's ardent and far-reaching impulse made him its immortal founder and great leader. Mistral deserves rightly the qualificative of great, for he personifies, and is a cause and effect of an epoch; he is one of those few men in the history of the world who can say of themselves, as Dante did: "I am a million, I am a whole nation, I am its whole hope and pain, its death and triumph, I am the whole period of history."

Frederi Mistral—his name is that of the wind which blows occasionally but violently on the shores of the Mediterranean Sea—was born in 1830 in the heart of Provence, in a village called Maiano, situated at the foot of the Alps, near Arlès and the Rhône not far from Aix, by Saint-Rémy renowned for its Roman monuments, and by Baux, the marvellous mediæval town of Southern France. Usually we confuse in our minds Provence with the South of fashion, the South of luxury, *la Côte d'azure* with its new towns and cosmopolitan population, the productive and commercial South, the country situated to the West of the Rhône where they cultivate the vine and live well—when the year is full of abundance—on the fertile soil. This is not Mistral's Provence. The true Provence is a *canton* bounded by the Rhône, the sea, and the first heights of the Alps, with its capitals Arlès and Aix, a narrow country as was Greece, and as poor as was ancient Hellas, a country with a few valleys and the alluvial plain of Camargue, a rocky country where rises in narrow terraces the land saved from land-slips, on which they grow mean olive and almond trees, whose vernal flowers are often nipped by freezing mistral; but also like Greece, it is a country where

the dazzling sun is never clouded, a country with pure and blue sky, a country resplendent with light, a country with white houses and dusty roads, with mountains painted at sunset with all the colours of the rainbow; a country full of perfume, where rocks disappear under evergreen genista, scented thyme, blooming heather, odorous lavender, and pungent rosemary; a country of *farniente,* of delightful laziness, of sobriety and simplicity; a country of songs, of carelessness, and of love.

In his **Memoirs** Mistral describes with great simplicity his childhood spent on his father's farm, living an antique life, *en famille* with domestics, sharing with them the work in the fields, the care of beasts of burden, the vigils during which the heart, the imagination and the sentiments played freely and gracefully. It was in that rustic, familiar, and traditional surrounding that Mistral was formed, his only distractions being the recital of the events and adventures of his father's campaign, the excursions to old places in the country, the description of a fair at Beaucaire when grandfather returned from it, and especially the continual contact with things of the land, with beings, the trees, the flowers, of which he was very fond during his free and healthy life in the open-air. In that book—his last work—Mistral tells us also about his father's marriage, accomplished under circumstances which much resemble that of Ruth and Boaz, and calls his sire the Sage, the Patriarch, the Lord-father, the respected and austere Master, whilst his mother is *la Maîtresse, ma mère belle.* Certainly, there was no luxury in his mode of living, but it mattered not to his superior mind; his talents and achievements were above attention to such distinctions. *Nec te quaesieris extra.*

Although, like many other remarkable men, it was not college, but family life and Nature that developed and made Frederi Mistral great, they took care to give *une education bourgeoise* to the youthful son of the farmer of Maiano. He was then ten years of age. The history of the boy, who became a fervent admirer of the ancients and their successor, is the history neither of a very diligent student, nor of a submissive and docile schoolboy. Whilst at Maiano he played truant so well and so often that his father said one day, "He must be locked up"; and he carried out his word by placing him in the boarding-school of Saint Michel at Frigolet, in an old monastery; and then at Avignon—his first great journey—with M. Millet, where he had a sad time, for teachers and comrades alike made fun of his *patois.* Of his *patois* he was very fond, thanks to his charming mother, who in order to amuse her only son would sing to him beautiful Provençal songs and recite wonderful tales. He soon ran away from Avignon and came to Maiano, where he was sent to M. Dupuy's school, and became acquainted with Joseph Roumanille, whose influence decided his future career. Roumanille was twelve years older than Mistral, and he had already published his first poetical attempt, called *Li Margarideto,* in *Boni Abeisso,* a Provençal journal issued in Marseilles. He told his new pupil and friend no less truthfully than poetically that he began to write poetry in French, but when he recited it to his mother she cried, because knowing only Provençal she could not understand her dear boy's effusions, and he promised himself not to write except in the language which his mother spoke. In that manner the new poetry was born from the tears of a woman who seemed to personify the little country much neglected and almost forgotten by her big sister.

Roumanille loved the melodious speech of the Rhône valley, and his enthusiasm for it he was able to communicate to "the sublime child," as he called Mistral, who said of him: "Scarcely had he shown me in their spring-time freshness these lovely field-flowers, when a thrill ran through my being and I exclaimed: 'This is the dawn my soul awaited to awaken to the light!' " From that time the two boys made a compact to work and to save the *lengo d'or* from the overwhelming influence of the northern speech, and to restore to it its former lustre. This work Mistral continued with still better results at Aix, where he was sent to study law, for in that ancient city of Provence he found abundant material in the old books. His first work in the Provençal language was a poem called **"Li Meissoun,"** Provençal georgics in four songs, when he was but seventeen years of age. When, in 1851, he returned home from Aix with the degree of *licencié en droit,* and was left free to choose his career, he unhesitatingly decided not only to create a new and independent literature, but also to effect a complete renascence of the mental life of Southern France, to reconquer for Provence her ancient prominence, and to cause France, to which she was united on terms of equality four hundred years ago, to look at her with admiration. The first step towards this vast and ambitious purpose was to develop and expand the dialect of Saint Rémy into a beautiful literary language. In this he followed Dante, who made the language of Florence the basis of the Italian tongue. The primary work consisted in epuration and fixation. The epuration meant elimination of all French words, for which he substituted the corresponding Provençal expressions. The fixation of the language was produced under the modest aspect of making the orthography stable. In reality, however, it was the phonetics and the morphology of the literary language that ruled the orthography constituted by Roumanille and Mistral, and was applied in the whole work of Felibres after the first publication of the *Armana prouvençan.* To this double work of epuration and fixation, which is rather negative, one should add, in order to understand better how important was Mistral's achievement, a positive work of enrichment. Into the idiom which he took for basis he introduced words gathered from outside the restricted limits of that idiom, modifying them a little in their form when necessary, which seemed to him expressive of new shades of action or sensation. For this purpose he sought out the old expressions, familiar and bold, which had no equivalent in French. These he found, not in the old books, but in the language of the people, and if he was archaic in that respect, he was not so after the manner of an antiquary, who pretends to revive words, forms, and constructions which have been abolished; he was like an amateur anxious to preserve what the present has of the old but still living.

Mistral's intelligent work and boundless enthusiasm vigorously furthered the Provençal renascence that was developed during the Congresses at Arlès in 1852, at Aix in 1853, and the famous gathering in Castel de Font-Segugne

in 1854, when he and his poet-friends constituted themselves into a permanent society under the old and enigmatic name of *Felibre*. These poets—Paul Giéra, Joseph Roumanille, Théodore Aubanel, Anselme Mathieu, Eugène Garcin, Brunet, Alphonse Tavan, and Frederi Mistral—*en pleine primevère de la vie et de l'an*—raised the flag of the linguistic, literary, and social resurrection of the South. Such was the beginning of this remarkable movement—the *Felibrige*—through which the inertia of the Provençals themselves has been overcome. A new intellectual life in the Rhône valley was started, and the fame of the *Felibres* and their work of consequence and weight has gone abroad into distant lands.

It was Mistral alone, however, who understood that eloquent manifestoes, theoretical discussions, and pretty poems were not sufficient to prove to France, and then to the world, that the language of the Troubadours is still living and is capable of having its own literature. For this it was necessary to produce a work of great literary and poetical value. And Mistral, tall and erect, elegant in his little *jaquette,* with his flowing cravat of *foulard,* wearing a *mousquetaire* soft hat, carrying a malacca with a silver handle, a light overcoat on his arm, his eyes full of resolve, his Olympian forehead, with something martial and imperial about it, crowning his radiant visage, leading a well-balanced life, free from the vain and petty occupations by which so many lives are consumed and in which too often the time and the talents of many writers and artists are wasted, "feasting not with the old leaven, nor with the leaven of malice and wickedness, but with the unleavened bread of sincerity and truth" [Epist. I. Cor. v. 7-8], gave himself wholeheartedly to writing an epic poem *Mirèio.* He alone, too, understood that, no matter how important his work might be, it must be appreciated in the first place in Paris, before it could be cherished in Provence, before the Provençal literature could claim its place amongst literatures of the world. This was done through an effort of the unfortunate, but noble, poet, Adolphe Dumas, Mistral's friend, who at once understood the value of his work. It was he who forced the leading Parisian critics to study the masterpiece, and introduced the young poet to Lamartine, who, after having read *Mirèio,* not only spoke of it with great enthusiasm, but wrote a long critique in *Cours familier de littérature.* "I read *Mirèio,*" wrote Lamartine to Reboul, "and was so smitten in my heart and mind that I am writing an *Entretien* about this poem. Yes, since the time of the Homeridæ of the Archipelago the world has not seen such a fountain of primitive poetry. Like you, I cried out: 'He is a Homer!' " Meanwhile, there came forth eulogistic appreciations from other critics, who compared Mistral to Virgil, Dante and Theocritus, one of them saying that the beautiful idyll ending the first canto of *Mirèio* reminded him of the purest breath of the "Song of Songs." However, the broadest, if not the most literary, was the welcome of Villemain, who said that "France is rich enough to have two literatures."

The story of the poem is very simple: the reciprocal love of two young people, with an impediment of social conditions, the consequence of which is a tragical end. But with this sentimental and ordinary basis, so often repeated but

Mirèio **is undoubtedly Mistral's greatest masterpiece, for, while being a purely Provençal work, both in its spirit and character, it has also immutable human characteristics, which can be understood by everybody, without consideration of time, race, or language.**

—The Count de Soissons

universally human, and therefore always new and interesting for the sympathy it ever awakens in human hearts, the author has interwoven so many scenes from the life of the people, has described in so masterly a fashion their work, their beliefs and traditions, their superstitions and legends, their joys and sorrows and aspirations, that the whole constitutes an unrivalled performance. He has done all this with an archaic simplicity, so that the art of writing seems to be totally absent, whilst the pictures exhibited before the enchanted eyes of the reader's soul seem to speak to him directly. In reading *Mirèio* one feels as if one were living in the places, conditions, and surroundings evoked by the magic power of the author. There are scenes quite ordinary in themselves, on which one looks without any emotion, presented with realism, but at the same time pervaded by an elusive charm. The atmosphere of an ideal, so difficult to describe, here enwraps everything and is felt everywhere. This ideal *Stimmung* is manifested towards the end of the poem in a rapture of pure mysticism worthy of the primitive writers and artists. In all this, the author's great personality is so concealed that it seems to be, as are the primitive heroic poems, born directly of the spirit and genius of the people.

Mirèio is undoubtedly Mistral's greatest masterpiece, for, while being a purely Provençal work, both in its spirit and character, it has also immutable human characteristics, which can be understood by everybody, without consideration of time, race, or language. For this reason *Mirèio* should be counted amongst those few works that are the property of all mankind. No *résumé,* or even translation, can furnish a notion of the beauty of *Mirèio,* of its musical qualities, its brightness of narration, its vivacity and harmony between words and sense, its graceful succession of rhymes and the cadence of its stanzas. Mistral's success was complete when the Academy crowned his poem and Gounod composed music to it. He had now shown by his work of unassailable beauty that he was fully conscious of the goal towards which he was working and leading his disciples and his province, the purpose of raising the people of the South of France to a conception of their individuality as a race, of the re-birth of the Latin race and the laying of the foundation of a great Latin union.

Mirèio is not the only work of Mistral. After this popular period, more or less contemporary with the poet, there followed a heroic, legendary poem, *Calendau,* reminding one of *Chansons de geste,* a work of value, although less known and appreciated outside Provence, because of its allegory

and its scholarly allusions. With regard to the performance, it is as good and as masterly as *Mirèio* because of the same musical verse, the same richness of expression, and the same originality. When his third poem *Nerto* was published, Mistral was rightly likened to Ariosto, a comparison justified by the serious touches here and there, and by its charming style and lively vein. It is a story of the time of Benedict XIII. (1394), and it presents a very sprightly picture of the papal court of those times. The poetic quality of *Lou Pouèmo dóu Rose* suffers from too much realism—a usual and just penalty in works of art—through the medium of which is imaged the life on the river. It differs from Mistral's other poems in this, that it is written in blank verse—the line being exactly that of the *Divina Commedia*—and there is a conscious avoidance, not only of rhyme, but of assonance as well; the rhythm of the line is marked, and it produces an effect on the ear like that of English iambic pentameters hypercatalectic. On the other hand, it is remarkably objective, like his other poems. But Mistral's unbounded enthusiasm concerning Provence leads him into exaggeration, and whilst he is masterly and poetic in describing nature, and especially in evoking the past, he is often superficial in serious questions and deep verities. The complete expression of his poetical ideas is to be found in the collection of poems published under the title of *Lis Isclo d'or,* in which one finds gems of the best and purest poetry. It is an enthusiastic appeal for life and light, for strength and energy addressed to his well-beloved Provence and its inhabitants. *La Reino Jano* was a failure as a drama. It was never performed, and proved again that there can be no dramatic literature in the language of the Troubadours, even in its modern revival. Whilst the above-mentioned works testify to Mistral's great poetical gift, his dictionary of the Provençal language, published under the title of *Trésor dóu Felibrige,* at which he worked for twenty years, shows how great was his erudition. That important work is not merely an agglomeration of words with their meanings, but it is frequently interpolated with historical facts, fables, proverbs, and legends, which throw light on the primitive meanings of many of the words. No wonder, therefore, that it was received enthusiastically by the scholars of the world.

I think I have shown that Mistral's whole work is uplifting. There is in it no concession to the fashions prevailing either in literature or custom: there is no calculation for a momentary success. His achievement belongs to that limited number of works which neither grow old nor die, for rising above the passing exigencies of changeable, intellectual taste, it expresses sentiments and passions essential to human nature, and it is consequently always capable of producing an echo in the human soul; it glorifies only what is really beautiful, noble, and sublime; it constitutes an ideal, after which the human spirit longs, even in the greatest degradation, and of which it will never cease to dream. There are some critics who speak of the exteriority of his method in presenting human nature, lamenting that he is not a poet whose work is a reflection of his own soul, and that he reproduces too vividly the gestures and words of his Southern people; they say that he is not deep enough in treating of the theme of love. Such critics evidently belong to that phalanx of writers who prefer what is difficult to what is beautiful, and against whom the great connoisseur of art, Winckelmann, warns us:

> Seek not to detect deficiencies and imperfections in a work of art, until you have previously learnt to recognise and discover beauties. This admonition is the fruit of experience, of noticing daily that the beautiful has remained unknown to most observers—who can see the shape, but must learn the higher qualities of it from others—because they wish to act the critic, before they have begun to be scholars. As it is easier to assume a negative than an affirmative position, so imperfections are much more easily observed and found than perfections.

And the affirmative attitude towards Mistral will suggest that his work should be much praised and admired for its degree of *Heiterkeit,* which is an important element in a work of art, and that the author of *Mirèio,* being a Latin, must be quite different from those who cherish Germanic obscurity as against Latin lucidity. Yes, Mistral seems to defend Latin countries against the pernicious influence of the North, which for more than a century has imposed its nebulous and subversive philosophy on Latin art in favour of the complexity and want of precision of Germanic music, and of Norwegian thought, *inintelligente et désenchantée,* and which threatens to corrupt our pure and clear genius. Mistral is, above all, a Latin; he loves Greco-Latin culture, and the date of issue of *Mirèio* is not only an unforgettable epoch because of the publication of a masterpiece; but it is also a historical point of time, in which there reappeared from behind the fog of Romanticism the classical tradition in art and thought. Mistral's works show us how to substitute the unbridled imagination by the luminous manner of looking on the world, and how to master our mind in order to produce works of art full of transcendental serenity.

Mistral's life, in its simple oneness and its astounding success, teaches those who seek restlessly and eagerly only for wealth and luxury, that after a certain not very excessive material welfare has been attained, then what most count in our sublunary existence are the things pertaining to the province of spirit. Gold is desirable to a certain degree, but far more valuable than wealth is the love of the transcendental, the love of the beautiful, the love of virtue, the love of man for woman and of woman for man, the love of lofty endeavour, the love of daring emulation: all these should be more cherished than ugly business, frantic industrialism and exhausting activity, for these alone can never bring happiness either to the individual or to the nation.

By the death of Frederi Mistral on March 25th of this year, not only France, but the whole world lost its greatest poet. During his lifetime a statue was erected in his honour at Arles. His mortal remains were deposited for their eternal rest in the little rustic cemetery of his village, in which he spent almost the whole of his most fruitful life. The inscription on his tombstone, engraved according to his wish, reads thus:—

> Non nobis Domine, non nobis,
>   Sed nomini tuo
> Et Provinciæ nostræ
>   Da gloriam.

However, notwithstanding his praiseworthy modesty, his name will remain surrounded with a great and amaranthine glory, for such lofty poets and such noble leaders of men are rarely inscribed on the pages of history. (pp. 669-77)

> The Count de Soissons, "Frederi Mistral," in Contemporary Review, *Vol. 105, No. 581, May, 1914, pp. 669-77.*

Jean Carrère   (essay date 1922)

[*In the excerpt below, Carrère asserts that "Mistral brought about the classical renaissance in France" and likens the craftsmanship of his verse and his moral mission as a poet to that of such classical writers as Horace, Dante, and Vergil.*]

[The] classical spirit, with all the light, serenity, strength, lightness of spirit, and inspiration which it involves, was restored in France half a century ago. And the man whose sunny genius gave us once more the pure light of Hellenism is to-day in the full radiance of his glory and the full vigour of his influence: Frédéric Mistral. It was Mistral who brought about the classical renaissance in France, and it is fitting to express to-day the gratitude which French literature owes him.

I say advisedly "French literature," and I ought to add "the French language," however strange these phrases may at first seem to superficial minds. They will be astonished to hear that the French language and literature can owe anything to a man who seems to have lived in revolt against them, even in hostility to them: to a poet who deliberately tried to create a literature alongside of, even rival to, our national literature, and to bring back to life beside our great language an idiom that had fallen out of use.

Yet it is unquestionably true, and it is enough to study impartially the work and life of Mistral to realise the whole of the inspiration they have given to a new generation of French writers. Destiny seems, at first sight, to have impenetrable secrets, and they seem, when we discover them, to be due to some sort of superhuman irony. Perhaps Mistral himself was rather surprised at the results of his work upon us. If he was, his surprise would not last long, for he is the exact opposite of an unconscious genius. He sees with marvellous clearness the effect which his writings and conduct may have in the future.

We have to agree with him. The Provençal renaissance brought about by Mistral is responsible for the renaissance of the pure French spirit; which proves that no effort is ever wasted. No poet in the whole history of letters was more completely, more purely, more naturally saturated with the Hellenic spirit—more *classical,* in a word—than Mistral. He belongs to the same great, luminous family as Homer, Plato, Vergil, Dante, Petrarch, and Racine. Of all his intellectual ancestors the one he approaches most nearly in spirit and form is Vergil. It seems as if the same breath, purified by the snow of the Alps, vivified by the breezes of the Mediterranean, animated the mind of the two poets, born almost in the same latitude: the one on the banks of a tributary of the Po, the other on a tributary of the Rhone. These two Gallo-Romans, one of Cisalpine, and one of Transalpine Gaul, both nourished by the purest Hellenic sap, displayed in their twin styles the fairest and brightest flowers of human poetry.

Mistral is, like Vergil, irreproachable in his choice of words, in the clearness and simplicity of his figures of speech, and in the crystalline limpidity of his language, so transparent that at first it seems to have no depth, yet so full of meaning that, after long consideration, one hardly sees the bottom of it. And what measure, what tact, what truth in his magnificent idyllic pictures! What sustained harmony! What faultless purity! In French letters only Racine and Fénelon have this marvellous limpidity; but the Provençal tongue, like the Latin, has, in addition, some taste of the sun that is lacking in our less coloured and less concrete tongue.

Such, during fifty years, without faltering, has the fine classic poet of *Mireille* and *Calendal* developed. But he has not only restored to us the clear speech and luminous visions of the Helleno-Roman civilisation. He is also an incarnation of the balanced wisdom, the free boldness, and the robust serenity of imperishable Hellenism. He is wholly and entirely classical, in spirit as well as form.

Mistral had the noblest ideal of the poet which it is possible to have. He has been the shepherd of peoples, the moral guide of the generations in which he lived, the teacher of energy to future generations. Never perhaps had the *os magna sonaturum* of Horace a more striking application. He sang only of beautiful things, he extolled only fine sentiments, and he evoked only great thoughts, because he himself, naturally, from inborn nobleness, could attempt nothing that was not great. He is unquestionably of that elect body which Vergil makes Æneas meet in the woods of his Elysian fields:

> Quique pii vates et Phœbo digna locuti.

Listen, for instance, to this splendid appeal, worthy of Vergil or Dante, with which Mistral begins his *Calendal*:

> Soul of my country—thou who dost shine in all its story and its tongue—when the barons of Picardy, of Germany, and of Burgundy—swarmed round Toulouse and Beaucaire—thou who didst fire on every side—against the black riders—the men of Marseilles and the sons of Avignon.

> By these great memories of the past—thou who dost save and hope—thou who, in our youth, still warmer and more generous—in spite of death and the digger, dost bring back the blood of our fathers—thou, inspirer of the sweet troubadours—and like the *mistral* dost later make the voice of Mirabeau roar.

> For the seas of the ages—and their storms and their horrors—in vain mix the nations and their frontiers efface; our mother-earth, nature, still feeds her sons—with the same milk; her hard breast still gives its fine oil to the olive.

> Soul ever rising anew,—joyous and proud and alive—who dost neigh in the noise of the Rhone and its wind;—soul of the woods full of harmony—and of the sunny bays—pious soul of my country—I call upon thee, incarnate thyself in my Provençal verse!

Do not these accents of pride and strength take us far away from the lamentable effusions of sickly love or sterile dream and all the individualist follies which Romanticism extolled in the last century? And what poet has better expressed the great ideal of classic poetry than the man whose whole poetic art is summed up in these two simple and sublime verses of his *Chant de la coupe*?

> Pour out the poet's wine,
>   Singing of man and God,
> For 'tis the food divine
>   That lifts the human clod.
>
> Grant us the power to know
>   Things good and true and brave,
> And every joy bestow
>   That laughs e'en at the grave.

Compare this conception of the poet with, for instance, the following from Musset:

> Madder than fair Ophelia with rosemary crowned,
> Sillier than page who for love of fairy has swooned,
> Played the tambourine on his shattered headgear.

Or with this of Verlaine:

> The fine shade! The fine shade!
> 'Tis that alone marries
> The dream to the dream, and the flute to the horn.

Passing from pure poetry to history we find that Mistral, both in his lyric and his epic poems, displays, whenever he conjures up the harmonious evolution of his beautiful country, the perfect balance of imagination and reason, the blend of wisdom and energy, which are the essence of the classical spirit. It is he who (in his *Ode aux poètes catalans*) wrote these two lines:

> For now it is plain, now at last do we know,
> That in the order divine all things work for good.

To this lofty ideal of the poet as the shepherd of nations, Mistral was faithful all his life, without the least lapse, without any Utopia, in virtue of the perfect balance of his genius. That is why his beautiful work, the reflection of his beautiful life, was not merely a matter of literature; it was a matter of conduct. He was not flute-player: he was a torch-bearer. At the end of the nineteenth century and the beginning of the twentieth this villager of Maillane dared to recall the solar mission of the poet, the descendant of Orpheus, the guide of the multitude, and of Amphion, the builder of cities.

But Mistral did more than express the mission of the poet in his fine verses. He realised it. Every poem of his is a fruitful act. Just as Vergil made the *Æneid* the guiding work of Roman thought, as Dante brought on the reawakening of Italy by his *Divine Comedy,* so Mistral, in his *Mireille,* his *Calendal,* and his *Îles d'or,* brought about the renaissance of the Provençal race; then, by repercussion, that of the provinces of France; and finally, as a natural consequence, the reawakening of the classical spirit in the whole of France.

No poet in the whole history of letters was more completely, more purely, more naturally saturated with the Hellenic spirit—more *classical,* in a word—than Mistral. He belongs to the same great, luminous family as Homer, Plato, Vergil, Dante, Petrarch, and Racine.

—Jean Carrère

It was impossible for such a man to live anywhere on French soil without the radiation from his work gradually stimulating the generation that grew up around him. What! In the height of a period of naturalism and exaggerated Romanticism, at a time when at Paris all the morbidities of the dream and all the ugliness of brutal realism formed the substance of the literature that was in vogue, in this age of unquestioned decadence, there was a rival of Vergil and Dante in Provence, and a genius of this character could be without influence on France itself? That would be to deny the most essential laws of intellectual development.

As regards the French language, in the first place, we may say that it owes to Mistral as much as the Provençal tongue does. After the invasion of disturbed ideas and disorderly styles which Romanticism had let into our literature by opening wide our doors to the barbarism of the north, we needed purification from the Mediterranean; we needed the bracing tonic of the Græco-Roman sun. France, let us not forget, belongs to the Latin family, and, if it is not to renounce its own genius, it must preserve entire the inheritance it has received from Greece. The *langue d'oïl* and the *langue d'oc* were twin births from the soil which the Gallo-Roman civilisation had fertilised.

From the eleventh century, the golden age in Occitania, to the seventeenth century, the golden age in the Île de France, through Thibault de Champagne, Froissart, Commines, Charles d'Orléans, Villon, Ronsard, Rabelais, and Montaigne, the *langue d'oc* and *langue d'oïl* had so mingled their sap, like two robust plants closely connected, that they had produced a single fruit: the fine classical style of the seventeenth century.

But a day came when this fruit seemed to rot on the parched branches, and in recent times one would have thought that it was all over with the fresh vegetation of France. Our language and style had, as it were, lost their race, and parasitic growths fastened upon the old tree of France, strangling it down to its very roots. Then came Mistral with his fertilising stream, issuing from the living wells of the *Æneid* and the *Odyssey,* and at one and the same time he restored life to the southern olive and the northern oak, which seemed about to perish.

Sustained by his sunny and limpid work, the newcomers in literature, especially those who had been fortunate enough to have been born in the lands glorified by Mistral, cherished a new regard for clear and harmonious form, on the one hand, and, on the other, a love of general ideas and noble and uplifting conceptions. In short, owing to the paramount influence of the author of *Mireille*—an influence that penetrated slowly, but with the calm sureness of a sun rising upon the horizon—all the young men of the new generation felt that they were impregnated with the classical spirit. Even those who did not know Mistral, who had never read him, felt on their foreheads, without knowing or wishing it, the purifying wind that came, by the southern roads, from the Rome of Vergil and the Greece of Plato. (pp. 239-45)

> *Jean Carrère, "The Renaissance of the Classical Spirit (Frederic Mistral)," in his* Degeneration in the Great French Masters: Rousseau, Chateaubriand, Balzac, Stendhal, Sand, Musset, Baudelaire, Flaubert, Verlaine, Zola, *translated by Joseph McCabe, 1922. Reprint by Books for Libraries Press, Inc., 1967, pp. 231-46.*

Vernon Loggins (essay date 1924)

[*Loggins was an American educator, editor, essayist, and biographer who wrote several works on American, English, and French authors. In the essay below, he considers several ways in which Mistral may be viewed as a significant figure in the nineteenth century, particularly discussing his broad appeal as a patriot and folk poet.*]

Frédéric Mistral died in 1914, just four months before the beginning of the World War. He had lived for nearly eighty-four years, and had seen his life-work the success which the most extravagant dreams of his youth could hardly have pictured. He had been famous since the age of twenty-nine, and had received such honors as few men of letters know in their lifetime. Again and again he had been offered a seat in the French Academy. He had been awarded the Nobel Prize in literature. Poetry-lovers and philologists from all parts of the world had sought him out in his simple home in the remote village of Maillane. But what pleased him most was the love accorded him by his own people of Provence. I once heard a fervent Provençal say: "Ah, 1914—that was a dark year! Our Master Mistral died and the horrible war began." No disaster, however great, could overshadow in the eyes of true sons of Provence the catastrophe which the death of Mistral meant to their *pays.*

In the year 1900 there was published at Marseilles a *Mistraliana* bibliography, containing hundreds of titles. Little just criticism is found in any article named in this bibliography. The *Félibres,* as the members of the society for the advancement of letters in the original languages of the Midi call themselves, were wonderful propagandists, and most of the talk about their chief poet had been only publicity for which they themselves were mostly responsible. But French thought has gone through an exacting test during the past nine years, and a crystallization of ideas has resulted. Critics are now giving real reasons for the greatness of Frédéric Mistral. They are pointing out that in any one of four ways he might be studied as a significant figure of the nineteenth century.

First, he might be considered as a patriot. His love for the land was something mystic, something not to be explained. It was not a love for Provence alone. Mistral was first of all a Provençal, but he never forgot that as such he was also a Frenchman. He never lost an opportunity to resent the charge often brought against the *Félibres* that they sought to bring about the secession of the Midi from the rest of France. Second, he may be looked upon as a defender of the classic tradition. Homer and Vergil, not the Troubadours nor Petrarch nor Dante, were Mistral's great gods. His view of life was the healthful, rounded view of the firm classicist. His technique was Vergilian. M. Jean Carrère, in his provocative book translated into English under the title of *Degeneration in the Great French Masters,* hurls diatribes at all the romanticists from Rousseau to Paul Verlaine, and then ends his book with a chapter glorifying Frédéric Mistral, hailing him as the greatest hope for the revival of real strength in French literature. Third, he is important as a philologist. *Le Trésor du Félibrige,* his stupendous dictionary of the languages of the Midi, is arousing more and more attention from those interested in Romance philology. This work cost Mistral ten years of his time and much of his poetic inventiveness, but there are many who consider it his strongest contribution towards the advancement of the cause to which he devoted his life. Fourth, he is being classed with the foremost poets of the soil, such as Robert Burns and John Synge. Some have ranked him with the Vergil of the *Georgics,* with Theocritus, and with the Goethe of *Hermann und Dorothea.*

It is certain that whatever broad appeal Mistral may make must be as patriot and poet of the soil. The two are in reality one. Nothing but a man's great love for his land and people can urge him to write about them with the rhapsodic enthusiasm which we find in the poems of Mistral. True, his enthusiasm often led him into exaggeration and extravagance; but, as Alphonse Daudet has so charmingly shown us, exaggeration and extravagance are natural traits of the Provençal. It would be hard to find a Provençal trait of character not brought out somewhere in the works of Mistral. In fact, it is such completeness that gives him his distinction. John Synge's sojourns in the Arran Islands and elsewhere among the Irish peasantry were adventures. They resulted in some of the most outstanding plays of modern times, but no one would proclaim these plays as a comprehensive depiction of present-day Celtic life. Synge was struck by the picturesque only; Mistral saw all Provence as picturesque, and tried to convince us that it really exists as he saw it. Robert Burns was a part of the world he wrote about, but take away the language he used and there remains little of actual eighteenth-century Scotland in his poetry. The aims of Vergil in the *Georgics,* and of Theocritus in the *Idylls* were the same: they produced conventional pastorals. As for *Hermann und Dorothea,* it is the work of a student of character rather than of an enthusiastic folk-poet. Mistral may have lacked the divine genius for song found in some of these masters, but none of them had his intensity,—an intensity growing out of a nobly sincere patriotism.

One must know something of the geography of the *pays* of Mistral if the work of the poet is to be understood. The Provence which he loved and sang about is not the broad south-eastern corner of France commonly known as Provence. The stretch of country embracing Avignon on the north and extending to the sea, with Nîmes included on the west and the Alpilles on the east, is the Provence of Mistral. Although the section is small, it has a varied topography and an enchanting history. There are two large rivers, the Durance and the Rhône; there is a rocky, desert-like plain around Les Baux, called the Crau; there are hills and mountains; there are the salty marshes at the mouth of the Rhône, known as the Camargue. Besides Avignon and Nîmes and Les Baux, there are the towns of Arles, Beaucaire, Tarascon, Saint-Remy, Maillane, Font Vielle, and Les Saintes Maries,—all important in legend and history.

In his three epics, Mistral aimed to give a full impression of this much-varied section as it existed in the middle of the nineteenth century. *Mirèio* (1859) is devoted mainly to the plains and the marshes; in *Calendau* (1867) we have the mountains and the sea; and *Lou Pouèmo dóu Rose* (1897) is a glorification of the great river of Provence. In *Nerto* (1884), a romantic narrative, and in *La Rèino Jano* (1890), a tragedy, the poet turned back to the flamboyant past of Provence, the period of the Troubadors and of the Avignon popes. *Lis Isclo d'Or* (1875) and *Lis Oulivado* (1912) are made up of miscellaneous lyrics, most of which are passionate outbursts of patriotism.

It is *Mirèio,* Mistral's first work and his masterpiece, that shows best his strength as poet of the soil. Throughout the poem there is a youthful enthusiasm which approaches ecstasy. There is a spontaneity that causes the reader to forget the epic machinery. The beginning of the invocation sets a mood which is always maintained, a mood of simplicity and *naïveté,* pronounced characteristics of the Provençal. The following translation may give some idea of the beautiful effect of artlessness found in the original and in Mistral's own French translation:—

> With Homer as my guide I sing!
> I sing a maid of my Provence.
> In all her virgin loves,
> Across the Crau, among the wheat,
> Down to the margin of the sea,
> I follow her.
> She is a soul of the soil,
> The very Crau itself is in her blood;
> And who would sing the maid must also sing the Crau.
> Well that she is resplendent only with the glow of youth!
> Well that she wears no golden diadem, nor royal cloak!
> My song shall raise her to the glory of a queen.
> I will praise her in our homely tongue;
> For, first of all, it is to you I sing,
> O workers in the fields and shepherds of Provence!

Then follows a prayer to the Saviour, "who was born among shepherds," to the Saviour of the *patrie.* The invocation ends with a folk-symbol: the aim to which the poet aspires is likened to a tender branch high on a fig-tree.

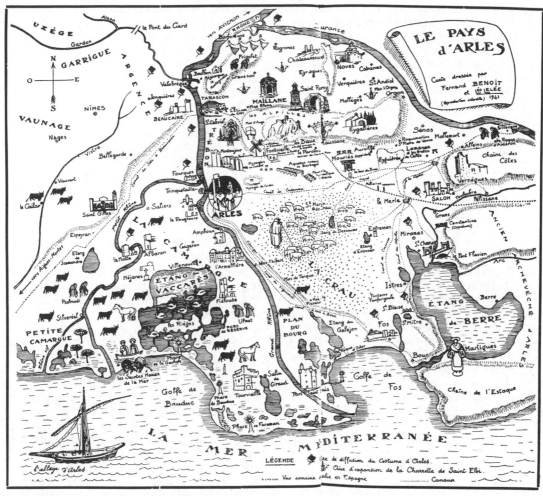

A map of Provence by Fernand Benoit and Léo Lelée, 1941.

The simple plot unfolds slowly, a plot too well known through Gounod's opera *Mireille* to be retold here. That which fascinates is not the story: it is the mass of digressions which make up the picture of Provence.

The most striking characteristic of the nature of Provence is the sun. The Provençal believes that it is his sunshine which has given him his peculiar temperament, and it is very likely that he is right. At any rate, **Mirèio** shows a full recognition of the poetical possibilities of this theory. The story opens with a description of a sunset. From this point on the idea of the sun becomes a leading *motif.* The eighth canto, which relates the flight of the heroine across the Crau to the shrine of the holy Maries, is a grand fugue treatment of the splendor of the Provençal sunshine on a summer day. In the tenth canto, the sun actually becomes a protagonist in the plot. Mirèio is struck by the piercing rays, and as a result of the stroke the holy Maries can appear to her in person, and in the end she can die and realize the true love which she is seeking.

The Provençaux prefer to think of **Mirèio** as allegorical. They like to fancy Mirèio herself as representing Provence. The sun stands for the all-consuming beauty towards which Provence dares to aspire. That she dares

means that she falls. Thus, any decadence which might be ascribed to Provence in that she is not an independent nation can be prettily explained away.

Another indication of the mystic way in which the Provençaux regard their sunshine is seen in the fact that the chief emblem of the *Félibres* is the *cigale.* It is an insect, much like our cicada, which sings only when the sun is shining. Since it is the sunshine of Provence which makes her poets sing, naturally the *cigale* is looked upon as a fitting emblem for the society organized to encourage literary production.

Although in **Mirèio** Mistral emphasizes the sun in portraying the nature of Provence, he does not overlook other aspects. The Rhône becomes a character in the action when Ourrias, the one villain in the story, is tricked to his death by the phantom boatmen of the mighty river. One of the most lyrical passages in the entire epic is the description of the waters of the Rhône at dawn, which appears at the beginning of the tenth canto. The Alpilles and the overlooking heights of the Ventour are mentioned again and again as watchmen over Provence. The hills of Les Baux and the mysterious Cave of the Fairies form the setting of the fascinating sixth canto, in which much of the profane folklore of Provence is related. It was a favorite theory of Mistral that Dante got his idea for his pictures of hell from a visit to the hills of Les Baux. Trees and flowers peculiar to Provence, such as the dwarf-oak, the olive, the fig, the mulberry, the salicorne and the tamarisk, are used in preference to plants found there but also found in other regions of France. The same may be said of the birds and animals made prominent in the poem.

Mistral always succeeded in making his nature-descriptions alive. This is partly due to the mood in which his poetry is written, the mood of simplicity and *naïveté* which I have spoken of as sounded in the very opening lines of *Mirèio.* Nothing but a childish fancy can personify the sun and mountains and rivers and trees and rocks and insects and spray from the sea, and at the same time make such personification convincing. An imaginative folk will do this sincerely and with effect. Mistral, as a true folk-poet, did it with great naturalness. A second reason for his effectiveness in the treatment of nature was his great sensitiveness to objects. He loved his Provence; therefore, he learned it. He knew it thoroughly, and everything of it and concerning it thrilled him. I recall a walk I had with an old inn-keeper at Les Baux. He was greatly interested in the *flora* of Provence, and took much delight in pointing out to me plant after plant, of which he would proudly pronounce the scientific name, the French name, and the Provençal name. I marvelled at his familiarity with such an enormous number of plants. "Ah," he said, "I know plants only. Our Master Mistral knew everything else in Provence just as well,—rocks, birds, beasts, fishes, rivers, hills, the sea!" A reading of *Mirèio* makes one confident that the inn-keeper was right. Mistral knew the nature of his Provence, he found it beautiful and rejoiced in it, and it was easily made alive in his poetry.

The characters in *Mirèio* represent as many Provençal types as the poet could well bring into the plot. In later poems the number is extended until his gallery of portraits becomes immense. It was Mistral's aim that no type found in his beloved Provence should be slighted. The leading characters are so idealized that they lose all illusion of reality. There are many young women in Provence to-day who imagine themselves Mirèios, but they could not exist as such and still be human and natural. In the minor characters, however, Mistral showed himself a master of portraiture. For instance, Mèste Ramoun, the wealthy *mas*-dweller (*mas* is the Provençal name for a farm-house) in *Mirèio* is drawn with such a faithful sense of realism that one who knows Provence immediately recognizes the character as taken from life. As a matter of fact, in Mèste Ramoun Mistral was painting his own father. The three suitors of Mirèio,—the young dreamer-shepherd, the gallant horseman of Camargue, and the brutal cattle-tender, are again types which are true to Provence. Mistral was weak in elaborating character, but where he had to give only a few strokes his pictures are sure and effective.

It is perhaps in the description of the folk customs that Mistral brings the true Provence closest to his readers. The picture of the evening meal before the *mas* of Mèste Ramoun in the first canto of *Mirèio* is unforgettable. We see the stone-hewn table, we see the master and his work-men and his vagabond guests gathered about it in the democratic fashion of Provence. Mirèio herself serves the food, "a salad made of greens of every sort and a large platter filled with beans." Those acquainted with the ways of Provence know that there must be singing before the meal is ended. And, surely enough, the venerable vagabond basket-maker sings in a most stirring manner a ballad of the Admiral Suffren, a popular Provençal hero. *Mirèio* abounds in such pictures. The picking of mulberry leaves for the silkworms, gossiping women assembled to "strip cocoons", shepherds in early spring driving their flocks to the mountains, the burning of the fires of Saint John and the dancing of the farandole on the eve of the harvesting season, gathering snails, threshing wheat on treading-floors,—all such customs are of the very soul of romantic and picturesque Provence.

The folk-poet must show how his people garb themselves. Mistral was much preoccupied with the idea of costume. It was one of his dreams that the traditional costume *du pays* should be made the standard of dress in Provence, especially among the women. On more than one occasion he urged the beauty and artistic grace of the Provençal coiffe and fichu and flowing skirt, and exhorted the women of Provence to cease trying to follow the fashions of Paris. The characters in his poems are usually described as wearing the costume *du pays,* and at times the costume is minutely depicted. When Mirèio gets herself ready for the flight to the shrine of the holy Maries, every detail of the dress (the traditional dress of the region around Saint Remy) which she adopts is set forth. The visitor to Provence to-day is usually impressed by the large number of natives who wear the coiffe and fichu; and, if he is fortunate enough to be present at a *fête* of the *Félibres,* he sees such a glory of costume that he feels Mistral's contentions fully justified. A few days ago I received a programme for what is characterized as the "Grand *Fêtes* of the City of Arles—for the year 1923—under the Patronage of Honor of Madam Marie Frédéric Mistral." Parades and processions, bull-fights and balls, even a performance of *Samson et Dalila,* are listed. But such a series of celebrations in Provence, and under the patronage of the widow of Mistral, could not be complete without a *fête du costume.* And indeed the programme promises such a *fête,* with a "Court of Love" and the "Floral Games", when there will be "songs, poems, tambourines, and farandoles." Provence has not forgotten Mistral's plea.

It has been said that only in Provence could a Mistral have been possible. This statement has been made because of the appeal of Provence to the temperament of a poet,—an appeal growing out of the natural beauty of the land, out of the quaint customs of the folk, and, probably most of all, out of the richness of the legends. The great imagination of the Provençal has been recognized since the times of the Troubadours. Out of such imagination came the stories which make so entrancing the poems of Mistral. Some have considered these stories as invented by the poet himself, but to look at them in this light would be a gross injustice to the faithful recorder of the life of his people which Mistral undoubtedly was.

There are so many legends in *Mirèio* alone that one wonders how more were found for the other poems. Yet, Mistral by no means exhausted his supply. Legends seem to grow up and flower in Provence overnight; and, although their development is quick, they are never forgotten. I happened to be in Arles once when there was being held a 'congress' of stenographers from the south-eastern section of France. One evening of the meeting was devoted to the unveiling of a tablet at the supposed birthplace in Trinquitaille, a suburb just across the Rhône from Arles, of Saint Gênet, a monkish scribe of the early Middle Ages and patron saint of stenographers. What the real story of Saint Gênet is I do not know, but I shall not forget the one which was invented for him on this occasion. It was said that he was very severe to his pupils, so severe that they grew to hate him. Finally, they were unable to endure his remonstrances any longer. They banded themselves together, secured swords, rushed upon their master while he was copying a manuscript, and decapitated him. Headless though the good Saint Gênet was, his skilled hands kept on writing! Many a story regarding Mistral himself has sprung up just as quickly and fixed itself in the minds of the Provençaux, ready to be handed down from generation to generation.

Since *Mirèio* was the first work of Mistral, he was free to bring into it the best legends which imaginative Provence had to offer. Some he told at length; others he summed up in a sentence or two. To one, the story of the holy Maries, one of the most precious of all Christian legends, he devoted two entire cantos. Moreover, he made it essential to the plot of the poem. According to the legend, certain disciples of Jesus, after the crucifixion of their Master, were driven from Palestine by their Jewish persecutors and set afloat on the sea in a worn barque, with neither sail nor oar. Driven by storms and threatened with destruction time after time, they were finally washed ashore on the coast of Provence, where stands to-day the sacred village of Les Saintes Maries. Among this company of disciples were Lazarus; his sisters, Mary and Martha, the latter of whom tamed the celebrated dragon of Tarascon; their servant, Sarah, patron saint of gipsies; Mary Magdalene; Trophime, who converted Arles; and Joseph of Arimethea, who went into England, but not, it is interesting to add, with the Holy Grail. The legend of these saints comes out of the very heart of mystic Provence. In *Mirèio* it becomes what it really is to the Provençaux,—a revelation and not a legend. It is told with an exaltation that carries us back to the religious fervor of the Middle Ages.

All the sacred legends as related by Mistral show this spirit of exaltation, but at the same time they lose none of the simplicity and charm of lifelikeness which make them truly Provençal. Remarkable for its *naïveté* is the story of Saint Trophime. He is represented as the oldest and wisest of the disciples who are stranded on the coast of Provence. In utter ignorance of their whereabouts, the wanderers, with Trophime as their leader, follow a roadway and finally arrive at the walls of Arles. They enter the gates and come upon the theatre, where a pagan festival is being celebrated. Trophime is filled with indignation when he sees a host of young girls, almost nude, dancing around an idol, a statue of Venus. In a loud voice he pronounces the name of Christ. The dancers immediately become still and hang

their heads in shame; the statue topples from its pedestal and falls to the ground. Then Trophime tells the story of the suffering of Jesus, and all the Arlesians repent, believe and are baptized. But the Provençal does not stop the legend at this point. He adds comment on the fallen statue. In spite of the fact that it is anti-Christian and a thing of abomination, Trophime and his fellow saints see that it is beautiful. It is, in fact, the famous Venus of Arles, accepted symbol of the splendor of ancient Provence, and in the eyes of every devoted Provençal a far better work of art than the Venus of Milo!

Some critics have pointed to the sixth canto of *Mirèio* as the most inspired piece of writing which Mistral ever accomplished. He approaches it hesitatingly; he even stops to invoke the aid of his fellow *Félibre* poets. But at length he takes his hero and heroine down into the Cave of the Fairies, and the fairy-lore of Provence is unfolded before them through the powers of the keeper of the Cave, Taven the sorceress. The many legends here introduced are briefly told, but they are probably as complete as they exist in the minds of the folk. Among the great number of goblins and elfs which are made to appear, one naturally meets universal types. There is a Robin Goodfellow, whose pranks are described as follows:—

> In his cheerful moods he will sweep your kitchen, triple the eggs of your hens, add sticks to your fire, and turn your roast. But let caprice possess him, and alas for you! He is a mischief-maker then. Into your porridge he will pour a peck of salt. . . . . If you are going to bed, he will put out your light. If you are going to vespers at Saint Trophime, he will spoil your Sunday dress.

There are Scaramouche and the Black Lamb and the Golden Goat. The two latter, however, are so localized that they seem to belong only to the fairy-lore of Provence. There are other types which are undoubtedly of pure Provençal origin. For instance, Taven points out an "ungainly creature" who is "tossing her head as though she were a poplar." The witch addresses her:—

> Then, you are the Laundress! When you stand on Mount Ventour, you are taken for a cloud. But shepherds know, and quick, quick, they lead their sheep to the fold. You amass the erring clouds around you, and when there are enough for the wash you raise your arms and you beat and beat. When you wring your clothes, water flows by the bucketful. The sea rises and roars, and pale sailors commend their ships to Notre Dame.

The canto ends with a riotous description of the Provençal Witches' Sabbath.

The legends of Provence which deal with the monuments form a class in themselves. There is every reason why the Provençal should be proud of his monuments; they are indeed magnificent. The Pont du Gard, the Maison Carrée and the Baths at Nîmes, the arenas at Nîmes and Arles, the Alyscamps and the Théâtre Antique at Arles, the Palace of the Popes and the supposed chapel of Petrarch's Laura at Avignon, the Mausoleum and Arch at Saint Remy, the church at Saint Gilles, the ramparts at Les

Baux,—the mention of the names of these monuments augurs romance. And to the Provençal they are romantic as his land itself is romantic. They are a part of it just as the hills and the plains and the rivers are a part of it. They have impressed him for centuries, and naturally legends and proverbs have grown up around them. I have already pointed out how the Théâtre Antique at Arles is made prominent in the legend of Saint Trophime. Much of *Nerto* is made up of stories concerning the Palace of the Popes. When a Provençal wants to show that something has great strength, he compares it with the pillars which support the Pont du Gard, to him giants always locked in a wrestle. Mistral made the most of this peculiar conception of monuments. As he tried to bring into his poems all types of persons found in Provence, in like manner his aim was to omit no monument. He presents each one to us with its age and its mystery and its legends, just as it appears to the Provençal who has always dwelt in its shadow.

Mistral called the Provençal Museum at Arles, known as the Museon Arleten, his last poem. It was inaugurated in 1899, mainly through the efforts of Mistral himself. Largely with the money received with the Nobel Prize in Literature, awarded to him in 1906, the poet secured for the museum the splendid seventeenth-century hôtel in which it is now housed. The collection is likely to strike the visitor as bizarre, but after it is studied it is recognized as perfectly characteristic of Provence and of Mistral himself. It is only another evidence of his determination to glorify his *patrie.* It is Provençal and at the same time it is French. And above all, it possesses that simple naturalness and charm so pronounced in the life of Provence and in the poems of Mistral. One finds as complete a representation of the nature of Provence as a museum could show. There are geological and botanical specimens. There are stuffed animals and birds and fishes. Some of the lifeless horses, fully caparisoned, do not exemplify the art of the taxidermist at its highest, but we smile at them as we do at the imperfections in Mistral's poems. One finds depicted the customs of the folk. There is a model of a typical *mas,* almost of natural size. There are implements used on the farms, vehicles of all sorts, and furniture. Costumes of different periods and of different sections of Provence are displayed. One of the traditional customs dearest to the heart of the Provençal, the feast of Noël, is shown in wax figures. Legends are told in paintings and by statues. One wax group shows the old Arlesian custom of the visit of the three women to the new mother and her first-born. The three are attired in the rich holiday costume of Arles, remarkable for the coiffe, the fichu, and the flowing skirt. One brings a match, symbolizing the desire that the child's body may be straight; another an egg, symbolical of fullness; and the third a lump of salt, symbolical of wisdom. The museum as a whole expresses in objects what the poems of Mistral express in verse. It is a summary of his life-work. As a museum it is unique, just as *Mirèio* as a poem is unique. But after all it is a beautiful and sincere expression of the life and spirit of a people, and its creator was justified in calling it a poem.

The best evidence that Mistral is a true poet of the soil is the fact that his poems are known and loved by thousands who cannot read them in the language in which they were written. The poet of the soil does best when he writes in the idiom of his people. Burns recognized this truth, and so did Synge. Mistral, too, recognized it, but he met a problem much greater than that of Burns or Synge. Their people used a dialect; his spoke a distinct language, once a language of highest repute but dropped, at the time of Mistral's boyhood, to the level of a vulgar *patois.* The young poet did not hesitate in making up his mind. He determined to make it a part of his work of patriotism to restore to the native language of Provence its former dignity. This determination met the strong encouragement of Joseph Roumanille, the oldest of the *Félibre* poets and Mistral's teacher and lifelong friend. The success which the *Félibres* met in carrying out this Dante-like scheme does not concern us in estimating Mistral as a universal poet of the soil. What does concern us is that his work soon attracted attention outside of Provence and that translations had to be provided. It is through these translations that Mistral is broadly known. One of the best tests of a work of literature is how well it will stand in translation. We undoubtedly miss much of Mistral when we read him in French or in any other language than Provençal; at the same time we know that we are getting much.

The best evidence, again, of the sincerity of Mistral as a patriot is the reverence, hardly short of worship, with which he is remembered in Provence. If he had not shown such an abundant love for his people, they in turn would not have honored him so highly. That a prophet is without honor in his own country is indeed not true in the case of Mistral. In the year 1909 a grand *fête* was held in Arles in celebration of the fiftieth anniversary of the publication of *Mirèio.* All Provence, from aristocrat to peasant, entered with zest into the celebration, and the memory of it will be treasured for long. A statue of the poet was unveiled. Calvé was there to sing his *Magali.* Mounet-Sully was brought down from the *Comédie Française* to recite favorite passage from his poems. A gala performance of Gounod's opera of *Mireille* was given in the old Roman arena, with a cast of the most prominent singers in France. It was a tribute of Provence to her aged poet while he was still alive. Now, nine years after his death, there are tributes to his memory. They are simpler, perhaps, than the *fête* of 1909; but they are more sincere, because they are as likely as not to be initiated by a group of peasants. Actual pilgrimages are made to his home and grave in Maillane, and to places mentioned in his poems. By far the most honored person in Provence to-day is Madame Mistral, the widow of the poet. The Courts of Love and the Floral Games, which the *Félibres* hold from time to time, are now devoted mainly to recitations from the works of Mistral; and there seems to be no marked regret that there is no poet in Provence to-day upon whose shoulders his mantle could fall. So much could not be expected of the gods. Charles Rieu, a peasant, is considered the most significant poet now writing in Provençal, and he is always thought of as a lesser member of Mistral's group. Instead of fostering new production, the Provençaux prefer to remain under the influence of the magnetic personality of Mistral and to revel in the idea that he was truly one of them. They follow with renewed devotion all the old customs which he loved and praised. The patriotism which was so deeply a part of his being has been translated into them. He revealed Provence in a new light, and now they love it in the same mystic way in which he loved it. But they do not forget to whom belongs the reward for the revelation.

When I was at Avignon, I had a talk with an antiquarian, an intelligent old woman, who had known Mistral very well. "Provence", she said,

> has given three great names to modern art,— Alphonse Daudet, Paul Cézanne, and Frédéric Mistral. Daudet went away to Paris and made fun of us. But we love him because he was so clever and witty and genial, and he really never forgot that he was a Nîmois. Besides, he wrote the most exquisite Provençal prose. Cézanne! Well, we don't understand his paintings. What he accomplished by his sojourns at Les Baux we don't know. His sunshine is just as much that of Brittany as of Provence. But Mistral! He was different. He was a Provençal in every way. He put our real spirit into his poetry. If you want to know Provence, learn Mistral. You will not only be studying Provence, but the one modern poet who is worthy of a place with Homer and Vergil and Dante.

Such an opinion is that of Provence as a whole to-day. If it shows more enthusiasm than critical judgment, it nevertheless expresses the truth of devotion. The patriot and the poet of the soil could not have a more worthy monument. (pp. 54-68)

Tudor Edwards on Mistral's regionalism and patriotism:

Mirèio (*Mireille*), published early in 1859, was Mistral's first and most celebrated epic poem. Mistral made it clear that in this he was attempting to do for Provence what Homer had done for Greece, and indeed Lamartine on reading the poem exclaimed *"C'est Homère!"* Yet the entire revival of Provençal art and letters was essentially Romantic in spirit, and affinities have been found between Mistral and both Burns and Scott. While the Scott findings are convincing enough if based purely on qualities of regional patriotism, the parallel with Burns is quite striking—both were sons of humble farmers, both recreated their native tongue and the local ballads, both inspired a rare and lasting *mystique.* Mistral, however, in writing his rustic epic illustrating the rhythm of life and work and passion in a rural community, dealing with the ill-starred love of Mireille and Vincent the basket-maker, with patriarchal shepherds, fishermen and *gardians,* against the background of the Rhone valley, the Alpilles and the salty wastes of the Camargue, achieved a unity and coherence such as produce a living traditional epic like *Pan Tadeusz,* and indeed Mickiewicz comes to mind when reading *Mirèio.* Mistral was a regionalist in the best sense. The true regional writer is a local dedicated patriot, writing to preserve a still existing if declining traditional way of life—Hardy in Dorset, Gabriel Miró in Spanish Murcia, C. F. Ramuz in the Swiss Valais.

Tudor Edwards, "Mistral's Centenary," in The Contemporary Review, *June, 1959.*

Vernon Loggins, "Frédéric Mistral: Poet of the Soil," in The Sewanee Review, *Vol. XXXII, No. 1, January, 1924, pp. 54-68.*

Rob Lyle   (essay date 1953)

[*In the following excerpt, Lyle offers a comparative discussion of* Mirèio, Calendau, Lou pouèmo dóu Rose, *and* Lis Oulivado *in which he evaluates the merits of each work.*]

In 1851, Mistral started to write *Mirèio.* This poem was not completed until 1858, when he gave the first reading of it to a group of friends, including the poet Aubanel who, as a critic has said, is to Mistral what Catullus was to Virgil. It is the first, and perhaps the finest flower of that civilization into which he was born and in which he grew up.

Mirèio is an epic, the poem of a country and a people, but it is a rustic epic: its Achilles is a poor and humble young man, the son of a wandering basket-maker, and its Helen a simple country girl, the daughter of a farmer. It is written in twelve books, and composed in an original seven-line stanza, in the first of which the poet is at pains to explain that he is attempting to do for Provence what Homer did for Greece, and at the same time to make clear that he is to do this, not through some exalted character, 'with golden diadem and damask mantle', but, as befits one who 'sings only for you, shepherds and people of the farms', through the person of a typical maiden of his beloved countryside, in whom it is not difficult to see a recollection of that young girl whom his father wooed, the mayor's daughter, standing alone amid the alien corn:

> A maiden of Provence I sing.
> In the love of her youth's spring,
> A simple, country girl whom now,
> Though to the outside world unknown,
> By Homer's great example borne
> I wish to trace, amid the corn,
> Towards the sea, across the Crau.

This introduction is followed by an invocation to Christ, 'born among shepherds', from whom is all inspiration, and to whom the poet's prayer rises, that, like the birds, on the wings 'of our Provençal tongue', he may attain to that branch whose fruits lie beyond the reach of the pickers. Then the tale begins.

Mèste Ambròsi, the basket-maker, and his son, Vincèn, ask hospitality at the *Mas di Falabrego,* the Farm of the Mulberries, where Mirèio, daughter of Mèste Ramoun, makes them welcome. Mèste Ambròsi is prevailed upon by the farm-labourers to sing an old ballad, and Vincèn, questioned by Mirèio, tells of youthful sports and contests. As a result, love opens in her heart, as sweetly and naturally as a flower in spring.

Between our world and Mirèio's, Freud has let fall the cold fog of his puritanical analysis, and has reduced to the dead level of sexual appetite the sharp peaks of youthful passion, with their snow-caps of sunlit joys and their *alpenrot* of transitory despairs. For, in Mirèio's world, though they be touched with the shadow of Original Sin, its characters are not yet warped by the revolt of a much greater presumption; theirs is a world wherein it is permitted to children to be young, and to old men to be wise.

And what delightful children they are; this Mirèio:

> Fifteen summers had Mirèio—
>   And the blue coast of Font-Vieio,
> You hills of Baux, you plains of Crau,
>   You've never seen such loveliness!
>   The sun had granted it such grace,
>   And, fresh and innocent, her face
> With dimpled cheeks like flowers did blow.
>
>   Her look was dew upon the leaf
>   That dissipates all sign of grief—
> Starlight is less sweet and pure:
>   It shone in those black locks whose flow
>   Fashioned its ringlets on her brow
>   And her rounded breast was now
> A double peach, still immature.

and this Vincèn:

> Vincèn was not as yet sixteen
> But in his form and face was seen
> Fine youth, and promise in his glance—
>   Burned brown, it's true . . . but the black earth
> To the best vintage will give birth
> And from the raisin dark as dearth
> There comes the wine to make you dance.

These children are real beings: persons. We have met them, however briefly, in the surroundings of Mistral's own upbringing. They are not the ideals of a romantic imagination, or the compensating symbols of a 'reactionary' dreamer. When, in the second canto, Mirèio and Vincèn declare their love for each other, in one of the most delicately sweet love-scenes in all literature, they do so with all the reverent eagerness of people imbued with the idea that one's neighbour is uniquely and irreplaceably valuable; they do so with a kind of awe at this perennial but ever fresh exposure of divinity—the eternal love and grace—somehow manifesting itself under the symbols of dark eyes, and red lips, and the inexplicable tenderness of line which defines the onset of human passion, that sweet cry in the ominous hush of our existence whose echoes sound through the eternal silences, for ever and ever.

This scene, of pure enchantment, is introduced, and interrupted, by a refrain which delicately paints in the background to the human drama; for it is the time of the mulberry-picking:

> Sing, *magnanarello,* sing!
>   For to harvest is to sing!
> The silkworm its third crop secretes;
>   The mulberry trees are full of girls,
>   Round whom the sunny weather swirls—
>   A flight of golden bees that whirls
> To rob the rosemary of its sweets!

Mistral is particularly happy in his landscapes and scene-painting, and he is sensitive to every mood and variation of nature, but, unlike many northern poets, he does not exalt nature at the expense of man; for him the human being is the centre of creation, and his nature-poetry nearly always exists only to enhance a human situation, or provide a setting appropriate to some play of character which occupies the foreground.

In the next canto, devoted to the talk of the women, the background is the gathering of the cocoons which the silkworms have spun. The range of reference is wide, and touches many aspects of Provençal history and geography: it ends with the singing of the ballad of *Magali,* which has all the quality of an original folk-song.

In the third canto, the time was spring: in the fourth it is summer, and, as if with the growing heat, the drama intensifies. Three suitors appear, to beg Mirèio's hand; and the first is a shepherd, Alàri.

Mistral exploits the introduction of Alàri to describe him, as he leads his huge herd of sheep up to the hill-pastures, crook in hand and with his white sheep-dogs, a dignified figure from the pastoral age, biblical and timeless, in one of those superb pictures which remind one of Rubens.

The second suitor is Véran, the *gardian,* or herdsman, of the Camargue, and through him we are given a vision of the wild horses of the plain, which roam there to this day, watched over by the cowboys with their tridents, or triple-pronged lances.

Finally, there comes the *toucadou,* Ourrias, the breeder of fighting bulls. In stanzas of great vigour, Mistral describes the rounding up of the herd for branding; the epic contest between Ourrias and one of the bulls, which he eventually overturns by the horns; and his final goring, by another bull, which leaves him with a long and sinister scar.

While each suitor has been used to elaborate on an aspect of Provençal life, the story has been suspended: but each suitor is rejected, and with the refusal of Ourrias, it begins to move forward quickly again. For, unlike the others, Ourrias cannot reconcile himself to the blow.

Angry and sullen, he turns homeward over the desolate Crau. There he meets Vincèn, coming towards him: Ourrias insults him, and they fight. Ourrias is beaten, but when Vincèn spares him Ourrias treacherously strikes him with his trident and leaves him for dead. He hurries on his way which leads him to the banks of the Rhône. Crossing in the ferry, he sees, upon the further bank, the St Medard's night procession, composed of the souls of those who have been drowned in the river: and he too must drown, for it is a phantom boat in which he is crossing and it slowly sinks beneath him.

The fight between Vincèn and Ourrias is characteristic of Mistral's reading of life. His hero must be a man and prove worthy of his beloved; for, in that world, lovely girls desire marriage, and a large family, and fine sons. The epic hero is usually, of necessity, almost super-human, a man of destiny, for he must be a symbol as well as a leader of men. In *Mirèio,* Mistral combines, in Vincèn, the qualities required of an epic hero with those common to any spirited young man of his country. In that vision of the world which the Mediterranean seems to impose on its sons, the keynote is clarity. Line and colour combine to limit, to order, to define. The individual takes on a special significance, and his functions are more precisely ordered than elsewhere. It is the same with the person's relations with his neighbour: these too must be clarified; each must have his place and his function, for the ultimate aim is harmony, between men and men, between men and women, between man and nature, between man and God. Hence Vincèn, who defeats evil in the form of Ourrias, is not acting in an exceptional way, for the sake of a literary tradition: he is reflecting, idealistically if you will, a code of action, a code of honour, characteristic of his race and of the Catholic culture of which he is the product. Mistral on to the old epic tradition of the Aegean has grafted the shoot of a living religious ethos, filling out the form of the classical hero with the richer content of the Christian interpretation of man; with the Roman reading of life.

In the same way, he follows the usual device of introducing the supernatural into his narrative, but, in place of the ancient Gods—to which even as late as Camoëns the epic poet had recourse—he introduces Christian mysticism, in this episode of the crossing of the Rhône, combined with a local religious tradition, so that, while attaching himself to an ancient literary precedent, he contrives to give it a Christian form, at the same time localising it by reference to a folk-belief characteristic of his own country.

Vincèn is found by swineherds and carried back to the farm. The sixth canto tells how he is restored to health by the witch, Taven, who lives in a cave in the Alpilles. It is a characteristic record of local legend and folk-lore, which, however, somewhat holds up the action.

This is resumed in the next canto, wherein Vincèn prevails upon his father to visit Mèste Ramoun and ask, on his son's behalf, for Mirèio's hand. He arrives at the farm with a group of harvesters, and all are royally entertained by the master. When these two old men, so like each other in many ways, and both of them made in the image of the poet's remarkable father, François, are finally alone, Ambròsi has his say; the suit is rejected.

This set-back, so necessary to the whole story, is the one romantic element in the poem, and is reminiscent of that Troubadour tradition which insisted that the highest love is unsatisfied and frustrated by circumstance, if not by the will of its protagonists, as is the case in the legend of Tristram and Iseult.

Ambròsi departs: night falls: and the canto closes with another scene worthy of Rubens. It is Midsummer night, the night of St John, patron of harvest; and round the blazing log fire the harvesters dance the farandole in honour of their patron saint:

> With proud heads high and free of care,
> Tumbling in the vibrant air,
> As one, they jumped and struck the ground
> As into the farandole they sped.
> The great flame crackled and was spread
> To strike reflections from each head
> By the great wind that whirled around.
>
> A swirl of sparks soars furiously
> Like unleashed stars, into the sky,
> As in the flame the fire-wood tumbles,
> While mingling with the tumult goes
> The gay and playful flute that blows
> Like a tree-sparrow in the boughs—
> St John, for you the pregnant country trembles!

> The furnace sparked and danced with joy,
> The tambourine monotonously
> Droned, buzzed and muttered like the sea
> When in the deep with peaceful beat
> It murmurs round earth's rocky feet,
> While the burned dancers, dark with heat,
> Brandished their shining blades on high.
>
> Then, with enormous jumps, three times
> They fire off muskets through the flames
> And over the red blaze they gyre,
> While from one tress of corn they glean the
> Husks into the dying ember
> Clasping St John's Wort and verbena,
> Blessed in the purifying fire:
>
> 'St John! St John! St John!' they cried.
> And then it seemed the hills had died
> And stars through all the shades were pouring,
> The while a wilful gust had brought
> Air from the hills with incense fraught
> Which, with the glow the fire had wrought,
> Through the blue dusk towards the Saint went
>   soaring.

These descriptive frescoes are common in Mistral, especially in his early work. The poet has constructive power of an unusual order for, while he builds up his scenes with many realistic details, these are successfully subordinated to the whole, which, at the end, emerges vivid and complete, standing out in the mind's eye like a piece of sculpture. Mistral has applied the plastic genius of the south, its visual sense and its sense of form, which is almost tactile, to poetry, the art of time, with marvellous results. Only Dante, among poets, excels him in this quality; but Dante's method, and his purpose, are quite different.

Meanwhile, Mirèio remembers Vincèn's advice, to call on the aid of *Li Santo,* the Holy Marys, if ever she be in trouble. She decides to set out, and leaves the house secretly. The eighth canto describes the first part of her journey across the barren Crau, a place of pitiless heat and waterless wastes. Eventually she comes across some Rhône fishermen who shelter her for the night.

Back at the farm, Mèsté Ramoun has discovered her absence. He organises a search, sending a runner to ask news of all the labourers. By this perfectly logical device, we are given a picture of the whole farm and all who work on it, for the runner passes from the mowers to the ploughmen, from the ploughmen to the harvesters, and ends up, on the boundaries of the farm, with the solitary shepherds, keeping watch over their flocks. One old shepherd saw Mirèio pass by before dawn, and heard the name of *Li Santo* on her lips. Her parents, hearing this, set off in pursuit.

This ninth canto is a marvel of observation, organisation, and description, a feast of colour and energy. At the same time it is formally perfect: nothing is introduced which is not appropriate to the theme and to the development of the central drama. Each scene, each episode, is even linked, as in a piece of music, by the recurring refrain of the runner's anxious question.

But Mirèio has crossed the Rhône, to continue her terrible journey. She sets out again in the early morning, sped on her way by the fisherman, and surrounded by the sweetness of the dawn upon the great river, which forms a poetic, and pitiless, contrast to the horror of heat which is to follow:

> As he was speaking, on the Rhône,
> Resplendent with the rosy tone
> Shed by the morning light, the barges
> Sailed slowly up, and from the sea
> The wind with their white sails grew free
> And pressed them on, as easily
> As shepherdess her snowy charges.

She passes on into the flat waste, among the tamarisks, and the cruel mirage. She has sunstroke, but fortified by the sight of the distant sea, at last she reaches the church, Les Saintes Maries de la Mer, and flinging herself down and summoning her last reserves of strength, calls upon the Saints:

> O Holy Marys dear,
> Who can change the tear
> Into the flower,
> Hear my prayer
> In this dark hour!
>
> Alas! when you will see
> My great agony
> And all my care,
> You will comfort me
> With piteous air.
>
> I am a young girl
> Who loves a boy,
> Vincèn the beautiful!
> Dear Saints I love him, he
> Is all my joy.
>
> I love him! I love him
> Even as the rill
> Delights to run,
> Or the strong bird will
> Soar in the sun. . . .
>
> But, have faith in what I say!
> Give me my Vincèn;
> When, full of joy and gay
> We will both come back then,
> To see you once again.

(pp. 11-18)

Mirèio's prayer is answered by the appearance of the Marys who come to bring her comfort and strength and, to this end, tell her, in the eleventh canto, the story of their own troubles, of their persecution in the Holy Land, their long journey to Provence, and their conversion of her country.

Once again, Mistral is able to use the passionate and uncomplicated faith of his countrymen and women to raise his narrative to another level of experience, illuminating the old and worn-out mechanism of epic powers with a delicate Christian mysticism.

Meanwhile, Mirèio's parents have arrived and found her in a state of collapse. She is carried up to the roof, where are the relics of the Saints. At last Vincèn too arrives from over the Crau. Torn with grief he kneels at her side and she welcomes him, trying, because she is herself consoled by her vision, to comfort him. The chant of the attendants rises, and Mirèio has her last vision: the Marys appear, borne over the blue waves of the Mediterranean in their boat that carries no sail, to fetch her away to eternal blessedness and the joyous contemplation of the beatific vision. 'What is this death that daunts you, but a mist that dissolves?'

She leaves a scene of weeping and lamentation which is finally overwhelmed by the rising chant from the church below: 'If it be peace that they need, the poor sinners who lament at your door, O white flowers of our salted plains, give them peace in abundance!'

From its first appearance this poem had an astonishing success; for it made no concessions to the spirit of the times. Its triumph in Provence was to be expected, but in Paris it was acclaimed by Adolphe Dumas, who likened its author to Virgil, and by Lamartine, who compared him with Homer. Its beauty and freshness have never faded: on the contrary, its popularity has constantly grown. Since its first triumph it has been translated into more than a dozen languages. And Mirèio herself has become a part of our civilized consciousness; another Antigone, another Beatrice, another Juliet; only 'un chato de Prouvenço', but a country maiden, for all that, of an unsurpassed purity, beauty, and heroism, who is, and must forever be, the shining symbol of the country in which she was conceived. The desert Crau had miraculously flowered again, and with the fairest flower of all.

Mistral's first epic was published at Avignon in 1859; but he had been active in other ways during the period of its composition.

In 1852, a group of Provençal poets had met together at Arles, at the instigation of Mistral, Roumanille and Gaut. A similar meeting took place at Aix in the following year, and in 1854, at Font-ségugne, this association of poet-patriots was officially born, and baptised the Felibrige.

The foundation of the Felibrige marks the beginning of Mistral's political life, for this association carried with it patriotic as well as poetic implications. These were to emerge more clearly after the success of *Mirèio,* which conferred a sudden lustre and authority upon the group.

It was certainly required, for, with minor exceptions, the Provençal poets of the time were undistinguished: they needed, above all things, the leadership and example of genius. There was, too, some confusion in the growth of the movement. The great Romantics embraced the cause of regionalism principally for political reasons—the tendency dates from 1848—and, with characteristic inconsistency, sentimentalised over 'worker-poets'; although their leader, Reboul, while not much of a poet, was a passionate adherent of the cause of Henri V.

Mistral's attitude, by contrast, is from the start entirely consistent, and he moves step by step in the formulation of his *politik.* From the beginning he is, then, a regionalist, desiring to see put into effect that degree of decentralization which will preserve local language, custom, and tradition. He is therefore in opposition to the Empire. At the same time he has vision: he is not a separatist. He understands very well that a chain is as strong as its weakest link; that the distinct provinces of a great country will be all the stronger, and more loyal, by virtue of their independence. The wise ruler, sure of his authority and position, can afford to allow his subjects a large measure of freedom, his peoples a large measure of autonomy; they will be all the healthier, all the more united, for these concessions. But the weak ruler, or the tyrant, must draw the reins of government (and he must work through a centralised bureaucracy) ever more tightly into his hands. Mistral, always balanced, clear, and serene, desired above all harmony, the equilibrium of conflicting forces for their individual and mutual benefit. Thus he was, to all intents and purposes, a federalist.

The liberal opposition, to which Mistral was at that time attached, was overwhelmed in 1851, and only gradually recovered its force during the next fifteen years. In the meantime, he had written his second epic, *Calendau,* which was completed in 1866.

This poem is very different from *Mirèio,* and reflects Mistral's current preoccupation with political problems. It is much more a regional, even a nationalist, poem that *Mirèio,* and for that reason alone has never enjoyed the success of its predecessor: the action is continually suspended by historical and topographical digressions, delightful in themselves but injurious to the shape of the whole: no character with the actuality of Mirèio emerges, the persons are symbols rather than portraits, mouthpieces for a dissertation on the wines of the country, or the fish which can be caught round its coasts. At the same time it contains passages of superb poetry; stanzas of a fervour and sublimity unsurpassed in all the poet's work. We are plunged into one as we begin to read.

This time, it is a simple fisherman to whom we are introduced in the first stanza. The scene has moved from the farms and the pastures to the coast. Then, without pause, follows the great invocation to the soul of Provence:

> *. . . soul of my native land*
>
> You that flamed forth and came to be
> Both in her speech and history
> When German, Picard and Burgundian,
> Besieged Toulouse, and then Beaucaire,
> You who did kindle everywhere
> Against the dark invaders there
> Men of Marseilles and Avignon;
>
> You who by force of memory
> Preserved our hope in days to be,
> You who, despite the grave and death,
> Fairer, more fruitful, more on fire,
> Did still the Troubadours inspire,
> Rejuvenating sage and sire
> Till Mirabeau spoke with the Mistral's breath;
>
> . . . The inundations of the years
> And all their tempests and their fears
> In vain mix race and boundary;
> For nature and the earth, our mother,
> Will feed us, sister, son and brother,
> With the same milk; their breasts discover
> The good oil to the olive tree.
>
> Soul eternally reborn,
> Noble, joyful, full of scorn,

> That in the Rhône and Rhône-wind neighs!
> Great soul of the harmonious wood,
> Of inlets where the sun's rays brood,
> Dear soul of our Provençal blood,
> I call thee! Live within my lays!

This passage is accompanied by a long and important note, which throws much light on the poet's outlook at the time, and reveals an interesting historical preoccupation which in all probability Mistral never abandoned, but which in any case is especially relevant to the composition of *Calendau.*

The line 'Quand li baroun picard, aleman, bourguignoun' is, as the note explains, a reference to the Albigensian crusade, which Mistral saw as an aggressive movement spurred on by racial rather than by religious feeling. He refers to the Crusaders as 'the invaders from the north'. The peoples of Languedoc, from the Alps to the Gulf of Gascony, from the Loire to the Ebro, have always been, the poet asserts, drawn together by a similarity of climate, instincts, customs, beliefs, law and language, with their nationality revealed and propagated by the Troubadours. One thing only was needed to effect a unity: a common enemy; but when, in crusader's dress, he appeared, he did so armed by the Church and in overwhelming force. The defeat of the peoples of Languedoc, as Mistral rightly notes, marked the beginning of the development of modern France; but he is insistent that these peoples desired rather a 'federal state', which is, to put it mildly, doubtful. Mistral is attributing to his ancestors national sentiments which were only born into consciousness in his own epoch. It is certain, however, that these peoples had a distinct existence, and, once this is granted, it is difficult not to agree with the poet's solution: but the federal idea, for which Mistral doubtless drew sustenance from the example of Alexander Hamilton, in America, and from the Swiss Republic, is a comparatively modern one, even today by no means accepted.

While, therefore, we may take exception to aspects of Mistral's historical interpretation, the principle upon which he has seized, and to which he adheres, is one which reveals him a practical visionary, and places him, politically, well in advance of his time. In the light of which, and before following him further along this road, we may return to the consideration of *Calendau.*

Calendau, the fisherman of Cassis, a little fishing-village near Toulon, loves Esterello, a girl of noble blood, a descendant of that race of eagles, *Les Baux,* who once lived in the eyrie of that name, now ruined, and, swooping from time to time from their heights like birds of prey, terrorised the surrounding countryside. A proud and daring race, not unlike a typical family of the Italian Renaissance—Gonzaga, or Este—they are described by Esterello in the first canto of the poem, together with other aspects of her history which, overflowing into the next canto, include her meeting and marriage with Lou Comte Severan, who turns out to be a bandit and a monster. From him, in horror, Esterello flees, by night, to take refuge in a cave in the mountains, and to be identified by local superstition with the fairy 'Esterello' (we are never told her real name) and, subsequently, to meet with Calendau, who, having heard all, sets out in search of the Count.

He crosses Provence, and his journey is used as a pretext to enlarge on the beauties of the country; its vistas; its hills, valleys and rivers; its trees and fruits. At last he meets with Severan, to whom he recounts the story of his life and exploits, with the object of provoking him.

'I am from Cassis, by the sea', he begins, and proceeds to describe it, not forgetting to mention its wine:

> Oh! could you taste it, you would see
> It's sweeter than the honey-bee,
> Scented with rosemary, diamond clear,
> The heather and myrtle that do grow
> Over our hills, enrich it so,
> It dances in the glass—I know
> I'd drain a flagon, were one here.

and to enumerate the fish which may be caught in its waters and the nets which are used to catch them. Every detail of the fishing is described, against the perfect backcloth of a summer night:

> It is a clear, a summer night:
> A whirl of stars falls from the height
> Into the deep; a lovelier arises.
> Soft to the oar the ocean grows
> And shimmering and sprawling flows
> And to the far horizon glows . . .
> It is a magic scene, that e'er surprises.

Calendau then speaks, in the fourth canto, of his father, and of Provence, home of his Ligurian ancestors: he tells of the Phoceans who brought to Provence the arts of civilization; of the Roman colonies at Agatha (Agde), Antipolis (Antibes), and Nicoa (Nice), and of Marseilles, whose inhabitants embraced the cause of Pompey against Caesar; of the coming of Christianity; of his country's independence and *effloraison* under the rival dynasties of the Raimonds de Toulouse and the Raimonds-Bérengers, when Province, as Mistral tells us in a note, from the Midi to Catalonia, 'attained a degree of political independence, of literary culture, of religious tolerance, of elegant custom and of material prosperity, superior to the general condition of the rest of Europe'. This is Provence's Medicean or Periclean age. Then comes the Albigensian crusade, the invasion from the north, and the Inquisition. Provence—and the Provençal tongue—sustain a mortal blow.

Calendau then tells of his meeting with Esterello, of his declaration, and its rejection, and of his departure, determined to perform such deeds as will conquer this disdain.

His first labour (Calendau is the Hercules of Provence) is the acquisition of riches, by means of a fabulous fishing expedition, a descriptive opportunity which the poet exploits to the full. But Esterello is not satisfied: her suitor must learn the vanity of mere gold, and she draws his attention to the example of the Troubadours, of Rudel, Foulquet, Vidal, Guillaume de la Tour, whose prowess was of a purer and altogether more exalted nature.

The sixth canto, something of an intermezzo, shows us Cassis *en fête*. There follows a description of certain Provençal dances, *Li Courdello, Li Pastourello, Li Mouresco,*

Li Triho, Lis Ouliveto, and, of course, *La Farandoulo.* In a note on these dances and their like, Mistral has this to say: '. . . our fathers excelled in clothing life with poetry. This idealisation of daily labour . . . contributed not a little to making each one love the condition and the country into which God had caused him to be born.'

This is a concrete and obvious example of an attitude to life typical of Mistral, which continually bears poetic fruit in the harmony and universality of so many of the episodes, descriptions and scenes in his epics. He is giving stylised expression to a world of experience, of thought, and of imagination, which itself is composed of countless stylised gestures. The poet himself, as we have seen, grew up against a background of such almost ritualistic gestures, of unconscious expressions of love, reverence, comradeship, compassion, interdependence, and hospitality, refined and hallowed by custom; no mere empty forms, but living conventions because illuminated by mutual trust and understanding, and by a common faith.

Nothing happens in isolation. The disintegration of the atom is paralleled by the disintegration of society and even of the human personality itself. Our society is collapsing for want of a common purpose and a common belief. Men can no longer speak to each other, for want of common premises. They talk different languages and inhabit a Babel of the spirit; while our men of genius no longer speak for, or to, the people. Our society has become inarticulate because it has ceased to be a community.

A healthy communal life expresses itself, externalises its beliefs, feelings, hopes, fears, ambitions and sorrows, through the mediums of folk-song and folk-lore; communal dances; customs, especially those surrounding the great events of childbirth, marriage and death; the shared ritual of religion; and the folk-arts, such as embroidery, which may, as in the Balkans, express the whole soul of a people in terms of highly abstract and elaborate design.

But a community which presumes to abandon its beliefs, and, in defiance of religious restraint, sets no bounds to the acquisition of material prosperity, substituting a gullible and superstitious reverence for science for the belief of an immortal soul in a personal God, destroys itself. Our mechanical society, having thus made a God of Humanity, has forgotten how to sing, to dance, to worship, to love, to tell stories, to think—in short, to live—and, for self-expression, is reduced to the bald raising of a clenched fist, and the raucous reiteration of stereotyped slogans. Even at its most intelligent, it can only express itself, and then esoterically, in terms of a *Waste Land* or—climax of inverted buffoonery—a *Ulysses.*

Mistral, by contrast, has something different to offer: the sublimation, in terms of great and idealistic art, of a community as it should be, whole, healthy, and harmonious; giving permanent shape to its lineaments, concrete form to its ideals, and ardent expression to its latent aspirations. He was, of course, fortunate in his material; it lay ready to his hand; but the transmutation of base, if fine, metal into gold was his achievement; and when he spoke, he spoke for a people, a race, a way of life, and, ultimately, for Western civilization—born, like himself, of the Mediterranean—with as natural an expression as the dances which he describes through the mouth of his national hero Calendau.

Calendau, meanwhile, has gone on to describe the joust without which no such fête would be complete. This exciting sport, the descendant of the old Roman water-games, the *Naumachia,* is practised enthusiastically to this day. The protagonists face each other on floating platforms, raised high over the water and drawn by multi-oared barges: they are armed with long lances and, as they collide, attempt to 'unseat' each other. Team competes against team, each drawn from a port or fishing village.

Calendau emerges victorious and relates the story of his exploit to Esterello who, though this time visibly moved, exhorts him with a greater example—*Lis Aliscamp,* the battle fought by Guillaume au Court Nez against the Saracens, and named after the famous cemetery at Arles, said (probably by *un vrai Marseillais*) to have been blessed by Christ himself; it was celebrated in a thirteenth-century French poem.

In the seventh canto, the hero sets out once more, this time to cut down the larches on Mont Ventoux, and, not content with that, to travel on to the Nesque valley, rob the hives of the Rocher du Cire of their honey and return with a portion of it to Esterello. She is not impressed and, quite rightly, rates him for undertaking tasks so destructive, even in the pursuit of glory.

Repentant, Calendau goes on a pilgrimage to the Sainte-Baume where he meets with two parties of the Compagnons du Tour de France, about to engage in a fight. He reconciles these representatives of ancient trades and at last succeeds in pleasing Esterello, who declares her love for him but, fearing that his may decline from a surfeit of happiness, sets before his eyes a still higher ideal: to rid the country of a monstrous bandit, Marco-mau, which exploit occupies the ninth canto.

He leads Marco-mau to Aix, in chains, and is received *coume un prince,* and fêted by the whole city, whose characteristically elaborate and symbolic pageant is minutely described. He ends his recitation with a peroration on pure love which enrages Severan, who takes him to his castle, the *Castelet d'Eiglun;* and, in the eleventh canto, called *The Orgy,* entices him with *un festin sardanapalen.* At last, outraged, Calendau overturns the table and challenges Severan to mortal combat, but one of the bandits fells him with a blow on the head and he is flung into a dungeon. He is helped to escape by a woman from Severan's band, and as the twelfth and last canto opens, hastens back to Esterello to defend her against Severan who has in the meantime set out to capture her. He returns by sea and passes by the islands of the coast, Les Iles de Lerius, and Les Iles d'Or, near Hyères with its oranges and pomegranates, *Coume un Jardin dis Esperido;* isles as remotely beautiful as a scene from Homer, heavy with legend, lying in the brilliant blue sea, hazy and nostalgic, with the pines leaning down over the waters of their gentle bays; isles heady with the scent of herbs, and loud with the sawing of the cicadas. Passing Toulon, he at last sights Lou Gibau and that coast of olives and oaks and terebinths 'where the wave fringes the golden beach with silver', the site of the parent town of Marseilles, the Greek city of Taurentum. He reaches Esterello, and, uttering a superb invocation, which begins:

> Trees of Mount Gibau! Pines, and you
> Myrtle-woods, juniper, and yew!
> And you, O sunset! you, O heath so calm!
> Great ocean! In my agony
> I take you, now, as testimony—
> Witness my love's eternity! . . .
> Birds of the forest, sing my wedding psalm!

he prepares to meet Severan's assault, hurling rocks down the mountainside until the bandit is at last consumed in the flames of the burning pine forests to which he himself has set fire.

Such a bare description of the action is sufficient to show the elaboration of incidental detail in this poem, and to point the difference from Mistral's earlier epic. This attention to description not essential to the action in fact violates one of the first principles of the epic form, which asserts that everything must be subordinated to the narrative. We miss here the harmonious perfection of *Mirèio,* its symmetry and frieze-like shape, so vital and plastic that it seems almost tangible. We miss too those great carved tableaux, in which time seems to stand still and a multitude of actions appear almost simultaneously before our eyes, so perfectly organised is the material. Not least, we miss the revelation of human character. The leading figures in *Calendau* are little more than ciphers, mouthpieces for passionate meditations on every aspect of the poet's beloved country. For these reasons it can perhaps never have the universal appeal—as it has certainly never had the success—of its predecessor. When that is said, however, it remains a tremendous achievement, a national hymn of great power, with passages of unsurpassed poetry, and with informative descriptions of scenes and customs of a luminous precision. (pp. 18-27)

[The first of Mistral's epic poems], *Mirèio,* is the poem of the countryside, of the farms and the plains; the second, *Calendau,* sings the mountains and the sea; while the last, *Lou Pouèmo dóu Rose,* is the poem of a great river, the Rhône.

In contrast to its predecessors it is composed in unrhymed decasyllables, divided into *laisses* like the *Chanson de Roland,* and recalling the early poem, **"Li Meissoun."** It describes the journey of a barge down the river in the days of horse navigation, and this theme, which is treated with a greater realism than the poet had ever previously employed, is combined with another of the highest fantasy, involving two characters, the one legendary, the other unearthly. But the real hero is the mighty river itself, and the very lines seem, as one reads, to reflect the various moods of the undulating and ever-moving waters. *Lou Pouèmo dóu Rose,* unlike the other poems, begins without ceremony:

> They are leaving Lyons at first light,
> The watermen who rule over the Rhône.
> These Condrillots are mighty-muscled men,
> Light-hearted, lusty, and a race who stand
> Ever bolt-upright on their rafts of fir,

Their faces gilded to the hue of bronze
By the sun's heat and by the river's glare.
But then, I tell you, more than ever now,
Was seen that kind of heavy-bearded giant,
Huge, bulky, powerful, like a forest oak,
Could lift a beam as though it were a straw—
From poop to prow they bellowed and they
    swore
Both loud and long, to warm each other's hearts,
From their great vats deep-swilling the red wine
    down
And from the pot drawing juicy hunks of meat.
There was a fine din all the river's length,
From north to south, without a break or pause,
'Turn her downstream now, ho! Royaume! Em-
    pire!
Prow upstream! On, now! Pull on the tow-ropes!'

The lives and homes of the boatmen are described in this straightforward way, until suddenly the poet falls into a vein of reverie, lamenting the passing of this open and vigorous life:

O the old times, so simple and so gay,
When all life seemed to bubble on the Rhône
When we came down as children to see pass
The proud Condrillots, on the broad water,
Hands to the tiller! Then the Rhône, thanks to
    them,
Was a huge beehive, full of noise and work.
Today, all that is silence, huge and dead,
Alas! and of that movement all that's left
Is but a trace, and the corroded furrow
That some old cable rubbed into the stone.

There follows a description of the various barges, including the *Caburle,* which is to play a leading part in the poem: its master is Apian, a typical Mistralian patriarch:

Patron Apian himself upon the poop
Directs the operations from the rail.
He has long hair that hangs in grey locks braided
And round about his temples curls and falls,
And two big, golden rings that are suspended
Down from his ears. And he is tall of stature
And his bright eyes dwell now upon each boat
To see that all goes well and is in order
As one after another, linked in file
By the long cable that holds them all together,
Clearing the shore amid the gurgling water,
All now in line, the barges sail away.

and, at length, the long convoy of barges sets sail for Beaucaire, as Apian recites the Lord's Prayer.

The theme of fantasy is introduced in the second canto, with the appearance of Guihén, Prince d'Aurenjo, or William, Prince of Orange and son of the King of Holland, who boards the boat at Vernaison. Young, fair, and almost spectral, he has about him a quality of dreamy romanticism which recalls Troubadours like Rudel. He has set out to seek his ideal under the symbol of the *Zwanenbloem,* or swan's flower of his own country, and the mention of it introduces a reference to the 'heroine', *L'Angloro,* a mysterious figure, the Undine of de la Motte Fouqué, the Ondine of Ravel:

. . . that is the 'flower of the Rhône', my good
    prince,

The flowering rush that grows beneath the wave
And which L'Angloro loves so much to pluck!

The rest of the canto is concerned with the arrival at and departure from Condrieu, where the boatmen meet their families, and with those easy and natural conversations of which Mistral is a master and which serve him on the one hand for exposition and on the other to describe the habits and customs of the watermen and the technicalities of their trade. So, starkly contrasted, realism and dream alternate in the gently flowing and flexible verse through the third canto and the fourth, in which the barge takes on three Venetian women who go to the great fair at Beaucaire to practise that calling for which the ladies of Venice are so justly famous. One of their number sings a ballad which evokes in the Prince a memory of the barcarolles that, sung in the summer evening, drift up from the waters of the Grand Canal: they were no doubt in Mistral's mind too, for he had visited Venice, with his wife . . . and while there had heard, to his great grief, of the death of Roumanille.

The leisurely movement of the poem grows more tense in the fifth canto with the appearance of L'Angloro. In this character the two themes, the realistic and the fantastic, meet and merge: for, when the barge arrives at the point where the Ardèche joins the Rhône, she is standing there on the shore, and turns out to be a gold-washer, who with her precarious gains helps to support her father. This simple and even humble person lives upon two levels, the matter-of-fact and the legendary, for she is the vehicle for the poet's immaterial reverie. Much courted by the watermen, she will have none of them and seems to prefer her lonely independence. There is much good-natured back-chat between her and the crew and it is not until the sixth canto that we see the other side of her nature: for this peasant girl is a child of the river and her mind is filled with dreams and visions of its mysterious divinity, *Lou Dra,* a kind of protean dragon, a green serpent who lures mortal women down beneath the waves to his watery home. Had she not herself seen him, and felt him, one summer night when she went swimming in the river?

The whole scene is a masterpiece of description and suggestion, which is broken off abruptly as the seventh canto begins and we return to the train of barges. It has reached Malatra where L'Angloro comes on board with her father, and the moment she sees the Prince she reacts with the classic swiftness of the romantic character who meets with her predestined lover. Pale and trembling,

'It's he! It's he!' she cried like one gone mad

and Guihèn replies:

I recognize thee,
Flower of the Rhône that blooms upon the wave!
Flower of delight half-glimpsed as in a dream
    . . .

and decisively she answers him:

I recognize thee, O Dra! whom I have seen
With that same flowering rush beneath the
    water . . .

Guihèn gives her the flower, and their fate is sealed:

> For love grows fast,
> Once they are in the boat that bears them on,
> Foredoomed, upon the wave.

Meanwhile the convoy moves on its way down-stream:

> The arcades
> Of the Pont St Esprit, with splendid sweep,
> Passed by in soaring triumph overhead . . .
> . . . Provence appeared; for she is heralded
> By the Pont St Esprit with its vast piles,
> Its twenty royal arches that are set
> Like a great coronet upon the Rhône.
> This is the holy and triumphant gate
> Of the land of love! And the olive trees,
> And the pomegranate, proudly flowering,
> And the millet with its abundant hair
> Already deck the marges and the banks.
> The plain spreads out, the verge grows ever
>   greener,
> And in the limpid, paradisal air,
> Are seen the northern slopes of Mont
>   Ventour . . .

The legendary atmosphere returns and is maintained as L'Angloro tells the company of the oracle at the fountain of Tourne, where there is a Mithraic monument, depicting with the usual symbols, the sacrifice of the bull by the young God, a sacrifice which is renewed to this day in the ritual of the bullfight. L'Angloro had drunk of the waters of this fountain and repeats a prophecy she had heard from the old witch who lived there. She interpreted the carvings on the monument to mean that a young man would bring disaster to the river and cause the sailors to be drowned, while the Dra will be driven from the river for ever. This alarms the boatmen for they have heard rumours of fireboats and steamships that can sail up-stream without horses. Thus does the legendary symbolism take on a deeper meaning in this poem which is a hymn to the great river that dominates the poet's country.

The next canto is however still idyllic, as the lovers indulge their dreams, until the calm is shattered by a whistle, and they see pass by a vessel carrying convicts to Toulon: an evil omen. They pass Orange, and arrive at Avignon where there is a diversion in the form of a treasure-hunt, organised by the Venetians. The last part of the eighth and the first part of the ninth canto consist in snatches of conversation, descriptions, and technical matters, until at last the convoy arrives at Beaucaire.

Here the great fair is in full swing, and through its intricacies the lovers wander, in a protracted intermezzo slightly reminiscent of the fair-scene in Gottfried Keller's *Romeo und Julia auf dem Dorfe,* where the lovers, Sali and Vrenchen, are likewise depicted before they are touched by the shadow of tragedy: for romantic love can only be fulfilled by death, by the *Liebestod.*

Meanwhile, the fair and its wares are described in homely detail, until, their business complete, the Condrillots harness the horses to the *Caburle* for the return journey to Lyons. There is a last meal, at which the Prince eulogises the great traditions of the waterway, now threatened, as he instinctively feels; but his words are brave; there is no use lamenting a lost cause, let us rather drink to the Rhône and the harvest sun, let us drink the wine of Genestet despite the vanquishers,

> And let the Bull-Rhône bellow in Rouanesso!

Evening is falling as he finishes speaking:

> And over Nîmes the sun was going down
> And spreading out along the splendid river
> The folds of its soft mantle drenched with blood,
> And letting fall the last gleam of its rays
> Over the Castle of Tarascon whence
> King René, at his window, seemed to bless
> The Rhône in its supreme and last upheaval.

As the eleventh canto opens, it is dawn, and the ascent begins. The method of moving upstream is described in detail, and over all the great figure of Apian presides. He invokes the blessing of God and the Holy Virgin,

> And under the branches of the white poplars,
> In the silence of the valley of the Rhône,
> And in the splendour of the rising sun,
> Behind the beautiful straining horses
> Who were pouring out vapour from their nos-
>   trils,
> The first carter took up the prayer . . .

but although, in this canto, there seems to be a calm, it is only the calm before the storm, and their prayers are in vain. The Mistral is blowing hard as the last canto opens.

But L'Angloro and Guihèn, oblivious, are talking of the marriage they will celebrate at the foot of the Mithraic monument at the *font de Tourno;* for they cannot be married as others are:

> Sun of Provence
> O god who brings to birth the grey lizards,
> And calls forth the cicadas from the earth,
> Who in my pallid, melancholy veins
> Brings to life the red blood of my forebears,
> Rhône-god that the Dra in his convolutions
> Entwines at Bourg, at Lyons and at Arles
> And to whom to-day, in the arenas,
> Unconscious sacrifice of the black bull
> Is offered, God who gaily scatters the shadows,
> God whose altar by an unknown shore
> To-day beholds deserted, with its rite
> Abandoned and forgotten—I, a savage,
> I, perhaps the last of your believers,
> Wish to offer on your altar the first-fruits
> Of my happiness, my nuptial night!

The mystic dialogue continues, while, as the climax draws nearer, the weather calms, the sun appears, and the heat becomes oppressive. The motion of the poem has now become as sluggish as that of the mighty river, somnolent and menacing. They have just passed the arches of the Pont St-Esprit when the first steamboat to be seen upon the Rhône appears suddenly round a bend, and tears into the line of barges, upsetting them and their crews, and dragging the horses into the water by which the whole convoy is swept against the arches of the bridge. When the Condrillots assemble upon the bank, they have lost their whole fleet and the Prince and L'Angloro are missing. 'Saint Nicholas has saved our lives', exclaims Apian, 'we will say a mass to him at Condrieu': but *Lou Dra* has carried off L'Angloro to his depths.

The poem ends briefly, on a note of humble resignation, as the survivors, with what they have been able to salvage about them, turn their steps homewards, *senso mai dire.*

On the whole the mixture of elements in this poem is extraordinarily successful. Despite the weight of symbolism which they have to bear, the characters are very real and hold our interest. Some have drawn attention to the 'northern' quality of this work; but, in truth, this quality is not so much northern as gnostic. The love of the principals, and the mithraic symbolism in which the development of the drama is clothed, have a strong gnostic colouring. This flavour, indeed, is strong in Provence, where despite every vicissitude, racial memory is comparatively pure. This flavour is well caught in the lyrical epilogue to Henry de Montherlant's fine novel, *Les Bestiaires,* which is built round a mithraic poem by the Marquis of Baroncelli-Javon. No part of Europe has such a strong association with gnosticism as Languedoc, whither it was brought, in its mithraic form at least, by the Roman soldier, whose works still play a part in the public life of the people. Nowhere has Catholicism been more powerfully touched by local tradition; and Mistral's own faith is inseparable from his patriotism, as can be seen from his attitude to the Albigensians—a gnostic sect—and the Avignonese papacy.

At the same time, as in *Mirèio* the poet restores and rejuvenates the old machinery of the primitive epic by the use of Christian powers, so here, in this poem, he uses to the same end this religious tradition, often associated with the Troubadours, which is still part of the racial consciousness of his people. For this reason alone the fantasy, however, irrational, never seems wholly fantastic and, far from being isolated, is merely enhanced by the realistic treatment of the details: the poem is therefore a reading of life, of a true epic breadth, and never a literary exercise, or a poetic *tour de force.*

But, when all is said, the final greatness of this last epic lies in its superb embodiment of a great river, with its life, its moods, its traditions and its inmost character which has influenced for centuries those who live by it: and, if we miss the symmetry and sculpture of *Mirèio,* or the fervent invocations of *Calendau,* we have instead something softer, more mysterious, more melodious; something as reflective as the deep and ever-moving water; something, perhaps, more profound.

For, in *Lou Pouèmo dóu Rose,* the Rhône speaks; and in its pages a mighty river sings forever.

. . .

Lis Oulivado appeared in 1912, when Mistral was eighty-two years of age, and as its name implies—for the olive-gathering is the last harvest of the Provençal year—was to be his final word. As he says at the beginning: 'As the weather grows cold and the sea rough, I feel that winter has come for me and that I must without delay gather my olives and offer my virgin oil on God's altar.'

On the whole less impressive than *Lis Isclo d'Or,* it nonetheless contains some great poems, including the sonnet for his own tomb: 'That is the tomb of a poet who fash-ioned songs for a beautiful Provençale called Mirèio'; and "Evo" ("Eve") which is a delightful hymn to physical beauty:

> What is the pearl
> That is born of the swirl
> In the kingdom of Amphitrite,
> If it do not shine
> On the ear divine
> Of the pearl-born Aphrodite!
>
> What are the grains
> The gold-washer gains
> Where the pregnant water swirls,
> If in pretty tresses
> The ore never graces
> Your nape with golden curls!
>
> What is the rose
> Whose buds unclose
> In the dews of a morning in May,
> If it wake not from sleep,
> If it wake not to weep
> On thy breast that is still more lovely!
>
> What is the cape
> That can undrape
> Its rainbow's hues in the sky,
> If on your whiteness
> Its falling brightness
> In long folds does not lie!
>
> What is the bait
> That makes us elate
> With longing to feel thy fire,
> If the King of the sky
> In his majesty
> Has not made thee for desire!
>
> All homage be
> To your royalty,
> And may all that brings delight,
> Smile upon thee
> And be offered thee . . .
> But never art thou so bright
>
> As in glory's hour
> When you burst into flower,
> Without dress or finery,
> As fateful and bare
> As once you were
> When God's hand fashioned thee!

In this poem all Mistral's joy and delight in, and his thoroughly Latin love for, the human face and form, the body radiant with the soul that inhabits it, shine forth in all their sweetness.

But perhaps the greatest poem in this collection—and one of the poet's greatest lyrics—is **"Lou Parangoun"** (**"The Archetype"**). The Archetype is Provence, which is seen now, through the haze of time, as a great ideal but, like all great ideals, a dream:

> My faith is but a dream: that much I know,
> But still a dream that seems enveiled in gold,
> A honey that can never cease to flow,
> A gulf whence I, myself in love, would go
> Bearing this Beauty that my arms enfold.

He reviews the forces that play upon this dream which he

has raised up to protect his faith against the ambitions, negations and illusions that threaten to devour it.

> But in the azure, my pellucid pall,
> In the sky's depth and blazing in my eyes,
> The type of my Provence, the beautiful,
> With her breast trembling where the sun's rays
> fall
> And Gyptis' cup in hand, I see arise.

The history of Provence then passes before his eyes:

> And now the fair Phoceans she distills,
> Crowned with wild olive and with myrtle dark:
> Under the cliffs, beneath the wooded hills,
> While her sweet song my spellbound hearing
> fills
> As it accompanies the pilot's barque.

Her fortunes rise with Rome, with the Troubadours and the Courts of Love: at last the Papacy comes to Avignon. And then begins the sad decline, and all seems lost and buried in dust:

> But Santo Estello in the empyrean height
> Performed a miracle one fair May morning:
> The endless Crau saw bloom in new delight
> Mireille—Provence, with Paradise alight,
> You've flowered again, fresh fragrance your
> adorning!

Though all be vanity, and Time pass onward, relentlessly wielding his scythe, faith, at last, is not illusion, but shall have its reward. (pp. 47-56)

> *Rob Lyle, in his* Mistral, *Yale University Press, 1953, 68 p.*

Thomas R. Hart   (essay date 1991)

[*In the following essay, Hart summarizes Mistral's aims as a writer and evaluates his success in documenting and preserving Provençal culture and popularizing Provençal literature.*]

The Provençal poet Frédéric Mistral is the most important of France's nineteenth-century regional writers. In 1904 he became the second Frenchman to receive the Nobel Prize for Literature. His name does not, however, appear in most histories of French literature. Yet the proper context for Mistral's poetry is surely nineteenth-century French literature and historiography rather than writing in Modern Provençal, limited both in range and in quantity, or the poetry of the troubadours, which has little relevance to his work. Conversely, our understanding of nineteenth-century French literature remains incomplete without some attention to regionalist literary movements, of which the Félibrige, the movement Mistral founded, is by far the most important. Its importance is not limited to France; the most recent edition of *The Oxford Companion to English Literature* reminds us that the Félibrige 'has served as an inspiration to a number of more recent movements favouring dispossessed languages and cultures'.

For the French Romantics, language and nationality were inseparably linked. Michelet asserts near the beginning of the *Tableau de la France* that forms Book 3 of his *Histoire de France* that 'la langue est le signe principal d'une nationalité.' For Mistral, too, 'uno lengo . . . es lou retra de tout un people, es la Biblo de soun istòri, lou mounumen vivènt de sa persounalita.' Mistral's chosen mission was to give back to Provençal its status as a literary language. In a letter of 15 September, 1894 to the philologist Gaston Paris, he insists that

> Je n'ai jamais travaillé ni chanté pour la gloire. Ma vraie muse a été une passion extraordinaire pour ma race, ma langue, mon pays; c'est pour les relever, les sauver, les glorifier, que je me fis poète, glossateur, grammairien, propagandiste, etc.

Dozens of similar passages are found in Mistral's letters and in his published works. They are summed up in the Latin epitaph he chose for his tombstone: *Non nobis sed Provinciae nostrae da gloriam.* One need not agree with Charles Mauron that the epitaph proves that Mistral was not an egoist, but this does not mean that he was a hypocrite. His conviction that he had dedicated his life to the service of Provence and its language must have made it difficult for him to separate his own prestige as a writer from that of Provençal as a newly revived literary language.

Mistral's first major work was a long narrative poem, *Mirèio,* published in 1859 when he was 29. The first edition included a facing French translation by the poet himself. All the later editions of *Mirèio*—there have been more than twenty—are bilingual, as are those of Mistral's other major works. It is usually assumed that the French translations reveal Mistral's ambition to be recognized as a poet by Parisian readers. [In his *Le Romantisme II 1843-1869,* 1979] Claude Pichois, for example, says of *Mirèio* that 'la traduction littérale en regard disait bien le désir d'être lu à Paris.' Theodore Zeldin similarly says [in *France 1848-1945: Intellect and Pride,* 1980] that 'Mistral . . . was not content simply to be the poet of Provence. He always had an eye on Paris.' In fact, however, the question is a little more complicated.

When *Mirèio* appeared in 1859, a large part of the Provençal bourgeoisie had already abandoned the language. Gaston Paris, in a long essay on Mistral first published in the *Revue de Paris* in 1894, noted that even the members of Mistral's own literary school, the Félibrige, usually spoke to one another in French. Many passages in Mistral's prose works make it clear that it is not just Parisians who scorn Provençal. So does a letter to Saint-René Taillandier, thanking him for his review of *Mirèio* in *Revue des Deux-Mondes:* 'Quant à ma traduction, ce qui me donne l'air d'avoir voulu l'écrire pour Paris, c'est que je l'ai faite surtout pour rapprendre à la classe aisée et citadine de nos contrées la langue qu'ils cherchaient en vaine a désapprendre.' Mistral's reference in *Mirèio* to 'our despised language', *nosto lengo mespresado,* may refer to its lack of prestige among people of his own class.

Recounting the founding of the Félibrige in his autobiography, written nearly half a century after the publication of *Mirèio,* Mistral recalls that 'As usual at dinner we spoke again of what was needed to raise our language from the neglect in which it lay ever since the bourgeois had betrayed the honour of Provence and reduced it to a menial condition.' The English version hardly conveys the tone of the original. Mistral does not speak of the neglect of Provençal but of the captivity in which it lay, '[lou] cativié mounte jasié', and the matter-of-fact assertion that 'the bourgeois . . . had reduced it to a menial condition' fails to capture the scorn for the bourgeois and the emotional involvement with the fate of Provençal in Mistral's words: 'li moussu l'avien redu, pecaire, à servi mèstre.'

Mistral's dislike for those he calls 'li moussu' or 'li moussurot' is apparent in many pages of his *Discours e dicho.* No doubt it has something to do with his humiliation by children brought up in town when he was sent away to boarding school. Despite his assertions to the contrary Mistral was not a man of the people but a village bourgeois. He could not forgive the members of his own class for abandoning Provençal, leading one of them to regret that Mistral had written *Mirèio* in 'la langue de nos domestiques'. Mistral's decision not to practice law may have been prompted in part by his refusal to identify himself with a class he despised for having rejected Provençal.

Mistral asserts near the beginning of *Mirèio* that he composed the poem solely for shepherds and country people: *cantan que pèr vautre, o pastre e gènt di mas.* The line may be interpreted in at least two different ways, which do not necessarily exclude one another. First, Mistral wants his work to be intelligible to the country people for whom Provençal was still a first language. But *pèr vautre,* in Provençal, like *pour vous* in French, can mean both 'for your sake, intended for you' and 'in your place, as a surrogate for you'. If we choose the second interpretation, Mistral is saying that he wants to act as a spokesman for the peasants who lack the schooling needed to write a work like *Mirèio.* Mistral seems never to have considered allowing the peasants to speak for themselves by collecting folktales or folksongs as Fauriel had done for Modern Greek or as Villemarqué claimed that he had done for Breton. His position recalls that of Michelet. Lionel Gossman says [in his *Between History and Literature,* 1990] that the historian 'never doubted that the people had to be led or that its books had to be written *for* it . . . The people was inarticulate, *infans,* and could attain self-awareness and self-expression only through the mediation of one who was both of it and beyond it, like Michelet himself.'

If Provençal was to take its place beside French as a literary language then literature in Provençal had to be brought to the attention of the French-speaking bourgeoisie, both in the Midi and in Paris. For this reason Mistral, apparently with some reluctance and on the advice of friends in Provence, journeyed to Paris to find an established French writer to sponsor his poem. In a letter of 12 August, 1858 to his friend Roumieux he says that 'I am going to leave for Paris next week; I'm going to try to get a preface from some literary bigwig (*quaque gros catau de la literaturo*).' Mistral's first choice was George Sand, whose use of the dialect of her native Berry in her *romans champêtres* must have interested him.

Sand explores some of the problem of using dialect in the *Avant-propos* of her novel *François le Champi,* first pub-

lished in 1848 and reissued a half-dozen times before the appearance of *Mirèio* in 1859. She observes that

> Le sentiment que j'ai de la simplicité rustique ne trouve pas de langage pour s'exprimer. Si je fais parler l'homme des champs comme il parle, il faut une traduction en regard pour le lecteur civilisé, et si je le fais parler comme nous parlons, j'en fais un être impossible, auquel il faut supposer un ordre d'idées qu'il n'a pas.

Mistral, of course, was free to solve the problem in the way Sand rejects. His decision to publish his work together with a French translation probably contributed to the complaints, which began to be heard during his lifetime, that his poems were unintelligible to the shepherds and country people, *[li] pastre e gènt di mas,* for whom he claimed to have written them. Mistral's opponents charged that his Provençal was both too literary and too different from other dialects to be easily understood and that he used rare words or words of his own invention. Jules Arnoux, for example, asserted in 1889 [in *Les troubadours et les félibres du Midi*] that '[les Félibres] ne sont pas compris des pauvres gens, et les lettrés eux-mêmes ne peuvent les lire sans le secours d'une traduction française.' Even Mistral's close friend Roumanille felt that a bilingual edition of *Mirèio* was indispensable because of the difficulty of the Provençal text.

Mistral, for his part, insisted that every word he used was alive among the people and stubbornly refused to concede that they found his work unintelligible. In a letter of 21 November, 1894, to Gaston Paris, he quotes the line 'Car cantan que pèr vautre, o pastre e gènt di mas!' and asserts that 'on a prétendu qu'il n'y avait là qu'une formule littéraire et sans conviction. C'est au contraire une de mes plus vieilles et plus durables sincérités. Je n'ai pas fait un vers de *Mireille* ou un vers de tel autre de mes poèmes sans me dire instantanément: "est-ce qu'un indigène illettré pourrait comprendre cela?" ' In another letter to Gaston Paris, of 3 October 1894, Mistral insists that 'c'est une erreur absolue (contre laquelle les félibres ont toujours dédaigné de protester) de croire que notre poésie n'est compréhensible au populaire qu'en partie. Nous sommes au contraire les poètes de France et d'Europe les plus rapprochés de la compréhension populaire.' Mistral would never have conceded, like Michelet, that 'sa langue [la langue du peuple], sa langue, elle m'était inaccessible. Je n'ai pas pu le faire parler.' To be understood by the people is, of course, not the same thing as identifying with them. Later in the same letter to Gaston Paris Mistral refers to the four thousand *paysans* who had listened to him recite his *Ode to the Catalans* at Saint-Rémy in 1868 as 'ces primitifs'.

Mistral's French version of *Mirèio* does more than just make his poem available to readers unfamiliar with Provençal. Sometimes he adds an explanatory phrase, for example when he translates 'l'home aloubati' by 'l'homme, avide comme un loup'. Elsewhere he introduced a neologism, often italicized, or adds a note to explain the figurative sense of a phrase, as he does with *li mirau soun creba,* literally 'the mirrors are broken', and *quand Marto fielavo,* 'when Martha used to spin'. All of these devices are surely meant to suggest that Provençal offers expressive riches that have no counterpart in French. They are an implicit rebuke to those Provençaux of Mistral's own class who believe that their mother tongue is only an impoverished patois, unfit for use in serious literature.

George Sand's experiments with dialect in her *romans champêtres* probably interested Mistral less than her idealistic treatment of rural life. As Naomi Schor has observed in an excellent article on Sand, ['Idealism in the Novel: Recanonizing Sand', in Joan DeJean and Nancy K. Miller's *Displacements: Women, Tradition, Literatures in French,* 1991], 'Realism in the nineteenth century signified *only* in relation to idealism, so much so that to consider one term in isolation from the other is to deplete, even distort, its significance.'

Sand's attitude is made clear in the first chapter, a preface addressed to the reader, of her novel *La Mare au diable,* first published in 1846:

> Certains artistes de notre temps, jetant un regard sérieux sur ce qui les entoure, s'attachent à peindre la douleur, l'abjection de la misère, le fumier de Lazare . . . Nous croyons que la mission de l'art est une mission de sentiment et d'amour, que le roman d'aujourd'hui devrait remplacer la parabole et l'apologue des temps naïfs, et que l'artiste a une tâche plus large et plus poétique que celle de proposer quelques mesures de prudence et de conciliation pour atténuer l'effroi qu'inspirent ses peintures. Son but devrait être de faire aimer les objets de sa sollicitude, et au besoin, je ne lui ferais pas un reproche de les embellir un peu. L'art n'est pas une étude de la réalité positive; c'est une recherche de la vérité idéale.

The series of rustic novels Sand began in 1845 was in part a reply to Balzac, who had portrayed peasants as surly, greedy brutes in *Les Paysans* (1844). John Ardagh speaks for many twentieth-century readers when he asserts [in *Writers' France: A Regional Panorama,* 1989] that Sand's

> portrayal of the peasantry is far too starry-eyed and simplistic: her idealized cardboard characters, however poor and uneducated, are always pure, good and noble, and even their toil is one long idyll, while little attempt is made to show the darker side of their lives and behaviour.

Although Mistral probably shared George Sand's views on idealistic fiction, his treatment of rural life in **Mirèio** is much darker.

In a fine study of the pastoral tradition [entitled *The Country and the City,* 1973], Raymond Williams observes that the ancient poets did not limit themselves to idealized scenes of rural peace and contentment. They contrast 'summer with winter; pleasure with loss; harvest with labour.' Virgil in his *Eclogues* and *Georgics* could still find room for 'the whole of a working country life'. In Renaissance adaptations, 'these living tensions are excised, until there is nothing countervailing, and selected images stand as themselves: not in a living but in an enamelled world.' Williams's counter-pastoral, exemplified by such works as George Crabbe's *The Village,* in which the poet asserts that he 'paint[s] the Cot, / As Truth will paint it, and as Bards will not', marks a return to Virgil's comprehensive

vision of rural life in opposition to Pope's insistence that 'to render a Pastoral delightful' the poet must expose 'the best side only of a shepherd's life, . . . concealing its miseries'.

Mirèio combines elements of the European pastoral tradition with elements of the tradition Williams calls counterpastoral. Mistral makes no attempt to conceal the tension between those who own land and those who do not. Our first glimpse of the *mas di Falabrego,* the farm on which Mirèio lives, is through the eyes of two poor basketmakers, father and son, who stress its wealth as one of the richest estates in the region, 'un tenamen di pus fort de la Crau'. Much later, the son, Vincèn, with whom Mirèio falls in love, begs his father to ask Mirèio's father Mèste Ramoun to allow her to marry him. Vincèn insists that one should ask whether a man is good and not whether he is poor: 'l'on dèu s'enchaure / Se l'ome es brave e noun s'es paure'. Vincèn's father, Mèste Ambròsi, reprimands him for his presumption, reminding him that he is only a *pauras,* a wretched pauper, but finally yields to the pleading of his son and daughter and goes to see Mirèio's father. He is rejected after a heated argument in which Mirèio herself takes part. Mirèio's parents make it perfectly clear that they will never accept anyone who lacks land or some other form of wealth as a match for their daughter. Her mother shows only contempt for Vincèn and treats Mirèio's desire to marry him as tantamount to a wish to run away and live among the gypsies. No doubt she would have reacted in the same way if Mirèio had fallen in love with one of the farmworkers, most of them seasonal employees rather than permanent members of the household. The happy hierarchy of the farm does not extend to those outside it and lasts only as long as the hierarchical order is respected.

Mistral's poem conspicuously lacks the social harmony that governs most contemporary representations of rural life. Ronald Hubscher's survey of the textbooks used in nineteenth-century French primary schools ['Modèle et anti-modèle paysans' in Yves Lequin's *Histoire des Francais XIXe-XXe siècles,* 1983] shows that they treat the peasants fundamentally as George Sand had done in her novels of rural life. The schoolbooks offer 'une vision paisible, rassurante, de la société . . . Explicitement, chaque leçon contient une morale, qui reflète évidemment le modèle idéologique dominant: sobriété, économie, satisfaction du devoir accompli, acceptation de sa condition.'

In nineteenth-century French painting, too, according to Richard and Caroline Brettell [in their *Painters and Peasants in the Nineteenth Century,* 1938] 'some of the fundamental values of bourgeois society—work, family, religion, and patriotism—were embodied time and time again in the peasant image'. Mistral invokes all of these values repeatedly in the speeches he made as *capoulié,* leader of the Félibrige, and constantly links them to the fate of the Provençal language. In a speech given in Montpellier in March 1875 Mistral contends that

> Lou grand patrioutisme nais de l'estacamen que l'on a pèr son endré, pèr si coustumo, pèr sa famiho . . . Se voulèn releva nosto pauro patrìo, releven ço que fai greia li patrioto: la religioun,

li tradicioun, li souvenenço naciounalo, la vièio
lengo dóu païs.

(True patriotism comes from the affection one
feels for the place where he was born, for its traditions, for his family . . . If we wish to renew
our poor fatherland, let us renew those things
that breed patriots: religion, traditions, national
memories, the old language of the region.)

All four of the values the Brettells mention—work, family,
religion, patriotism—are present in *Mirèio* and offset the
counter-pastoral elements in the poem.

Like many nineteenth-century painters, Mistral usually
presents his farm workers engaged in communal activity
like the harvest, or relaxing after the day's work is done,
as he does in Canto 1 when the men listen to Ambròsi's
ballad about the eighteenth-century Provençal naval hero
Suffren. Mistral, moreover, presents the work of the *mas*
in a way that hides the opposition between work and play,
as in his picture of the *descoucounarello,* the young women
who join Mirèio in gathering the cocoons of the silk-
worms, in Canto 1. Most of them, certainly all those mentioned by name, with the exception of the sorceress Taven,
are apparently on the same social level as Mirèio herself:
they are not peasant girls, but the daughters of landowners.

We do not know what George Sand thought of *Mirèio.*
Mistral did not succeed in getting her to write a preface
for his poem and there is good reason to doubt that she
ever read it. The task of introducing Mistral's poem to Parisian readers fell instead to the ageing romantic poet Alphonse de Lamartine.

Mistral visited Lamartine on his first trip to Paris in the
summer of 1858. Apparently Mistral did not ask him to
write a preface for *Mirèio,* perhaps because he was still
waiting for a reply from George Sand. He made a second
trip to Paris in the spring of 1859, soon after the publication of *Mirèio,* and again visited Lamartine. By now, of
course, it was too late to think of a preface, since *Mirèio*
had already been published, but Lamartine came to Mistral's aid in another, perhaps more effective way by devoting an entire number of his *Cours familier de littérature*
to *Mirèio.*

The *Cours familier,* which appeared in monthly instal-
ments from 1856 to 1869, was written entirely by Lamartine, who also supervised subscriptions and distribution.
It was frankly intended to make money, one of a number
of projects Lamartine undertook in a desperate attempt to
pay off a crushing accumulation of debts. Each number is
devoted to a single subject, usually an individual writer.
Lamartine calls them *entretiens* and they are indeed written in a familiar conversational style. The *entretiens* are
laced with autobiographical references, including remarks
on Lamartine's poverty and the fortitude with which he
bore it. They were based on hasty and superficial research
and are often filled out by long quotations. All of these
qualities are apparent in the fortieth *entretien,* devoted to
Mirèio, which appeared early in May, 1859.

Lamartine's praise for Mistral places the author of *Mirèio*
at a distance from contemporary Parisian fashion; he is

'un poète né, . . . un poète primitif'. If his poem is Homeric, it is the result of nature and not of study: 'son père,
comme tous les riches cultivateurs de la campagne, qui rê-
vent follement pour leurs fils, une condition supérieure,
selon leur vanité, à la vie rurale' had provided him with
a classical education. 'Heureusement', however, Mistral,
after his father's premature death 'se hâta . . . d'oublier
les langues savantes et importunes dont on avait obsédé sa
mémoire'.

The note of condescension is unmistakable; Lamartine repeatedly refers to Mistral's youth though the poet was 29
when *Mirèio* appeared in 1859. (Lamartine, incidentally,
says that he was twenty-five.) He carefully distinguishes
Mistral from 'ces hommes de vanité, plus que de génie,
qu'on appelle les poètes populaires' and praises him for
knowing his place: when Lamartine received him, the
young poet 'ne cherchait ni à s'enfler, ni à s'élever plus
haut que nature'. Lamartine insists that

nous ne sommes pas fanatique . . . de la soi-
disant démocratie dans l'art; nous ne croyons à
la nature que quand elle est cultivée par
l'éducation; nous n'avons jamais goûte avec un
faux enthousiasme ces médiocrités rimées sur
lesquelles des artisans dépaysés dans les lettres
tentent trop souvent, sans génie ou sans outils,
de faire extasier leur siècle; excepté *Jasmin*
. . . ; excepté *Reboul de Nîmes* . . . nous
n'avons vu, en général, que des avortements
dans cette poésie des ateliers. Que chantent-ils,
ceux qui ne voient la nature que dans la guingette? Il pourrait en sortir des Béranger; mais des
Homère et des Théocrite, non!

Lamartine's reference to the *guingette* is revealing: these
suburban restaurants, like their rivals the *cafés-concerts,*
were frequently denounced for promoting the indiscriminate mixing of persons drawn from different social classes.

Lamartine praises *Mirèio,* along with the poetry of Jasmin
and Reboul, as safe reading for the masses:

Voilà des livres tels qu'il en faudrait au peuple
de nos campagnes pour lire à la veillée après les
sueurs du jour . . . Voilà de ces livres qui bénis-
sent et qui édifient l'humble foyer où ils entrent!
voilà de ces épopées sur lesquelles les grossières
imaginations du peuple inculte se façonnent, se
modèlent, se polissent, et font passer avec des récits enchanteurs, de l'aïeul à l'enfant, de la mère
à la fille, du fiancé à l'amante, toutes les bontés
de l'âme, toutes les beautés de la pensée, toutes
les saintetés de tous les amours que font un sanc-
tuaire du foyer du pauvre! Ah! qu'il y a loin d'un
peuple nourri par de telles épopées villageoises
à ce pauvre peuple suburbain de nos villes, assis
les coudes sur la table avinée des guingettes, et
répétant à voix fausse . . . un refrain grivois de
Béranger . . . !

Lamartine goes on to say that if he were rich or Minister
of Public Instruction he would have six million copies of
Mirèio printed for free distribution

à toutes les portes où il y a une mère de famille,
un fils, un vieillard, un enfant capable d'épeler
ce catéchisme de sentiment, de poésie et de

vertu, que le paysan de Maillane vient de donner à la Provence, à la France et bientôt à l'Europe. Les Hébreux recevaient la manne d'en haut, cette manne nous vient d'en bas; c'est le peuple qui doit sauver le peuple.

Earlier, he had asserted that

> ces poëtes du soleil ne pleurent même pas comme nous; leurs larmes brillent comme des ondées pleines de lumière, pleines d'espérance, parce qu'elles sont pleines de religion. Voyez Reboul . . . ! Voyez Jasmin . . . ! Voyez Mistral dans sa mort des deux amants!

The last sentence again reveals Lamartine's haste or carelessness. Only Mirèio dies at the end of the poem; Mistral does not suggest that Vincèn's grief kills him too.

Lamartine's repeated assertions that Mistral owes more to his natural genius than to his education fail to do justice to an important aspect of *Mirèio.* As a schoolboy Mistral won prizes for both Latin and Greek. In nineteenth-century French schools, Greek and Latin literary texts were not merely objects of study but also models for imitation. The teacher or the manual proposed an 'argument' that the pupil would flesh out and ornament by recourse to the arsenal of rhetorical figures studied in class. For the more gifted students these schoolroom exercises became their first 'original' works. Mistral's first major composition, which was not published until after his death, was a poem in four cantos, **"Li Meissoun" ("The Harvests")**, strongly influenced by Virgil's Eclogues.

The opening lines of *Mirèio,* 'Cante uno chato de Prouvènço / Dins lis amour de sa jouvènço', clearly recall Virgil's 'Arma virumque cano' and at the same time announce that Mistral's subject is quite different. He will present a young woman in love, not a man and his achievements in war. His heroine is only a simple country girl, scarcely remembered outside her immediate surroundings: 'coume èro / Rèn qu'uno chato de la terro, / En foro de la Crau se n'es gaire parla.' The presence of Virgil, and of Homer as well, is felt at many other points in *Mirèio.* The cup that the shepherd Alàri carves as a gift for Mirèio in Canto 4 recalls Virgil's Third Eclogue, while the footrace at Nîmes that Vincèn describes to her in Canto 1 has a clear antecedent in Book 5 of the *Aeneid.* The fight between Vincèn and Ourrias in Canto 5 evokes episodes in the fifth book of the *Aeneid* and in the twenty-third book of the *Iliad.* There are, however, also striking differences. One of them is Mistral's use of images drawn from the animal world to underscore both the sexual rivalry between Vincèn and Ourrias and the ferocity of the struggle in which Vincèn is treacherously wounded. Mistral's most elaborate reworking of Virgil is Vincèn's visit to the cave of the sorceress Taven after his fight with Ourrias. It is, of course, modelled on Book 6 of the *Aeneid* and Mistral devotes the whole of his sixth canto to it.

Lamartine does not mention most of these reminiscences of Virgil. He insists that Mistral is unaware that he is following in the footsteps of Homer and Virgil: 'O jeune homme de Maillane . . . tu as été homérique et virgilien quand tu l'as voulu, sans y penser!' Lamartine does not even note that Vincèn's visit to Taven is based on Aeneas's descent to the underworld, though his recognition of Mistral's debt to Virgil may have contributed to his insistence that Mistral would have done better to omit the whole canto: 'Quant à nous, nous déchirerions ce chant tout entier sans rien regretter dans le poème.'

Lamartine's reluctance to acknowledge the use Mistral made of his classical education may be linked to his account of the poet's relations with his father and mother. Lamartine declares that Mistral's father died young and that he was brought up by his mother, who inspired his love for the Provençal language. In fact, Mistral's father died, at the age of 77, in 1855 when the poet was 25; both his parents were Provençal speakers. Lamartine's error is surely due primarily to haste and to his habitual carelessness in preparing the *Cours familier,* but it may also reflect his view of the relationship between Provençal and French. Lamartine, born in 1790, remains faithful to the dominant eighteenth-century view that dialect is opposed to language as nature is to culture. Dialect represents the world of women and feeling; language, the world of men, law and letters. Although Lamartine recognizes that Mistral has created a language out of a mere dialect, *un patois vulgaire,* he refuses to concede that he has done so by bringing all the resources of his education to writing in his mother tongue and thus effectively erasing the opposition between nature and culture. Mistral continues another strain in eighteenth-century thought, one that has been well analysed by Lionel Gossman [in *Between History and Literature*]:

> In certain novels and even, more modestly, in certain historical writings of the eighteenth century, there are significant signs of a revalorization both of the private, domestic sphere and of maternal origins, as opposed to paternal culture and law. It is as though a stratum of the bourgeoisie, conscious of its links to those origins—to the people and their material life—wished to rehabilitate them and to find a place for them in culture rather than to exclude and repress them as the other of culture . . . Culture remained, even for those who in the eighteenth century were curious about their mother tongue—or about folk poetry or local antiquities—a precious and precarious achievement of labor and effort, constantly threatened by the danger of regression into the supposedly undifferentiated world of nature, the mothers, and the people, and defended primarily by literary education.

Mistral's use of classical models in *Mirèio* is perhaps a sign of the persistence of this attitude, as is his fondness for citing classical analogues to Provençal folk beliefs in the notes to his poem. But of course he goes much further in the direction Gossman calls 'the rediscovery and rehabilitation of the primitive world of origins . . . and the creation of a unified and total culture without ruptures or exclusions [that] was a major enterprise of Romantic poetry, historiography, and philology'. *Mirèio* could not have been written in the eighteenth century.

No contemporary reader, so far as I know, perceived the tension between pastoral and counter-pastoral in *Mirèio.* Certainly Lamartine did not. He interpreted Mistral's poem as if it were a verse counterpart to George Sand's rustic novels. Indeed, Lamartine goes beyond Sand and turns Mistral's poem into a reassuring social message. His essay is too superficial to throw much light on Mistral's poem. It is interesting chiefly because it reveals social and political prejudices that Lamartine no doubt shared with other middle-class readers.

Mistral's speeches as leader of the Félibrige and the autobiography he wrote near the end of his life suggest that he interpreted *Mirèio* in much the same way as Lamartine. In a speech of 23 May 1886, honouring the patron saint of the Félibrige, he recalls that 'quand *Mirèio* pareiguè, i'a deja proun tèms d'acò, en vesènt lou bèu gàubi emé la gaiardiso de nosto parladuro, noste grand e bon mèstre Lamartine, diguè: "C'est le peuple qui doit sauver le peuple"' ('when *Mirèio* appeared long ago, our great and good master Lamartine, recognizing the grace and strength of our speech, said "It is the people that must save the people."') Like Lamartine, Mistral believed that persuading country people not to leave the country in order to seek their livelihood in the city was an urgent task, and he thought that encouraging the use of Provençal was one means of accomplishing it:

> Voulèn que nòsti chato, au liò d'estre elevado dins lou desden de nòsti causo de Prouvènço. . . continùnion de parla la lengo de soun brès, la douço lengo de si maire, e que demoron, simplo, dins lou mas ounte nasquèron . . .

> (We want our daughters, instead of being brought up to spurn our Provençal ways . . . , to continue to speak the language of their cradles, the sweet language of their mothers, and to remain, unspoiled, on the farms where they were born . . .)

Mistral has only scorn for people who want to leave their farms in order to rise into the urban bourgeoisie:

> lis enfant de la terro que volon plus la boulega, li fiéu di pescadou que volon plus prene la mar, li cago-nis di meisterau que volon tóuti èstre moussu!

> (children of the land who no longer want to till it, fishermen's sons who no longer want to go to sea, sons of craftsmen who all want to be gentlemen)

Mistral's affection for the common people is not in doubt, but it is clear that he does not feel himself to be one of them.

Mistral's timidity in exploring social issues limited his achievement as a realistic writer, just as his insistence on following classical models limited his attempt to make Provençal something more than a language used only for a certain kind of literature. These limitations explain in part why he failed to accomplish the lasting results achieved by the contemporary movement of literary and linguistic revival in Catalonia, which in its early stages was closely associated with the Félibrige. (pp. 175-86)

> *Thomas R. Hart, "Creating a Literature: Mistral and Modern Provençal," in* Journal of European Studies, *Vol. 21, No. 83, September, 1991, pp. 175-88.*

FURTHER READING

Biography

Baussan, Charles. "Mistral and His Work." *The Catholic World* XCVI, No. 573 (December 1912): 379-84.
Positive and highly descriptive discussion of Mistral's Provençal background, his Catholic faith, and his success as a poet.

Carter, Barbara Barclay. "Frédéric Mistral 1830-1914." *The Bookman* LXXII, No. 3 (November 1930): 274-79.
Assesses Mistral's career as a poet.

Daudet, Alphonse. "Mistral." *The Century Magazine* VIII, No. 3 (July 1885): 416-22.
Discusses his friendship with Mistral.

Maud, Constance E. "The Patriot Poets of Provence: Some Personal Memories." *Nineteenth Century and After* LXXX, No. CCCCLXXIII (July 1916): 58-72.
Comments on Mistral's role as a Provençal patriot and describes a meeting with him.

"Frédéric Mistral: Some Account of the Poet and His Work." *The Outlook* 126 (11 April 1914): 797-98.
Describes Mistral's last appearance at the Festival of Sainte-Estelle at Aix-en-Provence.

Sergeant, Elizabeth Shepley. "Frédéric Mistral." *Century* 90, No. 3 (July 1915): 465-73.
Recalls memories of Mistral and considers the future of Provençal literature following his death.

Criticism

Aldington, Richard. *Introduction to Mistral.* Carbondale: Southern Illinois University Press, 1960, 209 p.
A biographical and critical discussion of Mistral's major works.

Bartlett, Phyllis. "George Meredith on Mistral's *Mirèio.*" *The Yale University Library Gazette* 38, No. 2 (October 1963): 67-74.
Presents a review, which originally appeared in *Pall Mall Gazette* in 1869, of H. Crichton's translation of *Mirèio.*

Dargan, E. Preston. "Frédéric Mistral." *The Nation* XCVIII, No. 2,544 (2 April 1914): 360.
Offers brief commentary on Mistral's career and major works and praises his loyalty to Provence.

Henry, Stuart. "Frédéric Mistral." In his *French Essays and Profiles,* pp. 303-10. New York: E. P. Dutton & Co., 1921.
Briefly discusses various perspectives on Mistral's career, lifestyle, political views, and personality.

Logan, Olive. "Mistral and the Language of the Troubadours." *The Bookman* XXV (March 1907): 91-3.
Discusses the Félibre movement and considers the future of Provençal language and literature.

Marble, Annie Russell. "Frédéric Mistral: Poet of Provence." In her *The Nobel Prize Winners in Literature,* pp. 31-41. New York: D. Appleton and Co., 1925.

Surveys Mistral's career and briefly assesses his major works, concluding that Mistral was a poet "of the soil" who "created anew the life of his rural people; he touched daily incidents with poetic beauty."

Review of *Mes origines: Mémoires et récits de Frédéric Mistral,* by Frédéric Mistral. *The Nation* LXXXIV, No. 2,168 (17 January 1907): 65.

Positive review of Mistral's memoirs, concluding that "the qualities of Mistral's prose, as revealed by this book, are so surpassingly fine that it is impossible not to feel a half-regret that he did not devote his life to French prose instead of to Provençal poetry."

Review of *The Memoirs of Frederic Mistral,* by Frédéric Mistral. *The New York Times Book Review* XCI, No. 48 (30 November 1986): 23.

Provides a brief review of Mistral's *Memoirs,* commenting on Mistral's agrarian idealism and noting the historical value of his works.

O'Shea, John J. "A Provençal Renascence." *The American Catholic Quarterly Review* XXX, No. 118 (April 1905): 268-83.

Discusses the Provençal dialect and the role of the troubadours in Provençal culture and asserts that Mistral is "the embodiment of an ideal" in his evocation of the chivalrous qualities of the Provençal language.

"Frédéric Mistral's Memories of His Early Life." *The Outlook* 85 (2 March 1907): 521-22.

Presents an overview of Mistral's *Memoirs* and praises Mistral for offering "the rare and edifying spectacle of a life in perfect harmony with his creative work."

Additional coverage of Mistral's life and career is contained in the following source published by Gale Research: *Contemporary Authors,* Vol. 122.

L. M. Montgomery

1874-1942

(Full name Lucy Maud Montgomery Macdonald) Canadian novelist, short story writer, nonfiction writer, poet, and journalist.

INTRODUCTION

Best known for her novel *Anne of Green Gables*, Montgomery is one of the most celebrated authors in Canadian literature. In her works she often documented the vicissitudes of young girls who have been orphaned. Montgomery's protagonists typically display a precocious intelligence, courage, and sense of moral values, while at the same time possessing the childlike qualities of impulsiveness and spirited mischief.

Montgomery was born on Prince Edward Island, where she was raised by her grandparents. She began writing at the age of nine and was first published at sixteen. Early in her career she wrote poetry, essays, and short stories which were printed in various Canadian and American periodicals. Montgomery's first novel, *Anne of Green Gables*, was an immediate success, leading to a sequel and later to a series of novels featuring the character Anne Shirley. After the publication of the second novel of this series, *Anne of Avonlea*, Montgomery remarked: "If I'm to be dragged at Anne's chariot wheels the rest of my life, I'll bitterly repent having 'created' her." Nevertheless, Montgomery continued writing about Anne and other youthful heroines, including Sara Stanley in *The Story Girl*, Pat Gardiner in *Pat of Silver Bush*, and Jane Stuart in *Jane of Lantern Hill*. She also produced a trilogy about Emily Byrd Starr, an aspiring young author. *Emily of New Moon*, *Emily Climbs*, and *Emily's Quest* are considered autobiographical, reflecting Montgomery's struggles as a female Canadian author. She died in 1942.

Critics observe that Montgomery's novels follow a pattern in which a young female protagonist, through her vibrant personality and self-directed actions, influences her rigid guardians to become more compassionate and receptive. In *Anne of Green Gables*, Anne is sent by mistake to Matthew and Marilla Cuthbert, who had asked to adopt a boy. Utilizing her innate perceptiveness, she shows her elders and peers the fallacies of their narrow beliefs and becomes loved and accepted for herself. Such later works as *Anne of Avonlea* and *Anne's House of Dreams* depict her life as a schoolteacher, doctor's wife, and mother of six. Many of Montgomery's other stories feature Anne's children and the people in her town.

While some critics maintain that none of Montgomery's subsequent works equalled her achievement in *Anne of Green Gables*, most commend her as a storyteller whose charm transcends her faults. They praise her evocative

picture of the landscape and culture of Prince Edward Island and are especially impressed with her attacks on prejudice, lack of imagination, and tyranny over the young. Above all, critics applaud Montgomery's understanding of children as evidenced by her characterization of Anne, a heroine described by Mark Twain as "the dearest and most moving and delightful child since the immortal Alice."

PRINCIPAL WORKS

Anne of Green Gables (novel) 1908
Anne of Avonlea (novel) 1909
The Story Girl (short stories) 1911
Chronicles of Avonlea (novel) 1912
Anne of the Island (novel) 1915
The Watchman, and Other Poems (poetry) 1916
Anne's House of Dreams (novel) 1917
Rainbow Valley (novel) 1920
Rilla of Ingleside (novel) 1921

Emily of New Moon   (novel)   1923
Emily Climbs   (novel)   1924
Emily's Quest   (novel)   1927
Pat of Silver Bush   (novel)   1933
Courageous Women   (sketches)   1934
Anne of Windy Poplars   (novel)   1936; also published as
    Anne of Windy Willows
Jane of Lantern Hill   (novel)   1937
Anne of Ingleside   (novel)   1939
The Alpine Path   (autobiography)   1974
The Doctor's Sweetheart, and Other Stories   (short stories)   1979
The Selected Journals of L. M. Montgomery. 2 vols.
    (journal)   1985-87
The Poetry of Lucy Maud Montgomery   (poetry)   1987
Akin to Anne: Tales of Other Orphans   (short stories)   1988

CRITICISM

L. M. Montgomery   (essay date 1917)

[*In the following excerpt from* The Alpine Path, *originally published in the Toronto magazine* Everywoman's World *between June and November 1917, Montgomery reflects on her literary career, particularly the writing of* Anne of Green Gables.]

Many years ago, when I was still a child, I clipped from a current magazine a bit of verse, entitled "To the Fringed Gentian," and pasted it on the corner of the little portfolio on which I wrote my letters and school essays. Every time I opened the portfolio I read one of those verses over; it was the keynote of my every aim and ambition:

> Then whisper, blossom, in thy sleep
> How I may upward climb
> The Alpine path, so hard, so steep,
> That leads to heights sublime;
> How I may reach that far-off goal
> Of true and honoured fame,
> And write upon its shining scroll
> A woman's humble name.

It is indeed a "hard and steep" path; and if any word I can write will assist or encourage another pilgrim along that path, that word I gladly and willingly write. (p. 10)

[The] incidents and environment of my childhood . . . had a marked influence on the development of my literary gift. A different environment would have given it a different bias. Were it not for those Cavendish years, I do not think *Anne of Green Gables* would ever have been written.

When I am asked "When did you begin to write?" I say, "I wish I could remember." I cannot remember the time when I was not writing, or when I did not mean to be an author. To write has always been my central purpose around which every effort and hope and ambition of my life has grouped itself. I was an indefatigable little scrib-

bler, and stacks of manuscripts, long ago reduced to ashes, alas, bore testimony to the same. I wrote about all the little incidents of my existence. I wrote descriptions of my favourite haunts, biographies of my many cats, histories of visits, and school affairs, and even critical reviews of the books I had read.

One wonderful day, when I was nine years old, I discovered that I could write poetry. (pp. 52-3)

Poems, however, were not all I wrote. Very soon after I began to write verses I also began to write stories. The "Story Club" in *Anne of Green Gables* was suggested by a little incident of schooldays when Janie S—, Amanda M— and I all wrote a story with the same plot. I remember only that it was a very tragic plot, and the heroines were all drowned while bathing on Cavendish sandshore! Oh, it was very sad! It was the first, and probably the last, time that Janie and Amanda attempted fiction, but I had already quite a library of stories in which almost everyone died. (p. 57)

Nowadays, my reviewers say that my forte is humour. Well, there was not much humour in those early tales, at least, it was not intended there should be. Perhaps I worked all the tragedy out of my system in them, and left an unimpeded current of humour. I think it was my love of the dramatic that urged me to so much infanticide. In real life I couldn't have hurt a fly, and the thought that superfluous kittens had to be drowned was torture to me. But in my stories battle, murder and sudden death were the order of the day. (p. 58)

A story I had written in a prize competition was published in the Montreal *Witness,* and a descriptive article on Saskatchewan was printed in the Prince Albert *Times,* and copied and commented on favourably by several Winnipeg papers. After several effusions on "June" and kindred subjects appeared in that long-suffering *Patriot,* I was beginning to plume myself on being quite a literary person.

But the demon of filthy lucre was creeping into my heart. I wrote a story and sent it to the New York *Sun,* because I had been told that it paid for articles; and the New York *Sun* sent it back to me. I flinched, as from a slap in the face, but went on writing. You see I had learned the first, last, and middle lesson—"Never give up!" (p. 59)

After leaving Prince of Wales College I taught school for a year in Bideford, Prince Edward Island. I wrote a good deal and learned a good deal, but still my stuff came back, except from two periodicals the editors of which evidently thought that literature was its own reward, and quite independent of monetary considerations. I often wonder that I did not give up in utter discouragement. At first I used to feel dreadfully hurt when a story or poem over which I had laboured and agonized came back, with one of those icy little rejection slips. Tears of disappointment *would* come in spite of myself, as I crept away to hide the poor, crimpled manuscript in the depths of my trunk. But after a while I got hardened to it and did not mind. I only set my teeth and said "I will succeed." I believed in myself and I struggled on alone, in secrecy and silence. I never told my ambitions and efforts and failures to any one.

Down, deep down, under all discouragement and rebuff, I knew I would "arrive" some day.

In the autumn of 1895 I went to Halifax and spent the winter taking a selected course in English literature at Dalhousie College. Through the winter came a "Big Week" for me. On Monday I received a letter from *Golden Days,* a Philadelphia juvenile, accepting a short story I had sent there and enclosing a cheque for five dollars. It was the first money my pen had ever earned; I did not squander it in riotous living, neither did I invest it in necessary boots and gloves. I went up town and bought five volumes of poetry with it—Tennyson, Byron, Milton, Longfellow, Whittier. I wanted something I could keep for ever in memory of having "arrived."

On Wednesday of the same week I won the prize of five dollars offered by the Halifax *Evening Mail* for the best letter on the subject, "Which has the greater patience—man or woman?"

My letter was in the form of some verses, which I had composed during a sleepless night and got up at three o'clock in the wee sma' hours to write down. On Saturday the *Youth's Companion* sent me a cheque for twelve dollars for a poem. I really felt quite bloated with so much wealth. Never in my life, before or since have I been so rich!

After my Dalhousie winter I taught school for two more years. In those two years I wrote scores of stories, generally for Sunday School publications and juvenile periodicals. The following entry from my journal refers to this period:

> I have grubbed away industriously all this summer and ground out stories and verses on days so hot that I feared my very marrow would melt and my gray matter be hopelessly sizzled up. But oh, I love my work! I love spinning stories, and I love to sit by the window of my room and shape some "airy fairy" fancy into verse. I have got on well this summer and added several new journals to my list. They are a varied assortment, and their separate tastes all have to be catered to. I write a great many juvenile stories. I like doing these, but I should like it better if I didn't have to drag a "moral" into most of them. They won't sell without it, as a rule. So in the moral must go, broad or subtle, as suits the fibre of the particular editor I have in view. The kind of juvenile story I like best to write—and read, too, for the matter of that—is a good, jolly one, "art for art's sake," or rather "fun for fun's sake," with no insidious moral hidden away in it like a pill in a spoonful of jam!

It was not always hot weather when I was writing. During one of those winters of school teaching I boarded in a very cold farmhouse. In the evenings, after a day of strenuous school work, I would be too tired to write. So I religiously arose an hour earlier in the mornings for that purpose. For five months I got up at six o'clock and dressed by lamplight. The fires would not yet be on, of course, and the house would be very cold. But I would put on a heavy coat, sit on my feet to keep them from freezing and with fingers so cramped that I could scarcely hold the pen, I would write my "stunt" for the day. Sometimes it would

be a poem in which I would carol blithely of blue skies and rippling brooks and flowery meads! Then I would thaw out my hands, eat breakfast and go to school.

When people say to me, as they occasionally do, "Oh, how I envy you your gift, how I wish I could write as you do," I am inclined to wonder, with some inward amusement, how much they would have envied me on those dark, cold, winter mornings of my apprenticeship. (pp. 60-2)

In June, 1902, I returned to Cavendish, where I remained unbrokenly for the next nine years. For the first two years after my return I wrote only short stories and serials as before. But I was beginning to think of writing a book. It had always been my hope and ambition to write one. But I never seemed able to make a beginning.

I have always hated beginning a story. When I get the first paragraph written I feel as though it were half done. The rest comes easily. To begin a book, therefore, seemed quite a stupendous task. Besides, I did not see just how I could get time for it. I could not afford to take the time from my regular writing hours. And, in the end, I never deliberately sat down and said "Go to! Here are pens, paper, ink and plot. Let me write a book." It really all just "happened."

I had always kept a notebook in which I jotted down, as they occurred to me, ideas for plots, incidents, characters, and descriptions. In the spring of 1904 I was looking over this notebook in search of some idea for a short serial I wanted to write for a certain Sunday School paper. I found a faded entry, written many years before: "Elderly couple apply to orphan asylum for a boy. By mistake a girl is sent them." I thought this would do. I began to block out the chapters, devise, and select incidents and "brood up" my heroine. Anne—she was not so named of malice aforethought, but flashed into my fancy already christened, even to the all important "e"—began to expand in such a fashion that she soon seemed very real to me and took possession of me to an unusual extent. She appealed to me, and I thought it rather a shame to waste her on an ephemeral little serial. Then the thought came, "Write a book. You have the central idea. All you need do is to spread it out over enough chapters to amount to a book."

The result was ***Anne of Green Gables.*** I wrote it in the evenings after my regular day's work was done, wrote most of it at the window of the little gable room which had been mine for many years. I began it, as I have said, in the spring of 1904. I finished it in the October of 1905.

Ever since my first book was published I have been persecuted by the question "Was so-and-so the original of such-and-such in your book?" And behind my back they don't put it in the interrogative form, but in the affirmative. I know many people who have asserted that they are well acquainted with the "originals" of my characters. Now, for my own part, I have never, during all the years I have studied human nature, met one human being who could, as a whole, be put into a book without injuring it. Any artist knows that to paint *exactly* from life is to give a false impression of the subject. *Study* from life he must, copying suitable heads or arms, appropriating bits of character, personal or mental idiosyncrasies, "making use of the real to perfect the ideal."

But the ideal, his ideal, must be behind and beyond it all. The writer must *create* his characters, or they will not be life-like.

With but one exception I have never drawn any of my book people from life. That exception was "Peg Bowen" in *The Story Girl.* And even then I painted the lily very freely. I have used real places in my books and many real incidents. But hitherto I have depended wholly on the creative power of my own imagination for my characters.

Cavendish was "Avonlea" to a certain extent. "Lover's Lane" was a very beautiful lane through the woods on a neighbour's farm. It was a beloved haunt of mine from my earliest days. The "Shore Road" has a real existence, between Cavendish and Rustico. But the "White Way of Delight," "Wiltonmere," and "Violet Vale" were transplanted from the estates of my castles in Spain. "The Lake of Shining Waters" is generally supposed to be Cavendish Pond. This is not so. The pond I had in mind is the one at Park Corner, below Uncle John Campbell's house. But I suppose that a good many of the effects of light and shadow I had seen on the Cavendish pond figured unconsciously in my descriptions. Anne's habit of naming places was an old one of my own. I named all the pretty nooks and corners about the old farm. I had, I remember, a "Fairy-land," a "Dreamland," a "Pussy-Willow Palace," a "No-Man's-Land," a "Queen's Bower," and many others. The "Dryads Bubble" was purely imaginary, but the "Old Log Bridge" was a real thing. It was formed by a single large tree that had blown down and lay across the brook. It had served as a bridge to the generation before my time, and was hollowed out like a shell by the tread of hundreds of passing feet. Earth had blown into the crevices, and ferns and grasses had found root and fringed it luxuriantly. Velvet moss covered its sides and below was a deep, clear, sunflecked stream.

Anne's Katie Maurice was mine. In our sitting-room there had always stood a big book-case used as a china cabinet. In each door was a large oval glass, dimly reflecting the room. When I was very small each of my reflections in these glass doors were "real folk" to my imagination. The one in the left-hand door was Katie Maurice, the one in the right, Lucy Gray. Why I named them thus I cannot say. Wordsworth's ballad had no connection with the latter, for I had never read it at that time.

Indeed, I have no recollection of deliberately naming them at all. As far back as consciousness runs, Katie Maurice and Lucy Gray lived in the fairy room behind the book-case. Katie Maurice was a little girl like myself, and I loved her dearly. I would stand before that door and prattle to Katie for hours, giving and receiving confidences. In especial, I liked to do this at twilight, when the fire had been lit and the room and its reflections were a glamour of light and shadow.

Lucy Gray was grown-up and a widow! I did not like her as well as Katie. She was always sad, and always had dismal stories of her troubles to relate to me; nevertheless, I visited her scrupulously in turn, lest her feelings should be hurt, because she was jealous of Katie, who also disliked her. All this sounds like the veriest nonsense, but I cannot describe how real it was to me. I never passed through the room without a wave of my hand to Katie in the glass door at the other end.

The notable incident of the liniment cake happened when I was teaching school in Bideford and boarding at the Methodist parsonage there. Its charming mistress flavoured a layer cake with anodyne liniment one day. Never shall I forget the taste of that cake and the fun we had over it, for the mistake was not discovered until tea-time. A strange minister was there to tea that night. He ate every crumb of his piece of cake. What he thought of it we never discovered. Possibly he imagined it was simply some newfangled flavouring.

Many people have told me that they regretted Matthew's death in *Green Gables.* I regret it myself. If I had the book to write over again I would spare Matthew for several years. But when I wrote it I thought he must die, that there might be a necessity for self-sacrifice on Anne's part, so poor Matthew joined the long procession of ghosts that haunt my literary past.

Well, my book was finally written. The next thing was to find a publisher. I typewrote it myself, on my old second-hand typewriter that never made the capitals plain and wouldn't print "w" at all, and I sent it to a new American firm that had recently come to the front with several "best sellers." I thought I might stand a better chance with a new firm than with an old established one that had already a preferred list of writers. But the new firm very promptly sent it back. Next I sent it to one of the "old, established firms," and the old established firm sent it back. Then I sent it, in turn, to three "Betwixt-and-between firms", and they all sent it back. Four of them returned it with a cold, printed note of rejection; one of them "damned with faint praise." They wrote that "Our readers report that they find some merit in your story, but not enough to warrant its acceptance."

That finished me. I put *Anne* away in an old hat-box in the clothes room, resolving that some day when I had time I would take her and reduce her to the original seven chapters of her first incarnation. In that case I was tolerably sure of getting thirty-five dollars for her at least, and perhaps even forty.

The manuscript lay in the hatbox until I came across it one winter day while rummaging. I began turning over the leaves, reading a bit here and there. It didn't seem so very bad. "I'll try once more," I thought. The result was that a couple of months later an entry appeared in my journal to the effect that my book had been accepted. After some natural jubilation I wrote: "The book may or may not succeed. I wrote it for love, not money, but very often such books are the most successful, just as everything in the world that is born of true love has life in it, as nothing constructed for mercenary ends can ever have.

"Well, I've written my book! The dream dreamed years ago at that old brown desk in school has come true at last after years of toil and struggle. And the realization is sweet, almost as sweet as the dream."

When I wrote of the book succeeding or not succeeding,

I had in mind only a very moderate success indeed, compared to that which it did attain. I never dreamed that it would appeal to young and old. I thought girls in their teens might like to read it, that was the only audience I hoped to reach. But men and women who are grandparents have written to tell me how they loved **Anne,** and boys at college have done the same. The very day on which these words are written has come a letter to me from an English lad of nineteen, totally unknown to me, who writes that he is leaving for "the front" and wants to tell me "before he goes" how much my books and especially **Anne** have meant to him. It is in such letters that a writer finds meet reward for all sacrifice and labor.

Well, **Anne** was accepted; but I had to wait yet another year before the book was published. Then on June 20th, 1908, I wrote in my journal:

"To-day has been, as Anne herself would say, 'an epoch in my life.' My book came to-day, 'spleet-new' from the publishers. I candidly confess that it was to me a proud and wonderful and thrilling moment. There, in my hand, lay the material realization of all the dreams and hopes and ambitions and struggles of my whole conscious existence—my first book. Not a great book, but mine, mine, mine, something which I had created." (pp. 71-7)

With the publication of **Green Gables** my struggle was over. I have published six novels since then. . . .

The Story Girl was written in 1910 and published in 1911. It was the last book I wrote in my old home by the gable window where I had spent so many happy hours of creation. It is my own favourite among my books, the one that gave me the greatest pleasure to write, the one whose characters and landscape seem to me most real. All the children in the book are purely imaginary. The old "King Orchard" was a compound of our old orchard in Cavendish and the orchard at Park Corner. "Peg Bowen" was suggested by a half-witted, gypsy-like personage who roamed at large for many years over the Island and was the terror of my childhood. (p. 78)

[The] story of Nancy and Betty Sherman was founded on fact. The story of the captain of the *Fanny* is also literally true. The heroine is still living, or was a few years ago, and still retains much of the beauty which won the Captain's heart. **"The Blue Chest of Rachel Ward"** was another "ower-true tale." Rachel Ward was Eliza Montgomery, a cousin of my father's, who died in Toronto a few years ago. The blue chest was in the kitchen of Uncle John Campbell's house at Park Corner from 1849 until her death. We children heard its story many a time and speculated and dreamed over its contents, as we sat on it to study our lessons or eat our bed-time snacks. (p. 79)

The "Alpine Path" has been climbed, after many years of toil and endeavor. It was not an easy ascent, but even in the struggle at its hardest there was a delight and a zest known only to those who aspire to the heights. (p. 95)

L. M. Montgomery, in her The Alpine Path: The Story of My Career, *Fitzhenry & Whiteside Limited, 1974, 96 p.*

Ephraim Weber   (essay date 1944)

[*Weber was a Canadian author who wrote to Montgomery because he admired her poetry. They only met three times but established a friendship through steady correspondence that lasted for forty years. In the following excerpt, he argues that Montgomery's principal talent was her ability to create realistic and engaging characters.*]

To write with third-rate interest about the common people and their daily doings is easy; to write about them with second-rate interest is not extra hard; but to do it with first-rate interest is surprisingly difficult. L. M. Montgomery has depicted the common people of Prince Edward Island with first-rate interest; for, having grown up among them, she knows their ways, their traditions, their souls, as Dickens knows *his* islanders. And yet some of her critics are not won over; one of them, reviewing the later Canadian literature some years ago, called the Montgomery novels "the nadir of Canadian fiction." Of course the thrilling romantic plot is missing. To a reader of the old school, addicted to those far-spun yarns of romance vibrating with heroic excitement, the humbler affairs of the community novel may well be piddling neighborhood fusses. But many of the best late novels, highly rated and widely read, are quite without large-scale plot interest. What, no terrific tenseness between mighty antagonistic forces! No Himalayas scaled in pursuit of the villain! No war over the duchess! Well then, has the community novel any compensating substitute? The compensating substitute in the first-rate community novel is the interest of *reality.*

The interest of reality in the new Canadian novel is mainly *character* interest, heightened by concentrated regional setting; and not far behind is the interest of *incident.* To make up in this way for lack of plot structure is obviously no easy assignment. Before you know it, you have the dry rot of dullness—unless you scrape into unsavory realism. Then, too, this kind of fiction, far more than the heroic romance, attracts the spoiling imitator. Even so, if your author knows his kind and knows his art, the interest of reality fills the bill excellently.

Every day we meet people who have read a few of the "Anne" books, and there are those who have made a clean sweep of the Montgomery shelf, or have re-read parts of it. (pp. 64-5)

A German Mennonite girl of eleven comes to my study these times twice a week for a next "Anne" story, because "At the public library "Anne" books are always out, and the last one I had was all worn out and dirty." I quiz her a bit on these stories; her knowledge is surprising. What is there in them that fascinates this child, who is being brought up in a different social world and on a different language? It is surely her heart's response to the author's friendly human note and the living vividness of it all. "Montgomery girls," reported a bright tenth grade lass I was quizzing, "act just like we girls act; they're just so many of *us*. They just step out of the book and are with us." Her gusto in saying it showed how this middle-'teener enjoyed the illusion of reality. Herein is our author's opportunity: her upward trend and idealization of life is so naturally veiled as entertainment that our girls are off guard against being made better, and so *are* made better. (pp. 65-6)

So, are these Montgomery tales not nearer the zenith than the nadir? Can so many people of so many kinds in so many lands be charmed by *cheap* fiction with its anaemic reality? The adverse critics can still keep their souls in clover on ripping adventure, dashing romance, bigwig intrigue and unlimited realism.

Though it is still the Creator's secret how a talent produces its precise effects, let us visit the Montgomery study and see at least what distinguishing elements, what salt and savor, this creator puts into her characters. No, this is not an interview. Delicately sensitive to personality, she gets sharp impressions of people's inner selves, and is downright happy in exercising her resourceful inventiveness on all kinds of circumstances in which to show their behavior in action and to let us feel their atmosphere. To get us perfectly acquainted with her Island folks, she treats us to a liberal range of incidents, all the more engaging for their local color: Scotch Presbyterian and such. The reason her machinery does not creak is that she never proceeds by a technique she is learning, but just by an original instinct for her characters. Warm with emotion and animated by zest, she enters into them like a dramatist.

How she understands Matthew Cuthbert of **Green Gables**! When this lonely, taciturn soul speaks, he has something to say; his few words, so coolly spoken, make impressions. About such self-suppressing persons there emanates an aura of pathos, which we feel in this rude Scotchman, long-haired old farmer bachelor with a refined soul, a fair type of our pioneering bushwhackers. He has no one to love but a freckled, carrot-haired little thing of an orphan—and is afraid it may be discovered! (p. 68)

Quite as convincing a reality is Marilla, his old-maid sister. Are there, or have there ever been, such stern, dour, uncommunicative Scotch Presbyterians? Well, isn't this their very race-brand back a generation or two? Not on their sleeves but in their deep dense interiors they wear, or wore, their hearts. Added to years of the orphan's softening presence, it took Matthew's funeral to make Marilla confess she loved the child, loved her like her own flesh and blood; and in spite of her crabbed discipline she managed to tell her, "You've been my joy and comfort ever since you came to Green Gables." Her Scotch stubbornness—or shall we graciously call it her dogged consistency with her original grudge against the child for being a girl?—was sturdy stuff, backed up by the traditional asceticism, which supported her hard attitude; backed further by Matthew's secret love of the girl. The complexity is left nicely veiled, and makes good reading for those who know the old Scotch temperament. Though Marilla's earlier scoldings and denials give us heartache, we do not find it hard to forgive her in the end: "It's never been easy for me to say things out of my heart." Even some of us not exactly Scotch might give the old spinster a brotherly handshake on that if we could get ourselves to do it. But what a clean job she made of it once she got round to it! What a mother heart now has room to expand in her bosom! A reader told the author she regretted Matthew's early death; the author replied she had come to feel the same way, explaining her

object had been to bring Anne a needed sacrifice. Right or wrong, one fine thing accomplished by it is the highly-due humanization of Marilla. (pp. 68-9)

After a closer look at [Anne], all this about Marilla and Matthew needs to be re-read. Let us see what kind of energy, what sweetness and light, we can find in this World-Anne, whose major early troubles, next to her homelessness, were her carrot hair, her freckled nose, and the abomination of seeing her name without an *e*. (p. 69)

[At] the very start of the "Anne" fiction we have first class interest between humble character and humble circumstance: the anguish this sensitive child endures because she is a mistake and is to be driven out of her Eden to make room for a boy. An insipid character in this fine suspense would be boring. . . . Next comes the process of mistress bringing up ward—and ward "bringing up" mistress. "Father" had been brought up while listening to Anne's charming chat during the long buggy ride home. The old ascetic restraint and the new rebellion against it carry on the action, until by degrees the mistress is nine-tenths conquered and doesn't know it, at least hates to own it, even to herself. Not that the ward plotted it; her unconscious influence brought it about. Not Anne's outbreaks, but her quiet innate force liberalized the old-school Calvinist into healthy discipline. Still, the early strictness, though marred by harshness, had the effect of giving the child a compensating appreciation of life's blessings. Interesting reciprocity!

Anne is charming when she gets stormy. The abuses she suffers win her our tender feelings, which make her outbursts all the more startling. When the too neighborly Mrs. Rachel Lynde discharged her blunderbuss at her over her freckles, skinniness and carrot hair, she was "properly horrified" at the response she got; and nobody who was at Avonlea School the day Gilbert Blythe made fun of Anne's hair before the whole room when school was on will ever forget the scene she put up in dealing with him. Small events, these, but character and incident cooperate to make appealing young people's literature of them in their contexts; and appealing young people's literature makes no dull reading for older generations.

The "Anne" series of the Montgomery novels has as its main interest the development of this scrawny, sensitive orphan into a toughened and enlightened mother. To those who have not read **Green Gables,** the initial volume, this may sound blank and bleak, but only to those. Across the territory of these volumes her personality runs like a power line, distributing energy and light and love, right and left, wherever there is human material that can take the current. Naturally and satisfyingly her presence dominates the whole sequence. In letting such a mite evolve to such a power, the author has nowhere strained the laws and ways of reality to contrive an artificial perfection. Evolution has no grudge against the unlucky. To see Anne through her girlhood, 'teens and mature life is a great way for a girl to learn what unfading satisfaction can be got out of life without either sinking into drudging ambitionlessness or chafing to soar into flighty careering in public life and high society. Here we have that basic middle course which circles enduringly and fulfillingly about a woman's centre of gravity: a childhood home with nature's health and refinement playing about; enough choring to learn housekeeping; preparatory school, then college with its enlarging culture; a spicy nip of public life (school principal); a lovely courtship—such letters!—a fine married life &c. with its creative mystery; and in time that pleasant easing-off into lighter duties. (pp. 69-71)

Anne's unique originality, lively imagination, precocious wisdom, optimistic energy, versatile hearty serviceableness—all these in peculiar combination may well make her stand out. . . . (p. 71)

Reporting to the author on my complimentary copy of *Anne of Ingleside,* I noted how my wife and I were further impressed by her understanding of children, and how at spots our mellow smiles became 'teenish laughs; for the story was a delightfully undulating streak of entertainment. She replied I needn't have been so nice with my compliments: the yarn, spun to order as a fill-gap in Anne's life, was mainly padding. "But yarn and eiderdown, not hay," I retorted, bound to have the last word, "make nice padding." If this story lacks strict organic unity, it has at any rate the continuity of family raising, and such a family! Anne's, of course. One must know them, see them in action, overhear their remarks, be asked their questions, and feel the atmosphere, to get all there is.

As to gap-fillers: the Montgomery novels fall mainly into the "Anne," the "Emily," and the "Pat" groups. The first in each is written out of fascination for the dominating heroine, succeeding ones came at the insistence of readers and publishers of the first. L. M. M. did not experience heavenly joy in writing them all. . . . It is hard to think the author got no enjoyment out of the writing once she got warmed up to it; there is a live glow in it all. (pp. 71-2)

Are not these "Anne" stories as interesting as the coarse thrillers—to all but the sophisticated Smart Set and their following? The characters, Dog Monday and all, are normal and walk the plane we tread. After re-reading the books, can you imagine Anne as *fiction*? This Anne whose unconscious influence liberated, liberalized Marilla, Mrs. Lynde, Miss Barry; who stood her ground against the Pyes, the Sloanes, the Pringles; who meant so much to groping little Elizabeth and Paul, to gray-haired lonely Matthew, rugged Captain Jim, love-sick Charlotta the Fourth, gruff old Rebecca Dew; this Anne who, while making herself pluck roosters, roamed the Milky Way—can you doubt that if your daughters got to know her well, they would feel a stimulating lift from her toward becoming the girls they would like to be? (p. 73)

> *Ephraim Weber, "L. M. Montgomery's 'Anne'," in* The Dalhousie Review, *Vol. 24, No. 1, April, 1944, pp. 64-73.*

F. M. Frazer   (essay date 1975)

[*In the following essay, Frazer discusses Montgomery's short fiction in* The Road to Yesterday.]

Partisan Prince Edward Islanders, whose "How do you like our beautiful island?" is as automatic as other people's "How do you do", are understandably fond of all L. M. Montgomery's works and fanatical about *Anne of Green Gables.* Montgomery's picture of the island as a semi-magical, sea-girt garden is naturally appealing to patriots.

But they are far from alone in their enthusiasm. The most gifted English major graduating from the University of P. E. I. in 1973, a young woman now working toward a Ph.D. at the University of London, came to the Island university from Virginia because of *Anne.* And hers is only one testimony among thousands, though a particularly striking one, to the far-reaching and enduring power of Montgomery's first novel. The musical version by Donald Harron and Norman Campbell continues to draw overflowing audiences to every performance at the Charlottetown Summer Festival, where it has played for ten consecutive seasons. It was similarly successful at Expo 70 in Japan, and in England, where it won the London critics' award as the best musical of the 1968-69 crop. Admittedly, the stage show is now well launched as an independent entity, but fairly clearly the novel is the seminal draw.

Faced with such widespread and lasting love for one of her novels, one might expect a new book by Montgomery to be hailed as a literary event, the sort of thunderbolt, albeit of much smaller voltage, that we would recognize in the discovery of the concluding numbers of *Edwin Drood.* But *The Road to Yesterday,* a collection of fourteen stories unearthed by her son and now published for the first time, is unlikely to make much public impact. In other words, it is a consistent sequel to the other twenty books she wrote after *Anne,* and readers may well feel that she should have paid more attention to her Captain Jim of *Anne's House of Dreams* (1918) when he said, "A writing woman never knows when to stop; that's the trouble. The p'int of good writing is to know when to stop."

Austere readers, that is. For the rest of us, from the softhearted and sweet-toothed to the downright soppy, the book undoubtedly has touches of the old magic that flashed most frequently in *Anne* but also flickered intermittently in most of Montgomery's subsequent works. It is a magic composed of some honourable and some ignoble appeals. On the positive side are a few deft characterizations of lively, likeable characters like the early Anne of the "brisk mental processes", gorgeous imaginings, and penchant for "lifelong sorrows"; and some powerfully irritating portrayals of such unlovables as Anne's early antagonist, the appalling Josie Pye.

None of the protagonists in the current book rivals young Anne in either attractiveness or credibility, but there are several winning people, and the gallery of the nonheroic is not unimpressive. Perhaps the most memorable of the nonheroines is Myrtle Shelley, the grim old spinster of the story **"The Reconciliation"**. Decades ago, Miss Shelley lost her only beau, a glib, shallow fellow, to her best friend, the equally shallow but goodnatured Lisle. The jilting was abrupt and definite, and Miss Shelley's reaction was similarly emphatic: she slapped her rival's smiling face. Now, inspired by a revered minister's sermon on forgiveness, she sets out to make a great gesture of magnanimity. But charming, lightheaded Lisle, still charming in late middle age, long since married and widowed by someone else entirely, has quite forgotten the incident, and is merrily forgiving when reminded.

> To be forgiven when you came to forgive!
>
> Myrtle Shelley stood up. Her face had turned a dull crimson. Her faded blue eyes flashed fire. Deliberately she slapped Lisle Rogers across her smiling face—a hard, no-nonsense-about-it, tingling slap.
>
> "You didn't remember that first slap," she said. "Perhaps you will remember this one."

In fact, for all her saccharine maunderings about enchanted blue castles, white ways of delight, and latterday dryads by P. E. I. ponds, there is a streak of tough, humorous realism in L. M. Montgomery, and a broader conception of the capabilities and proclivities of human minds and spirits than she is normally given credit for. Early in *Anne of Green Gables,* Anne is compelled to apologize to Mrs. Lynde for repaying heedless adult cruelty with outraged reproach and rudeness. At first merely forced and persuaded, she soon warms to her task and indulges in such an orgy of self-abasement that even commonsensical Marilla is uneasy, though Anne herself is quite content. Occasionally Montgomery illuminates the uncomforting truth that it is possible to smile and smile and be a villain—or a fool, or something else not quite admirable—without ever realizing it oneself. So, in *The Road to Yesterday,* predatory relatives woo the eight-year-old heir to a fortune (**"The Cheated Child"**) with scarcely a glimmer of recognition that they don't really like him. And the ostensibly mourning relatives of **"A Commonplace Woman"**, putting in a long vigil as their Aunt Ursula dies, are comfortably conscious of their rectitude even as they fume with impatience.

Again on the positive side, Montgomery had a gift, though she sometimes betrayed it, for terse, telling phrases and effectively specific, tart dialogue. The cheated child's governess has a voice "as cold as rain". The raddled madwoman of **"A Dream Come True"** glares at her erstwhile admirer "in a way that made his skin crinkle". In **"A Commonplace Woman"** the heroine's perfunctory mourners try for appropriate sentiments:

> "Aunt Ursula was the best hand at a sponge cake I ever knew," said Uncle Alec.
>
> "What an epitaph!" said Emmy.

Then there are the less legitimate appeals, like the constant wish-fulfilments. If justice is not absolute in L. M. Montgomery's fiction, it comes incredibly close to that ideal state. Virtuous characters and sympathetic readers must suffer a little in the interest of plot—and so that the splendid compensations with compound interest will be particularly satisfying. But like the lady who simply couldn't manage to work in her doctor's diet allowances between her regular meals, Montgomery is considerably more interested in feasting than in fasting. And like enormous chocolate creams, her happy endings are individually delightful but cumulatively rather sickening.

On the face of it, a succession of just and beautiful endings

should be hard to sustain, and as I've said, Montgomery is in many ways a realist. Sometimes in this book she simply shifts key into quasi-fantasy or coyly invokes Divine Providence. Misty little Esmé of **"Fancy's Fool"**, a most insipid heroine, throws over a wealthy worldling and is rewarded with the reincarnation of a ghostly lover she once "met" in childhood when she accompanied her crazed (or enchanted) aunt into a haunted garden. Lincoln Burns, the amiable, hag-ridden bachelor of **"A Fool's Errand"**, succumbs obliquely to his sister's nagging insistence that he take a wife. He makes a pilgrimage to the distant beach where once long ago he proposed to a friendly little girl and bade her wait for him. She did wait. "He was not surprised to see a woman standing at the end of the sandy road, looking out over the sea. Somehow, it all fitted in, as if it had been planned ages ago."

Most often Montgomery pays her dues to credibility by sketching in the long sentences of sorrow or deprivation her protagonists have already served when she takes up their stories. Her philosophy seems to be that into every life a little sunshine must fall—only she chooses to bestow veritable sunbursts of blessings, monetary as well as spiritual.

Perhaps this need to mix realism with sugared romanticism, as much as her preoccupation with the past, accounts for the large number of late lovers' reunions in Montgomery's fiction. Half this collection of stories deals with present resolutions of old love affairs, one-sided or mutual.

Another kind of questionable nostalgia invests all fourteen stories, a kind identified by Montgomery's manuscript title for the book: "The Blythes are Quoted". The Blythes—Anne, Gilbert, their children, and their factotum Susan Baker—make fleeting appearances in the stories, or are at least quoted or considered. Presumably Montgomery hoped to invoke the old allure effortlessly exerted by young Anne but rarely approached by the subdued, gracious, queenly, birch-tree-kissing, conventionally romantic heroine she supposedly became. If so, the hope was worse than vain. For all the good-humoured tolerance of her infrequent remarks, Mrs. Blythe comes across as a painfully perfect goody-good. The moral conditions of characters are immediately signalled by their reactions to her. Admirers are obviously fine folk, and doubters are in spiritual peril. Decriers, envious and semirespectful though they tend to be, are plainly mad or bad. A kind of goddess, with Susan Baker as her priestess, Anne dwells apart, discussed but seldom seen by mere mortals. The effect is sadly stilted. Like Mazo de la Roche in the later Jalna books, Montgomery seems afraid to move a very popular character lest she jar the public's enchantment.

All in all, *The Road to Yesterday* has its charms, some dated and some not, some specious and some valid. But it is unlikely to appeal to a wide audience. The stories are not aimed at children, and are unlikely to attract teen-aged readers, now accustomed to rougher realism. They are certainly too novelettish to suit modern adult tastes. The chorus of the Harron-Campbell musical will probably carol "Anne of Green Gables, never change" to appreciative ears for years to come, while Montgomery's later books, including this posthumous one, leave scarcely an echo. For all Montgomery's real story-telling powers, the song underlines what seems to me a valid literary judgment. It ends, "Anne of Green Gables, in our hearts you are forever young." (pp. 89-92)

F. M. Frazer, "Scarcely an End," in Canadian
Literature, No. 63, Winter, 1975, pp. 89-92.

Mary Rubio (essay date 1975)

[*In the following excerpt, Rubio compares* Anne of Green Gables *to Mark Twain's* Tom Sawyer *(1876) and* The Adventures of Huckleberry Finn *(1884) and speculates on the aspects of Montgomery's novel that have brought it such lasting popularity.*]

It is interesting to speculate on what aspects of *Anne of Green Gables* have brought forth such a continuingly favourable response from so many people of varying ages and locales, with different degrees of literary sophistication. . . . Conceived as an adolescent novel, *Anne of Green Gables* surprised its author by appealing to young and old alike. In her letters to Ephraim Weber, Montgomery notes that the *Bookman* listed *Anne* as one of the six best-sellers in ten different major cities. Also, she summarizes the substance of a number of some sixty initial reviews, fifty-five of which are favourable. She tells Mr. Weber that Bliss Carman wrote a "flattering epistle" about the novel, but the greatest honour was receiving a letter from one of North America's most famous authors, Mark Twain, who wrote her "that in Anne I had created 'the dearest, and most lovable child in fiction since the immortal Alice'."

One of the only negative reviews of *Anne* appeared in the *New York Times.* The reviewer stated that the novel had "A mawkish, tiresome impossible heroine, combining the sentimentality of an Alfred Austin with the vocabulary of a Bernard Shaw." (It boggles the imagination to speculate on Shaw's response to any inference that he and Anne Shirley were at the same vocabulary level.) One thing is certain—had this reviewer been correct in his assessment of the novel, Montgomery would *not* have received such praise from Mark Twain. For in his own immensely popular novels of boyhood (*Tom Sawyer,* 1876; *The Adventures of Huckleberry Finn,* 1884,) Twain had directed devastating satire at any attitude or literary work which smacked of overblown romanticism or sentimentality. . . . Whatever criticism may be directed at *Anne,* one cannot dismiss it as typical of the overblown romantic fiction which was churned out for the popular markets of the day, the genre in which the *New York Times* reviewer puts it. (pp. 27-8)

Montgomery's publisher brought out Eleanor H. Porter's best-selling novel *Pollyanna* four years after *Anne of Green Gables.* On the surface, their heroines may appear comparable: both Anne and Pollyanna believe in the power of positive thinking. But *Pollyanna,* temporarily popular though it was, is an excellent example of a sentimental tear-jerker. The realism and genuine characterization in *Anne* become very apparent by comparison.

It is likely that Twain responded to Montgomery's novel partly because of its realism in presenting Anne and the psychological relationships between her and the external world. In addition, one can assume that an important factor in his response was his recognition of Montgomery's treatment of a socio-religious climate he knew well—small town Scotch-Presbyterianism. She, like he himself in both *Tom Sawyer* and *Huckleberry Finn,* had used hypocritical and distorted religious views and behaviour as the serious basis for comedy.

Both he and Montgomery shared the comic touch of the ironist. Very like Twain's hometown of Hannibal, L. M. Montgomery's hometown of Cavendish (fictionally depicted as Avonlea) was a small town inhabited by dignified and rigid Scotch-Presbyterians, upon whose character she maintained considerable perspective. She wrote Weber in March 1908 that she wondered if "religion has been a curse or a blessing to the world." In a delightful ironic sketch in the same letter, she describes

> an old lady who is one of the sweetest creatures alive. She would not harm a fly and I have seen her weep bitterly over the sufferings of a wounded cat. But it puts her in a simple fury to even hint that a merciful and loving God will hardly burn for all eternity the great majority of his creatures. I cannot understand this attitude on the part of so many. Nothing seems to enrage some people so much as any attempt to take away or mitigate their dearly beloved hell.

(pp. 28-9)

Both Montgomery and Twain had grown up with exposure to a distinctive variety of "Sunday school literature," a genre of 18th and 19th century writing which pretended to record the short life-history and sayings of child saints who lived perfect lives and died young, often after much suffering. Such literature, which had grown originally out of the Puritan concern for children's souls, was given *raison d'être* by the fact that infant mortality rates were so high. The Methodist and Sunday School movements of the 19th century prolonged the distribution of this type of children's literature, and the moralism present in it is also present in much of the secular fiction of the 19th century. It is reasonable to suspect that Twain's original impetus to create "bad" boys who steal and lie, but who are likeable in spite of their "sins" was the result of a childhood overdose of fictional "good" boys whom he found unpalatable. L. M. Montgomery comments that reading about little earthly saints convinced her that she could never be as good as they, so she might as well not try. (p. 29)

Such similarities in background may be responsible for the many ways in which Montgomery's and Twain's novels resemble each other. In each the central tension derives from the difference in perception between the adult and the child. The first character we meet in *Anne* is Mrs. Rachel Lynde, her house appropriately positioned where she can witness everything that goes on in the village. Montgomery presents her as the norm in the village, and Marilla is caught unwillingly in the middle trying to bring Rachel and Anne Shirley closer together in perception of acceptable behaviour. Anne, maturing, brings her own perspectives more in line with those of the village by the end of the novel, and Mrs. Lynde becomes less rigid. Likewise, Tom Sawyer and his Aunt Polly as well as Huck Finn and the Widow Douglas (and Miss Watson) have perspectives which are at odds with each other. Montgomery emphasizes the imaginative nature of the child-vision, whereas Twain focuses on its innocence; but whichever the focus, the child and the adult view the world from very different vantage points. And, it is from this discrepancy in viewpoint that the humour and the reality in each novel arise.

For instance, both authors show the adult vision of the world to be partly rooted in the Calvinistic Scotch-Presbyterian framework. Adults in all three novels are a relatively humourless bunch who take themselves and their lives very seriously. They distrust pleasure and frivolity, even if it is manifested in such harmless things as puffy sleeves and flowers on Sunday hats. The sparse, bare room which Anne enters at Green Gables reflects the no-frill nature of Marilla's personality, and Montgomery contrasts the icy-white of the room with Anne's perception of the glorious white of nature's blossoms outside.

At the beginning of *Anne,* Matthew is clearly the product of a repressive society: his personality is locked, inarticulate, within him. He is not afraid merely to express his opinions, he is afraid even to have them. During his four-year association with Anne, her spontaneity and love gradually draw him out, and his final fulfillment before his death comes in his being able to articulate his love for her in words. The simplicity of his words makes them even more touching: "Well now, I'd rather have you than a dozen boys, Anne . . . It was a girl—my girl—that I'm proud of."

In *Tom Sawyer* it is Aunt Polly who gives Tom little indication, verbal or otherwise, that she truly values and loves him. Though she is an extremely kind person, the natural and the spontaneous are repressed in her. She does cruel things to Tom in the belief that he will be bettered by a little suffering; worse, she fails to express her love for him. Only when she believes him dead does she express the extent of her affection. Fortunately for him and their future relationship, Tom has the emotional satisfaction of seeing her weeping for him.

Twain and Montgomery criticize the way religion is practised at various points in their works. Anne remarks that "Some people are naturally good, you know, and others are not. I'm one of the others. Mrs. Lynde says I'm full of original sin." Later she tells Marilla "When I'm with Mrs. Lynde I feel desperately wicked and as if I wanted to go and do the very thing she tells me I oughtn't to do. . . . Do you think it's because I'm really bad and unregenerate?" Fortunately, these spiritual worries don't oppress Anne's lively nature long. Tom Sawyer and Huck Finn—especially Huck—are not so fortunate: Huck labours under his conscience throughout the whole novel as he tries to reconcile the position of religious yet slave-holding adults with his own naive and supposedly 'wicked' view that being cruel to Negroes is wrong. Finally his "sound heart and deformed conscience" lead him to choose going to Hell as the result of freeing a slave above accepting the religious hypocrisy of adults.

Likewise, the matter of prayers gives Montgomery and Twain a source of more comedy. When scolded by Marilla for failure to say her prayers, Anne replies, "Mrs. Thomas told me that God made my hair red *on purpose,* and I've never cared about Him since. And anyhow I'd always be too tired at night to bother saying prayers. People who have to look after twins can't be expected to say their prayers." Anne's practical and childishly literal approach to prayer is reminiscent of Huck's: as he tells it, Miss Watson "told me to pray every day, and whatever I asked for I would get it. But it warn't so. I tried it. Once I got a fish-line, but no hooks. It warn't any good to me without hooks."

Some of the funniest incidents in both **Anne** and *Tom Sawyer* grow out of the adult conviction that a certain amount of suffering and humiliation in punishment is good for children. Anne's apology to Mrs. Lynde becomes unacceptable even though it is a very sincere apology because Anne enjoys delivering it. She becomes so caught up in doing it well with big words and dramatic gestures that she positively enjoys her own performance as one does an onerous task done well. Clearly it is not the act of apology, or the repentance it represents, but the suffering attendant upon it which is important. Likewise, had Aunt Polly realized the way in which Tom turned fence white-washing into a task full of positive enjoyment as well as profit, she would have been outraged rather than pleased at his cleverness and ingenuity. In each case humour comes through the reader's recognition that the adult position is slightly unreasonable; thus the situation becomes comic when the children outmaneuver the adults. There is delightful comic irony evoked by any such situation.

Thus, religion serves behind the scenes as a basis for humour: the religious background is the source of much of the tension in the novel, tension upon which the surface comedy can be built. It is the discrepancy between the outlandish behaviour of child heroines and heroes (Tom, Huck, Anne Shirley) and the acceptable norm in a quite small town (St. Petersburg and Avonlea) which creates the humour. Although childhood spontaneity can be repressed by many factors other than by distorted religiosity, in these three novels the adult perspective to a large extent results from a code of behaviour established by the literalism of small town and small-minded churchgoers. Neither Twain nor Montgomery attack religion: they use distortions of it for comedy. But to dwell any longer on aspects of religious satire in Anne would be to distort the focus of Montgomery's work.

Both Montgomery and Twain, writing from mature perspectives, treat their respective communities and characters with humour and affection. Each had an eye for the incongruous, the comic dimension in human behaviour which results when adults and children alike take themselves too seriously and affect pompousness in language or action. Montgomery makes use of the difference between Anne's level of diction and her level of understanding: Anne's phrases, taken from her reading of sentimental fiction apparently, far exceed her level of maturation and understanding. Likewise, Tom Sawyer's imagination also is full of many undigested novels about pirates and robbers.

Huck Finn, a much more complex work, uses a slightly converse situation. Huck's verbal abilities are moderate, but, naive as he may seem, his level of intuitive understanding is high. In each case, the reader is aware of the ironic contrast between level of diction and level of comprehension, a contrast which achieves both humour and satire.

Both authors enjoy setting their characters in formal, ritualistic situations and then deflating the ritual with a grossly inappropriate but plausible event. Marilla's dignified meal for the stylish Mr. and Mrs. Chester Ross is devastated by Anne's horrified shriek that the pudding sauce being served is one from which she had removed a drowned mouse earlier in the day. Likewise, in Twain, people fall accidentally into graves during the most solemn moments, dogs howl in the middle of pompous funeral orations, interminable church services are disrupted by the yelps of unfortunate dogs who sit on pinching bugs, and so on.

Aside from *Anne*'s comic and satiric elements, what has been responsible for its initial and continuing success? In spite of parallels between *Anne* and Twain's two novels of boyhood, Montgomery's work owes its success to elements distinctively its own: Anne is not a female Twain character. There are, in Anne, other areas which deserve comment: Montgomery's combination of realism and romanticism, her treatment of the imagination, and her perceptive dealing with the psychological needs of humans, both children and adults.

Anne of Green Gables is best considered as an example of literary realism, despite the fact that it contains such elements as haunted woods which are typical of romance. One of the realities which children can build up is a world of imaginative romance and dreams, and we must keep in mind that most of the highflown romance in *Anne* exists because Anne creates it in her mind. Her imagination takes over early in the book, and it is primarily from her point-of-view that we see much of Avonlea. She may be a pretentious little girl who has read too much without digesting it, but as such she represents a type of precocious adolescent who is familiar and realistic. Montgomery places her in a specific and realistic setting, and we finish the book with a good sense of what it was like to be a child living in a small Prince Edward Island town around 1900.

Anne Shirley uses the worst sentimental clichés when she talks. These serve a greater function than to create humour or to characterize her, however: through Anne's overly dramatic and flowery speech, Montgomery is able to satirize romance. Montgomery, writing of her own childhood, tells us that she was brought up with such "Literary pablum" as *Godey's Lady's Book,* which she always "devoured ravenously, crying my eyes out in delicious woe over the agonies of heroines who were all superlatively good and beautiful." Montgomery, who also spent a considerable amount of her own time doing hack writing for money, was obviously quite aware of the distinction between fresh and hackneyed expression. Anne's overripe diction is clearly intended to be comic, not only because it is inappropriate speech for a girl her age, but also because it is very trite and hackneyed in itself. Montgomery is clearly satirizing the popular literary taste for sentimen-

tal cliches just as Twain does in *Huck Finn* when he exposes us to the poetry of sweet little dead Emmeline Grangerford, poetry which outdoes the worst of the sentimental female versifiers who were then popular. (pp. 29-33)

Perhaps another of the factors which has made *Anne of Green Gables* so successful both with adults and children is Montgomery's treatment of the imagination. The term "imagination" was a prominent one in the 18th and 19th centuries. By the time Montgomery used the term, it had become quite ambiguous through application to many contexts. At its worst it had come to mean pure escapism; at its best, it was a faculty by which man ordered the world into a complex set of symbols, both verbal and spatial, and determined his own relationship to them. To have an imagination (then and now) designated an ability to create dimensions to one's internal landscape into which one could go, alone or with companions, to explore fully the meaning of being human; it was a place where one ordered sensory experience to give it meaning; where one came to terms with himself, determined his own identity, and emerged as a human being with a vision more profound.

The term "imagination" is one of the key words and concepts in *Anne of Green Gables.* What, however, does Montgomery mean when she speaks of it?

Anne possesses imagination in both the worst and the best of senses. When we first meet her she retreats to imaginary worlds from an unhappy real world. But she also possesses an unique ability to take ordinary sensory data from the external landscape of Avonlea and arrange it within her own imagination into a fascinating world. Whereas Anne looks through a window and sees a world that is "wonderful" outside, Marilla looks through the same window at the same time and sees only a big tree that "blooms great, but the fruit . . . [is] small and wormy." Most people are very much influenced by the constructions which other people place on reality; a political orator, a popular singer, an evangelist—each can completely catch us up in his own perception of reality. We can enter his imagination and see the world defined by his mood and by his particular arrangement of symbols. Some people perceive the world as a place of great struggle and probable defeat for them; external objects in their environment become threats. Other people regard the world as a challenge and a pleasure; the same factors which threatened the first group are a stimulus to the second. Anne Shirley possesses a perception of the world close to the second: readers love her for it.

The "imagination" has been much maligned by religion. Certainly we can see Marilla's distrust of it: "I don't believe in imagining things different from what they really are," she says; "When the Lord puts us in certain circumstances He doesn't mean for us to imagine them away." What Marilla's literal mind fails to discern is the difficulty of determining how things *really* are in reality. The external world does not exist for us until our senses gather data and our minds interpret it. Marilla might well reflect that a literal reading of the Bible tells us that one of the first requirements which God made of man after creation was that man use his imaginative faculty to name the animals which He had created.

Like Adam, Anne Shirley's first important act after coming to Avonlea is to rename the external world which she finds. "The Avenue," a stretch of blooming apple trees, is rechristened "the White Way of Delight," and "Barry's Pond" becomes "The Lake of Shining Waters." The names she chooses show us the particular quality of her perception of reality. She takes the commonplace and makes it beautiful. Marilla and Matthew do not have enough literary sophistication to realize that the particular phrases which Anne chooses to externalize her vision are somewhat hackneyed—they are merely enchanted with the positive nature of the vision itself.

Anne's stay in Avonlea is a fascinating study of how one's imaginative perception of the world can in effect metamorphose the actual structure of the world. One of the most exciting and satisfying aspects of the novel is Anne's transformation of an ordinary farm into a fairyland and of an inarticulate old bachelor and a cheerless old maid into people who can articulate their love.

Dour old Aunt Josephine Barry, in her selfish way, speaks for many readers when she summarizes her responses to Anne: "She makes me like her because she is interesting." Most humans are a little short on imagination and, like Aunt Josephine, enjoy being lifted out of commonplace lives by a free spirit like Anne.

I think that ultimately what readers respond to in *Anne* is not the mementary, amusing diversion of Anne's imaginative flights of fancy, but rather something far more powerful—the recognition that our perception of reality often becomes the blueprint for our lives. Our expectations can create our future. . . . Anne herself is aware of the importance of one's own perception of reality. She says "I read in a book once that a rose by any other name would smell as sweet, but I've never been able to believe it. I don't believe a rose *would* be as nice if it was called a thistle or a skunk cabbage."

That the vision of the individual imagination gave existence and shape to the external world was a tenet of literary romanticism; it is also, in the 1970's, an idea being explored by modern psychologists who have demonstrated, for instance, that a child who perceives himself as a failure is quite likely to become one, no matter how great his native abilities may be. But in 1908 when *Anne of Green Gables* appeared, such a doctrine ran counter to the sociological and biological determinism of the age. Other contemporary literary heroines of serious adult fiction had little or no ability to control the direction of their lives. Maggie, in Stephen Crane's *Maggie, A Girl of the Streets* (1896), is doomed by her environment from the beginning; Dreiser's heroine in *Sister Carrie* (1900, 1912) is a "little soldier of fortune," buffeted by fate and forces totally beyond her control. In an intellectual climate where people were presented as helpless either because of their own biological make-up or because of the social atmosphere in which they lived, novels such as *Anne of Green Gables,* suggested that one's imagination could influence the external world.

Today, children of the Anne Shirley age (11-15 in the novel) are beginning to test their wings outside the family.

They can watch Anne manipulate her environment. When she first meets Marilla and Matthew they are most unpromising parents; all humanity in them seems to be repressed, and what is more, they don't want her because she is a girl. Yet, they are better than the alternative, and Anne determines to find warmth and human kindness in them. At first, her manipulations are obvious—she tells Matthew and Marilla that she is an orphan that nobody ever loved and that she expects to be treated as badly by them as by everyone else. But her ability to control her environment is achieved by far more than such obvious manipulation: she presents herself as an interesting and impulsive child, one the Cuthberts need because she can furnish them with the psychological, emotional, and imaginative dimensions which are lacking in their own lives. And she does the same for us, the readers. (pp. 33-5)

Mary Rubio, "Satire, Realism, and Imagination in 'Anne of Green Gables'," in Canadian Children's Literature, No. 3, 1975, pp. 27-36.

Thomas E. Tausky (essay date 1983)

[*In the following excerpt, Tausky contends that the Emily trilogy* (Emily of New Moon, Emily Climbs, *and* Emily's Quest) *is a "spiritual autobiography" that traces the corresponding ecstasy and despair that the protagonist experiences as she attempts to dedicate herself to art and yet conform to society.*]

[*Emily of New Moon, Emily Climbs,* and *Emily's Quest*] can be read as the fictionalized confession of a troubled personality alternating between confidence in creativity and despairing self-doubt. Before the first of these novels was completed, Montgomery confided to a friend that Emily was an autobiographical character. . . . Critics have subsequently remarked upon the abundant parallels between Montgomery's literary career and the "Alpine Path" climbed by Emily. The comparison extend to deeper matters of the spirit, as is indicated by the juxtaposition of Montgomery's January 8, 1908 letter to [G. B.] MacMillan with a passage from Emily's diary in *Emily's Quest:*

> Do you take the "blues" too . . . I cannot fully describe these experiences . . . They *are dreadful,* far worse than physical pain. In so far as I can express my condition in words, I feel a great and awful *weariness*—not of body or mind but of *feeling,* coupled with a strange dread of the future—*any* future, even a happy one—nay, a happy one most of all for in this strange mood it seems to me that to be happy would require more *emotional energy* than I will possess.

> Gloom settles on my soul. I can't describe the feeling. It is dreadful—worse than any actual pain. In so far as I can express it in words I feel a great and awful weariness—not of body or brain but of *feeling,* coupled with a haunting dread of the future—*any* future—even a happy one—nay, a happy one most of all, for in this strange mood it seems to me that to be happy would require more effort—more buoyancy than I shall possess.

The duplication of phrasing in passages written more than a decade apart is astounding. Montgomery was in the habit of making one set of reflections serve more than one correspondent, and in this instance one must suspect that she attributed her innermost feelings to Emily by referring either to the original letter or to her personal diaries. In any event, the passages certainly demonstrate Montgomery's sense of identification with her protagonist.

Emily's story does not always take such a melancholy turn. Indeed, it follows the pattern of Montgomery's life in being on the surface a story of triumph. Emily finds a place in her family and community despite the opposition of disagreeable relatives and narrow-minded fellow citizens; she succeeds as an author, first with money-making potboilers and then with more artistic works, despite negative reactions from both family and publishers; she achieves happiness in love despite malicious attempts to separate her from her partner. Yet throughout all three books, as much emphasis is placed on the obstacles to success (both external and within Emily herself) as upon the ultimate victories.

Emily of New Moon concentrates on Emily's integration within the Murray family, and on her initial attempts to make herself into an artist. As the story of an isolated individual finding a new self-definition within a family, *Emily of New Moon* superficially resembles *Anne of Green Gables:* in both cases an orphan learns how to gain the affection she desperately craves, and in return transforms the character of her guardians. Yet, in several respects, the process of mutual adjustment is more complex and troubled in *Emily* than in the earlier novel. Anne quickly wins Matthew Cuthbert's heart, and although her conquest of Marilla is more gradual, it is evident from an early stage that Marilla has the warmth of heart to respond to Anne's charm. Emily has an ally corresponding to Matthew in Cousin Jimmy Murray, but in Elizabeth and Laura Murray, she has to contend with the two sides of Marilla's personality split into separate characters: Laura is all sympathy but ineffectual, and Elizabeth, the dominant spirit in the New Moon household, is cold, moralistic and self-righteous. Marilla's increasing acceptance of Anne is clearly indicated before the middle of *Anne,* whereas the turning-point of Emily's relationship with Elizabeth does not occur until *Emily* is nearly at its conclusion. When Elizabeth chooses to read unflattering descriptions of herself contained in Emily's confessional "letters" to her dead father, the resulting confrontation is presented at a level of seriousness altogether lacking in *Anne.* . . . (pp. 5-7)

For much of *Emily of New Moon,* our heroine is not even certain she wants to be accepted as a Murray. Here again, she differs from Anne, who has nothing but bitter memories to serve as an alternative to life with the Cuthberts. Emily can think of herself as a Starr, her father's child, and it is not until the aftermath of her quarrel with Elizabeth that she gives up the allegiance to her father implicit in her habit of writing letters to him.

Douglas Starr leaves a lasting imprint on his daughter in another respect: he constitutes her first image of the life of a writer. . . . Speaking to Emily on his deathbed, he has to admit that "from a worldly point of view I've cer-

tainly been a failure," . . . but takes consolation in the idea that "You have my gift . . . you will succeed where I have failed." . . . The prophecy proves to be correct, partly because Emily is determined to play out the role her father has cast for her. The image of the artist as an alienated outcast, financially insecure and scornfully regarded as a failure, is established through the character of Douglas Starr in the trilogy's opening pages, and is never completely abandoned in the nine hundred pages that follow. (p. 7)

If the oppressive events of real life can threaten to snuff out Emily's artistic flame, writing itself can sometimes counteract the pains of reality. Over and over again, Emily assuages the humiliation of a public defeat by retreating to the private world of her imagination. Her capacity to weave the distorted elements of reality into a healing fantasy often gives a necessary boost to morale in her vulnerable early years. Moreover, it is an indication of the talent Montgomery ascribes to her heroine that in the process of working out her tales, Emily moves from simple wish-fulfillment to a genuine absorption in the imagined world. . . . So far, fiction has simply cured Emily of her distress. But the entry into a creative world is suggested immediately afterwards, in the paradox of artistry that "she forgot the Murrays although she was writing about them."

The seriousness of Emily's self-image as a writer is particularly evident in *Emily of New Moon*'s final pages. Emily is determined not to give up her art, even when ordered to do so by her aunt. . . . Emily's consciousness of the similar dedication of her artist friends strengthens her resolve. . . . Montgomery also chooses to make Emily's compulsion to write the subject of the novel's concluding scene, in a chapter revealingly entitled "Emily's Great Moment." She nervously submits her work to Mr. Carpenter, a stern judge. He acidly denounces the failings of her poetry; however, like both Father Cassidy and Dean Priest before him, he is less concerned with the modest achievement of the present than with the character of the artist: "I think there's *something* trying to speak through you—but you'll have to make yourself a fit instrument for it." . . . He cross-examines her on her basic motivation, and only when she assures him that apart from loving to write she feels she *has* to write does he utter his benediction, urging her to "go on—climb!" . . .

Father Cassidy had already advised Emily to "keep on" . . . but the metaphor of ascent is given a more prominent place in the novel, as it seems to have had a more prominent place in Montgomery's own imagination. Montgomery had already chosen *The Alpine Path* as the title of her autobiographical sketch . . . , and the phrase is mentioned innumerable times throughout the *Emily* trilogy. . . . [The] poem does provide an external sanction for Emily's own guiding principles: the reliance upon Nature, the need for determination, confidence that literary success constitutes a worthy goal. (pp. 9-10)

Emily Climbs, the second volume of the trilogy, shows Emily making considerable progress along the literary slopes. . . . This success is achieved, however, in the face of obstacles every bit as discouraging as those encountered in *Emily of New Moon.* (p. 10)

In *Emily of New Moon,* becoming a artist was not, on the whole, incompatible with becoming a Murray; in *Emily Climbs,* however, the necessity for Emily to make painful choices becomes evident.

The inner drive to escape the suffocating confinement of a conventional milieu is a common subject in novels of the *bildungsroman* type. In *Emily Climbs,* Shrewsbury and Aunt Ruth are certainly all one could wish as a justification for shaking the red dust of the Island from one's feet. Yet Emily does not go; indeed, in the major scene of the novel, she consciously rejects an opportunity to go. In taking this decision, she makes a gesture similar to Anne's loyalty to Green Gables, but Emily does not face the tangible crisis that overwhelms the Cuthberts; hers is a totally voluntary act of renunciation. This episode gives *Emily Climbs* its greatest interest. Though this novel, more than its companions, often seems shapeless, it ultimately turns into a meditation upon inner freedom, particularly the freedom of the artist.

The choice is created for Emily when a Shrewsbury native who has become a successful New York editor offers to introduce her to the literary life of the big city. Until the moment of choice, Emily develops a sense of identification with and loyalty towards the Murray tradition, all the while preserving, with equal passion, the sense of detachment, the aloneness, of the artist. The intrinsic contradictions in Emily's values are revealed in a passage a few chapters before the appropriately-named Miss Royal arrives with her autocratic summons to literary glory. Emily reproaches herself on one page for confiding too much in Ilse because "it is not a Murray tradition to turn your soul inside out," . . . in the same diary entry, however, she complains bitterly about the obstacles to freedom:

> Nobody is free—never, except just for a few brief moments now and then, when the flash comes . . . All the rest of our years we are slaves to something—traditions—conventions—ambitions—*relations.*
>
> (pp. 11-12)

Emily's rejection of the temptation offered by Miss Royal appears at first sight to be a vote in favour of the Philistine Murray tradition, and even against literary aspiration. Miss Royal argues, plausibly enough, that "you mustn't waste your life here. . . . You must have . . . the training that only a great city can give." . . . The basis for Emily's response seems clear enough: "I belong to New Moon—I stay among my own people." . . . Yet on close examination, Emily's decision is not as unequivocal as it seems. Miss Royal offers herself, not just as a friendly adviser, but as a surrogate guardian. . . . Indeed, the repeated suggestion that Miss Royal has a penchant for attractive girls implies the interest of a sublimated Lesbian as well as substitute mother and frustrated author. In short, Emily has reason to suspect that Miss Royal would pose a greater threat than any Murray to her creative and personal independence. Just before Emily makes her final decision, her meditations show that she has come to feel that freedom

and stimulus to the imagination are to be associated with New Moon, not New York:

> Would the Wind Woman come to her in the crowded city streets? Could she be like Kipling's cat there? "And I wonder if I'll ever have the flash in New York," she thought wistfully.
>
> (p. 12)

It is appropriate that Emily should think of Kipling's cat at this crucial moment, for she has already used this literary animal as a symbol of her need for independence. The allusion is to "The cat that walked by himself," from *Just So Stories;* it is necessary to recall the fable briefly in order to evaluate its significance for Emily. The Cat desires the comforts of cave life, and yet will not give up his separateness. After a series of tough negotiations with the Woman, he agrees to provide needed services, and gains the privileges he desires. But he continues to insist on his lack of attachment to humanity, and at the end the narrator affirms his victory:

> But when he has done that, and between times, and when the moon gets up and night comes, he is the Cat that walks by himself, and all places are alike to him. Then he goes out to the Wet Wild Woods or up the Wet Wild Trees or on the Wet Wild Roofs, waving his wild tail and walking by his wild lone.

Much of Emily's character and behaviour can be understood in the light of the Kipling passage. Like the Cat, Emily has a need to make an alliance with human society; like the Cat, she brings benefits with her coming. But she is resentful of attacks upon her freedom, and remains faithful (like the Cat in the quoted passage) to a kinship with Nature in its untamed aspect.

Emily is given to associating herself with the Cat as a means of bolstering her identity when it is under attack from the Murrays. In the aftermath of the scene in which Aunt Elizabeth outlaws fiction, Emily defines her consciousness of being different from a Murray:

> I'm like Kipling's cat—I walk by my wild lone and wave my wild tail where so it pleases me. That's why the Murrays look askance at me. They think I should only run with the pack. . . .

The same allusion is used later on when Emily finds herself in disgrace with the Murrays yet again:

> I hate to go mincing through life, afraid to take a single long step for fear somebody is watching. I want to "wave my wild tail and walk by my wild lone." . . .

In an introspective passage of a letter to [Ephraim] Weber, Montgomery reveals that Emily's emotional identification with Kipling's cat springs from her own feeling:

> I have generally been considered a "good mixer" myself—but I am *not.* I am only an excellent imitation of one—compelled to play the part by the circumstances of my existence. In reality I detest "good mixers" and despise myself for aping them . . . The only people I ever knew who were really worth while were cats who walked by

themselves, rejoicing in their own peculiar brand of cathood and never pretending to be Maltese if they were tortoise shell.

The vehement tone of this passage and the image it develops, as much as its content, are indications that Emily's creator had very much at heart her protagonist's struggle to assert independence in the face of the circumstances of her existence.

Emily's Quest, the third volume of the trilogy, explores the consequences of Emily's decision to wave her wild tail in New Moon. Emily is not, however, allowed in the end to walk by her wild lone; the novel concludes with the marriage, not exactly a surprise to the reader, between Emily and Teddy Kent. Though *Emily's Quest* is more tightly knit than *Emily Climbs,* and contains much psychological interest, it subordinates Emily as artist to Emily as lover, and thereby disappoints some of the expectations aroused by the earlier books.

Yet there are some episodes and introspective passages in which Emily's dedication to her craft returns with the former seriousness. For example, the effects of a diseased love upon creativity are dramatized when Dean Priest deliberately condemns Emily's newly written first novel in order to claim her undivided heart. Montgomery underlines the magnitude of the evil inherent in this design by having Emily burn her manuscript . . . and then blunder into a fall that nearly costs her life: physical danger symbolizes the danger to the soul. When Emily recovers and forces herself to contemplate marriage with Dean, he wins an apparent victory in that she temporarily turns against writing; it is only after she frees herself from the incubus of Dean that the "miracle" . . . of a return to creativity occurs.

After this crisis has been resolved, Emily is finally able to reap the benefits of her long apprenticeship to art. A second novel is accepted by a very prominent publisher. Within her family, Emily is finally forgiven for being a writer: "It was better to have won her standing with the New Moon folks than with the world." . . . The opinion of the literary judges Emily values most is also favourable: Dean is won over, and Miss Royal is forced to admit that "You could never have written *The Moral of the Rose* here [i.e. in New York]." . . . With this concession, Emily can feel that the decision to remain at New Moon, which she herself questions through much of *Emily's Quest,* has been justified in literary as well as personal terms.

So, after many stumbles, Emily has climbed her Alpine Path. Nevertheless, for the young woman Montgomery portrays in *Emily's Quest* (quite a different person from the girl of the two earlier novels), literary success alone is no guarantee of happiness. Montgomery has Emily avow throughout the final novel that Teddy means more to her than the Alpine Path. Just before Teddy returns to provide the necessary happy ending, Emily feels utterly abandoned. . . . The character who had once resolved never to marry and to be *"wedded to my art"* . . . (emphasis Montgomery's) has certainly changed her outlook.

Montgomery's own changes of heart about the trilogy, as revealed in her correspondence, help to explain the shift

in direction one may detect in *Emily's Quest.* Her mood while at work on *Emily of New Moon* is strongly enthusiastic. . . . But when she turns to *Emily Climbs,* she comments

> I am working on a second Emily book now and later there will be a third. These two will be only hack-work. But I enjoyed writing *Emily of New Moon* and I do think it is good *of its kind.* The charm went out when I finished it and cannot be recaptured for a whole series.

This passage was written well before *Emily Climbs* was published; in retrospect, when she got stuck attempting to finish *Emily's Quest,* Montgomery came to feel that the task of writing *Emily Climbs* was not so bad after all:

> I wrote *Emily of New Moon* with intense pleasure. I wrote *Emily Climbs* not unenjoyably. But I have written Emily III so far with reluctance and distaste. So it will not amount to anything.

One reason for Montgomery's gloom is that as an author no less than as a minister's wife, she feels compelled to meet public expectations she is not inclined to satisfy. . . . In another complaint, Montgomery blames her own incapacity, rather than external pressures, for her difficulties with *Emily's Quest:*

> You ask about my literary activities. Well, just now I am trying to marry Emily off and am finding her a bit of a handful. Not because of any special perversity on her part—but simply because—alack!—I can't write a young-girl-romantic-love story. My impish sense of humour always spoils everything.

We do not have to accept without qualification Montgomery's somewhat contradictory expressions of despondency about the last two volumes of the trilogy. Writers have often disparaged some of their best work. In this instance, I think Montgomery was right to feel that *Emily of New Moon* was the best novel in the trilogy, and *Emily's Quest* the least satisfactory, but the falling off does not seem to be quite as dramatic as she believed it to be. It does appear evident, however, that Montgomery's view of the restrictive conventions she faced and the limited success she was achieving greatly affected the tone of the final volume. Emily's despair is her despair, just as Emily's earlier delight in "the flash" was Montgomery's own tribute to the joy of life and literary creation. The emotional depths of *Emily's Quest* are sounded, not in the exhilaration Emily still sometimes feels as a creator or even in her happiness when finally united with Teddy, but rather in the passages nakedly revealing moods of profound depression.

Yet another factor in Montgomery's complex attitude towards her work in this period appears to have been a feeling of guilt about her failure to develop a more ambitious project. She blamed herself, in essence, for not attempting to climb a higher Alpine Path. Even in her initial enthusiasm for *Emily of New Moon* she writes that the novel is "along the old lines" because she does not have the "unbroken leisure I want for a more serious attempt." . . . Four years later, Weber attempts to compliment Montgomery by suggesting that *The Blue Castle* is her adult

> **In the *Emily* novels, Montgomery wrote her own spiritual autobiography, and these works would have been even finer achievements if their author had realized that in writing them she had climbed the Alpine Path to heights as lofty as any she might have attained by composing an "adult novel."**
>
> *—Thomas E. Tausky*

book, but she will not be flattered. She finally reveals the exact nature of her cherished *magnum opus:*

> I take this to be a reference to a long-ago confession of mine that I wanted some day to write a book for adults. Oh, no, this is not the book of my ambition . . . "The" book is still unwritten. Though I hope to write it still: a book portraying the life among the big "clan" families of the Maritimes. I come of three of them . . . and I know the life from A to Z if I can only get it on paper *alive.*

Montgomery's view of herself as an unwilling slave of public taste whose best work remains unwritten cannot have worked to the advantage of the trilogy. There is a sad irony in all of this: the *Emily* books are far more a personal expression, far less the product of external pressures, than their author seems to have realized. Whatever the potential merit of her projected saga, it could not possibly have contained much more of Montgomery's inner spirit, or even of her particular insight into Island society, than may be found in the *Emily* trilogy.

The mixture of reverence for literary creation and persistent melancholy that we find in the *Emily* novels is, I have tried to show, related to Montgomery's character and conception of herself. No writer is an island, however; in Montgomery's case, the effect of the literary backgrounds one can associate with her—the inheritance of Romanticism, the situation of the woman writer, the influence of the Canadian milieu—may well have been to reinforce the tendency toward soul-searching and sorrow in her work.

The *Emily* novels are intensely Romantic works. Especially in *Emily of New Moon,* the protagonist's delight in Nature (which extends to symbolic identification: she is called a star, a skylark, a young eagle and a wild cherry tree) and joy in the "flash" define her being. In one extended and passionate scene, the narrator uses the Romantic vocabulary of Nature-worship as religion and poet as priest to describe Emily's emotions upon gazing at the Northern lights. . . . (pp. 12-17)

When Romantic visions fade, however, there are also specifically Romantic forms of depression. In a passage which in its entirety alludes to both the "Intimations Ode" and "Tintern Abbey," Emily wonders whether she might lose "the flash." . . . In sympathy with Shelley's lament that "the mind in creation is as a fading coal," Emily regrets

that "*Nothing* ever seems . . . as beautiful and grand . . . when it is written out, as it does when you are thinking or feeling about it." . . . In the account of Emily's "great and awful weariness" of the soul, already quoted, one can find a parallel with the "grief without a pang" of Coleridge's "Dejection: An Ode," particularly since Emily, like Coleridge, attributes tragic utterances to the wind. . . .

If Romantic poets fear the loss of visionary power, women novelists (or fictional women novelists) may have cause to fear the harmful consequences of divided interests. . . . At the conscious level, Emily experiences little of this conflict, since Teddy is himself an artist, and interests himself in her work. Yet, as we have seen, love for Teddy gets in the way of Emily's devotion to her art; even more fundamentally, Emily's feeling for Teddy is directly contrary to the state of mind which best suits her Romantic art. As an artist, Emily needs to walk by her wild lone; as a lover, Emily literally comes to Teddy's whistle, feeling "in the mad ecstasy of the moment" . . . that she is "helpless—dominated" . . . and reveling in her abasement.

Yet, if in this episode Emily's conduct seems to recall the behaviour of the Victorian heroine, she also may be linked with the women novelists who were contemporary with her creator. In her influential book, *A Literature of Their Own,* Elaine Showalter suggests that women novelists of the 1920s "found themselves pulled apart by the conflicting claims of love and art." Consequently, novels of Montgomery's own time portray heroines subject to the kind of distress from which Emily suffers in much of *Emily's Quest.* . . . Like her creator, Emily seems half-Victorian, half-modern; half-submissive, half self-sufficient; half the socially acceptable public mask, half the intensely private creative personality. The conventional ending of *Emily's Quest* does not really unify these divided selves.

To add to Emily's plight, she has to bear the burden of being a Canadian artist. This aspect of her misfortune is not strongly emphasized on the surface, but it emerges if one compares her trials with the difficulties other artist figures in Canadian fiction have to face. Like David Canaan or Philip Bentley, Emily has to live among rural people whose imaginations are shown to be limited, and whose sympathies are narrow. Like David Newman of Patricia Blondal's *A Candle to Light the Sun* and the artist heroines of Margaret Laurence's fiction, Emily has to struggle to define her own individuality while groping with ambivalent feelings about the stern representatives of the Celtic tradition in Canada. Like Rose, the protagonist of *Who Do You Think You Are?,* Emily learns to adopt disguises as the best defence against public scorn of the unconventional sensibility.

Emily shares with most of the characters already mentioned the representative dilemma of the Canadian artist figure: on the whole, she is not in harmony with the local society of her upbringing, yet she cannot bring herself to shake off its influence. . . . To satisfy herself or public expectations (or both) Montgomery allows Emily to have both artistic success and loyalty to her culture. The happy ending enabled Montgomery to experience vicariously the delights of the road not taken: Montgomery herself, after all, had forsaken P.E.I. for Ontario manses, and had come to feel that "a certain part of my soul" had been "long starved" in "years of exile." Emily's choice to remain at New Moon can be viewed more generally as representing the Romantic's preference of the rural to the urban world, the traditional heroine's preference of the familiar to the unknown, and the Canadian artist's inability to break free.

For Kipling's untamed cat, "all places are the same." For Emily and her fellow Canadian artists, attachment to place can mean both spiritual discipline and spiritual confinement. Emily's triumphant self-mastery and conquest of the outer world reflect the lessons learned by her creator, who could write of herself:

> Yes, I agree with you that all the trials of an un-congenial environment should be regarded as *discipline* . . . I used to be a most impulsive, pas-sionate creature . . . It was a very serious defect and injurious to me in many ways, mentally, morally, physically. I see now that it needed to be corrected and the life I have had to live has been of all others the one best calculated to cor-rect it.

The darker passages of the *Emily* trilogy tell another story. The penalty of bondage to more limited minds is inevitable alienation, an unbridgeable gap between the real and the ideal. In another letter, Montgomery writes:

> So, as a rule, I am very careful to be shallow and conventional where depth and originality are wasted. When I get very desperate I retreat into my realms of cloudland. . . .

The ecstasy and despair of a life dedicated to art and hindered by social pressures is the real subject of the *Emily* trilogy. This is an ambitious theme; moreover, it is also the underlying theme of Montgomery's own life. In the *Emily* novels, Montgomery wrote her own spiritual autobiography, and these works would have been even finer achievements if their author had realized that in writing them she had climbed the Alpine Path to heights as lofty as any she might have attained by composing an "adult novel." (pp. 17-19)

> Thomas E. Tausky, "L. M. Montgomery and 'The Alpine Path, So Hard, So Steep'," in Ca-nadian Children's Literature, No. 30, 1983, pp. 5-20.

T. D. MacLulich   (essay date 1985)

[*In the following essay, MacLulich compares Montgom-ery's characters Anne and Emily to other heroes and heroines in children's literature and places them within a larger literary context.*]

L. M. Montgomery has reported how, shortly after *Anne of Green Gables* (1908) was first published, she was pleased to receive a congratulatory note from Mark Twain, who described Anne as "the dearest, and most lov-able child in fiction since the immortal Alice." Twain, of course, was himself renowned as a creator of memorable fictional children. In fact, it seems possible that Twain had

recognized some points of affinity between Montgomery's novel and his own famous boys' book, *The Adventures of Tom Sawyer.* One particularly striking similarity between the two books is the protagonist's fondness for play-acting and self-dramatization. Tom's imaginative life is shaped by his reading of lurid adventure stories. Anne, for her part, is infatuated with sentimental ladies' fiction. Anne's penchant for casting herself as an actor in romantic adven-tures—which leads, for example, to her disastrous imper-sonation of the Lady Elaine—is a feminine analogue of Tom's compulsion to play out scenarios based on the ad-venture stories that are his favorite reading. We should not press this comparison too far, however. Montgomery's story, in which Anne eventually puts aside her personal ambitions in order to take care of the failing Marilla, dif-fers significantly from the fantasy of irresponsible adven-tures and unearned rewards that Twain creates.

The link between Montgomery and Twain may be tenu-ous, but it does provide a convenient way of introducing [my] main argument. . . . I want to suggest that relative-ly little attention has been paid to the literary context within which Montgomery's books took shape. Montgom-ery inherited a tradition of juvenile fiction that had be-come prominent in the later years of the nineteenth centu-ry, and was well-established by the time she began to write. It is quite natural that Montgomery's novels should bear a closer resemblance to nineteenth-century girls' books than they do to the boys' books written by Twain and other male authors. In fact, Montgomery's two best books, *Anne of Green Gables* and *Emily of New Moon* (1923), belong to a tradition that descends from one the most important books in nineteenth-century children's lit-erature, Louisa May Alcott's *Little Women* (1868). The heroines of Montgomery's two books are examples of a particularly interesting character who was first introduced into children's fiction in Alcott's story, the aspiring young writer or literary heroine.

In a general way, the emergence of children's fiction dur-ing the nineteenth century can be traced to an important shift in the prevailing view of children and of childhood itself. Philippe Ariès in *Centuries of Childhood* has de-scribed the process whereby childhood was recognized as a distinct phase in the cycle of human development, and children ceased to be regarded simply as small adults. This acceptance of childhood and adolescence as distinct phases in the human life cycle eventually affected the liter-ature that was written specially for children. Throughout much of the nineteenth century, ordinary fiction—the novels of Dickens are a leading example—often showed sympathy for the child's viewpoint, and a recognition that children could not be expected to conform to impossibly perfect standards of behaviour. By the latter half of the century, however, authors of children's books even started to judge society by how well it treated the children in its midst, rather than judging children by how well they adapted themselves to society's expectations.

The nineteenth century, then, virtually created the idea of a "literature" that was specially written with children's needs in mind. Before that, children had been forced to borrow occasional books from adult literature (outstand-

The first manuscript page of Anne of Green Gables.

ing examples are *Pilgrim's Progress, Robinson Crusoe,* and *Gulliver's Travels*), or sustain their imaginations on the meagre fare contained in the didactic tales and moral verses that their elders considered suitable for young readers. This overtly didactic literature was written without regard for the real imaginative needs of its proposed readers. As a result, very few of the early works written for children are still read today. Indeed, out of all the books written specifically for children and published prior to 1800, Lillian H. Smith can find only one work, Oliver Goldsmith's *Goody Two Shoes,* that has survived to become a children's classic.

During the nineteenth century, however, a significant change took place. In the latter half of the century, an increasing number of authors of children's books began to depict their juvenile heroes and heroines as neither paragons of virtue nor examples of vice incarnate. The authors of these books must have shared the attitudes Alcott attributes to Jo March in *Good Wives* (1869), the continuation of *Little Women.* Alcott tells us that Jo could not bring herself to use the simple didactic patterns expected in stories for young readers: "much as she like to write for children, Jo could not consent to depict all her naughty boys as being eaten by bears or tossed by mad bulls, because they did not go to a particular Sabbath-school, nor all the good infants, who did go, as rewarded by every kind of bliss, from gilded gingerbread to escorts of angels, when they departed this life with psalms or sermons on their lisping tongues."

Little Women was a landmark in the development of fiction for children. The four March sisters have been described as "unique in the children's literature of their time, for they are not perfect, but neither are they wholly depraved" [Ruth K. MacDonald, *Louisa May Alcott*]. The March sisters "are the first 'naughty' children allowed to survive and prosper in American children's literature. After them comes a long line of literary children who are accepted and loved in spite of their faults: Katy Carr in *What Katy Did* by Susan Coolidge (1872); Tom Bailey in *The Story of a Bad Boy* by Thomas Bailey Aldrich (1870); and most important, Mark Twain's *Tom Sawyer* (1876) and *Huckleberry Finn* (1884)." That is, along with boys' books such as *The Story of a Bad Boy* and *The Adventures of Tom Sawyer,* girls' books such as *Little Women* and *What Katy Did* helped to pioneer the creation of a children's literature that was realistic rather than moralistic.

Despite Alcott's very real understanding of children's psychological make-up, her book ultimately judges human conduct by a standard that is moral rather than psychological. Indeed, *Little Women* is structured as an illustration of the moral allegory contained in Bunyan's *Pilgrim's Progress.* Each of the March sisters has a "burden" which she must learn to overcome before she can become worthy of happiness. That is, Jo and her sisters are presented as "little women" with exactly the same moral responsibilities as adults. Their immature years do not entitle them to special consideration when they err.

On the other hand, Alcott's male contemporaries allow their heroes a much greater degree of freedom than Alcott and other woman writers grant to their heroines. In other words, the attitudes that shaped girls' fiction remained more conservative than did the attitudes that shaped boys' fiction. For every story like Susan M. Coolidge's *What Katy Did,* whose heroine "tore her dress every day, hated sewing, and didn't care a button about being called 'good'," there was a book like Martha Finley's *Elsie Dinsmore* (1868), whose heroine remains an insufferable prig in the old-fashioned manner. And even the rambunctious Katy Carr rather quickly turns into the proud and capable chatelaine of her father's home. The heroines of girls' books, then, could not enact the dreams of adventure and temporary escape from society that were permitted to the heroes of boys' books as a matter of course.

Tom Sawyer, for example, is able to evade his Aunt Polly's supervision virtually at will, and whenever he desires he joins the happily irresponsible Huck Finn. Of course, Tom's rebellion against society (unlike Huck's) is not deep-seated or lasting. In fact, although Tom often joins the disreputable Huck Finn, he is drawn to the daughter of a member of the town's social elite. And Twain eventually rewards Tom for his youthful adventures by providing him with money, the key to Tom's acceptance into middle-class respectable society. In girls' fiction, however, the heroine seldom leaves the domestic setting, and she earns the greatest adult approval by acting as a homemaker. In other words, there exists in children's fiction a counterpart of the gender gap that has often been pointed out in conventional fiction.

A surprising number of the major landmarks in the male-dominated mainstream of nineteenth-century American literature possess a sort of dual citizenship: although they are monuments in the elite or high culture, they are also fixtures on the shelf of children's classics. The most outstanding examples are Cooper's Leatherstocking tales and Twain's *The Adventures of Huckleberry Finn*. These books present variations on a theme that is particularly congenial to the American male imagination: the flight from a restrictive civilization that is perceived as female-dominated, and the dream of finding ideal male companionship in some place far removed from conventional society.

At the same time as male authors such as Cooper, Melville, and later Twain were producing the books that have made them famous, a great many female authors were writing sentimental domestic melodramas, often centred on homes in which men are conspicuously weak or absent. These books have not been acknowledged as "high art," nor have they been accepted as enduring children's classics. But they have an interest of their own, and some of the attitudes they expressed were incorporated into the tradition of girls' fiction that stems from Alcott's best-known novel.

According to Nina Baym, the sort of "women's fiction" exemplified by Susan Warner's *The Wide, Wide World* enjoyed an extraordinary vogue in pre–Civil War America. Most of these novels, Baym writes, "tell, with variations, a single tale. In essence, it is the story of a young girl who is deprived of the supports she had rightly or wrongly depended on to sustain her throughout life and is faced with the necessity of winning her own way in the world" [*Women's Fiction: A Guide to Novels by and about Women in America*]. Whatever the details of her story, the heroine's dilemma stems from the vicissitudes of sexual politics: "Her dilemma, simply, was mistreatment, unfairness, disadvantage, and powerlessness, recurrent injustices occasioned by her status as female and child. The authors' solutions are different from case to case and somewhat less simple than the dilemma, but all involve the heroine's accepting herself as female while rejecting the equation of female with permanent child."

Baym argues that a quietly subversive ideology underlies much of this fiction. The authors assume "that men as well as women find greatest happiness and fulfillment in domestic relations, but which are meant not simply spouse and parent, but the whole network of human attachments based on love, support, and mutual responsibility. Domesticity is set forth as a value scheme for ordering all of life, in competition with the ethos of money and exploitation that is perceived to prevail in American society." This domestic ideology is opposed to the values that prevailed in most fiction by men, for "to the extent that woman dominated the home, the [domestic] ideology implied an unprecedented historical expansion of her influence, and a tremendous advance over her lot in a world dominated by money and market considerations, where she was defined as a chattel or sexual toy."

The domestic ideology began to lose currency after the Civil War. Baym suggests: "The Civil War had demonstrated the feebleness of the affectional model of human relationships, and the Gilded Age affirmed profit as the motive around which all of American life was to be organized." But woman authors did not give up all hope of changing their society. The ravages of war and the ensuing ravages of capitalism conclusively demonstrated the faults inherent in the male-dominated social system. Although women could not immediately reform society because grown men were already too firmly set in their ways, perhaps women could use their control of the domestic environment to influence the values of the next generation. Perhaps, through a combination of educational reform and domestic influence, women could help to shape a new sort of man, who would adhere more closely to the humane values of the domestic ideology. Such an idea seems to lie behind Alcott's series of novels about Jo March. In *Little Women* and *Good Wives* Jo absorbs her mother's gentle ideals, and later in *Little Men* (1873 and *Jo's Boys* (1886) she collaborates with her husband in creating an unconventional school where affection and understanding transform potential delinquents into upright and generous young men and women.

Although Jo's management of Plumfield makes her the centre of a rather large "family," Alcott's heroine is not a typical representative of her sex. As a child, she is more enterprising and active, as well as more outspoken and spontaneous, than the common run of girls. Moreover, she gets into far more mischief than girls normally create for themselves. In short, she is a tomboy. In effect, Jo's conduct expresses a rebellion against the restrictive conception of proper feminine conduct that prevailed in Alcott's society. Yet in the end, as Patricia Meyer Spacks points out [in her *The Female Imagination*] *Little Women* endorses a viewpoint that equates femininity with submission, self-restraint, and service to others. As a result, Jo eventually learns to restrain precisely those traits that make her character so distinctive and interesting. Yet Jo does retain one trait that distinguishes her from most of the other juvenile heroines of her day: in late adolescence she earns money and at the same time asserts her independence by embarking on a literary career. Jo March is thus the earliest example in nineteenth-century girls' fiction of that character I have already labelled the literary heroine.

Jo March's literary aspirations are undoubtedly in part a response to the enormous popularity attained by woman authors in nineteenth-century America. Baym points out that the woman's fiction of mid-century "was by far the most popular literature of its time, and on the strength of that popularity, authorship in America was established as a woman's profession, and reading as a woman's avocation." Although later in the century woman's fiction gave way to other "more androgynous" forms of the novel, the link between women and authorship remained strong, for literature offered women of the middle classes one of their very few respectable alternatives to a career as wife and mother.

The writers of girls' books often used literary ambition as a clear sign of a heroine's reluctance to submit to all the restrictions imposed by her society. In consequence, the literary heroine usually experiences a conflict between her desire for personal autonomy and her reluctance to upset her family by opposing the conventional social proprieties. The literary heroine is therefore a potential rebel, for the logical outcome of her youthful protests would be a systematic rejection of the values and attitudes that prevail in the heroine's male-dominated society. But the literary heroine's rebellion is never carried through into adult life. Instead, she resolves her inner conflict in favour of submission to social convention. That is, although the creators of literary heroines attach considerable importance to the right of children to follow their own bent without undue restraint, they cannot allow adult women the same freedom to express themselves in socially unconventional ways.

Even Jo March, the most original of all literary heroines, moves towards conventionality as she ages. The lapse into propriety is even more striking in the stories of subsequent literary heroines. The most conspicuous of Jo's successors are probably Rebecca Rowena Randall in Kate Douglas Wiggin's *Rebecca of Sunnybrook Farm* (1903) and Anne Shirley in Montgomery's **Anne of Green Gables.** Like Jo March, these heroines are also given to impulsive behaviour and occasional acts of rebellion. But as they grow older, Rebecca and Anne increasingly yield to social pressures. Above all, they start to take care of other people, as respectable women are supposed to do. In later life, then, the unconventionality of these literary heroines narrows to a single trait, a penchant for literary self-expression. And in the end, like most other fictional heroines, even Rebecca and Anne must be married off—although this conventional denouement is postponed to the sequels of the stories in which these literary heroines make their debuts.

It seems likely that the popularity of Wiggin's book provided the stimulus that prompted Montgomery to tell the story of her vivacious orphan child. There are even a few phrases in **Anne of Green Gables** that may be verbal echoes of Wiggin's book. For example, both Rebecca's Aunt Miranda and Anne's guardian Marilla Cuthbert use the distinctive phrase "what under the canopy." At one point, when Rebecca's aunts are debating whether to return Rebecca to her family, Aunt Miranda remarks grimly: "We have put our hand to the plough, and we can't turn back." Marilla remarks at one crisis in Anne's upbringing, "I've put my hand to the plough and I won't look back." Perhaps these verbal echoes may simply result from the imitation of regional speech patterns. But it seems less likely that the numerous and striking parallels between Anne's story and Rebecca's story are purely coincidental. Rebecca and Anne are both poetic spirits set down in a pragmatic community; they are about the same age when the reader first meets them; they both come to live with elderly, unmarried guardians, whose emotions have particlly atrophied, and both girls reawaken their guardians' interest in life; both girls attend a one-room local school, where they encounter an unsympathetic teacher; later they both move on to a collegiate in a nearby town, where they prove their intellectual mettle in a wider arena. Most importantly, both girls become embroiled in a series of scrapes that exasperate their staid and conventional guardians; and eventually the guardians of both girls suffer from illness, and must be looked after by their wards, now grown almost to adulthood. Many of these details have a basis in the events of Montgomery's own life; but not until Wiggin's novel had appeared did she feel emboldened to make them the basis of her own fiction.

Wiggin and Montgomery do not make their fiction illustrate a systematic feminist theory, as Alcott did. Wiggin does make her youthful heroine complain: "Boys always do the nice splendid things, and girls can only do the nasty dull ones that get left over. They can't climb so high, or go so far, or stay out so late, or run so fast, or anything." But Rebecca, and Anne as well, soon abandon their incipient feminism as they approach maturity. Yet Wiggin and Montgomery are not entirely innocent of ideas. Examined carefully, their fiction embodies a view of human nature that differs markedly from Alcott's view. I mean that Montgomery and Wiggin understand their heroines primarily from a psychological perspective, whereas Alcott understood her characters primarily in moral terms. In other words, Rebecca and Anne are not presented as "little women" but as children: they are part of a separate class of humanity, with special emotional and intellectual needs that adults have a duty to meet. However, Rebecca and Anne lose their privileged status as they approach maturity; Wiggin and Montgomery could never allow an adult the latitude that they permit to their juvenile protagonists.

When **Anne of Green Gables** was first published, one American reviewer astutely described it as "a sort of Canadian 'Rebecca of Sunnybrook Farm'." But Montgomery has done more than imitate Wiggin's successful formula. She has improved on her model. Montgomery takes a more penetrating look than Wiggin does at the feelings of rejection and the longing for approval and love that childhood insecurities can create. Montgomery also displays greater literary skills, particularly in her use of irony, than Wiggin does. For example, Wiggin's book includes a great deal of effusive emotional posturing, of the sort Montgomery makes into an object of humour when she satirizes the stereotyped language and idealized emotions that Anne has learned from her reading of sentimental popular fiction. The divergence in tone between the two books can be readily illustrated. Wiggin describes Rebecca's offering of a public prayer as "an epoch in her life." Montgomery allows Anne to describe her visit to Diana's Aunt Josephine in Charlottetown as "an epoch in my life," but Montgomery clearly intends her readers to recognize that Anne's phrasing is naively borrowed from her reading.

Montgomery also shows a greater sociological acuity than Wiggin does in depicting the sometimes oppressive nature of life in a small rural community. Consider just the novel's opening scene, in which Mrs. Rachel Lynde is described as the self-appointed watchdog of Avonlea society. Mrs. Rachel is effectively portrayed as a busybody and a gossip; and she is self-righteous and offensive into the bargain. The narrator later tells us: "Mrs. Rachel was one of those delightful and popular people who pride themselves

TWENTIETH-CENTURY LITERARY CRITICISM, Vol. 51

on speaking their mind without fear or favour." We meet this Avonlea avatar of Mrs. Grundy even before we meet Marilla, Matthew, or Anne. That is, we are immediately introduced to the restrictive nature of Avonlea society, where convention and custom rule all conduct. Marilla and Matthew have never left their family home; their inhibited natures are the natural product of this convention-bound society. The effervescent Anne supplies what Marilla and Matthew—and Avonlea in general—have been missing. Like Rebecca, Anne has a salutary impact on many of the adults she meets—think of her enlivening effect not only on Marilla and Matthew but also on other adults, such as Diana's imperious Aunt Josephine.

One of the great strengths of Montgomery's book is her ability to present events from Anne's point of view. In the scenes in which Anne confronts adult authority, we invariably side with Anne rather than with her older opponent. Even Anne's most childish enthusiasms are accorded a dignified treatment, for Montgomery wants her readers to remember the overwhelming importance that children can attach to trifles such as wearing puffed sleeves, attending a community concert, eating ice cream, or sleeping in a spare room bed. If these things are important to any child, they are doubly significant to Anne, who has never done any of them before.

Anne's sufferings are treated very lightly. She was three months old when she was orphaned, and she tells Marilla "nobody wanted me even then." We are told: "Evidently she did not like talking about her experiences in a world that had not wanted her." But we can infer the urgency of her need for a home of her own when she tells Matthew: "Oh, it seems too wonderful that I'm going to live with you and belong to you. I've never belonged to anybody—not really." Marilla and Matthew, as well, quickly find that Anne fills a void in their lives. Matthew starts to accept Anne from the moment he first sees her, and finds: "He could not tell this child with the glowing eyes that there had been a mistake." He soon finds her lively conversation enchanting, and Marilla is not far behind: "She *is* kind of interesting, as Matthew says. I can feel already that I'm wondering what on earth she'll say next. She'll be casting a spell over me, too. She's cast it over Matthew." It is clear that Montgomery approves of her heroine's wide-eyed approach to life. In fact, Anne's exuberant outlook is held out by Montgomery as a fruitful way for adults to meet the world—or at least as a healthy corrective to the overly sombre outlook adopted by most adults in Avonlea.

Despite its attractiveness for adult readers, *Anne of Green Gables* is fundamentally a children's book. In *Emily of New Moon,* on the other hand, Montgomery may have aspired to higher things. Certainly, *Emily of New Moon* rather than the overtly "adult" novel *A Tangled Web* (1931) is Montgomery's closest approach to the serious study of Maritime clan life that she once expressed the ambition to write. But in *Emily of New Moon* Montgomery has not managed to work the sort of transformation on children's fiction that Twain achieved in *The Adventures of Huckleberry Finn.* Like Twain's book, Montgomery's novel often reveals the shortcomings of the adult world

seen by her young protagonist; however, Montgomery's book avoids the satire and the social criticism that Twain injects into his story. Moreover, Huck's adventures lead to his estrangement from society, but the first volume of the Emily series culminates in Emily's heart-warming reconciliation with her previously unsympathetic guardian. Both of Montgomery's best novels, then, remain children's books, whereas Twain's best novel crosses over into the category of "adult" fiction.

In the shape of its plot, *Emily of New Moon* resembles *Anne of Green Gables.* Like Anne Shirley, Emily Byrd Starr eventually finds a secure and affectionate home, and Emily displays a contagious vitality that enables her to enrich the lives of the emotionally reticent adults who reluctantly take her in. But the two novels differ considerably in tone. *Anne of Green Gables* is a far sunnier book than is *Emily of New Moon.* Anne begins to feel at home virtually from the moment she arrives at Green Gables; Matthew immediately takes her side, and Marilla is not far behind in extending her affection to the winsome orphan. In *Emily of New Moon,* however, Montgomery looks more deeply into the emotional consequences of being left as an unwanted burden with virtual strangers. Emily is not made welcome by Aunt Elizabeth Murray, the imperious relative who dominates life at New Moon. Although Cousin Jimmy and Aunt Laura ease Emily's discomfort, the stern Aunt Elizabeth is only won over after Emily has endured several confrontations with her strong-willed guardian, and demonstrated that she possesses an equally strong determination herself.

The differences between the books also mean that *Anne of Green Gables* is suited for younger audiences than is *Emily of New Moon.* For example, at seven years of age my own daughter enjoyed having Anne's story read to her. She could even perceive that the rhetoric in some of Anne's speeches was overdone and made Anne appear momentarily ridiculous. *Emily of New Moon,* on the other hand, is best suited for readers who are themselves nearing or passing through the turmoil of adolescence. Throughout the novel, Emily is pressured by her relatives to give up her literary ambitions, and adopt a more conventional outlook. Moreover, Emily is urged by nearly everyone she knows—by her relatives, by the eccentric Old Kelly, and by the vindictive Aunt Nancy Priest—to define her identity through her relationships with men.

In Emily Byrd Starr, the heroine of *Emily of New Moon,* Montgomery has created a literary heroine who is a worthy successor of Alcott's Jo March. All of Emily's most striking assertions of her individuality revolve around her determined pursuit of her literary ambitions. When Emily insists that she simply must write—the need to express herself is part of her very being—she is defending herself against those who view her as little more than another piece of family property. Like Anne, Emily is given to imagining romantic fantasies, which she projects into her youthful literary efforts. But Emily's literary ambitions are central to her being in a way that Anne's are not. Anne's writing is not meant to be taken very seriously. Anne has learned to spin romantic stories as compensation for the bleakness of her life before she arrived at

Green Gables, and once she begins to feel secure in the emotional support of her new home she feels less need for a private fantasy world. Emily's emotional scars are less easily healed, and she can only express her feelings of isolation and loss by projecting them into her writing so that the progress of her various literary efforts becomes an integral part of her story.

Montgomery has skillfully arranged her plot so that Emily's need to express herself by writing precipitates a series of conflicts with adults, especially with the imperious Aunt Elizabeth. The first such incident occurs when Aunt Elizabeth discovers the notebook in which Emily has recorded her earliest attempts at literature. " 'You mustn't read that, Aunt Elizabeth,' she [Emily] cried indignantly, 'that's mine,—my own *private property'*." Emily's assertion of children's rights makes no impact on Aunt Elizabeth, for whom children are little better than a rather troublesome kind of chattel, the property of whoever is charged with their upbringing:

> "Hoity-toity, Miss Starr," said Aunt Elizabeth, staring at her, "let me tell you that I have a right to read your books. I am responsible for you now. I am not going to have anything hidden or underhanded, and understand that. You have evidently something there that you are ashamed to have seen and I mean to see it. Give me that book."

Emily, however, has other ideas. She burns the book in the stove rather than let Aunt Elizabeth read it. Her writing is identified with her innermost being. She cannot let an unsympathetic stranger invade her personal identity in this way.

Later in the novel, the vindictive teacher, Miss Brownell, discovers that Emily has been writing a poem instead of doing her arithmetic. Sarcastically she tells the class, "Really, children, we seem to have a budding poet among us." Emily's pain is acute when Miss Brownell makes fun of her poem before the class:

> Miss Brownell held up the slate and read Emily's poem aloud, in a sing-song nasal voice, with absurd intonations and gestures that made it seem a very ridiculous thing. The lines Emily had thought the finest seemed the most ridiculous. The other pupils laughed more than ever and Emily felt that the bitterness of the moment could never go out of her heart.

Moreover, this is not the end of the incident. When Miss Brownell is informed that Emily has more poems in her desk, she immediately takes possession of them, over Emily's protests. Again, Emily's poetic efforts are held up to ridicule. Despite her humiliation, Emily retains sufficient presence of mind to snatch her papers back before Miss Brownell can throw them in the fire. "You are an unjust, tyrannical *person,*" she tells her teacher. When Miss Brownell tells this story to Aunt Elizabeth, Emily is forced to apologize without being given an opportunity to explain her side of the incident. Yet Emily does gain a small recognition of her right to personal dignity, when Aunt Elizabeth—prompted by Cousin Jimmy's apt Bibli-

cal citation—relents on her initial command that Emily kneel before the triumphant Miss Brownell.

Emily's writings often serve her as an emotional outlet. This is particularly true of the letters she addresses to her dead father, whom she salutes as "Mr. Douglas Starr, On the road to heaven." Emily's first letter to her father is written immediately after her humiliation by Miss Brownell, and the effort to articulate her grievances proves to be therapeutic. When Emily has finished writing, she regains her equanimity: "she had emptied out her soul and it was once more free of evil passions. She even felt curiously indifferent to Miss Brownell." These letters to her father serve several purposes: they enable Emily to vent her hostile feelings towards people, usually adults, who treat her unfairly; and they help her overcome the loneliness she feels at New Moon. In addition, as she writes her letters Emily feels a renewed companionship with her father, who was once her sole confidant.

Emily's letters to her father come to an end as a direct result of another confrontation with Aunt Elizabeth. Relations between the two are already strained because Aunt Elizabeth disapproves of Emily's insistence on writing fiction. Then Aunt Elizabeth discovers the place where Emily has hidden the letters, and reads them:

> Elizabeth Murray would never have read any writing belonging to a grown person. But it never occurred to her that there was anything dishonourable in reading the letters wherein Emily, lonely and—sometimes—misunderstood, had poured out her heart to the father she had loved and been loved by, so passionately and understandingly. Aunt Elizabeth thought she had a right to know everything that this pensioner on her bounty did, said, or thought. She read the letters and found out what Emily thought of her—of her, Elizabeth Murray, autocrat unchallenged, to whom no one had ever dared to say anything uncomplimentary.

Aunt Elizabeth summons Emily, intending to scold and punish her, but Aunt Elizabeth meets an unexpected response from Emily, who reacts to this invasion of her privacy in words that echo her earlier refusal to let Aunt Elizabeth peer into her private papers. Emily feels as though "Sacrilege had been committed—the most sacred shrine of her soul had been profaned," and she is indignant: " 'How dare you?' she said. 'How dare you touch *my private papers?*' "

When Emily snatches back her papers, Aunt Elizabeth is overcome by an unfamiliar emotion: "a most unpleasant doubt of her own conduct suddenly assailed her—driven home perhaps by the intensity and earnestness of Emily's accusation. For the first time in her life it occurred to Elizabeth Murray to wonder if she had done rightly." Aunt Elizabeth's immediate response to this disquieting idea is a defensive anger, and Emily is convinced that she will be sent away from New Moon. But when Aunt Elizabeth comes to Emily's room, something surprising happens. Aunt Elizabeth says, "Emily, I had no right to read your letters. I admit I was wrong. Will you forgive me?" The emotional release that follows clears the air on both sides, and reveals to Emily that the undemonstrative Aunt Elizabeth, despite her forbidding exterior, does love Emily. The next time Emily tries to write to her father, she finds that she is unable to do so. This happens because the revelation of Aunt Elizabeth's affection has completed the process by which New Moon has become a real home for Emily. She no longer needs to feel close to her ghostly father; she is secure now in the affections of her surrogate parents.

The two subsequent volumes of the Emily series are rather disappointing. The most interesting moments occur when Emily's literary ambitions bring her into conflict with her family's very circumscribed conception of the options open to women. As she grows older, however, Emily's story turns into a disappointing series of abortive courtships, which only end when Emily finally recognizes her attachment to her childhood companion, the painter Teddy Kent. It is small compensation that Montgomery makes Emily's soul-mate an artist, who will—presumably—allow her to continue her literary career. As she approaches maturity, Emily confides to her diary: "I don't like the thought of my life belonging to any one but myself." It is a definite comedown for her to finish as an ordinary romantic heroine, however unconventional some of the details of the romance may be.

Like Anne, Emily becomes both less assertive and less interesting as she grows older. After her marriage to Gilbert Blythe, Anne subordinates herself to the former classmate with whom she once competed on terms of equality. In the Emily series, Montgomery tries to avoid the problem of waning reader interest by ending Emily's story when her marriage becomes certain. Montgomery's ploy is not entirely successful, for once the Murray family accept Emily's literary vocation—and write her off as a permanent spinster—most of the sparkle goes out of Emily's tale. Emily no longer has to defend her personal identity against the assaults of society, and she experiences no inner conflict that can sustain an intense reader interest.

Montgomery wrote most effectively when she dealt with juvenile heroines, whose difficulties appeared to be associated with a special phase of life. Privately, in her journals and letters, she sometimes chafed against the restrictions that both publishers and readers imposed on the writer of children's fiction. However, she never attempted to break free from the conventions that hedged the form in which she cast the great majority of her work. As a result, Montgomery never made her fiction a vehicle for expressing a mature criticism of society. Social criticism entered her work principally when she protested against the overly strict and repressive way that adults sometime treated children. Her stories of literary heroines contain her strongest assertions of an individual's right to pursue her own course in life. But in her fiction she seldom expressed her awareness that grown women, too, could be subjected to constraints that were very similar to those she criticized when they were inflicted upon children. (pp. 5-16)

> *T. D. MacLulich, "L. M. Montgomery and the Literary Heroine: Jo, Rebecca, Anne, and Emily," in* Canadian Children's Literature, *No. 37, 1985, pp. 5-17.*

Elizabeth R. Epperly   (essay date 1985)

[Epperly is an American-born educator and author now living and teaching on Prince Edward Island. In the following essay, she examines Montgomery's use of language in Anne's House of Dreams.*]*

To L. M. Montgomery enthusiasts certain words and expressions have become familiar from long association. Again and again in the twenty L. M. Montgomery novels we find these words and images: spicy scent of ferns, tricksy winds, apple-green sunset skies, the fragrance of trampled mint. In fact, Montgomery, somewhat like her beloved novelist Anthony Trollope, had a penchant for repetition. She had favourite poets she liked to quote: Kipling, Tennyson, Keats, Bliss Carman, Longfellow, Thomas Gray, Milton; favourite situations she loved to conjure—lustrous-eyed, spirited girls struggling against insensitive and unthinking adults or peers. But unlike the prose-minded Trollope, L. M. Montgomery always yearned to be a poet rather than a novelist. This desire shaped her most interesting novels, for the repeated images and allusions that failed her in poetry helped to create atmosphere, enrich character, and generally modulate the tone of her prose.

Some descriptions in her novels are overdrawn or sentimental, but many do achieve a poetic harmony that eluded her successfully in poetry itself. In 1916, L. M. Montgomery published her only book of poetry, *The Watchman and Other Poems,* a tame volume that shows all too clearly that she did, as she freely admitted to Ephraim Weber, fit in the rhymes later with the help of a rhyming dictionary. In 1917, she produced another novel, (what was to be in the completed series the fifth Anne book), *Anne's House of Dreams,* potentially the most sentimental of any of her books since it deals with the long-awaited marriage of Anne Shirley and Gilbert Blythe. It is remarkably interesting and readable. Its success as a book is not found in Anne's and Gilbert's honeymoon, nor even primarily in the presence of spry Captain Jim or mysterious Leslie Moore, but in its tone. The same kinds of images and expressions used in numerous poems of *The Watchman* reappear in *Anne's House of Dreams,* but in the novel, they work.

L. M. Montgomery was passionately fond, as all the *Watchman* poems show, of the colour purple, of skies like cups of flagons, of flowers as cups, of "elfin" and "silver" and "gold" and "crystal." Many of the ninety-three poems, songs to the sea, hills, and woods, are marred by an ill-judged concentration of archaic or descriptive words borrowed liberally from Tennyson and Browning ("flagon," "gramarye," "shallop," "wold," "elfin," "weklin"). In *Anne's House of Dreams* a preoccupation with the sea and the woods and hills also produces descriptions full of colour, jewels, stars, airy wine, and elfin things. Some of the word choices, admittedly, are as irksome as they are in the poems. For example, once when Captain Jim visits Anne, the narrator carols: "The garden was full of moist, scented air of a maritime spring evening. There was a milk-white mist on the edge of the sea, with a young moon kissing it, and a silver gladness of stars over the Glen." More often, however, the love of metaphors, similes, jewels, and colours that stifled her poetry, brings life to the prose.

Four Winds, the Glen, the House of Dreams itself, and the lighthouse have charm because L. M. Montgomery uses vivid language to reveal them. Her fascination with the sea, sunsets, and the music from Tennyson's "horns of Elfland faintly blowing!" is often contagious. The profusion of colour in this early description is typical: "It was a gracious evening, full of delectable lights and shadows. In the west was a sky of mackerel clouds—crimson and amber-tinted, with long strips of apple-green sky between. Beyond was the glimmering radiance of a sunset sea, and the ceaseless voice of many waters came up from the tawny shore." In the prose the jewels and cups and colours of the poetry seem to well up naturally with Anne's enthusiasm for her new life:

> Her new home could not yet be seen; but before her lay Four Winds Harbour like a great, shining mirror of rose and silver . . . Beyond the bar the sea, calm and austere, dreamed in the afterlight. The little fishing village, nestled in the cove where the sand-dunes met the harbour shore, looked like a great opal in the haze. The sky over them was like a jewelled cup from which the dusk was pouring; the air was crisp with the compelling tang of the sea, and the whole landscape was infused with the subtleties of a sea evening. A few dim sails drifted along the darkening, fir-clad harbour shores. A bell was ringing from the tower of a little white church on the far side; mellowly and dreamily sweet, the chime floated across the water blent with the moan of the sea.

The verbs "dreamed," "nestled," "infused," "floated," and "blent" weave together the familiar "rose and silver," "opal," "jewelled cup," and "moan of the sea." The atmosphere of Anne's and Gilbert's first home is completed by more familiar and somehow freshly pleasing expressions: the house itself is like a "creamy seashell" and the sentinel poplars (Montgomery's favourites) stand in "stately, purple silhouette" while the fishing village across the harbour is "gemmed with lights." We interpret the rich tints and images as manifestations of the young married couple, and especially of Anne.

Special events in the novel are marked by appropriately joyous or sombre nature descriptions—Montgomery used pathetic fallacy extensively. For example, the arrival of Anne's first baby is happy (though the infant quickly dies): "One evening, when the sky's limpid bowl was filled with a red glory, and the robins were thrilling the golden twilight with jubilant hymns to the stars of evening, there was a sudden commotion in the little house of dreams." Conversely, when Owen Ford confesses to Anne his (then) hopeless love for Leslie Moore, the very breezes are sorrowful, and yet the aspen (like Leslie) stands apart as a reminder of nature's healing beauty: "The wind of evening in the poplars sounded like some sad, weird, old rune—some broken dream of old memories. A slender shapely young aspen rose up before them against the fine maize and emerald and paling rose of the western sky, which

brought out every leaf and twig in dark, tremulous, elfin loveliness."

Throughout the novel, we respond to a technique of alternating tones in the descriptions. The images are either colourful and vibrant or silvery, starry, and cool: the flames of crimson sunset are off-set by the shadows of stars. The tone or language of the descriptions is meant to enhance characterization, and it is no accident that the passion and coolness of the scenes are reconciled in a chief character in the story. The beautiful Leslie Moore gives mystery and romance to the quiet harbour life. For years she has lived with her imbecile husband, wasting her youth and passion on the moonlit sandshores of Four Winds. Anne is captivated by the contradiction in Leslie's looks and manner—something about the vivid woman exudes warmth, while her gestures are stiff and repelling. The initial description of her incorporates the red and the star: "She was hatless, but heavy braids of burnished hair, the hue of ripe wheat, were twisted about her head like a coronet; her eyes were blue and star-like; her figure, in its plain print gown, was magnificent; and her lips were as crimson as the bunch of blood-red poppies she wore at her belt."

Anne determines to befriend Leslie, and Captain Jim and Miss Cornelia aid the growth of confidence between the fulfilled and the thwarted woman. The semi-tragedy of Leslie's life provides welcome relief from the too nearly perfect happiness of Anne and Gilbert. If we appreciate much of the landscape through Anne's contented eyes, we also feel the undercurrents of sorrow and magic in the sea and shore because of Leslie's more complex life. The description of the sun striking Leslie's house suggests Leslie's importance to the tone of the story: "To the right, it fell on the old house among the willows up the brook, and gave it for a fleeting space casements more splendid than those of an old cathedral. They glowed out of its quiet and grayness like the throbbing, blood-red thoughts of a vivid soul imprisoned in a dull husk of environment."

Bitterness has made Leslie cold; she fears pity more than hatred and from habit retreats from the warmth and gentleness of intimacy. We compare the glare of a winter's day to Leslie's hopeless life when this description is closely followed by the appearance of Venus's shadow:

> The sky was sharp and blue; the snow diamonds sparkled insistently; the stark trees were bare and shameless, with a kind of brazen beauty; the hills shot assaulting lances of crystal. Even the shadows were sharp and stiff and clear-cut, as no proper shadows should be. Everything was either handsome or ugly. There was no soft blending, or kind obscurity, or elusive mistiness in that searching glitter.

The harsh, piercing crystal is then mellowed by "Venus, glorious and golden," the "brilliant star of evening." Anne exclaims over the beauty of the star's shadow, and Leslie herself interprets its significance: " 'I have heard that you can see the shadow of Venus only once in a lifetime, and that within a year of seeing it your life's most wonderful gift will come to you,' said Leslie. But she spoke rather hardly; perhaps she thought that even the shadow of Venus could bring her no gift of life." The gift of life does come to Leslie, first in Owen Ford's love and then in freedom from her marriage when an operation reveals that Leslie's "husband" is really a look-alike cousin (who had been on his way to tell Leslie of her real husband's death when he was overtaken in a brawl and then by fever). Leslie belongs to the warm star of Venus, not to the frigid glints of snow, and Owen Ford, a sensitive writer, is the one to appreciate her kinship to the beauty of the harbour: " 'And her eyes—they are as deep and blue as the gulf out there. I never saw such blueness—and gold! Did you ever see her hair down, Mrs. Blythe?' " Leslie's suppressed passion can now become the warmth of fulfillment, bringing her closer to Anne and restoring a down-to-earth normalness to the story.

Glimpses of Leslie's hidden warmth, and indeed the protective warmth of the entire story, are found through Captain Jim and the lighthouse beacon, emblem of his cheerful vigilance. This lighthouse has none of the subtle artistic power of Virginia Woolf, but it does serve to unify our impressions of the human revolvings within its ken. When Gilbert first describes the house to Anne, he tells of the beacon: " 'You'll love that Four Winds light, Anne. It's a revolving one, and it flashes like a magnificent star through the twilights. We can see it from our living room windows and our front door.' " Anne's first view of Four Winds is under its light: "The great revolving light on the cliff at the channel flashed warm and golden against the clear northern sky, a trembling, quivering star of good hope." The similarities between the beacon and Captain Jim's spiritual flame are deliberate. A few pages later he and Anne meet, and "Kindred spirit flashed recognition to kindred spirit." Captain Jim is homely, but no one ever thinks of his looks, for "the spirit shining through that rugged tenement beautified it so wholly." Through their first winter Captain Jim becomes a close friend and the lighthouse, its beacon dark during months when the harbor is frozen, is the center for Anne's and Leslie's growing intimacy.

For a while, the mysterious shadow of Venus takes the beacon's place as a force in the characters' lives. But in the spring, "again the Four Winds light begemmed the twilights" and Anne and Leslie are finally bound together when Anne's baby dies. The baby's death initiates Anne into adult grief, and she is then able to share Leslie's love and to hear the story of Captain Jim's sad romance, "Lost Margaret." As the benevolent light revolves, Captain Jim's life wish comes true, his life-book is written by Owen Ford; Anne bears a healthy baby; Leslie is released from her "dull husk of environment" to join Owen Ford. On the night before Owen comes to tell his love to Leslie, Anne reminds Leslie that "The omen of the shadow of Venus did come true for you" and Leslie "watched the great revolving light bestarring the short hours of the summer night, and her eyes grew soft and bright and young once more."

Toward the end of the novel, when Captain Jim (having read the completed life-book Owen Ford sends him), "crosses the bar" (allusion to another favourite Tennyson poem), the lighthouse is again our focus: "The long fields by the shore were dewy and fresh in that first fine, purely-tinted light. The wind came dancing and whistling up the channel to replace the beautiful silence with a music more beautiful still. Had it not been for the baleful star on the white tower that early walk would have been a delight to Anne and Gilbert. But they went softly with fear." Captain Jim's gentle spirit, like the lighthouse, continues to influence the harbour and Four Winds people. Anne hates to leave the house of dreams for the larger, more convenient home Gilbert has bought in the Glen, and uses as her reason " 'You can't see the lighthouse star from it.' " It is as though she identifies the beacon with all the joys she has known during her newlywed years. Owen and Leslie decide to buy the House of Dreams as a summer home, and Anne leaves for her new house assured that the spirit of the Four Winds life will be preserved. On the last page, the narrator says: "She went out, closing and locking the door behind her. Gilbert was waiting for her with a smile. The lighthouse star was gleaming northward. The little garden, where only marigolds still bloomed, was already hooding itself in shadows." Anne and Gilbert thus set out to greet a new life with their own "little Jem."

Anne's House of Dreams is not wholly made up of starshine, vibrant colours, and beacon flashes, nor is it merely a prettily illustrated tale of love and fulfillment. In it, as in all of her good novels, L. M. Montgomery catches life. She heightens the colours occasionally and indulges in favourite images and elements, but she knows how to make the characters breathe. In this book the rapturous songs of sea, wood, and hill are balanced by humorous characters and incidents so that poetry and everyday life rest comfortably together. The characters themselves are frequently laughing, and two sober-faced ones, Susan Baker and Miss Cornelia Bryant, unconsciously provide mirth for other characters and for the reader. In her descriptions of them, Montgomery makes fun of her own self-conscious style and keeps her writing from becoming embarrassingly sentimental or self-indulgent.

Susan Baker with her "that you may tie to" and "Susan is at the helm" is a welcome Dickensian comic relief figure. She bustles around Anne, and when waiting to hear how Anne fares in her first difficult delivery: " . . . Marilla paced the garden walks between the quahog shells, murmuring prayers between her set lips, and Susan sat in the kitchen with cotton wool in her ears and her apron over her head . . . "

It is Miss Cornelia, however, who insistently brings reality to the fancy and the romance. She is a homespun Betsey Trotwood and takes great delight in puncturing the male ego. Walking into the garden after Owen has tearfully confessed to Anne his love for Leslie, she overhears the end of Owen's inspired observations about our "prisoned infinite" and the "kindred infinite" and remarks: " 'You seem to have a cold in the head. Better rub some tallow on your nose when you go to bed . . . ' " Her language is peppered with lively expressions: of an offended church member, she says " 'But that family always thought they were much bigger potatoes than they really were' "; over the likelihood that Dick Moore did *not* get his head injured in a drunken brawl, " 'Pigs *may* whistle, but they've poor mouths for it.' "

Best of all is that L. M. Montgomery can use matter-of-fact Miss Cornelia, who "personates the comedy that ever peeps around the corner at the tragedy of life," to smile at her own effusiveness:

> Miss Cornelia sailed down to the little house one drowsy afternoon, when the gulf was the faint, bleached blue of hot August seas, and the orange lilies at the gate of Anne's garden held up their imperial cups to be filled with the molten gold of August sunshine. Not that Miss Cornelia concerned herself with painted oceans or sun-thirsty lilies. She sat in her favourite rocker in unusual idleness. She sewed not, neither did she spin.

The vague allusions to Coleridge and the Bible give the irony a double edge, commenting playfully on the straightforward character and the fanciful narrator.

Anne's House of Dreams, potentially mawkish because of its subject, works as a novel because L. M. Montgomery is able to control its tone throughout. The familiar poetic expressions and favourite pictures of nature help to unite the characters with their physical surroundings. Leslie is the sea mists and red poppies; Captain Jim is the light-house beacon and the gentle harbour sunsets; Anne is the brilliant colours and the quiet shadows. At the same time, Cornelia Bryant, Susan Baker, and steady young Dr. Blythe himself are constant reminders that prose, too, has its advantages. (pp. 40-5)

> *Elizabeth R. Epperly, "L. M. Montgomery's 'Anne's House of Dreams': Reworking Poetry," in* Canadian Children's Literature, *No. 37, 1985, pp. 40-6.*

Rea Wilmshurst   (essay date 1985)

[*Wilmshurst is a Canadian writer notable for her critical work on Montgomery. In the following essay, she explores the function of cooking in Montgomery's fiction.*]

A good cook will vary her menu; a good author will serve us a fresh and nourishing range of scenes, characters, and themes. L. M. Montgomery was both good cook and good writer, and in her stories we see a wonderful example of the way a real professional can shift ingredients into new forms effecting changes and surprises without any loss of wholesomeness or pleasure. Appropriately, one of her own staple narrative ingredients was the subject of cooking itself.

All readers who are fond of Anne of Green Gables will have suffered with vicarious embarrassment when her cake, made especially for Mr. and Mrs. Allan, turns out to have been flavoured (accidentally) with anodyne liniment rather than with vanilla. Anne eventually becomes an excellent cook, but cooking (not necessarily disastrous) continues to play a role in the subsequent novels devoted to her career: the tea for Mrs. Morgan in *Anne of Avonlea,* and Anne's first Christmas dinner in *Anne's House of Dreams,* for example. Reflecting on Montgomery's ten other novels, one realizes that cooking is also from time to time a matter of importance in them. In *The Story Girl* and *The Golden Road,* much is made of the Story girl's attempts to learn to cook. And her many disasters. Sara

Stanley (the Story Girl) is only partly comforted for her many failures when her cousin and teacher, Felicity, uses toothpowder to raise rusks for the Governor's wife and is eternally mortified as a result. (But the rusks did rise!) It is one of the marks of eleven-year-old Jane's maturity and level-headedness that she is prepared to take on summer housekeeping for her father at Lantern Hill, and that she takes it in her stride and becomes an excellent cook. There is a male cook, too, in *A Tangled Web:* Little Sam, whose excellent pea soup is renowned in the clan, but whose taste in *Objets d'art* makes for one of the entertaining subplots in that family chronicle.

Montgomery undoubtedly realized that stories having significant culinary details would appeal to readers young and old. From 1893 to 1910 she published at least sixteen stories in which cooking plays a major part, but none of them has been reprinted in the four collections of her short stories. By no means did Montgomery write up only bad experiences, however. As she did in her novels, Montgomery used the basic theme of cooking in many ways. Through a study of these short stories we gain insights not only into the diet of turn-of-the century Canadians, but also into social conventions, economic pressures, family tensions, and pre-adolescent psychology. I propose here to summarize some of these "cooking" stories, but I have not discussed each one in detail. . . .

Five stories that deal with mistakes in cooking also contain the idea of reward for recognition of worth. This may seem a contradiction, but Montgomery is skilled at saving the day for her cooks. Perhaps the most interesting is **"A New-Fashioned Flavoring,"** since it is the prototype for Anne's misadventure. Ivy, aged fifteen, and her brother Edmund, sixteen, are caring for their six younger siblings in the absence of their mother. They long for music lessons and college respectively, but have given up their hopes since the recent death of their father has left the family badly provided for. Their estranged uncle arrives for a surprise visit, and Ivy, in spite of a bad cold, bakes a cake for tea. It is flavoured with liniment (kept in an old vanilla bottle), unnoticed by her because of her cold. (Anne had a cold, too.) However, the uncle, who has been greatly diverted by the four-year-old *enfant terrible* of the family, manfully eats his cake and says nothing. He writes later to say he is sending Ivy a violin and will pay for lessons, and will send Edmund to college. His reasoning is not explained, but presumably he was thinking of a reconciliation when he paid his visit in the first place.

A better motivated reward in spite of error is illustrated in **"Dora's Gingerbread."** Ten-year-old Dora's Aunt Anna promises her a trip to town if she is able to bake good gingerbread. Dora works hard and confidently, refusing to go off to play with her neighbour, Tommy. The gingerbread looks fine, but has been flavoured with mustard, not ginger. The trip is cancelled, and Dora overwhelmed with humiliation. The next day Dora discovers Tommy bewailing the fact that he has no cake to take to his class outing. She bakes him an especially delicious and attractive one and is surprised when he is rather taken aback by her gift. Ten minutes later he is marching up to Aunt Anna to confess that he switched the mustard for ginger through the kitchen window (he knew the mustard was in an old ginger can) to pay back Dora for not coming to play with him. Now he feels remorseful and asks that Dora be allowed her reward. After a short cross-examination Aunt Anna relents—and invites Tommy to accompany them on the trip to town. A reward for recognition of worth for two, in this case.

Dora is a young girl, and Montgomery's young girls are often capable cooks at a tender age. Remember how Marigold, alone in the house and under pressure of company, was capable of whipping up the special Cloud of Spruce cake. "The Story of a Pumpkin Pie" is a revelation to those of us whose fillings for such items come in tins. In this story two ten-year-olds, Polly and Patty, who are staying with their grandmother, must entertain the minister in her absence. He is fond of, and visits every Sunday after his sermon to partake of, their grandmother's pumpkin pie. They resolve he shall have one in spite of her absence. They must go to the field, choose the pumpkin, lug it home, peel it, stew it, strain it, and then concoct the pie. It is a great success (although one of them had a nightmare about flavouring it with mustard).

Clearly it often happened that kitchen spices lived in mislabeled containers. Just as clearly, all these mistakes would have been avoided if this had not been the case. Cooks of the present day are facing again the situation of their grandmothers. We have started to buy our spices in bulk as they did and must be careful that they are sorted and labeled carefully on our return from shopping. Take heed from Montgomery's girls!

A more unusual ingredient is used in "The Locket That Was Baked," the same story that Peter includes in "Our magazine" in *The Golden Road*. Ten-year-old Josie Taylor volunteers to stay alone in her family's isolated house and do the family bread-making so her mother can go visiting. Her aunt allows her to wear an expensive locket as a reward. After the adults have left, a tramp comes to the door, and Josie is afraid that he will steal the necklace. There is nowhere to hide it but the bread, so she reaches up, breaks the chain, and kneads the locket into a loaf. The bread is in the oven while she gets the tramp a meal and he rummages about the house for money. After he leaves Josie is so upset that she lets the bread burn, but her aunt is very pleased with her courage and resourcefulness and gives her the locket to keep.

"A New-Fashioned Flavoring" demonstrated that members of a family can be reconciled through the medium of food. This reconciliation is often, however, inadvertent. Prissy Wood, in "The Cake That Prissy Made," is another ten-year-old who is a good cook. Her mother allows her to bake a cake all by herself to welcome a new minister's family. By the end of her labours she is so exhausted that she doesn't even scrape out the icing bowl. She should have, because—her first mistake—she had used saleratus (i.e., baking soda) instead of icing sugar for the frosting. Her second mistake, while not her fault, was to get wrong directions to the minister's house. She delivers her cake to Mrs. Stanleigh rather than to Mrs. Stanley. Mrs. Stanleigh is pleased with the story behind the gift, especially when she hears Prissy's name, but after her first mouthful of

cake she leaves the room rather hurriedly. She returns and finishes the piece, but leaves the icing. Prissy had brought the cake—through her second error—to a long-estranged friend of her mother's. The two women had long wished to be reconciled, but each had been too proud to take the first step until Prissy broke the ice. Prissy was the agent of more good will than she had intended in baking the new minister's wife a cake.

In "Uncle Richard's New Year's Dinner," another Prissy, aged seventeen, keeps house for her widowed father. In the same village lives his estranged brother, Richard. In the general store Prissy overhears her Uncle Richard say he has to be away that morning and will return to a cold dinner. Since her father is out of town she decides to cook dinner for her uncle as a surprise, planning on leaving before his return, of course. He catches her in his kitchen, invites her to help eat his dinner, and confesses to having wanted to be reconciled with her father for a long time. This Prissy, too, while intending one good deed, has achieved more than she expected.

Prissy's decision to please her uncle in spite of the brothers' estrangement is suggestive of her strength of character. Similar strength of character helps other Montgomery heroines in earning a living. "Lilian's Business Venture" tells how Lilian, when she and her mother are left very poor at her father's death, decides to try baking as a means of making some money. She starts in a small way for one or two neighbours, and has to steel herself to bear the sneers of several erstwhile "friends." However, after a year of hard work she has many customers, shows a profit, and can happily say that she is on her way to a successful career. She has built her character and her business at the same time, and the new friends she has made in the process are more worth her while.

Another of Montgomery's young women learns much about herself and the worth of things on the basis of a dinner. In "Elizabeth's Thanksgiving Dinner," we learn that Elizabeth and her widowed mother will be alone for Thanksgiving, their large circle of relatives being unable, at the last minute and for various reasons, to make their regular annual visit. Elizabeth at first decides to invite her girlfriends to dinner to help eat up the many prepared goodies, but on a last-minute shopping expedition she realizes that there are many young women in her town who are much more in need of pleasant surroundings and a comfortable one-day holiday. The table is finally surrounded with a shop assistant or two, a seamstress, two schoolteachers, and half a dozen other "working girls." Elizabeth feels she has gained much more satisfaction from this dinner than from many she has enjoyed with her usual girlfriends, and determines to continue helping and befriending this unfamiliar group.

Cooking as a step to romance is only represented once in these stories, an unexpected proportion, perhaps, for a writer who penned many romances, in several of which, moreover, appears the dictum that the way to a man's heart is through his stomach. Gilbert tells Miss Cornelia, in *Anne's House of Dreams,* that his grandmother's second rule for managing a husband was "Feed him well." "With enough pie," responds Miss Cornelia. "A Baking of Gingersnaps" is one of Montgomery's earliest stories, written before she had quite decided on L. M. Montgomery as her *nom de plume,* and published under the name "Maude Cavendish." Bessie and Alma are baking for their Aunt Clem's visitors and receive a last-minute order from her for gingersnaps. When a curious neighbour drops in, the girls are distracted by her questions, and the first batch is nearly all burnt. Knowing well their aunt's horror of waste, they hide all the cookies (even the few unburnt ones) in an old tree stump near the river, then fly back to whip up another batch before the company arrives. A day or so later, at a friend's dinner party, they meet two young men who tell a tale of finding gingersnaps in a tree stump and devouring the few good ones. One of the young men swears to marry the girl who made them, if he can find her, and the ending suggests that he will succeed in both ventures.

None of these stories is without a good share of humour, as is to be expected with Montgomery, but perhaps the most amusing is **"Uncle Chatterton's Gingerbread."** Not many men in Montgomery's works, besides Little Sam in *A Tangled Web,* are cooks. (In *Anne of Avonlea* Anne and Diana assist poor Mr. Blair in the baking of a cake, and he thanks them with a donation towards the painting of the village hall, but he certainly does not cook on a regular basis.) Uncle Chatterton's days are not complete unless he has found fault with his wife's cooking, and she has come to expect his criticisms and indeed is anxious about his health if they are not forthcoming. But a bold niece who is visiting them suggests, when he complains about the gingerbread at afternoon tea, that he make some himself.

Astonishingly enough, he agrees to do so and, just as astonishingly, does it very deftly. His creation comes out of the oven looking "as light and puffy as golden foam" (a repeated Montgomery description of cakes). However, in spite of a kitchenful of witnesses he had managed to flavour his gingerbread with mustard, and the first mouthful is the last.

Family gatherings, afternoon calls, and parties were important social occasions and all required a "bewildering variety" of good things to eat. Young Grandmother and Mother were appalled at the thought that there had been company at Cloud of Spruce in their absence, and that there had been no cake. "No company had ever found Cloud of Spruce cakeless." A good housekeeper was known by her table; even when Anne managed to convince Marilla that the table should be a "feast for the eye as well as the palate," the latter insisted that Anne leave enough room for the plates and food. Hot and fluffy biscuits, preserves, and several kinds of cake and pie were necessary concomitants to any visit.

A good amount of humour, a sprinkling of sentiment, and just a dash of well-chosen moralizing make Montgomery's stories just as successful as the baking of most of her heroines. She has given us a variety of stories, each with its own flavour and spice. (pp. 47-51)

Rea Wilmshurst, "Cooking with L. M. Montgomery," in Canadian Children's Literature, *No. 37, 1985, pp. 47-52.*

The "Green Gables" house, located in Prince Edward Island National Park. Designed to represent the Cuthbert home from Anne of Green Gables, *it actually belonged to Montgomery's uncle. Now a popular museum, the house is close to her childhood residence and gravesite.*

Kevin McCabe   (essay date 1985)

*[In the following essay, McCabe explores the personal
nature of Montgomery's poetry.]*

One of the happiest effects of the renewed interest in Canadian Literature has been the re-discovery of aspects of leading authors which had often been ignored by the literary world. The recent publication of some of Archibald Lampman's love poems is one example of how our appreciation of a standard author has been enlarged. The human tendency to "take as read" or "take as understood" authors who have seldom been thoroughly read or understood is thus being combatted by a number of recent scholarly works.

Among Canadian authors few have been so persistently typecast as Lucy Maud Montgomery. Known world-wide for **Anne of Green Gables,** she is usually described as the author of one good children's classic and as a writer who continued to work the same vein with diminishing returns, although, as I write, considerable research is beginning on her work. The first installment of her journals is in press, and two major bibliographical projects on her are nearing completion. Until the present time, however, Montgomery has been quite neglected, and her short stories and other writings have been very sparsely represented in anthologies. In the same way her poetry has been so totally eclipsed by her novels that until recently it was not considered necessary for any account of her career to give more than passing reference to the poems.

It is, therefore, very exciting to learn that L. M. Montgomery wrote poetry not only in large quantity, but generally of good quality. Her admirers will be especially pleased to learn that her verse possesses many of the qualities of her best prose writing, and demonstrates her characteristic interests in scenes of nature, human feelings, family conflicts, and the stages of life. In some ways her verse shows a wider range than her prose since it is less limited in subject matter and literary models. She herself wrote of her poetry: "I don't know whether I call verse my speciality or not. I know that I touch a far higher note in my verse than in prose. But I write much more prose than verse because there is a wider market for it, especially among the juvenile publications." As time went on the demand for prose gradually squeezed out her time for verse, although she continued to prefer writing verse, and did so whenever she could snatch time or inspiration.

Coming to L. M. Montgomery's poetry for the first time, I was rather surprised by its relative simplicity of style and lack of ornate poetic diction. It resembles more the simpler lyrics of Longfellow than the heavier style of the pre-Raphaelites and some of our Canadian "Confederation Poets." Although she does have a few favourite "poetical" words such as "adown" and "athwart" such affectations are usually limited, especially in her earlier poetry. Her tendency to see natural objects in human terms ("pathetic fallacy") is with her not simply a literary affectation, since it often is present in her private correspondence. In her poetry there is frequent use of what we might call "The Cloud" mode (after Shelley's poem) in which an inanimate object addresses the reader. We might remember

that L. M. Montgomery and some of her favourite models were pantheistic—that is, they believed, or half-believed, that all things possessed souls and were part of the expression of the nature divine. Thus nature is definitely in the foreground of their work.

Readers of large quantities of Victorian verse are often distressed by the rather uninspired nature and repetitiveness of much of it. Only a few Canadian poets from the period are now read often, namely Bliss Carman, Pauline Johnson, and Robert Service. Part of the reason for this decline in interest is the routine nature of much "magazine verse" of the period. Poems on certain set topics—the sea, the seasons, boy's life, courage and endeavour, the family circle, etc.—were used as fillers by popular magazines which were bought chiefly by women, children, and casual readers. The long term effect of producing quantities of verse on a limited number of subjects was often a vague and general style which took refuge in "poetical" phrasing and literary platitudes. Poets such as Tennyson and Masefield who attempted to write verses every day showed a progressive decline in poetic verve and expressiveness. L. M. Montgomery is no exception to the rule that the demand for quantity rather than quality eventually showed itself in repetitiveness and undistinguished work. Since, however, she switched her energies to prose fairly early in her career the effects are not as blatant as might be expected. Her genuine enjoyment of verse and the thrill of self-expression were only somewhat diminished by her marketing of poetry.

The freshness of much of L. M. Montgomery's verse is perhaps best explained by the remarkable correspondence between the markets she wrote for and her own loves and enthusiasms. The magazines wanted poems about fishing boats and storms at sea. She was born within walking distance of the Gulf of St. Lawrence and always loved sea and shore in all their moods. The magazines wanted poems about spring and meadows and woods. She loved the outdoors and spent most of her free time among the trees, brooks, and fields. Thus Miss Montgomery was not obliged to tear at her hair in order to meet the editors' requirements. Perhaps these did have an influence, however, in that there are very few detailed descriptions in her nature poems. She usually sketches a scene in outline and does not enumerate the names of flowers, plants, and trees, as does, for example, Lampman. In her letters, however, she often describes natural scenes in detail, proving that she was quite familiar with the names of things. It may be that she was inclined to think that poetry should lean toward the general and universal.

L. M. Montgomery wrote of her childhood "I had *no* companionship except that of books and solitary rambles in wood and fields." With respect to books her home did not provide many companions. There were few novels or magazines, and Lucy Maud learned early to revel in poetry. Longfellow, Tennyson, Whittier, Scott, Byron, Milton, and Burns were read and reread and became part of her world. She remained true to her first loves and, years later (February 1896), when she received her first cheque for her writing she used the money to buy the poems of Tennyson, Byron, Milton, Longfellow and Whittier. Her sincere appreciation for some often rather middling poets—Longfellow, Whittier, Scott, Ingelow, and Hemans—no doubt aided her contentment in following the same path herself.

She recollected having written her first verses when she was nine, and first submitting a poem to an editor at the age of twelve. In August 1890 (aged 15) Lucy Maud journeyed by train to Prince Albert, Saskatchewan, to live with her father and his second wife. She stayed there one year and her experiences in the new setting and her regular correspondence with friends at home seem to have given considerable impetus to her writing. That year also saw her first appearance in print—namely, a poem entitled **"On Cape Le Force"** printed in the Charlottetown *Daily Patriot,* November 26, 1890. Before the year was out she had several more pieces in print, which reinforced her interest in writing. The attempt to be reunited with her father, however, was at best a partial success, and she gladly returned to Cavendish in August 1891. The verses from this year show considerable technical ability and human interest, but also a certain bookishness and verbal infelicity which she was soon to leave behind.

Lucy Maud continued her writing back in P.E.I., although she also gave heed to preparing herself to teach in the local schools. In 1894 (aged 19) she first broke into the wider North American literary market with a poem in *The Ladies' World,* a popular American magazine for women. The two subscriptions she received as payment for this poem were the first tangible reward for her writing.

A year at Dalhousie College in Halifax (1895-6) was both an academic and literary success and marks a new era in her self-confidence and literary verve. We are told that "she always maintained that her contacts with Professor [Archibald] MacMechan inspired her, and enabled her to write with greater facility and effectiveness than before." In one week of February 1896 work of hers was accepted by three different editors for publication and for all three pieces she was paid. Perhaps the proudest achievement was the acceptance of her poem **"Fisher Lassies"** by the *Youth's Companion,* possibly the leading juvenile publication in America; the resulting cheque was for twelve dollars.

The work accepted that week showed considerable competence, and a growing talent for making the most of any theme or suggestion. Her verses on "Which has the most patience under ordinary cares and trials of life—man or woman?" are worth quoting in part for their new freedom in thought and expression.

> If a man's obliged to wait
> For some one who's rather late,
> No mortal ever got in such a stew,
> And if something can't be found
> That he's sure should be around,
> The listening air sometimes grows fairly blue
> . . .
>
> Some point to Job with pride
> As an argument for their side!
> Why, it was so rare a patient man to see,
> That when one was really found,
> His discoverers were bound

To preserve for him a place in history!

She returned to school-teaching in P.E.I. with a renewed determination to succeed in the literary world. She developed the habit of rising early each morning in order to get in some time for writing before facing her teaching duties. These years (1896-8) were productive of much good verse, and Miss Montgomery gradually added new names to the list of journals which were accepting her work. The death of her grandfather in March 1898 required her to return to Cavendish to help and care for her grandmother and her property. Lucy Maud remained situated at Cavendish with her grandmother until the latter's death in March 1911, except for one job as reporter-writer for the Halifax *Daily Echo* from October 1901 till June 1902. In Cavendish she continued to write poetry but began concentrating more on prose because of the larger market for it, and her need to supplement the limited family income.

Her work on the *Daily Echo,* I suspect, had a negative effect on the freshness and individuality of her poetry. In Halifax she taught herself to write verse amidst all the noises and distractions of a newspaper office. Her friend Ephraim Weber admired her ability to write a poem like **"Sea Gulls"** in a printing office. Yet we may wonder if her talent for producing something to order on any subject wasn't stretched too far under these circumstances. After 1901 her verse seems increasingly to rely on generalized memories and technical facility rather on direct and immediate feelings or impressions. At any rate as the first decade of this century proceeds we find more and more literary touches in her poems that we might wish away and fewer markedly individualized sentiments. By 1906 it is not uncommon to find her writing such garishly poetical posings as the following piece entitled **"Twilight"**:

> From vales of dawn hath Day pursued the Night
> Who mocking fled, swift-sandalled, to the west,
> Nor ever lingered in her wayward flight
> With dusk-eyed glance to recompense his guest,
> But over crocus hills and meadows gray
> Sped fleetly on her way.
>
> Now when the Day, shorn of his failing strength,
> Hath fallen spent before the sunset bars,
> The fair, wild Night, with pity touched at length,
> Crowned with her chaplet of out-blossoming stars
> Creeps back repentantly upon her way
> To kiss the dying Day.

Another factor was at work which may be noted in the verses of many middling poets. They often begin by writing about what they know and their own experiences. Gradually those scenes, ideas, and incidents which are of real interest to the writer and have real literary possibilities are used up. At this point the writer tends to become increasingly repetitive and starts to compensate by verbal dexterity and literary ingenuity for the absence of fresh inspiration. It is at this point (about 1904) that L. M. Montgomery turned more and more to prose and, in fact, began to write what later became *Anne of Green Gables.*

Many of the poems which L. M. Montgomery wrote between 1891 and 1901 do reflect the life she lived in Cavendish and are the more interesting for that. As one of her strongest talents lay in evoking the past, she continued to use these memories in her poems and novels. A typical early poem is **"The Gable Window"** (published 1897) which begins:

> It opened on a world of wonder,
> When summer days were sweet and long:
> A world of light, a world of splendour,
> A world of song.
>
> 'Twas there I passed my hours of dreaming.
> 'Twas there I knelt at night to pray:
> And, when the rose-lit dawn was streaming
> Across the day,
>
> I bent from it to catch the glory
> Of all those radiant silver skies
> A resurrection allegory
> For human eyes!
>
> The summer raindrops on it beating,
> The swallows clinging 'neath the eaves,
> The wayward shadows by it fleeting,
> The whispering leaves . . .

In such a poem Miss Montgomery was able to combine real experience with her love for dreaminess and evocation of the past. The descriptive passages in these early poems often seem particularly graphic and homey, as in the poem **"I Wonder"** (published 1896).

> The sun is set, it is faintly light.
> The pink in the west is chill and bright.
> Voices are somewhere, the air is still,
> A fox is barking on Crow Nest Hill.
> Through the long dim lane, to the pasture bars,
> John drives the cows 'neath the early stars.
> He is looking up through the trees at the Hall.
> "The grand old house is ablaze with light;
> The heir gives his birthday ball tonight.
> The captain's sons are home from town.
> They have brought their dogs and horses down.
> There's no lack of dinners and balls and wine,
> For their city friends, white-handed and fine.
> I saw the heir as he rode today,
> Scented, and trim on his prancing bay.
> Disease on his form and left its trace,
> And a frown disfigured his thin, dark face.
> I wonder if he would give his wealth.
> For my brown-limbed strength and ruddy
>   health.
> I wonder," says John. "I wonder."

Her early nature poetry also has an energy sometimes lacking in her later work, as in lines from **"In Haying Time"** (published 1897):

> The fields at dawn are silver-white,
> And wet with their baptismal dew;
> They ripen in the long, rare noons,
> Beneath a dome of cloudness blue.
> And in the twilight's purple dusk,
> How solemn, hushed, and dim they lie!
> At night the mellow moon looks down
> From silent, star-sown depths of sky.
>
> Each passing hour of night and day
> Some new and rare enchantment brings,
> In flowers that bloom and winds that blow,

> And joy of shy, blithe, living things
> That hide within the meadows green,
> Or murmur in the drowsy fields;
> And all the golden air is sweet
> With incense rose-red clover yields.

The demand for her stories, serials, and novels took away most of her time for writing verse. On November 10, 1907, she wrote to Ephraim Weber: "Do you know I haven't written a single line of verse since July. I'm going to try to write a poem tomorrow." Following the success of **Anne of Green Gables** (1908), L. M. Montgomery turned increasingly to writing novels, resolving to give up all "hack work." She had little trouble now publishing her verses and in 1916 brought out a collection entitled **The Watchman and Other Poems.** As this is the only book of her poems yet printed, it is a little unfortunate that it is somewhat unrepresentative since it omits many of her early poems, and includes most of her later more ambitious and "literary" pieces. No second edition was required and Miss Montgomery's reputation as a poet has declined steadily since that time.

It would be a mistake, however, to divide Miss Montgomery's poetical work into an early and satisfactory period and a later and unsatisfactory period. Inspiration comes and goes, and much of her earlier poetry is poor while some of her later poetry is quite good. She continued to write verse almost up to her death, and took great pleasure in it. One later poem which shows both inspiration and technical maturity is **"Night"** (published 1935):

> A pale enchanted moon is sinking low
> Behind the dunes that fringe the shadowy lea,
> And there is haunted starlight on the flow
> Of immemorial sea.
>
> I am alone and need no more pretend
> Laughter or smile to hide a hungry heart,
> I walk with solitude as with a friend
> Enfolded and apart.
>
> We tread an eerie road across the moor
> Where shadows weave upon their ghostly looms,
> And winds sing an old lyric that might lure
> Sad queens from ancient tombs.
>
> I am a sister to the loveliness
> Of cool, far hill and long-remembered shore,
> Finding in it a sweet forgetfulness
> Of all that hurt before.
>
> The world of day, its bitterness and cark
> No longer have the power to make me weep,
> I welcome this communion of the dark
> As toilers welcome sleep.

For L. M. Montgomery writing poetry was more than a literary activity; it was almost a form of Holy Communion. To read poetry was to glimpse into the realm of ideal beauty. God spoke to man through Poetry and Nature. In this trinity God was the most remote and inscrutable member. Indeed because we only see God darkly through his creation and the writings of great men, all dogmas (said the Transcendentalists) are merely human products. The poet is then a kind of priest who interprets the universe to men, who unfortunately are not wise enough to acclaim their insights.

There was a distinct element of snobbery in this new religion, for in order to be a transcendentalist it was almost a requirement to be either a writer or an artist. Lucy Maud herself often wrote sarcastically about the homely Presbyterianism of her background, although she carefully maintained the forms of Christianity all her life. Indeed Jesus was merely transformed into a wise and poetical teacher—one of the many precursors of Emerson.

One unfortunate effect of transcendentalism in literary circles was a distinct division of everything into either beautiful, poetical, spiritual and intellectual, or ugly, commonplace, materialistic, and stupid. Most aspects of the world around us, including people and institutions, tended to fall into the latter group. Among people only a few "kindred spirits" transcended the usual prosaic and unideal modes of existence. The poet was foremost among those who aspired to a truer and more beautiful life and scorned the mundane realities of everyday living. Miss Montgomery approvingly quoted Emerson on ideal *versus* real life: "In the actual—this painful kingdom of time and chance—are Care, Canker and Sorrow: with thought, with the ideal, is immortal hilarity—the rose of joy; round it all the Muses sing."

It is easy to see how such a philosophy could fall into a rather self-indulgent escapism, and this is sometimes the case in her poetry. It also provided the seeds for developing an aloof, critical, and even hostile attitude towards people in the mass. The distinction which Lucy Maud made between herself and others in her neighbourhood is hinted at when she writes of her neighbours' response to **Anne of Green Gables:** "If you have lived all your life in a little village where everybody is every whit as good and clever and successful as everybody else, and if you are foolish enough to do something which the others in the village cannot do, especially if that something brings you in a small modicum of fame and fortune, a certain class of people will take it as a personal insult to themselves, will belittle you and your accomplishment in every way and will go out of their way to make sure that you are informed of their opinions." She often contrasts the beauty of nature with the drabness of the lives she sees around her. She rarely can detail any spark of spirituality or glimmer of romance or intellect in her neighbours or in their faith and thought. "As a rule," she writes, "I am very careful to be shallow and conventional where depth and originality are wasted. When I get very desperate I retreat into my realms of cloudland and hold delightful imaginary dialogues with the shadowy, congenial shapes I meet there."

As with many Romantic writers and some of their modern descendants, she sometimes seems to put a higher premium on writing well than on living well. Energy which she could well have used in her everyday living, especially as she grew older, was applied towards her next poem, story, or novel. Her readers are the beneficiaries of this pursuit of good literary standards. She tried to put herself into her work and often succeeds better than one would expect. Although she confessed disbelief in the deity of Jesus, her poems on the incarnation and resurrection are by no means mere formal exercises, or without feeling. Her imaginative power often flashes forth in the unlikeliest

places and gives a brief splendour to even the weakest parts of her work.

"No man can serve two masters; for either he will hate the one, and love the other, or else he will hold to the one and despise the other" [Matthew 7:24]. In spite of her yearning for an ideal, spiritual, and poetical life, L. M. Montgomery was closely tied to some very worldly realities by her need for affection, respect, and recognition. The early death of her mother and her father's subsequent departure for Saskatchewan undoubtedly created a void in her life, and a need for reassurance and praise from her family and close associates. Her maternal grandparents were not easy to please and tended to be gruff and undemonstrative towards their granddaughter. Lucy Maud's pursuit of excellence was perhaps partly motivated by a desire to convince both her family and herself of her own value. She went to great lengths to gain the small-town respectability which privately she scorned. Her services as church organist, Sunday-school teacher, and later minister's wife all went against the grain, yet she agreed to marry a minister, and quickly came to regret it. To her correspondent Ephraim Weber she never tires of enumerating the magazines which accept her work, and how much they pay. In her first letter to G. B. MacMillan she proudly tells how much she earns by writing, although she would have been shocked if one of her neighbours had asked her about it. The only way which she could justify her passion for writing to her family, to her community, and even to herself was by earning money from it, and she set out doggedly to accomplish this.

Poetry began for her as a natural, almost instinctive passion, given impetus by lack of free communication with close family members or suitable companions. Eventually it became a tool for an introduction into the wider world or into the marketplace. But it always retained a confessional element for her, and its importance as an avenue of self-expression remained, especially when the novel became her dominant public medium. This explains in part why her earlier poetry is somewhat fresher, before it had become more of a product for the market, and why she returned to poetry again as she grew older to express some of her deeper feelings.

Poetry was at the centre of Montgomery's life and when we read her verses with this in mind it illuminates both her own experience and that of the era in which she lived.

—*Kevin McCabe*

We have already compared her work with the lyric parts of Henry Wadsworth Longfellow's poems, and the comparison is instructive. Like Longfellow she blends the ongoing Romantic literary tradition with popular interests and contemporary enthusiasms in a way that was very attractive to large numbers of people. As with Longfellow there is also an element of the school-teacher—the desire to impart information or attitudes—in her writing. There is also a very personal element in both poets—a nostalgia sometimes combined with a sense of bereavement. Both Longfellow and Montgomery were much influenced by the death or illnesses of friends and family members as well as by the depressing aspects of national or world politics. A kind of wistful sadness often possesses them for what might have been or for what could never be. Longfellow, of course, had a larger range of interest than Montgomery. A Longfellow poem, however, such as "The Day Is Done" shows close resemblances to hers both in thought and style. It begins with a reference to the bittersweet restlessness that both writers sometimes felt:

> I see the lights of the village
> Gleam through the rain and the mist:
> And a feeling of sadness comes o'er me
> That my soul cannot resist:
>
> A feeling of sadness and longing,
> That is not akin to pain,
> And resembles sorrow only
> As the mist resembles the rain.

Longfellow goes on to state a kind of "credo" for the middling poet. He argues that the "humbler poet" performs a function which the greater poets are unable to do—namely to provide soothing songs for the care-worn. Their power is attributed to the natural simplicity of the "humbler poet" who has this gift of singing "wonderful melodies":

> Come read to me some poem
> Some simple and heartfelt lay,
> That shall soothe this restless feeling,
> And banish the thoughts of day.
>
> Not from the grand old masters,
> Not from the bards sublime,
> Whose distant footsteps echo
> Through the corridors of Time.
>
> For, like strains of martial music,
> Their mighty thoughts suggest
> Life's endless toil and endeavour;
> And tonight I long for rest.
>
> Read from some humbler poet,
> Whose songs gush'd from his heart,
> As showers from the cloud of summer,
> Or tears from the eyelids start;
>
> When through long days of labour,
> And nights devoid of ease,
> Still heard in his soul the music
> Of wonderful melodies.
>
> Such songs have the power to diet
> The restless pulse of care,
> And come like the benediction
> That follows after prayer.

Longfellow and L. M. Montgomery both belonged to "Young America" when pioneering was still a contemporary phenomenon and urbanization could still be overlooked. Miss Montgomery's generation was perhaps the last to be dominated by rural or small-town writers. Ar-

chibald Lampman grew up in small towns such as Morpeth, Perrytown, Gore's Landing, and Cobourg. Charles G. D. Roberts spent his most impressionable years in Westcock, N. B., while Wilfred Campbell lived in Wiarton for some years. Wilson MacDonald was born in Cheapside, and Pauline Johnson grew up a few miles from Brantford. The chief centres of Canadian writing at the turn of the century were Fredericton and Ottawa.

The total lack of sympathy between these late Romantics and the modernist school results partly from this rural-urban split. Modernism in poetry derives almost entirely from the metropolitan centres—Paris, London, New York, and Chicago—and its chief practitioners have neither experience of nor interest in the world of nature. Such leaders as T. S. Eliot and Ezra Pound were in fact expatriates. Modernism naturally took as its chief theme the alienation of urban man, thus invoking its own nemesis. When modernism reached Canada it naturally gravitated to the largest centres—Montreal and Toronto—from where it carried on warfare against the tradition of nature poetry and popular verse.

The split between late Romanticism and Modernism was also one of feeling *versus* intellect. The Romantics loved poetry partly as a way of expressing their feelings and as a mode of vicariously enjoying the feelings of others. L. M. Montgomery wrote to G. B. MacMillan regarding her admiration for Robert Burns: "What a magnificent creature he was: I've loved his poetry ever since I was a baby. A great many poets appeal only or almost only to the intellect. Burns appeals to the heart and in this I think is the secret of his power. He makes his verses *live* with the richness of his own nature . . . He gave voice to the song that sings itself in *all* human hearts . . . " Burns represents a high point in the early Romantic movement, a level which later poets such as Montgomery often attempted to reach but with varying success. The continuing popularity of Romantic verse reinforces the Romantic claim to speak to and for large numbers of people. It may perhaps be said that people tend to be united by feelings and divided by philosophies.

L. M. Montgomery's own best poetry is usually an overflow of her feelings or an expression of her moods. In a good example of this is the poem which express her joy on the birth and infancy of her first son Chester. Further inspired by a visit of her dear cousin and friend, Fredericka Campbell, the two conspired to write humorous verses: "Fredericka and I have such fun in the mornings when I bathe and dress him in the kitchen while she is washing the breakfast dishes. We talk the most delicious nonsense to him, make all the funny impromptu rhymes we can about him, and act the fool generally, none daring to make us afraid. Here for example is this morning's classic on **"The Pirate Wag"**—which is one of Frede's nicknames for him:

> There was a pirate known as Wag
> Whose Sunday name was Punch;
> He sailed upon the raging main
> And ate his aunts for lunch.
>
> He liked them fricasseed and stewed;
> But sometimes for a change,

He broiled them nice and tenderly
Upon his kitchen range.

But he preferred them piping hot
Served up in a tureen,
Fried in deep fat a golden brown
And decked with paisley green.

And when an aunt was saucier
Than usual Waggy said,
'I'll have you made into a hash
You gristly old Aunt Frede.'

But when Aunt Stella was served up
Wag wouldn't touch a bite,
He said, 'If I et her I'd have
Most awful dreams tonight.'

When his supply of aunts ran out
Wag used to eat his fists,
And when he went to bed he put
His stockings on his wrist.

It is difficult for us even to imagine the importance of poetry to L. M. Montgomery and many of her contemporaries, and its unquestioned role in their lives. She describes the visit of an old friend to their home—they had been schoolmates forty or so years earlier—and wrote of their happy reunion: "Sometimes we quoted poetry. Nora would voice the first line of a couplet and I would finish it. Once in this alternate way we recited the whole of Wordsworth's 'Ode on the Intimations of immortality', lingering over the lines 'Our birth is but a sleep and a forgetting.' " Poetry was at the centre of Montgomery's life and when we read her verses with this in mind it illuminates both her own experience and that of the era in which she lived. (pp. 68-79)

> *Kevin McCabe, "Lucy Maud Montgomery: The Person and the Poet," in* Canadian Children's Literature, *No. 38, 1985, pp. 68-80.*

John Ferns   (essay date 1986)

[*In the following essay, Ferns analyzes the defining qualities of Montgomery's poetry.*]

> It came to him in rainbow dreams,
>   Blent with the wisdom of the sages,
> Of spirit and of passion born;
>   In words as lucent as the morn
> He prisoned it, and now it gleams,
>   A jewel shining through the ages,
>   **"The Poet's Thought"**
>   Lucy Maud Montgomery

Writing in *The Globe and Mail* on May 26, 1984, Judith Finlayson mentioned that Louisa May Alcott, the author of *Little Women,* was also the author of a neglected, but now republished, feminist novel. Readers of *Canadian Children's Literature* will be equally pleased to learn of another rediscovered work: Lucy Maud Montgomery of **Anne of Green Gables** fame was also the author of over 500 poems. Though many of these poems were published in magazines during Lucy Maud Montgomery's lifetime, yet she only published a slim selection of her verse in **The Watchman and Other Poems** (1916). Kevin McCabe and I have now prepared for publication a much wider selection of L. M. Montgomery's poetic works.

To characterise Lucy Maud Montgomery's poetry briefly is to say that she wrote largely in the Victorian-Edwardian style. Romanticism is strongly present in her work. As one reads through the 500 poems one is reminded often of Wordsworth's ideas, in particular of his concern with the goodness and innocence of childhood, a concern which Lucy Maud Montgomery shares. With Wordsworth, too, she shares a sense that nature has lessons to teach us. Of the other English romantics, her verse is strongly reminiscent of Keats, particularly in her sensuous descriptions of nature. Scott's Gothic narratives and Byron's melancholy lyricism also come to mind in reading her work. For both these poets she reveals an admiration.

Of the English Victorians, Tennyson (with Keats often mediated through him) is surely the strongest influence, though interestingly her most ambitious poem **"The Watchman"** is a dramatic monologue in Browning's manner. The Pre-Raphaelites were also an influence, as were such American romantic-transcendentalist poets as Longfellow, Whittier and Emerson.

If we accept Roberts, Carman, Lampman and D. C. Scott as our major Confederation poets, reading Lucy Maud Montgomery's poetry is like discovering another Confederation poet even though she is of a slightly later generation. She shares Roberts' Wordsworthianism, his philosophical and moral turn of mind and also his love of Eastern Canadian land—and seascapes. She resembles Carman in her metrical lyricism and Lampman in her Keatsian-sensuous dwelling upon the luxuriance of nature.

Her poems, from which we have chosen about 150 as worthy of republication, fall naturally into sections such as nature poems, poems of morality and religion, sea poems and elegiac and love poems. To attempt to group the poems in the way just described, however, immediately raises the issue of the arbitrariness and limitation of such groupings in that the best of the poems defy them and cry out instead for inclusion in more than one group. To illustrate what I mean—her best poems are often those that speak about nature in the language of religion as was frequently the case in nineteenth-century romantic poetry. Before providing illustrative examples of her best work in each of the groups mentioned, I would like to indicate why it appears best to present her work in this way. Montgomery wrote most of her poetry between the years 1890 and 1915 and then as she wrote more fiction she wrote less poetry. Even within this twenty-five year period, her work does not reveal important changes and developments. Indeed, the central event in the poet's life seems to have been the loss of her mother, who died when Lucy Maud Montgomery was about twenty-one months old. Many of her poems concern loss of a loved one—a theme not directly related to events in her life between 1890 and 1915. Therefore, a thematic rather than a chronological organization of a selection of her poems appears to be most appropriate.

Nature poems certainly constitute the largest section. Her first interest as a poet seems to have been the desire to express her love of the beauty of nature often, as noted, in the language of religion. Her poem **"After Drought"** which appeared in the *Christian Advocate* on October 1, 1908, provides a simple example of what I mean:

Last night all through the darkling hours we
heard
   The voices of the rain,
And every languid pulse in nature stirred
   Responsive to the strain;
The morning brought a breath of strong sweet
air
   From shadowy pineland blown,
And over field and upland everywhere
   A new-born greenness shone.
The saintly meadow lilies offer up
   Their white hearts to the sun,
And every wildwood blossom lifts its cup
   With incense overrun;
The brook whose voice was silent yestereve
   Now sings its old refrain,
And all the world is grateful to receive
   The blessing of the rain.

Perhaps it is the Biblical subject of drought or the Christian idea of rebirth that provokes the increasing use of religious language as the poem proceeds. "Darkling" is a word typical of nineteenth-century verse. Its use by Keats ("Ode to a nightingale"), Arnold ("Dover Beach") and Hardy ("The Darkling Thrush") will be familiar to most readers. Indeed, the lines "And every languid pulse in nature stirred / Responsive to the strain" are further reminiscent of Hardy's poem ("The ancient pulse of germ and birth / Was shrunken hard and dry.") though we have no certainty that Lucy Maud Montgomery could have read it. The mysterious (possibly divine) source of the "breath of strong sweet air" is a further possible source of the germination of religious language in the poem. Certain it is (whatever the source) that religious language grows as the poem develops. "The saintly meadow lilies," "wildwood blossom lifts its cup / With incense overrun," the brook hymn-like "Now sings its old refrain" and "The blessing of the rain" confirms this. Indeed, the metaphoric expression of one order of experience in terms of another lies at the root of poetry as an art of language.

Further instances of Lucy Maud Montgomery's use of this technique in some of her best poems can be found in poems like **"The Gable Window"** (which appeared originally in the April 1897 issue of *Ladies Journal*) or **"Night in the Pastures"** (*New England Farmer,* October, 1898). Or we find the technique reversed in a poem like **"In Planting Time"** in which natural imagery is used to express religious-moral sentiments and ideas. The first two stanzas of the poem depict the end of winter and the preparation of the land for sowing in the spring. The idea of sowing is then linked to moral living through the remaining five stanzas of the poem. Here is the third stanza:

Now, here's a thought for you and me: our
planting time is here,
In this bright spring of youth and hope, the best
time of the year!
And don't you think that we should be most
careful what we sow,
Since in the fair, wide fields of life our seeds will
surely grow?

"The Gable Window" which appeared in the April 1897 issue of *Ladies' Journal* is as characteristic an example as there is of a nature poem that, in its Bliss Carman and Pre-

Raphaelite reminiscences, again employs the language of religion. Indeed, Lucy Maud Montgomery seems to read nature for religious significances as Jerome Bump in his recent study indicates that Gerard Manley Hopkins did:

It opened on a world of wonder,
   When summer days were sweet and long,
A world of light, a world of splendor,
   A world of song.
Twas there I passed my hours of dreaming,
   Twas there I knelt at night to pray;
And when the rose-lit dawn was streaming
   Across the day.

I bent from it to catch the glory
   Of all those radiant silver skies—
A resurrection allegory
   For human eyes!

The summer raindrops on it beating,
   The swallows clinging 'neath the eaves,
The wayward shaddows [sic] by it fleeting
   The whispering leaves;

The birds that passed in joyous vagrance,
   The echoes of the golden moon,
The drifting in of subtle fragrance
   The wind's low croon;

Held each a message and a token
   In every hour of day and night;
A meaning wordless and unspoken,
   Yet read aright.

I looked from it o'er bloomy meadows
   Where idle breezes lost their way
To solemn hills whose purple shadows
   About them lay.

I saw the sunshine stream in splendour
   O'er heaven's utmost azure bars,
At eve the radiance, pure and tender
   Of white-browed stars.

I carried there my childish sorrows,
   I wept my little griefs away;
I pictured there my glad to-morrows
   In bright array.

The airy dreams of child and maiden
   Hang round that gable window still
As cling the vines, green and leaf-laden
   About the sill.

And though I lean no longer from it,
   To gaze with loving reverent eyes,
On clouds and amethystine summit,
   And star-sown skies,

The lessons at its casement taught me,
   My life with rich fruition fill;
The rapture of the peace they brought me
   Are with me still!

The poem in its form, imagery, style and tone is a direct result of Tennyson's dominance in nineteenth-century poetry.

One of Lucy Maud Montgomery's best poems finds its place in the section of moral religious poems. **"What Know We?"** appeared in *Churchman, Christian Advocate* for August 21, 1902, and was also reprinted in the *First*

Baptist Monthly. The poem shows Lucy Maud Montgomery's characteristic preference for stanzaic forms. Again the poem emerges directly from the popular tradition of Victorian religious verse that often took the form of hymn writing:

> What know we of the gnawing grief
>   That dims perchance our neighbor's way,
> The fretting worry, secret pain
>   That may be his from day to day?
> Then let no idle word of ours
>   Sting to his heart with more dismay.
>
> What know we of temptations deep
>   That hover round him like the night?
> What bitter struggles may be his,
>   What evil influences blight?
> Then be not hasty to condemn,
>   If he have strayed from paths of right.
>
> We know so little of the hearts
>   That everywhere around us beat,
> So little of the inner lives
>   Of those whom day by day we greet,
> Oh, it behooves us one and all
>   Gently to deal with those we meet!
>
> Gently to deal and gently judge,
>   With that divinest charity
> That thinks no evil but would seek
>   The good in every soul to see,
> Measuring not by what it is
>   But by that which it strives to be.

Lucy Montgomery's nature poetry is written frequently in a Tennysonian-Keatsian ornate style that derives from Shakespeare and Spenser. Her moral and religious poetry by contrast is often written (as here) in a plainer style which we can trace back through eighteenth-century poetry to Ben Jonson. Here, in **"What Know We?"**, we feel the anguish of human isolation, our inability often to recognise or fully sympathise with the sufferings of others. We sense here Lucy Maud Montgomery's moral feeling for the lot of other human beings. This is what gives strength to the poem.

Other moral and religious poems of interest include **"I Asked of God"**, **"Could We But Know"**, **"One of the Shepherds"**, **"The Only Way"**, **"A Prayer"**, **"The Revelation"** and, of course, **"The Watchman"** which is, in many ways, her most ambitious single poem and which gave its title to and held first place in her only volume of verse. It is a dramatic monologue that uses the method so frequently employed by Robert Browning. A Roman soldier, Maximus, speaks to his lover Claudia about how he stood guard over Christ's tomb and witnessed the resurrection. The result is that his pride in battle has changed to a desire to protect the suffering and weak. We are reminded strongly of Browning's "Epistle of Karshish" in which Karshish longs for belief like the Christian belief in life after death. Maximus concludes:

> I care no more for glory; all desire
> For honor and for strife is gone from me,
> All eagerness for war. I only care
> To help and save bruised beings, and to give
> Some comfort to the weak and suffering;
> I cannot even hate those Jews; my lips

> Speak harshly of them, but within my heart
> I only feel compassion; and I love
> All creatures, to the vilest of the slaves,
> Who seem to me as brothers. Claudia,
> Scorn me not for this weakness; it will pass—
> Surely 'twill pass in time and I shall be
> Maximus strong and valiant once again,
> Forgetting that slain god. And yet . . . and
>   yet . . .
> He looked as one who could not be forgot!

The final irony is that Maximus is not yet fully aware of his Christian conversion. When we take this poem together with **"The Gable Window"** we see the extent of Lucy Maud Montgomery's debt to Tennyson and Browning and to the conventions of Victorian verse. Lucy Maud Montgomery was no poetic innovator like Gerard Manley Hopkins. A major writer of Canadian children's fiction she was, but in her adherence to convention, a minor poet. She neither altered her style nor broke new poetic ground.

Although Lucy Maud Montgomery grew up on Prince Edward Island and knew the countryside and the sea at first hand, she writes more convincingly, and consequently better, about fields and woods than she does about the sea. Perhaps this is because she found the countryside more attractive and secure. It was a womb that Lucy Maud Montgomery could retreat into, in which she could find escape and peace. The sea, in contrast, was dangerous, associated with death and with her central obsessional subject—the loss of her mother. Her sea poems include **"Before Storm"**, **"Along Shore"**, **"On Cape Le Force"**, **"On the Gulf Shore"**, **"Out o' Doors"**, **"The Sandshore in September"**, **"Sea Song"**, **"When the Fishing Boats Go Out"**, **"When the Tide Goes Out"** and **"The Wreck of the 'Marco Polo'—1883,"** a remarkable early poem, written in August 1891, when Lucy Maud Montgomery was only seventeen. Typically enough (and to prove the point about the sea's association with loss) it concerns marine disaster.

"Before Storm" is one of the most successful of Lucy Maud Montgomery's sea poems:

> There's a grayness over the harbour like fear on
>   the face of a woman.
>   The sob of the waves has a sound akin to a
>   woman's cry,
> And deeps beyond the bar are moaning with evil
>   presage
>   Of a storm that will leap from its lair in that
>   dour northeastern sky.
>
> Slowly the pale mists rise, like ghosts of the sea,
>   in the offing,
>   Creeping all wan and chilly by headland and
>   sunken reef,
> And a wind is wailing and keening like a lost
>   thing 'mid the islands,
>   Boding of wreck and tempest, plaining of
>   dolour and grief.
>
> Swiftly the boats come homeward, over the grim
>   bar crowding,
>   Like birds that flee to their shelter in a hurry
>   and affright,
> Only the wild gray gulls that love the cloud and
>   the clamour

> Will dare to tempt the ways of the ravening
>   sea to-night.
>
> But the ship that sailed at the dawning, manned
>   by the lads that love us,
>   God help and pity her when the storm is
>   loosed on her track!
> Oh, women, we pray tonight and keep a vigil of
>   sorrow
>   For those we sped at the dawning and may
>   never welcome back!

The storm in stanza one is presented as a wild animal and the sea in stanza three is described as "ravening." Central to the poem's structure and meaning, however, is the use of simile which in its incomplete comparison adds to the poem's sense of division, the separation between the praying women on shore and "the lads that love us," who are at sea. In these similes we see further the way in which Lucy Maud Montgomery associated the sea with danger and loss. Immediately, in stanza one, the ominous grayness of the approaching storm is likened to "fear on the face of a woman." The same technique is repeated in stanza two in which "the pale mists rise, like ghosts of the sea, in the offing," and in the third line of the same stanza "a wind is wailing and keening like a lost thing 'mid the islands." In stanza three Montgomery again uses simile to draw her picture yet enforce a sense of separateness even in comparison, "Swiftly the boats come homeward, over the grim bar crowding, / Like birds that flee to their shelter in a hurry and affright." However, in stanza four simile is absent. Its place is taken by prayer, "God help and pity her [the ship] when the storm is loosed on her track." This is one of Lucy Maud Montgomery's most successful poems because in it she writes simply, directly and with feeling. She avoids the Victorian Romantic diction, the "adorns," "athwarts" and "amethystines" that in their archaic literariness clot and muffle her less successful poems.

The fourth and final section into which Lucy Maud Montgomery's selected poems can, for convenience, be placed is a section of poems that concern loss and love. In many ways loss and love are Lucy Maud Montgomery's central subjects. When she writes of nature, for example, her most frequent subject, she often writes indirectly of the pain-filled realities of losing and loving. Lucy Maud Montgomery's poems of loss are more particularly poems of mother loss. As already mentioned, the early loss of her mother seems to have been the most important formative event in her life, more important to her inner life than the later success of **Anne of Green Gables.** Doubtless, that was a wonderful confirmation, bringing popularity to off-set, to a degree, her life-long sense of loneliness. But in terms of the formation of Lucy Maud Montgomery's essential character, inseparable from her work as a writer, the loss of her mother is more important. In her poems she writes continuously (directly or indirectly) of this experience.

In **"Down Home"** the mother's presence is imagined:

> Down home to-night the moonshine falls
>   Across a hill with daisies pied,
> The pear-tree by the garden gate
>   Beckons with white arms like a bride.
>
> A savor as of trampled fern

> Along the whispering meadow stirs
> And, beacon of immortal love,
>   A light is shining through the firs.
>
> To my old gable-window creeps
>   The night wind with a sigh and song,
> And, weaving ancient sorceries
>   Thereto the gleeful moonbeams throng.
>
> Beside the open kitchen door
>   My mother stands, all longingly,
> And o'er the pathways of the dark
>   She sends a yearning thought to me.
>
> It seeks and finds my answering heart
>   Which shall no more be peace-possessed
> Until I reach her empty arms
>   And lay my head upon her breast.

"The pear-tree by the garden gate" is reminiscent of "holds the pear to the gable wall" in Tennyson's "Mariana." The similarity of the poem to Tennyson's *In memoriam* is particularly striking. Both are poems of yearning. Throughout, Lucy Maud Montgomery's elegiac and love poems are intimately related, because the love she feels for her mother is simultaneously associated with both loss and love. Thus, one of her more moving love poems is called **"The Light in Mother's Eyes."** Written in April 1897, it appeared in the *Family Story Paper* for December 1898. In this poem the lost mother is first recreated by Montgomery then her loss is described. It is as if poetry provides a means through which Lucy Maud Montgomery can wrestle with the problem of grief that obsesses her:

> . . . In hours when all life's sweetest buds
>   Burst into dewy bloom;
> In hours when cherished hopes lay dead
>   In sorrow and in gloom;
> In evening's hush, or morning's glow,
>   Or in the solemn night
> Those mother eyes still shed on me
>   Their calm, unchanging light.

In this poem Lucy Maud Montgomery first attempts to escape from and then confronts the problem of her grief. The critic Andrew Brink contends that poetry provides "symbolic repair" for loss, and that creativity is reparative. We indeed see the writing of poetry as providing for Montgomery "help for pain" in that relief is found through writing the grief out. But, finally, in the poem's last stanza the mother's death is accepted and consolation found in the Christian idea of reunion beyond death in "fields of Paradise."

In conclusion, I would like to consider three further poems by Lucy Maud Montgomery: **"In Church"** as an example of a poem in which all her concerns come together, **"The First Snowfall"** as an instance of the way in which her preoccupation with death and loss is shot through her nature poetry, and finally **"The Piper"** one of her last poems which was first published after her death.

"In Church" was published in *Ladies' Journal* in March, 1898:

> The wind blew in at the open window,
>   Sweet with the breath of the field's perfume,
> And the sunlight showered its benediction

Till the dim air burst into golden bloom.
Far up, we caught a blue glimpse of heaven
    And fancied we saw as we knelt in prayer,
The white-winged angels coming and going
    In the infinite deeps of untroubled air.

Our mother sat in the old dim corner
    With a holy light in her gentle eyes
As though she, too, saw with clearer vision
    The silver wings on the far-off skies
And as we sat with out small hands folded
    In the strange hushed calm of the sacred place
Dreaming of angels astray from heaven
    We always gave them our mother's face.

The choir sang and the music drifted
    Over our heads like a wordless prayer—
We knew it floated to pearly portals
    And left the praise of our spirits there.
Little recked we of the preacher's sermon.
    It was for people old and grown
But the mother-smile and the sunshine blessing
    And our dreamy fancies were all our own.

And ours were the voices that always whispered
    Softly above us of wondrous things
We knew that the angels were hovering near us
    Poised on the sweep of their shining wings.
Ah! we are never so near to heaven
    Now we are grown, as in days of yore;
We are wiser, perhaps, than in childhood's moments
    But the visions come to us nevermore.

The poem combines Lucy Maud Montgomery's love of nature, her interest in religion and her pre-occupation with mother-loss. Indeed, it brings together all her concerns. The poem concludes with a strong reminiscence of Wordsworth's "Immortality Ode" in its expression of the loss of childhood vision. We recall, of course, that Wordsworth lost his parents at an early age. The way in which Lucy Maud Montgomery associates her mother and the angels is particularly striking, "Dreaming of angels astray from heaven / We always gave them our mother's face."

In **"The First Snowfall"** which in many respects is a representative nature poem we can see the way that Lucy Maud Montgomery's preoccupation with death and loss suffuses a poem in which we do not immediately expect their presence:

A bitter chill has fallen o'er the land
    In this dull breathlessness of afternoon:
Voiceless and motionless the maples stand,
    Heart-broken, with each other to commune
In silent hopelessness. The cold grey sky
    Has blotted out the mountain's misty blue,
The nearer hills are palled in sombre guise
    Where shivering gleams of fitful light fall
    through.

Then comes the snowfall, as pale Autumn folds
    A misty bridal veil about her hair,
And lingers waiting in the yellowed wolds
    Until her wintry bridegroom greet her there.
The hills are hidden and we see the woods
    Like hosts of phantoms in the waning light.
The grassless fields, the leaf-strewn solitudes
    Grow dim before the fast oncoming night.

The lovely meadows pale and whiten swift,
    The trees their tracery of ermine weave,
Like larger flakes dim flocks of snowbirds drift
    Across the fading landscape of the eve.
Darkness comes early and beneath its wings
    We see a wraith-like world with spectres
    filled—
Naught but cold semblances of real things
    As though Earth's breathing were forever
    stilled.

Such words as "Heart-broken," "palled," "sombre" in stanza one, phrases such as "the woods / Like hosts of phantoms and "a wraith-like world with spectres filled" in stanzas two and three suggest suffering and death. Indeed, at the end of the poem the earth covered with the first snowfall is likened to a dead body, "Naught but cold semblances of real things / As though Earth's breathing were forever stilled." So in the midst of nature we are in death. In fact, a strikingly large number of Lucy Maud Montgomery's five-hundred poems concern loss and death either directly or indirectly.

In *Saturday Night* volume 57 for May 2, 1942, a poem called **"The Piper"** appeared. It was prefaced by a brief article under the caption "L. M. Montgomery's last poem" which ran as follows:

The sudden and lamented death of L. M. Montgomery (Mrs. Ewan Macdonald), the beloved author of *Anne of Green Gables,* lends a poignant additional interest to the verses which *Saturday Night* received from her only three weeks before her death, and which were scheduled for publication in this issue before her death was announced. In the letter which forwarded them the author wrote:

In one of my books, *Rilla of Ingleside,* a poem is mentioned, supposed to have been written and published by Walter Blythe before his death in the Great War. Although the poem had no real existence hundreds of people have written me asking me where they could get it. It has been written but recently, but seems to me even more appropriate now than then."

This is not the place to investigate the relation between Lucy Maud Montgomery's verse and prose, though no doubt the relationship would provide a subject for fruitful study. **"The Piper"** is printed immediately beneath the brief article:

One day the Piper came down the glen,
Sweet and long and low played he . . .
The children followed from door to door
No matter how those who loved might implore,
So wiling the song of his melody
As the song of a woodland rill.
Some day the Piper will come again
To pipe to the sons of the maple tree . . .
You and I will follow from door to door,
Many of us will come back no more!
What matter that if Freedom still
Be the crown of each native hill?

(pp. 29-39)

John Ferns, " 'Rainbow Dreams': The Poetry

of Lucy Maud Montgomery," in Canadian Children's Literature, *No. 42, 1986, pp. 29-40.*

Bonnie Ryan-Fisher (essay date 1988)

[*In the following review, Ryan-Fisher explores the theme of faith in Montgomery's short fiction collection* Akin to Anne: Tales of Other Orphans.]

In this collection of L. M. Montgomery's rediscovered stories, all but two of the nineteen tales were written between 1900 and 1908, before the publication of **Anne of Green Gables,** her first novel. After their first appearance in a variety of forgotten magazines, these stories had been lost to the reading public. Here they are reprinted, complete with original illustrations when such were available. . . . Rea Wilmshurst's discovery and consequent publication of these stories in a gift to this new generation of children and to all of us who ever were children. Into our 1980's world of harsh reality, where the-search-for-truth prevails in the guise of cynicism, these tales reintroduce some of the magic of believing.

Montgomery's own mother died when she was an infant and her father moved west where he eventually remarried, leaving his daughter to be raised by her aging maternal grandparents, strict Presbyterians. This less than idyllic childhood left the young Maud perpetually in search of a mother, of love and a real home, much like the orphan girl Charlotte, in **"Charlotte's Quest"**, which opens this collection. Charlotte turns to a witch for help in finding a mother while Montgomery herself works her own creative magic. In her stories, orphans successfully find all that they could wish for.

As Anne, Montgomery's best known heroine, so often demonstrated, the key to hope in the face of misfortune is simply to have imagination. Imagination and optimism shine through in L. M. Montgomery's tales. In the warm, story-book world she creates, nothing is impossible. Kin will find kin, and like hearts be united.

These stories are peopled with virtuous, dreamy-eyed orphans, and with women like Marilla who hide soft and generous hearts beneath gruff, business-like exteriors. In these Cinderella-plots, the beautiful are rich, and the poor are kind, and dreaming is a reasonable escape from harsh reality. Justice prevails, for virtue is unfailingly rewarded and mischief leads only to wholesome learning and never to disaster.

When Montgomery's orphans find love, they inevitably find security. A place to call home and freedom from financial worry are synonymous with happiness for her orphans, regardless of their age. Hardship and poverty may be endured from necessity or for the sake of love. Still, the meek shall inherit the earth, and Montgomery's heroes and heroines do reap earthly reward.

In these tales, children find blood kin who love them; grown brothers and sisters are reunited; adult orphans create family and home together; and talent discovers both mentor and protector in one.

The longest story included, **"The Running Away of Ches-**ter"**, is also perhaps the most moving in this collection. Young Chester takes it upon himself to escape the loveless protection of his Aunt Harriet Elwell, his father's stepsister. Like Anne, Chester "possesses imagination" and so he is able to endure the hardships that beset him as he seeks a livelihood. Chester's goodness, like Anne's, is tempered by mischief. And the tale itself centers around the struggle he faces with his conscience. When he finds love and security with a "rosy lady", he learns that virtue is not easily achieved. Does he confess to his benefactress that he has misled her? Should he risk losing the happiness he has found? Montgomery's answer, of course, is yes, for happiness based on falsehood is tainted. Still, honesty will find its own reward and Chester's dilemma is happily resolved once he confesses his past.

This type of internal struggle of conscience is frequent in **Tales of Other Orphans.** But Montgomery believes unapologetically that goodness does prevail. Her characters often wonder aloud if they may be dreaming or compare their good fortune with something out of a storybook, for often meetings and turnings in their lives are stunningly coincidental. Still, isn't it true that when fortune, good or bad, touches our lives heavily, we often see where the smallest of acts or incidents tipped the scale: an impetuous decision, a careless word, an unexpected change of heart? In Montgomery's tales, this truth is used again and again to illustrate that hope is always feasible and happiness indeed a possibility, no matter what present circumstances may suggest. (pp. 67-8)

Still it is ultimately the characters and their tales that make this book worth reading. A rediscovery of Montgomery in **Tales of Other Orphans** is a rediscovery of hope: a welcome thing in our anxious world. (p. 68)

> Bonnie Ryan-Fisher, "The Magic of Believing," in Canadian Children's Literature, *No. 52, 1988, pp. 67-8.*

Rosamond Bailey (essay date 1989)

[*In the following essay, Bailey compares Montgomery's protagonists Mary Vance from* Rainbow Valley *and Anne Shirley.*]

L. M. Montgomery's **Rainbow Valley**—a novel without a protagonist—contains a strong anti-heroine in the ragged waif Mary Vance, who not only dominates much of the book but also represents a bold, battered version of Anne Shirley.

Rainbow Valley is supposedly about "Anne's children growing up", their mother being little more than a background figure. Yet the story is really about the Meredith family: in particular, the efforts of the manse children to protect their father from parish criticism. At first, the impulsive and quick-tempered Faith Meredith, who is continually getting into scrapes, seems intended as a successor to the Green Gables heroine. "Just like me. I'm going to like your Faith", Anne Blythe remarks. As the book progresses, however, Faith's timid sister Una becomes increasingly important, acting on several occasions with the desperate courage known only to the very shy. [In her "Lucy

Maud Montgomery 1874-1942," *Canadian Children's Literature,* 1975] Elizabeth Waterston notes that in comparison with "the motherless brood at the nearby manse" the young Blythes are "shadowy". The sole exception here is the bookish Walter, who briefly abandons the realm of literature to defend his mother and Faith with his fists. In structuring **Rainbow Valley** around the adventures and misadventures of a group of children, Montgomery looks back to **The Story Girl** and its sequel **The Golden Road.** Like the Story Girl's cousins, the young Merediths and Blythes find themselves enthralled by a child with strange tales to tell (though Mary Vance and Sara Stanley have very little else in common). Perhaps the author realized that something was needed to inject vigour into the anticlimactic first meeting between the Blythe and Meredith children. The newcomers are accepted immediately into the Rainbow Valley circle, sharing a sacramental meal of dry bread and fried fish. "When the last trout had vanished, the manse children and the Ingleside children were sworn friends and allies. They had always known each other and always would. The race of Joseph recognized its own." Such absolute harmony among eight children is admirable, but it makes dull reading. Fortunately, Montgomery was inspired to introduce an additional outsider: the half-starved runaway who, once discovered in the old barn, proceeds to occupy the next four chapters.

Now the centre of an admiring and horrified group, Mary recounts her ill-treatment at the hands of Mrs. Wiley:

> "She's an awful woman. . . . She worked me to death and wouldn't give me half enough to eat, and she used to larrup me 'most every day. . . . She licked me Wednesday night with a stick. . . . 'cause I let the cow kick over a pail of milk. How'd I know the darn old cow was going to kick?"

She reveals her confused theology:

> "Hell? What's that?"

> "Why, it's where the devil lives," said Jerry. "You've heard of him—you spoke about him."

> "Oh, yes, but I didn't know he lived anywhere. I thought he just roamed round. Mr Wiley used to mention hell when he was alive. He was always telling folks to go there. I thought it was some place over in New Brunswick where he come from."

And on a later occasion she vents her rage at the overdressed lisping Rilla Blythe:

> "You think you're something, don't you, all dressed up like a doll? Look at me. My dress is all rags and *I* don't care! I'd rather be ragged than a doll baby. Go home and tell them to put you in a glass case. Look at me—look at me—look at me!"

In an effort to shift this colourful interloper and return to her central characters, Montgomery gets Mary out of the manse and into the home of Miss Cornelia. Yet even after having been cleansed, clothed, fine-tooth-combed, and set to learning the catechism, Mary persists in reappearing to disturb the serenity of Rainbow Valley. In her new role as self-appointed critic of her former playmates, she acts as catalyst for much of the subsequent action of the book.

No matter how hard the manse children try to avoid disgracing their father before his congregation, they generally make matters worse. Mary, echoing the officious Miss Cornelia, provides a constant and maddening refrain: "The talk is something terrible. I expect it's ruined your father in this congregation. He'll never be able to live it down, poor man. . . . You ought to be ashamed of yourselves." The Merediths never consider that the situation might be exaggerated by Mary, that accomplished teller of tall stories.

For example, it is Mary who breaks the news that Faith and Una have acted scandalously in staying home from church on Sunday in order to clean house. Faith is accordingly inspired to explain the mistake—in church:

> "It was all Elder Baxter's fault"—sensation in the Baxter pew—because he went and changed the prayer meeting to Wednesday night and then we thought Thursday was Friday and so on till we thought Saturday was Sunday. . . . And then we thought we'd clean house on Monday and stop old cats from talking about how dirty the manse was—."

Again, Mary brings word that the well-off and influential Mrs. Davis has left the church. Summoning her courage, Faith confronts the fearsome Norman Douglas to request that he attend church and pay towards her father's salary. He turns on her in fury: "If you wasn't such a kid I'd teach you to interfere in what doesn't concern you. When I want parsons or pill-dosers I'll send for them." But Norman is not to get off scot-free: Montgomery turns the situation around. Her temper aroused, Faith retaliates with a vigour worthy of Anne:

> "I am not afraid of you. You are a rude, unjust, tyrannical, disagreeable old man. Susan says you are sure to go to hell, and I was sorry for you, but I am not now. Your wife never had a new hat for ten years—no wonder she died. . . . Father has a picture of the devil in a book in his study, and I mean to go home and write your name under it."

Faith's winning-over of Norman, who admires her "spunk", provides temporary relief from the ever-present fear that the Rev. Meredith will lose his church. Mary Vance, however, keeps reappearing with further accounts of the manse children's dreadful behaviour (such as holding a praying competition in the Methodist graveyard). The Merediths are eventually goaded into forming a Good-Conduct Club—from which Mary is to be excluded:

> "We agree to punish ourselves for bad conduct, and always to stop before we do anything, no matter what, and ask ourselves if it is likely to hurt dad in any way, and any one who shirks is to be cast out of the club and never allowed to play with the rest of us in Rainbow Valley again."

Heretofore the efforts of the manse children to defend their father have had relatively harmless—and comic—

results. On two occasions, however, the stern judgments handed down by the Good-Conduct Club result in near-tragedy. The delicate Una collapses during a fast day endured by the children as punishment for having sung "Polly Wolly doodle" in the graveyard during a Methodist prayer-meeting. A short time later, Carl nearly dies of pneumonia following an all-night vigil "on Mr. Hezekiah Pollock's tombstone". By running from what he thought was a ghost, Carl has acted like a coward and thereby brought disgrace upon the family. Mary Vance has been indirectly responsible for this incident: it was her vivid account of Henry Warren's ghost that caused Carl and his sisters to run screaming from the supposed apparition.

Mary's lurid imagination has also caused trouble in another quarter. Local speculation concerning the possible remarriage of the Rev. Meredith leads Mary to warn her friends: "It'll be awful if you get a stepmother . . . the worst of stepmothers is, they always set your father against you." Una in particular becomes terrified at the prospect of her father's marrying Rosemary West, especially since Mary seems unable to leave the subject alone. "Mary has told me blood-curdling things about [stepmothers]. She says she knew of one who whipped her husband's little girls on their bare shoulders till they bled, and then shut them up in a cold, dark, coal cellar all night. She says they're *all* aching to do things like that." At the end of the book, the reconciliation of John Meredith and Rosemary West is made to depend ultimately on Una's overcoming her fears and facing the woman who (according to Mary) is a potential Wicked Stepmother. Rosemary is quick to dismiss Mary as "a silly little girl who doesn't know very much." Nevertheless this silly little girl has figured prominently in the novel, despite the author's efforts to keep her in her place. In contrast, Anne Blythe (the nominal heroine) is almost completely passive. It is Mary who fulfills, however imperfectly, the role that Mrs. Blythe supposedly adopts: sympathetic friend and champion of the Meredith family.

At the beginning we discover Anne, upon hearing of these motherless newcomers, "beginning to mother them already in her heart." We never actually see her with these children; we must take on trust Faith's averral that Mrs. Blythe "always understands—she never laughs at us." What we do witness, on the other hand, is Mary Vance immediately taking over the disordered manse household, cleaning and mending and tidying, even chasing the poor minister out of his study. We see Mary informing the Meredith children of their disgraceful behaviour, in the lofty tone of someone four times their age. Blunt, tactless, and eminently practical, Mary Vance is the one who actually "mothers" the manse family. Even allowing for her love of exaggeration, there is considerable truth in her warnings, which come as a shock to the children. Apparently Anne Blythe, who disdains to repeat gossip, has never thought to caution her protegés about the dangers of antagonizing the "old cats" in the congregation. Anne defends the children in private, soothing the agitated Miss Cornelia, who rushes to Ingleside after every fresh scandal to wail "What is to be done?" As though tired of this constant refrain, Anne eventually asserts herself, announcing that she would like to speak out in defense of the Mere-

diths before the community. Saying she would "like to" is as far as she goes. Mary Vance, on the other hand, does not hesitate to lock horns with the formidable Mrs. Davis:

> "Mrs. Elliott [Miss Cornelia] says she never saw the like of me for sticking up for my friends. I was real sassy to Mrs. Alec Davis about you and Mrs. Elliott combed me down for it afterwards. The fair Cornelia has a tongue of her own and no mistake. But she was pleased underneath for all, 'cause she hates old Kitty Alec and she's real fond of you. *I* can see through folks."

Mary's defense naturally counts for little—who will heed a nobody of an orphan? But at least she is not afraid to "stick up for her friends", while the more socially prominent Mrs. Dr. Blythe remains silent. The once lively Anne, as Elizabeth Waterston points out, has been "reduced to some cliché gestures". [In "The Decline of Anne: Matron v. Child," *Canadian Children's Literature,* 1975] Gillian Thomas suggests that Anne's reticence as a matron stems from the realization that she "must behave appropriately for her role as 'Mrs. Dr.' "; but total passivity scarcely seems appropriate in a woman who has achieved such status. Anne Blythe is curiously reluctant to express any opinions at all; it is almost as though she still feels herself the friendless orphan on probation before the community. As we have seen, Mary Vance—who is actually in this position—has no such qualms at first. As the story progresses we find the shadows of the prison-house of respectability beginning to close about her. "I simply feel that I can't associate with you any longer," she tells Faith unhappily. (Faith has disgraced herself by appearing at church without stockings.) "It ain't that I don't want to . . . [but] I'm in a respectable place and trying to be a lady." Compare Anne's rueful "we must be conventional or die, after we reach what is supposed to be a dignified age."

Mary Vance, whether or not intended as a substitute for Mrs. Blythe, is presented as the exact opposite of that more famous orphan Anne Shirley. That both children come from Hopetown Orphanage seems a coincidence meant to heighten the subsequent contrasts. Anne twice remarks that she too was once a "homeless little orphan"; Miss Cornelia on one occasion retorts, "I don't think this Mary-creature is or ever will be much like you." Elizabeth Waterston recognizes Mary as a different breed of orphan—"a brassy, skinny, pale-eyed, pugnacious one". There are, however, many surprising similarities between these children, and even the contrasts often suggest Mary as an inverted double for the Green Gables heroine: a rough, street-wise Anne.

Mary's initial description seems to set her apart from her predecessor. Anne is discovered more or less respectably outfitted for her journey and calmly awaiting Matthew at the station; Mary, wearing nothing except a ragged dress, is found cowering in a hayloft. Her "lank, thick, tow-coloured hair and very odd eyes—'white eyes' " are an unattractive contrast to Anne's red braids and large green-gray eyes. Note, however, that both children have braided hair; both are garbed in dresses "much too short and tight"—the typical hand-me-down wear of an orphan; both are equally skinny. Anne is eleven, Mary approximately twelve. Anne has a striking and expressive countenance; Mary's face is "wizened", unchildlike. Drain the colour from Anne's hair and eyes, and (more important) eradicate from her face the hope and innocence and love of life—and what might be left? Mary Vance.

Mary, despite her pale colouring, is far from insipid. Fortified by a square meal, she reverts to her "natural vivacity", dominating her rescuers almost at once. She is slangy, ungrammatical, near-profane; she is boastful and bossy among the other children; she is impudent to adults. Montgomery has gone to great lengths to create in this bold orphan the antithesis of the well-spoken and (usually) well-mannered Anne. Not that the Green Gables heroine is shy or withdrawn; she has a spirited nature of her own, a tongue and temper as quick as Mary's. Both heredity and environment appear to be responsible for making one child a hellion, the other a lady. The author supplies Mary with parents far different from those of Anne:

> "I was two years in the asylum. I was put there when I was six. My ma had hung herself and my pa had cut his throat."

> "Holy cats! Why?" said Jerry.

> "Booze," said Mary laconically.

In the same matter-of-fact way she adds that her parents used to beat her. More extreme opposites for those tragic lovers Walter and Bertha Shirley, who cherished their infant daughter, would be hard to imagine. Again, the child-battering Mrs. Wiley seems intended as a contrast to Anne's former guardians, who overworked and neglected her but stopped short of active ill-treatment. Or at least we assume so: Anne, normally so talkative, is reticent about her early life. "I know they meant to be just as good and kind as possible," she tells Marilla. "And when people mean to be good to you, you don't mind very much when they're not quite—always". We hear, almost in passing, of Mrs. Thomas's telling Anne that she was "desperately wicked"; of Mr. Thomas's habit of smashing things when he was "slightly intoxicated". Anne escapes the memories of drunken rages or verbal abuse by retreating into her fantasy-world; Mary, lacking such inner resources, boasts of her traumatic childhood. "She divined that the manse children were pitying her for her many stripes and she did not want pity. She wanted to be envied."

Given her long history of abuse, Mary's tough and belligerent exterior is believable. What is unrealistic, by comparison, is Anne's educated vocabulary and ladylike deportment. A child reared first by a scrubwoman with an alcoholic husband and then by a large backwoods family might be expected to turn out speaking, if not behaving, more like Mary Vance than Anne Shirley. The latter has actually had less formal education than her counterpart: four months in the orphanage as against Mary's two years, plus an even more sketchy attendance at public school. And neither the Thomas nor Hammond household seems to have contained books. The explanation for this striking contrast in behaviour between the two orphans lies in the wide social gulf established by Montgomery. [In "But What About Jane?" *Canadian Children's Literature*, 1975] Jean Little points out that Anne, "although definitely an orphan, is discovered to have sprung from genteel stock. By their relatives shall ye know them". Contrast Anne's polite opening speech, "I suppose you are Mr. Matthew Cuthbert of Green Gables?" with Mary's wail of "I haint had a thing to eat since Thursday morning, 'cept a little water from the brook out there." That "haint" immediately suggests Mary's social level. Her ancestors may have had pretensions—such as the rich grandfather who was a "rascal"—but they exist now only in her overloaded name, her sole legacy: "Mary Martha Lucilla Moore Ball Vance". Mary would doubtless scorn Anne's plain, single Christian name which the owner herself must embellish "with an *e*." A genteel background presumably accounts also for Anne's quickly acquired love of literature. Mary's domestic talents again place her on a lower plane: she seems actually to relish doing servants' work.

Regardless of their origins, both Anne and Mary find that to be an orphan is to be at a social disadvantage. The myth of the Wicked Orphan who poisons wells and sets farms afire (one of Mrs. Lynde's favourite topics) is given a comic application in *Anne of Green Gables:* Anne not only gets Diana drunk but also offers the minister's wife a cake flavoured with liniment. In *Rainbow Valley* the community of Glen St. Mary is suspicious of "home children". "You know yourself what that poor little creature the Jim Flaggs had, taught and told the Flagg children", Miss Cornelia warns the Rev. Meredith. But Mary, another such poor little creature, is surprisingly restrained in her speech: "If you knew some of the words I *could* say if I liked you wouldn't make such a fuss over darn." Gossip is her downfall; the ill effects of her wagging tongue have already been pointed out. (We may recall, in this connection, that Anne Shirley is reprimanded by Marilla for bringing home tales about the schoolmaster and Prissy Andrews.) Unwanted at first, both children are eventually accepted into the homes of strong-minded, spinsterish women. Miss Cornelia, who retains her maiden title, is a former old maid who married an old bachelor (see *Anne's House of Dreams*). Her mild, long-suffering husband Marshall echoes Matthew in encouraging the adoption of the orphan. Mary, however, goes into no Anne-like raptures at the prospect. Unable to visualize a home in which she might be wanted or even loved, she is content to know that she will not be beaten. Miss Cornelia admits, "I've no fault to find with Mary. . . . she's clean and respectful—though there's more in her than *I* can fathom. She's a sly puss." Mary is shrewd enough to learn almost overnight the best way of getting along with her new guardian—how different from the impulsive, blundering Anne! The relationship between Mary and Miss Cornelia reflects a mutual, if grudging, respect, rather than the genuine affection that develops between Anne and Marilla.

Indeed, Miss Cornelia seems the nearest thing to a "kindred spirit" that Mary encounters. "We was made for each other. . . . She's pizen neat, but so am I, and so we agree fine." Among her contemporaries Mary seeks no bosom friend; she prefers to be at the centre of the group, bossing, bragging, telling her horrific yarns. Oddly enough, only the introverts Walter Blythe and Una Meredith have any real influence over her. And even Una, once her confidante, is eventually provoked into resentful envy over the new velvet cap and squirrel muff that Mary flaunts. Fine feathers, for Mary, seem more important than friendship. On the very day she is rescued she turns on Faith for having made an unwise remark about the ragged dress: "When I grow up I'm going to have a blue sating dress. Your own clothes don't look so stylish." She chases Rilla Blythe—with dried codfish—simply for being better attired (although the author admits there was some provocation, Rilla being all too aware of her finery). Anne Shirley is also capable of rage over slurs on her appearance—witness the famous attacks upon Mrs. Lynde and Gilbert—and she has her own vanities: she longs for raven-black hair and fashionable puffed sleeves. Yet behind this attitude is a strong desire to be loved. She is convinced that no one wants an ugly child: "If I was very beautiful and had nut-brown hair would you keep me?" Having acquired her stylish clothes, she does not show them off quite as Mary does. Mary, whose emotional development has been stunted by ten years of abuse, craves status: she must feel superior even to her friends. Would Anne, in the same circumstances, still be capable of putting affection first—or would she, too, settle for good clothes and respectability as her highest goals?

It is hardly surprising that both Anne and Mary, neglected upon earth, should place little confidence in a loving Deity. Hopetown Orphanage has provided some religious instruction: Anne can recite the catechism flawlessly, while Mary has learnt "an old rhyme" to repeat at bedtime. Anne, however, has never said any prayers: "Mrs. Thomas told me that God made my hair red *on purpose,* and I've never cared about Him since." Mary is more tolerant:

> "Mind you, I haven't got anything against God, Una. I'm willing to give Him a chance. But, honest, I think He's an awful lot like your father—just absent-minded and never taking any notice of a body most of the time, but sometimes waking up all of a sudden and being awful good and kind and sensible."

The good ladies Marilla and Cornelia endeavour to overcome the ignorance of these little near-heathens by conventional methods: Anne is given the Lord's Prayer to learn, Mary the Shorter Catechism. Neither orphan is thereby transformed into a pious child of the Elsie Dinsmore variety. Instead, we find Anne moved to "irreverent" delight over a picture of Christ blessing little children: "I was just imagining . . . I was the little girl in the blue dress, standing off by herself in the corner as if she didn't belong to anybody, like me." Once she finds she is to remain at Green Gables, she finds it easy to pray. On the other hand, Mary—despite the kind efforts of the Rev. Meredith—remains dubious. She even speculates that it might be wise to ask the devil not to tempt her, thereby unconsciously paraphrasing part of the Lord's Prayer. Her subsequent model behaviour at Miss Cornelia's appears, as previously suggested, to be due to expediency rather than religious conversion.

Finally, Mary—although created as Anne's opposite—is by no means lacking in imagination. We find her moved almost to tears by Walter's prophecy of the Piper who will one day lead the boys away to war; we find her terrified at the prospect of going to hell because of her lies. She entertains the Rainbow Valley children with accounts of ghosts and superstitions and cruel stepmothers, much after the manner of Riley's Little Orphant Annie. The young Anne also enjoys Gothic horrors: her misadventure in the Haunted Wood has its parallel in the incident of Henry Warren's ghost, which Mary herself claims to have seen. Mary's imaginings are almost invariably morbid: we find no Snow Queens, no dryads, no Lady Cordelias. Like Anne, she enjoys self-dramatization, but rather than playing romantic heroines like Elaine the Lily Maid, she draws from her own history, presenting herself as the victim of Mrs. Wiley (that real-life Wicked Witch). Mary might be accused of exaggeration here, were it not that she bears actual bruises. For she is less careful of the truth than is Anne (whose constant refrain of "I'll imagine" as a preface to every fantasy becomes somewhat tedious after the first few chapters). Mary swears to have witnessed apparitions "all in white with skellington hands and heads" and actually to have met the Wandering Jew. The Merediths are charitable about these yarns. Nevertheless Mary has told actual untruths, thereby committing one of the worst childhood sins in the Montgomery canon. She is given some excuse: she lied to avoid further ill-treatment from the Wileys. (She is not a malicious troublemaker like Emily's false friend Rhoda in *Emily of New Moon,* or Nan's playmate Dovie in *Anne of Ingleside.*) Once informed of her wickedness, Mary repents. She continues, however, to confuse fiction with falsehood, calling Walter's readings "int'resting lies". There are some indications here that she might develop some appreciation of literature, given the opportunity. She will never, of course, be permitted by the author to reach Anne's cultural level. Mary belongs to a lower order, spiritually as well as socially.

Mary Vance is one of Montgomery's best comic characters. Considerable insight is shown as well in this portrait of a child warped both emotionally and intellectually by a brutal environment. Yet the author seems never to have considered that psychological abuse might have been just as harmful for Anne, destroying the capacity for affection and the rich imaginative vision that make her what she is. Matthew and Marilla might well have been confronted with a Mary Vance: but that is a story L. M. Montgomery never wrote. (pp. 8-16)

> Rosamond Bailey, "Little Orphan Mary: Anne's Hoydenish Double," in Canadian Children's Literature, *No. 55, 1989, pp. 8-17.*

FURTHER READING

Ellis, Sarah. "News from the North." *The Horn Book Magazine* (September-October 1988): 663-66.
    Review of *The Selected Journals of L. M. Montgomery.*

Sorfleet, John Robert, ed. *Canadian Children's Literature: A Journal of Criticism and Review* 1, No. 3 (Autumn 1975).

Special issue devoted to Montgomery's life and work, including several critical articles on her fiction.

Additional coverage of Montgomery's life and career is contained in the following sources published by Gale Research: *Children's Literature Review,* Vol. 8; *Contemporary Authors,* Vols. 108, 137; *Dictionary of Literary Biography,* Vol. 92; *Major Authors and Illustrators for Children and Young Adults;* and *Yesterday's Authors of Books for Children,* Vol. 1.

George Orwell

1903-1950

(Pseudonym of Eric Arthur Blair) English essayist, critic, novelist, and journalist.

The following entry presents criticism of Orwell's essays. For information on Orwell's complete career, see *TCLC*, Volumes 2 and 6; for discussion of his novel *Nineteen Eighty-Four*, see *TCLC*, Volume 15; for discussion of his novel *Animal Farm*, see *TCLC*, Volume 31.

INTRODUCTION

Best known for his political allegory *Animal Farm* and his dystopian novel *Nineteen Eighty-Four*, Orwell is also one of the most celebrated essayists in the English language. Both as an individual and as a writer, he was committed to the ideal of truth without allegiance to a particular party, movement, or school of thought, and his essays reflect his highly independent view of modern society, politics, and literature. In addition, Orwell's prose style in his essays is considered exemplary for its lucid and forceful presentation of often complex ideas and observations.

Orwell was born in India to a lower middle-class English family who struggled to provide him an education. At age eight he was sent to a well-known preparatory school in England where, despite his scholastic accomplishments, he felt himself inferior because of his low social standing. In his essay "Such, Such Were the Joys" Orwell explained that his sense of inferiority resulting from English class structure fostered his extreme sensitivity to social victimization. After studying at Eton on a scholarship, Orwell did not attend either Oxford or Cambridge, as was customary for Eton graduates, but instead took a position in the Indian Imperial Police. Stationed in Burma, he encountered the brutalities and inequities of colonial rule, which he vividly evoked in the essays "Shooting an Elephant" and "A Hanging."

Orwell left the police after five years to live in self-imposed poverty. He drew on his experiences to write the essay "How the Poor Die" and the autobiographical narrative *Down and Out in Paris and London*. As Orwell became more deeply involved in politics he wrote two more books combining autobiography and social criticism: *The Road to Wigan Pier*, commissioned by the socialist Left Book Club, and *Homage to Catalonia*, which, along with the essay "Looking Back on the Spanish War," details the causes and progress of the Spanish Civil War, in which Orwell fought in a militia unit. In 1940 he published *Inside the Whale, and Other Essays*, arguing in the title essay that writers had an obligation to be politically aware and engaged. Some of Orwell's most acclaimed essays on literature and popular culture were published in *Critical Essays*, including "Raffles and Miss Blandish," "The Art of Don-

ald McGill," and "Boys' Weeklies." One of Orwell's most important later essays, "Politics and the English Language," is an exploration of the way in which language may be politically manipulated, a subject Orwell expanded upon in his novel *Nineteen Eighty-Four*.

Orwell's prose style, especially that of his essays, has become a model for students of writing because of its precision, clarity, and vividness. Many of his essays, which combine observation and reminiscence with literary and social criticism, are considered modern masterpieces. Irving Howe reflected the critical consensus when he called Orwell "the best English essayist since Hazlitt."

PRINCIPAL WORKS

Down and Out in Paris and London (novel) 1933
Burmese Days (novel) 1934
A Clergyman's Daughter (novel) 1935
Keep the Aspidistra Flying (novel) 1936
Homage to Catalonia (nonfiction) 1938

CRITICISM

Q. D. Leavis (essay date 1940)

[*Leavis was a twentieth-century English critic, essayist, and editor. Her professional alliance with her husband, F. R. Leavis, resulted in several literary collaborations, including the successful quarterly periodical* Scrutiny, *in which she published many critical essays. Leavis stressed that "literary criticism is not a mystic rapture but a process of the intelligence," suggesting that a responsible critic should remain objective and eschew impressionistic responses to a work. Most importantly, she asserted, a work should not be judged on the basis of its moral value. In the following excerpt, Leavis discusses Orwell's literary criticism in* Inside the Whale.]

Mr. Orwell has not hitherto appeared as a literary critic, except incidentally, but as a novelist, a social thinker and a critic-participator in the Spanish War. Now he has published three literary essays which, promisingly, are all quite different. One is an examination of Dickens, another an analysis on not altogether original lines of boys' school stories, and the third a piece of contemporary criticism. From his other books we could deduce that he was potentially a good critic. For instance, he takes his own political line—starting from an inside knowledge of the working-class, painfully acquired, he can see through the Marxist theory, and being innately decent (he displays and approves of bourgeois morality) he is disgusted with the callous theorising inhumanity of the pro-Marxists. His explanation . . . of the conversion to Russian Communism of the young writers of the 'thirties is something that needed doing and could hardly have been done better. And he drives home his point with a piece of literary criticism, an analysis of a stanza of Auden's *Spain*. Again, he has lived an active life among all classes and in several countries, he isn't the usual parlour-Bolshevik seeing literature through political glasses; nor is he a literary gangster, his literary criticism is first-hand. These are exceptional qualifications nowadays. Without having scholarship or an academic background he yet gives the impression of knowing a surprising amount about books and au-

thors—because what he knows is live information, not card-index rubbish, his knowledge functions. A wide field of reference (provided it is not gratuitous), outside as well as inside literature proper, is a sure sign of an alert intelligence. While Mr. Orwell's criticism is discursive his pages are not cluttered up with academic 'scholarship' nor disfigured with the rash of the exhibitionistic imposters who displayed in *The Criterion*. His writings are not elegant, mannered or polite, or petty either; his style is refreshing, that of the man whose first aim is to say something which he has quite clear in his head—like the pamphleteering Shaw without the irresponsibility (which produced the paradoxes and the cheap effects). He really knows the stuff he is writing about (for instance, Dickens) and has not got it up in a hurry for the occasion (like Spender on Henry James in *The Destructive Element*).

This is his most encouraging book so far, because while his previously successful books have been ***The Road to Wigan Pier*** and ***Homage to Catalonia,*** not only timely but valuable in themselves, they had not seemed to lead anywhere. Mr. Orwell must have wasted a lot of energy trying to be a novelist—I think I must have read three or four novels by him, and the only impression those dreary books left on me is that nature didn't intend him to be a novelist. Yet his equivalent works in non-fiction are stimulating. It is the more evident because his novels are drawn from his own experience (***Burmese Days*** is based on his five years in the Indian Imperial Police service in Burma, others on his experiences as a down-and-out and so on). Yet these novels not only lack the brutal effectiveness of B. Traven's for instance, they might almost have been written by Mr. Alec Brown. You see what I mean. He has even managed to write a dull novel about a literary man, which is a feat—an attempt to do *New Grub Street* up-to-date, but Gissing was an artist and Mr. Orwell isn't. What an impressive book Mr. Orwell made out of his experiences in the Spanish War (***Homage to Catalonia***), but that isn't a novel; in spite of its patches of spleen and illogicality, what insight, good feeling and practical thinking are revealed in ***The Road to Wigan Pier*** (for sponsoring which the Left Book Club earned one of its few good marks), but if it had been a novel one can't believe it would have been as stimulating and convincing. It looks as though if he would give up trying to be a novelist Mr. Orwell might find his *métier* in literary criticism, in a special line of it peculiar to himself and which is particularly needed now. He is evidently a live mind working through literature, life and ideas. He knows what he is interested in and has something original to say about it. His criticism is convincing because his local criticisms are sound (always a test), and though his is not primarily a literary approach he is that rare thing, a non-literary writer who is also sensitive to literature. Thus his criticism of Dickens, while a lot of it is beside the point from *Scrutiny's* point of view, contains nuggets of literary criticism, and you can see his superior literary sensibility on the one hand to the Marxist critics of Dickens (*pro* or *con*) and on the other to the Hugh Kingsmill type. He is not sufficiently disciplined to be a considerable literary critic, he is and probably always will be a critic of literature who, while not a Communist, has nevertheless corresponding preoccupations, but the great thing is, he has a special kind of honesty, he corrects any astygmatic tendency in himself because in literature as in politics he has taken up a stand which gives him freedom. He can say just the right things about Comrade Mirsky's nasty book on *The Intelligentsia of Great Britain,* he can tick off Mac-neice in a characteristic attitude, expose Upward's puerile theorising, diagnose Auden & Co., and 'place' the school of Catholic-convert apologists. Even his enthusiasms—another test—turn out to be sound criticism. Thus, you may think that the only thing wrong with the title-essay of this book is that he seems to think Henry Miller a great novelist, but it turns out after all that he doesn't. He claims for *Tropic of Cancer* no more than that it is an example of the only kind of tolerably good novel that can be written now ('a completely negative, unconstructive, amoral writer, a passive accepter of evil')—and expects, as you and I do, that Miller will 'descend into unintelligibility, or into charlatanism' next.

Whether he will come to anything as a literary critic will probably depend on whether he can keep clear of the atmosphere of Bloomsbury and the literary racket. And there are other dangers. He reminds one of Mr. Robert Graves in his promising period in the 'twenties, and Mr. Graves's history since, from the standpoint of literary criticism, has been rather a sad one. Probably the best thing for him and the best thing for us would be to export him to interpret English Literature to the foreign student, instead of the yes-men who generally land the chairs of English abroad. Everyone would benefit; though one doesn't see him accepting such an offer. But one thing above all there is to his credit. If the revolution here were to happen that he wants and prophesies, the advent of real Socialism, he would be the only man of letters we have whom we can imagine surviving the flood undisturbed. (pp. 174-76)

Q. D. Leavis, "Mr. George Orwell," in Scrutiny, *Vol. IX, No. 2, September, 1940, pp. 173-76.*

Stuart Hampshire   (essay date 1946)

[*In the following review, Hampshire favorably assesses* Critical Essays.]

Mr. Orwell is a moralist-critic and not an aesthete; he is interested in attitudes to Life rather than in Beauty. His own writing is forthright and vigorous, but never noticeably fine or elaborated; and in the prose literature which he criticises he distinguishes diseases of the mind and political attitudes rather than differences of style. The strength and brilliance of his criticism come from his confidence in his own sanity; he never fails to dig out and expose the perversions and affectations of others, applying a test of enlightened good sense. This robust self-confidence might make a blunt and philistine critic; in fact, it does not, because Mr. Orwell's writing always seems to reflect new and entirely independent thinking. His writing follows his thought, which is untrammelled by fashion or prejudice. He seems to live by himself intellectually and to come out to spray poison on "the smelly little orthodoxies" which he finds growing like weeds around him.

The most brilliant and typical of the ten essays in [*Critical Essays*] is that on Rudyard Kipling, the longest and most satisfying on Charles Dickens. Mr. Orwell exults in savage over-statements of the unpopular view; and he is never happier in his writing than when he is affronting the genteel illusions of what he calls "the pansy-left." He is carried away by his pleasure in belabouring the soft lump of civilised prejudice which he finds before him, and is betrayed into rough epigrams, some of which are blatantly untrue. His critical attitude seems to have been formed by reaction against the intellectual fashions of his time; and the reactions have been violent, as though from doctrines intimately known and half-accepted and therefore rejected with a greater sense of liberation. It is not true that his judgement is perverted by the individualist's pride in being in a minority; but the sanity and justice of his critical attitude can only be appreciated against the particular background of Mr. Orwell's dislikes. Someone who did not know this background—a French reader, for instance—would not understand why the familiar principles of educated liberalism should be stated with such an accompaniment of aggressive exaggeration. "A humanitarian is always a hypocrite"; "No one, in our time, believes in any sanction greater than military power"—the fact that neither of these statements is literally true does not invalidate the extremely subtle and original argument about Kipling in which they occur. But such ferocious over-statements are puzzling unless they are understood in the context of a particular intellectual history and predicament; and this history and predicament are peculiar to intellectuals of the last two decades.

The predicament, which provokes these over-statements and sometimes contradictions, is roughly this: Suppose that one has been convinced by experience that imperialism is evil, and that Marx's analysis of capitalist society was generally correct; suppose also that one hates tyranny and suppression of the truth in any form; then who are one's friends? After 1939—and all these essays were written in or after 1939—it has not been an easy question. Charles Dickens perhaps, with very many qualifications, which are most carefully and ingeniously elaborated. H. G. Wells, who did not understand violence, is shown to have been no help since 1920. Yeats is a magnificent enemy; Koestler a confused and uncertain friend; Kipling an honest enemy.

"All art is propaganda," says Mr. Orwell, and one cannot discuss his criticism without discussing his politics. Three of the essays deal with the political and social implications of popular art—boys' weeklies, comic postcards and thrillers. There is also an entirely convincing defence of the harmlessness and genuine inanity of P. G. Wodehouse, and a rational appraisal of Salvador Dali. Nowhere in any of these essays is one conscious of any tension between Mr. Orwell's penetration and integrity as a critic and the framework of his political beliefs and preferences. He seems to have absorbed the doctrines on which the "little orthodoxies" are founded, and particularly Marx and Freud, but to have remained open-minded and empirical; he has so placed himself in an assured position above and beyond the warring of the sects, and is in consequence potentially the most authoritative and interesting of English critics. Unfortunately, literary mass-observation—the boys' weeklies, thrillers, post-cards—seem to have deflected him from writing anything which is comparable to the work of Mr. Edmund Wilson, the distinguished American critic who has similar if greater authority for the same reasons. The literary mass-observation is amusing and useful, but is easily forgotten, because the conclusions are obvious and already known and only the particular instances are new. They cannot be re-read in [re-issue] with the same pleasure as the essays on Dickens, Kipling and Wells.

Mr. Orwell's thought and method are so consistent that one could not have guessed, if it had not been stated, that this book represents the products of journalism in the last six years. Almost everybody who reads it will enjoy it and be stimulated by it; it is easily and forcefully written, and, in addition to its intellectual brilliance, has all the qualifications for great popularity—including a barely concealed impatience with highbrows and a suggestion of insularity. Nevertheless, highbrows will enjoy it most. (pp. 250, 252)

> *Stuart Hampshire, "A Redoubtable Critic," in*
> The Spectator, *Vol. 176, No. 6141, March 8,*
> *1946, pp. 250, 252.*

Eric Bentley (essay date 1946)

[*In the following review, Bentley praises Orwell's analysis of popular culture in* Dickens, Dali, and Others.]

[*Dickens, Dali and Others*] introduces to the American public a very talented English critic. Talented and symptomatic. George Orwell's career seems to have been a brave attempt to live down his Anglo-Indian and Etonian background (the Etonian part of which was all too vividly described in Cyril Connolly's *Enemies of Promise*). As policeman, school-teacher, bum, Spanish Loyalist, Home Guardsman, radical editor, and foreign correspondent for a Conservative paper he has kept himself on the go and, like another Koestler, has sought experiences which would bring him close to the central events of our time.

How has he come through? With flying colors, some will say, as a champion of liberty and of everything that is of good report. Personally I find the outcome more complex and more ambiguous.

The theme of *Dickens, Dali and Others* I take to be that in the past forty years—the span of Mr. Orwell's lifetime—a vast revolution has taken place in Western life, that Mr. Orwell is painfully aware of all its characteristics and complications, and that he is very angry because many people are so little aware of the revolution that they can go on living—culturally at least—in a nineteenth-century world that has no "objective" existence. Mr. Orwell's anger is all the greater because he too prefers nineteenth-century values and wishes we could really get back to them.

In protest against his background Mr. Orwell is a radical, but as the product of his background he is embarrassed by radicalism. To some extent this embarrassment is a good thing, since it makes Mr. Orwell acutely aware of silliness and eccentricity on the left. And it has driven him to adopt a splendid forthrightness of manner; his style is a model for all who would write simply and forcefully. But behind

the fine front of plainness is a malaise as marked as Mr. Connolly's. As with Koestler, the subjective element in the radicalism is far too large. The pressure of an almost personal resentment too often makes itself felt. A too evident *anxiety* prevents Mr. Orwell's satire on Russia—*Animal Farm*—from being more than an outburst. The result is bigotry. If one section of the left has as its motto "Stalin can do no wrong" the other, to which Mr. Orwell belongs, is just as obsessively concerned to show that Stalin can do no right.

In our world, where can a revolted Etonian turn? Mr. Orwell looks around him and sees our popular culture—the boys' magazines, the "naughty" postcards, the detective stories, nearly all of them refusing to acknowledge that anything has happened since 1910. (But "I for one should be sorry to see them vanish," says Mr. Orwell of the "naughty postcards.") He looks at a "modernistic" artist—Dali—and finds him false. What an age to live in! "Freud and Machiavelli have reached the outer suburbs." How much nicer it must have been when Freud and Machiavelli had got no further than Bloomsbury! So Mr. Orwell turns to some of our older contemporaries. Unfortunately Shaw and Laski are looking at Europe through the wrong end of the telescope. Wells is still living in the world of his youth. Kipling? Worth feeling wistful about, worth envying, but "a Conservative, a thing that does not exist nowadays." The study of Yeats brings Mr. Orwell to the woebegone conclusion: "By and large the best writers of our time have been reactionary in tendency." The only essay in Mr. Orwell's book that is full of enthusiasm is equally full of nostalgia. It is an essay on Charles Dickens, who is portrayed as an Orwell before the flood—"a nineteenth-century liberal, a free intelligence, a type hated with equal hatred by all the smelly little orthodoxies which are now contending for our souls." *Dickens, Dali and Others* might be read as a dirge for nineteenth-century liberalism. But if Orwell is a bit of a Zola, it is a pity that the best Dreyfus he can find is P. G. Wodehouse.

The most impressive feature of the book is not its unwitting revelation of its author but its keen analysis of popular culture. If Mr. Orwell has the worries, the tics, and the yearnings of the old-fashioned liberal doomed to live in this utterly illiberal century, he has also the old liberal's best qualities: straightforwardness, generous intelligence, and a serious devotion to culture. In America the critic who most closely resembles him is Edmund Wilson. Both men practise an admirable style that is close to good reporting and good debate—the heritage of the liberal's free press and free discussion. They have the same political attitude (anti-Russian leftism) and similar literary interests (Dickens, Kipling, Yeats). They are both at their best in territory where sociology and literature overlap.

Mr. Orwell at least—I will not say Mr. Wilson—is distinctly shaky in purely political and purely literary criticism—in *Animal Farm* and in his study of Henry Miller ("**Inside the Whale**"). Avoiding these two poles *Dickens, Dali and Others* is Orwell at his best. Which is saying a great deal. Few people have ever said better things about the culture of the masses. I would specify as little masterpieces the following essays: "**Boys' Weeklies**," "**The Art** of Donald McGill," and "Raffles and Miss Blandish." I hope they stimulate American critics to analyze the comic-strips and the pulps. The brilliance of Mr. Orwell's pioneer effort should put them on their mettle.

Eric Bentley, "Young Man Out of His Time," in The Saturday Review of Literature, Vol. 29, No. 19, May 11, 1946, p. 11.

Evelyn Waugh   (essay date 1946)

[*From the publication in 1928 of his novel* Decline and Fall *until his death in 1966, Waugh was England's leading satirical novelist. In such works as* Vile Bodies *(1930),* Scoop *(1938), and* The Loved One *(1948), he skewered such targets as the bored young sophisticates of the 1920s, the questionable values of the British press, and the American commercial trivialization of death. Considered a major Catholic author after his conversion in 1930, Waugh is best known today for his novel* Brideshead Revisited *(1945), which examines the lives of the members of a wealthy Catholic family. Much of Waugh's post-conversion writings reflect the author's often-maligned Tory values of the preeminence of wealth, privilege, and proper insouciance. In the following review, first published in 1946, Waugh provides a mixed assessment of* Critical Essays.]

The *Critical Essays* of Mr George Orwell comprise ten papers of varying length, written between 1939 and 1945, which together form a work of absorbing interest. They represent at its best the new humanism of the common man, of which Mass Observation is the lowest expression. It is a habit of mind rather than a school. Mr Edmund Wilson in the United States is an exponent and perhaps it is significant that two of Mr Orwell's ten subjects have been treated at length by him. The essential difference between this and previous critical habits is the abandonment of the hierarchic principle. It has hitherto been assumed that works of art exist in an order of precedence with the great masters, Virgil, Dante and their fellows, at the top and the popular novel of the season at the bottom. The critics' task has been primarily to preserve and adjust this classification. Their recreation has been to 'discover' recondite work and compete in securing honours each for his own protégé. This, I believe, is still the critic's essential task, but the work has fallen into decay lately through exorbitance. Critics of this popularly dubbed 'Mandarin' school must be kept under discipline by a civilized society whose servants they should be. For the past thirty years they have run wild and countenanced the cults of Picasso and Stein, and the new critics, of whom Mr Orwell is outstandingly the wisest, arrive opportunely to correct them. They begin their inquiry into a work of art by asking: 'What kind of man wrote or painted this? What were his motives, conscious or unconscious? What sort of people like his work? Why?' With the class distinctions the great colour-bar also disappears; that hitherto impassable gulf between what was 'Literature' and what was not. Vast territories are open for exploitation. Indeed the weakness of the new criticism lies there; that, whereas the 'Mandarins' failed by presumptuously attempting to insert cranks and charlatans into the ranks of the immortals, the new hu-

manists tend to concentrate entirely on the base and ephemeral. Mr Orwell's three most delightful essays deal respectively with comic postcards, 'penny-dreadfuls' and Mr James Hadley Chase. He treats only once of a subject that is at all recondite, W. B. Yeats's philosophic system, and then, I think, not happily.

The longest essay is on Charles Dickens and is chiefly devoted to refuting the opinions of Chesterton and Mr T. A. Jackson. (In this connection Mr Orwell should note, what is often forgotten, that Chesterton became a Catholic late in life. Most of his best-known work was written while he was still groping for his faith, and though it bears the promise of future realization, contains opinions which cannot be blithely labelled 'Catholic'.) He is entirely successful in his refutation and he fills his argument with brilliantly chosen illustrations many of which are entirely new, at any rate to me. I had never before reflected on the profound fatuity of the future life of the characters implied in their 'happy ending'.

There follows an ingenious analysis of the *Gem* and *Magnet* magazines and their successors. At my private school these stories were contraband and I read them regularly with all the zeal of law-breaking. (The prohibition was on social, not moral grounds. *Chums, The Captain* and the *BOP* were permitted. These again were recognized as 'inferior' to *Bevis, Treasure Island* and such books, which my father read aloud to me. Thus was the hierarchic system early inculcated.) I think Mr Orwell talks nonsense when he suggests that the antiquated, conservative tone of these stories is deliberately maintained by capitalist newspaper proprietors in the interest of the class structure of society. A study of these noblemen's more important papers reveals a reckless disregard of any such obligation. Here, and elsewhere, Mr Orwell betrays the unreasoned animosity of a class-war in which he has not achieved neutrality.

'The Art of Donald McGill' is, perhaps, the masterpiece of the book, an analysis of the social assumptions of the vulgar postcard. This and **'Raffles and Miss Blandish'** exemplify the method in which the new school is supreme. Every essay in the book provokes and deserves comment as long as itself. Lack of space forbids anything more than notes. I think Mr Orwell has missed something in his **'Defense of P. G. Wodehouse.'** It is, of course, insane to speak of Mr Wodehouse as a 'fascist', and Mr Orwell finely exposes the motives and methods of the Bracken-sponsored abuse of this simple artist, but I do find in his work a notable strain of pacifism. It was in the dark spring of 1918 that Jeeves first 'shimmered in with the Bohea'. Of all Mr Wodehouse's characters Archie Moffam alone saw war service. Of the traditional aspects of English life the profession of arms alone is unmentioned; parsons, schoolmasters, doctors, merchants, squires abound, particularly parsons. Serving soldiers alone are absent, and this is the more remarkable since, so far as the members of the Drones Club correspond to anything in London life, they are officers of the Brigade of Guards. Moreover, it is not enough to say that Mr Wodehouse has not outgrown the loyalties of his old school. When Mr Orwell and I were at school, patriotism, the duties of an imperial caste, etc., were already slightly discredited; this was not so in Mr

Wodehouse's schooldays, and I suggest that Mr Wodehouse did definitely reject this part of his upbringing.

The belief that Kipling 'sold out to the upper classes' which Mr Orwell shares with Mr Edmund Wilson, is not, I think, sound. What I know of Kipling's private life suggests that he had no social ambitions except so far as in his day the attention of the great was evidence of professional ability. The sinister thing about Kipling was his religion, a peculiar blend of Judaism, Mithraism and Mumbo-jumbo-masonry which Mr Orwell ignores. And here, I think, is found the one serious weakness of all his criticism. He has an unusually high moral sense and respect for justice and truth, but he seems never to have been touched at any point by a conception of religious thought and life. He allows himself, for instance, to use the very silly expression: 'Men are only as good' (morally) 'as their technical development allows them to be.' He frequently brings his argument to the point when having, with great acuteness, seen the falsity and internal contradiction of the humanist view of life, there seems no alternative but the acceptance of a revealed religion, and then stops short. This is particularly true of his criticism of M. Dali, where he presents the problem of a genuine artist genuinely willing to do evil and leaves it unexplained, and in his essay on Mr Koestler, where he reaches the brink of pessimism. I suspect he has never heard of Mgr Knox's *God and the Atom,* which begins where he ends and in an exquisitely balanced work of art offers what seems to me the only answer to the problem that vexes him. He says with unseemly jauntiness: 'Few thinking people now believe in life after death.' I can only answer that *all* the entirely sane, learned and logical men of my acquaintance, and more than half those of keen intelligence, do in fact sincerely and profoundly believe in it.

Mr Orwell seems as unaware of the existence of his Christian neighbours as is, say, Sir Max Beerbohm of the urban proletariat. He assumes that all his readers took Mr H. G. Wells as their guide in youth, and he repeatedly imputes to them prejudices and temptations of which we are innocent. It is this ignorance of Catholic life far more than his ignorance of the classic Catholic writers which renders Mr Orwell's criticism partial whenever he approaches the root of his matter.

It remains to say that Mr Orwell's writing is as readable as his thought is lucid. His style is conversational. Sometimes it lapses into the barrack-room slang of the class-war, as when he uses the word 'intellectual' to distinguish, merely, the man of general culture from the manual labourer instead of, as is more accurate, to distinguish the analytic, logical habit of mind from the romantic and aesthetic. It is a pity, I think, to desert the *lingua franca* of polite letters for the jargon of a coterie.

Perhaps in a journal largely read by the religious, it should be mentioned that one of the essays, **'Some Notes on Salvador Dali',** was suppressed in a previous publication on grounds of obscenity. There and elsewhere Mr Orwell, when his theme requires it, does not shirk the use of coarse language. There is nothing in his writing that is inconsistent with high moral principles. (pp. 304-07)

Evelyn Waugh, "A New Humanism," in The Essays, Articles and Reviews of Evelyn Waugh, *edited by Donat Gallangher, Little, Brown and Company, 1984, pp. 304-07.*

Stephen Spender   (essay date 1953)

[*Spender is an English man of letters who rose to prominence during the 1930s as a Marxist lyric poet and as an associate of W. H. Auden, Christopher Isherwood, C. Day Lewis, and Louis MacNeice. Like many other artists and intellectuals, Spender became disillusioned with communism after World War II, and although he may still occasionally make use of political and social issues in his work, he is more often concerned with aspects of self-knowledge and depth of personal feeling. His poetic reputation has declined in the postwar years, while his stature as a prolific and perceptive literary critic has grown. Spender believes that art contains "a real conflict of life, a real breaking up and melting down of intractable material, feelings and sensations which seem incapable of expression until they have been thus transformed. A work of art doesn't say 'I am life, I offer you the opportunity of becoming me.' On the contrary, it says: 'This is what life is like. It is even realer, less to be evaded, than you thought. But I offer you an example of acceptance and understanding. Now, go back and live!' " In the following excerpt, Spender favorably reviews* Such, Such Were the Joys.]

George Orwell is an extremely English writer. He is a man with a grouse. He holds forth about his grievances—the intelligentsia, the rich, the Stalinists, nationalists of every kind. He has simple views about matters which more learned men have not been decided about: for example, he thinks that God and belief in immortality are nonsense. The views of nearly everyone except himself, especially those of writers who are religious, he seems to attribute to a desire to be fashionable, if not to bad faith. All the same, he is real and has a real point of view. The strength of his position as against most of his intellectual opponents is that they have been irresponsible, even if they have not actually betrayed our freedoms; whereas he has practised what he preached. He is a social democrat who has fought for his beliefs and voluntarily lived like a poor man.

More than this he cares simply and passionately for intellectual freedom. His real grievance against his fellow writers is that they have not paid the price of freedom. He does not blame them so much for changing sides as for not sticking consistently to one or two values and being prepared to live and die for them. These values really are *habeas corpus* and the duty to be honest as a writer, even though as a citizen one has to take sides in a political conflict. In a revealing passage, he says that the writer should, in our political age, "split himself into two compartments," the artist who recognizes "objective truth" and the political partisan.

[*Such, Such Were The Joys*] is happily chosen. In the course of it, Orwell states simply and clearly all his main ideas, and the reader is able to see how these have roots in his personal experience. For example, the resemblance of the world of his preparatory school to that of *1984* is striking. Crossgates was in fact a miniature police state in which Sim, the headmaster, was Big Brother, and there were tortures and confessions. All the same, curious obsessions crop up in Orwell's childhood which it is difficult to explain. For example, one day walking outside the school, he saw a man looking at him, and immediately he concluded that this man must be a spy employed by the headmaster to report on the activities of the boys out of school; he remarks that it would not have seemed extraordinary to him that the headmaster would employ a whole army of spies. Then, after a list of very genuine grievances about the conditions which the sons of the upper-class British endure at public schools, he complains that Eton schoolboys have fried fish for supper, as though this were as bad as all the other things.

The shadow of *1984* lies, indeed, over the whole volume, till the reader begins to realize that Orwell's last work resulted from the accumulated experience of years and was not just a bitter outburst of disillusionment after the Second World War. *1984* had roots in the First World War, and in the school experiences I have mentioned, which go back before then. For *1984* is based simply on the idea of a kind of arithmetic progression of horror; we discover this when, in the essay entitled **"Looking Back on the Spanish Civil War,"** written in 1943, Orwell asks who would have imagined in 1925 that twenty years hence slavery would return to Europe. Elsewhere he shows his conviction that the area of freedom is diminishing, that the growth of the police state is inevitable, that the kinds of freedom to which we attach importance will be unthinkable in terms of the ideologies of tomorrow, that the writer in the liberal tradition is a mere survival, and that if there are writers at all in a totalitarian world of tomorrow they will be an entirely different kind of animal, unimaginable to us who are living today. The very illuminating essay **"Inside the Whale,"** on Henry Miller's *Tropic of Capricorn,* is a curious foreshadowing of the love affair between Winston Smith and the girl secretary in *1984.* Orwell writes:

> From now onwards the all-important fact for the creative writer is going to be that this is not a writer's world. That does not mean that he cannot help bring the new society into being, but he can take no part in the process *as a writer . . .* It seems likely, therefore, that in the remaining years of free speech any novel worth reading will follow more or less along the lines that Miller has followed.

Then he adds the curious prophecy about Miller himself: "Sooner or later I should expect him to fall into unintelligibility or charlatanism."

"Looking Back on the Spanish War" is the central essay in the book: Spain—as for so many others—is the turning point in Orwell's disillusionment. Here again we are in the world of *1984.* The truth about the Spanish War is perhaps already irrecoverable, because it has been hidden under so much untruthful propagandist thinking on both sides. He adds that he is frightened lest "the very concept of objective truth is fading out of the world."

Only two things remain for Orwell. One is the hope that the workers are too firmly grounded in the short-term day-to-day solid preoccupations of their lives to be taken in by what he would have called not "The Age of Anxiety" but "The Age of Lies." The other is a patriotic faith in the power of England somehow to survive. Both these hopes he upholds against the Intelligentsia.

There is a great deal of fun and entertainment to be derived from this book, but very little that is comforting. From his grave, Orwell accuses the intellectuals of cowardice and irresponsibility, and he certainly says enough to give some of us, myself included, bad consciences. He does though show a way of intellectual honesty combined with decent public spiritedness which can be followed, if we are prepared to pay the price of not escaping into easy material conditions and tricky positions. Immediately after reading this book I read the most recent number of a leading literary review and felt extraordinarily depressed. (pp. 18-19)

> Stephen Spender, "One Man's Conscience," in The New Republic, *Vol. 128, No. 11, March 16, 1953, pp. 18-19.*

An excerpt from *Why I Write*

All writers are vain, selfish and lazy, and at the very bottom of their motives there lies a mystery. Writing a book is a horrible, exhausting struggle, like a long bout of some painful illness. One would never undertake such a thing if one were not driven on by some demon whom one can neither resist nor understand. For all one knows that demon is simply the same instinct that makes a baby squall for attention. And yet it is also true that one can write nothing readable unless one constantly struggles to efface one's own personality. Good prose is like a window pane. I cannot say with certainty which of my motives are the strongest, but I know which of them deserve to be followed. And looking back through my work, I see that it is invariably where I lacked a *political* purpose that I wrote lifeless books and was betrayed into purple passages, sentences without meaning, decorative adjectives and humbug generally.

George Orwell, in his Why I Write, *Secker and Warburg, 1968.*

Henry Popkin   (essay date 1954)

[*In the following review, Popkin praises Orwell as a social historian and autobiographer in* Such, Such Were the Joys.]

One more posthumous volume of George Orwell's essays is a new reminder that Orwell was always, equally, a social historian and an autobiographer. The social history is usually on the surface. It starts with the 19th Century, a time of poverty, hard work, and faith in the future. This faith began to be realized early in the 20th Century, but World War I put an end to progress. The precise moment of change may be different in different essays; it may be the Boer War or World War I—1910, 1914, or 1918. The "I" of *Coming Up for Air* has trouble distinguishing: "Before the war, and especially before the Boer War, it was summer all the year round." In America, the highwater mark seems to have been reached just before the Civil War, but the point is always that things were better "before the war." Following the 1920's, "a period of irresponsibility," the 'thirties fostered poverty, which had now become meaningless because it was unnecessary; totalitarianism, which is unlike any of the older, gentler, Victorian or Edwardian forms of conservatism; and bully-worship, a product of totalitarianism and of the weak moral fibre of left-wing intellectuals. The future is just as certain a part of the historical pattern as the past, for the worst is yet to come: the spread of world totalitarianism, bringing with it the death of culture and freedom.

Almost every word Orwell ever wrote records one stage or another of this chronicle of incipient chaos. Most of the essays in *Dickens, Dali, and Others* examine such evidence of the early, happy period as the hopeful reformism of Dickens and the Edwardian origins of Wells, Wodehouse, Kipling, and others. In the essays gathered in the posthumous books and in his earlier novels, Orwell pictured our present woes, tempered a little by hope and nostalgia. The terrible future is the subject of the last novel, *1984.*

Social history requires a place as well as time, and Orwell's place is England, the center of his world. The happy life of the first decade of this century is seen as distinctively English, as in *Coming Up for Air:*

> The old English order of life couldn't change. For ever and ever decent God-fearing women would cook Yorkshire pudding and apple dumplings on enormous coal ranges, wear woollen underclothes and sleep on feathers, make plum jam in July and pickles in October.

One of the essays in *Such, Such Were the Joys* offers a catalog of the English virtues: patriotism, a simple code of decent conduct, respect for law, belief in liberty, individualism, love of flowers, and lack of artistic talent. This is a handy list because it shows where Orwell the autobiographer is joined to Orwell the social historian. These are precisely Orwell's virtues. In respect to the last and oddest of the virtues, one recalls Lionel Trilling's assertion, "He was not a genius." Mr. Trilling demonstrates that possession of this quality is entirely in Orwell's favor, just as Orwell himself managed to compliment the English people on their lack of talent. The other virtues are precisely the English traits and ethical rules of thumb that Orwell championed in his writings, in all the years that he complained of the death of patriotism and of "bedrock decency" or urged his readers to plant trees and love flowers. They are the deadly virtues from which the protagonists of three of Orwell's novels flee and to which they half-gladly, half-resignedly return.

Orwell's social history, like his English loyalty, only partially conceals a substructure of autobiography. He was born in 1903, and his childhood therefore coincided with the Edwardian Era, which, by an effort of will, he sometimes extended to 1914 or 1918. He was particularly revealing about the nature of these loyalties in his essay on Dickens, where he observed that "nearly everyone feels a

sneaking affection for the patriotic poems he learned as a child." After applying nostalgia as a literary criterion, he accused himself: "And then the thought arises, when I say I like Dickens, do I simply mean that I like thinking about my childhood?" He found the question unanswerable.

Another key passage occurs in *Coming Up for Air:*

> 1913! My God! 1913! The stillness, the green water, the rushing of the weir! It'll never come again. I don't mean that 1913 will never come again. I mean the feeling inside you, the feeling of not being in a hurry and not being frightened, the feeling you've either had and don't need to be told about, or haven't had and won't ever have the chance to learn.

As a matter of fact, Orwell *did* mean that 1913 will never come again. The character in the novel was twenty in 1913, but Orwell was ten. Surely the emotions here described belong to the security of childhood: "the feeling of not being in a hurry and not being frightened." They are not the exclusive property of the children of 1913; they were possible even to the children of the troubled 'thirties, and they will be shared by the children of the 'fifties, if they are permitted to grow up.

Such passages as these help to explain Orwell's preferences, in literature as in life. He loved everything Edwardian, everything he had first encountered before 1918: good bad poetry and good bad novels, Raffles, the boys' weeklies, Kipling's thin red line of Empire-builders, H. G. Wells's dream of the future, even P. G. Wodehouse's spats-wearing heroes. All of these seemed right, natural, and defensible to Orwell because they were supremely right and natural when he first knew them. It is no great exaggeration to say that Orwell frequently let nostalgia overpower his judgment, but, in listing these private reasons why he felt as he did, we must not forget one additional indispensable reason why he considered World War I the great watershed of our century: apparently it was.

Orwell's Edwardian leanings help to explain the unresolved dilemma of his later years—the conflict between his socialism and the pessimism that found its fullest expression in *1984.* In the essay **"Inside the Whale,"** in [*Such, Such Were the Joys*], Orwell made some useful observations about another literary exponent of nostalgia—especially useful, that is, when we measure them against Orwell himself. He remarked that D. H. Lawrence was basically pessimistic even though his heart leaped up when he beheld primitive peoples—Indians, Etruscans, and others:

> But what he is demanding is a movement away from our mechanized civilisation, which is not going to happen. Therefore his exasperation with the present turns once more into idealism of the past, this time a safely mythical past, the Bronze Age. When Lawrence prefers the Etruscans (*his* Etruscans) to ourselves it is difficult not to agree with him, and yet, after all, it is a species of defeatism, because that is not the direction in which the world is moving.

Orwell was too modern to be nostalgic about the Bronze

Age. Instead he idealized the Edwardians—which was almost equally a species of defeatism. I say almost because the Edwardians themselves were not defeatists, and no good sentimental-Edwardian could be pledged entirely to the past. This paradox mirrors the full complexity of Orwell's alternating hopes and fears for the future: hopes because the Edwardians, like Shaw and Wells (both of whom Orwell ultimately disowned), looked ahead—and fears because Edwardian hopefulness was booby-trapped in World War I and nothing can get us back to the Edwardian Eden of 1913. It is a genuine dilemma, as impossible to resolve as Orwell's self-questioning about his fondness for Dickens.

What Orwell really wanted was 1913 and not the unlikely socialist Utopia that might lie beyond 1984. We are told that the totalitarians will take over and that perhaps, sometime, somehow, they will be dislodged. Orwell knew Jack London's *The Iron Heel,* a novel that predicts just such a future for the world. Neither London nor Orwell could suggest how the dislodgment of totalitarianism might come to pass. In *1984,* the only note of hope is in the efforts of Emmanuel Goldstein, Big Brother's nemesis. Goldstein, like Orwell, is an old Edwardian, for he writes:

> The world of today is a bare, hungry, dilapidated place compared with the world that existed before 1914, and still more so if compared with the imaginary future to which the people of that period looked forward. In the early twentieth century, the vision of a future society unbelievably rich, leisured, orderly and efficient—a glittering antiseptic world of glass and steel and snow-white concrete—was part of the consciousness of nearly every literate person.

This is, of course, Orwell's nostalgia, complete with its Edwardian Utopianism. But Goldstein's reality is brought into question, and his would-be follower, Winston Smith, becomes a devout believer in Big Brother. Orwell evidently resolved his dilemma by concluding that a probably permanent catastrophe for the free world was inevitable.

Why, then, did Orwell go on? Why did he continue to warn and to threaten the left-wing intellectuals who were, he could observe, too stupid to understand him? Because he was an indignant man, because he had discovered at an early age that he had "a power of facing unpleasant facts" and that he felt the need to record them. Like Keats's Hyperion, he became one of "those to whom the miseries of the world / Are misery, and will not let them rest." He was angry even when anger had no logical place in his unhappy *Weltanschauung.*

This bitter, critical strain is visible even when, in the title essay of *Such, Such Were the Joys,* Orwell is recalling his education at a private school. He provides a detailed narrative not only of what happened but also of what he thought and felt—his fear that some "Mrs. Form" (the sixth form) was going to beat him, that he was at fault for revealing that a caning had not hurt him, that he was again at fault when his master broke a riding crop while beating him. Both the past humiliation and the present indignation are startlingly real, although Orwell wrote his account of these events almost forty years after they took place. On the other hand, look at Cyril Connolly's record of the same school days in the same school. He describes the same happenings, the same tyrants, and the same petty tyrannies. Although he must have been equally wretched at St. Wulfric's, he is now willing to let bygones be bygones. He understands at last what necessity and what insecurity forced the headmaster and his wife to be so vicious; the welts have healed, and the indignities are forgiven. It was not so with Orwell, who not only harbored but treasured his resentments. His humiliation at school was evil, and, though complaint is now futile, Orwell could no more ignore it than he could ignore the inanities of the left-wing intellectuals' line on world politics and on Spain.

Remembering his school in this way was a real test for Orwell. His school days fell in the period that his nostalgia romanticized. He could sentimentalize about the art of the time—especially the popular art—but his most rigorous standards were always reserved for life and not art. He was primarily a critic of life, and, unlike that softer Edwardian, Connolly, he would not, for the sake of nostalgia, relax his standards of humanity.

The chief target of Orwell's honest anger was the anti-Orwell, a sort of negative photograph of himself: the left-wing intellectual, whose defects corresponded exactly to Orwell's Edwardian, English virtues. The left-wing intellectual underestimates the national spirit, worships foreign bullies, and thinks that smelling flowers dissipates energy that ought to go into the revolution. If this portrait of the intellectual sounds like caricature, Orwell's never does. Actually, Orwell became unconvincing only when, by straying into a sometimes embarrassing praise of the common man, he tried to offer an alternative. (He seems to have been happily unaware of the American cult of the common man.) Since Orwell agreed with Lionel Trilling that there is no conservative intelligentsia, "Down with the leftist intellectual!" must mean "Up with the noble worker!" Orwell therefore wrote a poem in honor of a soldier who "was born knowing what I had learned / Out of books and slowly." In the essay **"Looking Back on the Spanish War,"** he assailed the treachery of the intellectuals and praised the workers who kept up the struggle after the others quit. Finally, this belated Rousseauism makes everything just a little too simple.

Orwell's attacks on the left-wing intellectuals, like his account of his school days, are best appreciated when we have a negative touchstone for comparison; Peter Viereck, with *The Shame and Glory of the Intellectuals,* is conveniently at hand. Both Orwell and Viereck are made uncomfortable by most modern writing, but, whenever the topic came up, Orwell would disclaim any knowledge of literary criteria and get on to something else. He never identified modern, or modernist, literary attitudes with his principal enemy, Stalinism. He left that gaucherie to Mr. Viereck, who has created that strange hybrid, Gaylord Babbitt, a "Stalinoid" (Mr. Viereck's word), who quotes the *Partisan Review*! It is a relief to turn to Orwell's honesty and good sense. In the decade when Auden and other poets of his generation were Marxists, it must have been tempting to lump Stalinism and aestheticism together, but Orwell was as honest a debater as he was a reporter. He fought his separate battles separately. There were not many names that he did not call the left-wing intellectual, but he never called him "aesthete."

Doubtless Orwell was not a genius, but it is not as easy as it looks to do what Orwell did so very well. If it looks easy to write personal recollections, to attack left-wing intellectuals, or to interpret the popular arts, then consider, respectively, the tepidity of Cyril Connolly, the intemperate rage of Peter Viereck, and the flounderings of Leo Gurko (in the recent *Heroes, Highbrows, and the Popular Mind*). We need these negative touchstones to remind us that Orwell, for all his nostalgia and for all his unresolvable dilemmas, was personally—and it is practically impossible to put this on any other basis—superior to his political and literary commitments, to anything he ever did, even to his skill as an essayist. We praise the honest, angry man revealed in these essays more even than the essays that reveal the man. (pp. 139-44)

> Henry Popkin, "Orwell the Edwardian," in The Kenyon Review, Vol. XVI, No. 1, Winter, 1954, pp. 139-44.

John Wain   (essay date 1954)

[*Wain is an English novelist, poet, and critic. Central to his critical stance is his belief that, in order to judge the quality of a piece of literature, the critic must make a moral as well as an imaginative judgment. James Gindin has called him "an excellent literary critic, intelligent, perceptive, and able to analyze and explain what he sees clearly and cogently." In the following essay, Wain asserts that Orwell's essays will outlive his novels in popular and critical appeal.*]

Orwell's essays are obviously much better than his novels. As a novelist he was not particularly gifted, but as a controversial critic and pamphleteer he was superb, as good as any in English literature. The novels do not add any new dimension to the ideas already put forward in the essays; they merely start them moving, like clockwork toys, in the hope of catching the attention of passers-by. Thus it comes as a shock to discover, for instance, that *Down and Out in Paris and London* is an earlier work than *The Clergyman's Daughter;* the novel is so inept, so obviously the product of inexperience and a lack of interest in the form it belongs to, the pamphlet so mature, balanced and successful. Finally, of course, Orwell came into his enormous popular success with two books that were not novels at all. *Animal Farm* is not even fiction, since the 'story' was there already in contemporary history, only waiting to be transposed into a fable.

Thus it is not in any provocative or paradoxical spirit that one says, quite simply, that *Critical Essays* is a better book than *1984,* or that the essay on *King Lear* will ultimately have more readers than *Animal Farm.* Orwell was pushed into writing fiction by the appalling imbalance of modern literary taste, which dictates that no book shall have more than a handful of readers unless it is a novel. But when his purely contemporary vogue has died down, his reputation will be in the hands of bookish and thoughtful people, who do not share the mania for fiction above all else, and then

the essays will rise to the top and the novels sink to the bottom. Already it is clear that the best strategy for Orwell's enemies is to concentrate on the novels, and keep quiet, as far as possible, about the fact that he was an essayist. For instance Mr Hopkinson, who with extraordinary astuteness managed to get his bitter attack on Orwell published and advertised by the British Council as one of their series 'Writers and their Work'—a stroke of genius worthy of the Florentine—gives most of his space to picking holes in the novels, and mentions the essays only in grudging asides. The result is as meaningful as a criticism of Eliot which gave most of its attention to the plays, on the grounds that more people have seen Eliot's plays than have read his poems or essays. There is no need for us to make the same false distribution of weight: and therefore it is in order to say at once that a new volume of Orwell's essays is more important than the discovery of an unpublished novel would be.

Of course one must fairly admit that *England Your England* is substantially less interesting than the two volumes of essays already in print. Orwell was a man of comparatively few ideas, which he took every opportunity of putting across, and a collection of his essays which gets anywhere near completeness will obviously contain the same ideas expressed a number of times with rather little variation. The selection from his occasional writings which he made himself (*Critical Essays,* 1946) has very little direct repetition; the first posthumous volume, *Shooting An Elephant,* contains echoes of *Critical Essays* and also internal echoes; while this third volume is, inevitably, a collection of scraps presenting almost nothing that was not said better elsewhere in Orwell's works.

This does not mean, however, that it is superfluous. On the contrary, it is a work of commanding interest, and not only for the obvious reason, that it is by Orwell. For one thing, the selectors have admitted the principle of reprinting passages from his early and unobtainable books; for another, it contains a long essay which Orwell himself rejected, and it is always interesting to ask why an author suppresses work that had seemed good enough to publish not long before. Let me deal with these two points in turn.

The unobtainable books drawn on are *The Road to Wigan Pier* and *The Lion and the Unicorn.* Selecting passages in this way is a thankless task, and obviously the selectors could not hope to please anyone but themselves; but even so I must confess that the golden opportunity seems to me to have been missed. It is clear enough that this will be the last volume of barrel-scrapings from the Orwell stock, so that anything not included here will have small chance of emerging in the future. Hence, no doubt, the excellent decision to include extracts from his books as well as a round-up of scattered articles. The trouble is that this decision was implemented in too feeble a way. *Wigan Pier,* for instance, is often said to be Orwell's worst book; but, even supposing this to be true, an author's best paragraphs or pages, even his best chapter, might occur in his worst book. (This is especially true of an author interested primarily in ideas.) The first part of *Wigan Pier* contains passages that Orwell never again equalled, but one would never think so from the two snippets reprinted here. The first two chapters should have been reproduced entire; they consist of a description of life in the industrial north during the depression, and their purpose is to serve as an introduction, a kind of preliminary barrage, for the political argufying that takes up the body of the book. In other words, these two chapters are a *Down and Out* in miniature, or, if you prefer to look at it another way, an expanded version of the kind of descriptive essay he gave us in **"How The Poor Die."** They contain unforgettable portraits (it is always the *real* people, from the Italian militiaman in *Catalonia* to Paddy and Bozo in *Down and Out,* who are most vivid in Orwell); we ought at least to have been given the sketch of Mr and Mrs Brooker, who kept the tripe shop and took in boarders—Mrs Brooker lying in bed all day and wiping her mouth on strips of newspaper, and Mr Brooker 'always moving with incredible slowness from one hated job to another. . . . In the mornings he sat by the kitchen fire with a tub of filthy water, peeling potatoes at the speed of a slow-motion picture.' (I quote from memory, and, being out of England with no access to books, had better apologize here and now for the lack of precise references in what follows.) The Brookers and their lodgers are better examples of Orwell's power of human portraiture than anything in the novels, and the descriptions of various features of working-class life in England at that period have a sting of pity and anger so urgent that to find anything comparable one has to go back to Langland. But one looks in vain for any sample in this book; *Wigan Pier* has missed its chance, and will now sink, with the bad passages dragging the good ones down to the satisfaction, no doubt, of Mr Hopkinson. Again, the early novels, poor as they are, contain some set pieces which could have been extracted with no loss of intelligibility. An obvious choice would have been the chapter in *The Clergyman's Daughter* where Orwell suddenly breaks into dramatic form, abandoning the realistic method of the rest of the book, in order to draw his nightmare picture of a night spent in Trafalgar Square; and possibly the description of a typical day's hop-picking in Kent, from the same book, would have interested many readers. All in all, one cannot but be disappointed that passages like these have been pushed out to make room for comparatively lightweight essays which repeat things Orwell had already hammered home.

The second point I mentioned above, that the book contains a long essay which Orwell himself virtually suppressed, is, happily, a good mark for the editors. (I put the word in the plural instinctively, because these things are usually done by a sort of informal committee.) When Orwell issued his *Critical Essays,* he reprinted two of the three long pieces which make up *Inside the Whale;* the title essay, which he dropped, is given here; and, while it is not one of his classic pieces of criticism, it is interesting to read it with an eye to the reasons for his having allowed it to go out of print.

To begin with, it is obviously written from the depths of despair, a despair more convincing than that of *1984,* because it was based on a straight reading of the omens without the complicating factor of fatal illness. The essay is chiefly concerned with Henry Miller, and in order to make out a case for Miller it includes a long retrospect of twenti-

eth-century literature, from the standpoint of 'tendency'. Orwell considers in turn the Georgians, the cosmopolitan 'twenties, and the political 'thirties, and in turn he rejects them. The Georgians are the simplest case, as he takes it for granted that no post-1918 reader can feel anything for them but contempt; Housman 'just jingles', Brooke's *Grantchester* is 'a sort of accumulated vomit from a stomach stuffed with place-names', and as for the Squires and Shankses, well, 'The wind was blowing from Europe, and long before 1930 it had blown the beer-and-cricket school naked, except for their knighthoods.' When he turns to the dominant writers of the 'twenties, Orwell is inclined to take them very seriously; indeed he pays their work the highest compliment he ever did pay to a work of literature; he said it was likely to survive. (It was one of the weaknesses of Orwell's literary criticism that he declared survival 'the only test worth bothering about', thereby sidestepping the really important questions.) But from this point of view, these writers stand convicted of 'a too Olympian attitude, a too great readiness to wash their hands of the immediate problem.' He felt that there was something heartless about the lifelong devotion to an æsthetic ideal (Joyce), the worship of primitivism in a world that was obviously becoming more and more industrial and urbanized (Lawrence), the 'Christian pessimism which implies a certain indifference to human misery' (Eliot).

Passing to the 'thirties, Orwell again found disappointing results. Here, indeed, was 'purpose', but in his view it was too facile, too orthodox, and above all, too soft and unrealistic. The characteristic writers of the period are all 'the kind of person who is always somewhere else when the trigger is pulled'. (Surely he was right about this, by the way; witness that characteristic figure of our time, the man who was a left-wing poet in the 'thirties and married a rich wife in the 'fifties.)

The conclusion to which he was driven was therefore one of utter pessimism for the future of literature. If the 'twenties were too loftily standing apart from the dogfight, 'the literary history of the 'thirties seems to justify the opinion that a writer does well to keep out of politics'. Yet on an earlier page he had said, 'a novelist who simply disregards the major public events of his time is generally either a footler or a plain idiot', and there is not much sign of wavering from this position as the essay unfolds itself. *Therefore* Miller is an important writer. He has stepped aside from political 'awareness' without joining 'the huge tribe of Barries and Deepings and Dells who simply don't notice what is happening.'

> I should say that he believes in the impending ruin of Western Civilization much more firmly than the majority of 'revolutionary' writers; only he does not feel called upon to do anything about it. He is fiddling while Rome is burning, and, unlike the enormous majority of people who do this, fiddling with his face towards the flames.

This is obviously the product of that despair which quite naturally overtook a man of letters when the bombers began to stream down the runways in 1939. Miller, who under normal conditions can be seen as a writer with about the same allowance of talent as, say, Robert Ross, is suddenly puffed up into a major figure because he provides an 'objective correlative' for Orwell's disgust and disappointment. (The reason he did not feel 'called upon' to do anything about the break-up of Western Civilization was because he belonged to a neutral country and knew perfectly well that there was no reason why he should ever hear a shot fired in anger in his life.) But for Orwell it was different, and when the end of the war found him, to his own surprise, still alive and writing, and even planning new books, the whole thing began, in retrospect, to look silly. But there was a more personal reason for withdrawing the essay. Not merely because it had praised an author who was not, on the whole, worth praise; but because both implicitly, by boosting Miller, and explicitly, in statements like the following, it had denied the possibility of writing books such as the ones Orwell was going to write during the rest of his life.

> The passive attitude will come back, and it will be more consciously passive than before. Progress and reaction have both turned out to be swindles. Seemingly there is nothing left but quietism—robbing reality of its terrors by simply submitting to it. . . . A novel on more positive, 'constructive' lines, and not emotionally spurious, is at present very difficult to imagine.

Clearly it was impossible for Orwell to continue holding this kind of opinion after the first dazed condition of shock and hopelessness had worn off. It would have left him with nothing to live for. His life was devoted to battling for human justice and decency, and in defence of the underdog; and it may be all very well for Miller, or someone like him, to declare that it doesn't matter if things fall to pieces altogether and there are no ideals left. When things fall to pieces it is always the underdog who suffers and the bully, the toady, and the clever liar who come out on top, and Orwell saw this clearly enough. If the imaginative writer abdicates his minimal human responsibility, his duty to put in a word on the right side now and again, his position is ultimately intolerable; however you may choose to rephrase it, the old idea of 'profit with delight', i.e. moral instruction made palatable, has got to stay.

It was this realization that made Orwell so concerned, in his later years, with the problems of honesty and truthfulness in the writer. He was born into a world where, on the whole, there was very little censorship of the printed word, and grew up in a worsening atmosphere until, by the time of his death in 1950, it had actually become difficult to speak the truth even in minor matters—difficult because of the psychological pressures on the writer. Hence Orwell's first concern, to which he can be seen anxiously returning on page after page of this volume, is the writer's duty to keep his mind free of fetters. Very briefly his point is this: if you accept anything on trust, if you give up your mental independence and submit to any orthodoxy, you are disqualified as an author. You may be a journalist, an ad. man or a party hack, but an author you cannot be. If there is even one subject on which you cannot be perfectly frank, that means there will be a paralysed corner of your mind, and the paralysis is always likely to spread. Everyone is familiar with Orwell's endless jeering at Russophile writers and politicians who have to change their funda-

mental beliefs every time the Moscow line is switched, and his love of repeating stories like the one about the 'Comrade' who went out to the lavatory during a meeting, to find that a surprise news bulletin over the radio had caused the 'line' to be changed during his absence. But while all this is admirable, while we accept Orwell eagerly as a great ally in the Cold War, we should not overlook the fact that in his eyes *every* orthodoxy was hateful. He spoke of '*all* the smelly little orthodoxies which are contending for our souls', not just *some* of them. In this connexion it is a pity that the editors did not give us a chance to reconsider the remarkable essay on Eliot's *Four Quartets,* which he published in *Poetry London* during the war. I have not the article by me, of course, but briefly the gist is this. Orwell is casting about for some explanation of what he considers the falling-off in Eliot's poetic powers since the *Waste Land* period, and comes to the conclusion that the poet's conversion to Anglo-Catholicism is at the roof of it, since, by embracing the doctrines of the Church, Eliot has found himself committed to believing, or pretending to believe, theories as to the origin of the world, the nature of life, etc., which nobody really holds. A simple Spanish peasant, who believes in Heaven and Hell as literally as he believes in New York, though he has never seen New York, can hold his belief without damage to his imagination; but when a subtly-thinking modern man of letters joins the Church, he does so for a complex of reasons, some of which are social, and henceforth he is to some extent blinkered. His vision becomes less acute because he is not free to look in any direction he chooses. There is, of course, an argument against this; for one thing it is arguable that by preferring *The Waste Land* to the *Quartets* Orwell is falling into a similar trap, allowing his imagination to be headed off by his intellect with its anti-religious bias; but it is a pity that the challenge is not taken up by some critic who is honest enough to consider the issue seriously. Certainly the lady who was put up to 'answer' Orwell in the same issue of the magazine did not make a very satisfactory job of it, and it is disappointing that the editors of this volume ran away from their obligation to bring this essay into the light.

The other major point that Orwell hammered home was again one that would occur to a sceptic more readily than to a believer: namely, the falsification of history. 'Truth will prevail,' said someone, I think Patmore, 'When no one cares if it prevail or not'; but, as Orwell pointed out, when both sides are busy faking the historical records to show that they have been in the right all along, you can easily reach a stage when the facts are simply not available. His major exercise on this theme is, of course, the 'Ministry of Truth' business in *1984,* but it is all there in the piece about the Spanish war in this book. After discussing a specific example—the presence or non-presence of a Russian force in Spain—he says:

> The implied objective of this line of thought is a nightmare world in which the Leader, or some ruling clique, controls not only the future but *the past.* If the Leader says of such and such an event, 'It never happened'—well, it never happened. If he says that two and two are five—well, two and two are five. This prospect frightens me much more than bombs.

Christians would retort that Truth has an existence of its own outside our world; but unless they are right, it is certainly true that heroic actions can be performed, saintly lives led, and great thoughts written down, and nobody need ever know anything about it.

And so this carelessly produced book is a major event. It is for us to keep Orwell's example constantly before us. So let us end on a personal note. 'When I was about sixteen,' he tells us in **"Why I Write,"**

> I suddenly discovered the joy of mere words, i.e. the sounds and associations of words. The lines from *Paradise Lost*—
>
> So hee with difficulty and labour hard
> Moved on: with difficulty and labour hee,
>
> which do not now seem to me so very wonderful, sent shivers down my backbone.

I think I can guess why. (pp. 71-8)

> John Wain, "The Last of George Orwell," in
> The Twentieth Century, *Vol. CLV, No. 923,
> January, 1954, pp. 71-8.*

Wayne Warncke   (essay date 1968)

[*In the following essay, Warncke examines Orwell's critical approach to literature.*]

No one would deny that George Orwell was a writer of his age. Whether he was any more conscious of the political crisis that the Western world has faced during the past several decades than many other writers have been is doubtful, but his own involvement in the struggle for human freedom and decency is unquestionable; and it is the most important single factor influencing his essays on literature from the briefest reviews to the more extended and better known studies of writers like Dickens and Henry Miller. Orwell's literary criticism at the very outset is a reaction against the practice of doctrinaire criticism— against the blatant shouting of creeds, the intellectual coercion and falsification of truth that Orwell found especially evident in the left-wing writing of his time. His response to this particular moral failure developed, however, into more than an appeal for honest literary criticism on the part of the orthodox Left. It extended to a general attack on the narrowness of all orthodoxy, political or religious, and undoubtedly made it difficult for him to find a position in his own literary criticism that would allow him the broadest critical point of view, yet allow too a *modus operandi* and a standard of judgment compatible with his attitude toward literature as a sociopolitical and thus moral force. The writer, at least any self-respecting one, could be neither totally committed to his aesthetic sensibility, nor to his social concern, and Orwell recognized the issue as a writer himself: "The job is to reconcile my ingrained likes and dislikes with the essentially public, non-individual activities that this age forces on all of us."

Orwell's initial problem as a critic of literature is clear enough: the pull toward an acknowledgement of any world view as a source of "good" literature met the counterpull toward acceptance of only a world view that was politically conscious and preferably liberal. Orwell could claim that "today, for example, one can imagine a good book being written by a Catholic, a Communist, a Fascist, a pacifist, an anarchist, perhaps by an old-style Liberal or an ordinary Conservative," but he could not imagine "a good book being written by a spiritualist, a Buchmanite or a member of the Ku-Klux-Klan." Though he stressed the importance of the writer's individuality and freedom, and the validity of one's own truth ("the imaginative writer is unfree when he has to falsify his subjective feelings, which from his point of view are facts"), he took many a writer to task for omitting in his work consideration of the social or political conditions of the life he was depicting. He criticized Graham Greene for not mentioning in *The Heart of the Matter* what would be naturally in the principal character's mind—the racial conflict between blacks and whites and the struggle against the local nationalist movement in the West African setting of Greene's novel. For the short story writer H. E. Bates to treat "the tiny misfortunes of over-sensitized people" during a period of total war seemed to Orwell unbelievable; and though Katherine Mansfield's "character touches" were "exquisite," Orwell added the observation that throughout her work there was a complete lack of social criticism, even implied; all her interest was centered on "individual and tiny gradations of conduct."

Orwell suggests a solution to the problem of the writer's responsibility by a repeated emphasis on the importance of a writer's sincerity: his being able to care, his really believing in his beliefs; and by equating literary talent with conviction:

> It seems therefore that for a creative writer possession of the "truth" is less important than emotional sincerity. Even Mr. Upward would not claim that a writer needs nothing beyond a Marxist training. He also needs talent. But talent, apparently, is a matter of being able to *care*, of really *believing* in your beliefs, whether they are true or false.

Yet even the application of this assertion became problematical when, for example, he evaluated the work of Yeats—a writer whose political and moral tendencies were, from Orwell's point of view, irresponsible. One suspects that Orwell reluctantly gave his concept of sincerity an altered emphasis in order to acknowledge (perhaps less unwillingly) his recognition of a great talent:

> Perhaps for a writer common sense matters less than sincerity, and even sincerity, in the ordinary moral and intellectual sense, less than something that might be called artistic sincerity. Yeats may have held some absurd or undesirable beliefs, and he may have laid claim to a mystic wisdom that he did not possess, but he would never in any circumstances have committed what he would have regarded as an aesthetic sin.

Despite the inconsistencies that are suggested by his all too brief theoretical commentary concerning literature, his practical criticism shows invariably and without confusion that the writer's responsibility is first to certain basic human values (indeed, including sincerity), which go unchanged whatever political or religious ideology makes claims for the infallibility of its doctrines. The general result in Orwell's criticism is an analysis of the quality of human response expressed in a writer's work. In the largest sense, Orwell's critical way is a finding and applying of human values, and the man as well as the critic shoulders this task, leaving indelible imprints of personality in the process.

Orwell's attitude toward literature is essentially pragmatic; literature is a force in the world for good or evil. Though Orwell is very much concerned with literature as a reflection of man and society, the concern itself derives from a belief that the significance of literature is the effect it has had or will have on the quality of human life. In this characteristic, Orwell is much closer to Dr. Johnson than to John Crowe Ransom; his attitude is more closely in line with a traditional view that goes back at least to Horace than it is with contemporary objective theories of art that have dominated literary criticism in the first half of this century. Nowhere does Orwell overtly state that instruction should take precedence over enjoyment or that enlightenment should precede entertainment, but this is an attitude that underlies his criticism; and it is evident that he sees the importance of literature as a means to an end, and that the end is the place where a responsible and significant literature will be discovered.

Yet Orwell's critical approach to literature differs at important points from both traditional literary pragmatism as practiced, for example, by the dominant neoclassical critics of the eighteenth century, and the special variety of pragmatic criticism illustrated by contemporary Marxist critics. Orwell's approach has, for one thing, a less prescriptive bent. He is unconcerned with rules which the writer must follow in order to achieve certain prescribed effects upon his audience, and he refuses to acknowledge "social realism" as the primary criterion of literary value, as the Marxists have commonly done. Orwell has a broad enough imagination not to become tied to a narrow view of what constitutes artistic truth, and too liberal a viewpoint to follow any mechanical set of critical principles.

Like both the Marxist and the traditional pragmatic critic, he emphasizes the responsibility of the artist to the reader and sees the aim of the artist in relation to the well-being of man in society, but he differs in his idea of precisely what that relationship is. Whereas the typical Marxist values literature insofar as it promotes the proletariat or the classless society, and the traditional pragmatic critic has tended to evaluate according to the degree that literature reaches the happy balance of both delighting and inducing "virtue" (a now dubious, if not impossible concept), Orwell values literature insofar as it is a free and sincere expression of a human truth, the only prescription being that artistic truth be verifiable in the daily life of humankind—that it have traceable roots in reality. The aim of the artist, or better his responsibility, is to be true ultimately to his own nature, to his own vision of man and society, for only in this way will he achieve the end that literature must essentially serve in society: if not the enhancement, at least the maintenance of human freedom and human truth.

Orwell's criticism is distinguished from the traditional, though not so much from the contemporary, pragmatic

approach in another important respect. Orwell is very much concerned with the source of literature. Although in this characteristic he is close to the Marxist critic in having a vital concern for the mind of the writer and the subject matter of his work, he differs again by not being restricted to an exclusive economic or class accounting for the derivation of the character of literature. With the belief that "above a quite low level, literature is an attempt to influence the viewpoint of one's contemporaries by recording experience," Orwell quite naturally would and, indeed, does concern himself chiefly with both source and effect, and less with form; his procedure as a critic is a combined analysis and evaluation of both the source and end of creative literary works.

The writer's "tendency" is as important to Orwell's criticism as the work's "literary qualities," and although he does not confuse these two aspects of literature in his evaluation by either dismissing or accepting a work because of its ideological tendency, the largest proportion of any one of his critical essays is given over to an analysis of what he called a writer's "message," or more accurately, the writer's beliefs. Yet Orwell's concern for effect is equally apparent in his essays. In his evaluation of literary qualities, there is a strong emphasis on the factor that increases human knowledge and human awareness. One of his major critical evaluations of Dickens' novels, for example, is that "except in a rather round-about way, one cannot *learn* very much from Dickens," and in the attendant comparisons of Dickens' characters and those of Tolstoy, Orwell points to the cause as a failure of truth to life: Tolstoy's characters are "struggling to make their souls, whereas Dickens's are already finished and perfect." "Dickens's characters have no mental life. They say perfectly the thing that they have to say, but they cannot be conceived as talking about anything else. They never learn, never speculate"—and so Tolstoy can tell us much more about ourselves than can Dickens.

In a slightly different way this same emphasis can be noted in Orwell's attitude toward the mixing of burlesque and realism in the English novel:

> English writers from Chaucer onwards have found it very difficult to resist burlesque, but as soon as burlesque enters the reality of the story suffers. Fielding, Dickens, Trollope, Wells, even Joyce, have all stumbled over this problem.

The implication of this brief critique is borne out in Orwell's evaluation of Gissing as the best novelist the English people have produced:

> It is obvious that Dickens, Fielding and a dozen others are superior to him [Gissing] in natural talent, but Gissing is a "pure" novelist, a thing that few gifted English writers have been. Not only is he genuinely interested in character and in telling a story, but he has the great advantage of feeling no temptation to burlesque. It is a weakness of nearly all the characteristic English novelists, from Smollett to Joyce, that they want to be "like life" and at the same time want to get a laugh as often as possible.

Presumably, Gissing's genuine interest in character is the

development of fictional figures in the manner of Tolstoy, and being "like life" clearly takes precedence in Orwell's mind over "natural" talent which suggests a careless facility and lack of serious concern. Orwell's point of view, in part, is a regard for unity of tone ("very few English novels exist throughout on the same plane of probability") and does not necessarily reflect an outright dismissal of the value of humor. In fact, Orwell stresses that Thackeray was by nature a burlesque writer, one who depicts "a world where no one is good and nothing is serious," and that his best work was purely burlesque. In "A Little Dinner at Timmins's" we have "one of the best comic short stories ever written" because Thackeray is really doing the same thing as he did in *Vanity Fair* without the disturbing mixture of comic and serious elements: "One feels that the folly of social ambition has been more conclusively demonstrated than it is by *Vanity Fair.*" Yet Orwell's concern for unity here is not for unity in and for itself, that is, as a principle of form, but for the effect this quality has in assuring a valid depiction of a serious human truth; and his tendency to value the "serious" writer, the more "scrupulous," as he referred to Gissing, over the writer who had "the instinct to play the fool" is clearly a leaning toward the especial importance of the moral effect of the novel, the idea that instruction rather than delight is the essential purpose of literature. Even Dickens is "funniest when he is discovering new sins," and his "comic genius is dependent on his moral sense," a clear moral code, which, incidentally, Orwell found lacking in Thackeray.

Orwell's dual critical concerns for both the source and the effect of art make up the heart of his criticism and are perhaps most clearly illustrated in his essays on the traditional English writers, Dickens, Kipling, and Swift. An idea of his fundamental critical approach, however, can be gained by examining in broad outline his general procedure as a critic and the basic premise which underlines his critical point of view. All of Orwell's major criticism follows roughly the same pattern of description and evaluation; in the first instance, through the use of historical, sociological, and psychological methods, literature supports the development of an analysis of the writer's world view; in the second instance literature becomes the subject of an evaluation of the writer's specific literary qualities.

These procedures are, of course, important to Orwell's ultimate evaluation of the end the writer's work serves in terms of the human truth it offers to an audience of the majority of men whose response is both empathetic and sympathetic. This conclusive phase of his criticism, particularly developed in his treatment of traditional writers, depends a great deal on his own personal response, formed by the peculiar exigencies of his age. Nevertheless, it is evident from his essays that he did not believe he was responding merely for himself or, indeed, for a select or specialized group, but rather for the majority of mankind. Thus Orwell is, in a sense, speaking from "the emotional overlap between the intellectual and the ordinary man," to which he referred in his essay on Kipling, and the assumptions that he makes in the name of both the ordinary man and the intellectual are always cogent, always humanly perceptive. It would be difficult to disagree with his

sense of what constitutes the universal appeals of writers to whom he gave his most extensive critical attention.

With an approach that places so great an emphasis on a writer's human orientation, it is not strange that the central concept of Orwell's criticism is the writer's "world view," a term used interchangeably with "tendency," "message," and "purpose" in Orwell's phraseology. Orwell is one of the chief representatives of a critical point of view which attaches most importance to the writer's attitude toward life. At the core of every writer's work is a fundamental vision of life, something analogous to the soul of the writer's being, and Orwell's major criticism centers in this unifying element of both the author and his art.

In Dickens, Orwell finds central a generosity of mind, a quasi-instinctive siding with the oppressed against the oppressors, a sound moral sense, but a narrow intellectual and imaginative vision of human progress; in Kipling, a sense of responsibility to England's ruling power which acted and made necessary decisions; in Swift, a simple refusal of life, a refusal to see anything in human life except dirt, folly, and wickedness, and a disbelief in the possibility of human happiness or the capability of improving earthly existence; in Eliot (after 1930), a gloomy Pétainism which turns its eyes to the past, accepts defeat, writes off earthly happiness as impossible, and mumbles about prayer and repentance; in Koestler (in 1944), a short-term pessimism at the base of which is a hedonistic longing for the Earthly Paradise; in Yeats, a hatred of modern Western civilization and a desire to return to the Bronze Age or perhaps to the Middle Ages; in Jack London, a natural urge towards the glorification of brutality, an almost unconquerable preference for the strong man against the weak man, coupled with a contrasting sympathy for human suffering under industrial capitalism; and in Henry Miller, an enjoyment of the process of life, an acceptance of civilization as it is. Orwell's major critical essays are neither more nor less than an elaboration upon these central concepts, and his critical procedure is to clarify and to evaluate each world view in its pertinent manifestations: as each is expressed through certain categories of the writer's life and as each is translated into certain characteristics of his art.

Orwell's treatment of the first major manifestation of the writer's world view is always extensive, suggesting something of the importance he attached to it. Significant to this phase of his criticism are the categories he selects for his descriptive analysis. These categories indicate Orwell's special sense of literature's close relationship to life as well as his own worldly perspective. His most important classification is the political. In stressing this descriptive device, he reveals his sense of the inevitable relationship between a serious creative work and its author's vision of the kind of society men should strive for. The absence of a positive political position is as significant as its presence, a fact which Orwell makes plain in his discussion of Dickens who distrusts politics and has the "half-belief" that government is unnecessary, and in his treatment of Henry Miller whose lack of "public-spiritedness" and disregard for the major public events of the moment go far toward explaining his passive acceptance of the world as it is.

Swift, on the other hand, has a reactionary and authoritarian cast of mind, and coupled with his intermittent anarchistic viewpoint, a vision of society which shows strong totalitarian tendencies. Orwell describes both Kipling and T. S. Eliot in terms of their conservatism, but Kipling is a Conservative of a type that is now extinct or perhaps impossible in an age of totalitarianism when what was formerly a positive and vital position becomes automatically a negative political view of society of the type evidenced in Eliot's "conservatism of the half-hearted modern kind." Jack London's "better angel is his Socialist convictions"; his outlook is democratic, and intellectually he envisions a society without exploitation and hereditary privilege, a world where the meek inherit the earth. "Translated into political terms, Yeat's tendency is Fascist," and he sees the "new civilization" as aristocratic and hierarchical.

What is important to note in all of these classifications is that they are not mechanically made, and that Orwell is not simply applying a narrow and absolute category that rules out the recognition of distinctly individual characteristics or even contradictory political tendencies. For example, Orwell observes that Swift shows a progressive strain which is not congruous with his central reactionary orientation. There are moments when he is constructive and advanced, and while he sees utopia as a strongly centralized society, he can also attack totalitarianism. An important quality that Orwell finds in Jack London is a Fascist streak, an instinct which "lay towards acceptance of a 'natural aristocracy' of strength, beauty and talent." The complicating factor in London (though it made him a good storyteller) is a "temperament" which is not in accord with his democratic outlook. Orwell is not merely labelling, but pointing out the nuances of each writer's political views; and his awareness of relativity and inconsistency, illustrated by his analysis within a category, is equally apparent in the variety of descriptive categories he applies. Other classifications that Orwell uses at different times and with different emphasis to bring out a writer's world view are the social, intellectual, and religious.

What such an analysis amounts to is a revelation of the writer's mind in terms of his attitudes, opinions, alignments, and beliefs, developed from biographical and historical facts, and by examining the writer's social, economic, geographical and psychological origins—all reflected in and supported by the writer's work. But the effect of the analysis and description is more than a clarification of the writer's world view; it is a judgment of that view as well. There is little doubt that Orwell is personally against the political reactionary and for the political progressive; that he opposes class snobbery and has egalitarian sympathies; that he values intellectual curiosity and a broad human awareness; and that he accepts an essential Christian morality, but rejects the beliefs of traditional Christian doctrine. In a sense this phase of Orwell's criticism is an arraignment, a calling to account, from Orwell's point of view, of the extent and quality of the writer's humanity as it is expressed in his work: the writer's anxiety for man's well-being both as an individual and as a member of the social community; the writer's attention to the process of life and concern for the surface of the earth; and the writer's attitude toward the ultimate value of human existence.

The importance of this phase of Orwell's criticism to the second phase, a treatment of world view translated into art, is inestimable because the interrelation of the two is the foundation of Orwell's specific literary analysis. The relationship can be seen in the method that Orwell follows, based on a fundamental critical premise: a writer's world view has a profound effect on the literary aspects of his work. That Orwell proceeds on this reasoning is illustrated throughout his criticism, but at several points in his essays he specifically states this critical principle and suggests additionally how a writer's outlook is actually translated into art.

In his essay on Dickens, while apologizing for not paying close enough attention to Dickens' literary qualities, he writes: "But every writer, especially every novelist, has a 'message,' whether he admits it or not, and the minutest details of his work are influenced by it." The principle is equally applicable to poetry, as Orwell explains in an article on T. S. Eliot: "It is fashionable to say that in verse only the words count and the 'meaning' is irrelevant, but in fact every poem contains a prose-meaning, and when the poem is any good it is a meaning which the poet urgently wishes to express. All art is to some extent propaganda." And again in his essay on Yeats, he states that "a writer's political and religious beliefs are not excrescences to be laughed away, but something that will leave their mark even on the smallest detail of his work." In this particular article Orwell even goes so far as to suggest that a connection exists between a writer's "tendency" and his literary style: "In the case of Yeats, there must be some kind of connection between his wayward, even tortured style of writing and his rather sinister vision of life." But his development of the connection is too brief and general to be conclusive in any sense; it extends only to remarks about an "artificial" manner of writing and a tendency present in all except Yeats's best passages of importing "a feeling of affectation." Orwell is more successful in the same article, however, in his attempt to point out that certain lines from Yeats's *The Hour-Glass,* though beautiful, are "profoundly obscurantist and reactionary"; thus Orwell demonstrates a relationship and, at the same time, implies what is admittedly a questionable evaluation.

With some writers Orwell is notably perceptive in analyzing both literary qualities and their causes, especially when he is capable of a sympathetic understanding of the writer's attitude toward life, as he is in his criticism of Kipling, for example. Kipling's world view, Orwell points out, was conservative, but his responsible attitude (an attitude Orwell believed to be the source of effective literary expression) toward the Empire gave him opportunities to observe Indian life and, consequently, to record what Orwell calls the best literary picture we have of nineteenth-century Anglo-India. With other writers, as the previous example of Yeats indicates, Orwell is evidently hampered by an inability to enter fully into the literary experience he is examining. This is most noticeable in his approach to T. S. Eliot, whose religious orientation and related poetry of meditation are alien to Orwell's sensibilities and belong to a realm of reality that Orwell does not care to recognize.

Orwell's overall treatment of poetry, especially contemporary poetry, is instructive, nevertheless; for it only more firmly corroborates his pragmatic attitude toward literature and suggests a particular relevancy in his basic aesthetic criterion. His discussion of Eliot's later poetry offers a ready example of a criticism largely directed by what can be called a "political" view of literature. The emphasis that Orwell places on the inadequacy of Eliot's poetic impulse in the first three poems from *Four Quartets* is a result of seeing Eliot's poetry ultimately from the broader context of the contemporary situation, that, if understood correctly as the crisis of the Western liberal culture, determines values germane not only to society but to literature as well. Behind Orwell's sense of Eliot's poetic ineffectiveness is a fundamental antagonism between Eliot's ambivalent tone (a good example would be the line: "But the faith and the love and the hope are all in the waiting") and Orwell's belief in the *doing* and not in the *waiting,* in an active response, indeed of any positive kind—in the type of vital response that can come from even a conservative orientation to life. "It is at least imaginable," Orwell states, "that if Eliot had followed wholeheartedly the anti-democratic, anti-perfectionist strain in himself he might have struck a new vein comparable to his earlier one."

What matters, then, even more than "truth" in Orwell's approach to the specific aesthetic effectiveness of Eliot's or any writer's work is Orwell's sense that the writer has honestly confronted his material. Thus, any world view, freely and sincerely held and not insane in a medical sense, as Orwell phrased it, can produce a genuine work of art. Orwell's ultimate aesthetic criterion is the intellectual and emotional validity of the writer's work, measured in large part by the intensity with which the writer has lived the content of his work; and this criterion saved Orwell most of the time from the blunders of doctrinaire critics he repeatedly condemned throughout his writing career.

Where Orwell's critical approach to literature shows particular strength is in a kind of hard core, relentless exposing of a writer's total human response. Perhaps Swift has never received such an unveiling as Orwell gives him, nor has Dickens been so sharply scrutinized and at the same time so sympathetically understood. Kipling is revealed in all his commonness and impalatable glorifying of a now defunct British military ideal, yet Orwell's essay is one of the most just and perceptive discussions of Kipling's mind and the large ramifications of his work that have been written. Fortunately, Orwell usually chose to write extendedly on authors into whom he had a special insight. Jack London, for example, is a contemporary writer Orwell seems to have understood completely. His analysis of London's dual strains: an intellectual bent toward the common man's struggle for survival and a temperamental or instinctual tendency toward a glorification of brutality and strength, is particularly pointed, especially when he shows that London's best work comes out of an interaction of both strains, as in certain of his short stories. An equally keen critical discernment of a contemporary writer is to be seen in his treatment of Arthur Koestler, whose

political attitudes were in certain respects similar to Orwell's own, but whose conclusions were much different.

At times Orwell's revelations are overdrawn and often disconcerting to the reader who is looking for a more aesthetically oriented criticism, but they are to a large degree valid, perhaps disconcerting because of their validity. Where Orwell fails is in the sin of omission, in an overemphasis on the political, social, and moral implications of literature that deprives his criticism of a sense that literature is something in itself, whose purposes are often wholly expressive, self-contained and not less valuable for being so.

The essential quality of such a criticism depends on what the critic conceives of as being explicitly human; how broad and far-reaching his own mind is in his attitude toward humanity and art; how openminded and tolerant he himself is toward his fellow beings; how fully he realizes the variousness and complexity of human experience. Orwell's criticism is adequate within the limited boundaries he sets, the standards he applies, and the distance he goes with them; but by its very nature his criticism denies the efficacy in literature of what one might describe as mythic vision—what E. M. Forster calls "prophecy"—and it is indifferent to the power Yeats' mystical philosophy had in forming his verse and the comparable effect the Christian faith had on Eliot's work after 1930. In emphasizing the reality of man's "points of attachment to the physical world," the "day-to-day struggle," Orwell was led to underrate the modern literature that has explored other realities, other problems than social and political. From Orwell's point of view, the most responsible and therefore valuable literature expresses the author's emotional and intellectual perception of the objective world and the individual's physical struggle for life rather than the author's introspection of a subjective world and the dark night of the human soul. The realities of the former world take precedence in Orwell's mind over the realities of the latter world; indeed, without freedom from political tyranny and social oppression, literature itself might cease to exist:

> Prose literature as we know it is the product of rationalism, of the Protestant centuries, of the autonomous individual. And the destruction of intellectual liberty cripples the journalist, the sociological writer, the historian, the novelist, the critic, and the poet, in that order. In future it is possible that a new kind of literature, not involving individual feeling or truthful observation, may arise, but no such thing is at present imaginable. It seems much likelier that if the liberal culture that we have lived in since the Renaissance actually comes to an end, the literary art will perish with it.

The crisis of the moment governed the significance of literature's subject matter and the creative writer's special concern for the individual. How cogent was Orwell's analysis? How urgent was the emergency that led to his critical emphasis? Despite his limitations, the direction of his criticism was necessary in the time of crisis; perhaps there will always be a place for it—at least the threat to human freedom has not abated. (pp. 484-97)

Wayne Warncke, "George Orwell's Critical

Approach to Literature," in The Southern Humanities Review, *Vol. II, No. 4, Fall, 1968, pp. 484-98.*

Alfred Kazin   (essay date 1968)

[*A highly respected American literary critic, Kazin is best known for his essay collections* The Inmost Leaf *(1955) and* Contemporaries *(1962), and particularly for* On Native Grounds *(1942), a study of American prose writing since the era of William Dean Howells. Having studied the works of "the critics who were the best writers—from Sainte-Beuve and Matthew Arnold to Edmund Wilson and Van Wyck Brooks" as an aid to his own critical understanding, Kazin has found that "criticism focussed many—if by no means all—of my own urges as a writer: to show literature as a deed in human history, and to find in each writer the uniqueness of the gift, of the essential vision, through which I hoped to penetrate into the mystery and sacredness of the individual soul." In the following excerpt, Kazin reviews* The Collected Essays, Journalism and Letters of George Orwell *in light of the American political climate of the 1960s.*]

[For] many of us it is still the age of Orwell. By this I mean that for many readers and writers, for people likely to be reading this, for people generally more interested in understanding things than in forcibly changing the destiny of whole classes of people, it is a tragic age when human values are dominated by force, when literature seems entirely under the domain of political *concern* yet has no influence on the political decisions that move us on. Orwell was a brilliantly topical novelist, an obstinately rational pamphleteer who with intense feeling brought the art of argument to the highest possible clarity not by writing down to his readers but by thinking in behalf of them as fellow citizens who could be endangered by false logic and demagogic appeals. He was a passionately level-headed reviewer and essayist who loved good literature above all things, but felt with his usual sense of nemesis that literature was coming to an end. As he put it in an essay on Henry Miller, **"Inside the Whale"** (1940):

> Almost certainly we are moving into an age of totalitarian dictatorships. . . . literature, in the form in which we know it, must suffer at least a temporary death. . . . The literature of liberalism is coming to an end and the literature of totalitarianism has not yet appeared and is barely imaginable. . . . The writer . . . is merely an anachronism, a hangover from the bourgeois age. . . .

This is the note of grim clarity—after us, the ice age!—that Orwell always took in discussing literature as a dying art, in defending democracy against Stalinists and Fascists, "this England" against the snotty Socialists of the *New Statesman and Nation.* Orwell was an old Etonian who loved England but hated its snobbery and imperialism, an anti-Fascist who was badly wounded in Spain but hated the Communists for murdering Anarchists and Trotskyites, a thoroughly radical intellectual who despised English radical intellectuals for admiring totalitarian Russia. He was a democratic socialist who said from the first that the Moscow purge trials were completely fraudulent. Since the Tories were usually in charge of poor old broken-down England, he hated the Tories. But "since there is no real reconstruction that would not lead to at least a temporary drop in the English standard of life, left-wing politicians and publicists are people who earn their living by demanding something that they don't genuinely want. . . . " So he was always in opposition, always outside all the parties, groups and groupings—poor and increasingly sick, naturally, for he *was* sickened by "an age like this." He was a writer dominated by politics, but he believed, with Karl Marx, that only when socialism has solved the economic problem will modern man get to his real problem: his disbelief in personal immortality.

It is so much rationality, clarity, hopelessness on the part of a humanist who felt that his world was going to hell—surely political despair helped to kill him at forty-seven—that makes the age of Orwell, then and now, so sad. But ours is not the age of Orwell, ours is not a sad age for Mark Rudd, Leonid Brezhnev, the Beatles, Marshall McLuhan, Timothy Leary and all assorted activists, swingers, rabble-rousers, acid heads, amateur yogis and hippies, who recognize that ours is an age of riches, chemicals, freedom, love and possibility. It is not the age of Orwell for Abbie Hoffman, founder of the Yippies, who explained the other day—

> I don't consider myself a leftist. Say I'm a revolutionary artist. Our concept of revolution is that it's fun. The left has the concept that you have to sacrifice. Who the hell is going to buy that product? A lot of the left is into masochistic theater, if you ask me.

Abbie has something there. [*The Collected Essays, Journalism and Letters of George Orwell* is] a magnificent tribute to the probity, consistency and insight of Orwell's topical writings. Orwell forbade any biography of him, but these two thousand pages make up a remarkable self-portrait, precisely because he was the writer most involved in his age. And yet one does not have to agree with C. P. Snow, who thought *Nineteen Eighty-Four* showed a desire that the future "not exist," to see that Orwell, like so many earlier 20th-century radicals, did not expect his side to win. In the end Orwell wanted only to be personally authentic, to remain himself in a bad time, to keep some old-fashioned liberty in England.

The age of Orwell was the age of Hitler and Stalin, of mass unemployment cured only by mass wars, of genocide and atomic warfare, of utopian hopes for the working class as the vanguard of humanity. It was haunted by poverty and unemployment. It began with the postwar slump of the 1920s, and it continued into England's postwar slump after 1945. (Orwell, who died in 1950, did not even have the satisfaction of outliving Stalin.) So it was an age in which the most sensitive consciences knew what it is to live every day with despair for others—an age, as Camus said, in which finally one struggled to keep certain values alive without any illusion that they would triumph. The sense of Orwell's struggle is overwhelming in these painfully clear pages. The necessity of struggle—against commercialism, against rant, against the lying propaganda of

Stalin and Hitler, against the re-writing of history by the one and the destruction by the second of history as a human ideal, against the destruction of so many human beings, so many ancient cities, so many cultural traditions, so many valuable habits of moderation and exactness in language (always a prime issue for Orwell)—explains why Orwell always writes here with such burning clarity, such intellectual fervor, such respect for logic as the commonweal of human intelligence. . . .

[The] New Left has the virtues of the affluent society that produced it: it is not wedded to depression, social or personal, and in a society bursting with abundance, it may practice austerity as a personal gesture again—one's own thing—but admirably doesn't believe in poverty as a way of life or defeat as a political habit. Orwell certainly practiced one and believed in the other. As everyone knows who has read *Down and Out in Paris and London* and *The Road to Wigan Pier,* Orwell, the old Etonian and ex-policeman, liked to visit squalor, to see "how the poor die." There was a lot of self-punishing there, for reasons that a biographer might make clear and that his collected papers don't. And though Orwell cared for literature beyond everything else, one reason that literature is "dying" is that Orwell's generation may have made too much of literature as an expression of and substitute for political defeat. Nowadays professors who were once radicals themselves like to praise themselves as "rational" and to condemn their radical students as "irrational." But the "rationality" of these middle-aged contemplatives seems to consist in the belief that literature is not a form of action in itself but a defense against action, not a form of power but a neutralization of power, not even an image of natural violence but a protection against all violence. The logic of this is always lonely and rather vain: there is not much communal life to it and certainly not much fun, by which I mean the energy that youth properly makes so much of as a political virtue.

Orwell certainly practiced poverty, loneliness, logic and defeat. Admittedly, he was an intellectual, not a great imaginative artist: even his brilliant critical essays on great 19th-century novelists, Dickens and Tolstoy, display a characteristic tendency to show them up as bad thinkers even when the final point is that they were too immensely gifted to *need* intellectual logic. Still, Orwell felt himself alone, pushed and punished himself for unknown reasons. It is to the point that from these four volumes one learns virtually nothing about his parents or his first wife, Eileen; nothing to explain why he left Eton for the imperial police in Burma. Orwell once told Anthony Powell that he had taken a girl to the park to make love to her because there was nowhere else to take her. That is especially interesting because of his conscious poverty and because Orwell, who occasionally lost his temper at the "pansy Left" and the "cosmopolitan scum," obviously had as strong a sense of propriety as he did of poverty, and managed to make ordinary English life in the Thirties seem even grimmer than it was. When a reader of his column in the left-wing *Tribune* observed that Orwell always found everything worse than it used to be, Orwell answered that the rosebushes that Woolworth's sold for sixpence were still very good.

Orwell was a loner as a novelist, which may be partly why he was so captious about Evelyn Waugh, who liked to play the country gentleman and playfully joined the Commandos. But he was also a loner in England's Left circles—"not one of us," a Labor Party bureaucrat pompously said to me during the war. I would suggest that Orwell was a mystery to himself. From the more than two thousand pages I have just admiringly read—and often re-read with the greatest interest—I can remember very little about the *characters* of other people, such as a novelist ordinarily delights in. What one finds most here is a remarkable gift for analyzing *other* people's favorite propositions, for spotting dishonesty in public figures and moral faults in intellectuals. Orwell certainly knew how to evoke the traditional intellectual loyalties of the English conscience. He had a great gift for dissecting whatever shocked his conscience. He had the critic's born sense of reaction and opposition, to whatever he saw in the England of his time—and the politics of his time—that he disliked.

In short, he never saw himself in a position of leadership, as many young radicals do in our day. Orwell saw himself as a man whose only treasure was his moral judgment, and for this he needed to stay poor. The frontispieces to the last two volumes bring back Orwell with the fierce crease lines down his cheeks, the writer's colored shirt and shabby tweed jacket, in all his suffering and grim honesty. He said in 1944 that

> . . . to make life liveable is a much bigger problem than it recently seemed. Since about 1930 the world has given no reason for optimism whatever. Nothing is in sight except a welter of lies, hatred, cruelty and ignorance, and beyond our present troubles loom vaster ones which are only now entering into the European consciousness.

He went on from that to describe certain reasons for hope, and he beautifully said that although "all revolutions fail, they are not the *same* failure." But the real basis of his tragic sense was his commitment to solitude: secular man feels utterly alone in the face of death and writing is too much the activity of a man alone.

One reason for the greater feeling of hope among radicals in the post-Orwell age is that the new technology makes for more community than did the old. Another is that many young intellectuals are not writers, don't live by literature or for it, as Orwell did, don't have his sense of solitude. Still another is that the young are so used to having things work that they can't imagine "politics" not working either; Orwell was a product of the agonizing period between the wars when it seemed as if unemployment would never end. But above all, Orwell's solitude represents a writer who knew how much he embodied something that was visibly passing. His life was unbearably filled with the poignance of mortality because he could always see *himself* being swept away as an historical moment.

But of how many radical pundits today will one want to read two thousand pages in another generation? (pp. 1, 3)

Alfred Kazin, "He Felt His World Was Going

to Hell—and It Was," in Book World, *October 27, 1968, pp. 1, 3.*

Ruth Ann Lief   (essay date 1969)

[*In the following excerpt, Lief examines Orwell's philosophy that art, literature in particular, must be created with a higher social or political motivation than "art simply for art's sake."*]

What a writer, in the way of confession or clarification, says of his motives for writing and his purposes in particular works perhaps matters little except to curiosity-seekers. Robinson Jeffers, who was clearly a poet but who has been miscalled many things, inclined briefly to his critics and declared, in verse, that he could "tell lies in prose." George Orwell may have had a similar flash of cynicism when he declared, in fiction, "it *is* fun when you have good food and good wine inside you—to demonstrate that we live in a dead and rotting world." But Orwell was too honest to be cynical of motives he made a matter of public record, as he did in an essay entitled bluntly **"Why I Write"**:

1) "sheer egoism": an attempt perhaps to secure "personal immortality" in an age of disbelief, a quest which he names in **"Looking Back on the Spanish War"** as "the major problem of our time."

2) "esthetic enthusiasm": which he evinces, for example, in his tribute to Kipling's verse: "A good bad poem is a graceful monument to the obvious."

3) "historical impulse": the desire "to see things as they are, to find out true facts and store them up for the use of posterity."

4) "political purpose": to "push the world in a certain direction, to alter other people's ideas of the kind of society that they should strive after."

Orwell's assurance that the first three motives "outweigh the fourth" seems to conflict with assertions he made in this essay and in others:

> . . . no book is genuinely free from political bias. The opinion that art should have nothing to do with politics is itself a political attitude.

> . . . every writer, especially every novelist, *has* a "message". . . . All art is propaganda.

> In our age there is no such thing as "keeping out of politics." All issues are political issues. . . .

He insisted that because they "leave their mark even on the smallest detail of his work," a writer's "political and religious beliefs are not excrescences to be laughed away." His own "lifeless books . . . purple passages, sentences without meaning, decorative adjectives and humbug generally" he attributes to lack of political purpose and declares, "Every line of serious work that I have written since 1936 has been written, directly or indirectly, *against* totalitarianism and *for* democratic socialism, as I understand it."

Orwell's two most intensely political novels are, without doubt, his most distinguished; without them, his fame today might be modest, if not obscure. His ideal from the beginning was to do what he did "with full consciousness" in *Animal Farm:* "to fuse political purpose and artistic purpose into a whole."

Not only as a novelist but, understandably, as a critic, Orwell refused to approach art simply for art's sake, but his critical essays show that it cost him a struggle to remain convinced that art was handmaiden to something more important than itself. Like writers in other times who evolved elaborate justifications for a profession so patently pleasurable and sedentary as to seem frivolous in the eyes of the world, Orwell was conscience-stricken for himself, for anyone who sat aside from the current of events and pushed a pen. Surrounded not only by the age-old iniquities and inequities of the human condition but by terrors peculiar to an age that has the secret of total power, he did not entirely trust the pen to be mightier than the sword. The triumph of totalitarianisms meant the disappearance of certain old assumptions—among them the assumption that evil defeats itself in the long run and good triumphs, the assumption, in fact, that good and evil can even be distinguished. Evil could be vanquished neither by itself—since it had finally found the secret of eternal life—nor by novelists but only by a military force commensurate to it. The "invasion of literature by politics" was bound to seem to Orwell a phenomenon peculiar to his generation, a generation forced by its environment to make a protective adaptation, to enlarge its conscience at the expense of faculties less suited to survival:

> we have developed a sort of compunction which our grandparents did not have, an awareness of the enormous injustice and misery of the world, and a guilt-stricken feeling that one ought to be doing something about it, which makes a purely esthetic attitude towards life impossible. No one, now, could devote himself to literature as single-mindedly as Joyce or Henry James.

For Orwell, certainly, political commitment was a deeply moral matter in an age of superstates embodying "evil." After his experience in the Spanish war—from 1936 onwards—Orwell may have suspected that it was already too late to stop ideological movements which were unhampered by a respect for current or historical fact, let alone a respect for human life. But, like any dedicated fighter, he believed one should try to stop them by *all means,* whether the means were military or intellectual. In an all-out struggle, art could not be regarded as an end in itself but as one means toward a desirable end.

Fiction and poetry, however, are notoriously non-utilitarian, even when they are written by men of strong political convictions. That propagandists use them as means to an end does not alter their essential nature. The artists admired by the Nazis may have been temporarily discredited in the eyes of anti-Nazis during the second world war, but the Allied cause did not suffer materially by having literary and musical antagonists in the libraries and concert halls of Germany. It is misleading even to say that the Nazis misused works of art. Short of being used as wrapping paper or as fuel, a novel or a painting has no practical value. What it does have transcends ideological squabbles and is affected by them only if, in the course of conflict or as a result of official policy, the work of art is destroyed completely.

Unlike works of art, propaganda has *only* practical value. It is used up ceaselessly as a means to an end and is never preserved for its own sake. The writing which interested Orwell, even when it was good *bad* writing, was not propaganda; and, although the distinction between art and propaganda is blurred in some of his shocking and quotable pronouncements, Orwell's criticism shows that he did know the difference between them, however much he denied the existence of objective criteria. To the end of his life he maintained that literary judgments, at best, rested on "trumped-up" reasons for irrational preferences. The most he would admit was a difference between a "literary" and a "non-literary" reaction to a book. "I like this book," he cautiously declares in **"Writers and Leviathan,"** is not "a non-literary reaction":

> the non-literary reaction is "This book is on my side, and therefore I must discover merits in it." Of course, when one praises a book for political reasons one may be emotionally sincere, in . . . that one does feel strong approval of it, but also it often happens that party solidarity demands a plain lie.

Orwell promptly enough gave the lie to the guardians of British solidarity who in 1945 were hanging P. G. Wodehouse in verbal effigy for his broadcasts in collaboration with the Germans, and who were getting ready to burn his novels on the assumption that their author must have been a traitor all along. In this case, Orwell goes to work, as a critic should, to examine the evidence. He finds it inconceivable, from a study of Wodehouse's novels, that their author ever imagined problems more complex than those faced by boys in public schools and their fathers in private clubs. Wodehouse was simply a political innocent, and his fiction, far from showing treasonable tendencies, was an anachronism of peculiarly English stamp. The characters in this fiction might be fools or cads, but their notions of superiority did not exempt them—as comparable notions exempted the Nazis—from the consequences of their deeds. Had Wodehouse been a really effective propagandist for supermen, modern or old-fashioned, Orwell might have found it harder to forgive him; but it was clear to Orwell that a man whose political development had been arrested in the "Edwardian age" could hardly be taken seriously as a traitor to England in the 1940's. The public hangmen might be sincere enough in their strong feelings of disapproval, but their attempt to incriminate Wodehouse on the basis of his fiction was nothing but "humbug," however sincere.

Modern war, to be sure, was no game of cricket, and Orwell was far less tolerant of what he considered fascist tendencies in writers who, whether or not they had a chance to use German radio facilities, deprecated and feared the "human equality" cherished by freedom-loving men. Writing of William Butler Yeats, Orwell tasks the Marxist critics for not having established the connection between an author's politics and his style. Impatient with Yeats' mysticism, which he sees as a cowardly excuse for denying the possibility of progress, and sensing that Yeats was a "great hater of democracy," Orwell sets out to hang him

for no less an offense than insincerity. After citing one or two unconvincing examples of Yeats' artificial or "quaint" diction, Orwell wearies of the job, leaving it for some more thorough Marxist. His failure to prove the case does not alter his conviction that it could and should be proved—as though pretentious diction and insincerity were crimes against democracy.

It is clear in this essay and in others Orwell wrote that "literary fascism" is easier to intuit than to establish by textual analysis. It is also clear that Orwell is troubled by a double standard which even he is obliged to resort to in judging artists. That he and Yeats (a genius capable of moving him) should be on opposite sides when the barricades were raised, and that Wodehouse (whom he outgrew in boyhood) should be his ineffectual ally! Perhaps it only confused the issue to know how a poet voted in elections or how he treated his housekeeper. Perhaps, also, it was not safe to let anyone push the world in the direction he wanted it to go—to propagandize under cover of fiction or, as a commissar of public morality, to decree which yogis were politically safe.

Nevertheless, the persuasive power of the written word, the urgency even of fictional prose, was a power Orwell could not help wanting to enlist in the struggle against the oppressors of mankind. There was a subtle kind of propaganda in good fiction and poetry just as there was in good bad fiction and poetry. In essay after critical essay Orwell attempted to define the extent of an artist's responsibility not to his craft but to the human race as a whole, that is, his political responsibility.

Had Orwell declared that instead of being propaganda, all art is moral, he would have raised fewer eyebrows, and had he postulated that every act today is a moral act—including trivial acts that were once decently obscured from public view—he would have made his political point. As it is, he said something even clearer philosophically and practically about writers in a world dedicated to its own destruction: "you can only create if you can *care.*" Caring about art for its own sake was not enough with the world in a state that threatened creative artists even more directly than it threatened progress toward economic goals. In his essay on Charles Dickens Orwell concedes that it is "not necessarily the business of a novelist, or a satirist, to make constructive suggestions." But in any fiction worth taking seriously there is an implicit view of the world which is essentially moral; and a "merely moral criticism of society," Orwell suggests, may be "just as 'revolutionary' . . . as the politico-economic criticism which is fashionable at this moment."

Orwell's criticism surely reflects less the "politico-economic" bent of his socialism than his moral preoccupations. He was distinctly uncomfortable, he confesses, with a writer like D. H. Lawrence who sympathized "about equally" with good and bad characters. He was much more comfortable with Dickens, whom he commends for siding with the underdog. Quite apart from his literary merits, Dickens was right as a human being. He was generously aroused by injustice, and his "bourgeois mentality," although it contrived no panacea for the world, took for granted the redeeming power of common decency. Orwell calls Dickens a "nineteenth-century liberal, a free intelligence, a type hated with equal hatred by all the smelly little orthodoxies which are now contending for our souls."

In **"Raffles and Miss Blandish"** Orwell remembers with fondness a "gentleman" burglar, one Raffles, fictitious product of a time "when people had standards, though they happened to be foolish standards." In the English manner of Raffles, would-be gentleman, what is done or what is not done is as irrational, Orwell admits, as a primitive taboo but has the same binding force: "everyone accepts it." He experiences a sharp sense of moral dislocation when, in contrast to Raffles (who was out to make a haul solely to secure his shaky social status) he comes across the characters of a more recent English "who done it," *No Orchids for Miss Blandish.* They are motivated uniformly to pursue power, in variously violent forms, for the sake of power. As though this pursuit were not senseless enough in itself, Orwell perceives that the distinction between the law-abiders and the law-breakers no longer separates the good guys from the bad. He had naively supposed that if "one must worship a bully, it is better that he should be a policeman than a gangster" and that the problem of "how to prevent power from being abused"—a problem admittedly unsolved—should be decided on the side of law and order, that is, common assent and social stability, rather than on the supposition that might makes right. (pp. 3-9)

Although Orwell did not make it explicit, implicit in the body of his writing is a distinction between "orthodoxy" and "ideology" on the one hand and, on the other, "standards" (both of taste and of conduct) and "law." A self-proclaimed socialist, he was not a predictable partisan and, if given the choice between anarchy and orthodoxy in politics or morals, quite likely would have chosen anarchy. It was better to be in doubt than to see doubt vanish from human affairs. But he did not like anarchy—a state in which nothing is illegal. A world where anything goes seemed as reprehensible to him as a world where everything is curtailed. It troubled him that there were no laws to govern the artist except the undefined internal laws that were alleged to govern the particular created world of a painting or a novel. He attacked violence and immorality in the subject matter of art as energetically as he attacked them in the world of men and governments without distinguishing one as a conceptual or symbolic construction of pigment or words and the other as the place where men inescapably lived and suffered. He was concerned that the artist be morally, if not politically, correct and only late in his life disabused himself of this notion and consigned it "to the nursery" along with the "lingering belief that every choice, even every political choice, is between good and evil, and that if a thing is necessary it is also right."

"Benefit of Clergy: Some Notes on Salvador Dali" is particularly symptomatic of Orwell's unwillingness to separate artistic excellence from subject matter and from the ethical tenor of the artist's life. He attacks Dali not for any political penchant but for a "direct, unmistakable assault on sanity and decency," on "life itself"—for crimes against humanity, so to speak. That Dali, in faction-torn

Orwell with his adopted son Richard. 1946.

Spain, played both ends against the middle and, during World War II, cared about nothing but eating well was enough to alert Orwell to his political irresponsibility; but Orwell relates the egoism of the man to the failure of the artist. He puts the man on trial in order to condemn the artist, much as the Americans (whom Orwell contemns for it) jailed Al Capone for income-tax evasion because they could not apprehend him for murder. Orwell grants that Dali has "exceptional gifts" and an exceptional capacity for hard work. But Dali's autobiography "stinks" in his fairly fastidious nostrils. It reveals what Orwell expects: that Dali is unworthy of his exceptional gifts—in fact, an "undesirable" in the human community. Should Dali's stature as an artist entitle him to benefit of clergy? Not if, as an artist, he works hard to a harmful end.

But, as Dali's accuser, Orwell finds himself in company he dislikes and devotes a considerable part of his critique to baiting the "high-brow baiters." He disassociates himself from their crude tactic of impugning what they can't understand. But if Scylla lies there, Charybdis lies to the other side, and he disassociates himself as vehemently from the art-for-art's-sakers, who were, in his view, "highbrows." Orwell names his own dilemma in steering a course between these alternatives—both of which seem to him humbug. "Obscenity is a very difficult question to discuss honestly. People are too frightened either of seeming to be shocked or of seeming not to be shocked, to be able to define the relationship between art and morals." Again he tasks the Marxist critics for failing in the essential work of critical definition. They are quick enough to smell what "stinks" and to label it bourgeois degeneracy, but name-calling, Orwell complains, is not enough. One should be able to say, "at least in imagination," that a book or picture is good, *and* that "it ought to be burned by the public hangman."

In trying to turn what one *should* be able to do into what one *can* do, Orwell draws an untenable analogy between artists who encourage "necrophilic reveries" and common criminals, maintaining the first do more harm than the latter. Yet he concludes that he would not, after all, burn Dali's pictures, because they "probably cast useful light on the decay of capitalist civilisation." Dali's diseased intelligence then becomes Exhibit I in Orwell's case against the "world's illness." Private vices become public virtues.

Here Orwell is in no better case than the brother who assures Browning's Fra Lippo Lippi that his painting "serves its purpose": in a kind of two-minutes hate, the "pious people" vent their rage upon the painting which depicts the villainous slaves who turn the "Deacon's spit." So Orwell permits Dali's art to stand as an object lesson in necrophilic preoccupations.

One feels, however, that Orwell is enraged with Dali because he disobeyed Fra Lippo's private injunction: to paint the "beauty and the wonder and the power, / Changes, surprises" in the world and "count it crime / To let a truth slip." For that, art is given, so that those with exceptional gifts can lend their vision to the ungifted. Dali obviously did not care for the spiritual or political health of the world. Orwell obviously did. Why, then, if the world was fatally sick—perhaps even "dead and rotting"—did Orwell himself write novels which did not "necessarily" have any power to cure or to resurrect? Why did he devote so much attention to the nonpolitical writing of his contemporaries and predecessors? Why, even if his devotion to literary matters was not as exclusive as James' or Joyce's, was he a man of letters and not a man of public affairs?

There is no dissembling in Orwell's urging a relationship between art and politics. What he cared about was a world politically safe not only for democracy but for the autonomy of the artist; and the world in which the artist worked and to which he bequeathed the enduring products of his work was menaced as never before in history, menaced by a new breed of men who were pre-eminently the enemies of mankind. When Orwell could not fight them with a sword, he fought them with a pen. His starting point, he declares in **"Why I Write,"** was "always a feeling of partisanship, a sense of injustice. When I sit down to write a book, I do not say to myself, 'I am going to produce a work of art.' I write it because there is some lie that I want to expose, some fact to which I want to draw attention, and my initial concern is to get a hearing." In so far as Orwell was a partisan, he took the part of the true against the false, the sincere against the insincere, the weak

against the strong, the life-lovers against the death-wishers, the artist against the hangman.

Even Orwell's "esthetic enthusiasm" is a partisan concern. As long as he lived, he promises in **"Why I Write,"** he would "feel strongly about prose style." "Good prose is like a window pane," he writes, and orthodoxy "of whatever color" in its demand for a "lifeless, imitative style" is its arch-enemy. Orwell's insistence upon clarity is bound up not only with his "esthetic enthusiasm" but with his "historical impulse" to make a true account of things for posterity and with his moral concern that the truth be reverenced for its own sake. In **"Politics and the English Language"** he holds insincerity responsible for the deterioration of English, whether that insincerity is unconscious—that is, merely *thoughtless,* as it is likely to be in an age of ready-made phrases that predetermine content—or deliberate, as with those who have motives for obfuscation. The hardening of language into cliché, the abuse of language in verbiage, abbreviation, ugly synthetic locutions, and the cynical perversion of language to say *"the thing which is not"* horrified Orwell esthetically and ethically. He grieved to see the variety, subtlety, and nuance of English lost, just as he grieved to see the dreariness of public architecture and the depersonalization of private housing.

But a loss of flexibility and variety meant also a loss of precision and expressiveness, a constriction of the range of concepts one could articulate, a loss feelingly described in the appendix of *1984,* which examines the political *raison d'être* of Newspeak: the prevention of "thoughtcrime." The concern of official etymologists (there is no other kind in *1984*) is to make literally unthinkable any heretical thought by ridding language not only of ideologically offensive concepts ("bad-think") but of vocabulary in excess of the most rudimentary utilitarian exchanges. Since much human talk is non-utilitarian, this destruction of words makes incommunicable and eventually inconceivable a number of previously cherished and significant experiences. In political oratory ("largely the defense of the indefensible") "duckspeak" is perfected: the brain idles while appropriate political noises issue from the larynx. The purpose of language is thus perverted, the symbols devised solely for the urgency of expressing meaning are rendered void of meaning, and the "reduced state of consciousness" necessary to perfect orthodoxy is assured. "Orthodoxy," as Syme explains in *1984,* "means not thinking—not needing to think." Huxley's brave new world achieves much the same result with soma; but the outstanding feature of Orwell's superstate is a monumental inefficiency, the purpose of which is to ensure the futility of all human endeavor and, in effect, to rob existence of its organic semblance: growth, becoming. "Nothing is efficient in Oceania except the Thought Police."

An "esthetic enthusiasm" for language is a care to keep it alive, that is, responsive to man's expressive needs. The death of language in prospect, its noticeable atrophy in present use, agitated and dismayed Orwell both as a private man with an emotive life demanding expression and as a political animal, capable of reason and unwilling to be deprived of his distinctive birthright: the tools of logical thought and the means of preserving an accurate record of his life and times. (pp. 11-15)

In his defense of Rudyard Kipling as a spokesman for British imperialism, Orwell discerns that those who rule are obliged to confront practical realities and decide not upon theoretic panaceas but upon *what to do*—an obligation government oppositions are *not* under. Stiff-necked and unimaginative as imperialist policy might have been, Orwell observes, it made one simple, unquestioned assumption, which was moral as well as political: the leaders who assumed responsibility had to bear it, however distasteful the acts consequent upon that responsibility might be. Kipling, like the imperialism with which he was allied in spirit, had this "sense of responsibility" to an eminent degree.

From his early role as subdivisional police officer in Burma, Orwell knew how fatal sensibility and imagination could be in one who ruled. Called upon to deal with an elephant which endangered the community and all too sensible of the conflicting pressures upon him, Orwell learned that to be responsible was to act, and to act was to be damned, whatever he did. The dilemma posed itself in purely emotional terms at the time: he was paralyzed between "hatred of the empire" he served and his "rage against the evil-spirited little beasts who tried to make [his] job impossible." Because of the uniform he wore and because of the mob of natives at his back waiting for him to inflict upon a possibly manageable animal the death that his rifle symbolized, he was driven to the expedient of acting like a sahib, however irrational or unjust such a course might prove. He had forfeited his right to be a spectator to someone else's mistakes. He had lost his freedom from political responsibility, and later in his life, when occasion arose, he could admire the honest if limited, sincere if unexamined assumptions that underlay Kipling's fictional world. The sahib was understandably the butt of ridicule and criticism among circles of refinement and discernment at home, but Kipling at least saw "clearly that men can only be highly civilised while other men, inevitably less civilised, are there to guard and feed them." Orwell had an abiding contempt for men who bit the hand that fed and sympathized with the enemies of those that guarded them.

Even before the English socialists had shown their colors in the Spanish struggle and the second world war Orwell sensed what their ideology meant to them. In *Keep The Aspidistra Flying* Ravelston's girlfriend, secure in her money and modernism, assures the worried editor: "Of course I know you're a Socialist. So am I. I mean we're all Socialists nowadays. . . . You can be a Socialist *and* have a good time, that's what I say." And in the same novel Gordon Comstock, whose political sympathies are as ambiguous as his social status, is suspicious of ideologies that get implemented. "There's only one objection to Socialism," he taunts Ravelston, "and that is that nobody wants it." What *would* Socialism mean in practice?

> Oh! Some kind of Aldous Huxley *Brave New World;* only not so amusing. Four hours a day in a model factory, tightening up bolt number 6003. Rations served out in grease-proof paper

at the communal kitchen. Community-hikes from Marx Hostel to Lenin Hostel and back. Free abortion-clinics on all the corners.

Socialism, like the Catholic Church and suicide, Comstock says, is simply a "standing temptation to the intelligentsia." The first world war, the monstrous industrial and political developments after it, the unspeakable meaninglessness of life in England, were enough, George Bowling declares in *Coming Up For Air,* to start anyone thinking, if not to make a Bolshie out of him. In fact, "every intelligent boy of sixteen is a Socialist. At that age one does not see the hook sticking out of the rather stodgy bait." If between the two major wars of the twentieth century no socialist program appeared on the political scene in England, it was because "no one genuinely wanted any major change" and revolutionary politics was largely a "game of make-believe."

The left-wing intellectuals—paradoxically those who gave evidence in writing of wanting to push the world in a particular direction—come again under Orwell's bitter attack in his essay on Henry Miller, **"Inside the Whale."** Here Orwell examines, almost as though against his will, the alternatives for a writer in an age when all issues seem political, "and politics itself is a mass of lies, evasions, folly, hatred, and schizophrenia." The year is 1940, and the state of the world is perilous if not intolerable for the writing of novels: the "age of totalitarian dictatorships—an age in which freedom of thought will be at first a deadly sin and later on a meaningless abstraction"—will destory the writer's world. "For *as a writer* he is a liberal, and what is happening is the destruction of liberalism." The novel (a "Protestant form of art"), because it is a "product of the free mind, of the autonomous individual," can be written only by "people who are *not frightened.*" It will not be written, therefore, by the "orthodoxy sniffers, nor by people who are conscience-stricken about their own orthodoxy."

But the question with Miller is not even one of orthodoxy. Because Miller is completely apolitical, he seems to Orwell to acquiesce in the state of the world. And yet *Tropic of Cancer* Orwell pronounces a "remarkable book" and pauses to consider the incongruity of his reaction.

> When *Tropic of Cancer* was published the Italians were marching into Abyssinia and Hitler's concentration-camps were already bulging. . . . It did not seem to be a moment at which a novel of outstanding value was likely to be written about American dead-beats cadging drinks in the Latin Quarter.

In the same decade other writers busied themselves hammering Marxism "into a new shape" every time Stalin "swapped partners." Their political commitment was that of men uprooted from a traditional orthodoxy: God was dead, but Stalin, thank god, lived; and, having experienced nothing but "liberalism" in their own country, Orwell charges, they swallowed the stodgy bait of Marxism. Unlike these "orthodoxy sniffers" so afraid to offend the political air over Moscow, Miller remained unperturbed by noises to the left or the right. He chose, says Orwell, to dwell inside the whale, in the veritable womb of Leviathan. He made, in effect, a "declaration of irresponsibility" and preserved a quietism just "short of being dead."

Although, Orwell concedes, "a novelist is not obliged to write directly about contemporary history," he who "simply disregards the major public events of the moment is generally either a footler or a plain idiot." Since *Tropic of Cancer* has convinced him that its author is neither, Orwell proposes two explanations for Miller's quietism: "either complete unbelief or else a degree of belief amounting to mysticism." For a creative writer, he reasons, "possession of the 'truth' is less important than emotional sincerity." An "untrue belief" in literature may be more "sincerely held than a 'true' one." Novels, he concludes, present merely the "truth about the individual reaction."

Miller's voice, to Orwell's ears, is that of the "ordinary, non-political, non-moral, passive man," the "human voice." He supposes that like the common man Miller is passive by political choice, content to keep his own house in order but as helpless against historical forces as against the elements.

T. S. Eliot, whose political and religious principles Orwell surely considered the result of an "untrue belief," nevertheless receives in this essay on Miller the most exalted of Orwell's critical encomiums. As a creative writer during the troubled teens and twenties of the century, "by simply standing aloof and keeping touch with pre-war emotions," Eliot did more to carry on the "human heritage" than those "committed" writers of the thirties who played *Simon Says* with Stalin. Orwell recognizes finally the necessity for a writer to be, above all, with no "sermons," true to the "subjective truth." And on the basis of this subjective truth, Orwell conjectures incredulously, "apparently, it is still possible for a good novel to be written." As though a good novel were ever written on any other basis!

But despite this affirmation of the artistic as distinct from the journalistic or historic truth, Orwell pronounces what he considers Miller's withdrawal as a *politically* significant act, a willful retreat from the only *seemingly* different "swindles" of progress and reaction, a defeatism which robs reality of its terrors by simply submitting to them.

> Get inside the whale. . . . Give yourself over to the world-process, stop fighting against it or pretending that you control it; simply accept it, endure it, record it. That seems to be the formula that any sensitive novelist is now likely to adopt.

Orwell's reluctance to accept this formula makes the word *sensitive* almost pejorative. The novelist who abjures his political responsibility to stand and be counted—or shot down—can't 'take it.' He is good for nothing, by implication, *except* writing novels. Like the cat in *Animal Farm,* he votes on both sides of the issue, or if he does not equivocate, simply escapes, he is like Mollie, who prefers blue ribbons and sugar lumps to "volunteer" labor for the common good.

Orwell's ambivalence toward the writer's role in these essays is obvious. He defends Dickens, Kipling, Wodehouse, Miller and T. S. Eliot apparently because he sees something in them that he cares about—that deserves championing against charges of social irresponsibility. His role of

devil's advocate eventually, of course, drove him to consider more and more directly the case he was pleading. In **"Politics vs. Literature"** he asks to what extent one's enjoyment of a particular work of art depends upon one's agreement with its author's opinions. Although he is unwilling to admit that literary excellence is a thing fully separable from its subject matter, he concedes that a certain "intellectual detachment" enables one to "disagree" with a writer and yet perceive his merits. Enjoyment, however, is another question: sheer literary talent cannot persuade one to enjoy, he says, a book which is "truly wounding or shocking." For purposes of argument, he grants that there may be "such a thing as good or bad art." And, if there is, then the excellence or lack of it must inhere "in the work of art itself." If a book seems "really pernicious" and "likely to influence other people in some undesirable way," Orwell suggests skeptically, one simply devises esthetic standards to disprove its literary merits. "And yet," he admits, upon occasion, "enjoyment can overwhelm disapproval, even though one clearly recognizes that one is enjoying something inimical."

Orwell's instance to prove the possibility is his own perennial enjoyment of *Gulliver's Travels.* He does not for a moment deny Swift's literary ability (although even here he puts *good* in disclaiming quotation marks) but refuses to attribute his "enjoyment" solely to that. Wounding and shocking as *Gulliver's Travels* is, he decides, and diseased as Swift's world view is, one feels the partial truth Swift enunciates: "the part which he abstracts from the whole does exist," however one shrinks from recognizing it.

Can a book, then, be "good" if it expresses "a palpably false view of life"? The "best books of any one age," Orwell observes,

> have always been written from several different viewpoints, some of them palpably more false than others. In so far as a writer is a propagandist, the most one can ask of him is that he shall genuinely believe in what he is saying, and that it shall not be something blazingly silly. . . . The views . . . must be compatible with sanity, in the medical sense, and with the power of continuous thought: beyond that what we ask of him is talent, which is probably another name for conviction.

In *Gulliver's Travels,* because of the intensity of Swift's conviction, a "world view which only just passes the test of sanity is sufficient to produce a great work of art."

Orwell's ambivalence toward "great works of art" the world view of which he disapproved might have been dispelled had Orwell admitted the distinction between the discrete disciplines of art and history, or art and ethics for that matter. His failure to distinguish the separate areas of human experience these disciplines are bound to be true to is the unimportant failure of a writer who would have scorned the role of esthetician and never presumed to be a philosopher. Neither, for all his protests, was he a propagandist. What moved him to write—essay or novel—was what he cared about. He knew which truth he was after instinctively, if not theoretically, and his apparent guilt about writing merely novels may have sprung from his sense that novels were true only to the "subjective reaction," a reaction which, without verification from one's fellow men, might be a form of insanity. Relentless, Orwell pursued the elusive truth of historical fact, returned in exposition to what was verifiable by document and eyewitness. The created realities of the novel must have seemed sham to him. After all, unlike the "facts" of history, they held still. They were always the same. They were eternal. And today they alone assure Orwell's immortality—a difficult enough achievement in a world encroached upon by anonymity, meaninglessness and death.

However misdirected in particulars, the intensity of conviction in Orwell's own world view produced in his critical writing a discernment of artistic sincerity and in his fiction a subjective sense of the world imperiled by malign forces. He cared and, without a boundless fund of inventive ingenuity, he created, achieving the final luminosity of *Animal Farm* and the political novel *par excellence, 1984:* a tragedy of personal heroism in a mechanical "world-process" which mangles the individual as purposelessly and cruelly as ever the ancient fates kept Oedipus alive in order to teach him he was dead.

In some way that had nothing to do with subject matter, however, Orwell sensed that a novelist, by virtue of what he produced ("the product of rationalism, of the Protestant centuries, of the autonomous individual"), was in the simple practice of his craft "*against* totalitarianism" as much as any democratic socialist. And what the artist bequeathed to the world strengthened the world by proclaiming the human essence. In much the symbolic way the coral embedded in crystal subtly threatens the Party in *1984* and incriminates him who owns it, imagination and a love of truth in writers (even a love of prose style) destined them to be the inveterate heretics of ideologies and orthodoxies. Explicitly political or not, they would be suspect under a totalitarian system.

The relation between art and politics, if we judge by the two rich essays he devoted to the subject in the late forties, tantalized Orwell to his dying day. In **"The Prevention of Literature"** he reaffirms his belief that "[a]bove a quite low level, literature is an attempt to influence the viewpoint of one's contemporaries by recording experience." Freedom of expression, he argues, concerns the "most 'unpolitical' imaginative writer" as vitally as the expositor. Censorship of the news, proscriptive and prescriptive regulations of journalistic freedom, had become controversial even in democratic countries obliged to weigh the whole truth and nothing but the truth against the expedients of national security and partisan loyalties. Not only the journalist but his readers were conscious of the "unfreedom" in news media which threatened, in addition to the professional integrity of these media, in the long run any reliable historical accounting of events.

But Orwell's main interest in **"The Prevention of Literature"** (1946) and **"Writers and Leviathan"** (1948) is the plight of the creative artist, who is "unfree" in a less spectacular way if he is compelled "to falsify his subjective feelings"—the "facts" which constitute his subject matter.

> He may distort and caricature reality in order to make his meaning clearer, but he cannot misrep-

resent the scenery of his own mind; he cannot say with any conviction that he likes what he dislikes, or believes what he disbelieves. If he is forced to do so . . . his creative faculties dry up.

Can the "imaginative writer" get inside the whale—merely observe, record and remain noncommittal? Not in an age in which all issues are political issues. Under repressive conditions one's private feelings may be the most controversial subject of all. There is, Orwell reasserts, "no such thing as genuinely non-political literature"; "fears, hatreds, and loyalties" are inextricable from the modern political atmosphere. "Even a single taboo can have an all-round crippling effect upon the mind, because there is always the danger that any thought which is freely followed up may lead to the forbidden thought." It is one thing for a politician to switch his loyalties; his activity is inevitably bound into a network of compromise and expedience. But a writer who is forced to switch his loyalties must "tell lies about his subjective feelings, or suppress them altogether. In either case he has destroyed his dynamo. Not only will ideas refuse to come to him, but the very words he uses will seem to stiffen under his touch."

Sincerity, again, is Orwell's touchstone for the creative writer. He foresaw that even a Yeats or a Dali, compelled to rejoice in a workers' paradise of equality, sobriety, and propriety, might suffer an atrophy of creative gifts which would render those gifts nugatory. The imagination, Orwell concludes, "like certain wild animals, will not breed in captivity."

It is significant that Orwell, against his egalitarian instinct and his aversion to benefit of clergy, here devises a special category for the artist and distinguishes the creative writer even from the journalist as a species which can thrive only under the most inviolable autonomy. One should be able, in theory at least, to demand that the artist comply with prevailing standards of morality and decency and objective standards of social and political truth. But more precious than such public government of conduct and belief was the thing that ruled private feeling with an absolute tyranny of its own: total honesty or nothing. The artist was different from his fellow men. For most people the problem of personal integrity and public allegiance, Orwell writes, does not even arise:

> . . . their lives are split already. They are truly alive only in their leisure hours, and there is no emotional connection between their work and their political activities. Nor are they generally asked, in the name of political loyalty, to debase themselves as workers. The artist, and especially the writer, is asked just that—in fact, it is the only thing that politicians ever ask of him. . . . But his writings, in so far as they have any value, will always be the product of the saner self that stands aside, records the things that are done and admits their necessity, but refuses to be deceived as to their true nature.

The artist, then, whatever civic role he plays (in war or in elections, for instance) must keep "inviolate" the self which makes his work possible.

Orwell in these two essays also entertains the possibility

that in an "age of faith" there might exist no disruptive conflict between the artist and the prevailing orthodoxy. Perhaps, he concedes, an orthodoxy which had been long enough established to be taken indifferently would leave "large areas" of a writer's mind unhampered by his official beliefs. Totalitarianism, however, Orwell fears, promises not so much "an age of faith as an age of schizophrenia," in which neither the stability of objective truths nor the "emotional sincerity . . . literature demands" can be tolerated. The prevailing orthodoxy would be *totalitarian,* that is, totally proscriptive and prescriptive not only of subject matter and attitudes but of the language in which they might be couched. For all its purposes, book-writing machines, fed on formulas and prefabricated phrases, would do a more reliable job than writers; and, since tyranny is one of the themes that "cannot be celebrated in words," the writer would have to choose between "silence and death."

Believing that, even in countries dominated by no official ideologies, political responsibility had become synonymous with "yielding oneself over to orthodoxies and 'party lines,' with all the timidity and dishonesty that implies," Orwell confronts the paradox that his own critical and personal creed as a writer made inevitable; and he declares unequivocally that "acceptance of *any* political discipline" is "incompatible with literary integrity." A writer's political and religious beliefs—even if they are as seemingly apolitical as pacifism and personalism—are "poisonous to literature. . . . Indeed, the mere sound of words ending in -ism seems to bring with it the smell of propaganda. . . . As soon as they are allowed to have any influence, even a negative one, on creative writing, the result is not only falsification, but often the actual drying-up of the inventive faculties."

Here Orwell makes it clear that all art is *not* propaganda, that the two are, in fact, irreconcilable: "To yield subjectively, not merely to a party machine, but even to a group ideology, is to destroy yourself as a writer." What, then, is the answer? To abjure politics? Emphatically not: "To lock yourself up in the ivory tower is impossible and undesirable" in an age like ours. Orwell pleads simply for a "sharper distinction" between political and literary loyalties and suggests a kind of bifurcation of functions for the writer as creator and as political animal. Political responsibility has little to do with ultimate truth, and political action is of necessity expedient—a means to an end, a doing of "certain distasteful but necessary things" without the concomitant "obligation to swallow the beliefs that usually go with them." What is necessary is not necessarily "right." Political decisions propose ugly alternatives,

                    10a Mortimer Crescent
                    London NW 6
                    17.2.44

        Dear Mr Struve,

                        Please forgive me for not writing
    earlier to thank you for the very kind gift of "25 Years of Soviet
    Russian Literature", with its still more kind inscription. I am
    afraid I know very little about Russian literature and I hope your
    book will fill up some of the many gaps in my knowledge. It has
    already roused my interest in Zamyatin's "We", which I had not heard
    of before. I am interested in that kind of book, and even keep making
    notes for one myself that may get written sooner or later. I wonder
    whether you can tell if there is an adequate translation of Blok?
    I saw some translated fragments about ten years ago in "Life and
    Letters", but whether they were any good as a translation I do not
    know.

                I am writing a little squib which might amuse you when it
    comes out, but it is so not O.K. politically that I don't feel
    certain in advance that anyone will publish it. Perhaps that gives
    you a hint of its subject.

                Yours sincerely

                Geo. Orwell

A letter from Orwell to Gleb Struve.

and one is forced to choose "which of two evils is the less." One can resolve the dilemma frequently only "by acting like a devil or a lunatic."

> When a writer engages in politics he should do so as a citizen, as a human being, but not *as a writer.* I do not think he has the right, merely on the score of his sensibilities, to shirk the ordinary dirty work of politics. . . . But whatever else he does in the service of his party, he should never write for it.

In effect, what Orwell demands of the writer is no less than "most people" have already accommodated themselves to: political assent, even co-operation, in the means to necessary ends, and at the same time rejection of the ideology which envisions these ends. On the one hand, the writer must fearlessly pursue thoughts he knows to be heretical and scorn the risk of being condemned. On the other hand, when his "writings and his political activities . . . actually contradict one another" and when such contradiction seems "plainly undesirable," Orwell does not suggest that the writer abstain from political action—certainly not that he "falsify [his] impulses." The remedy, Orwell says, is "to remain silent."

Orwell impales himself on both horns of the dilemma here. Because politics is a mass of lies and a choice of evils, because right and wrong are forever relative in the sphere of action, all honest men, not just writers, it would seem, must be schizophrenic, and the difference among them dependent solely on whether they consciously suffer the discrepancy between their impulses and their actions or, without admitting the discrepancy, slip painlessly into lunacy. The paradox comes up again and again in Orwell's writing and is perhaps its single most powerful generative idea. Committed himself to the goal of the left orthodoxy—"a viable form of society which large numbers of people actually want"—he realized that his fellow travelers toward this goal could not admit their ideological "falsities" nor discuss openly the problems that give rise to them. Modern men, Orwell maintains, are all to some extent victims of "perfectionist philosophy" and become obscurantist when actuality belies their beliefs. "Hence there has arisen a sort of schizophrenic manner of thinking, in which words like 'democracy' can bear two irreconcilable meanings, and such things as concentration camps and mass deportations can be right and wrong simultaneously." An orthodoxy always contains "unresolved paradoxes." One can reason from empirical data to valid conclusions only "if one is privately disloyal to the official ideology."

We will probably never know on how many or how serious occasions Orwell himself, noting the discrepancy between his private conclusions and official ideology, remained "silent." But one is persuaded by the number of times he attacked the orthodox and insisted upon seeing the discrepancy between the private truth and the public lie that he seldom followed his own "remedy." For to have remained "silent" would have been to do away with his inviolate self as effectually as a public hangman might; and one doubts that, after all Orwell had to say about the pernicious effects of self-censorship, he acquiesced in this schizophre-nic tyranny beyond concessions to tactfulness in direct confrontation or patriotism in England's dark hours.

There is certainly little evidence in Orwell's critical essays that the partisan feeling out of which he said he wrote distorted the evidence he examined. At most, that feeling abstracted and gave shape to the moral questions that arise from the total import of an artist's work. In Orwell's fiction, partisan causes invariably yield to the created life of his characters, who may have come into being originally as denouncers of imperialism, capitalist exploitation, or commercial depredations, but who in the end obey "private feelings" that have nothing to do with official beliefs.

If in his fiction and criticism Orwell fused "political purpose and artistic purpose," it was because he cared about the human essence and feared its enemies. In the mundane drama he conceived, the "great death wish of the modern world" is personified as a gigantic robot of man's invention, foot poised to smash the face of the sleeping protagonist. What would rouse the sleeper? The sound of exploding bombs? The duckspeak of political oratory?

The silent, ageless mirror held up to life—which never so much as clouded with the sleeper's breath—might have no power to alarm or to make constructive suggestions, but by keeping touch with men's emotions it carried on the "human heritage." The artists preserved the subjective truth of being. The historians preserved the notable deeds and words of men for the "use of posterity." The polemicists pushed the world in the direction they wanted it to go. But before any of these could operate people had to be kept alive, and this specifically political task occasionally curtailed or forfeited the freedom of artists, historians and polemicists alike.

For there were those who created because they cared and those who destroyed because they hated. Much as he dreaded the hardening of heartfelt truths into official dogma, Orwell had the political sense to know that history abhors a vacuum and that the commissars would rush in where yogis feared to tread. Precisely because it was a necessary evil, because it took precedence over what outranked it in the scale of values, the political sphere required the utmost vigilance, lest the guardians of public safety and morality became the inquisitors of private conscience and delivered into the hands of the hangman not only the criminal but those who slept inside the whale.

In a democracy, Orwell could admit no freedom from political responsibility, even for the artist, but he did come to see that art was a means to a political end only because its truth was a recording of subjective feeling—from the merest visceral twinge to the magnificent, barely sane obsessions of mystical insight—and such truth was "*against* totalitarianism." The artist's work, however, was a "thing apart" from politics, and his autonomy as a worker had to be guaranteed by political means; for he, of all the workers of the world, was as a worker the most easily debased. (pp. 20-33)

Ruth Ann Lief, in her Homage to Oceania: The Prophetic Vision of George Orwell, *Ohio State University Press, 1969, 162 p.*

Roberta Kalechofsky   (essay date 1973)

[*Kalechofsky is an American critic, educator, and fiction writer. In the following essay, she relates Orwell's essays on popular culture to his novel* Coming Up for Air.]

Orwell knew that the past, like the machine, was useful and dangerously alluring. Anachronism is a distinct evil in his moral paradigm. He faults men like P. G. Wodehouse, H. G. Wells, the colonel Blimps and the upper-class tories, for continuing to live in the mental world of the 1920s at a time when Hitler was marching across Europe. In his essay on Wells, Orwell comments that "The energy that actually shapes the world springs from emotions—racial pride, leader-worship, religious belief, love of war. . . . " At the end of the essay he sums up Wells as "too sane to understand the modern world."

This is almost a nihilistic statement about the faculties of intellect and judgment and man's ability to control his world. It expresses Orwell's feeling at that time that political behavior is not subject to rational laws. From 1943 to 1945 Orwell was literary editor of the *Tribune* and wrote a weekly column for it called, **"As I Please."** (He continued to contribute to it irregularly until April 1947.) In the 29 November 1946 contribution he wrote, " . . . we shall get nowhere unless we start by recognizing that political behavior is largely nonrational, that the world is suffering from some kind of mental disease which must be diagnosed before it can be cured."

The world into which Orwell was born in 1903 was one in which science was exploding and influencing everyone's political thinking. The age was an optimistic one. At the same time the possessors of wealth had reached a new zenith in irresponsibility and vulgarity. By the 1930s it was clear that the vices of the early part of the twentieth century, imperialism and class oppression, were ever present, while the virtues of this early era were no longer adequate for the contemporary world. A new mental attitude was required, and Orwell hoped that socialism would be the means to generate this new attitude. Other things being equal, he could tolerate Kipling's assumptions about imperialism because they had integrity in Kipling's time. What Orwell could not forgive were values, institutions, and mental habits that had lived on past their time. His final criticism of the class system in England was that it was an anachronism. Orwell attacked irresponsibility and mental laziness, not authority.

Progress, change, the growth and decay of institutions, particularly the development of a moral climate, are part of Orwell's sense of history. When belief in progress is one side of the coin, anachronism as an evil is the other side. By progress Orwell did not mean improvement in leaps and bounds, but a tortuous inching forward. "Say what you will, things *do* change," is the refrain in his political thinking. At various times he pointed to the upgrading of manners, the development of a more critical attitude toward cruelty, even to the advent of technology, to prove his point.

When Orwell wrote *Coming Up for Air* in 1938 it was his one flirtation with a past age. It set the keynote for his stocktaking of past and present for the next few years. He was beginning to tally the score between what had been lost and what had been gained. The question behind the revolution in *Animal Farm* is whether societal progress is a reality.

Orwell's era and his development in it have been summed up nicely by John Wain in *The World of George Orwell.* "Most of what seem to be the paradoxes in Orwell's thinking and writing can be explained by the fact that he was born into an age in which the really suffocating nonsense was talked by reactionaries, and lived on into an age in which it was talked by progressives." What Orwell would have liked was a culture that combined the optimism of Wells and the responsibility of Kipling with a socialist platform.

The identification of conservatism and evil with the past, and radicalism and good with the future is intellectually unsound. Every culture of any duration has contained a mixture of good and evil, and future ones will be no different. The Sumerian king, Hammurabi, almost five thousand years ago, formulated a principle that crimes committed by members of the upper class were to be more stringently punished than similar crimes committed by members of the lower class. He assumed that privilege conferred responsibility. If such a premise were to be put into law today, would we be going forward or backward?

Tom Hopkinson said that Orwell was without historical perspective. This is partially true; Orwell's historical perspective was a foreshortened one. He was not interested in remote antiquities, biblical times, or, the so-called classical ages. He had no romantic associations with history. But his sense of the movement of history from the mid-nineteenth century to his own time was keen. One suspects that this historical perspective is related to his feeling for experience and secularism. He was attached to phenomenological reality and, except for some observations on Shakespeare, Swift, Smollett, and Tolstoy, did not like to go outside his personal range of experience.

Coming Up for Air contrasts the age of Orwell's childhood with the present age in which its narrator, George Bowling, lives. This is the age of the late 1930s, on the edge of World War II. The threat of war hovers everywhere in the book. It is a militarized, overmechanized age of synthetic and packaged foods, air-conditioned rooms, and uncontrollable hatreds. "Everything comes out of a carton or a tin, or it's hauled out of a refrigerator or squirted out a tap or squeezed out of a tube."

George Bowling bites into a frankfurter and discovers that it is made of fish. "It gave me the feeling that I'd bitten into the modern world and discovered what it was really made of." The modern world is ersatz. Nothing is made of what it seems to be.

For Orwell this lack of reality in things is related to our present moral instability. The assumption in *Coming Up for Air* is that the early twentieth century had been in possession of a world view, a moral standard in which both nature and man had their place and a relationship to each other. His picture of Bowling's childhood suggests that the focus on the eternal cycle of birth, life, and death did provide man, whatever its lacks, with a mighty definition of himself that could be grasped by the lowest and the highest intellects as "the scheme of things," while contemporary man has neither this nor any world view and is morally adrift.

Orwell resembles Joyce Cary in this novel, in his apprehension of societal dissolution and instability. On several occasions a character in a novel by Cary remarks that the modern world makes one feel as if the ground were shifting underneath. In *Coming Up for Air,* Orwell says of George Bowling's parents, "Their good and evil would remain good and evil. They didn't feel the ground they stood on shifting under their feet."

George "Fatty" Bowling is the protagonist in the novel. Indeed, the other characters, Bowling's wife, Porteous the intellectual, Bowling's old girlfriend, are either background caricatures or clichés. Bowling is virtually the only developed character in a novel that is more a sequence of Orwell's observations on the modern scene than a novel.

As a character Bowling grew out of Orwell's interest in the creation of a literature of the common man, out of his enthusiasm for James Joyce's *Ulysses* and Henry Miller's *Tropic of Cancer.* This enthusiasm and Orwell's interest in the lower class, even his creation of Fatty Bowling, rested on what Woodcock called Orwell's obsession with finding "a natural way of living." But like the character of Gordon Comstock in *Keep the Aspidistra Flying,* George's character is not integrated with plot and theme. His observations are clearly those of Orwell.

The book was begun in Marrakech in 1938, where Orwell had gone for his health. Off and on, from 1936 until the outbreak of World War II he lived in Wallington, Hertfordshire where, in addition to writing and vegetable gardening, which he enjoyed, he ran a small store. It was here that he lived with Eileen O'Shaughnessy after they were married. It was probably this experience that enabled him to create the youth of George Bowling with its atmosphere of small shopkeepers and simple economics.

There is a cluster of essays that Orwell wrote between 1939 and 1945 around the theme of popular culture, which are related to *Coming Up for Air.* These essays are **"Charles Dickens," "Boys' Weeklies," "The Art of Donald McGill," "Nonsense Poetry,"** and **"Good Bad Books."** The essays were collected in 1946 under the title, *Dickens, Dali and Others: Studies in Popular Culture.* The title is relevant to Orwell's analysis of modern literature as comprised of two main directions. The first direction is represented by Dickens, who can be pathetic, middle-class, bourgeois, finicky about proletarian revolutions, but who was read by the proletarian as few other writers were because he affirmed the moral outlook of the working class. The second direction is represented by Dali, whom Orwell regarded as morally degenerate.

Dali represented for him the immoral artist as Pound represents the fascist literary genius. Art and literature did not become golden calves for Orwell to which he was ready to sacrifice other virtues. With reservations, he felt that Pound should be given the Bollingen prize for literature, but he condemned him for his broadcasts on behalf of the fascists. Orwell did not confuse the issue between a writer's morality and a writer's craft, or think that a man should be forgiven for his sins as a person because he wrote well.

His essays on Tolstoy, Swift, Kipling, Dickens and other literary figures reveal that he was conscious of a writer both as writer and as human being—a person with particular values, who possesses a potential for good and evil. He explained Dali in terms of the decay of capitalist civilization. He saw him as essentially an Edwardian product, particularly attached to the year 1900 and to the fin de siècle mood of eroticism and madness. Dali represented for Orwell the trend in the early twentieth century toward irresponsible wealth, "when every European capital swarmed with aristocrats and *rentiers* who had given up sport and politics and taken to patronizing the arts. If you threw dead donkeys at people, they threw money back."

Orwell's analysis of Dali indicated his interest in the sociological implications of a writer or an artist and his work. Orwell stressed the relationship between writer and moral climate. For example, **"Boys' Weeklies"** studies the effect books and magazines have on adolescent boys. It concerns the kind of fiction few intellectuals would notice. The boys' weeklies are serial stories about the adventures of wealthy private-school boys. The serials were read, however, largely by those who could not afford to go to such schools. Still, the appeal in the stories was to snobbery and fantasies of wealth. They celebrated the social atmosphere of 1910—laissez faire economics, ridicule of foreigners, trust in the empire.

Orwell took the formation of the imagination very seriously. He believed that the books read earliest in life leave the most vivid impression. Young boys who grew up on a diet of wealth-fantasy would be poor consumers of left-wing thought.

On the other hand, **"The Art of Donald McGill"** (Donald McGill was probably a trade name) is an art designed to appeal to the better-off working class and the lower middle class. The essay concerns the humorous obscene postcard frequently found in tourist shops or at the seashore.

In his study of this art, Orwell reached several conclusions about the proletariat. The humor in this type of postcard, when Orwell wrote about it, had not changed in forty years, which indicates continuity and stability in working-class culture: ". . . what you are really looking at is something as traditional as Greek tragedy, a sort of sub-world of smacked bottoms and scrawny mothers-in-law which is part of Western European consciousness."

The humor is not pornographic. Orwell compared it to the kind of ribaldry that goes on at a village wedding, such as sewing bells to the bridal bed. The standard sexual jokes are about nakedness, illegitimate children, newly married couples, and old maids. Nagging wives, drunkenness, and mothers-in-law make up the rest of the subject matter. The important point is that these jokes indicate a strict marriage code.

The "swell" and the slum dweller are equally figures of fun. So are the subjects of free love, nudism, and feminism.

Orwell's analysis of this type of art confirmed the observation made in *The Road to Wigan Pier* about the conservatism of the proletariat. By the time he wrote *1984* he had a consistent view of this class.

His further studies in popular literature revealed to him that pre-1914 popular literature could be snobbish and conservative, but post-1914 popular literature, such as the comic book, revels in undisguised brutality and the pursuit of power. The pursuit of status and wealth may have been the substance of fantasy for a poor boy at the turn of the century, but it had been replaced by the pursuit of power as the substance of most people's fantasies. Orwell regarded this type of literature, which made brutality attractive, as an American phenomenon, rooted in the gangster films of the 1930s, and in an "equivocal attitude towards crime." The essay to read on this subject is **"Raffles and Miss Blandish."**

Orwell's interest in subliterature is connected to his concern with literature as a reflection of the moral health of a nation. As a literary critic, he avoided coterie subjects and coterie arguments. His socialist values determined an approach to literature that was sociological and egalitarian. He took pains to avoid arguments based on standards or ideas of taste. A "high" and a "low" literature, a "good" and a "bad" literature, frequently imply the varieties of social status. In his search for an egalitarian standard he preferred to write about such topics as **"Nonsense Poetry"** and **"Good Bad Books."**

His avoidance of traditional literary assumptions rests too on his feeling that statements about literary standards were, like religious statements, beyond proof. Like Samuel Johnson, he accepted "the test of time" as the only proof of the worth of a work of literature. Tolstoy had written a pamphlet bitterly attacking Shakespeare. In his essay, **"Lear, Tolstoy and the Fool,"** Orwell asks, "And with what result? Forty years later, Shakespeare is still there completely unaffected. . . . "

Literature is sustained by the principle of ipso facto. Critics and criticism exert little influence. Virginia Woolf may be demonstrated to be a better writer than Harriet Beecher Stowe, but what does that matter? *Uncle Tom's Cabin* had broader appeal than anything Virginia Woolf wrote. Questions of the structure of the work and the stature of the writer are irrelevant. The relationship between a literary work and the public is ultimately indefinable. Orwell believed that the success, not just commercially, of a work of literature was basically mysterious, and the study of literature was as close as he ever came to being interested in something he regarded as mysterious.

Coming Up for Air evolved out of his concern with the creation of a literature that could "cast a kind of bridge across the frightful gulf which exists, in fiction, between the intellectual and the man-in-the-street," as he wrote in a review on *Tropic of Cancer* in 1936. Orwell's novel is an extension of the world described in **"The Art of Donald McGill."** George Bowling's wife, Hilda, is a middle-class variant of the nagging wife. Hilda, their friends, and their neighborhood are almost a spiteful distillation of middle-class venality and consumerism. The central activity in

Hilda's life is bargain-hunting. Objects have only monetary value.

George Bowling's sexual peccadilloes that embroider his marriage contribute to what there is of plot, which is little. Indeed, there is little plot in any of Orwell's novels, except *Burmese Days.* In *Coming Up for Air* the plot evolves from the fact that Bowling, an insurance man, wins some money at the track that his wife knows nothing about. Instead of spending it on a woman which he might have done at another time, he decides to "sneak off " to go back to visit the town in which he was raised. Ironically, Bowling's wife suspects him of infidelity, when Bowling is searching for integrity and faith in life. Can he convince her of the truth of this particular trip? Would it matter if he could, since their relationship is so negligible to begin with?

Orwell's description of this marriage has some similarity to his description of marital humor in **"The Art of Donald McGill."** Hilda Bowling is described as going into the slump of middle age right after marriage, withering "off like a flower that's set its seed." In **"The Art of Donald McGill,"** Orwell wrote, "One of the very few authentic class differences, still existing in England is that the working classes age very much earlier . . . they do lose very early their youthful appearance." Orwell, who was influenced by his studies of proletarian values, thereafter criticized the middle-class effort to sustain youth and avoid aging.

Four conventions of the McGill postcards operate in *Coming Up for Air:* Marriage only benefits the woman; it is a victory for her and a trap for the man. "Sex-appeal vanishes at about the age of twenty-five." (An effort is made to make Bowling unattractive. He is not only fat at forty, but wears false teeth.) There is no such thing as a happy marriage. No man ever gets the better of a woman in an argument.

It is still possible to find comedians today whose jokes revolve around these conventions, but it is becoming rare. It is only recently that the mother-in-law figure and the drunken husband sneaking home at night have become obsolete as subjects of humor. Middle-class humor now has a political context; it has broadened its base, it has become more dissident and less domestic. Society has replaced the family as the source of humor.

But in Orwell's age domestic strife was among the leading humorous subjects. Certainly Orwell thought that the working class found domestic strife a comic subject. This assumption may have influenced his decision to write a book that was a commentary on the contemporary world from the point of view of the beleaguered husband. Unfortunately, this experiment in writing literature by an intellectual for the common man has the drawback of a television family skit. The language and episodes are banal. The familiarity of the domestic scenes is dreary. The dialogues between Hilda and George are all alike.

> "But look here, Hilda! You've got this all wrong. It isn't what you think at all. You don't understand."
>
> "Oh, yes, I do, George, I understand *perfectly.*"

"But look here, Hilda—!"

This type of dialogue between them almost never varies in the novel.

James Joyce, as everyone knows, solved the problem of banality by creating an extraordinarily uncommon language. Such a solution was not possible for Orwell because, if for no other reason, he would take pains to avoid linguistic eccentricities.

The best writing in *Coming Up for Air* is the description of George's rural youth. Here we are in the world of **"Riding down from Bangor"** and **"Helen's Babies,"** two essays by Orwell that reflect life in the nineteenth century in the United States and in England, a life characterized by strong family ties and piety. In *Coming Up for Air* Orwell's description of George's mother kneading dough exhibits his appreciation for the domestic skills that were part of this world.

His account of the tools, baits, and techniques used in fishing illustrate his love of fact. George's early affection for fishing plays a part in the theme which is intended to contrast the present with the past. In Bowling's present world "There's time for everything except the things worth doing." Bowling's lament, like Thoreau's observation, is that work usurps a man's life. Chief among the compulsions in modern life "is an everlasting, frantic struggle to sell things." Orwell's use of Bowling's position as an insurance salesman is ironic. The struggle to sell keeps Bowling hopping with insecurity, while it is security he is supposed to sell.

Before becoming an insurance salesman he had been a traveling salesman. He worked on commission and sold just about everything—cutlery, soap powder, corkscrews, can openers, and office accessories. Orwell's description of the life of the traveling salesman recalls Arthur Miller's *Death of a Salesman*. Surely the salesman is a representative type of our century.

> The cross-country journeys, the godless places you fetched up in, suburbs of midland towns that you'd never hear of in a hundred normal lifetimes. The ghastly bed-and-breakfast houses where the sheets always smell faintly of slops and the fried egg at breakfast has a yolk paler than a lemon. And the other poor devils of salesmen that you're always meeting, middle-aged fathers of families in moth-eaten overcoats and bowler hats, who honestly believe that sooner or later trade will turn the corner and they'll jack their earnings up to five quid a week.

George Bowling's existence is replete with the shabbiness and boring repetitiveness depicted in *Keep the Aspidistra Flying.* George asks, "Do you know the road I live in—Ellesmere Road, West Bletchley? Even if you don't, you know fifty others exactly like it." The themes of loss of individuality and the boredom of the quotidian are mirrored in the architecture. Bowling observes that the status of the people who live here is illusionary. They don't own the houses they think they own; the banks own them. They only imagine they have something to lose. Like anachronisms, they are out of step with reality. Curiously, Or-

well's point that money is power is a capitalistic notion, contrary to the aristocratic notion that status is power.

The intention of the novel, however, is not a critique of the middle class, for the book makes clear that George's parents inhabit a likable middle-class world, the world of small shopkeepers in a small town. The critique is directed toward the modern world; the contrast is not between one class and another, but between the same class as it existed in the past and as it exists in the present. The marital and domestic world of George's middle-class parents have virtue, but George's contemporary domestic world does not. His mother is an idealization. Her favorite form of relaxation is to read about the latest murder. Her tastes represent Orwell's observation about lower class values in his essay, **"Decline of the English Murder."** George's wife is the subject of a joke about overbearing women. Her entertainment is got from food-fads, admission-free public meetings, free lectures on hypnotism, theosophy, or yogi cookery. She is the subject of lower-class humor as Orwell analyzed that humor in **"The Art of Donald McGill."**

The trajectory of time in the novel, however, is not from the past to the present, but from the past to the future. The antiutopia of *1984* was already implicit in George Bowling's view of the future: "But it isn't the war that matters, it's the afterwar. The world we're going down into, the kind of hate-world, slogan-world. The coloured shirts, the barbed wire, the rubber truncheons."

George confronts Porteous, West Bletchley's intellectual, with his presentiments. He asks him what he thinks of Hitler. Porteous, pipe in hand, responds, "I see no reason to pay any attention to him. A mere adventurer. These people come and go. Ephemeral, purely ephemeral." Bowling, the common man, is not sure what ephemeral means, but he knows what Hitler and Joe Stalin mean. Porteous, like Ravelston, is one of Orwell's too few fictive projections of the intellectual, a type of individual that he describes elsewhere and often. In a review of *Beggar My Neighbour* by Lionel Fielden, Orwell wrote, "In the last twenty years western civilisation has given the intellectual security without responsibility, and in England, in particular, it has educated him in skepticism while anchoring him almost immovably in the privileged class."

Porteous, however, is not a skeptic; he is an anachronism. His mental world is Crete or Mycenae. He has plenty of imagination for the past, but none for the modern world. He has been enfeebled by history and poetry. Bowling reflects that his mind probably stopped "about the time of the Russo-Japanese war." Porteous's particular sin is his paralysis. As Bowling observes, " . . . all the decent people are paralyzed."

Bowling's past has disappeared; the modern world has taken it over. A rubbish dump occupies the site of the old fishing hole; a modern housing development, designed in fake Tudor to make it look like the past, has replaced the woods; the supermarket has replaced the small shops. What Bowling learns from his return to the past is that his present age, the decade of the 1930s, is drifting toward a holocaust, that his present civilization is resting on very thin ice. "My dear fellow!" Porteous says, "There is nothing new under the sun." Yes, there is, George Bowling says, "Old Hitler's something different. So's Joe Stalin." (pp. 82-97)

Roberta Kalechofsky, in her George Orwell, *Frederick Ungar Publishing Co., 1973, 149 p.*

David Lodge   (essay date 1977)

[*Lodge is an English critic, educator, and novelist. In the following essay, he discusses differences in reader response to Orwell's semi-fictional essay "A Hanging" and a journalistic account of an execution.*]

George Orwell's **'A Hanging'**, is undoubtedly part of 'English Literature' but surely . . . it is a factual document, and to say that it is literature because we can read it as if it were fiction can only deprive it of its main claim to be valued, namely that it is telling the truth, making us 'face the facts' of capital punishment.

When I first read **'A Hanging'** I certainly assumed that it was a true story, an eye-witness account. The more I studied it, the more I suspected that Orwell had added or altered some details for literary effect, but I did not doubt that the piece was essentially factual and historical. I think this is probably the response of most readers of **'A Hanging'**—certainly nearly all the published commentary on it assumes that it is, like its companion piece **'Shooting an Elephant'**, a true story based on Orwell's own experience. The exception is the interesting biography of Orwell's early years, *The Unknown Orwell* (1972) by Peter Stansky and William Abrahams. They have interviewed Orwell's friend Mabel Fierz, who was largely responsible for getting *Down and Out in London and Paris* (1933) published and whom he met in 1930. They report:

> he appears to have told her things he told no-one else—from a literary point of view, the most sensational confidence was that his essay **'A Hanging'** which came out in the *Adelphi* the next winter was not, as it purported to be, an eye-witness account but a work of the imagination, for (she remembers him telling her) he had never been present at a hanging.

Stansky and Abrahams have also talked to Orwell's colleagues in the Burmese police force, who agreed that

> It would have been most unusual, though not impossible . . . for him to have been present at a hanging. As Headquarters ASP [Assistant Superintendent of Police] at Insein his duties would not normally require his presence there.

Writing in *The Road to Wigan Pier* (1937) about his experience of administering the British Empire, Orwell says, 'I watched a man hanged once. It seemed to me worse than a thousand murders'—which appears to be a fairly clear reference to, and authentication of, **'A Hanging'**. But Stansky and Abrahams show that Orwell, like most of us, did not always tell the strict truth, either in conversation or in print. So there is at least an element of doubt about the eye-witness authenticity of **'A Hanging'**, a possibility that it is a fiction.

To entertain this possibility may be a shock at first, involv-

ing a sense of having been deceived. But on reflection we can see, I think, that the factors which made us read the text as an eye-witness account are mainly *external* to the text. First, most of us read it, no doubt, in a volume of Orwell's essays, a context which implies that is a factual, rather than a fictional account. The volumes of essays in which it appeared, *Shooting an Elephant* (1950) and *Collected Essays* (1961) were, however, posthumous publications: Orwell himself was not responsible for placing **'A Hanging'** in this non-fiction context. In his lifetime the piece was published only twice—in the *Adelphi* for August 1931 and in the *New Savoy* in 1946. Secondly, we read **'A Hanging'** knowing that George Orwell was a police officer in Burma, a job which he grew to detest and repudiate, but one that would plausibly enough involve him in witnessing an execution. We may, indeed, read **'A Hanging'** with that reference in *The Road to Wigan Pier* at the back of our minds.

The original readers of **'A Hanging'** in the *Adelphi* had no such knowledge of its author. 'Eric A. Blair', as the piece was signed (he did not adopt the name George Orwell until 1933) was known to them only as the author of a few book reviews in the same periodical and of a first-person sketch of a weekend spent in an English workhouse—**'The Spike'**—published in April 1931, and later incorporated into *Down and Out in Paris and London.* The text of **'A Hanging'** itself gives no information about the 'I' figure who narrates: no explanation of why he is present at the hanging, or what his function is supposed to be. This absence would have been more striking to the original readers than it is to us, who read back into the text all the biographical information we have acquired about George Orwell/Eric Blair, much of which he himself supplied in his books from 1936 onwards. Stansky and Abrahams observe the same ambiguity about the 'I' figure in **'The Spike'** and in *Down and Out,* which Orwell was writing at about the same time. They argue that the invention of this narrator, originally in **'The Spike'**, was the crucial technical breakthrough in Eric Blair's early struggles to find a style for himself that was not hopelessly derivative and conventionally 'literary'.

> The material he had accumulated until now had to be reinvented if he was to use it truthfully—which meant not a surface honesty but to get under the surface (any honest reporter could take care of the surface) and get down to the essence of it. He began to write in the first person without intervention: simply, I was there.

But since the focus was to be on *'there'*, the personal history of *'I'* had to be rigorously curtailed. (Stansky and Abrahams plausibly suggest that Blair adopted the pseudonym 'George Orwell' when *Down and Out* was published not, as he claimed, because he feared the book would be a failure, but to reinforce the anonymity of the narrator. They also show how he rather clumsily attempted to conceal the fact that he had collected much of the material by deliberately posing as a down-and-out).

It is very unlikely, at this date, that we shall ever be able to establish definitely whether Orwell attended a hanging or not, and more or less impossible that we should ever be able to check the particular circumstances of **'A Hanging'** against historical fact. It may be completely factual, it may be partly based on experience, or partly on the reported experience of others, or partly fictional, or wholly fictional—though the last possibility seems to me the least likely. The point I wish to make is that it doesn't really matter. As a text, **'A Hanging'** is self-sufficient, self-authenticating—autotelic, to use the jargon word. The internal relationships of its component parts are far more significant than their external references. In fact, when we examine the text carefully we see that these external references—to time, place, history—have been kept down to a minimum. There are no proper names except 'Burma' and the Christian name of the head warder. There are no dates. There is no explanation of the prisoner's crime. And it is because the external references of the text are reduced in this way that the internal relationships of its component parts . . . are correspondingly important, as I shall show.

'A Hanging' is literature, therefore, not because it is self-evidently fictional, but because it does not need to be historically verifiable to 'work'. Although it is possible, and perhaps natural in some circumstances, to read **'A Hanging'** as history, the text will, I believe, survive the undermining of that assumption. It is equally satisfying, equally successful read as a true story or as a fiction or as something in between, and nothing we might discover about its relationship to history will affect its status as literature.

It may seem that I am making too simple a distinction here between fiction and history, and taking a naively positivistic view of the latter. But while it is true that historians construct fictions in the sense that they inevitably select and interpret 'the facts' according to conscious or unconscious ideological predilections, no neutral or total reconstruction of the past being possible, nevertheless history is based on the assumption that there is a body of facts to be selected from and interpreted, and that our understanding of an event can be improved or revised or altered by the discovery of new facts or the invalidation of old ones. There is no way in which our understanding of **'A Hanging'** could be improved or revised or altered by the discovery of new facts. In this respect it contrasts instructively with an account of a hanging by Michael Lake that appeared in the *Guardian* for 9 April, 1973 under the title 'Michael Lake Describes What the Executioner Actually Faces'. This text has many features in common with **'A Hanging'** and superficially the same narrative design: the procession to the scaffold, the numbed state of the condemned man, the abrupt operation of the gallows, the whisky and the macabre joking of the officials afterwards, the narrator's residual sense of guilt. 'Michael Lake Describes . . .' seems to me a good piece of journalism, and as a polemic against capital punishment perhaps more effective than Orwell's piece. But it *is* journalism, and remains this side of literature. Its effectiveness depends on our trust that it is historically verifiable. If we discovered that there was no such person as Walter James Bolton, or that Michael Lake had never attended a hanging, the text would collapse, because it would be impossible to read it, as one can read **'A Hanging'**, as an effective piece of fiction. Once its external references were cut, the comparative weakness of its internal structure would become all too evident. We should become aware of clichés, opportu-

nities missed, a lack of variety in tempo and in intensity of feeling. Details like 'Mr Alf Addison, an old friend of mine' would no longer have any function and would become irritating irrelevancies. And perhaps we should feel we were being bullied into the desired response by crudely sensationalist means.

Correspondingly, **'A Hanging'** has certain qualities which 'Michael Lake Describes . . . ' hasn't got: a narrative structure, for instance, that is more than a mere sequence. The structure of Michael Lake's report is a chain of items linked in chronological order and suspended between an opening statement of polemical intent and a closing statement of personal feeling. The structure of **'A Hanging'** is also chronological, but it is more complex: the inevitable movement towards the death of the condemned man is deliberately but unexpectedly retarded at two points: first by the interruption of the dog and secondly by the prisoner's invocation of his god. These delays heighten the tension, and they allow the moral protest against capital punishment to emerge out of the narrative instead of being merely signalled at the beginning and end. Another structural difference is that Orwell's piece goes on proportionately longer after the actual execution, enforcing the double concern of the writer: not only with what the execution does to the executed but also what it does to the executioners. In a sense, this extended ending is another form of retardation, since it retards the expected termination of the text.

'Retardation' is one of the basic devices that, according to the Russian Formalist Victor Shklovsky, enable narrative art to achieve the effect of 'defamiliarization' which he held to be the end and justification of all art:

> Habitualization devours objects, clothes, furniture, one's wife and the fear of war. 'If all the complex lives of many people go on unconsciously, then such lives are as if they had never been.' Art exists to help us recover the sensation of life; it exists to make us feel things, to make the stone *stony*. The end of art is to give a sensation of the object as seen, not as recognized. The technique of art is to make things 'unfamiliar', to make forms obscure, so as to increase the difficulty and the duration of perception. The act of perception in art is an end in itself and must be prolonged. *In art, it is our experience of the process of construction that counts, not the finished product.*

Although the last statement leads logically to Shklovsky's celebration of *Tristram Shandy* as the supreme example of narrative art, the quotation in the second sentence is from the diary of Tolstoy, from whom Shklovsky draws several of his illustrations. In other words, there is no incompatibility between the theory of 'defamiliarization' and realistic writing of the kind Orwell practiced—indeed **'A Hanging'** illustrates the theory very well, for what Orwell is doing is defamiliarizing the idea of capital punishment—the idea, not the experience of it, since only the first is 'familiar'.

Michael Lake is trying to do the same thing, but by the comparatively crude method of filling out the familiar idea with unfamiliar details. He selects and describes aspects of the event he witnessed which will make us recoil from it: the possibility of Bolton's head being torn off by his own weight, the hypocrisy and/or irrelevance of the chaplain's prayers, the macabre fancy-dress of the executioner's get-up, Bolton's inarticulateness, and so on. But these details belong to quite disparate emotive categories—some are nauseating, some ironic, some pathetic—and Lake makes no attempt to relate them to each other. He fires the details at us on the principle of the shotgun: if a few miss the target, enough will hit it to make the desired effect. It would be difficult to say, on the evidence of the text, exactly what aspect of the proceedings was to him the most significant or indeed what it is, precisely, that makes capital punishment inhuman in his view.

There is no such difficulty in the Orwell text. The central paragraph makes clear what the narrator feels to be wrong about capital punishment (though it is an 'unspeakable wrongness' he in fact proceeds to speak it). Interestingly, it is not the most gruesome or solemn part of the proceedings that provokes this realization, but a gesture so small and ordinary that most people, perhaps including Mr. Lake, would never have noticed it (always supposing, of course, that it actually happened): the prisoner side-stepping the puddle. Why is this gesture so pregnant with meaning for the narrator? Because in the context of imminent death, it makes him understand what it is to be alive. Orwell has thus defamiliarized the idea of capital punishment by defamiliarizing something in fact much more familiar, much more veiled by habit: simply being alive. Implicitly the incident reveals that there is all the difference in the world between knowing *that* we shall die and knowing *when* we shall die. Human life exists in an open-ended continuum. We know that we shall die, but if we are healthy our minds and bodies function on the assumption that we shall go on living, and indeed they cannot function in any other way. The man instinctively avoids the trivial discomfort of stepping in the puddle on his way to the scaffold. His nails continue growing even as he falls through the air with a tenth of a second to live. So he is in the intolerable position of having to behave as if he is going to go on living, but knowing that he isn't going to. And the spectator is correspondingly impressed by the grim irony that all present are inhabiting the same continuum of experience, but that for one person it is not open-ended: 'he and we were a party of men walking together, seeing, hearing, feeling, understanding the same world'— the present participles emphasize the notions of continuity and community—'and in two minutes, with a sudden snap, one of us would be gone—one mind less, one world less.'

There is then, in this central paragraph, an emphasis on the idea of time in relation to life and death. 'Time is life, and life is time,' runs the lyric of a modern song. 'Death,' said Wittgenstein, 'is not an event *in* life. We do not live to experience death.' At the level of maximum abstraction that is what **'A Hanging'** is about: the paradoxical relationships between the concepts death, life and time, in the context of capital punishment. For capital punishment in a sense seeks to subvert the logic of Wittgenstein's assertion, to force the experience of death into life. That is why it is, or may be held to be, inhuman and obscene. Michael

Lake is dimly aware of these paradoxes—at least I think that is why he is shocked and incredulous that the chaplain is reading aloud the Burial Service over the living man. But he hasn't quite worked out what is shocking about it, and without Orwell's piece for comparison we might not have worked it out either. (pp. 9-15)

> David Lodge, "George Orwell's 'A Hanging', and 'Michael Lake Describes'," in his The Modes of Modern Writing: Metaphor, Metonymy, and the Typology of Modern Literature, *Cornell University Press, 1977, pp. 9-16.*

Jefferson Hunter   (essay date 1979)

[*In the following essay, Hunter discusses common themes and techniques in Orwell's essays, including his "expanded essays"* Down and Out in Paris and London, The Road to Wigan Pier, *and* Homage to Catalonia.]

George Orwell's last book was published thirty-two years ago. The nightmarish events imagined there, which in 1949 seemed reassuringly distant, lie a scant five years in the future, or so his title proclaims: *1984.* That is a date to be approached warily, one would think; and yet even those of us who admire Orwell deeply have grown used to anticipating it complacently, convinced as we are that Orwell wrote the book when embittered and dying, that he knew too little about the economic dependencies of modern industrial states, that he had too little trust in mankind. Whether complacency is justified remains to be seen. Orwell's own advice on literary judgments was to await the verdict of time, and if we do so we will soon have the evidence of our senses to tell us whether the telescreens are peering into our lives, whether the clocks on bright cold April afternoons are striking thirteen.

In the meantime Orwell's apparent failure as prophet has not damaged his reputation as writer, if only because the future he so melodramatically imagined seems less important than the present which his prose may help us survive. Much of his work, to be sure, is dated: newsletters, broadcasts, arguments for now forgotten causes, reviews of books which once were important. Events forced him, in the words of an Auden poem which he severely criticized, to expend his powers on the flat ephemeral pamphlet and the boring meeting. But in his most characteristic work, the formal essays and books—***Down and Out in Paris and London, The Road to Wigan Pier, Homage to Catalonia***— which are essentially expanded essays, he diagnoses political diseases from which we are not yet fully recovered. Examining the abuses of rhetoric, he implicates our present evasions; writing about himself, he finds the permanent sources of human decency.

Especially since the publication of his collected essays and journalism in 1968 Orwell has been regarded as a latter-day Dr. Johnson telling writers to clear their minds of the modern varieties of cant: technical obfuscation, meaningless words, the hackneyed political metaphor, the callous euphemism. To claim, as Orwell does in **"Politics and the English Language,"** that phrases like "rectification of frontiers" or "elimination of undesirable elements" dehumanize their users is a form of moral perception. Orwell approaches this and other tasks of cleansing language with the utmost seriousness, for the fact which the rectifier of frontiers prefers not to see is the fact of human suffering. But accompanying Orwell's moral rigor is an aesthetic fastidiousness, a feeling for "words and their right arrangement. Pleasure in the impact of one sound on another, in the firmness of good prose or the rhythm of a good story" (**"Why I Write,"** 1946). Sometimes discussed openly, sometimes only hinted at by choice of metaphor, one idea consistently underlies Orwell's attacks on the propagandists: they are betrayers of the craft of writing and the comeliness of language. He denounces the lazy stylists who let "the ready-made phrases come crowding in"; again and again he returns to images of jerry-built and mass-produced writing, words in the form of hard objects: "phrases tacked together like the sections of a prefabricated hen-house," "strips of words which have already been set in order by someone else," "prefabricated phrases bolted together like the pieces of a child's Meccano set."

The mechanical process is taken to an extreme in Newspeak, in which a "warm and valued compliment" like "doubleplusgood duckspeaker" jams Oldspeak words together, depriving them of connotation. Dealing in such locutions is symptom and cause of the party mentality: "What was slightly horrible was that from the stream of sound that poured out of his mouth, it was almost impossible to distinguish a single word. Just once Winston caught a phrase—'complete and final elimination of Goldsteinism'—jerked out very rapidly and, as it seemed, all in one piece, like a line of type cast solid." The line of type, however, is not the perfected form which orthodoxy may be expected to take. Like the orators Swift describes in *A Tale of a Tub,* whose words are "Bodies of much Weight and Gravity, as is manifest from those deep Impressions they make and leave upon us," Orwell's Newspeakers turn rhetoric into weaponry: "a Party member called upon to make a political or ethical judgement should be able to spray forth the correct opinions as automatically as a machine gun spraying forth bullets."

Such reductive similes, together with the careful analyses of propaganda provided in many Orwell essays, amount to a lesson about what language can destroy. For that much alone we can be grateful, but Orwell is disserved if his works are taken merely as warnings, as exposés of what not to do. Everything he wrote, even the earliest reportage, exemplifies the potentiality of language for good, for political honesty as well as political lying. To the prefabricated phrases he opposes a moral vision and a means of expressing it in vigorous and flexible prose, and to value the vision properly we must make two inquiries into the prose: how the Orwellian virtues are actually achieved in the detailed operations of writing and rewriting; how Orwell's style allows him to discover—forces on him—an appropriate form for his most original discourse.

On February 11, 1936, Orwell noted in his diary some impressions of unemployed men he had met in the Brookers' lodging house in Warrington Lane, Wigan. (Like other left-wing travelers in the thirties, he was keeping a careful record of what he saw in the lower depths.) This comment is typical:

> Joe, another lodger, single. Unemployed on 17/-a week. Pays 6/-a week for his room and sees to his own food. Gets up about 8 to give his bed up to "our Joe" [the Brookers' son] and remains out of doors, in Public Library etc most of day. A bit of an ass but has some education and enjoys a resounding phrase. Explaining why he never married, he says portentously, "Matrimonial chains is a big item." Repeated this sentence a number of times, evidently having an affection for it.

This is an entry in a long catalogue of victims, and is characteristic of Orwell only in its meticulous factuality (he adds a footnote to correct 17/-to 15/-). It became a character sketch in **The Road to Wigan Pier** (1937), the book which resulted from his fact-finding tour:

> Joe, like the Scotchman, was a great reader of newspapers and spent almost his entire day in the Public Library. He was the typical unmarried unemployed man, a derelict-looking, frankly ragged creature with a round, almost childish face on which there was a naively naughty expression. He looked more like a neglected little boy than a grown-up man. I suppose it is the complete lack of responsibility that makes so many of these men look younger than their ages. From Joe's appearance I took him to be about twenty-eight, and was amazed to learn that he was forty-three. He had a love of resounding phrases and was very proud of the astuteness with which he had avoided getting married. He often said to me, "Matrimonial chains is a big item," evidently feeling this to be a very subtle and portentous remark. His total income was fifteen shillings a week, and he paid out six or seven to the Brookers for his bed. I sometimes used to see him making himself a cup of tea over the kitchen fire, but for the rest he got his meals somewhere out of doors; it was mostly slices of bread-and-marg and packets of fish and chips, I suppose.

The sketch is clearly more sympathetic to Joe than Orwell's diary: "sympathetic" in the sense that it enters fully into Joe's world without forcing any kind of commiseration from the reader. The published version fleshes him out, makes him an individual ("naively naughty," "frankly ragged"). There is a new weight of meaning given Joe which can elicit sympathy or other, possibly more complex, responses: Orwell is as amused by Joe's pretension as he is distressed by his childishness. The presentation is not of sociological fact but of a man for whom it is possible to feel affection and a certain contempt at the same time, the former being in a sense validated by the latter: Joe is not an idealized proletarian and not even unique, as the typifying language ("these men") makes clear. But Orwell's superiority to Joe is not simple, as it was in the diary ("a bit of an ass"). In **The Road to Wigan Pier** the remnants of love and pride in Joe are carefully preserved. Orwell expands "sees to his own food" with a phrase that sets Joe to work ("making himself a cup of tea over the kitchen fire"). In the enforced idleness of unemployment any gesture of activity, however slight, is significant enough to be reported.

Joe is made noticeable both particularly and generally by an unremarkable alternation between individual details and the ills of an entire class: that is, Joe looks twenty-eight but is really forty-three: the lack of responsibility makes all the unemployed look and act young. Such balancings of detail with generalities are less typical of Orwell than passages built around a single telling detail which elicits a generalization—which has, in other words, the function of metaphor, the compression of meaning within specific, readily apprehensible limits. The meaning is most compressed and telling when it is discovered in apparently negligible facts, victims, or forms of working life. The detail in a passage from *The Road to Wigan Pier* reveals what ought to be, but is not, in front of everyone's nose: "Of the five pay-checks . . . no less than three are rubber-stamped with the words 'death stoppage.' When a miner is killed at work it is usual for the other miners to make up a subscription, generally of a shilling each, for his widow, and this is collected by the colliery company and automatically deducted from their wages. The significant detail here is the *rubber stamp.*" The ordinary forms of working language are also scrutinized. Richard Rees recorded an Orwellian observation that brilliantly revived a dead metaphor: "When socialists told him that under socialism there would be no such feeling of being at the mercy of unpredictable and irresponsible powers, he commented: 'I notice people always say *under* socialism.' "

Orwell's details move toward general implications as part of a reported personal movement from raw experience to understanding. With scrupulous honesty he admits that he himself needs a sharp detail of memory to recover the significance of an event or place. That is why his essays so often begin by insisting on concrete details: "First of all the physical memories, the sounds, the smells and the surfaces of things." "Whenever I read phrases like 'war guilt trials,' 'punishment of war criminals,' and so forth, there comes back into my mind the memory of something I saw in a prisoner-of-war camp in South Germany." The surfaces of things are set against mere verbiage, a process of writing like the sudden emotional discovery made by Gordon Comstock, the hero of Orwell's novel *Keep the Aspidistra Flying* (1936). Gordon gets his girl pregnant but scarcely realizes what he has done until she begins talking about money for an abortion and that talk suddenly pulls him up: "For the first time he grasped, with the only kind of knowledge that matters, what they were really talking about. The words 'a baby' took on a new significance. They did not mean any longer a mere abstract disaster, they meant a bud of flesh. . . . It was the squalid detail of the five pounds that brought it home." For the emotionally crippled Gordon, but no less for a professional writer, "there is often need of some concrete incident before one can discover the real state of one's feelings" (**"Revenge Is Sour,"** 1945).

"The real state of one's feelings." Feelings are particularly pertinent to Orwell as essayist because he directly participates in his reported scenes. In *The Road to Wigan Pier* his reactions to what he sees are in one sense typical (hence his repeated identification of himself as a middle-class observer) and in another sense exemplary. The unspoken directive of his book is "share my anger and compassion." Orwell's self-consciousness thus has strict uses, or is meant to have them, for his reactions are not always fitted tactfully into the scene. *The Road to Wigan Pier,* though much more straightforward and honest as autobiography than its predecessor *Down and Out in Paris and London,* reveals doubts about what he is doing (is his journey to Wigan only a slumming expedition, an expiation of class guilt?) which render the closing chapters on socialism uneasy and shrilly abusive. Orwell's prose is not sufficiently under control to give coherence to a work which badly needs it (*Homage to Catalonia,* published in 1938, is his first formally satisfactory book), but in isolated passages of *The Road to Wigan Pier* and even in earlier essays he succeeds in making his relation to what he observes a demonstrably important part of his subject.

"A Hanging" (1931), for example, portrays an observer intimately involved with a victim. The observer is in fact a victimizer. The essay begins abruptly, with details—a sodden Burmese morning, the condemned cells of a prison, the waiting warders. The straightforward impersonal tone suggests that hanging is a matter best treated with mechanical efficiency. The British police officers, including Orwell, supervise the handcuffing of the prisoner, a bugle calls "desolately thin in the wet air," and the superintendent gruffly orders the procession to start. Then Orwell, following the prisoner, sees him step around a puddle:

> It is curious, but till that moment I had never realised what it means to destroy a healthy, conscious man. When I saw the prisoner step aside to avoid the puddle, I saw the mystery, the unspeakable wrongness, of cutting a life short when it is in full tide. This man was not dying, he was alive just as we were alive. All the organs of his body were working—bowels digesting food, skin renewing itself, nails growing, tissues forming—all toiling away in solemn foolery. His nails would still be growing when he stood on the drop, when he was falling through the air with a tenth of a second to live. His eyes saw the yellow gravel and the grey walls, and his brain still remembered, foresaw, reasoned—reasoned even about puddles. He and we were a party of men walking together, seeing, hearing, feeling, understanding the same world; and in two minutes, with a sudden snap, one of us would be gone—one mind less, one world less.

The personal reaction is strong because it is delayed. The pacing of Orwell's observations is under tight control throughout the essay, and in this paragraph a like control is exerted over the style: it grows more emotive only in response to the accumulating insights that force Orwell to realize that the man was not simply dying. Beginning with a single observation, the detail of the puddle, Orwell moves back and forth between the language of moral order ("the mystery," "the unspeakable wrongness") and the language of contingency ("a sudden snap"). Figurative phrases like "in full tide" are followed by the justifying particulars—the bowels, the skin, the nails. Orwell shows us specifically what the condemned man is seeing, in order to make him more pathetically an individual who cannot stop observing the outside world he still shares with his warders. The gravel, walls, and puddle, by suggesting exactly what "the same world" means, prepare us for the key argument, which is put very simply: ("He and we were a party of men walking together . . . one of us would be gone"), and then for the sudden turn which makes the loss of a mind into the loss of a world. The paragraph concludes with a metaphor made convincing by the care with which its evolution is traced.

As Alex Zwerdling noted in a recent study of Orwell, it is only by taking the condition of the victim and the psychological state of the victimizer with equal seriousness that class hatred can be broken down. By moving in **"A Hanging"** from puddle to shared humanity, from casual curiosity to full emotional commitment, Orwell demonstrates the breakdown of his own class and racial hatred. But to make that breakdown general a third participant needs to join the scenes from which Orwell draws political or social significance: the reader. His understanding must be guaranteed, his allegiance gained, his relation to observed and observer defined. The author-reader bond in Orwell's essays is an arrangement between equals. His direct addresses are invitational ("When you go down a coal-mine . . . "), not dictatorial or patronizing. They break off when they have served their purpose and before they come to seem manipulative. Consider a scene not of injustice but of contentment:

> The year is 1910—or 1940, but it is all the same. You are at Greyfriars, a rosy-cheeked boy of fourteen in posh, tailor-made clothes, sitting down to tea in your study on the Remove passage after an exciting game of football which was won by an odd goal in the last half-minute. There is a cosy fire in the study, and outside the wind is whistling. The ivy clusters thickly round the old grey stones. The King is on his throne and the pound is worth a pound. Over in Europe the comic foreigners are jabbering and gesticulating, but the grim grey battleships of the British Fleet are steaming up the Channel and at the outposts of Empire the monocled Englishmen are holding the niggers at bay. Lord Mauleverer has just got another fiver and we are all settling down to a tremendous tea of sausages, sardines, crumpets, potted meat, jam and doughnuts. After tea we shall sit round the study fire having a good laugh at Billy Bunter and discussing the team for next week's match against Rookwood.

This parody of the *Gem* and the *Magnet* (**"Boys' Weeklies,"** 1940) shifts from signs of exclusiveness ("posh, tailor-made clothes") to a shared experience ("having a good laugh at Billy Bunter"). Just at the moment when continued use of "you" might make the reader feel unfairly thrust into a ridiculous past, Orwell changes to "we." The absurdly sheltered world turns out to be worth joining, at least momentarily, because its effect is to break down the solitude in which Orwell thought all men lived.

The opening of **The Road to Wigan Pier** similarly establishes an investigative partnership between Orwell and his reader:

> The first sound in the mornings was the clumping of the mill-girls' clogs down the cobbled street. Earlier than that, I suppose, there were factory whistles which I was never awake to hear.
>
> There were generally four of us in the bedroom, and a beastly place it was, with that defiled impermanent look of rooms that are not serving their rightful purpose. . . . There was a once-gaudy carpet ringed by the slop-pails of years, and two gilt chairs with burst seats, and one of those old-fashioned horsehair armchairs which you slide off when you try to sit on them.

"Beastly" is an Etonian's instinctive response to something unpleasant and an immediately noticeable sign of Orwell. The "that" in "that defiled impermanent look," however, casually associates this squalor with beastly appearances the reader has previously known and so keeps Orwell's disgust from seeming merely private. The old-fashioned armchairs, described a little later in the paragraph, turn out to be "those" armchairs "which you slide off when you try to sit on them." By the time we read the first two paragraphs we find ourselves, perhaps without realizing the means that have gotten us there, with Orwell in a place where we do not really belong but where we now seem to be uncomfortably at home. That is a first step, of course, toward wishing to abolish such places as a home for anyone.

The sense of familiarity is qualified by the reader's awareness that Orwell is in fact at one remove from actual suffering. An irony surrounds his relation to the dwellers in Wigan: "Earlier than that, I suppose, there were factory whistles which I was never awake to hear." Describing the elderly mechanic in the adjacent bed, which was placed so close to the foot of Orwell's that the latter had to sleep with his legs doubled up, Orwell comments, "Luckily he had to go to work at five in the morning, so I could uncoil my legs and have a couple of hours' proper sleep after he was gone." In spite of being close enough to the Brookers and their lodgers to count himself one of the "four of us in the bedroom," Orwell goes out of his way to note the difference between writer and laborer.

The situation of both created scenes, Greyfriars study and Wigan slum, is sympathy expressed at an inevitable distance—a situation provided again and again in Orwell's works. With the reader at his side he looks through a clear window at suffering he cannot heal ("He was dying, very slowly and in great agony, but in some world remote from me where not even a bullet could damage him further"), at contentment he cannot share, or—as in **"Looking Back on the Spanish War"**—at a past he cannot recover. He is on the outside looking in, like Dorothy Hare, the heroine of his 1935 novel *A Clergyman's Daughter,* who enviously watches Cockney families boiling tea over crackling fires of hop-bines, or like Gordon Comstock, who from the windswept street stares longingly into the steamy windows of a pub. "Good prose is like a window pane," Orwell once wrote. The windowpane is too modest a figure for his own good prose, windows being most virtuous when they are least noticed, but it is profoundly appropriate as a symbol separating him, and the reader whom he makes to be present, from the unreachable pain or joy on the other side.

At the key points of Orwell's essays and books it is a face he sees through the figurative window—the face of a deformed ex-SS prisoner in **"Revenge Is Sour,"** the faces of a peasant woman and a black soldier in **"Marrakech,"** the nearly human face of a dying animal in **"Shooting an Elephant,"** the generously angry face of Charles Dickens, the face of Numéro 57 in **"How the Poor Die,"** the face of Joe. *Homage to Catalonia* records Orwell's encounter with an Italian militiaman in the Lenin barracks in Barcelona: "Something in his face deeply moved me. It was the face of a man who would commit murder and throw away his life for a friend—the kind of face you would expect in an Anarchist, though as likely as not he was a Communist." Orwell was deeply enough moved by the meeting to write one of his rare poems about it. The final stanza is "But the thing I saw in your face / No power can disinherit: / No bomb that ever burst / Shatters the crystal spirit." Moments of perception (and self-revelation) like these are always temporary, as Orwell admits with deliberate bathos ("But I also knew that to retain my first impression of him I must not see him again; and needless to say I never did see him again. One was always making contacts of that kind in Spain"). But they are nevertheless the certainties to which his mind keeps returning; they generate all of his political emotions and his most important literary method. From them he derives an ideal of communication between individuals that leads to an ideal of communicative prose. What the militiaman and Orwell share the reader and Orwell can also share.

The momentariness of these key encounters gives Orwell's accounts of them a formal separateness and strength which he put to good use. The moments become the focal points of the books and long essays, just as specific details become the focal points of his paragraphs. *Homage to Catalonia* begins with Orwell's meeting the Italian militiaman, and similar scenes later in the book introduce all the major themes. Moreover the moments, when only slightly more elaborated, become works in themselves: short essays or narratives in which meaning is conveyed to the reader not in an analytical or logical structure but rather in a sudden discovery. The suddenness is nearly always a part of Orwell's personal experience: The phrase *It struck me then* recurs constantly in these short pieces, which have the concision and shapeliness ordinarily associated with fiction rather than reportage or political argument.

An **"As I Please"** column in 1947 consists of a lesson learned and then taught in four paragraphs. With no introduction but a brief distancing in time (he is looking through the windowpane into his past), Orwell plunges into narrative: "Nearly a quarter of a century ago I was travelling on a liner to Burma." In sketching the ship and its sailors he puts the reader casually on the scene ("One of those old sailors on whose back you almost expect to see barnacles growing"), and then explains his relation to the quatermasters as that of mere passenger to godlike beings. Then one day he sees the most impressive of these men scuttling along the deck holding a half-eaten custard pudding, an illicit leftover from the passengers' tables. "At one glance," in a "sudden revelation," Orwell sees the political lesson in the man's face ("the man's air of guilt made it unmistakeable"), so that at the very moment when the observer recognizes the social gulf between passenger and crewman he comes closer to the quartermaster than he has ever been. As momentary intimates they exchange the shameful fact that "a highly skilled craftsman, who might literally hold all our lives in his hands, was glad to steal scraps of food from our table." "Across more than twenty years" Orwell feels the shock of astonishment: the telling of the episode has brought him closer to his past and so overcome one other kind of separation. All the essays devoted to scenes of human community, even those in which the community is thwarted or possible only for seconds, stem from an ideal which Orwell felt more deeply than any political doctrine. In celebrating moments of communication among all the parties to a written work— the author's past and present self, the subject, the reader— he writes with greatest and most elusive power, his "style" on these occasions being not a separate definable quality but an indistinguishable part of his subject and form—less a manner of putting words on the page than a way of presenting himself as a man.

A final example from *The Road to Wigan Pier.* A much-quoted portrait of suffering in that book is of a slum-girl

Orwell's National Union of Journalists membership card.

seen from a train. Orwell first wrote about her in the diary he was keeping in 1936, and thus we have two versions of what she meant to him:

> Passing up a horrible squalid side-alley, saw a woman, youngish but very pale and with the usual draggled exhausted look, kneeling by the gutter outside a house and poking a stick up the leaden waste-pipe, which was blocked. I thought how dreadful a destiny it was to be kneeling in the gutter in a back-alley in Wigan, in the bitter cold, prodding a stick up a blocked drain. At that moment she looked up and caught my eye, and her expression was as desolate as I have ever seen; it struck me that she was thinking just the same thing I was.
>
> The train bore me away, through the monstrous scenery of slag-heaps, chimneys, piled scrap-iron, foul canals, paths of cindery mud crisscrossed by the prints of clogs. This was March, but the weather had been horribly cold and everywhere there were mounds of blackened snow. As we moved slowly through the outskirts of the town we passed row after row of little grey slum houses running at right angles to the embankment. At the back of one of the houses a young woman was kneeling on the stones, poking a stick up a leaden waste-pipe which ran from the sink inside and which I suppose was blocked. I had time to see everything about her—her sacking apron, her clumsy clogs, her arms reddened by the cold. She looked up as the train passed, and I was almost near enough to catch her eye. She had a round pale face, the usual exhausted face of the slum girl who is twenty-five and looks forty, thanks to miscarriages and drudgery; and it wore, for the second in which I saw it, the most desolate, hopeless expression I have ever seen. It struck me then that we are mistaken when we say that "It isn't the same for them as it would be for us," and that people bred in the slums can imagine nothing but the slums. For what I saw in her face was not the ignorant suffering of an animal. She knew well enough what was happening to her—understood as well as I did how dreadful a destiny it was to be kneeling there in the bitter cold, on the slimy stones of a slum backyard, poking a stick up a foul drain-pipe.

Some changes in the published version are such as we might expect any careful writer to make in the course of revision—scrapping imprecise adjectives ("horrible squalid") and awkward repetitions ("in the gutter in a back-alley in Wigan, in the bitter cold"), adding details ("kneeling on the stones"). Orwell reorders the stages of the encounter for rhetorical emphasis, postponing the second mention of "poking a stick" to the end of the description, where it will have the greatest effect, and supporting the final sentence with alliteration and a marked rhythm.

What is the point of changing "she looked up and caught my eye" to "I was almost near enough to catch her eye"? Of placing himself on a train that is bearing him away? (In the diary Orwell is walking when he passes the back alley.) These fictions create a dramatic scene in which communication between unequals is barely achieved. A man on a train passes by a woman he can see only for a second—and yet a second is time enough to see everything about her. Readily understandable because she has so little opportunity to be different, this woman with her usual exhausted face is a dweller not in Wigan but in "the slums."

In contrasting the dreary generality of suffering with the sharp momentariness of the insight Orwell exposes the meaning of the encounter. This meeting is severely limited, not so treasured a symbolic act as his shaking hands with the Italian militiaman; but it at least permits him to see something in her face and consequently in her mind. She knows what is happening to her. Indeed in the published version she knows "how dreadful a destiny" she is enacting. The formal phrase is something joining her with Orwell and the reader, who have already been linked in a common ignorance which it is one purpose of the scene to overcome ("we are mistaken when we say . . . "). All three participants in the scene—Orwell, the woman, and the reader—are united in opposition to the snobbery which deals in clichés and comfortably divides the world into "them" and "us." The train will pass on; in this section of *The Road to Wigan Pier* Orwell is escaping to a more amenable landscape of springlike weather and rooks treading. But the moment of union and separation is preserved.

Any discussion of Orwell's prose is likely to dwell on the sympathy, frankness, and clarity with which he observes injustice. The sense of humor which saves him from angry hectoring and emotional indulgence, though just as typical of his style, evades definition, slips through the most earnest analyses of memorable passages. His age gave Orwell an ample abyss in which to gaze, but he saw in that fact no reason to let the abyss gaze into him; fashionable writers, as he notes about the twenties in **"Inside the Whale"** (1940), fulfilled Nietzsche's prediction by toppling into the abyss in droves: "It was an age of eagles and of crumpets, facile despairs, backyard Hamlets, cheap return tickets to the end of the night." A less humorous, less flexible Orwell could not have satirized this posturing, much less turned on himself—as Orwell the chronicler of social injustice, the honest broker, the castigator of literary follies, so often turns on himself, noting his errors, his pretensions, and his prejudices.

There is a single Orwellian style, whether it presents us with coal-miners or the comic excesses of its creator's social conscience. Orwell is a writer whose voice remains remarkably constant as it modulates from form to form, from novel to essay, and even as it shifts and varies its tone: moving from flat exposition to rhetorical urgency, from sensitive exegesis to reductive translation, it flexibly accommodates statistics, invective, description, social theory, comedy, characterization, political vision, and self-parody into a recognizable style which, whether it is angry or compassionate, is always ready to adapt itself to different purposes, which never takes itself too seriously.

For this suppleness in Orwell's prose there is no better place to look than an essay which at first seems hardly serious. **"Some Thoughts on the Common Toad,"** which was published in the same month (April 1946) as **"Politics and the English Language,"** announces the pleasant discovery that elder trees are sprouting on a bombed-out site, that nature goes on "existing unofficially" in the heart of a desolated London. Orwell quietly sets his own cheerfulness against the asceticism of revolutionaries who believe that mankind ought to be discontented, who suspect that a liking for nature in the machine age is backward-looking and ridiculous, and who insist on an inflexible and cliché-ridden style ("the shackles of the capitalist system," "a class angle"). The conclusion of the essay lets nature have the upper hand and suggests an appropriate moral about human limitation:

> At any rate, spring is here, even in London N. 1, and they can't stop you enjoying it. This is a satisfying reflection. How many a time have I stood watching the toads mating, or a pair of hares having a boxing match in the young corn, and thought of all the important persons who would stop me enjoying this if they could. But luckily they can't. So long as you are not actually ill, hungry, frightened or immured in a prison or a holiday camp, spring is still spring. The atom bombs are piling up in the factories, the police are prowling through the cities, the lies are streaming from the loudspeakers, but the earth is still going round the sun, and neither the dictators nor the bureaucrats, deeply as they disapprove of the process, are able to prevent it.

Orwell's repeated "you" puts the reader in the frightening prison or the comic holiday camp, and joins him with Orwell on the side of common humanity, apart from "they," the important persons. His exaggeration at the close ("deeply as they disapprove of the process") renders the dictators superfluous. And finally his colloquial tone ("This is a satisfying reflection") is in itself a refusal to accede to political asceticism. Orwell's paragraph is a denial of the ruthless intellectual will, of that species of madness which [Samuel Johnson's] *Rasselas* diagnoses: "Hear, Imlac, what thou wilt not without difficulty credit. I have possessed for five years the regulation of the weather and the distribution of the seasons; the sun has listened to my dictates, and passed from tropic to tropic by my direction; the clouds, at my call, have poured their waters, and the Nile has overflowed at my command; I have restrained the rage of the dog star and mitigated the fervors of the crab." The effort of Johnson and Orwell is to save man from arrogance. Whatever the important persons decree, the earth Orwell describes so well will still be going around the sun. Whatever lies stream from the loudspeakers, people can still be told about toads mating or a pair of hares having a boxing match in the young corn.

Orwell knew that the power of language is limited. It can remind us of what is in front of our noses, it can make us conscious of suffering, it can deflate grandiloquence (including one's own grandiloquence), it can join individuals; but it cannot organize mankind into perfect consistency. The best explanation of the motives behind his prose is a single sentence from the last major essay he wrote, his partly admiring but chiefly critical meditation on saintliness, **"Reflections on Gandhi,"** which was finished in the autumn of 1948, just before Orwell went into the tuberculosis sanitarium for the last time: "The essence of being human is that one does not seek perfection, that one *is*

sometimes willing to commit sins for the sake of loyalty, that one does not push asceticism to the point where it makes friendly intercourse impossible, and that one is prepared in the end to be defeated and broken up by life, which is the inevitable price of fastening one's love upon other human individuals." At his most serious Orwell takes pains to be disconcerting. The prose of what amounts to a final statement on life is full of surprising turns. The essence of being human is not what we have been told, he insists, not the striving for perfection saints have preached. "Sin" and "loyalty" belong in the same sentence. The precise "asceticism" jostles the casual "friendly intercourse." In the most surprising turn of all, Orwell's knowledge that he is going to be defeated and broken up by life, which could easily seem self-pitying or ostentatiously stoical, is made to arise from love. Warmth suddenly emerges from defeat: a Spanish officer shakes Orwell's hand, Gordon Comstock marries his girl and makes something of his life, elders sprout in the crater, spring toads arise, like Persephone, from the dead. The price of living is not to be forgotten—everything Orwell wrote is meant to remind us of the pain of suffering, and the pain of accepting responsibility for suffering—but in reading him we discover why the price is worth paying. Without writers like Orwell to teach us how to fasten love upon other human individuals we would not know how to suffer or rejoice. (pp. 436-54)

Jefferson Hunter, "Orwell's Prose: Discovery, Communion, Separation," in The Sewanee Review, *Vol. LXXXVII, No. 3, Summer, 1979, pp. 436-54.*

Sant Singh Bal   (essay date 1981)

[*In the following excerpt, Bal discusses the connection between ethics and aesthetics in Orwell's prose style.*]

Though Orwell's life and thought . . . are shaped by his moral values, it is his prose style which brings out best the essential nature of his ethical imagination. No wonder, whenever we think of Orwell as a writer, our most characteristic response is to the language he honed and fashioned for himself. In a period of literary affectation, Orwell developed so simple a prose style that its excellences pass unperceived. "Orwell, apart from being anything else," says Malcolm Muggeridge, "was the perfect twentieth-century stylist. His dry sentences with their splendid clarity and smoldering indignation convey better than any other contemporary writer the true mood of our times." English is a difficult language, and few succeed in writing it well. But Orwell manages it with great skill and with a carpenter's grip on "jagged particularities," concentrates his energies on expository prose. The language came so very easily to him. In **"Why I Write,"** he says: "I knew that I had a facility with words and a power of facing unpleasant facts. . . ." There is a straight, conversational tone about his prose style, which writers such as Swift and Defoe carry on from Bunyan, and Orwell belongs to this tradition. His hatred of cant and current clichés, his puritanical avoidance of the luxury of sentimental and purple prose, his distrust of all abstractions are essentially moral concerns, and they link up with the qualities of courage, patience, honesty and simplicity. He might as well have said with Keats: "I am certain of nothing but of the holiness of the Heart's affections and the truth of imagination."

Orwell's style and his vision are one. His attack on imperialism and on all forms of totalitarianism, capitalism and orthodoxies, political as well as religious, stems from deeply-held moral values. Orwell is an impressive witness, an honest man who writes clearly and with a wealth of detail from firsthand experience. He values personal opinions, and stresses the supreme value of the individual above society. Confidence in the authenticity of his personal moral sense is a *sine qua non* in the affirmation of individualist aesthetics and ethics. The following observation of Lara in *Doctor Zhivago* reflects a vision basically akin to Orwell's: "The great misfortune, the root of all the evil to come, was the loss of faith in the value of personal opinions. People imagined it was out of date to follow their own moral sense, that they must all sing the same tune in chorus and live by other people's notions . . . " Out of his personal experiences of class, oppression and poverty, Orwell evolved the deeply-held personal values that give his prose style, besides the power to render the multi-dimensionality of a particular event or situation, a unique kind of moral flavour. In fact, Orwell's style grows so near to the subject that we no longer think of it as a style. His art and his individualist ethics confirm each other, and become inextricable. In his essay, **"Culture and Democracy,"** Orwell affirms his belief in the indissoluble unity of art and life in a single sentence: "Literature as we know it is inseparable from the sanctity of the individual;" and his commitment, born of his personal experience and personal vision gets so completely absorbed into the texture of his world-view that in the words of Woodcock, "it became the inner subject of his books, around which the action played like a continuous allegory in various forms, and even of his briefest and most occasional essays."

Again, in the case of Orwell, style is but a disposition, his characteristic address whereby he notifies his inner being and his moral vision. It is a style which imposes upon a human situation a political ideal and seeks to order the world in pursuit of ethical norms and values. His aim was to expose the evils of his society and to raise "political writing into an art." **"Why I Write"** is a self-conscious attempt to reconcile political motives and aesthetic achievement, and in many other essays and journalistic writings, he testifies to his concern for style and purity of language. Orwell's style is consciously and scrupulously subordinated to his ideas. While the plots of his novels are constructed to prove a definite thesis, the style and language in his pamphlets, essays and reviews are strictly in accordance with the subject in hand which is invariably argued from a moral point of view. It can be easily seen how Orwell's convictions about men and politics lead to ideas about the use of words. Not only his art, but also his ideas about art, have political bases. Orwell defends his choice of subjects by arguing his political purposes and the inevitability of politics. "In our age," he writes, "there is no such thing as 'keeping out of politics.' All issues are political issues . . . " This is Orwell's way of affirming the moral value of his work. He tells us: "And looking back through my work, I see that it is invariably where I lacked a politi-

cal purpose that I wrote lifeless books and was betrayed into purple passages, sentences without meaning, decorative adjectives and humbug generally." But it is important to note that Orwell never supported any kind of political orthodoxy. In his view, the writer cannot be chained to any political party. He was himself a rebel, and wrote for a cause from a rebel's point of view. In his essays on political subjects, Orwell's approach is objective and analytical rather than propagandistic. It is this fact and his use of language that isolate him from other pamphleteers and political propagandists.

He was conscious of the fact that in writing for a cause in an age of political upheavals, clear prose could be a very effective weapon. This brings us to Orwell's views on the purity and morality of language. The use of language, he believes, is both a political and a moral act. In few modern writers, there is such a conscious, vigilant and rigorous regard for the purity of English language as in Orwell. His whole personality is undoubtedly involved in ensuring its health and vitality. Between 1944 and 1948, Orwell was obsessed with the problem of political writing. During this period he wrote, amongst other things, **"The Prevention of Literature," "Politics and the English Language," "Why I Write," "Writers and Leviathan," "Politics versus Literature: An Examination of Gulliver's Travels."** He also edited, with Reginald Reynolds, an anthology of political pamphlets from the past, called *British Pamphleteers.* Something in the spirit of these pamphleteers spoke to his imagination. Their militancy and pugilistic tone, in most cases, bespoke a temperament that would have no truck with expediency and immoral compromises. Their language thus had a certain sincerity and authenticity which Orwell found hard to match in the prose of his time. "The present political chaos," says Orwell, "is connected with the decay of language, and that one can probably bring about some improvement by starting at the verbal end." His own efforts to achieve that "improvement" are evident in his essays on language, in his own careful style, and most elaborately in the principles of Newspeak in *Nineteen Eighty-Four.* On the morality of language, Orwell, the artist, and Orwell, the polemicist, come closest to a unified vision. To quote E. M. Forster, Orwell "was passionate over the purity of prose . . . for if prose decays, thought decays and all the finer roads of communication are broken. Liberty, he argues, is connected with prose, and the bureaucrats who want to destroy liberty tend to write and speak badly." Orwell believes that if men write and speak clearly, they are likelier to think clearly and remain comparatively free. The language of free men must be candid, vivid and truthful. Those who take refuge in vagueness do so because they have something to hide. Clear writing and clear thinking are impossible in a totalitarian state, and Orwell constantly pleaded for people to recognize that there was a very close connection between the decay of language and the stifling of freedom. Orwell connects obscurity in language, in particular, with Fascism. "Prose literature as we know it," Orwell tells us in **"The Prevention of Literature,"** "is the product of rationalism, of the Protestant centuries, of the autonomous individual. And the destruction of intellectual liberty cripples" a writer. In some ways, Orwell's thought appears to be somewhat simplistic and reductive. Though obscurity in language or style is no virtue in itself, quite often it becomes a genuine mode of expression as in Henry James or in William Faulkner. On the other hand, bare, clinical prose such as Hemingway's does not necessarily support an egalitarian or liberal vision. Nevertheless, Orwell has a point. Obscurity in language and obscurantism tend to go hand in hand, particularly amongst second-rate writers.

Orwell concluded that the English language was in a bad way, largely through its misuse by politicians, and that political writing in our time consists almost entirely of prefabricated phrases bolted together like the pieces of a child's Meccano set. It is the unavoidable result of self-censorship. To write in plain vigorous language, one has to think fearlessly, and if one thinks fearlessly one cannot be politically orthodox. He surveys the British history and observes that in the past, at any rate through the Protestant centuries, the idea of rebellion and the idea of intellectual integrity were mixed up. A heretic—political, moral, religious, or aesthetic—was one who refused to outrage his own conscience. In fact, the individual's right to prove all things and hold fast to that which is good is believed by Orwell to be the source of the distinctive literature of the past four centuries. He believes that the whole of European literature of this period is built on the concept of intellectual honesty. Orwell is also convinced that so long as there is a gap between one's real and one's declared aims, one turns to long words and exhausted idioms. "The great enemy of clear language is insincerity." Immoral politics would certainly affect language adversely. Orwell says: "In our time, political speech and writing are largely the defence of the indefensible. . . . Millions of peasants are robbed of their farms and sent trudging along the roads with no more than they can carry: this is called *transfer of population* or *rectification of frontiers.* People are imprisoned for years without trial, or shot in the back of the neck or sent to die of scurvy in Arctic lumber camps: this is called *elimination of unreliable elements.* Such phraseology is needed if one wants to name things without calling up mental pictures of them." Simone Weil, a writer who occupies in France a position similar to Orwell's in England, also attacks the immoral use of language in much the same way as Orwell. She writes: " . . . when empty words are given capital letters, then on the slightest pretext, men will begin shedding blood for them and piling up ruin in their name . . . " Orwell believes that there is a definite relationship between language, honesty of purpose and political commitment. Besides politicians, the immediate enemies of truthfulness, he feels, are the Press lords, the film magnates and the bureaucrats. He draws our attention to the fact that many of our inane comic-strips, sex novelettes and sadistic crime stories are nothing but half cousins to the "prolefeed" flooding from "Pornosec" in "minitrue's" Fiction Department.

As a moralist, Orwell immediately set about deciding how the beauty and purity of the English language might be preserved. Many other writers have advocated the purity of language from time to time, but they have done so from an aesthetic standpoint. In Orwell's case, however, the aesthetic instinct always gave way to the polemical on moral grounds. At its best, it was both an aesthetic and

ethical experience for him to use words with accuracy. To have done otherwise would have offended not only his conscience, but his sense of artistic integrity. He loved the English language for its range of tone, its grammatical simplicity, its large vocabulary, and its adaptability. But he was concerned that it was being polluted by politicians and American borrowings. In the essay, **"The English People,"** the language assumes the character of a simple, honest Englishman who finds himself exposed to temptations from the outside world. Orwell's general attitude is conservative and ethical, and he urges a purer and more English usage. Even during his last illness, his interest in the purity of language did not flag. T. R. Fyvel found him reading the newspapers and carefully noting any instances of journalistic misuse of words. In **"Politics and the English Language"** which has become a classic, Orwell has produced not only an acute analysis of the linguistic maladies, but also suggested some important rules for bringing the language back to good health. The health and vitality of the English language over the centuries was, for Orwell, primarily an ethical question. In its growth and maturity, he discerned patterns of a rational sensibility in search of moral and social stability. If the rough-hewn and wind-swept profile of Anglo-Saxon prose indicated the moral energies of an adventurous and sea-faring people, the gentle wash and swell of the prose in the King James *Bible* brought out, among other things, their spiritual yearnings.

Intellectual vigour and moral clarity are at the back of Orwell's lucid and powerful prose style. For instance, in his essay **"Lear, Tolstoy and the Fool,"** he says: "Give away your lands if you want to, but don't expect to gain happiness by doing so. Probably you won't gain happiness. If you live for others, you must live *for others,* and not as a roundabout way of getting an advantage for yourself." In fact, the morality of his language is almost instinctive, and his deepest literary commitment is to crystalline prose—prose "like a window pane"—which would not conceal truth. Therefore, he deliberately seeks to use what William Wordsworth described as "a selection of the language really used by men." Keith Alldritt in *The Making of George Orwell: An Essay in Literary History,* and John Wain in *Essays on Literature and Ideas* maintain that Orwell's simplicity results from the fact that his subject matter is simple. But I feel that in part his simplicity arises from one of the most praiseworthy features of his mind—his determination to see things in their essential reality and contingency. Most of the literary frills, accretions and encrustations were, in his view, a screen to hide the poverty of thought and experience. A mere froth of words indicated moral confusion. Paul Potts, therefore, is justified in claiming that the clarity of Orwell's literary style was the direct result of his genuine search for freedom. It is a consciously pure style, stripped and yet polished. It may be noted that honesty of presentation was for Orwell the fusion of an accurate and unprejudiced eye with a language that was simple, exact and elegant. Not since Swift, has there been a prose more powerful, lucid, flexible and eloquent than Orwell's.

Again, the myth of the proletariat leads him to conclude that "language ought to be the joint creation of poets and manual workers," and to the belief that when the educated classes lose touch with the working classes, the language suffers. Orwell says that the working classes are in contact with physical reality, and that they usually use simple, concrete language, and think of metaphors that really call up a visual image. In my view, by attempting to mix the lower class idiom with that of the upper classes, Orwell wants to achieve a kind of emotional integration between these two classes. Sociologically speaking, it is an effort to impregnate the language of the upper classes with energy and earthiness, and thus to keep the conduits of the English language flowing. Many sociologists and analysts believe that the energy of the working class idiom keeps a language from becoming dainty and effete. Slang and colloquial expressions, being down to earth, have at once a chromatic quality and an auditory appeal. This is a language straight from the pit or the solar plexus. However, Orwell's own language is not proletarian as such. Nor does he use slang and colloquialisms except, of course, in the dialogues involving working-class characters. What probably he suggests is the necessity of keeping the proletarian practice in mind. He would have, of course, liked the formal language of thought and argument to retain proletarian verve and concreteness.

Orwell emphasizes the importance of stylistic care, clarity and precision, or what Swift calls "proper words in proper places." The words chosen are those which say most about the important and serious things he has to say; and nothing comes between the reader and Orwell's intention. At its best, Orwell's prose has a plate-glass transparency, affirming the integrity of his world-view. This is particularly true of the essays and passages dealing with nature, animals, school days, tramping and the like. Whenever he has to describe an object or a person or an incident that falls directly in the line of his vision—**"Shooting an Elephant"** being a good example—, he shows a unique talent for precision, atmosphere and economy. No interregnum then intervenes to subvert, camouflage or circumvent the thought or emotion thus aroused. A perfect linguistic correlative is found to do the job. What he sees turns into a picture; and it has an *affective* truth about it. The craftsmanlike clarity which characterizes his prose was intended to portray with vividness the character of the visible world as he saw it, that almost Keatsian world where beauty and truth become each other's revelation in the same way as, in Orwell's view, the quality of prose is inextricably linked with the intention of sincerity. Orwell could render the sensuous aspect of a scene or a situation with a kind of studied elegance and economy. The apparent richness is achieved through a judicious interplay of sounds, sights and colours.

He knows that the style makes the beauty of prose. In his Notebooks and in **"Politics and the English Language,"** Orwell supports the view of Samuel Butler that a writer ought to take a great deal of pains to write "clearly, tersely and euphoniously." Orwell wrote many a sentence three or four times over. Thus, he tempered his style into a strong, fine, supple instrument and mastered the art of transparent style, brought it to a high degree of ease and confidence, and always wrote fluently and plentifully. He acknowledged in 1940: "I believe the modern writer who has influenced me most is Somerset Maugham, whom I admire for his power of telling a story straight-forwardly and without frills." But there was a prose of another order also, as he discovered and responded to in the stories of D. H. Lawrence, a prose that was written with greater intensity than Butler or Maugham allowed for. The influence of D. H. Lawrence is discernible in the vivid descriptions of landscape in **Burmese Days** and in his essays embodying his nostalgia for the past.

Orwell's imagination evokes a peculiar reverence for what is physical and factual. That is why, his most memorable scenes are those in which he depicts human misery, humiliation and defeat. **Down and Out in Paris and London, The Road to Wigan Pier** and many of his essays are full of such scenes. Again, his metaphors and tropes, drawn from the more concrete and intimate experiences of life, give his language and style a certain degree of earthiness. "The truth is," he writes in a review of Henry Miller's *Black Spring,* "that the written word loses its power if it departs too far, or rather if it stays away too long, from the ordinary world where two and two make four." A conscious contact with nature, "the world of appearances, facts, and laws" is morally so essential to him. He believes that to abandon nature is not only to debase the spiritual life, but to destroy the authenticity of the "autonomous individual." It is our contact with nature which alone can keep us simple, sane and humble. (pp. 184-94)

Orwell's ethics has a very specific influence not only on the content and form of his writings, but also on their reciprocal relationship. His autobiographical essays such as **"A Hanging," "Shooting an Elephant," "How the Poor Die," "Such, Such were the Joys,"** etc., and his autobiographical documentaries, **Down and Out in Paris and London, The Road to Wigan Pier** and **Homage to Catalonia** arise from an urgent moral feeling of the requirement to give expression to certain thoughts and impressions. John Mander writes that these essays and documentaries enabled Orwell to bring his real gifts into play. They represent, he says, "his most satisfactory achievement; the kernel of his creative work as a writer." Like most writers of autobiography, Orwell tampers with facts in the interest of artistic and aesthetic proportion and ethical emphasis. In each case, Orwell describes a situation or an event which is generally based on his personal experience, and then builds up his theme strictly from an ethical point of view, eventually narrowing the whole analysis down to moral-political polemics.

In **"A Hanging,"** Orwell identifies himself with the prisoner marching to the gallows: "He and we were a party of men walking together, seeing, hearing, feeling, understanding the same world; and in two minutes, with a sudden snap, one of us would be gone—one mind less, one world less." After the hanging, all have a drink together, native and European alike. The dead man is "a hundred yards away". Orwell suggests that it is only after a shocking incident that the white and the native can come out of their rigid psychical ruts and meet like human beings. By combining his falcon's power of observation and his keen but controlled humanism, Orwell gives his essay the shape of a tragic poem. The aim is to expose the protected victimizer to his victim, to make the white races and the ruling classes see and feel exactly what life in the "other world" is like. The nameless Indian coolie becomes a human being with the shift from "he and we" to "one of us" in the sentence quoted above. By creating a sudden and vivid bond between the condemned man and those on this side of the law, Orwell has, by an act of the imagination, drawn the reader into the orbit of his sympathies. Later in *The Road to Wigan Pier* he was to write: "I watched a man hanged once. It seemed to me worse than a thousand murders."

The whole atmosphere is vividly evoked mainly through an effective use of metaphor and irony, and this appeals to our moral sensibility. The essay begins and ends with description rather than argument. The subtle use of animal imagery is another remarkable feature of Orwell's style in this essay. When the prisoner raises the cry of "Ram! Ram! Ram! Ram!," the dog which has suddenly appeared on the scene, answers "the sound with a whine." It appears as if the world of nature were condemning the inhuman proceedings of the humans. Thus, the essay, despite its small scale, is a complete work of art, and the effect that Orwell creates reminds us of such writers as Camus and Kafka.

In the same way, in **"Shooting an Elephant,"** Orwell records a moment of sudden revelation—"the futility of the white man's dominion in the East"—which is characterized by a moral dilemma. The contradictions in the author's thoughts and the situation are skilfully depicted, through a nexus of ambiguities. ". . . All I knew was that I was struck between my hatred of the empire I served and my rage against the evil-spirited little beasts (the Burmese) who tried to make my job impossible." Although Orwell's attitude to his subject is complex, in the final analysis, it is a firm and subtle condemnation of imperialism. He dramatizes the real nature of imperialism, which is, that the wielder of tyrannical power is himself enslaved and brutalized in the process. Thus, driven by the collective will of the Burmese, he kills the elephant "solely to avoid looking a fool." The moral predicament of the author is symbolic of the moral position of the white races in the East. To achieve the whole effect, Orwell condemns a part of himself, of his experience and background. The subject and style become one. The style in this essay is, on the whole, simple, strong, economical, and capable of being adapted to a variety of uses—exposition, description, argument, criticism. To quote Tom Hopkinson, **"Shooting an Elephant"** ranked within his lifetime as a classic, and "gives an example of his prose style at its most lucid and precise." I may add that in point of the coalescence of autobiography, style and ethics, **"Shooting an Elephant"** is a seminal essay, and points forward to the mature essays of the forties.

Again, in **"How the Poor Die"** which is a sort of epilogue to *Down and Out in Paris and London,* Orwell's style and ethics are inextricably linked. In February 1929, Orwell fell ill with pneumonia while in Paris, and was hospitalized there. It was during this period that he got the subject-matter for this essay. The bureaucratic admission routine, the prison-like indifference, the unspeakable food, the dirt, the vermin, the smell, everything is described in min-

ute detail. Orwell comments on the condition of the poor in a hospital and exposes the callousness of doctors, nurses and medical students who regarded the poor patients as "specimens" for conducting their experiments. He tells us that there were many beds past which the doctor walked day after day, and many a time "followed by imploring cries,"; the medical students lacked all perception that the patients were human beings, while a nurse would stand beside the bed of a patient, "whistling, as grooms are said to do with horses." It is through such vivid pictures that Orwell authenticates his moral horror. The style is clean, vivid, taut and muscular. The situations and characters appear like etchings and carvings in stone. The moments of agony and shame and guilt have been caught as in a frieze.

The real subject of **"Such, Such were the Joys"** is what goes on in a child's mind: "A child which appears reasonably happy may actually be suffering horrors which it cannot or will not reveal. It lives in a sort of alien under-water world which we can only penetrate by memory or divination." But this subject is connected with the defective education system, and the evils of class-division. The division of the essay into sections shows the richness and variety of Orwell's thought. Autobiography interprets the past, and the author's life becomes the centre of the conflict and contradictions inherent in the Edwardian society, a society of which the Crossgates is a microcosm. In his characteristic simple but forceful style, Orwell succeeds in conveying the idea that tyranny succeeds in the world because

---

An excerpt from *Review of Henry Miller's* Tropic of Cancer

One result of the breakdown of religious belief has been a sloppy idealisation of the physical side of life. In a way this is natural enough. For if there is no life beyond the grave, it is obviously harder to face the fact that birth, copulation, etc are in certain aspects disgusting. In the Christian centuries, of course, a pessimistic view of life was taken more or less for granted. "Man that is born of woman hath but a short time to live and is full of misery", says the Prayer Book, with the air of stating something obvious. But it is a different matter to admit that life is full of misery when you believe that the grave really finishes you. It is easier to comfort yourself with some kind of optimistic lie. Hence the tee-heeing brightness of *Punch,* hence Barrie and his bluebells, hence H. G. Wells and his Utopiae infested by nude schoolmarms. Hence, above all, the monstrous soppification of the sexual theme in most of the fiction of the past hundred years. A book like *Tropic of Cancer,* which deals with sex by brutally insisting on the facts, swings the pendulum too far, no doubt, but it does swing it in the right direction. Man is not a Yahoo, but he is rather like a Yahoo and needs to be reminded of it from time to time. All one asks of a book of this kind is that it shall do its job competently and without snivelling—conditions that are satisfied in this case, I think.

George Orwell, "Review of Henry Miller's Tropic of Cancer," *in his* The Collected Essays, Journalism and Letters of George Orwell, *Secker and Warburg, 1968.*

most of its victims lack a voice. Orwell gives words to the world's silent victims. (pp. 195-98)

Sant Singh Bal, in his George Orwell: The Ethical Imagination, *Arnold-Heinemann, 1981, 254 p.*

Salman Rushdie　(essay date 1984)

[*An Indian-born English novelist, critic, and nonfiction writer, Rushdie is most widely known for his novel* The Satanic Verses *(1988), a symbolic and allegorical narrative that explores themes relating to good and evil, religious faith and fanaticism, illusion and reality, and the plight of Indians who have relocated to Great Britain. The book's publication sparked riots and controversy around the world, resulting in Rushdie's forced hiding because of death threats from various Muslim leaders who considered the novel blasphemous. In the following excerpt from his essay* "Outside the Whale," *Rushdie disputes the assessment of the relationship between politics and literature in Orwell's* "Inside the Whale".]

The title ["Outside the Whale"] derives, obviously, from that of an earlier piece (1940) by . . . Mr Orwell. And as I'm going to dispute its assertions about the relationship between politics and literature, I must of necessity begin by offering a summary of that essay, **'Inside the Whale'.**

It opens with a largely admiring analysis of the writing of Henry Miller:

> On the face of it no material could be less promising. When *Tropic of Cancer* was published the Italians were marching into Abyssinia and Hitler's concentration camps were already bulging . . . It did not seem to be a moment at which a novel of outstanding value was likely to be written about American dead-beats cadging drinks in the Latin Quarter. Of course a novelist is not obliged to write directly about contemporary history, but a novelist who simply disregards the major public events of the moment is generally either a footler or a plain idiot. From a mere account of the subject matter of *Tropic of Cancer,* most people would probably assume it to be no more than a bit of naughty-naughty left over from the twenties. Actually, nearly everyone who read it saw at once that it was . . . a very remarkable book. How or why remarkable?

His attempt to answer that question takes Orwell down more and more tortuous roads. He ascribes to Miller the gift of opening up a new world 'not by revealing what is strange, but by revealing what is familiar.' He praises him for using English 'as a spoken language, but spoken *without fear,* i.e., without fear of rhetoric or of the unusual or poetic word. It is a flowing, swelling prose, a prose with rhythms in it.' And most crucially, he likens Miller to Whitman, 'for what he is saying, after all, is "I accept".'

Around here things begin to get a little bizarre. Orwell quite fairly points out that to say 'I accept' in life in the thirties 'is to say that you accept concentration camps, rubber truncheons, Hitler, Stalin, bombs, aeroplanes, tinned food, machine-guns, *putsches,* purges, slogans, Be-

daux belts, gas masks, submarines, spies, provocateurs, press censorship, secret prisons, aspirins, Hollywood films and political murders.' (No, I don't know what a Bedaux belt is, either.) But in the very next paragraph he tells us that 'precisely because, in one sense, he is passive to experience, Miller is able to get nearer to the ordinary man than is possible to more purposive writers. For the ordinary man is also passive.' Characterizing the ordinary man as a victim, he then claims that only the Miller type of victim-books, 'nonpolitical, . . . non-ethical, . . . non-literary, . . . noncontemporary', can speak with the people's voice. So to accept concentration camps and Bedaux belts turns out to be pretty worthwhile, after all.

There follows an attack on literary fashion. Orwell, a thirty-seven-year-old patriarch, tells us that 'when one says that a writer is fashionable one practically always means that he is admired by people under thirty.' At first he picks easy targets—A. E. Housman's 'roselipt maidens' and Rupert Brooke's 'Grantchester' ('a sort of accumulated vomit from a stomach stuffed with place-names'). But then the polemic is widened to include 'the movement,' the politically committed generation of Auden and Spender and MacNeice. 'On the whole,' Orwell says, 'the literary history of the thirties seems to justify the opinion that a writer does well to keep out of politics.' It is true he scores some points, as when he indicates the bourgeois, boarding-school origins of just about all these literary radicals, or when he connects the popularity of Communism among British intellectuals to the general middle-class disillusion with all traditional values: 'Patriotism, religion, the Empire, the family, the sanctity of marriage, the Old School Tie, birth, breeding, honour, discipline—anyone of ordinary education could turn the whole lot of them inside out in three minutes.' In this vacuum of ideology, he suggests, there was still 'the need for something to believe in,' and Stalinist Communism filled the void.

Returning to Henry Miller, Orwell takes up and extends Miller's comparison of Anaïs Nin to Jonah in the whale's belly.

> The whale's belly is simply a womb big enough for an adult . . . a storm that would sink all the battleships in the world would hardly reach you as an echo . . . Miller himself is inside the whale, . . . a willing Jonah . . . He feels no impulse to alter or control the process that he is undergoing. He has performed the essential Jonah act of allowing himself to be swallowed, remaining passive, *accepting.* It will be seen what this amounts to. It is a species of quietism.

And at the end of this curious essay, Orwell—who began by describing writers who ignored contemporary reality as 'usually footlers or plain idiots'—*embraces* and *espouses* this quietist philosophy, this cetacean version of Pangloss's exhortation to *'cultiver notre jardin.'* 'Progress and reaction,' Orwell concludes, 'have both turned out to be swindles. Seemingly there is nothing left but quietism—robbing reality of its terrors by simply submitting to it. Get inside the whale—or rather, admit you are inside the whale (for you *are,* of course). Give yourself over to the world-process . . . simply accept it, endure it, record it.

That seems to be the formula that any sensitive novelist is now likely to adopt.'

The sensitive novelist's reasons are to be found in the essay's last sentence, in which Orwell speaks of 'the *impossibility* of any major literature until the world has shaken itself into its new shape.'

And we are told that fatalism is a quality of Indian thought.

It is impossible not to include in any response to **'Inside the Whale'** the suggestion that Orwell's argument is much impaired by his choice, for a quietist model, of Henry Miller. In the forty-four years since the essay was first published, Miller's reputation has more or less completely evaporated, and he now looks to be very little more than the happy pornographer beneath whose scatological surface Orwell saw such improbable depths. If we, in 1984, are asked to choose between, on the one hand, the Miller of *Tropic of Cancer* and 'the first hundred pages of *Black Spring'* and, on the other hand, the collected works of Auden, MacNeice and Spender, I doubt that many of us would go for old Henry. So it would appear that politically committed art can actually prove more durable than messages from the stomach of the fish.

It would also be wrong to go any further without discussing the senses in which Orwell uses the term 'politics'. Six years after **'Inside the Whale',** in the essay **'Politics and the English Language'** (1946), he wrote: 'In our age there is no such thing as "keeping out of politics". All issues are political issues, and politics itself is a mass of lies, evasions, folly, hatred and schizophrenia.'

For a man as truthful, direct, intelligent, passionate and sane as Orwell, 'politics' had come to represent the antithesis of his own world-view. It was an underworld-become-overworld, Hell on earth. 'Politics' was a portmanteau term which included everything he hated; no wonder he wanted to keep it out of literature.

I cannot resist the idea that Orwell's intellect, and finally his spirit, too, were broken by the horrors of the age in which he lived, the age of Hitler and Stalin (and, to be fair, by the ill health of his later years). Faced with the overwhelming evils of exterminations and purges and fire-bombings, and all the appalling manifestations of politics-gone-wild, he turned his talents to the business of constructing and also of justifying an escape-route. Hence his notion of the ordinary man as victim, and therefore of passivity as the literary stance closest to that of the ordinary man. He is using this type of logic as a means of building a path back to the womb, into the whale and away from the thunder of war. This looks very like the plan of a man who has given up the struggle. Even though he knows that 'there is no such thing as "keeping out of politics",' he attempts the construction of a mechanism with just that purpose. Sit it out, he recommends; we writers will be safe inside the whale, until the storm dies down. I do not presume to blame him for adopting this position. He lived in the worst of times. But it is important to dispute his conclusions, because a philosophy built on an intellectual defeat must always be rebuilt at a later point. And undoubtedly Orwell did give way to a kind of defeatism and despair. By the time he wrote *Nineteen Eighty-Four,* sick and cloistered on Jura, he had plainly come to think that resistance was useless. Winston Smith considers himself a dead man from the moment he rebels. The secret book of the dissidents turns out to have been written by the Thought Police. All protest must end in Room 101. In an age when it often appears that we have all agreed to believe in entropy, in the proposition that things fall apart, that history is the irreversible process by which everything gradually gets worse, the unrelieved pessimism of *Nineteen Eighty-Four* goes some way towards explaining its status as a true myth of our times.

What is more . . . , the quietist option, the exhortation to submit to events, is an intrinsically conservative one. When intellectuals and artists withdraw from the fray, politicians feel safer. Once, the right and left in Britain used to argue about which of them 'owned' Orwell. In those days both sides wanted him; and, as Raymond Williams has said, the tug-of-war did his memory little honour. I have no wish to reopen these old hostilities; but the truth cannot be avoided, and the truth is that passivity always serves the interests of the status quo, of the people already at the top of the heap, and the Orwell of **'Inside the Whale'** and *Nineteen Eighty-Four* is advocating ideas that can only be of service to our masters. If resistance is useless, those whom one might otherwise resist become omnipotent.

It is much easier to find common ground with Orwell when he comes to discuss the relationship between politics and language. The discoverer of Newspeak was aware that 'when the general [political] atmosphere is bad, language must suffer.' In **'Politics and the English Language'** he gives us a series of telling examples of the perversion of meaning for political purposes. 'Statements like "Marshal Pétain was a true patriot," "The Soviet Press is the freest in the world," "The Catholic Church is opposed to persecution" are almost always made with intent to deceive,' he writes. He also provides beautiful parodies of politicians' metaphor-mixing: 'The Fascist octopus has sung its swan song, the jackboot is thrown into the melting pot.' Recently, I came across a worthy descendant of these grand old howlers: *The Times,* reporting the smuggling of classified documents out of Civil Service departments, referred to the increased frequency of 'leaks' from 'a high-level mole'.

It's odd, though, that the author of ***Animal Farm,*** the creator of so much of the vocabulary through which we now comprehend these distortions—doublethink, thought-crime, and the rest—should have been unwilling to concede that literature was best able to defend language, to do battle with the twisters, *precisely by entering the political arena.* The writers of the Group 47 in post-war Germany, Grass, Böll and the rest, with their 'rubble literature' whose purpose and great achievement it was to rebuild the German language from the rubble of Nazism, are prime instances of this power. So, in quite another way, is a writer like Joseph Heller. In *Good as Gold* the character of the presidential aide Ralph provides Heller with some superb satire at the expense of Washingtonspeak. Ralph speaks in sentences that usually conclude by contradicting their beginnings: 'This administration will back you all the way until it has to', 'This President doesn't want yes-men. What we want are independent men of integrity who will agree with all our decisions after we make them.' Every time Ralph opens his oxymoronic mouth he reveals the limitations of Orwell's view of the interaction between literature and politics. It is a view which excludes comedy, satire, deflation; because of course the writer need not always be the servant of some beetle-browed ideology. He can also be its critic, its antagonist, its scourge. From Swift to Solzhenitsyn, writers have discharged this role with honour. And remember Napoleon the Pig.

Just as it is untrue that politics ruins literature (even among 'ideological' political writers, Orwell's case would founder on the great rock of Pablo Neruda), so it is by no means axiomatic that the 'ordinary man', *l'homme moyen sensuel,* is politically passive. We have seen that the myth of this inert commoner was a part of Orwell's logic of retreat; but it is nevertheless worth reminding ourselves of just a few instances in which the 'ordinary man'—not to mention the 'ordinary woman'—has been anything but inactive. We may not approve of Khomeini's Iran, but the revolution there was a genuine mass movement. So is the revolution in Nicaragua. And so, let us not forget, was the Indian revolution. I wonder if independence would have arrived in 1947 if the masses, ignoring Congress and the Muslim League, had remained seated inside what would have had to be a very large whale indeed. (pp. 93-9)

Salman Rushdie, "Outside the Whale," in his Imaginary Homelands: Essays and Criticism 1981-1991, *Granta Books, 1984, pp. 87-101.*

Paul Fussell   (essay date 1988)

[*Fussell is an American critic, educator, and nonfiction writer. In the following excerpt, he discusses Orwell's commonsensical approach to criticism in his literary essays.*]

Doubtless many theatergoers imagine that one of T. S. Eliot's most characteristic and important works is *Old Possum's Book of Practical Cats,* just as numerous TV-watchers must conceive that *Brideshead Revisited* represents Evelyn Waugh's talent at its most distinguished. Certainly middlebrow consensus has long celebrated *The Old Man and the Sea* as Hemingway's greatest achievement. A similar fate has fallen upon Orwell. His two works most vociferously celebrated are **Nineteen Eighty-Four** and **Animal Farm,** despite their demonstrating precisely his lack of great talent for either science-romance narrative or animal fable. In both, his anxiety that the essayistic message get across regardless occasions frequent narrative stoppage, overall clumsiness, and even something like archness. And indeed, the parts of **Nineteen Eighty-Four** one remembers with admiration are not narrative but strictly expository—the descriptions of the government and customs of Oceania, for example, or the mock-philological Appendix on "The Principles of Newspeak." Orwell is by nature an essayist, and even in his more engaging novels, like **Keep the Aspidistra Flying** and **Coming Up for Air,** essays keep breaking in.

An essayist obsessed with values: that's a fair working definition of a critic in general, and it's a good description of Orwell in particular. Although not immense, his critical output is large and impressive, and the kind of writers he has chosen to work on suggests at once his critical leanings. He's drawn to satirists and malcontents, like Swift and Smollett, and to "manly" novelists, writers like Kipling and Gissing, Conrad and Charles Reade and H. G. Wells. No one could tax Henry Miller with effeminacy, and Orwell's enthusiasm for the rude demotics of *The Tropic of Cancer* constitutes one of the most persuasive tributes Miller has ever received. Orwell's frequent adversions to Lawrence and Joyce suggest his susceptibility to the solid and downright, the "daily," as well as the soundness of his taste for contemporary work. The list of authors in whom he shows little interest is as significant: he dilates on no Romantic poets, no Renaissance writers except Shakespeare, no Henry James or Virginia Woolf. Almost no Americans except Mark Twain. No Gide, no Proust, no Mann. A little bit of Russian novel, but not much. Little contemporary poetry except Yeats (Fascist tendencies noted) and Eliot (a great poet: too bad his piety makes him so silly). It's impossible to imagine him being interested in Wallace Stevens. He notices no literary theorists, philosophers, or aestheticians. In addition to essays on single authors, he performs numerous workouts in literary sociology, like the considerations of boys' weeklies and lewd seaside postcards and bookshop culture; and the treatments of the pamphlet as a genre and of Good Bad Books, of the psychology of the reviewer, and the respective attractiveness of books vs. cigarettes as things to spend money on. And preeminently, the essay **"Politics and the English Language,"** which, widely anthologized, is now as familiar to hundreds of thousands of American college students as James Harvey Robinson's "Four Kinds of Thinking" used to be.

One can learn a lot about a critic by inferring his favorite substantive of disapprobation. For example, Ben Jonson's might be *indecorum.* Dryden's, *dullness.* Samuel Johnson's, *unnaturalness.* Wordsworth's, *artifice.* Coleridge's, *incoherence.* Arnold's, *provincialism.* Eliot's, *romanticism.* There's no doubt about Orwell's, for he uses it frequently and forcefully: it is *humbug.* For all its weaknesses, he loves *Tropic of Cancer* because he detects no humbug in it, another way of saying that Miller registers without affectation "everyday facts and everyday emotions." Literary pomposity and mental dishonesty are Orwell's constant targets, and his aim is sharp partly because he knows the book business so well. It is not every critic who has had the advantage of working in a bookshop and seeing at firsthand the wide difference between what people praise and what they read. Orwell's street-smart instinct for the facts of books recalls Johnson's, and there are numerous Orwellisms fit to be compared with Johnson's observation, "People seldom read a book which is given to them." Satirizing one Martin Walter, a commercial "teacher of writing" who has claimed that his formulas for "plotting" have produced many successful writers, Orwell asks, "Who are these successful writers whom Mr. Walter has launched upon the world? Let us hear their names, and the names of their published works, and then we shall know where we are." The tone is that of Johnson asking James

Macpherson to produce the Ossianic manuscripts, as well as that of Johnson observing of Macpherson, said to have argued that there is no difference between virtue and vice, "If he does really think that there is no distinction between virtue and vice, why, Sir, when he leaves our houses, let us count our spoons." Orwell's nose for literary pretentiousness and cant is as acute as Johnson's sniffing out Thomas Gray's bogus classicism. "For anyone who wants a good laugh," Orwell writes, "I recommend . . . I. A. Richard's *Practical Criticism,*" that classic exposé of the pretentiousness and incapacity of a selection of Cambridge students of literature. Orwell did not attend a university.

Immersed in the book trade, observing all day behavior in the bookshop and the rental library, Orwell grows naturally into a skeptical and empirical critic. Confronting the great piles of remainders, he can't help noticing the ultimate fate of books pronounced, on their first appearance, masterpieces. He sees that their pages serve finally as food for worms, their dusty tops the graves of bluebottles. As he says in **"Confessions of a Book Reviewer,"** "It is almost impossible to mention books in bulk without grossly overpraising the great majority of them. Until one has some kind of professional relationship with books one does not discover how bad the majority of them are." Nor does one learn other things that a good critic must know, like the frequency with which the title of an essay or book is the creation of an editor, not the author, and even that elements of the author's text are often the result of an editor's insisting that you can't *say* that. As if he ate and slept with *A Tale of a Tub* by his side, Orwell shares Swift's vision of the relation of literature to the book trade, and he perceives in a very eighteenth-century way that although literature is many other things as well, one thing it surely is, is a social institution, that every act of reading is an implicit social transaction. Thus he likes to speculate about the social causes and contexts of literary phenomena, "the *external* conditions that make certain writers popular at certain times." Why, for example, was Housman all the rage in the teens and twenties? For one thing, he could be regarded as a "country" poet, purveying a form of nostalgic compensation to newly urbanized readers of the "*rentier*-professional class," as well as gratifying their snobbery about "belonging to the country and despising the town." Fake-civilized people, Orwell notes, "enjoy reading about rustics (key phrase, 'close to the soil') because they imagine them to be more primitive and passionate than themselves." The collapse of religion also lies behind the vogue of Housman, who was seen to be "satisfyingly anti-Christian." A few years later, after the Great War, anthropological pessimism came in (like plus fours). One read Spengler and went Abroad. Money was easy, and "Everyone with a safe £500 a year turned highbrow and began training himself in *tædium vitae.*" And so it goes. Literature is less the result of inexplicable subjective impulse than of compensatory social urges. Instructed by honest observation, Orwell learns in the bookshop about "the rarity of really bookish people," the frequency with which Austen and Thackeray are toted home from the shop but never opened. The opening chapter of **Keep the Aspidistra Flying,** depicting young Gordon Comstock's ennui and disdain working in Mr. McKechnie's bookshop and rental

library, is probably as good a guide as any to the essence of Orwell's critical understanding and method. "If we did get a writer worth reading, should we know him when we saw him, so choked as we are with trash?" He is fascinated by the pathology of literary bad taste and loves to display ironically the names of novelists (Ethel M. Dell, Hugh Walpole, Warwick Deeping) once thought as attractive as Herman Wouk, Leon Uris, and James A. Michener. (pp. 82-7)

When in **"England Your England"** Orwell specifies as characteristic of the English "the lack of philosophical faculty, the absence . . . of any need for an ordered system of thought or even for the use of logic," he comes close to autobiographical description. A vigorous independence of mind, a freedom from all critical theory and "schools," is Orwell's hallmark. He can't even be designated a Socialist critic, because his Socialism is constantly succumbing to an aristocratic awareness that quality and freedom matter terribly. In his essay **"The Prevention of Literature"** he sketches a description of the traditional good writer as necessarily a heretic: formerly, he says, "His outlook was summed up in the words of the Revivalist hymn:

> Dare to be a Daniel,
> Dare to stand alone;
> Dare to have a purpose firm,
> Dare to make it known."

"To bring this hymn up to date," he adds, "one would have to add a 'Don't' at the beginning of each line." For all Orwell's distance from conventional religion, his is the spirit of British Dissent, and when he is playing Daniel it is difficult not to think of Bunyan, Milton, or Blake. This is why there's no critic like him.

He is certainly in what he recognizes as "the Liberal tradition," but if he rather resembles Edmund Wilson in the breadth of his curiosity and the firmness of his principles, his is a much more political imagination—Wilson seems hardly to have recognized that the Second World War was taking place. And if he has quite a lot in common with Lionel Trilling, with whom he shares a similar social-moral sense, his impulses are more activist. "No one can embrace Orwell's works," says E. M. Forster, "who hopes for ease," and no one can go to his criticism with any hope of extracting a formula, dialectic, or method. For those now weary of the successive orthodoxies of neo-Marxism, structuralism, and deconstruction, he is a distinct relief. His only tools are sensitivity and intelligence, and they inform him that books are written by human beings who hope to make a "statement" about something, that "propaganda in some form or other lurks in every book," that "our aesthetic judgments are always colored by our prejudices and beliefs." Orwell knows that even poems are, willy-nilly, about something: that's why they stop when they've finished being about what they're about. His legacy to succeeding critics can be summed up in a word: sense. His awareness of the irrational element in humanity, in politics, and in writing and art keeps him from imposing rationalistic expectations that invite the erection of a structure of critical assumptions. In **"Wells, Hitler, and the World State"** he accurately locates H. G. Wells's defect: he can't conceive how people can be so irrational as to follow Hitler. "Wells is too sane," Orwell concludes, "to understand the modern world."

Just as he often echoes Johnson in tone and texture, so in his general critical approach. When Voltaire denigrated Shakespeare for his inattention to the classical unities and for the mess and irrationality of his works, Johnson defended him vigorously and Britishly: literature is what works empirically, not what assumes proper shapes. Likewise Orwell defends Shakespeare on the same grounds from the attacks of Tolstoy, who demands of a great author some highminded view, philosophical or religious, of life in general, together with a nearer approach than Shakespeare shows to an orderly, systematic, sensible technique. Tolstoy demands in an author, Orwell says, "dignity of subject-matter, sincerity, and good craftsmanship. . . . As Shakespeare is debased in outlook, slipshod in execution and incapable of being sincere even for a moment, he obviously stands condemned." But now Orwell brings up "a difficult question": "If Shakespeare is all that Tolstoy has shown him to be, how did he ever come to be so generally admired?" Orwell's answer, like Johnson's, is to invoke the irrational but human nature of the common reader. "There is no argument by which one can defend a poem. It defends itself by surviving, or it is indefensible." On that firm skeptical hook Orwell, quintessential British empiricist as he is, hangs all his criticism.

Because one's critical operations are not rational, one can honestly take pleasure in writings one knows to be artistically defective. "Art is not the same thing as cerebration," Orwell observes in his little essay on **"Good Bad Books."** "One can be amused or excited or moved by a book that one's intellect simply refuses to take seriously." For Orwell, critical systems are a totalitarianism, a menace in literature as in life. While wondering how a second-rater like H. G. Wells achieved such a powerful hold on the young of his generation, Orwell drops in a significant *systematically:*

> Back in the nineteen-hundreds it was a wonderful experience for a boy to discover H. G. Wells. There you were, in a world of pedants, clergymen, and golfers, with your future employers exhorting you to "get on or get out," your parents *systematically* warping your sexual life, and your dull-witted schoolmasters sniggering over their Latin tags; and here was this wonderful man . . . who *knew* that the future was not going to be what respectable people imagined.

The *ad hoc* is thus always preferable to any system. Orwell's loyalty to the empirical in part reflects his almost neurotic sensitivity to physical reality. His critical sensibility is nourished by the details of life—chairs and tables, coins, type sizes, printed ephemera, ordinary people. "Not uninteresting" is a phrase that recurs. His behavior illustrates Terence's *Homo sum; humani nil a me alienum puto.* "For casual reading—in your bath, for instance, or late at night when you are too tired to go to bed, or in the odd quarter of an hour before lunch—there is nothing to touch a back number of the *Girl's Own Paper.*" For him, the trouble with literary people, theoretical critics, and the "left intelligentsia" is "emotional shallowness": they "live in a world of ideas and have little contact with physical

reality." When the reference book *Twentieth Century Authors* solicited an autobiographical note, he declared that his business was to "write books and raise hens and vegetables." Indeed, "Outside my work the thing I care most about is gardening, especially vegetable gardening." What other literary critic would include, as part of his career, experience as a tramp and a resident of "Common Lodging Houses"? Of what other critic writing in the early forties could it be said, as Frederic Warburg, his editor and publisher, has said of Orwell, "He was . . . a very keen Home Guard sergeant"? We can begin to infer some critical obligations identifiable as Orwellian:

1. The critic should read everything all the time—labels, signs, pamphlets, corporate reports, college catalogs, poems, novels, plays, "non-fiction," press releases—the lot. His business is language and its behavior in relation to human beings and their desires. The critic should beware generic snobbery—literature has its social classes just like life.

2. He should go in fear of any orthodoxy, political, religious, nationalistic, or literary.

3. Skeptical of orthodoxies, the critic should exercise his sense of humor and proportion and develop his capacity to take pleasure, sheer pleasure, in reading and writing.

4. He should be interested in everything: the love life of toads, the way tortoises drink and the poor die, the dynamics of anti-Semitism, the differences between Caslon and sans-serif types, the motives impelling ordinary people to read, why books get written at all, the price of food, the reason women do not as a rule become stamp collectors, and the reason shipwrecks and trial scenes are literary staples. The critic should be able, like Orwell, to get an idea of the riches of the New World by noting of Mark Twain's America that the smallest coin then circulating was equivalent not to a British penny but a British shilling.

5. In his critical writing he should strive for absolute honesty, even at the cost of occasional personal humiliation. "To see what is in front of one's nose needs a constant struggle," he says, and he knows that many of one's youthful enthusiasms would sorely embarrass the mature critic. As Orwell puts it: "I think that any critic . . . must have many passages in his youth that he would willingly keep dark." (How often do we hear from a critic that at one time he greatly admired e e cummings or Somerset Maugham?) "Lies" really bother him, and Gordon Comstock's indictment of advertising as nothing but lying is heartfelt Orwell, a foretaste of his later outraged assault on the language of political duplicity. The main thing he admires in Smollett is his "outstanding intellectual honesty." He exhorts intellectuals to look into themselves without equivocation for traces of anti-Semitism, having noticed that the writer deploring it most often "fails to start his investigation in the one place where he could get hold of some reliable evidence—that is, in his own mind."

Anatomized this way, Orwell might seem merely bluff and simpleminded, strong, to be sure, but wanting in subtlety and artistic guile. But actually he is a master of the kind of critical discourse that turns on itself, that plays with the reader, establishing a tactical dynamics of ambiguity, surprise, dualism, even fruitful contradiction. For example: in the early part of his essay on Dickens, he seems to invite us to patronize Dickens as something close to "a reactionary humbug" who counts on "a change of heart" to ameliorate the human condition. And the reader comfortably settles into this position. But actually, Orwell goes on, looked at from a slightly different angle, Dickens appears a thoroughgoing hater of tyranny and thus a genuine, though "moral," revolutionary: "It is not at all certain that a merely moral criticism of society may not be just as 'revolutionary'—and revolution, after all, means turning things upside down—as the politico-economic criticism which is fashionable at this moment [1939]." In real life and in Dickens—and we can add in Orwell as well— "The moralist and the revolutionary are constantly undermining each other." Hence the necessity of ambiguity and complication.

Orwell performs a similar operation in his essay on Kipling. First, he attacks him with all the usual charges: he is undeniably a sadist, a "pre-Fascist," an imperialist. But the "turn" to a less moralistic, self-righteous view of Kipling operates as an invitation to the reader to peer into himself:

> We all live by robbing Asiatic coolies, and those of us who are "enlightened" all maintain that those coolies ought to be set free; but our standard of living, and hence our "enlightenment," demands that the robbery shall continue.

And as Orwell proceeds, he turns Kipling around until the reader is obliged to see another side: Kipling the hater of war and the writer of some of the best good bad poetry in English, from which no one but "a snob and a liar" could deny receiving pleasure. Kipling had "a certain grip on reality," and it was not his fault that reality was what it was. If it is true that he identified himself with a fatuous ruling class, "he gained a corresponding advantage from having at least tried to imagine what action and responsibility are like." Furthermore, "It is a great thing in his favor that he is not witty, not 'daring,' has no wish to *épater les bourgeois.*" Conducted through these twists and turns of balancing and weighing, the reader has been brought to discrimination. He is finally asked to confront this critical paradox and to make of it what he may: "Kipling deals in thoughts which are both vulgar and permanent." Like Shakespeare, but of course not as good. Here as everywhere, dogmatic, monolithic certainty is the critical enemy. Is it a good thing to be, like Henry Miller, inside the whale, protected by one's "art" from noticing the larger troubles of the outside world? Well, yes, in one way, any appearance at all of "the autonomous individual" being a refreshing sight in a world of totalitarians and zombies. In another way, of course, not at all. In fact, quite irresponsible. And yet—

Such complicated unwillingness to decide absolutely finds a corollary in one of Orwell's most notable stylistic techniques. He will often combine two quite contradictory rhetorical gestures, one, as it were, giving, the other taking away. On the one hand, an enactment of total sincerity, as in the *earnestly* in "I earnestly counsel anyone who has not done so to read . . . *Tropic of Cancer.*" Or sometimes

recourse to the "sincere" second-person address: "You never walk far through any poor quarter of any big town without coming upon a small newsagent's shop." Or, after quoting an apparently odd utterance by Cyril Connolly: "When you read the second sentence in this passage, your natural impulse is to look for the misprint." But on the other hand, while such gestures of intimate honesty are going on, an equal but opposite movement will begin to take place: obvious exaggeration and overstatement and even "lying," as in the *never* and the *anys* in the sentence about the newsagent's shop. One passage in **"Inside the Whale"** very clearly exemplifies this characteristic double movement. It begins with what appears to be honest confession, motivated by a sincere desire to be accurate and fair, an opponent of exaggeration:

> Some years ago I described Auden as "a sort of gutless Kipling." As criticism this was quite unworthy, indeed it was merely a spiteful remark, but it is a fact that in Auden's work, especially his earlier work, an atmosphere of uplift— something rather like Kipling's *If* or Newbolt's *Play up, Play up and Play the Game!*—never seems to be very far away.

Thus far honest discrimination. Now for the opposite, the irresponsible, misleading exaggeration, pivoting on words like *pure* and *exact.*

> Take, for instance, a poem like "You're leaving now, and it's up to you boys." It is pure scoutmaster, the exact note of the ten-minutes' straight talk on the dangers of self-abuse.

The effect is of course comic, and one impression given off is that criticism is an activity too human for solemnity. Or inappropriate exactitude.

Such a glance at Orwell's verbal technique may prompt the question, How well should a critic write? F. R. Leavis, says Lachlan Mackinnon, "was doggedly determined not to write well," and one hardly goes to Kenneth Burke, William Empson, W. K. Wimsatt, or the later R. P. Blackmur for the pleasures of their prose. Orwell, on the other hand, asserts in **"Why I Write"** that writing an essay would be insupportable if it were not, in addition to an intellectual, "also an esthetic experience." "I shall continue," he says, "to feel strongly about prose style," and his feeling strongly about it makes his prose the clearest and least pompous in modern criticism. As he sees it, there are two moral defects which issue in bad writing: one is laziness, the other pretentiousness. He implies an immunity to both when, in **"Politics and the English Language,"** he comes out with the phrase "the work of prose-construction" to suggest what it takes to write well and goes on to list the techniques by which such hard work is "habitually dodged": dying metaphors, jargony verbs ("render inoperative"), passive voice, meaningless words, needless multiplication of syllables ("the fact that"). So flagrant are these techniques not just in political rhetoric but in art and literary criticism, he finds, that "it is normal to come across long passages which are almost completely lacking in meaning." For Orwell, one contributor of meaninglessness is the popularity among critics of terms which are mere emotional triggers. *Sentimental* was one in his day. "I once began making a list of writers whom the critics called 'sentimental.' In the end it included nearly every English writer. The word is in fact a meaningless symbol of hatred. . . . " Today he might zero in on *reductive,* or *simplistic,* or *authentic,* terms as offensive as *beautiful* in Orwell's day. The cause of bad writing, especially of criticism, is specifically "literary society." Things might improve, he suggests, if novels could be reviewed not by "reviewers" but by amateurs: "A man who is not a practiced writer but has just read a book which has deeply impressed him is more likely to tell you what it is *about* than a competent but bored professional."

Just as Pound (not one of Orwell's idols) was learning to write poems by the technique of excision, cutting everything not strictly necessary, Orwell was learning to do the same in prose. Rigorously jettisoning unnecessary words (usually prepositions or *gradus* modifiers) in order to let the meaning leap forth is one of his devices for achieving clarity, and at the same time suggesting a special sincerity and honesty. As he writes Roger Senhouse in 1948, "I may be wrong, but my instinct is simplicity every time." Thus he is proud to write **Coming Up for Air** without using a single semicolon, "an unnecessary stop." Warburg testifies that "nothing had to be done" with Orwell's copy. "Really nothing. Orwell as a writer was less trouble I should think than anybody I've ever met," which is to say that no one had to spend time cutting inert adjectives and removing padding from his sentences.

A critic's impulse to be simple and clear may be taken as a sign of personal generosity, evidence of a hope that many will be able to share his perceptions unimpeded. Orwell's personal generosity was remarkable, and it was fearless. In one of his London Letters to *Partisan Review* (Winter 1945) he invited all readers of that magazine visiting London (they would be American soldiers, largely) to look him up and talk literature and politics. He reminds them that during working hours he can be found at the offices of the *Tribune.* He then adds: "But failing that my home number is CAN 3751." I find that astonishing. Imagine any other well-known critic risking boredom by inviting hundreds of earnest aspirants to drop in anytime. If it's hard to imagine in 1945, it's harder to imagine today. Alfred Kazin just might do that. So might Irving Howe. Most American critics would not, including specifically Edmund Wilson.

But "saints should always be judged guilty until they are proved innocent," as Orwell says at the beginning of his essay on Gandhi. Orwell certainly has his defects and limitations. For one thing, once he goes much further back than the middle of the nineteenth century, his historical imagination fails him. He has trouble understanding a society which is not Liberal. This is the main reason he's not satisfying on *Gulliver's Travels.* While recognizing its context in "politics," he ignores its context in religious politics, missing, for example, the reason Swift satirizes the Dutch so vigorously—they were famous for religious toleration, which to Swift meant they were really crypto-atheists. As a religious skeptic and socialist, Orwell is a sucker for the Houyhnhnms and takes them as seriously as they do themselves. Skilled at some kinds of satire himself, he doesn't always seem to understand that satire is by nature negative and destructive, just as, say, pastoral is positive. It's Orwell's strong sense of justice that gets in the way. Humor fails him, for example, when he instances one of Swift's (or rather Gulliver's) wildly comic "lists" as evidence of Swift's "irresponsible violence." Gulliver asserts that his reconciliation with the Yahoo kind back in England

> might not be so difficult if they would be content with those vices and follies only which nature hath entitled them to. I am not in the least provoked at the sight of a lawyer, a pickpocket, a colonel, a fool, a lord, a gamester, a politician, a whoremonger, a physician, an evidence, a suborner, an attorney, a traitor, or the like.

Missing the point entirely, Orwell explains with weary, literal-minded patience: "The list lumps together those who break the conventional code, and those who keep it. For instance, if you automatically condemn a colonel, as such, on what grounds do you condemn a traitor? Or again, if you want to suppress pickpockets, you must have laws, which means that you must have lawyers." He concludes of Swift's performance here: "One has the feeling that personal animosity is at work." To which the only answer is, Yes. Orwell is too goodhearted to be trusted with eighteenth-century satire, and sometimes he talks as if the world always should have been modern, as if through some oversight it failed to be modern until the nineteenth century. In his essay on Dickens he seems disappointed that Dickens is not more like Jack London. And sometimes he allows his rage for justice to overcome his tact, as in his essay **"Looking Back on the Spanish War."** Most of it is written precisely in the rabble-rousing idiom ("the lords of property and their hired liars and bumsuckers") reprehended in **"Politics and the English Language."** And even in "politics" he sometimes exhibits astonishing blindness. For one thing, until the end of the war he can't conceive that the Germans are simply killing off the Jews. He is too nice to imagine that. As late as 1943 he understands that the vignette of "elderly Jewish professors flung into cesspools" conveys an image of extreme Nazi misbehavior and that adversion to "pogroms and deportations" virtually sums up the matter. What prevents his suspecting the worst is simply his insufficiently developed sense of evil. Wholly secular, he lacks an equivalent of the conception of original sin.

On the other hand, with contemporary writing he is wonderfully sound. Although he doubtless overrates Henry Miller—largely, one suspects, because he constitutes a stench in genteel nostrils—he knows that Lawrence and Joyce are good and that Sean O'Casey is not. He recognizes Eliot's distinction while condescending to his religion and despising his politics. He knows that the "modern" part of Quiller-Couch's *Oxford Book of English Verse* is a national disgrace. Acutely, he senses that something's the matter with Aldous Huxley, that his work will survive as little as Wells's. Orwell made as few mistakes as anyone in estimating the ultimate value of his contemporaries.

At this moment, as literary criticism grows daily more pretentious, more afflicted with delusions of power and authority, more "theory"-ridden and remote, Orwell is a refreshing counterweight, with his eye focused on such actual operative literature as Boys' Weeklies and seaside postcards. His example has doubtless encouraged a reawakened interest in the generic conventions of kinds of writing not normally in high repute as literature—travel books, memoirs, histories, and the like—as well as literary forms too daily and commonplace to be considered artistic, like letters to the editor and "personal," i.e., lonely hearts, classified ads. Their inevitable and touching element of self-praise ("Clever non-smoking intellectual man desires friendship with a woman who thinks and jogs") Orwell was entirely free of. He lived only forty-six years, and when tuberculosis killed him he died without self-pity or complaint, or even wonder. I think that, as well as his critical performance, sets a good example. (pp. 88-102)

Paul Fussell, "George Orwell: The Critic as Honest Man," in his Thank God for the Atom Bomb and Other Essays, *Summit Books, 1988, pp. 82-102.*

FURTHER READING

Alldritt, Keith. *The Making of George Orwell.* London: W&J Mackay, 1969, 187 p.
 Contains a section on the autobiographical aspects of Orwell's essays.

Brander, Laurence. "Literary Essays." In *George Orwell*, pp. 37-57. London: Longmans, Green and Co., 1954.
 Discusses Orwell's literary essays in light of his politics.

Calder, Angus. "Orwell: The Rarer Animal." *New Statesman* 76, No. 1960 (4 October 1968): 429-30.
 Reviews *The Collected Essays, Journalism and Letters of George Orwell*, focusing on the collection's biographical usefulness.

Elliott, George P. "A Failed Prophet." *The Hudson Review* X, No. 1 (Spring 1957): 149-54.
 Asserts that Orwell failed to construct an alternative ethos "because of the materialist rationalism which has been the binding spirit and philosophy of the age of science and which has at no time or place been stronger than during Orwell's generation in England."

Harris, Harold J. "Orwell's Essays and *1984.*" *Twentieth Century Literature* 4, No. 4 (January 1959): 154-61.

Illustrates how Orwell expanded upon the "raw materials" in his essays to create *1984*.

Meyers, Jeffrey. "George Orwell: The Honorary Proletarian." *Philological Quarterly* XLVII, No. 4 (October 1969): 526-49.
 Explores the relationship between Orwell's self-imposed poverty and the social and political agenda recurrent in his essays and semifictional writing.

——, ed. *George Orwell: The Critical Heritage.* London: Routledge, 1975, 392 p.
 Collection of critical essays and reviews of Orwell's work.

Spender, Stephen. "A Measure of Orwell." *The New York Times Book Review* (29 October 1950): 4.
 Reviews *Shooting an Elephant, and Other Essays*, remarking that Orwell "exists in his books like a rather flat but honest character-part, uttering stimulating and at times wonderful monologues, in a clear, hard prose."

Sypher, Wylie. "The Free Intelligence." *The Nation* 162, No. 21 (25 May 1946): 630-32.
 Mixed review of *Dickens, Dali, and Others*.

Thompson, E. P. "Outside the Whale." In *Out of Apathy*, edited by E. P. Thompson, pp. 141-94. London: New Left Books, 1960.
 Provides a Marxist interpretation of *Inside the Whale*, calling it "an apology for quietism."

Watson, George. "Facing Unpleasant Facts: George Orwell's Reports." *The Sewanee Review* XCVI, No. 4 (Fall 1988): 644-57.
 Asserts that Orwell created "existential literature" by "[reporting] an experience deliberately chosen, usually because of its hardship and danger, with a view to authorship."

Wilson, Angus. "Orwell and the Intellectuals." *The Observer* (24 January 1954): 8.
 Reviews *England, Your England, and Other Essays*, pointing out that the collection "illustrates admirably [the] combination of aesthetic devotion and political honesty which made [Orwell] so powerful a prophet, but . . . also illustrates certain serious blindnesses which are no less important."

Woodcock, George. *The Crystal Spirit: A Study of George Orwell.* New York: Schocken Books, 1966, 366 p.
 Contains a lengthy examination of Orwell's prose style in his essays.

James Whitcomb Riley

1849-1916

American poet, journalist, essayist, and playwright; also wrote under the pseudonym Benjamin F. Johnson of Boone.

INTRODUCTION

Riley was a popular poet best known for works about life in small-town and rural America. Born and raised in Indiana, Riley wrote about the people and places he observed during his travels in that state. Although many critics have maintained that Riley's poetry is sentimental and inartistic, others have applauded his ability to capture the essence of midwestern life in a style that engages a broad audience.

The son of a prominent lawyer, Riley was born in Greenfield. An uninterested student, Riley left school when he was sixteen, studied law briefly with his father, and then worked at a series of odd jobs, including summer employment as a sign and house painter and a musician with a patent medicine show. During this period Riley incorporated rhymes into the advertisements he painted and later read his poems as part of the medicine show. Returning to Greenfield, Riley began to contribute poetry and prose sketches to various newspapers and in 1877 was hired as a staff writer for the *Anderson Democrat.* Provoked by the ridicule of his poems in a rival newspaper, Riley perpetrated a hoax to prove that the only thing a poem needed to gain critical praise was the byline of a famous writer. Riley composed a poem, "Leonainie," which he claimed was discovered on the flyleaf of one of the notebooks of Edgar Allan Poe. Published in the *Kokomo Dispatch,* the poem created a furor among booksellers, critics, and scholars, who overwhelmed the newspaper with requests for the original manuscript of the newly discovered work. Riley's employers at the *Democrat* became angry with him for publishing his work in a competing newspaper, thereby depriving the *Democrat* of profitable publicity, and asked him to resign. Soon afterward Riley secured a position with the *Indianapolis Journal,* where he was a contributing writer from 1877 to 1885. During his employment with the *Journal,* Riley wrote some of his most famous poems, including "When the Frost Is on the Punkin," "Little Orphant Annie," and "The Raggedy Man," and he began to give readings of his works throughout the United States. His success as a poet and public orator brought him great notoriety, and his numerous speaking engagements made him one of the wealthiest American poets in history. He died in 1916.

In 1883 Riley published *The Old Swimmin' Hole, and 'Leven More Poems,* a collection of verse he had written for the *Indianapolis Journal.* Featuring pastoral settings and "country folk," these poems were written in the dialect of small-town Indiana. *The Old Swimmin' Hole* and Riley's other collections, including *Pipes O' Pan at Zekesbury* and *Green Fields and Running Brooks,* were praised for their combination of humor and pathos and their appealing portrayal of midwestern life. Critics maintain that Riley's best poems capture the essence of an era in American life characterized by a spirit of optimism. Although such earlier critics as J. C. Squire found Riley's themes simplistic, his rhymes hackneyed and forced, and his use of dialect cumbersome, later commentators have found his rendering of nineteenth-century midwestern dialect accurate and his treatment of small-town characters and settings vivid and appropriate, if somewhat idealistic. Riley's observations of quaint people, places, and language endeared him to large audiences and helped popularize poetry among American readers. As Indiana state senator Albert J. Beveridge remarked in 1908, "Riley speaks our tongue. His works are the language of the people. He is the interpreter of the common heart."

PRINCIPAL WORKS

The Old Swimmin' Hole, and 'Leven More Poems (poetry) 1883
Afterwhiles (poetry) 1887
Nye and Riley's Railway Guide [with Edgar W. Nye] (sketches) 1888
Old-Fashioned Roses (poetry) 1888
Pipes O' Pan at Zekesbury (poetry) 1888
Rhymes of Childhood (poetry) 1890
The Flying Islands of the Night: A Fantastic Drama in Verse (drama) 1891
Neighborly Poems (poetry) 1891
Green Fields and Running Brooks (poetry) 1892
Poems Here at Home (poetry) 1893
Armazindy (poetry) 1894
The Days Gone By, and Other Poems (poetry) 1895
A Tinkle of Bells, and Other Poems (poetry) 1895
A Child-World (poetry) 1897
The Poems and Prose Sketches of James Whitcomb Riley, 16 vols. (poetry and sketches) 1897-1914
Rubáiyát of Doc Sifers (poetry) 1897
Riley Love Lyrics (poetry) 1899
Home-Folks (poetry) 1900
The Book of Joyous Children (poetry) 1902
His Pa's Romance (poetry) 1903
Riley Songs O' Cheer (poetry) 1905
While the Heart Beats Young (poetry) 1906
The Boys of the Old Glee Club (poetry) 1907
Morning (poetry) 1907
Old School Day Romances (poetry) 1909
A Hoosier Romance, 1868 (poetry) 1910
Fugitive Pieces (poetry) 1914
Letters of James Whitcomb Riley (letters) 1930
The Complete Poetical Works of James Whitcomb Riley (poetry) 1937

CRITICISM

The Overland Monthly (essay date 1891)

[*In the following excerpt, the critic notes Riley's ability to represent childhood experiences using both dialect and "good English."*]

Poems of childhood are always sure of popularity. There is no feeling more universal in its application than that of sympathy with childish things. Not the sympathy that gives interest in the same thing a child finds interest in. It is rather a sympathy with those acts and feelings of childhood which attract us because of the simple humanity they display. Most of such actions and feelings are unconsciously experienced by the child, and would not probably interest him as they do older people. It is only when the older child looks back and judges them in the light of later experience that they seem either amusing or of special value.

From this standpoint James Whitcomb Riley's *Rhymes of Childhood* would be pronounced as addressed to grown people, rather than to children of the age and experience of those whose thoughts and feelings figure in these pages. It is a delightful book from cover to cover, and displays a rare insight into the habits of mind of the child. The dialect, too, is true to nature, and seldom if ever overdrawn.

But the success of the poems depends on an appreciation of the man in the boy, the detection of the beginning of the shrewdness and judgment of age in the apparently unconscious childish actions. The child himself would never be conscious of this, and would find his interest in simpler, more direct action. But if there is nothing else, there is for every one a tender reminiscence in the simple philosophy, the unconscious pathos, the secure trustfulness of childhood. The Raggedy Man bids fair to become a classic in literature. He is drawn in such broad lines that any one can fit him to a recollection of some "hired man" who made his young life happier; and who does not find an understanding of the human nature in the following?

Wunst we went-a fishin'—Me
An' my Pa an' Ma all three,
When they was a picnic, 'way
Out to Hanch's Woods one day.

An' they was a crick out there,
Where the fishes is, an' where
Little boys 't aint big and strong
Better have their folks along!

My Pa he ist fished an' fished!
An' my Ma she said she wished
Me an' her was home; an' Pa
Said he wished so worse 'n Ma.

Pa said, Ef you talk er say
Anything, er sneeze, er play,
Haint no fish, alive er dead,
Ever go' to bite! he said.

Purt' nigh dark in town when we
Got back home; an' Ma says she,
Now she'll have a fish for shore!
An' she buyed one at the store.

Now at supper Pa he won't
Eat no fish, an' says he don't
Like 'em.—An' he pounded me
When I choked! . . . Ma, did n't he?

. . . . .

You better not fool with a Bumble-bee!—
Ef you don't think they can sting—you'll see!
They're lazy to look at, an' kindo' go
Buzzin' an' buzzin' aroun' so slow,
An' ac' so slouchy an' all fagged out,
Danglin' their legs as they drone about
The holly hawks 'at they can't climb in
'Ithout ist a-tumble-un out agin!
Wunst I watched one climb clean 'way
In a jim'son blossom, I did, one day,—
An' I ist grabbed it—an' nen let go—
An' *"Ooh-ooh! Honey! I told ye so!"*
Says the Raggedy Man; an' he ist run
An' pullt out the stinger, an' don't laugh none,
An' says: "They *has* been folks, I guess,

'At thought I was predjudust, more or less,—
Yit I maintain 'at a Bumble-bee
Wears out his welcome too quick for me!"

There is another side—free from dialect—that is presented by this volume. In good English Mr. Riley has done some serious work that is worthy of attention. He has a good ear for melody, and a delicacy of expression that makes him expert at cradle songs and lullabies. His love for nature is the out-of-door affection of a boy. **"The Tonic of the Spring"** moves him and brings back

> The shadow of the open door,
> And dancing dust and sunshine blent,
> Slanting the way the morning went,
> And beckoning my thoughts afar
> Where reeds and running waters are;
> Where amber-colored bayous glass
> The half drowned weeds and wisps of grass;
> Where sprawling frogs in loveless key,
> Sing on and on incessantly.

And occasionally, in more pensive vein, one comes across a thing like this:—

> Lord! Kind Lord!
>   Gracious Lord! I pray
> Thou wilt look on all I love
>   Tenderly today!
> Weed their hearts of weariness;
>   Scatter every care
> Down a wake of angel-wings
>   Winnowing the air.
> Bring unto the sorrowing
>   All release from pain;
> Let the lips of laughter
>   Overflow again;
> And with all the needy
>   O divide, I pray,
> This vast treasure of content
>   That is mine today!

(pp. 657-58)

A review of "Rhymes of Childhood," in The Overland Monthly, *Vol. XVII, No. 102, June, 1891, pp. 657-58.*

William Morton Payne (essay date 1893)

[*The longtime literary editor for several Chicago publications, Payne reviewed books for twenty-three years at the* Dial, *one of America's most influential journals of literature and opinion in the early twentieth century. In the following excerpt, he maintains that Riley's nondialect poems are of higher quality than his works in dialect.*]

Mr. Riley's [*Green Fields and Running Brooks*] is largely in dialect, and dialect so treated as to open many a glimpse into the workings of homely human nature. But, excellent of its kind as all this work is, the author's talent appears to us better employed in efforts of a more serious sort. Is it not almost a waste of poetic energy to expend upon the restricted realism of dialect composition a power that commands, as Mr. Riley's does, the broader horizons of soul-life, and surprises the secrets of universal nature. Such a poem as the following two-stanzaed pearl is worth

many a string of dialect beads. The verses are of **"The Singer."**

> While with Ambition's hectic flame
>   He wastes the midnight oil,
> And dreams, high-throned on heights of fame,
>   To rest him from his toil,—
>
> Death's Angel, like a vast eclipse,
>   Above him spreads her wings,
> And fans the embers of his lips
>   To ashes as he sings.

Mr. Riley's insight into natural beauty is sympathetic and true. His **"Ditty of No Tone,"** "piped to the Spirit of John Keats," seems at the first glance a mere echo, but a closer study of its imagery shows the work to be essentially the author's own. We quote the second of three stanzas:

> Deep silences in woody isles wherethrough
>   Cool paths go loitering, and where the trill
> Of best-remembered birds hath something new
>   In cadence for the hearing—lingering still
> Through all the open day that lies beyond;
>   Reaches of pasture-lands, vine-wreathen oaks,
>   Majestic still in pathos of decay;—
> The road—the wayside pond
>   Wherein the dragon-fly an instant soaks
>   His filmy wing-tips ere he flits away.

Note the entire absence of predication—so marked a characteristic of modern poetry. Note also the exquisite selection of material and felicity of diction. Such poetry deserves very high praise.

Riley as a public speaker:

Riley's talent as a reader (he disliked the term recitationist) was hardly second to his creative genius. As an actor—in such parts, for example, as those made familiar by Jefferson—he could not have failed to win high rank. His art, apparently the simplest, was the result of the most careful study and experiment; facial play, gesture, shadings of the voice, all contributed to the completeness of his portrayals. So vivid were his impersonations and so readily did he communicate the sense of atmosphere, that one seemed to be witnessing a series of dramas with a well-set stage and a diversity of players. He possessed in a large degree the magnetism that is the birthright of great actors; there was something very appealing and winning in his slight figure as he came upon the platform. His diffidence (partly assumed and partly sincere) at the welcoming applause, the first sound of his voice as he tested it with the few introductory sentences he never omitted—these spoken haltingly as he removed and disposed of his glasses—all tended to pique curiosity and win the house to the tranquillity his delicate art demanded. He said that it was possible to offend an audience by too great an appearance of cock-sureness; a speaker did well to manifest a certain timidity when he walked upon the stage, and he deprecated the manner of a certain lecturer and reader, who always began by chaffing his hearers.

Meredith Nicholson, in her The Man in the Street: Papers on American Topics, *1921.*

William Morton Payne, in a review of "Green Fields and Running Brooks," in The Dial, *Chicago, Vol. XIV, No. 165, May 1, 1893, p. 282.*

Hamlin Garland   (interview date 1894)

[*An American novelist, short story writer, and essayist, Garland was a close friend of Riley. In the following excerpt, Riley and Garland discuss Riley's life and literary influences.*]

Riley's country, like most of the State of Indiana, has been won from the original forest by incredible toil. Three generations of men have laid their bones beneath the soil that now blooms into gold and lavender harvests of wheat and corn.

The traveller to-day can read this record of struggle in the fringes of mighty elms and oaks and sycamores which form the grim background of every pleasant stretch of stubble or corn land.

Greenfield, lying twenty miles east of Indianapolis, is to-day an agricultural town, but in the days when Whitcomb Riley lived here it was only a half-remove from the farm and the wood-lot; and the fact that he was brought up so near to the farm, and yet not deadened and soured by its toil, accounts, in great measure at least, for his work.

But Greenfield as it stands to-day, modernized and refined somewhat, is apparently the most unpromising field for literature, especially for poetry. It has no hills, and no river nor lake. Nothing but vast and radiant sky, and blue vistas of fields between noble trees.

It has the customary main street with stores fronting upon it; the usual small shops, and also its bar-rooms, swarming with loungers. It has its courthouse in the square, half-hid by great trees—a grim and bare building, with its portal defaced and grimy. The people, as they pass you in the street, speak in the soft, high-keyed nasal drawl which is the basis of the Hoosier dialect. It looks to be, as it is, half-way between the New England village and the Western town.

The life, like that of all small towns in America, is apparently slow-moving, purposeless, and uninteresting; and yet from this town, and other similar towns, has Whitcomb Riley drawn the sweetest honey of poesy—honey with a native delicious tang, as of buckwheat and basswood bloom, with hints of the mullein and the thistle of dry pastures.

I found Mr. Riley sitting on the porch of the old homestead, which has been in alien hands for a long time, but which he has lately bought back. In this house his childhood was passed, at a time when the street was hardly more than a lane in the woods. He bought it because of old-time associations.

"I am living here," he wrote me "with two married sisters keeping house for me during the summer; that is to say, I ply spasmodically between here and Indianapolis."

I was determined to see the poet here, in the midst of his native surroundings, rather than at a hotel at Indianapolis.

I was very glad to find him at home, for it gave me opportunity to study both the poet and his material.

It is an unpretentious house of the usual village sort, with a large garden; and his two charming sisters with their families (summering here) give him something more of a home atmosphere than he has had since he entered the lecturer's profession. Two or three children—nephews and nieces—companion him also.

After a few minutes' chat Riley said, with a comical side glance at me: "Come up into my library." I knew what sort of a library to expect. It was a pleasant little upper room, with a bed and a small table in it, and about a dozen books.

Mr. Riley threw out his hand in a comprehensive gesture, and said: "This is as sumptuous a room as I ever get. I live most o' my time in a Pullman car or a hotel, and you know how blamed luxurious an ordinary hotel room is."

I refused to be drawn off into side discussions, and called for writing paper. Riley took an easy position on the bed, while I sharpened pencils, and studied him closely, with a view to let readers of *McClure's* know how he looks.

He is a short man, with square shoulders and a large head. He has a very dignified manner—at times. His face is smoothly shaven, and, though he is not bald, the light color of his hair makes him seem so. His eyes are gray and round, and generally solemn, and sometimes stern. His face is the face of a great actor—in rest, grim and inscrutable; in action, full of the most elusive expressions, capable of humor and pathos. Like most humorists, he is sad in repose. His language, when he chooses to have it so, is wonderfully concise and penetrating and beautiful. He drops often into dialect, but always with a look on his face which shows he is aware of what he is doing. In other words, he is master of both forms of speech. His mouth is his wonderful feature: wide, flexible, clean-cut. His lips are capable of the grimmest and the merriest lines. When he reads they pout like a child's, or draw down into a straight, grim line like a New England deacon's, or close at one side, and uncover his white and even teeth at the other, in the sly smile of "Benjamin F. Johnson," the humble humorist and philosopher. In his own proper person he is full of quaint and beautiful philosophy. He is wise rather than learned—wise with the quality that is in proverbs, almost always touched with humor.

His eyes are near-sighted and his nose prominent. His head is of the "tack-hammer" variety, as he calls it. The public insists that there is an element of resemblance between Mr. Riley, Eugene Field and Bill Nye. He is about forty years of age and a bachelor—presumably from choice. He is a man of marked neatness of dress and delicacy of manner. I began business by asking if he remembered where we met last.

"Certainly—[Rudyard] Kipling's. Great storyteller, Kipling. I like to hear him tell about animals. Remember his story of the two elephants that lambasted the one that went 'must'?"

"I *guess* I do. I have a suspicion, however, that Kipling was drawing a long bow for our benefit, especially in that story of the elephant that chewed a stalk of cane into a swab to wind in the clothing of his keeper, in order to get him within reach. That struck me as bearing down pretty hard on a couple of simple Western boys like us."

"Waive the difference for genius. He made it a good story, anyway; and, aside from his great gifts, I consider Kipling a lovely fellow. I like him because he's natively interested in the common man."

I nodded my assent, and Riley went on:

"Kipling had the good fortune to get started early, and he's kept busy right along. A man who is great has no time for anything else," he added in that peculiarity of phrase and solemnity of utterance which made me despair of ever dramatizing him.

"He's going to do better," I replied. "The best story in that book is 'His Private Honor.' That's as good as anybody does. What makes Kipling great is his fidelity to his own convictions and to his own conditions, his writing what he knows about. And, by the way, the Norwegians and Swedes at the World's Fair have read us a good lesson on that score. They've put certain phases of their life and landscape before us with immense vim and truth, while our American artists have mainly gone hunting for themes—Breton peasants and Japanese dancing-girls."

Riley sternly roused up to interrupt: "And ignoring the best material in the world. Material just out o' God's hand, lying around thick"—then quick as light he was Old Man Johnson again:

> Thick as clods in the fields and lanes
> Er these-ere little hop-toads when it rains.

"American artists and poets have always known too much," I went on. "We've been so afraid the world would find us lacking in scholarship, that we've allowed it to find us lacking in creative work. We've been so very correct, that we've imitated. Now, if you'd had four or five years of Latin, Riley, you'd be writing Latin odes or translations."

Riley looked grave. "I don't know but you're right. Still, you can't tell. Sometimes I feel that I am handicapped by ignorance of history and rhetoric and languages."

"Well, of course, I ought not to discuss a thing like this in your presence, but I think the whole thing has worked out beautifully for the glory of Indiana and Western literature."

There came a comical light into his eyes, and his lips twisted up in a sly grin at the side, as he dropped into dialect: "I don't take no credit for my ignorance. Jest born thataway," and he added, a moment later, with a characteristic swift change to deep earnestness: "My work did itself."

As he lay, with that introspective look in his eyes, I took refuge in one of the questions I had noted down: "Did you ever actually live on a farm?"

"No. All I got of farm life I picked up right from this distance—this town—this old homestead. Of course, Greenfield was nothing but a farmer town then, and besides, fa-

ther had a farm just on the edge of town, and in corn-plantin' times he used to press us boys into service, and we went very loathfully, at least I did. I got hold of farm life some way—all ways, in fact. I might not have made use of it if I had been closer to it than this."

"Yes, there's something in that. You would have failed, probably, in your perspective. The actual work on a farm doesn't make poets. Work is a good thing in the retrospect, or when you can regulate the amount of it. Yes, I guess you had just the kind of a life to give you a hold on the salient facts of farm life. Anyhow, you've done it, that's settled."

Riley was thinking about something which amused him, and he roused up to dramatize a little scene. "Sometimes some real country boy gives me the round turn on some farm points. For instance, here comes one stepping up to me: 'You never lived on a farm,' he says. 'Why not?' says I. 'Well,' he says, 'a turkey-cock gobbles, but he don't ky-ouck as your poetry says.' He had me right there. It's the turkey-hen that ky-oucks. 'Well, you'll never hear another turkey-cock of mine ky-ouckin',' says I."

While I laughed, Riley became serious again. "But generally I hit on the right symbols. I get the frost on the pumpkin and the fodder in the shock; and I see the frost on the old axe they split the pumpkins with for feed, and I get the smell of the fodder and the cattle, so that it brings up the right picture in the mind of the reader. I don't know how I do it. It ain't me."

His voice took on a deeper note, and his face shone with a strange sort of mysticism which often comes out in his earnest moments. He put his fingers to his lips in a descriptive gesture, as if he held a trumpet. "I'm only the 'willer' through which the whistle comes."

"The basis of all art is spontaneous observation," I said, referring back a little. "If a man is to work out an individual utterance with the subtlety and suggestion of life, he can't go diggin' around among the bones of buried prophets. I take it you didn't go to school much."

"No, and when I did I was a failure in everything—except reading, maybe. I liked to read. We had McGuffey's Series, you know, and there was some good stuff there. There was Irving and Bryant and Cooper and Dickens—"

"And 'Lochiel's Warning'—"

He accepted the interruption. "And 'The Battle of Waterloo,' and 'The Death of Little Nell'—"

I rubbed my knees with glee as I again interrupted: "And there was 'Marco Bozzaris,' you know, and 'Rienzi.' You recollect that speech of Rienzi's—'I come not here to talk,' etc.? I used to count the class to see if 'Rouse, ye Slaves,' would come to me. It was capitalized, you remember. It always scared me nearly to death to read those capitalized passages."

Riley mused. "Pathos seems to be the worst with me. I used to run away when we were to read 'Little Nell.' I knew I couldn't read it without crying, and I knew they'd all laugh at me and make the whole thing ridiculous. I couldn't stand that. My teacher, Lee O. Harris, was a friend to me and helped me in many ways. He got to understand me beautifully! He knew I couldn't learn arithmetic. There wasn't any gray matter in that part of my head. Perfectly empty! But I can't remember when I wasn't a declaimer. I always took natively to anything theatrical. History I took a dislike to, as a thing without juice, and so I'm not particularly well stocked in dates and events of the past."

"Well, that's a good thing, too, I guess," I said, pushing my point again. "It has thrown you upon the present, and kept you dealing with your own people. Of course, I don't mean to argue that perfect ignorance is a thing to be desired, but there is not distinction in the historical poem or novel, to my mind. Everybody's done that."

Riley continued: "Harris, in addition to being a scholar and a teacher, was, and is, a poet. He was also a playwright, and made me a success in a comedy part which he wrote for me, in our home theatricals."

"Well, now, that makes me think. It was your power to recite that carried you into the patent-medicine cart, wasn't it? And how about that sign-painting? Which came first?"

"The sign-painting. I was a boy in my teens when I took up sign-painting."

"Did you serve a regular apprenticeship?"

"Yes, learned my trade of an old Dutchman here, by the name of Keefer, who was an artist in his way. I had a natural faculty for drawing. I suppose I could have illustrated my books if I had given time to it. It's rather curious, but I hadn't been with the old fellow much more than a week before I went to him and asked him why he didn't make his own letters. I couldn't see why he copied from the same old forms all the time. I hated to copy anything."

"Well, now, I want to know about that patent-medicine peddling."

Something in my tone made him reply quickly:

"That has been distorted. It was really a very simple matter, and followed the sign-painting naturally. After the 'trade' episode I had tried to read law with my father, but I didn't seem to get anywhere. Forgot as diligently as I read. So far as school equipment was concerned, I was an advertised idiot: so what was the use? I had a trade, but it was hardly what I wanted to do always, and my health was bad—very bad—bad as *I* was!

"A doctor here in Greenfield advised me to travel. But how in the world was I to travel without money? It was just at this time that the patent-medicine man came along. He needed a man, and I argued this way: 'This man is a doctor, and if I must travel, better travel with a doctor.' He had a fine team, and a nice-looking lot of fellows with him; so I plucked up courage to ask if I couldn't go along and paint his advertisements for him."

Riley smiled with retrospective amusement. "I rode out of town behind those horses without saying good-by to any one. And though my patron wasn't a diploma'd doctor, as I found out, he was a mighty fine man, and kind to his horses, which was a recommendation. He was a man of good habits, and the whole company was made up of good straight boys."

"How long were you with him?"

"About a year. Went home with him, and was made same as one of his own lovely family. He lived at Lima, Ohio. My experience with him put an idea in my head—a business idea, for a wonder—and the next year I went down to Anderson and went into partnership with a young fellow to travel, organizing a scheme of advertising with paint, which we called 'The Graphic Company.' We had five or six young fellows, all musicians as well as handy painters, and we used to capture the towns with our music. One fellow could whistle like a nightingale, another sang like an angel, and another played the banjo. I scuffled with the violin and guitar."

"I thought so, from that poem on **'The Fiddle'** in *The Old Swimmin' Hole.*"

"Our only dissipation was clothes. We dressed loud. You could hear our clothes an incalculable distance. We had an idea it helped business. Our plan was to take one firm of each business in a town, painting its advertisements on every road leading into the town: 'Go to Mooney's,' and things like that, you understand. We made a good thing at it."

"How long did you do business?"

"Three or four years, and we had more fun than anybody." He turned another comical look on me over his pinch-nose eyeglasses. "You've heard this story about my travelling all over the State as a blind sign-painter? Well, that started this way. One day we were in a small town somewhere, and a great crowd watching us in breathless wonder and curiosity; and one of our party said: 'Riley, let me introduce you as a blind sign-painter.' So just for mischief I put on a crazy look in the eyes and pretended to be blind. They led me carefully to the ladder, and handed me my brush and paints. It was great fun. I'd hear them saying as I worked, 'That feller ain't blind.' 'Yes, he is, see his eyes.' 'No, he ain't, I tell you, he's playin' off.' 'I tell you he *is* blind. Didn't you see him fall over a box there and spill all his paints?' "

Riley rose here and laughingly reenacted the scene, and I don't wonder that the villagers were deceived, so perfect was his assumption of the patient, weary look of a blind person.

I laughed at the joke. It was like the tricks boys play at college.

Riley went on. "Now, that's all there was to it. I was a blind sign-painter one day, and forgot it the next. We were all boys, and jokers, naturally enough, but not lawless. All were good fellows. All had nice homes and good people."

"Were you writing any at this time?"

"Oh, yes, I was always writing for purposes of recitation. I couldn't find printed poetry that was natural enough to speak. From a child I had always flinched at false rhymes and inversions. I liked John G. Saxe because he had a jaunty trick of rhyming artlessly; made the *sense* demand the rhyme—like

> 'Young Peter Pyramus—I call him Peter,
> Not for the sake of the rhyme or the metre,
> But merely to make the name completer.'

I liked those classic travesties, too—he poked fun at the tedious old themes, and that always pleased me." Riley's voice grew stern, as he said: "I'm against the fellows who celebrate the old to the neglect of our own kith and kin. So I was always trying to write of the kind of people I *knew,* and especially to write verse that I could read just as if it were being spoken for the first time."

"I saw in a newspaper the other day that you began your journalistic work in Anderson."

"That's right. When I got back from my last trip with 'The Graphic Company,' young Will M. Croan offered me a place on a paper he was just connecting himself with. He had heard that I could write, and took it for granted I would be a valuable man in the local and advertising departments. I was. I inaugurated at once a feature of free doggeral advertising, for our regular advertisers. I wrote reams and miles of stuff like this:

> 'O Yawcob Stein,
> Dot frent of mine,
> He got dot Cloding down so fine
> Dot effer'body bin a-buyin'
> Fon goot old Yawcob Stein.' "

"I'd like to see some of those old papers. I suppose they're all down there on file."

"I'm afraid they are. It's all there. Whole hemorrhages of it."

"Did you go from there to Indianapolis?"

He nodded.

"How did you come to go? Did you go on the venture?"

"No, it came about in this way. I had a lot of real stuff, as I fancied, quite different from the doggerel I've just quoted; and when I found something pleased the people, as I'd hold 'em up and *read* it to 'em, I'd send it off to a magazine, and it would come back quite promptly by return mail. Still I believed in it. I had a friend on the opposition paper who was always laughing at my pretensions as a poet, and I was anxious to show him I could write poetry just as good as that which he praised of other writers: and it was for his benefit I concocted that scheme of imitating Poe. You've heard of that?"

"Not from any reliable source."

"Well, it was just this way. I determined to write a poem in imitation of some well-known poet, to see if I couldn't trap my hypercritical friend. I had no idea of doing anything more than that. So I coined and wrote and sent 'Leonainie' to a paper in a neighboring county, in order that I might attack it myself in my own paper and so throw my friend completely off the track. The whole thing was a boy's fool trick. I didn't suppose it would go out of the State exchanges. I was appalled at the result. The whole country took it up, and pitched into me unjustifiably."

"Couldn't you explain?"

"They wouldn't *let* me explain. I lost my position on the paper, because I had let a rival paper have 'the discovery!' Everybody insisted I was trying to attract attention, but that wasn't true. I simply wanted to make my critic acknowledge, by the ruse, that I *could* write *perfect* verse, so far as *his* critical (?) judgment comprehended. The whole matter began as a thoughtless joke, and ended in being one of the most unpleasant experiences of my life."

"Well, you carried your point, anyway. There's a melancholy sort of pleasure in doing that."

Riley didn't seem to take even that pleasure in it.

"In this dark time, just when I didn't know which way to turn—friends all dropping away—I got a letter from Judge Martindale of the *Indianapolis Journal,* saying, 'Come over and take a regular place on the *Journal,* and get pay for your work.' "

"That was a timely piece of kindness on his part."

"It put me really on my feet. And just about this time, too, I got a letter from Longfellow, concerning some verses that I had had the 'nerve' to ask him to examine, in which he said the verses showed 'the true poetic faculty and insight.' This was high praise to me then, and I went on writing with more confidence and ambition ever after."

"What did you send to him?"

"I don't remember exactly—some of my serious work. Yes, one of the things was **'The Iron Horse.'** " He quoted this:

> No song is mine of Arab steed—
> My courser is of nobler blood
> And cleaner limb and fleeter speed
> And greater strength and hardihood
> Than ever cantered wild and free
> Across the plains of Araby.

"How did Judge Martindale come to make that generous offer? Had he been contributing to the *Journal?*"

"Oh, yes, for quite a while. One of the things I had just sent him was the Christmas story, **'The Boss Girl,'** a newsboy's story. He didn't know, of course, that I was in trouble when he made the offer, but he stood by me afterwards, and all came right."

"What did you do on the *Journal?*"

"I was a sort o' free-lance—could do anything I wanted to. Just about this time I began a series of 'Benjamin F. Johnson' poems. They all appeared with editorial comment, as if they came from an old Hoosier farmer of Boone County. They were so well received that I gathered them together in a little parchment volume, which I called *The Old Swimmin' Hole and 'Leven More Poems,'* my first book."

"I suppose you put forth that volume with great timidity?"

"Well, I argued it couldn't break me, so I printed a thousand copies—hired 'em done, of course, at my own expense."

"Did you sell 'em?"

"They sold themselves. I had the ten-bushel box of 'em down in the *Journal* office, and it bothered me nearly to death to attend to the mailing of them. So when Bowen & Merrill agreed to take the book off my hands, I gladly consented, and that's the way I began with them."

"It was that little book that first made me acquainted with your name," I said. "My friend and your friend, Charles E. Hurd, of the *Boston Transcript,* one day read me the poem 'William Leachman,' which he liked exceedingly, and ended by giving me a copy of the book. I saw at once you had taken up the rural life, and carried it beyond Whittier and Lowell in respect of making it dramatic. You gave the farmer's point of view."

"I've tried to. But people oughtn't to get twisted up on my things the way they do. I've written dialect in two ways. One, as the modern man, bringing all the art he can to represent the way some other fellow thinks and speaks; but the 'Johnson' poems are intended to be like the old man's *written* poems, because he is supposed to have sent them in to the paper himself. They are representations of written dialect, while the others are representations of dialect as manipulated by the artist. But, in either case, it's the other fellow doin' it. I don't try to treat of people as they *ought* to think and speak, but as they do think and speak. In other words, I do not undertake to edit nature, either physical or human."

"I see your point, but I don't know that I would have done so without having read **'The Old Swimmin' Hole,'** and the **'Tale of the Airly Days.'** "

I quoted here those lines I always found so meaningful:

> Tell of the things just like they was,
>   They don't need no excuse.
> Don't tech 'em up as the poets does.
>   Till they're all too fine for use!

Riley rose to his feet, and walked about the room. "I don't believe in dressing up nature. Nature is good enough for God, it's good enough for me. I see Old Man Johnson, a living figure. I know what the old feller has read. I'd like to have his picture drawn, because I love the old codger, but I can't get artists to see that I'm not making fun of him. They seem to think that if a man is out o' plumb in his language he must be likewise in his morals."

I flung my hand-grenade: "That's a relic of the old school, the school of caricature—a school that assumes that if a man has a bulbous nose he necessarily has a bulbous intellect, which doesn't follow. I've known men with bulbous noses who were neither hard drinkers nor queer in any other particular, having a fine, dignified speech and clear, candid eyes."

"Now, old Benjamin looks queer, I'll admit. His clothes don't fit him. He's bent and awkward. But that don't prevent him from having a fine head and deep and tender eyes, and a soul in him you can recommend."

Riley paused, and looked down at me with a strange smile. "I tell you, the crude man is generally moral, for Nature has just let go his hand. She's just been leading him through the dead leaves and the daisies. When I deal with such a man I give him credit for every virtue; but what he does, and the way he does it, is his action and not mine."

He read at this point, with that quaint arching of one eyebrow, and the twist at the side of the mouth with which he always represents "Benjamin F. Johnson":

> " 'My Religen is to jest
> Do by all my level best,
>   Feelin' God'll do the rest—
> Facts is, fur as *I* can see,
> The Good Bein', makin' me.
> 'Ll make me what I *ort* to be—' "

And that's the lovely Old Man Johnson talkin', and not *me*—but I'm *listenin'* to him, understand, yes, and keepin' still!"

The tender side of the poet came out here, and I said: "I had a talk with your father yesterday, and I find that we're in harmony on a good many reform topics. He's a populist and a greenbacker. Do you have any reform leanings?"

"Father is a thinker, and ain't afraid of his thinkin' machine. I'm turned away from reform because it's no use. We've got to *con*form, not *re*form, in our attitude with the world and man. Try reformin', and sooner or later you've got to quit, because it's always a question of politics. You start off with a reform idea, that is, a moral proposition. You end up by doing something politic. It's in the nature of things. You can, possibly, reform just one individual, but you can't reform the world at large. It won't work."

"All reforms, in your mind, are apparently hopeless, and yet, as a matter of fact, the great aggregate conforms to a few men every quarter of a century."

This staggered Riley, and he looked at me rather helplessly. "Well, it's an unpleasant thing, anyhow, and I keep away from it. I'm no fighter. In my own kind of work I can do good, and make life pleasant."

He was speaking from the heart. I changed the subject by looking about the room. "You don't read much, I imagine?"

He turned another quizzical look on me. "I'm afraid to read much, I'm so blamed imitative. But I read a good deal of chop-feed fiction, and browse with relish through the short stories and poems of to-day. But I have no place to put books. Have to do my own things where I catch time and opportunity."

"Well, if you'd had a library, you wouldn't have got so many *people* into your poems. You remind me of Whitman's poet, you tramp a perpetual journey. Where do you think you get your verse-writing from?"

"Mainly from my mother's family, the Marines. A characteristic of the whole family is their ability to write rhymes, but all unambitiously. They write rhymed letters to each other, and joke and jim-crow with the Muses."

"Riley, I want to ask you. Your father is Irish, is he not?"

"Both yes and no. *His* characteristics are strongly Irish, but he was born a Pennsylvania Dutchman, and spoke the German dialect before he spoke English. It has been held that the name Riley probably comes from 'Ryland,' but there's an 'O'Reilly' theory I muse over very pleasantly."

I saw he was getting tired of indoors, so I rose. "Well, now, where's the old swimmin' hole?"

His face lighted up with a charming, almost boyish, smile. "The old swimmin' hole is right down here on Brandy-wine—the old 'crick,' just at the edge of town."

"Put on your hat, and let's go down and find it."

We took our way down the main street and the immensely dusty road towards the east. The locusts quavered in duo and trio in the ironweeds, and were answered by others in the high sycamores. Large yellow and black butterflies flapped about from weed to weed. The gentle wind came over the orchards and cornfields, filled with the fragrance of gardens and groves. The road took a little dip towards the creek, which was low, and almost hidden among the weeds.

Riley paused. "I haven't been to the old swimmin' hole for sixteen years. Wc used to go across there through the grass, all except the feller with the busted toenail. He had to go round." He pointed at the print of bare, graceful feet in the dust, and said:

> We could tell, by the dent of the heel and the
>   sole,
> There was lots of fun on hand at the old swim-
>   min' hole.

As we looked out on the hot mid-summer landscape, Riley quoted again, from a poem in his forthcoming book—a poem which he regards as one of his very best:

> The air and the sun and the shadows
>   Were wedded and made as one,
> And the winds ran o'er the meadows
>   As little children run:
>
> And the winds flowed over the meadows,
>   And along the willowy way
> The river ran, with its ripples shod
>   With the sunshine of the day:
>
> O, the winds poured over the meadows
>   In a tide of eddies and calms,
> And the bared brow felt the touch of it
>   As a sweetheart's tender palms.
>
> And up through the rifted tree-tops
>   That signalled the wayward breeze
> I saw the hulk of the hawk becalmed
>   Far out on the azure seas.

Riley recited this with great beauty of tone and rhythm— such as audiences never hear from him, hearing only his dialect.

As we walked on we heard shouts, and I plucked Riley's sleeve: "Hear that? If that isn't the cry of a swimming boy, then my experiences are of no value. A boy has a shout which he uses only when splashing about in a pond."

Riley's face glowed. "That's right, they're there—just as we used to be."

After climbing innumerable fences, we came upon the boys under the shade of the giant sycamore and green thorn-trees. The boys jiggled themselves into their clothes, and ran off in alarm at the two staid and dignified men, who none the less had for them a tender and reminiscent sympathy.

All about splendid elm-trees stood, and stately green thorn-trees flung their delicate, fern-like foliage athwart the gray and white spotted boles of tall, leaning syca-mores. But the creek was very low, by reason of the dry weather.

We threaded our way about, seeking out old paths and stumps and tree trunks, which sixteen years of absence had not entirely swept from the poet's mind. Then, at last, we turned homeward over the railroad track, through the dusty little town. People were seated in their little back-yards here and there, eating watermelon, and Neighbor Johnson's poem on the "Wortermelon" came up:

> Oh, wortermelon time is a-comin' 'round agin,
> And they ain't no feller livin' any tickleder'n me.

We passed by the old courthouse, where Captain Riley, the poet's father, has practised law for fifty years. The cap-tain lives near, in an odd-looking house of brick, its turret showing above the trees. On the main street groups of men of all ranks and stations were sitting or standing, and thcy all greeted the poet as he passed by with an off-hand: "How are ye, Jim?" to which the poet replied: "How are you, Tom?" or "How are you, Jack? How's the folks?" Personally, his townsmen like him. They begin to respect him also in another way, so successful has he become in a way measurable to them all.

Back at the house, we sat at lunch of cake and watermel-on, the sisters, Mrs. Payne and Mrs. Eitels, serving as hostesses most delightfully. They had left their own homes in Indianapolis for the summer, to give this added pleasure to their poet-brother. They both have much of his felicity of phrase, and much the same gentleness and sweetness of bearing. The hour was a pleasant one, and brought out the simple, domestic side of the man's nature. The sisters, while they showed their admiration and love for him, ad-dressed him without a particle of affectation.

There is no mysterious abyss between Mr. Riley and his family. They are well-to-do, middle-conditioned Ameri-cans, with unusual intellectual power and marked poetic sensibility. Mr. Riley is a logical result of a union of two gifted families, a product of hereditary power, coöperating with the power of an ordinary Western town. Born of a gentle and naturally poetic mother, and a fearless, uncon-ventional father (lawyer and orator), he has lived the life common to boys of villages from Pennsylvania to Dakota, and upon this were added the experiences he has herein related.

It is impossible to represent his talk that night. For two hours he ran on—he the talker, the rest of us the irritating cause. The most quaintly wise sentences fell from his lips in words no other could have used; scraps of verse, poetic images, humorous assumptions of character, daring figures of speech—I gave up in despair of ever getting him down on paper. He read, at my request, some of his most beautiful things. He talked on religion, and his voice grew deep and earnest.

"I believe a man prays when he does well," he said. "I believe he worships God when his work is on a high plane; when his attitude towards his fellow-men is right, I guess God is pleased with him."

I said good-night, and went off down the street, musing upon the man and his work. Genius, as we call it, defies conditions. It knows no barriers. It finds in things close at hand the most inexhaustible storehouse. All depends upon the poet, not upon materials. It is his love for the thing, his interest in the fact, his distribution of values, his selection of details, which makes his work irresistibly comic or tender or pathetic.

No poet in the United States has the same hold upon the minds of the people as Riley. He is the poet of the plain American. They bought thirty thousand dollars' worth of his verse last year; and he is also one of the most successful lecturers on the platform. He gives the lie to the old saying, for he *is* a prophet in his own country. The people of Indiana are justly proud of him, for he has written **Poems Here at Home.** He is read by people who never before read poetry in their lives, and he appeals equally well to the man who is heart-sick of the hollow conventional verse in imitation of some classic.

He is absolutely American in every line he writes. His schooling has been in the school of realities. He takes things at first-hand. He considers his success to be due to the fact that he is one of the people, and has written of the things he liked and they liked. The time will come when his work will be seen to be something more than the fancies of a humorist.

As I walked on down the street, it all came upon me with great power—this production of an American poet. Everything was familiar to me. All this life, the broad streets laid off in squares, the little cottages, the weedy gardens, the dusty fruit-trees, the young people sauntering in couples up and down the sidewalk, the snapping of jack-knives, and the low hum of talk from scattered groups. This was Riley's school. This was his material, apparently barren, dry, utterly hopeless in the eyes of the romantic writers of the East, and yet capable of becoming world-famous when dominated and mastered and transformed, as it has been mastered and transformed by this poet of the people.

In my estimation, this man is the most remarkable exemplification of the power of genius to transmute plain clods into gold that we have seen since the time of Burns. He has dominated stern and unyielding conditions with equal success, and reflected the life of his kind with greater fidelity than Burns.

This material, so apparently grim and barren of light and shade, waited only for a creative mind and a sympathetic intelligence; then it grew beautiful and musical, and radiant with color and light and life.

Therein is the magnificent lesson to be drawn from the life and work of the Hoosier poet. (pp. 219-34)

Hamlin Garland, in a conversation with James Whitcomb Riley in McClure's Magazine, *Vol. II, No. 3, February, 1894, pp. 219-34.*

Bliss Carman   (essay date 1898)

[*Carman was a Canadian poet and essayist. In the following essay, he praises Riley's poetry for its lyrical quality and universal themes.*]

Even if Mr. Riley's poetry . . . had no claim to distinction in itself, the fact of its unrivaled popularity would challenge consideration. But, fortunately, his work does not depend on so frail a tenure of fame as the vogue of a season or the life of a fad. The qualities which secure for it a wider reading and a heartier appreciation than are accorded to any other living American poet are rooted deep in human nature; they are preëminently qualities of wholesomeness and common sense, those qualities of steady and conservative cheerfulness which ennoble the average man, and in which the man of exceptional culture is too often lacking. Its lovers are the ingenuous home-keeping hearts, on whose sobriety and humor the national character is based. And yet, one has not said enough when one says it is poetry of the domestic affections, poetry of sentiment; for it is much more than that.

Poetry which is free from the unhappy spirit of the age, free from dejection, from doubt, from material cynicism, neither tainted by the mould of sensuality nor wasted by the maggot of "reform," is no common product, in these days. So much of our art and literature is ruined by self-consciousness, running to the artificial and the tawdry. It is the slave either of commercialism, imitative, ornate, and insufferably tiresome, or of didacticism, irresponsible and dull. But Mr. Riley at his best is both original and sane. He seems to have accomplished that most difficult feat, the devotion of one's self to an art without any deterioration of health. He is full of the sweetest vitality, the soundest merriment. His verse is not strained with an overburden of philosophy, on the one hand, nor debauched with maudlin sentimentalism, on the other. Its robust gayety has all the fascination of artlessness and youth. It neither argues, nor stimulates, nor denounces, nor exhorts; it only touches and entertains us. And after all, few things are more humanizing than innocent amusement.

It is because of this quality of abundant good nature, familiar, serene, homely, that it seems to me no exaggeration to call Mr. Riley the typical American poet of the day. True, he does not represent the cultivated and academic classes; he reflects nothing of modern thought; but in his unruffled temper and dry humor, occasionally flippant on the surface, but never facetious at heart, he might stand very well for the normal American character in his view of life and his palpable enjoyment of it. Most foreign critics are on the lookout for the appearance of something novel and unconventional from America, forgetting that the laws of art do not change with longitude. They seize now on this writer, now on that, as the eminent product of democracy. But there is nothing unconventional about

Mr. Riley. "He is like folks," as an old New England farmer said of Whittier. And if the typical poet of democracy in America is to be the man who most nearly represents average humanity throughout the length and breadth of this country, who most completely expresses its humor, its sympathy, its intelligence, its culture, and its common sense, and yet is not without a touch of original genius sufficient to stamp his utterances, then Mr. James Whitcomb Riley has a just claim to that title.

He is unique among American men of letters (or poets, one might better say; for strictly speaking he is not a man of letters at all) in that he has originality of style, and yet is entirely native and homely. Whitman was original, but he was entirely prophetic and remote, appealing only to the few; Longfellow had style, but his was the voice of our collegiate and cultivated classes. It is not a question of rank or comparison; it is merely a matter of definitions. It is the position rather than the magnitude of any particular and contemporary star that one is interested in fixing. To determine its magnitude, a certain quality of endurance must be taken into account; and to observe this quality often requires considerable time. Quite apart, then, from Mr. Riley's relative merit in the great anthology of English poetry, he has a very definite and positive place in the history of American letters as the first widely representative poet of the American people.

He is professedly a home-keeping, home-loving poet, with the purpose of the imaginative realist, depending upon common sights and sounds for his inspirations, and engrossed with the significance of facts. Like Mr. Kipling, whose idea of perpetual bliss is a heaven where every artist shall "draw the thing as he sees it, for the God of things as they are," Mr. Riley exclaims:—

> Tell of the things jest like they wuz—
>   They don't need no excuse!
> Don't tetch 'em up as the poets does,
>   Till they're all too fine fer use!

And again, in his lines on a Southern Singer:—

> Sing us back home, from there to here:
> Grant your high grace and wit, but we
> Most honor your simplicity.

In the proem to the volume ***Poems here at Home*** there occurs a similar invocation, and a test of excellence is proposed which may well be taken as the gist of his own artistic purpose:—

> The Poems here at Home! Who'll write 'em
>   down,
> Jes' as they air—in Country and in Town?—
> Sowed thick as clods is 'crost the fields and lanes,
> Er these 'ere little hop-toads when it rains!
> Who'll "voice" 'em? as I heerd a feller say
> 'At speechified on Freedom, t'other day,
> And soared the Eagle tel, it 'peared to me,
> She was n't bigger 'n a bumble-bee!
>
> What We want, as I sense it, in the line
> O' poetry is somepin' Yours and Mine—
> Somepin' with live-stock in it, and out-doors,
> And old crick-bottoms, snags, and sycamores!
> Putt weeds in—pizenvines, and underbresh,
> As well as johnny-jump-ups, all so fresh

> And sassy-like!—and groun'-squir'ls,—yes, and
>   "We,"
> As sayin' is,—"We, Us and Company."

In the lines **"Right here at Home"** the same strain recurs, like the very burden of the poet's life-song:—

> Right here at home, boys, is the place, I guess,
> Fer me and you and plain old happiness:
> We hear the World's lots grander—likely so,—
> We'll take the World's word for it and not go.
> We know *its* ways ain't *our* ways, so we'll stay
> Right here at home, boys, where we *know* the
>   way.
>
> Right here at home, boys, where a well-to-do
> Man's plenty rich enough—and knows it, too,
> And's got a' extry dollar, any time,
> To boost a feller up 'at *wants* to climb,
> And's got the git-up in him to go in
> And *git there,* like he purt' nigh allus kin!

It is in this spirit that by far the greater part of his work, the telling and significant part of it, is conceived. The whole tatterdemalion company of his Tugg Martins, Jap Millers, Armazindys, Bee Fesslers, and their comrades, as rollicking and magnetic as Shakespeare's own wonderful populace, he finds "right here at home;" nothing human is alien to him; indeed, there is something truly Elizabethan, something spacious and robust, in his humanity, quite exceptional to our fashion-plate standards. In the same wholesome, glad frame of mind, too, he deals with nature,—mingling the keenest, most loving observation with the most familiar modes of speech. An artist in his ever sensitive appreciation and impressionability, never missing a phase or mood of natural beauty, he has the added ability so necessary to the final touch of illusion,— the power of ease, the power of making his most casual word seem inevitable, and his most inevitable word seem casual. It is in this, I think, that he differs from all his rivals in the field of familiar and dialect poetry. Other writers are as familiar as he, and many as truly inspired; but none combines to such a degree the homespun phrase with the lyric feeling. His only compeer in this regard is Lowell, in the brilliant Biglow Papers and several other less known but not less admirable Chaucerian sketches of New England country life. Indeed, in humor, in native eloquence, in vivacity, Mr. Riley closely resembles Lowell, though differing from that bookman in his training and inclination, and naturally, as a consequence, in his range and treatment of subjects. But the tide of humanity, so strong in Lowell, is at flood, too, in the Hoosier poet. It is this humane character, preserving all the rugged sweetness in the elemental type of man, which can save us at last as a people from the ravaging taint of charlatanism, frivolity, and greed.

But we must not leave our subject without discriminating more closely between several sorts of Mr. Riley's poetry; for there is as much difference between his dialect and his classic English (in point of poetic excellence, I mean) as there is between the Scotch and the English of Burns. Like Burns, he is a lover of the human and the simple, a lover of green fields and blowing flowers; and like Burns, he is far more at home, far more easy and felicitous, in his native Doric than in the colder Attic speech of Milton and Keats.

This is so, it seems to me, for two reasons. In the first place, the poet is dealing with the subject matter he knows best; and in the second place, he is using the medium of expression in which he has a lifelong facility. The art of poetry is far too delicate and too difficult to be practiced successfully without the most consummate and almost unconscious mastery of the language employed; so that a poet will hardly ever write with anything like distinction or convincing force in any but his mother tongue. An artist's command of his medium must be so intimate and exquisite that his thought can find adequate expression in it as easily as in the lifting of a finger or the moving of an eyelid. Otherwise he is self-conscious, unnatural, false; and, hide it as he may, we feel the awkwardness and indecision in his work. He who treats of subjects which he knows only imperfectly cannot be true to nature; while he who employs some means of expression which he only imperfectly controls cannot be true to himself. The best art requires the fulfillment of both these severe demands; they are the cardinal virtues of art. Disregard of the first produces the dilettante; disregard of the second produces the charlatan. That either of these epithets would seem entirely incongruous, if applied to Mr. Riley, is a tribute to his thorough worth as a writer.

His verse, then, divides itself sharply into two kinds, the dialect and the conventional. But we have so completely identified him with the former manner that it is hard to estimate his work in the latter. It may be doubted, however, whether he would have reached his present eminence, had he confined his efforts to the strictly regulated forms of standard English. In poems like **"A Life Term"** and **"One Afternoon,"** for instance, there is smoothness, even grace of movement, but hardly that distinction which we call style, and little of the lyric plangency the author commands at his best; while very often in his use of authorized English there is a strangely marked reminiscence of older poets, as of Keats in **"A Water Color"** (not to speak of **"A Ditty of No Tone,"** written as a frankly imitative tribute of admiration for the author of the "Ode to a Grecian Urn"), or of Emerson in "The All-Kind Mother." In only one of the dialect poems, on the other hand, so far as I recall them, is there any imitative note. His **"Nothin' to Say"** has much of the atmosphere and feeling as well as the movement of Tennyson's "Northern Farmer." But for the most part, when Mr. Riley uses his own dialect, he is thoroughly original as well as effective. He has not only the lyrical impetus so needful to good poetry; he has also the story-teller's gift. And when we add to these two qualities an abundant share of whimsical humor, we have the equipment which has so justly given him wide repute.

All of these characteristics are brought into play in such poems as **"Fessler's Bees,"** one of the fairest examples of Mr. Riley's balladry at its best:—

> Might call him a bee-expert,
> When it come to handlin' bees,—
> Roll the sleeves up of his shirt
> And wade in amongst the trees
> Where a swarm 'u'd settle, and—

> Blamedest man on top of dirt!—
> Rake 'em with his naked hand
> Right back in the hive ag'in,
> Jes' as easy as you please!

For Mr. Riley is a true balladist. He is really doing for the modern popular taste, here and now, what the old balladists did in their time. He is an entertainer. He has the ear of his audience. He knows their likes and dislikes, and humors them. His very considerable and very successful experience as a public reader of his own work has reinforced (one may guess) his natural modesty and love of people, and made him constantly regardful of their pleasure. So that we must look upon his verses as a most genuine and spontaneous expression of average poetic feeling as well as personal poetic inspiration.

Every artist's work must be, necessarily, a more or less successful compromise between these two opposing and difficult conditions of achievement. The great artists are they who succeed at last in imposing upon others their own peculiar and novel conceptions of beauty. But these are only the few whom the gods favor beyond their fellows; while for the rank and file of those who deal in the perishable wares of art a less ambitious standard may well be allowed. We must have our balladists as well as our bards, it seems; and very fortunate is the day when we can have one with so much real spirit and humanity about him as Mr. Riley.

At times the pathos of the theme quite outweighs its homeliness, and lifts the author above the region of self-conscious art; the use of dialect drops away, and a creation of pure poetry comes to light, as in that irresistible elegy **"Little Haly,"** for example:—

> "Little Haly, little Haly," cheeps the robin in the
>   tree;
> "Little Haly," sighs the clover; "Little Haly,"
>   moans the bee;
> "Little Haly, little Haly," calls the kill-dee at
>   twilight;
> And the katydids and crickets hollers "Haly" all
>   the night.

In this powerful lyric there is a simple directness approaching the feeling of Greek poetry, and one cannot help regretting the few intrusions of bad grammar and distorted spelling. They are not necessary. The poem is so universal in its human appeal, it seems a pity to limit the range of its appreciation by hampering it with local peculiarities of speech.

At times, too, in his interpretations of nature, Mr. Riley lays aside his drollery and his drawling accent in exchange for an incisive power of phrase.

> The wild goose trails his harrow

is an example of the keenness of fancy I refer to. Another is found in the closing phrase of one of the stanzas in **"A Country Pathway"**:—

> A puritanic quiet here reviles
>   The almost whispered warble from the
>   hedge,
> And takes a locust's rasping voice and files
>   The silence to an edge.

In *The Flying Islands of the Night* Mr. Riley has made his widest departure into the reign of whimsical imagination. Here he has retained that liberty of unshackled speech, that freedom and ease of diction, which mark his more familiar themes, and at the same time has entered an entirely fresh field for him, a sort of grown-up fairyland. There are many strains of fine poetry in this miniature play, which show Mr. Riley's lyrical faculty at its best. In one instance there is a peculiar treatment of the octosyllabic quatrain, where he has chosen (one cannot guess why) to print it in the guise of blank verse. It is impossible, however, to conceal the true swing of the lines.

> I loved her. Why? I never knew. Perhaps
> Because her face was fair. Perhaps because
> Her eyes were blue and wore a weary air.
> Perhaps! Perhaps because her limpid face
> Was eddied with a restless tide, wherein
> The dimples found no place to anchor and
> Abide. Perhaps because her tresses beat
> A froth of gold about her throat, and poured
> In splendor to the feet that ever seemed
> Afloat. Perhaps because of that wild way
> Her sudden laughter overleapt propriety;
> Or—who will say?—perhaps the way she wept.

It almost seems as if Mr. Riley, with his bent for jesting and his habit of wearing the cap and bells, did not dare be as poetical as he could; and when a serious lyric came to him, he must hide it under the least lyrical appearance, as he has done here. But that, surely, if it be so, is a great injustice to himself. He might well attempt the serious as well as the comic side of poetry, remembering that "when the half-gods go, the gods arrive." (pp. 424-28)

> *Bliss Carman, "Mr. Riley's Poetry," in* The Atlantic Monthly, *Vol. LXXXII, No. CCC-CXCI, September, 1898, pp. 424-28.*

Meredith Nicholson (essay date 1900)

[*In the following excerpt, Nicholson examines the style and subject matter of Riley's poetry.*]

[Riley's] first marked recognition followed the publication in the *Journal* of a series of poems signed "Benj. F. Johnson, of Boone," which not only awakened wide interest, but gave direction to a talent that had theretofore been without definite aim. He encouraged the idea that the poems were really the work of a countryman, and prefaced them with letters in prose to add to their air of authenticity, much as Lowell introduced the "Biglow Papers." This series included **"Thoughts fer the Discuraged Farmer," "When the Frost is on the Punkin,"** and **"To My Old Friend, William Leachman,"** which were winningly unaffected and simple, bearing out capitally the impression of a bucolic poet celebrating his own joys and sorrows. The charm of the "Benj. F. Johnson" series lay in their perfect suggestion of a whimsical, lovable character, and wherever Mr. Riley follows the method employed first in those pieces, he never fails of his effect.

It should be remembered, in passing from Riley masquerading as "Benj. F. Johnson" to Riley undisguised, that two kinds of dialect are represented. The Boone County poet's

contributions are printed as the old farmer is supposed to have written them, not as reported by a critical listener. There is a difference between the attempt of an illiterate man to express his own ideas on paper, and a transcript of his utterances set down by one trained to the business— the vernacular as observed and recorded by a conscious artist. In every community there is a local humorist, a sayer of quaint things, whose oddities of speech gain wide acceptance and circulation, and Mr. Riley is his discoverer in Indiana. Lowell, with his own New England particularly in mind, said that "almost every county has some good diesinker in phrase, whose mintage passes into the currency of the whole neighborhood"; and this may be applied generally to the South and West. Mr. Riley writes always with his eye on a character; and those who question his dialect do not understand that there is ever present in his mind a real individual. The feeling and the incident are not peculiar to the type; they usually lie within the range of universal experience; but the expression, the manner, the figure of the subject, are suggested in the poem, not by speech alone, but by the lilt of the line and the form of the stanza. Mr. Riley is more interested in odd characters, possessing marked eccentricities, than in the common, normal type of the farm or the country town, and the dialect that he employs often departs from the usual vocabulary of the illiterate in the field he studies, and follows lines of individual idiosyncrasy. The shrewdly humorous farmer who is a whimsical philosopher and rude moralist delights him. This character appears frequently in his poems, often mourning for the old times, now delighting in "noon-time an' June-time, down around the river"; and again expressing contentment with his own lot, averring that "they's nothin' much patheticker 'n just a-bein' rich." To these characters he gives a dialect that is fuller than the usual rural speech: *ministratin'* (ministering), *resignated* (resigned), *artificialer* (more artificial), *competenter* (more competent), *tractabler* (more tractable), and *familiously* (familiarly), not being properly in the Hoosier *lingua rustica,* but easily conceivable as possible deviations. Mr. Riley has been criticised for imputing to his characters such phrases as "when the army broke out" and "durin' the army," referring to the Civil War, and many careful observers declare that he could never have heard these phrases; but very likely he has heard them from the eccentric countrymen for whom he has so strong an affinity; or he may have coined them outright as essential to the interpretation of such characters. In the main, however, he may be followed safely as an accurate guide in the speech of the Southeastern element of the population, and his questionable usages and inconsistencies are few and slight, as the phrase "don't you know," which does not always ring true, or "again" and "agin," used interchangeably and evidently as the rhyme may hint. The abrupt beginning of a sentence, frequently noticed in Mr. Riley's dialect verses, is natural. The illiterate often experience difficulty in opening a conversation, expressing only a fragment, to which an interlocutor must prefix for himself the unspoken phrases. There is no imposition in Mr. Riley's dialect, for his amplifications of it are always for the purpose of aiding in the suggestion of a character as he conceives it; he does not pretend that he portrays in such instances a type found at every cross-roads. "Doc Sifers" and "The Raggedy Man" are not peculiar to Indiana, but have their respective counterparts in such characters as Mark Twain's "Pudd'n-head Wilson" and the wayside tramp, who has lately been a feature of farce comedy rather than of our social economy. **"Fessler's Bees," "Nothin' to say," "Down to the Capital," "A Liz-town Humorist,"** and **"Squire Hawkins's Story"** show Mr. Riley at his happiest as a delineator of the rural type. In these sketches he gives in brief compass the effect of little dramas, now humorous, now touched with simple and natural pathos, and showing a nice appreciation of the color of language which is quite as essential in dialect as in pure English. But it matters little that the *dramatis personæ* change, or that the literary method varies; the same kindliness, the same blending of humor and pathos, and the same background of "green fields and running brooks" characterize all. "The crude man is," the poet believes, "generally moral," and the Riley Hoosier is intuitively religious, and is distinguished by his rectitude and sense of justice.

Mr. Riley made his work effective through the possession of a sound instinct for appraising his material, combined with a good sense of proportion. His touch grew steadily firmer, and he became more fastidious as the public made greater demands upon him; for while his poems in dialect gained him a hearing, he strove earnestly for excellence in the use of literary English. He has written many poems of sentiment gracefully and musically, and with no suggestion of dialect. Abundant instances of his felicity in the strain of retrospect and musing might be cited. The same chords have been struck time and time again; but they take new life when he touches them, as in **"The All-Golden"**:—

> I catch my breath, as children do
> In woodland swings when life is new,
> And all the blood is warm as wine
> And tingles with a tang divine. . . .
> O gracious dream, and gracious time,
> And gracious theme, and gracious rhyme—
> When buds of Spring begin to blow
> In blossoms that we used to know,
> And lure us back along the ways
> Of time's all-golden yesterdays!

It is not the farmer alone whose simple virtues appeal to him; but rugged manhood anywhere commands his tribute, and he has hardly written a more touching lyric than **"Away,"** whose subject was an Indiana soldier:—

> I cannot say, and I will not say
> That he is dead—He is just away!

He has his own manner of expressing an idea, and this individuality is so marked that it might lead to the belief that he had little acquaintance with the classic English writers. But his series of imitations, including the prose of Scott and Dickens and the characteristic poems of Tennyson and Longfellow, are certainly the work of one who reads to good purpose and has a feeling for style. When he writes naturally there is no trace of bookishness in his work; he rarely or never invokes the mythologies, though it has sometimes pleased him to imagine Pan piping in Hoosier orchards. He is read and quoted by many who are not habitual readers of poetry—who would consider it a sign of weakness to be caught in the act of reading poems of any

kind, but who tolerate sentiment in him because he makes it perfectly natural and surrounds it with a familiar atmosphere of reality. The average man must be trapped into any display of emotion, and Mr. Riley spreads for him many nets from which there is no escape, as in **"Nothin' to say, my daughter,"** where the subject is the loneliness and isolation of the father whose daughter is about to marry, and who faces the situation clumsily, in the manner of all fathers, rich or poor. The remembrance of the dead wife and mother adds to the pathos here. The old man turns naturally to the thought of her:—

> You don't rickollect her, I reckon? No; you
>   wasn't a year old then!
> And now yer—how old *air* you? W'y, child, not
>   *'twenty'*! When?
> And yer nex' birthday's in Aprile? and you want
>   to git married that day?
> I wisht yer mother was livin'!—but I hain't got
>   nothin' to say!
> Twenty year! and as good a gyrl as parent ever
>   found!
> There's a straw ketched onto yer dress there—
>   I'll bresh it off—turn round.
> (Her mother was jest twenty when us two run
>   away.)
> Nothin' to say, my daughter! Nothin' at all to
>   say!

The drolleries of childhood have furnished Mr. Riley subjects for some of his most original and popular verses. Here, again, he does not accept the conventional children of literature, whom he calls "the refined children, the very proper children—the studiously thoughtful, poetic children"; but he seeks "the rough-and-tumble little fellows 'in hodden gray,' with frowzly heads, begrimed but laughing faces, and such awful vulgarities of naturalness, and crimes of simplicity, and brazen faith and trust, and love of life and everybody in it!" It is in this spirit that he presents now the naïve, now the perversely erring, and again the eerie and elfish child. He is a master of those enchantments of childhood that transfigure and illumine and create a world of the imagination for the young that is undiscoverable save to the elect few. He does not write patronizingly to his audience; but listens, as one should listen in the realm of childhood, with serious attention, and then becomes an amanuensis, transcribing the children's legends and guesses at the riddle of existence in their own language. "The Raggedy Man" is not a romantic figure; he is the shabby chore-man of the well-to-do folk in the country town, and the friend and oracle of small boys. His mind is filled with rare lore, he—

> Knows 'bout Giunts, an' Griffuns an' Elves
> An' the Squidgicum-Squees 'at swallers ther-
>   selves!

And he may be responsible, too, for "Little Orphant Annie's" knowledge of the "Gobbleuns," which Mr. Riley turned into the most successful of all his juvenile pieces. He reproduces most vividly a child's eager, breathless manner of speech, and the elisions and variations that make the child-dialect. Interspersed through **"The Child World,"** a long poem in rhymed couplets, are a number of droll juvenile recitatives; but this poem has a much greater value than at first appears. It presents an excellent picture of domestic life in a western country town, and the town is Mr. Riley's own Greenfield, on the National Road. This poem is a faithful chronicle, lively and humorous, full of the local atmosphere, and never dull. The descriptions of the characters are in Mr. Riley's happiest vein: the father of the house, a lawyer and leading citizen; the patient mother; the children with their various interests, leading up to "Uncle Mart," the printer, who aspired to be an actor—

> He joyed in verse-quotations—which he took
> Out of the old "Type Foundry Specimen Book."

The poem is written in free, colloquial English, broken by lapses into the vernacular. It contains some of his best writing, and proves him to possess a range and breadth of vision that are not denoted in his lyrical pieces alone. *The Flying Islands of the Night, a fantastic drama in verse,* his only other effort of length, was written earlier. It abounds in the curious and capricious, but it lacks in simplicity and reserve—qualities that have steadily grown in him.

Humor is preëminent in Mr. Riley, and it suggests that of Dickens in its kinship with pathos. It seems to be peculiar to the literature of lowly life that there is heartache beneath much of its gayety, and tears are almost inevitably associated with its laughter. Mr. Riley never satirizes, never ridicules his creations; his attitude is always that of the kindly and admiring advocate; and it is by enlisting the sympathy of his readers, suggesting much to their feeling and imagination, and awakening in them a response that aids and supplements his own work, that Mr. Riley has won his way to the popular heart. The restraints of fixed forms have not interfered with his adequate expression of pure feeling. This is proved by the sonnet, **"When She Comes Home Again,"** which is one of the tenderest of his poems. In the day that saw many of his contemporaries in the younger choir of poets carving cherry stones of verse after French patterns he found old English models sufficient, and his own whim supplied all the variety he needed. Heroic themes have not tempted him; he has never attained sonority or power, and has never needed them; but melody and sweetness and a singular gift of invention distinguish him.

Many imitators have paid tribute to Mr. Riley's dialect verse, for most can grow the flowers after the seed have been freely blown in the market-place. Perhaps the best compliment that can be paid to Mr. Riley's essential veracity is to compare the verse of those who have made attempts similar to his own. He is, for example, a much better artist than Will Carleton, who came before him, and whose "Farm Ballads" are deficient in humor; and he possesses a breadth of sympathy and a depth of sincerity that Eugene Field did not attain in dialect verse, though Field's versatility and fecundity were amazing. There is nowhere in Mr. Riley a trace of the coarse brutality with which Mr. Hamlin Garland, for example, stamps the life of a region lying farther west. There is no point of contact between Lowell and Mr. Riley in their dialectic performances, as civic matters do not interest the Indianian; and his view of the Civil War becomes naturally that of the countryman who looks back with wistful melancholy, not to the national danger and dread, but to the neighborhood's

glory and sorrow, as in **"Good-by, Jim."** It might also be said that Mr. Riley has never put the thoughts of statesmen into the mouths of countrymen, as Lowell did, consistency being one of his qualities. There has sprung up in Mr. Riley's time a choir of versifiers who are journalistic rather than literary, and who write for the day, much as the reporters do. Mr. Riley, more than any one else, has furnished the models for these, and it would seem that verses could be multiplied interminably, or so long as such refrains as "When father winds the clock" and "The hymns that mother used to sing" can be found for texts.

With the publication of the "Benj. F. Johnson" poems in a paper-covered booklet, Mr. Riley's literary career began. The intervening years have brought him continuous applause; his books of verse have been sold widely in this country and in England, and that, too, in "the twilight of the poets," with its contemporaneous oblivion for many who have labored bravely in the paths of song. He early added to his reputation as a writer that of a most successful reader of his own poems, and on both sides of the Atlantic his work and his unique personality have won for him the friendship of many distinguished literary men of the day. It is to be said that the devotion of the people of his own State to their poet, from first to last, has been marked by a cordiality and loyalty that might well be the envy of any man in any field of endeavor. No other Western poet has ever occupied a similar place; and the reciprocal devotion, on the other hand, of the poet to his own people, is not less noteworthy or admirable. He has always resented the suggestion that he should leave Indiana for Boston or New York, where he might be more in touch with the makers of books; and in recent years he purchased the old family residence at Greenfield, to which he returns frequently for rest and inspiration. For fifteen years he has been the best-known figure in Indianapolis, studying with tireless attention the faces in the streets, nervously ranging the book-stores, and often sitting down to write a poem at the desk of some absentee in the *Journal* office. His frequent reading and lecturing tours have been miserable experiences for him, as he is utterly without the instinct of locality, and has timidly sat in the hotels of strange towns for many hours for lack of the courage requisite for exploration. Precision and correctness have distinguished him in certain ways, being marked, for example, in matters of dress and in his handwriting; his manuscripts are flawlessly correct, and the slouch and negligence of the traditional poet are not observed in him.

His long list of books includes *Afterwhiles* (1887); *Pipes of Pan at Zekesbury* (1888); *Old-fashioned Roses* (1889); *Rhymes of Childhood* (1891); and *Poems Here at Home* (1897); and he has known the luxury of a cosmopolitan edition of his writings in a series that embraced the definitive Stevenson. Fame came to Mr. Riley when he was still young, and it is only a fair assumption that he has not exhausted his field, but that he will grow more and more secure in it. Serious work it has not always been possible for him to do, for his audience learned to expect humor in all his verses, and refused to be disappointed; but his ambition lies beyond humorous dialect, though he finds no fault with the public preference. All that he writes is welcome, for he is a preacher of sound optimism and a sincere believer in the final good that comes to all. (pp. 160-76)

> *Meredith Nicholson, "The Hoosier Interpreted: James Whitcomb Riley," in her* The Hoosiers, *The Macmillan Company, 1900, pp. 156-76.*

Harriet Monroe   (essay date 1916)

[*As the founder and editor of* Poetry, *Monroe was a key figure in the American "poetry renaissance" that took place in the early twentieth century.* Poetry *was the first periodical devoted primarily to the works of new poets and to poetry criticism, and from 1912 until her death Monroe maintained an editorial policy of printing "the best English verse which is being written today, regardless of where, by whom, or under what theory of art it is written." In the following essay, she reflects on Riley's poetic accomplishment.*]

Riley was one of the poets of power in that it was given to him to "tell the tale of the tribe." He was keen enough in imagination, fine enough in sympathy, and creative enough in art, to apprehend his fellow-countryman and fix his type. He arrived during his life at this high distinction—that he speaks for Indiana, and Indiana is what he made it. Still more, he has widened the bounds of Indiana, made it absorb its middle-western neighbors to right and left so far as their country people and village people are true to his type. And he made the world love his Indiana—his cheerful, whimsical, unassuming, shrewd and sentimental neighbors, the democratic people of the plains, people strongly individualized and yet one not more than t'other, all measuring up to the same standard of extremely human feelings and failings. He has given to a big state a personality—in a sense his own personality because he was of its essence. By thus revealing its people to themselves, he has given them power and pride—"a smiling pride," as George Ade calls it, in their own character—and something of power to throw off the poses and pretences dear to every community, and to live sincerely, without fear or shame.

It was humanity that interested him, not nature. One gets a general effect of plain fertile farming country as the background of his neighbors' lives, but he does not see details of land or sky. Perhaps those large round glasses covered visual vagueness; at any rate such a poem as "**Knee-deep in June**" expresses a general human ecstasy in a beautiful day, but it does not express that love of the earth, and identification with its forces, that intimate knowledge of every phase of earth-life which we get, for example, from John Muir's prose, and which we are beginning to feel in a few of the younger poets. Riley's interest was in human beings—yes, and in dogs and other familiar animals.

His art, like the character of the people he spoke for, was simple and direct. If it yielded often to the temptation of a too obvious sentimentality, it rose in strong moments to a poignant tenderness, or even to a veiled suggestion of heroic beauty. And always, between both extremes it was iri-

descent with humor—humor always gentle and tender, never grim or grotesque or sardonic.

He was, of course, to a degree unusual even among poets, a child. And out of a rare sympathy with fellow-children he was able to produce masterpieces of child-character like "**Little Orphant Annie**," "**The Raggedy Man**," "**The Bear Story**" and other familiar ballads of eternal youth. But beyond this, he was able to see grown-ups almost with a child's direct and untroubled vision, and to sketch them vividly in a few swift lines. As Edith Wyatt wrote . . . : (pp. 305-07)

> Among Mr. Riley's many distinguished faculties of execution in expressing, in stimulating, "an exquisite appreciation of the most simple and universal relations of life," one faculty has been, in so far as I know, very little mentioned—I mean his mastery in creating character. Mr. Riley has expressed, has incarnated in the melodies and harmonies of his poems, not merely several living, breathing human creatures as they are made by their destinies, but a whole world of his own, a vivid world of country-roads, and country-town streets, peopled with farmers and tramps and step-mothers and children, trailing clouds of glory even when they boast of the superiorities of "Renselaer"; a world of hard-working women and hard-luck men, and poverty and prosperity, and drunkards and raccoons and dogs and grandmothers and lovers. To have presented through the medium of rhythmic chronicle, a world so sharply limned, so funny, so tragic, so mean, so noble, seems to us in itself a striking achievement in the craft of verse.

An advertisement for one of Riley's public readings in 1886.

It is even more—it is to be immortal. Riley has captured a region and an era, and so handled and molded and stamped it that he is inextricably bound up with it—an ancestor of all who are born in it. It is a smaller region than the one Mark Twain mapped out with epic grandeur and explored with abysmal laughter—in a sense it is one of its neighborhoods. Smaller also than Spoon River, for it is all on the surface of the earth, amid summer suns and storms, while Spoon River digs deep to the earth's centre, where all nations are neighbors. It is a little world that Riley gives to us, but a world very human and funny and brotherly, and his best poems speak from the heart of it with its authentic lyric voice. (p. 307)

> *Harriet Monroe, "James Whitcomb Riley," in* Poetry, *Vol. VIII, No. VI, September, 1916, pp. 305-07.*

Edith Wyatt   (essay date 1917)

[*In the following excerpt, Wyatt contends that Riley's poetry embodies a distinctly American language and outlook.*]

In a delightful conversation quoted in an essay entitled "The Dusk of the Gods" in a recent *Atlantic Monthly*, George Moore says,

> If there be a future for the English language, which I doubt, it is in America. A great deal of your speech is Elizabethan, and what is not you have invented. You are still inventing a language, while we have stopped; we take what additions foreigners and our savage subjects supply us, but that is all. Perhaps in America another language will arrive, adapted to literary usage . . . out of your slang, your dialects.

Appearing almost on the morrow of the death of our most accomplished singer of dialect lyrics, these penetrating words brought to mind one of the most beautiful endowments of James Whitcomb Riley.

Like *Uncle Remus* he was an inventor of language, and his unique singing speech has contributed to human expression. He brought words from life into letters. Familiar phrases which had vibrated as mere blatant discords at the touch of a lesser writer, were at the hands of his skill harmonies from the strings of his spirit's lute. He was a magician who could use terms such as "Looky there!" and "Lawzy!" in a manner that lent a biting reality to tragedy, and echoed in your memory like the tale of something an acquaintance has looked on in life.

> Pore folks lives at Lonesomeville;
>   Lawzy! but they're pore!
> Houses with no winders in,
>   And hardly any door:
> Chimbly all tore down, and no
>   Smoke in that at all—
> Ist a stovepipe through a hole
>   In the kitchen-wall!
>
> Pump that's got no handle on;
>   And no woodshed—And *wooh!*
> Mighty cold there, choppin' wood,
>   Like pore folks has to do!

> Winter-time, and snow and sleet
>   Ist fairly fit to kill!—
> Hope to goodness *Santy Claus*
>   Goes to Lonesomeville!

Music enters at the spaces left by all those hard g's and guttural word-endings he cuts out so gracefully. The reproduction of illiteracy is generally a mere verbatim copy of ignorance; but James Whitcomb Riley's reproduction is a subtle enhancement of the tone of the sound he modulates. I suppose no one will deny that "shadder" sounds longer and thinner and more alarming than "shadow" or that "saranade" has a more harmonic air than "serenade."

> And when the boys u'd saranade, I've laid so still
>   in bed
> I've even heard the locus'-blossoms droppin' on
>   the shed
> When "Lily Dale" er "Hazel Dell," had sobbed
>   and died away—
>
> . . . I want to hear the *old* band play.

Besides the lovely musical web he wove of our unpromising Middle Western colloquialisms, he has given us innumerable words of his own improvisation, as in "the kyouck and gobble of the struttin' turkey-cock" and the description of the boy standing up and driving, who

> —comes skallyhootin' through
>   Our alley, with one arm
> A-wavin' Fare-ye-well to you—!

Widely enjoyed and beloved, the poetry of James Whitcomb Riley will probably always in our lifetime encounter a species of objection in the minds of many Americans. His poetry sings. Its force is emotional. Its sincere charm is absolute, and depends not at all on being something like something else—on the audience's recollection of Greek verse, or familiarity with Japanese art, or impressionistic landscape. To the kind of reader for whom a recognizable, musical idea limits, instead of greatly liberating, the communicative faculty of poetry, to the kind of reader who thinks of poetry as a species of more tight-mouthed and cryptic prose, to the kind of reader who is worried by poets who will not give him, so to speak, any reliable library references for their inspiration—to such American readers as these James Whitcomb Riley's poetry must always seem all wrong and misguided. Anyone can understand his songs. People have always been cutting them out of the newspapers and reciting them at ice cream sociables and church benefits. They are a part of the national consciousness. To Brahmins of poetry these are disquieting manifestations inclining them to the Brahminical error of supposing that poetry which is commonly understood and enjoyed cannot be supposed to be of beauty or value.

The reader of **"A Small Boy and Others"** will recall a charming passage descriptive of a relative of the James family who investigated an inherited estate in remote fastnesses of our land typified by Henry James as "the Beaver Kill." This large, humorous phrase seemed to indicate, in Henry James absorbing recollections, all in our country that rose west of the Allegheny mountains, all that was not turned towards the east, just as in the American Indian phrase the words "High-Muck-a-Muck" denote all manner of persons of constituted authority among other races—expressions both of them fascinating to consider, defining as they do a comprehensive, but clearly and even agreeably acknowledged ignorance expressed with child-like recoursefulness.

Undoubtedly the wisdom and beauty of James Whitcomb Riley can never sing to the ears of those of our compatriots who readily adopt the ignorance of sophistication without troubling themselves to learn its knowledge; and on account of the fact that his poetry belongs to the Beaver Kill it must remain undistinguished for the whole range of taste, so pleasantly disparaged by George Moore, which does not care for indigenous expression but only for expression derived.

"If a shipload of Elgin marbles," he says,

> had been landed at Yokohama in the seventeenth century there would have been no more Japanese art. They would have said, 'This is the thing to do,' and they would have done it—badly.
>
> When European art did come to Japan, it killed the Japanese formula. The Japanese now go to Paris to paint, and a pretty mess they make of it; or they stay at home and try to imitate their own handicraft of two hundred years ago; but the inward vision has vanished from Japan.

Innumerable, doubtless, are those dwellers in the country of Lincoln's familiar habitation who possess a hopeless faith or fancy that the Middle West has been blessed by the presence of an inward vision unnamable. Rock-shod rivers, brown prairies, friendly towns, the wide run of grain fields and corn-bottoms must seem always for the lovers of that lay of land the natural home of a spirit inexpressibly spacious, plain and free. The air that forever comforts you and breaks your heart and assuages you again with pleasurable pain in James Whitcomb Riley's poetry is the melody that tells you that you are a part of that spirit of life. You may have dropped beneath it a hundred and a thousand times. But you have known its wild and infinitely endearing grace. Your soul has felt the shadows of its might. You, too, have lived these staunchnesses and dreams that are the last realities, and heard the band play in the square and seen the neighbors bring home *Coon Dog Wess.*

I once had occasion to read to an English night class of young Russian and Polish people, James Whitcomb Riley's **"Raggedy Man."** In their pleasure in its sincerity and quiet intangible delight I felt a tribute to a certain magic of interpretation in the poem I had never really appreciated before.

> O the Raggedy Man! He works for Pa;
> An' he's the goodest man you ever saw!
> He comes to our house every day,
>   An' waters the horses, an' feeds 'em hay;
> An' he opens the shed—an' we all ist laugh
> When he drives out our little old wobble-ly calf;
> An' nen—ef our hired girl says he can—
>   He milks the cow for 'Lizabuth Ann—
>   Ain't he a' awful good Raggedy Man?
>   Raggedy! Raggedy! Raggedy Man!

> The Raggedy Man—one time, when he
> Wuz makin' a little bow'-n'-erry fer me,
> Says, "When you're big like your Pa is,
> Air *you* go' to keep a fine store like his—
> An' be a rich merchant—an' wear fine clothes?
> Er what *air* you go' to be, goodness knows?"
> An' nen he laughed at 'Lizabuth Ann,
> An' I says, " 'M go' to be a Raggedy Man!—
>   I'm ist go' to be a nice Raggedy Man!
>   Raggedy! Raggedy! Raggedy Man!"

Something of our own, not like the spirit of other lands, something better far indeed than we are often able to be, and better than our thoughts or any of the formulae, but somehow like our best fleet instincts, spoke truly to alien listeners in the genius of this poem sung as lightly as the wind blew down the locust blossoms on the shed roof.

When all our ways and days are vanished, and far-off people hardly distinguish the memory of Henry George from that of George Washington, what will tell the nameless spirit we live, to distant listeners? Some such word as this, one may hope—simple and brief and true out of the silence.

Nothing has been said here of James Whitcomb Riley's remarkable gift in characterization—so that not a creature appears in his brief lyric tales, from the thoroughly disagreeable wife of *Mylo Jones* to the heroic *Coon Dog Wess,* but is fully individualized. Nothing has been said of his nonsense poems or his enchanting parodies, or his verse not in dialect. For some of us—or rather for me, at least—James Whitcomb Riley's poetry has become a part of the country of one's mind; and one walks about in it without thinking of the names of the different places there; and hears—

> The echoes of old voices, wound
>   In limpid streams of laughter where
> The river Time runs bubble-crowned,
> And giddy eddies ripple there;
>   Where roses, bending o'er the brink,
>   Drain their own kisses as they drink
>   And ivies climb and twine and cling
>   About the song I never sing.—

and listens to the song one never sings oneself.

Here are poems made of the living word. In the mortality of their maker, it is a comfort to turn back to their charm and truth that sing so far in the surrounding night—

> Sing on! sing on, you gray-brown bird,
> Sing from the swamps, the recesses—pour your
>   chant from the bushes,
> Limitless out of the dusk, out of the cedars and
>   pines.

(pp. 182-90)

Edith Wyatt, "James Whitcomb Riley," in her Great Companions, *D. Appleton and Company, 1917, pp. 182-90.*

Solomon Eagle [pseudonym of J. C. Squire]   (essay date 1920)

[*Squire was an English man of letters who, as a poet, lent his name to the "Squire-archy," a group of poets who struggled to maintain the Georgian poetry movement of the early twentieth century. Typified by such poets as Rupert Brooke and John Drinkwater, Georgian poetry was a reaction against Victorian prolixity, turn-of-the-century decadence, and contemporary urban realism. Squire and the Georgians wished to return to the nineteenth-century poetic tradition of William Wordsworth and the Lake Poets, concerning themselves primarily with the traditional subjects and themes of English pastoral verse. Squire was also a prolific critic who was involved with many important English periodicals; he founded and edited the* London Mercury, *served as literary and, later, acting editor of the* New Statesman, *and contributed frequently to the* Illustrated London News *and the* Observer. *His criticism, like his poetry, is considered traditional and good-natured. In the following essay, he offers a negative assessment of Riley's poetry.*]

In bed, with a high temperature, and all the repellent attributes of forehead, eyes, mouth, and back which are described in patent medicine advertisements, I had not lived, during the week, a strenuous intellectual life. At rare intervals, and for two or three minutes at a time, my leaden eyelids had lifted and I had taken in a few lines of *Buried Alive* and *A Rebours,* which, for some, or no, reason, found themselves side by side on my table. Being utterly incapable of thought, I was just wondering from which of these two books I should quote a few passages which, with some perfunctory praise or condemnation, would fill a yawning page, when one came into my bedroom and told me that the *Times* had an obituary notice of James Whitcomb Riley. The old man, it seems, had joined the great majority a few days before myself; and I had my selections from Riley brought up, as also a volume of the *Encyclopædia,* to refresh my memory. For the only line of Riley's that I could recall in my condition was one which I have quoted before: "The beetle booms adown the glooms and bumps along the dusk," and which could scarcely be considered representative.

Riley, like Joaquin Miller and other American bards of the type, probably had many amiable qualities. I should think he would have made a very kind, though a too voluble, grandfather. But he was a very bad writer. And his badness was "of various kinds." In the volume I open the first poem is called **"A Life Lesson."** It begins:—

> There! little girl, don't cry!
> 　They have broken your doll, I know;
> 　　And your tea-set blue,
> 　　And your play-house, too,
> 　Are things of the long ago;
> But childish troubles will soon pass by—
> 　There! little girl, don't cry!

In the next verse it is her slate that is broken; in the last (need I say it?), her heart. Perhaps what the *Encyclopædia* writer calls his "naïve humour and tenderness" may be held to be illustrated here. But naïveté may be carried too far. A few pages later on there is a lyric called **"A Song,"** which, though it might elicit storms of applause in a Westend music-hall, could hardly be held, by even the most tolerant of critics, to justify a claim to immortal bays. The text is:—

> There is ever a song somewhere, my dear;
> 　There is ever a something sings alway.

And the chorus is certainly as good a model for that kind of journalist who is, like myself, paid by space, as anything I've ever seen:—

> There is a song somewhere, my dear,
> 　Be the skies above or dark or fair,
> There is ever a song that our hearts may hear,
> 　There is ever a song somewhere, my dear,
> 　There is ever a song somewhere!

On the whole I think I prefer Riley's dialect poems, even though they do occasionally present an English reader with such problems as the word "lightning-bug," which I very timidly hazard may be Hoosier for glowworm, though without confidence enough to bet on it. The more conventional poems are free from this kind of difficulty, though I am rather puzzled by a being with:—

> 　　　　a plume of red,
> That spurted about in the breeze and bled
> In the bloom of the every lad.

As a rule the difficulty with these poems does not lie in particular words. Where it does lie may be indicated if I quote the last stanza of an endeavour to expand and presumably to improve the nursery rhyme of **"Curly Locks"**:

> And feast upon strawberries, sugar and cream
> From a service of silver, with jewels agleam.
> At thy feet will I bide, at thy beck will I rise,
> And twinkle my soul in the light of thine eyes!

Well, really! Goodness only knows what sort of picture the poet meant to "conjure up" by that last line. Is "twinkle" here a verb transitive or intransitive?

Take this again: the first two stanzas of **"The Funny Little Fellow"**:—

> 'Twas a Funny little Fellow
> 　Of the very purest type,
> For he had a heart as mellow
> 　As an apple over-ripe;
> And the brightest little twinkle
> 　When a funny thing occurred,
> And the lightest little tinkle
> 　Of a laugh you ever heard!
>
> His smile was like the glitter
> 　Of the sun in tropic lands
> And his talk a sweeter twitter
> 　Than the swallow understands;
> Hear him sing—and tell a story—
> 　Snap a joke—ignite a pun,
> 'Twas a capture—rapture—glory,
> 　And explosion—all in one!

I cannot enter into details, or it might be possible to inquire whether it is really complimentary to a person to compare his smile to a tropical sun, or his heart to an *over-ripe* apple. Whether the poet intended the additional dubious compliment of comparing his friend's singing to an explosion can only be decided by an authoritative elucidation of his rather hectic punctuation. But the stanzas illustrate very well what was really wrong with Riley; it was not that he was too naïve, but that he wasn't naïve enough. He was sophisticated without being intelligent. He was always self-conscious, whether he was attempting to write as he conceived that other poets had written, or whether he was setting out to interpret the feelings of the strong and simple folk of the prairie.

I find that the *Encyclopædia* appears to regard as one of Riley's principal feats an imitation of Poe that he published in the Anderson *Democrat*. It had the initials "E. A. P." under it; it was alleged by the editor to have been found "on the fly-leaf of an old Latin-English dictionary" then owned by "an uneducated and illiterate man" in Kokomo, who had received it from his grandfather, in whose tavern, near Richmond, Va., it had been left by "a young man who showed plainly the marks of dissipation"; and it deceived many distinguished critics. I have not seen this work, though I can quite well imagine what it must be like. But I cannot conceive that anything of Riley's could really make it worth the *Times'* while to speculate, as it did, whether Riley would live or not. Its conclusion, that he has as much chance of living as many others, was at least cautious, but on the whole I incline to think that the *Times* writer, like myself, had had to go to the *Encyclopædia* for his facts, and that, unlike myself, he had never read any Riley. For the sober truth is that the "Hoosier poet" was neither a better nor a worse writer than Mrs. Wheeler Wilcox, and that both owe their popularity to the same qualities. Mr. G. R. Sims is at least as good, though he doesn't borrow quite so many conventional pretty-pretties to adorn his verse. (pp. 163-68)

> Solomon Eagle [pseudonym of J. C. Squire], "James Whitcomb Riley," in his Books in General, second series, *Alfred A. Knopf, 1920, pp. 163-68.*

Edgar Lee Masters   (essay date 1928)

[*Masters was one of the first major twentieth-century American authors to use the theories of modern psychology to examine human thought and motivation. A prolific writer, he is best known for the monumental poetic cycle* Spoon River Anthology, *a collection of free-verse epitaphs on the men and women buried in a small-town churchyard. With its sardonic attack on provincial dullness and spiritual sterility,* Spoon River Anthology *strongly influenced the literature of the 1920s. In the following excerpt, he studies the idealization of American rural life in Riley's poetry.*]

The County Fair of Middle Western America was not a Vanity Fair to the people themselves. The balloon ascent was thrilling enough, and no one dreamed of the aëroplane. There were side-shows of performing Chinese, fire-eaters and the like; wheels of fortune, and barkers selling razors, can-openers and glass-cutters. The event attracted the country fiddlers, some of whom played for the platform dancers. Under the big trees beyond the race-track the shadows and the grass invited the farmer people and the villagers with their lunches, and the fire blazed for the making of coffee. For a week the same people walked the grounds ruining the grass and making paths to the sheds where the live stock was exhibited, or the products of the soil.

One saw for all this time, day by day the same faces, the same roisterers, the same old notables wearing stove-pipe hats and doe-skin coats; the same couples paired for the occasion, and soon to be paired for life. Every day the merry-go-round whirled to some melodic air that the boys were soon whistling, and which, after the Fair was closed, became the memorial voice of the ended carnival. A neighborhood flavor and character was developed in that one happy week, as it does in a town, as it did in fact in Indiana, which became a Fair with a spirit all its own.

A few other things must be added to the allegory. The Fair draws to its side the Muse of Memory. The old are present, those who have made the county, held office and waged the wars. The young sit on the grass with them at the lunch hour, and learn the tales of an earlier day. Queer characters, rural wits, men happy in drink, move amid the throngs, or stand about regaling each other with neighborhood news. By them may be standing bright-eyed youths with aptitudes for character and humor; and one of these may be a future James Whitcomb Riley feeding his genius on idiomatic turns of speech, odd sayings, and pictorial episode. In fact this very thing happened to Riley. Indiana was a happy County Fair to him, which he saw under unusual advantages, and with eyes peculiarly gifted for gathering in what was quaint and joyous and innocent in country and village life. His State and his people had developed a culture distinctive of the first pioneer days; they had a spirit of their own of which such politicians as Voorhees was one expression, and Lew Wallace, Charles Major, Meredith Nicholson and Booth Tarkington were another; and Riley in poetry was still another. Each had his individual voice; but the overtone was this Indiana, this beautiful State carved from the old Northwest, with its admixture of southern feelings and ways of life, and its alertness to business, means of prosperity, politics, learning, books and the romantic outlook, transmuted from adventure, land hunting, the log-cabin, and the happiness of primitive living.

Riley did not wish, even if he could have done so, to go behind the happy appearances of the Fair. He might mention at times that there were fights, that some one was "stobbed"; but he did not penetrate to dramatic reasons. The old fiddler was always lovable, never trivial or clownish. The pioneers were heroic figures of the land-clearing days, of the trials of the wilderness, of the log-cabin with its happy simplicities. If they were prudent and sagacious old land traders who made good use of their chances, that was not for poetical treatment. He showed the Fair and its personages in their holiday dress, gay and amiable, laughing and feasting; if grieving or wounded, tenderly attended, and if ludicrous, still lovable. At the Fair he found the Aunt Marys, the Orphant Annies, the philosophical cobblers, the happy crippled boys. He did not probe for secrets and for causes; for to him, diagnosis was a form of cruelty. He may have learned something from Hogarth, whose life he studied with diligence as a boy and young man. If so he applied what he admired in the work of that painter to character depiction of amiable humor and tender sympathy. He did not gather stories in Vanity Fair. Aunt Mary's faults, if any, remain unveiled; the crippled boy's father is dismissed with a humorous line. When he became famous he gave his creed to the younger Cawein for him to follow too, confiding in him the secret of the great truth which the poet sees and should guard from any touch too merely human. "Give nothing to it," he wrote, "but pure joy and beauty, and compassion and tenderness: a Christ-like laying on of hands on brows that ache, and wounds that bleed, fainting from pain, and worn and weary."

What Riley did in his more than twenty books, was to give pure joy and compassion and tenderness, and very often great beauty to the Fair that he knew, to the life of Indiana of the pioneer days down to the dawn of the twentieth century. He put Indiana as a place and a people in the memory of America, more thoroughly and more permanently than has been done by any other poet before or since his day for any other locality or people. This challenging comparison will evoke the claims of other poets: Whittier and Bret Harte, for example. But Riley created many more types than Whittier did; and he did it with greater variety and charm, and truer to the atmosphere of the fair. Riley was more of the people than Whittier was, for he had a richer *wanderjahre;* but if he was not more of the people, Riley's people were more to be with than Whittier's. The stocks of Scotch-Irish and English and Germans which poured into Indiana during the first half of the nineteenth century from the Carolinas, Virginia, Pennsylvania, from Tennessee and from Kentucky, were a more vital, human and picturesque people than the New Englanders with whom Whittier dealt, and who for two centuries before his day, had lived in a state of unchanged and arrested activity. Bret Harte succeeded with a few strokes of satiric genius, the "Heathen Chinee," in chief, perhaps; but all in all, Bret Harte merely made a report of the American adventurer who absorbed a Spanish colony into the body of American life. The California of Bret Harte is a land that came and went as a camp, pitched and taken down. The Indiana of Riley was the spread of a people who founded a State and populated it before he was born. His first vision of it showed him what it was at first, and what it had grown from without greatly changing its character. (pp. 342-45)

In classifying Riley's total output, making allowance first for the fact that many of his poems belong in two or more columns, for example that many of his child-poems are also dialect poems, it will be found that he wrote 223 poems about or for children; 141 poems of nature; 139 love poems; 136 humorous poems in dialect; 119 poems of tribute or for occasions; 77 poems of reflection; 74 narrative or dramatic poems; 70 poems of bereavement; 60 poems of backward turning fancy to old days; 40 poems on the various holidays; 25 on friendship and 22 on patriotism. The love poems have tenderness; a few approach to a certain passion, but they are not really passionate. They belong to the chivalric days of America when it was believed that women were better than men—to the days of the angelic woman. At the first he wrote a good many poems to inamoratas, but they are romantically mild. In 1875 he published **"An Old Sweetheart of Mine"**:

> As one who cons at evening o'er an album all
>   alone,

And muses on the faces of the friends that he has
  known;
So I turn the leaves of fancy, till in shadowy design,
I find the smiling features of an old sweetheart
  of mine.

To quote this and drop the subject would be unfair to Riley. He did vastly better than this over and over again. In 1885, for example, he wrote a sonnet entitled **"When She Comes Home,"** a beautiful celebration of domestic reunion after absence. In the same key of intensity is **"The Wife Blessed,"** a lyric of exquisite refinement which sings marital happiness. But of passion that overwhelms with disaster and suffering, but with ecstasy too, he wrote no line. Men and women separated by tragic circumstances, trusting souls reduced by faithlessness to misery, could not have escaped his observation. And for dramatizing such souls he had before him Byron and Browning; yet Riley held to his creed of "laying Christlike hands on brows that ache and wounds that bleed." That creed belonged to the nature of the man who was enraptured of hollyhocks and old-fashioned roses, but whom the beauty of woman led neither to memorable romance nor to matrimony.

His mild and chivalrous treatment of romantic love might be analyzed until its causes were traced to their source; but it suffices here to mention the fact alone. Neither Longfellow nor the poetical fashions of his day would have held him to the course he pursued if it had been in him to follow another. And similarly Hogarth, whom he read about so diligently in youth, left him uninfluenced for the contemplation and report of Hogarthian types, men or women, who were so much before his eyes in Indiana, look where he would to avoid seeing them. He took note of raggedy men, rural loafers at the country store, tramps, and such types, but he depicted them lightly and humorously; their deeper tragedies he never touched. He had vivid powers of character-drawing; but had he had capacity for more searching drama, which he did not have, the brake which he really put on his genius, and the blinders which he fastened over his eyes, kept him from portraying other than the rural mirth and the innocent sorrows of the Fair.

Looked at another way, his work divides itself between poems written in conventional English and in a variety of measures; and poems written in dialect, but chiefly in the Hoosier dialect. When he wrote sonnets and lyrics in the traditional manner of the great English poetry he spoke for himself. When he wrote in dialect his characters spoke. They were a more authentic voice of his genius than his own voice was. Though his sonnets at their best were as effectual as those his American contemporaries produced, they lacked the unified condensation, the crystal summation which makes a sonnet a thing of memorable perfection. To enforce this point comparison may be made between his sonnet on a cricket and Keats's. Keats was a great master of the sonnet, to be sure; but the fact that Riley was not can be proved by placing their sonnets side by side. Stepping to a lower level of comparison, Riley's lyrics at their best are not inferior, and perhaps they are not equalled by those of any American poet of his day; and this is true in spite of the fact that sometimes only Riley's childlike sincerity saves them from over tenderness, from the unrestraint which blinds sympathy to reality.

At times he attempted work that in no way belonged to him, such as *The Flying Islands of the Night.* Indeed many of his poems in standard English give the impression of Aunt Mary dressed for some great occasion, and who looks odd to us in her silk gown, too fine and yet not fine enough. It may have been that the critical attacks made upon him for the use of dialect caused him to show the world what he could do in the Keats, Longfellow or Swinburne manner. But he was sustained in many ways for his use of dialect, by the example of Burns for one thing, and Tennyson for that matter. And certainly when Lowell and Howells called his successes in dialect indisputable poetry, he was justified in heeding them more than his critics, who were nothing but poetical scribes at best. Lastly he must have known that in this field of poetry he was a master, and one of the few conspicuous masters of the world. **"Out to Old Aunt Mary's," "Griggsby's Station," and "Little Orphant Annie," "Jim," and "The Happy Little Cripple,"** are not surpassed for pathos in the English language; and they have great beauty—the beauty of the Indiana hills and fields, of hollyhocks and yellow roses, and the song of the robin, in no wise impugned by a preference for the majesty of mountains or the ecstasy of the skylark.

But his work of incomparable merit, of unmatched excellence, was in the field of childhood delineation. Here he has no equal, and no one to be mentioned in the same breath with him. Here he was pure genius. The work of other poets in this domain is artificial compared to Riley's. It is but tin toys prettily made and brightly painted and varnished when placed by the side of Riley's flesh and blood creations, native to a spot and a life of America—now vanished! His success with poems of children was largely due to the fact that he really loved them, and by reason of his child-like heart entered into their secrets. For humor one will look far to find anything in verse to excel **"A Liz Town Humorist," "Joney," "Doc Sifers," "An Idiot," "Jap Miller," "Thoughts on the Late War," "The Raggedy Man," "Our Hired Girl," "Some Scattering Remarks of Bub," "Rubáiyat of Doc Sifers," "His Pa's Romance,"** and many besides these. They make a whole gallery of American types, too priceless ever to be lost. They are distinctively our own.

Satire and irony do not conduce to "pure joy and beauty and compassion"; but they were not among Riley's gifts. Neither did the experiences of his life, his early conditioning prepare him to use them. Saving a romantic pining for the "airly days," America suited and pleased him. The religious atmosphere around him gave him no disturbance; the course of the country politically met his approval. He venerated such figures as McKinley and Harrison who was one of the poet's friends and admirers. His man with the hoe owned a farm; there was no emptiness of the ages in his face, but it was lighted with smiles, and the jaw was not let down and not brutal; it was square and strong and told of the forests which had been felled, and the fields which had been cultivated. Riley's fallen in the Philippines had served the country patriotically, and they had joined the son of Katy, with whom Riley could sympathize "as

she reads all his letters over, writ from the war,"—from the camp at Gettysburg. The liberty that Whitman chanted did not interest Riley; and if he may be classed with Burns as a singer of the wildwoods and of simple hearts, he has no part with the saturnine Scotchman when he flamed forth with such searing satire upon hypocrisy, privilege and cant. Riley lived and wrought in what might be termed the Old Gold Age of American life; and his best work was done when he was about fifty, and the twentieth century dawned. When he was thirty-seven he sang:

> Tell me a tale of the timberlands,
> And the old time pioneers—
> Somepin a pore man understands
> With his feelin's well as ears.

To the last he looked back wistfully at a halcyon past, as if, after all, his present was not everything he made himself believe it was. Well for him that he did not see much of the Age of Steel, which had begun to build factories and blasts, at the very gates of the County Fair! (pp. 357-62)

Edgar Lee Masters, "James Whitcomb Riley," in Essays of Today: 1926-1927, *edited by Odell Shepard and Robert Hillyer, The Century Co., 1928, pp. 342-62.*

Riley's acquaintance with country life:

The country lore that Riley had collected and stored in youth was inexhaustible; it never seemed necessary for him to replenish his pitcher at the fountains of original inspiration. I have read somewhere a sketch of him in which he was depicted as walking with Wordsworthian calm through lonely fields, but nothing could be more absurd. Fondly as he sang of green fields and running brooks, he cultivated their acquaintance very little after he established his home at Indianapolis. Lamb could not have loved city streets more than he. Much as Bret Harte wrote of California after years of absence, so Riley drew throughout his life from scenes familiar to his boyhood and young manhood, and with undiminished sympathy and vigor.

Meredith Nicholson, in her The Man in the Street: Papers on American Topics, *1921.*

Horace Gregory and Marya Zaturenska (essay date 1946)

[*Gregory was an American poet, critic, educator, and editor; Zaturenska, his wife, was a Russian-born American poet, critic, and editor. In the following excerpt, they argue that the popularity of Riley's poems rested on their nostalgic portrayals of small-town life.*]

Although contemporary historians of American poetry tend to grow uneasy or shy at the mention of James Whitcomb Riley . . . , it would be an error of self-conscious embarrassment to underrate the phenomenon of his popularity and its significance. Of recent years, his reputation has been linked with the notoriety achieved by Ella Wheeler Wilcox (1855-1919), whom he admired, and it is all too easy to see why the mechanical optimism which flows so freely through the verse of both poets has brought to light an acceptable if not profound association. It is also true that both were born in the Middle West during a period when literary reputations owed their existence to the encouragement received from editors and readers of small-town newspapers and when the yearning for culture spread like a low prairie wind over the land; yet Riley's verse sustained and has continued to sustain its hold upon the popular imagination with greater tenacity than the work of any newspaper poet in his generation. (p. 59)

Though it would be unwise to overestimate the quality of Riley's verse on the mere evidence of its popularity, it is also clear that his gifts aroused a public response that is seldom if ever earned by grace of empty rhyming and familiar music. Those who read through the bulky volume of his letters, edited by William Lyon Phelps in 1930, will be impressed by a native shrewdness, by a mature as well as boyish energy and sly humor, by a touch of gentleness that, however worldly, remains unspoiled, and by a kind of literary cultivation that was self-taught and yet well disciplined. He had taken as his motto "The heart is all," and he kept his ear tuned to the music that stirred the heart of his native state and, later, the whole nation. Perhaps because he, like "O. Henry," was a true provincial, and because the large cities of the nation were filled with men and women from small towns and villages, he found a national audience. To them his verse contained accurate and beloved pictures of Indiana pastures and farmyards, of side roads that led to hidden streams and ponds, and these were re-created in the speech of provincial characters, who were recognized not only on Middle Western small-town streets, but in all small towns—they were the people who stayed at home, who loved the familiar sight of things at home, who were tenacious of old ways and were moved by simple sentiment. When someone questioned Riley concerning the accuracy of his Hoosier dialect, he admitted that its sources were in the memory of his own childhood, a childhood which had been spent during the same years that welcomed the publication of the second series of *The Biglow Papers*. Perhaps it was not surprising that Riley's own rules for writing dialect verse were of but the slightest variation from the Yankee idiom of Birdofredum Sawin and Ezekiel Biglow; Lowell had fixed the literary pattern for the speech and attitudes of small-town characters in America, and the sentiment of "The Courtin'" with its lines,

> All kin' o' smily roun' the lips
> An' teary roun' the lashes . . .

set the standard in which provincial America saw itself reflected as in a mirror.

Riley was obsessed by childhood, as some greater poets have been, and it is easy to see why someone once said of him that all his verses read as if they had been written by the very old and the very young against the middle-aged. In his obituary address on Riley before The Academy of Arts and Letters, Hamlin Garland said: "He expressed something of the wistful sadness of the middle-aged man who is looking back on the sunlit streams of his boyhood." (pp. 60-1)

Riley tested the value of his verses by the response from his audiences and learned through their physical reactions how to gauge the taste of a larger, national public. Riley himself told how on one of his first lecture tours, he read his lines to **"A Happy Little Cripple,"** a composition artfully contrived to bring an immediate response from those who heard it. He saw two people in the audience suddenly get up and walk out. In making inquiries he discovered that the verses had affected his two listeners too deeply, and that they had a crippled child waiting for them at home. This incident distressed Riley profoundly, who took great care to recite lines that would not depress his audiences, nor strike too deeply into the darkness of their fears and doubts. He had a great dread of the darker places in the soul, and of the sinister or complicated recesses of the mind. Coupled with his dread of darkness was his deep and genuine dislike of Whitman; and William Lyon Phelps remarked that on this subject in private conversation he often gave way to unprintable language. "A cult-reputation," Riley once wrote of Whitman, "he began by writing bad verses for magazines. These attracted no attention, so he decided to write something startling and eccentric." He also insisted, and not without justice, that Whitman lacked a sense of humor. Though Riley admired Poe, he also thought him much too "morbid." Ambrose Bierce was another writer who offended every instinct by which he lived, who was miles away from Riley's world of circus parades, of village bands, of small white clapboard houses set off by wide lawns and shaded by heavy trees, his world of a remembered childhood in which the emotions of pathos could be felt, if not fully understood, and which by its childlike character held no room for tragedy.

It might be said that to those who read and heard him, Riley never failed to hearten and console. It was not for nothing that his Indianapolis neighbors seeing him leave the yellow and white frame house on Lockerbie Street, faultlessly attired, gold-headed cane in hand, stopping to call children by name and sometimes giving them copper one-cent pieces, called him "Sunny Jim." And it was not for nothing that he had dedicated one of his books to "all Americans who were ever boys, to all at least who had the good luck to be country boys, and to go barefoot." (pp. 62-3)

As his own admirers were never tired of repeating, Riley had kept intact the heart, the emotions of a boy; and it was his unquestioning faith in the essential goodness of boyish work and play that continued to win the hearts of his many readers. If he sang of the old swimming hole, the old trundle bed, the old haymow, the old glee club, and going out again to visit old Aunt Mary—and recited each stanza as though it had been written for the millions of children who also recited verse on Thursday afternoons in public schools—every note he struck found an answering response in the breasts of those who stopped to listen to the song. What he had found and brought to light in a remembered childhood may not have been what childhood was, but to those who heard him, it was what childhood should have been in a world that was slowly drifting toward the instabilities which preceded and came after the First World War. The drift was noted in certain undercurrents of unrest that were to lead toward disillusionments and to an embittered analysis of the same milieu in the *Winesburg, Ohio* of Sherwood Anderson and the *Spoon River Anthology* of Edgar Lee Masters.

Meanwhile and throughout the first decade of a self-consciously American twentieth century, Riley continued to supply his publishers with scores of poems written in two languages, the first in what came to be known as a "Hoosier dialect," and the second in the readily acceptable idiom of conventional magazine verse. There were times when Riley himself preferred the latter idiom and was fond of recalling an anecdote in which a Browning Club member asked him whether or not he enjoyed reading dialect verse. "Some of it," Riley replied. "Eugene Field's is all right. But the other day I read some verse by a fellow named Chaucer, and I think he went altogether too far." This touch of wit, carefully phrased so as to offend no one, was characteristic of the particular craftsmanship he employed, as well as the not unworldly elegance in dress and manner that was so brilliantly reflected in the Sargent canvas which became his official portrait.

More than all else, he was the versifier of the long, bright summer holiday:

> With all your harvest stores of olden joys,
> Vast overhanging meadow-lands of grain . . .
> ["An Old Friend"]

> The yearning cry of some bewildered bird
> Above an empty nest, and truant boys

> Along the river's shady margin heard,
> A harmony of noise.
> ["August"]

> And down the woods to the swimmin' hole
> Where the big white hollow old sycamore
> grows . . .
> ["A Backward Look"]

And through the image of a summer's day, again and again, Riley's insistent longing for the past appears; and this emotion has never been more fortunately expressed than in his **"Where-Away"**:

> Children at the pasture-bars,
> Through the dusk, like glimmering stars,
> Waved their hands that we should bide
> With them over eventide:
> Down the dark their voices failed
> Falteringly, as they hailed,
> And died into yesterday—
> Night ahead and—Where-Away?

It is for the clear statement of this emotion, accompanied by his thumbnail sketches of small-town characters, that Riley's verse has been remembered and among the *fabulae* of American literature it may endure. For twenty years he was the poet of American family life in the same sense that Booth Tarkington became the novelist of the humorously perceived and yet idealized American home. And from the oblique position of his bachelorhood, for Riley never married, it is perhaps significant that his frequent spokesman was the man of all work and odd jobs, "the Raggedy Man," who was the traditional figure of the American

"Uncle," as well as the romantic "Tramp" of Ridgely Torrence's "Eyewitness."

Riley, in a letter of advice to the young Booth Tarkington, told him that his stories should be "Godlike, Manlike, Childlike," and this instruction was, of course, a rule that he had tried to follow in the writing of his own verse. (pp. 63-5)

> *Horace Gregory and Marya Zaturenska, "The Barefoot Boy of Indiana: James Whitcomb Riley," in their* A History of American Poetry, 1900-1940, *Harcourt Brace Jovanovich, Inc., 1946, pp. 59-66.*

If James Whitcomb Riley were here today I should take him by the hand and say, "Beloved poet, you have known how to touch the great heart of the people quickly and deeply. That is what we must all do, if we are to succeed. . . . Teach us the way."

—*Arthur E. Bostwick, in his* Library Essays: Papers Related to the Work of Public Libraries, *1920.*

James T. Farrell   (essay date 1951)

[*Farrell was an American novelist, short story writer, and critic who is best known for his grim Studs Lonigan trilogy, a series of novels depicting the life of a lower middle-class man from Chicago. Influenced primarily by the author's own Irish-Catholic upbringing on Chicago's rough South Side, and by the writings of Theodore Dreiser, Marcel Proust, and James Joyce, Farrell's fiction is a naturalistic, angry portrait of urban life. His writings explore—from a compassionate, moralistic viewpoint—the problems spawned of poverty, circumstance, and spiritual sterility. Farrell has written: "I am concerned in my fiction with the patterns of American destinies and with presenting the manner in which they unfold in our times. My approach to my material can be suggested by a motto of Spinoza which I have quoted on more than one occasion: 'Not to weep or laugh, but to understand'." In the following excerpt, he studies the manifestations of the American frontier myth in Riley's poetry.*]

"The world of childhood," William Dean Howells said, "the childhood of that vanished West, which lay between the Ohio and the Mississippi, and was, unless memory abuses my fondness, the happiest land there ever was under the sun."

James Whitcomb Riley held sentiments about pre-Civil War Midwestern childhood similar to those of Howells. He was born in 1849 in Greenfield, Indiana. All during his life, he looked backward with nostalgic and sentimental eyes upon his own childhood days in Indiana. He referred

TWENTIETH-CENTURY LITERARY CRITICISM, Vol. 51

to this time of his life again and again in his verse. He turned the yearnings of childhood, the unfulfilled dreams of boyhood into cliché after cliché. In one poem, he wrote:

> Dreaming again, in anticipation,
> The same old dreams of our boyhood days
> That never came true . . .

This quotation is illustrative of what Riley later felt about his childhood. Personal statements of his, made to his biographer, Marcus Dickey, match what he said in his verse.

When Riley was a boy, there was still an enormous frontier. Metaphorically speaking, it was just beyond the horizon of Greenfield, Indiana. As a lad, Riley could see the new pioneers passing along the National Road. He could watch the new waves sweep on, and as he did, his eye would be held, most especially, by those who seemed eccentric, and who might be wearing raggedy clothes.

Many have observed that the migration into the American wilderness was not like the migrations of barbarians in the past. It was a movement from civilization into wilderness. This can be seen more concretely, perhaps, if we try to think of Riley gazing out of his schoolroom window in Greenfield and seeing the wagons going by, watching all kinds and types of human beings as they moved on to penetrate farther into the American West. Those who had come earlier, those who were of the same generation as Riley's father and grandfather, had built schoolhouses similar to the one from which the boy, James Whitcomb Riley, looked out. And this great migration of human beings from civilization into the wilderness, beginning long before Riley's birth and continuing during his boyhood days, was practically unprecedented in history.

The settlers brought with them not only the tools of civilization, but also their ideas of civilization; and in some of their wagons there were books. They came from a background of democratic political experiences. They desired to be free. They were going forth, individually, to find their fortunes, and, socially, to conquer and build a continent. As they moved on, they passed the schoolhouses and courthouses that their pioneer predecessors had already built. Culturally as well as economically, they were to have a part in the shaping of new destinies. Frederick Jackson Turner, commenting on just such matters in *The Frontier in American History,* wrote: "The conception was firmly fixed in the thirties and forties that the West was the coming power in the Union, that the fate of civilization was in its hands . . ."

The Mississippi Valley, during the Jacksonian days, and immediately after them, was not a new Athens. But it was an area in which a vigorous new society lived. And there were books in this area. Marcus Dickey, in *The Youth of James Whitcomb Riley,* remarked on this fact. He pointed out that Scott, Dickens, and other writers were known and read on the frontier. One frequently comes on letters of the pioneers that suggest a level of culture as well as idealism and dreams of an American future. In fact, there is pathos in some of these letters when we read them with the advantages of hindsight. For we are still so far from reaching even an approximation of some of the early dreams and promise of American life.

The role of books in this transplanted culture is most dramatically personified in the career of Abraham Lincoln. And especially for those so-called practical men who scoff and sneer at books, it is pertinent to emphasize the fact that without books Lincoln could not have risen and developed to become the great and humane man whose memory is so honored. Lincoln's ambitions were stimulated by the world of books, not by that of crass Philistines: Lincoln's ideas and his emotional and intellectual development were intimately bound up with books.

A later era turned the image of American promise into the Horatio Alger figure, who is thrifty and provident but not intellectually curious. However, the real personification of the promise of American life at its best is Abraham Lincoln. And the story of Lincoln includes the picture of Lincoln reading and studying by candlelight in a log cabin. This image has been sentimentalized, and the significance of the book in this Lincoln picture has been reduced. However, in this image of Lincoln, the book is central. The picture loses all meaning if the book is lost sight of. Abraham Lincoln developed because there were pioneers who brought ideas, democratic hopes and books, as well as tools and arms, with them into the American wilderness. James Whitcomb Riley wrote of Lincoln in this connection:

> Lincoln was a rich man. He lived in the American woods. . . . How rich he was with that handful of seven books by the cabin fire. What value he attached to his visit to this world: every day a day of discovery, a new survey of facts and principles, every day reaching out like widespreading trees around him for soil and water. I would rather see what he saw and loved than see the skyline of a great city.

Mark Twain's career is also bound up with the frontier. The story of Riley's own life indicates that he identified himself with both Lincoln and Twain, but especially with the latter. He often cited Tom Sawyer and Huckleberry Finn and tried to read something of their fictional lives into his own memories of boyhood. And he commented on the fact that he, like Mark Twain, had opposed his father. (pp. 63-70)

. . . . .

One of the problems of cultural history and analysis which is all too infrequently dealt with in America is this—how does the consciousness of writers evolve, develop, take shape in this country? Here, however, I can only suggest that such a problem should be posed and dealt with, and that it is also pertinent to the works of James Whitcomb Riley.

The analysis presented above should suggest the kind of cultural climate in which Riley grew up. Riley spoke at length of his boyhood, and his remarks are copiously quoted in Marcus Dickey's, *The Youth of James Whitcomb Riley.* Riley loved nature. He loved the streams, the fields. He hated and resented school. In after years, he spoke of school with contempt, because of the discipline of the three R's, the whippings, the floggings, and the boresomeness of the appeal to pure verbal authority.

"Omit the schoolmarm from my history entirely," he said to Marcus Dickey, "and the record of my career would not be seriously affected." Reading this and other and longer statements which he made to Marcus Dickey, I am inclined to suspect that he was overstating his resentment, and that there is in his words something of the affected note of a man consciously speaking to impress an audience by an appeal to stereotyped attitudes.

However, I do believe that there was no such affectation in another of his remarks to Mr. Dickey when he said of himself that he "was a timid boy as I have been a bashful man." To me, the over-crystallized nostalgia for his own boyhood at a time when dreams and anticipations never came true strongly suggests timidity. Likewise, his stereotyped poems sentimentally dismissing the attractions of fame, suggest the desire for fame on the part of one who, while bashful and timid, is also highly self-centered and ambitious.

However, these remarks can lead us into psychological speculation. Let it suffice for our purposes here that we accept his own statement about his timidity.

Marcus Dickey remarked of Riley that "The pioneer past was a rich landscape for" him. At the time Riley attended school—school that was pretty much of a closed and narrowed universe for him—there was that continuing flow of new pioneers, roustabouts, itinerants, nondescripts and others, past the schoolhouse. School and knowledge signified a discipline of the three R's imposed by adults. But outside the wagons flowed on to the West.

Besides, there was that world of nature he loved. Here was a rich and open world of material to feed the senses of boys. The world of pioneer America was a rich one for boys because there was so much upon which the senses could feed, so much upon which the imagination could fasten. There was the awesome beauty of nature, there was a sense of space, there was the animal world, and there was the opportunity for free and wide-ranging play.

Along with this, there was a social world of building, of motion, which embodied a genuine confidence in the future. Careers were open. To the West there was free land. Many who were dissatisfied could pick up and move on. These boys were the sons or the grandsons of those who had left their homes to forge ahead through the Cumberland Gap and over the Alleghenies to this new world.

We see then that there was a social basis for the kind and quality of dreams and experiences of many boys in the American Midwest, prior to the Civil War. All of us are, more or less, nostalgic for our childhood. This note of nostalgia for childhood, which was expressed by Howells, by Mark Twain, and which was one of the major, if stereotyped, themes of James Whitcomb Riley, can, in the light of these remarks, become doubly understandable to us.

I have mentioned James Whitcomb Riley's resentment of school. This seems to be part of a commonplace and possibly affected resentment of authority which we can find in his life, but not in his work. The Rileys were poor in the post-Civil War days. Riley's father, a village lawyer, never recouped what he lost by serving in the Union Army.

Riley's self-portrait at age fourteen.

One night in his youth, Riley dressed up to go out: he was dressed very shabbily. His father, noticing this, told him that he could come into the garden and hoe. Riley obeyed. But suddenly, he threw his hoe over the fence and into the garden of a neighbor. This was his declaration of independence.

At a later date, when speaking of this incident in his life, he said: "I used language that would sear the walls of a synagogue. I resolved never to work with a hoe again—and I never did." After throwing the hoe over the fence, Riley marched off, resolute and angry. From this time on, his relationships with his father were strained.

During this youthful period, he worked at various jobs, and then he became an itinerant. When he first began to write verse, his father believed that this was not a proper career for a young man. But while Riley avowed that he had no objection, per se, to working with a hoe, he did not want this kind of work for himself.

We cannot attempt to analyze this action of Riley's fully, but we can note that involved in it was the dawning of cultural aspiration. And this dawning of cultural aspiration in American youth is something much more common than many may be aware of. There have been American youths throwing away their hoes, literally or symbolically, for many decades. This is a natural, normal, and fairly characteristic aspect of American experiences. Riley's action here forms the pattern for the actions of many American writers of widely varying degrees of talent and achievement. (pp. 81-7)

Riley's verse emphasizes a feeling for security. It gives almost endless expression to received sentiments. It tends to ritualize human emotions in terms of accepted sentimentalities. I have already spoken of the awesomeness of the open world of pioneer America. Life was, as it were, very new and very young and it was changing and full of motion. But there is, also, much evidence to suggest that many hungered for security. The history of the building of the American continent shows how many went so far, emigrated, set up their stakes in a new place and there settled down, wanting, for themselves, no more change and uncertainty.

This desire for security has permeated small town life. The sentimentality of Riley—at times his verse became like a fog of sentimentality—seems to me to be but one of many expressions of this feeling for security. The emotions which he expressed are usually safe. They are lost in nostalgia, quilted in formalized reveries, and they are rarely spontaneous.

Insecurity, adventure, freedom is expressed, largely, in the image of the ragged and shabby itinerant who is a stage or typed character. Riley's verses are highly self-centered, and again and again, satisfaction is expressed in terms of cliché. In particular, love is rendered into a cozy cliché. Thus, these concluding stanzas from **"An Old Sweetheart of Mine"**:

> When we should live together in a cozy little cot
> Hid in a nest of roses, with a fairy garden spot,
> Where the vines were ever fruited, and the
>   weather ever fine,
> And the birds were ever singing for that old
>   sweetheart of mine.
> When I should be her lover forever and a day
> And she my faithful sweetheart till the golden
>   hair was gray;
> And we should be so happy that when either's
>   lip were dumb
> They would not smile in Heaven till the other's
>   kiss had come.

Many favor Riley's dialect poems and value them more highly than his formal verse. These offended such an Easterner as Thomas Bailey Aldrich [who wrote, "The English language is too rich and sacred a thing to be mutilated and vulgarized"]. In these, something of the life and interests of the farmers and of small town life creeps into the lines, but these are also usually stereotyped. They contain lines which are also fresh or perceptive, but as a whole, this dialect poetry is contrived and artificial. However, it does reveal something of the life, the character, the social relationships and interests of the farmers and small town people of his time. It gives a mirror—often distorted by sentimentality and artificiality, however—of the times.

Donald Culross Peattie, in his Preface, "Riley as a Nature Poet," to *The Complete Poetical Works of James Whitcomb Riley,* divided nature poets into two schools: ". . . those who find in Nature, a reflection of their own moods or a sermon for human betterment, like Wordsworth, and that rarer sort that tries to echo Nature with her own

voice. It is a comparatively easy and pleasant thing to talk about one's self; apparently it is harder, as the naturalists already know, to report Nature." Peattie, in this brief Preface, was setting up a misleading contrast here, for he used this contrast in order to establish Riley's reputation as a nature poet.

This is unnecessary, and like most such comparisons and contrasts, when used to hail a writer, it lacks validity. It is open to question as to whether or not we can say that nature has moods. The major illustration from Riley's poems which Peattie cited, was a descriptive one, delineating a blue jay. Peattie's inconsistency here suggests the misleading character of his unnecessary comparison with Wordsworth. I should agree with Peattie that Riley was a nature poet. His observation of phases of nature, of birds, of trees, fields, streams and sky was often very clear. And he, at times, registered seasonal changes with high suggestive power. I would here especially cite his poem, **"August."**

But Riley talked about himself in his nature poetry, as much as, if not more than, did Wordsworth. And usually he talked about himself less interestingly. He often used nature as a means of alluding to banal reveries which he allegedly had. He marred his nature poetry with accounts of his ever-recurrent and weak nostalgia for the boyhood and the boyhood dreams and visions, which "never came true."

Riley's poetry is part of the regional literature of the Midwest, generally characterized by Frederick Jackson Turner in the quotation which I have cited above. It was largely "imitative and reflective of common things in a not uncommon way." It contained, in some of the dialect poetry, especially **"Little Orphant Annie,"** elements of a new expression, and of native humor. And it contained passages of true nature poetry, revealing feeling for the barnyards, fields, trees, streams, and skies of Indiana. This contrasted with his many crystallized sentimentalities.

Furthermore, he was, at times, bumptious and bucolic. His feeling of individualism at times approaches a rigid self-centeredness, as well as a confidence about the community in which he lived. This spilled over into parochialism. His work can be related to that of such writers as George Ade and Booth Tarkington, but this is a task that must be left for another occasion.

Riley can also be seen as a Midwestern phenomenon at a time of change. There is, in my mind, a sociological significance in his sentimentality, in his demonstration of a will for security in a world of change. He reveals an inner world at great variance with a changing outer world. He drew on the sources of culture brought into the West with the pioneers, and added to these touches of the new and evolving life which was being created all about him.

But he closed out of his verse more of this new world than he let into it. Again and again he tamed this world, and locked it up safely in his clichés of emotion, as Whitman and as Mark Twain did not do. We can here note how he reveals the dissociation which I have commented on above. He drew on resources from without, from English literature in particular, but only to make of these an imputation which was not individualized, not used as a cultural heritage to be assimilated as part of the cultural background from which the New World culture would be created.

After all, he wrote very many poems like **"A Life-Lesson,"** which I quote in full:

> There! little girl; don't cry!
> They have broken your doll, I know;
> And your tea-set blue,
> And your play-house too,
> Are things of the long-ago;
> But childish troubles will soon pass by—
> There! little girl; don't cry!
>
> There! little girl; don't cry!
> They have broken your slate, I know;
> And the glad, wild ways
> Of your schoolgirl days
> Are things of the long ago;
> But life and love will soon come by—
> There! little girl; don't cry!
>
> There! little girl; don't cry!
> They have broken your heart, I know;
> And the rainbow gleams
> Of your youthful dreams
> Are things of the long ago;
> But Heaven holds all for which you sigh—
> There! little girl; don't cry!

The "long ago" of Riley was usually the dreamed-of "never was," which walled out the spontaneous welling up of dream and feeling and emotion and aspiration which is, or should be, part of every human life. The "long ago" was a dream of false inner security. (pp. 88-96)

We are familiar enough with the general nature of the changes which have come about, not only in America but in the entire world, during the hundred years since James Whitcomb Riley was born. These have come "on a scale of the impulses of the elements." Thus, the beginnings of the discovery concerning the use of atomic energy.

We seem more than a century away from our forbears of 1851. Our inner world seems to us to be different from theirs. Collectively, we possess much more power than they possessed: individually, we feel much less confident, much less secure than they felt. Collectively, we live in a world of greater danger and menace than they did: individually and in a temporary social sense, we seem to be more secure from visible dangers. We face no dangers of the wilderness. Our wilderness is ourselves, our emotions, our fears, our anxieties, our despairs, our individual and lonely fears, in the face of the collective power of man to utilize the very "impulses of the elements" in a way that can destroy us all.

Materially, we have seen the day when many of the promises of American life have been fulfilled. Socially, and in a human sense, we are far, very far from achieving even an approximation of these promises. Some of the best of our modern American literature, for instance the work of Theodore Dreiser and of Sherwood Anderson, has dramatized this fact. It has dramatized something of the story of what the development of American civilization has cost in terms of the quality of ideals in America, and in terms,

also, of what this has meant emotionally and psychologically.

The type of security which was reflected in Riley's writings—and about which I have commented above—is nonexistent. His verse here might be described as an unreal little dream village in a world of social and psychological wilderness. And this social and psychological wilderness might also be described as the new American frontier of our day.

When Riley was born, there was a great physical and material unknown not far beyond the Indiana horizon. Today, we can say that there is a great psychological and social unknown and that it is in ourselves, and in each and every "single, solitary soul." America was discovered by Columbus. It was conquered and built up to its present state of power and greatness by the pioneers and by many of the sons and daughters of the pioneers. The new discovery of America, the re-discovery of America, awaits us and our children. And this re-discovery must involve the winning of a greater sense of what all of this has meant, and what all of this felt like, not only to masses, but again, to the single, solitary soul, to many single solitary souls. And literature is one of the most powerful of human inventions which permit us to make such revelations. (pp. 100-03)

> *James T. Farrell, "The Frontier and James Whitcomb Riley," in* Poet of the People: An Evaluation of James Whitcomb Riley, *by Jeannette Covert Nolan, Horace Gregory, and James T. Farrell, Indiana University Press, 1951, pp. 61-106.*

Dale B. J. Randall   (essay date 1960)

[*Randall is an American educator and critic. In the following essay, he analyzes Riley's use of dialect.*]

An admirer of James Whitcomb Riley has claimed that 'for his dialect poetry he kept notebooks as accurate as a scientist's. . . . The philologist of the future, studying Middle-Western colloquialisms of the late-nineteenth century, may depend on Riley's transcription of them as the most exact ever made.' Yet another reader maintains that Riley's dialect verse depicts ersatz Hoosiers who speak 'a dubious dialect as yet unidentified by any philologist.' As such comments suggest, no very diligent search is necessary to find Riley criticisms ranging over the entire spectrum of opinion and prejudice. Since no study of the poet's dialect, so far as I know, has ever been undertaken, and since a sound evaluation of his work must involve a knowledge of his language, I offer here a brief analysis of his dialect usage. Let us consider the following kinds of evidence: opinions concerning Riley's dialect; his *modus operandi;* his own comments and poems; and the nature of Hoosier speech.

Perhaps early criticisms of Riley are best approached with the recollection that Americans at the close of the last century had not only what seemed an innate enthusiasm for American writing, but also the remnants of a feeling that dialect in literature was not wholly respectable. The Brahminical smile of H. W. Boynton, who refers to Riley's 'momentary lapses into English,' is merely one expression of the idea that 'the men and women who speak dialect are not worth portraying in literature.'

Riley felt called on to attack the idea. Even Chaucer, he wrote in an article for the *Forum,* 'when his song was at best pitch,' was writing dialect. In fact, it is always a good writer's duty to permit 'his rustic characters to think, talk, act and live, just as nature designed them.' Hence, 'the real master must not only know each varying light and shade of dialect expression, but he must as minutely know the inner character of the people whose native tongue it is, else his product is simply a pretence—a wilful forgery, a rank abomination.' At its best, well-written dialect will 'convey to us a positive force of soul, truth, dignity, beauty, grace, purity, and sweetness, that may even touch us to the tenderness of tears.'

For some readers, of course, this sort of rationalization was unnecessary. To William Dean Howells, among others, Riley seemed worthy of favorable comparison with Burns and Wordsworth. 'The Hoosier parlance which he has subdued to rhyme,' wrote Howells, 'has not the consecration which time has given the Scottish dialect in Ramsay and Burns, but it says things as tenderly and as intimately, and on the lips of this master it is music.' On the whole, in fact, Middle Westerners contemporary with Riley tended to regard his Hoosier very favorably. Edward Eggleston, himself a student of earlier Indiana speech, observed in a letter to Brander Matthews that Riley's Hoosier was 'a little thin,' but he also said that 'there is not a false note in it. . . . As dialect it is perfectly sound Hoosier . . .' Eggleston reasoned that Riley learned it 'more among villagers than among rustics,' and that by the time he came along 'the tremendous . . . vigor of the public school system in Indiana must have washed the color out of the dialect a good deal.' Moreover, unlike Lowell, who uses dialect 'with a full appreciation of its linguistic and philosophical relations,' Riley, according to Eggleston, uses it

> *only so far as it contributes to his effect* of pathos or humor. Of its nicer shades, its half-tints he is as yet unconscious. This is inevitable in a man of his age and in one who has continued to live where he cannot know any other rustic speech for comparison.

In more recent years, literary historians have tended either to ignore Riley or to dismiss him with a patronizing remark or two. In 1938, for instance, Richard A. Cordell wrote that the poet 'reports the uneducated Hoosier's bad grammar rather than his dialect.' Far more persuasive are the words of Horace Gregory, who in 1951 expressed the opinion that Riley wrote

> a language that has all the marks of literary and not literally spoken invention; in it we hear echoes of a speech that has its origin in *The Biglow Papers* . . . in the Far Western gold rush stories of Bret Harte, and in the dialect verses of John Hay. The Hoosier dialect as Riley wrote it was a variation of all these, a skillful combination. . . . [It is an] unliteral dialect that has behind it a span of literary precedent, and as Riley

wrote it, it extended the span of a nineteenth century convention.

On the other hand, one also finds modern writers who continue to champion Riley. R. E. Banta, for example, did not hesitate to claim in 1949 that in Riley's 'great talent for the accurate hearing and the true recording of dialect he was unsurpassed in his time. His Hoosier was perfection itself . . .'

It seems clear that there is no such thing as a general opinion on Riley's dialect. Significantly, however, the poet was nearly universally praised for his accuracy by Middle Westerners of his own day who had had a chance to hear the language he tried to record. Although such spokesmen were surely swayed to some degree by pride of location, the sheer volume of their voices drowns out such mild complaints as Eggleston's.

In attempting an estimate of our own, we shall be aided by a knowledge of how Riley worked. William Lyon Phelps, a personal friend of Riley, echoes such writers as Banta, Carman, Tevis, and the Russos by saying that the poet 'always took infinite pains with his verse, considered carefully its technique and the weight of every word.' Another source on the subject is George Hitt, who not only knew Riley for many years, but shared an office with him when they both worked on the Indianapolis *Journal.* Hitt writes:

> As we were both Hoosiers, born and bred, and had heard the same kinds of dialect, we drifted into the habit of using it with each other without thought or comment. Wherever we were, whether traveling, or in our office, or at my home, Riley, assuming the old farmer, or some other character, with me for a mere foil, would keep up long conversations, trying out new phrases and terms of speech, which afterwards would appear in his verse or prose. He was constantly studying and determining the values of the common-talk that we heard on trains or in towns or out in the open country; hence, there is nothing artificial in his dialect—he knew it at first hand.

Nor was Riley's interest in dialect a late development. Another friend, Minnie Mitchell, reports that even as a child the poet took careful note of the dialect of rustic clients who came in to see his father, a lawyer. In other words, Riley did not stumble over fame while strolling through the 'medder' one day. No matter what one decides about the accuracy of his dialect or the value of his verse, there are numerous witnesses to testify that he was a painstaking craftsman both in the gathering and the use of his materials.

Further evidence concerning language is available from Riley himself. In a letter dated August 4, 1880, we find him taking a stand on the question of so-called 'poetic diction.' To a would-be writer, Mrs. R. E. Jones, he reveals that:

> It has been, and is, my effort to avoid all phrases, words or reference to the old-time order of literature; and to avoid, too, the very acquaintance of it—because we are apt to absorb more or less of the peculiar ideas, methods, etc., of those au-

thors we read; and as everything is right in its place—so the old authors are right in the past—while new ones must be here in the present—see?

He even abrogates the syntax of the old school. In a letter to Madison Cawein on September 19, 1891, he says:

> Don't—don't—*Don't* ever becloud your beautiful ideas by too intricate—too long, or too involved sentences. . . . And don't—don't—*Don't* invert! No matter though every classic master whose winy verse you ever jabbed your beak in has inverted, don't you do it. You improve on them by getting there directly . . .

Of course, not all of Riley's edicts are negative. To Lucy Furman in February, 1893, he writes as follows:

> In dialect be as conscientious as in your purest English—seeing to it always, with most vigilant minuteness, that your unlettered characters are themselves in thought, word and deed. . . . If anything be not plausible as Nature, reject it—scratch it out.

Perhaps the most telling of the passages in his correspondence appears in a letter to Benjamin Parker (August 29, 1897). Here he reveals his attitude toward dialect, his chief goal, and a nicety of insight which might surprise his detractors. Riley writes, 'I most conscientiously believe . . . there is a legitimate use for it [dialect], and as honorable a place for it as for the English, pure and unadulterated. The only trouble seems to be its misuse . . . ' Later he observes that 'once in a while . . . some finished critic discriminates and estimates the dialectic purpose exactly.' He cites as an example a critic of his **'Nothin' to Say'** who has written that the poem 'is an illustration of the only possible excuse for this sort of work,' namely, that 'the tender and touching little poem does not depend on the dialect,' but that 'the feeling, the homely pathos of the verse makes it of value, and the dialect is simply its strongest and most fitting expression.' Riley adds: 'That is the highest praise I seek or my ambition desires . . .'

Hamlin Garland is also helpful in rounding out the evidence concerning Riley's views on language. He quotes the poet as saying that he has written dialect in two ways:

> One, as the modern man, bringing all the art he can to represent the way some other fellow thinks and speaks; but the 'Johnson' poems [Riley used this pseudonym for such verses as **'When the Frost Is on the Punkin'**] are intended to be like the old man's *written* poems, because he is supposed to have sent them in to the paper himself. . . . But, in either case, it's the other fellow doin' it. I don't try to treat of people as they *ought* to think and speak, but as they do think and speak. In other words, I do not undertake to edit nature, either physical or human.

And, as a matter of fact, we learn elsewhere that the famous refrain of **'When the Frost Is on the Punkin'** was taken verbatim from an old-timer who lived near Greenfield.

Although Riley's long-held aims incline one to believe in the accuracy of his dialect, a man's reach may exceed his grasp. Because Riley's poems themselves must be examined before a judgment can be made, I have gone to the collection known as *Riley Farm-Rhymes,* an obvious choice for our present purpose, since we may well ignore such trembly pieces as **'Dream'** or any of Riley's other kinds of verse. Of the twenty-seven selections contained in this volume about 70 percent are in Riley's Hoosier dialect, about 22 percent in a fairly simple, straightforward language that we might call General American or Refined General American (using 'Refined' to indicate the scarcity of colloquialisms), and 4 percent (one poem) in a sort of hybrid language, part General and part 'Poetic.' It may come as a bit of a shock that the book also contains a poem in what surely may be called 'Poetic English.' A verse entitled **'June'** opens thus:

> O QUEENLY month of indolent repose!
> I drink thy breath in sips of rare perfume,
> As in thy downy lap of clover-bloom
> I nestle like a drowsy child and doze . . .

In succeeding lines we come across 'zephyr,' 'damask-work,' 'e'er,' and 'glade,' and in the concluding line we even find so heinous a remnant of the past as 'All hail the Peerless Goddess of the Year!'

In order to understand the nature of the Hoosier poet's more famous language I have chosen five poems from *Farm-Rhymes:* **'When the Frost Is on the Punkin'; 'Mylo Jones's Wife'; 'Griggsby's Station'; 'Old-fashioned Roses';** and **'A Tale of the Airly Days.'** (pp. 36-41)

That many expressions in [Riley's poems] were current in Indiana, both in Riley's time and before, few will doubt. For all of the differences between the two men, one finds Eggleston in *The Hoosier Schoolmaster* using numerous words which occur in the five Riley poems under examination. As one might expect, Eggleston's hickory-smoked dialect smacks more strongly of the backwoods, but he, too, uses *back-log, 'low, tuck* (cf. Riley's *was tuck*), *Pap, Mirandy* (cf. Riley's *Marindy*), *feller, tomorry, a-comin', wunst* (cf. Riley's *onc't*), etc.

Perhaps even more helpful than Eggleston's work, however, is a glossary of Hoosierisms compiled about 1906 by O. W. Hanley. Lists of expressions current in Indiana today may furnish helpful clues to what Riley was trying to do, but the radio if not the television set has penetrated deeply enough into even the back-farm society of Indiana to preclude any but the most infrequent occurrence of such unadulterated old-time talk. Hence the value of a compilation such as Hanley's, which records expressions typical of the then-isolated portions of the Wabash Valley. Words mentioned by Hanley and listed from Riley include *'low, allus, ast, kyarpet, airly* (pronounced, says Hanley, 'with *e* as in *hen*'), *ef, ellum, feller, jest* for 'just,' *man* meaning 'husband,' *pap* for 'father,' etc.

Still another source of information about old-time Hoosier dialect is the correspondence of semiliterate, nineteenth-century Indianians. Here, eventually, one might find all or nearly all the expressions that Riley uses. Certainly one finds many words remindful of Riley's eye dialect—e.g. *sed, thay, hartey,* and *tho.* Here, too, are Rileyesque slips in grammar—'you was' and 'we was' and 'n[e]ver got . . . nor.' Here are country expressions such as 'cuting . . .

stomach teeth' and 'I am coming . . . abiling.' And here, too, is the honest reporting of *felars, gether, bin, git, thorte, aheep, agoing, saplins, learnt,* and *fur* (for), every one of which was set down by writers as the word sounded to them. Of course, many such expressions could be found in contemporary writing from other states, but the point here is simply that they were used both by unself-conscious Indianians and by Riley.

Despite his occasional lapses, Riley's claim to accuracy also tends to be substantiated by the work of modern scholars. Because of the period in which he wrote, of course, evidence probably will remain fragmentary even after the appearance of the long-awaited Atlas of the North-Central States. A. L. Davis, however, makes it clear not only that southern Illinois, Indiana, and Ohio still retain terms not found elsewhere, but that such Riley words as *relations* and *poison vine* are especially common in Indiana. Mrs. McDavid furnishes, in addition to evidence already cited, information concerning the use of *growed, heerd, run* (pret.), *tuk, writ,* and other forms that appear in the Riley poems analyzed. (pp. 46-7)

[Nonetheless] I have set aside no words as 'Hoosier.' The reason is simply that—as the author of *The Hoosier Schoolmaster* long ago recognized—'in nothing is the student of American folk-speech so liable to error as in assigning geographical limits to a word or phrase.' Riley surely seems accurate enough to justify saying that most of his expressions belong to the main core of rural Indiana speech. He himself realized that no two persons speak a dialect in just the same way, and yet there is an Indiana quality to such words as *man* (husband), *Pap,* and *gether,* and (elsewhere in **Farm-Rhymes**) *hay-rick, pop-paws,* and *pizenvine.* The fact remains, however, that Eggleston applied the term 'Hoosier' to the language not only of Indiana, but of parts of Ohio, Kentucky, and Illinois; even Riley, speaking to a group in Chicago, referred to 'the dialect that is peculiar to our Western American country'; and an Eastern reviewer of Eggleston's *Schoolmaster* observed coolly that 'almost none of the dialectic forms was unfamiliar, that none was of much rarity, but all had been very well known as existent.' In fact, a sufficiently diligent search will turn up some record of a non-Indiana usage of every Riley expression considered here. From Ohio, Kentucky, Illinois, Arkansas, Missouri, and Kansas, from Pennsylvania, Massachusetts, and New Hampshire, come records of *ga'nts, gether, kyarpet, womern,* and *chinkin'.* Riley's *t'other* goes back to a Ben Jonson more rare than he of Boone County, his *afore* to Shakespeare, and his *yit* to Chaucer. This is not to say that Riley does not use words truly characteristic of Indiana speech, that he does not report Hoosier dialect. But *ga'nts* and *gether* do not now and never did stop at the Indiana border. In 1905 two investigators felt 'compelled to confess . . . that, in spite of considerable search, they have been unable to find a single provincialism which they would be willing to assert is at present confined to Indiana alone.'

That the language Riley tried to record is an amalgamation, of course, in no wise affects the quality of his performance. But certain other matters do. Having recognized the more convincing qualities of such a poem as **'Mylo

Jones's Wife,'** one should also consider such matters as Riley's use of the apostrophe. Surely Benj. F. Johnson of Boone would never have written *whoopin'* nor *s'pose* unless he was far more wise in the ways of punctuation than his real-life counterparts. At the first appearance of **'When the Frost Is on the Punkin,'** Johnson made the same literate blunder of writing *clackin', cluckin', risin',* and *appetizin',* an error corrected neither in **Farm-Rhymes** nor in the editions of Riley's collected works in 1913 and 1916. Both in this poem and others the Riley-Johnson use of the hyphen is also questionable; although it is phonetically unobtrusive (as in *a-preachin'*), I have not yet found it substantiated by the practice of any Hoosier letter writers. Subsequent to the poem's first appearance, moreover, Riley learned that no turkey cock ever 'kyoucks,' and yet he continued to refer to 'the kyouck . . . of the struttin' turkey-cock.' In the same poem, however, he tidily changed *its* to *it's* and (as we have seen) *somepin* to *something*—perhaps forgetting that in **'A Tale of the Airly Days'** Johnson was allowed to retain his *somepin'* from first to last. More understandable—and far more prominent among the revisions which Riley made both here and elsewhere—are those which lead away from literacy. *Early* becomes *airly; blossoms, blossums; rustle, russel;* and *their, theyr.* In the stanza which was added, however, the poet allowed both *their* and *theyr* to remain in a single line.

Riley's inflection and phrasing are also important. Part of the effect of a poem like **'Mylo Jones's Wife'** is achieved by strategic italics and numerous dashes. In such a work Riley suggests a conversational cadence which no analysis of individual words can ever touch. It was an instinct for rightness in such matters which led him to alter 'night of gracious rest' to the more natural 'night of peaceful rest' in **'When the Frost Is on the Punkin,'** although the word *gracious* might seem appropriate in some other Hoosier phrase. Nevertheless, the over-all syntactical authenticity of such poems should in fairness be regarded together with such less convincing locutions as appear in **'Old-fashioned Roses.'** Perhaps no flesh-and-blood Hoosier farmer would claim, as does the speaker here, that his dying wife's eyes 'whispered with a smile,' much less that they gave him burial instructions. And perhaps no farmer would say, as does the narrator of **'How John Quit the Farm,'** 'I noticed, with a sigh' or 'my happiness, that evening, with the settin' sun went down.' The colloquial *settin'* is simply not enough to deceive us into thinking such lines literally authentic.

To deplore the matter, however, especially considering the relative scarcity of this sort of phraseology, is to ignore the basic fact that if Riley had recorded literally the speech of the back-country Hoosiers (as he perhaps thought he was doing), he would not have been able to write in verse at all. It is surely a rare person, Hoosier or otherwise, who speaks in rhymed and rhythmic lines; and possibly it is an even rarer person who would find it a pleasure to struggle through phonetically faithful verse. Of course, Riley's writing was not scientific transcription. It was founded on selection and dependent on suggestion. And considerable tact and insight were involved. It is a bit shortsighted, therefore, to complain that Riley allows one of his farmers to notice something 'with a sigh.' The more important fact is that the poem as a whole achieves its effect, ultimately, not in spite of such phrases but partly because of them, or at least because of the principle they represent.

Whatever we may conclude concerning the quality of Riley's verse, there is evidence of various kinds to indicate that by his use of 'plane words' he suggested Hoosier speech and suggested it well. Though he was by no means infallible, his own reiterated claim to accuracy is for the most part supported by men and women who knew the dialect at firsthand, by those who observed his working habits, by letters of nineteenth-century Indianians, and by scholarly lists and studies. Riley did not invariably 'tell of the things jest as they was,' nor did he really

> tetch' em up like the poets does,
> Tel theyr all too fine fer use!

But touch them up he did. As a writer of verse he could scarcely have done otherwise. (pp. 47-50)

> Dale B. J. Randall, "Dialect in the Verse of 'The Hoosier Poet'," in American Speech, Vol. XXXV, No. 1, February, 1960, pp. 36-50.

Richard H. Crowder   (essay date 1978)

[*Crowder was an American educator, critic, and author of* Those Innocent Years: The Legacy and Inheritance of a Hero of the Victorian Era, James Whitcomb Riley *(1957). In the following essay, Crowder considers the eroticism in Riley's sonnets.*]

Among the nearly 1,500 Riley poems, I count 84 sonnets. Thirty-four of them have some level of sexual reference, and only nine of these were written outside the ten-year span of 1878-87. During this period the poet showed interest in several women, including Ella Wheeler, Lizzie Kahle of Pennsylvania, Clara Bottsford of Greenfield, and Booth Tarkington's sister, Haute. These connections were broken for a variety of reasons; but, generally, Riley was searching for an ideal that simply could not exist. How much these liaisons, Platonic or otherwise, influenced the nature of the eroticism in his sonnets it is impossible to surmise. The majority of the poems are in the first person, but may have been written, as Peter Revell suggests, to flutter the pulses of his uncritical readers and thus maintain his popularity. To examine a few of these sonnets might contribute to a change of attitude toward the Riley canon.

In a fairly early sonnet in this decade, **"Dearth,"** about not giving all to love, the voice speaks in the immediacy of the present tense. It is night, the girl's hand is shaking in the man's, her teary eyes seem to say that she regrets having strayed. Her lover has a feeling that her passion has previously been released elsewhere. She is able, however, to make him forget her past betrayal in present ecstasy. The poet uses the imagery of ripe grapes:

> I forget,
> While crimson clusters of your kisses press
> Their wine out on my lips, my royal fare
> Of rapture, since blind fancy needs must guess
> They once poured out their sweetness other-
> where,

> With fuller flavoring of happiness
> Than e'en your broken sobs may now declare.

In thoughts as wordly weary as Edna St. Vincent Millay's, the man expresses his feeling that the lady protests too much.

The theme of the sonnet **"Sleep"** is not actual physical contact with a woman, but the imagery is nevertheless purely erotic, approaching the lascivious. Drowsiness and the act of letting go as the speaker falls asleep are compared to the "languor" of sinking into some "ocean-depth of love." The male speaker compares himself to an Argonaut (a *machismo* parallel) who with tremendously willing cooperation falls into a passionate embrace with a siren obviously lying beneath him, for her seductive eyes are, as he says, "upturned to mine," and her arms "coil their sorcery / About my neck." The poem closes with reference again to the depths of the ocean, with the addition of details of wanton abandon. In consequence of the siren's "kisses so divine,"

> The heavens reel above me, and the sea
> Swallows and licks its wet lips over me.

Such amorousness would make the simple act of falling asleep almost too exciting for the necessary relaxation. The reader is reminded of passionate passages in Whitman's "Song of Myself" and "Children of Adam." (Incidentally, Riley would have nothing to do with the seeming free-form structure of Whitman's verse. Like Frost, he demanded the challenge of a net for his game of tennis.)

The early part of the poem centers on the figures of satyrs—no pikers themselves in a sexual way. Addressed to Sleep as a god, the poem pictures him as lethargically watching the *persona* himself

> lave my soul as in enchanted streams
> Where reveling satyrs pipe along the brink,
> And, tipsy with the melody they drink,
> Uplift their dangling hooves and down the
> beams
> Of sunshine dance like motes.

This inspired image, mingling wine, dance, and song, is, if not openly sexual, at least peripherally sensual—that is, just at "the brink." The uplifting of the "dangling hooves" of the "reveling satyrs" is marvelously suggestive. The combination of "enchanted streams" and the "wet lips" of the sea with the love-play of the Argonaut and the siren, added to the orgiastic prancings of the drunken godlings, make one forget the sentimentalities of **"An Old Sweetheart of Mine."**

In **"My Night"** Riley responds to Keats's "Ode to a Nightingale." He speaks to his heart, correcting Keats:

> You do not guess how tender is the Night,
> And in what faintest murmurs of delight
> Her deep, dim-throated utterances flow
> Across the memories of long-ago!

The heart may imagine that it hears "the exquisite / Staccatos of a bird," but the speaker says it is mistaken: no nightingale here, nor any bird at all; rather the poet returns to the aphrodisiac imagery of lips and water, a sensuality more intimate than the Romantic dream of Keats or the Victorian chasteness of Riley's beloved Longfellow's "Hymn to the Night": this is not Keats's "embalmed darkness" or Longfellow's "calm, majestic presence." Instead, the speaker assures his heart that the sounds in the darkness are

> a blur
> Of misty love-notes, laughs and whisperings
> The Night pours o'er the lips that fondle
> her. . . .

Already this sonnet is more suggestive than either of the other poems. The breeze, faint but fragrant, is the breath of Night quavering like a lover's. The concluding couplet invokes the lover's caress to induce the ultimate reaction to carnal gratification:

> O blessed sweetheart, with thy swart, sweet-kiss,
> Baptize me, drown me in black swirls of bliss.

If this image of passion is not drawn from actual experience, Riley's fantasy life was assuredly realistic and vivid. The constantly repeated secretive s sound, the mystery of the kiss in the dark, and then the physicality of the whirlpool express orgasmic climax as neither Longfellow nor Keats attempts to do. Though baptism and drowning do not approach the near-lewdness of the sea's licking lips, they signify acts of inundation just as submissive to the act of love.

"When She Comes Home" presents a picture of trust and confidence quite absent from **"Dearth,"** though here too are trembling and sobbing, now on the man's part. He will touch the woman's hand tentatively as he did the first time, when he could not bring himself to look into her eyes. "Distress" was followed by "silence," the adolescent awkwardness of the incommunicable. He recalls (and at the same time looks forward to) the fragrance of her clothes. He knows the experience will have a dizzying effect, marked by misty eyes. (Even his soul will become hazy, for he will momentarily lose control of his senses.) He will give way to tears and a lump in his throat because he knows he is unworthy of her arms. All will end well as the lovers are at last "hidden in the old embrace," obviously to be enjoyed by sweethearts too long separated.

J. W. Lever says that "Wyatt's best love poetry was really out-of-love poetry." We have already considered Riley's **"Dearth,"** in which there is a suspicion that the woman is "out of love." There are a half dozen other such sonnets, though not necessarily Riley's "best," for some of them fall readily into the bathos of rejection.

The earliest of these was written about three months after Riley's disappointing call on Ella Wheeler. The details of **"Let Us Forget"** do not match those of the Wheeler episode, but the poet's fantasies could have been at work. The gist of the sonnet is that, though the lovers have experienced a romantic attachment some time before, it has all come to nothing; the sensible move would be to forget. The sestet describes their last meeting: they have made gestures of love, but without passion. They may be weeping for a lost love, but it is better forgotten; for it is futile to summon up empty emotions. The two of them are mutually "out of love":

> But yesterday I kissed your lips, and yet
> Did thrill you not enough to shake the dew
> From your drenched lids—and missed, with
> no regret,
> Your kiss shot back, with sharp breaths failing
> you:
> And so, to-day, while our worn eyes are wet
> With all this waste of tears, let us forget!

If **"False and True"** is filled with rejecting females, it has a happy ending for the long-suffering male, who has heard vows of fidelity from the lips of many now gone from him. He finds delight, however, in the fact that one woman is loyal. Mostly, the poem is devoid of erotic gesture, except that the second unfaithful one "sighed tremulously" as in her "dainty way" she would

> fawn
> About my face, with mellow fingers drawn
> Most soothingly o'er brow and drooping
> head.

The poet admits to many such mistresses—living elsewhere now:

> and yet I make
> No bitter moan above their grassy graves—
> Alas! they are not dead for me to take
> Such sorry comfort!

Sentimental phrases are plentiful in this poem, but with ironic purpose: e.g., such woman's vows as "Till my breath is fled / Know I am faithful," and the poet's own non-existent "bitter moan," "grassy graves," "sorry comfort." Rather, the *persona* here is pointing up the ultimate flatness of sentimentality. The woman still true to him has never descended to such excessive affectation. He describes his own reaction to her with a lovely comment (worthy of George Herbert): "my heart behaves / Most graciously." (In spite of the many desertions, this really qualifies as an "in-love" poem, for faithfulness is victorious.)

The male speaker of **"The Lost Thrill"** sounds like a sated voluptuary: he admits to experiencing all the "sweets of ecstasy" that his fancy has ever envisioned. He describes vividly what he means:

> The caress that clings—
> The lips that mix with mine in murmurings
> No language may interpret, and the free,
> Unfettered brood of kisses, hungrily
> Feasting in swarms of honeyed blossomings
> Or passion's fullest flower.

This is not objective summation. In the first person, it shows love-making in increasing intensity: the clinging caress, the initial locking of lips, the utterance of indistinct sounds beyond the understanding of normal thinking; then the kisses coming in a hungry flood until they reach the peak of passion. The thrill, however, is gone. Sexual satisfaction is easily available; what is missing is freshness and discovery as

> in the first kiss
> A lover ever poured through lips of mine,

an experience so heavenly, so "subtle," that no poem could ever adequately communicate its "essence."

Three sonnets are used to develop the situation in the Poe-like **"Has She Forgotten?"** Riley has lowered the bars to let in some conventional sentimentality, especially in sonnets I and II, the first of which is replete with "birds and bees" (yes, really), "tombs . . . cold and gray," and so on. The lover's voice is setting the scene: Maytime in an old cemetery, a proposed trysting place. But the woman has not come. The final lines are fuel for incremental repetition at the close of the two remaining sonnets:

> Has she forgotten life—love—every one—
> Has she forgotten me—forgotten me?

The significance is not yet clear. All we know is that the two lovers have met here before and were to meet again today. "Has she forgotten *life*" is the clue, not yet developed. In the midst of sentimental excrescences Riley is practicing a certain reserve, an economy.

Sonnet II moves the situation ahead. Again, it is difficult for the modern reader to accept what Huck Finn would label "tears and flapdoodle":

> Mine arms clutch now this earthen heap
> Sodden with tears that flow on ceaselessly
> As autumn rains the long, long, long nights weep
> In memory of days that used to be—. . . .

(The pathetically fallacious "autumn rains" weeping for the past is going overboard.) Then comes the repetition, altered to suit the progress of the situation:

> Has she forgotten these?
> And in her sleep,
> Has she forgotten me—forgotten me?

Now the truth is out: "her sleep" is obviously death. Well might she have "forgotten life." The lover is speculating on cognition after death. This second sonnet has opened with half-promises of life-like realism:

> Low, low down in the violets I press
> My lips and whisper to her.

He thinks of this gesture in terms of

> the old caress
> That made our breath a quickened atmosphere.

In the final sonnet he regards the coming night in such erotic imagery as to create in his fantasy the ultimate act of love with this woman brought back from her burial place. He now reveals his Poe-derived necrophilia, though he realizes it will be only "pretense," not the real thing,

> old love's awful dawn-time when said we,
> "To-day is ours!"

Riley uses oxymoron to express the paradoxes of passion: ease and tension, languor and appetite:

> To-night, against my pillow, with shut eyes,
> I mean to weld our faces. . . .

He expects the "tense ease / Of every longing nerve of indolence. . . ." Then comes the vividly overt statement of intention—making love to a corpse, if only in imagination:

> Lift from the grave her quiet lips, and stun
> My senses with her kisses—draw the glee
> Of her glad mouth, full blithe and tenderly,
> Across my own. . . .

Even through the overworked Riley diction, the sensuality of these lines is at the verge of shocking. So real is the lover's longing that the poet's punctuation of the refrain is no longer question marks, but the exclamation points of disbelief:

> Ah, Heaven! can it be
> She has forgotten me—forgotten me!

There are other similarly suggestive poems in this form, but we must end with a brief look at the second of two sonnets combined under the title **"Time"** in the Biographical Edition. This is the outcry of a love-starved male who cannot sleep. Seven exclamation points accent the lover's desires and the painful agonizing as he flings himself about on his lonely bed, praying, in desperation, that God will grant him just one kiss to match the passion of his coursing blood. Feeling guilty, he draws away from what might be blasphemy, apparently trying to separate physical desire from reverence:

> . . . A wild prayer!—bite thy pillow, praying so—
> Toss this side, and whirl that, and moan for dawn . . .

He prays now only that morning will bring the distractions of day and closes the sestet with "Pray on!" as if to say "A lot of good that will do!"

With the addition to Riley commentary of Jared Carter's "Defrosting the Punkin" in [the Fall 1977] issue of *Indiana Writes,* we are daring to discover a new Riley in American literature. In part, my purpose here has been to correct the opinion that Riley was a writer only of dialect verse, of children's poems, and of nostalgic recollections of a world that had never been. Though I can make no case for biographical parallels of these sonnets, nevertheless, if Riley did not have the experience of genuine passion, his fantasies at least, even though perhaps for the gently cynical purpose of making money, moved incontrovertibly from time to time in the direction of the fleshly. (pp. 143-50)

> *Richard H. Crowder, "Sexuality in the Sonnets of James Whitcomb Riley," in* The Old Northwest, *Vol. 4, No. 2, June, 1978, pp. 143-50.*

FURTHER READING

Bibliography

Russo, Anthony J., and Russo, Dorothy R., eds. *A Bibliography of James Whitcomb Riley.* Indianapolis: Indiana Historical Society, 1944, 351 p.

The most comprehensive descriptive bibliography of Riley's works.

Biography

Cagle, William R. "James Whitcomb Riley: Notes on the Early Years." *Manuscripts* XVII, No. 2 (Spring 1965): 3-11.
    Provides information on Riley's early life and career.

Crowder, Richard. *Those Innocent Years: The Legacy and Inheritance of a Hero of the Victorian Era, James Whitcomb Riley.* Indianapolis: Bobbs-Merrill, 1957, 288 p.
    Comprehensive but uncritical biography.

Dickey, Marcus. *The Youth of James Whitcomb Riley: Fortune's Way with the Poet from Infancy to Manhood* and *The Maturity of James Whitcomb Riley: Fortune's Way with the Poet in the Prime of Life and After.* Indianapolis: Bobbs-Merrill, 1919-22.
    The fullest biography of Riley. These two volumes are, however, uncritical and replete with sentimental adulation.

Eitel, Edmund Henry. "James Whitcomb Riley—A Sketch." In his *The Complete Works of James Whitcomb Riley,* edited by Edmund Henry Eitel, pp. 367-87. Indianapolis: Bobbs-Merrill, 1913.
    Outlines Riley's life and career.

French, Florence. " 'Dear Man!': Bluff Letters of Literary Friendship from James Whitcomb Riley to Hamlin Garland." *Ball State University Forum* 20, No. 2 (Spring 1979): 38-43.
    Excerpts from correspondence between Riley and Garland, with commentary by French.

Garland, Hamlin. "Vernacular Poets and Novelists" and "In Riley's Country." In his *Roadside Meetings,* pp. 90-108, pp. 224-39. New York: Macmillan, 1930.
    Reminiscences about Garland's long friendship with Riley.

Phelps, William Lyon. Foreword to *Letters of James Whitcomb Riley,* edited by William Lyon Phelps, pp. 1-9. Indianapolis: Bobbs-Merrill, 1930.
    Biographical overview and introduction to Riley's letters. Phelps comments: "[These letters] have the peculiar flavor of [Riley's] personality; they reveal his innermost nature in an incomparable manner. They are thus more valuable than any prepared autobiography."

Criticism

Beers, Henry A. "The Singer of the Old Swimmin' Hole." In his *The Connecticut Wits, and Other Essays,* pp. 31-43. New Haven, Conn.: Yale University Press, 1920.
    Characterizes Riley as the great poet of the American people.

Beveridge, Albert J. "James Whitcomb Riley—Poet of the People." In his *The Meaning of the Times, and Other Speeches,* pp. 254-59. Indianapolis: Bobbs-Merrill, 1908.
    Celebrates Riley's firm optimism and talent for capturing human emotion.

Dunn, Waldo H. "James Whitcomb Riley and Donald G. Mitchell." *Publications of the Modern Language Association* XLI, No. 3 (September 1926): 767-69.
    Refutes the accounts in Marcus Dickey's *The Youth of James Whitcomb Riley* of Riley's association with Donald G. Mitchell, former editor of the periodical *Hearth and Home.*

Review of *Rhymes of Childhood,* by James Whitcomb Riley. *Harper's New Monthly Magazine* LXXXII, No. CCCCXCII (May 1891): 965-66.
    Positive assessment of Riley's honesty and vivid imagery in *Rhymes of Childhood.*

Monahan, Michael. "Our Best-Loved Poet." In his *New Adventures,* pp. 169-86. New York: George H. Doran, 1917.
    Praises Riley as an artist who "never pretended to write above the heads and hearts of the plain people."

Nolan, Jeannette Covert; Gregory, Horace; and Farrell, James T. *Poet of the People: An Evaluation of James Whitcomb Riley.* Bloomington: Indiana University Press, 1951, 106 p.
    Three essays assessing Riley's career and works. The essay by Farrell is excerpted above.

Review of *Green Fields and Running Brooks,* by James Whitcomb Riley. *The Overland Monthly* XXII, No. 132 (December 1893): 659.
    Favorable review. The critic notes that *Green Fields and Running Brooks* shows greater depth of emotion than Riley's earlier works.

Revell, Peter. *James Whitcomb Riley.* New York: Twayne, 1970, 174 p.
    Survey of Riley's career.

Additional coverage of Riley's life and career is contained in the following sources published by Gale Research: *Contemporary Authors,* **Vols. 118, 137;** *Major Authors and Illustrators for Children and Young Adults;* **and** *Something about the Author,* **Vol. 17.**

Bruno Schulz

1892-1942

Polish short story writer and critic.

For further information on Schulz's career, see *TCLC*, Volume 5.

INTRODUCTION

Schulz is considered one of twentieth-century Poland's greatest writers. His reputation rests on a small body of extant work: the short story collections *Sklepy cynamonowe* (*The Street of Crocodiles*) and *Sanatorium pod klepsydra* (*Sanatorium under the Sign of the Hourglass*). An amalgam of autobiography, fantasy, and philosophy, Schulz's stories are often compared to the dreamlike works of Surrealism, Symbolism, and Expressionism while at the same time representing a highly individual achievement in world literature.

Schulz was born in Drohobycz, a provincial town that became part of Poland when that country regained independence from the Austro-Hungarian Empire in 1918. The youngest son of a Jewish textile merchant, Schulz studied architecture for three years at Lvov Polytechnikum. While he did not attain a degree at the Polytechnikum, his proficiency in graphics later earned him a teaching post at a high school in Drohobycz. According to his biographer, Jerzy Ficowski, Schulz loathed his job and devoted his spare time to writing and drawing. Somewhat reclusive, Schulz rarely left his hometown and relied on correspondence for much of his communication with other writers and artists. Among his correspondents was Deborah Vogel, a poet who edited the literary journal *Cuszjtar*. In his letters to Vogel he included strange and fantastic narratives based on his childhood experiences. At Vogel's suggestion Schulz shaped these stories into his first book, *The Street of Crocodiles*. Published in 1934, this volume impressed the Warsaw literati and won a golden laurel from the Polish Academy of Letters. Schulz published only one more book in his lifetime, *Sanatorium under the Sign of the Hourglass*, although he had been working on a novel entitled *Mesjaz* (which translates as "The Messiah") when he was fatally shot by a soldier in Nazi-occupied Drohobycz in 1942. The manuscript is believed to have been lost or destroyed during World War II.

The Street of Crocodiles and *Sanatorium under the Sign of the Hourglass* have been compared to the fiction of Franz Kafka and Marcel Proust. In their fiction Kafka and Schulz transform banal places, people, and events into highly symbolic and often grotesque narratives. For example, in *The Street of Crocodiles*, the narrator tells of his father's physical and mental deterioration through symbolic

metamorphoses into a bird, cockroach, and crab. Many critics contend that Schulz's writing resembles Proust's in its obsession with childhood and time. In his stories Schulz devotes much attention to the narrator's impressions of his past and to the process of memory itself.

Unlike *The Street of Crocodiles*, which focuses primarily on the narrator's peculiar father, *Sanatorium under the Sign of the Hourglass* deals mostly with the experiences of the narrator himself, who resides in a chimerical world where time and space are mutable. In one episode, for instance, the narrator visits his dead father in a strange sanatorium, where the older man carries on a posthumous existence. Of *Sanatorium under the Sign of the Hourglass* Emil Breiter observed that "[Schulz] tears the mask off the world by depriving it of the principle of causality, both temporal and spatial. In the apparent chaos that rules in 'supernumerary time' . . . or in illusory space, . . . the writer preserves such discipline in reasoning, shaping, and observation that one would think he existed in the clearest of realms, one perfectly ordered and free from contradictions."

PRINCIPAL WORKS

Sklepy cynamonowe (short stories and novella) 1934
   [*The Street of Crocodiles,* 1963; published in England
      as *Cinnamon Shops, and Other Stories,* 1963]
Sanatorium pod klepsydra (short stories) 1937
   [*Sanatorium under the Sign of the Hourglass,* 1978]
Letters and Drawings of Bruno Schulz: With Selected Prose
   1988
The Complete Fiction of Bruno Schulz (short stories and
   novella) 1989

CRITICISM

Colleen M. Taylor   (essay date 1969)

[*In the excerpt below, Taylor explores the theme of the
return to childhood in several of Schulz's stories.*]

There are definite psychological similarities between
[Marcel Proust and Bruno Schulz]: both were sickly, neurotic, sexually abnormal (Schulz was a self-admitted mas-
ochist), introspective, and shared a fear of "le néant"
which they sought to eliminate through art, by, as Sartre
said, "creating the feeling that (they) are essential in relation to the world, that is, essential to (their) creation."
Both sought through art a confirmation of their existence.
Proust, according to [Leo Bersani], "had a fearful fantasy
of losing the self unless it could be fixed in some external
picture," while Schulz, who "leaned toward nothingness"
(Gombrowicz) and hated the present, looked back to his
childhood as a period of authenticity when he was not yet
alienated from himself and the external world. And although Schulz, like Proust, used a narrator, Józef, distinct
in name from himself, *Cinnamon Shops* was, he wrote, "an
autobiography . . . or rather a genealogy of the soul."

Nevertheless, the works of Schulz and Proust are quite different in form, in style, and in their authors' reactions to
the past. In sheer size, the difference is striking: Schulz
wrote only one purely autobiographical work, *Cinnamon
Shops* a small (about one hundred pages) collection of fifteen loosely connected stories, while only eight of the thirteen stories of *Sanatorium under the Water Clock* are autobiographical in nature. Proust approaches the past with
the powerful, rational intellect of the mature writer; he
carefully analyzes his past experiences, reproducing in detail the external world and his past perceptions of it and,
on this basis, draws general conclusions about his experience, his personality, and the human condition. Schulz's
treatment of the past, on the other hand, is neither analytical, intellectual, nor realistic. Rather, he describes the
world as he saw it *during* his childhood in a highly lyrical,
emotionally charged prose, without drawing conclusions
or offering explanations; he returns in his creative imagination to that time when the dividing line between imagination and external reality has not been drawn and the
mind is not yet trapped in what Rimbaud called "the pris-

on of reason." Hence his art is often of a fantastic, surrealistic nature: his father is changed into a crab, a cockroach,
and a bird, his aunt becomes a pile of ashes, while rooms
fill with strange vegetable growths, fiery bars appear in the
air, and even time is speeded up and slowed down. These
are among the occurrences in the world of "festivals and
miracles" which Schulz describes and which in many respects is the diametric opposite of the world in which
Schulz, as a child and as an adult, actually lived.

For Schulz's return to childhood in his art represents, on
one level, a reaction against the historical and social conditions of his era, especially the physical and moral ugliness of twentieth-century industrial life. . . . The stores
of the Street of Crocodiles were filled with cheap shoddy
goods—*landeta* 'trash,' a word which is frequently met
with in interwar Polish literature as a symbol of the ugliness, pretension, and moral decay of the postwar world.
Contrasted to it, Schulz presents his ideal—the world of
the Cinnamon Shops, so called for their rich mahogany
panelling, in which rare, beautiful wares were sold: Bengal
lights, parrots, mandrake roots, homunculi in jars, old
folio volumes. This world is also identified with his father,
a silk merchant of the old school who is eventually ruined
by the rise of the unscrupulous merchants of the Street of
Crocodiles, becomes physically and mentally ill, and dies.
In the story **"Martwy sezon"** (**"The Dead Season"**), he
writes:

> Horrified by the spreading dissipation, he shut
> himself up in the lonely service of a high ideal.
> His hands never let go of the reins, he never al-
> lowed himself to relax the rigor, to lapse into
> comfortable certainty.
>
> Balanda, Ska, and those other dilettantes of the
> guild could allow themselves that, for the hun-
> ger for perfection, the asceticism of high mas-
> tery, was alien to them. My father looked with
> pain upon the decline of the guild. Who among
> the present-day generation of silk merchants still
> knew the fine traditions of the past art . . . who
> of them could reach the extreme finesse of style
> in the exchange of notes, memoranda, and let-
> ters? Who still knew all the charm of commer-
> cial diplomacy, the diplomacy of the good old
> school?

The rise of a crude but vigorous class of capitalists at the
expense of the old, dignified merchantry is a familiar
theme in European literature of the early twentieth century: *Buddenbrooks* by Thomas Mann (whose works Schulz
knew well and with whom he corresponded) is perhaps the
best example. Indeed, much of the literature of the postwar period was a reaction against the ugliness and misery
of modern urban life. The French Surrealists were in rebellion against the smug philistinism of the French bourgeoisie, while certain of the German Expressionists attacked the squalor of the city and the cruelty of the ruling
industrial class. Some of the latter hoped for a brave new
world in the future; Schulz's utopia, however, was in the
past, in the world of his childhood. Schulz's paintings especially reveal striking affinities with those of the Expressionists, especially Georg Grosz and Max Beckmann, by
their distorted Gothic figures, mask-like faces, and the

"demonic" nature of their subject matter (to use St. I. Witkiewicz's word), which reveals the "evil based in the human soul." Expressionism had been introduced into Poland by Przybyszewski and the Zdrój group, and Schulz studied for six months at the Vienna Academy of Fine Arts in 1910. Schulz's prose, too, has certain Expressionist characteristics: the emotional lyricism, which borders on rhetoric, his preoccupation with sex, and its extreme subjectivity.

But Schulz's rejection of the present was also motivated by his own psychological and economic problems. After his father's death in 1905, he was forced to discontinue his art studies and support his family: his mother, his aunt, and, later, his older sister. After some difficulty he found a job teaching at the local gymnasium in Drohobycz, a job for which his natural shyness made him unfit. He hated both his work and the lack of domestic privacy. . . . (pp. 456-58)

Thus, lonely and oppressed by his environment, Schulz sought relief in memories of a happier time. As he said to a student, Andrzej Cheiuk: "The most beautiful and most intimate thing in a man are his memories from youth, from childhood. Yes, rather from childhood. People without childhoods to which they can return in memory are color-blind. How wonderful it is that layers of memories can be unfolded before our eyes . . . as when a flower in a movie, growing slowly, is speeded up. Memory is an element: at times we curse it, at times bless it." Schulz sought to recreate these memories in his art. But his childhood was not "realistically" portrayed; rather, Schulz emphasizes its most attractive features, especially in *Cinnamon Shops.* It is as if a spotlight were turned upon certain things while the background remains in darkness. Such an analogy is not out of place here, for one of the distinctive features of Schulz's style in his use of light and color: he literally "paints" with words, which reflects his artistic training.

Colors have strong emotional connotations and perform a symbolic function in Schulz's work. Bright colors are associated with those things that Schulz values and loves: the Cinnamon Shops, his father's aviary, nature, and his hero Maximilian in **"Wiosna"** (**"Spring"**) which begins with a panegyric to the color red. . . . (p. 459)

On the other hand, the most damning epithet in Schulz's lexicon is "grey" or "colorless." He writes of the "grey days of winter, hardened with boredom," the "grey world" of his villain, the Emperor Franz Joseph, who bans the color red from his court (**"Spring"**). In **"The Street of Crocodiles"** he writes: "Only a few people noticed the peculiar characteristic of that district: that fatal lack of color, as if that shoddy, quickly growing area could not afford the luxury of it. Everything was grey there, as in black-and-white photographs or in cheap illustrated catalogues." (p. 459)

Schulz occasionally describes members of his family in his work, as he does in **"August"**; **"Pan Karol"** and **"Dodo"** (his cousin) are the other major examples of this. But his work is dominated by one figure: that of his father, Jakub, the central personage in approximately half of Schulz's

stories. The beginning of his father's physical and mental illness marked the end of Schulz's childhood. . . . (p. 460)

Schulz's attitude toward his father has little in common with that of Kafka, although the importance of the father in their works is often pointed out by critics as proof of the writers' essential kinship. Kafka feared and hated his practical, domineering father, while Schulz felt only love and admiration for his father as an impractical "defender of the lost cause of poetry."

And this admiration took on a special form in his work. In an article entitled **"Mityzacja rzeczywistości"** (**"The Mythologization of Reality"**) Schulz states: "All poetry is mythologization and aspires to the restoration of myths about the world. The mythologizing of the world is not yet finished." . . . The figures of Adela, the family maid, the archetype of "woman as destroyer," his aunt, the local half-wit Touya, and other characters in his work can be regarded as attempts to raise the specifics of his private life to the level of the universal.

But the most important example of Schulz's "mythologization of reality" is his elevation of his father to the status of a semi-divine figure: Jakub is compared, among other things, to a Heresiach, an Old Testament Prophet, Atlas, a magus, and St. George. Many of these comparisons are from the Old Testament, for Schulz, although not a practicing Jew, was fascinated by the ritual and tradition of Judaism. In the story **"Noc wielkiego sezonu"** (**"Night of the Great Season"**) Old Testament imagery is prevalent: his father in his shop is compared to a prophet blowing a shofar against the background of the "folds and valleys of a fantastic Canaan" (the bales of cloth which are "touched with the wand of Moses"), while the "worshippers of Baal"—the greedy customers—stand at the "bottom of that Sinai which rose from my father's anger." . . . And at the end of the story **"Dead Season"** his father is visited by a mysterious black-bearded man who, "like the angel with Jacob," engages in a deadly struggle with him. "Of what?" asks the narrator. "Of the name of God? Of the Covenant?" No one knew, although from that day on began "seven long years of harvest for the store."

But Schulz's father is identified with another world: with those "doubtful, risky, and equivocal regions which we shall call for short the Regions of the Great Heresy." This is manifested in two ways: in his pagan-like closeness to the animal world and in his theories on Demiurgy by which he seeks to emulate the Creator Himself.

Perhaps what Schulz most admired in his father was his unending battle against the boredom and stagnation of the provincial town and his own household. . . . [In **"Ptaki"** (**"Birds"**)] his father imports exotic birds' eggs from all over the world to construct a brilliant aviary, pulsating with life, color, and motion. His father's passionate interest in animals was that of the huntsman and the artist, notes Schulz, but also the result of a "deeper biological sympathy of one creature for another" which was to have "uncanny, complicated, essentially sinful and unnatural" results. For Schulz's father is, in fact, so near to the world of animals that the narrator cannot distinguish them. His father resembles a certain stuffed condor, which even uses his chamber pot, so that after his father's death, the narrator is convinced he has been reincarnated as the stuffed bird. He also suspects that his father has become a cockroach and, later, a crab in **"Ostatnia ucieczka ojca" ("The Last Flight of Father")**.

However, we must point out that these "metamorphoses" are different from those in the work of Kafka. Gregor Samsa's transformation into an insect in "Metamorphosis" is sudden, apparently without cause, and can be interpreted as an externalization of his feelings of guilt and worthlessness. Kafka narrates the story in a simple, matter-of-fact style, without explanation, and almost from Samsa's point of view, so that the reader accepts the basic premise and the subsequent events of the story as real events. The reader of Schulz's work, however, is not sure whether a metamorphosis did occur—that is, whether Schulz expects us to assume the reality of the event, as does Kafka, or whether he is simply re-creating a child's imaginative processes. That is, the narrator in Schulz's work cannot be regarded as a reliable reporter on external, *objective* reality. Moreover, in Schulz's work a metamorphosis is never a sudden change, but rather the end result of a gradual process, the culmination of the "fermentation of material" for which "ordinary objects were only masks." Spiritual forces in Schulz's world can materialize: the father's resemblance to the condor increased with time because of his sympathy for the noble bird and ends in his reincarnation in his form.... Schulz again is mythologizing by returning to a pagan view of the world in which the line between animals and men is not yet finely drawn, and, as in the old myths, men and gods change into animals, and vice versa.

Schulz's father enters the "Regions of the Great Heresy" in another way: he is also a creator and, in his theories, is the double of Schulz the writer. In **"Traktat o manekinach" ("Treatise on Tailors' Dummies")**, a series of three lectures made by Jakub to Adela and some sewing girls, Schulz expresses his own views on art and creativity. Jakub says: "We have lived for too long under the terror of the matchless perfection of the Demiurge. For too long the perfection of his creation has paralyzed our own creative instinct. We don't wish to compete with him. We have no ambition to emulate. We wish to be creators in our own, lower sphere; we wish to have the privilege of creation, we want creative delights, we want—in one word—Demiurgy." That is, the artist is an independent creator who constructs in his work a reality distinct from external reality, so that art is no longer a reproduction of existence, but rather an addition, a supplement to it. Art was not to be mimetic or "realistic": Jakub proposes the creation of a "*generatio aequivoca . . . a* species half organic, pseudo-fauna and pseudo-flora, the result of a fantastic fermentation of matter." This concept of art is again close to that of the Expressionists with their slogan "Los von der Natur" and the Surrealists who "saw art as a building process, not an expression or statement of existence as it is" [Anna Balakian]. And Schulz's own art exemplifies his theory, for in it he has created a self-contained, independent universe governed by immanent laws. Metamorphoses occur, objects take on lives of their

own, while even physical laws are suspended. Schulz's representation of time and space is especially unusual in that time is given physical properties: it can be stretched, expanded, shrunk. . . . (pp. 460-63)

Without lapsing into pseudo-Freudian theorizing, one might submit that Schulz's later devotion to his father in his art stems in part from his feelings of guilt because of his childhood attraction to his mother, his "siding with the enemy." But more important is the love, nostalgia, and gratitude he must have felt toward this strange, ill, lonely man waging his heroic struggle against the boredom and stagnation of life in his family and in Drohobycz. The gratitude may also stem from the writer's belief that his own gifts of imagination and creativity are inherited from the defender of the "lost cause of poetry."

Schulz's return in his art to the period of childhood is motivated not only by nostalgia and a desire to escape present reality: he also sought to regain his childhood consciousness and the freshness of vision which lies at the roots of the creative process. (p. 466)

Childhood is the time of man's most active relationship to reality, which is not systematized by experience or custom, but is seen for the first time in a fresh and individual way. Schulz once wrote to a friend, "My ideal is 'to mature' into childhood. That would be a true maturity." And the child's creative vision of reality is the subject of the first two stories of *Sanatorium under the Water Clock:* **"The Book"** and **"The Genial Epoch."** (p. 467)

The story **"Emeryt" ("The Retired Man")** is one of Schulz's most unusual treatments of the return to childhood. It reveals not so much the influence of Western European literary developments, but the impact of Schulz's friend and colleague, Witold Gombrowicz. The two contemporaries could hardly have been more dissimilar. Gombrowicz, with his customary arrogance, wrote, "Bruno worshipped me. I did not worship him," and admitted that he was never able to finish reading even one of Schulz's stories. But he also admitted that it was Schulz alone who understood his character and his art; he praised Schulz's review of his novel *Ferdydurke.* He and Schulz did share one thing: their concern for experimentation with form, which meant to them more than merely the structure and style of a work of art—it concerned the total relationship of man to himself and to his world. For both writers, the time of childhood offered revelation of the central problem.

Schulz's story **"The Retired Man"** is narrated in the first person by a retired office worker (one of the rare cases when the author is not himself the narrator) who begins by talking about his strange "condition": "a great sobriety . . . a lack of all burdens, a lightness, irresponsibility, levelling of differences. . . . Nothing holds me and nothing ties me down, a lack of support, limitless freedom. . . ." His problem is ontological: deprived of work and society by retirement, he can no longer define himself; his existence, "like that of all retired people," is precarious, and he fears that the fall winds may carry him away. He dreams of becoming a pastry seller, a chimney sweep, even a tree, for these "know the boundaries of their conditions and what is suitable for them." To return to his old office and be knocked about *po koleżeńsku* by the director is pleasant, for it confirms his existence. But the retired man finds a solution to his problem and relief for his existential anguish. While watching children playing in the park, he was "confused and delighted at their fresh, lively behavior . . . their impetuous *savoir vivre.*" Hence he himself goes to the local gymnasium and enrolls in the first class as a student. The director, a pompous pedagogue reminiscent of Gombrowicz's Professor Pimko, tells him: "A very laudatory and worthy decision. I understand you want to rebuild your education from the roots up, from the basics. I always maintain that grammar and the multiplication table are the basis of character building." He asks the retired man a multiplication question, and when he cannot answer, he happily realizes that at last he has returned to the state of total ignorance and innocence. The children accept him, and he becomes their leader, the center of countless intrigues and pranks. The culmination of his delight is his beating by the director, when he can only lisp helplessly. "I was really now a child," he says. But the ending of the story is enigmatic: he is carried away into the air by the winds he had earlier feared. What this probably means is that his existence is still inauthentic, for a mere adoption of the forms of childhood is not a valid means of self-definition; his existence is still precarious. Childhood, Schulz implies, is the happiest, most creative period of life—but its physical reality is lost, and can be recaptured only temporarily in imagination, dreams, and art. Moreover, in this story he reveals the negative side of childhood: the helplessness and passivity of a child before the forces of adult authority (although the retired man-child enjoys his beating by the director). (pp. 468-70)

[Both] Schulz and Gombrowicz recognize the superiority of childhood over maturity in terms of freedom from externally imposed modes of being. But the two writers emphasize different aspects of childhood: Schulz looks with nostalgia on the child's freshness of vision and imaginative power, while Gombrowicz tends to stress the absence of moral and social values and categories. But both regard childhood as a lost Paradise of spontaneity, freedom, and a "sense of the endless possibilities of existence." (p. 470)

Against the world of boredom, conventions, and form— the Austro-Hungarian Empire, the dreary vulgarity of Drohobycz and the Street of Crocodiles, the school where he taught, the lack of privacy and his own psychological fears and weaknesses—Schulz in his work opposes the world of the artist and the child, the world of his father and the Cinnamon Shops, where reality is not restricted but rather freed through the power of man's imagination. Indeed, when reading Schulz one is convinced of the truth of Baudelaire's famous dictum: "Genius is childhood recaptured at will." (p. 471)

> *Colleen M. Taylor, "Childhood Revisited: The Writings of Bruno Schulz," in* Slavic and East-European Journal, *Vol. XIII, No. 4, Winter, 1969, pp. 455-72.*

John Updike   (essay date 1979)

[*Considered a perceptive observer of the human condition and an extraordinary stylist, Updike is one of America's most distinguished men of letters. In the following excerpt from an introduction first published in the 1979 Penguin Edition of* Sanatorium under the Sign of the Hourglass, *he outlines salient stylistic traits and themes in Schulz's short fiction.*]

I. B. Singer, a pleasanter genius from the same between-the-wars Poland, said of Schulz, "He wrote sometimes like Kafka, sometimes like Proust, and at times succeeded in reaching depths that neither of them reached." The striking similarities—Marcel Proust's inflation of the past and ecstatic reaches of simile, Franz Kafka's father-obsession and metamorphic fantasies—point toward an elusive difference: the older men's relative orthodoxy within the Judeo-Christian presumptions of value, and the relative nakedness with which Schulz confronts the mystery of existence. Like Jorge Luis Borges, he is a cosmogonist without a theology. The harrowing effort of his prose (which never, unlike that of Proust or Kafka, propels us onward but instead seems constantly to ask that we stop and reread) is to construct the world anew, as if from fragments that exist after some unnamable disaster.

What might this disaster be? His father's madness, I would guess. "Madness" may be too strong a term— "retreat from reality," certainly. "In reality he was a Drogobych merchant, who had inherited a textile business and ran it until illness forced him to abandon it to the care of his wife. He then retired to ten years of enforced idleness and his own world of dreams": thus Celina Wieniewska, who has so finely translated Schulz's two volumes into English, outlines the facts of the case in her preface to *The Street of Crocodiles.* In that volume the story **"Visitation"** says of the father's retirement: "Knot by knot, he loosened himself from us; point by point, he gave up the ties joining him to the human community. What still remained of him—the small shroud of his body and the handful of nonsensical oddities—would finally disappear one day, as unremarked as the gray heap of rubbish swept into a corner, waiting to be taken by Adela to the rubbish dump." The many metamorphoses of Schulz's fictional father-figure, culminating in the horrifying crab form he assumes in **"Father's Last Escape,"** the sometimes magnificent delusional systems the old man spins, and the terrible war of diminishment versus enlargement in the imagery that surrounds this figure have their basis in an actual metamorphosis that must have been, to the victim's son, more frightening than amusing, more humiliating than poetic.

In Kafka, by contrast, the father threatens by virtue of his potency and emerges as less frail than he at first seems. In both cases the father occupies the warm center of the son's imagination. The mother is felt dimly and coolly and gets small thanks for her efficiency and sanity. At least, however, Schulz's mother is not entirely absent from his recreated world; in the writings of Søren Kierkegaard—yet another bachelor son of a fascinating, if far from reassuring, father—the mother is altogether absent. From the mother, perhaps, men derive their sense of their bodies;

from the father, their sense of the world. From his relationship with his father Kafka construed an enigmatic, stern, yet unimpeachable universe; Schulz presents an antic, soluble, picturesque cosmos, lavish in its inventions but feeble in its authority. In **"Tailors' Dummies"** (from *The Street of Crocodiles*) he has his father pronounce: "If, forgetting the respect due to the Creator, I were to attempt a criticism of creation, I would say 'Less matter, more form!' "

Sensitive to formlessness, Schulz gives even more attention than Samuel Beckett to boredom, to life's preponderant limbo, to the shoddy swatches of experience, to dead seasons, to those negative tracts of time in which we sleep or doze. His feeling for idle time is so strong that the adamant temporal medium itself appears limp and fickle to him:

> We all know that time, this undisciplined element, holds itself within bounds but precariously, thanks to unceasing cultivation, meticulous care, and a continuous regulation and correction of its excesses. Free of this vigilance, it immediately begins to do tricks, run wild, play irresponsible practical jokes, and indulge in crazy clowning. The incongruity of our private times becomes evident.

"The incongruity of our private times"—the phrase encapsulates a problematical feature of modern literature, its immurement in the personal. Abandoning kings and heroes and even those sagas of hearsay that inspired Joseph Conrad and Thomas Hardy, the writer seems condemned to live, like the narrator of **"Loneliness"** (in *Sanatorium under the Sign of the Hourglass*), in his old nursery. Limited, by the empirical bias of this scientific age, to incidents he has witnessed, to the existence he has lived minute by drab minute, the writer is driven to magnify, and the texture of magnification is bizarre. More purely than Proust or Kafka Schulz surrendered to the multiple distortions of obsessed reflection, giving us now a father as splendid as the glittering meteor, "sparkling with a thousand lights," and in other places a father reduced to rubbish.

Schulz's last surviving work, the small novella **"The Comet"** (published at the end of *The Street of Crocodiles*), shows Father himself at the microscope, examining a fluorescent homunculus that a wandering star has engendered in the quiet of the stove's pitch-dark chimney shaft, while Uncle Edward, whom Father's sorcery has transformed into an electric bell, sounds the alarm for the end of the world, which does not come. In these vivid, riddling images an ultimate of strangeness is reached, and a degree of religious saturation, entirely heterodox, unknown in literature since William Blake. Indeed, Schulz's blazing skies, showing "the spirals and whorls of light, the pale-green solids of darkness, the plasma of space, the tissue of dreams," carry us back to the pagan astronomers, their midnight wonder and their desolate inklings of a superhuman order. (pp. 492-95)

Schulz's verbal art strikes us—stuns us, even—with its overload of beauty. But, he declares, his art seeks to serve truth, to fill in the gaps that official history leaves. "Where is truth to shelter, where is it to find asylum if not in a place where nobody is looking for it . . . ?" Schulz himself was a hidden man, in an obscure Galician town, born to testify to the paradoxical richness, amid poverty of circumstance, of our inner lives. (p. 497)

> *John Updike, "Eastern Europeans: Polish Metamorphoses," in his* Hugging the Shore: Essays and Criticism, *Alfred A. Knopf, Inc., 1983, pp. 491-97.*

C. P. Ravichandra (essay date 1985)

[*In the excerpt below, Ravichandra analyzes the imagery in "August."*]

Bruno Schulz's **"August"** poses a new problem of analysis. The skein of semantics is not easily unravelled in spite of the vivid experiential content, a fast moving narrative. The clue lies, perhaps, in the choice of primal images. The difficulty of interpretation could also lie in the alter-identity of the author as the central character of the story.

The story, which hardly runs to eight pages, in English translation, has in it what embodies modernism: the ability to form whorl after whorl a complex system of analogous experience. The power of suggestion is realized through a variety of syntactical experiments to drive home the apposed sensibility of a child in a garish world.

August is an adumbrating presence with its febrile aspect. The world is encysted by the month. The child is seen slowly metastasizing in this atmosphere, from an obfuscated condition to the vitiating adult world. August is the mandrel on which the child is turned, milled.

Placed in the total scheme of Schulz's collection, *The Street of Crocodiles,* the opening lines of **"August"** gain a telescoped nuance: "In July my father went to take the waters and left me, with my mother and elder brother, a prey to the blinding white heat of summer days." The tone and the mood of the story is set by these lines. The child cannot get out of it. The conjunctive "and" succeeded by the objective case "left me" denotes an irreparable situation at once isolating the child in its company. The protective shield is not the mother but the father. Now that he is absent, the child is almost desolate. From then on all events of life start growing strangely meaningful as the child has to, by itself, interpret all encounters. The patriarch will not anymore lead the child through the labyrinth.

Schulz draws from the vast repertory of linguistic skill at his command the necessary tools to oppose the mood created by the earlier sentence. The next lines are of pure joy, of great celebration: "Dizzy with light, we dipped into that enormous book of holidays, its pages blazing with sunshine and scented with the sweet melting pulp of golden pears." It is not always possible to effectively juxtapose the inanimate and the animate. But therein lies Schulz's strength. For him, words are like marbles that come alive in the fingers of a child. Like in a game of marbles, his words strike each the other to explode into a universe of meanings not obscure but opulent. The child is tempted into forgetting the absence. Almost Keatsian in its effusiveness, the images flood the scene and cloy the senses.

The delirious passage quoted above comes with a sudden turn from the sober narrative of the first line. As in all works of any poetic merit, in this too, the associational element provides a richness and helps in adding to the structural evolution of the story. Such effulgence is seen leading Schulz to create the character of Adela. She is the Pomona of this world, returning from the market with a basket full of season's spoils and splendour. Schulz weaves a fascinating web of her description into the design of the story. She at once evokes both wonder and a feeling of revulsion. She is associated simultaneously with plenty and butchery, her basket holding fruits and "the raw material of meals with a yet undefined taste, the vegetative and terrestrial ingredients of dinner, exuding a wild and rustic smell." The adumbrative use of both romantic, surrealistic, and the harsh, almost horrific descriptions on one hand help to exalt and on the other puncture the exalted in a subtle manner. Another interesting aspect of Adela is the fact that it is through her that the child is exposed to the richness of the month, also it is she who diffuses the harsh glare of the August sun by drawing shades on the window. Perhaps, it is Adela who, after the father, offers in her being, some sort of a shelter to the child who is seen emerging from the cocoon of innocence into the world of sensational experience.

The next stage of significance is the one where the child emerges from within the house out on to the street for a walk with its mother. Schulz's black humour reaches one of its many heights in the following description of the child's observation of the effect of sunlight on the people crowding Stryjska Street:

> The passers-by, bathed in melting gold, had their eyes half closed against the glare, as if they were drenched with honey. Upper lips were drawn back, exposing the teeth. Everyone in this golden day wore that grimace of heat—as if the sun had forced his worshippers to wear identical masks of gold. The old and the young, women and children, greeted each other with these masks, painted on their faces with thick gold paint; they smiled at each other's pagan faces—the barbaric smiles of Bacchus.

The entire universe of Schulz's story now changes into a paganistic celebration with a touch of the phantasmal. The celebration reverberates with silence—a silence that descends on the reader with all its import of the underworld. Such is the metamorphoses which Schulz achieves.

The next paragraph exposits how the eye also observes, paradoxically, that the "Market square was empty and white-hot, swept by hot winds like biblical desert." August, divested of all its enchanting, alluring aspect, now manifests in all its harsh nature. The only objects that appear alive in such a world are the acacias. And rightly so. All else is garbed in emptiness. What relieves this atmosphere is a bunch of indolent youth who play at an inscrutable game.

Thus the contrastive pictures and the evoked stillness commingle to intimate in unmistakable terms the act of growing up in that one predestined act of stepping out of the shaded room.

The first section of the story ends with child passing the urban part of Stryjska Street and entering the suburban section. Here the child faces a very different world. Now, it is the heartland of August in this suburbia. And the description gathers momentum with the striking metaphor of the sunflower. Undoubtedly, it is the patriarch who is the enormous sunflower, towards the end of his days. And the blue bells and dimity flowers are the family which remains insensitive to the tragic import of his life. The sunflower image is the actuated expression of the child's nonverbalized fears. It is only apparent when it is seen in the context of the entire of *The Street of Crocodiles.*

The second section begins in an impressionistic manner. The richly dramatized syntax almost lulls the reader to perceive everything in a benign fashion. But what Schulz attempts, and quite successfully at that, is to show how August has merely produced, with all its potency, a proliferation in weeds. Now, it is Touya, the half-wit girl, who seems to usurp the crown of August from Adela. The half-wit and the season thus grow to be the apotheosis of each other. Curiously, Touya, we see, is the offspring of Maria, the saffron-yellow woman, who scrubs everything with saffron. What we do not forget is the fact that August dusts all under its sky with a golden tint. The ironic reversal effected here through Maria to subvert the aspect of August is but obvious.

Schulz's mockery finds an expression through a new device as he makes Adela the agent who summons the child to the strange world of Maria and Touya—the kingdom of death and the world of anoetic sexuality. If Maria's death implies, for the child, a certain evil presence in the world, Touya's sexual propinquity without any real objective reference is an element which cannot be comprehended for what it is by the child. We see the child's sensibility altering in a determinate manner only when confronted with Maria's death. The syntax picks up pace and flows like an erruption of lava: "And, as if taking advantage of her sleep, the silence talked, the yellow, bright, evil silence delivered its monologue, argued and loudly spoke its vulgar maniacal soliloquy." The reflective sentence that follows the account of Maria's death is in reality a note on the oppressive month that August has grown to be.

In the third section, the child enters the magical world of Aunt Agatha. At the outset the portals of Agatha's house seem to offer a way out from the world of death and of sterile force. The all absorbing mind of the child now attempts to grasp in realistic terms the ethereal world of Agatha. That perhaps signifies an attempt on the part of any growing consciousness to come to terms with whatever is mystical, and/or beyond the physical. The child is susceptible to what at first appears to be a surrealistic idyll of Agatha's world. The "lush green" garden yields to an ephemeral world: "In these pink, green, and violet balls were enclosed bright shining worlds, like the ideally happy pictures contained in the peerless perfection of soap bubbles." The pity is that whatever concrete identity such a world possesses is as that of the soap bubbles.

The doors of Agatha's house exert an influence of their own. They are living presences by crossing which one enters a new sphere of experience. And what cannot be wished away is the knowledge that these doors are always open like those of hell. And Agatha in all her stateliness is the Proserpina of this world. It is only in her stateliness that Agatha is in contrast with the emaciated Maria. For Agatha's fertility is ultimately not much different from that of Touya, "It was an almost self-propagating fertility, a feminity without rein, morbidly expansive." But if Touya's morbid sexual urge which remains unfulfilled is due to her warped nature, Agatha's unrequitted sexuality is due to the inadequacy of the male (rather, she renders the male inadequate). She is "the heroism of womanhood triumphing by fertility over the shortcomings of nature, over the insufficiency of the male." Such is her nature. Uncle Mark is the epitome of her contempt for the male.

Schulz's gibe at Agatha is directed through her children. Lucy sees in the most innocent of queries a "secret allusion to her most sensitive maidenhood." Her uncontrolled blushings, an abnormal cephalic condition, and a generally unwholesome appearance are all a logical result of Agatha's own aberrated existence. And Emil at first appears as exotic as the far off places which he has visited. The child craves for his attention and gets it in plenty. For, Emil's globe trotting has resulted in his being a voyeur and a pervert.

Thus Schulz evolves an entire universe of perversity. In such a world the unsuspecting mind for ever grows a victim to the process of unnaturalization. It is a world where the awakening consciousness is forever confined and subjected to a terrible isolation. The "finger-thumb opposition" leads in such a climate not to the logical develop-ment of a heightened dexterity but to "a shiver of uneasiness," the result of a comprehension of the febrile nature of the world in which one lives. And that is the theme song of August. (pp. 1-6)

> *C. P. Ravichandra, "The Febrile World of Bruno Schulz: An Analysis of 'August'," in* The Literary Criterion, *Vol. XX, No. 3, 1985, pp. 1-6.*

Russell E. Brown   (essay date 1985)

[*In the following essay, Brown examines the theme of metamorphosis in Schulz's short stories, particularly as it applies to the fictional father figure.*]

Bruno Schulz (1892-1942) wrote two collections of fiction, **The Street of Crocodiles** (**Sklepy cynamonowe** 1934) and **Sanatorium under the Sign of the Hourglass** (**Sanatorium pod klepsydra** 1937), plus a few separately published short stories. Their central theme is the presentation of his father, a loving, but also ambivalent, description of the last years of the textile merchant of Drohobycz (1846-1915) and especially of his relations with his son, called Joseph in the stories. These are not chronologically arranged, but represent independent efforts to describe and assess the central figure in the author's life. Many of the stories do not even mention his father, but are devoted to other family members and to fringe members of the Galician provincial city. Yet Schulz's main purpose is an elegy to the father, only secondarily a portrayal of family and community. The narrator Joseph himself is strangely passive, content to observe and report the life of his fascinating father, not himself in action, hardly even evaluating or judging him.

Far from creating a realistic and historically exact protrayal of his childhood world, as might be found in Proust or Thomas Mann's *Buddenbrooks* (1901), Schulz transforms the autobiographical base of his work into myths of origins, lifework, illness and death, which are strikingly original and beautiful even in the unchained literature of the twentieth century. For example, his father's physical and mental decline is expressed in a number of magical transformations into lower life forms—like a bird, cockroach, or crab—and thus after his death the son can visit him in a sanatorium where the father reconstructs a feeble image of his former existence.

Schulz's use of the motif of animal transformations recalls to modern readers Franz Kafka's story, *The Metamorphosis* (1912). Indeed the use of this device, along with the preoccupation with his father, has been enough to earn Schulz the dubious title of the Polish Kafka, a title many critics are quick to deny.

The transformation of Gregor Samsa occurs to a son, not to a father as in Schulz, and as a specific punishment for an inadequate and guilty life, corresponding to the death sentence of Kafka's *The Trial* from the same period. The *Ungeziefer* (vermin) which Samsa becomes is the "appropriate punishment" applied in Greek mythology to humans like Narcissus, turned into a flower because of his vanity.

Schulz on "reality" in *Cinnamon Shops*:

Cinnamon Shops proposes a certain formula for reality; it posits a special kind of substance. The substance of that reality is in a state of continual fermentation, germination, latency. There are no inanimate, durable, or fixed objects. Everything trespasses beyond its own limits, persists in a given form only long enough to quit it. Life there is conducted by the precept of pan-masquerade. Reality assumes certain forms for show, for sport, for the fun of it. One person may be a human, another a cockroach; but these are forms only, they do not get to the quick of it; they are but skins that in a moment will be shed. Postulated here is a radical monism by which everything is reduced to mask. Life means the conscription of innumerable masks; the migration of forms is its very essence. An aura of pan-irony emanates from that backstage atmosphere where the actors, after quitting their costumes, mock the pathos of their parts. There is an inherent irony, a tease, a clownish ribbing in the very fact of individual existence. . . .

Whether any meaning is left to a reality freed from all illusion is not for me to say. I can only testify that it could not be endured if it did not afford compensation in some other dimension. In a way, we derive a deep satisfaction from this loosening of reality; we have an interest in this bankrupcy of reality.

Bruno Schulz, in "An Interview with Bruno Schulz," Cross Currents *6, 1987.*

Schulz applies his animal transformations not to himself, but to his beloved father. They are not punishment for a crime or false way of life, or part of a father-son conflict, for Schulz admires and emulates his fictional father, who produces imaginative attempts to create artistic universes, even discourses on the nature of modern art—which the biographical cloth-merchant of Galicia never could have delivered. Rather than punishment or condemnation of his father, the various metamorphoses accompany, exemplify, or demonstrate his illness, insanity, even his bankruptcy in business and in marriage. Since there are a number of transformations, usually ending in death, scattered throughout the two collections of stories, a certain provisional playful quality obtains. Having expressed a certain aspect of his father's personal and spiritual downfall, each can then be revoked, superseded by the next poetic version of his suffering, alienation and disappearance.

The father's transformation may also arise as a wilful and revolutionary accompaniment to his creative efforts, for example in **"Birds."** There he begins by collecting eggs of exotic birds, then hatches them to create a fantastic aviary in the attic of birds which are at once beautiful and deformed, extravagant products of a fevered, desperate vision. They are justified as part of the war against boredom, a defense of "the lost cause of poetry." Accompanying this artistic project the father himself becomes, or merges with, one of the birds, a condor, which is kept in the attic where it is recognized to "be" the father by both Joseph and his mother, "although we never discussed the subject." In an earlier story, **"Visitation,"** the father had imitated the pose of the large stuffed vulture hanging on the apartment wall. And in a later story, **"Cockroaches,"** the stuffed bird, now again called a condor, survives in deteriorating condition after the father has perished. So, disregarding chronology, Schulz shows first the creation of the birds in the attic area, with the father joining them as a live condor; "later" father and stuffed vulture coexist in the family living quarters, and still later a stuffed condor outlives the father.

Olga Lukashevich interprets the condor choice of birds as an illustration of the father's failure to become a more splendid and beautiful bird—although it may be noted that none of the birds created by the father are healthy specimens. As she points out, "the condor—the largest of the vultures—is a scavenger who does not hunt but feeds on carrion; and he is ordinarily associated with death and decay." ("Bruno Schulz's 'The Street of Crocodiles.' A Study in Creativity and Neurosis" in *The Polish Review* 13 (1968), p. 69).

Joseph's father himself "explains" the preservation of the dead or transformed family member within the home by means of the practices of primitive peoples:

> Ancient mythical tribes used to embalm their dead. The walls of their houses were filled with bodies and heads immured in them: a father would stand in a corner of the living room— stuffed, the tanned skin of a deceased wife would serve as a mat under the table.
> **("Treatise on Tailors' Dummies: Conclusion")**

Thus Schulz's use of ancient myth is not naive or uncon-

scious, but a sophisticated system of allusion and modern adaptation. The father predicts his own "future" fate as a stuffed bird or crab tolerated long after his death within the family home. Of course Schulz's transformed fathers have a chameleon aspect not seen in primitive folklore: they can revive, escape to still further metamorphoses.

But to return to the episode of bird creation: driven from the attic by Adela in a fit of spring-cleaning and philistine contempt for the artist or just for men, the birds return to the city in the last story of *The Street of Crocodiles,* **"Night of the Great Season"** in nightmare fashion, crippled and blind:

> Nonsensically large, stupidly developed, the birds were empty and lifeless inside. All their vitality went into their plumage, into external adornment. They were like exhibits of extinct species in a museum, the lumber room of a birds' paradise.

These lines contain a manifest level of allusion to works of art, like Schulz's own stories, which he thereby characterizes himself internally in an ironic, self-deprecating mode. The invasion of birds is greeted with stone-throwing by the general populace, by "merry-makers," and soon "the plateau was strewn with strange, fantastic carrion." Just as Adela drove the birds from the attic, the public is hostile to the beautiful flawed products of an admittedly mad creator.

But then, in **"Cockroaches,"** the father who "was then no more with us," survives as the stuffed condor of the aviary; he stands on a shelf in the living room, sadly deteriorated, moth-eaten and without eyes, sawdust emerging from the sockets. Here, the bird-form of the father lacks the parallel reference to artistic creation seen in **"The Birds,"** it refers only to mortality of a family member and to the attitudes of the survivors.

In this story also, the mother is joined with Adela in a conspiracy of women against the helpless, disintegrating father. After she refuses to answer the question of whether the stuffed bird is really the father, Joseph asks her "What is the meaning then of all the stories and the lies which you are spreading about Father?" The embarrassed mother, not above being "coy like a woman with a strange man," weakly changes the subject to cockroaches, another example of transformation the father has undergone which is less incriminating for her and Adela.

This bird example of animal metamorphosis is the most fully developed in Schulz's work, displaying the aspect of artistic creativity and fantasy which is a model for Schulz's own art, along with the aspect of a symbolic treatment of the real father's own real decline and fall. It also shows the usually muted theme of feminine hostility, and the son's feeble attempt to come to his father's rescue.

Other transformations such as that of the cockroaches included in the same story are less complete and rich. The cockroaches have not been created by the father, who initially shares the revulsion of other family members for them, wildly stabbing them with a javelin, until he falls under their spell, hiding as they do, crawling like them, his body stained with black spots "like the scales of a cockroach." In a reductionist "explanation" Schulz writes:

> My father at that time no longer possessed that power of resistance which protects healthy people from the fascination of loathing. Instead of fighting against the terrible attraction of that fascination, my father, a prey to madness, became completely subjected to it.

Although in both cases, the birds and the cockroaches, the father's own change is triggered by the appearance of many of the species he is to become, in the former case the change is benign, beautiful and linked to artistry, while the latter case is pure nightmare without redeeming features or meanings. Therefore the mother interrupts a discussion of the stuffed condor for father's more horrible cockroach metamorphosis which she believes Joseph would be able neither to defend nor to identify with.

In line with the arbitrariness, interchangeability and temporary quality of these transformations—against which a Kafka can appear elementary—she finally denies he has been transformed at all:

> Don't torture me, darling; I have told you already that Father is away, travelling all over the country; he now has a job as a commercial traveler. You know that he sometimes comes home at night and goes away again before dawn.

Thematically related to the cockroach transformation are the father's becoming a fly in **"Dead Season"** (*Sanatorium*) and a gnat in **"Eddie"** (*Sanatorium*), both as a temporary reaction to these insects pestering him. In the former example, the narrator gives another gratuitous explanation of the change:

> Yet, looking at it dispassionately, one had to take my father's transformation *cum grano salis.* It was much more the symbol of an inner protest, a violent and desperate demonstration from which, however, reality was not absolutely absent. One has to keep in mind that most of the events described here suffer from summer aberrations . . .

Thus various "minor" transformations of the father occur to which even the narrator warns us not to attach much significance. Taken as a group they show the vulnerability and dissolution of a formerly integrated bourgeois personality as the father descends through madness and illness into death. Although Joseph may defend the father, as in **"Cockroaches,"** he is just as likely to display the same embarrassment, the averting of eyes which other family members display. At such moments he is far indeed from the solidarity of his pre-mother mythic origins in **"The Book"** or the perception of the father in **"Birds"** as a prototype artist and forerunner to the writer Bruno Schulz himself.

Only one other animal transformation of the father is imbued with mythopoeic significance, that into a crab in **"Father's Last Escape,"** the story which concludes *Sanatorium.*

"Last" is not meant here in a final sense temporally, as there is even a kind of survival from this extreme example of death transformation; for Joseph in another story, **"Sanatorium,"** now again in human form, visits his father after death. In **"Father's Last Escape,"** Joseph's mother brings a crab (or a large scorpion) in from the stairs. He is recognized as the father: surrealistically, "in spite of the metamorphosis, the resemblance was incredible." As in other cases, such as his transformation to a cockroach, the father continues to haunt the family for a long time, even insisting on appearing at dinnertime and narrowly avoiding being stamped on by a visiting uncle.

But now an "unbelievable deed" takes place. Whereas the other transformations of the father were voluntary, self-generated, and self-terminated, the mother now intervenes to finish off the father. She cooks him and serves him for dinner. When all refuse in horror to eat him, he is put in the sitting room, on a table next to the album of family photographs. He even gradually comes back to life after *this* ordeal.

> One morning, we found the plate empty. One leg lay on the edge of the dish, in some congealed tomato sauce as aspic that bore the traces of his escape. Although boiled and shedding his legs on the way, with his remaining strength he had dragged himself somewhere to begin a homeless wandering and we never saw him again.

Here Schulz, after various evocations of the animal-transformation motif, has achieved a new level of symbolic statement, discovering a new myth that was buried in the metaphors of his father's fall. Father becomes a human sacrifice, which in primitive rituals is to be eaten by the tribe, as echoed in the Christian Eucharist ritual.

Father's death is not a purely personal event, it is a sacrifice for the family, who could now, like Joseph, absorb and incorporate his magical, god-like qualities through eating him. It would also be a way finally to put a halt to the endless series of transformations, to his long drawn-out process of dying, freeing the family and Joseph for other interests and activities. Since they do not actually accept the proposal of the mother, the father is neither released from his torments, nor does the son win the potency and other god-like attributes his father possessed. But, as in the case of the original father-son union which preceded the materialization of the mother, Schulz has here achieved an archetypal recall of primitive ritual which transcends the autobiographical commonplace situation of a father's sickness and death.

The mother's act of cooking the father—or preparing him for sacrificial consumption—is momentarily challenged by the aghast son, who, nevertheless, soon retreats from "she" to the "we" of family unity, implying an acceptance of personal responsibility, as a member of the murderous family, for his father's sacrifice. And yet he, and the others, are too civilized to actually eat him, to carry out to the end the primeval ritual of becoming a father, a leader, a powerful warrior, by consuming his body.

Joseph could thereby again reach the primitive myth level of the story of his origins, **"The Book,"** where a father has a son without a mother: that of the ancient Greek gods who ate one another. He also would have thereby achieved that union he so desired to recapture—"alone in our room"—the father in his own body literally, a room which the mother, in spite of her seductive, treacherous ways, could then never enter. Maleness would be linked to maleness; the son would be the father in a way which could never be reversed. Instead Joseph has to make the lonely trip to the sanatorium of his dead father where he will neither be satisfactorily united with his father nor from which he will ever return to the normal world. This is the myth of Orpheus, of the trip to the underworld.

Before leaving the topic of animal transformations, however, it should be noted that these are not employed only for the father. In Schulz's cosmology, where matter and time are both freed of their normal common-sense predictability and regularity, all life and even lifeless matter is always capable of sudden, self-directed spurts of metamorphosis. These casual, cosmic changes generally lack the poignant, tragic quality of the father's changes since the narrator Joseph and the author Schulz have no particular emotional commitment to the subject of their transformations.

Thus Aunt Perasia, otherwise not mentioned in the two books, appears during the **"Gale"** *(The Street of Crocodiles).* Angered at the clumsy preparation of a chicken for cooking, which results in its brief return to life while being scorched, as well as by the general confusion of the terrible storm, Aunt Perasia, like the father with roaches, assumes the role of the creature which has irritated her. First she shrinks to chicken size, then makes stilts out of two splinters to approximate chicken legs, whereupon she scampers about the kitchen like a bird. She then repeats the scorching episode: "became smaller and smaller, black and folded like a wilted, charred sheet of paper, oxidized into a petal of ash, disintegrating into dust and nothingness." This surrealistic end of a relative is noted by the family merely "with regret"; they soon return to their activities "with some relief." The father also had disintegrated, a "gray heap of rubbish," after another transformation, in **"Visitations."**

The father himself describes another transformation, this time from human to inanimate object, in the **"Treatise on Tailors' Dummies."** His brother "as a result of a long and incurable illness" has turned into the "rubber tube of an enema" carried about on a cushion by a cousin who has to sing lullabies to him.

In **"The Comet,"** a story published separately (1938) after the two books of stories, the father becomes a mad scientist, engaging in experiments in chemistry and mesmerism. Out of the ornate carvings on the back of a dining room chair he creates a relative, Aunt Wanda **"The Comet,"** published together with *The Street of Crocodiles.* He then turns Uncle Edward into a bell or buzzer which his wife often activates, "in order to hear that loud and sonorous sound in which she recognized the former timbre of her husband's voice in moments of irritation."

But these caprices, transformations of human beings to inanimate objects, applied mostly to minor relatives from the endless supply of uncles and aunts, have little to do with Schulz's recreation of archaic myth-materials in the

Czaki and Mickiewicz Streets, where Schulz was killed by the Gestapo agent Karl Güenther.

saga of his father. Instead, they are surrealist fantasies of a modern quality, connected with Schulz's and others' speculations about the nature of matter and time.

A last example: the firemen in **"My Father Joins the Fire Brigade"** (*Sanatorium*) spend their winters curled up in chimneys, like cocoons, or hibernating animals: "They sleep upright, drunk with raspberry syrup . . . You must pull them out by their ears and take them back to their barracks . . . " Here the metamorphosis is temporary, seasonal, and reversible. We are far from the sentimental protrayals of the father's dilemma.

Schulz's portrayals of his father's metamorphoses are like fairytales in that the victim is guiltless, but the transformations are not capricious, being appropriate signs of both the father's mortality and his creativity. Therefore, here more like the classical fables, no rescue is possible: the loving son cannot rescue his father from the nightmare of kaleidoscope transformations, which although sometimes self-healing or self-cancelling, are all steps in an inevitable procession to the land of the dead, the sanatorium where the father lives among the ruins of his former way of life.

Furthermore, the alienation between son and father also precludes any fairytale type rescue; indifference, boredom, embarrassment, even occasional gestures of hostility prevent Joseph from seriously trying to reestablish the mystical father-son harmony of that so-distant time before the appearance of the mother. Having early abandoned hope of a return to the pre-mother paradise of "our room, which at that time was as large as the world" (**"The Book"**), Joseph seeks the recovery of The Book alone, at the degenerate forms which are the only ones available to him: the mail-order catalogue, Rudolph's stamp collection (**"Spring"**), his drawings (**"The Age of Genius"**). Meanwhile the transformations of his father, which prefigure both the son's mortality and creativity are chronicled in the main with a bemused detachment. The mixture of ambivalence and resignation in face of, on the whole, admirable, heroic efforts of the father, while autobiographically anchored by the death of the father in reality twenty years before, is nevertheless a puzzling feature in the fiction of

Bruno Schulz. The ancient father-son materials lead either to a dual or to a reunion. (pp. 373-80)

> *Russell E. Brown, "Metamorphosis in Bruno Schulz," in* The Polish Review, *Vol. XXX, No. 4, 1985, pp. 373-80.*

Russell E. Brown   (essay date 1987)

[*In the excerpt below, Brown analyzes Schulz's use of the myth of traveling to an underworld after death in "Sanatorium under the Sign of the Hourglass."*]

One of the archaic myths which Bruno Schulz employs in his poetic reconstruction of the father-son relationship is a visit to the underworld, the land of the dead. Unlike other myths, especially the animal transformations illustrating the father's disintegration which occur throughout Schulz's two books of fiction [*The Street of Crocodiles* and *Sanatorium under the Sign of the Hourglass*], the myth of a visit to the land beyond death is contained in a single story, **'Sanatorium under the Sign of the Hourglass'**, the title story of his second book.

One of the great archetypes of world literature, such visits range from the Greek Orpheus and Odysseus and the Babylonian *Gilgamesh* through Dante's *Divine Comedy* and Goethe's *Faust* (Part Two), to many modern examples. The purpose of the perilous journey may be to visit or rescue a deceased loved one, as in the cases of Orpheus and Gilgamesh, or to get information about how to proceed in some specific earthly project (Odysseus), about man's fate after death in general (Dante), or even about the future of living men or nations on earth. Schulz's Joseph visits the land beyond death for the first reason.

Whereas the entry to this world in the great models of world literature was either down, beneath the earth's surface (as in Dante, *Gilgamesh* or *Faust*) or in Greek-Roman models, across a body of water by boat, Joseph proceeds by railroad to the sanatorium where his father now resides. This substitution of modern technology is familiar from modern versions like Kasack's *Die Stadt hinter dem Strom* (1949) or Thomas Mann's *Der Zauberberg* (1924)—if the latter can be considered in this tradition—where Schulz, who was influenced by Mann, especially in his modern adaptations of myth, may have even found the 'sanatorium' setting since it is not thematically consistent with his hometown, family-based work. But aside from minor features, like the arrival by train, the empty corridors, perhaps the immediate visit to the sanatorium restaurant and the long periods of sleep, Schulz's sanatorium fable bears little resemblance to Thomas Mann's, where a broad panorama of (living) European society is assembled on a Swiss mountain for the treatment of tuberculosis. Joseph's father, on the other hand, seems to be the only patient in his sanatorium. It might be noted that Schulz's father died of tuberculosis, along with cancer.

Hans Castorp unexpectedly remains on the magic mountain for seven years, achieving a kind of *Bildung* in the process; Joseph's planned brief visit is also lengthened indefinitely. In a way he, too, is treated as a patient, or an extension of his father the patient, sharing the same room, even the same bed.

Joseph's journey to the sanatorium, which begins with a train ride, continues with a foot march through a forest (Dante?) where he crosses a foot-bridge into the main entrance of the sanatorium. The foot-bridge, which separates the world of the living from that of the dead, may be a kind of brief homage to Kafka—*Das Schloss* begins in the same way—or it suggests the river borders to the underworld of classical mythology, the Styx, Acheron, Lethe. It is part of the proliferation of entry-motifs to the underworld (train, hill, dark forest, foot-bridge), which Schulz builds between the normal world and the special mythic area, like a summary of the beginnings of related epics.

Jerzy Ficowski in a summary of mythological elements in the Sanatorium story says, 'The Sanatorium is Hades transplanted to this side of the Styx and at the same time a metaphor of art—Schulz's art—as the redeemer of the past' ('The Schulzian Tense, or the Mythic Path to Freedom' in *Polish Perspectives* 10 (1967) Nr. 11).

The 'classic' matter of a Bruno Schulz story is the recall, reconstruction, or mythopoeic heightening of scenes from the author's childhood, particularly as the childhood scenes commemorate and elegize the central figure of his life: his father Jacob. Bruno, who is named Joseph in the exclusively first-person narratives, experiences the world as a child and it is the child's intensity of perception, as well as the child's freedom from convention and mechanical ways of organizing reality which justify the fantastic metaphors and transformations, the flights of fancy which make Schulz's work unique and memorable. Here Schulz is working in a literary context beyond his own personal formula.

The narrator of **'Sanatorium'** is also not the boy of other stories, recording the fall of his father within the family circle as a child might experience it. Joseph is now a grown man as various erotic incidents reveal; he has ordered a pornographic book by mail, or in discussing the manners of young women he calls himself parenthetically 'a young man who still has a certain amount of interest in such things.' And yet, characteristic of the blurred chronology of Schulz's work, his dead father is wearing a suit 'which he had made only the previous summer.' That is, the father's death occurred less than a year ago, when Joseph's perceptions, as recorded in stories of that period, were still those of a child.

In spite of such temporal inconsistencies, however, the narrator is now clearly an adult; his father even asks him to help out in the family business, a possibility never contemplated in his father's last days. **'Sanatorium'** is written from the perspective of Schulz at the time of composition, rather than the time twenty years earlier (in 1915) when his father died.

The visit to the underworld myth of the story, uprooted from Schulz's 'natural' setting of his own childhood on the market square of Drohobycz with his father's textile business, the servant girl Adela, and an endless series of aunts and uncles, is alien to Schulz's central concern: the return to, and recovery of the, past. Perhaps he chose it as an experiment in an attempt to move beyond the compulsive confines of his initial subject matter. If Schulz's career as a writer had continued normally without the catastrophe of World War Two and the destruction of Poland, Drohobycz, and the extermination of the Jews, he would have had to move into new fictional territory, as Kafka did in the twelve years left to him after his 'breakthrough' of 1912. Schulz in this transitional work has freed the narrator from the child perspective, has changed the setting from the purely autobiographical local home setting to a world-myth underworld, and still is able to write about his father, now receding and diminishing, 'curled up, small as a kitten.'

Schulz has assembled a number of familiar elements from the epic monuments of underworld visits as well as the superstitions connected with death. A good example of the latter occurs when Joseph looks into a mirror in his father's room at the sanatorium and is unable to see his own reflection. In the language of popular Gothic tradition or the ghost story, this means that Joseph himself is already dead. But this suggestion is never followed up; indeed Joseph is able to flee the sanatorium later and return to the railroad-link to the world. Thus he is not dead yet, although he is never able actually to get back home; in an allusion to another topos, conceivably inspired by Kafka's *Ein Landarzt,* Joseph ends as an eternal traveller like the wandering Jew.

Along with the oppressive darkness of the area around the sanatorium, a special kind of sweet air pervades in the adjoining city, causing inebriation, indolence, sleepiness. Suggestive of fleshly decay, it also recalls the special air of the courts in Kafka's *Der Prozess,* which Schulz and his fiancee translated into Polish. The darkness is also echoed in the 'black vegetation,' including a black fern displayed prominently everywhere where one expects flowers. Schulz has tacked this phenomenon onto a description of the way young women act in the region, to which the black ferns have no connection, as if he suddenly decided to add another Gothic feature to the original myth.

Upon Joseph's arrival at the sanatorium he is told that everybody is asleep. When he points out that it is daytime, not night, the chambermaid says, 'Here everybody is asleep all the time . . . Besides, it is never night here.' Later Joseph describes life 'in this town' as full of people sleeping everywhere not only in bed but in restaurants, cabs, even standing up when out for a walk. The motif of the dead as sleepers, of Lethos, the stream of forgetfulness of the Underworld, is here pushed to comic absurdity. We also note in the maid's statement the absence of day and night, the eternal twilight of Hades.

Perhaps the most striking classical motif-borrowing occurs in the appearance of a fierce black dog guarding the sanatorium entrance. This is Cerberus, the (three-headed) guard-dog whom Odysseus and other heroes have to overcome to gain passage into the underworld. In Schulz's story he is treated with unexpected kindness by the frightened Joseph and as a result assumes human form. In classical mythology, Cerberus can be tamed by offering him cake, as do Psyche and Aeneas. Hercules even captures the dog and brings him to the world of the living briefly

(12th task), while Joseph brings the dog-man to his father's room. Another interpretation of this creature will be offered below.

Having established the main myth, the visit to the underworld in **'Sanatorium'** and characteristic motifs associated with this archetypal situation, one may point to a complementary, if not opposed, level of interpretation.

In most mythological versions of the land beyond death, great numbers of souls are assembled, either in sad boredom or suffering the torments of endless punishment. But Joseph's father lives in a sanatorium where he is the only patient Joseph ever sees during his stay. Although there are corridors of numbered rooms, a restaurant with uncleared tables, even tips left behind, Joseph never meets any other occupants of the sanatorium and begins to suspect his father is the only patient. Of the presumably large staff that would be needed for such an institution, only a chambermaid and the chief doctor ever materialize. An elaborate system of deception seems in operation to prevent Joseph from learning the true state of affairs.

Near the Sanatorium, however, there is a well-populated town, where Joseph's father has started a new textile business. Inviting Joseph to visit him there, he assumes Joseph has a prior knowledge of the town. And indeed he finds his way easily: 'What a strange, misleading resemblance it bore to the central square of our native city!' The magical reconstruction of their hometown is immediately rationalized by Joseph: 'How similar, in fact, are all the market squares in the world! Almost identical houses and shops!' But Joseph's father has passed away into a world which is a copy of his own lifetime world, a more rundown or deteriorating version perhaps, but nevertheless an environment where he can for a time continue his former life of selling cloth. His shop is full of customers, his shop assistants hurry about even more than in the 'old days' at home. As American Indians imagined a 'happy hunting ground' in the life after death, where some activities of their former life, like hunting and fishing, would continue, so Schulz here shows the dead merchant starting a new business in an almost identical town beyond the grave.

And yet the father's condition is not permanent or stabilized. A further physical deterioration is taking place in him, so that he will soon be too weak to continue the business. He seems to hope Joseph will be willing to take his place:

> You should look into the store more often, Joseph. The shop assistants are robbing us. You can see that I am no longer equal to the task. I have been lying here sick for weeks, and the shop is being neglected, left to ruin itself.

Not only do we have a mirror image of the city and business in the other world, but the father is in the same condition of failing health and sanity as he was at home. He was dying there, and here he is also dying. We may ask where he will be sent after this second death, since he is *already* in the place after death, the underworld. However, classical myths of life after death also include this idea of final disappearance of the soul after a stay in Hades.

The linkage of these two worlds, before and after death,

is further demonstrated by the fact that a system of communication apparently functions between them. Not only is there a railroad connection in *and out* but the father can ask if there was any mail from home. Back in normal life Joseph had ordered a pornographic book from a bookseller who now inexplicably sends him a package direct to this father's new business address.

These facts all suggest that another level of meaning for the sanatorium world is that it is simply the same world the family has always lived in, a new metaphorical arrangement of the familiar materials Schulz has always worked with: life at home in Drohobycz. At least in the business and public aspects of the life of father and son there is only a continuation, thus undermining the 'visit to the underworld' mythic theme.

Joseph, now admittedly older, in his description of life in this 'new' place gives the above-mentioned characterization of the air of superiority which young women display in public, an analysis which has absolutely nothing to do with male-female relations in the afterlife, but corresponding to the author's mistress-slave syndrome of dominant women and servile men, seen in Schulz's art work and also in stories like **'Treatise on Tailors' Dummies.'** Schulz here apparently 'forgets' that he is in the world of the dead, interrupting his ghost story for a normal (for him) evocation of the mysterious power of women, especially the magnetism of feet, 'shapely and graceful in their spotless footwear.' Such attractions can hide blemishes, especially in the face, an observation which one finds also, for example, in the 'home' world of *The Street of Crocodiles.*

Furthermore, the invasion of an enemy army, as well as the appearance of native fascist militia in the town, undermine the level of mythic visit to the underworld. Nothing seems more incompatible with a society of the dead than war or political unrest in such a setting. As in the analysis of young ladies' charms, Schulz is interpolating in a 'naive' way untransformed material from his own (real-life) situations, dropping the mask of allegory or archetype. Rather than an inconsistency or mistake on the author's part, these features may lead us to a different way of reading the story. Schulz is really writing about the real world through a facade of allusion to myth, a fantasy-reorganization of autobiography which can, however, be abandoned at will. The dead father who has left Drohobycz, is found again in the same world, still on the point of final decline to death—after he supposedly has already died. **'Sanatorium'** belongs to the whole set of stories about father's death, none of which precludes a new later story.

If in the town there is 'business as usual', what of the sanatorium? Surely that is an element irreconcilable with a mere fantasy reconstruction of autobiographical reminiscence. If locale and business are normally 'in place,' the sanatorium, which is where father (and son) sleep in a single bed, must correspond to the home, the living quarters of the diminished family. As in the idyll of **'The Book,'** at the beginning of Joseph's life, female characters while present, are remote, do not penetrate the room itself which father and son share.

The fact that there seem to be no other patients living at the sanatorium thus would no longer be a confusing bit of mystification, as Joseph believes, but would correspond to the real situation which the sanatorium masks. As Joseph's home was the place where the sick and dying father was kept (the sole patient there), so is he kept here in the appropriate substitute building of a hospital.

The flirtatious chambermaid, criticized for neglecting her duties as she hurries about on mysterious errands, corresponds to Adela, the seductive, dominating maid servant of the home-world stories. Adela attracted all the males in her proximity, even the sexually latent Joseph; here the corresponding maid, while acting seductively is not shown actually winning the attention of the few men present in the sanatorium environment. But Joseph who is now interested in pornography interprets her breathless appearance as follows: 'She had run out of a room, as if having torn herself from someone's importuning arms . . . She was only awaiting an opportunity to leap behind the half-opened door.' The voyeuristic Joseph used to watch Adela at home, speculating about her relations with men. As the chambermaid leads Joseph to the doctor one may be reminded of the promiscuous Leni, the servant of Joseph K.'s lawyer in *Der Prozess,* which Schulz, as noted, transmitted to Polish readers.

Even though the father, perhaps senile, is now indifferent to her charms, the chambermaid provides the same erotic impulse from the socially inferior servant level, so commonly received by bourgeois men before the First World War, reflected in Schulz's work as well as in that of Kafka or of Thomas Mann. In many a tale of middle-class families, sexual initiation is provided by female servants (*Amerika, Felix Krull*).

Another part of the sexual constellation is, of course, the 'proper' woman, both a mother and a wife, from the same social class. She is perceived either as essentially neuter in an erotic sense or as a tyrant who inhibits natural animal expressions of all kinds in the immediate related males, as for example Aunt Agatha with Uncle Mark in **'August'** (*The Street of Crocodiles*).

Without the hypothesis that the sanatorium may be, aside from a place for the dead, a poetically transformed version of home, the appearance of Joseph's mother in the corridors would be totally perplexing, as indeed it is to Joseph:

> "Mother!" I exclaim in a voice trembling with excitement, and my mother turns her face to me and looks at me for a moment with a pleading smile. Where am I? What is happening here? What maze have I become entangled in?

What Joseph does not understand in his conscious purpose of narrating a mythical visit to the underworld, but nevertheless unwittingly reveals to us, is that the sanatorium on another level is really an alternative image of life at home, in Drohobycz, *before* the death of the father. For here in the underworld the father is still dying, still losing his textile business; both the seductive maid and the ineffectual mother are present.

The next problem is the role of Dr. Gotard. In this world he has taken over many of the functions the father used to perform at home, going for long walks with Joseph, holding philosophical discourse similar to the 'Treatise' maintaining the primary relation with the female servant (they are the only two staff members visible). His beard, the enema bottle he hurries past with in the night, and his excessive periods of sleep—not necessary for a supernatural 'official' of Hades—relate him to Joseph's father, for example, in **'Visitation'** (*Crocodiles*). The father and Dr. Gotard are both authority figures, the head men of enterprises, the textile shop and the sanatorium respectively. The two are linked in Joseph's chain of thought as well: 'My father was somewhere in the thick of a revolution or in a burning shop' is followed, illogically, by 'Dr. Gotard was unavailable.' The logic for Joseph is that they are in effect the same person: if the father is busy, Dr. Gotard is 'unavailable.' Since Joseph's mother is next mentioned, Dr. Gotard is also placed within a listing of family members.

The father is thus doubled, present in two manifestations, the original familiar one and another incorporating many of his features and habits. So too is the son, who also has a *Doppelgaenger* in the sanatorium: the guard dog who becomes, or really always was, a man.

It is interesting to watch Joseph, or Bruno Schulz, shifting gears in the description of the fearful dog. Having introduced him originally as a motif from the Hades myth, he now discovers the potential the tormented creature has as a variation of Joseph himself. When the dog has stretched his chain to the limit and is unable to reach Joseph, the latter is able to identify him for the first time:

> . . . only now did I see him clearly. How great is the power of prejudice! How powerful the hold of fear! How blind I had been! It was not a dog, it was a man. A chained man, whom, by a simplifying metaphoric wholesale error, I had taken for a dog. I don't want to be misunderstood. He was a dog, certainly, but a dog in human shape. The quality of a dog is an inner quality and can be manifested as well in human as in animal shape.

Thus Joseph admits to what he wittily calls 'a simplifying metaphoric wholesale error'; the simplification was to view the dog solely as one kind of metaphor, that deriving from the archetype, and not to see until now that he is also a man like Joseph, as we will see, another Joseph.

The dog has been explained above as a mythic component, the classical three-headed dog Cerberus. His other function is to express aspects of the son, to provide a variant son for the father. Just as the son and his lost friend in *Das Urteil* of Kafka can be viewed as aspects of the same person (the businessman Kafka by day, the artist Kafka by night) so the fierce dog whom Joseph initially fears may be reduced to an alternative Joseph.

Firstly, he is chained to the institution of the sanatorium and its chief, as Joseph is dependent on the family business and its fascinating head, even following him beyond his demise on the difficult journey to the underworld. He looks initially like 'an intellectual or a scholar,' 'wearing a black suit,' and the narrator thinks he might be 'Dr. Gotard's unsuccessful elder brother.' This hypothesis is psychologically revealing: a brother of the chief doctor may be equated with the son of a textile business owner; the dog-man is unsuccessful like Joseph, and like Schulz himself (who had a highly successful elder brother, Izydor, in real-life).

Schulz seems to be inviting us here to consider the possible identification of Joseph and the dog-man with such parallels, but he quickly withdraws the statements made thus far: 'the first impression was false . . . he looked more like a bookbinder, a tubthumper, a vocal party member.' These speculations, along with his description as exceedingly primitive and ugly, produce a new set of new ironic associations with Joseph and especially with the author Bruno Schulz. Schulz is a writer of books, which a bookbinder then binds; he is also part of the literary process, either completing or inhibiting the art of Schulz. The term party-member is also meaningful if we think of the party as a family; in Schulz's family he was indeed the vocal one, writing the chronicle of his family, which would otherwise be forgotten.

The ugliness which is stressed ironically only reflects Schulz's own image of himself physically as shown in the self-caricatures of his art work. The ferocity the dog-man seems to possess may reflect the anger which Schulz felt at losing his father, first from the prefemale paradise of his earliest memories, then to sickness and death, anger at his inability to marry or otherwise lead a sexually fulfilling life, and finally anger at failure in his own adult career, as contrasted to that of his *successful* older brother.

The bookbinder was wearing a decent black suit, but had bare feet. Like father and doctor he wears the uniform of conventional propriety and authority, but his feet reveal an incomplete socialization. He is still partly a primitive savage, a person too poor to be able to afford shoes, or a child too small to need them. Joseph summarizes: 'I must drop this horrible friendship with a bookbinder who smells of dog and who is watching me all the time.' Friendship, watching, are indicators of the interchangeability and interdependency of the two; the smell of dog is ironically self-depreciating, like the dog's ugliness.

Desperate to escape this creature, which shows more of Joseph to himself than he wishes to see, perhaps providing the self-image he sought in the mirror unsuccessfully ('I must ask for a new looking glass') he leads the dog-man to his father's room where, promising to get him some cognac, Joseph rushes away to the railway station. On the way he imagines the father's return to his room and 'his confrontation with the terrible beast.' But these reflections and the act itself are vindictive only if the dog-man and Joseph are two separate characters; Cerberus and the visitor from the living world in the archetype, respectively. For in the second system of interpretation what Joseph has done in taking the dog-man to his father's room is neither illogical nor cruel. It is natural for Joseph, or this part of him, to go back to his father, to whom his anger will be no more a threat than it has ever been; it is also natural that a part of Joseph wants to escape a full confrontation between father and son, the *union mystico* of sleeping together in the same bed, their practice at the sanatorium. His fears for his father's safety, after betraying him, are hypocritical but unnecessary in the parrallel-world context: the father's fate may be death and disappearance, even from this second world, but it will not be at the hands of a son.

In addition to the use of a single black guard-dog, which has the double function of being a classical underworld motif, Cerberus, and of being an *alter ego,* a part of Joseph, a variation of the black dog motif occurs:

> Packs of black dogs are often seen in the vicinity of the sanatorium. Of all shapes and sizes they run at dusk along the roads and paths, engrossed in their own affairs, silent, tense, and alert.

Here the dogs are a political and social phenomenon, an animal parallel to the enemy and the local armed civilians. Again, the initial intention of the author to provide a modern reworking of the archetypal visit to the land of the dead is interrupted for the incompatible purpose of evoking the world of the living. But though they have nothing to do with the Cerberus motif, they do relate to the other use of the black dog-man: as a repressed diabolic component of Joseph himself. Beyond the individual analysis, men in society have both a predatory animal locked within, and a herd instinct, a susceptibility to mass hysteria and insanity. Thus they can be motivated by fascist or militaristic ideologies to threaten civilized society, running through the streets on silent, as yet unrevealed missions of violence. Here the black colour, which relates the packs of dogs to Cerberus-Joseph is probably also a reference to the black shirts of European fascism.

Aside from the guarding-of-Hades aspect then, Schulz uses threatening black dogs, both singly and in groups, to refer to evil, sub-human tendencies in modern man, in the narrator and in society in general, which threaten the family and the state. Joseph specifically links the two examples of the beast within man in the text: 'Nothing is to be done about this plague of dogs, but why does the management of the Sanatorium keep an enormous Alsatian on a chain . . . ' Here Joseph, without consciously realizing the symbolism of each example of black dogs which the author intended, implicity denies the possibility of meaningful action against fascist-military threats to society, but ponders the relevance of the sanatorium dog, which will soon be revealed to be an enraged man, another son to be placed in his father's room.

Thus the sanatorium which Schulz constructed as a modern, mythopoeic reworking of the ancient archetype of a visit to the land of the dead can also be read as a poetic masking of his normal field of interest, with the usual cast of characters, occupations, and relationships, with the father not yet dead but still on the verge of death (as he was in real life for ten years). But in this apparently merely literary setting, this mythopoeic revival of a well-known archetypal situation, Schulz may split himself into two actors, to reveal the angry beast which lurks behind his childish apathy and voyeurism and also to show himself as a coward who flees the spectacle of his father's tragic fate. For while the dog-man is only an imaginary threat (his father, for example, 'walks past the beast with indifference whenever we go out together') he does express a secret wish of the son: to attack and destroy his father personally. The father and his business are actually much more in danger from the invading army and the local uprising in the city; but even these, a foreshadowing of the destruction of Poland and the Jews, will not touch him, since they were still twenty-five years away at the time of his death in 1915, when Schulz's real father died at the age of sixty-nine. The invading army was to spell the doom rather of the son, the author who instead of riding endlessly on a train, singing songs to earn a little money, was to lose his poetic voice in the collapse of Poland, and then his life at the hands of the Gestapo in 1942. (pp. 35-46)

> *Russell E. Brown, "Bruno Schulz's Sanatorium Story: Myth and Confession," in* Polish Perspectives, *Vol. XXX, No. 3, March, 1987, pp. 35-46.*

V. S. Pritchett   (essay date 1990)

[*A contemporary English writer, Pritchett is respected for his mastery of the short story and for what critics describe as his judicious, reliable, and insightful literary criticism. In the following essay, he examines comic aspects in the stories in* The Street of Crocodiles.]

The ridiculous or preposterous father is a subject irresistible to the comic genius. The fellow is an involuntary god, and the variety of the species extends over the knockabout and the merely whimsical to the full wonder of incipient myth. To this last superior class the fantastic father invented by Bruno Schulz in **The Street of Crocodiles** belongs; the richness of the portrait owes everything to its brushwork and to our private knowledge that the deepest roots of the comic are poetic and even metaphysical.

Few English-speaking readers have ever heard of Schulz, and I take from his translator, Celina Wieniewska, and the thorough introduction by Jerzy Ficowski, the following notes on a very peculiar man. Schulz came of a Jewish family of dry goods merchants in the dull little town of Drogobych in Poland—it is now in the USSR—where he became a frustrated art master in the local high school and lived a solitary and hermetic life. The family's trade separated them from the ghetto; his natural language was Polish. The only outlet for his imagination seems to have been in writing letters to one or two friends, and it is out of these letters that his stories in this and other volumes grew. They were a protest against a boredom amounting to melancholia. He became famous, but found he could not live without the Drogobych he hated and he was caught there when the war began and the Nazis put him into the ghetto. It is said that a Gestapo officer who admired his drawings wangled a pass for him to leave the ghetto; one night when he took advantage of his freedom and was wandering among the crowds in the streets he was recognised and shot dead in a random shooting-up of the crowd. He was fifty years old.

It is not surprising to find comic genius of the poetic kind in serious and solitary men, but to emerge it has to feed on anomalies. We might expect—or fear—that Schulz would be a Slavonic droll in the Polish folk tradition, but he is not. Distinctly an intellectual, he translated Kafka's *The Trial* and was deep in *Joseph and His Brothers*—to my mind the most seminal of Thomas Mann's works; hence his sense of life as a collusion or conspiracy of improvised myths. Note the word 'improvised'.

Drogobych had suddenly become an American-type boom town owing to the discovery of oil, and the fantasy of Schulz takes in the shock of technology and the new cult of things and the pain of the metamorphosis. His translator is, rightly I think, less impressed by his literary sources in Kafka or surrealism than by the freedom of the painter's brush—his prose, she says, has the same freedom and originality as the brush of Chagall.

'Our Heresiarch'—as Schulz calls his secretive father, in *The Street of Crocodiles*—blossoms into speeches to his family or the seamstresses and assistants in his dress shop. He rambles into theories about the Demiurge and our enchantment with trash and inferior material. He discourses on the agonies of Matter:

> Who knows . . . how many suffering, crippled, fragmentary forms of life there are, such as the artificially created life of chests and tables quickly nailed together, crucified timbers, silent martyrs to cruel human inventiveness. The terrible transplantation of incompatible and hostile races of wood, their merging into one misbegotten personality.

Misbegetting is one of his obsessions.

> Only now do I understand the lonely hero who alone had waged war against the fathomless, elemental boredom that strangled the city. Without any support, without recognition on our part, that strangest of men was defending the lost cause of poetry.

The awed seamstresses cutting out dresses to fit the draper's model in their room are told the model is alive.

Where is poetry born? In the solitary imagination of the child who instantly sees an image when he sees a thing, where the wallpaper becomes a forest, the bales of cloth turn into lakes and mountains. In this way, the father has the inventive melancholy of Quixote. The delightful thing about him is that he is the embarrassing, scarcely visible nuisance in shop and home. It is hard to know where he is hiding or what he is up to. He is an inquiring poltergeist, coated with human modesty; even his faintly sexual ventures, like studying a seamstress's knee because he is fascinated by the structure of bones, joints, and sinews, are as modest as Uncle Toby's confusion of the fortress of Namur with his own anatomy. A minor character, like Adela the family servant, sets off the old man perfectly. She comes to clean out his room.

> He ascribed to all her functions a deeper, symbolic meaning. When, with young firm gestures, the girl pushed a long-handled broom along the floor, Father could hardly bear it. Tears would stream from his eyes, silent laughter transformed his face, and his body was shaken by spasms of delight. He was ticklish to the point of madness. It was enough for Adela to waggle her fingers at him to imitate tickling, for him to rush through all the rooms in a wild panic, banging the doors after him, to fall at last flat on the

bed in the farthest room and wriggle in convulsions of laughter, imagining the tickling which he found irresistible. Because of this, Adela's power over Father was almost limitless.

This is a small matter compared with his ornithological phase when he imports the eggs of birds from all parts of the world and hatches them in the loft. The birds perched on curtains, wardrobes, lamps. (One—a sad condor—strongly resembles him.) Their plumage carpeted the floor at feeding time. The passion in due course took an 'essentially sinful and unnatural turn'.

> . . . my father arranged the marriages of birds in the attic, he sent out matchmakers, he tied up eager attractive brides in the holes and crannies under the roof, . . .

In the spring, during the migration, the house was besieged by whole flocks of cranes, pelicans, peacocks. And father himself, in an absent-minded way, would rise from the table,

> wave his arms as if they were wings, and emit a long-drawn-out bird's call while his eyes misted over. Then, rather embarrassed, he would join us in laughing it off and try to turn the whole incident into a joke.

It is a sign of Schulz's mastery of the fantastic that, at the end of the book, he has the nerve to describe how after many years the birds returned to the house—a dreadful spectacle of miscegenation, a brood of freaks, degenerate, malformed:

> Nonsensically large, stupidly developed, the birds were empty and lifeless inside. All their vitality went into their plumage, into external adornment . . . Some of them were flying on their backs, had heavy misshapen beaks like padlocks, were blind, or were covered with curiously coloured lumps.

In a curious passage the father compares them to an expelled tribe, preserving what they could of their soul like a legend, returning to their motherland before extinction—a possible reference to the Diaspora and the return.

Like an enquiring child, the father is wide open to belief in metamorphoses as others are prone to illness: for example he has a horror of cockroaches and, finding black spots on his skin, prepares for a tragic transformation into the creature he dreads by lying naked on the floor. But it is in the father's ornithological phase that we see the complexity of Schulz's imagination. The whole idea—it is hinted—may spring from a child's dream after looking at pictures of birds; it is given power by being planted in the father; then it becomes a grotesque nightmare; and finally we may see it as a parable, illustrating the permutations of myths which become either the inherited wastepaper of the mind or its underground. Incidentally—and how recognisable this is in childish experience—there is an overwhelming picture of the ragged idiot girl of the town sleeping on the rubbish heap, who suddenly rises from the fly-infested dump to rub herself in terrible sexual frenzy against a tree.

Under the modesty of Schulz the senses are itching in disguise. Each episode is extraordinary and carried forward fast by a highly imaged yet rational prose which is especially fine in evoking the forbidden collective wishes of the household or the town: when a comet appears in the sky and a boy comes home from school saying the end of the world is near, the whole town is enthusiastic for the end of the world. When a great gale arrives, the town becomes a saturnalia of *things* at last set free to live as matter wants to live. There is the admonitory farce when loose-living Uncle Edward agrees to reform and to submit to the father's discovery of mesmerism and the magic of electricity. Uncle Edward is eager to shed all his characteristics and to lay bare his deepest self in the interests of Science, so that he can achieve a 'problem-free immortality'.

> The dichotomy 'happy/unhappy' did not exist for him because he had been completely integrated.

Schulz's book is a masterpiece of comic writing: grave yet demented, domestically plain yet poetic, exultant and forgiving, marvellously inventive, shy and never raw. There is not a touch of whimsy in it. (pp. 128-32)

> *V. S. Pritchett, "Bruno Schulz: Comic Genius," in his* Lasting Impressions: Selected Essays, *Chatto & Windus, 1990, pp. 128-32.*

Susan Miron   (essay date 1992)

[*In the excerpt below, Miron assesses Schulz's short fiction and its influence on contemporary writers on the occasion of the centenary year of his birth.*]

Bruno Schulz, the morbidly shy, reclusive, hypersensitive Polish-Jewish writer, would surely be stunned to find he had, in his centenary, become as mythical a literary presence as the exotic entourage he so ingeniously invented in his own drawings and short stories. This unlikely object of nearly cultish adulation would most likely find this fame as puzzling as his admirers have found him. The recent flurry of books by Schulz that have appeared in the space of two years—the volume of drawings, his letters, and his collected fiction—shock, confound, overwhelm, and astonish with their abundance of sensory data, voluptuous prose, and hallucinatory splendor. Yet, despite this impressive triptych [**The Complete Fiction of Bruno Schulz, The Drawings of Bruno Schulz,** and **Letters and Drawings of Bruno Schulz: with Selected Prose**], the man behind these images seems as much a mystery as ever, an enigma whose essence is better translated into fiction than biography, as his surfacing in several contemporary novels attests. Cynthia Ozick's bewitching novel, *The Messiah of Stockholm,* is a deeply felt and brilliantly imagined homage to Schulz and to his lost novel, *The Messiah,* rescued and reimagined here if only for a moment of fictional time. A. B. Yehoshua uses part of a Schulz story as an epigraph in *A Late Divorce,* and David Grossman devotes some hundred pages to "Bruno" in *See Under: Love.*

Singled out for murder by an SS agent on "Black Thursday," November 19, 1942, Schulz was buried by a friend late that evening in the Jewish cemetery in his small town of Drohobycz (then part of Poland, earlier part of the Austro-Hungarian Empire, now part of the Soviet Union). In *See Under: Love,* Grossman imagines the Schulz of **The Street of Crocodiles** eluding his killers by jumping into the sea at Danzig and turning into a salmon. In reality, both his grave and the graveyard, like the manuscript of his lost novel, *The Messiah,* have disappeared, perhaps fittingly for an artist whose life, death, drawings, and stories have themselves become the mythical threads out of which other writers' stories have since been woven. How ironic that the writer who lived all his life in a small provincial town, who kept at a distance even those he loved, allowing them access only through the gateway of letter-writing, has so touched his readers that many cannot bear the thought of his death and, in protest, have rewritten and reimagined his fate, launching what he would have called "a counter-offensive of fantasy" against reality itself.

Schulz owes his posthumous reputation not only to the tireless Jerzy Ficowski, who for forty years has conducted a treasure hunt for Schulz's lost writings and drawings, but also to Philip Roth, who, as general editor of Penguin's *Writers of the Other Europe Series* introduced Schulz to American readers. (In dedicating *The Messiah of Stockholm* to Roth, Cynthia Ozick thanked him for introducing her to Schulz.) Ficowski has claimed that Schulz's work "was so distinctive that it had no precedents in Polish and European literature nor any worthy followers or successors." Yet Schulz certainly knew German literature: he loved Thomas Mann (his letters to Mann are lost), wrote a brilliant afterword to *The Trial,* and adored Rilke. He certainly knew and reviewed with great insight modern Polish literature. Danilo Kis, the recipient just before his death of the Bruno Schulz Prize, given to a writer underrecognized in the United States, does seem a successor of sorts. Kis, whose fiction is as father-fixated as Schulz's, once quipped to John Updike, "Schulz is my god." Even Kis's choice of title for his novel *Hourglass* is reminiscent of Schulz's second novel, **Sanatorium at the Sign of the Hourglass.** (pp. 161-62)

Schulz did not have his first book of stories, **Cinammon Shops,** published until he was forty. The stories began life as a series of postscripts dropped off into a mailbox, part of a correspondence now lost, with a Polish-Jewish writer, Debora Vogel. Eventually the postscripts broke free of their epistolary moorings and were discovered by another influential Polish woman, Zofia Nalkowska, who became Schulz's patroness and persuaded the publishing house of Rój to publish this unknown writer from the provinces. By contrast, from an early age he impressed teachers, friends, and galleries with his artwork.

Schulz began to illustrate his stories some ten years before his literary debut. He designed the dust jackets for **Cinnamon Shops** (1934) and **Sanatorium under the Sign of the Hourglass** (1937), and he created drawings for each book, although only the thirty-three for **Sanatorium** were used. Jerzy Ficowski believes that Schulz himself wrote the copy on the original dust jacket of **Sanatorium.**

> The author illustrates his work himself. This very striving to finish the task with his own hands makes us think about the inspiration of priests and craftsmen of the Middle Ages.

During the Nazi occupation of Drohobycz, Schulz was hired as a "house Jew" by the Gestapo officer Felix Landau, to paint signs and family portraits and perform light carpentry. Although Schulz was given false documents to help him escape, he never got the chance to use these "Aryan papers." Walking in the ghetto on the way to buy food, he was shot twice in the head by Landau's rival, Karl Guenther. Schulz was kept alive for a year serving Landau, who boasted he had a Jewish artist-slave that he sustained with a slice of bread and a bowl of soup. One of Schulz's tasks at Landau's was to decorate Landau's son's room with fairy tales, later described by one of Schulz's former students (quoted in the *Drawings*):

> Even then Schulz remained faithful to his artistic method: the figures of kings, knights, and squires painted in a fantastic, legendary scenery in the house of the Gestapo officer displayed distinctively non-Aryan features. Those were the people Schulz were living with at the time. Their emaciated, tormented faces were rendered with unbelievable resemblance. And those miserable people, transferred by Schulz's imagination from the world of tragic reality, reappeared in his paintings with splendor and glory as kings seated in their thrones in sable furs and crowns, as knights on white horses surrounded by their squires, as sovereign rulers riding in their golden carriages . . .

In much the same way that Schulz's letters expose his fragile emotional make-up and his frequent descents into near-malfunctioning, his drawings, so many of which are self-portraits, reveal even more striking obsessions and neuroses; one feels a discomfort watching this artist go public under the misguided assumption that he is portraying nothing terribly offensive or grotesque. While looking at the volume of his artwork can induce queasiness or even embarrassment, one cannot easily put it down. Utterly spellbinding, it offers a glimpse into a tormented soul fixated on degradation, whose prose only alludes to tendencies which spring into full bloom under the art pen. As a reviewer of his own writing, Schulz's self-perception dazzles us; he sent this description to the Italian publisher of a translation of *Cinnamon Shop:*

> The keynote to *Sanatorium* is the dream of renewal of life through the power of delight, the unleashing of inspiration, the primeval human belief that the dammed-up loveliness of things, hampered and hidden though it is, only awaits an inspired being to break its bonds and release a flood of happiness over all the world . . . Those reveries about shuffling off the coils of the body, about a revaluation of life through poetry, have found in Schulz a new homeland, a climate of their own, in which, watchful, they burgeon forth in tropical vegetation: a legendary childhood of wonder, elation, and metamorphosis.

Schulz's letters, too, are full of explanations about his mythologizing of reality, the role of art ("to be a probe sunk into the nameless"), and his need for isolation, which so directly conflicted with his need for "a friend, a kindred spirit, a partner for voyages of discovery." Reading these confessions, one often feels the same sense of trespassing that occurs while looking at the drawings: beneath what Adam Zagajewski has called "the captivating sentences of his downy prose," there lurked tremendous anguish, frustration, and sense of failure, "something like the collapse of my whole personality."

It is rare that one finds a critical piece or blurb about Schulz which does not mention Kafka; some have even dubbed him "the Polish Kafka." Like Kafka's, Schulz's letters seem to answer a need to communicate while remaining alone; "isolated from the stuff of daily life," Schulz put it. Each wrote far more letters than fiction. Both were surprisingly candid about their infirmities and neuroses in their letters; both sustained long and involved correspondences with fiancées whom they never married, instead living their adult lives with family members, working at jobs which left them little time for writing. The uncanny likenesses between these two men's lives, letters, and fiction of father-fixations and unforgettable metamorphoses is striking. While Kafka, in his notorious letter to his father, declared, "All my writing is about you," Schulz might have said something similar, having in his fiction created one of literature's most outlandish and fantastic fathers, whose own metamorphosing adventures make Gregor Samsa's seem almost pedestrian.

Schulz is credited as having helped to introduce Kafka's fiction to Poland. He wrote a lengthy and incisive afterword to *The Trial,* which appeared only in the 1936 edition. He lent his name to the translation done by Jozefina Szelínska, to encourage its publication, although he is often mistakenly credited with the translation itself. If Kafka was obsessed by space, Schulz was similarly obsessed by time. In one letter he admits to being dominated by:

> . . . the virginity of time. Just as for some rajah of melancholy and insatiable disposition any woman brushed by a male glance is already tainted and thereby unfit for anything but the silken noose, so for me any piece of time someone has laid claim to, has even casually mentioned in passing, is already marred, spoiled, unfit for consumption. I can't stand people laying claim to my time. They make the scrap they touched nauseating to me. I am incapable of sharing time, of feeding on somebody's leftovers.

Time is examined and transmogrified throughout Schulz's fiction, where it occupies a starring role alongside Father, who undergoes as many mutations and transformations (crab, cockroach, horsefly) as Schulzian time. Neither Father nor time can stay put in their original format. They exist in a state of constant flux, mutating and disappearing at will. Time appears in **"The Night of the Great Season"** as "that great eccentric" which "begets sometimes other years, different, prodigal years which—like a sixth, smallest toe—grow a thirteenth month . . . a hunchback month, a half-wilted shoot, more tentative than real." In **"The Age of Genius,"** Schulz explains that while ordinary events are arranged within time, strung along its length as on a thread, other events have occurred too late, that is, "after the whole of time has been distributed, divided, and allotted." What is to be done with these events:

. . . hanging in the air, homeless, errant? Could it be that time is too narrow for all events? Could it happen that all seats within time might have been sold? Is there perhaps some kind of bidding for time?

Time, and the "framework of uninterrupted chronology" with our "scrupulous habit of reporting on used-up hours" are all but forsaken in the hilarious story, **"Sanatorium under the Sign of the Hourglass,"** where the "quick decomposition of time" ceases to interest people, who, instead, accept time free of vigilance. "It immediately begins to do tricks, play irresponsible jokes, and indulge in crazy clowning." The staff of the sanatorium have put back the clock, reactivating time past, with all its possibilities, so that which might have happened in "ordinary time" can be undone. Thus, Father, dead in other locales, is offered a possibility of recovery, although the staff admits that his death "throws a certain shadow on his existence here." In a letter to a critic who had written about *Cinnamon Shops,* Schulz claims that the kind of art he cares about is "precisely a regression, childhood revisited. My ideal goal is to 'mature into childhood.' " Schulz's fiction and artwork act as extended elegies to childhood, his family, and Drohobycz, keeping each alive through spectacular acts of metamorphoses. (pp. 163-66)

> *Susan Miron, "Bruno Schulz Redux," in* Partisan Review, *Vol. LIX, No. 1, Winter, 1992, pp. 161-66.*

FURTHER READING

Criticism

Baranczak, Stanislaw. "His First Short Story Was a Postscript." *Los Angeles Times Book Review* (11 February 1990): 2, 10.

> Positive review of *The Complete Fiction of Bruno Schulz* in which the critic states: "Schulz's work appears the extreme consequence of 20th-Century fiction—its evolution toward the lyrical rather than the epic, the fantastic rather than the realistic, the subjective rather than the objective modes of narration and vision."

Brown, Russell E. "Bruno Schulz and World Literature." *Slavic and East European Journal* 34, No. 2 (1990): 224-46.

> Establishes Schulz's place "in the literary universe *outside* his native Polish language and culture." The critic also discusses major influences on Schulz's writing.

Budurowycz, Bohdan. "Galicia in the Work of Bruno Schulz." *Canadian Slavonic Papers* 28, No. 4 (December 1986): 359-68.

> Explores the significance of Schulz's native Galicia to his fiction.

Iribarne, Louis. "On Bruno Schulz." *Cross Currents: A Yearbook of Central European Culture,* No. 6 (1987): 173-77.

> Introduction to four previously unpublished fictional writings and one letter, which Iribarne translated. He comments: "[Each] of these pieces can be read as a Schulzian commentary on the art of writing, on a poesy that seeks to reunite the sublime and the base."

Klawans, Stuart. "Metamorphoses: Bruno Schulz's Hothouse Flowers." *VLS,* No. 70 (December 1988): 12-15.

> Appreciative overview of Schulz's literary output and life.

Ozick, Cynthia. "The Phantasmagoria of Bruno Schulz." In her *Art & Ardor,* pp. 224-28. New York: Alfred A. Knopf, 1983.

> Highly praises *The Street of Crocodiles,* comparing Schulz's writing to that of Isaac Babel, I. B. Singer, and Franz Kafka.

Robins, Nicholas. "The Golem." *London Magazine* 32, Nos. 9-10 (December-January 1993): 50-8.

> Detailed view of Schulz's personal life and its relationship to his fiction.

Schulz, Bruno. "An Essay for S. I. Witkiewicz." In *Four Decades of Polish Essays,* edited by Jan Kott, pp. 106-10. Evanston, Ill.: Northwestern University Press, 1990.

> Schulz reveals the imagery, symbolism, and themes of his early drawings and their importance to his fiction.

Edith Somerville
1858-1949

Martin Ross
1862-1915

(Full name Edith Anna Œnone Somerville; also wrote under the pseudonym Guilles Herring; Martin Ross is the pseudonym of Violet Florence Martin) Anglo-Irish novelists, short story writers, essayists and memoirists.

INTRODUCTION

In their many works of fiction, Somerville and Ross explored class conflicts of turn-of-the-century Ireland. Although best known for a series of comic short stories collectively known as *The Irish R.M.,* Somerville and Ross are also widely regarded as the most important chroniclers of the vanished Anglo-Irish gentry.

Somerville was born on the island of Corfu. The oldest of eight children, she grew up on the Somerville family estate in Cork, where she developed a great love for the Irish countryside, people, and pastimes. Educated primarily at home, Somerville displayed a talent for painting and drawing while young. In her late teens she studied at the South Kensington School of Art, and later in art schools on continental Europe. She returned home in 1886, and shortly after met her cousin Violet Martin, who also belonged to a landed Protestant family. Somerville later referred to this meeting as "the hinge of my life, the place where my life, and hers, turned over." The two women discovered a shared enthusiasm for writing, and within a year of meeting each other, they were at work on a novel together, despite their families' conviction that writing was not respectable work for young ladies of good breeding. During their literary partnership, which lasted twenty-eight years, Somerville and Ross wrote five novels together, as well as short stories, travel essays, and memoirs.

After Ross's death in 1915 of an inoperable brain tumor, Somerville at first had no intention of further pursuing her literary career. However, she resumed writing after a spiritualist friend convinced her that she could still contact Ross's spirit through automatic writing. Nearly all of Somerville's subsequent works were published under the joint signature of Somerville and Ross. Following Ross's death, Somerville wrote three more novels of critical significance: *Mount Music, An Enthusiast,* and *The Big House of Inver.* For some of these works, Somerville made use of notes and drafts that Ross had left behind. She also published a series of essays Ross had written alone, along with some of her own, in a collection called *Irish Memories.* In her later years, Somerville toured the United States, and her paintings and drawings were exhibited in American and European galleries. She died in 1949.

Somerville and Ross's first novel, *An Irish Cousin,* was published in 1889 and contains many of the elements that characterize their subsequent work: portrayals of tensions

Edith Somerville (left) and Martin Ross in 1894.

between various social classes, vivid descriptions of gentry life, and a sharp rendering of dialect. In 1894 Somerville and Ross published *The Real Charlotte,* which most critics still consider their masterpiece and among the finest Irish novels of the period. This work chronicles the plottings and manipulations of Charlotte Mullen, a plain, middle-class woman determined to ascend Ireland's social ladder. Though some early critics decried what they considered the novel's vulgarity, later commentators admired its accurate portrayal of Ireland's social strata and its uncompromising realism. As Conor Cruise O'Brien has observed: "Evil has often been more dramatically exhibited, but I do not think it has ever been more convincingly worked out in humdrum action, or brought home with such a terrible cumulative effect as an element in everyday life."

Much of Somerville and Ross's work during the final years of the nineteenth century was geared to commercial tastes, because both women were trying to raise money for the upkeep of their faltering family estates. They sold a number of short stories about foxhunting to sporting magazines as well as travel essays and other short pieces. The authors' greatest commercial success came in 1908 with *Some Experiences of an Irish R.M.,* a collection of previously published short stories involving an English rural magistrate and his vain efforts to impose his nation's law and order on an Irish province. Filled with chases, mix-ups, and other comic conventions, the stories are brought to life with vivid Irish dialect. Enormously popular, this collection was followed by two sequels, *Further Experiences of an Irish R.M.,* and *In Mr. Knox's Country. The Irish R.M.* stories have been attacked by some commentators for what they believe are stereotypical depictions of Irish peasants as drunk, untrustworthy, and clownish. Other critics, however, observe that Somerville and Ross just as frequently satirize their own class. Many critics find that while the writers are best remembered for the *Irish R.M.* stories rather than for their realistic novels, their comic and serious fiction are complementary, looking at the same themes from a different angle. What is not disputed is the authors' flair for minute realistic detail, their often ironic sense of humor, and their gift for rendering Irish dialect on the printed page.

PRINCIPAL WORKS*

An Irish Cousin (novel) 1889

Naboth's Vineyard (novel) 1891

In the Vine Country (travel essays) 1893

Through Connemara in a Governess Cart (travel essays) 1893

The Real Charlotte (novel) 1894

Beggars on Horseback (travel essays) 1895

The Silver Fox (novel) 1898

Some Experiences of an Irish R.M. (short stories) 1899

All on the Irish Shore (short stories) 1903

Some Irish Yesterdays (reminiscences) 1906

Further Experiences of an Irish R.M. (short stories) 1908

Dan Russel the Fox (novel) 1911

In Mr. Knox's Country (short stories) 1915

Irish Memories (essays, sketches, and reminiscences) 1917

Mount Music (novel) 1919

Strayaways (essays) 1920

An Enthusiast (novel) 1921

Wheel-Tracks (essays, sketches, and reminiscences) 1923

The Big House of Inver (novel) 1925

French Leave (novel) 1928

The States through Irish Eyes (travel essays) 1930

An Incorruptible Irishman (biography) 1932

The Smile and the Tear (essays) 1933

Notes of the Horn: Hunting Verse, Old and New (folklore) 1934

The Sweet Cry of Hounds (essays) 1936

Sarah's Youth (novel) 1938

Records of the Somerville Family of Castlehaven and Drishane from 1174 to 1940 [with Boyle Somerville] (nonfiction) 1940

Notions in Garrison (essays) 1941

Happy Days (essays) 1946

Maria and Some Other Dogs (short stories) 1949

---

*Somerville cowrote with Martin Ross (pseudonym of Violet Martin) the books published through 1915, the year of Ross's death. The remaining volumes, with the exception of *Records of the Somerville Family,* were published under both authors' names, although Somerville wrote them herself.

CRITICISM

The Spectator (essay date 1899)

[*In the following review of the stories in* Some Experiences of an Irish R.M., *the critic praises Somerville and Ross's accurate rendering of Irish life and dialect as well as their sense of humor.*]

The literary alliance between Miss Somerville and Miss Martin ("Martin Ross") has already borne many admirable results, but in the quality and quantity of diversion provided none of their previous ventures has equalled **Some Experiences of an Irish R.M.,** a series of episodes which, after delighting the readers of the *Badminton* for the past year, have now been collected in volume form for the permanent entertainment of all Hibernophil readers. One needs to have lived in, or at least to have visited, Ireland to appreciate at its true worth the remarkable fidelity of the portraiture and the landscape painting, but only an uncompromising hater of all dialect could fail to be exhilarated by such irresistible fun as that which pervades the story of Bocock's Mare. The "R.M." and his pragmatic English visitor have, owing to a succession of disasters, failed to get more than half-way to a local race-meeting. Taking shelter from the rain at a publichouse, they hear an account of the races at second hand, and in particular of a steeplechase in which "Bocock's owld mare," ridden by one Driscoll, was matched against a horse ridden by another local worthy named Clancy. The narrator, after describing how he had planted himself at a convenient spot on the course to encourage the mare, proceeds to narrate his *modus operandi* when he saw Driscoll, her jockey, was riding a losing race:—

> ' "Skelp her, ye big brute!" says I. "What good's in ye that ye aren't able to skelp her?" . . . . . . Well, Mr. Flurry, and gintlemen . . . . . . I declare to ye when owld Bocock's mare heard thim roars she sthretched out her neck like a gandher, and when she passed me out she give a couple of grunts, and looked at me as ugly as a Christian. "Hah!" says I, givin' her a couple o' dbraws o' th' ash plant across the butt o' the tail, the way I wouldn't blind her, "I'll make ye grunt!" says I, "I'll nourish ye!" I knew well she was very frightful of th' ash plant since the winter Tommeen Sullivan had her under a sidecar. But now, in place of havin' any obligations to me, ye'd be surprised if ye heard the blaspheemious expressions of that young boy that was ridin' her; and whether it was over-anxious he was, turnin' around the way I'd hear him cursin', or whether it was some slither or slide came to owld Bocock's mare, I dunno, but she was bet up against the last obstackle but two, and before ye could say "Shnipes," she was standin' on her two ears beyant in th' other field! I declare to ye, on the vartue of me oath, she stood that way till she reconnoithered what side Driscoll would fall, an' she turned about then and rolled on him as cosy as if he was meadow grass!' Slipper stopped

short; the people in the doorway groaned appreciatively; Mary Kate murmured 'The Lord save us!'—'The blood was dhruv out through his nose and ears,' continued Slipper, with a voice that indicated the cream of the narration, 'and you'd hear his bones crackin' on the ground! You'd have pitied the poor boy.' 'Good heavens!' said Leigh Kelway [the English visitor] sitting up very straight in his chair. 'Was he hurt, Slipper?' asked Flurry casually. 'Hurt is it?' echoed Slipper in high scorn 'killed on the spot!' He paused to relish the effect of the *dénoûement* on Leigh Kelway. 'Oh, divil so pleasant an afternoon ever you seen; and indeed, Mr. Flurry, it's what we were all sayin', it was a great pity your honour was not there for the likin' you had for Driscoll.'

Of course the "kilt" man turns up to confound the narrator and mystify the Englishman still further. But it must not be thought that these stories are mere pieces of caricature. The various typical personages introduced—Mr. Flurry Knox, the squireen "M.F.H."; old Mrs. Knox, his relative who goes cub-hunting in a bath-chair; that accomplished horse-coper, Miss Bobbie Bennett; and Mrs. Cadogan, the "R.M.'s" housekeeper—are all drawn from the life of modern Galway and Cork. The dialogue is throughout rich in delicious Hibernianisms—*e.g.,* we read of whisky as "pliable as new milk," of a bandmaster who was "a thrifle fulsome after his luncheon," and of a horse who was a "nice flippant jumper." Indeed, if there were many women writers like Miss Martin and Miss Somerville, the discussion whether their sex is deficient in the sense of humour would be not merely otiose but impertinent. (pp. 788-89)

A review of "Some Experiences of an Irish R.M.," in The Spectator, *Vol. 83, No. 3726, November 25, 1899, pp. 788-90.*

C. L. Graves   (essay date 1913)

[*In the excerpt below, Graves explores the use of humor in both the comic and serious fiction of Somerville and Ross.*]

The literary partnership of Miss Edith Somerville and Miss Violet Martin—the most brilliantly successful example of creative collaboration in our times—began with *An Irish Cousin* in 1889. Published over the pseudonyms of 'Geilles Herring' and 'Martin Ross,' this delightful story is remarkable not only for its promise, afterwards richly fulfilled, but for its achievement. The writers proved themselves the possessors of a strange faculty of detachment which enabled them to view the humours of Irish life through the unfamiliar eye of a stranger without losing their own sympathy. They were at once of the life they described and outside it. They showed a laudable freedom from political partisanship; a minute familiarity with the manners and customs of all strata of Irish society; an unerring instinct for the 'sovran word,' a perfect mastery of the Anglo-Irish dialect; and an acute yet well-controlled sense of the ludicrous. The heroine accurately describes the concourse on the platform of a small Irish country station as having 'all the appearance of a large social gathering or *conversazione,* the carriages being filled, not by

those who were starting, but by their friends who had come to see them off.' When she went to a county ball in Cork she discovered to her dismay that all her partners were named either Beamish or Barrett:

Had it not been for Willy's elucidation of its mysteries, I should have thrown my card away in despair. "No; not *him*. That's *Long* Tom Beamish! It's *English* Tommy you're to dance with next. They call him English Tommy because, when his militia regiment was ordered to Aldershot, he said he was 'the first of his ancestors that was ever sent on foreign service.' " . . . I carried for several days the bruises which I received during my waltz with English Tommy. It consisted chiefly of a series of short rushes, of so shattering a nature that I at last ventured to suggest a less aggressive mode of progression. "Well," said English Tommy confidentially, "ye see, I'm trying to bump Katie! That's Katie," pointing to a fat girl in blue. "She's my cousin, and we're for ever fighting."

As a set-off to this picture of the hilarious informality of high life in Cork twenty-five years ago there is a wonderful study of a cottage interior, occupied by a very old man, his daughter-in-law, three children, two terriers, a cat, and a half-plucked goose. The conversation between Willy Sarsfield—who foreshadows Flurry Knox in *Some Experiences of an Irish R.M.* by his mingled shrewdness and *naïveté*—and Mrs Sweeny is a perfect piece of reproduction.

Mrs Sweeny was sitting on a kind of rough settle, between the other window and the door of an inner room. She was a stout, comfortable-looking woman of about forty, with red hair and quick blue eyes, that roved round the cabin, and silenced with a glance the occasional whisperings that rose from the children. "And how's the one that had the bad cough?" asked Willy, pursuing his conversation with her with his invariable ease and dexterity. "Honor her name is, isn't it?"—"See, now, how well he remembers!" replied Mrs Sweeny. "Indeed, she's there back in the room, lyin' these three days. Faith, I think 'tis like the decline she have , Masther Willy."—"Did you get the doctor to her?" said Willy. "I'll give you a ticket if you haven't one."—"Oh, indeed, Docthor Kelly's afther givin' her a bottle, but shure I wouldn't let her put it into her mouth at all. God knows what'd be in it. Wasn't I afther throwin' a taste of it on the fire to thry what'd it do, and Phitz! says it, and up with it up the chimbley! Faith, I'd be in dread to give it to the child. Shure if it done that in the fire, what'd it do in her inside?"—"Well, you're a greater fool than I thought you were," said Willy politely.— "Maybe I am, faith," replied Mrs Sweeny, with a loud laugh of enjoyment. "But if she's for dyin', the crayture, she'll die aisier without thim thrash of medicines; and if she's for livin', 'tisn't thrusting to them she'll be. Shure, God is good, God is good——"—"Divil's betther!" interjected old Sweeny, unexpectedly. It was the first time he had spoken, and having delivered himself of this trenchant observation, he relapsed into silence and the smackings at his pipe.

But the tragic note is sounded in the close of *An Irish Cousin*—Miss Martin and Miss Somerville have never lost sight of the abiding dualism enshrined in Moore's verse which tells of the tear and the smile in Erin's eye—and it dominates their next novel, *Naboth's Vineyard,* published in 1891, a sombre romance of the Land League days. Three years later they reached the summit of their achievement in *The Real Charlotte,* which still remains their masterpiece, though easily eclipsed in popularity by the irresistible drollery of *Some Experiences of an Irish R.M.* To begin with, it does not rely on the appeal to hunting people which in their later work won the heart of the English sportsman. It is a ruthlessly candid study of Irish provincial and suburban life; of the squalors of middle-class households; of garrison hacks and 'underbred, finespoken,' florid squireens. But secondly and chiefly it repels the larger half of the novel-reading public by the fact that two women have here dissected the heart of one of their sex in a mood of unrelenting realism. While pointing out the pathos and humiliation of the thought that a soul can be stunted by the trivialities of personal appearance, they own to having set down Charlotte Mullen's many evil qualities 'without pity.' They approach their task in the spirit of Balzac. The book, as we shall see, is extraordinarily rich in both wit and humour, but Charlotte, who cannot control her ruling passion of avarice even in a death chamber, might have come straight out of the pages of the *Comédie Humaine.* Masking her greed, her jealousy and her cruelty under a cloak of loud affability and ponderous persiflage, she is a perfect specimen of the *fausse bonne femme.* Only her cats could divine the strange workings of her mind:

> The movements of Charlotte's character, for it cannot be said to possess the power of development, were akin to those of some amphibious thing whose strong, darting course under the water is only marked by a bubble or two, and it required almost an animal instinct to note them. Every bubble betrayed the creature below, as well as the limitations of its power of hiding itself, but people never thought of looking out for these indications in Charlotte, or even suspected that she had anything to conceal. There was an almost blatant simplicity about her, a humorous rough and readiness which, joined with her literary culture, proved business capacity, and her dreaded temper, seemed to leave no room for any further aspect, least of all of a romantic kind.

Yet romance of a sort was at the root of Charlotte's character. She had been in love with Roddy Lambert, a showy, handsome, selfish squireen, before he married for money. She had disguised her tenderness under a bluff *camaraderie* during his first wife's lifetime, and hastened Mrs Lambert's death by inflaming her suspicions of Roddy's infidelity. It was only when Charlotte was again foiled by Lambert's second marriage to her own niece, that her love was turned to gall and she plotted to compass his ruin.

The authors deal faithfully with Francie FitzPatrick, Charlotte's niece, but an element of compassion mingles with their portraiture. Charlotte had robbed Francie of a legacy, and compounded with her conscience by inviting the girl to stay with her at Lismoyle. Any change was a godsend to poor Francie, who, being an orphan, lived in Dublin with another aunt, a kindly but feckless creature whose eyes were not formed to perceive dirt nor her nose to apprehend smells, and whose idea of economy was 'to indulge in no extras of soap or scrubbing brushes, and to feed her family on strong tea and indifferent bread and butter, in order that Ida's and Mabel's hats might be no whit less ornate than those of their neighbours.' In this dingy household Francie had grown up, lovely as a Dryad, brilliantly indifferent to the serious things of life, with a deplorable Dublin accent, ingenuous, unaffected and inexpressibly vulgar. She captivates men of all sorts: Roddy Lambert, who lunched on hot beefsteak pie and sherry; Mr Hawkins, an amorous young soldier, who treated her with a bullying tenderness and jilted her for an English heiress; and Christopher Dysart, a scholar, a gentleman, and the heir to a baronetcy, who was ruined by self-criticism and diffidence. Francie respected Christopher and rejected him; was thrown over by Hawkins whom she loved; and married Roddy Lambert, her motives being 'poverty, aimlessness, bitterness of soul and instinctive leniency towards any man who liked her.' Francie had already exasperated Charlotte by refusing Christopher Dysart: by marrying Lambert she dealt a death-blow to her hopes and drove her into the path of vengeance.

But the story is not only engrossing as a study of vulgarity that is touched with pathos, of the vindictive jealousy of unsunned natures, of the cowardice of the selfish and the futility of the intellectually effete. It is a treasure-house of good sayings, happy comments, ludicrous incidents. When Francie returned to Dublin we read how one of her cousins, 'Dottie, unfailing purveyor of diseases to the family, had imported German measles from her school.' When Charlotte, nursing her wrath, went to inform the servant at Lambert's house of the return of her master with his new wife, the servant inquired 'with cold resignation' whether it was the day after to-morrow:

> "It is, me poor woman, it is," replied Charlotte in the tone of facetious intimacy that she reserved for other people's servants. "You'll have to stir your stumps to get the house ready for them."—"The house is cleaned down and ready for them as soon as they like to walk into it," replied Eliza Hackett with dignity, "and if the new lady faults the drawing-room chimbley for not being swep, the master will know it's not me that's to blame for it, but the sweep that's gone dhrilling with the Mileetia."

Each of the members of the Dysart family is hit off in some memorable phrase; Sir Benjamin, the old and irascible paralytic, 'who had been struck down on his son's coming of age by a paroxysm of apoplectic jealousy'; the admirable and unselfish Pamela with her 'pleasant anxious voice'; Christopher, who believed that, if only he could 'read the "Field" and had a more spontaneous habit of cursing,' he would be an ideal country gentleman; and Lady Dysart, who was a clever woman, a renowned solver of acrostics in her society paper, and a holder of strong opinions as to the prophetic meaning of the Pyramids. With her 'a large yet refined bonhomie' took the place of tact, but being an

Englishwoman she was 'constitutionally unable to discern perfectly the subtle grades of Irish vulgarity.' Sometimes the authors throw away the *scenario* for a whole novel in a single paragraph, as in this compressed summary of the antecedents of Captain Cursiter:

> Captain Cursiter was "getting on" as captains go, and he was the less disposed to regard his junior's love affairs with an indulgent eye, in that he had himself served a long and difficult apprenticeship in such matters, and did not feel that he had profited much by his experiences. It had happened to him at an early age to enter ecstatically into the house of bondage, and in it he had remained with eyes gradually opening to its drawbacks, until, a few years before, the death of the only apparent obstacle to his happiness had brought him face to face with its realisation. Strange to say, when this supreme moment arrived, Captain Cursiter was disposed for further delay; but it shows the contrariety of human nature, that when he found himself superseded by his own subaltern, an habitually inebriated viscount, instead of feeling grateful to his preserver, he committed the imbecility of horsewhipping him; and finding it subsequently advisable to leave his regiment, he exchanged into the infantry with a settled conviction that all women were liars.

Nouns and verbs are the bones and sinews of style; it is in the use of epithets and adjectives that the artist is shown; and Miss Martin and Miss Somerville never make a mistake. An episode in the life of one of Charlotte's pets—a cockatoo—is described as occurring when the bird was 'a sprightly creature of some twenty shrieking summers.' We read of cats who stared 'with the expressionless but wholly alert scrutiny of their race'; of the 'difficult revelry' of Lady Dysart's garden party, where the men were in a hopeless minority and the more honourable women sat on a long bench in 'midge-bitten dulness.' Such epithets are not decorative, they heighten the effect of the picture. Where adjectives are not really needed Miss Martin and Miss Somerville can dispense with them altogether and yet attain a deadly precision, as when they describe an Irish beggar as 'a bundle of rags with a cough in it,' or note a characteristic trait of Roddy Lambert by observing that 'he was a man in whom jealousy took the form of reviling the object of his affections, if by so doing he could detach his rivals'—a modern instance of 'displiceas aliis, sic ego tutus ero.' When Roddy Lambert went away after his first wife's funeral we learn that he 'honeymooned with his grief in the approved fashion.' These felicities abound on every page; while the turn of phrase of the peasant speech is caught with a fidelity which no other Irish writer has ever surpassed. When Judy Lee, a poor old woman who had taken an unconscionable time in dying, was called by one of the gossips who had attended her wake 'as nice a woman as ever threw a tub of clothes on the hill,' and complimented for having 'battled it out well,' Norry the Boat replied sardonically:

> Faith thin, an' if she did die itself she was in the want of it; sure there isn't a winther since her daughther wint to America that she wasn't anointed a couple of times. I'm thinkin' the peo-

> ple th' other side o' death will be throuncin her for keepin' them waitin' on her this way.

Humour is never more effective than when it emerges from a serious situation. Tragedy jostles comedy in life, and the greatest dramatists and romancers have made wonderful use of this abrupt alternation. There are many painful and diverting scenes in *The Real Charlotte,* but none in which both elements are blended so effectively as the story of Julia Duffy's last pilgrimage. Threatened with eviction from her farm by the covetous intrigues of Charlotte, she leaves her sick bed to appeal to her landlord, and when half dead with fatigue falls in with the insane Sir Benjamin, to be driven away with grotesque insults. On her way home, she calls in at Charlotte's house only to find Christopher Dysart reading Rossetti's poems to Francie FitzPatrick, who has just timidly observed, in reply to her instructor's remark that the hero is a pilgrim, 'I know a lovely song called "The Pilgrim of Love"; of course it wasn't the same thing as what you were reading, but it was awfully nice too.' This interlude is intensely ludicrous, but its cruel incongruity only heightens the misery of what has gone before and what follows.

The Silver Fox, which appeared in 1897, need not detain us long, though it is a little masterpiece in its way, vividly contrasting the limitations of the sport-loving temperament with the ineradicable superstitions of the Irish peasantry. Impartial as ever, the authors have here achieved a felicity of phrase to which no other writers of hunting novels have ever approached. 'Imagination's widest stretch' cannot picture Surtees or Mr Nat Gould describing an answer being given 'with that level politeness of voice which is the distilled essence of a perfected anger.'

But the atmosphere of *The Silver Fox* is sombre, and a sporting novel which is at once serious and of a fine literary quality must necessarily appeal to a limited audience. The problem is solved to perfection in *Some Experiences of an Irish R.M.,* a series of loosely-knit episodes which, after running a serial course in the 'Badminton Magazine,' were republished in book form towards the close of 1899. There is only one chapter to cloud the otherwise unintermittent hilarity of the whole recital. The authors have dispensed with comment, and rely chiefly on dialogue, incident, and their intimate and precise knowledge of horses, and horse-copers of both sexes. An interested devotion to the noble animal is here shown to be the last infirmity of noble minds, for old Mrs Knox, who combined the culture of a *grande dame* with the appearance of a refined scarecrow, went cub-hunting in a bath chair. In such a company a young sailor whose enthusiasm for the chase had been nourished by the hirelings of Malta, and whose eye for points had probably been formed on circus posters, had little chance of making a good bargain at Drumcurran horse fair:

> "The fellow's asking forty-five pounds for her," said Bernard Shute to Miss Sally; "she's a nailer to gallop. I don't think it's too much."—"Her grandsire was the Mountain Hare," said the owner of the mare, hurrying up to continue her family history, "and he was the grandest horse in the four baronies. He was forty-two years of age when he died, and they waked him the same

as ye'd wake a Christian. They had whisky and porther—and bread—and a piper in it."—"Thim Mountain Hare colts is no great things," interrupted Mr Shute's groom contemptuously. "I seen a colt once that was one of his stock, and if there was forty men and their wives, and they after him with sticks, he wouldn't lep a sod of turf."—"Lep, is it!" ejaculated the owner in a voice shrill with outrage. "You may lead that mare out through the counthry, and there isn't a fence in it that she wouldn't go up to it as indepindent as if she was going to her bed, and your honour's ladyship knows that dam well, Miss Knox."—"You want too much money for her, McCarthy," returned Miss Sally, with her little air of preternatural wisdom. "God pardon you, Miss Knox! Sure a lady like you knows well that forty-five pounds is no money for that mare. Forty-five pounds!" He laughed. "It'd be as good for me to make her a present to the gentleman all out as take three farthings less for her! She's too grand entirely for a poor farmer like me, and if it wasn't for the long weak family I have, I wouldn't part with her under twice the money."—"Three fine lumps of daughters in America paying his rent for him," commented Flurry in the background. "That's the long weak family!"

The turn of phrase in Irish conversation has never been reproduced in print with greater fidelity, and there is hardly a page in the book without some characteristic Hibernianism such as 'Whisky as pliable as new milk,' or the description of a horse who was a 'nice flippant jumper,' or a bandmaster who was 'a thrifle fulsome after his luncheon,' or a sweep who 'raised tallywack and tandem all night round the house to get at the chimbleys.' The narrative reaches its climax in the chapter headed **'Lisheen Races. Second-hand.'** Major Yeates and his egregious English visitor Mr Leigh Kelway, an earnest Radical publicist, having failed to reach the scene, are sheltering from the rain in a wayside public-house where they are regaled with an account of the races by Slipper, the dissipated but engaging huntsman of the local pack of hounds. The close of the meeting was a steeplechase in which 'Bocock's owld mare,' ridden by one Driscoll, was matched against a horse ridden by another local sportsman named Clancy, and Slipper who favoured Driscoll, and had taken up his position at a convenient spot on the course, thus describes his mode of encouraging the mare:

> " 'Skelp her, ye big brute!' says I. 'What good's in ye that ye aren't able to skelp her?' . . . Well, Mr Flurry, and gintlemen . . . I declare to ye when owld Bocock's mare heard thim roars she sthretched out her neck like a gandher, and when she passed me out she give a couple of grunts, and looked at me as ugly as a Christian. 'Hah!' says I, givin' her a couple o' dhraws o' th' ash plant across the butt o' the tail, the way I wouldn't blind her, 'I'll make ye grunt!' says I, 'I'll nourish ye!' I knew well she was very frightful of th' ash plant since the winter Tommeen Sullivan had her under a sidecar. But now, in place of havin' any obligations to me, ye'd be surprised if ye heard the blaspheemious expressions of that young boy that was ridin' her; and

whether it was over-anxious he was, turnin' around the way I'd hear him cursin', or whether it was some slither or slide came to owld Bocock's mare, I dunno, but she was bet up agin the last obstackle but two, and before you could say 'Shnipes,' she was standin' on her two ears beyon in th' other field! I declare to ye, on the vartue of me oath, she stood that way till she reconnoithered what side Driscoll would fall, an' she turned about then and rolled on him as cosy as if he was meadow grass!" Slipper stopped short; the people in the doorway groaned appreciatively; Mary Kate murmured "The Lord save us!"—"The blood was dhruv out through his nose and ears," continued Slipper, with a voice that indicated the cream of the narration, "and you'd hear his bones crackin' on the ground! You'd have pitied the poor boy."—"Good heavens!" said Leigh Kelway sitting up very straight in his chair. "Was he hurt, Slipper?" asked Flurry casually. "Hurt is it?" echoed Slipper in high scorn; "killed on the spot!" He paused to relish the effect of the *dénouement* on Leigh Kelway. "Oh, divil so pleasant an afthernoon ever you seen; and indeed, Mr Flurry, it's what we were all sayin', it was a great pity your honour was not there for the likin' you had for Driscoll."

Leigh Kelway, it may be noted, is the lineal descendant of Mr Prettyman, the pragmatic English under-secretary in 'Charles O'Malley' who, having observed that he had never seen an Irish wake, was horrified by the prompt offer of his Galway host, a notorious practical joker, to provide a corpse on the spot. But this is only one of the instances of parallelism in which the later writers, though showing far greater restraint and fidelity to type, have illustrated the continuance of temperamental qualities, which Lever and his forerunner Maxwell—the author of 'Wild Sports of the West'—portrayed in a more extravagant form. On the other hand, it would be impossible to imagine a greater contrast than that between Lever's thrasonical narrator-heroes and Major Yeates, R.M., whose fondness for sport is allied to a thorough consciousness of his own infirmities as a sportsman. There is no heroic figure in *Some Experiences of an Irish R.M.,* but the characters are all lifelike, and at least half a dozen—'Flurry' Knox, his cousin Sally and his old grandmother Mrs Knox of Aussolas, Slipper, Mrs Cadogan and the incomparable Maria—form as integral a part of our circle of acquaintance as if we had known them in real life. *The Real Charlotte* is a greater achievement, but the *R.M.* is a surer passport to immortality.

The further instalment of *Experiences* published a few years later did not escape the common lot of sequels. They were brilliantly written; but one was more conscious of the excellence of the manner than in any of their predecessors. The two volumes of short stories and sketches, published in 1903 and 1906 under the titles of *All on the Irish Shore* and *Some Irish Yesterdays* respectively, show some new and engaging aspects of the genius of the collaborators. There is a chapter called **'Children of the Captivity'** in which the would-be English humorist's conception of Irish humour is dealt with faithfully—as it deserves to be. The essay is also remarkable for the passage in which are set down once and for all the true canons for the treatment of dialect. Pronunciation and spelling, as the authors point out, are after all of small account in its presentment:

> The vitalising power is in the rhythm of the sentence, the turn of phrase, the knowledge of idiom, and of, beyond all, the attitude of mind. . . . The shortcoming is, of course, trivial to those who do not suffer because of it, but want of perception of word and phrase and turn of thought means more than mere artistic failure, it means want of knowledge of the wayward and shrewd and sensitive minds that are at the back of the dialect. The very wind that blows softly over brown acres of bog carries perfumes and sounds that England does not know: the women digging the potato-land are talking of things that England does not understand. The question that remains is whether England will ever understand.

The hunting sketches in these volumes include the wonderful "Patrick Day's Hunt," which is a masterpiece in the the high *bravura* of the brogue. Another is noticeable for a passage on the affection inspired by horses. When Johnny Connolly heard that his mistress was driven to sell the filly he had trained and nursed so carefully, he did not disguise his disappointment:

> "Well, indeed, that's too bad, miss," said Johnny comprehendingly. "There was a mare I had one time, and I sold her before I went to America. God knows, afther she went from me, whenever I'd look at her winkers hanging on the wall I'd have to cry. I never seen a sight of her till three years afther that, afther I coming home. I was coming out o' the fair at Enniscar, an' I was talking to a man an' we coming down Dangan Hill, and what was in it but herself coming up in a cart! An' I didn't look at her, good nor bad, nor know her, but sorra bit but she knew me talking, an' she turned in to me with the cart. 'Ho, ho, ho!' says she, and she stuck her nose into me like she'd be kissing me. Be dam, but I had to cry. An' the world wouldn't stir her out o' that till I'd lead her on meself. As for cow nor dog nor any other thing, there's nothing would rise your heart like a horse!"

And if horses are irresistible, so are Centaurs. That is the moral to be drawn from *Dan Russel the Fox,* the latest work from the pens of Miss Somerville and Miss Martin, in which the rival claims of culture and fox-hunting are subjected to a masterly analysis.

The joint authors of the *R.M.* have paid forfeit for their popularity by being expected to repeat their first resounding success. Happily the pressure of popular demand has not impaired the artistic excellence of their work, though we cannot help thinking that if they had been left to themselves they might have given us at least one other novel on the lines of *The Real Charlotte.* Their later work, again, has been subjected to the ordeal, we do not say of conscious imitation, but of comparison with books which would probably have never been written, or would have been written on another plan, but for the success of the *R.M.* To regard this rivalry as serious would be, in the opinion of the present writer, an abnegation of the critical faculty. (pp. 30-42)

C. L. Graves, "The Lighter Side of Irish Life," in The Quarterly Review, Vol. 219, No. 436, July, 1913, pp. 26-47.

Orlo Williams   (essay date 1920)

[*In the following excerpt, Williams stresses the technical and literary merits of Somerville and Ross's comic fiction, which he finds superior to the authors' more serious works.*]

Few humorists who write merely to catch the passing fancy of the day can have been more successful or more popular [than Edith Somerville and Martin Ross]: in the merely temporary quality of effervescence they can compete with any of their contemporaries. The sportsman who hates art and loathes poetry has the *Irish R.M.* and its fellows in well-thumbed copies on his bookshelves; the man who only reads for laughter and never for improvement praises these authors as highly as the most discriminating, and those who would faint at the suspicion of becoming in any way involved in classic literature will joyfully immerse themselves in "Somerville and Ross," like thirsty bibbers quaffing a curious vintage for its exhilaration rather than its quality. Appreciation has poured in upon them from all sides, from those who know and delight in the comic sides of Irish life, when treated observantly and not fantastically, from those to whom hunting and horseflesh are almost the be-all and end-all of existence, from those who treat their brains to a good story as to a stimulative drug, as well as from those who bring more discrimination to their appraisement. The devotees will often claim that they alone can scent the subtler flavour from these hilarious pages. The Irishman, unless he be of the kind that despises all light-heartedness in writing of his country, will assert that none but he can get the exquisite appreciation of comparing the work of art with the reality which inspired it: the hunting fraternity will find it hard to suppose that one who knows not what it is to be

> Oft listening how the hounds and horn
> Clearly rouse the slumbering morn
> From the side of some hoar hill,
> Through the high wood echoing shrill,

can possibly enjoy the skill shown by these authors in describing the joy of horses and the thrill of hunting. Nevertheless, the books of Miss Somerville and Martin Ross are heartily enjoyed by a host of readers who are neither Irish nor hunting people, for the simple reason that they are prompted to an explosion of laughter whenever they take up one of these stories. The bulk of these readers would wish to go no further in their appreciation: they embrace the givers of present laughter with so full a measure of enjoyment that it would seem to them unnecessary to probe any further into the chemistry of such excellence, nor perhaps would they deem it possible that any higher praise than their freely-expressed enjoyment could be looked for by any authors. Yet to my mind it is possible. While including in one's general testimony all that can be said by the most extravagant of these admirers, the taster who is considering the cellar of English literature which is being laid down for posterity may discern qualities not so apparent to the quaffer for immediate exhilaration. It is hard to conceive it, but the bubbles may vanish: if they do, the question is, what will be left? My point is that the work of Miss Somerville and Martin Ross has the qualities of a wine that will keep.

It cannot be a great wine, for the vineyard is too restricted. The high winds of emotion have not swept over its soil, nor has the soft rain of tenderness moistened it. It will always be bright and rather dry like Vouvray, gay but with a little bite in it: posterity may even call it "curious." But they will recognise that it holds the authentic flavours that distinguish infallibly the finer products of English literary bins. The authors have chosen a small field, but they direct on it an accuracy of vision which is remarkable, and, seeing that they were two, a unity of vision which is a miracle. In the expression of this vision they display an unfailing sureness of touch and a precision which is perfect in its admirable economy. They handle our language with a deftness and flexibility which is a rarity in itself, and their style, though always original, is nourished by a recollection of great models both in prose and poetry. Theirs is a literary equipment of the first class, solidly framed, well clothed, attractive in appearance, and ornamented with taste. They touch nothing that they do not embellish: events by their unflagging narrative power, which goes as unfalteringly as one of their choicest hunters, character by their sympathetic insight, scenery by their love of natural beauty, dialogue by their dramatic sense. It is not all Ireland that they draw, let that be admitted; they prefer to laugh, letting others weep. Yet, if the whole heart of Ireland does not beat within their pages, a part of it is there, pulsing with true Irish blood and throbbing with truly Irish emotions. Their aspect is no more that of Mr. James Joyce or Mr. Synge or Mr. Yeats than it is that of Mr. George Moore or Mr. Devlin, but, if they are justly praised for their merits, that praise cannot be diminished because they looked on Ireland with laughing eyes through a West Carbery window. Their books are literature no less certainly than *Castle Rackrent* is literature, and for very similar reasons.

Well, let us taste. It is a bright dry wine, I have said. It is not, perhaps, the quality which the authors would ascribe to what they consider their best work, ***The Real Charlotte***—an estimate in which Mr. Stephen Gwynn agrees with them. This is a fine sombre story of a middle-aged woman's jealousy, for Charlotte is a kind of Irish Cousine Bette. But, if the subject is comparable to that of Balzac's novel, the treatment is certainly not so, and that is my reason for not regarding this as the work by which their achievement can best be judged. It is the work in which they have aimed highest, and the measure of their success is not small, but the theme of Charlotte's jealousy and the havoc in other lives which it caused needed for its convincing development all the powers of a great tragic artist. It is with no want of recognition of the authors' artistic aims or want of sympathy with their regret at abandoning them for others less lofty that this is said: but the work of an artist can best be judged from that part of it which most nearly reaches perfection. Miss Somerville and Martin Ross most nearly reached perfection in their lighter stories of Irish life, and it says much for their acumen that they saw the line on which their talent could naturally reach its maturity, courageously turning their backs on higher and more tragic paths likely to tax them beyond their capabilities. At the same time, it would be unjust not to point out that even in their best work comedy does not exclude the more poignant feelings. It would be the greatest mistake to regard these two writers as nothing more than jesters. Their humour is the true humour which runs hand-in-hand with pity, and the sympathy mingled with their laughter robs it of any taste of bitterness. There is a chapter in ***Some Irish Yesterdays*** which shows how their hearts were touched. It treats of marriage and love, death and birth among the peasantry in the south-west of Ireland with a delicacy of feeling which is beyond praise, and shows that the writers did not observe with the aloofness of an explorer among savages, but that for them seeing and describing alike were deeply-felt emotional experiences. The chapter opens with a memory of a wedding in the little Roman Catholic chapel of the village, a simple ceremony, after which the bridegroom hauled his wife up beside him on to a shaggy horse and started for home at a lumbering gallop. Then, in a brilliant transition by way of Tom Cashen's reflections on marriage and a glimpse of his married life, we are introduced at Tom Cashen's funeral to the bride of twenty-five years ago, "a middle-aged stranger in a frilled cap and blue cloak, with handsome eyes full of friendliness," with her ill-health, her profusion of children, and "himself" whose "nose glowed portentously above a rusty grey beard and beneath a hat-brim of a bibulous tint." Then listen to the passage which follows:

> The sunny Shrove Tuesday in early March lived again as she spoke, the glare of the sunshine upon the bare country brimming with imminent life, the scent of the furze, already muffling its spikes in bloom, the daffodils hanging their lamps in shady places. How strangely, how bleakly different was the life history summarised in the melancholy October evening! Instead of the broad-backed horse, galloping on roads that were white in the sun and haze of the strong March day, with the large frieze-clad waist to meet her arms about, and the laughter and shouting of the pursuers coming to her ear, there would be a long and miry tramping in the darkness, behind her spouse, with talk of guano and geese and pigs' food, and a perfect foreknowledge of how he would complete, at the always convenient shebeen, the glorious fabric of intoxication, of which the foundation had been well and truly laid at the funeral.

From the funeral we pass again to the cottage in which "the Triplets" are holding their reception, the three day-old babes cradled in the stuffy room, hazy with the smoke of the turf fire, the crowd in the doorway, the old woman rocking the cradle:

> Obscure corners harboured obscure masses, that might be family raiment, or beds, or old women; somewhere among them the jubilant cry of a hen proclaimed the feat of laying an egg, in muffled tones that suggested a lurking-place under a bed. Between the cradle and the fire sat an old man in a prehistoric tall hat, motionless in the stupor of his great age; at his feet a boy wrangled with a woolly puppy that rolled its eyes till the blue

whites showed, in a delicious glance of humour, as it tugged at the red flannel shirt of its playmate.

Such a passage in a Russian novelist would warrant ecstasies on the part of our *illuminati*: let us no less highly praise our own art when it is possible. The chapter concludes with some lights on the commercial methods of matrimony practised by the peasant class: the writers do not defend them but call attention to the surprising bloom that is apt to spring from them. "From them springs, like a flower from a dust heap, the unsullied, uneventful home-life of Western Ireland." "There is here no material of the accepted sort, for a playwright; no unsatisfied yearnings and shattered ideals, nothing but remarkable common sense, and a profound awe for the sacrament of Marriage. Marriage, humorous, commercial, and quite unlovely, is the first act; the second is mere preoccupation with an accomplished destiny; the last is usually twilight and much faithfulness." The dialogue is a masterpiece throughout, epigram, heart-piercing pathos, with humour, heavenly and inveterate, lubricating all. Of an elderly couple, married by a happy thought some thirty years before, it was said, as the authors' record, "their hearts were within in each other." This chapter, through which breathes all the soft beauty and humour of the soil, is a sufficient answer to those who would tax these writers with a uniform attitude of rather heartless derision or with following—what a blind criticism!—in the benighted footsteps of those who have given us the dreary horror of the traditional stage Irishman.

Then, again, there is another spirit that breathes delicately through these stories, tempering their outlines as the mists of the Atlantic those of the craggy western hillside. It is the spirit of natural beauty, which, to the hearts of Miss Somerville, herself an accomplished draughtsman, and Martin Ross, makes ever the sharpest appeal. They make the reader plainly feel that if the unconventional dignity and penetrating wit of the Irish folk clutches powerfully at their feelings, the inexhaustible beauty of its surroundings pierces to their very marrow. Quotation after quotation might be given to show their remarkable gift of rendering the scenery which has so moved their imaginations. I can only choose a few, embarrassed at the richness of the field of choice. The last chapter of *Some Irish Yesterdays* opens with an example which it is hard to surpass:

> The road to Connemara lies white across the memory—white and very quiet. In that far west of Galway, the silence dwells pure upon the spacious country, away to where the Twelve Pins make a gallant line against the northern sky. It comes in the heathery wind, it borrows peace from the white cottage gables on the hillside, it is accented by the creeping approach of a turf cart, rocking behind its thin grey pony. Little else stirs save the ducks that sail on a wayside pool to the push of their yellow propellers; away from the road, on a narrow oasis of arable soil, a couple of women are digging potatoes; their persistent voices are borne on the breeze that blows warm over the blossoming boglands and pink heather.

> Scarcely to be analysed is that fragrance of Irish

air; the pureness of bleak mountains is in it, the twang of turf smoke is in it, and there is something more, inseparable from Ireland's green and grey landscapes, wrought in with her bowed and patient cottages, her ragged walls, and eager rivers, and intelligible only to the spirit.

Here is another landscape, the **Irish R.M.**'s view of his own demesne:

> Certainly the view from the roof was worth coming up to look at. It was rough heathery country on one side. With a string of little blue lakes running like a turquoise necklet round the base of a firry hill, and patches of pale green pasture were set amidst the rocks and heather. A silvery flash behind the undulations of the hills told where the Atlantic lay in immense plains of sunlight.

What, again, could be a more delightful overture to the lifelike description of the regatta on Lough Lonen than the short paragraph which conveys in a few touches all the beauty of the scene?

> A mountain towered steeply up from the lake's edge, dark with the sad green of beech-trees in September; fir woods followed the curve of the shore, and leaned far over the answering darkness of the water; and above the trees rose the toppling steepnesses of the hill, painted with the purple glow of heather. The lake was about a mile long, and, tumbling from its farther end, a fierce and narrow river fled away west to the sea, some four or five miles off.

In these descriptions there is no striving for elaborate effect: the authors simply place the scene before our eyes with that aptness of language which is like the unerring needle of a master etcher. To travel on the wings of Miss Somerville and Martin Ross gives one constant thrills of amazement at their hawk-like swoops after a telling phrase: they catch an apt simile on the wing with an arresting suddenness which adds moments of breathlessness to the already exhilarating flight of their rapid narrative. Instances can be picked out from any of the stories like plums from a pudding.

> In the depths of the wood Dr. Hickey might be heard uttering those singular little yelps of encouragement that to the irreverent suggest a milkman in his dotage. . . .

> It was a gleaming morning in mid-May, when everything was young and tense, and thin and fit to run for its life, like a Derby horse. . . .

> I followed Dr. Hickey by way of the window, and so did Miss M'Evoy; we pooled our forces, and drew her mamma after us through the opening of two foot by three steadily, as the great god Pan drew pith from the reed. . . .

> Old McRory had a shadowy and imperceptible quality that is not unusual in small fathers of large families; it always struck me that he understood very thoroughly the privileges of the neglected, and pursued an unnoticed, peaceful and observant path of his own in the background. I

watched him creep away in his furtive, stupefied manner, like a partly-chloroformed ferret. . . .

Miss McRory's reins were clutched in a looped confusion, that summoned from some corner of my brain a memory of the Sultan's cipher on the Order of the Medjidie.

Like smuts streaming out of a chimney the followers of the hunt belched from the lane and spread themselves over the pale green slopes. . . .

Though the temptation is almost irresistible, I refrain here from displaying this incisive power applied to character, notably to Irish character. The success of our authors in this respect is so notorious that further testimony is superfluous. If we have any appreciation of their art at all, the Major and the gentle Philippa, his wife, Flurry and Sally Knox, old Mrs. Knox looking as if she had robbed a scarecrow, with her white woolly dog with sore eyes and a bark like a tin trumpet, against the inimitable background of her ramshackle mansion of Aussolas, scene of many wit-combats between her and Flurry, Miss Bobbie Bennett, the McRory family, John Kane, Mrs. Knox's henchman, and Michael the huntsman, all are as vivid to us as our dearest friends. It is worth pointing out, however, that an almost diabolical power of delineation is not the only compelling quality in these portraits. There is in their introduction of their characters that natural dramatic instinct which they have so humorously observed in their Irish neighbours. I need only instance the ingenuity by which Mrs. Knox is first heard "off," easily vanquishing in speech that doughty antagonist, an Irish countrywoman: or the introduction of John Kane in "the Aussolas Martin Cat," in two inimitable pages, which are followed by another perfect passage of comic drama, the entry into the old demesne of Aussolas of vulgar Mr. Tebbutts, the would-be tenant:

Away near the house the peacock uttered his defiant screech, a note of exclamation that seemed entirely appropriate to Aussolas; the turkey-cock in the yard accepted the challenge with effusion, and from further away the voice of Mrs. Knox's Kerry bull, equally instant in taking offence, ascended the gamut of wrath from growl to yell. Blended with these voices was another—a man's voice, in loud harangue, advancing down the long beech walk to the kitchen garden. As it approached the wood-pigeons bolted in panic, with distracted clappings of wings, from the tall firs by the garden wall in which they were wont to sit arranging plans of campaign with regard to the fruit. We sat in silence. The latch of the garden gate clicked, and the voice said in stentorian tones:

"My father 'e kept a splendid table."

Every gathering of their countrymen—the meet, the run, the horse show, the races, the regatta, the auction—has an intensity of motion and character which is achieved not by the tiresome enumerative methods of some modern realists, but by the skilful selection of the practised artist, and by a clever condensation of observations—their only

form of exaggeration—gathered over a wide range of times and places.

Finally—the word starts up all too soon—let us praise the powerful sweep of their narrative, for it is this rapidity and staying power which sets the crown on their achievement. When they are out with the hunt, whatever be the quarry, they are as "crabbed leppers" as ever moved the picturesque admiration of an Irish hunt following. They are off at the first cry of the hounds and nothing stops them, they drop over the slaty fences, change feet on the banks, thread the rocky paths of steep ascents and career down the craggy hills, like Flurry Knox's mounts to the discomfiture of staider Saxon hunters. With them, moreover, there is never a check; they gallop hot on the scent from first to last, and run the story to a triumphant death in an ecstasy of unquenchable laughter. Their climaxes are marvellous, led up to as they are by a brilliant and sustained crescendo. Think of the *mêlée* at the end of **"High Tea at McKeown's,"** or of the **"Dane's Breechin',"** with its exquisite interlude of the search for the "pin" in the village post-office; think of the finale to **"Philippa's Foxhunt,"** with the Irish clergy and Mrs. Knox pulling the small boy out of the drain: or of Lady Knox's ominous arrival at the end of **"Oh, Love! Oh, Fire!"** and the escape of Sally in Mrs. Knox's pony-chaise, or of the combined catastrophe that fell upon the Major's household in **"A Royal Command."** For pure art in narrative construction these finales are unexampled in English literature of to-day, all the more because they are free from all buffoonery. Here is one that starts a movement *conbrio:*

A shout from the top of the hill interrupted the amenities of the check. Flurry was out of the wood blowing shattering blasts upon his horn, and the hounds rushed to him, knowing the "gone away" note that was never blown in vain. The brown mare came out through the trees and the undergrowth like a woodcock down the wind, and jumped across a stream on to a more than questionable bank; the hounds splashed and struggled after him, and as they landed the first ecstatic whimpers broke forth. In a moment it was full cry, discordant, beautiful, and soul-stirring, as the pack spread and sped, and settled into line.

It is only one of many such. Let me send the reader to his shelf to take down *In Mr. Knox's Country,* and read **"Put Down Two and Carry One,"** with its account of the events which led to Miss McRory's riding pillion behind the Major into the scandalised sight of Lady Knox, or to expire once more over the mingling of Mrs. McRory's golden butterfly with Philippa's hat-trimming at the harvest festival (**"The Bosom of the McRorys"**). I am compelled to quote, for its rendering of the purely ludicrous, from the incident of Playboy's nocturnal rescue in **"The Conspiracy of Silence"** (*Further Experiences of an I.R.M.*). Major Yeates, as deputy master in Flurry Knox's absence, has taken the hounds over to hunt with Mr. Flynn, who, after a run full of incident, has connived at the secretion of Playboy, a fine hound of the old Irish breed, in a bedroom at the top of the house. The Major is warned of this by the youngest boy, whose gratitude he has earned by giving him a mount that day. The pair thereupon grope their way upstairs to raid the bedroom in its owner's absence:

> A dim skylight told that the roof was very near my head; I extended a groping hand for the wall, and without any warning found my fingers closing improbably, awfully, upon a warm human face.
>
> [It was the servant, Maggie Kane, bringing up a drumstick of a goose to pacify the hound. They open the door of the room, and Playboy is revealed tied to the leg of a low wooden bedstead.] He was standing up, his eyes gleamed green as emeralds, he looked as big as a calf. He obviously regarded himself as the guardian of Eugene's bower, and I failed to see any recognition of me in his aspect, in point of fact he appeared to be on the verge of an outburst of suspicion that would waken the house once and for all. We held a council of war in whispers that perceptibly increased his distrust; I think it was Maggie Kane who suggested that Master Eddy should proffer him the bone while I unfastened the rope. The strategy succeeded, almost too well, in fact. Following the alluring drumstick, Playboy burst into the passage, towing me after him on the rope. Still preceded by the light-footed Master Eddy, he took me down the attic stairs at a speed which was the next thing to a headlong fall, while Maggie Kane held the candle at the top. As we stormed past old Flynn's door I was aware that the snoring had ceased, but "the pace was too good to inquire." We scrimmaged down the second flight into the darkness of the hall, fetching up somewhere near the clock, which, as if to give the alarm, uttered three loud and poignant cuckoos. I think Playboy must have sprung at it, in the belief that it was the voice of the drumstick; I only know that my arm was nearly wrenched from its socket, and that the clock fell with a crash from the table to the floor, where, by some malevolence of its machinery, it continued to cuckoo with a jocund and implacable persistence. Something that was not Playboy bumped against me. The cuckoo's note became mysteriously muffled, and a door, revealing a fire-lit-kitchen was shoved open. We struggled through it, bound into a sheaf by Playboy's rope, and in our midst the cuckoo clock, stifled but indomitable, continued its protest from under Maggie Kane's shawl.

And now, if I may close with a recollection of what is, perhaps, the most brilliant of all these brilliant narratives, I will call to the reader's mind the story of **"The Pug-nosed Fox,"** from the same volume. Every gift of language, delineation, vigorous intensity, dramatic gradation, and swiftness of progress over a series of crises to a perfect culmination has been lavished by the authors on this story. From the misguided efforts of the photographer to take a picture of the hounds on a sweltering August day, all through the untimely chase of the old fox to the discovery of Tomsy Flood sewn up in a feather mattress in the loft of the McRorys' stable, and the raid of the hounds upon the wedding breakfast at the moment of the entry of the guests, there is not a moment in which to draw breath. It is life itself, with all the added quickness to its revolutions

'Mrs Knox extended a skinny hand'

My friend Slipper

Two of Somerville and Ross's most memorable characters from the Irish R.M. *stories: Old Mrs. Knox and Slipper, both drawn by Edith Somerville.*

and intensity to its vision that art can give. With this memory I must leave this little classic to its future, but so that art, rather than criticism, shall have the last word, a typical passage, showing the authors' ease of transition from beauty to comedy, shall close this grateful appreciation:

> At the top of the hill we took another pull. This afforded us a fine view of the Atlantic, also of the surrounding country and all that was therein, with, however, the single exception of the hounds. There was nothing to be heard save the summery rattle of the reaping-machine, the strong and steady rasp of a corn-crake, and the growl of a big steamer from a band of fog that was advancing, ghost-like, along the blue floor of the sea. Two fields away a man in a straw hat was slowly combing down the flanks of a haycock with a wooden rake, while a black-and-white cur slept in the young after-grass beside him. We broke into their sylvan tranquillity with a heated demand whether the hounds had passed that way. Shrill glamour from the dog was at first the only reply; its owner took off his hat, wiped his forehead with his sleeve, and stared at us.
>
> "I'm as deaf as a beetle this three weeks," he said, continuing to look us up and down in a way that made me realise, if possible, more than before, the absurdity of looking like a Christmas card in the heat of a summer's day.
>
> "Did ye see the HOUNDS?" shouted Michael, shoving the chestnut up beside him.
>
> "It's the neurology I got," continued the haymaker, "an' the pain does be whistlin' out through me ear till I could mostly run into the say from it."
>
> "It's a pity ye wouldn't," said Michael, whirling Moses round.

(pp. 556-64)

Orlo Williams, "A Little Classic of the Future," in The London Mercury, *Vol. I, No. 4, February, 1920, pp. 555-64.*

Ann Power (essay date 1964)

[*In the following excerpt, Power analyzes the strengths and weaknesses of Somerville and Ross's major novels.*]

> The sun was red in the west when our horses were brought round to the door. . . . In the darkened façade of the long grey house, a window, just over the hall-door, caught our attention. In it, for an instant, was a white face. Trails of ivy hung over the panes, but we saw the face glimmer for a moment and vanish. As we rode home along the side of the hills, we could talk and think only of the presence at the window. We had been warned of certain subjects not to be approached and knew enough of the history of that old house to realise what we had seen. An old stock, isolated from the world at large, wearing itself out in those excesses that are a protest of human nature against unnatural conditions, dies at last with its victims round its death-bed.

> Half-acknowledged, half-witted, wholly horrifying, living ghosts, haunting the house that gave them but half their share of life. . . . Little as we may have achieved it, an ideal of Art rose then for us, far and faint as the half-moon, and often, like her, hidden in clouds, yet never quite obscured or forgotten.

A glimpse of the tragedy behind the Anglo-Irish situation, a statement of serious artistic aims—the devotee of the *Irish R.M.* might be surprised to discover that this passage is from Edith Somerville's memoirs, describing how she and her cousin, Violet Martin ("Martin Ross") came to write their first novel. Indeed, many people might be surprised to discover that they wrote novels, or anything else besides the *Irish R.M.* books, but, in fact, apart from the three *Irish R.M.* books and many collections of stories and sketches, ten novels appeared under their joint signatures. Five of these they wrote together and five were written by Edith Somerville alone, after Violet Martin's death. And yet, of these novels, so little known, one is a masterpiece, and a second very nearly the great tragic novel of the Anglo-Irish. Even in their lesser novels they present a vivid and authentic picture of the Ireland of their day and in particular of the Anglo-Irish of the Big House, that race with no country, Irish in England, English in Ireland, tied to England by culture and politics, tied to the Ireland that rejected them by upbringing and sentiment.

Their subject is probably one of the chief reasons for their neglect, that, and their Unionist sympathies—two things that set them apart, not only in the literary sense, from their contemporaries of the Irish Revival. For though they were acquainted with Yeats and Lady Gregory and the other literary figures of their time, their opinions and their preference for a retired country life isolated them from the intellectual excitement of their period. For Somerville and Ross, though they held the Other Ireland in great affection and sympathy, were ultimately of the Big House in their outlook and reflect in their books the contradictory attitudes of admiration and patronage, of sympathy and distrust that are part of the split personality of Anglo-Ireland.

They published their first book, *An Irish Cousin,* in 1889, when Violet was twenty-seven and Edith thirty-one. The ease with which they worked together must have been due in no small measure to the fact that this was an attraction of opposites. Violet Martin was the intellectual of the two, shy, and with a strong vein of pessimism that was deepened by many years of ill-health. Edith Somerville was the extrovert, the optimist, not at all an intellectual and never one to probe too deeply into a problem, though she had a lively mind. Both women were suffragettes, of the constitutional rather than the militant type, and both, as might be guessed from their books, were very keen huntswomen—Edith Somerville was for many years M.F.H. of the West Carbery Hounds. Violet must have had a streak of recklessness in her retiring nature, for her chronic short sight made hunting a dangerous sport for her, as events were to prove.

From the moment their first book appeared (under a penname, since the formidable Mrs. Somerville considered writing books for publication was not an occupation for *les jeunes filles bien élevées*) Somerville and Ross were asked the inevitable question: what part did each of them play in the writing of their books? Let Edith Somerville answer this herself (since she lived to the age of ninety-one, she grew, finally, a little impatient of it). "The question . . . has ever been considered of the greatest moment, and, as a matter of fact, it was a point that never entered our minds to consider. To those who may be interested in an unimportant detail, I may say that our work was done conversationally. One or the other—not infrequently both, simultaneously—would state a proposition. This would be argued, combated perhaps, approved or modified; it would then be written down by the (wholly fortuitous) holder of the pen, would be scratched out, scribbled in again; before it found itself finally transferred into decorous MS it would probably have suffered many things, but it would, at all events have had the advantage of having been well aired." Later, in the last article that she wrote, for *Irish Writing* in 1946, she enlarged a little: "I think I am right in attributing to my cousin the more subtle and recondite adjective, the more knife-edged slice of sarcasm, the more poetic feeling for words and a sense of Style that seems to me flawless and unequalled."

Their first novel, while it is redeemed by some good character drawing and scenes of social comedy, suffers from a melodramatic plot and stylistic clichés. It was much improved when they revised it for another edition in 1903. It had some favourable notices which softened their mothers' attitude to their hobby and emboldened them to publish, two years later, *Naboth's Vineyard.* This is an interesting book, the odd-man-out of their novels, since it has a peasant setting. Stylistically it is a great advance on their first, and their control of the plot is far more sure. But the love affair between Rick and Ellen is altogether too much of a pastoral idyll and though they make a valiant attempt to get inside the minds of their peasant characters, they were, not surprisingly, unable altogether to make the intuitive leap that alone could render their characters convincing. The considerable technical problem of showing the workings of a mind unaware of its own processes, "living", in Patrick Kavanagh's phrase, "below the level of consciousness", proved too much for them. These two difficulties, the portrayal of the "peasant Irish" and the love-interest they never altogether solved, for reasons that were possibly more psychological than technical.

According to Geraldine Cummins, who knew Edith Somerville well and wrote her biography, Violet Martin enjoyed doing the love-scenes in their books, but for Edith there was a strong taboo on the whole subject of sex. "I sought diligently," says Miss Cummins, "for a romance in Edith's life. Neither in her books, nor in her conversations with me was there any indication that she ever had a love-affair." Acquaintances also commented that there was a streak of the aggressive feminist in Edith's make-up. Certainly, to judge from her memoirs, her upbringing left her with something of a grudge against the male sex. "Daughters were at a discount," she wrote, "they were permitted to eat of the crumbs that fell from their brothers' tables, and if no crumbs fell the daughters went unfed." In all their works Ireland is shown as "a man's world" and in their portraits of the men of the Big House,

there is no doubt which sex the authors regarded as the weaker. Their men-folk (and we gather that they were drawing on experience of their own families) are no match for their wives, who are superior to them morally, spiritually and intellectually—there are not many clever men in their books and those that are, usually employ their intelligence for unworthy ends. There is more than a shade of satire in their portraits of men—their touch only deserts them when they come to the romantic lead, the eligible young bachelor, who is a mere lay-figure. This leads to difficulties when they treat the love-interest in their books, and is particularly noticeable in the novels that Edith wrote alone.

It is not that they cannot handle the subject of love, for love unrequited provides some of their most perceptive passages; it is love requited that floors them. Only in *The Real Charlotte* are their lovers in any way convincing, and even here there are places where the writing shows signs of strain. We begin to suspect that if their eligible young bachelor seems unreal to the reader, it is because the authors couldn't believe in his existence either.

Somerville and Ross became famous through their humorous writing, through their comic masterpieces the *Irish R.M.* books, but in their novels the humour could more correctly be classed as satire. While they satirise many subjects, the English in Ireland, Society and sometimes, one suspects, even themselves, their main target is the *nouveau riche* and the middle classes on the make, satire which sometimes takes off altogether into farce, or which is sometimes too savage to be classed as humour at all. The social climber is a traditional butt for the satirist, and in the settled state of English society, the interplay of the different social classes is a legitimate subject for the comedy of manners. But there is always a touch of unease in the novels of Somerville and Ross; we are always aware that in an Irish setting this theme has tragic potentialities, so complex and so deep are the loyalties that divide the two nations of Ireland.

Those acquainted only with the *Irish R.M.* books may, in fact, be surprised to find that many of the Somerville and Ross novels are sombre, even tragic in tone. When they came to write of the Big House, it was already dying and the face at the ivy-covered window looks out through the pages of their novels. Closely linked with this theme of the decay of the Big House is that of an attraction between a child of the Big House and someone from the Other Ireland. Sometimes this is not much more than a *tendre,* sometimes it is a more serious involvement, but always the authors hint that it holds the possibility of disaster, something more than just the social implications of such a relationship. Although it is a fairly obvious theme for anyone writing about Ireland, it occurs in so many of their novels as to make one wonder if it had an unconscious significance for Somerville and Ross. Was it for them the symbol of the romantic appeal of the Irish point of view (an appeal to which they were not insensitive as many passages in their novels show) an attraction often felt by the Anglo-Irish, yet so often unacknowledged, because of the feelings of guilt that it must arouse? In *An Enthusiast* the underlying meaning of this theme (if I am right) is brought to the surface. The Enthusiast of the title is a son of the Big House who tries, out of genuine idealism, to reconcile the old enmities by co-operating with the New Ireland (this was written in 1921). In the end, he is deserted and defeated by both sides. The conclusion of *An Enthusiast* would seem to be that the gulf between the two nations is too great ever to be bridged in a general or lasting manner. There is a very sympathetic portrait in this book of an idealistic nationalist, Eugene Cashen, and it is he who provides the comment which we take as the authors' own: "It is the mixture of levity and brutality in the people that breaks my heart." This comment is most surprisingly paralleled in Canon Sheehan's book *The Graves of Kilmorna* and indeed, the whole section dealing with Eugene Cashen and his sister could have come directly from Canon Sheehan's book.

It may be questioned how far Somerville and Ross or the Anglo-Irish they represented either tried or wanted to bridge that gulf. In a very interesting correspondence with Violet Martin, in 1912, Stephen Gwynn takes her to task on this very point: "You know so much," he wrote, "you and yours stand for so much that is the very choice essence of Ireland, that it fills me with distress to see you all standing off there in your own paddock, distrustful and not even curious about the life you don't even touch."

The Anglo-Irish may have stood off in their own paddock, whether from choice or necessity, but Somerville and Ross can hardly be accused of lack of curiosity or of knowledge of the rest of Ireland. Their novels cover the whole range of Irish life—not always with equal success, this would be asking too much of women of their background and period, but the Big House itself and the life of the countryside and towns is portrayed with great accuracy. That they are capable of a sympathetic and realistic portrayal of the middle classes is shown by *The Real Charlotte* and sustained passages in all their novels. Their portrayal of peasant life, however, has come in for considerable criticism from Irish commentators and is the reason why many Irish people, even today, cannot read them without an uncontrollable rising of the hackles. These critics would be surprised to find that Violet Martin attacked that overworked English misconception, the Stage Irishman, in her articles, but it cannot be denied that Somerville and Ross have done much to perpetuate his image. However great their sympathy with the Irish attitude to life, however keen their appreciation of the Irish intelligence, there always creeps in that deadly touch of condescension, and even in the most affectionate portrait, is the fatal sense of displaying the Irish to an English reader— the trap which lies in wait, however cunningly hidden, for all Irish writers who address an English audience.

It is significant that this subtle distortion is least evident in their best novel, *The Real Charlotte.* This book was published in 1894, only five years after their first, *An Irish Cousin. The Real Charlotte* is such an outstanding novel that it is astonishing it should be so little known. In scope and social range it can be compared to George Eliot's *Middlemarch,* but its portrayal of character is at a deeper level, its range of emotion is greater and much subtler, and it is, *pace* Dr. Leavis, a considerably more intelligent book,

perhaps because Somerville and Ross have a sense of humour. The central character is Charlotte Mullen, daughter of a Protestant farmer, a plain, hearty woman, whose jovial manner conceals a ruthless determination that is the mainspring of her nature. The plot hinges on her love for Roderick Lambert, a good-looking, weak opportunist, and her revenge on him, when, after the death of his invalid wife, he marries, not Charlotte after all, but her young cousin Francie Fitzpatrick. Charlotte has been compared to La Cousine Bette, but neither of the authors had read Balzac's novel at the time and her character was partly based on that of a woman they had both known, dead some years before. They were dumbfounded to discover, after the book was published, that the love-affair they had invented for "Charlotte" and which had arisen solely out of the events of the novel, was "in almost every detail of Charlotte's relations with Lambert and his wife, incredibly, almost appallingly true."

This is a much more leisurely book than its two predecessors, and coming so soon after them, its complete technical assurance is unexpected. The plot is concerned with character rather than incident and its different strands are perfectly integrated into the whole. In this novel we find all their themes, the life of the Big House, caught in the moment just before it began to decline, Charlotte's passion for land, the infatuation of Christopher Dysart, the intelligent, indecisive son of the Big House for the lower middle-class Francie. Francie, introduced to the Dysarts by Charlotte, whose pawn and victim she is, embarks on an innocent and intoxicating infiltration of Big House society. Occupying as she does a position midway between the two worlds, Francie could have been treated sentimentally or satirically, but the balanced realism of the book prevents sentimentality and the encounters between Francie and the Dysarts are shown mainly from Francie's point of view, with a sympathy that largely precludes satire. The character of Francie in its whole painful development is shown with the greatest skill.

But Charlotte herself is their greatest achievement, a character absolutely real to the reader, treated with complete sureness of touch. Though every twist and turn of her ruthless nature are revealed to us, yet, most skilfully, we are obliged to see her with sympathy, particularly in the brief and subtle scene with Lambert when we first realise her feelings for him and the well-worn situation of the plain woman in love is given a new dimension. We are shown every facet of her complicated character without ever losing the sense of its unity. Her victims and her inferiors are in no doubt as to her real personality, but others are quite deceived by her "humorous rough and readiness". Only Francie's intuition warns her: "She held the conventional belief that Charlotte was queer, but very kind and jolly, but she had a fear of her that she could hardly have given a reason for. It must have been by that measuring and crossing of weapons that takes place unwittingly and yet surely in the consciousness of everyone who lives in intimate connection with another, that she had learned, like her great-aunt before her, the weight of the real Charlotte's will and the terror of her personality."

Somerville and Ross have been taken to task by various

critics for Francie's death at the end of the book—they are accused of killing her off out of snobbery. Because she was an interloper, it is inferred, she had to go. Edith deals with this point in *Irish Memories.* The first draft of the book was finished in 1892. "The most agitating scenes of Charlotte," says her diary, "finished Francie." Edith goes on: "We felt her death very much . . . when we began to know that there could be but one fate for Francie, it felt like killing a wild bird that had trusted itself to you. We have often been reviled for that, as for many other incidents in *The Real Charlotte,* but I still think we were right." And they were. Between Charlotte on the one hand and the ranks of the Big House on the other, one senses that Francie never really had a chance and subconsciously expects her death: all through the book one holds one's breath while Francie flutters her unsuspecting way, so little aware of the forces that oppose her. And so, her death has an artistic inevitability. Even were this not so, its justification lies in the masterly final scene, between Charlotte and Lambert, when the news of Francie's death, in one stroke of horrifying irony, brings retribution to Charlotte.

This book shocked their families and acquaintances. "All here loathe Charlotte," Mrs. Somerville wrote to her daughter, with her customary forthrightness. It upset the reviewers too: "The amours are mean, the people mostly repulsive and the surroundings depressing." But its perceptive realism was praised by a few discerning critics, notably Andrew Lang, and gradually the chorus of critical acclaim grew stronger, until even Mrs. Somerville began to revise her opinion. Edith always held that it was their best novel, but on trying to re-read it in old age, she found it "too tragic and painful. I am surprised," she said, "that Martin and I, young and happy as we were, should have written so unhappy a book."

The novel that followed this, *The Silver Fox,* was published in 1895. It was written in serial form, a structure which bothered the authors, and is something of a disappointment after *The Real Charlotte.*

In 1898 they were commissioned by *The Badminton Magazine* to do a series of humorous sketches with an Irish and, preferably, a hunting background. This series, published as *Some Experiences of an Irish R.M.* was to make them famous, but it is little known that it was written under circumstances of considerable difficulty. In November, when they had just finished the third story of the series, Violet Martin was seriously injured in a hunting accident. For several weeks she was in great pain, and her health remained permanently affected. It was ten years before she was able to hunt again and not till they wrote *Dan Russell the Fox,* published in 1911, was she strong enough for the sustained work necessary for a novel. In 1915, just after the publication of the third and last collection of *Irish R.M.* stories, *In Mr. Knox's Country,* Violet Martin died.

Edith Somerville continued to publish under the joint signature, but it is at once noticeable that Martin's sure critical sense is lacking. Edith's first novel, *Mount Music,* was planned and some scenes written, before her cousin's death, but Violet would never have allowed those coy archaisms and laboured circumlocutions that so mar the style. The impression left by this novel is that its serious theme, the relationship between Catholic and Protestant in Ireland, has been frivolously treated and the issues that it raised have been side-stepped by the violent ending. Edith's estimate of the part her cousin played in their authorship seems to have been correct, but she fails to give herself credit for the character drawing, which even in this imperfect book is unusually sure. *An Enthusiast,* published in 1921, is a very uneven book, and her next novel, *The Big House of Inver,* which came out in 1925, is therefore unexpected.

Edith Somerville was sixty-five when she wrote this tantalising book, a great tragic novel *manqué.* In structure and in theme, it owes much to Maria Edgeworth's *Castle Rackrent,* probably unconsciously, but its inspiration came from a letter that Martin wrote to Edith in 1912.

> Yesterday I drove to see X——House, a great cut stone house of three stories.
>
> Perfectly empty. It is on a long promontory by the sea and there rioted three or four generations of X——s, living with country women, occasionally marrying them, all illegitimate four times over. . . .
>
> Yesterday as we left, an old Miss X——, daughter of the last owner, was at the door in a little donkey trap. She lives near in an old castle and since her people died she will not go into X—— House or into the enormous yard or the beautiful old garden.
>
> She was a strange mixture of distinction and commonness, like her breeding and it was very sad to see her at the door of that great house.
>
> If we dared to write up that subject!

The book is dominated by Shibby Pindy, the illegitimate daughter of old Captain Jas Prendeville. She is a character of tragic stature, proud, shrewd, resourceful and loyal. Her whole life is devoted to her dream of restoring the Prendeville family, and the great empty Prendeville mansion, the Big House of Inver, to their former glory. It is her tragedy that she is defeated by the weakness of those she loves.

With the exception of one or two passages from the pen of that coy alter ego who was so disastrously at work in *Mount Music,* the first three-quarters of this novel are so impressive that the reader is bewildered when suddenly the impetus falters, the concentration slackens and even the style begins to slip, and although there are a couple of powerful scenes towards the end (Shibby's interview with Jimmy Connors is particularly good), the book never quite recovers.

This is probably due to Edith's Achilles heel, the mechanics of the plot. Three-quarters of the way through, she temporarily removes from the scene Shibby Pindy and her protegé, young Kit Prendeville, and embarks upon a long, semi-humorous digression which is essentially part of a sub-plot. This would not have mattered earlier in the book, but it is a fatal mistake to allow such slackening of the tension at the beginning of the crucial final quarter of the book, when everything should be directed towards the climax. It is possible the novel might have been improved had we been allowed to set the Big House and its occupants more in perspective, by seeing more of the village of Inver, and had the strong character of Shibby been counter-poised by greater stress on the Connor family. One could also fault it for occasional lapses of style and for the note of explication which sometimes creeps into the comments on Shibby. But had the pace and tension only been maintained, the novel could have taken these and other minor weaknesses in its stride. As it is, however, these flaws make themselves felt and in the final assessment *The Big House of Inver,* though so very impressive, remains only in potential a great book.

The Big House of Inver was followed in her old age by two lightweight, semi-autobiographical novels, which added nothing to her reputation. She died in 1949, at the age of ninety-one.

The novels of Somerville and Ross will always pose a question—their two best novels are so outstanding that we inevitably wonder why the others are, comparatively, disappointing.

Part of the answer will, I think, be found in their attitude to their work—which may unwittingly have been the legacy of Mrs. Somerville and perhaps also a result of their lack of contact with other writers or critical minds. I doubt whether a greater involvement with the Irish Revival would have benefitted them; they were not sufficiently in sympathy with its aims. Whatever the reason, it is evident that they fatally underestimated their talents. According to Edith Somerville's memoirs, they deliberately set out, in *The Real Charlotte* and *The Big House of Inver,* to write a "serious novel", and in forsaking this type of book for their lighter novels and humorous sketches, they forfeited the place they might have held among the European novelists. There are, of course, technical reasons which make these two novels so much more successful than their others. They both have something lacking in the other novels: the driving power in each of them is supplied by a remarkable and powerful central character, which gives concentration to the whole. In other respects, however, they are surprisingly different. *The Real Charlotte* is on a much larger scale than their other books and owes much of its power to the beautifully observed realism of its large canvas; its success is due, not only to the skill of the character drawing, but to the accumulative effect of carefully selected detail. *The Big House of Inver* on the other hand, has a narrow range, and, in the theme of the canny agent rising to prosperity at the expense of his employer, a well-shaped framework which did much to counteract the structural weakness evident in Edith Somerville's other novels.

The rest of the answer is probably a commonplace and practical one. They had just begun on the famous *Irish R.M.* stories, when Violet Martin had her hunting accident, and they were able to write only one more novel before she died. The success of the *Irish R.M.* books led them away from novel writing: Edith says that they put aside their plans for a serious novel, in order to write the last collection of *R.M.* stories. While nobody would

grudge the time they spent on the *Irish R.M.* books, one might grudge the time that they spent pot-boiling for various periodicals. When we come to consider the later novels it is, of course, useless to speculate on what they would have written had Violet Martin lived, but we can be reasonably sure that they would have written better. But it must be remembered, when considering the books written by Edith alone, that writing was only one of her many activities and it is doubtful if she was prepared, or able, to give as much time to her writing as Martin had done. During the decade after Martin's death (at the end of which *The Big House of Inver* was published) Ireland endured a revolution that was both political and social, and throughout this time Edith was very much occupied with the day-to-day problems of keeping the Somerville estates solvent. At the end of this period she was sixty-five, and the death-sentence, as she knew, had been passed on the world that she had lived in and written about. The audience she had written for, the English and the Anglo-Irish, had been obliged by recent events somewhat to revise their attitudes to Ireland: the Stage Irishman had his revenge at the last. Now, perhaps, she no longer knew who her audience was.

Their literary career presents us with tantalising might-have-beens. Had Martin only lived; had Edith been able to give more time to writing; had the *Irish R.M.* books, minor masterpieces though they are, been less popular: had they only appreciated their great talents—they were capable, to judge by their best work, of taking their place among the great novelists of the English language. But as it is, we cannot assess them on the strength of hypothetical work, only by what they did, in fact, produce. Their humorous masterpieces, the *Irish R.M.* books, and their two best novels must ensure them a permanent place not only in Anglo-Irish literature, but among the writers of the English-speaking world. (pp. 43-53)

> *Ann Power, "The Big House of Somerville and Ross," in* The Dublin Magazine, *Vol. 3, No. 1, Spring, 1964, pp. 43-53.*

Conor Cruise O'Brien (essay date 1965)

[*An Irish politician, historian, and critic, O'Brien served as Ireland's representative to the United Nations from 1955 to 1961 and has since held positions in the Irish government and in academia. He has written numerous studies of Irish history, of the United Nations, and of modern politics, and his works are often praised for their iconoclasm as well as their insight. Although O'Brien has concentrated his attention primarily on political and historical matters, his literary opinions are also highly esteemed and he has written important studies of Catholic writers and the influence of politics on literature. In the following excerpt, O'Brien defends the works of Somerville and Ross against the charge that they are "anti-Irish."*]

> The protest attending on an alien Ascendancy's
> callous caperings is of course always most active
> in a period of national revival.

This opinion is, of course, that of Professor Daniel Corkery and he makes it clear, in that interesting and curious work, *Synge and Anglo-Irish Literature,* that he would apply the description "an alien Ascendancy's callous caperings" to at least a great part of the work of Edith Somerville and her cousin Violet Martin who wrote as Martin Ross.

It would be pleasant in some ways, although perhaps a little dull, to bypass these formidable social, political and moral categories of Professor Corkery's, to dismiss them as "extra-literary considerations" and get down to a purely aesthetic discussion of the artistic merit of the novels and short stories of Somerville and Ross. But the novels and the stories themselves are full of extraliterary considerations and the Irish reader approaches them with his head buzzing with controversial bees. Anti-Irish . . . ? Stage-Irish . . . ? Snobs? These are stock responses—to use the language of Professor I. A. Richards—and therefore not particularly useful in literary criticism. But they cannot be ignored in any discussion of this body of work; they have to be confirmed, to the extent that they are true, or dismantled, to the extent that they are prejudices, before we can be heard saying something relevant about the merits of the books themselves.

On one of Professor Corkery's counts at least we must find a true bill. They were certainly ascendancy. They belonged to old established landed families, the Somervilles in West Cork and the Martins in Galway, and they flourished in a time when such families did in fact constitute an ascendancy. Most of their best work, indeed, was done or at least conceived in what might be called the Indian Summer of the Ascendancy, between the fall of Parnell in 1890 and the outbreak of the World War in 1914. The terrible eighties were behind, and the more terrible twenties undreamed of. There was honey still for tea, and there was hunting, plenty of hunting—and, of course, for the callous, capers. If there was a hint of future trouble in the air—a whiff of the acrid journalism of D. P. Moran, poison laid on certain lands, barbed wire across the path of the hunt—it was no more than lent tang and tension and distinction to the lives of high-spirited people like Edith Somerville and her cousin.

That they were snobs—in one sense of that word— followed naturally from the fact that they belonged to the Irish landed gentry. They had to look down on other people in order to see them. Or so they sincerely felt. And they wanted to see them clearly, to place them socially: "Catholic middle-class moving up"; "Protestant lower-middle-class, stuck"; "Gentleman run wild, with touch of brogue." They wrote on these matters with an almost pedantic care for accuracy, within social conventions which they thoroughly understood and thoroughly approved. Their approval is, to profane ears, often excessive, and one cannot help feeling that the ability to detach themselves from the conventional values of their class would have enriched their work. But their snobbery, as I think we must call it, was at least a live and intelligent system of social apprehension, strictly contemporary and even brisk. It is confusing to have to describe it by the same name as we must apply to the dreary and indiscriminate archaism of

certain modern writers, or the vicarious nostalgia of Mr. Evelyn Waugh.

Were they then aliens, colonial writers—to use, again, some of Professor Corkery's terminology—who exploited Ireland in their work for the amusement of the foreigner? This can only be tested by attention to the work itself. The work to which the reproach is most directed is the popular and comic *Irish R.M.* series of short stories—***Some Experiences of an Irish R.M., Further Experiences of an Irish R.M.*** and *In Mr. Knox's Country.* From among these I have selected—and have had to abridge—the extract which you are about to hear read. It is from a story called **"Lisheen Races, Second-hand."** A character called Slipper is describing to a crowd, including the R. M. and a pompous Englishman, a trick he played at the races on one Driscoll:

> 'Twas within in the same whisky tint meself was, with the bandmasther and a few of the lads, an' we buyin' a ha'porth o' crackers, when I seen me brave Driscoll landin' into the tint, and a pair o' thim long boots on him; him that hadn't a shoe nor a stocking to his foot when your honour had him picking grass out o' the stones behind in your yard. "Well," says I to meself, "we'll knock some spoort out of Driscoll!"
>
> "Come here to me, acushla!" says I to him; "I suppose it's some way wake in the legs y'are," says I, "an' the docthor put them on ye the way the people wouldn't thrample ye!"
>
> "May the divil choke ye!" says he, pleasant enough, but I knew by the blush he had he was vexed.
>
> "Then I suppose 'tis a left-tenant colonel y'are," says I; "yer mother must be proud out o' ye!" says I, "an' maybe ye'll lend her a loan o' thim waders when she's rinsin' yer bauneen in the river!" says I.
>
> "There'll be work out o' this!" says he, lookin' at me both sour and bitther.
>
> "Well indeed, I was thinkin' you were blue moulded for want of a batin'," says I. He was for fightin' us then, but afther we had him pacificated with about a quarther of a naggin' o' sperrits, he told us he was goin' ridin' in a race.
>
> "An' what'll ye ride?" says I.
>
> "Owld Bocock's mare," says he.
>
> "Knipes!" says I, sayin' a great curse; "is it that little staggeen from the mountains; sure she's somethin' about the one age with meself," says I. "Many's the time Jamesy Geoghegan and meself used to be dhrivin' her to Macroom with pigs an' all soorts," says I; "an' is it leppin' stone walls ye want her to go now?"
>
> "Faith, there's walls and every vari'ty of obstackle in it," says he.
>
> "It'll be the best o' your play, so," says I, "to leg it away home out o' this."
>
> "An' who'll ride her, so?" says he.

"Let the divil ride her," says I.

There was no great delay afther that till they said there was a race startin' and the dickens a one at all was goin' to ride only two, Driscoll, and one Clancy.

"Stand aisy now by the plantation," says I; "if they get to come as far as this, believe me ye'll see spoort," says I, "an' 'twill be a convenient spot to encourage the mare if she's anyway wake in herself," says I, cuttin' somethin' about five feet of an ash sapling out o' the plantation.

Well, I hadn't barely thrimmed the ash plant when I heard the people screechin', an' I seen Driscoll an' Clancy comin' on, leppin' all before them, an' owld Bocock's mare bellusin' and powdherin' along, an' bedad! whatever obstackle wouldn't throw *her* down, faith, she'd throw *it* down, an't there's the thraffic they had in it.

"I declare to me sowl," says I, "if they continue on this way there's a great chance some one o' thim'll win," says I.

"Ye lie!" says the bandmasther, bein' a thrifle fulsome after his luncheon.

Well, when I seen them comin' to me, and Driscoll about the length of the plantation behind Clancy, I let a couple of bawls.

I declare to ye when owld Bocock's mare heard them roars she sthretched out her neck like a gandher, and when she passed me out she give a couple of grunts, and looked at me as ugly as a Christian.

"Hah!" says I, givin' her a couple o' dhraws o' th' ash plant across the butt o' the tail, the way I wouldn't blind her; "I'll make ye grunt!" says I, "I'll nourish ye!"

Well whether it was over-anxious he was, turnin' around the way I'd hear him cursin', or whether it was some slither or slide came to owld Bocock's mare, I dunno, but she was bet up agin the last obstackle but two, and before ye could say "shnipes," she was standin' on her two ears beyond in th' other field! I declare to ye, on the vartue of me oath, she stood that way till she reconnoithered what side would Driscoll fall, an' she turned about then and rolled on him as cosy as if he was meadow grass!

The blood was dhruv out through his nose and ears and you'd hear his bones crackin' on the ground! You'd have pitied the poor boy.

"Was he hurt, Slipper?"

"Hurt is it? Killed on the spot! Oh, divil so pleasant an afthernoon ever you seen; and indeed, Mr. Flurry, it's what we were all sayin', it was a great pity your honour was not there for the likin' you had for Driscoll."

That is callous enough, if you take it literally, and I suppose it could be called capering to amuse the foreigner. Certainly the *Irish R.M.* books must have been read by more English people than Irish: after all, there are more

of the English and I am afraid they read more books. But I suggest that it is time, in this matter of literary criticism, that we should apply the essential principle of Sinn Fein. I mean by that that we should judge a book not by how we think it may affect a hypothetical foreigner, but solely by how it actually does affect ourselves. In short, if Slipper's story and the *Irish R.M.* books in general do seem funny to us, they need no other justification. They will not, of course, seem funny if we feel, for instance, that their idiom is divorced from any living Irish speech or that the scenes and traits of character that they describe have no roots in Irish life. But this is not the case with Somerville and Ross; they exaggerate, obviously, as every comic writer does, but their exaggeration is firmly based on Irish ground which they knew well and which in their own way they loved deeply. They lived in Ireland for almost all their writing lives and they had, as a writing team, a sensitive ear and a penetrating, humorous eye. If their writing is not part of the literature of Ireland, then Ireland is a poorer place than many of us believe it to be.

Let us get back to Driscoll, for a moment, whom we left for dead under his horse. The end of that story is that Driscoll appears, at the climax of Slipper's story, with a face like "a red-hot potato in a bandage" and thirsting for vengeance on Slipper. Does that remind you of any other scene in our literature? It seems to me to resemble rather strikingly the return of the supposedly murdered da in Synge's *Playboy of the Western World*. There is something of the same rodomontade, there is the same macabre relish for violent death, the same vengeful return from the dead. I do not know whether the parallel has been pointed out before—such writers on Synge as I have consulted do not mention it. In any case the *Irish R.M.* was published in 1899, and *The Playboy* was written in 1905-6, so it is at least possible—I think myself it is probable—that **"Lisheen Races, Second-hand"** was at the back of Synge's mind as he wrote. The world of Somerville and Ross may not be quite as remote from the world of the Literary Revival as we sometimes suppose. I make a present of the point to Professor Corkery; it suits his thesis; indeed I cannot think why he missed it. Could it be that he has never read the *Irish R.M.*?

Martin Ross died in 1915, and in 1915 also the last collection of *Irish R.M.* stories appeared. Edith Somerville continued to write as Somerville and Ross—and in fact maintained that the collaboration extended beyond the grave—but Slipper and Flurry Knox appeared no more. Probably the survivor in the partnership, which was also a close friendship and affinity, felt she could no longer maintain the lighthearted mood of the *R.M.* stories; also the grimmer climate which set in in 1914 might have been less kind to Slipper and his friends. But there had from the beginning been a tragic side to the work of Somerville and Ross. This had predominated in such early novels as *An Irish Cousin*; *Naboth's Vineyard*, which contains one of the best descriptions of boycott that have been left to us; *The Real Charlotte*, which is generally regarded as their masterpiece; and *The Silver Fox*, to which we shall return. All of these novels were published before 1899, the year in which the first *Irish R.M.* scored its immense success with, as Professor Corkery would wish me to point out, the English public. From that date until the death of Martin Ross in 1915 the tragic vein almost disappears from their writing, although signs of it may occasionally be glimpsed even in the *R.M.* series. After that date it reappears in two important novels, *Mount Music* in 1919 and *The Big House of Inver* in 1925, and in the less successful but interesting *An Enthusiast* (1921), which deals with "the troubles." *The Big House of Inver* is their last important work, although there were many occasional publications, and one rather slight novel, *French Leave,* between then and Edith Somerville's death in 1949, in her ninetieth year. Those who are interested in her long life and remarkable character and in the nature of her literary partnership with Martin Ross should read Miss Geraldine Cummins's valuable biography, published in 1952.

Three novels are more important than the rest—*The Real Charlotte, Mount Music,* and *The Big House of Inver.* Mr. Stephen Gwynn, speaking out of his wide knowledge of the subject, has said that *The Real Charlotte* is one of the most powerful novels of Irish life ever written. Its central figure, Miss Charlotte Mullen, is certainly a massive and formidable concentration of evil intent working in commonplace detail, without any thunderclaps or blue flame. Evil has often been more dramatically exhibited, but I do not think it has ever been more convincingly worked out in humdrum action, or brought home with such a terrible cumulative effect as an element in everyday life. The people on whom she brings ruin—the common, pretty Francie Fitzpatrick, and common, swaggering Lambert the agent—are satisfactory enough as experiments in ruin, but somehow the class convention—which is particularly hard and disdainful in this book—comes between them and our pity, and between the book as a whole and complete success. Francie and Lambert are not wellbred, not therefore quite human. Charlotte Mullen is of course of the same class, but one feels her to have attained a certain aristocracy of evil like Satan in Pandemonium:

> by merit rais'd
> To that bad eminence.

The middle class—which is, by the way, here a Protestant middle class—occupies the centre of attention—a circumstance which is unique in the work of Somerville and Ross. Above is a highly idealized Ascendancy family, the Dysarts; below are the peasants, who are in this book a collection of grotesques envisaged bleakly and without sympathy. For the rest, the book is exceedingly well and sparely written and more carefully constructed than any of their other novels—although the pace at the finish is, as is usual with them, recklessly forced. *The Real Charlotte* is generally considered the best of their novels, and I think it is so. It is also, unfortunately, the one most marred by evidence of lack of sympathy with outsiders. Professor Corkery, in a striking phrase, denounces the presence in our literature of "an alien ascendancy streaked with the vulgarity of insensibility." The verdict itself has a little streak of the same, and its harshness is unjust, as far as most of the work of Somerville and Ross is concerned. But in *The Real Charlotte* the streak is noticeable and it harms an otherwise splendid achievement. That does not mean, however, that I think *The Real Charlotte* is un-Irish.

There is nothing un-Irish about aristocratic pride; a great part of our Gaelic literature throbs with a full and blue-blooded contempt for the lowborn.

The two other main novels, *Mount Music* and *The Big House of Inver,* are much more loosely written, but with more generous feeling. The ice has melted—there are twenty-five years after all between *The Real Charlotte* and *Mount Music*—and the style has lost some of its edge, the edge that I think Martin Ross put on it, for good and ill. The central theme of *Mount Music* is one of which Irish writers have in general tended to fight rather shy, that of religious intolerance, on the part of both Protestants and Catholics. Miss Somerville calls it, cheerfully enough, the Spirit of the Nation and follows its devious workings and its double language with remarkable detachment. The whole subject is of course now utterly out of date, and such a spirit can scarcely be conceived by the modern Irish reader, who positively drips with tolerance. Nonetheless the book may be read for its antiquarian interest.

Although both *Mount Music* and *The Big House of Inver* lack style as compared with *The Real Charlotte* they have not lost the power of generating a daemonic force in a credible character. Such is Dr. Francis Mangan in *Mount Music*; such, in *The Big House of Inver,* is Shibby Pindy, the illegitimate greathearted daughter of a gentle family, who has had a peasant upbringing, but whose passion is to restore, through her half-brother, the glories of *The Big House,* which stands empty at the beginning of the novel and is in flames at the end. *The Big House of Inver,* were it not for something a little blurred and loose in the writing, would surpass *The Real Charlotte.* I am not indeed quite sure that it does not surpass it as it is, for if there is a blur in the writing, there is no such smudge of meaningless character as in the Dysart family group in the earlier novel.

What we regret, then, among so much that we admire, is that, as imaginative sympathy deepened, style declined. The youthful arrogance which somewhat blunted the moral perception yet carried itself extremely well. The quality of unwavering intelligence was in the writing—an intelligence not worried by clichés, but never allowing a cliché to come between it and the reality of the given moment. This alertness flags in the later works, which have wider vision but a less precise one. Perhaps had it not been for the success of the *R.M.* stories, which diverted them for so many and such important years from their vein of tragedy, Somerville and Ross might have given us a work of their maturity which would have been as alert as it was humane.

You have heard, near the beginning of this talk, a passage from the *Irish R.M.* illustrating the comic side, which is the better-known side, of Somerville and Ross. I want you to hear, before the talk ends, a passage in their tragic vein. The passage I have selected is from one of the less-known works, a short novel called *The Silver Fox,* which appeared in 1897, three years after *The Real Charlotte,* and two years before the first of the *R.M.* books. It was the last novel of tragic temper published in the lifetime of Martin Ross. As a story it is not fully thought out—probably the minds of the two writers were already beginning to turn towards the *Irish R.M.*—but it has certain scenes where we glimpse that balance of alertness and humanity which is never quite sustained in any of their major novels. The passage which you are going in a few moments to hear Miss Lynch read is one of these rare scenes, or so it seems to me. *The Silver Fox* is about hunting and about the supernatural; the fox itself is an unearthly creature, of which the peasantry stand in terror and which the hunt vainly and ruinously pursues. Maria Quin belongs to a peasant family and she has lost her brother and her father because, she believes, of the fox and of the hunt. As the hunt passes near the house in which her brother lies dead she rushes out "full of a blind indignation against those who, for their own amusement, had wrecked the fortunes of a family, and now came to gallop past the house of death, guided by that grey and ill-omened thing." She finds that a horse and rider, having cleared a high bank, have fallen deep into an unsuspected cleft. She manages to rescue the rider, an Englishwoman, Lady Susan French, who had on the previous day seen her brother Tom Quin's body lifted from the river.

> "Is the horse killed?" [Lady Susan] said hoarsely, scrambling on to her feet and looking down through the naked branches that fringed the long cleft.
>
> Even the first glance could certify that Solomon had met his death in an instant. He lay in a heap in the obscurity forty feet below, on loose rocks among dark water; his head was doubled under his chest at an impossible angle that told the tale of a broken neck. The uttermost effort of a good horse had not been enough to save him, when he had tried to jump out from the top of the high bank across a chasm nearly twenty feet wide. That endeavour and all his simple and gallant life seemed expressed in the wreck of strength and intelligence that lay below, with the water washing over the flap of the saddle, over the shapely brown fetlocks, over the thin and glossy mane.
>
> It was mysterious water, an underground stream that slid out of the dumb and sightless caverns of the rock, and passed away into them again with a swirl, a stealthy swift thing, escaping always from the eye of day, and eating the foundations of the limestone walls that sheltered it.
>
> Lady Susan still held the hand that had rescued her; it led her through the brushwood to open ground, till the short wet grass was under her foot and the mist blew in her face. She turned her head away, and the sobs broke from her. Any one who has loved horse or dog will know how and where they touch the heart and command the tear. Let us trust that in some degree it is known to them also, that the confiding spirit may understand that its god can grieve for it.
>
> Maria Quin looked at Lady Susan with eyes that were as dry as glass. The Irish peasant regards the sorrow for a mere animal as a childishness that is almost sinful, a tempting of ill fate in its parody of the grief rightly due only to what is described as "a Christhian"; and Maria's heart glowed with the unwept wrongs of her brother.

> "What happened him?" she asked, and the knot of pain and outrage was tight in her voice.
>
> "I tried to pull him back when I saw what was coming," said Lady Susan, with difficulty. "I couldn't stop him; he had too much way on. I only did harm. I think he would have got across only for that." She stopped and gulped down the sob. It was dreadful to her to cry before an inferior. "He all but got over, but he dropped his hind legs into it and fell back. I somehow caught those branches just as he was going, and he dropped away from under me, and I hung there. I couldn't climb up. Then you came." She recovered herself a little, and turned towards her rescuer. "I haven't thanked you yet. It was awfully good and plucky of you."
>
> Their eyes met, and it seemed as if till then Lady Susan had not recognized Maria Quin. She visibly flinched, and her flushed face became a deeper red, while the hand that had begun to feel for her purse came out of her pocket empty.
>
> "Little ye cried yestherday whin ye seen my brother thrown out on the ground by the pool," said Maria, with irrepressible savageness, "you that's breakin' yer heart afther yer horse."

Lady Susan, you remember, is an Englishwoman, and the dialogue between her and Maria is, in the full sense, an Anglo-Irish dialogue; a dialogue also in the writers' hearts, torn by irreconcilable things. As long as England and Ireland are neighbours I think that dialogue must continue in some form, and the work of Somerville and Ross will not easily go out of date. (pp. 106-15)

> *Conor Cruise O'Brien, "Somerville and Ross,"*
> *in his* Writers and Politics, *Pantheon Books,*
> *1965, pp. 106-15.*

Sean McMahon   (essay date 1968)

[*In the excerpt below, McMahon praises the realism of* The Real Charlotte *and examines the class-consciousness of its authors.*]

It is for the *R.M.* stories that [Somerville and Ross] are world famous. The three books *Some Experiences of an Irish R.M.* (1899), *Further Experiences of an Irish R.M.* (1908), and *In Mr. Knox's Country* (1915) belong to the class of highly popular, middle-brow, sub-classics. Like the Sherlock Holmes stories, they are read with uncritical fervour and recurring enjoyment by all but, possibly, extreme Irish nationalists, in whose craw there would be much to stick. Thus a modern Irish reader finds himself, on the one hand, laughing helplessly at the extremely funny stories and admiring the elegance and the skill of the language and, on the other hand, seething at the bland assumptions behind the facade of the writing. To quote Lionel Fleming again, talking of his cousin Edith:

> I find her books (though I really should say "their" books) marvellously evocative of Ireland, and very, very funny. There are no other works which I can pick up to read in London that can so instantly give me back that feeling of furze-bushes and ragged stone walls; of moisture

dripping from tall trees; of flat, slated mansions; and of the sea-mist creeping in from the Atlantic. . . . But like so many others of her class, she would not concede that the scene she chronicled *was* a passing one.

From a literary point of view their best work together was a novel *The Real Charlotte* (1894) which critics, from Andrew Lang (at the time of its publication) through Lord David Cecil to V. S. Pritchett, in 1968, have claimed as "perhaps the best that ever came out of Ireland." It is a long novel—long enough to have been issued on first publication in the traditional three volumes of Victorian fiction. Some trace of the formality of the time still lingers about the book. The writing is perhaps a little bit precise; the chapters, of fairly regular size, change vantage point as automatically as the slide-mechanism of a magic-lantern changed the picture. The authors had not quite developed the suppleness which makes the *R.M.* stories so timeless, but all their other virtues of wit, compassion, and marvelous characterization are there. The novel presents an absolutely unblinking view of the people and the period—in which the confined and narrow Ireland is preserved like a fly in amber.

They had the advantage of writing about the only settled cultural order in what had been a primitive peasant land, and what was soon to become an unsettled revolutionary state. The native Catholic Irish were not in a position to write about themselves yet (though with Joyce, Corkery and MacNamara they were soon to begin). Even then they were bound to be "primitives" compared with the products of Big House breeding: The comedy of manners, implying an experience and control of the subtleties of class and society, could only come from this solipsistic example of formal society in Ireland. This organized and deep-rooted structure, confined in its sphere and with its best days long gone, was being eroded, on the one hand, by the slow rough movement of the peasantry and, on the other, by the first assaults of the technocrats from the cities. Thus, though the novel is superficially a record of the events of one year in the lives of a few characters, one is conscious of the same clash and engagement of strong systems as is to be found in Mrs. Gaskell's novel, *North and South.*

The action takes place in the west of Ireland in country much like that around Ross House. The Dysarts of Bruff still hold their tennis parties and picnics; the red jackets of the soldiers make a brave show at Sunday service in Lismoyle church. True, Sir Benjamin Dysart is a senile cripple, and his eldest son Christopher is not what the area (nor, indeed, the fashionable London season) understands by the Master. They much prefer the style, looks and language of Roddy Lambert, the Dysart's agent, who had the impeccably good taste to marry an ailing, rich widow whom he can dominate completely. Of the other people of the district the most important is Charlotte Mullen who, on the surface, is a bluff, kindly, well-read creature liked by many acquaintances, including Lady Dysart. But underneath is a cold and clever financier (the *real* Charlotte) whose only weakness is her affection for Lambert.

In the late eighteenth-century the peasantry divided the

Edith Somerville (left) and Martin Ross.

gentry into three classes: half-mounted gentlemen, gentlemen every inch of them, and gentlemen to the backbone. By this rule of thumb, Charlotte Mullen would have been a half-mounted lady and Roddy Lambert, as in Michael Arlen's self-description, every other inch a gentleman. Into this brittle society comes Francie Fitzpatrick, a beautiful, unsophisticated young woman whose charm and physical presence compensate for the vulgarity of her upbringing and the naivete of her social behavior. Translated from the comparatively egalitarian milieu of Dublin, North Side, she finds life in Lismoyle completely entrancing. The cousin of Charlotte, she is the daughter of a rather unfortunate marriage in which Isabelle Mullen married beneath her. Charlotte, the legal beneficiary of Francie's grandmother, has promised to look after the child and it suits her sense of economy to combine duty with profit. She hopes to marry Francie to young Dysart and at the same time to increase her own stock, both real and metaphorical, so that Roddy will fall into her ample arms when his ailing wife dies. She brings the same careful strategy to this affair as to the dispossessing of Julia Duffy of Gurthnamuckla, secure in the knowledge that any false move or wrong emphasis will be written off as part of her brusque but essentially good-hearted nature. Francie falls for the most handsome and most feckless of the officers, Lieutenant Gerald Hawkins (who is a latter-day Mr.

Wickham), rejects Christopher and is banished to Bray and her former associates by a wrathful and frustrated Charlotte. That lady is restored to good humor by the death of Mrs. Lambert, which she herself helped precipitate by showing the extent of Lambert's love for Francie. This, too, turns sour when Lambert marries Francie.

It is characteristic of Charlotte that she knows something damaging about most people in the district. Stray words and incidents noted and cross-referenced in magnificent filing-system of her brain eventually form dossiers. It is from a chance remark of Dinny Lydon's wife about the rent of Gurthnamuckla pasture, which her cousin Jim McDonagh has at fee, that she learns that Lambert has been cheating his employer. She denounces him to Dysart but he, still in love with Francie, cannot bring himself to prosecute. He even considers allowing him to make good the missing money and to keep his position. It is typical of Francie's self-centered innocence that she has no idea of the extent of Christopher's generosity in not proceeding against Lambert and the novel ends with the death of Francie who falls from a horse on her way to meet Hawkins. Before the news is out Charlotte and Lambert have a final confrontation. All illusions are shattered and each is left contemplating the other's ugliness. The woman, bereft of the one piece of softness in her nature, is hard and ugly, the man miserably superficial and selfish. It is at this moment that they hear of the accident and it is clear to the reader that their common reaction is one of guilt.

One of the most striking things about the novel is the characterization of the women and the animals. (The men are inevitably less successful. It is perhaps trivial to consider the treatment of the non-humans. The authors would have argued the point. One fact which emerges from their most recent biography is that they were certain that their many pets were as like to attain to a heavenly reward as humans. . . . The account of Max and Dinah, "the indoor dogs" at Bruff, shows the same accuracy of observation and humor as in the description of the humans). Charlotte is, of course, the dominating character in the novel. She is as lifelike and as lovingly observed as Anna Karenina or Emma Bovary, though there are not many obvious points of similarity.

Charlotte is not so romantic or so foolish as either, but her weakness is of the same kind as theirs. The only flaw in her cold ambition is her love for Roddy Lambert which began in the days when they sat side by side in the Bruff estate office and when her small unpaid loans to Lambert were rewarded by kisses. This aside, her life is a continuing process of improving her position. She is remarkably consistent in that her romantic ambition dovetails with her social and territorial aspirations. Her ideal is to be lady of a more substantial house than her modest legacy Tally-ho, and to live in it as the loving wife of Roderick Lambert. The house best suited to her taste is the fine if deteriorating mansion, Gurthnamuckla, at the time held by a decayed lady of some quality, whose father had married his own milkmaid. This aspect of the Big House file seems to have both repelled and fascinated Somerville and Ross from their earliest association. As readers of *Eire-Ireland* will remember from Benedict Kiely's dissertation *The Great*

Gazebo, Martin wrote to Edith about an old woman she had seen, the last of her line:

> Yesterday as we left, an old spinster, daughter of the last owner, was at the door in a little donkey-tray. She lives near in an old castle, and since her people died she will not go into The House, or in the enormous yard, or the beautiful old garden. She was a strange mixture of distinction and commonness, like her breeding, and it was very sad to see her at the door of that great house. If we dared to write up that subject. . . .

Julia Duffy of Gurthnamuckla is such an old lady.

Charlotte proceeds against her, in Thomas Flanagan's expression, "like a force of nature." The old woman, ill and driven to distraction by Charlotte's machinations, dies in the asylum, and Charlotte becomes the new mistress of Gurthnamuckla.

One of the reasons for her excessive social ambition is her good reception at Bruff House, where the idiosyncratic Lady Dysart finds her a cultural if not a social equal in the desert of Lismoyle. The Dysart children are too well-bred to show their distaste of her loud persistence, but they are misled as the others in believing that her good nature is more than skin deep. Only her inferiors, her servants and the wretched tenants of her lakeside hovels, know the true harshness of her tongue and the unsentimentality of her nature. Only in her passion for Lambert is she vulnerable, only here does her intelligence waver so that she is genuinely surprised when he marries Francie. Her feelings which have caused her so much embarrassment turn to hatred, in which she is implacable.

Lambert, like many Somerville and Ross men, does not ring completely true. Edith had manifestly no time for men and though Martin had at least one minor love affair before meeting Edith she had none afterwards. Lambert is essentially the "cad" of the later melodrama, handsome, vain, spendthrift and stupid. His power over women we have to take on trust and one is disappointed to find him so stock a character compared with the flesh-and-blood creation, Charlotte. We respect and never quite lose sympathy for this woman. Her sins are scarlet but her blood is red.

The other main character, Francie, is a delightful creation, gentle and vulnerable, doomed like a butterfly to be crushed by forces she does not understand. The remarkable sympathy of the writers for a girl whose commonness should horrify them help to increase the pathos. Her social failings are not spared, however. The catalog of her gaffes is given in full: the unaristocratic taking of tea with sugar; her enthusiasm for and lack of discrimination with wine ("Gorman was regaling his fellows in the servants' hall with an account of how Miss Fitzpatrick had eaten her curry with a knife and fork, and her Scotch woodcock with a spoon, and how she had accepted every variety of wine that he had offered to her, and taken only a mouthful of each . . . "); her lack of taste in clothes.

But Francie is not the only one who comes in for domestic censure. *The Real Charlotte* is many leagues away from the surrealism of the *R.M.* stories: There is none of the overstatement nor are there as many nasty little digs at the emerging middle-class. Yet the upper-class attitudes of the authors keep coming through. The novel is a kind of handbook for the Ireland of the non-Celtic twilight. Consider the following description of a shop cake served by Charlotte at afternoon tea:

> Christopher, having cut the grocer's cake, and found it was the usual conglomerate of tallow, saw-dust, bad eggs, and gravel, devoted himself to thick bread and butter. . . .

This has all the asperity of experience, but there are wider social implications. The inferiority of the quality of the cake would have been forgiven, but not the error of serving it. To resort to a bought cake suggested a grave lack of skill on the part of the mistress or of training in her servants. At the same meal Charlotte in her impatience stirred her tea with the sugar tongs while Francie and Hawkins played with the tea-spoons. Even the tea-table had been laid for breakfast, "a truly realistic touch being conferred by two eggs standing in the slop-basin." These departures from social behavior are taken to be symbolical of greater inadequacy. Charlotte's self-education is pilloried at the expense of the easily carried gloss of Eton and Winchester. In the view of the authors the combination of kind hearts and coronets was perfection. Anything short of this may have been worthy but not adequate.

It is probably well to remember that to ladies of their class the posture of the newly rich middle-class was genuinely funny. One of the more savage stories in *Further Adventures of an Irish R.M.* is **"The Pug-nosed Fox,"** which introduces for the first time the terrible McRorys of Temple Braney. (Their later awful adventures are related in *In Mr. Knox's Country.*) The main comment in the early story is, to modern eyes, a particularly hurtful one: according to Major Yeates' cook, Mrs. Cadogan, "Wild pigs in America wouldn't be treated worse than what Mrs. McRory treated her servants." An element of the same deadly wit is to be found in *The Real Charlotte,* in the description of Mrs. Beattie's midsummer party.

> Mrs. Beattie had trawled Lismoyle and its environs with the purest impartiality: no one was invidiously omitted, not even young Redmond the solicitors clerk, who came in thick boots and a suit of dress clothes so much too big for him as to make his trousers look twin concertinas.

The effect may not be quite what the authors intended. In fact, the writer overcomes the aristocrat and the impression of the party is of a marvelous Dickensian gaiety, leaving no bad taste in the modern Irish mouth. Somerville and Ross would like to have been thought of in the way in which they described Lady Dysart—whose "serene radicalism ignored the inequalities of a lower class." They admired and respected their own loyal tenants and saw many of their good points, but condemned with some superciliousness their lack of organization and hygiene. The jolly, childlike servants of the *R.M.* stories—Mrs. Cadogan, Slipper and the rest—smack of white Uncle-Tomism. One feels that the authors' true feelings emerge in such a sentence (from *The Real Charlotte*) as, "Washerwomen do not, as a rule, assimilate the principles of their trade."

Preoccupations with class aside, the book is pure gold. One remembers the description of lake and bog scenery:

> But in the second or third mile the face of the country changed. The blue lake that had lain in the distance like a long slate of lapis lazuli, was within two fields of them now, moving drowsily in and out of the rocks, and over the coarse gravel of the shore. The trees had dwindled to ragged hazel and thorn bushes; the fat cows of the comfortable farms round Lismoyle were replaced by lean, dishevelled goats, and the shelves and flags of grey limestone began to contest the right of the soil with the thingrass and grey brushwood. We have said grey limestone, but that hard worked adjective cannot at all express the cold, pure blueness that these boulders take under the sky of summer. Some word must yet be coined in which neither blue nor lilac predominate, and in which the steely purple of a pigeon's breast shall not be forgotten.

To read the novel beside such a lake in summer weather is to realize how little some things, at any rate, have changed.

Another very characteristic side to the book is the vein of gothic atmosphere which can intrude into the gayest page. In the same way as the waters of Ross lake could turn grey and unwholesome when the sun went behind a cloud, or a quarter of a mile could change the landscape from rich pasture to bog and bracken, so the mood of the novel can suddenly alter. The preoccupation with the dark side of the curtain seems to have been Martin's. The marvelous description of the gloom and decay of Gurthnamuckla was wrung fresh from her memories of the return to Ross after an absence of sixteen years. The authors' first published work was *An Irish Cousin* which was written at Castletownshend and incorporated the locale of Drishane House and some of the scenery round Ross. During the writing it was referred to as *The Shockeraun,* an obvious pun on Boucicault's melodrama *Con The Shaughraun.* It had its share of gothic trappings—a lone heroine, a large, disturbing house, madness, disinheritance and poetic justice. Such decor would have been out of place in a realistic piece like *The Real Charlotte* but the story of Julia Duffy and her dispossession from Gurthnamuckla brings in the note of gloom. On the journey from Lismoyle to her house (described above) the landscape changes symbolically. The woman herself, the pitiful remains of what had once been a splendid family, alone and friendless, living in the crumbling remains of a great house is an excellent symbol for the hidden decay all around. A feature of the older melodramas was the neatness of their denouements when all loose ends were woven into a completed tapestry. *The Real Charlotte* shows a similar but much more subtle tying-in. As Francie in near hysteria leaves her house to elope with Hawkins, she passes the funeral of Julia Duffy which, by old custom, is brought by the deceased person's home. As she whips her horse past the hearse, the wailing and flapping of the keening women's cloaks cause the horse to rear and she is thrown at the gate of Gurthnamuckla. The moment is one of considerable horror and it is a characteristic Martin touch.

Apart from the account of the marriage of convenience between gentry and peasant, when (as V. S. Pritchett states in his review of the Collis biography) "Gentry and peasant dissembled, averting their eyes from the real situation, and played a kind of game with their remarkable tongues," *The Real Charlotte* is remarkable also for a very clear account of life in Protestant Dublin. Martin had lived there for many years (1872-1888) and the description of the *longeurs* of summer Sundays in the city—"epitome of all that is hot, arid, and empty"—forms the first chapter of the book. The deadliness of the genteel drudgery of Francie's exile in Bray, such a contrast to the life she knew at Lismoyle, makes her acceptance of Lambert inevitable. The description of the winter promenade has all the detail and the sadness of a lithograph:

> It was a very bright clear afternoon, and touch of frost in the air gave the snap and brilliancy that are often lacking in an Irish winter day. On such a Sunday Kingstown pier assumes a fair semblance of its spring and summer gaiety; the Kingstown people walk there because there is nothing else to be done at Kingstown, and the Dublin people come down to snatch what they can of sea air before the short afternoon darkens, and the hour arrives when they look out for members of the St. George's Yacht Club to take them in to tea.

The reader is reminded again of the separate kind of life led in the city and of the disengagement of the majority of the population from nationalism. In the crowds thronging the sea-front—in a place no one then knew as Dun Laoghaire—we can see much the same kind of people who, twenty years later, on Easter Monday, 1916, went off to Fairyhouse Races unaware of the terrible beauty of modern Ireland aborning.

But, by then, Martin was dead and Edith had begun to live out the rest of her long life without her dear friend, in a convulsively changed country. Before she died, the Government of Ireland Act (1947) had severed the last ties of Unionism. Her life had been a kind of fighting compromise, making the best of the new order and stifling or, at least, muting her regrets at the passing of the old. The many books she wrote on her own (with Martin's spiritual assistance) lack the control of the terrestial Martin. It is likely, had she lived, that *The Big House of Inver* would have their monument. As things are, the *R.M.* stories have recently been reissued in one volume, and while these are the works that will keep their authors' names as alive as Conan Doyle's and Mark Twain's (for the same kind of reason) their great achievement, both as a psychological study of greed and innocence and as a social document of striking historical interest, remains *The Real Charlotte.* It is sixty years since it was first published. The Ireland that they knew has changed, but the essentials remain: Sixty years is a short time in the history of a country as torpid as Ireland. Somerville and Ross had the genius to recognize and preserve these essentials. One of the best and most recent tributes comes from the witty and perceptive writer, Terence de Vere White, in the latest of the anatomies of the country:

> If one were to confine one's reading about Ireland to a single book, more is to be learned about the country from *The Real Charlotte* than from any other.

(pp. 126-35)

Sean McMahon, "John Bull's Other Ireland: A Consideration of 'The Real Charlotte' by Somerville and Ross," in Eire-Ireland, *Vol. III, No. 4, 1968, pp. 119-35.*

John Cronin (essay date 1969)

[*In the following excerpt, Cronin discusses the major themes of four Somerville and Ross novels, challenging the perception of the authors as "anti-Irish."*]

The Ascendancy novel has long been suspect in Ireland, for reasons which are as historically obvious as they are critically wrong-headed. The first quarter of the present century saw Ireland involved in a convulsive effort of national rediscovery and self-assertion. The period had a generous share of violence in it and was richly productive of passionate attitudes. It was a period of traumatic, political change and it was unlikely perhaps that literature would during such an historical maelstrom remain the object of calm scrutiny. Much modern Irish criticism would be the despair of any 'New Critic' who bothered to attend to it, since all too often Irish critics have been prescriptive in their approach rather than exploratory, bringing to bear on books demands which are essentially irrelevant to literature. Too often such critics have approached books with a preconceived notion of what is fitting in an Irish novel and, if a narrowly chauvinistic prescription is not filled, the work is found guilty and condemned out of hand. Since the best books, tiresomely but inevitably, refuse to march to anyone's tune but their own, a great deal of worthwhile material has either been forgotten or ignored. It is an extraordinary and entirely regrettable fact that at this moment not one of the novels of Edith Somerville and Violet Martin is in print. In the critical field they have been only slightly better served. Geraldine Cummins's biography of Edith Somerville, though affectionate and well-intentioned, is chattily discursive, unmethodical and idiosyncratic. It is a source of great pleasure to me personally that the first really perceptive article by an Irish critic on these writers came from the pen of one of my former teachers. I refer to Dr B. G. MacCarthy, herself a writer and critic of repute and lately Professor of English at University College, Cork. More recently, there have been interesting articles in the *Dublin Review* [by Ann Power] and the *Kenyon Review* [by Thomas Flanagan] but no full-scale study of the writings of Somerville and Ross has yet appeared.

Somerville and Ross belong to a rich tradition of the Irish novel which, beginning with Maria Edgeworth, includes such writers as the Banims, Gerald Griffin, William Carleton, Charles Lever and George Moore. A healthy critical curiosity would surely concern itself not with deploring the formative influences of this tradition, but with exploring the dynamic nature of its essential tensions. Somerville and Ross were daughters of the Ascendancy and their principal concern as writers is with their own class. To fault them for this and to dub them colonial or alien is to ignore their work in favour of critically irrelevant, extraliterary considerations. They were part of a small and powerful Ascendancy enclave, not part of the larger Ireland, and their books are redolent of what Conor Cruise O'Brien has called [in *Writers and Politics,* 1965] the 'Indian Summer of the Irish Ascendancy'.

The dominant themes of the 'Ascendancy' novel in Ireland have been related to the tradition's attempts to define itself and its place in its society. The painful crux of the Anglo-Irish, Irish to the English and English to the Irish, led to a curiously bi-focal vision which is not without its compensations. If the Anglo-Irish writer was often cut off from the mass of the people by religious and class divisions of a formidable kind, he was, too, often united with them by a shared love of the countryside over which an accident of history had given him and his kind command. The future dilemma of the class had been foreshadowed in the difficulties of the early colonists when it was found that English settlers showed a deplorable tendency to marry the Irish and settle down with them, and laws had to be enacted to avert this threat to the racial purity of the colonizing forces. As far back as 1366, the preamble to the Statutes of Kilkenny had spelt out the problem:

> Whereas at the Conquest of the land of Ireland and for a long time afterwards, the English of the said land used the English language, mode of riding, and apparel, and were governed, both they and their subjects, called betaghs, according to the English law . . . now many English of the said land, forsaking the English language, manners, mode of riding, laws and usage, live and govern themselves according to the manners, fashions and language of the Irish enemies, whereby the said land and the liege people thereof, the English language, the allegiance due to our Lord the King, and the English laws are put into subjection and decayed, and the Irish enemies exalted and raised up contrary to reason.

There followed a long list of enactments, prohibiting intermarriage, use of the Irish language, Irish surnames, Irish customs and so on. It was hopeless. Religiously, socially, matrimonially, the two sides of this strange historical mixture were to be hopelessly entangled and intertwined. The separatist attempts of the early legislators were as absurd in their way as the later intolerances of doctrinaire Irish critics. Neither showed much sense of how human beings really function. The characteristic tensions of the Ascendancy novel, then, are the product of this unique historical merger and Somerville and Ross are among its finest exponents.

In point of time, they slightly predate the Irish Literary Revival. Their finest novel, *The Real Charlotte,* was published in 1894, and they were already literary figures of international repute during the pioneering days of the Abbey Theatre. They knew many of the great figures of the new movement, notably Lady Gregory and Yeats. However, they kept themselves aloof from the Dublin-based movement quite consciously and although there may have been some element of social withdrawal in this, it is, perhaps, easy to overstate it. The principal figures of the Irish Literary Revival were, after all, as firmly of the Ascendancy as they were themselves. Yeats, Lady Gregory, Synge, George Moore—none of these was 'mere' Irish and none was a Catholic (except Moore, who felt it necessary to assert his preference for Protestantism in a celebrated letter to the *Irish Times*). John Synge's family deplored his association with theatrical folk and, if there was something of the same kind of social reaction in the attitude of Somerville and Ross to the new movement, there may also have been a strong artistic instinct for survival at work. For it was not to be the destiny of these two to explore the legends of the past in search of Celtic twilight. They had relevant material more ready to their hands to which they were powerfully drawn. When Somerville and Ross saw an old woman going down the path, she might not have the walk of a queen but she was quite likely to have a remarkably vivid tongue in her head and a striking individuality. In the essay already referred to above, Conor Cruise O'Brien quotes a long passage from the R.M. story, **'Lisheen Races, Second Hand',** and speculates as to whether Synge may not have been indebted to parts of it when writing *The Playboy of the Western World.* 'The world of Somerville and Ross may not be quite as remote from the world of the Literary Revival as we sometimes suppose,' he suggests. It is certainly noticeable that the incidental, cultural activities of Somerville and Ross were strikingly similar to those of Synge and Lady Gregory. Like them, they attended classes in the Irish language—like them, they foraged among the country people in search of phrases and habits of speech. They had in common with the leading figures of the Irish Literary Revival their ear for rich, fully-flavoured language. Their novels and stories abound in examples of splendidly accurate Anglo-Irish speech and they are, without question, the supreme exponents of the Anglo-Irish speech of the province of Munster. But while their talents and even many of their interests coincided with those of their great contemporaries, the focus of their literary curiosity was to be different.

It is necessary, therefore, to stand the usual critical attitude on its head and to state firmly of Somerville and Ross that their strength as writers and as observers of the Irish scene derives precisely from the firmness with which they were rooted in their class and that, paradoxically, they are most revealing of the other Ireland when they are most firmly entrenched in their own setting. There is a scene in **The Real Charlotte** which is to the point here. It occurs late in the book when Charlotte visits the local tailor, Dinny Lydon, who has been turning a coat for her. She calls on him for a fitting, and also to wheedle out of him some information which she will use against Roderick Lambert. The wary exchange between Charlotte and the Lydons is beautifully observed. At one point, Mrs Lydon speaks briefly to her husband in Irish:

> 'Arrah, dheen dheffeth, Dinny, thurrum cussoge um'na.' 'Yes, hurry on and give me the coat, Dinny,' said Charlotte, displaying that knowledge of Irish that always came as a shock to those who were uncertain as to its limitations.

In this and in the chapter generally what is evoked with remarkable power and expressed with notable economy of style is the peculiarly complex nature of this brief encounter between the masterful, vulgar Charlotte and her warily amiable, social inferiors. The final turn of her screw on them is that she even knows some of their private language, how much exactly they cannot guess. There is suggested here, with fine economy, a whole, menacing hinterland of unknown resentments.

This imaginative perception is typical of this splendid novel, the fine flower of the writers' joint achievement. It is a book in which setting and period are perfectly realized and a group of finely conceived characters set in motion within a carefully constructed plot. The resulting novel compels attention on its own terms and blossoms, too, into a telling, symbolic analysis of a crumbling Ascendancy group. The world of the novel is a Protestant, Ascendancy world. The native Catholic Irish impinge only as servants or as an occasional threat to the perfection of a family tree. The writers are not struggling here, as they had done in the earlier novel, *Naboth's Vineyard,* to understand an alien, national psyche. This is a brilliant novel about people who are wholly understood, moving in a setting which is completely realized. It is a triumph of realistic fiction. If it is interpretative of the social conditions from which it sprang, it is so because it is, first of all, a fine novel, a fully imagined, sympathetically conceived story of people whose aspirations and despairs the writers either understood directly or reached towards with a fine creative intuition. The book is everywhere characterised by the imaginative perfection proper to such an achievement. Time and again one is struck to admiration by the writers' sureness of touch. *The Real Charlotte* grows into a magnificent exposé of the essential irrelevance of true vulgarity. It is a remarkable tribute to the writers' sense of evil and their power to depict it that when, in Chapter 34, Francie and Charlotte face each other in anger and the cat Susan jumps on Charlotte like a familiar, the bizarre suggestion of witchcraft is entirely acceptable and appropriate in relation to this coarse and unscrupulous creature.

Charlotte Mullen is at the centre of the book. Her hunger for land and social advancement sets the plot in motion. Her greedy desire to possess the dying Julia Duffy's once fine estate of Gurthnamuckla involves her with Roderick Lambert whom she also wants to possess, desiring him with all the fierce, concealed passion of an ugly, ageing, intelligent, determined woman. One social extreme of the novel is represented by the Dysart family, an amusingly conceived group of aristocratic hybrids—Lady Dysart carefully planting her flower-beds full of the chickweed plants which she has mistaken for asters; Pamela, her daughter, decent and doomed to spinsterdom; Christopher, the slightly epicene and introspective son and heir who is almost but not quite quickened into life by his love for Francie, and Sir Benjamin, an invalid trapped in a wheel-chair, an elderly, aristocratic daftie, who bellows at visitors and is rapidly removed from the scene when necessary by his attendant, James Canavan. Together they represent a composite picture of sterility and decay at the top of the social hierarchy. Charlotte is a vulgar, lower-middle class woman clawing her way up the ladder; Roderick Lambert is a nobody, who, in the book's own words, attains 'brevet rank as a country gentleman' by acquiring the agency for the Dysart estate. The book is passionately concerned throughout with rank and social status. Charlotte,

according to her memorably caustic servant, Norry the Boat, wants to go and live in Gurthnamuckla and 'let on she's as grand as the other ladies in the counthry'. Local society is presented to us with an Austenian precision. We meet the mamas and their hopeful daughters and those important figures, 'the Lismoyle officers', at a series of memorable picnics and dances and tennis parties. The novel is rich in vivid scenes that quiver with the vigour of credibility. One recalls Lady Dysart's comprehensive tennis party in Chapter 3 which provides a panorama of the social group we are to be concerned with, or the hilarious theatricals in Chapter 20 where Francie incurs the displeasure of Lady Dysart by flirting with Captain Hawkins, or the boat trip in Chapter 14 which almost ends in disaster and highlights the rivalry between Christopher Dysart and Roderick Lambert. Charlotte figures in a series of grimly memorable encounters; her greedy vigil by her aunt's death-bed in Chapter 2, her vulture-visit to the ailing Julia Duffy in Chapter 10, and Chapter 32 in which she, for all practical purposes, causes the death of Roderick Lambert's wife. Vivid as these scenes are, none of them is a mere setpiece; each is as functional as it is brilliant. The novel throughout possesses a moral and philosophic profundity and a power of psychological penetration which cause one to wonder to what heights these writers might not have attained had the tremendous popularity of the *R.M.* stories not shortly diverted them to other pursuits and had not death soon after intervened for one of them. *The Real Charlotte* has tenderness and strength and a quite unusual perceptiveness and richly deserves Lord David Cecil's description of it as 'a master-piece, a classic'. It is pre-eminently the novel in which Somerville and Ross realized with an unforgettable totality the dying world of the Anglo-Irish Ascendancy, aspects of which only were to be tackled in the other novels.

Since this is the finest work they achieved together, this may be the point at which to refer briefly to the much discussed question of their writing partnership. The whole problem of their remarkable collaboration has been frequently investigated and discussed. Sir Patrick Coghill, who was privileged to see them at work, has given an authoritative account of their working methods in an address delivered to the Friends of the Library at Trinity College Dublin in 1951, subsequently published in *Hermathena* in the following year. Edith Somerville herself, in the very last article she wrote, **'Two of a Trade'** (published in *Irish Writing* in 1946), discussed the matter once again and tried good-humouredly to suggest the nature of the separate contributions. It is altogether a fascinating subject and one on which the critical last word has perhaps not yet been said, but I am now concerned with it only to the extent of pointing to an aspect of the collaboration which immediately interests me. Edith Somerville went on putting the two names to her work after Violet Martin's death. In several prefatory notes she wrote with great warmth and affection of her former collaborator and it would be easy to see all this simply as affectionate tribute to a beloved cousin and fellow-writer. But in one subsequent novel at least, the finest she achieved with her own pen and one of the finest of all Irish historical novels *The Big House of Inver,* Edith did have Violet Martin again as her collaborator, in the sense that the novel was the ultimate outcome of a letter written by Violet Martin a dozen years before the book's publication and three years before Violet's death. An extract from the letter appears at the end of the novel and reads as follows:

> March 8, 1912
>
> Yesterday I drove to see X- House. A great cut stone house of three stories . . . Perfectly empty. . . . It is on a long promontory by the sea, and there rioted three or four generations of X . . .s, living with countrywomen, occasionally marrying them, all illegitimate four times over . . . About one hundred and fifty years ago, a very grand Lady . . . married the head of the family and lived there, and was so corroded with pride that she would not allow her two daughters to associate with the neighbours of their own class. She lived to see them marry two of the men in the yard . . .
>
> Yesterday, as we left, an old Miss X, daughter of the last owner, was at the door in a little donkey-trap.
>
> She lives near in an old castle, and since her people died she will not go into X. House, or into the enormous yard, or the beautiful old garden.
>
> She was a strange mixture of distinction and commonness, like her breeding and it was very sad to see her at the door of that great house.
>
> If we dared to write up that subject . . .!
>
> Yours ever,
> 'Martin'

Edith Somerville so dared in *The Big House of Inver* and, in doing so, pursued one of the great, informing curiosities of these writers and, indeed, one of the great central themes of the Ascendancy novel generally. The book is in direct line of descent from Maria Edgeworth's *Castle Rackrent,* that great seminal chronicle of the ruin of a once splendid family. The parallels between Miss Edgeworth's roistering Rackrents and Edith Somerville's playboy Prendervilles is clear. Both writers convey with splendid vigour the special combination of bravura and folly which will bring down a Big House in ruin and admit the scavenging profiteers who await its end. But Edith Somerville gives to the old form a new dimension which the earlier novelist might well have admired and envied, for, in the figure of Shibby Pindy, she created a memorable character conceived and executed on the grand scale. Shibby, watching over the decay of the line of which she herself is but a by-blow, is surely one of the most memorable of all figures in the Anglo-Irish novel. Her quixotic efforts to restore the Prenderville fortunes by marrying her adored half-brother Kit to a suitable heiress, are doomed to failure—the family has brought down its own ruin on its own head through many rioting generations of irresponsibility and moral indifference and Shibby's semi-savage innocence seems their most powerful rebuke. Her pathetic furnishing of the splendid rooms of the Big House with tawdry, gimcrack rubbish purchased with her heart's blood at local auctions carries the powerful drive of a greatly conceived symbol, worthy of the imagination of a Dickens. Her ignorant, simple determination is the necessary

moral counterbalance to the cynical, frivolous irresponsibility of the line she is trying to restore. That ruin is finally brought upon the Big House of Inver by old Jas Prenderville himself who sells it and then accidentally burns it to the ground, is fitting; whom the gods wish to destroy they first make mad and the Prendervilles create their own destruction.

If *The Real Charlotte* and *The Big House of Inver,* their finest work without a doubt, represent together the writers' vision of their society and its historical context, it is safe to say, in spite of the justly renowned humour of their short stories, that they are essentially writers of powerful tragic vision. Daughters of the Ascendancy they were, and themselves part of the world of the Big House but they were never less than seriously critical of it all. In them the eye of love is also the eye of judgement.

In several other interesting books, Edith explored aspects of the Ascendancy dilemma. In *Mount Music* she tackles the theme of intermarriage between Catholic and Protestant at Big House level and canvasses the issues with notable fairness and a great deal of perception. Mount Music, the Big House which gives the book its title has fallen on evil days. Its owner, Richard Talbot-Lowry, stubbornly refuses to join his fellow landowners in selling his land to the tenants:

> At Mount Music, where once the milk and honey had flowed with effortless abundance each year brought increasing stress. The rents grew less, the expenses greater, that large and omnivorous item known as 'keeping up the place' was as exacting as ever, the minor problems of household existence more acute. There had been a time when the Mount Music tenants had vied with each other in the provision of sons and daughters for service in the Big House, when bonfires had blazed for the return of 'the young gentleman' and offerings of eggs had greeted 'the young ladies'. Now the propitiatory turkey that heralded a request, the goose that signalised a success, gained with the help of the hereditary helpers, had all ceased. Alien influences had poisoned the wells of friendship. Such rents as were paid were extracted by the hard hand of the law, and the tenants held indignation meetings against the landlord who refused to resign to them what they believed to be theirs, and he was equally convinced was his.

Edith Somerville describes Richard Talbot-Lowry and his class with a sort of impatient affection:

> In the days when Christian Talbot-Lowry was a little girl, that is to say between the eighties and nineties of the nineteenth century, the class known as Landed Gentry was still pre-eminent in Ireland. Tenants and tradesmen bowed down before them, with love sometimes, sometimes with hatred, never with indifference. The newspapers of their districts recorded their enterprises in marriage, in birth, in death, copiously, and with a servile rapture of detail that, though it is not yet entirely withheld from their survivors, is now bestowed with an equal unction on those who, in many instances, have taken their places, if not their place, socially, in Irish every-

day existence. There is little doubt but that after the monsters of the Primal Periods had been practically extinguished, a stray reptile, here and there, escaped the general doom, and as Mr Yeats says of his lug-worm, may have sung with 'its grey and muddy mouth' of how 'somewhere to North or West or South, there dwelt a gay, exulting, gentle race' of Plesiosauridae or Pterodactyli.

This image of the Pterodactyl pervades the book, and Richard Talbot-Lowry is the supreme example of the species. The language of the passage I have just quoted surely implies a criticism of the system which is described. Servility was not a quality rated high by Edith Somerville and, although she depicts Richard Talbot-Lowry as a benevolent despot, she indicates that she is aware that the day of even the most benevolent of despots is over and that a realist would admit this. The Talbot-Lowry's hasty departure from Mount Music at the end of all is not sentimentalized or glamourized. This is a retreat in bad order and the novel shows this ruthlessly:

> On Monday morning Christian saw her father and mother start, too agitated by their coming journey to have a spare thought for sentiment; too much beset by the fear of what they might lose, their keys, their sandwiches, their dressing-boxes, to shed a tear for what they were losing, and had lost.

On the other hand, the character of Big Doctor Mangan who schemes in a manner almost worthy of Charlotte Mullen herself to get his daughter married 'into the gentry' and who gets Richard Talbot-Lowry into his clutches by lending him money, until eventually he becomes himself the owner of Mount Music, is treated with a kind of tolerant admiration. He is a schemer and a social climber but he is big and generous in heart and a real strength of understanding goes into his creation. In this novel the technique may be noticeably slacker than in the best of the work these writers achieved together but the book's heart is in the right place and a great deal of intelligent detachment is combined with an honestly acknowledged involvement. And what a contemporary ring we hear in a passage like the following from Chapter 30:

> The roofs of Cluhir made a dark profile in the middle distance, the lower part of the houses hidden in the steaming mist, and the beautiful outline of the twin crests of Carrigaholt was like a golden shadow in the sky above them. The spire and the tower of the two churches of Cluhir rose on either side of the pale radiance of the river, with the slender arch of the bridge joining them, as if to show in allegory their inherent oneness, their joint access to the water of life. Religion counted for but little with Larry in those days, yet as the wonder of beauty sank into his soul . . . the thought of what it would mean for Ireland if the symbol of the linking bridge had its counterpart in reality sprang into his eager mind.

An Enthusiast, the novel which followed *Mount Music,* pursued these aspirations to unity into the political field. Its hero Dan Palliser is a young man of idealistic bent,

who hopes to solve Ireland's problems by economic means, by improved farming methods, by the introduction of properly run creameries and co-operative societies. Unhappily for him the year is 1920 and the political malaise has gone too far. The new Ireland is about to prey upon itself, rumour has taken the place of truth and rational counsel is being rejected in place of party slogans. This is an Ireland, as the book puts it, 'of burning police barracks and Irishmen murdered by their brothers'. It is the period of the Black and Tans, of raid and counter-raid. Dan Palliser is distrusted by his social equals because of his friendly relations with people suspected of Sinn Fein sympathies and distrusted by the local farmers because of his Ascendancy background. It is a time for taking sides, not for taking thought and Dan's sanity makes him an unhappy odd-man-out in his locality and in his period. He is, at the end, shot to death by one of his own guests during an arms raid by Republican forces on his old family home. He dies in the open, clutching his father's old Crimean sword, a suitable symbol of the way time and events have passed him by.

Both *Mount Music* and *An Enthusiast* end in tragedy, as though the problems posed are incapable of solution—yet when we set this sombreness against the warmth and humanity of the books themselves, the conclusion does not, somehow, seem quite so inescapable.

Violet Martin died in 1915, one year before modern Ireland's baptism of fire. Edith Somerville lived to a great age and died in 1949, the year in which the Irish Free State declared itself a Republic, thus breaking its last ties with the established order into which these two talented women were born and in which they grew to maturity. Out of the chaos and flux of their times they have left us much to be grateful for—in *The Real Charlotte* a great realistic novel, in *The Big House of Inver* one of Ireland's finest historical novels, in the *R.M.* stories a whole comic universe for our delight. They possessed the gifts of the great novelists in abundance—they created and peopled a world for us and, with their world and their people they amuse us, they entertain us, they delight us, they fascinate us and, quite often, they make us think beyond the event and its circumstances to motives and causes. They have richly enfleshed for us in brilliantly human terms a whole era which, in the history books, might seem merely a sequence of hatreds and animosities. Cut off from the majority of the people of their country by great barriers of religion and tradition, they yet knew that these barriers were not to remain insuperable. It is their awareness of this and their brightly talented efforts to weave a fable to fit the change which gives them their relevance for an Ireland which is, even now, only painfully struggling at last to come to terms with a blend of traditions.

The works of Somerville and Ross do not merely demand our attention. They deserve it. (pp. 8-18)

John Cronin, "Dominant Themes in the Novels of Somerville and Ross," in Somerville and Ross: A Symposium, *The Queen's University, 1969, pp. 8-19.*

F. S. L. Lyons (essay date 1970)

[*In the following excerpt, Lyons praises the works of Somerville and Ross for their accurate portrayal of Irish life and subtle sense of tragedy.*]

[Of the three novels *The Real Charlotte, Mount Music,* and *The Big House of Inver,*] only the first—in most judgements incomparably the best—was written before the death of Martin Ross, which may explain why it is that although *The Real Charlotte* was a very early work (published in 1894), whereas the other two appeared after the displacement of the gentry had become an accomplished fact, it is this book which penetrates most deeply into the change that was taking place in Irish society. What *The Real Charlotte* portrays is not only the decadence of a southern ruling family—the Dysarts—but the thrusting ambition of a rural bourgeoisie (it sounds a strange mixture but Ireland was able to produce it) which besides seeking to add field to field and farm to farm, aimed also at usurping the social prestige and dominance that had belonged to the Ascendancy until the Land War and the land legislation had together loosened their hold upon the countryside. It is true that the authors make their female land-grabber, Charlotte Mullen, a Protestant (one wonders how much significance they attached to having given her what in Ireland is usually a Catholic name), but in her ruthlessness and greed she symbolizes, if in an exaggerated form, the energy and ability that were driving out the old and bringing in the new.

The Real Charlotte was a remarkable achievement, not only as the literary masterpiece it can claim to be, but as a work of profound historical insight. Edith Somerville, when she came to publish *Mount Music* and *The Big House of Inver* (in 1919 and 1925 respectively) had had time to weigh the full devastation wrought upon her people by the storm that had begun to break in 1916, and although the action of both books takes place before 1914 the emphasis on futility and decay is even more apparent. Of the two, *The Big House of Inver* is the more impressive, and it is perhaps significant that the idea for the book had been conceived by Martin as far back as 1912 after a visit to an old and derelict family mansion. 'A great cut stone house of three stories,' she wrote. 'Perfectly empty . . . It is on a long promontory by the sea, and there rioted three or four generations of X's, living with the countrywomen, occasionally marrying them, all illegitimate four times over . . . About one hundred and fifty years ago, a very grand Lady . . . married the head of the family and lived there, and was so corroded with pride that she would not allow her two daughters to associate with the neighbours of their own class. She lived to see them marry two of the men in the yard.' The theme of *The Big House of Inver* is precisely the degradation of such a family, worked out with that feeling for the social nuances of the Irish countryside that Edith Somerville and Martin Ross both had to an almost uncanny degree.

Nowadays it is the deep, underlying pessimism of these books, combined with the stoic determination of the authors to see their world as nearly as possible as it actually was, that most impress the observer. Yet it is only right to remember that this view of Somerville and Ross is a very recent one and that until a few years ago nearly all appraisals of their work were distorted by the immense success of their three volumes of stories, *Some Experiences of an Irish R.M.* (1899), *Further Experiences of an Irish R.M.* (1908), and *In Mr. Knox's Country* (1915). This distortion has tended to occur in two quite different ways. On the one hand, generations of readers, captivated by the vividness, humour and sheer high spirits of the stories, have agreed in establishing them as classics of the hunting-field and in placing the two ladies firmly in the same stable as Surtees, forgetting that the stable was never more than an outlying appendage to the Big House which was their real habitation, with the ironic result that to this day the *R.M.* stories are the only work of Somerville and Ross to be found regularly in print. But, on the other hand, nationalist critics have generally seen in the undoubted 'Ascendancy' tone of the stories a kind of heartless arrogance, a deliberate emphasis upon the stage-Irishman in the vein of *Handy Andy* and all those other Anglo-Irish novels which set out, in Yeats's phrase, to exploit rather than to express the people.

With the innocent amusement of the general reading public we are not here concerned, except perhaps to regret that the unending demand for more of the Irish R.M. almost certainly diverted Edith and Martin from further experiments of the calibre of *The Real Charlotte.* But the charge of Handy Andyism is more serious and more difficult to refute. In a sense, indeed, it cannot be refuted. The Somervilles and Martins were acutely aware of belonging to a governing class and both ladies—especially Edith—were very much alive to the frontier between acquaintance and familiarity. In much of their writing—and this is as evident in the *R.M.* stories as in their more serious work—there is a distinct tone of *de haut en bas,* which, at least to those *en bas,* was all the more irritating because it was almost unconscious. It is perfectly true that they measured social gradations with almost pedantic accuracy, but it has to be said that what they measured did actually exist. However lamentable, however injurious to patriotic pride, the historical evidence is unmistakable that landlords *were* dominant, tenants *were* servile, servants *were* unreliable, dirty and dishonest, different standards *did* prevail for different strata of society.

Yet, it may still be argued, granted that social differentiation of this kind existed, was it necessary to make the Irish peasant a caricature of his true self by putting into his mouth a flow of language which to the outsider may seem richly funny, but which to others may be no more than a grotesque parody of the real thing? But is the peasant language of Somerville and Ross a grotesque parody, are the tenants and grooms and servants no more than caricatures? On the contrary, there are strong indications that the truth is very different. It is apparent from many of the extracts from the letters and diaries of the two ladies printed by Mr Collis that from their earliest days as writers both Edith and Martin not only had an infallible eye for the drolleries (and discomforts) of life in rural Ireland at the turn of the century, but also had a quite exceptionally exact ear for the speech—undeniably vivid and racy as it was—that surrounded them in their impressionable youth and which they reproduced time after time, in the novels as well as in the *R.M.* stories, with astonishing fidelity. Indeed, one might go further and say that with them, unlike, say, Synge, or even Lady Gregory, one has a sense not of a speech that is deliberately contrived to be poetic or dramatic, but rather of something flowing naturally out of the environment and recorded with all the tender precision of a folk-lorist. What Somerville and Ross did have, of course, and what folk-lorists generally don't, was a highly developed sense of the ridiculous and the ability to extract the maximum amusement out of the most mundane and trivial occasions. For that, surely, they do not need to be forgiven.

It was this feeling of being close to the sources of their material, without the necessity of having to invent a style, that separated Somerville and Ross so decisively from the literary renaissance that was proceeding simultaneously with their own development. They came to know most of the leading figures of that renaissance, and even to win through to a rather grudging respect for Yeats as the chief of them, but all attempts to corral them into any of the movements active in the Ireland of their prime are doomed to failure. They worked happily in their own medium and were content to leave others to work in theirs, but they were a world removed from the aesthetic and political preoccupations of Dublin. This again was partly a consequence of their never-sleeping class-consciousness—they had no wish to attach themselves to a group which seemed to them to have conspicuously few 'gentlemen' in it. But their aloofness reflected also their instinctive distrust of the attempt that Yeats and some of his friends were making to come to terms with nationalism. Edith and Martin were uncompromising Unionists and never saw any reason to change their views. Edith, indeed, had the strongest reasons for not doing so, for not only did she live through the period in the 1920's when many Big Houses were destroyed and many Ascendancy families harried into exile, but in 1936 her own brother, Admiral Boyle Somerville, was shot on the door-step of his house in Castle Townshend for no other reason apparently than that he had helped a number of local young men to join the Royal Navy.

In the last analysis, what gave them their special distinction was a proud refusal to abandon the views and standards of their youth even while seeing so clearly the weakness and vulnerability of the caste to which they belonged. It is not merely that they caught so exactly the quality of Anglo-Irish life in the twenty years or so before the First World War, it is also that they realized its transience. This is why the fashion of dismissing them simply as comic writers fails utterly to do them justice. Comedy was there, of course, and often in the very forefront of their work, but when that work is viewed as a whole the note of tragedy is inescapable. And if we are to sum up their art in a single sentence it is surely this—that they carried into literature more completely and more perceptively than any of their contemporaries the essence of the Anglo-Irish dilemma. It is the dilemma of those who stand between two traditions—the native and the alien—and can never become completely assimilated to either. Certainly, it could be argued—and often has been argued—that the Anglo-Irish, with their wide-ranging service to the Empire in all sorts

of capacities, had assimilated themselves to the alien tradition all too well, and the nationalist gibe that an Anglo-Irishman is an Englishman who happens to have been born and/or lived in Ireland dies hard. This, however, is a superficial view of a complex phenomenon, assuming, as it seems to do, that many generations of living in the country have made no difference to the 'colonial' or 'alien' stock. But in reality even the most expatriate of Anglo-Irishmen have generally regarded themselves as other than English, and the more they have lived among the English the more important to them this otherness has tended to become.

Yet there remained—and still remains—the apparently insoluble problem of the second assimilation, assimilation with the native tradition. Not for nothing was the Big House set apart from the village, surrounded by its high stone walls, leading its own quite separate life. For the physical isolation in which most of the Anglo-Irish grew up was no more than the visible manifestation of the intellectual and spiritual isolation in which they were condemned—it is not too strong a word—to live. No doubt many of them were unconscious of the fact and right up to the end fleeted the time carelessly as of old. No doubt, also even for those who were intelligent enough to understand what was happening to them the ambivalence of their situation cannot have seemed all loss, since their very detachment bred that ironic temper which permeates their writings and may perhaps have been their greatest intellectual strength. But when all is said the price they paid was a high one. To be born in a country and to grow up to love it, but never fully to possess it, never completely to belong to it, may create not just great literature but also unhappy men and women. Of such, Somerville and Ross stand as the truest and most compassionate interpreters. (pp. 117-22)

> *F. S. L. Lyons, "The Twilight of the Big House," in* Ariel: A Review of International English Literature, *Vol. 1, No. 3, July, 1970, pp. 110-22.*

John Cronin   (essay date 1972)

[*In the following excerpt, Cronin analyzes the strengths and weaknesses of individual stories from* The Irish R.M. *books, and also discusses the novel* Dan Russel the Fox.]

[*Some Experiences of an Irish R.M.*] was a huge success and brought [Somerville and Ross] international fame. The first edition of three thousand copies sold out in a month and a second edition was called for. The first dozen of the *R.M.* stories brought the cousins the sort of general acclaim which even their finest novel, published five years earlier, had not earned them.

In the *R.M.* stories, Edith and Martin suspend their awareness of the historical inevitabilities which attend their class and present us with a comic universe seen with the eye of love. Their earlier work, as has been indicated, had given ample evidence of a darker vision, but in their most celebrated stories they flee reality and take happy refuge in a world compounded of outrageously funny acci-

Martin Ross, c. 1900.

dents and extravagant Irish talk. To the making of this comic universe they brought their dual sense of the ridiculous and their marvellous ear for Munster speech. All their lives they had moved between two Irelands and had talked with double tongue. From the day-to-day encounters of their two worlds and the rich ambiguities born of the clash of two languages they produced a whirl of farce and chatter which moves at its own exciting pace, according to its own laws or absence of them, scorning the drabness of literal representation and pausing not for sober judgements. To ask of their comic world that it conform to rules entirely irrelevant to it is mere folly. We do not visit the world of Jeeves and Bertie Wooster in search of profound social comment; we do not quarry in a Feydeau farce for the grim realities of the French middle-class. Nor should we approach the *R.M.* stories as though they ought to be a repository of the truth about late-nineteenth-century Ireland. What we must bring to our enjoyment of them is our sense of the essential daftness of circumstance, our joy in linguistic nuance, our delight in things going wonderfully wrong, our tolerance of two and two's everlasting failure to make a symmetrically satisfactory four, in short, a sense of humour sharpened by experience.

The stories do not set out to be profound explorations of character or telling analyses of social or political structures. They are comedy of incident realized within a stiff convention. The extremes of the convention are provided by the "gentry" at the top and the locals and servants at the bottom. We accept this without protest for the purposes of the comedy, just as we accept the essential absur-

dity of the Bertie Wooster-Jeeves relationship as the basis of the idiotic events in which they become involved together, and, as with the Bertie-Jeeves relationship, a large part of the comedy lies in the frequency with which the master-servant relationship is reversed. As long as the convention works to embroil both master and servant in a mutual comic debacle, all is well. Uneasy moments in regard to the motivation of real characters, such as have sometimes occurred in the early novels, are avoided in a situation where character has, as it were, been arbitrarily frozen so that a whirl of funny happenings can be set in motion. Real uneasiness arises only in relation to the no-man's-land between the extremes: the territory occupied by the Flynns and the McRorys, nouveau-riche social climbers who try to cross the "boundery-line" that divides the elect from their social inferiors. In the stories in which these characters appear, as will be seen later, the writers' control over their material tends to waver somewhat.

The opening story, **"Great Uncle McCarthy,"** is highly effective in introducing us to the *milieu* and to a whole range of the characters, while yet remaining a brisk, comic story in its own right. We enter into the R.M.'s new world with the R.M. himself newly arrived in Skebawn and hunting for a house. The fine note of pervasive paradox is struck from the very beginning when Major Yeates, though desperately anxious to escape from Mrs. Raverty's dreadful hotel into his new home, finds himself giving both the carpenter and the plumber seven days without the option of a fine. As though he has not suffered enough, he has as his landlord Florence McCarthy Knox, the celebrated Flurry who "looked like a stable boy among gentlemen, and a gentleman among stableboys" and who appropriately makes his first entrance on the stage when he comes to sell his new tenant a horse. Flurry is, of course, one of the great creations of the whole *R.M.* series. He appears in most of the stories, sometimes as the manipulator, sometimes as himself the butt. His clan of relatives ranges from Sir Valentine Knox of Castle Knox down to the auctioneer Knox known as "Larry the Liar." If Major Yeates is, for the writers' purpose, the perfectly conceived innocent abroad, Flurry is his perfect cicerone, a kind of quietly manic Man Friday who leads his Crusoe by the nose into ever stranger scrapes. Philippa broods over the story as an unseen wife-to-be. All the horrors of the house combine to suggest the shock which awaits her arrival since Philippa, unlike the Major, is wholly English and, therefore, likely to find the logic of Skebawn not to her taste. We await her arrival with appalled glee. The superb climax in which Flurry is made to look memorably silly by running his mother's first cousin to ground in the attic, thereby uncovering the McCarthy Gannons who have been secretly squatting in the Major's house and shooting his foxes, splendidly synthesizes the themes of the series. It is altogether appropriate that the amiable scavengers among whom he is to live should quarter themselves on the Major from the beginning and that his servants should be complicatedly in league with them. The roguery of Skebawn lies in wait for Major Yeates in the heart of his own house. How right it is, also, that the hunt, which is going to be so important a part of his life from now on, should pursue its first quarry right into the very house itself. All the themes and all the people and all the wickedly hilarious contrivances come to roost under the Major's roof for our splendid delectation, in this first, compendious story. Here is God's plenty, with the comfortable assurance of more to come. (pp. 52-6)

The *R.M.* stories are the comic obverse of novels like *The Real Charlotte* and *The Big House of Inver.* The backgrounds are the same—tea-parties and boating expeditions, hunting and dancing, picnics and sports-days, flirtations and matchmakings. Only the angle of vision is different. The amusing trip in Bernard Shute's yacht, *Eileen Oge,* which ends with the slaughter of Dr. Fahy's cockatoo, recalls the near-disaster which overtakes Roderick Lambert, Francie Fitzpatrick and Christopher Dysart in the ill-fated *Daphne.* Lady Knox sounds remarkably like the Lady Dysart of Bruff who bewails the superfluity of women in her party. It is the same world but, this time, sunny side up.

The best of the stories partake of the confidence and sureness of touch which inform the best of the novels. It is, as always, a world of masters and servants but one in which the roles are, more often than not, comically reversed. At times the humor arises out of the doings of "the gentry," the Major, Mrs. Knox, Flurry, Sally etc. At other times it arises out of the gentry's unsuccessful encounters with the locals, as in **"The Holy Island,"** where Major Yeates and the other representatives of law and order are made to look silly by the machiavellian Mr. Canty. Major Yeates moves through the series as the perfect exponent of the Anglo-Irish experience, the Englishman in him outraged by the lunacies of his encounters, the Irishman in him warmly responding to it all, the magistrate lost in the man and his desperate efforts after official propriety scattered to the winds by his English wife's delighted laughter.

Special scorn is reserved, as always with these writers, for one species only, the uncomprehending English tourist, most memorably embodied in the unhappy Leigh Kelway of **"Lisheen Races, Second-Hand."** This beautifully constructed story reduces the smugness of the visiting Briton to shreds in a series of tightly controlled declensions. As we jolt with him through the countryside in a series of doomed journeys, fated never to reach the race-meeting and increasingly embroiled in the murkiness of Irish events and Irish speech, we rejoice in the uproarious overthrow of all his English simplicities. Never has race-meeting been so memorably unvisited, never has the English failure to understand the Irish been so completely and good-humouredly demonstrated. There lie behind the story both a wealth of technical expertise on the part of the writers and the controlled, colonial resentment of an entire class. Leigh Kelway, a sort of Miss Hope-Drummond in trousers, comes to Ireland to write up "the liquor question" and moves inexorably to the dreadful, country pub where Slipper delivers his celebrated description of the Lisheen Races and Driscoll's "death." His final undoing, as the outraged Lord Waterbury surveys him lying in the ruins of two coaches on the roadside, is a superbly contrived climax to a brilliantly managed narrative.

This first volume of *R.M.* stories contains one of a tragic nature, **"The Waters of Strife,"** a story written during the second half of the November in which Martin sustained her severe fall. It is fourth in the series and appeared in the January 1899 issue of the *Badminton Magazine.* A quarrel after a local regatta leads to a fight in which Bat Callaghan kills Jim Foley. The murderer disappears and the police, though they succeed in satisfying themselves of Callaghan's guilt, fail to find the murderer. Callaghan pays a mysterious midnight visit to Major Yeates's house to inform him of the whereabouts of his victim's corpse and Mrs. Callaghan, Bat's mother, solicits the Major's assistance to keep her out of court. Time passes and the affair is gradually forgotten. Later, Major Yeats is invited to a stag-party by his old regiment who wish to make him a presentation in honour of his forthcoming marriage. While he is a guest at the regiment's quarters, one of the sentries, an Irishman named Harris, shoots at a face which is staring at him from the top of a high wall. When the face continues to stare at him, Harris goes mad and shoots himself. Next morning Major Yeates recognizes "Harris" as Bat Callaghan, done to death by the ghost of his victim who has been conjured up by his guilty conscience.

The story is quite unlike anything else in this first volume of *R.M.* stories in that it concerns itself seriously with a tragedy which takes place outside the secure world of the Major and Flurry and Mrs. Knox. No very profound exploration of this world, which is seen as one of violence and superstition, **"The Waters of Strife"** is nevertheless held together and given a certain validity by the economical and effectively pathetic depiction of Bat's mother, the Widow Callaghan. Her letter, found in the dead man's pocket, has a ring of accuracy about it reminiscent of Synge. This darker world, on the periphery of the jocund arena in which the majority of the *R.M.* stories are played out, is allowed to intrude but rarely into the sunny center of things. In the second volume of *R.M.* stories, the earlier part of **"Oweneen the Sprat"** shows the Major's comfortable world being intimidated by menace from the darker periphery, the Major himself being the culprit on this occasion. However, this later story is resolved in a comic exposure of the blackmailers and the Major's universe is restored to its customary serenity. Inside the laager, the common people appear as supple-tongued servants, outside they are, usually, amiable adjuncts to the comedy but very occasionally, as in **"The Waters of Strife,"** a discordant note intrudes. There is just enough of this darker mode to hint at the writers' awareness of the fragile unreality of the world of comedy they are spreading before us.

The first volume of the *R.M.* stories ends in triumphant comedy with Flurry Knox's wedding to Sally Knox and the resolving of the dispute between old Mrs. Knox and Lady Knox. **"Oh Love, Oh Fire!"** is a merry mélange of dancing and devious dalliance which winds up the book on a suitable note of lovers' meetings at journey's end. This last story appeared in the *Badminton Magazine* in September 1899, and a mere two months later the series was put into book form by Longmans. The speed with which they moved to publication is a tribute to the popularity of the stories as they appeared and to the publishers' conviction that the series made a satisfactory unit. As invariably happens with such sets of stories, a few, while functioning adequately within the group, work less well on their own account. One recalls how this occurs even in Joyce's *Dubliners,* where "After the Race" is clearly a thinner story than many of the others, one which more requires the support given to it by its context in the group of which it is part. Similarly, in the first *R.M.* book, **"The Policy of the Closed Door,"** while furthering the courtship of Flurry and Sally Knox, does little else of real interest or value. Because it is so dependent on its setting in the series as a whole, it is less artistically autonomous than many of the other stories.

Major Yeates is the key to the book's success. He is the perfect guide to the world we explore with him, the most genial and likeable of hosts. Maurice Collis, in a felicitously Anglo-Irish lapse, surely caused by a nudge from Slipper's ghost, tells us that "Major Yeates is partially of Irish abstraction, but the Irish scene is quite new to him." Yes, indeed! Later on, of course, when the Irish scene is no longer quite so new to him, the major is rather less "abstracted" but he remains at all times entirely "partial." It is his partiality which woos and wins us. (pp. 57-61)

[In] the autumn of 1908 *Further Experiences of an Irish R.M.* was published by Longmans and sold extremely well, new editions being constantly called for.

In this second series, Major Yeates is rather less the neophyte than he has previously been. In fact, we learn in the opening story, **"The Pug-Nosed Fox,"** that he is actually deputy M.F.H. in place of Flurry Knox, during the latter's absence with the Irish Yeomanry at the South African War. The Major is still wax in the hands of the locals but he scores over Flurry on quite a number of occasions, notably in the concluding story, **"The Whiteboys,"** where he is allowed to triumph in Flurry's special, canine province. The Major is now the proud but harassed father of two rather pestilential boys who are given to taking fright at the slightest strange incident, a habit which would seem to render them peculiarly unfitted for the hectic universe they are called upon to inhabit. Children are not the *forte* of these writers, any more than passionate love scenes.

One of the finest of the *R.M.* stories is **"Poisson D'Avril,"** in which the Major, on his way to a family wedding at the English home of their relative, Alice Hervey, undergoes a series of hilarious adventures in improbable trains and crowded country hotels. Edith and Martin, who spent a good deal of time on various temperamental Irish trains, are particularly amusing when they describe the vicissitudes of rail travel. The cheerless waiting rooms where the fires smoke but do not burn, the unexplained halts at unidentified spots on the line, the angry English travellers who find it all quite intolerable, the highly individualistic railway officials who are prepared to advise passengers on the buying of salmon but profess to know nothing about timetables—over it all broods what the story calls "the inveterate supremacy in Ireland of the personal element." Inevitably, the Major misses his connection with the Mail Train and finds himself stranded at Loughranny. The town is thronged for an Irish festival of music and dance and Major Yeates is lucky to get a bed on a palliasse under the billiard-table in the local hotel. His early-morning encounter with the First Prize for Reels, who has spent the night on top of the billiard table and whose feet are "like

three-pound loaves with the dint of the little dancing-shoes I had on me in the competition last night," is entirely a delight. His eventual arrival at Alice Hervey's very English home with quite the wrong sort of parcel provides one of the best climaxes in the series. As in **"Lisheen Races, Second Hand,"** this story of another comic journey is beautifully constructed with a fine balance of comic incident and dialogue. There is no straining after effect, no uneasiness in the handling of the characters. The Major is at his most endearing as he struggles with his perennial task of reconciling the demands of his two universes and comes inevitably to grief. Another equally effective story is **"The Last Day of Shraft."** In this, the Major finds himself burdened with a troublesome visitor in the shape of Philippa's elderly stepbrother, Maxwell Bruce, who is an Irish-language and folklore enthusiast. The series of misadventures by which the Major, local representative of law and order, and his serious-minded brother-in-law find themselves warmly entrapped in Mrs. Brickley's shebeen in a fume of illicit whiskey and old Irish song is delightfully contrived. The humor is worthy of a Flann O'Brien.

Much less happy are the effects achieved in the story **"Sharper Than a Ferret's Tooth,"** in which we once again encounter the McRory family, whom we have previously met in **"The Pug-Nosed Fox."** The McRorys are cheerful parvenus who have been socially accepted (after a struggle) because the sons are handsome, the daughters pretty and cheerful and the mother good-humoredly prepared to buy generously at local bazaars. In the clumsily-titled **"Sharper Than a Ferret's Tooth,"** Philippa and Miss Shute are trying to marry off Bernard Shute to the Major's niece, Sybil Hervey. Sybil is, unfortunately, more interested in the handsome Curly McRory. As a result of a minor mishap in a boat, the Major's entire party finds itself stranded in the McRory house, dripping wet, in need of clothes and hot food and drink. All these things are provided instantly by the open-handed McRorys who entertain the whole party royally. The snag is that Sybil is thrown into Curly's willing arms, thus frustrating Philippa's and Miss Shute's matchmaking plans for Bernard. The situation is an anticipation, on the comic level, of aspects of Edith's later novel, *Mount Music.* In fact, Mrs. McRory is clearly the prototype of Mrs. Mangan in the later work. It would seem to be the writers' aim to depict the McRorys (as Edith later depicts the Mangans) as cheerful vulgarians. The trouble is that it is the "gentry" group whose vulgarity is here most clearly exposed. The McRorys' only sin is that they rescue the dripping voyagers, clothe them, feed them, entertain them and captivate the "lady" intended for Bernard Shute. The complacent vulgarity of the "gentry" group is exposed in a fashion which can hardly, one feels, have been the writers' intention. Philippa, Sally Knox and Miss Shute jeer at Mrs. McRory's taste in clothes and sneer when they are offered "a choice of about eighty silk blouses." Even the Major is allowed a mild sneer at the immaculate "Lounge Suit" lent to him by the handsome Curly. The elaborate meal offered by the McRorys is made the subject of further mockery: the food is of the wrong kind, wrongly served and there is too much of it anyhow. The whole point is that "real gentry" can afford to do without this kind of crude excess, that money is no substitute for blood. Unfortunately, bad manners are no substitute for courtesy. The writers, on this occasion, actually make us dislike the Major's family group and their associates, a bad error which conflicts with the whole nature of the series and shatters the convention within which they are working. The comedy of situation at which they excel has momentarily broken down and something unpleasant from the real world has briefly intruded. On the whole, Edith was to handle such complications more tolerantly and more acceptably in her later novels. (pp. 63-6)

. . . . .

The seven years between the publication of the second volume of *R.M.* stories and the death of Violet Martin produced only two further works of any importance, the rather lightweight novel, ***Dan Russel the Fox,*** in 1911 and the third and final volume of the *R.M.* stories published in the year of Martin's death, 1915, under the title ***In Mr Knox's Country.*** It is matter for genuine regret that the partners had not, with the creative confidence engendered in them by ***The Real Charlotte,*** moved on from that fine novel to even greater fictional heights. Their failure to do so may be explained in various ways. Pinker, who had become their literary agent in 1896, and Longmans, pleased by the success of the *R.M.* stories, constantly pressed them to produce more work of that nature and the cousins' need for money forced them to comply with this request instead of devoting to their fictions the slow and careful preparation which had gone to the making of ***The Real Charlotte.*** (pp. 67-8)

Dan Russel the Fox had been begun as early as 1904, while the writers were at Amélie-les-Bains in the interests of Martin's health; but they had abandoned the novel after a few chapters and did not resume it until 1909 when they were at Portofino with Hildegarde and a friend, Miss Nora Tracey. It is a longer novel than ***The Silver Fox*** and handles the same themes in a more straightforward manner, omitting the element of fantasy. Wealthy, young English heiress, Katherine Rowan, on holiday at Aix-les-Bains with a friend, Mrs. Masterman, has an encounter with a dapper and engaging little Irishwoman, Mrs. Delanty, as a result of which she comes to Ireland for an extended stay. The visit turns into the usual process of discovery of the strange land. Katherine becomes a devotee of the hunt and the book broadens into a series of hunting scenes which are portrayed with great vigor. Katherine, having fallen in love with the hunt, now proceeds to make the mistake of falling in love also with the huntsman, one John Michael Fitz-Symons, younger brother of the Master of the Hunt. John Michael is handsome and inarticulate and Katherine's involvement with him infuriates her other suitor, a writer named Ulick Adare. Adare proposes to Katherine, in a scene where the girl's embarrassment seems to reflect the authors' inability to handle such passages:

> "You might be as rude to me as you liked; it would be better than torture." The last word was almost inaudible.
>
> Katherine took a step backwards, so sudden was the shock, and so strangely mixed with it the instinct to get away from him.

> "That's putting it rather strongly," she said, red to the roots of her hair, but still trying hard to be commonplace.

Mrs. Delanty, the neat, capable little Irishwoman responsible for attracting Katherine to Ireland, is, however, a successful creation and her gulling of the silly Fanshawe is amusingly handled. John Michael, a combination of sex appeal and stupidity, is a sort of inarticulate Mellors who insists on confining his attention to game-keeping (or, in John Michael's case, to hounds). The writers' inability to follow through to any kind of logical conclusion the consequences of Katherine's sexual interest in the unresponsive John Michael produces a number of awkward scenes, culminating in a tortuously contrived climax at the Fitz-Symons' house. Mrs. Fitz-Symons urges her stolid son to propose marriage to Katherine and he recoils in horror from the suggestion, loudly asserting that he would "sooner sweep a kennel in America" than offer himself in marriage to the lady. Katherine overhears his unflattering protestations and is abruptly restored by the shock to the safety of the bosom of her own class. As the novel closes, she is back once more on the continent, convalescing safely at Portofino, and Ulick Adare is about to sail into her life once again:

> As for Ireland, Ireland was a tradition, a grey spot astray upon a misty ocean. In a remote past things had happened there; she thought of them as little as possible, but sometimes they sprang upon her unawares, and made her understand that we may regret our sins, but we agonize over our follies.

The progress of the novel, lively enough at times, is badly flawed by the writers' unwillingness to pursue the implications of the sexual motifs they sound. Even when Mrs. Delanty, who is no English lady but merely a vulgar and calculating little Irish nobody with a good figure, offers herself to the incredible John Michael, reluctance is the response of the writers as well as the swain:

> "Johnny!" she cried, beginning to sob, "wouldn't you stay for my sake? Don't you know how fond I am of you?"
>
> What more she said neither she nor John Michael can ever clearly remember, nor do they desire to do so, but in that insane moment of surrender and self-forgetfulness, the small, second-rate, egotistical soul of Mrs. Delanty found wings, and spread them in a larger air.
>
> It was over in an instant, and she knew that she had given herself away for nothing. They were standing opposite each other in suffocating tension and embarrassment.

Mrs. Delanty is forced to console herself by marrying the equally egregious but conveniently infatuated Fanshawe.

In a sense, we are unhappily back once more with the grosser simplicities of some of the earlier fiction. English heiresses do not marry Irish huntsmen, and if they are indiscreet enough to lust after them then they must be shepherded away to safer places, however gauche the contrivance which ensures their deliverance. Violet Powell describes the novel as "well-constructed" but many of the characters are mere stereotypes. In *Dan Russel the Fox* the R.M. world is being uneasily used for the exploration of character and motive. The weakness of the novel is caused by a clash of conventions and the writers' unwillingness or inability to write frankly about sex. (pp. 69-72)

The year 1915, which was to rob Edith of her collaborator, saw the publication of the third and final volume of *R.M.* stories. Shortly afterwards, in *Irish Memories,* she described the circumstances in which this volume came into being:

> I suppose it was the result of old habit, and of the return of the hounds, but, for whatever reason, during the years that followed the appearance of *Dan Russel the Fox,* Martin and I put aside the notions we had been dwelling upon in connection with "a serious novel," and took to writing *R.M.* stories again. These, six couple of them (like the first draft of the re-established pack), wandered through various periodicals, chiefly *Blackwood's Magazine,* and, in July, 1915, they were published in a volume with the title of *In Mr Knox's Country.*

One of the stories in this collection, **"When I First Met Dr Hickey,"** harks back, as its title suggests, to the early days of Major Yeates's stay in Ireland. When Edith later edited a full collection of the *R.M.* stories she placed this one immediately after the opening story, **"Great Uncle McCarthy."** It is a pleasant story, which moves at a brisk pace and has a suitably uproarious climax. In general, however, the stories in this last volume depict both an ageing major and an ageing Ireland. The Major and Flurry Knox are greying and the large estates have passed, through a series of Land Acts, out of the possession of the gentry. In **"The Finger of Mrs Knox"** the mood is mordantly nostalgic. The Major and Mrs. Knox sit by the fire in the hall of Aussolas Castle, reminiscing about the past and are visited by Stephen Casey, the son of one of Mrs. Knox's former tenants. Casey is in the clutches of Goggin, a local "gombeen," a figure similar to Jeremiah Donovan of *Naboth's Vineyard.* Unable to pay his debt to Goggin, Stephen Casey runs the risk of having his cattle seized in settlement of his debt and appeals to Mrs. Knox for assistance. Her bitter reply reveals the change in the times:

> "I have no tenants," replied Mrs. Knox tartly; "the Government is your landlord now, and I wish you joy of each other!"

With suitably touching loyalty, Casey protests his preference for the old paternalistic order of things and is sent round to the servants' hall for his tea, while the lady of the manor broods over his problem. In the event, she prevails against Goggin on Casey's behalf and the stark issues of the situation are dissolved in a comic hunting debacle, with the Major acting as a convenient catalyst. In spite of the comedy, however, there is no mistaking the presence of a sunset touch. The old days are gone for ever and a new and less congenial order is taking the place of the hereditary ascendancy.

Not all the stories carry these ominous overtones. **"The Bosom of the McRorys"** and **"The Comte de Pralines"** are cheerful romps in the series' most relaxed manner. In **"The Friend of Her Youth"** the central figure of Chichester recalls the unfortunate Leigh Kelway of **"Lisheen Races Second Hand."** He is "an elderly young man, worn smooth by much visiting in country houses" and he is made to come to grief among a hearty yachting set, a milieu which recalls parts of *The Real Charlotte* and of earlier *R.M.* stories. Altogether, this last collection of *R.M.* stories, though intermittently very funny, has in it both overtones of bitterness and a strong sense of *déjà-vu.* The writers fall back on situations often exploited before and there is not, in this book, any sense of a coherent chronological progress such as governs the other two in the series. (pp. 72-4)

> *John Cronin, in his* Somerville and Ross, *Bucknell University Press, 1972, 111 p.*

Wayne E. Hall   (essay date 1980)

[*In the excerpt below, Hall examines Somerville and Ross's views on the political reforms occurring in Ireland at the time their novels were written. Hall also discusses* The Irish R.M. *stories and* The Real Charlotte *as reflections on the vanishing way of life of the Anglo-Irish upper class.*]

The most complete fictional account of the decline of the landed gentry in nineteenth-century Ireland comes from the novels of Somerville and Ross, writers who had almost no contact with the "official" members of the Irish Renaissance, who, in fact, regarded such organizations as the Gaelic League as "secretly highly disloyal." Yet their combined experiences brought to their collaborations an epic breadth that depicts the Protestant Ascendancy in relation to every other major social force in Ireland and that produced, in *The Real Charlotte* (1894), perhaps the greatest Irish novel of the nineteenth century. The Somervilles of Drishane and the Martins of Ross, the house whose name Violet Martin attached to her share of the authorship, both suffered the economic and political losses that systematically eliminated the Irish landed gentry. The two cousins recognized the place their own families occupied in the decisive social transition—within the span of only three generations, Ross House slipped from financial stability into abandonment and near ruin. In writing of such processes, Somerville and Ross maintain a realistic, detached, often ironic tone. But the fiction cannot overcome a deeply felt regret for the lost way of life; their sympathies and point of view remain bound to those of the Big House.

The latter part of the nineteenth century is portrayed most completely in the novel Edith Somerville rightly called the "best of our books," *The Real Charlotte.* The novel preserves the atmosphere of an aristocracy in the brilliant and idle autumn of its power. The Dysarts of Bruff, wealthy Protestant landholders and the center of social activity in the town of Lismoyle, host and attend a season's worth of teas, picnics, tennis parties, and outings on the lake with the British officers. The Dysarts form only the top layer of a society that includes wealthy farmers and land agents, extends down through shopkeepers and tradesmen, and reaches to the servants and finally to the beggars. The authors range widely. But always they control the separate elements with familiarity and realism; with a precisely directed prose style; with contrasts that balance one class against another; and also with the complex strength of one central character, Charlotte Mullen.

Charlotte unites the novel's cross section of classes and interests. Closely involved in all the shifting balances of power, she uses her shrewd plots to influence the fortunes of many other characters, for good as well as for ill. She converses as easily with the inner circle of Bruff's aristocracy as she does with the Catholic tenants and beggars. Early in the novel she inherits a sizable amount of money that provides much of the capital behind her swift rise in the society, from the level of tenant to that of an actual landed proprietor. Even more than on the useful financial backing, however, Charlotte relies for her successes on a powerful will, intelligence, and social audacity. When she ultimately fails, therefore, the loss cuts deeply into every level of the society whose fate she has linked with her own. She may resort to underhanded tactics or bully her opposition into acquiescence, but her most ambitious scheme has the sensible and sympathetic goal of marrying her cousin Francie into the Dysart family and thus continuing the aristocratic line. Her inability to carry through her plan both results from and helps perpetuate the decay weakening the whole society—the declining fortunes of the Protestant Ascendancy.

Somerville and Ross follow most of the Irish writers of this period in attaching more weight to the internal decay of the Ascendancy than to the newly emerging economic and political structures beyond its control. Although Charlotte does not belong to that class, she represents a rejuvenating strength that might succeed in restoring the power of the Big House. The gains of the Irish middle class came in large part out of the pockets and privileges of the upper class. In their opposition to these gains, the authors depreciate the value of Charlotte's materialistic goals and cause her ultimately to fail at what she wants most. Yet the hope that Charlotte's vital practicality may unite with and inspire the Ascendancy balances the authors' suspicion of the rising middle class and brings to Charlotte's character a unity of attractive and repulsive traits that is psychologically and aesthetically effective. Charlotte's plan for her cousin's marriage holds out the distinct promise of success and renewal. Human action, however, has little effect on restoring the dwindling power of the Big Houses; the old feudal order cannot be joined to new sources of energy. With the old values extinct, no one wins any meaningful control over Ireland's future, not the gentry, and not the middle classes who acquire a material power that has lost its moral worth. The authors can finally only stand back and observe this failure, much as they did within their own families, with an attitude of sometimes amused, sometimes horrified, dismay. (pp. 64-6)

Even as she continued to support the old economic system, therefore, Somerville also recognized the part that the gentry had played in its own ruin. Her 1925 novel, *The Big House of Inver*, uses the Prendeville estate to chronicle the entire history of the Protestant Ascendancy of the

nineteenth century. From its earliest beginnings in nobility and splendor, the family line soon became corrupted by marriages into the lower class and, even more so, by its own brilliant but debilitating extravagance. She does not withhold admiration for the aristocratic gallantry of their lives, for all the epic waste; yet she feels the tragedy of it as well. The landed class had dealt too recklessly with its resources and by the end of the century had none left to fall back on. Never feeling as committed as Violet Martin to the old way of life, Somerville wrote in 1917:

> Things are better now. . . . Inspectors, instructors, remission of rents, land purchase, State loans, English money in various forms, have improved the conditions in a way that would hardly have been credible thirty years ago, when, in these congested districts, semi-famine was chronic.

Yet the deep-rooted sympathies and instinctive assumptions that had shaped *The Real Charlotte* in 1894 remained firm throughout both their lives. Prosperity for the large mass of people and bureaucratic thoroughness do not necessarily create moral ideals or provide acceptable substitutes for the cast-off traditional values. Somerville and Ross could understand the passage of the old order into history and appreciate the new social institutions; but their first and strongest loyalties remained always with the Big House.

They recognized, years before most members of their landed class, that the old system of land ownership and social privileges was nearing its end, paralyzed by its own feudal sensibilities and extravagances. Yet historical perception formed only one part of the authors' sense of their class. Literature also gave them a way of evoking the past and using it to measure and judge the new, rising interests. Their recreation of the old social order continues to mourn the loss of that way of life, even as it admits the loss. With all its strengths and limitations, the vantage point of the Protestant Ascendancy serves as the dominating center of their work. They accurately describe the fate of many once great estates, yet their work passes, perhaps too lightly, over the fate of the large mass of the peasantry. While estates might go bankrupt, the tenants faced eviction and starvation. People who remembered these harsher sacrifices more vividly than the relief payments, emergency supplies, and financial losses of the gentry increasingly saw the Big Houses of Ireland as a symbol of exploitation rather than protection. (pp. 69-70)

Until Martin's death in 1915, the two writers frequently lived and traveled together, sometimes gathering material for a book or article on their excursions. Even when separated, as during Martin's efforts with her mother to reopen and restore the poorly managed Ross mansion in 1888, the two regularly corresponded on various writing projects. Their first novels, *An Irish Cousin* (1889) and *Naboth's Vineyard* (1891), rely heavily on sinister family intrigues that threaten sentimental love affairs. Critics took little notice of the works, although the *Lady's Pictorial* printed the second novel as well as two of the travel books that brought the authors the most attention in the early 1890s. Their greatest success came with the publication in 1899 of *Some Experiences of an Irish R.M.*, reprinted five times the year it appeared. Two other collections of R.M. stories followed: *Further Experiences of an Irish R.M.* (1908), still riding the wave of the earlier work's popularity, had a first edition of 10,000 copies; *In Mr. Knox's Country* (1915) completed the series of marvelously comic stories. (p. 71)

Major Yeates, the Resident Magistrate (or R.M.), is a decent and innocent Englishman assigned to judicial duty in an Ireland that persistently defies his reason and comprehension. The first account of his adventures, *Some Experiences of an Irish R.M.,* opens with his acquisition of one of the marginally less dilapidated country houses in the West. Unknown to him, the squatters who previously enjoyed the house move to the attic and, fortified now with the Major's whiskey as well as the game from his estate, go on with their poaching practice. Their activities inevitably and hilariously come to light, but the pattern continues to plague Yeates throughout the book: even in the comparative safety of his own home, he is not immune from the shrewd but questionable schemes of the native Irish. The well-meaning representative of legal authority, he fails to keep even himself from becoming an accomplice, unwilling or unwitting, in later plots of dubious legal or moral nature.

Because of his professional status, Major Yeates is also compelled to participate in frequent social events not of his choosing or liking. His wife Philippa organizes many of these, in blithe disregard for her husband's longing for a little peace and quiet. In his marriage as well as in his dealings with the neighbors, Yeates most commonly finds himself manipulated by life's circumstances. He does enjoy fox hunting, however, and in their attention to complicated, madcap action in this work, Somerville and Ross achieve their most poetic effects in the many descriptions of the hunt. The Irish Literary Revival could easily dismiss them as witty observers of gentry sporting-life. For their many readers, on the other hand, the hunting scenes became the most characteristic and best-loved feature of the *R.M.* stories.

Part of the work's appeal, outside Ireland, lay in its reinforcement of the stage-Irish characters previously found in Charles Lever or William Carleton. The peasantry can be very helpful on hunts, battering down rough walls for the horses or hysterically shrieking directions for the riders. In other affairs, however, they resemble old Handy Andy—unreliable but good natured, untrustworthy but colorful in their voluble explanations. One story, **"The Holy Island,"** recounts the predictable fate of a shipwrecked cargo of rum. Despite the best efforts of the police, the peasants manage to loot the casks and either get totally drunk or sneak the plunder off for a profitable resale to the pubs. Ireland is a holy island, the authors ironically suggest, only in the minds of the most naive of its inhabitants.

The character of Flurry Knox unites these stories as much as that of the Major. His main occupation is horse dealing, for Flurry can scheme and maneuver with the best. Unlike Yeates, but similar to Charlotte Mullen, Flurry makes things happen, moving easily up and down the various levels in his society as circumstances require. He changes

over the course of the stories, however. Just as Yeates becomes more the knowledgeable local, Flurry becomes more domesticated and serious. His marriage is the final event in the work, another intricate scheme that accompanies his inheritance of his grandmother's large estate. On the wedding day the shockingly cultivated dress and behavior of Slipper, the omnipresent idler and notorious poacher, suggest huge changes in the state of the world. Normality quickly returns to the landscape, however. Slipper is discovered the next day, drunk as usual, his trappings of respectability scattered in the ditch.

The world of the Irish R.M. resists change, and therein lay a good part of its appeal, both to the English readers and to Somerville and Ross themselves. Their Irish people exist in an innocent and good-humored past, in an imagined period before such characters as resident magistrates had become the intensely hated alien representatives of English law. In *Wheel-Tracks,* a 1923 collection of earlier pieces and autobiographical sketches, Somerville described the Irishman who had supplanted those like Slipper.

> America and National Schools have created a new variety of Irishman, with his sense of humour drugged by self-conceit, with not enough education to reveal to him his ignorance, and with the bad manners inspired, apparently, by Democracy, which seems to act as an autointoxicant, with a result that is an indifferent substitute for the generous power of hero-worship.

The Irish of the *R.M.* stories, for all their exasperating foibles, at least kept their sense of humor. And, more importantly, they kept their place. With an epic scope more complete than that of any other writer of the Irish Renaissance, Somerville and Ross captured the dilemma of the Protestant Ascendancy, its apprehensive and indefinite position between the native Irish and alien English. Their own sense of humor, however, came under increasing strain. In late 1898 Martin took a fall from a horse and suffered the severe back injury from which she never wholly recovered. Her health made the sustained and taxing effort of another serious work like *The Real Charlotte* seem out of reach for the remaining years of their collaboration. The depleted resources of Ross and Drishane further demanded more of the *R.M.* stories that had proven so successful commercially. The fate of the old social order, turning increasingly to the tragedy that had marked *The Real Charlotte,* instead helped lead the two writers deeper into the comic world of the R.M.

The Real Charlotte began as a skeleton scenario in 1889. A year later Somerville and Ross were hard at work on the novel and finished it in the summer of 1892; revising and editing took another year. Publishers proved reluctant to take the manuscript, but Ward and Downey finally bought the rights for £250 and published it in three volumes in May 1894. Uneasy about their first three-decker and their most serious and ambitious work so far, the authors felt disappointed by some of the first reviews and the reactions among members of the two families, who disliked the "unpleasantness" of the novel. Within a year, however, the initial opposition gave way before the critics who acclaimed the work as perhaps the finest Irish novel of the century.

The Real Charlotte is about failure and loss (or, "unpleasantness"). It studies a broad section of Irish society of the late nineteenth century and finds that society characterized by decline, victim to a relentless string of defeats and dispossessions. No one gains anything substantial through his or her efforts, and only a few characters just manage to break even. The staggering record of failure needs emphasis early in a discussion of the novel because of the ease with which we as readers overlook it. In one measure of its success, the novel lures us into the same kind of ill-fated dreams that entangle the characters. The frequently light, witty tone conceals the underlying darkness, as do the dreams themselves, many of them attractive and sensible, seemingly within reach. But always a plan that has such promise ends in shambles, or a sympathetic character fails at some crucial point. Until the very end we believe that something will turn out right. And as events sweep aside even the final hope, we, like the servant who brings the last piece of tragic news, like the authors themselves, can only turn aside helplessly from the ruin.

In leading up to each failure or loss, the novel frequently creates situations of contrast: someone's external appearance versus his inner motivations, or his present status versus his past, or his own behavior versus that of another character who, although in similar circumstances, belongs to a different social group. The contrasts partially define by negation and elimination, by determining what a character is not. "Washerwomen do not, as a rule, assimilate the principles of their trade." This statement contains much that is characteristically Somerville and Ross. The artificially elevated diction and point of view establish an ironic contrast between language and experience. The qualifier "as a rule" adds to the irony and also gently tempers the directness of an already indirect statement. The authors distance themselves through such techniques from the world of the novel just enough to prevent too complete an identification with any character. As detached, critical, slightly amused observers, they finally refuse an entanglement in the potentially disappointing outcome. No character, therefore, earns unqualified admiration and sympathy. For us, the irony, the qualifiers, and the statements of negation, the whole manner of definition, reveal enough through indirection to make the characters engagingly attractive, bad habits and all. Only gradually do we learn of the futility of their efforts, something the authors have foreseen all along.

The novel emphasizes the differences common to many characters between their inner and outer selves. With the definitions of character originating from such a distanced point of view, Charlotte requires the most attention. Because of her more complex motives and more intelligent schemes, the "real" Charlotte emerges only after a wide range of observations, and then only dimly. She resembles

> some amphibious thing, whose strong, darting course under the water is only marked by a bubble or two, and it required almost an animal instinct to note them. . . . but people never thought of looking out for these indications in

Charlotte, or even suspected that she had anything to conceal.

She thus functions as a limiting force on the other characters in the novel; if one could succeed in comprehending Charlotte, in charting the subsurface movements of her nature, then one could exercise some control over the various influences pressing in on the society. Action could become effective. Instead, only rare and easily overlooked signs hint to the others that the real Charlotte differs from what she seems.

One of the most vividly realistic of the early pictures of her reveals Charlotte keeping a lonely watch over the sick-bed of her dying aunt:

> Probably at no moment of her forty years of life had Miss Charlotte Mullen looked more startlingly plain than now, as she stood, her squat figure draped in a magenta flannel dressing-gown, and the candle light shining upon her face. . . . The lines about her prominent mouth and chin were deeper than usual; her broad cheeks had a flabby pallor; only her eyes were bright and untired, and the thick yellow-white hand that manipulated the hair-pin was as deft as it was wont to be.

The description follows the sequence of other characters' perceptions of Charlotte. Her unattractive shapelessness at first appears pathetic and vulnerable, the candle light and deep-red dressing gown only emphasizing a loveless existence that will never lure a man to her bedroom. Yet Charlotte's eyes betray her intensity and strength. In a novel whose characters so often lack energy and the ability to act decisively, her deft competence arouses our interest and makes her increasingly sympathetic and attractive as the central figure.

Charlotte directs her usually successful schemes with a quick intelligence, but even more with her powerful will. In the most straightforward of her major plans, she wants ownership of Gurthnamuckla, a particularly valuable holding on the Dysarts' large estate. Julia Duffy occupies the farm but has let it slide progressively deeper into ruin, thus completing the decay of her family's position, a loss of respectability even more humiliating in comparison to Charlotte's rise in society. Although Charlotte claims that at one time her ancestors ranked with the Dysart family, Julia and the Lismoyle society rather think of her as the daughter of a national schoolmistress and the granddaughter of a "barefooted country girl."

Beneath its veneer of poverty, Gurthnamuckla remains an attractive piece of property. With it, Charlotte could become even more important in Lismoyle as a landed proprietor and the "lady of the manor." The farm's pastures offer rich grazing land and an opportunity to work more closely with Roderick Lambert, to "stable our horses together," as Lambert suggests. Formerly a pupil in her father's house, he managed to acquire the position of land agent for the Bruff estate. Her long, deeply felt love for him has proven "more costly to Charlotte than any other thing that had ever befallen her." The passion she has had to repress when Lambert once rejected her brings to Charlotte's plots even more emotional intensity. For a woman of her position, intelligence, and abilities, Ireland in the 1880s would have offered few opportunities outside the financial consolidations of a shrewd marriage. As an example of what women had to face in other professional endeavors, Charlotte could have taken a lesson from Parnell's perfunctory suppression of the Ladies' Land League in 1882, an organization headed by his own sisters.

Lambert thus becomes the highly desired object in a further major scheme, and marriage seems a real possibility when his wife dies. Charlotte simultaneously hopes to arrange a marriage of her first cousin, Francie Fitzpatrick, to Christopher Dysart and that family fortune. The highflown, at times outrageous, ambition of these schemes actually detracts little from our agreement with Charlotte that they make a lot of sense. Lambert is a cheap, flashy opportunist, and a petty embezzler besides; but he's more pathetic than evil or despicable. Despite his conviction that he has "raised himself just high enough from the sloughs of Irish middle-class society to see its vulgarity" and to feel slightly repulsed by Charlotte, he has already wed once for money. Marriage could break the spiral of disappointment in Charlotte's personal life. And through the second plotted match, Francie could inspire Christopher to shake off his personal lethargy, his lack of "confidence in anything about himself except his critical ability," in a marriage that would both renew and carry on the Dysart family line.

But too many forces work against success, and nothing turns out right. Francie rejects Christopher and thus occasions one of those spasms of fury when "the weight of the real Charlotte's will, and the terror of her personality" burst through to the surface. Charlotte's strength of will later faces a much harsher test with the news of Lambert's betrayal: he has somehow won Francie's hand. The first loss leaves society the poorer; the second cuts Charlotte personally and goads her truly to revenge. Her last and most inspired plot, fueled by her despair and rage, finishes by destroying Lambert, Francie, even Charlotte herself. She not only gains crushing financial power over Lambert, she offers to Francie the possibility of leaving him and running off with the superficially romantic British officer Hawkins. Lambert finally realizes the horror of what Charlotte has done to him, but their confrontation, and the novel, end abruptly with news that appalls them both: Francie has been killed in a fall from a horse. Charged in her aunt's dying wish to care for Francie with the inheritance that Charlotte instead used primarily to foster her own social advancement, Charlotte must now confront her most awesome personal failure.

Francie offered the cheeriest possibility for a happy ending of some sort. She possesses boundless energy and charm and an irrepressible optimism that more than compensate for her lack of seriousness and cultivated taste. An orphan, raised in Dublin, she brings the city's intensity to Lismoyle when she comes under Charlotte's care. Vulgarity, one of the novel's recurrent concepts, clashes with the more traditional standards of the agrarian community, but Francie injects some badly needed imagination and freshness into a fading society. Somerville wrote of her: "We knew her best; we were fondest of her." Her fatal

spill, the last of five deaths, seems the most tragic, especially when we recall the energy and success that characterized her initial escapades.

The frequent social events provide contrasts between many characters. Their breeding and cultivated poise, or lack of those crucial qualities, emerge from such affairs as the tea party given by the Beatties. We first see how Lady Dysart manages her lawn tennis party and thus can more accurately gauge the Beatties' upper-middle-class affair, the awkward uncertainty beneath their show of gentility. Charlotte's tea party falls to a lower level still, and even the servants have their social rituals. The comparisons, the details peculiar to each level, define a good part of the class differences and also suggest the relative worth of each. Francie, riding on her background in such democratic institutions as the Dublin Sunday School, which "permeates all ranks," proves capable of shifting freely from one class to the next. The unaffected luxury and quiet, meditative elegance of Bruff not only awes her, it offers her a way of life the authors see as qualitatively better.

The ease with which Christopher Dysart becomes fascinated with Francie and then idealizes her abilities and talents suggests the possibility that she might well move among the aristocracy as his wife some day. In teaching her about poetry, "he had found out subtle depths of sweetness and sympathy that were, in their responsiveness, equivalent to intellect." The irony does not entirely mask the sexuality of the language. Even though Christopher continues to appear "infinitely remote" in Francie's mind, "her pliant soul rose through its inherited vulgarities, and gained some vision of higher things." She can shed the limitations of her class more easily than she can her fascination with Hawkins, however. Although the suave, irresponsible officer once seemed to her a star "of unimagined magnitude," Francie finds him more comprehensible than Christopher. Feeling comfortable within the conventional language he uses in their love scenes, she allows herself to be overpowered by his sheer animal charm. Christopher, by comparison, speaks often of kindness in wooing Francie. He respects her more than does Lambert and his smothering, selfish concern. When she puts up a front of independence, therefore, one that Hawkins would have brushed straight through and Lambert stubbornly waited out, Christopher acknowledges it.

Lambert, least likely of the three, finally marries Francie. Her flirtation with Hawkins resulted in her expulsion from Bruff, followed by Charlotte's anger that Francie refused Christopher's proposal. Packed off in disgrace, Francie suffers the final blow when she learns that Hawkins, more in need of money than love, has returned to an original betrothed who will pay off all his debts. Lambert, dull but persistent, represents to her the only link to the happy summer in Lismoyle and an escape from the drudgery and poverty of her aunt and uncle's house in Bray. In his role as savior, however, Lambert has very limited range. After he had earlier capsized his yacht and was floundering helplessly in the lake, Christopher was the one to save Francie from drowning. The lake is much more his element than Lambert's; or Cursiter's, who chugs meaninglessly back and forth across it in a steam launch; or Hawkins', who runs the launch aground. Why, then, does Christopher, with his hidden strength, with his unselfish concern for Francie, rate "small claim to respect or admiration" from the authors?

The judgment belies much of the respect and affection Somerville and Ross have for Christopher but does point to what they see as crucial inadequacies. He is a failed artist, a creature "so conscious of its own weakness as to be almost incapable of confident effort." In his hobby of photography he seeks a mechanical proficiency otherwise immobilized by his own self-doubts.

> His fastidious dislike of doing a thing indifferently was probably a form of conceit . . . it brought about in him a kind of deadlock. . . . Half the people in the world were clever nowadays, he said to himself with indolent irritability, but genius was another affair.

Frustrated by the conviction that he lacks superior qualities, Christopher refuses halfway measures and insulates himself from any risks, social or emotional. Yet both the social and the emotional situations call for strong, decisive action. Francie represents one way, seemingly the only way, for Christopher to break free of his paralyzed isolation. As with other characters, notably Lambert, scenes of natural beauty signal a fairly conventional mood of lyrical reverie for Christopher. But while Lambert accepts these emotions and momentarily escapes from convention, Christopher always questions his feelings as "mere self-conscious platitudes." Francie changes that, arousing in him renewed faith in "the mysteries of life into which he had thought himself too cheap and shallow to enter." She complements his failings, transforms him into a stronger, more decisive and active person, allows him success. And equally important to the novel, marriage would assure his family line.

Several factors contribute to Christopher's failure. One is simply his personal weakness, his inability to win Francie even from someone as shallow as Hawkins. And the tremendous pressure of circumstances proves too complex, too firmly locked into a downward-turning spiral. The collapse of his relationship with Francie cuts even deeper into the power of an already failing landed class. Attractive as Christopher may be, he shares in the debilitating weakness and ineffectuality paralyzing the Protestant Ascendancy and dooming it to ever greater decay. Nor does the future of the newer, rising classes appear substantially brighter. In her victories over both Julia Duffy and Lambert, Charlotte resorts to the hated methods of the Irish "gombeen men," usury and financial coercion, to drive her victims into ruin. Yet her gains cost her a great deal and fail to bring her what she wants most.

The choice of a spinster as a main character raises biographical issues closely related to the social character of *The Real Charlotte.* The novel relies on many obvious biographical details, such as the resemblance of Lough Moyle to Lough Corrib, the Galway lake marking one edge of Ross estate. Gurthnamuckla housed a Ross tenant, a widow in arrears on rent. And Somerville explained that her mother provided the model for Lady Dysart: "She, as we said of Lady Dysart, said the things that other people were afraid to think." Charlotte only seems to practice such honesty. More speculative, and more crucial to the novel, is the resemblance of Robert Martin, Violet's brother, to Christopher Dysart. Robert wrote plays requiring the participation of the whole family, as does Christopher's younger brother Garry. He frequently sailed Ross Lake. He had the romanticism and sensitivity that mark Christopher as eccentric. And his reluctance to carry on the Ross estate after James Martin's death in 1872 necessitated its abandonment. In their ambivalence about Christopher, Somerville and Ross temper their affection with the judgment that, like all the other men in the novel who have abdicated responsibility or proven ineffectual, he is not the strong, masculine hero needed to carry on the Dysart family line.

His sister Pamela, too, we sense, will never marry. Spinsterhood proves an accurate metaphor in defining the dilemma of the landed gentry. And marriage fails to offer any successful alternative. As an institution, it takes a relentless beating in *The Real Charlotte,* with one character after another demonstrating, whether by word or in practice, that wives and husbands have a miserable time of it together. The unmarried states of Pamela and Christopher coincide with the internal weakness of the gentry, its failure to propagate its aristocratic tradition and values. With Charlotte, spinsterhood points up an even broader deficiency in the society, the inability of vital, decisive action to reverse the decline of the old way of life.

There remains a vast gulf separating Christopher from those who possess, as do Francie or Charlotte, the energy of renewal and who offer him an escape from his paralysis. The personal weakness preventing him from winning Francie also makes him no match for Charlotte's brisk practicality and business schemes. At their meeting to discuss the affairs of the Bruff estate, he and Charlotte appear together as "two incongruous figures on the turf-quay, one short, black, and powerful, the other tall, white, and passive." Christopher can master the surface of the lake, can even save Francie from its depths. But he can never hope to comprehend the murky, mysterious forces suggested by the turf-quay hidden along the shore and whose dark recesses Charlotte, as distinctively Irish as the Dysarts are British, knows so well.

The universality of failure in the novel serves a warning to those in Ireland who value too much the kinds of materialistic gains Charlotte wants. Such a rise in society can bring nothing but disappointment; the middle classes should therefore seek more idealistic and spiritual goals than those that serve only self-interest and that so often come at the expense of the gentry. Even more importantly, Somerville and Ross see failure as the distinguishing feature of their own dilemma, and of the whole state of crisis within the landed class. Feeling that they themselves could never marry, they could at least create a literary character who attempts marriages for other people. In the interests of their class, they hold out the hope that such matchmaking will restore the fading power of the landed families. In the interest of their art, and demanding from themselves a clearer vision of their experience, they had no alternative but to depict such hopes as futile.

Edith Somerville recorded an incident from her years with Violet Martin that struck them both, at the beginning of their literary career, with the force of a supernatural vision. They were leaving from a visit to the family of an old estate when they glimpsed, in a secluded window of the mansion, a white face:

> An old stock, isolated from the world at large, wearing itself out in those excesses that are a protest of human nature against unnatural conditions, dies at last with its victims round its death-bed. Half-acknowledged, half-witted, wholly horrifying; living ghosts, haunting the house that gave them but half their share of life, yet withheld from them, with half-hearted guardianship, the boon of death.

The shock seemed to them an inspiration, a signpost towards the kinds of realism and authenticity they should strive for in their work. The theme of the lonely figure on the margins of his society became more pronounced in Yeat's writing from the 1890s, and over and over in the literature of this decade there recurs the image of the person trapped between life and death, the real and the ideal, the waking nightmare and the visionary dream. The landed gentry in late nineteenth-century Ireland found themselves isolated in just such a fashion. An alien class in their own society, heirs to a noble past and a desolate future, they felt unable to repair their failing fortunes, yet felt equally unable to accept the lot that history offered them. (pp. 72-82)

> *Wayne E. Hall, "Somerville and Ross," in his* Shadowy Heroes: Irish Literature of the 1890s, *Syracuse University Press, 1980, pp. 64-82.*

Hilary Robinson   (essay date 1980)

[*In the following excerpt, Robinson analyzes the themes and characterization in four of the minor novels of Somerville and Ross.*]

[*An Irish Cousin*] is a sombre book despite its many comic scenes. Contemporary critics found it too gloomy, but Edith Somerville believed that it owed its success with the public to the very fact that it was 'first in the field of Irish country life which did not rollick'. The gloom is not simply that of the sensational gothic sort—though there are elements of that too, but emanates from the mists and rains and winds sweeping in from the Atlantic over the desolate West of Ireland, so that the lonely inhabitants are driven almost mad by the natural conditions and their own isolation. It is still a polite society and their indulgences are hid beneath a veneer of manners which makes the sins more awful as well as more interesting. So secret are some of the sins however that the reader is never quite sure of the truth. Uncle Dominick's plotting to get the house and estate from his elder brother is clear enough, but his relationship with Mad Moll is not. She believes herself to be the illegitimate daughter of an uncle of Dominick—that is, his cousin. This claim seems to have been respected by the family; she has been allowed to live in the house as a kind of housekeeper. Unfortunately she becomes Dominick's mistress. When he marries she is

turned out and married to a tenant. Dominick's wife dies in childbirth and Moll, who has given birth to a child at the same time (presumably Dominick's?) becomes the child's foster mother. Moll's own daughter falls in love with her foster-brother (and presumably her half-brother) and during the course of the novel marries him. The somewhat intricate plot is unrolled somewhat shakily with a few creaks, by way of a brass memorial plaque in the church, reminiscences of old tenants, the discovery of a diary and the revelation of an unposted letter.

Although the tale and characters are uncannily similar to Sheridan Le Fanu's *Uncle Silas,* the novel is more worthy of attention because it is more serious. It is not just a supernatural tale written for effect. There are phantom carriages and hauntings but there is also social and psychological realism. It began indeed as a 'shilling shocker' and what turned it from that into a novel is extremely interesting. It was an experience which was in itself, ironically, sensational—much closer to Catherine Morland's than Jane Austen's idea of reality. It is also the first appearance of the subject which is to interest them for the rest of their lives as writers, and to provide them with endless material for stories and novels:

> The sunset was red in the west when our horses were brought round to the door, and it was at that precise moment that into **An Irish Cousin** some thrill of genuineness was breathed. In the darkened facade of the long grey house, a window, just over the hall-door, caught our attention. In it, for an instant, was a white face. Trails of ivy hung over the panes, but we saw the face glimmer there for an instant and vanish.
>
> As we rode home along the side of the hills, and watched the fires of the sunset sink into the sea, and met the crescent moon coming with faint light to lead us home, we could talk and think only of that presence at the window. We had been warned of certain subjects not to be approached, and we knew enough of the history of that old house to realise what we had seen. An old stock, isolated from the world at large, wearing itself out in those excesses that are a protest of human nature against unnatural conditions, dies at last with its victims around its death-bed. Half-acknowledged, half-witted, wholly horrifying; living ghosts, haunting the house that gave them but half their share of life, yet withheld from them with half-hearted guardianship, the boon of death.

In the novel this kind of distress is made vivid and put into perspective by the point of view: everything is seen through the eyes of a Canadian cousin who is in Ireland for the first time. She is quite unaware of there being Irish and Anglo-Irish: 'In fact, had my uncle and cousin met me on the pier, clad in knee-breeches and tail-coats, and hailed me with what I believed to be the national salutation, "Begorra!" I should scarcely have been taken aback.' Ireland to her is a remote corner of the British Empire and she arrives saying 'I am thankful to get back to Great Britain again!' Through her eyes we see a countryside of a sad and wild beauty made ugly by man. The nearest village, Rathbarry, is the first of many similar villages in their work, a single street of low, dirty cottages interspersed with grubby shops. In the vicinity there are three Big Houses: the O'Neills' home, Clashmore Hall, where life is orderly and things are looked after and cared for; the Jackson-Crolys' house where dirt is swept under the carpet; and Durrus, the Sarsfields' house where there is never any sweeping done at all. Durrus is overrun with rats, its walls furred with damp, thick layers of dust and cobwebs settled over everything. When Theo finds her hairbrush used to support the window because the sash is gone she finds it 'eminently characteristic of the slipshod manner of life at Durrus'. When a latch is broken on a gate, a stone is used to prop the gate shut; nothing is ever mended. Peach trees grow out through the broken windows of the greenhouse. The rest of the kitchen garden is a wilderness with unpruned trees, overgrown paths and lichen-covered bushes. But, there is nothing charming or romantic about this neglect:

> Certainly I had never before seen anything like the mixture of prosperity and dilapidation in these solid stone buildings, with their rickety doors and broken windows. Through the open coach-house door I saw an unusual amount of carriages, foremost among them the landau in which I had driven from Esker, with a bucket placed on its coach-box in order to catch a drip from the roof. A donkey and a couple of calves were roaming placidly about, and, though there was no lack of stable-helpers and hangers-on, everything was inconceivably dirty and untidy.

In such descriptions the setting transcends gothic gloom; the physical decay of the house and environs expresses the moral degeneracy of its inhabitants. When Moll, struck dumb by some nameless horror, pirouettes before the house at night, with curtsies and dumb prayers as she kneels motionless, hands crossed on breast, pale face beseeching the sky for justice, or peers through the ivy covered window, and creates such an effect that the whole countryside seems to catch her agony, 'the patches of grey lichen on the trees repeated in the growing twilight the effect of the grey face at the darkened window' we are in the realm of popular Victorian fiction, but always intermingled with these scenes is mundane carelessness, ordinary slackness and dilapidation that inject life into the book.

Night and the weather are used poetically to reflect the suppressed guilt and subconscious fears of the characters. When Theo and Dominick confront Moll, indoors, 'It was getting darker, and the rain came driving in from the sea in ghost-like white clouds'; as the human suffering increases so the storm comes inland to them. It rushes in from the Atlantic hurling down trees, throwing itself against the Big House with such force that they cannot open the shutters in day time: 'I sat in the semidarkness of the library, trying to read, and looking from time to time through the one unshuttered window out onto the gravel sweep . . . A great sycamore had fallen across the drive a little below the house, and the other trees swung and writhed as if in despair at the long stress of the gale.' When Willy allows himself to be blackmailed into marrying his foster sister and so gives up all hope of making anything of his life, his misery is in tune with the gale: ' "It's all over now," he said. "Everything's gone to smash." A

rush of wind shivered through the laurels, and shook a quick rattle of drops from the shining leaves.' When Dominick commits suicide, nature is a fitting backdrop:

> There was weight in the air, the sky was low and foreboding, and a watery streak of yellow lay along the horizon behind the bog. A rook rustled close over my head with a subdued croak; I dully watched him flying quietly home to the tall elms by the lodge; he was still circling round them before settling down, when a long, wavering cry struck upon my ear, a sound that once heard is never forgotten, the cry of a woman keening.

The tenantry play an important part in this novel. We see them and the Anglo-Irish through Theo's eyes. She goes to the birthday party the tenants hold for Willy and comes upon quite another way of life. Instead of Corelli and Schubert played on piano and violin, there is a hunchback on a donkey playing jigs on his bagpipes, which to her strange ears sounds like 'a succession of grunts and squeals of varying discordancy'. Surrounded by men in knee-breeches and tail-coats who are drinking porter she feels for the first time since she has been in Ireland a complete foreigner: 'in spite of my Sarsfield blood, a stranger in a strange land'. When she goes to the town with Willy she finds her horse the focal point for beggars and groups of women who discuss her lineage and looks as if she were deaf or an inhabitant of a different planet. The Irish funeral on the Strand of the Dead again makes her feel her otherness: she watches the boats arrive with the coffin, sees the women beating their breasts and chanting and keening. With the burial over they go to their own family graves to pray and tell their beads; she looks at them in their blue cloaks, with the grey headstones the pale blue sky behind them as if they are in a picture. When they talk to her it is with a pleasing mixture of ease and formality; lively talk which ends graciously, 'Good-evening to your honour, miss. May the Lord comfort your honour long, and that I may never die till I see you well married.' The townspeople, on the other hand, are far more constrained—Willy and Theo are expected to want a room by themselves for tea in the hotel, and the traveller already in the dining room leaves at a word from the boots as soon as they enter.

Sweeney's cottage is a realistic picture of such an abode. There is the proverbial hospitality and good manners side by side with the barbaric cruelty to animals: Mrs Sweeney is busy plucking a live goose when they arrive. When Willy talks to her he automatically adopts an accent and vocabulary close to her own. He remembers the names of her children and their various ailments but he does not patronise her and she does not pander to him. He tells her she is 'a greater fool than I thought you were' and that her senile father-in-law has more sense than she has. When she says goodbye to them, she gives them a bowl of eggs and tells Willy to carry them home for Theo's breakfast, and then gives him a hearty slap on the back: ' "Och, there's no fear but he'll mind!" she said, winking at me. "He'd do more than that for yourself, and small blame to him!" ' The difference between the two Irish communities is not ignored but one is not held up to ridicule more than the other. We do laugh at the servants sometimes, as when

Edith Somerville in riding attire, 1905.

Theo's dress is inspected by the Durrus servants as she leaves for the ball. To her astonishment she finds them lined up in the hall: ' "Well, miss," began Mrs Rourke in tones of solemn conviction, "ye might thravel Ireland this night, and ye wouldn't find her aiqual! Of all the young ladies ever I seen, you take the sway!"

"Glory be to God! 'tis thrue!" moaned the kitchen-maid in awe-stricken assent.' This is more good natured perhaps than the comedy of the Jackson-Crolys' annual dance. The master of the house stands at the foot of the stairs to welcome his guests, 'a small, bald-headed gentlemen, moving in an agitated way from leg to leg, and apparently engaged in alternately putting on and taking off his gloves.' The style of dancing is aggressive, consisting of couples trying to knock each other over, a mode which one of Theo's partners explains by saying the one he's trying to bump is his cousin Kate. She reflects, 'There seemed at the time nothing very incongruous about this explanation. There was a hilarious informality about the whole entertainment that made it unlike any I had ever been at before. Every one talked and laughed at the full pitch of their lungs.' At supper she overhears one lady saying, 'Now, captain, if you say that again, I'll pelt me patty at you!' When the popular 'Sweethearts' is played on the piano the pianist and all the dancers sing the refrain together:

'Oh, lo-*ove* for a year,
A we-*eek*, a day,'

The chaperones take it in turn to be pianist, and are applauded according to the vigour with which they bang the piano. At supper-time the doctor goes in two or three times, each time working his way down the table like a mowing machine. The social comedy veers on the savage as Theo sees: '. . . a convivial party of lunatics . . . Mobcaps, night-caps, fools'-caps and sunbonnets nodded in nightmare array round the table.' The description of the ball struck Sir William Gregory as a little too realistic. He admired the book very much but wrote to Mrs Martin that Violet should be reprimanded for that: 'By the way I ought to scold her for giving the idea that our Irish county balls are of the ramshackle nature described—though I should not be surprised if my narration of one in this County may have lingered in her mind. But what will Co. Cork folk say?'

The language in the book is precise; adjectives are used with discrimination, and images though rare are witty. When Theo meets Mrs Barrett she finds, 'a monumental old lady, who having been established by Willy in the most reliable chair in the room, remained there in mammoth silence, motionless, save for her alert eyes, which wandered from face to face, and suggested to me the idea of a restless intelligent spirit imprisoned in a feather bed.' Dominick's nature is apparent in the phrase which describes his manner as 'glacial geniality' and his voice as being 'of a mellifluous not to say alarming propriety'. Willy's nature and state of education is captured in the description of his speech as 'ungrammatical gallantry'. Theo's self-contained coolness is always present in her style: she reports the palmist who says she has 'no sense of humour, and homicidal tendencies combined with unusual conscientiousness'; and she describes her feelings about the seasickness she has recently suffered as: 'But for me it has only two aspects—the pathetic and the revolting; the former being the point of view with which I regard my own sufferings, and the latter having reference to those of others.'

The poised narration is Theo's personal tone of voice; each of the other characters has his own voice. Dominick's English is almost eighteenth-century in its politeness; the rector of Rathbarry has such a strong Cork accent that Theo can hardly understand the sermons. Mimi Burke, a fearless hunting lady, with a deep voice which breaks out in 'booming cadences' has a sort of half-way speech. Her accent is basically Co. Cork but Theo says no system of spelling would give any idea of it; briefly, ' "fie" she pronounced "foy", and "Sarsfield" in her sonorous tones became "Sorsefield" '. Her speech is sprinkled with imagery which makes it more colourful than that of most of the Anglo-Irish characters; it is closer to the peasantry. She tells Mrs Jackson-Croly: 'Why, you're a grand woman! We'd all be dying down with dullness only for you!' Mrs Jackson-Croly's snobbery is reflected in her speech as she tells how she has to take her daughters to Southsea (where the military are) to stop them from getting an accent: 'I loathe a Cork brogue! My fawther took me abroad every year; he was so alormed lest I'd aquire it, and I assure you, when we were children, he used to insist on mamma's putting cotton wool in our ears, when we went to old Mr Flannagan's church, for fear we'd ketch his manner of speaking.' The speech of the tenants is lively and authentic, depending as much on the rhythm of the sentences as on the vocabulary.

The main characters are Dominick Sarsfield, the two cousins, and Nugent O'Neill. Dominick shares many characteristics with Uncle Silas: he is a gentleman; he speaks with the greatest courtesy; he is a snob and he is utterly self-engrossed. Where Uncle Silas is a secret opium addict, Uncle Dominick imbibes more than a bottle of brandy a day. Selfishness is responsible for his neglect of his son Willy. He lacks the money to send him to an English public school, so he lets him grow up with a level of education far below his own. Unable to provide Willy with any companions of his own standing he lives in dread that Willy will disgrace himself by befriending the young girl in the lodge, but he is too lethargic to think of any alternative. At the first mention of the pretty lodge girl, Moll's daughter, he flares up, 'When people in that class of life are taken out of their proper places they at once begin to presume.' His classic speech about the breakdown of the class system is as fiery as it is because he is involved personally, through his fear of what Willy will do:

> 'I cannot believe that any sane person can honestly hold such absurd theories. What! do you mean to tell me that one of my tenants, a creature whose forefathers have lived for centuries in ignorance and degradation, is my equal?'

> 'His degradation is merely the result of injustice,' said Miss O'Neill, coolly adjusting her *pince-nez*.

> 'I deny it,' said my uncle loudly. His usually pale face was flushed, and his eyes burned. 'But that is not the point. What I maintain is, that any fusion of classes such as you advocate would have the effect of debasing the upper while it entirely failed to raise the lower orders. If you were to marry your coachman, as, according to your theories of equality, I suppose you would not hesitate to do, do you think these latent instincts of refinement that you talk about would make him a fit companion for you and your family? You know as well as I do that such an idea is preposterous. It is absurd to suppose that the natural arrangement of things can be tampered with. This is a subject on which I feel very strongly, and it shocks me to hear a young lady in your position advance such opinions!'

In his eyes it is far worse for Willy to marry the lodge girl than to take her as his mistress; the latter is possible without taking her out of her class. When Willy disobeys him, his malicious spite is singularly well conveyed; he speaks slowly: '. . . the words falling from his lips like drops of acid. "You mean to say she is your wife?" ' His fury is inflamed by his own guilt and fear of exposure as well as his snobbery and cold sense of rightness; his expression of it is exact in the mixture of controlled hatred and sarcasm: ' "And your bride? May I ask if she has done me the honour of coming here?" He wiped a thin foam from his lower lip with trembling hand. "Or is she perhaps at her father's residence?" ' Icy sarcasm alternates with animal ravings

as he decides that his son shall be cut off penniless rather than let his new bride profit by her marriage. But, convincingly enough, he is polite to Theo even when at the height of his alcoholic ravings; she is a lady. He is passionately determined to get a door opened; she cannot do it, and his reaction is the elegant: ' "No, my dear, I see it is no use trying tonight. You are tired, and so am I."—he sighed deeply, and put his hand to his chest—"this oppression that I am suffering from tries me terribly. I will go to my room and see if I can get a little rest. I need rest badly." ' When his mind gives way, the mellifluousness of tone, and the grammatical propriety is kept. It is a most convincing picture of a mad old gentleman: Theo tells him he looks tired.

> 'Do I? Well, to tell you the truth, I have been quite unable to sleep lately. I am so much disturbed by these hackney carmen who make it a practice to drive past the house at all hours of the night; I hope they do not annoy you? I have told them several times to go away but they simply laugh at me. And the strange thing is,' he continued, leaning over the rail of the corridor, and looking suspiciously down into the hall, 'that though I gave orders that the lodge gates should always be locked at night, it does not stop them in the least—they just drive through them. Well, goodnight, my dear,' he said, nodding at me in a friendly way.

Willy is the Irish cousin of the title, but the centre of interest is shared between him and the narrator, Theo. She is an unconventional heroine. At the start of the book she is suffering from seasickness; as for looks, we are told that when she has a riding hat on she looks just like her father did when he was a boy. She is often muddy from playing with wet dogs; she goes ferreting; the rats in the house do not bother her at all; she wraps an old carriage rug around her shoulders and puts on a cap of her cousin Willy's when she goes for a walk. She prides herself on being clear-headed and sensible, and though she is romantic about Ireland and the new life it may hold for her, she is not hoping to fall in love. She never deceives herself about Willy, whom she finds such an excellent companion. He is immense fun but she notes, 'he could not be said to be either very cultured or refined.' Her naïvety makes her shock at finding out Willy's love for her very credible: she is so upset that he is suffering and that all their good times are over, and yet she is made to recognise that much as she likes him and sorry as she is for his sorrow, nothing will make her feel differently. Time will not change her: 'every feeling in me rose in sudden revolt at the idea with a violence that astonished myself'. She is equally surprised at the suddenness with which she recognises she is in love with the arrogant Nugent: 'I could not understand how this improbable, this incredible thing had come about.' Like the usual heroine she turns to her diary to see when she began to notice Nugent, but there is nothing there: only one entry after a day's hunting, 'Mr O'Neill piloted me. Dull and conceited.' Nugent is the silent stiff man of principle.

Nugent, the heroine's choice, is not easy to like; like Darcy he will not flirt, nor try to please: when Theo tries small talk with him he gives perfunctory answers; he is not a polite man. And he is patronising, 'I have always heard that Canadian young ladies had a very gay time,' and 'ladies do not generally get on very well without shops and dances'. He only begins to be polite when Theo shows an interest in music. Again there is Mr Darcy's kind of superiority—when Theo offers to accompany him, ' "Oh, thanks very much; my sister always accompanies me," he responded coolly.' Theo finds his deliberate self-possession extremely exasperating. He has 'frigid, uninterested civility'. At the dinner party when he has to entertain Theo he annoys her by being so unexcited, so quiet, and yet with a humorous turn to his sentences which she finds interesting despite herself. He is utterly poised and self-contained. When Willy petulantly intrudes on a speech of Nugent's the latter ignores Willy until he's finished his sentence, 'Then, with a tolerating smile . . . asked him what he had said.'

Willy is a delightful portrait of a young man full of potential who is the victim of circumstances: his father, and the isolation of Durrus. 'There's no sound I hate like that row the groundswell makes out there at the point. If you're feeling any way lonely, it makes you want to hang yourself. . . . I tell you you've no notion what this place is like in the winter. Sometimes there's not a creature in the country to speak to from one month's end to another.' All the responsibility of the house and farm falls on him. He runs it all. He is well-dressed, amiable, eager to please and to make his cousin feel at home: he sees that there is a fire in her room and puts pen and paper there for her letters; he gives her tea as soon as she arrives. Theo finds him an excellent host, 'He plied me with everything on the table, eating his own breakfast, and talking all the time with unaffected zest and vigour, and I began to feel as if the time I had known him could be counted in months instead of hours.' He has the seemingly feminine ability to sit over a fire and talk for hours about nothing in particular; he adores gossiping, but without any malice; and he has as well 'quite a special gift of recounting small facts with accuracy and detail'; indoors and out he is an excellent companion for Theo. When he falls in love with her his already sharp observation and sensitivity to others is even heightened so that he 'appeared to be able to take in my doings with the back of his head.' Nothing is too much trouble for him, and throughout the novel *he* is the charming and amusing young man, not Nugent. In an episode similar to the necklace one on the day of the ball in *Mansfield Park*, our sympathies are with Willy not Nugent. The latter sends Theo a gorgeous spray which he has made himself out of splendid yellow chrysanthemums and feathery maidenhair fern. Willy goes out in the pouring rain to look for the first violets, and gives her a bedraggled little bunch. Like Fanny Price she solves the predicament by taking both; she wears the violets and carries the bouquet, but feels 'somehow Willy's bunch of violets had taken away most of my pleasure [in the hot-house flowers]'.

Through Theo's relationship with her Irish cousin and Nugent O'Neill the authors begin to explore the nature of romantic passion, giving it a background of alcoholism, murder and suicide. All Willy's goodness is vanquished when Theo tells him that she cannot love him 'like that'; he flings her flowers into the fire; he grabs hold of her and forces kiss after kiss upon her. As if he knows his case is doomed he always unerringly chooses the most unsalubrious place to talk to her of his feelings for her. First a dreary, tasteless study, then the dark, dank hole of the commercial room in the local hotel, where the tea is red and 'the bread and butter and the china were alike abnormally thick', these things being somehow an image of what life with Willy would be like. Nugent talks to her in the midst of music and potted plants, elegant drawing-rooms and pleasant perfumed conservatories. If there is any kind of rationale in her choice of Nugent it is simply that she is too fastidious to accept Willy, much as she likes him. The scenes of passion are well done: Willy, having been blackmailed into marrying the lodge girl, comes to say goodbye to Theo and still cannot leave her if there is a chance that she has changed her mind. When she kisses his cheek he misunderstands and will not let her go until she is forced to say, 'I meant that I was fond of you, but I never was in love with you.' Before he goes she is in tears and then so is he: 'He snatched my hand again, and kissed it many times; he was crying too. "God help us both!" he said. "Goodbye." ' Willy's suffering is brought on by this unrequited love, but it is deepened and made entirely hopeless because of his earlier affair with the lodge girl and his father's sins of greed and sexual exploitation. Willy is not strong enough to overcome the disadvantages of his environment. His voluntary exile to Australia is the only attempt at putting things right he can make. Theo might be able to inspire passion in others, but she is not capable of it herself. Without Willy's complications her falling in love with Nugent would be entirely sweet and creditable.

Naboth's Vineyard was commissioned in 1889 for a literary magazine which was intent on publishing writing of various political and religious opinions. But the commissioner, Langbridge, changed his mind and decided to publish it in a 'cycle of newspapers' as he feared it would lead to partisan feelings over the Land League question. Somerville & Ross refused to let it appear in newspapers, so Langbridge bought the copyright for £30, and brought it out as a novel in 1891. To the authors' amazement it was treated as a serious work about the political situation, and given solemn reviews by *The Spectator, The Times* and the *Saturday Review*. Later Edith Somerville was always derogatory about the book: 'I have long realised that Martin and I made a very great mistake in writing ***Naboth's Vineyard.*** Not a bad plot, but quite unreal characters.' She said that the characters were 'ladies and gentlemen who talk in brogue—quite a good brogue, only that "Judy O'Grady" has "the Colonel's lady" under *her* skin . . .' She really did believe that one could only write about the social class one belonged to! As it is, the characters in this book are very uneven, and most of them are stage Irish figures. Ellen Leonard is a stock colleen of the Irish melodrama, pretty, simple and innocent. The stock villain is there in the gombeen man who is also the president of the local branch of the Land League; hence he is able to use his position there in order to better himself and grab more land. Rick O'Grady is the conventional hero, the returned emigrant, who has made his fortune in the States and returned in time to shelter the distressed colleen and perform acts of bravery for her sake: he breaks the boycott, swims a brimming river, puts out a farmyard fire single-handed, and marries her in the end. Even the landlord is the traditional absentee who is hated because of his absence; when his woods are on fire the men will not stir themselves, 'If he wouldn't live in the counthry and mind his place, let him lose it and be d——d to him!' The half-idiot boy, Dan, who is eaten up with two passions, love for Ellen and hatred of the gombeen man, does belong to the melodramatic: there is the macabre scene where he sees the gombeen man's corpse in the river, and bends to shake hands with him to say farewell and then as he bends suffers one of his epileptic fits:

> He tried to shake the hand up and down, but it felt as heavy as lead. It seemed to him as if it were pulling him down; blackness came before his eyes and he screamed. But the hand still drew him down, and he fell forward and lay, face downwards, in the mud.

> There was great quietness after this, and before long the startled sandpipers and curlews were hopping and running about, and digging their long bills into the mud, not twenty yards from where the two figures lay.

The easing of the facile emotion with the description of the natural life reasserting itself does slightly mitigate the macabre, but it is still magazine stuff. Better are the scenes of Dan's wooing of Ellen; he cannot think, but is motivated by simple emotions of desire or hatred, and he is embarrassingly pathetic in the love scenes. Ellen's mother is partly the stock widow with the pretty daughter whose virtue she must protect, but she is given some vitality by her passion for her land. She is a woman of fierce determination who will take on the gombeen man and the whole Land League to keep her land. And it is not for the sake of her daughter. 'If there wasn't a one left in this house only meself and the Lord Almighty I'd stay in it if the town of Rossbrin came to put me out!'

It is however with the other strong woman, Harriet Donovan, wife of the gombeen man and old girl friend of the hero, Rick O'Grady, that they transcend stage Irish characters. Harriet is the first of their women characters who is motivated by both good and evil impulses. She has married for money instead of waiting for the man she loved to come home, and she has to stand by and watch him fall in love and marry a much younger girl. Because her emotions have never become involved with her husband she cannot see that her relationship with Rick is completely different from what it was before she was married. She still loves Rick and because of the strength of her emotions she believes she has every right to love him. She cannot see that she has changed and that instead of the gentle soft girl she was seven years ago when Rick went off to make his fortune, she is a ruthless married woman, eaten up with frustrated passion and thwarted desires. Throughout she has a commonness which is consistent: it was that which made her marry Donovan for comfort and security and then made her incapable of accepting her lot. Her first words are full of irritation and pent-up emotion: when her husband asks her why she has come out into the countryside, even though she *is* guilty of an ulterior motive she cannot resist getting in a jibe about the disagreeable house she has to live in, 'What'd keep me in the town? I came

up here to get out of the smell of them beastly fish!' Their horrible married life is clearly depicted; his rough desire for her and her hatred of him: jealous of Rick, he tells her that Rick fancies the girl Ellen. Harriet's loathing is vivid: 'She felt she could kill him as she looked down on him, stretched out in sodden comfort before the fire, with an egotistical smile on his heavy face, and his fat hand caressing his tumbler of whiskey and water.' There is an awful scene when he discovers that she has invited Rick to the house; husband and wife glare at each other like wild animals, and he attacks her with his stick and then manages to stop himself and breaks the stick in half before rushing out; she, undaunted, is still spitting her malicious remarks at him as he goes. So wrought up is she that with Rick she cannot be sensible. She has no idea of playing her cards carefully. She knows that he condemns her malice and dislikes her for it, but she cannot help herself. Jealousy gets the better of her and when there is a chance to belittle the young girl she takes it. She sneers at her for wearing a shawl instead of a hat; she pretends that the village idiot is engaged to be married with the girl.

At the height of her jealousy she is driven into the forest in a storm, grappling with the question of whether Rick loves the girl or not. The furious storm matches her own inner turmoil, and in this heightened emotional state she lets her husband fall to his death when she could have saved him. This almost-murder is again to be used in later books to show the kind of evil which a very ordinary person can be guilty of. Harriet has a moment of choice, her first impulse is to save him but, 'before her lips opened some devil's messenger of a thought shot lucidly through her mind' and she obeys it. 'Her husband's step was on the bridge; she became rigid and numb, and all things seemed as unreal as a dream.' She lets him fall and then rushes to the bridge, too late of course: 'She turned, and, not knowing what she did, fled away through the woods.' Throughout the action she is living on two different levels of knowledge. In her heart she knows that Rick does not love her any more and is attracted by the young girl, but she cannot bring this knowledge into her daily mind. She convinces herself that Rick befriends the girl out of a mixture of personal and political motives, 'out of antagonism to her husband and a high-handed contempt for authority'. She persuades herself that she lets her husband die partly out of a desire to protect Rick, turning the awful deed into an opportunity for self-advancement in the field of passion: 'She would call to him and stop him; he would know how true she had been to him.' In a final painful scene she throws herself about Rick's neck saying, 'I forgive ye, Rick . . . they'll never know it, and you and me that loves one another will be happy in the end.' The conventionality of the ending—her retreat into the convent—is slightly mitigated by her lack of repentance. Even now she cannot subdue her passion; she spends her last night 'kneeling at her bedside, her remorse and penitence put by for a future day, weeping fierce, unsatisfied tears, with Rick O'Grady's photograph pressed to her lips.' It is their first picture of a woman at the mercy of her passion, their first study of the triumph of evil.

When Longmans thought of reissuing *Naboth's Vineyard* in 1916, Edith Somerville was not enthusiastic 'The subject is very tragic and, just now especially, I doubt whether a Land League story would be popular. Undoubtedly people just at present prefer stories of a cheerful character.' *Naboth's Vineyard,* like *An Irish Cousin,* is potentially tragic not because of its picture of the political situation but because of its depiction of a life in which evil predominates over good. (pp. 57-72)

. . . . .

The Silver Fox was written for serialisation, and plot and characters are extremely simple. It is similar to Thomas Hardy's *Mayor of Casterbridge* in so far as it is a study of an old way of life which is being destroyed by modern civilisation and its new values.

> The ring of the trowel travelled far on the wind across the heather, a voice of civilisation, saying pertinent, unhesitating things to a country where all was loose, and limitless, and inexact. Up here, by the shores of Lough Turc, people had, from all ages, told the time by the sun, and half-an-hour either way made no difference to anyone; now—most wondrous of all impossibilities—the winter sunrise was daily heralded by the steely shriek of an engine whirling truckloads of men to their work across the dark and dumb boglands.

The book also attempts to assess the nature of the Anglo-Irish race, by comparing it with the English and the Irish races. The story unites the two themes: the English come bringing their more advanced techniques into the Irish way of life. The catalyst by which we know the racial reactions is a silver fox. The point of view is that of an omniscient narrator who is usually quite detached, but at times descends into scornful generalisations. The scales are always weighted against the English characters: 'With Mr Glasgow, as with most of his countrymen, smartness came next to cleanliness and considerably in advance of godliness.' This rather clumsy scorn was probably a reaction to a review of *The Real Charlotte.* Edith Somerville has said that *The Silver Fox* was inspired by T. P. O'Connor's remarks on the earlier novel, and she quotes his words, 'hard and pitiless censors, as well as sardonic, squalid, and merciless observers of Irish life', commenting: 'We felt this to be so uplifting that we lost no time in laying the foundations of a further "ferocious narrative".' But in the same review O'Connor condemned them for caricaturing Irish people:

> Not a gleam of their kindness, tenderness, and loyalty; and it is only class prejudice which could induce such a picture of the Irish servant . . . It is not accident that, while every Irishman and Irishwoman in the story is fiercely exposed, the few English characters have nearly all the virtues . . . I regard it as one of the vulgarist traits in the character of the 'Shoneens', that, while they have so microscopic an eye for the faults of their own land and their own people, they can see nothing but virtue and excellence in any person with English blood.

Wrong as his comments are—Hawkins and Miss Hope-Drummond are 'exposed' as much as any character—they must have rankled. In *The Silver Fox,* Lady Susan and the

Glasgows are faulted much more than any of the others. Glasgow is more of a bounder than Hawkins, eager to have an affair with the virginal Slaney and then quick to forget all about her in the excitement of an affair with the married Lady Susan, 'He remembered only as a transient caprice the moment, unforgettable for her, that had given her life its first touch of passion'. With Mrs Glasgow the narrative poise is lost and she comes over as the stock loose woman of melodrama: 'Her hair was straw-coloured, and drooped in nauseous picturesqueness over her coal-black eyebrows; her face was fat and white, her dress was a highly-coloured effort at the extreme of the latest fashion but one; the general effect was elderly.'

Characters are of two kinds: minor ones who partake in the story, and major ones who are necessary for the themes as well. The minor ones are almost entirely comic and are given in neat sketches; they are static and judged as they are made. Three humorous sentences tell us all there is to know about Slaney's uncle. 'The Honourable Charles Herrick was an elderly and prosperous bachelor, whose blameless life was devoted to two pursuits, gardening and writing controversial letters to the Church papers. He was a small, dry gentleman, very clean, and not in the least deaf. Strangers always experienced a slight shock in finding that he was not a clergyman.' We laugh at his attempt to convert the pantry boy to Protestantism, and at his complaints about the Canon's papish practice of turning to the east for the Creed. Major Bunbury is to marry the heroine but he is given the same comic treatment. His solid masculinity is gently made fun of when he reads the newspaper as if he were serving his country, 'No woman can hope to read *The Times* as though it were a profession; it is a masculine gift, akin to that of dining'. And his capacity for romantic love is held in check by the comic tone. He looks at Slaney and the narrator comments, 'Major Bunbury felt that his special sister (who read Carlyle and played Scarlatti) would like to meet her. Although he hunted six days a week, he kept a soul somewhere, and his sister knew where it was.' The two major characters are women whose roles are to carry the themes of the two ways of life, and the two races: Lady Susan is English and modern, Slaney is Anglo-Irish and traditional. The Irish point of view is given by a third woman, Maria Quin. The barriers between them are not too simple: Lady Susan and Maria share an abandonment which Slaney's quietness and reserved manner spare her from. Lady Susan ignores everyone else in the hotel dining room by taking the best position at the fire and doing her hair in the looking glass; when she has eaten all she wants she flings her napkin at her husband's head, and snatches Major Bunbury's plate from him—regardless of the fact that he is still eating—and gives it to the cat. This sort of behaviour is as foreign to Slaney as is Maria Quin's when she ignores the roomful of people, and throws herself across the table in convulsions of grief when they come to nail down her father's coffin.

The contrast between the traditional values and the modern ones is made mainly through the characters of Slaney and Lady Susan. The English woman wears too much makeup, dyes her hair red, drinks too much, smokes too often, and laughs too loud. She is shrill and arrogant and pretends to be even more so. She poses as an emancipated woman and a frivolous one, hence all her talk about disliking poetry, and her professed ability to play cards for hours on end. At all costs she will be fashionable. Beside Lady Susan, Slaney is dowdy and dull. She cannot ice-skate or ride a bicycle; she plays the piano instead of strumming on a mandolin. Given the choice she will spend a free afternoon reading Swinburne's *Atalanta in Calydon*. She says her prayers every night. At the start of the story the one is trivial and superficial, the other solemn and idealistic; both are modified by events. Slaney develops from the 'guileless egotist' who is incapable of seeing through Glasgow, into the young woman who loves and marries the very ordinary Major Bunbury. Lady Susan learns to love and respect her husband. Lady Susan and the new railway both threaten to undermine the traditional values of the Irish community. Her casual affair with Glasgow, and the way in which the railway destroys the fairy hill are of a piece. Neither belong in the Irish country side: when she is flirting with Glasgow in the new railway station the simple description is telling: 'Behind her the empty window framed gaunt mountain peak, a lake that frittered a myriad sparkles from its wealth of restless silver, and the grey and faint purple of the naked wood beyond it. It seemed too great a background for her powdered cheek and her upward glances at her host.' When the crucial accident occurs on the railway the blow is struck simultaneously for Lady Susan and the railway. The truck crashes and her escape with Glasgow is stopped.

The analysis of racial characteristics is made primarily by the ways the characters react to the possibility of the supernatural, or at least to the possibility that a view of life which excludes the mysterious is severely limited. The Irish reaction to the rumour of the silver fox is explicit—they are terrified. In Irish folklore the silver fox is a witch or fairy, and his appearance at the time in which the railway is disturbing a fairy hill is doubly portentous. He is united with the prophecy of trouble if Cahirdeen hill is thrown into the bog of Tully. Two Irish men die haunted to death by the silver fox, and consumed with guilt for their part in touching the hill. The young man is simple, 'he was always innocent like, and when he was a child not a word out of him the longest year ever came only talkin' of God and the fairies, and the like o'that'. But the old man is not, and his reaction to the fox is thoroughly credible, his wife describes his agony in her own words which add to the credibility: he 'felt like a wind from the say coming bechuxt his skin and his blood afther he seeing the same fox'. The reaction of the whole Irish community is unanimous, 'Bether for him not to be intherfarin' with the likes o'that place'. When Maria Quin meets the fox she does not stop to wonder about its reality, instead she automatically falls on her knees and prays. The English response is quite different. Glasgow is a rational man and simply denies that there is anything outside the control of man. Lady Susan thinks the whole business about the fox 'Such rot!' The Anglo-Irish do not laugh at the fox story; Hugh, Lady Susan's husband, not only comes face to face with the animal but he sees Danny Quin's ghost reliving his death. Slaney respects the beliefs of the country people; she is as open to the psychic as Hugh but like Maria Quin

she is still able to pray. One night she is bothered when saying her prayers by Lady Susan's carrying on with Glasgow while Hugh is away:

> She remained for a long time on her knees, with a blank, spent mind, soothed in some dull way by the suggestions of her attitude, till a slight sound on the terrace, under her open window, made her lift her head and listen.
>
> The sound came and went, and Slaney was roused to put aside the curtains and look down. There was nothing to be seen but the fog that had risen out of the sea and settled on the land, with frost and moonlight blended in its whiteness; all the world seemed arrested and tranced, all the air charged with its cold and mysterious presence.

The next moment the Quins' collie slips by on the trail of the fox.

The differences in attitude to the supernatural are made to relate to the whole moral consciousness of the characters. It is made to seem better to believe. Glasgow's failure as a man—so that he will think nothing of adultery for example—and his failure as a business man, both stem from his belief that reason is supreme. The Irishmen cannot be treated as rational facts so Glasgow's economic calculations are wrong and he is made bankrupt. Lady Susan's failure as Hugh's wife, and her complete lack of sympathy, are a part of the obtuseness which makes her blind to the druids' stones and so almost cause her death and Hugh's. The standing stones which tell the Irish and Anglo-Irish of a huge cleft in the rocks say nothing to the English. Maria Quin tells Lady Susan scornfully, 'While ye live ye'll mind yerself whin ye see them. I thought everyone in the counthry knew this place. But sure what are you but a sthranger!' The authors' belief in the sensitivity of the Celtic people to the other world, compared with the opacity of the Saxon race, does lead them to oversimplification.

Where it is a question of contrasting the Irish and English nations the dice is rather heavily loaded by showing us the English race through the eyes of the romanticised Slaney. In the early chapters the ice-skating on the Thames and the champagne luncheon is contrasted with the Irish wake. In the dialogue the Irish are far superior, Lady Susan's strident soprano and shrill silliness have none of the vigour of the peasants. When Danny Quin is said to have 'sustained fatal injuries' the response is, ' "Arrah, what fatal injuries?" returned the old woman with scorn; "no, but to break his neck was what he done. Didn't he walk out over the brink o'the big sand-pit in Cashel the same as one that wouldn't have the sight, an' he a fine soople man no more than seventy years?" ' The judgment on this whiskey-sodden group is undermined because it is made by Glasgow, ' "What swine they are," he thought,' with whom we hate to agree. Whereas we *are* tempted into agreeing with the sensitive and refined Slaney that the English scream 'inanities to each other', and that their talk is 'either babyish or vulgar', and they themselves 'overdressed and artificial'. When the Quin boy commits suicide Glasgow and Slaney are brought together and once again there is no doubt where our sympathies are directed:

'It would be simpler if you said at once that honest or sane people had better give up having any dealings with the Irish,' he returned hotly.

'Do you mean English people? They certainly have not been eminently successful so far.'

There is a more balanced picture of the two nations when Slaney is not involved. The scene for example between Lady Susan and Maria Quin, where the former is grieving for the death of her horse, and the Irish girl has absolutely no understanding of her sorrow:

> Maria Quin looked at Lady Susan with eyes that were as dry as glass. The Irish peasant regards the sorrow for a mere animal as a childishness that is almost sinful, a tempting of ill-fate in its parody of the grief rightly due only to what is described as 'a Christian'; and Maria's heart glowed with the unwept wrongs of her brother . . .

> 'Little ye cried yestherday whin ye seen my brother thrown out on the ground by the pool,' said Maria, with irrepressible savageness, 'you that's breakin' yer heart afther yer horse.'

The Anglo-Irish are seen to have the best characteristics of both races, but so far as education and civilisation are concerned, they are closer to the English. Slaney's marriage to Major Bunbury carries this point. It is inconceivable that she should marry an ordinary Irishman. From the Irish people's point of view they belong together too. When Maria Quin is angered by the hunt riding through their yard, while her brother's corpse is there she makes no distinction between the riders. She is 'maddened by their brutal self-engrossment, their cheery and inconsequent voices', and Hugh himself despite all his visionary capacities is the M.F.H.

There are too many themes in the story and the attempt to make Slaney develop from 'the guileless egoist' to a young woman 'with a new and strong understanding of herself' is too ambitious for the length of the tale. We are told that her knowledge of her happiness with Major Bunbury came 'with all the tenderness and strong romance that were hidden in her nature, with all the comprehension of herself that had grown out of bitter experience'. But we have to take it on trust, we do not see the self-knowledge nor the suffering. We do see a change in Lady Susan, the potentially passionate character. She learns to love her husband, and to show solicitude and affection, and to recognise that there might after all be something in 'bad luck, and everything'.

The movement of the whole is different from any of their previous works in so far as it moves from the ill-fated gloom of desolate Co. Galway into the light and sweetness of a happy ending. There is harmony and peace at the end, at the polo-ground in Phoenix Park:

> The afternoon was more balmy sweet as the shadows lengthened and the coolness came; beyond the beautiful miles of grass and trees the western sky was gathering the warmth of sunset; opposite in the east, the brown smoke of Dublin stained the tranquil heaven, and above it a ghost-ly half-moon stood like a little white cloud in the depths of blue.

(pp. 118-25)

Ulick Adare, the hero of **Dan Russel the Fox,** expresses the authors' opinion when he says, 'there's no such thing in literature as a Sporting Novel. The two things are incompatible.' For them the division between their novels and their sporting stories was clear, and all the time they were writing the **Irish R.M.** stories, they were planning to write a novel which would be very different from the stories. **Dan Russel** was started in 1904, then put to one side for six years. When they returned to it they were thinking of it for serialisation. It was mainly Pinker's encouragement which kept them at it, and which kept it light and sporty. When it was finished there was difficulty placing it, and they feared that they might have made a business error as well as an artistic mistake. Pinker tried to persuade Edith Somerville to illustrate it, but she refused, 'I detest an illustrated novel.' There seems to have been some confusion about this, because Violet Martin wrote to Lady Gregory saying that it was meant to have been a book of coloured pictures with stories appended, and that without the pictures it was a very light sporting story. She insisted that it was not a novel because a novel was a story 'that cannot be split up into isolated incidents', and this one had too obviously been written for serialisation. She even apologises when she returns proofs, 'It is, as a novel, a slight piece of work. We began it with a divided mind and an idea of short hunting sketches—but we hope it will read pleasantly.' Edith Somerville is equally lacking in confidence, and writes to a brother, 'We fear that everyone will be disappointed: the serious because it is sporting and the sporting because it is serious. I think about six people may like it'.

Violet Martin's wish, 'please goodness we need not write another hunting novel', was answered. And of all their work this is the one that is most concerned with the horse and the hound. It is so enthusiastic about hunting that it is almost a plea for the sport which took up so much of their time and energy. It is hunting from the point of view of avid enthusiasm. But, the enthusiasm is held in check by their literary talents, and the poise of the narrative does give detachment. Those who live merely for hunting are judged and in the judgment the book transcends the sporting story. The sub-title, 'An Episode in the Life of Miss Rowan' should not be forgotten. Miss Rowan, the protagonist, falls in love with John Michael, the personification of hunting, while Ulick Adare, the literary man, her social and mental equal, is cast to one side. The story of her relationships with these two men is quite different from anything in the sporting stories. The social background to the story is also done more seriously than anything in the tales.

Ulick Adare is hostile to hunting, which he sees as a waste of time, and to hunting people whom he sees as bores. He is Anglo-Irish but lives in London where his journalism earns him enough to keep his widowed mother and his Wicklow estate. Whereas his poetry is romantic and full of sentiment, he is ironic and detached, his friendships are intellectual. He enjoys Katharine's arguments and conversation, until she is rendered helpless by a fall and he falls in love with her. She belongs to his world; she is a writer too, and Ulick respects her literary judgments. After her fall from a horse, her first words on gaining consciousness are 'How much the mental consciousness is in advance of the physical!' When she is able to stand up she recalls a picture in *Punch* and mutters, 'And there be t'owd mare, and she be stearin' too, surely!'; two reactions which are quite lost on John Michael, he just does not understand their language. When Katharine meets Ulick unexpectedly in the middle of the Irish countryside he seems like her saviour, 'She was suddenly aware that she felt as might a marooned seaman, who, surrounded by friendly natives, sees a man-o'-war's boat arrive at his coral beach.' She admires Ulick's writing and his sensitive perceptions of life. She is an heiress, supremely confident and hypercritical, and yet through the lure of hunting she throws over all her literary friends, all civilised company (Mrs Masterman can hardly believe the uncouth community she enters, 'I have never before been in any part of Ireland where there was not so much as *one* white person,') and becomes as one with those who share her passion for the chase. 'Those of Katharine's friends who were wont to accuse her of excessive and wilful fastidiousness, would have been entertained at beholding her, wind-ruffled, flushed and voluble, riding along a bog-road with two buckeens of low degree, deeply immersed in the affairs of a cultureless, not to say barbarous community.'

John Michael has the looks of a Spanish gypsy and not an idea in his head beyond hunting. Mrs Masterman, who as her name implies is not very susceptible to the charms of the other sex, can only see him as 'that fox-hunting yokel; whose solitary means of expression is to blow a horn!' But for Katharine he is 'like Saint George on horseback . . . courage found its best expression in horsemanship, and horsemanship was summed up in John Michael'. When he is riding she actually purports to see his halo and begins to string together words 'about Grace and Courage and Speed'. He is unfortunately stupid and lacking in all imagination. The differences between the two characters, and the difference between John Michael as he actually is and John Michael as he appears to Katharine are shown dramatically and with humour. He is immensely shy, and at his mother's tea party he perches on a piano stool so tense with nerves that Katharine feels 'if so much as a twig cracked he would melt into the upright piano, even as Daphne was merged in the laurel.' After she has made efforts at conversation he at last screws up courage to talk to her:

> 'I suppose you were never at Cahirmee?' said John Michael with an effort that wrung a creak from the music-stool.
>
> Katharine felt that she was witnessing the awakening of a social conscience. It was unfortunate that she was obliged to answer the question in the negative.
>
> 'Well, it's a chancey place to buy a colt.'

At this stage she can still see clearly, 'He's a nice gentle thing, . . . When I die I'm going to endow a hospital for the Shy, and there shall be a John Michael ward.' But as she falls deeper into the passion of hunting, her vision dims.

When the three main characters are together their relationships are expressed with comic contrasts. John Michael is hunting rabbits when he comes across Ulick reading his poetry to Katharine. She at once switches her enthusiasm from the poetry to the previous day's hunting, ending her rhapsody, 'One crowded hour of glorious life!' John Michael's reply, 'It was more than an hour, I made it an hour and seventeen minutes,' is all that Ulick could wish. When Katharine, to annoy Ulick, goes on to wish they were hunting on such a beautiful day, John Michael is as literal as before, 'I'm afraid there wouldn't be much of a scent.' To Katharine this naïvety and simple mindedness is attractive, 'She was in the mood to feel the charm of simplicity.' His limited consciousness and his one-track mind do give him a sincerity which Katharine is sophisticated enough to respect. What she fails to see is that his lack of complication, imagination and awareness of his own sexual attractiveness, is a kind of sub-normality. He is, as Captain Bolger says, 'A kind of a nun of a fellow' because he has no sense of people as being in any way different from his hounds. When he is at his most gentle he looks at Katharine, 'almost as kindly as if she were a hound'. When his mother tells him that Katharine would like to marry him he is most upset, 'angry, violently angry . . . to say a low, dirty thing like that about a lady'. He has no concept of marriage as being different from the mating of hounds, 'I'd hate to be married, I'd sooner sweep a kennel in America.'

The scenes of the misery of unrequited love are well done; all of Ulick's and Katharine's reading of love poetry is of no help to them. When he tells her of his love it is nauseating to her, deeply in love as she is with John Michael, 'it was not beautiful to her, nor eloquent, nor compelling; worst of all, it failed to enlist her sympathy. It was merely bewildering, and immensely distasteful.' She cannot help but cringe away from Ulick and deal 'helplessly and conventionally with the greatest miracle of all'. This scene is counterpointed with the one of Mrs Delanty confessing her love to John Michael. He knows that something is up, 'Suspicion, reasonless and deep, like that of a woodland animal, kept him silent', but he just does not know how to respond on a personal level. She begs him to stay in Ireland:

> 'You and me would run the whole show between us!'
>
> Her cheeks were hot and her voice was changed and wavering.
>
> 'It'd be like old times when we were friends first!'
>
> John Michael was aware of a pang approaching physical terror, and, by some sub-connection of ideas, saw before his eyes an ornate cigarette case, bestowed upon him four Christmases ago by Mrs Delanty, and never since revealed to human eye, an object at once abhorrent and alarming to him.
>
> 'Thank you,' he said hurriedly, 'I don't think that would do very well.'

When she seizes hold of him and bursts into tears asking him to stay for her sake, he is paralysed with tension and embarrassment. Whereas Katharine is alarmed at Ulick's suffering and deeply sorry for him, and does her best to tell him the truth as gently as she can, John Michael, in a similar situation, says nothing. When Mrs Delanty has gone he begins to stir the hounds' pudding dragging the shovel round and round and says, 'Oh, my goodness! That was awful!' In their different ways the characters here do feel much more than any of those in *The Irish R.M.* stories. There is none of the agony of the passion of the novels, and compared with *The Real Charlotte* the suffering is not deep, but Katharine, Ulick and John Michael do each get involved emotionally. The novel does prove Ulick wrong when he denies the existence of the sporting novel because, 'Sentiment, romance, character, even humour, they simply don't exist where sport is concerned.' Sentiment and romance there are in plenty, character and humour too.

The most striking minor characters are all women. Katharine's travelling companion and Ulick's cousin, a wealthy English matriarch whose husband is tucked away in India, strides through the book dominating all, and amused by Ulick and Katharine. The plight of an unmarried penniless woman is dramatically presented in the character of Miss Scanlan. She, the eldest of eighteen, acts as cook and maid to her married sister, grateful for being given a home; 'education, especially for females, was deemed a superfluity, and the family talent for marriage not being bestowed upon her, she had spent her life as unpaid nurserymaid, unpaid dressmaker, and unpaid sick nurse to her relations. Having no money she had no influence, standing or significance.' Mrs Delanty whose share of the family's talent for marriage was to run away at the age of seventeen with a ne'er do well, is a young and attractive widow. She has life under control now and is eminently capable and self-sufficient. She can save money by turning her hand to most things, and by economising stringently she can keep a horse and hunt. She is on the look-out for a second husband, and she never overlooks a chance of personal advancement. But her vitality and gift of expression lift her far above her English equivalent, 'Of course Gus is an old friend of mine, but I must say I never liked him very much.' It is the voice of Francie Fitzpatrick we hear in Aix-les-Bains (where Mrs Delanty is an elderly woman's companion) when she takes her first sip of white wine:

' "Oh, Heavenly Powers!" she gasped, and the South of Ireland lay bare, "that's awful! That's the ugly wine! For gracious' sake, is it poison?" ' Despite all her common sense she can do nothing about her hopeless love for John Michael, and makes a last bid for him even though it means risking losing the wealthy Englishman who is eating out of her hand. In her passion for the simple and beautiful John Michael, she herself is lifted above her life of calculations and economies, 'in that insane moment of surrender and self-forgetfulness, the small, second-rate, egotistical soul of Mrs Delanty found wings, and spread them in a larger air.'

Mrs Fitz-Symons, like Mrs Delanty and her sister, helps to give us the solid social background; John Michael's mother, she is very unlike him, being fat, coarse and extremely voluble with the Irish countrywoman's gift of the gab. When Mrs Masterman makes the perennial complaint about Irish servants, Mrs Fitz-Symons responds, 'I have one this minute, a great, good-natured-slob of a girl, that'd sit up all night with you if you were ill, and if you were well, maybe she wouldn't get out of her bed at all!' She is perfectly content with her lot in life, adores her son, John Michael, and really does not care whether her new neighbours bother to know her or not, 'I'm too old to go calling on grand English ladies like them! They wouldn't be bothered with me!' She is an excellent hostess and when Captain Bolger calls unexpectedly she immediately makes him very welcome, and sits down to talk to him.

> Mrs Fitz-Symons picked up a half-knitted stocking, and seating herself at the other side of the fire, began to knit in a comfortable and conversational manner. The fact that she had on her housekeeping apron, and a tweed cap that had been discarded by her younger son, did not disturb her in the least.

As for humour, the last ingredient which Ulick fears is swallowed up by the master passion sport, there is no shortage of that. The dialect is as humorous as in any of their writings. Mrs Delanty's servant girl, who is forced to wait at table, offers an omelette when there is no plate to put it on, and says afterwards, 'When a thing'd go wrong that way, an' I goin' round the ladies and gentlemen, I'd busht out shweatin'!' The blacksmith describes how weak he felt after having the flu, 'afther leaving the bed, if it was no more than the frivolity of putting on me little gansey, I'd be in a passpiration with the dint of it.' There is the conversation Katharine overhears on the boat as it draws near Kingstown; the stewardess asks, 'Will I get you some nice hot water to wash your hands?' and receives the memorable reply, 'Ah, thank ye, no. I'll not mind. I'm going to relations.' And there is the pervading humour of the whole, which presents the characters to us with detachment and holds the entire story, including the hunting episodes, in comic judgment. (pp. 139-46)

> *Hilary Robinson, in her* Somerville & Ross: A Critical Appreciation, *Gill and Macmillan, 1980, 217 p.*

Anthony Cronin   (essay date 1983)

[*In the following excerpt, Cronin analyzes the strong female characters in many of Somerville and Ross's more serious works.*]

The binding theme of the two best-known novels of Somerville and Ross is the attempt by a strong-minded woman to reverse or control circumstance; to acquire or defend property; to improve or enhance her own or her family's social position. Charlotte Mullen in *The Real Charlotte* has neither birth, nor breeding, nor, to begin with at least, money. Nor has she any of the "natural" weapons of her sex: grace, charm or good looks. A certain rough wit and readiness at repartee ensure her the form of acceptance as a "character" that is always available in Ireland, whatever the social milieu; but her comparative literacy and her undoubted intelligence give rise, if anything, to suspicion. A land-agent's daughter who inherits the property of the aunt with whom she has lived as a poor relation, she occupies an uneasy position in the hierarchies of Protestantism in and around the town of Lismoyle. Tally-Ho Lodge is far below Bruff Castle, the home of the Dysart family and the centre of everybody's social ambitions. But it is not so far below Bruff Castle as it is above the hovels of the fish-women to whom Charlotte lends money at exorbitant interest.

Charlotte has many schemes, but the instrument of one of them is to be her nineteen-year-old orphan cousin Francie Fitzpatrick, a common but pretty girl from Dublin. If she can be thrown together with Christopher Dysart in suitable circumstances a match may result. The prospects for Charlotte of such an alliance would be dazzling. What ruins the scheme are Christopher's ambiguous, gentlemanly qualities and Francie's all too unambiguous reaction to the male attractiveness of one of the officers of the garrison, Captain Hawkins. Christopher is a Hamlet *de nos jours,* with a streak of intelligent cynicism just strong enough to unfit him for everything in the big world, including the career in the diplomatic service he is supposed to be pursuing, and a dash of artistic sensibility just too weak to make an artist of him. Conor Cruise O'Brien, in his essay on Somerville and Ross in *Writers and Politics,* has seen the attitude of the authors to the Dysarts as reflecting a snobbery which gives a coldness to the book. Francie, he says, is "not well-bred, and therefore not quite human". The Dysarts are a "highly idealised ascendancy family". It is a strange judgment, for Christopher is a prig, his father a lunatic at large and his mother a nincompoop. Francie, on the other hand, is vibrant with youth and the desire for life, a miraculously convincing portrait of a young woman on whom biology has conferred a radiance which far outshines her vulgarity and ignorance. Common, in the pejorative, merely social sense she may be. If she is commonplace, then life itself is commonplace and a bore; but, though it often seems so to Christopher, the authors know otherwise.

And the case with Charlotte is something likewise. This ugly, "thick-set" woman, scheming with Lambert the agent for possession of Gorthnamuckla, a half-ruined "little big house" and its lands; plotting her own social advancement through Francie; ceaselessly and dangerously active among the semi-dormant inhabitants of a torpid pool, seems to Dr. O'Brien to be "evil". It is a suggestion which reminds us that he once wrote a book about the Catholic novel which committed him to a sympathetic understanding of the notion that human beings can be the instruments of supernatural purposes, can, as it were, take on, from above or below, a goodness or badness beyond the human scale.

Fortunately, however, the authors of *The Real Charlotte* held a more rational view of the world we live in. Charlotte is a graceless, greedy, unscrupulous, secretive and ambitious woman. She plots her own advantage in a scheme of things in which the Dysarts have already so many advantages as to have no necessity to plot; and, if the principle of the world is energy, she is superior to

them, as indeed she knows herself to be. To believe that they are superior to her in any mode of conduct or activity except those dependent on prior possession, is to convict oneself of snobbery.

And accordingly the tragedy of the book is hers and Francie's. There are flickerings of tragedy in Christopher Dysart's situation: he could, after all, had he been a more determined young man, and capable of knowing what he wanted, have taken for bride, almost as of right, a beautiful nineteen-year-old who had evoked in him a response to life that little else seemed likely to do. The alternative, what he probably does take outside the confines of the book, is amply summed up by the portrait of the societally acceptable Miss Hope-Drummond, who is languidly setting her cap at him.

But Francie's enormous, if latent, sexual drive is focussed on the worthless, philandering Captain Hawkins. She neither properly understands nor cares about the rigid social conventions of Lismoyle society. She is not as concerned with her own advantage as everybody naturally assumes her to be. She misses her chance.

And, strangely enough, Charlotte's schemes also go partly awry because even ugly, masculine-seeming women are capable of passion: in her case directed at another worthless male weakling, the Dysarts' self-centred and dishonest agent, Roddy Lambert. Her desire to possess this vulgar oaf, who is, because of his wife's money and position fractionally higher in the social scale than herself, but as low or lower in any possible human one, involves her in several miscalculations. Since the book is concerned with triangular relationships which cannot be resolved, misunderstandings, ludicrously ill-founded loves and ambitions, it is possible to see it as comedy; and indeed it has, often enough, been so described. In fact it is written with a depth of feeling and a tenderness towards the unavailing in human love, particularly where Francie is concerned, that give it an extraordinary quality; but its underlying theme is the defeat of two women, both of whom in one way or another represent the life-force, by societal convention and coldness.

The theme of ***The Big House of Inver*** is also the defeat of a woman, Shibby Pindy or Prendeville, whose ambition is, in the scheme of things, impossible of realisation. The book was published in 1925; but its conception went back to 1912; and it seems only right to regard it as a joint work, particularly since Edith Somerville wished it to be thought of as such.

The big Queen Anne house of the title had been built by Robert Prendeville, a smuggling Galway landowner, whose handsome son, Beauty Kit, marries a great prize but dies of the smallpox. After his death his aristocratic wife shuts herself up in the big house and there lives

> for long, lonely years, refusing, in arrogance, to know, or to let her children know, her neighbours, freezing herself into, as it were, an iceberg of pride, living to see, at last, her only son, Nicholas, marry the daughter of one of the Inver gamekeepers, and her two daughters, Isabella and Nesta, go off with two of her own grooms.

The glories and greatness of Inver therewith suffered downfall. Five successive generations of mainly half-bred and wholly profligate Prendevilles rioted out their short lives in the Big House, living with country women, fighting, drinking, gambling.

In the sixth generation comes Captain Jas, whose army career ends in disgrace; whose dissipations are, like Lord Kilgobbin's, such that he finds the company of village toadies more congenial than that of his equals; and who, after the fashion of his kind, fathers a daughter, Isabella or Shibby, on a village girl who dies in child-bed. Partly in order to dish a cousin who expects to inherit, Captain Jas marries, at sixty-three, a respectable, but penniless and acquiescent young woman from the neighbouring town. The fruit of this late union is Christopher, a dazzlingly handsome young man who resembles his ancestor, Beauty Kit, and inherits much of the family's tendency to drift and dissipation.

Shibby and this seventh generation Kit, are therefore half-brother and sister, though there are forty years between them. When the story properly begins the big house facing the sea is shuttered and empty. Kit and his father live in the old Norman tower with Shibby as house-keeper and unacknowledged member of the family. The demesne has been acquired, along with much of the land, by the Weldons, who are the Prendeville's agents. It has become Shibby's passion to restore her beloved, beautiful half-brother to his inheritance; and to that end, though she would prefer a more aristocratic match, even another Lady Isabella had such been suitable, she plots a marriage with the Weldon's daughter, Peggy.

She is defeated in the end because Kit has too much of the Prendevilles as well as something of the peasant in him. He too has become carelessly involved with a village girl, Maggie Connor; she becomes pregnant, and his attempts to cast her off are complicated by her madness. There is a curious echo here of the partnership's first book, *An Irish Cousin,* in which a mad peasant girl had played a mysterious and never quite explained part in the general Gothic atmosphere: and of *The Silver Fox* in which Maria Quin's grief for her brother who has been killed by the hunt vents itself in curses on the uncaring riders. The demented figure of Maggie Connor flits in and out of the book, cursing Kit and the Prendevilles; and we cannot but feel that there is something in this recurrent theme of the ascendancy's superstitious fear of the "natives" whom they had wronged; who spoke a mysterious language and had mysterious powers pertaining to their ancient possession of the soil, something of the Anglo-Indian and African settlers' fear of the native magic. Finally Maggie Connor's drunken brother Jimmy waylays Peggy Weldon and tells her that Kit has fathered a child on his sister. In her confusion her parents succeed in getting her to accept an offer of marriage from a wealthy English bore, Sir Harold Burbank; but Captain Jas and Kit have already betrayed Shibby by selling the big house to him behind her back. Her breaking is in proportion to her strength and single-mindedness, which far exceed those of the men of the Prendeville line which she has tried to restore.

Between the publication of *The Silver Fox* and their next major novel, *Mount Music,* in 1919, the friends published three volumes of the perennially popular *Irish R.M.* stories, the first appearing in 1899. [The] date is important for extraneous reasons. These were the years of the establishment of county councils, the Congested Districts Board, of the Wyndham Land Acts, of Balfour's decision to kill Home Rule by kindness; and, though self-government began to become a serious question again when the Liberals raised it in 1912, with a certain amount of acquiescence in defeat and in the fairly good bargain they had made, the ascendancy could for a while view Ireland again in the way in which they had always wanted to view it, and as much Irish literature has succeeded in viewing it in flagrant defiance of all the facts: that is, as a sort of comic Arcadia, where confusion and misrule are rife but nobody comes to much harm except in a comic, knockabout way. It is a view that is reflected in much of the minor literature of the time, notably the novels of George A. Birmingham, the stories of Lynn Doyle and the poems of Percy French; and it has its attractions for minor writers even to-day.

Which is not to say that the *R.M.* stories do not have their own kind of realism. They contain more peasant characters than anything else the authors wrote. The observation is exact and the ear for dialogue superb. Patrick Kavanagh used to say that Somerville and Ross had a better ear for Irish dialogue than anybody except James Joyce; and something of its quality is summed up in the answer the engine driver in **'Poisson D'Avril'** gives to the warning about the local train's delay on the line, since "the goods" is coming behind: "Let her come. She'll meet her match."

In 1919, four years after Violet Martin's death, *Mount Music* appeared. Again the surviving author claimed that, in its genesis and its early drafts, it owed much to her friend; and again it seems only fair to grant the wish that it should, in some sense or other, be regarded as a collaboration. The main part and the climax of the story is set in 1907, a matter of some importance because between 1903 and 1909 tenant purchase was an option, but it was not yet compulsory for landlords to sell, and the Irish Party was still factionalised, the re-unification achieved under John Redmond not having been the success anticipated in 1900. The unusual precision of the dating is necessary because a good deal hinges on these facts.

Again the most interesting, and, with one exception, in all senses the strongest character is a woman; this time, for a change, a young woman, Christian Talbot-Lowry. Her father, a martial hero of Indian and Afghan conflicts, is the owner of Mount Music, the big house of the title. In spite of the fact that his wife, the daughter of an English earl, had brought twenty thousand golden sovereigns with her to Ireland, his estate is heavily mortgaged. He exists on credit, but sale to the tenants under the government scheme would leave him with neither ancestral home nor ready money, an outcome that, with weak obstinacy, he refuses to contemplate, though the refusal to sell has made him unpopular to the extent that obstacles are put in the way of the hunt and a horse that Christian is riding is killed after a man armed with a hay-knife suddenly appears at a bank it is jumping.

The attitudes of this stubborn "pterodactyl", as the authors call him, are contrasted with those of his young cousin and neighbour Larry Coppinger, of Coppinger's Court. The son of another Indian army hero who married a member of an ancient Catholic family in the North of England, Larry has been brought up in his mother's communion. Furthermore he has read *The Spirit of the Nation* and is able to quote Thomas Davis. Worse (from Dick Talbot-Lowry's point of view anyway) he has set a bad example by selling to his tenants. And to cap all he decides to stand as a nationalist candidate.

In some ways he is Christopher Dysart all over again: a dilettante in art, politics and love. He paints sporadically and without much determination. His share of the spirit of the nation is scarcely enough to carry him through the sordidities of a by-election campaign; and in any case he chooses the wrong faction and is defeated. When he comes up against Talbot-Lowry's opposition to his engagement to Christian he gives in without a struggle. And on the rebound he allows himself to become, engaged, almost against his will, to Tishy Mangan, the daughter of the local doctor, who is a prominent small-town politician with immense ambitions.

Dr. O'Brien sees Mangan as evil too: at least he speaks of a "daemonic force in a credible character"; but if that is the case there must have been a lot of daemonism around in 1907. The worst we can say of him is that he has secretly been buying up the mortgages on Mount Music; that he has ambitions beyond her social station for his daughter; and that he confuses her social advancement with her happiness. The best is that he is the strongest-minded male in the book.

There is a contrived happy ending, brought about by Tishy's elopement with the fellow she really loves and by the usual novelist's device of killing off one of the characters, in this case the daemonic Dr. Mangan. Christian gets her Larry, with what ultimate result in happiness we know not. Maybe she had what marriage councillors call "strength enough for two".

The killing off of Dr. Mangan is a not untypical device. Somerville and Ross were not averse to doing in a character to round off a book. Their most entrancing and successful creation, Francie Fitzpatrick, is killed off at the end of *The Real Charlotte,* after Roddy Lambert's wife has already been got out of the way. Captain Jas dies amid the flames of the big house of Inver. They were novelists and they wrote the novel as it is written. At a crucial stage of *The Real Charlotte* Francie accidentally drops a letter and a photograph of Captain Hawkins on the floor in front of Christopher Dysart; and a great deal is made to hinge on Charlotte Mullen's discovery of Lambert's cheques and account books. They tell a story, often the sort of story in which the reader agonises for the outcome. Were it not for Dr. O'Brien's testimony that he finds the class convention comes between her and our pity, it would be difficult to imagine a reader who did not agonise for the fate of poor Francie Fitzpatrick.

But this ability of theirs to make a causative narrative construction hinges on more than a willingness to make unblushing use of passable chance or coincidence. The novel as it is written needs people who can go up or down the social ladder, who are anxious for social advancement or the retention of their position but conscious of social convention. There has to be the possibility not only of ruin but of lesser punishments, such as disgrace and ostracisation, often visited on the improperly ambitious.

As ascendancy writers Somerville and Ross had the advantage of having rigid social conventions to deal with. They also had wealth as a subject and the possibility of quite large-scale reversals and advancements of family fortune. They had a keen sense of social position and property, with what they thought of as its traditions, was an important theme to them. It has not been so to other Irish writers who were more infected by the general atmosphere which I have called in the chapter on William Carleton one of near-anarchic "sloth, cheer and despair." Of course in literature they were traditionalists too. For all these reasons they wrote novels, not fictive constructions like Joyce, Flann O'Brien and Beckett; imaginative transpositions of circumstance like Francis Stuart or George Moore, chronicles such as *Castle Rackrent,* or mélanges of anecdote such as Lever and Carleton delighted in. They wrote extended anecdotes in the three *R.M.* volumes all right; but in *The Real Charlotte* they wrote the only great Irish novel that is really and truly a novel and employs all the novelist's devices shamelessly but with finesse.

You can say that this lessens it if you like, but we must judge by results. I have spoken of their major, or binding theme; but there are riches and to spare within it and released by it, as one theme is released by another in great literature. It is an enormously sharp-witted and perceptive social drama, with tragic results for at least two of the participants to some extent dependent on the arbitrary conventions of the social code. It contains two of the most convincing and penetrating portraits of women in all literature, and in Francie's case one of the most enchanting. In Francie's marriage to Lambert, as in Peggy Weldon's and, to a lesser degree, Tishy Mangan's parentally inspired engagements, the situation of women who marry or become engaged under social and economic pressure evokes in the authors a deep, sympathetic response, which is part of their vision of the struggle between the life-force, in its often distorted forms, and its enemies in their often more acceptable ones.

But besides these things there are throughout it, as throughout the rest of their work, more evocative descriptions of the Irish landscape in its various moods than anyone else has written. And above all, perhaps, there is also, in its very depths, a heartbreaking awareness of the tiny chances and mischances, the moments of misapprehension and indecision, on which the huge, eternal destinies of lovers hang.

What actual experiences of these matters the authors may have had, we do not really know. From the accounts of their relationship and writing methods they gave there must have been a deep undercurrent of psychic sympathy between them. Let us hope, for their sakes, that there was something more, at least in the avowal. But, whether or no, they were still probably blessed beyond the ordinary. (pp. 78-86)

Anthony Cronin, "Edith Somerville and Martin Ross: Women Fighting Back," in his Heritage Now: Irish Literature in the English Language, *St. Martin's Press, 1983, pp. 75-86.*

Maureen Waters (essay date 1984)

[*In the excerpt below, Waters explores the depiction of comic Irish stereotypes that appear in the* Irish R.M. *stories.*]

The character of Major Yeates, the R.M. or Resident Magistrate, provides [the *Irish R.M.*] stories with an important unifying element since it is from his perspective that the comedy develops. Civil, modest and good natured, Yeates is spokesman for a legal system represented as equally benevolent. He is, however, continually frustrated by Gaels of every description, by the climate, the animals, the landscape, the physical stubborn quality of Ireland, itself. Moreover, Yeates discovers soon after his arrival at Shreelane, in the Southwest near Cork, that there is a mysterious dynamism at work, an energy, a palpable resistance to reason. The method which he attempts to apply is everywhere undermined by a mode of life that is distinctly alien. This is not to suggest that Yeates is doctrinaire in his thinking; he is generally tolerant and even humorous but, in the main, consistent in his behavior and attitudes and so becomes a perfect foil to the unpredictable countryman.

In his *Study of Celtic Literature* (1867), Matthew Arnold put an authoritative gloss on qualities attributed to Saxon and Celt during the nineteenth century. Although his intention—the establishment of a Chair of Celtic Studies at Oxford—was both magnanimous and successful, one result was the perpetuation of a stereotype which had an adverse effect on the Home Rule movement. On the one hand he postulated a balanced, rational Saxon with a genius for government and material prosperity; and on the other, an emotional, sensual Celt, wanting in "sanity and steadfastness," quick to rebel against the "despotism of fact." Such qualities were said to account for the failure of the latter to reach any "material civilization sound and satisfying and not out at elbows; poor, slovenly and half-barbarous." He wrote at length of the Celt's love of beauty, his spirituality and "penetrating melancholy." He pronounced the Celtic sensibility with its "nervous exaltation" to be "feminine" in quality and remarked on the "extravagance and exaggeration of the sentimental Celtic nature" before concluding that the Celt lacked "a promising political temperament."

The *Irish R.M.* stories may be read as a comic exposition of Arnold's thesis because the duality that he argues for is basic to the authors' conception of character. One difference worth emphasizing, however, is that Yeates, who bears the burden of reason and steadfastness, is Anglo-Irish and consequently more resilient than the merely English stereotype would allow.

Violet Powell has commented on the fact that "Great-Uncle McCarthy," the opening story in *Some Experiences of An Irish R.M.,* offers a paradigm of the relationship between Yeates and the country people. The dominant image in the story is the large old dilapidated house rented by Yeates, which he tries to make over according to his own standards. The house is drafty, damp and riddled with vermin. But the most disquieting element is the mysterious shuffling at night along the upper floors, a "pervading sub-presence," which Yeates is encouraged to believe is the ghost of his landlord's great-uncle McCarthy. He eventually discovers that he is the unwitting host of some elderly McCarthys who, with the aid of the housekeeper, have made themselves comfortable in the attic, helping themselves to Yeates's food and whiskey. The McCarthys, comic tattered ghosts of a once powerful clan, never concede any wrongdoing. They insist that the rights of kinship have precedence over any legal contract.

Yeates's struggle with that house and its inhabitants is the first stage of a continuing effort to domesticate and civilize, to bring order and harmony and cleanliness to the province of Shreelane. The local people resist by adhering to tribal rituals and loyalties which are inscrutable to the R.M. Wakened one night, he goes out into the garden where a dead crow falls at his feet. An odd enough circumstance, rendered all the more peculiar by the fact that the crow has been dead for some time. In Shreelane, however, a fact is not easily or necessarily linked to a definable cause.

In "Great-Uncle McCarthy," as in many of the stories that follow, Yeates is the butt of the joke. He is frequently duped by local people who know much more about a given situation than he does. They connive and collaborate all the while covering their tracks by a pretense of ignorance or ineptitude or superstitious fear. While they obviously reflect nineteenth century stereotypes of the Irish, to a certain extent they use these stereotypes to advantage, enjoying the game while profiting from Yeates's inability to check them even when he guesses the truth.

Through Yeates's eyes the Irish often appear vigorous and imaginative, but they are also unreliable, highly emotional, manipulative, verbally very clever clowns. They seem eager to please, but are, in fact, intractable and impervious to change. As a result, the Anglo-Irishman must suffer his property to deteriorate, must be prepared for discomfort and delay, and the continual intrusion of the "personal element" in all details of life. The perspective of Somerville and Ross is not completely one-sided, however. The vagaries of the pleasure loving Irish are to some extent balanced by those of the Anglo-Irish gentry who seem to have an infinite capacity for discomfort and boredom, much of it endured in the name of sport or social obligation. Yeates and his English wife, Philippa, are discreet, polite, conventional people, more fitted to accept than to alter circumstances. It often seems that the clash of cultures provides the only real excitement in their lives.

These cultural differences are best illustrated in the matter of law. As Resident Magistrate, Yeates attempts to render judgments on the basis of an objective examination of the evidence. The local people, on the other hand, openly flout the law when they cannot bend it to their own interests. Giving testimony in court is looked upon as an opportunity to demonstrate their powers of rhetoric and flair for the dramatic. This is vividly demonstrated in **"The Waters of Strife"** when the mother of a man accused of murder is called as a witness. She pretends great ignorance and humility, trembling before the lawyers with their "big rocks of English," sobbing into her handkerchief, but nonetheless quick to offer a bribe. On the stand she proves her mettle: "Bat Callaghan's mother had nothing to fear from the inquiry. She was by turns deaf, imbecile, garrulously candid, and furiously abusive of the principal witness." The case ends with the complete certainty that the accused is guilty, but the law is rendered helpless by the tactics of witnesses like Mrs. Callaghan. Justice is finally achieved when the guilty man dies of fright, imagining he is pursued by the ghost of his victim. It is notable that in this story, as in so much nineteenth century fiction, the Irish are regarded as primarily "superstitious" rather than "religious."

The circumvention of the law is also an important theme in **"The Holy Island"** and **"Oweneen the Sprat."** In these stories humor is generated by the legendary capacity of the Irish for hard liquor and linked to Yeates's futile efforts to establish order in the place of anarchy.

In **"The Holy Island"** a ship is wrecked off the coast of Shreelane and barrels of rum are washed ashore. The local people regard the whole thing as a great "spree," drinking up as much of it as they can get their hands on, despite Yeates's attempt to save the cargo. Some of the more enterprising make off with a sizable quantity of liquor, which is then concealed on the "holy island." Subsequent disturbances on that island are attributed to supernatural causes, and there is considerable rumor about the potency of the "holy water" to be had there. Before the police can investigate, however, the rum has been happily sent on to Cork attached to the bishop's funeral train.

In **"Oweneen the Sprat"** Yeates is threatened with a suit by a local character who fell, while drunk, in the path of his carriage. Although uninjured, Owen Twohig pretends to be crippled for life, and terrible tales of his sufferings and obscure threats of vengeance trickle back to Yeates's household, to be related with pleasurable hysteria by the Irish servants.

Yeates resists the growing pressure to capitulate, but his determination crumbles once he meets Mrs. Twohig, the mother of "Oweneen," and is forced to listen to an interminable account of the "hard life," that is, the unmerited suffering of her "little orphans" for the last thirty years. The details are strangely garbled, palpably false and delivered in a medley of words in which English has undergone a transformation of both sound and meaning. Not even Yeates's disgust at the squalor of her home, with its implication of idleness and poor management, frees him from her spell, from the unswerving righteousness of her manner, her apparent conviction that Oweneen will be "under clutches" ("on crutches") for the rest of his life. Conceding defeat, he offers her money and flees.

Yeates's dilemma is resolved just as he is about to abandon all efforts at a legal solution. He sets out laden with gifts, prepared to offer personal restitution when he surprises a group of men enjoying a bowling game. In hot pursuit of a ball, Oweneen runs straight into the arms of Yeates. Thus the duplicity is exposed, but the result is laughter. What better jest than to bring suit against a magistrate, to force him into a position from which neither the law nor his superior social advantage can extricate him?

In these stories the Irish continue to be judged purely in terms of establishment norms, and there is not the slightest hint that there might be any flaw in a legal structure which is inappropriate to and out of sympathy with local interests. The poverty of the Irish is typically linked to their unsteadiness of character, their indifference to material needs, to authority, to practical forms of organization. John Kelleher has pointed out that many of these so-called Celtic qualities, emphasized by Matthew Arnold and other Victorians like Somerville and Ross, were taken as virtues by the writers of the Revival.

The "Celtic imagination" is treated with some ambivalence by Somerville and Ross who enjoy a laugh even at their own expense but tend to see the Irish countryman as primarily manipulative and weak in moral judgment. This is evident in **"Lisheen Races, Second-Hand"** even though the butt of the joke turns out to be an Englishmen, Leigh Kelway, who is gathering material for a novel. The plot moves quickly through a series of mishaps which leave Kelway more and more gloomy, but which certainly afford him opportunity to study his subject at close hand. He is marooned for hours in a public house crammed with men drinking together after the races, where the "bread tasted of mice, the butter of turf-smoke, the tea of brown paper." The high points of the races are provided by Slipper who, in many respects, is a throwback to the simple clown. Dressed in ill fitting and oddly assorted garments, he is invariably drunk, self-effacing, unreliable. His humor reveals an "exulting pessimism" and a taste for extravagant detail, but the climax of the story, in which one of the riders is thrown, is a comic version of a near fatal injury suffered by Violet Martin:

> . . . "before ye could say 'shnipes,' the mare was standing on her two ears beyond in th' other field! . . . she stood that way till she reconnoithered what side would Driscoll fall an' she turned about then and rolled on him as cosy as if he was meadow grass!"
>
> Slipper stopped short; the people in the doorway groaned appreciatively; Mary Kate murmured: "The Lord save us!"
>
> "The blood was dhruv out through his nose and ears," continued Slipper, with a voice that indicated the cream of the narration "and you'd hear his bones crackin' on the ground! You'd have pitied the poor boy."
>
> "Good heavens!" said Leigh Kelway, sitting up very straight in his chair.
>
> "Was he hurt, Slipper?" asked Flurry casually.
>
> "Hurt is it?" echoed Slipper in high scorn; 'killed on the spot!'

The unfortunate rider eventually turns up "with a face like a red-hot potato tied up in a bandage."

In his classic essay, *On the Study of Celtic Literature,* Matthew Arnold suggested that the imagination and energy of the Celt be viewed as complements to the genius of Saxon and Norman and that a fruitful culture would emerge once these elements were properly understood. Somerville and Ross, speaking out of personal and historic circumstances, took a skeptical view. In their stories wily Irish clowns seem bent on pulling down every outpost of civilization. In the face of their contempt for English government and their adherence to a more primitive, but always more inspired, way of life, Yeates's system of reason and moral order is doomed to failure. The best he can do is maintain an ironic distance while bending to the inevitable. His decision is no doubt related to the fact that Somerville and Ross witnessed the collapse of their own familiar, privileged world. With the establishment of the Irish Free State in 1921, Edith Somerville (Violet Martin died in 1915) became a displaced person, forced to sell her family estate because of debt.

There is certainly a class consciousness and a racist consciousness at work in Somerville and Ross, and they undoubtedly contributed to the stereotype of the Irish countryman as a tricky clown, which has currency even today. It should be acknowledged, however, that their faults are outweighed by the merit of their best stories. On the whole their characters have wit and vitality, and the dialogue attributed to their country people, despite some stage Irishisms, is better and more accurate than that of most comic writers who preceded them. Like their contemporaries, John Synge and Augusta Gregory, they listened avidly and recorded local speech, and they made some attempt to learn Irish. In many instances their dialogue ("That one has a tongue that'd clip a hedge"; "I had to put the height of the house of curses to it before Mary would believe me") is an exact replica of this recorded speech. Rejecting the sentimental comedy of the previous era, Somerville and Ross wrote with a biting humor and satire which reflects their kinship with Jonathan Swift, Maria Edgeworth and John Synge.

Somerville and Ross have that firm grasp of detail and economy of plot essential to good satire. Their precisely polished prose is distinguished by metaphor which is often original and zany in character. Even their hunting stories, which seem tedious today, are redeemed by flashes of wit. Few writers are so successful in recording the distinctive qualities of dogs, horses, animals of all kinds.

In many stories, such as **"Oweneen the Sprat," "Poisson D'Avril"** and **"The House of Fahy,"** animals, objects, even the physical landscape take on an eccentric character of their own. The effect is to suggest the uncertainty of life in a way that is peculiarly modern because of its fusion of the comic and the grotesque. In the first story, for example, Yeates imagines the bicycle on which he travels a mountain road being transformed into "an opinionated and semi-paralyzed wheelbarrow." In **"Poisson D'Avril"** he takes a slow and difficult trip by a train which makes unscheduled stops to allow the crew to enjoy a card game.

Yeates has the additional burden of an enormous salmon which has been promised for a wedding feast:

> We had about fifteen miles to go, and we banged and bucketed over it in what was, I should imagine, record time. The carriage felt as if it were galloping on four wooden legs, my teeth chattered in my head, and the salmon slowly churned its way forth from its newspaper, and moved along the netting with dreadful stealth.

"The House of Fahy" begins with a voyage aboard a dingy yacht where Yeates has a premonition of the comic disaster which looms ahead: " . . . resting on the sea's rim, a purple bank of clouds lay awaiting the descent of the sun, as seductively and as malevolently as a damp bed at a hotel awaits a traveller." The night which finally envelops them is as "black as the inside of a cow."

Somerville and Ross underscore the limitations of human resources in the face of a reality which is faintly sinister but clearly absurd. In their work as a whole, however, the theme of the absurd—that unsettling and inexplicable "sub-presence"—is most consistently and forcibly linked with the Irish country people against whom the Sisyphean Yeates may persist but never prevail. (pp. 15-22)

Maureen Waters, "The Rustic Clown or Fool," in her The Comic Irishman, *State University of New York Press, 1984, pp. 9-27.*

Edith Somerville in 1948.

Harold Orel   (essay date 1987)

[*In the following excerpt, Orel analyzes some of the themes and characters in the* Irish R.M. *stories, and finds a positive, truthful representation of Irish life and culture.*]

The thirty-four stories of Somerville and Ross have been reprinted in one volume under an omnibus title, ***The Irish R. M. and His Experiences*** (1928). For three generations the authors have been censured for adopting wholeheartedly and uncritically the prejudices of the Ascendancy class (to which, indeed, Somerville and Ross belonged), but the fact that their narratives bubbled over with good cheer, and had little or nothing bad to say about the English who were grinding down the Irish remorselessly in everybody else's fictions, does not change the bases of their continuing appeal.

The accusation deserves re-examination, nevertheless. Most of the historians of Irish literature who omit E. OE. Somerville and Martin Ross from consideration—for example, Herbert Howarth's *The Irish Writers / Literature and Nationalism 1880-1940* (1958) has no index-entry for two of the most popular writers of the period he is considering—forget (or perhaps are ignorant of the fact) that Major Sinclair Yeates, the Resident Magistrate who tells all the stories in the first person, says that he is Irish himself. Major Yeates—educated at Sandhurst—has seen service in India, and is in his middle 30s when we first meet him; the time covered by the stories runs from shortly before the Boer War to a few years following the Great War, in other words, from the last of his bachelor days to at least the ninth birthday of his son.

It is true, of course, that Major Yeates is seldom wholly absorbed by the riotous events that take place in a Petty Sessions Court in southwestern Ireland. If Somerville and Ross had so chosen, they could have alluded more directly to the major events affecting Ireland between 1890 and 1920. Florence McCarthy Knox, or Flurry, Major Yeates's landlord and perhaps the most picturesque single character of the entire series, goes off to serve with the Irish Yeomanry during the South African War, but neither while fighting overseas nor after he returns to his "Black Protestant" tribe do we hear the slightest hint of a moral stance taken toward that particular conflict. Home Rule, so far as we can tell, is not an issue Major Yeates wants to think about. The one casual mention it receives is somewhat like thunder heard on a distant horizon; it is, at any rate, a long way from Shreelane, the Major's home, and from Skebawn, the nearby town. Indeed, if it were not for the Major's wife—Philippa—who has a lively sympathy for Irish problems, and who even tries to learn the Irish language from the National schoolmaster, we would not know that the Celtic Movement has infiltrated to this remote corner of Ireland. "My own attitude with regard to the Celtic movement," the Major writes in **"The Last Day of Shraft,"** "was sympathetic, but a brief inspection of the grammar convinced me that my sympathies would not survive the strain of tripthongs, eclipsed consonants, and synthetic verbs, and that I should do well to refrain from embittering my declining years by an impotent and humiliating pursuit of the most elusive of pronunciations."

The Major does not demur when Joseph Francis M'Cabe, in **"The Shooting of Shinroe,"** points out that the English are different from the Irish because they like to arrange things. But it is not clear that "arranging" things improves anybody's temper, or contributes to the good life. There is a logic inherent in the chaos of Irish life. In **"The Friend of Her Youth,"** the point is made that signposts do not exist in this remote corner of the world: "The residents, very reasonably, consider them to be superfluous, even ridiculous, in view of the fact that everyone knows the way, and as for strangers, 'haven't they tongues in their heads as well as another?' It all tends to conversation and an increased knowledge of human nature." Who can gainsay the conclusion?

The English need to be educated, since they know so little about Ireland. One of the most often anthologized stories, **"Lisheen Races, Second-hand,"** tells us of Yeates's fellow-student at Magdalene, Leigh Kelway, who is making his way steadily up the ladder of bureaucratic success (the Major notes that Kelway's eyes have acquired "a statesmanlike absence of expression"), and who is acting as private secretary to Lord Waterbury, a man intensely interested in "the Liquor Question in Ireland." Kelway thinks that the best way to proceed is to gather statistics, and the Major finds that the friend of his youth has turned into a dull dog indeed. What better way to help Kelway learn about the Irish first-hand than to take him to Mohona, "our champion village, that boasts fifteen public-houses out of twenty buildings of sorts and a railway station"; and to allow him to hear the prosecution of a publican for selling drink on a Sunday, "which gave him an opportunity of studying perjury as a fine art, and of hearing a lady, on whom police suspicion justly rested, profoundly summed up by the sergeant as 'a woman who had th' appairance of having knocked at a back door.'" Kelway does not know what to do with such data (which, of course, go to the heart of the matter that he and Lord Waterbury are investigating), and, as the Major sighingly reports, "The net result of these experiences has not yet been given to the world by Leigh Kelway."

The differences between England and Ireland are infinite in number, and obvious enough, and unbridgeable. The English like order, routine, the solace to be derived from a contemplation of iterative acts. The Irish refuse to be cabined, cribbed, confined. As the Major writes in **"Poisson d'Avril,"** even before the hilarious chain of unlikely events related to an eight-pound salmon has time to connect its first two links, "Before the train was signalled I realized for the hundredth time the magnificent superiority of the Irish mind to the trammels of officialdom, and the invetereate supremacy in Ireland of the Personal Element."

The Major comes down firmly on the side of the Irish way of doing things, even though he is frequently (and unpleasantly) surprised, discomfited, and even (when the hunt is in full swing and at its most unpredictable) terrified by how it's all turning out. In **"The Waters of Strife,"** the Major contemplates briefly, through the isinglass of memory, boat races at Oxford: "a vision of smart parasols, of gorgeous barges, of snowy-clad youths, and of low slim outriggers, winged with the level flight of oars, slitting the water to the sway of the line of flat backs." But that was Oxford, and no world is farther away in space and time than that of Lough Lonen, the scene of the regatta to which the Major has pledged his patronage:

> Certainly undreamed-of possibilities in aquatics were revealed to me as I reined in the Quaker on the outskirts of the crowd, and saw below me the festival of the Sons of Liberty in full swing. Boats of all shapes and sizes, outrageously overladen, moved about the lake, with oars flourishing to the strains of concertinas. Black swarms of people seethed along the water's edge, congesting here and there round the dingy tents and stalls of green apples and the club's celebrated brass band, enthroned in a wagonette, and stimulated by the presence of a barrel of porter on the box-seat, was belching forth "The Boys of Wexford," under the guidance of a disreputable ex-militia drummer, in a series of crashing discords.

How tame, how pallid, Oxford seems by contrast! How lively the Irish scene!

Part of what the Major enjoys is the courtesy extended to him, and part of that, to be sure, is his due as Resident magistrate (a post, by the way, that has long since been extinguished in the Republic); but most of the good manners and the politeness he encounters may be attributed to a natural Irish graciousness. Time after time, Yeates meets strangers who treat him as a prince, and speak fair and shining words to him. Indeed, the stories record an exuberance of language that has no natural counterpart in late Victorian literature on the other side of St. George's Channel or the Irish Sea. Who can forget (once he has been introduced to the expression) the subtle definition of the police sergeant who speaks of "parties" brought into court for violating the peace as "not to say dhrunk, but in good fighting thrim"? Equally memorable is the story of the way in which a two-gallon jar of potheen, thrown from a top back window to avoid seizure by the police who are searching the premises, falls on a goose, and kills it to the bone; "but the trouble was, that on account of falling on the goose the jar wasn't broken, so the bobbies got the potheen." When Slipper (a recurring colorful, and disreputable, character, the only one Somerville and Ross admitted had been drawn from the life) describes a horse falling over on its rider, "The blood was dhruv out through his nose and ears, and you'd hear his bones crackin' on the ground. . . . " Flurry, casually, asks whether the rider was hurt (Flurry knows how to discount this hyperbole). " 'Hurt is it?' " echoed Slipper in high scorn; " 'killed on the spot!' He paused to relish the effect of the *dénouement*. . . . 'Oh, divil so pleasant an afthernoon ever you seen. . . . ' " In **"The Whiteboys,"** the carman muses, "You wouldn't know [what ails old Mr. O'Reilly, who has been sick for a long time]. Sure he's very old, and that 'fluenzy has the country destroyed; there's people dying now that never died before."

It is equally difficult to forget the dapper young priest who disapproves of the appearance of a horse at the Poundlick

Races: "That horse is no good. Look at his great flat feet! You'd bake a cake on each of them!" And surely nobody has ever mistranslated the Latin expression, *"De gustibus non est disputandum,"* with as much gusto as the anonymous Irishman who renders it thus: "You cannot touch pitch without being disgusted."

No single quotation, however, can do justice to a fairly complicated set of attitudes toward Irish life and culture, but I think it is safe to say that Somerville and Ross weighed the Irish version of the culinary arts in the balance, and found it wanting. Every reference to food confirms this impression, beginning with the ubiquitous comments on the flavor of soot added to coffee, soup, and even the savoury. Fish seems to come to the table in its pristine condition, "amazingly endowed with bones." Sherry can burn the shell off an egg. The Major, with "a resignation born of adversity," swallows "the mixture of chicory and liquorice" which his housekeeper possesses the secret of distilling from the best and most expensive coffee. In one memorable meal, "the bread tasted of mice, the butter of turfsmoke, the tea of brown paper." Open-air holiday-making in Ireland inevitably features "crubeens," alias pigs' feet, "a grisly delicacy." One young lady, attempting "to try conclusions between a blunt knife and a bullet-proof mutton chop," delicately moves her potato dish so as to cover the traces of a bygone egg, and her glance lingers on the flies that drag their way across a melting mound of salt butter. "I like local colour," she adds quietly, "but I don't care about it on the tablecloth." In **"Holy Island,"** we read of potato cakes speckled with caraway seeds, swimming in salt butter, that are intended to be eaten "shamelessly and greasily," and to be washed down with hot whisky and water. The Irish so love dogs that they do not have it in their hearts to blame their canines for getting up on a table (in the absence of humans) and eating the roast beef intended for dinner. Mrs. Cadogan, the cook, passionately laments: "And I had planned that bit of beef for the luncheon, the way we wouldn't have to inthrude on the cold turkey! Sure he has it that dhragged, that all we can do with it now is run it through the mincing machine for the major's sandwiches." (At this "appetizing suggestion," the Major thinks it advisable to change the subject.) Perhaps the Irish draw the line at enjoying goat's milk in the tea; but only the Irish would think of using it for such a purpose, as in the story **"Occasional Licenses."**

Another memorable moment occurs in the story **"Oh Love! Oh Fire!"** when Flurry is given the responsibility for making the punch for a ball. The question is, what shall the punch be made in? The most readily available container is the boiler, and Flurry flinches only momentarily when he thinks of all the cockroaches in it. He goes at his task with genuine enthusiasm: "Well, then, here goes for the cockroaches! What doesn't sicken will fatten! Give me the kettle, and come on you, Kitty Collins, and be skimming them off!" (In all fairness to Flurry, there are no complaints of the punch when the brew is completed, and the dance thunders on "with a heavier stamping and a louder hilarity than before.")

In another narrative, **"The Man That Came to Buy Apples,"** we hear of the cuisine at Aussolas, Flurry's ancestral home, as being fraught "with dark possibilities, being alternately presided over by bibulous veterans from Dublin, or aboriginal kitchen-maids off the estate." Confronted with a choice between curry and Irish stew, the Major feels "as Fair Rosamond might have felt when proffered the dagger or the bowl," and only after he has chosen curry does Flurry volunteer the amiable observation that, since the Major has never eaten his grandmother's curry before, he is in for a treat: "Well, you'd take a splint off a horse with it." A typical meal at the Knockeenbwee dinner-table (in **"A Conspiracy of Silence"**) opens at six with "strong tea, cold mutton, and bottled porter," and continues past eight o'clock "in slow but unceasing progress, suggesting successive inspirations on the part of the cook." Pollock, which some might think a relatively inoffensive fish, rouses the special ire of Somerville and Ross, and is always mentioned scornfully; the Major has a long-formed opinion that eating pollock is like eating boiled cotton wool with pins in it. Even mulligatawny is dismissed as "a hell-broth of liquid mustard" in **The Bosom of the McRorys."** The consistency of these images suggests that Somerville and Ross experienced some difficulty in finding decent food to eat in Ireland.

Various sports and recreations form the heart of the subject matter in these stories, many of which are extended anecdotes dealing with fox-hunting, the shooting of grouse, fishing, sailing in a regatta, racing on sands, trotting-matches, yachting, games such as a tug of war, or dancing, auctions, and agricultural fairs; but the matters already touched on—the irreconcilable differences between the Irish and the English, the lovable disorder of Irish life, the strong conviction that good manners count for something in our brief existence, the vivid metaphors of Irish speech, and the over-optimistic expectations that perhaps tomorrow's dining may be better than today's—were, of course, important in turn-of-the-century Ireland. They are still important. There can be no doubt that Major Yeates's misadventures among his fellow-countrymen have as devoted an audience as Robert Smith Surtees's wonderful stories about Jorrocks, published during the first half of the nineteenth century, still have among the English; perhaps larger, because of the splendid adaptations prepared in Ireland and shown on public television channels in the U.S. very recently.

A great deal more deserves to be said about the tight pacing of the narratives, the canny exploitation of minor bits of information that unexpectedly become crucial in the final moments of a story, the conversational murmurs that suggest (with some justice) that every man and woman in Ireland is a wit worthy to sit at Richard Brinsley Sheridan's table, and the extraordinarily unsentimental view taken by Major Yeates toward dogs and horses. The Major knows that some are mean-tempered and fractious, and others lazy and unwilling to earn their keep; he sees them as individuals, and he never misstates his honest assessment of their worth, though he is remarkably forgiving, and neither he nor we as readers can imagine a universe without them; when they behave well or even nobly, the Major is the first to praise their merits. By the time he has finished talking about their behavior and misdeeds, a reader has met a fascinating cast of characters: Quaker,

Cruiskeen, Moonlighter, Maria, and many more, as rich in their diversity as the Irishmen and Englishmen who presume, unworthily, to "own" them.

But Knox, Flurry, and the Major deserve to be described, even if only briefly. Mrs. Knox, of course, is Flurry's grandmother, "a rag-bag held together by diamond brooches," eighty-three years old when we first meet her (in **"Trinket's Colt"**) and well into her nineties by the end of the series. Her voice, the Major notes, is so commanding that he believes he would clean forty pig-sties if she desired him to do so. She dresses eccentrically, but in a manner that forbids comment. Her conversation is cultured; indeed, one of the reasons she likes the Major is that he recognizes (and can on occasion complete) one of her poetical quotations. But she is argumentative, too, and Flurry has ample reason to respect her hard-driving business acumen. The two of them share a pride in family heritage, horse-flesh, and Irish traditions. Somerville and Ross emphasize her indestructibility. Woe to the Englishman who patronizes her, for she comes from a race that will enjoy the final triumph.

Flurry is quintessentially Irish, despite the fact that religious values do not shade his ethical practices. We learn early on (in **"Great Uncle McCarthy,"** first of the tales) that he seldom laughs, "having in unusual perfection the gravity of manner that is bred by horse-dealing, probably from the habitual repression of all emotion save disparagement." He does not like to have a practical joke played on himself, and takes it most unkindly when John Simpson-Hodges, an English gentleman who does everything with a flair, imitates a French count successfully, and exploits his status as guest during a fiercely competitive hunt. Flurry is a sour loser in various contests, given to blunt language ("There isn't a four-year-old in this country that I'd be seen dead with at a pig fair" is one of his more ingratiating remarks) and an occasional insult (he tells Miss Bennett, in **"A Misdeal,"** that an unruly hunter he has sold her uncle misbehaves because the size of her foot frightens him). He is even cynical about the possibility that perfect justice can be rendered through the laws of Ireland.

But Somerville and Ross seem to have had second thoughts about his character as one story succeeded another, and they gradually softened the harsh outlines of his blunt manner. Flurry knows his fellow-countrymen too well to hold a grudge for long, and he forgives their human weaknesses in a way that teaches Yeates how to temper justice with mercy. (Flurry is not only a Master of Foxhounds, but a Justice of the Peace.) He is also a romantic hero: his elopement is carried on most dashingly and makes him more human and, yes, more likable. The Major does not presume to understand him fully. As he remarks in **"The Aussolas Martin Cat,"** "Flurry was ambiguous and impenetrable; there were certain matters in which Flurry trusted nobody, knowing the darkness of his own heart and the inelasticity of other people's points of view."

Of the Major something has been said, and yet not enough. He is obviously a survivor, for he undergoes trials and exertions that would ruin a lesser man. He loves to hunt, but frequently ends the day "a muddy and dripping outcast," with his sodden clothes clinging clammily about himself, and the wind piercing them with "all the iciness of the boghole." He dances in a spectacularly unsuccessful way. In one story (**"The Bosom of the McRorys"**), he remembers a particular dance: "We were occasionally wrecked upon reefs of huddled furniture, and we sustained a collision or two of first-rate magnitude; after these episodes my partner imperceptibly steered me to a corner, in which I leaned heavily against whatever was most stable, and tried to ignore the fact that the floor was rocking and the walls were waving. . . . " More important, he can take a joke on himself. His sense of humor, aided by his wife's enthusiasm for living in this benighted land, helps him to triumph even over those moments when he realizes how Flurry has outwitted him still one more time. Nevertheless, Flurry respects him as a judge, a lover of good horses and friendly dogs, and an all-round good fellow. Mrs. Knox, Flurry, and the Major have interlinked destinies, and Somerville and Ross demonstrate, in story after story, how much they need each other, and how a willingness to compromise, to find the middle way, is essential for any kind of progress in Ireland. (pp. 17-23)

> *Harold Orel, "Some Elements of Truth in the Short Stories of Somerville and Ross: An Appreciation," in* English Literature in Transition: 1880-1920, *Vol. 30, No. 1, 1987, pp. 17-25.*

Ann Owens Weekes   (essay date 1990)

[*In the following excerpt, Weekes interprets* The Real Charlotte *as a feminist work.*]

The Real Charlotte, published in 1894, nearly one hundred years after *Castle Rackrent,* often evokes Maria Edgeworth, that "brilliant pioneer of Irish novelists," by its energy and astringent humor. In its narrational biases and calm acceptance of the unusual, **The Real Charlotte** recalls Edgeworth's narrator, Thady Quirk. The novel was greeted initially with aversion; Edith Somerville noted that a "distinguished London literary paper" pronounced it "one of the most disagreeable novels we have ever read." Soon, however, **The Real Charlotte** was recognized as a very rich and funny work. . . . After 1922, however, in an Ireland that saw the former ascendancy as a barrier to its full political independence, the work of Somerville and Ross was devalued and ignored. But time passes and attitudes change; the novel has been reprinted in recent decades to applause in both Ireland and England. Terence de Vere White, for example, finds **The Real Charlotte** second only to "the great whale" (Joyce's *Ulysses*), and V. S. Pritchett calls it [in "Hunting Ladies," *The New Statesman,* 24 May 1968] the best Irish novel of any period. Yet despite its success, the novel has not received detailed analyses: only the themes of the Big House and the declining race have been examined in detail, and the perceptive analysis of society therein has been applauded. Despite its emphasis on land and on the qualities of several houses, however, **The Real Charlotte** does not focus so much on the Big House as does a later novel by Somerville and Ross, **The Big House of Inver** (1925), which expands Edgeworth's theme by reaching into history to explain

contemporary events. Given American interest in exhuming valuable but forgotten work, it is surprising that **The Real Charlotte** remains virtually unknown in the United States.

One reason for the neglect may be the presence of certain resistant, almost inassimilable passages, which sprinkle the work with weedlike regularity and persistence. Another reason may be the narrational stance, often biased and sometimes heedless to or apparently unaware of human suffering. Not that one expects a naive identification with narrational values, but in a world increasingly aware of ethnic sensitivities the patronizing colonist's voice grates, especially in relation to the still unsolved problem of Irish/English relations. I suggest, however, that the difficult passages and the narrational stance are integral elements in **The Real Charlotte,** essential to any thorough analysis of the novel. These are indeed literary manifestations of the authors' personal and political situations and may finally be examples of the "formal experiment" Alicia Ostriker expects in women's texts. In depicting the crumbling of the Anglo-Irish ascendancy, Somerville and Ross reveal the connections between the society and the patriarchal family on which it is modeled; the source of disintegration in their beloved society mirrors and can be seen as a logical extension of the source of injustice in the equally beloved family. The arbitrariness of the access to power—political, economic, and social—which membership in the ascendancy ordained, reflects the arbitrariness of gender-specific roles ordained by membership in the patriarchal family. The injustice and destructiveness—the ignoble tragedy—of the class and gender system is revealed almost against the will of the narrators, who never fully condemn it and who frequently stand in the same difficult, ambivalent relationship to the text as do the authors to their society. (pp. 60-1)

The Real Charlotte overtly attempts to portray the fine values of the aristocracy and the meanness of the forces that oppose it—the corrupt agent, Roddy Lambert; the upstart land grabber, Charlotte Mullen; and the almost savage tenantry, represented by the miserable inhabitants of Ferry Row. The quiet of Lismoyle is shattered when the poor but very pretty Francie Fitzpatrick visits her cousin Charlotte. All the local men—Christopher Dysart, the lethargic heir to Bruff; Gerald Hawkins, the dashing British officer; and Roddy Lambert, the husband of an ailing widow and secret passion of Charlotte—dance around Francie's flame. Throughout a summer of tennis parties and boating outings, Francie flirts with her pursuers, much to the concern of the local matrons—especially Lady Dysart, who has her own plans for Christopher. Charlotte schemes all the while to acquire the land and house for which she thirsts, a property occupied by the ill Julia Duffy and guaranteed her for life by the now senile Sir Benjamin Dysart. She also plots to raise herself socially through Francie's marriage to Christopher and to assuage her arid passion by her own marriage to Roddy, after she hastens the final exit of his first wife. Things go wrong when Gerald, Francie's love, abandons her in the hopes of marrying an English girl and an English fortune. Angered by Francie's refusal of Christopher and enraged by her mocking of Charlotte's desire for Roddy, Charlotte puts Francie out of her house.

Ironically, by rendering Francie homeless, Charlotte places her in a position to accept reluctantly Roddy's proposal. Seeking revenge but feigning good will to the newly-weds, Charlotte in the role of chaperon plots to leave Francie alone with the returned and repentant Gerald. This precipitates the final tragedy, as Francie, torn between riding off with Gerald or riding to the comfort of her financially ruined husband, is thrown from her mare, which is frightened by Julia Duffy's funeral cortege. For Charlotte has succeeded in acquiring Julia's property, and Julia has gone rapidly from madness to death. Despite the ruthlessness of Charlotte and the dishonesty of Roddy, it is the weakness within the Big House—the senility of Sir Benjamin Dysart and the inertia of his son and heir—that makes the ascendancy easy prey. Recognizing this ambivalence, Thomas Flanagan sees Somerville and Ross as moved by "fierce though critical loyalty to the Big House and a harsh, often ungenerous opposition to its enemies. But," he notes, "they move steadily toward tragic knowledge, toward recognition of the fact that the Big House was not destroyed by the mutinous cabins but by its own weakness and capacity for self-deception" ["The Big House of Ross-Drishane," *Kenyon Review,* 1966].

The response to their personal situation as daughters in the patriarchal family of the Big House is more wrenching: "Daughters," Edith wrote, "were at a discount, . . . permitted to eat of the crumbs that fell from their brothers' tables, and if no crumbs fell the daughters went unfed." Marriage also evoked Edith's ambivalence. Reminiscing about the great-grandparents she and Violet shared, the artist Edith voices regret at the Lord Chief Justice's "marital complacency" in averring that his artist/wife on her marriage "devoted herself to 'making originals instead of copies.'" The persistent conflicts between affection and justice that gnawed at Somerville and Ross throughout their lives emerge in *The Real Charlotte*—as do the parodic, qualifying, conflicting voices M. M. Bakhtin described [in *Dialogic Imagination*] in his analysis of novelization—in both the difficult narrational stance and in those inassimilable passages that so frequently, in presenting a confusion of genders, emphasize the arbitrariness of gender-specific roles.

In this ignoble tragedy, whose subject is not so much the decline of the Big House as the destructive effects of these roles, the two passages on "apostolic succession" invite interpretation, for they point to what I call "narrational contamination," the conflicts and ambivalence that infect the authors also infecting both their characters and their narrators. Dividing Roman Catholics from Protestants, the maid Eliza Hackett from Mrs. Lambert and Charlotte, the doctrine of apostolic succession also implies an unnatural generation that excludes women, much as the law of primogeniture excludes the women who preserve the estates from inheriting them. In this connection, the scenes are replete with ironies. Lucy, the rich first wife of the spoiled Roddy Lambert, complains to Charlotte of her maid's impudence in attending mass and of her assertion "I consider the Irish church [Protestant Church of Ireland] hasn't the

Apostolic succession." Charlotte's indignation at Eliza's doctrinal position—"You don't tell me that fat-faced Eliza Hackett said that?"—reflects, of course, her contempt for servants and for what she sees as the presumption of Roman Catholics. It may also, however, reflect her unconscious or unverbalized indignation at all such male preserves. Charlotte is herself excluded from the world of business—the agentship of Bruff, for example—despite her excellent qualifications, by another such unwritten, "men only" law. (The Church of Ireland was also a male preserve, but only the Roman Catholic church enunciated the doctrine of the Apostles' male heirs so clearly.) But in the disintegrating, declining world of Anglo-ireland, despite the law of primogeniture, women—Charlotte, Mrs. Lambert, and Julia Duffy—are the sole survivors in their families and consequently do inherit property. Contrary to the apparent stability of church and property laws, then, the text suggests the inherent instability and contradiction in any exclusively male system of dissemination and generation.

The inherited male right, which apostolic succession decrees, both to disseminate and to interpret the word of the law is connected to a paradigm of authorship. The nineteenth century, as Sandra Gilbert and Susan Gubar show [in their *The Madwoman in the Attic*], envisioned the author as masculine, a reflection of the original Creator of the Word, "a father, a progenitor, a procreator, an aesthetic patriarch whose pen is an instrument of generative power like his penis." Like apostolic succession, this authorship postulates an exclusively male, therefore unnatural, generation. Since his authority is semantically and metaphorically connected to that of the original Father, the male author, by implication, is not only omniscient and omnipotent, creator and judge of his creatures, but also just and objective, modeled on a just and objective God. Somerville and Ross undermine this paradigm of objectivity throughout *The Real Charlotte*, especially in scenes referring to the apostolic succession.

The conclusion of the first of these passages draws our attention to the Word and, by extension, to any word as text and to its potential subversion by a disruptive feminine discourse. Mrs. Lambert completes her complaint against Eliza, appealing: "I ask you Charlotte, what could I say to a woman like that, that could wrest the Scriptures to her own purposes?" The narrators are ironic at Mrs. Lambert's expense, for Eliza's Roman Catholic church would not allow personal interpretation or wresting of Scripture, whereas Mrs. Lambert's and Charlotte's Church of Ireland would. Although the phrase will not be repeated for some one hundred fifty pages, the dark side of the religious conflict surfaces repeatedly, alerting the reader when the phrase recurs. Charlotte, for example, cautions Julia Duffy, daughter of a drunken, Protestant father and a dairymaid, Catholic mother, that the "poor Archdeacon frets about" Father Heffernan's luring Julia "into his fold!"

The phrase apostolic succession recurs as Francie, married by this time to the widower Roddy Lambert but still in love with the soldier Hawkins, strolls in the garden of Rosemount, attempting to avoid Hawkins and the temptation his visit would present. Eliza Hackett gathers spinach in a far corner of the garden, meditating, the narrators note, "with comfortable assurance on the legitimacy of Father Heffernan's apostolic succession, but outwardly the embodiment of solid household routine and respectability." The reader is jolted by the unexpected aside on a peripheral character, an aside which presents no new plot or character information but simply calls attention to the narrators. These narrators are not, or at least not consistently, the intrusive, guiding narrators of many nineteenth-century novels whose presence is always felt. We cannot predict the sympathies of the narrators of *The Real Charlotte.* In the descriptions of Lady Dysart's party, for example, they seem to depict objectively and journalistically, but they forsake this objectivity to comment unsympathetically on the unwashed denizens of Ferry Row, to plead finally for compassion for Charlotte, and to repeat the views of one of their creatures, the silly Mrs. Lambert. I would argue that this repetition is again an instance of the subtle emphasis Nancy Miller attributes to women writers in their delineation of their own stories, an emphasis which reinforces structural as well as thematic concerns in its underscoring of the sardonic, not to say prejudiced, narrating voice.

Inviting the reader to witness the narrational contamination in this instance, the authors imply a partiality and lack of objectivity endemic to all authors. Given the context of apostolic succession and its association with the paradigm of male authorship, the passage can be read as questioning the legitimacy of the traditional authorial metaphor. Eliza is subversive, but her subversion consists in adhering to a model of male privilege and female exclusion, much indeed as Somerville and Ross themselves adhere to the Anglo-Irish world whose laws exclude them from inheritance. In place of a stable world with fixed truths, the authors of *The Real Charlotte* present an inchoate world dying and forming at the same time, a Bakhtinian world in which the voice of authority—apostolic, paternal, social, or authorial—is constantly undermined by the parodic voices of those not fully suppressed. In place of the voice, which—given the metaphor of authorial generation—must be a single one, the narrators stress their "we" duality and suggest the essentially compromised nature of their text, an offspring that by its genesis must embody the sometimes conflicting elements of its dual inheritance. The authors' names on the title page, the male-sounding E. OE. Somerville and Martin Ross, complicate, as does Edgeworth's male narrator, the narrational stance and allow us to read all the narrational insensitivities and acceptances of female victimization as the representation by two women authors of women's view of the contemporary male perspective.

Narrational bias and inconsistency are nowhere more evident than in the indulgence extended Lady Dysart (who closely resembles Edith's mother) and the aversion extended Charlotte Mullen, the weed (to use an image from the novel) in the garden of Anglo-Ireland. Charlotte is introduced in one of the novel's many inassimilable passages, a moment that also draws attention to the arbitrariness of gender-specific roles. The narrators interrupt Norry the Boat's midnight vigil by a sharp bell:

A woman's short thick figure appeared in the doorway.

"The mistress wants to see *Susan,*" this person said in a rough whisper; "is *he* in the house?"

"I think he's below in the scullery," returned Norry; "but, my Law! Miss Charlotte, what does she want of him? Is it light in her head she is?"

"What's that to you? Go fetch him at once," replied Miss Charlotte, with a sudden fierceness. [my italics]

The reader suspects a misprint—who or what is he/Susan? Before our curiosity is satisfied, the narrators reveal Charlotte, a woman whose plainness and distasteful habits they constantly underscore. Brushing aside the dying woman's request to see her pretty niece Francie, Charlotte harshly insists that it was Susan the woman had asked for. But the dying voice reproves: "It isn't cats we should be thinking of now. God knows the cats are safe with you." Susan, we finally understand, is not Francie's female rival for the dying woman's attention but a tomcat, christened with the feminine nominative years before by the young Francie, who in so doing had disdained nominal gender conventions as she had also disdained behavioral conventions in tomboyishly leading the rampaging gang of children.

The same neglect of Victorian restriction is tragic for Francie the woman, Somerville and Ross's beloved "wild bird." Francie's pursuit of Hawkins, who has awakened her love, meets with Lady Dysart's disapproval and leads directly to Francie's dismissal from Bruff, where she had been visiting, and indirectly to her marriage with Lambert. The problem in *The Real Charlotte* is not an absence of love—indeed almost all the characters are "in love"—but rather it is the difficulty of achieving mutual love. This difficulty is exacerbated for women by the restrictive conventions: Pamela Dysart, for example, the model Anglo-Irish Victorian woman, cannot reveal her affection to Captain Cursiter, who lacks the courage to speak his own. Francie, however, is roundly condemned for her honesty. Pamela may thus be seen as the positive, passive woman of the tradition Alicia Ostriker condemns, and Francie, as a move toward the aggressive, negative figure. Somerville and Ross appear to adhere to convention in depicting Pamela positively and Francie negatively, but the picture is not so clear: Pamela, for example, is not rewarded with marriage, and years later Edith wrote that of all the characters she and Violet created Francie "was our most constant companion, . . . we were fondest of her." The conclusion of the Susan scene suggests the pathos of suppressed love, as Charlotte strokes and soothes the cat with unexpected, even quasi-erotic tenderness: "Be quiet, my heart's love, . . . be quiet."

The grotesqueness of the moment is heightened by the importance granted the female-named tomcat, a status bestowed on all the cats in Tally-Ho Lodge but particularly emphasized in Susan's case. Susan is the most important personage at Tally-Ho, his position in Charlotte's house peculiarly akin to that of Roddy Lambert, Charlotte's secret passion, in the house of the rich widow, Lucy. As Lambert is humored and cosseted by his wife, so Susan is by Charlotte. As Lambert expects the best, most comfortable chair after his rich meal, so Susan expropriates the best chair after a rich dish of cream. As Lambert, the independent, can walk off from dull Rosemount for entertainment and privacy, so Susan departs from Tally-Ho when the bustle of female activity infringes on his comfort and dignity. And finally, as Lambert cheats his employers, Sir Benjamin and Christopher Dysart, so Susan, the well-fed parasite, steals mackerel from Norry's kitchen.

Similarly the sexual rivalry of the eligible males—the heir, Christopher Dysart; the agent, Roddy Lambert; and the soldier, Gerald Hawkins—for Francie's favor is parodied by the hostility with its implication of jealousy between Lambert and the cats. On Charlotte's denying his visit to Francie, Lambert viciously kicks Mrs. Bruff, grandniece and female surrogate of Susan, who is himself a surrogate of Lambert, into the bushes. The final play on the identification between Lambert and Susan occurs when Charlotte and Francie quarrel over Lambert's affections. Furious at Francie's mocking jibes, which are like salt to her private passion, Charlotte attempts to strike the younger woman. But Susan intervenes, jumps on Charlotte en route to his usual perch on her shoulder, and receives to his astonishment the blow meant for Francie. The analogies between the human and animal behaviors serve to parody the former, and the confusion of Susan's gender calls attention to the arbitrariness, as irrational as Francie's childish naming of the cat, of gender-specific roles, roles that confer, among other privileges, the right, or at least the option, of pursuit to tomcats and men.

The tyranny of gender is again emphasized in the presentation of James Canavan, the one-time tutor of the Dysart family who is now tutor only to the young Garry and attendant to Sir Benjamin. Canavan has "from time immemorial been the leading lady in Garry's theatricals" and is thus given the part of Queen Elizabeth I in the presentation of *Kenilworth*. Having done his part to perfection, Canavan/Queen Elizabeth disappears from the stage as Leicester's love, Amy Robsart, is entombed. But to the surprise of the audience, the queen bounces back on stage with a cry of "discordant triumph." With Amy Robsart's white plume stuck in his crown, he jumps on the coffin flourishing the poker/scepter and continues his furious song and dance until he falls through, on top of the screaming Amy. Refusing to accept the part written for the queen by the male author, Canavan, the rejected queen, will not remain conveniently hidden but bounces on stage demanding that his pain be heeded. In effect, then, Canavan, by his persistent pursuit of his desire, Leicester, plays the role that male psychiatrists in the nineteenth and much of the twentieth centuries define as madness in women.

But madness in a woman is sanity in a man: Canavan's persistent pursuit is endemic to all the males. Christopher courts Francie despite her disinterest, Lambert seeks her even in his first wife's lifetime, and Hawkins's pursuit after her marriage leads to Francie's death. Although marriage is the only "vocation" open to women, they can play no part in seeking happiness therein. Lady Dysart was compelled to marry the elderly Sir Benjamin, the lovely Pame-

la can only drift aimlessly, Francie's attempts to be with Hawkins before her marriage to Lambert meet with Lady Dysart's unmitigated contempt, and the plain Charlotte's efforts to engage Lambert are ignored or ridiculed.

Although the Kenilworth scene continues the gender play, James Canavan's origins rather than his gender may be the source of his madness. The tutor, Violet Martin noted, is modeled on James Tucker, a hedge schoolmaster who had helped in the Martins' school during the famine, remaining as the family tutor and, like Canavan, acting in the children's theatricals. The colonized Canavan, like Maria Edgeworth's Thady, is, to use Elizabeth Janeway's term and paradigm, one of the weak whose powerlessness and dependence align him situationally with all the nineteenth-century women, Anglo- or Gaelic-Irish. Canavan's original, however, played the role not of female but of male lover in Robert Martin's theatricals. Perhaps thematic resonances dictated the inversion. The day following the play, Francie Fitzpatrick meets Canavan and Garry, and in a scene that confirms his madness, Canavan kills a rat. The resentful Garry reports that had Lady Dysart not interfered, Canavan would have gone on jumping on Amy until he had killed her. A victim of the patriarchal system herself, Lady Dysart, who had condemned Francie's attempt to elide the unfair rules of pursuit, again ends Canavan's mad attempt to destroy the system. Canavan's madness, depicted in his attempt to destroy his rival, Amy, parodies Charlotte's madness, which does in fact destroy her rival, Francie. Linked in *Castle Rackrent* by their dependence on the powerful, women and other colonized figures are linked in **The Real Charlotte** by the overt narrational perception of the madness in their pursuit of desire.

But madness, though continually repressed, is pervasive. The leaders of Lismoyle society, Sir Benjamin and Lady Dysart, are introduced in scenes that depict their imbecility. The narrators observe that the picture of Lady Dysart at work in the garden with her daughter, Pamela, might seem to be "worthy in its domestic simplicity of the Fairchild Family," but they add sardonically, a dachshund (that absurd parody of an animal) replaces the paterfamilias. And Lady Dysart, having mistaken the young chickweed in a seedling pan "for the asters that should have been there, was filling her bed symmetrically with the former, an imbecility that Mrs. Sherwood would never have permitted in a parent."

Lady Dysart's imbecility is more than horticultural, though given the respect paid gardeners in Anglo-Ireland, this is grievous. Lady Dysart invites too many women to her parties. She is unaware, being English, of the dialectical nuances and parochial behavioral patterns that mark Charlotte as vulgar. Additionally she has no sympathy for Francie, whom she regards as a "man-hunter" and a threat to her plans for Christopher. Affection transcends narrational irritation, however, and Lady Dysart is allowed to emerge unscathed, reminding the reader of Edith's combined affection and exasperation with her mother, the model for Lady Dysart. Indeed Mrs. Somerville's comments on Francie's death could be Lady Dysart's: "Francie deserved to break her neck for her vulgarity," she wrote, "and the girls *had* to kill her to get the whole set of them out of the awful muddle they had got into!"

Sir Benjamin is allowed to speak his own imbecility. Alone in the drawing room, Miss Evelyn Hope-Drummond, the English guest invited by Lady Dysart as a possible bride for Christopher, reaches to pick a rosebud.

> "Ha—a—ah! I see ye, missy! Stop picking my flowers! Push, James Canavan, you devil, you! Push!"
>
> A bath-chair, occupied by an old man in a tall hat, and pushed by a man also in a tall hat, had suddenly turned the corner of the house, and Miss Hope-Drummond drew back precipitately to avoid the uplifted walking-stick of Sir Benjamin Dysart.
>
> "Oh, fie, for shame, Sir Benjamin!" exclaimed the man who had been addressed as James Canavan. "Pray, cull the rose, Miss," he continued, with a flourish of his hand; "sweets to the sweet!"
>
> Sir Benjamin aimed a backward stroke with his oak stick at his attendant, a stroke in which long practice had failed to make him perfect, and in the exchange of further amenities the party passed out of sight.

Failing to strike Miss Hope-Drummond with the phallic cane, a symbol now of his impotence, Sir Benjamin turns on Canavan. Dressing and speaking in Sir Benjamin's own mode, refusing to do his employer's bidding, and usurping the latter's power with his invitation to the English guest, Canavan symbolically foreshadows the displacement to come that is suggested so vividly in the disturbing and frequent images of the barely repressed hordes of Ferry Row. Class and family converge in the head of Lismoyle society and the Dysart family only to be repudiated and rendered impotent by the dispossessed Canavan, the surrogate madwoman.

Sir Benjamin's viciousness to the English girl who might have been his son's bride is a reflection of the political schizophrenia of Anglo-Ireland, economically and politically aligned with England but emotionally tied to Ireland. What Somerville and Ross reveal is that this schizophrenia extended far beneath national politics to the family itself, the foundation, support, and model of the system. The hostility that Sir Benjamin exhibits to the guest from "across the water" is a pale, dulled reflection of the hostility he has cherished to his own English wife, Lady Dysart, who had been married in her youth "with a little judicious coercion" to this man, thirty years her senior, and who, "after a long and, on the whole, extremely unpleasant period of matrimony" was now freed from his companionship by the intervention of his stroke. And the Anglo-Irish hostility to the English brides is also characteristic of Christopher, who evades not only Evelyn but all the women his optimistic but obtuse mother invites. The relative paucity of narrational comment on the victimization of Lady Dysart is itself ironic—again reminiscent of Maria Edgeworth's male narrator who accepts the fate of the Rackrent wives almost as a condition of nature, which, as such, requires no comment.

The confusion of gender in the cases of Canavan and Susan highlights the confusion and effects of Charlotte's gender in this ignoble tragedy. Both the narrators and the other characters apply male adjectives or expectations to Charlotte. When she arrives at Lady Dysart's biannual party, for example, Charlotte is greeted by her hostess who bemoans the excessive number of women, treating Charlotte, as several critics note, as an honorary man. And Charlotte herself assumes the "brevet" rank throughout. Ignoring the "midge-bitten" rows of women, she joins a "fairly representative trio" of Anglo-Irish gentlemen who rail together about Irish politics and the pleasure it would give them "to pull the rope at the execution of a certain English statesman." Apparently equally upset by their land-leaguing tenants and by Gladstone's attempts to transfer land from the ascendancy to the tenants, the gentlemen seem incapable of anything but complaint. Declaring herself a better politician than any of them, Charlotte tells of the personal vengeance she extracted from her plumber, and Christopher Dysart acknowledges that "if anyone could understand the land Act," that person would be Charlotte. At the next party, the Beattie's, Charlotte, the narrators note, joins the "other heads of families" for a "gentlemanly glass of marsala." She creates, they tell us, a "gentleman's avenue" at her new home, Gurthnamuckla, does a man's job of repairing the potato loft, and acts like a "madman" in her altercation with Francie. It is surely no accident that one of her impoverished Ferry Row tenants, the most repressed group presented, addresses Charlotte as "Honoured Madman."

In Somerville and Ross's disintegrating world the confusion of gender is not only a symptom of the overt political disease that threatens the society but also an indication of how the accident of gender determines one's life, creating another, more fundamental, political dis-ease at the core of the social order. Susan has been christened by the young, naive Francie; the problem of the cat's textual gender is therefore the result of an accident. Charlotte's gender too is the result of a purely fortuitous interaction of biological elements. Charlotte is not only an avid and intelligent reader, one who realizes Christopher's foolishness in reading Rossetti to Francie, but she is also more capable than any man in Lismoyle in the business reserved for men. Charlotte's father had been the agent for Bruff, and the intelligent woman apparently picked up the workings of the agent-tenant system from accompanying her father to his office. When Lambert became her father's pupil, Charlotte helped him to learn his work, lending him money whenever necessary. The implication is that Charlotte, more astute than Lambert, had frequently saved him from trouble—first with her father, then with his employer. Yet as a woman Charlotte is not considered for the agentship of Bruff, whereas masculinity alone qualifies the mediocre Lambert.

The provisions of the land acts, which would eventually deprive Anglo-Ireland of much of its livelihood, are understood by Charlotte who, greedy for house and land, rents to the poor and buys for herself rather than selling to tenants as do her real-life Anglo-Irish compatriots. Desiring Julia Duffy's home, Charlotte is again the "master" of both Lambert and Christopher. All information is filed correctly and stored in her organized mind for easy access and cross-reference. Thus when Julia Duffy's tenant goes bankrupt, leaving Julia unable to pay her own rent to the Dysart estate, Charlotte is able to take over the house she has always wanted. Almost in the role of omniscient narrator, Charlotte understands Sir Benjamin's senility and inability to enforce the verbal promise of lifetime tenantship he had given Julia, Christopher's disinterest in and deplorable ignorance of his father's business that was soon to be his own, Julia's illness and her inability to make her case to Christopher, and Lambert's inability to force Julia out. Ethics aside, Charlotte's managerial competency, energy, and resourcefulness are the the equivalents of those women estate managers, Edith Somerville and Violet Martin. Indeed we might see in Charlotte a bitter and perhaps unconscious reflection of the authors' own status in their society, Charlotte serving both as scapegoat and authorial representative. Charlotte's intelligence, decisiveness, knowledge of the community and of human strengths and weaknesses, and her eminent qualifications to perform the jobs reserved for the incompetent males are ignored by her society and often by her narrators.

Had Charlotte been content to accept her position as honorary gentleman—feared by her servants and subordinates, avoided by the genteel Christopher and Pamela Dysart, appreciated for her humor (her vulgarity not understood) by the English Lady Dysart, ignored and hardly considered a woman by the eligible gentlemen, the soldiers, and by-times Lambert—she could have lived an emotionally sterile but, despite the gender restrictions, economically successful life. In other words, had Charlotte settled for the male individualism defined by [David] Bakan as the manifestation of "self-protection, self-assertion, and self-expansion," she might have been happy. Ironically, however, Charlotte seeks communion.

Born plain, Charlotte is yet imbued with some of the values and desires of her age. Since the business world, the public world, was male, fulfillment for a woman could only lie in marriage. The pervasiveness of this social more need hardly be argued; the ranks of the hopeful Beattie and Baker girls, the hopes of Francie, her friends, and Lady Dysart are ample evidence of the marriage market, the business in which women must compete, though they cannot make the rules. And indeed Charlotte's desire is not simply an acceptance of convention. In return for her help in the old days, the young, handsome Roddy Lambert had expressed his gratitude in an "ardent manner—a manner that had seemed cheap enough to him, at the time, but that had been more costly to Charlotte than any other thing that had ever befallen her." Encouraged by this fleeting episode, Charlotte nourishes a fervid passion for Lambert even through his marriage to the rich widow, realizing, Lambert thinks, with her "eminent common sense" the necessity of such a marriage for a poor but ambitious man. Throughout the years, the narrators note, Charlotte evidences her desire by provocative glances to which, "unfair as it may be," Lambert, had he seen them, would not have responded. In the epigraph to this chapter,

the narrators consider Charlotte after she has won everything but that which is most important to her—Lambert. They note the ignoble tragedy to which the trivialities of appearance assign a plain woman in their beloved and vicious world. For Charlotte's is the tragedy of gender. Born female, she cannot employ her "male" talents; born plain, she cannot compete in the only business open to women. Charlotte is the weed, placed by cultural codes involuntarily—even insanely—in the bed of asters, helpless to transform her drab colors and bulky shape into the glowing shades and elegant forms of the asters yet condemned, nevertheless, for being as she is.

Somerville and Ross depict a society whose hideous injustices, both personal and political, they recognize, but one that, given paradoxical human nature, they nevertheless cherish. As women suffragists who worked tirelessly for the vote, writers whose work supported the Big Houses destined for their brothers rather than themselves, and human beings whose affections and emotions turned to their own rather than to the opposite sex, Somerville and Ross stood in relation to their society as do their narrators to the society and text of *The Real Charlotte.* Critics have often noted the sympathy of the writers/narrators to the Dysart family, the effete and obtuse leaders of Lismoyle society. But the depth of that sympathy and its contamination of the narrators have not been observed. The code of good behavior, for example, which instinctively governs all the actions of the Dysart family, is constantly applied by the narrators also as a test of a character's appeal. Lambert's pretension to middle-class respectability and his consequent awareness of Charlotte's vulgarity is mocked, whereas Lady Dysart's unawareness is treated indulgently. Christopher's and Pamela's instinctive recoil from vulgarity receives narrational approval, even when such recoil renders Christopher impotent. Charlotte's obvious vulgarities of manner provoke both characters and narrators, and the latter join the Dysarts in observing and ridiculing the signs of Charlotte's ill-breeding, the "electroplated teaspoons" and the "grocer's cake." Indeed *vulgarity,* a word that constantly recurs, seems to be more than surface deep. Its presence in Francie's case, we understand, has not only limited her sensitivity and obscured and distorted her world view, but it also has, like a smothering parasite, stunted her moral development.

More important, however, are the implicit alignments. In the comic scene when the first Mrs. Lambert complains to Charlotte of Eliza's attending Catholic mass, the narrators note that one of Charlotte's "most genuine feelings was a detestation of Roman Catholics." This narrational assessment not only contributes to the humor of the occasion but also exposes the dark side of Charlotte's bigotry. Elsewhere the narrators note that Charlotte "affected a vigorous brogue, not perhaps being aware that her own accent scarcely admitted of being strengthened"; again they note the "guttural at the end of the word that no Saxon gullet could hope to produce." Sneering at her manner of dressing, they suggest she has the "Irish peasant's" habits. Finally, the narrators comment that "there was a strain of superstition in her that, like her love of land, showed how strongly the blood of the Irish peasant ran in her veins."

In ridiculing Charlotte thus, in aligning her with Celtic rather than Saxon gullets, peasants rather than landlords, the narrators simultaneously distance her from English and Protestant, or ascendancy, origins and link her to the Gaelic Catholic hordes she despises. Ironically, however, in thus aligning Charlotte, in thus ridiculing her origins, the narrators themselves share the religious prejudice of which they accuse her. Although the code that governs the Dysarts' behavior is insufficient (witness Lady Dysart's destructive obtuseness, Christopher's effete posturing and his almost inhuman detachment, and Pamela's complete loss of self in her role as angel-in-the-house), the narrators make no secret of their personal bias toward these sympathetic, charming, though perhaps useless relics of a past age.

The idea of art as mimesis is destroyed by Somerville and Ross's deliberate involvement with their characters. There can be no distinction between the object reflected in the glass and the glass itself. The properties of the glass and the skill of its makers (narrators and authors) determine, as they always have, the reflection. The assumption of objectivity that reflection implies is discarded, the vested interest and prejudice of every author and her fictional narrational representative being recognized in its place. *The Real Charlotte,* an ignoble tragedy of gender-specific roles, attacks by this narrative strategy the traditional assumptions of patriarchal texts. The notion of a male intelligence that can transcend its affections and prejudices, so palpably untrue in the social and political arenas, and that can fairly represent its own society is undermined by the intrusive biases of the narrators of *The Real Charlotte,* biases which often reflect those of the authors. The ideal of art Somerville and Ross offer seems diminished, but it is also more honest than that of traditional narrative. The biased narrational stance may have been deliberately conceived, but at times the authors, like Charlotte and like the narrators, may have been driven by subconscious impulses, by the subversive, parodic voices, to say more than they knew.

The appropriateness of the narrational stance is evident in any case from a reading of *The Real Charlotte,* whose very richness is in great part the result of the thematic recognition and the superb structural representation of the wayward, often tragic patterns of human affections. A passage near the end of the work summarizes Somerville and Ross's attitude to their own society:

> Civilization at Bruff had marched away from the turf quay. The ruts of the cart track were green from long disuse and the willows had been allowed to grow across it, as a last sign of superannuation. In old days every fire at Bruff had been landed at the turf quay from the bogs at the other side of the lake; but now, since the railway had come to Lismoyle, coal had taken its place. It was in vain that Thady the turf cutter had urged that turf was a far handsomer thing about a gentleman's place than coal. The last voyage of the turf boat had been made, and she now lay, grey from rottenness and want of paint, in the corner of the miniature dock.

Like Thady, the narrators of *The Real Charlotte* urge that

Edith Somerville (left) and Martin Ross in their studio with assorted pet dogs.

their society, the society of the Anglo-Irish ascendancy, is far handsomer than the emerging society of the Gaelic-Irish peasantry, and like Thady too the narrators have a vested interest in the preservation of this society. Overtly asserting this interest and surrendering the pose of authorial objectivity, *The Real Charlotte,* a tragedy in which women are defined and valued by their appearance, becomes itself the weed, the bristling chickweed, in the artificial aster garden of Anglo-Irish literature. (pp. 66-82)

> *Ann Owens Weekes, "Somerville and Ross: Ignoble Tragedy," in her* Irish Women Writers: An Uncharted Tradition, *The University Press of Kentucky, 1990, pp. 60-82.*

FURTHER READING

Biography

Collis, Maurice. *Somerville and Ross: A Biography.* London: Faber and Faber, 1968, 284 p.
   Chronicles the lives and partnership of Somerville and Ross, based on the letters and diaries of both women.

Cronin, John. *Somerville and Ross.* Lewisburg, Pa.: Bucknell University Press, 1972, 111 p.
> Briefly summarizes the lives of the authors and analyzes their major works.

Cummins, Geraldine. *Dr. E. OE. Somerville: A Biography.* London: Andrew Dakers, 1952, 271 p.
> The first published biography of Somerville, written by her personal friend and fellow spiritualist.

Lewis, Gifford. *Somerville and Ross: The World of the Irish R.M.* Harmondsworth: Viking, 1985, 251 p.
> Presents an interpretation of the authors' personal lives based on their published and private writings. This book challenges some of the more controversial assumptions of the Collis biography concerning the nature of Somerville and Ross's friendship.

Criticism

Corkery, Daniel. *Synge and Anglo-Irish Literature: A Study.* 1931. Reprint. New York: Russell & Russell, 1965, 247 p.
> Uses Somerville and Ross as examples of the "Colonial" strain in Anglo-Irish literature, in contrast to J. M. Synge's sympathies with the ordinary Irish. Corkery illuminates the debate that occurred during the lifetimes of Somerville and Ross about the nature of Anglo-Irish literature.

Gwynn, Stephen Lucius. *Irish Books and Irish People.* 1920. Reprint. Freeport, N. Y.: Books for Libraries Press, 1969, 120 p.

> Reprints a 1918 article, "Yesterday in Ireland," which explores the historical and political climate in which Somerville and Ross wrote.

Powell, Violet. *The Irish Cousins: The Books and Background of Somerville and Ross.* London: Heinemann, 1970, 214 p.
> Reviews the lives and literary career of Somerville and Ross, analyzing the relationship between the authors' work and their personal lives. Provides critical appraisals of some of the authors' shorter and lesser known works.

Pritchett, V. S. *The Living Novel and Later Appreciations.* New York: Vintage, 1967, 459 p.
> Contains a chapter on Somerville and Ross that compares *The Real Charlotte* to the more popular *Irish R.M.* stories. Pritchett finds the later works to be lacking the depth of *The Real Charlotte* and speculates whether working on the *R.M.* stories might have distracted the authors from achieving the artistic potential that is evident in the earlier work.

Quiller-Couch, Arthur. "Tribute to Ireland." In his *The Poet as Citizen and Other Papers,* pp. 218-26. New York: MacMillan, 1935, 226 p.
> Focuses on the family histories of Somerville and Ross.

Robinson, Hilary. *Somerville and Ross: A Critical Appreciation.* New York: St. Martin's, 1980, 217 p.
> Provides a short biography and detailed critical analysis of all the major works of Somerville and Ross.

Twentieth-Century
Literary Criticism

Cumulative Indexes
Volumes 1-51

How to Use This Index

Aldanov, Mark (Alexandrovich)
        1886(?)-1957 .... TCLC 23
    See also CA 118

Aldington, Richard 1892-1962...... CLC 49
    See also CA 85-88; DLB 20, 36, 100

Aldiss, Brian W(ilson)
        1925- .... CLC 5, 14, 40
    See also CA 5-8R; CAAS 2; CANR 5, 28;
        DLB 14; MTCW; SATA 34

Alegria, Claribel 1924-............ CLC 75
    See also CA 131; CAAS 15; HW

Alegria, Fernando 1918-.......... CLC 57
    See also CA 9-12R; CANR 5, 32; HW

Aleichem, Sholom .... TCLC 1, 35
    See also Rabinovitch, Sholem

Aleixandre, Vicente 1898-1984 ... CLC 9, 36
    See also CA 85-88; 114; CANR 26;
        DLB 108; HW; MTCW

Alepoudelis, Odysseus
    See Elytis, Odysseus

Aleshkovsky, Joseph 1929-
    See Aleshkovsky, Yuz
    See also CA 121; 128

Aleshkovsky, Yuz .... CLC 44
    See also Aleshkovsky, Joseph

Alexander, Lloyd (Chudley) 1924- .. CLC 35
    See also AAYA 1; CA 1-4R; CANR 1, 24,
        38; CLR 1, 5; DLB 52; MAICYA;
        MTCW; SATA 3, 49

Alfau, Felipe 1902-.............. CLC 66
    See also CA 137

Alger, Horatio, Jr. 1832-1899..... NCLC 8
    See also DLB 42; SATA 16

Algren, Nelson 1909-1981 .... CLC 4, 10, 33
    See also CA 13-16R; 103; CANR 20;
        CDALB 1941-1968; DLB 9; DLBY 81,
        82; MTCW

Ali, Ahmed 1910- .... CLC 69
    See also CA 25-28R; CANR 15, 34

Alighieri, Dante 1265-1321 .... CMLC 3

Allan, John B.
    See Westlake, Donald E(dwin)

Allen, Edward 1948-.............. CLC 59

Allen, Roland
    See Ayckbourn, Alan

Allen, Woody 1935- .... CLC 16, 52
    See also AAYA 10; CA 33-36R; CANR 27,
        38; DLB 44; MTCW

Allende, Isabel 1942- .... CLC 39, 57
    See also CA 125; 130; HW; MTCW

Alleyn, Ellen
    See Rossetti, Christina (Georgina)

Allingham, Margery (Louise)
        1904-1966 .... CLC 19
    See also CA 5-8R; 25-28R; CANR 4;
        DLB 77; MTCW

Allingham, William 1824-1889 ... NCLC 25
    See also DLB 35

Allison, Dorothy 1948-............ CLC 78

Allston, Washington 1779-1843.... NCLC 2
    See also DLB 1

Almedingen, E. M. .... CLC 12
    See also Almedingen, Martha Edith von
    See also SATA 3

Almedingen, Martha Edith von 1898-1971
    See Almedingen, E. M.
    See also CA 1-4R; CANR 1

Alonso, Damaso 1898-1990 .... CLC 14
    See also CA 110; 131; 130; DLB 108; HW

Alov
    See Gogol, Nikolai (Vasilyevich)

Alta 1942-...................... CLC 19
    See also CA 57-60

Alter, Robert B(ernard) 1935-...... CLC 34
    See also CA 49-52; CANR 1

Alther, Lisa 1944-.............. CLC 7, 41
    See also CA 65-68; CANR 12, 30; MTCW

Altman, Robert 1925-............. CLC 16
    See also CA 73-76

Alvarez, A(lfred) 1929-.......... CLC 5, 13
    See also CA 1-4R; CANR 3, 33; DLB 14,
        40

Alvarez, Alejandro Rodriguez 1903-1965
    See Casona, Alejandro
    See also CA 131; 93-96; HW

Amado, Jorge 1912-........... CLC 13, 40
    See also CA 77-80; CANR 35; DLB 113;
        MTCW

Ambler, Eric 1909-............ CLC 4, 6, 9
    See also CA 9-12R; CANR 7, 38; DLB 77;
        MTCW

Amichai, Yehuda 1924- ...... CLC 9, 22, 57
    See also CA 85-88; MTCW

Amiel, Henri Frederic 1821-1881 .. NCLC 4

Amis, Kingsley (William)
        1922- ...... CLC 1, 2, 3, 5, 8, 13, 40, 44
    See also AITN 2; CA 9-12R; CANR 8, 28;
        CDBLB 1945-1960; DA; DLB 15, 27,
        100; MTCW

Amis, Martin (Louis)
        1949- .... CLC 4, 9, 38, 62
    See also BEST 90:3; CA 65-68; CANR 8,
        27; DLB 14

Ammons, A(rchie) R(andolph)
        1926- .... CLC 2, 3, 5, 8, 9, 25, 57
    See also AITN 1; CA 9-12R; CANR 6, 36;
        DLB 5; MTCW

Amo, Tauraatua i
    See Adams, Henry (Brooks)

Anand, Mulk Raj 1905-........... CLC 23
    See also CA 65-68; CANR 32; MTCW

Anatol
    See Schnitzler, Arthur

Anaya, Rudolfo A(lfonso) 1937- .... CLC 23
    See also CA 45-48; CAAS 4; CANR 1, 32;
        DLB 82; HW; MTCW

Andersen, Hans Christian
        1805-1875 .... NCLC 7; SSC 6
    See also CLR 6; DA; MAICYA; WLC;
        YABC 1

Anderson, C. Farley
    See Mencken, H(enry) L(ouis); Nathan,
        George Jean

Anderson, Jessica (Margaret) Queale
        .... CLC 37
    See also CA 9-12R; CANR 4

Anderson, Jon (Victor) 1940- .... CLC 9
    See also CA 25-28R; CANR 20

Anderson, Lindsay (Gordon)
        1923-..................... CLC 20
    See also CA 125; 128

Anderson, Maxwell 1888-1959 ..... TCLC 2
    See also CA 105; DLB 7

Anderson, Poul (William) 1926- .... CLC 15
    See also AAYA 5; CA 1-4R; CAAS 2;
        CANR 2, 15, 34; DLB 8; MTCW;
        SATA 39

Anderson, Robert (Woodruff)
        1917-..................... CLC 23
    See also AITN 1; CA 21-24R; CANR 32;
        DLB 7

Anderson, Sherwood
        1876-1941 ...... TCLC 1, 10, 24; SSC 1
    See also CA 104; 121; CDALB 1917-1929;
        DA; DLB 4, 9, 86; DLBD 1; MTCW;
        WLC

Andouard
    See Giraudoux, (Hippolyte) Jean

Andrade, Carlos Drummond de ...... CLC 18
    See also Drummond de Andrade, Carlos

Andrade, Mario de 1893-1945..... TCLC 43

Andrewes, Lancelot 1555-1626 .... LC 5

Andrews, Cicily Fairfield
    See West, Rebecca

Andrews, Elton V.
    See Pohl, Frederik

Andreyev, Leonid (Nikolaevich)
        1871-1919 .... TCLC 3
    See also CA 104

Andric, Ivo 1892-1975 .... CLC 8
    See also CA 81-84; 57-60; MTCW

Angelique, Pierre
    See Bataille, Georges

Angell, Roger 1920-.............. CLC 26
    See also CA 57-60; CANR 13

Angelou, Maya 1928-.... CLC 12, 35, 64, 77
    See also AAYA 7; BLC 1; BW; CA 65-68;
        CANR 19; DA; DLB 38; MTCW;
        SATA 49

Annensky, Innokenty Fyodorovich
        1856-1909 .... TCLC 14
    See also CA 110

Anon, Charles Robert
    See Pessoa, Fernando (Antonio Nogueira)

Anouilh, Jean (Marie Lucien Pierre)
        1910-1987 ...... CLC 1, 3, 8, 13, 40, 50
    See also CA 17-20R; 123; CANR 32;
        MTCW

Anthony, Florence
    See Ai

Anthony, John
    See Ciardi, John (Anthony)

Anthony, Peter
    See Shaffer, Anthony (Joshua); Shaffer,
        Peter (Levin)

Anthony, Piers 1934-............. CLC 35
    See also CA 21-24R; CANR 28; DLB 8;
        MTCW

Antoine, Marc
    See Proust, (Valentin-Louis-George-Eugene-)
        Marcel

Austen, Jane
1775-1817 . . . . NCLC 1, 13, 19, 33
See also CDBLB 1789-1832; DA; DLB 116;
WLC

Auster, Paul 1947- . . . . CLC 47
See also CA 69-72; CANR 23

Austin, Frank
See Faust, Frederick (Schiller)

Austin, Mary (Hunter)
1868-1934 . . . . TCLC 25
See also CA 109; DLB 9, 78

Autran Dourado, Waldomiro
See Dourado, (Waldomiro Freitas) Autran

Averroes 1126-1198 . . . . CMLC 7
See also DLB 115

Avison, Margaret 1918- . . . . CLC 2, 4
See also CA 17-20R; DLB 53; MTCW

Axton, David
See Koontz, Dean R(ay)

Ayckbourn, Alan
1939- . . . . CLC 5, 8, 18, 33, 74
See also CA 21-24R; CANR 31; DLB 13;
MTCW

Aydy, Catherine
See Tennant, Emma (Christina)

Ayme, Marcel (Andre) 1902-1967 . . . CLC 11
See also CA 89-92; CLR 25; DLB 72

Ayrton, Michael 1921-1975 . . . . CLC 7
See also CA 5-8R; 61-64; CANR 9, 21

Azorin . . . . CLC 11
See also Martinez Ruiz, Jose

Azuela, Mariano 1873-1952 . . . . TCLC 3
See also CA 104; 131; HW; MTCW

Baastad, Babbis Friis
See Friis-Baastad, Babbis Ellinor

Bab
See Gilbert, W(illiam) S(chwenck)

Babbis, Eleanor
See Friis-Baastad, Babbis Ellinor

Babel, Isaak (Emmanuilovich)
1894-1941(?) . . . . CLC 73
See also CA 104; TCLC 2, 13

Babits, Mihaly 1883-1941 . . . . TCLC 14
See also CA 114

Babur 1483-1530 . . . . LC 18

Bacchelli, Riccardo 1891-1985 . . . . . CLC 19
See also CA 29-32R; 117

Bach, Richard (David) 1936- . . . . CLC 14
See also AITN 1; BEST 89:2; CA 9-12R;
CANR 18; MTCW; SATA 13

Bachman, Richard
See King, Stephen (Edwin)

Bachmann, Ingeborg 1926-1973 . . . . . CLC 69
See also CA 93-96; 45-48; DLB 85

Bacon, Francis 1561-1626 . . . . LC 18
See also CDBLB Before 1660

Bacovia, George . . . . TCLC 24
See also Vasiliu, Gheorghe

Badanes, Jerome 1937- . . . . CLC 59

Bagehot, Walter 1826-1877 . . . . . . NCLC 10
See also DLB 55

Bagnold, Enid 1889-1981 . . . . CLC 25
See also CA 5-8R; 103; CANR 5, 40;
DLB 13; MAICYA; SATA 1, 25

Bagrjana, Elisaveta
See Belcheva, Elisaveta

Bagryana, Elisaveta
See Belcheva, Elisaveta

Bailey, Paul 1937- . . . . CLC 45
See also CA 21-24R; CANR 16; DLB 14

Baillie, Joanna 1762-1851 . . . . NCLC 2
See also DLB 93

Bainbridge, Beryl (Margaret)
1933- . . . . CLC 4, 5, 8, 10, 14, 18, 22, 62
See also CA 21-24R; CANR 24; DLB 14;
MTCW

Baker, Elliott 1922- . . . . CLC 8
See also CA 45-48; CANR 2

Baker, Nicholson 1957- . . . . CLC 61
See also CA 135

Baker, Ray Stannard 1870-1946 . . . TCLC 47
See also CA 118

Baker, Russell (Wayne) 1925- . . . . . . CLC 31
See also BEST 89:4; CA 57-60; CANR 11,
41; MTCW

Bakshi, Ralph 1938(?)- . . . . CLC 26
See also CA 112; 138

Bakunin, Mikhail (Alexandrovich)
1814-1876 . . . . NCLC 25

Baldwin, James (Arthur)
1924-1987 . . . . . . CLC 1, 2, 3, 4, 5, 8, 13,
15, 17, 42, 50, 67; DC 1; SSC 10
See also AAYA 4; BLC 1; BW; CA 1-4R;
124; CABS 1; CANR 3, 24;
CDALB 1941-1968; DA; DLB 2, 7, 33;
DLBY 87; MTCW; SATA 9, 54; WLC

Ballard, J(ames) G(raham)
1930- . . . . CLC 3, 6, 14, 36; SSC 1
See also AAYA 3; CA 5-8R; CANR 15, 39;
DLB 14; MTCW

Balmont, Konstantin (Dmitriyevich)
1867-1943 . . . . TCLC 11
See also CA 109

Balzac, Honore de
1799-1850 . . . . NCLC 5, 35; SSC 5
See also DA; DLB 119; WLC

Bambara, Toni Cade 1939- . . . . CLC 19
See also AAYA 5; BLC 1; BW; CA 29-32R;
CANR 24; DA; DLB 38; MTCW

Bamdad, A.
See Shamlu, Ahmad

Banat, D. R.
See Bradbury, Ray (Douglas)

Bancroft, Laura
See Baum, L(yman) Frank

Banim, John 1798-1842 . . . . NCLC 13
See also DLB 116

Banim, Michael 1796-1874 . . . . . . NCLC 13

Banks, Iain
See Banks, Iain M(enzies)

Banks, Iain M(enzies) 1954- . . . . CLC 34
See also CA 123; 128

Banks, Lynne Reid . . . . CLC 23
See also Reid Banks, Lynne
See also AAYA 6

Banks, Russell 1940- . . . . CLC 37, 72
See also CA 65-68; CAAS 15; CANR 19;
DLB 130

Banville, John 1945- . . . . CLC 46
See also CA 117; 128; DLB 14

Banville, Theodore (Faullain) de
1832-1891 . . . . NCLC 9

Baraka, Amiri
1934- . . . CLC 1, 2, 3, 5, 10, 14, 33; PC 4
See also Jones, LeRoi
See also BLC 1; BW; CA 21-24R; CABS 3;
CANR 27, 38; CDALB 1941-1968; DA;
DLB 5, 7, 16, 38; DLBD 8; MTCW

Barbellion, W. N. P. . . . . TCLC 24
See also Cummings, Bruce F(rederick)

Barbera, Jack 1945- . . . . CLC 44
See also CA 110

Barbey d'Aurevilly, Jules Amedee
1808-1889 . . . . NCLC 1
See also DLB 119

Barbusse, Henri 1873-1935 . . . . TCLC 5
See also CA 105; DLB 65

Barclay, Bill
See Moorcock, Michael (John)

Barclay, William Ewert
See Moorcock, Michael (John)

Barea, Arturo 1897-1957 . . . . TCLC 14
See also CA 111

Barfoot, Joan 1946- . . . . CLC 18
See also CA 105

Baring, Maurice 1874-1945 . . . . TCLC 8
See also CA 105; DLB 34

Barker, Clive 1952- . . . . CLC 52
See also AAYA 10; BEST 90:3; CA 121;
129; MTCW

Barker, George Granville
1913-1991 . . . . CLC 8, 48
See also CA 9-12R; 135; CANR 7, 38;
DLB 20; MTCW

Barker, Harley Granville
See Granville-Barker, Harley
See also DLB 10

Barker, Howard 1946- . . . . CLC 37
See also CA 102; DLB 13

Barker, Pat 1943- . . . . CLC 32
See also CA 117; 122

Barlow, Joel 1754-1812 . . . . NCLC 23
See also DLB 37

Barnard, Mary (Ethel) 1909- . . . . CLC 48
See also CA 21-22; CAP 2

Barnes, Djuna
1892-1982 . . . CLC 3, 4, 8, 11, 29; SSC 3
See also CA 9-12R; 107; CANR 16; DLB 4,
9, 45; MTCW

Barnes, Julian 1946- . . . . CLC 42
See also CA 102; CANR 19

Barnes, Peter 1931- . . . . CLC 5, 56
See also CA 65-68; CAAS 12; CANR 33,
34; DLB 13; MTCW

Baroja (y Nessi), Pio 1872-1956 . . . . TCLC 8
See also CA 104

Baron, David
See Pinter, Harold

Baron Corvo
See Rolfe, Frederick (William Serafino Austin Lewis Mary)

Barondess, Sue K(aufman)
1926-1977 .... CLC 8
See also Kaufman, Sue
See also CA 1-4R; 69-72; CANR 1

Baron de Teive
See Pessoa, Fernando (Antonio Nogueira)

Barres, Maurice 1862-1923 ...... TCLC 47
See also DLB 123

Barreto, Afonso Henrique de Lima
See Lima Barreto, Afonso Henrique de

Barrett, (Roger) Syd 1946- .... CLC 35
See also Pink Floyd

Barrett, William (Christopher)
1913-1992 .... CLC 27
See also CA 13-16R; 139; CANR 11

Barrie, J(ames) M(atthew)
1860-1937 .... TCLC 2
See also CA 104; 136; CDBLB 1890-1914; CLR 16; DLB 10; MAICYA; YABC 1

Barrington, Michael
See Moorcock, Michael (John)

Barrol, Grady
See Bograd, Larry

Barry, Mike
See Malzberg, Barry N(athaniel)

Barry, Philip 1896-1949......... TCLC 11
See also CA 109; DLB 7

Bart, Andre Schwarz
See Schwarz-Bart, Andre

Barth, John (Simmons)
1930- ...... CLC 1, 2, 3, 5, 7, 9, 10, 14, 27, 51; SSC 10
See also AITN 1, 2; CA 1-4R; CABS 1; CANR 5, 23; DLB 2; MTCW

Barthelme, Donald
1931-1989 ...... CLC 1, 2, 3, 5, 6, 8, 13, 23, 46, 59; SSC 2
See also CA 21-24R; 129; CANR 20; DLB 2; DLBY 80, 89; MTCW; SATA 7, 62

Barthelme, Frederick 1943-........ CLC 36
See also CA 114; 122; DLBY 85

Barthes, Roland (Gerard)
1915-1980 .... CLC 24
See also CA 130; 97-100; MTCW

Barzun, Jacques (Martin) 1907- .... CLC 51
See also CA 61-64; CANR 22

Bashevis, Isaac
See Singer, Isaac Bashevis

Bashkirtseff, Marie 1859-1884 ... NCLC 27

Basho
See Matsuo Basho

Bass, Kingsley B., Jr.
See Bullins, Ed

Bassani, Giorgio 1916-............ CLC 9
See also CA 65-68; CANR 33; DLB 128; MTCW

Bastos, Augusto (Antonio) Roa
See Roa Bastos, Augusto (Antonio)

Bataille, Georges 1897-1962 .... CLC 29
See also CA 101; 89-92

Bates, H(erbert) E(rnest)
1905-1974 .... CLC 46; SSC 10
See also CA 93-96; 45-48; CANR 34; MTCW

Bauchart
See Camus, Albert

Baudelaire, Charles
1821-1867 .... NCLC 6, 29; PC 1
See also DA; WLC

Baudrillard, Jean 1929-........... CLC 60

Baum, L(yman) Frank 1856-1919 ... TCLC 7
See also CA 108; 133; CLR 15; DLB 22; MAICYA; MTCW; SATA 18

Baum, Louis F.
See Baum, L(yman) Frank

Baumbach, Jonathan 1933- ...... CLC 6, 23
See also CA 13-16R; CAAS 5; CANR 12; DLBY 80; MTCW

Bausch, Richard (Carl) 1945- ...... CLC 51
See also CA 101; CAAS 14; DLB 130

Baxter, Charles 1947-.......... CLC 45, 78
See also CA 57-60; CANR 40; DLB 130

Baxter, George Owen
See Faust, Frederick (Schiller)

Baxter, James K(eir) 1926-1972 .... CLC 14
See also CA 77-80

Baxter, John
See Hunt, E(verette) Howard, Jr.

Bayer, Sylvia
See Glassco, John

Beagle, Peter S(oyer) 1939-......... CLC 7
See also CA 9-12R; CANR 4; DLBY 80; SATA 60

Bean, Normal
See Burroughs, Edgar Rice

Beard, Charles A(ustin)
1874-1948 .... TCLC 15
See also CA 115; DLB 17; SATA 18

Beardsley, Aubrey 1872-1898 ..... NCLC 6

Beattie, Ann
1947- .... CLC 8, 13, 18, 40, 63; SSC 11
See also BEST 90:2; CA 81-84; DLBY 82; MTCW

Beattie, James 1735-1803 .... NCLC 25
See also DLB 109

Beauchamp, Kathleen Mansfield 1888-1923
See Mansfield, Katherine
See also CA 104; 134; DA

Beauvoir, Simone (Lucie Ernestine Marie Bertrand) de
1908-1986 .... CLC 1, 2, 4, 8, 14, 31, 44, 50, 71
See also CA 9-12R; 118; CANR 28; DA; DLB 72; DLBY 86; MTCW; WLC

Becker, Jurek 1937-............. CLC 7, 19
See also CA 85-88; DLB 75

Becker, Walter 1950-............. CLC 26

Beckett, Samuel (Barclay)
1906-1989 ...... CLC 1, 2, 3, 4, 6, 9, 10, 11, 14, 18, 29, 57, 59
See also CA 5-8R; 130; CANR 33; CDBLB 1945-1960; DA; DLB 13, 15; DLBY 90; MTCW; WLC

Beckford, William 1760-1844 .... NCLC 16
See also DLB 39

Beckman, Gunnel 1910-.......... CLC 26
See also CA 33-36R; CANR 15; CLR 25; MAICYA; SAAS 9; SATA 6

Becque, Henri 1837-1899........ NCLC 3

Beddoes, Thomas Lovell
1803-1849 .... NCLC 3
See also DLB 96

Bedford, Donald F.
See Fearing, Kenneth (Flexner)

Beecher, Catharine Esther
1800-1878 .... NCLC 30
See also DLB 1

Beecher, John 1904-1980........... CLC 6
See also AITN 1; CA 5-8R; 105; CANR 8

Beer, Johann 1655-1700............. LC 5

Beer, Patricia 1924-.............. CLC 58
See also CA 61-64; CANR 13; DLB 40

Beerbohm, Henry Maximilian
1872-1956...............TCLC 1, 24
See also CA 104; DLB 34, 100

Begiebing, Robert J(ohn) 1946-..... CLC 70
See also CA 122; CANR 40

Behan, Brendan
1923-1964 .... CLC 1, 8, 11, 15
See also CA 73-76; CANR 33; CDBLB 1945-1960; DLB 13; MTCW

Behn, Aphra 1640(?) 1689 .... LC 1
See also DA; DLB 39, 80, 131; WLC

Behrman, S(amuel) N(athaniel)
1893-1973 .... CLC 40
See also CA 13-16; 45-48; CAP 1; DLB 7, 44

Belasco, David 1853-1931 .... TCLC 3
See also CA 104; DLB 7

Belcheva, Elisaveta 1893- .... CLC 10

Beldone, Phil "Cheech"
See Ellison, Harlan

Beleno
See Azuela, Mariano

Belinski, Vissarion Grigoryevich
1811-1848 .... NCLC 5

Belitt, Ben 1911-................. CLC 22
See also CA 13-16R; CAAS 4; CANR 7; DLB 5

Bell, James Madison 1826-1902 ... TCLC 43
See also BLC 1; BW; CA 122; 124; DLB 50

Bell, Madison (Smartt) 1957- ...... CLC 41
See also CA 111; CANR 28

Bell, Marvin (Hartley) 1937-..... CLC 8, 31
See also CA 21-24R; CAAS 14; DLB 5; MTCW

Bell, W. L. D.
See Mencken, H(enry) L(ouis)

Bellamy, Atwood C.
See Mencken, H(enry) L(ouis)

Bellamy, Edward 1850-1898 .... NCLC 4
See also DLB 12

Bellin, Edward J.
See Kuttner, Henry

Belloc, (Joseph) Hilaire (Pierre)
        1870-1953 . . . . TCLC 7, 18
    See also CA 106; DLB 19, 100; YABC 1

Belloc, Joseph Peter Rene Hilaire
    See Belloc, (Joseph) Hilaire (Pierre)

Belloc, Joseph Pierre Hilaire
    See Belloc, (Joseph) Hilaire (Pierre)

Belloc, M. A.
    See Lowndes, Marie Adelaide (Belloc)

Bellow, Saul
        1915- . . . . . . CLC 1, 2, 3, 6, 8, 10, 13, 15,
                                      25, 33, 34, 63
    See also AITN 2; BEST 89:3; CA 5-8R;
        CABS 1; CANR 29; CDALB 1941-1968;
        DA; DLB 2, 28; DLBD 3; DLBY 82;
        MTCW; WLC

Belser, Reimond Karel Maria de
        1929- . . . . CLC 14

Bely, Andrey . . . . TCLC 7
    See also Bugayev, Boris Nikolayevich

Benary, Margot
    See Benary-Isbert, Margot

Benary-Isbert, Margot 1889-1979 . . . CLC 12
    See also CA 5-8R; 89-92; CANR 4;
        CLR 12; MAICYA; SATA 2, 21

Benavente (y Martinez), Jacinto
        1866-1954 . . . . TCLC 3
    See also CA 106; 131; HW; MTCW

Benchley, Peter (Bradford)
        1940- . . . . CLC 4, 8
    See also AITN 2; CA 17-20R; CANR 12,
        35; MTCW; SATA 3

Benchley, Robert (Charles)
        1889-1945 . . . . TCLC 1
    See also CA 105; DLB 11

Benedikt, Michael 1935- . . . . CLC 4, 14
    See also CA 13-16R; CANR 7; DLB 5

Benet, Juan 1927- . . . . CLC 28

Benet, Stephen Vincent
        1898-1943 . . . . TCLC 7; SSC 10
    See also CA 104; DLB 4, 48, 102; YABC 1

Benet, William Rose 1886-1950 . . . TCLC 28
    See also CA 118; DLB 45

Benford, Gregory (Albert) 1941-. . . . CLC 52
    See also CA 69-72; CANR 12, 24;
        DLBY 82

Bengtsson, Frans (Gunnar)
        1894-1954 . . . . TCLC 48

Benjamin, David
    See Slavitt, David R(ytman)

Benjamin, Lois
    See Gould, Lois

Benjamin, Walter 1892-1940 . . . . . TCLC 39

Benn, Gottfried 1886-1956. . . . . TCLC 3
    See also CA 106; DLB 56

Bennett, Alan 1934- . . . . CLC 45, 77
    See also CA 103; CANR 35; MTCW

Bennett, (Enoch) Arnold
        1867-1931 . . . . TCLC 5, 20
    See also CA 106; CDBLB 1890-1914;
        DLB 10, 34, 98

Bennett, Elizabeth
    See Mitchell, Margaret (Munnerlyn)

Bennett, George Harold 1930-
    See Bennett, Hal
    See also BW; CA 97-100

Bennett, Hal . . . . CLC 5
    See also Bennett, George Harold
    See also DLB 33

Bennett, Jay 1912- . . . . CLC 35
    See also AAYA 10; CA 69-72; CANR 11;
        SAAS 4; SATA 27, 41

Bennett, Louise (Simone) 1919-. . . . . CLC 28
    See also BLC 1; DLB 117

Benson, E(dward) F(rederic)
        1867-1940 . . . . TCLC 27
    See also CA 114

Benson, Jackson J. 1930-. . . . . CLC 34
    See also CA 25-28R; DLB 111

Benson, Sally 1900-1972 . . . . CLC 17
    See also CA 19-20; 37-40R; CAP 1;
        SATA 1, 27, 35

Benson, Stella 1892-1933. . . . . TCLC 17
    See also CA 117; DLB 36

Bentham, Jeremy 1748-1832 . . . . . NCLC 38
    See also DLB 107

Bentley, E(dmund) C(lerihew)
        1875-1956 . . . . TCLC 12
    See also CA 108; DLB 70

Bentley, Eric (Russell) 1916-. . . . . . . CLC 24
    See also CA 5-8R; CANR 6

Beranger, Pierre Jean de
        1780-1857 . . . . NCLC 34

Berger, Colonel
    See Malraux, (Georges-)Andre

Berger, John (Peter) 1926- . . . . . . CLC 2, 19
    See also CA 81-84; DLB 14

Berger, Melvin H. 1927- . . . . CLC 12
    See also CA 5-8R; CANR 4; SAAS 2;
        SATA 5

Berger, Thomas (Louis)
        1924- . . . . CLC 3, 5, 8, 11, 18, 38
    See also CA 1-4R; CANR 5, 28; DLB 2;
        DLBY 80; MTCW

Bergman, (Ernst) Ingmar
        1918- . . . . CLC 16, 72
    See also CA 81-84; CANR 33

Bergson, Henri 1859-1941 . . . . TCLC 32

Bergstein, Eleanor 1938- . . . . CLC 4
    See also CA 53-56; CANR 5

Berkoff, Steven 1937-. . . . . CLC 56
    See also CA 104

Bermant, Chaim (Icyk) 1929- . . . . . . CLC 40
    See also CA 57-60; CANR 6, 31

Bern, Victoria
    See Fisher, M(ary) F(rances) K(ennedy)

Bernanos, (Paul Louis) Georges
        1888-1948 . . . . TCLC 3
    See also CA 104; 130; DLB 72

Bernard, April 1956- . . . . CLC 59
    See also CA 131

Bernhard, Thomas
        1931-1989 . . . . CLC 3, 32, 61
    See also CA 85-88; 127; CANR 32;
        DLB 85, 124; MTCW

Berrigan, Daniel 1921-. . . . . CLC 4
    See also CA 33-36R; CAAS 1; CANR 11;
        DLB 5

Berrigan, Edmund Joseph Michael, Jr.
        1934-1983
    See Berrigan, Ted
    See also CA 61-64; 110; CANR 14

Berrigan, Ted. . . . . CLC 37
    See also Berrigan, Edmund Joseph Michael,
        Jr.
    See also DLB 5

Berry, Charles Edward Anderson 1931-
    See Berry, Chuck
    See also CA 115

Berry, Chuck. . . . . CLC 17
    See also Berry, Charles Edward Anderson

Berry, Jonas
    See Ashbery, John (Lawrence)

Berry, Wendell (Erdman)
        1934- . . . . CLC 4, 6, 8, 27, 46
    See also AITN 1; CA 73-76; DLB 5, 6

Berryman, John
        1914-1972 . . . . . . CLC 1, 2, 3, 4, 6, 8, 10,
                                      13, 25, 62
    See also CA 13-16; 33-36R; CABS 2;
        CANR 35; CAP 1; CDALB 1941-1968;
        DLB 48; MTCW

Bertolucci, Bernardo 1940- . . . . CLC 16
    See also CA 106

Bertrand, Aloysius 1807-1841 . . . . NCLC 31

Bertran de Born c. 1140-1215 . . . . . CMLC 5

Besant, Annie (Wood) 1847-1933 . . . TCLC 9
    See also CA 105

Bessie, Alvah 1904-1985. . . . . CLC 23
    See also CA 5-8R; 116; CANR 2; DLB 26

Bethlen, T. D.
    See Silverberg, Robert

Beti, Mongo. CLC 27
    See also Biyidi, Alexandre
    See also BLC 1

Betjeman, John
        1906-1984 . . . . CLC 2, 6, 10, 34, 43
    See also CA 9-12R; 112; CANR 33;
        CDBLB 1945-1960; DLB 20; DLBY 84;
        MTCW

Betti, Ugo 1892-1953. . . . . TCLC 5
    See also CA 104

Betts, Doris (Waugh) 1932-. . . . CLC 3, 6, 28
    See also CA 13-16R; CANR 9; DLBY 82

Bevan, Alistair
    See Roberts, Keith (John Kingston)

Beynon, John
    See Harris, John (Wyndham Parkes Lucas)
        Beynon

Bialik, Chaim Nachman
        1873-1934 . . . . TCLC 25

Bickerstaff, Isaac
    See Swift, Jonathan

Bidart, Frank 1939- . . . . CLC 33
    See also CA 140

Bienek, Horst 1930-. . . . . CLC 7, 11
    See also CA 73-76; DLB 75

Bierce, Ambrose (Gwinett)
1842-1914(?) ..... **TCLC 1, 7, 44; SSC 9**
See also CA 104; 139; CDALB 1865-1917;
DA; DLB 11, 12, 23, 71, 74; WLC

Billings, Josh
See Shaw, Henry Wheeler

Billington, Rachel 1942-.......... **CLC 43**
See also AITN 2; CA 33-36R

Binyon, T(imothy) J(ohn) 1936- .... **CLC 34**
See also CA 111; CANR 28

Bioy Casares, Adolfo 1914-.... **CLC 4, 8, 13**
See also CA 29-32R; CANR 19; DLB 113;
HW; MTCW

Bird, C.
See Ellison, Harlan

Bird, Cordwainer
See Ellison, Harlan

Bird, Robert Montgomery
1806-1854 .... **NCLC 1**

Birney, (Alfred) Earle
1904-.................. **CLC 1, 4, 6, 11**
See also CA 1-4R; CANR 5, 20; DLB 88;
MTCW

Bishop, Elizabeth
1911-1979 ...... **CLC 1, 4, 9, 13, 15, 32;**
PC 3
See also CA 5-8R; 89-92; CABS 2;
CANR 26; CDALB 1968-1988; DA;
DLB 5; MTCW; SATA 24

Bishop, John 1935-............... **CLC 10**
See also CA 105

Bissett, Bill 1939-................ **CLC 18**
See also CA 69-72; CANR 15; DLB 53;
MTCW

Bitov, Andrei (Georgievich) 1937-... **CLC 57**

Biyidi, Alexandre 1932-
See Beti, Mongo
See also BW; CA 114; 124; MTCW

Bjarme, Brynjolf
See Ibsen, Henrik (Johan)

Bjornson, Bjornstjerne (Martinius)
1832-1910 .... **TCLC 7, 37**
See also CA 104

Black, Robert
See Holdstock, Robert P.

Blackburn, Paul 1926-1971 ...... **CLC 9, 43**
See also CA 81-84; 33-36R; CANR 34;
DLB 16; DLBY 81

Black Elk 1863-1950 .... **TCLC 33**

Black Hobart
See Sanders, (James) Ed(ward)

Blacklin, Malcolm
See Chambers, Aidan

Blackmore, R(ichard) D(oddridge)
1825-1900 .... **TCLC 27**
See also CA 120; DLB 18

Blackmur, R(ichard) P(almer)
1904-1965 .... **CLC 2, 24**
See also CA 11-12; 25-28R; CAP 1; DLB 63

Black Tarantula, The
See Acker, Kathy

Blackwood, Algernon (Henry)
1869-1951 .... **TCLC 5**
See also CA 105

Blackwood, Caroline 1931- .... **CLC 6, 9**
See also CA 85-88; CANR 32; DLB 14;
MTCW

Blade, Alexander
See Hamilton, Edmond; Silverberg, Robert

Blaga, Lucian 1895-1961 .... **CLC 75**

Blair, Eric (Arthur) 1903-1950
See Orwell, George
See also CA 104; 132; DA; MTCW;
SATA 29

Blais, Marie-Claire
1939- .... **CLC 2, 4, 6, 13, 22**
See also CA 21-24R; CAAS 4; CANR 38;
DLB 53; MTCW

Blaise, Clark 1940-............... **CLC 29**
See also AITN 2; CA 53-56; CAAS 3;
CANR 5; DLB 53

Blake, Nicholas
See Day Lewis, C(ecil)
See also DLB 77

Blake, William 1757-1827 .... **NCLC 13**
See also CDBLB 1789-1832; DA; DLB 93;
MAICYA; SATA 30; WLC

Blasco Ibanez, Vicente
1867-1928 .... **TCLC 12**
See also CA 110; 131; HW; MTCW

Blatty, William Peter 1928-......... **CLC 2**
See also CA 5-8R; CANR 9

Bleeck, Oliver
See Thomas, Ross (Elmore)

Blessing, Lee 1949-............... **CLC 54**

Blish, James (Benjamin)
1921-1975 .... **CLC 14**
See also CA 1-4R; 57-60; CANR 3; DLB 8;
MTCW; SATA 66

Bliss, Reginald
See Wells, H(erbert) G(eorge)

Blixen, Karen (Christentze Dinesen)
1885-1962
See Dinesen, Isak
See also CA 25-28; CANR 22; CAP 2;
MTCW; SATA 44

Bloch, Robert (Albert) 1917-....... **CLC 33**
See also CA 5-8R; CANR 5; DLB 44;
SATA 12

Blok, Alexander (Alexandrovich)
1880-1921 .... **TCLC 5**
See also CA 104

Blom, Jan
See Breytenbach, Breyten

Bloom, Harold 1930- .... **CLC 24**
See also CA 13-16R; CANR 39; DLB 67

Bloomfield, Aurelius
See Bourne, Randolph S(illiman)

Blount, Roy (Alton), Jr. 1941- ..... **CLC 38**
See also CA 53-56; CANR 10, 28; MTCW

Bloy, Leon 1846-1917............. **TCLC 22**
See also CA 121; DLB 123

Blume, Judy (Sussman) 1938-... **CLC 12, 30**
See also AAYA 3; CA 29-32R; CANR 13,
37; CLR 2, 15; DLB 52; MAICYA;
MTCW; SATA 2, 31

Blunden, Edmund (Charles)
1896-1974 .... **CLC 2, 56**
See also CA 17-18; 45-48; CAP 2; DLB 20,
100; MTCW

Bly, Robert (Elwood)
1926- .... **CLC 1, 2, 5, 10, 15, 38**
See also CA 5-8R; CANR 41; DLB 5;
MTCW

Bobette
See Simenon, Georges (Jacques Christian)

Boccaccio, Giovanni 1313-1375
See also SSC 10

Bochco, Steven 1943-............. **CLC 35**
See also CA 124; 138

Bodenheim, Maxwell 1892-1954 ... **TCLC 44**
See also CA 110; DLB 9, 45

Bodker, Cecil 1927- .... **CLC 21**
See also CA 73-76; CANR 13; CLR 23;
MAICYA; SATA 14

Boell, Heinrich (Theodor) 1917-1985
See Boll, Heinrich (Theodor)
See also CA 21-24R; 116; CANR 24; DA;
DLB 69; DLBY 85; MTCW

Bogan, Louise 1897-1970..... **CLC 4, 39, 46**
See also CA 73-76; 25-28R; CANR 33;
DLB 45; MTCW

Bogarde, Dirk .... **CLC 19**
See also Van Den Bogarde, Derek Jules
Gaspard Ulric Niven
See also DLB 14

Bogosian, Eric 1953- .... **CLC 45**
See also CA 138

Bograd, Larry 1953-.............. **CLC 35**
See also CA 93-96; SATA 33

Boiardo, Matteo Maria 1441-1494 .... **LC 6**

Boileau-Despreaux, Nicolas
1636-1711 .... **LC 3**

Boland, Eavan 1944-........... **CLC 40, 67**
See also DLB 40

Boll, Heinrich (Theodor)
1917-1985 .... **CLC 2, 3, 6, 9, 11, 15, 27,**
39, 72
See also Boell, Heinrich (Theodor)
See also DLB 69; DLBY 85; WLC

Bolt, Lee
See Faust, Frederick (Schiller)

Bolt, Robert (Oxton) 1924-........ **CLC 14**
See also CA 17-20R; CANR 35; DLB 13;
MTCW

Bomkauf
See Kaufman, Bob (Garnell)

Bonaventura................... **NCLC 35**
See also DLB 90

Bond, Edward 1934-....... **CLC 4, 6, 13, 23**
See also CA 25-28R; CANR 38; DLB 13;
MTCW

Bonham, Frank 1914-1989.......... **CLC 12**
See also AAYA 1; CA 9-12R; CANR 4, 36;
MAICYA; SAAS 3; SATA 1, 49, 62

Bonnefoy, Yves 1923-........ **CLC 9, 15, 58**
See also CA 85-88; CANR 33; MTCW

Bontemps, Arna(ud Wendell)
1902-1973 .... CLC **1, 18**
See also BLC 1; BW; CA 1-4R; 41-44R;
CANR 4, 35; CLR 6; DLB 48, 51;
MAICYA; MTCW; SATA 2, 24, 44

Booth, Martin 1944- .... CLC **13**
See also CA 93-96; CAAS 2

Booth, Philip 1925- .... CLC **23**
See also CA 5-8R; CANR 5; DLBY 82

Booth, Wayne C(layson) 1921- ..... CLC **24**
See also CA 1-4R; CAAS 5; CANR 3;
DLB 67

Borchert, Wolfgang 1921-1947 ..... TCLC **5**
See also CA 104; DLB 69, 124

Borel, Petrus 1809-1859 .... NCLC **41**

Borges, Jorge Luis
1899-1986 ... CLC **1, 2, 3, 4, 6, 8, 9, 10,**
13, 19, 44, 48; SSC 4
See also CA 21-24R; CANR 19, 33; DA;
DLB 113; DLBY 86; HW; MTCW; WLC

Borowski, Tadeusz 1922-1951 ...... TCLC **9**
See also CA 106

Borrow, George (Henry)
1803-1881 .... NCLC **9**
See also DLB 21, 55

Bosman, Herman Charles
1905-1951 .... TCLC **49**

Bosschere, Jean de 1878(?)-1953 ... TCLC **19**
See also CA 115

Boswell, James 1740-1795 .... LC **4**
See also CDBLB 1660-1789; DA; DLB 104;
WLC

Bottoms, David 1949- .... CLC **53**
See also CA 105; CANR 22; DLB 120;
DLBY 83

Boucicault, Dion 1820-1890 ...... NCLC **41**

Boucolon, Maryse 1937-
See Conde, Maryse
See also CA 110; CANR 30

Bourget, Paul (Charles Joseph)
1852-1935 .... TCLC **12**
See also CA 107; DLB 123

Bourjaily, Vance (Nye) 1922- .... CLC **8, 62**
See also CA 1-4R; CAAS 1; CANR 2;
DLB 2

Bourne, Randolph S(illiman)
1886-1918 .... TCLC **16**
See also CA 117; DLB 63

Bova, Ben(jamin William) 1932- .... CLC **45**
See also CA 5-8R; CANR 11; CLR 3;
DLBY 81; MAICYA; MTCW; SATA 6,
68

Bowen, Elizabeth (Dorothea Cole)
1899-1973 ...... CLC **1, 3, 6, 11, 15, 22;**
SSC 3
See also CA 17-18; 41-44R; CANR 35;
CAP 2; CDBLB 1945-1960; DLB 15;
MTCW

Bowering, George 1935- .... CLC **15, 47**
See also CA 21-24R; CAAS 16; CANR 10;
DLB 53

Bowering, Marilyn R(uthe) 1949- ... CLC **32**
See also CA 101

Bowers, Edgar 1924- .... CLC **9**
See also CA 5-8R; CANR 24; DLB 5

Bowie, David .... CLC **17**
See also Jones, David Robert

Bowles, Jane (Sydney)
1917-1973 .... CLC **3, 68**
See also CA 19-20; 41-44R; CAP 2

Bowles, Paul (Frederick)
1910- .... CLC **1, 2, 19, 53; SSC 3**
See also CA 1-4R; CAAS 1; CANR 1, 19;
DLB 5, 6; MTCW

Box, Edgar
See Vidal, Gore

Boyd, Nancy
See Millay, Edna St. Vincent

Boyd, William 1952- .... CLC **28, 53, 70**
See also CA 114; 120

Boyle, Kay
1902-1992 ..... CLC **1, 5, 19, 58; SSC 5**
See also CA 13-16R; 140; CAAS 1;
CANR 29; DLB 4, 9, 48, 86; MTCW

Boyle, Mark
See Kienzle, William X(avier)

Boyle, Patrick 1905-1982 .... CLC **19**
See also CA 127

Boyle, T. Coraghessan 1948- .... CLC **36, 55**
See also BEST 90:4; CA 120; DLBY 86

Boz
See Dickens, Charles (John Huffam)

Brackenridge, Hugh Henry
1748-1816 .... NCLC **7**
See also DLB 11, 37

Bradbury, Edward P.
See Moorcock, Michael (John)

Bradbury, Malcolm (Stanley)
1932- .... CLC **32, 61**
See also CA 1-4R; CANR 1, 33; DLB 14;
MTCW

Bradbury, Ray (Douglas)
1920- .... CLC **1, 3, 10, 15, 42**
See also AITN 1, 2; CA 1-4R; CANR 2, 30;
CDALB 1968-1988; DA; DLB 2, 8;
MTCW; SATA 11, 64; WLC

Bradford, Gamaliel 1863-1932 ..... TCLC **36**
See also DLB 17

Bradley, David (Henry, Jr.) 1950- .. CLC **23**
See also BLC 1; BW; CA 104; CANR 26;
DLB 33

Bradley, John Ed 1959- .... CLC **55**

Bradley, Marion Zimmer 1930- ..... CLC **30**
See also AAYA 9; CA 57-60; CAAS 10;
CANR 7, 31; DLB 8; MTCW

Bradstreet, Anne 1612(?)-1672 .... LC **4**
See also CDALB 1640-1865; DA; DLB 24

Bragg, Melvyn 1939- .... CLC **10**
See also BEST 89:3; CA 57-60; CANR 10;
DLB 14

Braine, John (Gerard)
1922-1986 .... CLC **1, 3, 41**
See also CA 1-4R; 120; CANR 1, 33;
CDBLB 1945-1960; DLB 15; DLBY 86;
MTCW

Brammer, William 1930(?)-1978 .... CLC **31**
See also CA 77-80

Brancati, Vitaliano 1907-1954 ..... TCLC **12**
See also CA 109

Brancato, Robin F(idler) 1936- ..... CLC **35**
See also AAYA 9; CA 69-72; CANR 11;
SAAS 9; SATA 23

Brand, Max
See Faust, Frederick (Schiller)

Brand, Millen 1906-1980 .... CLC **7**
See also CA 21-24R; 97-100

Branden, Barbara .... CLC **44**

Brandes, Georg (Morris Cohen)
1842-1927 .... TCLC **10**
See also CA 105

Brandys, Kazimierz 1916- .... CLC **62**

Branley, Franklyn M(ansfield)
1915- .... CLC **21**
See also CA 33-36R; CANR 14, 39;
CLR 13; MAICYA; SAAS 16; SATA 4,
68

Brathwaite, Edward (Kamau)
1930- .... CLC **11**
See also BW; CA 25-28R; CANR 11, 26;
DLB 125

Brautigan, Richard (Gary)
1935-1984 .... CLC **1, 3, 5, 9, 12, 34, 42**
See also CA 53-56; 113; CANR 34; DLB 2,
5; DLBY 80, 84; MTCW; SATA 56

Braverman, Kate 1950- .... CLC **67**
See also CA 89-92

Brecht, Bertolt
1898-1956 ..... TCLC **1, 6, 13, 35; DC 3**
See also CA 104; 133; DA; DLB 56, 124;
MTCW; WLC

Brecht, Eugen Berthold Friedrich
See Brecht, Bertolt

Bremer, Fredrika 1801-1865 ..... NCLC **11**

Brennan, Christopher John
1870-1932 .... TCLC **17**
See also CA 117

Brennan, Maeve 1917- .... CLC **5**
See also CA 81-84

Brentano, Clemens (Maria)
1778-1842 .... NCLC **1**

Brent of Bin Bin
See Franklin, (Stella Maraia Sarah) Miles

Brenton, Howard 1942- .... CLC **31**
See also CA 69-72; CANR 33; DLB 13;
MTCW

Breslin, James 1930-
See Breslin, Jimmy
See also CA 73-76; CANR 31; MTCW

Breslin, Jimmy .... CLC **4, 43**
See also Breslin, James
See also AITN 1

Bresson, Robert 1907- .... CLC **16**
See also CA 110

Breton, Andre 1896-1966 ... CLC **2, 9, 15, 54**
See also CA 19-20; 25-28R; CANR 40;
CAP 2; DLB 65; MTCW

Breytenbach, Breyten 1939(?)- .. CLC **23, 37**
See also CA 113; 129

Bridgers, Sue Ellen 1942- .... CLC **26**
See also AAYA 8; CA 65-68; CANR 11,
36; CLR 18; DLB 52; MAICYA;
SAAS 1; SATA 22

Bridges, Robert (Seymour)
1844-1930 .... **TCLC 1**
See also CA 104; CDBLB 1890-1914;
DLB 19, 98

Bridie, James .... **TCLC 3**
See also Mavor, Osborne Henry
See also DLB 10

Brin, David 1950- .... **CLC 34**
See also CA 102; CANR 24; SATA 65

Brink, Andre (Philippus)
1935- .... **CLC 18, 36**
See also CA 104; CANR 39; MTCW

Brinsmead, H(esba) F(ay) 1922- .... **CLC 21**
See also CA 21-24R; CANR 10; MAICYA;
SAAS 5; SATA 18

Brittain, Vera (Mary)
1893(?)-1970 .... **CLC 23**
See also CA 13-16; 25-28R; CAP 1; MTCW

Broch, Hermann 1886-1951 .... **TCLC 20**
See also CA 117; DLB 85, 124

Brock, Rose
See Hansen, Joseph

Brodkey, Harold 1930- .... **CLC 56**
See also CA 111; DLB 130

Brodsky, Iosif Alexandrovich 1940-
See Brodsky, Joseph
See also AITN 1; CA 41-44R; CANR 37;
MTCW

Brodsky, Joseph .... **CLC 4, 6, 13, 36, 50**
See also Brodsky, Iosif Alexandrovich

Brodsky, Michael Mark 1948- ..... **CLC 19**
See also CA 102; CANR 18, 41

Bromell, Henry 1947- .... **CLC 5**
See also CA 53-56; CANR 9

Bromfield, Louis (Brucker)
1896-1956 .... **TCLC 11**
See also CA 107; DLB 4, 9, 86

Broner, E(sther) M(asserman)
1930- .... **CLC 19**
See also CA 17-20R; CANR 8, 25; DLB 28

Bronk, William 1918- .... **CLC 10**
See also CA 89-92; CANR 23

Bronstein, Lev Davidovich
See Trotsky, Leon

Bronte, Anne 1820-1849 .... **NCLC 4**
See also DLB 21

Bronte, Charlotte
1816-1855 .... **NCLC 3, 8, 33**
See also CDBLB 1832-1890; DA; DLB 21;
WLC

Bronte, (Jane) Emily
1818-1848 .... **NCLC 16, 35**
See also CDBLB 1832-1890; DA; DLB 21,
32; WLC

Brooke, Frances 1724-1789 .... **LC 6**
See also DLB 39, 99

Brooke, Henry 1703(?)-1783 .... **LC 1**
See also DLB 39

Brooke, Rupert (Chawner)
1887-1915 .... **TCLC 2, 7**
See also CA 104; 132; CDBLB 1914-1945;
DA; DLB 19; MTCW; WLC

Brooke-Haven, P.
See Wodehouse, P(elham) G(renville)

Brooke-Rose, Christine 1926- ...... **CLC 40**
See also CA 13-16R; DLB 14

Brookner, Anita 1928- ...... **CLC 32, 34, 51**
See also CA 114; 120; CANR 37; DLBY 87;
MTCW

Brooks, Cleanth 1906- .... **CLC 24**
See also CA 17-20R; CANR 33, 35;
DLB 63; MTCW

Brooks, George
See Baum, L(yman) Frank

Brooks, Gwendolyn
1917- ...... **CLC 1, 2, 4, 5, 15, 49; PC 7**
See also AITN 1; BLC 1; BW; CA 1-4R;
CANR 1, 27; CDALB 1941-1968;
CLR 27; DA; DLB 5, 76; MTCW;
SATA 6; WLC

Brooks, Mel .... **CLC 12**
See also Kaminsky, Melvin
See also DLB 26

Brooks, Peter 1938- .... **CLC 34**
See also CA 45-48; CANR 1

Brooks, Van Wyck 1886-1963 ...... **CLC 29**
See also CA 1-4R; CANR 6; DLB 45, 63,
103

Brophy, Brigid (Antonia)
1929- .... **CLC 6, 11, 29**
See also CA 5-8R; CAAS 4; CANR 25;
DLB 14; MTCW

Brosman, Catharine Savage 1934- .... **CLC 9**
See also CA 61-64; CANR 21

Brother Antoninus
See Everson, William (Oliver)

Broughton, T(homas) Alan 1936- ... **CLC 19**
See also CA 45-48; CANR 2, 23

Broumas, Olga 1949- .... **CLC 10, 73**
See also CA 85-88; CANR 20

Brown, Charles Brockden
1771-1810 .... **NCLC 22**
See also CDALB 1640-1865; DLB 37, 59,
73

Brown, Christy 1932-1981 .... **CLC 63**
See also CA 105; 104; DLB 14

Brown, Claude 1937- .... **CLC 30**
See also AAYA 7; BLC 1; BW; CA 73-76

Brown, Dee (Alexander) 1908- .. **CLC 18, 47**
See also CA 13-16R; CAAS 6; CANR 11;
DLBY 80; MTCW; SATA 5

Brown, George
See Wertmueller, Lina

Brown, George Douglas
1869-1902 .... **TCLC 28**

Brown, George Mackay 1921- .... **CLC 5, 48**
See also CA 21-24R; CAAS 6; CANR 12,
37; DLB 14, 27; MTCW; SATA 35

Brown, (William) Larry 1951- ...... **CLC 73**
See also CA 130; 134

Brown, Moses
See Barrett, William (Christopher)

Brown, Rita Mae 1944- .... **CLC 18, 43**
See also CA 45-48; CANR 2, 11, 35;
MTCW

Brown, Roderick (Langmere) Haig-
See Haig-Brown, Roderick (Langmere)

Brown, Rosellen 1939- .... **CLC 32**
See also CA 77-80; CAAS 10; CANR 14

Brown, Sterling Allen
1901-1989 .... **CLC 1, 23, 59**
See also BLC 1; BW; CA 85-88; 127;
CANR 26; DLB 48, 51, 63; MTCW

Brown, Will
See Ainsworth, William Harrison

Brown, William Wells
1813-1884 .... **NCLC 2; DC 1**
See also BLC 1; DLB 3, 50

Browne, (Clyde) Jackson 1948(?)-... **CLC 21**
See also CA 120

Browning, Elizabeth Barrett
1806-1861 ....·.... **NCLC 1, 16; PC 6**
See also CDBLB 1832-1890; DA; DLB 32;
WLC

Browning, Robert
1812-1889 ....,....... **NCLC 19; PC 2**
See also CDBLB 1832-1890; DA; DLB 32;
YABC 1

Browning, Tod 1882-1962 .... **CLC 16**
See also CA 117

Bruccoli, Matthew J(oseph) 1931- .. **CLC 34**
See also CA 9-12R; CANR 7; DLB 103

Bruce, Lenny .... **CLC 21**
See also Schneider, Leonard Alfred

Bruin, John
See Brutus, Dennis

Brulls, Christian
See Simenon, Georges (Jacques Christian)

Brunner, John (Kilian Houston)
1934- .... **CLC 8, 10**
See also CA 1-4R; CAAS 8; CANR 2, 37;
MTCW

Brutus, Dennis 1924- .... **CLC 43**
See also BLC 1; BW; CA 49-52; CAAS 14;
CANR 2, 27; DLB 117

Bryan, C(ourtlandt) D(ixon) B(arnes)
1936- .... **CLC 29**
See also CA 73-76; CANR 13

Bryan, Michael
See Moore, Brian

Bryant, William Cullen
1794-1878 .... **NCLC 6**
See also CDALB 1640-1865; DA; DLB 3,
43, 59

Bryusov, Valery Yakovlevich
1873-1924 .... **TCLC 10**
See also CA 107

Buchan, John 1875-1940 .... **TCLC 41**
See also CA 108; DLB 34, 70; YABC 2

Buchanan, George 1506-1582 .... **LC 4**

Buchheim, Lothar-Guenther 1918- ... **CLC 6**
See also CA 85-88

Buchner, (Karl) Georg
1813-1837 .... **NCLC 26**

Buchwald, Art(hur) 1925- .... **CLC 33**
See also AITN 1; CA 5-8R; CANR 21;
MTCW; SATA 10

Buck, Pearl S(ydenstricker)
1892-1973 .... **CLC 7, 11, 18**
See also AITN 1; CA 1-4R; 41-44R;
CANR 1, 34; DA; DLB 9, 102; MTCW;
SATA 1, 25

Buckler, Ernest   1908-1984. . . . . CLC 13
See also CA 11-12; 114; CAP 1; DLB 68;
SATA 47

Buckley, Vincent (Thomas)
1925-1988 . . . . CLC 57
See also CA 101

Buckley, William F(rank), Jr.
1925- . . . . CLC 7, 18, 37
See also AITN 1; CA 1-4R; CANR 1, 24;
DLBY 80; MTCW

Buechner, (Carl) Frederick
1926- . . . . CLC 2, 4, 6, 9
See also CA 13-16R; CANR 11, 39;
DLBY 80; MTCW

Buell, John (Edward)   1927-. . . . . CLC 10
See also CA 1-4R; DLB 53

Buero Vallejo, Antonio   1916- . . . CLC 15, 46
See also CA 106; CANR 24; HW; MTCW

Bufalino, Gesualdo   1920(?)-. . . . . CLC 74

Bugayev, Boris Nikolayevich   1880-1934
See Bely, Andrey
See also CA 104

Bukowski, Charles   1920-. . . . CLC 2, 5, 9, 41
See also CA 17-20R; CANR 40; DLB 5,
130; MTCW

Bulgakov, Mikhail (Afanas'evich)
1891-1940 . . . . TCLC 2, 16
See also CA 105

Bullins, Ed   1935- . . . . CLC 1, 5, 7
See also BLC 1; BW; CA 49-52; CAAS 16;
CANR 24; DLB 7, 38; MTCW

Bulwer-Lytton, Edward (George Earle Lytton)
1803-1873 . . . . NCLC 1
See also DLB 21

Bunin, Ivan Alexeyevich
1870-1953 . . . . TCLC 6; SSC 5
See also CA 104

Bunting, Basil   1900-1985. . . . CLC 10, 39, 47
See also CA 53-56; 115; CANR 7; DLB 20

Bunuel, Luis   1900-1983 . . . . CLC 16
See also CA 101; 110; CANR 32; HW

Bunyan, John   1628-1688 . . . . LC 4
See also CDBLB 1660-1789; DA; DLB 39;
WLC

Burford, Eleanor
See Hibbert, Eleanor Alice Burford

Burgess, Anthony
1917- . . . . . . CLC 1, 2, 4, 5, 8, 10, 13, 15,
22, 40, 62
See also Wilson, John (Anthony) Burgess
See also AITN 1; CDBLB 1960 to Present;
DLB 14

Burke, Edmund   1729(?)-1797. . . . . LC 7
See also DA; DLB 104; WLC

Burke, Kenneth (Duva)   1897- . . . . CLC 2, 24
See also CA 5-8R; CANR 39; DLB 45, 63;
MTCW

Burke, Leda
See Garnett, David

Burke, Ralph
See Silverberg, Robert

Burney, Fanny   1752-1840 . . . . NCLC 12
See also DLB 39

Burns, Robert   1759-1796 . . . . . . LC 3; PC 6
See also CDBLB 1789-1832; DA; DLB 109;
WLC

Burns, Tex
See L'Amour, Louis (Dearborn)

Burnshaw, Stanley   1906-. . . . . CLC 3, 13, 44
See also CA 9-12R; DLB 48

Burr, Anne   1937- . . . . CLC 6
See also CA 25-28R

Burroughs, Edgar Rice
1875-1950 . . . . TCLC 2, 32
See also CA 104; 132; DLB 8; MTCW;
SATA 41

Burroughs, William S(eward)
1914- . . . . CLC 1, 2, 5, 15, 22, 42, 75
See also AITN 2; CA 9-12R; CANR 20;
DA; DLB 2, 8, 16; DLBY 81; MTCW;
WLC

Busch, Frederick   1941- . . . CLC 7, 10, 18, 47
See also CA 33-36R; CAAS 1; DLB 6

Bush, Ronald   1946- . . . . CLC 34
See also CA 136

Bustos, F(rancisco)
See Borges, Jorge Luis

Bustos Domecq, H(onorio)
See Bioy Casares, Adolfo; Borges, Jorge
Luis

Butler, Octavia E(stelle)   1947- . . . . . CLC 38
See also BW; CA 73-76; CANR 12, 24, 38;
DLB 33; MTCW

Butler, Samuel   1612-1680 . . . . LC 16
See also DLB 101, 126

Butler, Samuel   1835-1902 . . . . . . TCLC 1, 33
See also CA 104; CDBLB 1890-1914; DA;
DLB 18, 57; WLC

Butler, Walter C.
See Faust, Frederick (Schiller)

Butor, Michel (Marie Francois)
1926- . . . . CLC 1, 3, 8, 11, 15
See also CA 9-12R; CANR 33; DLB 83;
MTCW

Buzo, Alexander (John)   1944-. . . . . . CLC 61
See also CA 97-100; CANR 17, 39

Buzzati, Dino   1906-1972 . . . . CLC 36
See also CA 33-36R

Byars, Betsy (Cromer)   1928-. . . . . . . CLC 35
See also CA 33-36R; CANR 18, 36; CLR 1,
16; DLB 52; MAICYA; MTCW; SAAS 1;
SATA 4, 46

Byatt, A(ntonia) S(usan Drabble)
1936- . . . . CLC 19, 65
See also CA 13-16R; CANR 13, 33;
DLB 14; MTCW

Byrne, David   1952-. . . . . CLC 26
See also CA 127

Byrne, John Keyes   1926-. . . . . CLC 19
See Leonard, Hugh
See also CA 102

Byron, George Gordon (Noel)
1788-1824 . . . . NCLC 2, 12
See also CDBLB 1789-1832; DA; DLB 96,
110; WLC

C.3.3.
See Wilde, Oscar (Fingal O'Flahertie Wills)

Caballero, Fernan   1796-1877. . . . . NCLC 10

Cabell, James Branch   1879-1958 . . . TCLC 6
See also CA 105; DLB 9, 78

Cable, George Washington
1844-1925 . . . . TCLC 4; SSC 4
See also CA 104; DLB 12, 74

Cabral de Melo Neto, Joao   1920-. . . CLC 76

Cabrera Infante, G(uillermo)
1929- . . . . CLC 5, 25, 45
See also CA 85-88; CANR 29; DLB 113;
HW; MTCW

Cade, Toni
See Bambara, Toni Cade

Cadmus
See Buchan, John

Caedmon   fl. 658-680. . . . . CMLC 7

Caeiro, Alberto
See Pessoa, Fernando (Antonio Nogueira)

Cage, John (Milton, Jr.)   1912- . . . . . CLC 41
See also CA 13-16R; CANR 9

Cain, G.
See Cabrera Infante, G(uillermo)

Cain, Guillermo
See Cabrera Infante, G(uillermo)

Cain, James M(allahan)
1892-1977 . . . . CLC 3, 11, 28
See also AITN 1; CA 17-20R; 73-76;
CANR 8, 34; MTCW

Caine, Mark
See Raphael, Frederic (Michael)

Calderon de la Barca, Pedro
1600-1681 . . . . LC 23; DC 3

Caldwell, Erskine (Preston)
1903-1987 . . . . CLC 1, 8, 14, 50, 60
See also AITN 1; CA 1-4R; 121; CAAS 1;
CANR 2, 33; DLB 9, 86; MTCW

Caldwell, (Janet Miriam) Taylor (Holland)
1900-1985 . . . . CLC 2, 28, 39
See also CA 5-8R; 116; CANR 5

Calhoun, John Caldwell
1782-1850 . . . . NCLC 15
See also DLB 3

Calisher, Hortense   1911-. . . . CLC 2, 4, 8, 38
See also CA 1-4R; CANR 1, 22; DLB 2;
MTCW

Callaghan, Morley Edward
1903-1990 . . . . CLC 3, 14, 41, 65
See also CA 9-12R; 132; CANR 33;
DLB 68; MTCW

Calvino, Italo
1923-1985 . . . . . CLC 5, 8, 11, 22, 33, 39,
73; SSC 3
See also CA 85-88; 116; CANR 23; MTCW

Cameron, Carey   1952-. . . . . CLC 59
See also CA 135

Cameron, Peter   1959-. . . . . CLC 44
See also CA 125

Campana, Dino   1885-1932. . . . . . . TCLC 20
See also CA 117; DLB 114

Campbell, John W(ood, Jr.)
1910-1971 . . . . CLC 32
See also CA 21-22; 29-32R; CANR 34;
CAP 2; DLB 8; MTCW

Campbell, Joseph 1904-1987 . . . . . . **CLC 69**
See also AAYA 3; BEST 89:2; CA 1-4R;
124; CANR 3, 28; MTCW

Campbell, (John) Ramsey 1946- . . . . **CLC 42**
See also CA 57-60; CANR 7

Campbell, (Ignatius) Roy (Dunnachie)
1901-1957 . . . . **TCLC 5**
See also CA 104; DLB 20

Campbell, Thomas 1777-1844 . . . . **NCLC 19**
See also DLB 93

Campbell, Wilfred . . . . **TCLC 9**
See also Campbell, William

Campbell, William 1858(?)-1918
See Campbell, Wilfred
See also CA 106; DLB 92

Campos, Alvaro de
See Pessoa, Fernando (Antonio Nogueira)

Camus, Albert
1913-1960 . . . . **CLC 1, 2, 4, 9, 11, 14, 32,
63, 69; DC 2; SSC 9**
See also CA 89-92; DA; DLB 72; MTCW;
WLC

Canby, Vincent 1924- . . . . **CLC 13**
See also CA 81-84

Cancale
See Desnos, Robert

Canetti, Elias 1905- . . . . . . **CLC 3, 14, 25, 75**
See also CA 21-24R; CANR 23; DLB 85,
124; MTCW

Canin, Ethan 1960- . . . . **CLC 55**
See also CA 131; 135

Cannon, Curt
See Hunter, Evan

Cape, Judith
See Page, P(atricia) K(athleen)

Capek, Karel
1890-1938 . . . . **TCLC 6, 37; DC 1**
See also CA 104; 140; DA; WLC

Capote, Truman
1924-1984 . . . . . . **CLC 1, 3, 8, 13, 19, 34,
38, 58; SSC 2**
See also CA 5-8R; 113; CANR 18;
CDALB 1941-1968; DA; DLB 2;
DLBY 80, 84; MTCW; WLC

Capra, Frank 1897-1991 . . . . **CLC 16**
See also CA 61-64; 135

Caputo, Philip 1941- . . . . **CLC 32**
See also CA 73-76; CANR 40

Card, Orson Scott 1951- . . . . **CLC 44, 47, 50**
See also CA 102; CANR 27; MTCW

Cardenal (Martinez), Ernesto
1925- . . . . **CLC 31**
See also CA 49-52; CANR 2, 32; HW;
MTCW

Carducci, Giosue 1835-1907 . . . . **TCLC 32**

Carew, Thomas 1595(?)-1640 . . . . **LC 13**
See also DLB 126

Carey, Ernestine Gilbreth 1908- . . . . **CLC 17**
See also CA 5-8R; SATA 2

Carey, Peter 1943- . . . . **CLC 40, 55**
See also CA 123; 127; MTCW

Carleton, William 1794-1869 . . . . . . **NCLC 3**

Carlisle, Henry (Coffin) 1926- . . . . . . **CLC 33**
See also CA 13-16R; CANR 15

Carlsen, Chris
See Holdstock, Robert P.

Carlson, Ron(ald F.) 1947- . . . . **CLC 54**
See also CA 105; CANR 27

Carlyle, Thomas 1795-1881 . . . . . . **NCLC 22**
See also CDBLB 1789-1832; DA; DLB 55

Carman, (William) Bliss
1861-1929 . . . . **TCLC 7**
See also CA 104; DLB 92

Carossa, Hans 1878-1956 . . . . **TCLC 48**
See also DLB 66

Carpenter, Don(ald Richard)
1931- . . . . **CLC 41**
See also CA 45-48; CANR 1

Carpentier (y Valmont), Alejo
1904-1980 . . . . **CLC 8, 11, 38**
See also CA 65-68; 97-100; CANR 11;
DLB 113; HW

Carr, Emily 1871-1945 . . . . **TCLC 32**
See also DLB 68

Carr, John Dickson 1906-1977 . . . . . . **CLC 3**
See also CA 49-52; 69-72; CANR 3, 33;
MTCW

Carr, Philippa
See Hibbert, Eleanor Alice Burford

Carr, Virginia Spencer 1929- . . . . **CLC 34**
See also CA 61-64; DLB 111

Carrier, Roch 1937- . . . . **CLC 13, 78**
See also CA 130; DLB 53

Carroll, James P. 1943(?)- . . . . **CLC 38**
See also CA 81-84

Carroll, Jim 1951- . . . . **CLC 35**
See also CA 45-48

Carroll, Lewis . . . . **NCLC 2**
See also Dodgson, Charles Lutwidge
See also CDBLB 1832-1890; CLR 2, 18;
DLB 18; WLC

Carroll, Paul Vincent 1900-1968 . . . . **CLC 10**
See also CA 9-12R; 25-28R; DLB 10

Carruth, Hayden 1921- . . . . **CLC 4, 7, 10, 18**
See also CA 9-12R; CANR 4, 38; DLB 5;
MTCW; SATA 47

Carson, Rachel Louise 1907-1964 . . . **CLC 71**
See also CA 77-80; CANR 35; MTCW;
SATA 23

Carter, Angela (Olive)
1940-1992 . . . . **CLC 5, 41, 76**
See also CA 53-56; 136; CANR 12, 36;
DLB 14; MTCW; SATA 66;
SATA-Obit 70

Carter, Nick
See Smith, Martin Cruz

Carver, Raymond
1938-1988 . . . **CLC 22, 36, 53, 55; SSC 8**
See also CA 33-36R; 126; CANR 17, 34;
DLB 130; DLBY 84, 88; MTCW

Cary, (Arthur) Joyce (Lunel)
1888-1957 . . . . **TCLC 1, 29**
See also CA 104; CDBLB 1914-1945;
DLB 15, 100

Casanova de Seingalt, Giovanni Jacopo
1725-1798 . . . . **LC 13**

Casares, Adolfo Bioy
See Bioy Casares, Adolfo

Casely-Hayford, J(oseph) E(phraim)
1866-1930 . . . . **TCLC 24**
See also BLC 1; CA 123

Casey, John (Dudley) 1939- . . . . **CLC 59**
See also BEST 90:2; CA 69-72; CANR 23

Casey, Michael 1947- . . . . **CLC 2**
See also CA 65-68; DLB 5

Casey, Patrick
See Thurman, Wallace (Henry)

Casey, Warren (Peter) 1935-1988 . . . **CLC 12**
See also CA 101; 127

Casona, Alejandro . . . . **CLC 49**
See also Alvarez, Alejandro Rodriguez

Cassavetes, John 1929-1989 . . . . **CLC 20**
See also CA 85-88; 127

Cassill, R(onald) V(erlin) 1919- . . . **CLC 4, 23**
See also CA 9-12R; CAAS 1; CANR 7;
DLB 6

Cassity, (Allen) Turner 1929- . . . . **CLC 6, 42**
See also CA 17-20R; CAAS 8; CANR 11;
DLB 105

Castaneda, Carlos 1931(?)- . . . . **CLC 12**
See also CA 25-28R; CANR 32; HW;
MTCW

Castedo, Elena 1937- . . . . **CLC 65**
See also CA 132

Castedo-Ellerman, Elena
See Castedo, Elena

Castellanos, Rosario 1925-1974 . . . . . **CLC 66**
See also CA 131; 53-56; DLB 113; HW

Castelvetro, Lodovico 1505-1571 . . . . . **LC 12**

Castiglione, Baldassare 1478-1529 . . . **LC 12**

Castle, Robert
See Hamilton, Edmond

Castro, Guillen de 1569-1631 . . . . **LC 19**

Castro, Rosalia de 1837-1885 . . . . . **NCLC 3**

Cather, Willa
See Cather, Willa Sibert

Cather, Willa Sibert
1873-1947 . . . . . . **TCLC 1, 11, 31; SSC 2**
See also CA 104; 128; CDALB 1865-1917;
DA; DLB 9, 54, 78; DLBD 1; MTCW;
SATA 30; WLC

Catton, (Charles) Bruce
1899-1978 . . . . **CLC 35**
See also AITN 1; CA 5-8R; 81-84;
CANR 7; DLB 17; SATA 2, 24

Cauldwell, Frank
See King, Francis (Henry)

Caunitz, William J. 1933- . . . . **CLC 34**
See also BEST 89:3; CA 125; 130

Causley, Charles (Stanley) 1917- . . . . . **CLC 7**
See also CA 9-12R; CANR 5, 35; CLR 30;
DLB 27; MTCW; SATA 3, 66

Caute, David 1936- . . . . **CLC 29**
See also CA 1-4R; CAAS 4; CANR 1, 33;
DLB 14

Cavafy, C(onstantine) P(eter) . . . . . . **TCLC 2, 7**
See also Kavafis, Konstantinos Petrou

Cavallo, Evelyn
See Spark, Muriel (Sarah)

Cavanna, Betty .... **CLC 12**
See also Harrison, Elizabeth Cavanna
See also MAICYA; SAAS 4; SATA 1, 30

Caxton, William 1421(?)-1491(?)..... **LC 17**

Cayrol, Jean 1911- .... **CLC 11**
See also CA 89-92; DLB 83

Cela, Camilo Jose 1916- ..... **CLC 4, 13, 59**
See also BEST 90:2; CA 21-24R; CAAS 10;
CANR 21, 32; DLBY 89; HW; MTCW

Celan, Paul .... **CLC 53**
See also Antschel, Paul
See also DLB 69

Celine, Louis-Ferdinand
.... **CLC 1, 3, 4, 7, 9, 15, 47**
See also Destouches, Louis-Ferdinand
See also DLB 72

Cellini, Benvenuto 1500-1571 .... **LC 7**

Cendrars, Blaise
See Sauser-Hall, Frederic

Cernuda (y Bidon), Luis
1902-1963 .... **CLC 54**
See also CA 131; 89-92; HW

Cervantes (Saavedra), Miguel de
1547-1616 .... **LC 6, 23; SSC 12**
See also DA; WLC

Cesaire, Aime (Fernand) 1913- .. **CLC 19, 32**
See also BLC 1; BW; CA 65-68; CANR 24;
MTCW

Chabon, Michael 1965(?)- .... **CLC 55**
See also CA 139

Chabrol, Claude 1930- .... **CLC 16**
See also CA 110

Challans, Mary 1905-1983
See Renault, Mary
See also CA 81-84; 111; SATA 23, 36

Challis, George
See Faust, Frederick (Schiller)

Chambers, Aidan 1934- .... **CLC 35**
See also CA 25-28R; CANR 12, 31;
MAICYA; SAAS 12; SATA 1, 69

Chambers, James 1948-
See Cliff, Jimmy
See also CA 124

Chambers, Jessie
See Lawrence, D(avid) H(erbert Richards)

Chambers, Robert W. 1865-1933... **TCLC 41**

Chandler, Raymond (Thornton)
1888-1959 .... **TCLC 1, 7**
See also CA 104; 129; CDALB 1929-1941;
DLBD 6; MTCW

Chang, Jung 1952- .... **CLC 71**

Channing, William Ellery
1780-1842 .... **NCLC 17**
See also DLB 1, 59

Chaplin, Charles Spencer
1889-1977 .... **CLC 16**
See also Chaplin, Charlie
See also CA 81-84; 73-76

Chaplin, Charlie
See Chaplin, Charles Spencer
See also DLB 44

Chapman, George 1559(?)-1634...... **LC 22**
See also DLB 62, 121

Chapman, Graham 1941-1989 ..... **CLC 21**
See also Monty Python
See also CA 116; 129; CANR 35

Chapman, John Jay 1862-1933 .... **TCLC 7**
See also CA 104

Chapman, Walker
See Silverberg, Robert

Chappell, Fred (Davis) 1936- .... **CLC 40, 78**
See also CA 5-8R; CAAS 4; CANR 8, 33;
DLB 6, 105

Char, Rene(-Emile)
1907-1988 .... **CLC 9, 11, 14, 55**
See also CA 13-16R; 124; CANR 32;
MTCW

Charby, Jay
See Ellison, Harlan

Chardin, Pierre Teilhard de
See Teilhard de Chardin, (Marie Joseph)
Pierre

Charles I 1600-1649 .... **LC 13**

Charyn, Jerome 1937- .... **CLC 5, 8, 18**
See also CA 5-8R; CAAS 1; CANR 7;
DLBY 83; MTCW

Chase, Mary (Coyle) 1907-1981 ...... **DC 1**
See also CA 77-80; 105; SATA 17, 29

Chase, Mary Ellen 1887-1973 .... **CLC 2**
See also CA 13-16; 41-44R; CAP 1;
SATA 10

Chase, Nicholas
See Hyde, Anthony

Chateaubriand, Francois Rene de
1768-1848 .... **NCLC 3**
See also DLB 119

Chatterje, Sarat Chandra 1876-1936(?)
See Chatterji, Saratchandra
See also CA 109

Chatterji, Bankim Chandra
1838-1894 .... **NCLC 19**

Chatterji, Saratchandra .... **TCLC 13**
See also Chatterje, Sarat Chandra

Chatterton, Thomas 1752-1770 .... **LC 3**
See also DLB 109

Chatwin, (Charles) Bruce
1940-1989 .... **CLC 28, 57, 59**
See also AAYA 4; BEST 90:1; CA 85-88;
127

Chaucer, Daniel
See Ford, Ford Madox

Chaucer, Geoffrey 1340(?)-1400 ..... **LC 17**
See also CDBLB Before 1660; DA

Chaviaras, Strates 1935-
See Haviaras, Stratis
See also CA 105

Chayefsky, Paddy .... **CLC 23**
See also Chayefsky, Sidney
See also DLB 7, 44; DLBY 81

Chayefsky, Sidney 1923-1981
See Chayefsky, Paddy
See also CA 9-12R; 104; CANR 18

Chedid, Andree 1920- .... **CLC 47**

Cheever, John
1912-1982 ...... **CLC 3, 7, 8, 11, 15, 25,**
64; SSC 1
See also CA 5-8R; 106; CABS 1; CANR 5,
27; CDALB 1941-1968; DA; DLB 2, 102;
DLBY 80, 82; MTCW; WLC

Cheever, Susan 1943- .... **CLC 18, 48**
See also CA 103; CANR 27; DLBY 82

Chekhonte, Antosha
See Chekhov, Anton (Pavlovich)

Chekhov, Anton (Pavlovich)
1860-1904 ...... **TCLC 3, 10, 31; SSC 2**
See also CA 104; 124; DA; WLC

Chernyshevsky, Nikolay Gavrilovich
1828-1889 .... **NCLC 1**

Cherry, Carolyn Janice 1942-
See Cherryh, C. J.
See also CA 65-68; CANR 10

Cherryh, C. J. .... **CLC 35**
See also Cherry, Carolyn Janice
See also DLBY 80

Chesnutt, Charles W(addell)
1858-1932 .... **TCLC 5, 39; SSC 7**
See also BLC 1; BW; CA 106; 125; DLB 12,
50, 78; MTCW

Chester, Alfred 1929(?)-1971....... **CLC 49**
See also CA 33-36R; DLB 130

Chesterton, G(ilbert) K(eith)
1874-1936 .... **TCLC 1, 6; SSC 1**
See also CA 104; 132; CDBLB 1914-1945;
DLB 10, 19, 34, 70, 98; MTCW;
SATA 27

Chiang Pin-chin 1904-1986
See Ding Ling
See also CA 118

Ch'ien Chung-shu 1910- .... **CLC 22**
See also CA 130; MTCW

Child, L. Maria
See Child, Lydia Maria

Child, Lydia Maria 1802-1880 .... **NCLC 6**
See also DLB 1, 74; SATA 67

Child, Mrs.
See Child, Lydia Maria

Child, Philip 1898-1978 .... **CLC 19, 68**
See also CA 13-14; CAP 1; SATA 47

Childress, Alice 1920- .... **CLC 12, 15**
See also AAYA 8; BLC 1; BW; CA 45-48;
CANR 3, 27; CLR 14; DLB 7, 38;
MAICYA; MTCW; SATA 7, 48

Chislett, (Margaret) Anne 1943- .... **CLC 34**

Chitty, Thomas Willes 1926- .... **CLC 11**
See also Hinde, Thomas
See also CA 5-8R

Chomette, Rene Lucien 1898-1981 .. **CLC 20**
See also Clair, Rene
See also CA 103

Chopin, Kate .... **TCLC 5, 14; SSC 8**
See also Chopin, Katherine
See also CDALB 1865-1917; DA; DLB 12,
78

Chopin, Katherine 1851-1904
See Chopin, Kate
See also CA 104; 122

Chretien de Troyes
c. 12th cent. - .... **CMLC 10**

Christie
See Ichikawa, Kon

Christie, Agatha (Mary Clarissa)
   1890-1976 . . . . . **CLC 1, 6, 8, 12, 39, 48**
   See also AAYA 9; AITN 1, 2; CA 17-20R;
   61-64; CANR 10, 37; CDBLB 1914-1945;
   DLB 13, 77; MTCW; SATA 36

Christie, (Ann) Philippa
   See Pearce, Philippa
   See also CA 5-8R; CANR 4

Christine de Pizan 1365(?)-1431(?) . . . . **LC 9**

Chubb, Elmer
   See Masters, Edgar Lee

Chulkov, Mikhail Dmitrievich
   1743-1792 . . . . **LC 2**

Churchill, Caryl 1938- . . . . **CLC 31, 55**
   See also CA 102; CANR 22; DLB 13;
   MTCW

Churchill, Charles 1731-1764 . . . . **LC 3**
   See also DLB 109

Chute, Carolyn 1947- . . . . **CLC 39**
   See also CA 123

Ciardi, John (Anthony)
   1916-1986 . . . . **CLC 10, 40, 44**
   See also CA 5-8R; 118; CAAS 2; CANR 5,
   33; CLR 19; DLB 5; DLBY 86;
   MAICYA; MTCW; SATA 1, 46, 65

Cicero, Marcus Tullius
   106B.C.-43B.C. . . . . **CMLC 3**

Cimino, Michael 1943- . . . . **CLC 16**
   See also CA 105

Cioran, E(mil) M. 1911- . . . . **CLC 64**
   See also CA 25-28R

Cisneros, Sandra 1954- . . . . **CLC 69**
   See also AAYA 9; CA 131; DLB 122; HW

Clair, Rene . . . . **CLC 20**
   See also Chomette, Rene Lucien

Clampitt, Amy 1920- . . . . **CLC 32**
   See also CA 110; CANR 29; DLB 105

Clancy, Thomas L., Jr. 1947-
   See Clancy, Tom
   See also CA 125; 131; MTCW

Clancy, Tom . . . . **CLC 45**
   See also Clancy, Thomas L., Jr.
   See also AAYA 9; BEST 89:1, 90:1

Clare, John 1793-1864 . . . . **NCLC 9**
   See also DLB 55, 96

Clarin
   See Alas (y Urena), Leopoldo (Enrique
   Garcia)

Clark, (Robert) Brian 1932- . . . . **CLC 29**
   See also CA 41-44R

Clark, Eleanor 1913- . . . . **CLC 5, 19**
   See also CA 9-12R; CANR 41; DLB 6

Clark, J. P.
   See Clark, John Pepper
   See also DLB 117

Clark, John Pepper 1935- . . . . **CLC 38**
   See also Clark, J. P.
   See also BLC 1; BW; CA 65-68; CANR 16

Clark, M. R.
   See Clark, Mavis Thorpe

Clark, Mavis Thorpe 1909- . . . . **CLC 12**
   See also CA 57-60; CANR 8, 37; CLR 30;
   MAICYA; SAAS 5; SATA 8, 74

Clark, Walter Van Tilburg
   1909-1971 . . . . **CLC 28**
   See also CA 9-12R; 33-36R; DLB 9;
   SATA 8

Clarke, Arthur C(harles)
   1917- . . . . . . **CLC 1, 4, 13, 18, 35; SSC 3**
   See also AAYA 4; CA 1-4R; CANR 2, 28;
   MAICYA; MTCW; SATA 13, 70

Clarke, Austin 1896-1974 . . . . **CLC 6, 9**
   See also CA 29-32; 49-52; CAP 2; DLB 10,
   20

Clarke, Austin C(hesterfield)
   1934- . . . . **CLC 8, 53**
   See also BLC 1; BW; CA 25-28R;
   CAAS 16; CANR 14, 32; DLB 53, 125

Clarke, Gillian 1937- . . . . **CLC 61**
   See also CA 106; DLB 40

Clarke, Marcus (Andrew Hislop)
   1846-1881 . . . . **NCLC 19**

Clarke, Shirley 1925- . . . . **CLC 16**

Clash, The . . . . **CLC 30**
   See also Headon, (Nicky) Topper; Jones,
   Mick; Simonon, Paul; Strummer, Joe

Claudel, Paul (Louis Charles Marie)
   1868-1955 . . . . **TCLC 2, 10**
   See also CA 104

Clavell, James (duMaresq)
   1925- . . . . **CLC 6, 25**
   See also CA 25-28R; CANR 26; MTCW

Cleaver, (Leroy) Eldridge 1935- . . . . **CLC 30**
   See also BLC 1; BW; CA 21-24R;
   CANR 16

Cleese, John (Marwood) 1939- . . . . . **CLC 21**
   See also Monty Python
   See also CA 112; 116; CANR 35; MTCW

Cleishbotham, Jebediah
   See Scott, Walter

Cleland, John 1710-1789 . . . . **LC 2**
   See also DLB 39

Clemens, Samuel Langhorne 1835-1910
   See Twain, Mark
   See also CA 104; 135; CDALB 1865-1917;
   DA; DLB 11, 12, 23, 64, 74; MAICYA;
   YABC 2

Cleophil
   See Congreve, William

Clerihew, E.
   See Bentley, E(dmund) C(lerihew)

Clerk, N. W.
   See Lewis, C(live) S(taples)

Cliff, Jimmy . . . . **CLC 21**
   See also Chambers, James

Clifton, (Thelma) Lucille
   1936- . . . . **CLC 19, 66**
   See also BLC 1; BW; CA 49-52; CANR 2,
   24; CLR 5; DLB 5, 41; MAICYA;
   MTCW; SATA 20, 69

Clinton, Dirk
   See Silverberg, Robert

Clough, Arthur Hugh 1819-1861 . . **NCLC 27**
   See also DLB 32

Clutha, Janet Paterson Frame 1924-
   See Frame, Janet
   See also CA 1-4R; CANR 2, 36; MTCW

Clyne, Terence
   See Blatty, William Peter

Cobalt, Martin
   See Mayne, William (James Carter)

Coburn, D(onald) L(ee) 1938- . . . . . . **CLC 10**
   See also CA 89-92

Cocteau, Jean (Maurice Eugene Clement)
   1889-1963 . . . . **CLC 1, 8, 15, 16, 43**
   See also CA 25-28; CANR 40; CAP 2; DA;
   DLB 65; MTCW; WLC

Codrescu, Andrei 1946- . . . . **CLC 46**
   See also CA 33-36R; CANR 13, 34

Coe, Max
   See Bourne, Randolph S(illiman)

Coe, Tucker
   See Westlake, Donald E(dwin)

Coetzee, J(ohn) M(ichael)
   1940- . . . . **CLC 23, 33, 66**
   See also CA 77-80; CANR 41; MTCW

Coffey, Brian
   See Koontz, Dean R(ay)

Cohen, Arthur A(llen)
   1928-1986 . . . . **CLC 7, 31**
   See also CA 1-4R; 120; CANR 1, 17;
   DLB 28

Cohen, Leonard (Norman)
   1934- . . . . **CLC 3, 38**
   See also CA 21-24R; CANR 14; DLB 53;
   MTCW

Cohen, Matt 1942- . . . . **CLC 19**
   See also CA 61-64; CANR 40; DLB 53

Cohen-Solal, Annie 19(?)- . . . . **CLC 50**

Colegate, Isabel 1931- . . . . **CLC 36**
   See also CA 17-20R; CANR 8, 22; DLB 14;
   MTCW

Coleman, Emmett
   See Reed, Ishmael

Coleridge, Samuel Taylor
   1772-1834 . . . . **NCLC 9**
   See also CDBLB 1789-1832; DA; DLB 93,
   107; WLC

Coleridge, Sara 1802-1852 . . . . **NCLC 31**

Coles, Don 1928- . . . . **CLC 46**
   See also CA 115; CANR 38

Colette, (Sidonie-Gabrielle)
   1873-1954 . . . . . . **TCLC 1, 5, 16; SSC 10**
   See also CA 104; 131; DLB 65; MTCW

Collett, (Jacobine) Camilla (Wergeland)
   1813-1895 . . . . **NCLC 22**

Collier, Christopher 1930- . . . . **CLC 30**
   See also CA 33-36R; CANR 13, 33;
   MAICYA; SATA 16, 70

Collier, James L(incoln) 1928- . . . . . **CLC 30**
   See also CA 9-12R; CANR 4, 33;
   MAICYA; SATA 8, 70

Collier, Jeremy 1650-1726 . . . . **LC 6**

Collins, Hunt
   See Hunter, Evan

Collins, Linda 1931- . . . . **CLC 44**
   See also CA 125

Collins, (William) Wilkie
1824-1889 .... **NCLC 1, 18**
See also CDBLB 1832-1890; DLB 18, 70

Collins, William 1721-1759 .... **LC 4**
See also DLB 109

Colman, George
See Glassco, John

Colt, Winchester Remington
See Hubbard, L(afayette) Ron(ald)

Colter, Cyrus 1910- .... **CLC 58**
See also BW; CA 65-68; CANR 10; DLB 33

Colton, James
See Hansen, Joseph

Colum, Padraic 1881-1972 .... **CLC 28**
See also CA 73-76; 33-36R; CANR 35;
MAICYA; MTCW; SATA 15

Colvin, James
See Moorcock, Michael (John)

Colwin, Laurie (E.)
1944-1992 .... **CLC 5, 13, 23**
See also CA 89-92; 139; CANR 20;
DLBY 80; MTCW

Comfort, Alex(ander) 1920- .... **CLC 7**
See also CA 1-4R; CANR 1

Comfort, Montgomery
See Campbell, (John) Ramsey

Compton-Burnett, I(vy)
1884(?)-1969 ...... **CLC 1, 3, 10, 15, 34**
See also CA 1-4R; 25-28R; CANR 4;
DLB 36; MTCW

Comstock, Anthony 1844-1915 .... **TCLC 13**
See also CA 110

Conan Doyle, Arthur
See Doyle, Arthur Conan

Conde, Maryse .... **CLC 52**
See also Boucolon, Maryse

Condon, Richard (Thomas)
1915- .... **CLC 4, 6, 8, 10, 45**
See also BEST 90:3; CA 1-4R; CAAS 1;
CANR 2, 23; MTCW

Congreve, William
1670-1729 .... **LC 5, 21; DC 2**
See also CDBLB 1660-1789; DA; DLB 39,
84; WLC

Connell, Evan S(helby), Jr.
1924- .... **CLC 4, 6, 45**
See also AAYA 7; CA 1-4R; CAAS 2;
CANR 2, 39; DLB 2; DLBY 81; MTCW

Connelly, Marc(us Cook)
1890-1980 .... **CLC 7**
See also CA 85-88; 102; CANR 30; DLB 7;
DLBY 80; SATA 25

Connor, Ralph .... **TCLC 31**
See also Gordon, Charles William
See also DLB 92

Conrad, Joseph
1857-1924 .... **TCLC 1, 6, 13, 25, 43;
SSC 9**
See also CA 104; 131; CDBLB 1890-1914;
DA; DLB 10, 34, 98; MTCW; SATA 27;
WLC

Conrad, Robert Arnold
See Hart, Moss

Conroy, Pat 1945-. .... **CLC 30, 74**
See also AAYA 8; AITN 1; CA 85-88;
CANR 24; DLB 6; MTCW

Constant (de Rebecque), (Henri) Benjamin
1767-1830 .... **NCLC 6**
See also DLB 119

Conybeare, Charles Augustus
See Eliot, T(homas) S(tearns)

Cook, Michael 1933- .... **CLC 58**
See also CA 93-96; DLB 53

Cook, Robin 1940- .... **CLC 14**
See also BEST 90:2; CA 108; 111;
CANR 41

Cook, Roy
See Silverberg, Robert

Cooke, Elizabeth 1948- .... **CLC 55**
See also CA 129

Cooke, John Esten 1830-1886 ..... **NCLC 5**
See also DLB 3

Cooke, John Estes
See Baum, L(yman) Frank

Cooke, M. E.
See Creasey, John

Cooke, Margaret
See Creasey, John

Cooney, Ray .... **CLC 62**

Cooper, Henry St. John
See Creasey, John

Cooper, J. California. .... **CLC 56**
See also BW; CA 125

Cooper, James Fenimore
1789-1851 .... **NCLC 1, 27**
See also CDALB 1640-1865; DLB 3;
SATA 19

Coover, Robert (Lowell)
1932- .... **CLC 3, 7, 15, 32, 46**
See also CA 45-48; CANR 3, 37; DLB 2;
DLBY 81; MTCW

Copeland, Stewart (Armstrong)
1952- .... **CLC 26**
See also Police, The

Coppard, A(lfred) E(dgar)
1878-1957 .... **TCLC 5**
See also CA 114; YABC 1

Coppee, Francois 1842-1908 ...... **TCLC 25**

Coppola, Francis Ford 1939- .... **CLC 16**
See also CA 77-80; CANR 40; DLB 44

Corcoran, Barbara 1911- .... **CLC 17**
See also CA 21-24R; CAAS 2; CANR 11,
28; DLB 52; SATA 3

Cordelier, Maurice
See Giraudoux, (Hippolyte) Jean

Corelli, Marie 1855-1924........ **TCLC 51**
See also Mackay, Mary
See also DLB 34

Corman, Cid. .... **CLC 9**
See also Corman, Sidney
See also CAAS 2; DLB 5

Corman, Sidney 1924-
See Corman, Cid
See also CA 85-88

Cormier, Robert (Edmund)
1925- .... **CLC 12, 30**
See also AAYA 3; CA 1-4R; CANR 5, 23;
CDALB 1968-1988; CLR 12; DA;
DLB 52; MAICYA; MTCW; SATA 10,
45

Corn, Alfred 1943- .... **CLC 33**
See also CA 104; DLB 120; DLBY 80

Cornwell, David (John Moore)
1931- .... **CLC 9, 15**
See also le Carre, John
See also CA 5-8R; CANR 13, 33; MTCW

Corrigan, Kevin .... **CLC 55**

Corso, (Nunzio) Gregory 1930-... **CLC 1, 11**
See also CA 5-8R; CANR 41; DLB 5,16;
MTCW

Cortazar, Julio
1914-1984 ...... **CLC 2, 3, 5, 10, 13, 15,
33, 34; SSC 7**
See also CA 21-24R; CANR 12, 32;
DLB 113; HW; MTCW

Corwin, Cecil
See Kornbluth, C(yril) M.

Cosic, Dobrica 1921- .... **CLC 14**
See also CA 122; 138

Costain, Thomas B(ertram)
1885-1965 .... **CLC 30**
See also CA 5-8R; 25-28R; DLB 9

Costantini, Humberto
1924(?)-1987 .... **CLC 49**
See also CA 131; 122; HW

Costello, Elvis 1955-.............. **CLC 21**

Cotter, Joseph S. Sr.
See Cotter, Joseph Seamon Sr.

Cotter, Joseph Seamon Sr.
1861-1949 .... **TCLC 28**
See also BLC 1; BW; CA 124; DLB 50

Coulton, James
See Hansen, Joseph

Couperus, Louis (Marie Anne)
1863-1923 .... **TCLC 15**
See also CA 115

Court, Wesli
See Turco, Lewis (Putnam)

Courtenay, Bryce 1933-........... **CLC 59**
See also CA 138

Courtney, Robert
See Ellison, Harlan

Cousteau, Jacques-Yves 1910-...... **CLC 30**
See also CA 65-68; CANR 15; MTCW;
SATA 38

Coward, Noel (Peirce)
1899-1973 .... **CLC 1, 9, 29, 51**
See also AITN 1; CA 17-18; 41-44R;
CANR 35; CAP 2; CDBLB 1914-1945;
DLB 10; MTCW

Cowley, Malcolm 1898-1989 .... **CLC 39**
See also CA 5-8R; 128; CANR 3; DLB 4,
48; DLBY 81, 89; MTCW

Cowper, William 1731-1800....... **NCLC 8**
See also DLB 104, 109

Cox, William Trevor 1928- ... **CLC 9, 14, 71**
See also Trevor, William
See also CA 9-12R; CANR 4, 37; DLB 14;
MTCW

Cozzens, James Gould
 1903-1978 .... **CLC 1, 4, 11**
  See also CA 9-12R; 81-84; CANR 19;
  CDALB 1941-1968; DLB 9; DLBD 2;
  DLBY 84; MTCW

Crabbe, George 1754-1832....... **NCLC 26**
  See also DLB 93

Craig, A. A.
  See Anderson, Poul (William)

Craik, Dinah Maria (Mulock)
 1826-1887 .... **NCLC 38**
  See also DLB 35; MAICYA; SATA 34

Cram, Ralph Adams 1863-1942.... **TCLC 45**

Crane, (Harold) Hart
 1899-1932 .... **TCLC 2, 5; PC 3**
  See also CA 104; 127; CDALB 1917-1929;
  DA; DLB 4, 48; MTCW; WLC

Crane, R(onald) S(almon)
 1886-1967 .... **CLC 27**
  See also CA 85-88; DLB 63

Crane, Stephen (Townley)
 1871-1900 ..... **TCLC 11, 17, 32; SSC 7**
  See also CA 109; 140; CDALB 1865-1917;
  DA; DLB 12, 54, 78; WLC; YABC 2

Crase, Douglas 1944- .... **CLC 58**
  See also CA 106

Craven, Margaret 1901-1980....... **CLC 17**
  See also CA 103

Crawford, F(rancis) Marion
 1854-1909 .... **TCLC 10**
  See also CA 107; DLB 71

Crawford, Isabella Valancy
 1850-1887 .... **NCLC 12**
  See also DLB 92

Crayon, Geoffrey
  See Irving, Washington

Creasey, John 1908-1973.......... **CLC 11**
  See also CA 5-8R; 41-44R; CANR 8;
  DLB 77; MTCW

Crebillon, Claude Prosper Jolyot de (fils)
 1707-1777 .... **LC 1**

Credo
  See Creasey, John

Creeley, Robert (White)
 1926- ..... **CLC 1, 2, 4, 8, 11, 15, 36, 78**
  See also CA 1-4R; CAAS 10; CANR 23;
  DLB 5, 16; MTCW

Crews, Harry (Eugene)
 1935- .... **CLC 6, 23, 49**
  See also AITN 1; CA 25-28R; CANR 20;
  DLB 6; MTCW

Crichton, (John) Michael
 1942- .... **CLC 2, 6, 54**
  See also AAYA 10; AITN 2; CA 25-28R;
  CANR 13, 40; DLBY 81; MTCW;
  SATA 9

Crispin, Edmund .... **CLC 22**
  See also Montgomery, (Robert) Bruce
  See also DLB 87

Cristofer, Michael 1945(?)- .... **CLC 28**
  See also CA 110; DLB 7

Croce, Benedetto 1866-1952 ...... **TCLC 37**
  See also CA 120

Crockett, David 1786-1836 .... **NCLC 8**
  See also DLB 3, 11

Crockett, Davy
  See Crockett, David

Croker, John Wilson 1780-1857 .. **NCLC 10**
  See also DLB 110

Crommelynck, Fernand 1885-1970 .. **CLC 75**
  See also CA 89-92

Cronin, A(rchibald) J(oseph)
 1896-1981 .... **CLC 32**
  See also CA 1-4R; 102; CANR 5; SATA 25,
  47

Cross, Amanda
  See Heilbrun, Carolyn G(old)

Crothers, Rachel 1878(?)-1958..... **TCLC 19**
  See also CA 113; DLB 7

Croves, Hal
  See Traven, B.

Crowfield, Christopher
  See Stowe, Harriet (Elizabeth) Beecher

Crowley, Aleister................. **TCLC 7**
  See also Crowley, Edward Alexander

Crowley, Edward Alexander 1875-1947
  See Crowley, Aleister
  See also CA 104

Crowley, John 1942-.............. **CLC 57**
  See also CA 61-64; DLBY 82; SATA 65

Crud
  See Crumb, R(obert)

Crumarums
  See Crumb, R(obert)

Crumb, R(obert) 1943-.......... **CLC 17**
  See also CA 106

Crumbum
  See Crumb, R(obert)

Crumski
  See Crumb, R(obert)

Crum the Bum
  See Crumb, R(obert)

Crunk
  See Crumb, R(obert)

Crustt
  See Crumb, R(obert)

Cryer, Gretchen (Kiger) 1935-...... **CLC 21**
  See also CA 114; 123

Csath, Geza 1887-1919........... **TCLC 13**
  See also CA 111

Cudlip, David 1933- .... **CLC 34**

Cullen, Countee 1903-1946 ..... **TCLC 4, 37**
  See also BLC 1; BW; CA 108; 124;
  CDALB 1917-1929; DA; DLB 4, 48, 51;
  MTCW; SATA 18

Cum, R.
  See Crumb, R(obert)

Cummings, Bruce F(rederick) 1889-1919
  See Barbellion, W. N. P.
  See also CA 123

Cummings, E(dward) E(stlin)
 1894-1962 ...... **CLC 1, 3, 8, 12, 15, 68;**
                                              PC 5
  See also CA 73-76; CANR 31;
  CDALB 1929-1941; DA; DLB 4, 48;
  MTCW; WLC 2

Cunha, Euclides (Rodrigues Pimenta) da
 1866-1909 .... **TCLC 24**
  See also CA 123

Cunningham, E. V.
  See Fast, Howard (Melvin)

Cunningham, J(ames) V(incent)
 1911-1985 .... **CLC 3, 31**
  See also CA 1-4R; 115; CANR 1; DLB 5

Cunningham, Julia (Woolfolk)
 1916- .... **CLC 12**
  See also CA 9-12R; CANR 4, 19, 36;
  MAICYA; SAAS 2; SATA 1, 26

Cunningham, Michael 1952- .... **CLC 34**
  See also CA 136

Cunninghame Graham, R(obert) B(ontine)
 1852-1936 .... **TCLC 19**
  See also Graham, R(obert) B(ontine)
  Cunninghame
  See also CA 119; DLB 98

Currie, Ellen 19(?)-............... **CLC 44**

Curtin, Philip
  See Lowndes, Marie Adelaide (Belloc)

Curtis, Price
  See Ellison, Harlan

Cutrate, Joe
  See Spiegelman, Art

Czaczkes, Shmuel Yosef
  See Agnon, S(hmuel) Y(osef Halevi)

D. P.
  See Wells, H(erbert) G(eorge)

Dabrowska, Maria (Szumska)
 1889-1965 .... **CLC 15**
  See also CA 106

Dabydeen, David 1955- .... **CLC 34**
  See also BW; CA 125

Dacey, Philip 1939- .... **CLC 51**
  See also CA 37-40R; CAAS 17; CANR 14,
  32; DLB 105

Dagerman, Stig (Halvard)
 1923-1954 .... **TCLC 17**
  See also CA 117

Dahl, Roald 1916-1990........ **CLC 1, 6, 18**
  See also CA 1-4R; 133; CANR 6, 32, 37;
  CLR 1, 7; MAICYA; MTCW; SATA 1,
  26, 73; SATA-Obit 65

Dahlberg, Edward 1900-1977... **CLC 1, 7, 14**
  See also CA 9-12R; 69-72; CANR 31;
  DLB 48; MTCW

Dale, Colin.................... **TCLC 18**
  See also Lawrence, T(homas) E(dward)

Dale, George E.
  See Asimov, Isaac

Daly, Elizabeth 1878-1967......... **CLC 52**
  See also CA 23-24; 25-28R; CAP 2

Daly, Maureen 1921- .... **CLC 17**
  See also AAYA 5; CANR 37; MAICYA;
  SAAS 1; SATA 2

Daniels, Brett
  See Adler, Renata

Dannay, Frederic 1905-1982 .... **CLC 11**
  See also Queen, Ellery
  See also CA 1-4R; 107; CANR 1, 39;
  MTCW

D'Annunzio, Gabriele
 1863-1938 .... **TCLC 6, 40**
  See also CA 104

Demijohn, Thom
See Disch, Thomas M(ichael)

de Montherlant, Henry (Milon)
See Montherlant, Henry (Milon) de

de Natale, Francine
See Malzberg, Barry N(athaniel)

Denby, Edwin (Orr) 1903-1983 . . . . . **CLC 48**
See also CA 138; 110

Denis, Julio
See Cortazar, Julio

Denmark, Harrison
See Zelazny, Roger (Joseph)

Dennis, John 1658-1734 . . . . **LC 11**
See also DLB 101

Dennis, Nigel (Forbes) 1912-1989 . . . . **CLC 8**
See also CA 25-28R; 129; DLB 13, 15;
MTCW

De Palma, Brian (Russell) 1940- . . . . **CLC 20**
See also CA 109

De Quincey, Thomas 1785-1859 . . . **NCLC 4**
See also CDBLB 1789-1832; DLB 110

Deren, Eleanora 1908(?)-1961
See Deren, Maya
See also CA 111

Deren, Maya . . . . **CLC 16**
See also Deren, Eleanora

Derleth, August (William)
1909-1971 . . . . **CLC 31**
See also CA 1-4R; 29-32R; CANR 4;
DLB 9; SATA 5

de Routisie, Albert
See Aragon, Louis

Derrida, Jacques 1930- . . . . **CLC 24**
See also CA 124; 127

Derry Down Derry
See Lear, Edward

Dersonnes, Jacques
See Simenon, Georges (Jacques Christian)

Desai, Anita 1937- . . . . **CLC 19, 37**
See also CA 81-84; CANR 33; MTCW;
SATA 63

de Saint-Luc, Jean
See Glassco, John

de Saint Roman, Arnaud
See Aragon, Louis

Descartes, Rene 1596-1650 . . . . **LC 20**

De Sica, Vittorio 1901(?)-1974 . . . . . **CLC 20**
See also CA 117

Desnos, Robert 1900-1945 . . . . **TCLC 22**
See also CA 121

Destouches, Louis-Ferdinand
1894-1961 . . . . **CLC 9, 15**
See also Celine, Louis-Ferdinand
See also CA 85-88; CANR 28; MTCW

Deutsch, Babette 1895-1982 . . . . **CLC 18**
See also CA 1-4R; 108; CANR 4; DLB 45;
SATA 1, 33

Devenant, William 1606-1649 . . . . . . **LC 13**

Devkota, Laxmiprasad
1909-1959 . . . . **TCLC 23**
See also CA 123

De Voto, Bernard (Augustine)
1897-1955 . . . . **TCLC 29**
See also CA 113; DLB 9

De Vries, Peter
1910- . . . . **CLC 1, 2, 3, 7, 10, 28, 46**
See also CA 17-20R; CANR 41; DLB 6;
DLBY 82; MTCW

Dexter, Martin
See Faust, Frederick (Schiller)

Dexter, Pete 1943- . . . . **CLC 34, 55**
See also BEST 89:2; CA 127; 131; MTCW

Diamano, Silmang
See Senghor, Leopold Sedar

Diamond, Neil 1941- . . . . **CLC 30**
See also CA 108

di Bassetto, Corno
See Shaw, George Bernard

Dick, Philip K(indred)
1928-1982 . . . . **CLC 10, 30, 72**
See also CA 49-52; 106; CANR 2, 16;
DLB 8; MTCW

Dickens, Charles (John Huffam)
1812-1870 . . . . **NCLC 3, 8, 18, 26**
See also CDBLB 1832-1890; DA; DLB 21,
55, 70; MAICYA; SATA 15

Dickey, James (Lafayette)
1923- . . . . **CLC 1, 2, 4, 7, 10, 15, 47**
See also AITN 1, 2; CA 9-12R; CABS 2;
CANR 10; CDALB 1968-1988; DLB 5;
DLBD 7; DLBY 82; MTCW

Dickey, William 1928- . . . . **CLC 3, 28**
See also CA 9-12R; CANR 24; DLB 5

Dickinson, Charles 1951- . . . . **CLC 49**
See also CA 128

Dickinson, Emily (Elizabeth)
1830-1886 . . . . **NCLC 21; PC 1**
See also CDALB 1865-1917; DA; DLB 1;
SATA 29; WLC

Dickinson, Peter (Malcolm)
1927- . . . . **CLC 12, 35**
See also AAYA 9; CA 41-44R; CANR 31;
CLR 29; DLB 87; MAICYA; SATA 5, 62

Dickson, Carr
See Carr, John Dickson

Dickson, Carter
See Carr, John Dickson

Didion, Joan 1934- . . . . . **CLC 1, 3, 8, 14, 32**
See also AITN 1; CA 5-8R; CANR 14;
CDALB 1968-1988; DLB 2; DLBY 81,
86; MTCW

Dietrich, Robert
See Hunt, E(verette) Howard, Jr.

Dillard, Annie 1945- . . . . **CLC 9, 60**
See also AAYA 6; CA 49-52; CANR 3;
DLBY 80; MTCW; SATA 10

Dillard, R(ichard) H(enry) W(ilde)
1937- . . . . **CLC 5**
See also CA 21-24R; CAAS 7; CANR 10;
DLB 5

Dillon, Eilis 1920- . . . . **CLC 17**
See also CA 9-12R; CAAS 3; CANR 4, 38;
CLR 26; MAICYA; SATA 2, 74

Dimont, Penelope
See Mortimer, Penelope (Ruth)

Dinesen, Isak . . . . **CLC 10, 29; SSC 7**
See also Blixen, Karen (Christentze
Dinesen)

Ding Ling . . . . **CLC 68**
See also Chiang Pin-chin

Disch, Thomas M(ichael) 1940- . . . **CLC 7, 36**
See also CA 21-24R; CAAS 4; CANR 17,
36; CLR 18; DLB 8; MAICYA; MTCW;
SAAS 15; SATA 54

Disch, Tom
See Disch, Thomas M(ichael)

d'Isly, Georges
See Simenon, Georges (Jacques Christian)

Disraeli, Benjamin 1804-1881 . . **NCLC 2, 39**
See also DLB 21, 55

Ditcum, Steve
See Crumb, R(obert)

Dixon, Paige
See Corcoran, Barbara

Dixon, Stephen 1936- . . . . **CLC 52**
See also CA 89-92; CANR 17, 40; DLB 130

Doblin, Alfred . . . . **TCLC 13**
See also Doeblin, Alfred

Dobrolyubov, Nikolai Alexandrovich
1836-1861 . . . . **NCLC 5**

Dobyns, Stephen 1941- . . . . **CLC 37**
See also CA 45-48; CANR 2, 18

Doctorow, E(dgar) L(aurence)
1931- . . . . . **CLC 6, 11, 15, 18, 37, 44, 65**
See also AITN 2; BEST 89:3; CA 45-48;
CANR 2, 33; CDALB 1968-1988; DLB 2,
28; DLBY 80; MTCW

Dodgson, Charles Lutwidge 1832-1898
See Carroll, Lewis
See also CLR 2; DA; MAICYA; YABC 2

Doeblin, Alfred 1878-1957 . . . . **TCLC 13**
See also Doblin, Alfred
See also CA 110; DLB 66

Doerr, Harriet 1910- . . . . **CLC 34**
See also CA 117; 122

Domecq, H(onorio) Bustos
See Bioy Casares, Adolfo; Borges, Jorge
Luis

Domini, Rey
See Lorde, Audre (Geraldine)

Dominique
See Proust, (Valentin-Louis-George-Eugene-)
Marcel

Don, A
See Stephen, Leslie

Donaldson, Stephen R. 1947- . . . . **CLC 46**
See also CA 89-92; CANR 13

Donleavy, J(ames) P(atrick)
1926- . . . . **CLC 1, 4, 6, 10, 45**
See also AITN 2; CA 9-12R; CANR 24;
DLB 6; MTCW

Donne, John 1572-1631 . . . . **LC 10; PC 1**
See also CDBLB Before 1660; DA;
DLB 121; WLC

Donnell, David 1939(?)- . . . . **CLC 34**

Donoso (Yanez), Jose
1924- . . . . **CLC 4, 8, 11, 32**
See also CA 81-84; CANR 32; DLB 113;
HW; MTCW

Dunne, Finley Peter 1867-1936.... TCLC 28
See also CA 108; DLB 11, 23

Dunne, John Gregory 1932-........ CLC 28
See also CA 25-28R; CANR 14; DLBY 80

Dunsany, Edward John Moreton Drax
Plunkett 1878-1957
See Dunsany, Lord; Lord Dunsany
See also CA 104; DLB 10

Dunsany, Lord................... TCLC 2
See also Dunsany, Edward John Moreton
Drax Plunkett
See also DLB 77

du Perry, Jean
See Simenon, Georges (Jacques Christian)

Durang, Christopher (Ferdinand)
1949-.................... CLC 27, 38
See also CA 105

Duras, Marguerite
1914-...... CLC 3, 6, 11, 20, 34, 40, 68
See also CA 25-28R; DLB 83; MTCW

Durban, (Rosa) Pam 1947-........ CLC 39
See also CA 123

Durcan, Paul 1944-........... CLC 43, 70
See also CA 134

Durrell, Lawrence (George)
1912-1990 .... CLC 1, 4, 6, 8, 13, 27, 41
See also CA 9-12R; 132; CANR 40;
CDBLB 1945-1960; DLB 15, 27;
DLBY 90; MTCW

Durrenmatt, Friedrich
.... CLC 1, 4, 8, 11, 15, 43
See also Duerrenmatt, Friedrich
See also DLB 69, 124

Dutt, Toru 1856-1877.......... NCLC 29

Dwight, Timothy 1752-1817...... NCLC 13
See also DLB 37

Dworkin, Andrea 1946-......... CLC 43
See also CA 77-80; CANR 16, 39; MTCW

Dwyer, Deanna
See Koontz, Dean R(ay)

Dwyer, K. R.
See Koontz, Dean R(ay)

Dylan, Bob 1941-...... CLC 3, 4, 6, 12, 77
See also CA 41-44R; DLB 16

Eagleton, Terence (Francis) 1943-
See Eagleton, Terry
See also CA 57-60; CANR 7, 23; MTCW

Eagleton, Terry................... CLC 63
See also Eagleton, Terence (Francis)

Early, Jack
See Scoppettone, Sandra

East, Michael
See West, Morris L(anglo)

Eastaway, Edward
See Thomas, (Philip) Edward

Eastlake, William (Derry) 1917-..... CLC 8
See also CA 5-8R; CAAS 1; CANR 5;
DLB 6

Eberhart, Richard (Ghormley)
1904-............... CLC 3, 11, 19, 56
See also CA 1-4R; CANR 2;
CDALB 1941-1968; DLB 48; MTCW

Eberstadt, Fernanda 1960-........ CLC 39
See also CA 136

Echegaray (y Eizaguirre), Jose (Maria Waldo)
1832-1916 .... TCLC 4
See also CA 104; CANR 32; HW; MTCW

Echeverria, (Jose) Esteban (Antonino)
1805-1851 .... NCLC 18

Echo
See Proust, (Valentin-Louis-George-Eugene-)
Marcel

Eckert, Allan W. 1931-........... CLC 17
See also CA 13-16R; CANR 14; SATA 27,
29

Eckhart, Meister 1260(?)-1328(?) .. CMLC 9
See also DLB 115

Eckmar, F. R.
See de Hartog, Jan

Eco, Umberto 1932-........... CLC 28, 60
See also BEST 90:1; CA 77-80; CANR 12,
33; MTCW

Eddison, E(ric) R(ucker)
1882-1945 .... TCLC 15
See also CA 109

Edel, (Joseph) Leon 1907-...... CLC 29, 34
See also CA 1-4R; CANR 1, 22; DLB 103

Eden, Emily 1797-1869 .... NCLC 10

Edgar, David 1948-............... CLC 42
See also CA 57-60; CANR 12; DLB 13;
MTCW

Edgerton, Clyde (Carlyle) 1944- .... CLC 39
See also CA 118; 134

Edgeworth, Maria 1767-1849...... NCLC 1
See also DLB 116; SATA 21

Edmonds, Paul
See Kuttner, Henry

Edmonds, Walter D(umaux) 1903-.. CLC 35
See also CA 5-8R; CANR 2; DLB 9;
MAICYA; SAAS 4; SATA 1, 27

Edmondson, Wallace
See Ellison, Harlan

Edson, Russell................... CLC 13
See also CA 33-36R

Edwards, G(erald) B(asil)
1899-1976 .... CLC 25
See also CA 110

Edwards, Gus 1939-.............. CLC 43
See also CA 108

Edwards, Jonathan 1703-1758........ LC 7
See also DA; DLB 24

Efron, Marina Ivanovna Tsvetaeva
See Tsvetaeva (Efron), Marina (Ivanovna)

Ehle, John (Marsden, Jr.) 1925-.... CLC 27
See also CA 9-12R

Ehrenbourg, Ilya (Grigoryevich)
See Ehrenburg, Ilya (Grigoryevich)

Ehrenburg, Ilya (Grigoryevich)
1891-1967 .... CLC 18, 34, 62
See also CA 102; 25-28R

Ehrenburg, Ilyo (Grigoryevich)
See Ehrenburg, Ilya (Grigoryevich)

Eich, Guenter 1907-1972 .... CLC 15
See also CA 111; 93-96; DLB 69, 124

Eichendorff, Joseph Freiherr von
1788-1857 .... NCLC 8
See also DLB 90

Eigner, Larry..................... CLC 9
See also Eigner, Laurence (Joel)
See also DLB 5

Eigner, Laurence (Joel) 1927-
See Eigner, Larry
See also CA 9-12R; CANR 6

Eiseley, Loren Corey 1907-1977..... CLC 7
See also AAYA 5; CA 1-4R; 73-76;
CANR 6

Eisenstadt, Jill 1963-............. CLC 50
See also CA 140

Eisner, Simon
See Kornbluth, C(yril) M.

Ekeloef, (Bengt) Gunnar
1907-1968 .... CLC 27
See also Ekelof, (Bengt) Gunnar
See also CA 123; 25-28R

Ekelof, (Bengt) Gunnar............. CLC 27
See also Ekeloef, (Bengt) Gunnar

Ekwensi, C. O. D.
See Ekwensi, Cyprian (Odiatu Duaka)

Ekwensi, Cyprian (Odiatu Duaka)
1921-....................... CLC 4
See also BLC 1; BW; CA 29-32R;
CANR 18; DLB 117; MTCW; SATA 66

Elaine.......................... TCLC 18
See also Leverson, Ada

El Crummo
See Crumb, R(obert)

Elia
See Lamb, Charles

Eliade, Mircea 1907-1986 .... CLC 19
See also CA 65-68; 119; CANR 30; MTCW

Eliot, A. D.
See Jewett, (Theodora) Sarah Orne

Eliot, Alice
See Jewett, (Theodora) Sarah Orne

Eliot, Dan
See Silverberg, Robert

Eliot, George
1819-1880 .... NCLC 4, 13, 23, 41
See also CDBLB 1832-1890; DA; DLB 21,
35, 55; WLC

Eliot, John 1604-1690 .... LC 5
See also DLB 24

Eliot, T(homas) S(tearns)
1888-1965 ...... CLC 1, 2, 3, 6, 9, 10, 13,
15, 24, 34, 41, 55, 57; PC 5
See also CA 5-8R; 25-28R; CANR 41;
CDALB 1929-1941; DA; DLB 7, 10, 45,
63; DLBY 88; MTCW; WLC 2

Elizabeth 1866-1941............. TCLC 41

Elkin, Stanley L(awrence)
1930- ... CLC 4, 6, 9, 14, 27, 51; SSC 12
See also CA 9-12R; CANR 8; DLB 2, 28;
DLBY 80; MTCW

Elledge, Scott..................... CLC 34

Elliott, Don
See Silverberg, Robert

Elliott, George P(aul) 1918-1980..... CLC 2
See also CA 1-4R; 97-100; CANR 2

Elliott, Janice 1931-.............. CLC 47
See also CA 13-16R; CANR 8, 29; DLB 14

Elliott, Sumner Locke 1917-1991 . . . **CLC 38**
See also CA 5-8R; 134; CANR 2, 21

Elliott, William
See Bradbury, Ray (Douglas)

Ellis, A. E. . . . . **CLC 7**

Ellis, Alice Thomas . . . . **CLC 40**
See also Haycraft, Anna

Ellis, Bret Easton 1964- . . . . **CLC 39, 71**
See also AAYA 2; CA 118; 123

Ellis, (Henry) Havelock
1859-1939 . . . . **TCLC 14**
See also CA 109

Ellis, Landon
See Ellison, Harlan

Ellis, Trey 1962- . . . . **CLC 55**

Ellison, Harlan 1934- . . . . **CLC 1, 13, 42**
See also CA 5-8R; CANR 5; DLB 8;
MTCW

Ellison, Ralph (Waldo)
1914- . . . . **CLC 1, 3, 11, 54**
See also BLC 1; BW; CA 9-12R; CANR 24;
CDALB 1941-1968; DA; DLB 2, 76;
MTCW; WLC

Ellmann, Lucy (Elizabeth) 1956- . . . . **CLC 61**
See also CA 128

Ellmann, Richard (David)
1918-1987 . . . . **CLC 50**
See also BEST 89:2; CA 1-4R; 122;
CANR 2, 28; DLB 103; DLBY 87;
MTCW

Elman, Richard 1934- . . . . **CLC 19**
See also CA 17-20R; CAAS 3

Elron
See Hubbard, L(afayette) Ron(ald)

Eluard, Paul. . . . . **TCLC 7, 41**
See also Grindel, Eugene

Elyot, Sir Thomas 1490(?)-1546 . . . . . **LC 11**

Elytis, Odysseus 1911- . . . . **CLC 15, 49**
See also CA 102; MTCW

Emecheta, (Florence Onye) Buchi
1944- . . . . **CLC 14, 48**
See also BLC 2; BW; CA 81-84; CANR 27;
DLB 117; MTCW; SATA 66

Emerson, Ralph Waldo
1803-1882 . . . . **NCLC 1, 38**
See also CDALB 1640-1865; DA; DLB 1,
59, 73; WLC

Eminescu, Mihail 1850-1889 . . . . . **NCLC 33**

Empson, William
1906-1984 . . . . **CLC 3, 8, 19, 33, 34**
See also CA 17-20R; 112; CANR 31;
DLB 20; MTCW

Enchi Fumiko (Ueda) 1905-1986 . . . . **CLC 31**
See also CA 129; 121

Ende, Michael (Andreas Helmuth)
1929- . . . . **CLC 31**
See also CA 118; 124; CANR 36; CLR 14;
DLB 75; MAICYA; SATA 42, 61

Endo, Shusaku 1923- . . . . . **CLC 7, 14, 19, 54**
See also CA 29-32R; CANR 21; MTCW

Engel, Marian 1933-1985 . . . . **CLC 36**
See also CA 25-28R; CANR 12; DLB 53

Engelhardt, Frederick
See Hubbard, L(afayette) Ron(ald)

Enright, D(ennis) J(oseph)
1920- . . . . **CLC 4, 8, 31**
See also CA 1-4R; CANR 1; DLB 27;
SATA 25

Enzensberger, Hans Magnus
1929- . . . . **CLC 43**
See also CA 116; 119

Ephron, Nora 1941- . . . . **CLC 17, 31**
See also AITN 2; CA 65-68; CANR 12, 39

Epsilon
See Betjeman, John

Epstein, Daniel Mark 1948- . . . . **CLC 7**
See also CA 49-52; CANR 2

Epstein, Jacob 1956- . . . . **CLC 19**
See also CA 114

Epstein, Joseph 1937- . . . . **CLC 39**
See also CA 112; 119

Epstein, Leslie 1938- . . . . **CLC 27**
See also CA 73-76; CAAS 12; CANR 23

Equiano, Olaudah 1745(?)-1797 . . . . . . **LC 16**
See also BLC 2; DLB 37, 50

Erasmus, Desiderius 1469(?)-1536 . . . . **LC 16**

Erdman, Paul E(mil) 1932- . . . . **CLC 25**
See also AITN 1; CA 61-64; CANR 13

Erdrich, Louise 1954- . . . . **CLC 39, 54**
See also AAYA 10; BEST 89:1; CA 114;
CANR 41; MTCW

Erenburg, Ilya (Grigoryevich)
See Ehrenburg, Ilya (Grigoryevich)

Erickson, Stephen Michael 1950-
See Erickson, Steve
See also CA 129

Erickson, Steve . . . . **CLC 64**
See also Erickson, Stephen Michael

Ericson, Walter
See Fast, Howard (Melvin)

Eriksson, Buntel
See Bergman, (Ernst) Ingmar

Eschenbach, Wolfram von
See Wolfram von Eschenbach

Eseki, Bruno
See Mphahlele, Ezekiel

Esenin, Sergei (Alexandrovich)
1895-1925 . . . . **TCLC 4**
See also CA 104

Eshleman, Clayton 1935- . . . . **CLC 7**
See also CA 33-36R; CAAS 6; DLB 5

Espriella, Don Manuel Alvarez
See Southey, Robert

Espriu, Salvador 1913-1985 . . . . **CLC 9**
See also CA 115

Espronceda, Jose de 1808-1842 . . . **NCLC 39**

Esse, James
See Stephens, James

Esterbrook, Tom
See Hubbard, L(afayette) Ron(ald)

Estleman, Loren D. 1952- . . . . **CLC 48**
See also CA 85-88; CANR 27; MTCW

Evan, Evin
See Faust, Frederick (Schiller)

Evans, Evan
See Faust, Frederick (Schiller)

Evans, Marian
See Eliot, George

Evans, Mary Ann
See Eliot, George

Evarts, Esther
See Benson, Sally

Everett, Percival
See Everett, Percival L.

Everett, Percival L. 1956- . . . . **CLC 57**
See also CA 129

Everson, R(onald) G(ilmour)
1903- . . . . **CLC 27**
See also CA 17-20R; DLB 88

Everson, William (Oliver)
1912- . . . . **CLC 1, 5, 14**
See also CA 9-12R; CANR 20; DLB 5, 16;
MTCW

Evtushenko, Evgenii Aleksandrovich
See Yevtushenko, Yevgeny (Alexandrovich)

Ewart, Gavin (Buchanan)
1916- . . . . **CLC 13, 46**
See also CA 89-92; CANR 17; DLB 40;
MTCW

Ewers, Hanns Heinz 1871-1943 . . . **TCLC 12**
See also CA 109

Ewing, Frederick R.
See Sturgeon, Theodore (Hamilton)

Exley, Frederick (Earl)
1929-1992 . . . . **CLC 6, 11**
See also AITN 2; CA 81-84; 138; DLBY 81

Eynhardt, Guillermo
See Quiroga, Horacio (Sylvestre)

Ezekiel, Nissim 1924- . . . . **CLC 61**
See also CA 61-64

Ezekiel, Tish O'Dowd 1943- . . . . **CLC 34**
See also CA 129

Fagen, Donald 1948- . . . . **CLC 26**

Fainzilberg, Ilya Arnoldovich 1897-1937
See Ilf, Ilya
See also CA 120

Fair, Ronald L. 1932- . . . . **CLC 18**
See also BW; CA 69-72; CANR 25; DLB 33

Fairbairns, Zoe (Ann) 1948- . . . . **CLC 32**
See also CA 103; CANR 21

Falco, Gian
See Papini, Giovanni

Falconer, James
See Kirkup, James

Falconer, Kenneth
See Kornbluth, C(yril) M.

Falkland, Samuel
See Heijermans, Herman

Fallaci, Oriana 1930- . . . . **CLC 11**
See also CA 77-80; CANR 15; MTCW

Faludy, George 1913- . . . . **CLC 42**
See also CA 21-24R

Faludy, Gyoergy
See Faludy, George

Fanon, Frantz 1925-1961 . . . . **CLC 74**
See also BLC 2; BW; CA 116; 89-92

Fanshawe, Ann . . . . **LC 11**

Flaubert, Gustave
 1821-1880 . . . . . NCLC 2, 10, 19; SSC 11
 See also DA; DLB 119; WLC

Flecker, (Herman) James Elroy
 1884-1915 . . . . TCLC 43
 See also CA 109; DLB 10, 19

Fleming, Ian (Lancaster)
 1908-1964 . . . . CLC 3, 30
 See also CA 5-8R; CDBLB 1945-1960;
 DLB 87; MTCW; SATA 9

Fleming, Thomas (James)   1927- . . . . CLC 37
 See also CA 5-8R; CANR 10; SATA 8

Fletcher, John Gould   1886-1950 . . . TCLC 35
 See also CA 107; DLB 4, 45

Fleur, Paul
 See Pohl, Frederik

Flooglebuckle, Al
 See Spiegelman, Art

Flying Officer X
 See Bates, H(erbert) E(rnest)

Fo, Dario   1926- . . . . CLC 32
 See also CA 116; 128; MTCW

Fogarty, Jonathan Titulescu Esq.
 See Farrell, James T(homas)

Folke, Will
 See Bloch, Robert (Albert)

Follett, Ken(neth Martin)   1949- . . . . CLC 18
 See also AAYA 6; BEST 89:4; CA 81-84;
 CANR 13, 33; DLB 87; DLBY 81;
 MTCW

Fontane, Theodor   1819-1898 . . . . . NCLC 26
 See also DLB 129

Foote, Horton   1916- . . . . CLC 51
 See also CA 73-76; CANR 34; DLB 26

Foote, Shelby   1916- . . . . CLC 75
 See also CA 5-8R; CANR 3; DLB 2, 17

Forbes, Esther   1891-1967 . . . . CLC 12
 See also CA 13-14; 25-28R; CAP 1;
 CLR 27; DLB 22; MAICYA; SATA 2

Forche, Carolyn (Louise)   1950- . . . . . CLC 25
 See also CA 109; 117; DLB 5

Ford, Elbur
 See Hibbert, Eleanor Alice Burford

Ford, Ford Madox
 1873-1939 . . . . TCLC 1, 15, 39
 See also CA 104; 132; CDBLB 1914-1945;
 DLB 34, 98; MTCW

Ford, John   1895-1973 . . . . CLC 16
 See also CA 45-48

Ford, Richard   1944- . . . . CLC 46
 See also CA 69-72; CANR 11

Ford, Webster
 See Masters, Edgar Lee

Foreman, Richard   1937- . . . . CLC 50
 See also CA 65-68; CANR 32

Forester, C(ecil) S(cott)
 1899-1966 . . . . CLC 35
 See also CA 73-76; 25-28R; SATA 13

Forez
 See Mauriac, Francois (Charles)

Forman, James Douglas   1932- . . . . . . CLC 21
 See also CA 9-12R; CANR 4, 19;
 MAICYA; SATA 8, 70

Fornes, Maria Irene   1930- . . . . . . CLC 39, 61
 See also CA 25-28R; CANR 28; DLB 7;
 HW; MTCW

Forrest, Leon   1937- . . . . CLC 4
 See also BW; CA 89-92; CAAS 7;
 CANR 25; DLB 33

Forster, E(dward) M(organ)
 1879-1970 . . . . . CLC 1, 2, 3, 4, 9, 10, 13,
                                       15, 22, 45, 77
 See also AAYA 2; CA 13-14; 25-28R;
 CAP 1; CDBLB 1914-1945; DA; DLB 34,
 98; DLBD 10; MTCW; SATA 57; WLC

Forster, John   1812-1876 . . . . NCLC 11

Forsyth, Frederick   1938- . . . . . . CLC 2, 5, 36
 See also BEST 89:4; CA 85-88; CANR 38;
 DLB 87; MTCW

Forten, Charlotte L. . . . . TCLC 16
 See also Grimke, Charlotte L(ottie) Forten
 See also BLC 2; DLB 50

Foscolo, Ugo   1778-1827 . . . . NCLC 8

Fosse, Bob . . . . CLC 20
 See also Fosse, Robert Louis

Fosse, Robert Louis   1927-1987
 See Fosse, Bob
 See also CA 110; 123

Foster, Stephen Collins
 1826-1864 . . . . NCLC 26

Foucault, Michel
 1926-1984 . . . . CLC 31, 34, 69
 See also CA 105; 113; CANR 34; MTCW

Fouque, Friedrich (Heinrich Karl) de la Motte
 1777-1843 . . . . NCLC 2
 See also DLB 90

Fournier, Henri Alban   1886-1914
 See Alain-Fournier
 See also CA 104

Fournier, Pierre   1916- . . . . CLC 11
 See also Gascar, Pierre
 See also CA 89-92; CANR 16, 40

Fowles, John
 1926- . . . . CLC 1, 2, 3, 4, 6, 9, 10, 15, 33
 See also CA 5-8R; CANR 25; CDBLB 1960
 to Present; DLB 14; MTCW; SATA 22

Fox, Paula   1923- . . . . CLC 2, 8
 See also AAYA 3; CA 73-76; CANR 20,
 36; CLR 1; DLB 52; MAICYA; MTCW;
 SATA 17, 60

Fox, William Price (Jr.)   1926- . . . . . CLC 22
 See also CA 17-20R; CANR 11; DLB 2;
 DLBY 81

Foxe, John   1516(?)-1587 . . . . LC 14

Frame, Janet . . . . CLC 2, 3, 6, 22, 66
 See also Clutha, Janet Paterson Frame

France, Anatole . . . . TCLC 9
 See also Thibault, Jacques Anatole Francois
 See also DLB 123

Francis, Claude   19(?)- . . . . CLC 50

Francis, Dick   1920- . . . . CLC 2, 22, 42
 See also AAYA 5; BEST 89:3; CA 5-8R;
 CANR 9; CDBLB 1960 to Present;
 DLB 87; MTCW

Francis, Robert (Churchill)
 1901-1987 . . . . CLC 15
 See also CA 1-4R; 123; CANR 1

Frank, Anne(lies Marie)
 1929-1945 . . . . TCLC 17
 See also CA 113; 133; DA; MTCW;
 SATA 42; WLC

Frank, Elizabeth   1945- . . . . CLC 39
 See also CA 121; 126

Franklin, Benjamin
 See Hasek, Jaroslav (Matej Frantisek)

Franklin, (Stella Maraia Sarah) Miles
 1879-1954 . . . . TCLC 7
 See also CA 104

Fraser, Antonia (Pakenham)
 1932- . . . . CLC 32
 See also CA 85-88; MTCW; SATA 32

Fraser, George MacDonald   1925- . . . . CLC 7
 See also CA 45-48; CANR 2

Fraser, Sylvia   1935- . . . . CLC 64
 See also CA 45-48; CANR 1, 16

Frayn, Michael   1933- . . . . . . CLC 3, 7, 31, 47
 See also CA 5-8R; CANR 30; DLB 13, 14;
 MTCW

Fraze, Candida (Merrill)   1945- . . . . . CLC 50
 See also CA 126

Frazer, J(ames) G(eorge)
 1854-1941 . . . . TCLC 32
 See also CA 118

Frazer, Robert Caine
 See Creasey, John

Frazer, Sir James George
 See Frazer, J(ames) G(eorge)

Frazier, Ian   1951- . . . . CLC 46
 See also CA 130

Frederic, Harold   1856-1898 . . . . . . NCLC 10
 See also DLB 12, 23

Frederick, John
 See Faust, Frederick (Schiller)

Frederick the Great   1712-1786 . . . . . . LC 14

Fredro, Aleksander   1793-1876 . . . . . NCLC 8

Freeling, Nicolas   1927- . . . . CLC 38
 See also CA 49-52; CAAS 12; CANR 1, 17;
 DLB 87

Freeman, Douglas Southall
 1886-1953 . . . . TCLC 11
 See also CA 109; DLB 17

Freeman, Judith   1946- . . . . CLC 55

Freeman, Mary Eleanor Wilkins
 1852-1930 . . . . TCLC 9; SSC 1
 See also CA 106; DLB 12, 78

Freeman, R(ichard) Austin
 1862-1943 . . . . TCLC 21
 See also CA 113; DLB 70

French, Marilyn   1929- . . . . . . CLC 10, 18, 60
 See also CA 69-72; CANR 3, 31; MTCW

French, Paul
 See Asimov, Isaac

Freneau, Philip Morin   1752-1832 . . NCLC 1
 See also DLB 37, 43

Friedan, Betty (Naomi)   1921- . . . . . . CLC 74
 See also CA 65-68; CANR 18; MTCW

Friedman, B(ernard) H(arper)
 1926- . . . . CLC 7
 See also CA 1-4R; CANR 3

Friedman, Bruce Jay 1930- . . . . **CLC 3, 5, 56**
See also CA 9-12R; CANR 25; DLB 2, 28

Friel, Brian 1929- . . . . **CLC 5, 42, 59**
See also CA 21-24R; CANR 33; DLB 13;
MTCW

Friis-Baastad, Babbis Ellinor
1921-1970 . . . . **CLC 12**
See also CA 17-20R; 134; SATA 7

Frisch, Max (Rudolf)
1911-1991 . . . . . **CLC 3, 9, 14, 18, 32, 44**
See also CA 85-88; 134; CANR 32;
DLB 69, 124; MTCW

Fromentin, Eugene (Samuel Auguste)
1820-1876 . . . . **NCLC 10**
See also DLB 123

Frost, Frederick
See Faust, Frederick (Schiller)

Frost, Robert (Lee)
1874-1963 . . . . **CLC 1, 3, 4, 9, 10, 13, 15,
26, 34, 44; PC 1**
See also CA 89-92; CANR 33;
CDALB 1917-1929; DA; DLB 54;
DLBD 7; MTCW; SATA 14; WLC

Froy, Herald
See Waterhouse, Keith (Spencer)

Fry, Christopher 1907- . . . . . . **CLC 2, 10, 14**
See also CA 17-20R; CANR 9, 30; DLB 13;
MTCW; SATA 66

Frye, (Herman) Northrop
1912-1991 . . . . **CLC 24, 70**
See also CA 5-8R; 133; CANR 8, 37;
DLB 67, 68; MTCW

Fuchs, Daniel 1909- . . . . **CLC 8, 22**
See also CA 81-84; CAAS 5; CANR 40;
DLB 9, 26, 28

Fuchs, Daniel 1934- . . . . **CLC 34**
See also CA 37-40R; CANR 14

Fuentes, Carlos
1928- . . . . . . **CLC 3, 8, 10, 13, 22, 41, 60**
See also AAYA 4; AITN 2; CA 69-72;
CANR 10, 32; DA; DLB 113; HW;
MTCW; WLC

Fuentes, Gregorio Lopez y
See Lopez y Fuentes, Gregorio

Fugard, (Harold) Athol
1932- . . . . **CLC 5, 9, 14, 25, 40; DC 3**
See also CA 85-88; CANR 32; MTCW

Fugard, Sheila 1932- . . . . **CLC 48**
See also CA 125

Fuller, Charles (H., Jr.)
1939- . . . . **CLC 25; DC 1**
See also BLC 2; BW; CA 108; 112; DLB 38;
MTCW

Fuller, John (Leopold) 1937- . . . . **CLC 62**
See also CA 21-24R; CANR 9; DLB 40

Fuller, Margaret . . . . **NCLC 5**
See also Ossoli, Sarah Margaret (Fuller
marchesa d')

Fuller, Roy (Broadbent)
1912-1991 . . . . **CLC 4, 28**
See also CA 5-8R; 135; CAAS 10; DLB 15,
20

Fulton, Alice 1952- . . . . **CLC 52**
See also CA 116

Furphy, Joseph 1843-1912 . . . . **TCLC 25**

Fussell, Paul 1924- . . . . **CLC 74**
See also BEST 90:1; CA 17-20R; CANR 8,
21, 35; MTCW

Futabatei, Shimei 1864-1909 . . . . . **TCLC 44**

Futrelle, Jacques 1875-1912 . . . . . . **TCLC 19**
See also CA 113

G. B. S.
See Shaw, George Bernard

Gaboriau, Emile 1835-1873 . . . . . . **NCLC 14**

Gadda, Carlo Emilio 1893-1973 . . . . **CLC 11**
See also CA 89-92

Gaddis, William
1922- . . . . **CLC 1, 3, 6, 8, 10, 19, 43**
See also CA 17-20R; CANR 21; DLB 2;
MTCW

Gaines, Ernest J(ames)
1933- . . . . **CLC 3, 11, 18**
See also AITN 1; BLC 2; BW; CA 9-12R;
CANR 6, 24; CDALB 1968-1988; DLB 2,
33; DLBY 80; MTCW

Gaitskill, Mary 1954- . . . . **CLC 69**
See also CA 128

Galdos, Benito Perez
See Perez Galdos, Benito

Gale, Zona 1874-1938 . . . . **TCLC 7**
See also CA 105; DLB 9, 78

Galeano, Eduardo (Hughes) 1940- . . . **CLC 72**
See also CA 29-32R; CANR 13, 32; HW

Galiano, Juan Valera y Alcala
See Valera y Alcala-Galiano, Juan

Gallagher, Tess 1943- . . . . **CLC 18, 63**
See also CA 106; DLB 120

Gallant, Mavis
1922- . . . . **CLC 7, 18, 38; SSC 5**
See also CA 69-72; CANR 29; DLB 53;
MTCW

Gallant, Roy A(rthur) 1924- . . . . **CLC 17**
See also CA 5-8R; CANR 4, 29; CLR 30;
MAICYA; SATA 4, 68

Gallico, Paul (William) 1897-1976 . . . **CLC 2**
See also AITN 1; CA 5-8R; 69-72;
CANR 23; DLB 9; MAICYA; SATA 13

Gallup, Ralph
See Whitemore, Hugh (John)

Galsworthy, John 1867-1933 . . . . **TCLC 1, 45**
See also CA 104; CDBLB 1890-1914; DA;
DLB 10, 34, 98; WLC 2

Galt, John 1779-1839 . . . . **NCLC 1**
See also DLB 99, 116

Galvin, James 1951- . . . . **CLC 38**
See also CA 108; CANR 26

Gamboa, Federico 1864-1939 . . . . . . **TCLC 36**

Gann, Ernest Kellogg 1910-1991 . . . . **CLC 23**
See also AITN 1; CA 1-4R; 136; CANR 1

Garcia, Christina 1959- . . . . **CLC 76**

Garcia Lorca, Federico
1898-1936 . . **TCLC 1, 7, 49; DC 2; PC 3**
See also CA 104; 131; DA; DLB 108; HW;
MTCW; WLC

Garcia Marquez, Gabriel (Jose)
1928- . . . . **CLC 2, 3, 8, 10, 15, 27, 47, 55;
SSC 8**
See also Marquez, Gabriel (Jose) Garcia
See also AAYA 3; BEST 89:1, 90:4;
CA 33-36R; CANR 10, 28; DA;
DLB 113; HW; MTCW; WLC

Gard, Janice
See Latham, Jean Lee

Gard, Roger Martin du
See Martin du Gard, Roger

Gardam, Jane 1928- . . . . **CLC 43**
See also CA 49-52; CANR 2, 18, 33;
CLR 12; DLB 14; MAICYA; MTCW;
SAAS 9; SATA 28, 39

Gardner, Herb . . . . **CLC 44**

Gardner, John (Champlin), Jr.
1933-1982 . . . . . **CLC 2, 3, 5, 7, 8, 10, 18,
28, 34; SSC 7**
See also AITN 1; CA 65-68; 107;
CANR 33; DLB 2; DLBY 82; MTCW;
SATA 31, 40

Gardner, John (Edmund) 1926- . . . . . **CLC 30**
See also CA 103; CANR 15; MTCW

Gardner, Noel
See Kuttner, Henry

Gardons, S. S.
See Snodgrass, W(illiam) D(e Witt)

Garfield, Leon 1921- . . . . **CLC 12**
See also AAYA 8; CA 17-20R; CANR 38,
41; CLR 21; MAICYA; SATA 1, 32

Garland, (Hannibal) Hamlin
1860-1940 . . . . **TCLC 3**
See also CA 104; DLB 12, 71, 78

Garneau, (Hector de) Saint-Denys
1912-1943 . . . . **TCLC 13**
See also CA 111; DLB 88

Garner, Alan 1934- . . . . **CLC 17**
See also CA 73-76; CANR 15; CLR 20;
MAICYA; MTCW; SATA 18, 69

Garner, Hugh 1913-1979 . . . . **CLC 13**
See also CA 69-72; CANR 31; DLB 68

Garnett, David 1892-1981 . . . . **CLC 3**
See also CA 5-8R; 103; CANR 17; DLB 34

Garos, Stephanie
See Katz, Steve

Garrett, George (Palmer)
1929- . . . . **CLC 3, 11, 51**
See also CA 1-4R; CAAS 5; CANR 1;
DLB 2, 5, 130; DLBY 83

Garrick, David 1717-1779 . . . . **LC 15**
See also DLB 84

Garrigue, Jean 1914-1972 . . . . **CLC 2, 8**
See also CA 5-8R; 37-40R; CANR 20

Garrison, Frederick
See Sinclair, Upton (Beall)

Garth, Will
See Hamilton, Edmond; Kuttner, Henry

Garvey, Marcus (Moziah, Jr.)
1887-1940 . . . . **TCLC 41**
See also BLC 2; BW; CA 120; 124

Gary, Romain . . . . **CLC 25**
See also Kacew, Romain
See also DLB 83

Gascar, Pierre .... CLC 11
See also Fournier, Pierre

Gascoyne, David (Emery) 1916- .... CLC 45
See also CA 65-68; CANR 10, 28; DLB 20;
MTCW

Gaskell, Elizabeth Cleghorn
1810-1865 .... NCLC 5
See also CDBLB 1832-1890; DLB 21

Gass, William H(oward)
1924- ... CLC 1, 2, 8, 11, 15, 39; SSC 12
See also CA 17-20R; CANR 30; DLB 2;
MTCW

Gasset, Jose Ortega y
See Ortega y Gasset, Jose

Gautier, Theophile 1811-1872 ..... NCLC 1
See also DLB 119

Gawsworth, John
See Bates, H(erbert) E(rnest)

Gaye, Marvin (Penze) 1939-1984 ... CLC 26
See also CA 112

Gebler, Carlo (Ernest) 1954- .... CLC 39
See also CA 119; 133

Gee, Maggie (Mary) 1948-......... CLC 57
See also CA 130

Gee, Maurice (Gough) 1931-....... CLC 29
See also CA 97-100; SATA 46

Gelbart, Larry (Simon) 1923- ... CLC 21, 61
See also CA 73-76

Gelber, Jack 1932-........... CLC 1, 6, 14
See also CA 1-4R; CANR 2; DLB 7

Gellhorn, Martha Ellis 1908- ... CLC 14, 60
See also CA 77-80; DLBY 82

Genet, Jean
1910-1986 ... CLC 1, 2, 5, 10, 14, 44, 46
See also CA 13-16R; CANR 18; DLB 72;
DLBY 86; MTCW

Gent, Peter 1942-................ CLC 29
See also AITN 1; CA 89-92; DLBY 82

George, Jean Craighead 1919-...... CLC 35
See also AAYA 8; CA 5-8R; CANR 25;
CLR 1; DLB 52; MAICYA; SATA 2, 68

George, Stefan (Anton)
1868-1933 .... TCLC 2, 14
See also CA 104

Georges, Georges Martin
See Simenon, Georges (Jacques Christian)

Gerhardi, William Alexander
See Gerhardie, William Alexander

Gerhardie, William Alexander
1895-1977 .... CLC 5
See also CA 25-28R; 73-76; CANR 18;
DLB 36

Gerstler, Amy 1956-.............. CLC 70

Gertler, T. .... CLC 34
See also CA 116; 121

Ghalib 1797-1869 .... NCLC 39

Ghelderode, Michel de
1898-1962 .... CLC 6, 11
See also CA 85-88; CANR 40

Ghiselin, Brewster 1903- .... CLC 23
See also CA 13-16R; CAAS 10; CANR 13

Ghose, Zulfikar 1935-............. CLC 42
See also CA 65-68

Ghosh, Amitav 1956- .... CLC 44

Giacosa, Giuseppe 1847-1906 ...... TCLC 7
See also CA 104

Gibb, Lee
See Waterhouse, Keith (Spencer)

Gibbon, Lewis Grassic .... TCLC 4
See also Mitchell, James Leslie

Gibbons, Kaye 1960- .... CLC 50

Gibran, Kahlil 1883-1931....... TCLC 1, 9
See also CA 104

Gibson, William 1914-............ CLC 23
See also CA 9-12R; CANR 9; DA; DLB 7;
SATA 66

Gibson, William (Ford) 1948- ... CLC 39, 63
See also CA 126; 133

Gide, Andre (Paul Guillaume)
1869-1951 .... TCLC 5, 12, 36
See also CA 104; 124; DA; DLB 65;
MTCW; WLC

Gifford, Barry (Colby) 1946-....... CLC 34
See also CA 65-68; CANR 9, 30, 40

Gilbert, W(illiam) S(chwenck)
1836-1911 .... TCLC 3
See also CA 104; SATA 36

Gilbreth, Frank B., Jr. 1911-....... CLC 17
See also CA 9-12R; SATA 2

Gilchrist, Ellen 1935-......... CLC 34, 48
See also CA 113; 116; CANR 41; DLB 130;
MTCW

Giles, Molly 1942- .... CLC 39
See also CA 126

Gill, Patrick
See Creasey, John

Gilliam, Terry (Vance) 1940-....... CLC 21
See also Monty Python
See also CA 108; 113; CANR 35

Gillian, Jerry
See Gilliam, Terry (Vance)

Gilliatt, Penelope (Ann Douglass)
1932- .... CLC 2, 10, 13, 53
See also AITN 2; CA 13-16R; DLB 14

Gilman, Charlotte (Anna) Perkins (Stetson)
1860-1935 .... TCLC 9, 37
See also CA 106

Gilmour, David 1949-............. CLC 35
See also Pink Floyd
See also CA 138

Gilpin, William 1724-1804....... NCLC 30

Gilray, J. D.
See Mencken, H(enry) L(ouis)

Gilroy, Frank D(aniel) 1925-........ CLC 2
See also CA 81-84; CANR 32; DLB 7

Ginsberg, Allen
1926- ...... CLC 1, 2, 3, 4, 6, 13, 36, 69;
PC 4
See also AITN 1; CA 1-4R; CANR 2, 41;
CDALB 1941-1968; DA; DLB 5, 16;
MTCW; WLC 3

Ginzburg, Natalia
1916-1991 .... CLC 5, 11, 54, 70
See also CA 85-88; 135; CANR 33; MTCW

Giono, Jean 1895-1970......... CLC 4, 11
See also CA 45-48; 29-32R; CANR 2, 35;
DLB 72; MTCW

Giovanni, Nikki 1943- ..... CLC 2, 4, 19, 64
See also AITN 1; BLC 2; BW; CA 29-32R;
CAAS 6; CANR 18, 41; CLR 6; DA;
DLB 5, 41; MAICYA; MTCW; SATA 24

Giovene, Andrea 1904-............ CLC 7
See also CA 85-88

Gippius, Zinaida (Nikolayevna) 1869-1945
See Hippius, Zinaida
See also CA 106

Giraudoux, (Hippolyte) Jean
1882-1944 .... TCLC 2, 7
See also CA 104; DLB 65

Gironella, Jose Maria 1917- .... CLC 11
See also CA 101

Gissing, George (Robert)
1857-1903 .... TCLC 3, 24, 47
See also CA 105; DLB 18

Giurlani, Aldo
See Palazzeschi, Aldo

Gladkov, Fyodor (Vasilyevich)
1883-1958 ....TCLC 27

Glanville, Brian (Lester) 1931- ...... CLC 6
See also CA 5-8R; CAAS 9; CANR 3;
DLB 15; SATA 42

Glasgow, Ellen (Anderson Gholson)
1873(?)-1945 ....TCLC 2, 7
See also CA 104; DLB 9, 12

Glassco, John 1909-1981 .... CLC 9
See also CA 13-16R; 102; CANR 15;
DLB 68

Glasscock, Amnesia
See Steinbeck, John (Ernst)

Glasser, Ronald J. 1940(?)-........ CLC 37

Glassman, Joyce
See Johnson, Joyce

Glendinning, Victoria 1937-........ CLC 50
See also CA 120; 127

Glissant, Edouard 1928-........ CLC 10, 68

Gloag, Julian 1930- .... CLC 40
See also AITN 1; CA 65-68; CANR 10

Gluck, Louise (Elisabeth)
1943- .... CLC 7, 22, 44
See also Glueck, Louise
See also CA 33-36R; CANR 40; DLB 5

Glueck, Louise................... CLC 7, 22
See also Gluck, Louise (Elisabeth)
See also DLB 5

Gobineau, Joseph Arthur (Comte) de
1816-1882 .... NCLC 17
See also DLB 123

Godard, Jean-Luc 1930-........... CLC 20
See also CA 93-96

Godden, (Margaret) Rumer 1907-... CLC 53
See also AAYA 6; CA 5-8R; CANR 4, 27,
36; CLR 20; MAICYA; SAAS 12;
SATA 3, 36

Godoy Alcayaga, Lucila 1889-1957
See Mistral, Gabriela
See also CA 104; 131; HW; MTCW

Godwin, Gail (Kathleen)
1937- .... CLC 5, 8, 22, 31, 69
See also CA 29-32R; CANR 15; DLB 6;
MTCW

Godwin, William 1756-1836...... **NCLC 14**
See also CDBLB 1789-1832; DLB 39, 104

Goethe, Johann Wolfgang von
1749-1832 .... **NCLC 4, 22, 34; PC 5**
See also DA; DLB 94; WLC 3

Gogarty, Oliver St. John
1878-1957 .... **TCLC 15**
See also CA 109; DLB 15, 19

Gogol, Nikolai (Vasilyevich)
1809-1852 ...... **NCLC 5, 15, 31; DC 1;
SSC 4**
See also DA; WLC

Gold, Herbert 1924-....... **CLC 4, 7, 14, 42**
See also CA 9-12R; CANR 17; DLB 2;
DLBY 81

Goldbarth, Albert 1948-........ **CLC 5, 38**
See also CA 53-56; CANR 6, 40; DLB 120

Goldberg, Anatol 1910-1982 .... **CLC 34**
See also CA 131; 117

Goldemberg, Isaac 1945- .... **CLC 52**
See also CA 69-72; CAAS 12; CANR 11,
32; HW

Golden Silver
See Storm, Hyemeyohsts

Golding, William (Gerald)
1911- ..... **CLC 1, 2, 3, 8, 10, 17, 27, 58**
See also AAYA 5; CA 5-8R; CANR 13, 33;
CDBLB 1945-1960; DA; DLB 15, 100;
MTCW; WLC

Goldman, Emma 1869-1940....... **TCLC 13**
See also CA 110

Goldman, Francisco 1955-........ **CLC 76**

Goldman, William (W.) 1931-.... **CLC 1, 48**
See also CA 9-12R; CANR 29; DLB 44

Goldmann, Lucien 1913-1970 ...... **CLC 24**
See also CA 25-28; CAP 2

Goldoni, Carlo 1707-1793 .... **LC 4**

Goldsberry, Steven 1949-.......... **CLC 34**
See also CA 131

Goldsmith, Oliver 1728-1774......... **LC 2**
See also CDBLB 1660-1789; DA; DLB 39,
89, 104, 109; SATA 26; WLC

Goldsmith, Peter
See Priestley, J(ohn) B(oynton)

Gombrowicz, Witold
1904-1969 .... **CLC 4, 7, 11, 49**
See also CA 19-20; 25-28R; CAP 2

Gomez de la Serna, Ramon
1888-1963 .... **CLC 9**
See also CA 116; HW

Goncharov, Ivan Alexandrovich
1812-1891 .... **NCLC 1**

Goncourt, Edmond (Louis Antoine Huot) de
1822-1896 .... **NCLC 7**
See also DLB 123

Goncourt, Jules (Alfred Huot) de
1830-1870 .... **NCLC 7**
See also DLB 123

Gontier, Fernande 19(?)- .... **CLC 50**

Goodman, Paul 1911-1972.... **CLC 1, 2, 4, 7**
See also CA 19-20; 37-40R; CANR 34;
CAP 2; DLB 130; MTCW

Gordimer, Nadine
1923- .... **CLC 3, 5, 7, 10, 18, 33, 51, 70**
See also CA 5-8R; CANR 3, 28; DA;
MTCW

Gordon, Adam Lindsay
1833-1870 .... **NCLC 21**

Gordon, Caroline
1895-1981 .... **CLC 6, 13, 29**
See also CA 11-12; 103; CANR 36; CAP 1;
DLB 4, 9, 102; DLBY 81; MTCW

Gordon, Charles William 1860-1937
See Connor, Ralph
See also CA 109

Gordon, Mary (Catherine)
1949- .... **CLC 13, 22**
See also CA 102; DLB 6; DLBY 81;
MTCW

Gordon, Sol 1923-................. **CLC 26**
See also CA 53-56; CANR 4; SATA 11

Gordone, Charles 1925-.......... **CLC 1, 4**
See also BW; CA 93-96; DLB 7; MTCW

Gorenko, Anna Andreevna
See Akhmatova, Anna

Gorky, Maxim.................... TCLC 8
See also Peshkov, Alexei Maximovich
See also WLC

Goryan, Sirak
See Saroyan, William

Gosse, Edmund (William)
1849-1928 .... **TCLC 28**
See also CA 117; DLB 57

Gotlieb, Phyllis Fay (Bloom)
1926- .... **CLC 18**
See also CA 13-16R; CANR 7; DLB 88

Gottesman, S. D.
See Kornbluth, C(yril) M.; Pohl, Frederik

Gottfried von Strassburg
fl. c. 1210-................. **CMLC 10**

Gottschalk, Laura Riding
See Jackson, Laura (Riding)

Gould, Lois .... CLC 4, 10
See also CA 77-80; CANR 29; MTCW

Gourmont, Remy de 1858-1915.... **TCLC 17**
See also CA 109

Govier, Katherine 1948-.......... **CLC 51**
See also CA 101; CANR 18, 40

Goyen, (Charles) William
1915-1983 .... **CLC 5, 8, 14, 40**
See also AITN 2; CA 5-8R; 110; CANR 6;
DLB 2; DLBY 83

Goytisolo, Juan 1931- .... **CLC 5, 10, 23**
See also CA 85-88; CANR 32; HW; MTCW

Gozzi, (Conte) Carlo 1720-1806 .. **NCLC 23**

Grabbe, Christian Dietrich
1801-1836 .... **NCLC 2**

Grace, Patricia 1937-............. **CLC 56**

Gracian y Morales, Baltasar
1601-1658 .... **LC 15**

Gracq, Julien.................. CLC 11, 48
See also Poirier, Louis
See also DLB 83

Grade, Chaim 1910-1982 .... **CLC 10**
See also CA 93-96; 107

Graduate of Oxford, A
See Ruskin, John

Graham, John
See Phillips, David Graham

Graham, Jorie 1951-............. **CLC 48**
See also CA 111; DLB 120

Graham, R(obert) B(ontine) Cunninghame
See Cunninghame Graham, R(obert)
B(ontine)
See also DLB 98

Graham, Robert
See Haldeman, Joe (William)

Graham, Tom
See Lewis, (Harry) Sinclair

Graham, W(illiam) S(ydney)
1918-1986 .... **CLC 29**
See also CA 73-76; 118; DLB 20

Graham, Winston (Mawdsley)
1910- .... **CLC 23**
See also CA 49-52; CANR 2, 22; DLB 77

Grant, Skeeter
See Spiegelman, Art

Granville-Barker, Harley
1877-1946 .... **TCLC 2**
See also Barker, Harley Granville
See also CA 104

Grass, Guenter (Wilhelm)
1927-.. **CLC 1, 2, 4, 6, 11, 15, 22, 32, 49**
See also CA 13-16R; CANR 20; DA;
DLB 75, 124; MTCW; WLC

Gratton, Thomas
See Hulme, T(homas) E(rnest)

Grau, Shirley Ann 1929-......... **CLC 4, 9**
See also CA 89-92; CANR 22; DLB 2;
MTCW

Gravel, Fern
See Hall, James Norman

Graver, Elizabeth 1964-.......... **CLC 70**
See also CA 135

Graves, Richard Perceval 1945- .... **CLC 44**
See also CA 65-68; CANR 9, 26

Graves, Robert (von Ranke)
1895-1985 ...... **CLC 1, 2, 6, 11, 39, 44,
45; PC 6**
See also CA 5-8R; 117; CANR 5, 36;
CDBLB 1914-1945; DLB 20, 100;
DLBY 85; MTCW; SATA 45

Gray, Alasdair 1934- .... **CLC 41**
See also CA 126; MTCW

Gray, Amlin 1946- .... **CLC 29**
See also CA 138

Gray, Francine du Plessix 1930-.... **CLC 22**
See also BEST 90:3; CA 61-64; CAAS 2;
CANR 11, 33; MTCW

Gray, John (Henry) 1866-1934 .... **TCLC 19**
See also CA 119

Gray, Simon (James Holliday)
1936-................... **CLC 9, 14, 36**
See also AITN 1; CA 21-24R; CAAS 3;
CANR 32; DLB 13; MTCW

Gray, Spalding 1941-............. **CLC 49**
See also CA 128

Gray, Thomas 1716-1771....... **LC 4; PC 2**
See also CDBLB 1660-1789; DA; DLB 109;
WLC

Grayson, David
See Baker, Ray Stannard

Grayson, Richard (A.) 1951- .... CLC 38
See also CA 85-88; CANR 14, 31

Greeley, Andrew M(oran) 1928- .... CLC 28
See also CA 5-8R; CAAS 7; CANR 7;
MTCW

Green, Brian
See Card, Orson Scott

Green, Hannah .... CLC 3
See also CA 73-76

Green, Hannah
See Greenberg, Joanne (Goldenberg)

Green, Henry .... CLC 2, 13
See also Yorke, Henry Vincent
See also DLB 15

Green, Julian (Hartridge)
1900- .... CLC 3, 11, 77
See also CA 21-24R; CANR 33; DLB 4, 72;
MTCW

Green, Julien 1900-
See Green, Julian (Hartridge)

Green, Paul (Eliot) 1894-1981...... CLC 25
See also AITN 1; CA 5-8R; 103; CANR 3;
DLB 7, 9; DLBY 81

Greenberg, Ivan 1908-1973
See Rahv, Philip
See also CA 85-88

Greenberg, Joanne (Goldenberg)
1932- .... CLC 7, 30
See also CA 5-8R; CANR 14, 32; SATA 25

Greenberg, Richard 1959(?)- .... CLC 57
See also CA 138

Greene, Bette 1934- .... CLC 30
See also AAYA 7; CA 53-56; CANR 4;
CLR 2; MAICYA; SAAS 16; SATA 8

Greene, Gael .... CLC 8
See also CA 13-16R; CANR 10

Greene, Graham
1904-1991 .... CLC 1, 3, 6, 9, 14, 18, 27,
37, 70, 72
See also AITN 2; CA 13-16R; 133;
CANR 35; CDBLB 1945-1960; DA;
DLB 13, 15, 77, 100; DLBY 91; MTCW;
SATA 20; WLC

Greer, Richard
See Silverberg, Robert

Greer, Richard
See Silverberg, Robert

Gregor, Arthur 1923- .... CLC 9
See also CA 25-28R; CAAS 10; CANR 11;
SATA 36

Gregor, Lee
See Pohl, Frederik

Gregory, Isabella Augusta (Persse)
1852-1932 .... TCLC 1
See also CA 104; DLB 10

Gregory, J. Dennis
See Williams, John A(lfred)

Grendon, Stephen
See Derleth, August (William)

Grenville, Kate 1950- .... CLC 61
See also CA 118

Grenville, Pelham
See Wodehouse, P(elham) G(renville)

Greve, Felix Paul (Berthold Friedrich)
1879-1948
See Grove, Frederick Philip
See also CA 104

Grey, Zane 1872-1939 .... TCLC 6
See also CA 104; 132; DLB 9; MTCW

Grieg, (Johan) Nordahl (Brun)
1902-1943 .... TCLC 10
See also CA 107

Grieve, C(hristopher) M(urray)
1892-1978 .... CLC 11, 19
See also MacDiarmid, Hugh
See also CA 5-8R; 85-88; CANR 33;
MTCW

Griffin, Gerald 1803-1840 .... NCLC 7

Griffin, John Howard 1920-1980.... CLC 68
See also AITN 1; CA 1-4R; 101; CANR 2

Griffin, Peter .... CLC 39

Griffiths, Trevor 1935- .... CLC 13, 52
See also CA 97-100; DLB 13

Grigson, Geoffrey (Edward Harvey)
1905-1985 .... CLC 7, 39
See also CA 25-28R; 118; CANR 20, 33;
DLB 27; MTCW

Grillparzer, Franz 1791-1872...... NCLC 1

Grimble, Reverend Charles James
See Eliot, T(homas) S(tearns)

Grimke, Charlotte L(ottie) Forten
1837(?)-1914
See Forten, Charlotte L.
See also BW; CA 117; 124

Grimm, Jacob Ludwig Karl
1785-1863 .... NCLC 3
See also DLB 90; MAICYA; SATA 22

Grimm, Wilhelm Karl 1786-1859 .. NCLC 3
See also DLB 90; MAICYA; SATA 22

**Grimmelshausen, Johann Jakob Christoffel
von** 1621-1676 .... LC 6

Grindel, Eugene 1895-1952
See Eluard, Paul
See also CA 104

Grossman, David 1954- .... CLC 67
See also CA 138

Grossman, Vasily (Semenovich)
1905-1964 .... CLC 41
See also CA 124; 130; MTCW

Grove, Frederick Philip .... TCLC 4
See also Greve, Felix Paul (Berthold
Friedrich)
See also DLB 92

Grubb
See Crumb, R(obert)

Grumbach, Doris (Isaac)
1918- .... CLC 13, 22, 64
See also CA 5-8R; CAAS 2; CANR 9

Grundtvig, Nicolai Frederik Severin
1783-1872 .... NCLC 1

Grunge
See Crumb, R(obert)

Grunwald, Lisa 1959- .... CLC 44
See also CA 120

Guare, John 1938- .... CLC 8, 14, 29, 67
See also CA 73-76; CANR 21; DLB 7;
MTCW

Gudjonsson, Halldor Kiljan 1902-
See Laxness, Halldor
See also CA 103

Guenter, Erich
See Eich, Guenter

Guest, Barbara 1920- .... CLC 34
See also CA 25-28R; CANR 11; DLB 5

Guest, Judith (Ann) 1936- .... CLC 8, 30
See also AAYA 7; CA 77-80; CANR 15;
MTCW

Guild, Nicholas M. 1944- .... CLC 33
See also CA 93-96

Guillemin, Jacques
See Sartre, Jean-Paul

Guillen, Jorge 1893-1984 .... CLC 11
See also CA 89-92; 112; DLB 108; HW

Guillen (y Batista), Nicolas (Cristobal)
1902-1989 .... CLC 48
See also BLC 2; BW; CA 116; 125; 129;
HW

Guillevic, (Eugene) 1907- .... CLC 33
See also CA 93-96

Guillois
See Desnos, Robert

Guiney, Louise Imogen
1861-1920 .... TCLC 41
See also DLB 54

Guiraldes, Ricardo (Guillermo)
1886-1927 .... TCLC 39
See also CA 131; HW; MTCW

Gunn, Bill .... CLC 5
See also Gunn, William Harrison
See also DLB 38

Gunn, Thom(son William)
1929- .... CLC 3, 6, 18, 32
See also CA 17-20R; CANR 9, 33;
CDBLB 1960 to Present; DLB 27;
MTCW

Gunn, William Harrison 1934(?)-1989
See Gunn, Bill
See also AITN 1; BW; CA 13-16R; 128;
CANR 12, 25

Gunnars, Kristjana 1948- .... CLC 69
See also CA 113; DLB 60

Gurganus, Allan 1947- .... CLC 70
See also BEST 90:1; CA 135

Gurney, A(lbert) R(amsdell), Jr.
1930- .... CLC 32, 50, 54
See also CA 77-80; CANR 32

Gurney, Ivor (Bertie) 1890-1937... TCLC 33

Gurney, Peter
See Gurney, A(lbert) R(amsdell), Jr.

Gustafson, Ralph (Barker) 1909- .... CLC 36
See also CA 21-24R; CANR 8; DLB 88

Gut, Gom
See Simenon, Georges (Jacques Christian)

Guthrie, A(lfred) B(ertram), Jr.
1901-1991 .... CLC 23
See also CA 57-60; 134; CANR 24; DLB 6;
SATA 62; SATA-Obit 67

Guthrie, Isobel
See Grieve, C(hristopher) M(urray)

Guthrie, Woodrow Wilson 1912-1967
See Guthrie, Woody
See also CA 113; 93-96

Guthrie, Woody . . . . **CLC 35**
See also Guthrie, Woodrow Wilson

Guy, Rosa (Cuthbert) 1928- . . . . **CLC 26**
See also AAYA 4; BW; CA 17-20R;
CANR 14, 34; CLR 13; DLB 33;
MAICYA; SATA 14, 62

Gwendolyn
See Bennett, (Enoch) Arnold

H. D. . . . . **CLC 3, 8, 14, 31, 34, 73; PC 5**
See also Doolittle, Hilda

Haavikko, Paavo Juhani
1931- . . . . **CLC 18, 34**
See also CA 106

Habbema, Koos
See Heijermans, Herman

Hacker, Marilyn 1942- . . . . **CLC 5, 9, 23, 72**
See also CA 77-80; DLB 120

Haggard, H(enry) Rider
1856-1925 . . . . **TCLC 11**
See also CA 108; DLB 70; SATA 16

Haig, Fenil
See Ford, Ford Madox

Haig-Brown, Roderick (Langmere)
1908-1976 . . . . **CLC 21**
See also CA 5-8R; 69-72; CANR 4, 38;
CLR 31; DLB 88; MAICYA; SATA 12

Hailey, Arthur 1920- . . . . **CLC 5**
See also AITN 2; BEST 90:3; CA 1-4R;
CANR 2, 36; DLB 88; DLBY 82; MTCW

Hailey, Elizabeth Forsythe 1938- . . . **CLC 40**
See also CA 93-96; CAAS 1; CANR 15

Haines, John (Meade) 1924- . . . . **CLC 58**
See also CA 17-20R; CANR 13, 34; DLB 5

Haldeman, Joe (William) 1943- . . . . . **CLC 61**
See also CA 53-56; CANR 6; DLB 8

Haley, Alex(ander Murray Palmer)
1921-1992 . . . . **CLC 8, 12, 76**
See also BLC 2; BW; CA 77-80; 136; DA;
DLB 38; MTCW

Haliburton, Thomas Chandler
1796-1865 . . . . **NCLC 15**
See also DLB 11, 99

Hall, Donald (Andrew, Jr.)
1928- . . . . **CLC 1, 13, 37, 59**
See also CA 5-8R; CAAS 7; CANR 2;
DLB 5; SATA 23

Hall, Frederic Sauser
See Sauser-Hall, Frederic

Hall, James
See Kuttner, Henry

Hall, James Norman 1887-1951 . . . **TCLC 23**
See also CA 123; SATA 21

Hall, (Marguerite) Radclyffe
1886(?)-1943 . . . . **TCLC 12**
See also CA 110

Hall, Rodney 1935- . . . . **CLC 51**
See also CA 109

Halliday, Michael
See Creasey, John

Halpern, Daniel 1945- . . . . **CLC 14**
See also CA 33-36R

Hamburger, Michael (Peter Leopold)
1924- . . . . **CLC 5, 14**
See also CA 5-8R; CAAS 4; CANR 2;
DLB 27

Hamill, Pete 1935- . . . . **CLC 10**
See also CA 25-28R; CANR 18

Hamilton, Clive
See Lewis, C(live) S(taples)

Hamilton, Edmond 1904-1977 . . . . **CLC 1**
See also CA 1-4R; CANR 3; DLB 8

Hamilton, Eugene (Jacob) Lee
See Lee-Hamilton, Eugene (Jacob)

Hamilton, Franklin
See Silverberg, Robert

Hamilton, Gail
See Corcoran, Barbara

Hamilton, Mollie
See Kaye, M(ary) M(argaret)

Hamilton, (Anthony Walter) Patrick
1904-1962 . . . . **CLC 51**
See also CA 113; DLB 10

Hamilton, Virginia 1936- . . . . **CLC 26**
See also AAYA 2; BW; CA 25-28R;
CANR 20, 37; CLR 1, 11; DLB 33, 52;
MAICYA; MTCW; SATA 4, 56

Hammett, (Samuel) Dashiell
1894-1961 . . . . **CLC 3, 5, 10, 19, 47**
See also AITN 1; CA 81-84;
CDALB 1929-1941; DLBD 6; MTCW

Hammon, Jupiter 1711(?)-1800(?) . . **NCLC 5**
See also BLC 2; DLB 31, 50

Hammond, Keith
See Kuttner, Henry

Hamner, Earl (Henry), Jr. 1923- . . . **CLC 12**
See also AITN 2; CA 73-76; DLB 6

Hampton, Christopher (James)
1946- . . . . **CLC 4**
See also CA 25-28R; DLB 13; MTCW

Hamsun, Knut . . . . **TCLC 2, 14, 49**
See also Pedersen, Knut

Handke, Peter 1942- . . **CLC 5, 8, 10, 15, 38**
See also CA 77-80; CANR 33; DLB 85,
124; MTCW

Hanley, James 1901-1985 . . . **CLC 3, 5, 8, 13**
See also CA 73-76; 117; CANR 36; MTCW

Hannah, Barry 1942- . . . . **CLC 23, 38**
See also CA 108; 110; DLB 6; MTCW

Hannon, Ezra
See Hunter, Evan

Hansberry, Lorraine (Vivian)
1930-1965 . . . . **CLC 17, 62; DC 2**
See also BLC 2; BW; CA 109; 25-28R;
CABS 3; CDALB 1941-1968; DA;
DLB 7, 38; MTCW

Hansen, Joseph 1923- . . . . **CLC 38**
See also CA 29-32R; CAAS 17; CANR 16

Hansen, Martin A. 1909-1955 . . . . . **TCLC 32**

Hanson, Kenneth O(stlin) 1922- . . . . **CLC 13**
See also CA 53-56; CANR 7

Hardwick, Elizabeth 1916- . . . . **CLC 13**
See also CA 5-8R; CANR 3, 32; DLB 6;
MTCW

Hardy, Thomas
1840-1928 . . . . . . **TCLC 4, 10, 18, 32, 48;
SSC 2**
See also CA 104; 123; CDBLB 1890-1914;
DA; DLB 18, 19; MTCW; WLC

Hare, David 1947- . . . . **CLC 29, 58**
See also CA 97-100; CANR 39; DLB 13;
MTCW

Harford, Henry
See Hudson, W(illiam) H(enry)

Hargrave, Leonie
See Disch, Thomas M(ichael)

Harlan, Louis R(udolph) 1922- . . . . . **CLC 34**
See also CA 21-24R; CANR 25

Harling, Robert 1951(?)- . . . . **CLC 53**

Harmon, William (Ruth) 1938- . . . . . **CLC 38**
See also CA 33-36R; CANR 14, 32, 35;
SATA 65

Harper, F. E. W.
See Harper, Frances Ellen Watkins

Harper, Frances E. W.
See Harper, Frances Ellen Watkins

Harper, Frances E. Watkins
See Harper, Frances Ellen Watkins

Harper, Frances Ellen
See Harper, Frances Ellen Watkins

Harper, Frances Ellen Watkins
1825-1911 . . . . **TCLC 14**
See also BLC 2; BW; CA 111; 125; DLB 50

Harper, Michael S(teven) 1938- . . **CLC 7, 22**
See also BW; CA 33-36R; CANR 24;
DLB 41

Harper, Mrs. F. E. W.
See Harper, Frances Ellen Watkins

Harris, Christie (Lucy) Irwin
1907- . . . . **CLC 12**
See also CA 5-8R; CANR 6; DLB 88;
MAICYA; SAAS 10; SATA 6, 74

Harris, Frank 1856(?)-1931 . . . . **TCLC 24**
See also CA 109

Harris, George Washington
1814-1869 . . . . **NCLC 23**
See also DLB 3, 11

Harris, Joel Chandler 1848-1908 . . . **TCLC 2**
See also CA 104; 137; DLB 11, 23, 42, 78,
91; MAICYA; YABC 1

Harris, John (Wyndham Parkes Lucas)
Beynon 1903-1969 . . . . **CLC 19**
See also CA 102; 89-92

Harris, MacDonald
See Heiney, Donald (William)

Harris, Mark 1922- . . . . **CLC 19**
See also CA 5-8R; CAAS 3; CANR 2;
DLB 2; DLBY 80

Harris, (Theodore) Wilson 1921- . . . . **CLC 25**
See also BW; CA 65-68; CAAS 16;
CANR 11, 27; DLB 117; MTCW

Harrison, Elizabeth Cavanna 1909-
See Cavanna, Betty
See also CA 9-12R; CANR 6, 27

Harrison, Harry (Max) 1925- . . . . **CLC 42**
See also CA 1-4R; CANR 5, 21; DLB 8;
SATA 4

Harrison, James (Thomas) 1937-
See Harrison, Jim
See also CA 13-16R; CANR 8

Harrison, Jim .... CLC 6, 14, 33, 66
See also Harrison, James (Thomas)
See also DLBY 82

Harrison, Kathryn 1961- .... CLC 70

Harrison, Tony 1937-............. CLC 43
See also CA 65-68; DLB 40; MTCW

Harriss, Will(ard Irvin) 1922-...... CLC 34
See also CA 111

Harson, Sley
See Ellison, Harlan

Hart, Ellis
See Ellison, Harlan

Hart, Josephine 1942(?)- .... CLC 70
See also CA 138

Hart, Moss 1904-1961 .... CLC 66
See also CA 109; 89-92; DLB 7

Harte, (Francis) Bret(t)
1836(?)-1902 ...... TCLC 1, 25; SSC 8
See also CA 104; 140; CDALB 1865-1917;
DA; DLB 12, 64, 74, 79; SATA 26; WLC

Hartley, L(eslie) P(oles)
1895-1972 .... CLC 2, 22
See also CA 45-48; 37-40R; CANR 33;
DLB 15; MTCW

Hartman, Geoffrey H. 1929-....... CLC 27
See also CA 117; 125; DLB 67

Haruf, Kent 19(?)- .... CLC 34

Harwood, Ronald 1934-........... CLC 32
See also CA 1-4R; CANR 4; DLB 13

Hasek, Jaroslav (Matej Frantisek)
1883-1923 .... TCLC 4
See also CA 104; 129; MTCW

Hass, Robert 1941-............ CLC 18, 39
See also CA 111; CANR 30; DLB 105

Hastings, Hudson
See Kuttner, Henry

Hastings, Selina................... CLC 44

Hatteras, Amelia
See Mencken, H(enry) L(ouis)

Hatteras, Owen................. TCLC 18
See also Mencken, H(enry) L(ouis); Nathan,
George Jean

Hauptmann, Gerhart (Johann Robert)
1862-1946 .... TCLC 4
See also CA 104; DLB 66, 118

Havel, Vaclav 1936-........ CLC 25, 58, 65
See also CA 104; CANR 36; MTCW

Haviaras, Stratis................. CLC 33
See also Chaviaras, Strates

Hawes, Stephen 1475(?)-1523(?) ..... LC 17

Hawkes, John (Clendennin Burne, Jr.)
1925- ...... CLC 1, 2, 3, 4, 7, 9, 14, 15,
27, 49
See also CA 1-4R; CANR 2; DLB 2, 7;
DLBY 80; MTCW

Hawking, S. W.
See Hawking, Stephen W(illiam)

Hawking, Stephen W(illiam)
1942- .... CLC 63
See also BEST 89:1; CA 126; 129

Hawthorne, Julian 1846-1934 ..... TCLC 25

Hawthorne, Nathaniel
1804-1864 .... NCLC 39; SSC 3
See also CDALB 1640-1865; DA; DLB 1,
74; WLC; YABC 2

Haxton, Josephine Ayres 1921- .... CLC 73
See also CA 115; CANR 41

Hayaseca y Eizaguirre, Jorge
See Echegaray (y Eizaguirre), Jose (Maria
Waldo)

Hayashi Fumiko 1904-1951...... TCLC 27

Haycraft, Anna
See Ellis, Alice Thomas
See also CA 122

Hayden, Robert E(arl)
1913-1980 ...... CLC 5, 9, 14, 37; PC 6
See also BLC 2; BW; CA 69-72; 97-100;
CABS 2; CANR 24; CDALB 1941-1968;
DA; DLB 5, 76; MTCW; SATA 19, 26

Hayford, J(oseph) E(phraim) Casely
See Casely-Hayford, J(oseph) E(phraim)

Hayman, Ronald 1932-............ CLC 44
See also CA 25-28R; CANR 18

Haywood, Eliza (Fowler)
1693(?)-1756 .... LC 1

Hazlitt, William 1778-1830...... NCLC 29
See also DLB 110

Hazzard, Shirley 1931- .... CLC 18
See also CA 9-12R; CANR 4; DLBY 82;
MTCW

Head, Bessie 1937-1986........ CLC 25, 67
See also BLC 2; BW; CA 29-32R; 119;
CANR 25; DLB 117; MTCW

Headon, (Nicky) Topper 1956(?)- ... CLC 30
See also Clash, The

Heaney, Seamus (Justin)
1939- .... CLC 5, 7, 14, 25, 37, 74
See also CA 85-88; CANR 25;
CDBLB 1960 to Present; DLB 40;
MTCW

Hearn, (Patricio) Lafcadio (Tessima Carlos)
1850-1904 .... TCLC 9
See also CA 105; DLB 12, 78

Hearne, Vicki 1946-............. CLC 56
See also CA 139

Hearon, Shelby 1931-............. CLC 63
See also AITN 2; CA 25-28R; CANR 18

Heat-Moon, William Least.......... CLC 29
See also Trogdon, William (Lewis)
See also AAYA 9

Hebert, Anne 1916- .... CLC 4, 13, 29
See also CA 85-88; DLB 68; MTCW

Hecht, Anthony (Evan)
1923- .... CLC 8, 13, 19
See also CA 9-12R; CANR 6; DLB 5

Hecht, Ben 1894-1964 .... CLC 8
See also CA 85-88; DLB 7, 9, 25, 26, 28, 86

Hedayat, Sadeq 1903-1951....... TCLC 21
See also CA 120

Heidegger, Martin 1889-1976 ...... CLC 24
See also CA 81-84; 65-68; CANR 34;
MTCW

Heidenstam, (Carl Gustaf) Verner von
1859-1940 .... TCLC 5
See also CA 104

Heifner, Jack 1946-.............. CLC 11
See also CA 105

Heijermans, Herman 1864-1924 ... TCLC 24
See also CA 123

Heilbrun, Carolyn G(old) 1926-..... CLC 25
See also CA 45-48; CANR 1, 28

Heine, Heinrich 1797-1856 .... NCLC 4
See also DLB 90

Heinemann, Larry (Curtiss) 1944- .. CLC 50
See also CA 110; CANR 31; DLBD 9

Heiney, Donald (William) 1921-..... CLC 9
See also CA 1-4R; CANR 3

Heinlein, Robert A(nson)
1907-1988 ...... CLC 1, 3, 8, 14, 26, 55
See also CA 1-4R; 125; CANR 1, 20;
DLB 8; MAICYA; MTCW; SATA 9, 56,
69

Helforth, John
See Doolittle, Hilda

Hellenhofferu, Vojtech Kapristian z
See Hasek, Jaroslav (Matej Frantisek)

Heller, Joseph
1923- .... CLC 1, 3, 5, 8, 11, 36, 63
See also AITN 1; CA 5-8R; CABS 1;
CANR 8; DA; DLB 2, 28; DLBY 80;
MTCW; WLC

Hellman, Lillian (Florence)
1906-1984 ...... CLC 2, 4, 8, 14, 18, 34,
44, 52; DC 1
See also AITN 1, 2; CA 13-16R; 112;
CANR 33; DLB 7; DLBY 84; MTCW

Helprin, Mark 1947- ..... CLC 7, 10, 22, 32
See also CA 81-84; DLBY 85; MTCW

Helyar, Jane Penelope Josephine 1933-
See Poole, Josephine
See also CA 21-24R; CANR 10, 26

Hemans, Felicia 1793-1835 ...... NCLC 29
See also DLB 96

Hemingway, Ernest (Miller)
1899-1961 .... CLC 1, 3, 6, 8, 10, 13, 19,
30, 34, 39, 41, 44, 50, 61; SSC 1
See also CA 77-80; CANR 34;
CDALB 1917-1929; DA; DLB 4, 9, 102;
DLBD 1; DLBY 81, 87; MTCW; WLC

Hempel, Amy 1951-.............. CLC 39
See also CA 118; 137

Henderson, F. C.
See Mencken, H(enry) L(ouis)

Henderson, Sylvia
See Ashton-Warner, Sylvia (Constance)

Henley, Beth .... CLC 23
See also Henley, Elizabeth Becker
See also CABS 3; DLBY 86

Henley, Elizabeth Becker 1952-
See Henley, Beth
See also CA 107; CANR 32; MTCW

Henley, William Ernest
1849-1903 .... TCLC 8
See also CA 105; DLB 19

Hennissart, Martha
See Lathen, Emma
See also CA 85-88

Hoffman, William M(oses) 1939- . . . **CLC 40**
See also CA 57-60; CANR 11

Hoffmann, E(rnst) T(heodor) A(madeus)
1776-1822 . . . . **NCLC 2**
See also DLB 90; SATA 27

Hofmann, Gert 1931- . . . . **CLC 54**
See also CA 128

Hofmannsthal, Hugo von
1874-1929 . . . . **TCLC 11**
See also CA 106; DLB 81, 118

Hogan, Linda 1947- . . . . **CLC 73**
See also CA 120

Hogarth, Charles
See Creasey, John

Hogg, James 1770-1835 . . . . **NCLC 4**
See also DLB 93, 116

Holbach, Paul Henri Thiry Baron
1723-1789 . . . . **LC 14**

Holberg, Ludvig 1684-1754 . . . . **LC 6**

Holden, Ursula 1921- . . . . **CLC 18**
See also CA 101; CAAS 8; CANR 22

Holderlin, (Johann Christian) Friedrich
1770-1843 . . . . **NCLC 16; PC 4**

Holdstock, Robert
See Holdstock, Robert P.

Holdstock, Robert P. 1948- . . . . **CLC 39**
See also CA 131

Holland, Isabelle 1920- . . . . **CLC 21**
See also CA 21-24R; CANR 10, 25;
MAICYA; SATA 8, 70

Holland, Marcus
See Caldwell, (Janet Miriam) Taylor
(Holland)

Hollander, John 1929- . . . . . . **CLC 2, 5, 8, 14**
See also CA 1-4R; CANR 1; DLB 5;
SATA 13

Hollander, Paul
See Silverberg, Robert

Holleran, Andrew 1943(?)- . . . . **CLC 38**

Hollinghurst, Alan 1954- . . . . **CLC 55**
See also CA 114

Hollis, Jim
See Summers, Hollis (Spurgeon, Jr.)

Holmes, John
See Souster, (Holmes) Raymond

Holmes, John Clellon 1926-1988 . . . . **CLC 56**
See also CA 9-12R; 125; CANR 4; DLB 16

Holmes, Oliver Wendell
1809-1894 . . . . **NCLC 14**
See also CDALB 1640-1865; DLB 1;
SATA 34

Holmes, Raymond
See Souster, (Holmes) Raymond

Holt, Victoria
See Hibbert, Eleanor Alice Burford

Holub, Miroslav 1923- . . . . **CLC 4**
See also CA 21-24R; CANR 10

Homer c. 8th cent. B.C.- . . . . **CMLC 1**
See also DA

Honig, Edwin 1919- . . . . **CLC 33**
See also CA 5-8R; CAAS 8; CANR 4;
DLB 5

Hood, Hugh (John Blagdon)
1928- . . . . **CLC 15, 28**
See also CA 49-52; CAAS 17; CANR 1, 33;
DLB 53

Hood, Thomas 1799-1845 . . . . **NCLC 16**
See also DLB 96

Hooker, (Peter) Jeremy 1941- . . . . . . **CLC 43**
See also CA 77-80; CANR 22; DLB 40

Hope, A(lec) D(erwent) 1907- . . . . **CLC 3, 51**
See also CA 21-24R; CANR 33; MTCW

Hope, Brian
See Creasey, John

Hope, Christopher (David Tully)
1944- . . . . **CLC 52**
See also CA 106; SATA 62

Hopkins, Gerard Manley
1844-1889 . . . . **NCLC 17**
See also CDBLB 1890-1914; DA; DLB 35,
57; WLC

Hopkins, John (Richard) 1931- . . . . . . **CLC 4**
See also CA 85-88

Hopkins, Pauline Elizabeth
1859-1930 . . . . **TCLC 28**
See also BLC 2; DLB 50

Hopley-Woolrich, Cornell George 1903-1968
See Woolrich, Cornell
See also CA 13-14; CAP 1

Horatio
See Proust, (Valentin-Louis-George-Eugene-)
Marcel

Horgan, Paul 1903- . . . . **CLC 9, 53**
See also CA 13-16R; CANR 9, 35;
DLB 102; DLBY 85; MTCW; SATA 13

Horn, Peter
See Kuttner, Henry

Hornem, Horace Esq.
See Byron, George Gordon (Noel)

Horovitz, Israel 1939- . . . . **CLC 56**
See also CA 33-36R; DLB 7

Horvath, Odon von
See Horvath, Oedoen von
See also DLB 85, 124

Horvath, Oedoen von 1901-1938 . . . **TCLC 45**
See also Horvath, Odon von
See also CA 118

Horwitz, Julius 1920-1986 . . . . **CLC 14**
See also CA 9-12R; 119; CANR 12

Hospital, Janette Turner 1942- . . . . . **CLC 42**
See also CA 108

Hostos, E. M. de
See Hostos (y Bonilla), Eugenio Maria de

Hostos, Eugenio M. de
See Hostos (y Bonilla), Eugenio Maria de

Hostos, Eugenio Maria
See Hostos (y Bonilla), Eugenio Maria de

Hostos (y Bonilla), Eugenio Maria de
1839-1903 . . . . **TCLC 24**
See also CA 123; 131; HW

Houdini
See Lovecraft, H(oward) P(hillips)

Hougan, Carolyn 1943- . . . . **CLC 34**
See also CA 139

Household, Geoffrey (Edward West)
1900-1988 . . . . **CLC 11**
See also CA 77-80; 126; DLB 87; SATA 14,
59

Housman, A(lfred) E(dward)
1859-1936 . . . . **TCLC 1, 10; PC 2**
See also CA 104; 125; DA; DLB 19;
MTCW

Housman, Laurence 1865-1959 . . . . . **TCLC 7**
See also CA 106; DLB 10; SATA 25

Howard, Elizabeth Jane 1923- . . . **CLC 7, 29**
See also CA 5-8R; CANR 8

Howard, Maureen 1930- . . . . . **CLC 5, 14, 46**
See also CA 53-56; CANR 31; DLBY 83;
MTCW

Howard, Richard 1929- . . . . . . **CLC 7, 10, 47**
See also AITN 1; CA 85-88; CANR 25;
DLB 5

Howard, Robert Ervin 1906-1936 . . . **TCLC 8**
See also CA 105

Howard, Warren F.
See Pohl, Frederik

Howe, Fanny 1940- . . . . **CLC 47**
See also CA 117; SATA 52

Howe, Julia Ward 1819-1910 . . . . . **TCLC 21**
See also CA 117; DLB 1

Howe, Susan 1937- . . . . **CLC 72**
See also DLB 120

Howe, Tina 1937- . . . . **CLC 48**
See also CA 109

Howell, James 1594(?)-1666 . . . . **LC 13**

Howells, W. D.
See Howells, William Dean

Howells, William D.
See Howells, William Dean

Howells, William Dean
1837-1920 . . . . **TCLC 41, 7, 17**
See also CA 104; 134; CDALB 1865-1917;
DLB 12, 64, 74, 79

Howes, Barbara 1914- . . . . **CLC 15**
See also CA 9-12R; CAAS 3; SATA 5

Hrabal, Bohumil 1914- . . . . **CLC 13, 67**
See also CA 106; CAAS 12

Hsun, Lu . . . . **TCLC 3**
See also Shu-Jen, Chou

Hubbard, L(afayette) Ron(ald)
1911-1986 . . . . **CLC 43**
See also CA 77-80; 118; CANR 22

Huch, Ricarda (Octavia)
1864-1947 . . . . **TCLC 13**
See also CA 111; DLB 66

Huddle, David 1942- . . . . **CLC 49**
See also CA 57-60; DLB 130

Hudson, Jeffrey
See Crichton, (John) Michael

Hudson, W(illiam) H(enry)
1841-1922 . . . . **TCLC 29**
See also CA 115; DLB 98; SATA 35

Hueffer, Ford Madox
See Ford, Ford Madox

Hughart, Barry 1934- . . . . **CLC 39**
See also CA 137

Hughes, Colin
See Creasey, John

Hughes, David (John) 1930- .... **CLC 48**
See also CA 116; 129; DLB 14

Hughes, (James) Langston
1902-1967 ..... **CLC 1, 5, 10, 15, 35, 44;
DC 3; PC 1; SSC 6**
See also BLC 2; BW; CA 1-4R; 25-28R;
CANR 1, 34; CDALB 1929-1941;
CLR 17; DA; DLB 4, 7, 48, 51, 86;
MAICYA; MTCW; SATA 4, 33; WLC

Hughes, Richard (Arthur Warren)
1900-1976 .... **CLC 1, 11**
See also CA 5-8R; 65-68; CANR 4;
DLB 15; MTCW; SATA 8, 25

Hughes, Ted
1930- .... **CLC 2, 4, 9, 14, 37; PC 7**
See also CA 1-4R; CANR 1, 33; CLR 3;
DLB 40; MAICYA; MTCW; SATA 27,
49

Hugo, Richard F(ranklin)
1923-1982 .... **CLC 6, 18, 32**
See also CA 49-52; 108; CANR 3; DLB 5

Hugo, Victor (Marie)
1802-1885 .... **NCLC 3, 10, 21**
See also DA; DLB 119; SATA 47; WLC

Huidobro, Vicente
See Huidobro Fernandez, Vicente Garcia

Huidobro Fernandez, Vicente Garcia
1893-1948 .... **TCLC 31**
See also CA 131; HW

Hulme, Keri 1947- .... **CLC 39**
See also CA 125

Hulme, T(homas) E(rnest)
1883-1917 .... **TCLC 21**
See also CA 117; DLB 19

Hume, David 1711-1776............ **LC 7**
See also DLB 104

Humphrey, William 1924- .... **CLC 45**
See also CA 77-80; DLB 6

Humphreys, Emyr Owen 1919-..... **CLC 47**
See also CA 5-8R; CANR 3, 24; DLB 15

Humphreys, Josephine 1945-.... **CLC 34, 57**
See also CA 121; 127

Hungerford, Pixie
See Brinsmead, H(esba) F(ay)

Hunt, E(verette) Howard, Jr.
1918- .... **CLC 3**
See also AITN 1; CA 45-48; CANR 2

Hunt, Kyle
See Creasey, John

Hunt, (James Henry) Leigh
1784-1859 .... **NCLC 1**

Hunt, Marsha 1946-.............. **CLC 70**

Hunter, E. Waldo
See Sturgeon, Theodore (Hamilton)

Hunter, Evan 1926- .... **CLC 11, 31**
See also CA 5-8R; CANR 5, 38; DLBY 82;
MTCW; SATA 25

Hunter, Kristin (Eggleston) 1931-... **CLC 35**
See also AITN 1; BW; CA 13-16R;
CANR 13; CLR 3; DLB 33; MAICYA;
SAAS 10; SATA 12

Hunter, Mollie 1922-.............. **CLC 21**
See also McIlwraith, Maureen Mollie
Hunter
See also CANR 37; CLR 25; MAICYA;
SAAS 7; SATA 54

Hunter, Robert (?)-1734............ **LC 7**

Hurston, Zora Neale
1903-1960 ...... **CLC 7, 30, 61; SSC 4**
See also BLC 2; BW; CA 85-88; DA;
DLB 51, 86; MTCW

Huston, John (Marcellus)
1906-1987 .... **CLC 20**
See also CA 73-76; 123; CANR 34; DLB 26

Hustvedt, Siri 1955-.............. **CLC 76**
See also CA 137

Hutten, Ulrich von 1488-1523...... **LC 16**

Huxley, Aldous (Leonard)
1894-1963 .. **CLC 1, 3, 4, 5, 8, 11, 18, 35**
See also CA 85-88; CDBLB 1914-1945; DA;
DLB 36, 100; MTCW; SATA 63; WLC

Huysmans, Charles Marie Georges
1848-1907
See Huysmans, Joris-Karl
See also CA 104

Huysmans, Joris-Karl.............. TCLC 7
See also Huysmans, Charles Marie Georges
See also DLB 123

Hwang, David Henry 1957-........ **CLC 55**
See also CA 127; 132

Hyde, Anthony 1946-............. **CLC 42**
See also CA 136

Hyde, Margaret O(ldroyd) 1917- ... **CLC 21**
See also CA 1-4R; CANR 1, 36; CLR 23;
MAICYA; SAAS 8; SATA 1, 42

Hynes, James 1956(?)-............ **CLC 65**

Ian, Janis 1951- .... **CLC 21**
See also CA 105

Ibanez, Vicente Blasco
See Blasco Ibanez, Vicente

Ibarguengoitia, Jorge 1928-1983.... **CLC 37**
See also CA 124; 113; HW

Ibsen, Henrik (Johan)
1828-1906 ..... **TCLC 2, 8, 16, 37; DC 2**
See also CA 104; DA; WLC

Ibuse Masuji 1898-............... **CLC 22**
See also CA 127

Ichikawa, Kon 1915-............. **CLC 20**
See also CA 121

Idle, Eric 1943-.................. **CLC 21**
See also Monty Python
See also CA 116; CANR 35

Ignatow, David 1914-...... **CLC 4, 7, 14, 40**
See also CA 9-12R; CAAS 3; CANR 31;
DLB 5

Ihimaera, Witi 1944- .... **CLC 46**
See also CA 77-80

Ilf, Ilya........................ TCLC 21
See also Fainzilberg, Ilya Arnoldovich

Immermann, Karl (Lebrecht)
1796-1840 .... **NCLC 4**

Inclan, Ramon (Maria) del Valle
See Valle-Inclan, Ramon (Maria) del

Infante, G(uillermo) Cabrera
See Cabrera Infante, G(uillermo)

Ingalls, Rachel (Holmes) 1940-..... **CLC 42**
See also CA 123; 127

Ingamells, Rex 1913-1955 .... **TCLC 35**

Inge, William Motter
1913-1973 .... **CLC 1, 8, 19**
See also CA 9-12R; CDALB 1941-1968;
DLB 7; MTCW

Ingelow, Jean 1820-1897 .... **NCLC 39**
See also DLB 35; SATA 33

Ingram, Willis J.
See Harris, Mark

Innaurato, Albert (F.) 1948(?)- .. **CLC 21, 60**
See also CA 115; 122

Innes, Michael
See Stewart, J(ohn) I(nnes) M(ackintosh)

Ionesco, Eugene
1912- .... **CLC 1, 4, 6, 9, 11, 15, 41**
See also CA 9-12R; DA; MTCW; SATA 7;
WLC

Iqbal, Muhammad 1873-1938 ..... **TCLC 28**

Ireland, Patrick
See O'Doherty, Brian

Irland, David
See Green, Julian (Hartridge)

Iron, Ralph
See Schreiner, Olive (Emilie Albertina)

Irving, John (Winslow)
1942- .... **CLC 13, 23, 38**
See also AAYA 8; BEST 89:3; CA 25-28R;
CANR 28; DLB 6; DLBY 82; MTCW

Irving, Washington
1783-1859 .... **NCLC 2, 19; SSC 2**
See also CDALB 1640-1865; DA; DLB 3,
11, 30, 59, 73, 74; WLC; YABC 2

Irwin, P. K.
See Page, P(atricia) K(athleen)

Isaacs, Susan 1943- .... **CLC 32**
See also BEST 89:1; CA 89-92; CANR 20,
41; MTCW

Isherwood, Christopher (William Bradshaw)
1904-1986 .... **CLC 1, 9, 11, 14, 44**
See also CA 13-16R; 117; CANR 35;
DLB 15; DLBY 86; MTCW

Ishiguro, Kazuo 1954- ...... **CLC 27, 56, 59**
See also BEST 90:2; CA 120; MTCW

Ishikawa Takuboku
1886(?)-1912 .... **TCLC 15**
See also CA 113

Iskander, Fazil 1929-............. **CLC 47**
See also CA 102

Ivan IV 1530-1584 .... **LC 17**

Ivanov, Vyacheslav Ivanovich
1866-1949 .... **TCLC 33**
See also CA 122

Ivask, Ivar Vidrik 1927-1992....... **CLC 14**
See also CA 37-40R; 139; CANR 24

Jackson, Daniel
See Wingrove, David (John)

Jackson, Jesse 1908-1983 .... **CLC 12**
See also BW; CA 25-28R; 109; CANR 27;
CLR 28; MAICYA; SATA 2, 29, 48

Jackson, Laura (Riding) 1901-1991 .. **CLC 7**
See also Riding, Laura
See also CA 65-68; 135; CANR 28; DLB 48

Jones, D(ouglas) G(ordon) 1929-.... **CLC 10**
See also CA 29-32R; CANR 13; DLB 53

Jones, David (Michael)
1895-1974 .... **CLC 2, 4, 7, 13, 42**
See also CA 9-12R; 53-56; CANR 28;
CDBLB 1945-1960; DLB 20, 100; MTCW

Jones, David Robert 1947-
See Bowie, David
See also CA 103

Jones, Diana Wynne 1934- .... **CLC 26**
See also CA 49-52; CANR 4, 26; CLR 23;
MAICYA; SAAS 7; SATA 9, 70

Jones, Edward P. 1951-........... **CLC 76**

Jones, Gayl 1949-.............. **CLC 6, 9**
See also BLC 2; BW; CA 77-80; CANR 27;
DLB 33; MTCW

Jones, James 1921-1977.... **CLC 1, 3, 10, 39**
See also AITN 1, 2; CA 1-4R; 69-72;
CANR 6; DLB 2; MTCW

Jones, John J.
See Lovecraft, H(oward) P(hillips)

Jones, LeRoi .... **CLC 1, 2, 3, 5, 10, 14**
See also Baraka, Amiri

Jones, Louis B. .... **CLC 65**

Jones, Madison (Percy, Jr.) 1925-... **CLC 4**
See also CA 13-16R; CAAS 11; CANR 7

Jones, Mervyn 1922- .... **CLC 10, 52**
See also CA 45-48; CAAS 5; CANR 1;
MTCW

Jones, Mick 1956(?)-............. **CLC 30**
See also Clash, The

Jones, Nettie (Pearl) 1941- .... **CLC 34**
See also CA 137

Jones, Preston 1936-1979 .... **CLC 10**
See also CA 73-76; 89-92; DLB 7

Jones, Robert F(rancis) 1934-....... **CLC 7**
See also CA 49-52; CANR 2

Jones, Rod 1953- .... **CLC 50**
See also CA 128

Jones, Terence Graham Parry
1942-...................... **CLC 21**
See also Jones, Terry; Monty Python
See also CA 112; 116; CANR 35; SATA 51

Jones, Terry
See Jones, Terence Graham Parry
See also SATA 67

Jong, Erica 1942-.......... **CLC 4, 6, 8, 18**
See also AITN 1; BEST 90:2; CA 73-76;
CANR 26; DLB 2, 5, 28; MTCW

Jonson, Ben(jamin) 1572(?)-1637...... **LC 6**
See also CDBLB Before 1660; DA; DLB 62,
121; WLC

Jordan, June 1936-.......... **CLC 5, 11, 23**
See also AAYA 2; BW; CA 33-36R;
CANR 25; CLR 10; DLB 38; MAICYA;
MTCW; SATA 4

Jordan, Pat(rick M.) 1941- .... **CLC 37**
See also CA 33-36R

Jorgensen, Ivar
See Ellison, Harlan

Jorgenson, Ivar
See Silverberg, Robert

Josipovici, Gabriel 1940-........ **CLC 6, 43**
See also CA 37-40R; CAAS 8; DLB 14

Joubert, Joseph 1754-1824 .... **NCLC 9**

Jouve, Pierre Jean 1887-1976...... **CLC 47**
See also CA 65-68

Joyce, James (Augustine Aloysius)
1882-1941 .... **TCLC 3, 8, 16, 35; SSC 3**
See also CA 104; 126; CDBLB 1914-1945;
DA; DLB 10, 19, 36; MTCW; WLC

Jozsef, Attila 1905-1937.......... **TCLC 22**
See also CA 116

Juana Ines de la Cruz 1651(?)-1695 ... **LC 5**

Judd, Cyril
See Kornbluth, C(yril) M.; Pohl, Frederik

Julian of Norwich 1342(?)-1416(?) .... **LC 6**

Just, Ward (Swift) 1935-........ **CLC 4, 27**
See also CA 25-28R; CANR 32

Justice, Donald (Rodney) 1925- .. **CLC 6, 19**
See also CA 5-8R; CANR 26; DLBY 83

Juvenal c. 55-c. 127 .... **CMLC 8**

Juvenis
See Bourne, Randolph S(illiman)

Kacew, Romain 1914-1980
See Gary, Romain
See also CA 108; 102

Kadare, Ismail 1936- .... **CLC 52**

Kadohata, Cynthia.................. **CLC 59**
See also CA 140

Kafka, Franz
1883-1924 .... **TCLC 2, 6, 13, 29, 47;
SSC 5**
See also CA 105; 126; DA; DLB 81;
MTCW; WLC

Kahn, Roger 1927-............... **CLC 30**
See also CA 25-28R; SATA 37

Kain, Saul
See Sassoon, Siegfried (Lorraine)

Kaiser, Georg 1878-1945 .... **TCLC 9**
See also CA 106; DLB 124

Kaletski, Alexander 1946-......... **CLC 39**
See also CA 118

Kalidasa fl. c. 400-............... **CMLC 9**

Kallman, Chester (Simon)
1921-1975 .... **CLC 2**
See also CA 45-48; 53-56; CANR 3

Kaminsky, Melvin 1926-
See Brooks, Mel
See also CA 65-68; CANR 16

Kaminsky, Stuart M(elvin) 1934- ... **CLC 59**
See also CA 73-76; CANR 29

Kane, Paul
See Simon, Paul

Kane, Wilson
See Bloch, Robert (Albert)

Kanin, Garson 1912-.............. **CLC 22**
See also AITN 1; CA 5-8R; CANR 7;
DLB 7

Kaniuk, Yoram 1930-............. **CLC 19**
See also CA 134

Kant, Immanuel 1724-1804 ...... **NCLC 27**
See also DLB 94

Kantor, MacKinlay 1904-1977 ...... **CLC 7**
See also CA 61-64; 73-76; DLB 9, 102

Kaplan, David Michael 1946- ...... **CLC 50**

Kaplan, James 1951- .... **CLC 59**
See also CA 135

Karageorge, Michael
See Anderson, Poul (William)

Karamzin, Nikolai Mikhailovich
1766-1826 .... **NCLC 3**

Karapanou, Margarita 1946-....... **CLC 13**
See also CA 101

Karinthy, Frigyes 1887-1938...... **TCLC 47**

Karl, Frederick R(obert) 1927- ..... **CLC 34**
See also CA 5-8R; CANR 3

Kastel, Warren
See Silverberg, Robert

Kataev, Evgeny Petrovich 1903-1942
See Petrov, Evgeny
See also CA 120

Kataphusin
See Ruskin, John

Katz, Steve 1935-................ **CLC 47**
See also CA 25-28R; CAAS 14; CANR 12;
DLBY 83

Kauffman, Janet 1945-............ **CLC 42**
See also CA 117; DLBY 86

Kaufman, Bob (Garnell)
1925-1986 .... **CLC 49**
See also BW; CA 41-44R; 118; CANR 22;
DLB 16, 41

Kaufman, George S. 1889-1961..... **CLC 38**
See also CA 108; 93-96; DLB 7

Kaufman, Sue .... **CLC 3, 8**
See also Barondess, Sue K(aufman)

Kavafis, Konstantinos Petrou 1863-1933
See Cavafy, C(onstantine) P(eter)
See also CA 104

Kavan, Anna 1901-1968........ **CLC 5, 13**
See also CA 5-8R; CANR 6; MTCW

Kavanagh, Dan
See Barnes, Julian

Kavanagh, Patrick (Joseph)
1904-1967 .... **CLC 22**
See also CA 123; 25-28R; DLB 15, 20;
MTCW

Kawabata, Yasunari
1899-1972 .... **CLC 2, 5, 9, 18**
See also CA 93-96; 33-36R

Kaye, M(ary) M(argaret) 1909-..... **CLC 28**
See also CA 89-92; CANR 24; MTCW;
SATA 62

Kaye, Mollie
See Kaye, M(ary) M(argaret)

Kaye-Smith, Sheila 1887-1956..... **TCLC 20**
See also CA 118; DLB 36

Kaymor, Patrice Maguilene
See Senghor, Leopold Sedar

Kazan, Elia 1909-........... **CLC 6, 16, 63**
See also CA 21-24R; CANR 32

Kazantzakis, Nikos
1883(?)-1957 .... **TCLC 2, 5, 33**
See also CA 105; 132; MTCW

Kazin, Alfred 1915-........... **CLC 34, 38**
See also CA 1-4R; CAAS 7; CANR 1;
DLB 67

Keane, Mary Nesta (Skrine) 1904-
See Keane, Molly
See also CA 108; 114

Keane, Molly.................... CLC 31
See also Keane, Mary Nesta (Skrine)

Keates, Jonathan 19(?)-.......... CLC 34

Keaton, Buster 1895-1966......... CLC 20

Keats, John 1795-1821...... NCLC 8; PC 1
See also CDBLB 1789-1832; DA; DLB 96,
110; WLC

Keene, Donald 1922-............. CLC 34
See also CA 1-4R; CANR 5

Keillor, Garrison.................. CLC 40
See also Keillor, Gary (Edward)
See also AAYA 2; BEST 89:3; DLBY 87;
SATA 58

Keillor, Gary (Edward) 1942-
See Keillor, Garrison
See also CA 111; 117; CANR 36; MTCW

Keith, Michael
See Hubbard, L(afayette) Ron(ald)

Kell, Joseph
See Wilson, John (Anthony) Burgess

Keller, Gottfried 1819-1890....... NCLC 2
See also DLB 129

Kellerman, Jonathan 1949-........ CLC 44
See also BEST 90:1; CA 106; CANR 29

Kelley, William Melvin 1937-...... CLC 22
See also BW; CA 77-80; CANR 27; DLB 33

Kellogg, Marjorie 1922-............ CLC 2
See also CA 81-84

Kellow, Kathleen
See Hibbert, Eleanor Alice Burford

Kelly, M(ilton) T(erry) 1947-....... CLC 55
See also CA 97-100; CANR 19

Kelman, James 1946-.............. CLC 58

Kemal, Yashar 1923-........... CLC 14, 29
See also CA 89-92

Kemble, Fanny 1809-1893....... NCLC 18
See also DLB 32

Kemelman, Harry 1908-........... CLC 2
See also AITN 1; CA 9-12R; CANR 6;
DLB 28

Kempe, Margery 1373(?)-1440(?) ..... LC 6

Kempis, Thomas a 1380-1471....... LC 11

Kendall, Henry 1839-1882....... NCLC 12

Keneally, Thomas (Michael)
1935-...... CLC 5, 8, 10, 14, 19, 27, 43
See also CA 85-88; CANR 10; MTCW

Kennedy, Adrienne (Lita) 1931-.... CLC 66
See also BLC 2; BW; CA 103; CABS 3;
CANR 26; DLB 38

Kennedy, John Pendleton
1795-1870 .... NCLC 2
See also DLB 3

Kennedy, Joseph Charles 1929-...... CLC 8
See also Kennedy, X. J.
See also CA 1-4R; CANR 4, 30, 40;
SATA 14

Kennedy, William 1928-... CLC 6, 28, 34, 53
See also AAYA 1; CA 85-88; CANR 14,
31; DLBY 85; MTCW; SATA 57

Kennedy, X. J..................... CLC 42
See also Kennedy, Joseph Charles
See also CAAS 9; CLR 27; DLB 5

Kent, Kelvin
See Kuttner, Henry

Kenton, Maxwell
See Southern, Terry

Kenyon, Robert O.
See Kuttner, Henry

Kerouac, Jack ..... CLC 1, 2, 3, 5, 14, 29, 61
See also Kerouac, Jean-Louis Lebris de
See also CDALB 1941-1968; DLB 2, 16;
DLBD 3

Kerouac, Jean-Louis Lebris de 1922-1969
See Kerouac, Jack
See also AITN 1; CA 5-8R; 25-28R;
CANR 26; DA; MTCW; WLC

Kerr, Jean 1923-................. CLC 22
See also CA 5-8R; CANR 7

Kerr, M. E. .... CLC 12, 35
See also Meaker, Marijane (Agnes)
See also AAYA 2; CLR 29; SAAS 1

Kerr, Robert .... CLC 55

Kerrigan, (Thomas) Anthony
1918-..................... CLC 4, 6
See also CA 49-52; CAAS 11; CANR 4

Kerry, Lois
See Duncan, Lois

Kesey, Ken (Elton)
1935-.......... CLC 1, 3, 6, 11, 46, 64
See also CA 1-4R; CANR 22, 38;
CDALB 1968-1988; DA; DLB 2, 16;
MTCW; SATA 66; WLC

Kesselring, Joseph (Otto)
1902-1967 .... CLC 45

Kessler, Jascha (Frederick) 1929-.... CLC 4
See also CA 17-20R; CANR 8

Kettelkamp, Larry (Dale) 1933- .... CLC 12
See also CA 29-32R; CANR 16; SAAS 3;
SATA 2

Keyber, Conny
See Fielding, Henry

Khayyam, Omar 1048-1131...... CMLC 11

Kherdian, David 1931-........... CLC 6, 9
See also CA 21-24R; CAAS 2; CANR 39;
CLR 24; MAICYA; SATA 16, 74

Khlebnikov, Velimir .... TCLC 20
See also Khlebnikov, Viktor Vladimirovich

Khlebnikov, Viktor Vladimirovich 1885-1922
See Khlebnikov, Velimir
See also CA 117

Khodasevich, Vladislav (Felitsianovich)
1886-1939 .... TCLC 15
See also CA 115

Kielland, Alexander Lange
1849-1906 .... TCLC 5
See also CA 104

Kiely, Benedict 1919-........... CLC 23, 43
See also CA 1-4R; CANR 2; DLB 15

Kienzle, William X(avier) 1928- .... CLC 25
See also CA 93-96; CAAS 1; CANR 9, 31;
MTCW

Kierkegaard, Soeren 1813-1855... NCLC 34

Kierkegaard, Soren 1813-1855.... NCLC 34

Killens, John Oliver 1916-1987..... CLC 10
See also BW; CA 77-80; 123; CAAS 2;
CANR 26; DLB 33

Killigrew, Anne 1660-1685.......... LC 4
See also DLB 131

Kim
See Simenon, Georges (Jacques Christian)

Kincaid, Jamaica 1949-........ CLC 43, 68
See also BLC 2; BW; CA 125

King, Francis (Henry) 1923-..... CLC 8, 53
See also CA 1-4R; CANR 1, 33; DLB 15;
MTCW

King, Stephen (Edwin)
1947-.............. CLC 12, 26, 37, 61
See also AAYA 1; BEST 90:1; CA 61-64;
CANR 1, 30; DLBY 80; MTCW;
SATA 9, 55

King, Steve
See King, Stephen (Edwin)

Kingman, Lee..................... CLC 17
See also Natti, (Mary) Lee
See also SAAS 3; SATA 1, 67

Kingsley, Charles 1819-1875..... NCLC 35
See also DLB 21, 32; YABC 2

Kingsley, Sidney 1906-............ CLC 44
See also CA 85-88; DLB 7

Kingsolver, Barbara 1955-......... CLC 55
See also CA 129; 134

Kingston, Maxine (Ting Ting) Hong
1940-.................. CLC 12, 19, 58
See also AAYA 8; CA 69-72; CANR 13,
38; DLBY 80; MTCW; SATA 53

Kinnell, Galway
1927-........... CLC 1, 2, 3, 5, 13, 29
See also CA 9-12R; CANR 10, 34; DLB 5;
DLBY 87; MTCW

Kinsella, Thomas 1928-......... CLC 4, 19
See also CA 17-20R; CANR 15; DLB 27;
MTCW

Kinsella, W(illiam) P(atrick)
1935-..................... CLC 27, 43
See also AAYA 7; CA 97-100; CAAS 7;
CANR 21, 35; MTCW

Kipling, (Joseph) Rudyard
1865-1936 .... TCLC 8, 17; PC 3; SSC 5
See also CA 105; 120; CANR 33;
CDBLB 1890-1914; DA; DLB 19, 34;
MAICYA; MTCW; WLC; YABC 2

Kirkup, James 1918- .... CLC 1
See also CA 1-4R; CAAS 4; CANR 2;
DLB 27; SATA 12

Kirkwood, James 1930(?)-1989 ...... CLC 9
See also AITN 2; CA 1-4R; 128; CANR 6,
40

Kis, Danilo 1935-1989 .... CLC 57
See also CA 109; 118; 129; MTCW

Kivi, Aleksis 1834-1872......... NCLC 30

Kizer, Carolyn (Ashley) 1925-... CLC 15, 39
See also CA 65-68; CAAS 5; CANR 24;
DLB 5

Klabund 1890-1928............. TCLC 44
See also DLB 66

Klappert, Peter 1942-............. CLC 57
See also CA 33-36R; DLB 5

Klein, A(braham) M(oses)
1909-1972 .... **CLC 19**
See also CA 101; 37-40R; DLB 68

Klein, Norma 1938-1989 .... **CLC 30**
See also AAYA 2; CA 41-44R; 128;
CANR 15, 37; CLR 2, 19; MAICYA;
SAAS 1; SATA 7, 57

Klein, T(heodore) E(ibon) D(onald)
1947- .... **CLC 34**
See also CA 119

Kleist, Heinrich von 1777-1811.... **NCLC 2**
See also DLB 90

Klima, Ivan 1931-................ **CLC 56**
See also CA 25-28R; CANR 17

Klimentov, Andrei Platonovich 1899-1951
See Platonov, Andrei
See also CA 108

Klinger, Friedrich Maximilian von
1752-1831 .... **NCLC 1**
See also DLB 94

Klopstock, Friedrich Gottlieb
1724-1803 .... **NCLC 11**
See also DLB 97

Knebel, Fletcher 1911-1993........ **CLC 14**
See also AITN 1; CA 1-4R; 140; CAAS 3;
CANR 1, 36; SATA 36

Knickerbocker, Diedrich
See Irving, Washington

Knight, Etheridge 1931-1991....... **CLC 40**
See also BLC 2; BW; CA 21-24R; 133;
CANR 23; DLB 41

Knight, Sarah Kemble 1666-1727 ..... **LC 7**
See also DLB 24

Knowles, John 1926- ...... **CLC 1, 4, 10, 26**
See also AAYA 10; CA 17-20R; CANR 40;
CDALB 1968-1988; DA; DLB 6; MTCW;
SATA 8

Knox, Calvin M.
See Silverberg, Robert

Knye, Cassandra
See Disch, Thomas M(ichael)

Koch, C(hristopher) J(ohn) 1932- ... **CLC 42**
See also CA 127

Koch, Christopher
See Koch, C(hristopher) J(ohn)

Koch, Kenneth 1925- .... **CLC 5, 8, 44**
See also CA 1-4R; CANR 6, 36; DLB 5;
SATA 65

Kochanowski, Jan 1530-1584........ **LC 10**

Kock, Charles Paul de
1794-1871 .... **NCLC 16**

Koda Shigeyuki 1867-1947
See Rohan, Koda
See also CA 121

Koestler, Arthur
1905-1983 .... **CLC 1, 3, 6, 8, 15, 33**
See also CA 1-4R; 109; CANR 1, 33;
CDBLB 1945-1960; DLBY 83; MTCW

Kogawa, Joy Nozomi 1935-........ **CLC 78**
See also CA 101; CANR 19

Kohout, Pavel 1928-.............. **CLC 13**
See also CA 45-48; CANR 3

Koizumi, Yakumo
See Hearn, (Patricio) Lafcadio (Tessima
Carlos)

Kolmar, Gertrud 1894-1943...... **TCLC 40**

Konrad, George
See Konrad, Gyoergy

Konrad, Gyoergy 1933- ...... **CLC 4, 10, 73**
See also CA 85-88

Konwicki, Tadeusz 1926-..... **CLC 8, 28, 54**
See also CA 101; CAAS 9; CANR 39;
MTCW

Koontz, Dean R(ay) 1945-......... **CLC 78**
See also AAYA 9; BEST 89:3, 90:2;
CA 108; CANR 19, 36; MTCW

Kopit, Arthur (Lee) 1937- .... **CLC 1, 18, 33**
See also AITN 1; CA 81-84; CABS 3;
DLB 7; MTCW

Kops, Bernard 1926-.............. **CLC 4**
See also CA 5-8R; DLB 13

Kornbluth, C(yril) M. 1923-1958.... **TCLC 8**
See also CA 105; DLB 8

Korolenko, V. G.
See Korolenko, Vladimir Galaktionovich

Korolenko, Vladimir
See Korolenko, Vladimir Galaktionovich

Korolenko, Vladimir G.
See Korolenko, Vladimir Galaktionovich

Korolenko, Vladimir Galaktionovich
1853-1921 .... **TCLC 22**
See also CA 121

Kosinski, Jerzy (Nikodem)
1933-1991 .... **CLC 1, 2, 3, 6, 10, 15, 53,
70**
See also CA 17-20R; 134; CANR 9; DLB 2;
DLBY 82; MTCW

Kostelanetz, Richard (Cory) 1940-.. **CLC 28**
See also CA 13-16R; CAAS 8; CANR 38

Kostrowitzki, Wilhelm Apollinaris de
1880-1918
See Apollinaire, Guillaume
See also CA 104

Kotlowitz, Robert 1924-............ **CLC 4**
See also CA 33-36R; CANR 36

Kotzebue, August (Friedrich Ferdinand) von
1761-1819 .... **NCLC 25**
See also DLB 94

Kotzwinkle, William 1938- ... **CLC 5, 14, 35**
See also CA 45-48; CANR 3; CLR 6;
MAICYA; SATA 24, 70

Kozol, Jonathan 1936-............ **CLC 17**
See also CA 61-64; CANR 16

Kozoll, Michael 1940(?)- .... **CLC 35**

Kramer, Kathryn 19(?)- .... **CLC 34**

Kramer, Larry 1935- .... **CLC 42**
See also CA 124; 126

Krasicki, Ignacy 1735-1801....... **NCLC 8**

Krasinski, Zygmunt 1812-1859 .... **NCLC 4**

Kraus, Karl 1874-1936............ **TCLC 5**
See also CA 104; DLB 118

Kreve (Mickevicius), Vincas
1882-1954 .... **TCLC 27**

Kristeva, Julia 1941- .... **CLC 77**

Kristofferson, Kris 1936-.......... **CLC 26**
See also CA 104

Krizanc, John 1956-.............. **CLC 57**

Krleza, Miroslav 1893-1981........ **CLC 8**
See also CA 97-100; 105

Kroetsch, Robert 1927- ...... **CLC 5, 23, 57**
See also CA 17-20R; CANR 8, 38; DLB 53;
MTCW

Kroetz, Franz
See Kroetz, Franz Xaver

Kroetz, Franz Xaver 1946- .... **CLC 41**
See also CA 130

Kroker, Arthur 1945-............. **CLC 77**

Kropotkin, Peter (Aleksieevich)
1842-1921 .... **TCLC 36**
See also CA 119

Krotkov, Yuri 1917-.............. **CLC 19**
See also CA 102

Krumb
See Crumb, R(obert)

Krumgold, Joseph (Quincy)
1908-1980 .... **CLC 12**
See also CA 9-12R; 101; CANR 7;
MAICYA; SATA 1, 23, 48

Krumwitz
See Crumb, R(obert)

Krutch, Joseph Wood 1893-1970.... **CLC 24**
See also CA 1-4R; 25-28R; CANR 4;
DLB 63

Krutzch, Gus
See Eliot, T(homas) S(tearns)

Krylov, Ivan Andreevich
1768(?)-1844 .... **NCLC 1**

Kubin, Alfred 1877-1959 .... **TCLC 23**
See also CA 112; DLB 81

Kubrick, Stanley 1928-............ **CLC 16**
See also CA 81-84; CANR 33; DLB 26

Kumin, Maxine (Winokur)
1925- .... **CLC 5, 13, 28**
See also AITN 2; CA 1-4R; CAAS 8;
CANR 1, 21; DLB 5; MTCW; SATA 12

Kundera, Milan
1929- .... **CLC 4, 9, 19, 32, 68**
See also AAYA 2; CA 85-88; CANR 19;
MTCW

Kunitz, Stanley (Jasspon)
1905- .... **CLC 6, 11, 14**
See also CA 41-44R; CANR 26; DLB 48;
MTCW

Kunze, Reiner 1933-.............. **CLC 10**
See also CA 93-96; DLB 75

Kuprin, Aleksandr Ivanovich
1870-1938 .... **TCLC 5**
See also CA 104

Kureishi, Hanif 1954(?)-.......... **CLC 64**
See also CA 139

Kurosawa, Akira 1910-............ **CLC 16**
See also CA 101

Kuttner, Henry 1915-1958........ **TCLC 10**
See also CA 107; DLB 8

Kuzma, Greg 1944-................ **CLC 7**
See also CA 33-36R

Kuzmin, Mikhail 1872(?)-1936 .... **TCLC 40**

Lawton, Dennis
See Faust, Frederick (Schiller)

Laxness, Halldor . . . . **CLC 25**
See also Gudjonsson, Halldor Kiljan

Layamon fl. c. 1200- . . . . **CMLC 10**

Laye, Camara 1928-1980 . . . . **CLC 4, 38**
See also BLC 2; BW; CA 85-88; 97-100;
CANR 25; MTCW

Layton, Irving (Peter) 1912- . . . . . **CLC 2, 15**
See also CA 1-4R; CANR 2, 33; DLB 88;
MTCW

Lazarus, Emma 1849-1887 . . . . **NCLC 8**

Lazarus, Felix
See Cable, George Washington

Lazarus, Henry
See Slavitt, David R(ytman)

Lea, Joan
See Neufeld, John (Arthur)

Leacock, Stephen (Butler)
1869-1944 . . . . **TCLC 2**
See also CA 104; DLB 92

Lear, Edward 1812-1888 . . . . **NCLC 3**
See also CLR 1; DLB 32; MAICYA;
SATA 18

Lear, Norman (Milton) 1922- . . . . . . **CLC 12**
See also CA 73-76

Leavis, F(rank) R(aymond)
1895-1978 . . . . **CLC 24**
See also CA 21-24R; 77-80; MTCW

Leavitt, David 1961- . . . . **CLC 34**
See also CA 116; 122; DLB 130

Leblanc, Maurice (Marie Emile)
1864-1941 . . . . **TCLC 49**
See also CA 110

Lebowitz, Fran(ces Ann)
1951(?)- . . . . **CLC 11, 36**
See also CA 81-84; CANR 14; MTCW

le Carre, John . . . . **CLC 3, 5, 9, 15, 28**
See also Cornwell, David (John Moore)
See also BEST 89:4; CDBLB 1960 to
Present; DLB 87

Le Clezio, J(ean) M(arie) G(ustave)
1940- . . . . **CLC 31**
See also CA 116; 128; DLB 83

Leconte de Lisle, Charles-Marie-Rene
1818-1894 . . . . **NCLC 29**

Le Coq, Monsieur
See Simenon, Georges (Jacques Christian)

Leduc, Violette 1907-1972 . . . . **CLC 22**
See also CA 13-14; 33-36R; CAP 1

Ledwidge, Francis 1887(?)-1917 . . . **TCLC 23**
See also CA 123; DLB 20

Lee, Andrea 1953- . . . . **CLC 36**
See also BLC 2; BW; CA 125

Lee, Andrew
See Auchincloss, Louis (Stanton)

Lee, Don L. . . . . **CLC 2**
See also Madhubuti, Haki R.

Lee, George W(ashington)
1894-1976 . . . . **CLC 52**
See also BLC 2; BW; CA 125; DLB 51

Lee, (Nelle) Harper 1926- . . . . . . **CLC 12, 60**
See also CA 13-16R; CDALB 1941-1968;
DA; DLB 6; MTCW; SATA 11; WLC

Lee, Julian
See Latham, Jean Lee

Lee, Lawrence 1903- . . . . **CLC 34**
See also CA 25-28R

Lee, Manfred B(ennington)
1905-1971 . . . . **CLC 11**
See also Queen, Ellery
See also CA 1-4R; 29-32R; CANR 2

Lee, Stan 1922- . . . . **CLC 17**
See also AAYA 5; CA 108; 111

Lee, Tanith 1947- . . . . **CLC 46**
See also CA 37-40R; SATA 8

Lee, Vernon . . . . **TCLC 5**
See also Paget, Violet
See also DLB 57

Lee, William
See Burroughs, William S(eward)

Lee, Willy
See Burroughs, William S(eward)

Lee-Hamilton, Eugene (Jacob)
1845-1907 . . . . **TCLC 22**
See also CA 117

Leet, Judith 1935- . . . . **CLC 11**

Le Fanu, Joseph Sheridan
1814-1873 . . . . **NCLC 9**
See also DLB 21, 70

Leffland, Ella 1931- . . . . **CLC 19**
See also CA 29-32R; CANR 35; DLBY 84;
SATA 65

Leger, (Marie-Rene) Alexis Saint-Leger
1887-1975 . . . . **CLC 11**
See also Perse, St.-John
See also CA 13-16R; 61-64; MTCW

Leger, Saintleger
See Leger, (Marie-Rene) Alexis Saint-Leger

Le Guin, Ursula K(roeber)
1929- . . . . **CLC 8, 13, 22, 45, 71; SSC 12**
See also AAYA 9; AITN 1; CA 21-24R;
CANR 9, 32; CDALB 1968-1988; CLR 3,
28; DLB 8, 52; MAICYA; MTCW;
SATA 4, 52

Lehmann, Rosamond (Nina)
1901-1990 . . . . **CLC 5**
See also CA 77-80; 131; CANR 8; DLB 15

Leiber, Fritz (Reuter, Jr.)
1910-1992 . . . . **CLC 25**
See also CA 45-48; 139; CANR 2, 40;
DLB 8; MTCW; SATA 45;
SATA-Obit 73

Leimbach, Martha 1963-
See Leimbach, Marti
See also CA 130

Leimbach, Marti . . . . **CLC 65**
See also Leimbach, Martha

Leino, Eino . . . . **TCLC 24**
See also Loennbohm, Armas Eino Leopold

Leiris, Michel (Julien) 1901-1990 . . . **CLC 61**
See also CA 119; 128; 132

Leithauser, Brad 1953- . . . . **CLC 27**
See also CA 107; CANR 27; DLB 120

Lelchuk, Alan 1938- . . . . **CLC 5**
See also CA 45-48; CANR 1

Lem, Stanislaw 1921- . . . . **CLC 8, 15, 40**
See also CA 105; CAAS 1; CANR 32;
MTCW

Lemann, Nancy 1956- . . . . **CLC 39**
See also CA 118; 136

Lemonnier, (Antoine Louis) Camille
1844-1913 . . . . **TCLC 22**
See also CA 121

Lenau, Nikolaus 1802-1850 . . . . . . **NCLC 16**

L'Engle, Madeleine (Camp Franklin)
1918- . . . . **CLC 12**
See also AAYA 1; AITN 2; CA 1-4R;
CANR 3, 21, 39; CLR 1, 14; DLB 52;
MAICYA; MTCW; SAAS 15; SATA 1,
27

Lengyel, Jozsef 1896-1975 . . . . **CLC 7**
See also CA 85-88; 57-60

Lennon, John (Ono)
1940-1980 . . . . **CLC 12, 35**
See also CA 102

Lennox, Charlotte Ramsay
1729(?)-1804 . . . . **NCLC 23**
See also DLB 39

Lentricchia, Frank (Jr.) 1940- . . . . . **CLC 34**
See also CA 25-28R; CANR 19

Lenz, Siegfried 1926- . . . . **CLC 27**
See also CA 89-92; DLB 75

Leonard, Elmore (John, Jr.)
1925- . . . . **CLC 28, 34, 71**
See also AITN 1; BEST 89:1, 90:4;
CA 81-84; CANR 12, 28; MTCW

Leonard, Hugh
See Byrne, John Keyes
See also DLB 13

**Leopardi, (Conte) Giacomo (Talegardo
Francesco di Sales Save**
1798-1837 . . . . **NCLC 22**

Le Reveler
See Artaud, Antonin

Lerman, Eleanor 1952- . . . . **CLC 9**
See also CA 85-88

Lerman, Rhoda 1936- . . . . **CLC 56**
See also CA 49-52

Lermontov, Mikhail Yuryevich
1814-1841 . . . . **NCLC 5**

Leroux, Gaston 1868-1927 . . . . **TCLC 25**
See also CA 108; 136; SATA 65

Lesage, Alain-Rene 1668-1747 . . . . . . **LC 2**

Leskov, Nikolai (Semyonovich)
1831-1895 . . . . **NCLC 25**

Lessing, Doris (May)
1919- . . . . . **CLC 1, 2, 3, 6, 10, 15, 22, 40;
SSC 6**
See also CA 9-12R; CAAS 14; CANR 33;
CDBLB 1960 to Present; DA; DLB 15;
DLBY 85; MTCW

Lessing, Gotthold Ephraim
1729-1781 . . . . **LC 8**
See also DLB 97

Lester, Richard 1932- . . . . **CLC 20**

Lever, Charles (James)
1806-1872 . . . . **NCLC 23**
See also DLB 21

Leverson, Ada 1865(?)-1936(?) . . . . **TCLC 18**
See also Elaine
See also CA 117

Long, Emmett
See Leonard, Elmore (John, Jr.)

Longbaugh, Harry
See Goldman, William (W.)

Longfellow, Henry Wadsworth
1807-1882 . . . . **NCLC 2**
See also CDALB 1640-1865; DA; DLB 1,
59; SATA 19

Longley, Michael 1939- . . . . **CLC 29**
See also CA 102; DLB 40

Longus fl. c. 2nd cent. - . . . . **CMLC 7**

Longway, A. Hugh
See Lang, Andrew

Lopate, Phillip 1943- . . . . **CLC 29**
See also CA 97-100; DLBY 80

Lopez Portillo (y Pacheco), Jose
1920- . . . . **CLC 46**
See also CA 129; HW

Lopez y Fuentes, Gregorio
1897(?)-1966 . . . . **CLC 32**
See also CA 131; HW

Lorca, Federico Garcia
See Garcia Lorca, Federico

Lord, Bette Bao 1938- . . . . **CLC 23**
See also BEST 90:3; CA 107; CANR 41;
SATA 58

Lord Auch
See Bataille, Georges

Lord Byron
See Byron, George Gordon (Noel)

Lord Dunsany . . . . **TCLC 2**
See also Dunsany, Edward John Moreton
Drax Plunkett

Lorde, Audre (Geraldine)
1934- . . . . **CLC 18, 71**
See also BLC 2; BW; CA 25-28R;
CANR 16, 26; DLB 41; MTCW

Lord Jeffrey
See Jeffrey, Francis

Lorenzo, Heberto Padilla
See Padilla (Lorenzo), Heberto

Loris
See Hofmannsthal, Hugo von

Loti, Pierre . . . . **TCLC 11**
See also Viaud, (Louis Marie) Julien
See also DLB 123

Louie, David Wong 1954- . . . . **CLC 70**
See also CA 139

Louis, Father M.
See Merton, Thomas

Lovecraft, H(oward) P(hillips)
1890-1937 . . . . **TCLC 4, 22; SSC 3**
See also CA 104; 133; MTCW

Lovelace, Earl 1935- . . . . **CLC 51**
See also CA 77-80; CANR 41; DLB 125;
MTCW

Lowell, Amy 1874-1925 . . . . **TCLC 1, 8**
See also CA 104; DLB 54

Lowell, James Russell 1819-1891 . . **NCLC 2**
See also CDALB 1640-1865; DLB 1, 11, 64,
79

Lowell, Robert (Traill Spence, Jr.)
1917-1977 . . . **CLC 1, 2, 3, 4, 5, 8, 9, 11,**
15, 37; PC 3
See also CA 9-12R; 73-76; CABS 2;
CANR 26; DA; DLB 5; MTCW; WLC

Lowndes, Marie Adelaide (Belloc)
1868-1947 . . . . **TCLC 12**
See also CA 107; DLB 70

Lowry, (Clarence) Malcolm
1909-1957 . . . . **TCLC 6, 40**
See also CA 105; 131; CDBLB 1945-1960;
DLB 15; MTCW

Lowry, Mina Gertrude 1882-1966
See Loy, Mina
See also CA 113

Loxsmith, John
See Brunner, John (Kilian Houston)

Loy, Mina . . . . **CLC 28**
See also Lowry, Mina Gertrude
See also DLB 4, 54

Loyson-Bridet
See Schwob, (Mayer Andre) Marcel

Lucas, Craig 1951- . . . . **CLC 64**
See also CA 137

Lucas, George 1944- . . . . **CLC 16**
See also AAYA 1; CA 77-80; CANR 30;
SATA 56

Lucas, Hans
See Godard, Jean-Luc

Lucas, Victoria
See Plath, Sylvia

Ludlam, Charles 1943-1987 . . . . . **CLC 46, 50**
See also CA 85-88; 122

Ludlum, Robert 1927- . . . . **CLC 22, 43**
See also AAYA 10; BEST 89:1, 90:3;
CA 33-36R; CANR 25, 41; DLBY 82;
MTCW

Ludwig, Ken . . . . **CLC 60**

Ludwig, Otto 1813-1865 . . . . **NCLC 4**
See also DLB 129

Lugones, Leopoldo 1874-1938 . . . . . **TCLC 15**
See also CA 116; 131; HW

Lu Hsun 1881-1936 . . . . **TCLC 3**

Lukacs, George . . . . **CLC 24**
See also Lukacs, Gyorgy (Szegeny von)

Lukacs, Gyorgy (Szegeny von) 1885-1971
See Lukacs, George
See also CA 101; 29-32R

Luke, Peter (Ambrose Cyprian)
1919- . . . . **CLC 38**
See also CA 81-84; DLB 13

Lunar, Dennis
See Mungo, Raymond

Lurie, Alison 1926- . . . . **CLC 4, 5, 18, 39**
See also CA 1-4R; CANR 2, 17; DLB 2;
MTCW; SATA 46

Lustig, Arnost 1926- . . . . **CLC 56**
See also AAYA 3; CA 69-72; SATA 56

Luther, Martin 1483-1546 . . . . **LC 9**

Luzi, Mario 1914- . . . . **CLC 13**
See also CA 61-64; CANR 9; DLB 128

Lynch, B. Suarez
See Bioy Casares, Adolfo; Borges, Jorge
Luis

Lynch, David (K.) 1946- . . . . **CLC 66**
See also CA 124; 129

Lynch, James
See Andreyev, Leonid (Nikolaevich)

Lynch Davis, B.
See Bioy Casares, Adolfo; Borges, Jorge
Luis

Lyndsay, Sir David 1490-1555 . . . . **LC 20**

Lynn, Kenneth S(chuyler) 1923- . . . . **CLC 50**
See also CA 1-4R; CANR 3, 27

Lynx
See West, Rebecca

Lyons, Marcus
See Blish, James (Benjamin)

Lyre, Pinchbeck
See Sassoon, Siegfried (Lorraine)

Lytle, Andrew (Nelson) 1902- . . . . . . **CLC 22**
See also CA 9-12R; DLB 6

Lyttelton, George 1709-1773 . . . . **LC 10**

Maas, Peter 1929- . . . . **CLC 29**
See also CA 93-96

Macaulay, Rose 1881-1958 . . . . . **TCLC 7, 44**
See also CA 104; DLB 36

MacBeth, George (Mann)
1932-1992 . . . . **CLC 2, 5, 9**
See also CA 25-28R; 136; DLB 40; MTCW;
SATA 4; SATA-Obit 70

MacCaig, Norman (Alexander)
1910- . . . . **CLC 36**
See also CA 9-12R; CANR 3, 34; DLB 27

MacCarthy, (Sir Charles Otto) Desmond
1877-1952 . . . . **TCLC 36**

MacDiarmid, Hugh . . . . . **CLC 2, 4, 11, 19, 63**
See also Grieve, C(hristopher) M(urray)
See also CDBLB 1945-1960; DLB 20

MacDonald, Anson
See Heinlein, Robert A(nson)

Macdonald, Cynthia 1928- . . . . . . **CLC 13, 19**
See also CA 49-52; CANR 4; DLB 105

MacDonald, George 1824-1905 . . . . . **TCLC 9**
See also CA 106; 137; DLB 18; MAICYA;
SATA 33

Macdonald, John
See Millar, Kenneth

MacDonald, John D(ann)
1916-1986 . . . . **CLC 3, 27, 44**
See also CA 1-4R; 121; CANR 1, 19;
DLB 8; DLBY 86; MTCW

Macdonald, John Ross
See Millar, Kenneth

Macdonald, Ross . . . . . **CLC 1, 2, 3, 14, 34, 41**
See also Millar, Kenneth
See also DLBD 6

MacDougal, John
See Blish, James (Benjamin)

MacEwen, Gwendolyn (Margaret)
1941-1987 . . . . **CLC 13, 55**
See also CA 9-12R; 124; CANR 7, 22;
DLB 53; SATA 50, 55

Machado (y Ruiz), Antonio
1875-1939 . . . . **TCLC 3**
See also CA 104; DLB 108

Machado de Assis, Joaquim Maria
1839-1908 .... TCLC **10**
See also BLC 2; CA 107

Machen, Arthur................... TCLC **4**
See also Jones, Arthur Llewellyn
See also DLB 36

Machiavelli, Niccolo 1469-1527 ...... LC **8**
See also DA

MacInnes, Colin 1914-1976...... CLC **4, 23**
See also CA 69-72; 65-68; CANR 21;
DLB 14; MTCW

MacInnes, Helen (Clark)
1907-1985 .... CLC **27, 39**
See also CA 1-4R; 117; CANR 1, 28;
DLB 87; MTCW; SATA 22, 44

Mackay, Mary 1855-1924
See Corelli, Marie
See also CA 118

Mackenzie, Compton (Edward Montague)
1883-1972 .... CLC **18**
See also CA 21-22; 37-40R; CAP 2;
DLB 34, 100

Mackenzie, Henry 1745-1831 .... NCLC **41**
See also DLB 39

Mackintosh, Elizabeth 1896(?)-1952
See Tey, Josephine
See also CA 110

MacLaren, James
See Grieve, C(hristopher) M(urray)

Mac Laverty, Bernard 1942-....... CLC **31**
See also CA 116; 118

MacLean, Alistair (Stuart)
1922-1987 .... CLC **3, 13, 50, 63**
See also CA 57-60; 121; CANR 28; MTCW;
SATA 23, 50

MacLeish, Archibald
1892-1982 .... CLC **3, 8, 14, 68**
See also CA 9-12R; 106; CANR 33; DLB 4,
7, 45; DLBY 82; MTCW

MacLennan, (John) Hugh
1907- .... CLC **2, 14**
See also CA 5-8R; CANR 33; DLB 68;
MTCW

MacLeod, Alistair 1936- .... CLC **56**
See also CA 123; DLB 60

MacNeice, (Frederick) Louis
1907-1963 .... CLC **1, 4, 10, 53**
See also CA 85-88; DLB 10, 20; MTCW

MacNeill, Dand
See Fraser, George MacDonald

Macpherson, (Jean) Jay 1931-...... CLC **14**
See also CA 5-8R; DLB 53

MacShane, Frank 1927-........... CLC **39**
See also CA 9-12R; CANR 3, 33; DLB 111

Macumber, Mari
See Sandoz, Mari(e Susette)

Madach, Imre 1823-1864 .... NCLC **19**

Madden, (Jerry) David 1933- .... CLC **5, 15**
See also CA 1-4R; CAAS 3; CANR 4;
DLB 6; MTCW

Maddern, Al(an)
See Ellison, Harlan

Madhubuti, Haki R.
1942- .... CLC **6, 73; PC 5**
See also Lee, Don L.
See also BLC 2; BW; CA 73-76; CANR 24;
DLB 5, 41; DLBD 8

Madow, Pauline (Reichberg) .... CLC **1**
See also CA 9-12R

Maepenn, Hugh
See Kuttner, Henry

Maepenn, K. H.
See Kuttner, Henry

Maeterlinck, Maurice 1862-1949 ... TCLC **3**
See also CA 104; 136; SATA 66

Maginn, William 1794-1842....... NCLC **8**
See also DLB 110

Mahapatra, Jayanta 1928-......... CLC **33**
See also CA 73-76; CAAS 9; CANR 15, 33

Mahfouz, Naguib (Abdel Aziz Al-Sabilgi)
1911(?)-
See Mahfuz, Najib
See also BEST 89:2; CA 128; MTCW

Mahfuz, Najib................. CLC **52, 55**
See also Mahfouz, Naguib (Abdel Aziz
Al-Sabilgi)
See also DLBY 88

Mahon, Derek 1941-.............. CLC **27**
See also CA 113; 128; DLB 40

Mailer, Norman
1923- ...... CLC **1, 2, 3, 4, 5, 8, 11, 14,
28, 39, 74**
See also AITN 2; CA 9-12R; CABS 1;
CANR 28; CDALB 1968-1988; DA;
DLB 2, 16, 28; DLBD 3; DLBY 80, 83;
MTCW

Maillet, Antonine 1929-........... CLC **54**
See also CA 115; 120; DLB 60

Mais, Roger 1905-1955 .... TCLC **8**
See also BW; CA 105; 124; DLB 125;
MTCW

Maitland, Sara (Louise) 1950-...... CLC **49**
See also CA 69-72; CANR 13

Major, Clarence 1936-....... CLC **3, 19, 48**
See also BLC 2; BW; CA 21-24R; CAAS 6;
CANR 13, 25; DLB 33

Major, Kevin (Gerald) 1949-....... CLC **26**
See also CA 97-100; CANR 21, 38;
CLR 11; DLB 60; MAICYA; SATA 32

Maki, James
See Ozu, Yasujiro

Malabaila, Damiano
See Levi, Primo

Malamud, Bernard
1914-1986 ...... CLC **1, 2, 3, 5, 8, 9, 11,
18, 27, 44, 78**
See also CA 5-8R; 118; CABS 1; CANR 28;
CDALB 1941-1968; DA; DLB 2, 28;
DLBY 80, 86; MTCW; WLC

Malcolm, Dan
See Silverberg, Robert

Malherbe, Francois de 1555-1628..... LC **5**

Mallarme, Stephane
1842-1898 .... NCLC **4, 41; PC 4**

Mallet-Joris, Francoise 1930-...... CLC **11**
See also CA 65-68; CANR 17; DLB 83

Malley, Ern
See McAuley, James Phillip

Mallowan, Agatha Christie
See Christie, Agatha (Mary Clarissa)

Maloff, Saul 1922-................ CLC **5**
See also CA 33-36R

Malone, Louis
See MacNeice, (Frederick) Louis

Malone, Michael (Christopher)
1942- .... CLC **43**
See also CA 77-80; CANR 14, 32

Malory, (Sir) Thomas
1410(?)-1471(?) .... LC **11**
See also CDBLB Before 1660; DA;
SATA 33, 59

Malouf, (George Joseph) David
1934- .... CLC **28**
See also CA 124

Malraux, (Georges-)Andre
1901-1976 ...... CLC **1, 4, 9, 13, 15, 57**
See also CA 21-22; 69-72; CANR 34;
CAP 2; DLB 72; MTCW

Malzberg, Barry N(athaniel) 1939-... CLC **7**
See also CA 61-64; CAAS 4; CANR 16;
DLB 8

Mamet, David (Alan)
1947- .... CLC **9, 15, 34, 46**
See also AAYA 3; CA 81-84; CABS 3;
CANR 15, 41; DLB 7; MTCW

Mamoulian, Rouben (Zachary)
1897-1987 .... CLC **16**
See also CA 25-28R; 124

Mandelstam, Osip (Emilievich)
1891(?)-1938(?) .... TCLC **2, 6**
See also CA 104

Mander, (Mary) Jane 1877-1949... TCLC **31**

Mandiargues, Andre Pieyre de....... CLC **41**
See also Pieyre de Mandiargues, Andre
See also DLB 83

Mandrake, Ethel Belle
See Thurman, Wallace (Henry)

Mangan, James Clarence
1803-1849 .... NCLC **27**

Maniere, J.-E.
See Giraudoux, (Hippolyte) Jean

Manley, (Mary) Delariviere
1672(?)-1724 .... LC **1**
See also DLB 39, 80

Mann, Abel
See Creasey, John

Mann, (Luiz) Heinrich 1871-1950... TCLC **9**
See also CA 106; DLB 66

Mann, (Paul) Thomas
1875-1955 .... TCLC **2, 8, 14, 21, 35, 44;
SSC 5**
See also CA 104; 128; DA; DLB 66;
MTCW; WLC

Manning, David
See Faust, Frederick (Schiller)

Manning, Frederic 1887(?)-1935 ... TCLC **25**
See also CA 124

Manning, Olivia 1915-1980 ...... CLC **5, 19**
See also CA 5-8R; 101; CANR 29; MTCW

Mano, D. Keith 1942- . . . . **CLC 2, 10**
See also CA 25-28R; CAAS 6; CANR 26;
DLB 6

Mansfield, Katherine. . . **TCLC 2, 8, 39; SSC 9**
See also Beauchamp, Kathleen Mansfield
See also WLC

Manso, Peter 1940- . . . . **CLC 39**
See also CA 29-32R

Mantecon, Juan Jimenez
See Jimenez (Mantecon), Juan Ramon

Manton, Peter
See Creasey, John

Man Without a Spleen, A
See Chekhov, Anton (Pavlovich)

Manzoni, Alessandro 1785-1873 . . **NCLC 29**

Mapu, Abraham (ben Jekutiel)
1808-1867 . . . . **NCLC 18**

Mara, Sally
See Queneau, Raymond

Marat, Jean Paul 1743-1793 . . . . **LC 10**

Marcel, Gabriel Honore
1889-1973 . . . . **CLC 15**
See also CA 102; 45-48; MTCW

Marchbanks, Samuel
See Davies, (William) Robertson

Marchi, Giacomo
See Bassani, Giorgio

Margulies, Donald. . . . . **CLC 76**

Marie de France c. 12th cent. -. . . . **CMLC 8**

Marie de l'Incarnation 1599-1672. . . . **LC 10**

Mariner, Scott
See Pohl, Frederik

Marinetti, Filippo Tommaso
1876-1944 . . . . **TCLC 10**
See also CA 107; DLB 114

Marivaux, Pierre Carlet de Chamblain de
1688-1763 . . . . **LC 4**

Markandaya, Kamala . . . . **CLC 8, 38**
See also Taylor, Kamala (Purnaiya)

Markfield, Wallace 1926-. . . . . **CLC 8**
See also CA 69-72; CAAS 3; DLB 2, 28

Markham, Edwin 1852-1940 . . . . . . **TCLC 47**
See also DLB 54

Markham, Robert
See Amis, Kingsley (William)

Marks, J
See Highwater, Jamake (Mamake)

Marks-Highwater, J
See Highwater, Jamake (Mamake)

Markson, David M(errill) 1927- . . . . **CLC 67**
See also CA 49-52; CANR 1

Marley, Bob. . . . . **CLC 17**
See also Marley, Robert Nesta

Marley, Robert Nesta 1945-1981
See Marley, Bob
See also CA 107; 103

Marlowe, Christopher
1564-1593 . . . . **LC 22; DC 1**
See also CDBLB Before 1660; DA; DLB 62;
WLC

Marmontel, Jean-Francois
1723-1799 . . . . **LC 2**

Marquand, John P(hillips)
1893-1960 . . . . **CLC 2, 10**
See also CA 85-88; DLB 9, 102

Marquez, Gabriel (Jose) Garcia. . . . . . **CLC 68**
See also Garcia Marquez, Gabriel (Jose)

Marquis, Don(ald Robert Perry)
1878-1937 . . . . **TCLC 7**
See also CA 104; DLB 11, 25

Marric, J. J.
See Creasey, John

Marrow, Bernard
See Moore, Brian

Marryat, Frederick 1792-1848 . . . . **NCLC 3**
See also DLB 21

Marsden, James
See Creasey, John

Marsh, (Edith) Ngaio
1899-1982 . . . . **CLC 7, 53**
See also CA 9-12R; CANR 6; DLB 77;
MTCW

Marshall, Garry 1934-. . . . . **CLC 17**
See also AAYA 3; CA 111; SATA 60

Marshall, Paule 1929- . . **CLC 27, 72; SSC 3**
See also BLC 3; BW; CA 77-80; CANR 25;
DLB 33; MTCW

Marsten, Richard
See Hunter, Evan

Martha, Henry
See Harris, Mark

Martin, Ken
See Hubbard, L(afayette) Ron(ald)

Martin, Richard
See Creasey, John

Martin, Steve 1945-. . . . . **CLC 30**
See also CA 97-100; CANR 30; MTCW

Martin, Violet Florence
1862-1915 . . . . **TCLC 51**

Martin, Webber
See Silverberg, Robert

Martin du Gard, Roger
1881-1958 . . . . **TCLC 24**
See also CA 118; DLB 65

Martineau, Harriet 1802-1876. . . . **NCLC 26**
See also DLB 21, 55; YABC 2

Martines, Julia
See O'Faolain, Julia

Martinez, Jacinto Benavente y
See Benavente (y Martinez), Jacinto

Martinez Ruiz, Jose 1873-1967
See Azorin; Ruiz, Jose Martinez
See also CA 93-96; HW

Martinez Sierra, Gregorio
1881-1947 . . . . **TCLC 6**
See also CA 115

Martinez Sierra, Maria (de la O'LeJarraga)
1874-1974 . . . . **TCLC 6**
See also CA 115

Martinsen, Martin
See Follett, Ken(neth Martin)

Martinson, Harry (Edmund)
1904-1978 . . . . **CLC 14**
See also CA 77-80; CANR 34

Marut, Ret
See Traven, B.

Marut, Robert
See Traven, B.

Marvell, Andrew 1621-1678. . . . . **LC 4**
See also CDBLB 1660-1789; DA; DLB 131;
WLC

Marx, Karl (Heinrich)
1818-1883 . . . . **NCLC 17**
See also DLB 129

Masaoka Shiki. . . . . **TCLC 18**
See also Masaoka Tsunenori

Masaoka Tsunenori 1867-1902
See Masaoka Shiki
See also CA 117

Masefield, John (Edward)
1878-1967 . . . . **CLC 11, 47**
See also CA 19-20; 25-28R; CANR 33;
CAP 2; CDBLB 1890-1914; DLB 10;
MTCW; SATA 19

Maso, Carole 19(?)- . . . . **CLC 44**

Mason, Bobbie Ann
1940- . . . . **CLC 28, 43; SSC 4**
See also AAYA 5; CA 53-56; CANR 11,
31; DLBY 87; MTCW

Mason, Ernst
See Pohl, Frederik

Mason, Lee W.
See Malzberg, Barry N(athaniel)

Mason, Nick 1945-. . . . . **CLC 35**
See also Pink Floyd

Mason, Tally
See Derleth, August (William)

Mass, William
See Gibson, William

Masters, Edgar Lee
1868-1950 . . . . **TCLC 2, 25; PC 1**
See also CA 104; 133; CDALB 1865-1917;
DA; DLB 54; MTCW

Masters, Hilary 1928- . . . . **CLC 48**
See also CA 25-28R; CANR 13

Mastrosimone, William 19(?)- . . . . . . **CLC 36**

Mathe, Albert
See Camus, Albert

Matheson, Richard Burton 1926- . . . **CLC 37**
See also CA 97-100; DLB 8, 44

Mathews, Harry 1930-. . . . . **CLC 6, 52**
See also CA 21-24R; CAAS 6; CANR 18,
40

Mathias, Roland (Glyn) 1915-. . . . . . **CLC 45**
See also CA 97-100; CANR 19, 41; DLB 27

Matsuo Basho 1644-1694. . . . . **PC 3**

Mattheson, Rodney
See Creasey, John

Matthews, Greg 1949- . . . . **CLC 45**
See also CA 135

Matthews, William 1942-. . . . . **CLC 40**
See also CA 29-32R; CANR 12; DLB 5

Matthias, John (Edward) 1941-. . . . . . **CLC 9**
See also CA 33-36R

Matthiessen, Peter
1927- . . . . **CLC 5, 7, 11, 32, 64**
See also AAYA 6; BEST 90:4; CA 9-12R;
CANR 21; DLB 6; MTCW; SATA 27

Maturin, Charles Robert
1780(?)-1824 . . . . **NCLC 6**

Medoff, Mark (Howard) 1940- ... **CLC 6, 23**
See also AITN 1; CA 53-56; CANR 5;
DLB 7

Meged, Aharon
See Megged, Aharon

Meged, Aron
See Megged, Aharon

Megged, Aharon 1920- .... **CLC 9**
See also CA 49-52; CAAS 13; CANR 1

Mehta, Ved (Parkash) 1934- .... **CLC 37**
See also CA 1-4R; CANR 2, 23; MTCW

Melanter
See Blackmore, R(ichard) D(oddridge)

Melikow, Loris
See Hofmannsthal, Hugo von

Melmoth, Sebastian
See Wilde, Oscar (Fingal O'Flahertie Wills)

Meltzer, Milton 1915- .... **CLC 26**
See also AAYA 8; CA 13-16R; CANR 38;
CLR 13; DLB 61; MAICYA; SAAS 1;
SATA 1, 50

Melville, Herman
1819-1891 ...... NCLC 3, 12, 29; SSC 1
See also CDALB 1640-1865; DA; DLB 3,
74; SATA 59; WLC

Menander
c. 342B.C.-c. 292B.C.... **CMLC 9; DC 3**

Mencken, H(enry) L(ouis)
1880-1956 .... **TCLC 13**
See also CA 105; 125; CDALB 1917-1929;
DLB 11, 29, 63; MTCW

Mercer, David 1928-1980.......... **CLC 5**
See also CA 9-12R; 102; CANR 23;
DLB 13; MTCW

Merchant, Paul
See Ellison, Harlan

Meredith, George 1828-1909 ... **TCLC 17, 43**
See also CA 117; CDBLB 1832-1890;
DLB 18, 35, 57

Meredith, William (Morris)
1919- .... **CLC 4, 13, 22, 55**
See also CA 9-12R; CAAS 14; CANR 6, 40;
DLB 5

Merezhkovsky, Dmitry Sergeyevich
1865-1941 .... **TCLC 29**

Merimee, Prosper
1803-1870 .... **NCLC 6; SSC 7**
See also DLB 119

Merkin, Daphne 1954- .... **CLC 44**
See also CA 123

Merlin, Arthur
See Blish, James (Benjamin)

Merrill, James (Ingram)
1926- .... **CLC 2, 3, 6, 8, 13, 18, 34**
See also CA 13-16R; CANR 10; DLB 5;
DLBY 85; MTCW

Merriman, Alex
See Silverberg, Robert

Merritt, E. B.
See Waddington, Miriam

Merton, Thomas
1915-1968 .... **CLC 1, 3, 11, 34**
See also CA 5-8R; 25-28R; CANR 22;
DLB 48; DLBY 81; MTCW

Merwin, W(illiam) S(tanley)
1927- ...... **CLC 1, 2, 3, 5, 8, 13, 18, 45**
See also CA 13-16R; CANR 15; DLB 5;
MTCW

Metcalf, John 1938-............. **CLC 37**
See also CA 113; DLB 60

Metcalf, Suzanne
See Baum, L(yman) Frank

Mew, Charlotte (Mary)
1870-1928 .... **TCLC 8**
See also CA 105; DLB 19

Mewshaw, Michael 1943-.......... **CLC 9**
See also CA 53-56; CANR 7; DLBY 80

Meyer, June
See Jordan, June

Meyer, Lynn
See Slavitt, David R(ytman)

Meyer-Meyrink, Gustav 1868-1932
See Meyrink, Gustav
See also CA 117

Meyers, Jeffrey 1939- .... **CLC 39**
See also CA 73-76; DLB 111

Meynell, Alice (Christina Gertrude Thompson)
1847-1922 .... **TCLC 6**
See also CA 104; DLB 19, 98

Meyrink, Gustav .... **TCLC 21**
See also Meyer-Meyrink, Gustav
See also DLB 81

Michaels, Leonard 1933-........ **CLC 6, 25**
See also CA 61-64; CANR 21; DLB 130;
MTCW

Michaux, Henri 1899-1984 ...... **CLC 8, 19**
See also CA 85-88; 114

Michelangelo 1475-1564............ **LC 12**

Michelet, Jules 1798-1874 ...... **NCLC 31**

Michener, James A(lbert)
1907(?)- .... **CLC 1, 5, 11, 29, 60**
See also AITN 1; BEST 90:1; CA 5-8R;
CANR 21; DLB 6; MTCW

Mickiewicz, Adam 1798-1855 ..... **NCLC 3**

Middleton, Christopher 1926- ...... **CLC 13**
See also CA 13-16R; CANR 29; DLB 40

Middleton, Stanley 1919-........ **CLC 7, 38**
See also CA 25-28R; CANR 21; DLB 14

Migueis, Jose Rodrigues 1901-..... **CLC 10**

Mikszath, Kalman 1847-1910 ..... **TCLC 31**

Miles, Josephine
1911-1985 .... **CLC 1, 2, 14, 34, 39**
See also CA 1-4R; 116; CANR 2; DLB 48

Militant
See Sandburg, Carl (August)

Mill, John Stuart 1806-1873..... **NCLC 11**
See also CDBLB 1832-1890; DLB 55

Millar, Kenneth 1915-1983 .... **CLC 14**
See also Macdonald, Ross
See also CA 9-12R; 110; CANR 16; DLB 2;
DLBD 6; DLBY 83; MTCW

Millay, E. Vincent
See Millay, Edna St. Vincent

Millay, Edna St. Vincent
1892-1950 .... **TCLC 4, 49; PC 6**
See also CA 104; 130; CDALB 1917-1929;
DA; DLB 45; MTCW

Miller, Arthur
1915- .... **CLC 1, 2, 6, 10, 15, 26, 47, 78;**
DC 1
See also AITN 1; CA 1-4R; CABS 3;
CANR 2, 30; CDALB 1941-1968; DA;
DLB 7; MTCW; WLC

Miller, Henry (Valentine)
1891-1980 .... **CLC 1, 2, 4, 9, 14, 43**
See also CA 9-12R; 97-100; CANR 33;
CDALB 1929-1941; DA; DLB 4, 9;
DLBY 80; MTCW; WLC

Miller, Jason 1939(?)- .... **CLC 2**
See also AITN 1; CA 73-76; DLB 7

Miller, Sue 1943- .... **CLC 44**
See also BEST 90:3; CA 139

Miller, Walter M(ichael, Jr.)
1923- .... **CLC 4, 30**
See also CA 85-88; DLB 8

Millett, Kate 1934-................ **CLC 67**
See also AITN 1; CA 73-76; CANR 32;
MTCW

Millhauser, Steven 1943-....... **CLC 21, 54**
See also CA 110; 111; DLB 2

Millin, Sarah Gertrude 1889-1968 .. **CLC 49**
See also CA 102; 93-96

Milne, A(lan) A(lexander)
1882-1956 .... **TCLC 6**
See also CA 104; 133; CLR 1, 26; DLB 10,
77, 100; MAICYA; MTCW; YABC 1

Milner, Ron(ald) 1938-............ **CLC 56**
See also AITN 1; BLC 3; BW; CA 73-76;
CANR 24; DLB 38; MTCW

Milosz, Czeslaw
1911- .... **CLC 5, 11, 22, 31, 56**
See also CA 81-84; CANR 23; MTCW

Milton, John 1608-1674............. **LC 9**
See also CDBLB 1660-1789; DA; DLB 131;
WLC

Minehaha, Cornelius
See Wedekind, (Benjamin) Frank(lin)

Miner, Valerie 1947- .... **CLC 40**
See also CA 97-100

Minimo, Duca
See D'Annunzio, Gabriele

Minot, Susan 1956- .... **CLC 44**
See also CA 134

Minus, Ed 1938-................. **CLC 39**

Miranda, Javier
See Bioy Casares, Adolfo

Miro (Ferrer), Gabriel (Francisco Victor)
1879-1930 .... **TCLC 5**
See also CA 104

Mishima, Yukio
.... **CLC 2, 4, 6, 9, 27; DC 1; SSC 4**
See also Hiraoka, Kimitake

Mistral, Frederic 1830-1914 ...... **TCLC 51**
See also CA 122

Mistral, Gabriela.................. TCLC 2
See also Godoy Alcayaga, Lucila

Mistry, Rohinton 1952-........... **CLC 71**

Mitchell, Clyde
See Ellison, Harlan; Silverberg, Robert

Mitchell, James Leslie 1901-1935
See Gibbon, Lewis Grassic
See also CA 104; DLB 15

Mitchell, Joni 1943-.............. CLC 12
See also CA 112

Mitchell, Margaret (Munnerlyn)
1900-1949 .... TCLC 11
See also CA 109; 125; DLB 9; MTCW

Mitchell, Peggy
See Mitchell, Margaret (Munnerlyn)

Mitchell, S(ilas) Weir 1829-1914 .. TCLC 36

Mitchell, W(illiam) O(rmond)
1914- .... CLC 25
See also CA 77-80; CANR 15; DLB 88

Mitford, Mary Russell 1787-1855.. NCLC 4
See also DLB 110, 116

Mitford, Nancy 1904-1973........ CLC 44
See also CA 9-12R

Miyamoto, Yuriko 1899-1951 ..... TCLC 37

Mo, Timothy (Peter) 1950(?)-...... CLC 46
See also CA 117; MTCW

Modarressi, Taghi (M.) 1931-...... CLC 44
See also CA 121; 134

Modiano, Patrick (Jean) 1945-..... CLC 18
See also CA 85-88; CANR 17, 40; DLB 83

Moerck, Paal
See Roelvaag, O(le) E(dvart)

Mofolo, Thomas (Mokopu)
1875(?)-1948 .... TCLC 22
See also BLC 3; CA 121

Mohr, Nicholasa 1935-............ CLC 12
See also AAYA 8; CA 49-52; CANR 1, 32;
CLR 22; HW; SAAS 8; SATA 8

Mojtabai, A(nn) G(race)
1938- .... CLC 5, 9, 15, 29
See also CA 85-88

Moliere 1622-1673 .... LC 10
See also DA; WLC

Molin, Charles
See Mayne, William (James Carter)

Molnar, Ferenc 1878-1952....... TCLC 20
See also CA 109

Momaday, N(avarre) Scott
1934- .... CLC 2, 19
See also CA 25-28R; CANR 14, 34; DA;
MTCW; SATA 30, 48

Monroe, Harriet 1860-1936....... TCLC 12
See also CA 109; DLB 54, 91

Monroe, Lyle
See Heinlein, Robert A(nson)

Montagu, Elizabeth 1917-........ NCLC 7
See also CA 9-12R

Montagu, Mary (Pierrepont) Wortley
1689-1762 .... LC 9
See also DLB 95, 101

Montagu, W. H.
See Coleridge, Samuel Taylor

Montague, John (Patrick)
1929- .... CLC 13, 46
See also CA 9-12R; CANR 9; DLB 40;
MTCW

Montaigne, Michel (Eyquem) de
1533-1592 .... LC 8
See also DA; WLC

Montale, Eugenio 1896-1981... CLC 7, 9, 18
See also CA 17-20R; 104; CANR 30;
DLB 114; MTCW

Montesquieu, Charles-Louis de Secondat
1689-1755 .... LC 7

Montgomery, (Robert) Bruce 1921-1978
See Crispin, Edmund
See also CA 104

Montgomery, L(ucy) M(aud)
1874-1942 .... TCLC 51
See also CA 108; 137; CLR 8; DLB 92;
MAICYA; YABC 1

Montgomery, Marion H., Jr. 1925-.. CLC 7
See also AITN 1; CA 1-4R; CANR 3;
DLB 6

Montgomery, Max
See Davenport, Guy (Mattison, Jr.)

Montherlant, Henry (Milon) de
1896-1972 .... CLC 8, 19
See also CA 85-88; 37-40R; DLB 72;
MTCW

Monty Python .... CLC 21
See also Chapman, Graham; Cleese, John
(Marwood); Gilliam, Terry (Vance); Idle,
Eric; Jones, Terence Graham Parry; Palin,
Michael (Edward)
See also AAYA 7

Moodie, Susanna (Strickland)
1803-1885 .... NCLC 14
See also DLB 99

Mooney, Edward 1951-........... CLC 25
See also CA 130

Mooney, Ted
See Mooney, Edward

Moorcock, Michael (John)
1939- .... CLC 5, 27, 58
See also CA 45-48; CAAS 5; CANR 2, 17,
38; DLB 14; MTCW

Moore, Brian
1921- .... CLC 1, 3, 5, 7, 8, 19, 32
See also CA 1-4R; CANR 1, 25; MTCW

Moore, Edward
See Muir, Edwin

Moore, George Augustus
1852-1933 .... TCLC 7
See also CA 104; DLB 10, 18, 57

Moore, Lorrie .... CLC 39, 45, 68
See also Moore, Marie Lorena

Moore, Marianne (Craig)
1887-1972 .... CLC 1, 2, 4, 8, 10, 13, 19,
47; PC 4
See also CA 1-4R; 33-36R; CANR 3;
CDALB 1929-1941; DA; DLB 45;
DLBD 7; MTCW; SATA 20

Moore, Marie Lorena 1957-
See Moore, Lorrie
See also CA 116; CANR 39

Moore, Thomas 1779-1852........ NCLC 6
See also DLB 96

Morand, Paul 1888-1976.......... CLC 41
See also CA 69-72; DLB 65

Morante, Elsa 1918-1985........ CLC 8, 47
See also CA 85-88; 117; CANR 35; MTCW

Moravia, Alberto....... CLC 2, 7, 11, 27, 46
See also Pincherle, Alberto

More, Hannah 1745-1833 .... NCLC 27
See also DLB 107, 109, 116

More, Henry 1614-1687............ LC 9
See also DLB 126

More, Sir Thomas 1478-1535 .... LC 10

Moreas, Jean................... TCLC 18
See also Papadiamantopoulos, Johannes

Morgan, Berry 1919-.............. CLC 6
See also CA 49-52; DLB 6

Morgan, Claire
See Highsmith, (Mary) Patricia

Morgan, Edwin (George) 1920-..... CLC 31
See also CA 5-8R; CANR 3; DLB 27

Morgan, (George) Frederick
1922-...................... CLC 23
See also CA 17-20R; CANR 21

Morgan, Harriet
See Mencken, H(enry) L(ouis)

Morgan, Jane
See Cooper, James Fenimore

Morgan, Janet 1945- .... CLC 39
See also CA 65-68

Morgan, Lady 1776(?)-1859...... NCLC 29
See also DLB 116

Morgan, Robin 1941-.............. CLC 2
See also CA 69-72; CANR 29; MTCW

Morgan, Scott
See Kuttner, Henry

Morgan, Seth 1949(?)-1990 .... CLC 65
See also CA 132

Morgenstern, Christian
1871-1914 .... TCLC 8
See also CA 105

Morgenstern, S.
See Goldman, William (W.)

Moricz, Zsigmond 1879-1942 ..... TCLC 33

Morike, Eduard (Friedrich)
1804-1875 .... NCLC 10

Mori Ogai .... TCLC 14
See also Mori Rintaro

Mori Rintaro 1862-1922
See Mori Ogai
See also CA 110

Moritz, Karl Philipp 1756-1793 ...... LC 2
See also DLB 94

Morland, Peter Henry
See Faust, Frederick (Schiller)

Morren, Theophil
See Hofmannsthal, Hugo von

Morris, Bill 1952-................ CLC 76

Morris, Julian
See West, Morris L(anglo)

Morris, Steveland Judkins 1950(?)-
See Wonder, Stevie
See also CA 111

Morris, William 1834-1896 .... NCLC 4
See also CDBLB 1832-1890; DLB 18, 35, 57

Morris, Wright 1910-... CLC 1, 3, 7, 18, 37
See also CA 9-12R; CANR 21; DLB 2;
DLBY 81; MTCW

Morrison, Chloe Anthony Wofford
See Morrison, Toni

Morrison, James Douglas 1943-1971
See Morrison, Jim
See also CA 73-76; CANR 40

Morrison, Jim .... **CLC 17**
See also Morrison, James Douglas

Morrison, Toni 1931- ..... **CLC 4, 10, 22, 55**
See also AAYA 1; BLC 3; BW; CA 29-32R;
CANR 27; CDALB 1968-1988; DA;
DLB 6, 33; DLBY 81; MTCW; SATA 57

Morrison, Van 1945- .... **CLC 21**
See also CA 116

Mortimer, John (Clifford)
1923- .... **CLC 28, 43**
See also CA 13-16R; CANR 21;
CDBLB 1960 to Present; DLB 13;
MTCW

Mortimer, Penelope (Ruth) 1918- .... **CLC 5**
See also CA 57-60

Morton, Anthony
See Creasey, John

Mosher, Howard Frank 1943- ...... **CLC 62**
See also CA 139

Mosley, Nicholas 1923- .... **CLC 43, 70**
See also CA 69-72; CANR 41; DLB 14

Moss, Howard
1922-1987 .... **CLC 7, 14, 45, 50**
See also CA 1-4R; 123; CANR 1; DLB 5

Mossgiel, Rab
See Burns, Robert

Motion, Andrew 1952- .... **CLC 47**
See also DLB 40

Motley, Willard (Francis)
1912-1965 .... **CLC 18**
See also BW; CA 117; 106; DLB 76

Mott, Michael (Charles Alston)
1930- .... **CLC 15, 34**
See also CA 5-8R; CAAS 7; CANR 7, 29

Mowat, Farley (McGill) 1921- ..... **CLC 26**
See also AAYA 1; CA 1-4R; CANR 4, 24;
CLR 20; DLB 68; MAICYA; MTCW;
SATA 3, 55

Moyers, Bill 1934- .... **CLC 74**
See also AITN 2; CA 61-64; CANR 31

Mphahlele, Es'kia
See Mphahlele, Ezekiel
See also DLB 125

Mphahlele, Ezekiel 1919- .... **CLC 25**
See also Mphahlele, Es'kia
See also BLC 3; BW; CA 81-84; CANR 26

Mqhayi, S(amuel) E(dward) K(rune Loliwe)
1875-1945 .... **TCLC 25**
See also BLC 3

Mr. Martin
See Burroughs, William S(eward)

Mrozek, Slawomir 1930- .... **CLC 3, 13**
See also CA 13-16R; CAAS 10; CANR 29;
MTCW

Mrs. Belloc-Lowndes
See Lowndes, Marie Adelaide (Belloc)

Mtwa, Percy (?)- .... **CLC 47**

Mueller, Lisel 1924- .... **CLC 13, 51**
See also CA 93-96; DLB 105

Muir, Edwin 1887-1959 .... **TCLC 2**
See also CA 104; DLB 20, 100

Muir, John 1838-1914 .... **TCLC 28**

Mujica Lainez, Manuel
1910-1984 .... **CLC 31**
See also Lainez, Manuel Mujica
See also CA 81-84; 112; CANR 32; HW

Mukherjee, Bharati 1940- .... **CLC 53**
See also BEST 89:2; CA 107; DLB 60;
MTCW

Muldoon, Paul 1951- .... **CLC 32, 72**
See also CA 113; 129; DLB 40

Mulisch, Harry 1927- .... **CLC 42**
See also CA 9-12R; CANR 6, 26

Mull, Martin 1943- .... **CLC 17**
See also CA 105

Mulock, Dinah Maria
See Craik, Dinah Maria (Mulock)

Munford, Robert 1737(?)-1783 .... **LC 5**
See also DLB 31

Mungo, Raymond 1946- .... **CLC 72**
See also CA 49-52; CANR 2

Munro, Alice
1931- .... **CLC 6, 10, 19, 50; SSC 3**
See also AITN 2; CA 33-36R; CANR 33;
DLB 53; MTCW; SATA 29

Munro, H(ector) H(ugh) 1870-1916
See Saki
See also CA 104; 130; CDBLB 1890-1914;
DA; DLB 34; MTCW; WLC

Murasaki, Lady .... **CMLC 1**

Murdoch, (Jean) Iris
1919- ...... **CLC 1, 2, 3, 4, 6, 8, 11, 15,
22, 31, 51**
See also CA 13-16R; CANR 8;
CDBLB 1960 to Present; DLB 14;
MTCW

Murphy, Richard 1927- .... **CLC 41**
See also CA 29-32R; DLB 40

Murphy, Sylvia 1937- .... **CLC 34**
See also CA 121

Murphy, Thomas (Bernard) 1935-... **CLC 51**
See also CA 101

Murray, Albert L. 1916- .... **CLC 73**
See also BW; CA 49-52; CANR 26; DLB 38

Murray, Les(lie) A(llan) 1938- ..... **CLC 40**
See also CA 21-24R; CANR 11, 27

Murry, J. Middleton
See Murry, John Middleton

Murry, John Middleton
1889-1957 .... **TCLC 16**
See also CA 118

Musgrave, Susan 1951- .... **CLC 13, 54**
See also CA 69-72

Musil, Robert (Edler von)
1880-1942 .... **TCLC 12**
See also CA 109; DLB 81, 124

Musset, (Louis Charles) Alfred de
1810-1857 .... **NCLC 7**

My Brother's Brother
See Chekhov, Anton (Pavlovich)

Myers, Walter Dean 1937- .... **CLC 35**
See also AAYA 4; BLC 3; BW; CA 33-36R;
CANR 20; CLR 4, 16; DLB 33;
MAICYA; SAAS 2; SATA 27, 41, 70, 71

Myers, Walter M.
See Myers, Walter Dean

Myles, Symon
See Follett, Ken(neth Martin)

Nabokov, Vladimir (Vladimirovich)
1899-1977 ..... **CLC 1, 2, 3, 6, 8, 11, 15,
23, 44, 46, 64; SSC 11**
See also CA 5-8R; 69-72;
CDALB 1941-1968; DA; DLB 2;
DLBD 3; DLBY 80, 91; MTCW; WLC

Nagai Kafu .... **TCLC 51**
See also Nagai Sokichi

Nagai Sokichi 1879-1959
See Nagai Kafu
See also CA 117

Nagy, Laszlo 1925-1978 .... **CLC 7**
See also CA 129; 112

Naipaul, Shiva(dhar Srinivasa)
1945-1985 .... **CLC 32, 39**
See also CA 110; 112; 116; CANR 33;
DLBY 85; MTCW

Naipaul, V(idiadhar) S(urajprasad)
1932- .... **CLC 4, 7, 9, 13, 18, 37**
See also CA 1-4R; CANR 1, 33;
CDBLB 1960 to Present; DLB 125;
DLBY 85; MTCW

Nakos, Lilika 1899(?)- .... **CLC 29**

Narayan, R(asipuram) K(rishnaswami)
1906- .... **CLC 7, 28, 47**
See also CA 81-84; CANR 33; MTCW;
SATA 62

Nash, (Frediric) Ogden 1902-1971 .. **CLC 23**
See also CA 13-14; 29-32R; CANR 34;
CAP 1; DLB 11; MAICYA; MTCW;
SATA 2, 46

Nathan, Daniel
See Dannay, Frederic

Nathan, George Jean 1882-1958 ... **TCLC 18**
See also Hatteras, Owen
See also CA 114

Natsume, Kinnosuke 1867-1916
See Natsume, Soseki
See also CA 104

Natsume, Soseki .... **TCLC 2, 10**
See also Natsume, Kinnosuke

Natti, (Mary) Lee 1919-
See Kingman, Lee
See also CA 5-8R; CANR 2

Naylor, Gloria 1950- .... **CLC 28, 52**
See also AAYA 6; BLC 3; BW; CA 107;
CANR 27; DA; MTCW

Neihardt, John Gneisenau
1881-1973 .... **CLC 32**
See also CA 13-14; CAP 1; DLB 9, 54

Nekrasov, Nikolai Alekseevich
1821-1878 .... **NCLC 11**

Nelligan, Emile 1879-1941 .... **TCLC 14**
See also CA 114; DLB 92

Nelson, Willie 1933- .... **CLC 17**
See also CA 107

Nemerov, Howard (Stanley)
1920-1991 .... **CLC 2, 6, 9, 36**
See also CA 1-4R; 134; CABS 2; CANR 1,
27; DLB 6; DLBY 83; MTCW

Neruda, Pablo
    1904-1973 ..... **CLC 1, 2, 5, 7, 9, 28, 62;**
                                                PC 4
    See also CA 19-20; 45-48; CAP 2; DA; HW;
    MTCW; WLC

Nerval, Gerard de 1808-1855...... **NCLC 1**

Nervo, (Jose) Amado (Ruiz de)
    1870-1919 .... **TCLC 11**
    See also CA 109; 131; HW

Nessi, Pio Baroja y
    See Baroja (y Nessi), Pio

Neufeld, John (Arthur) 1938- ...... **CLC 17**
    See also CA 25-28R; CANR 11, 37;
    MAICYA; SAAS 3; SATA 6

Neville, Emily Cheney 1919-....... **CLC 12**
    See also CA 5-8R; CANR 3, 37; MAICYA;
    SAAS 2; SATA 1

Newbound, Bernard Slade 1930-
    See Slade, Bernard
    See also CA 81-84

Newby, P(ercy) H(oward)
    1918-..................... **CLC 2, 13**
    See also CA 5-8R; CANR 32; DLB 15;
    MTCW

Newlove, Donald 1928- .... **CLC 6**
    See also CA 29-32R; CANR 25

Newlove, John (Herbert) 1938-..... **CLC 14**
    See also CA 21-24R; CANR 9, 25

Newman, Charles 1938-.......... **CLC 2, 8**
    See also CA 21-24R

Newman, Edwin (Harold) 1919- .... **CLC 14**
    See also AITN 1; CA 69-72; CANR 5

Newman, John Henry
    1801-1890 .... **NCLC 38**
    See also DLB 18, 32, 55

Newton, Suzanne 1936- .... **CLC 35**
    See also CA 41-44R; CANR 14; SATA 5

Nexo, Martin Andersen
    1869-1954 .... **TCLC 43**

Nezval, Vitezslav 1900-1958 ...... **TCLC 44**
    See also CA 123

Ngema, Mbongeni 1955- .... **CLC 57**

Ngugi, James T(hiong'o)........ **CLC 3, 7, 13**
    See also Ngugi wa Thiong'o

Ngugi wa Thiong'o 1938-.......... **CLC 36**
    See also Ngugi, James T(hiong'o)
    See also BLC 3; BW; CA 81-84; CANR 27;
    DLB 125; MTCW

Nichol, B(arrie) P(hillip)
    1944-1988 .... **CLC 18**
    See also CA 53-56; DLB 53; SATA 66

Nichols, John (Treadwell) 1940- .... **CLC 38**
    See also CA 9-12R; CAAS 2; CANR 6;
    DLBY 82

Nichols, Leigh
    See Koontz, Dean R(ay)

Nichols, Peter (Richard)
    1927- .... **CLC 5, 36, 65**
    See also CA 104; CANR 33; DLB 13;
    MTCW

Nicolas, F. R. E.
    See Freeling, Nicolas

Niedecker, Lorine 1903-1970.... **CLC 10, 42**
    See also CA 25-28; CAP 2; DLB 48

Nietzsche, Friedrich (Wilhelm)
    1844-1900 .... **TCLC 10, 18**
    See also CA 107; 121; DLB 129

Nievo, Ippolito 1831-1861 ...... **NCLC 22**

Nightingale, Anne Redmon 1943-
    See Redmon, Anne
    See also CA 103

Nik.T.O.
    See Annensky, Innokenty Fyodorovich

Nin, Anais
    1903-1977 ...... **CLC 1, 4, 8, 11, 14, 60;**
                                            SSC 10
    See also AITN 2; CA 13-16R; 69-72;
    CANR 22; DLB 2, 4; MTCW

Nissenson, Hugh 1933-........... **CLC 4, 9**
    See also CA 17-20R; CANR 27; DLB 28

Niven, Larry .... **CLC 8**
    See also Niven, Laurence Van Cott
    See also DLB 8

Niven, Laurence Van Cott 1938-
    See Niven, Larry
    See also CA 21-24R; CAAS 12; CANR 14;
    MTCW

Nixon, Agnes Eckhardt 1927-...... **CLC 21**
    See also CA 110

Nizan, Paul 1905-1940........... **TCLC 40**
    See also DLB 72

Nkosi, Lewis 1936-.............. **CLC 45**
    See also BLC 3; BW; CA 65-68; CANR 27

Nodier, (Jean) Charles (Emmanuel)
    1780-1844 .... **NCLC 19**
    See also DLB 119

Nolan, Christopher 1965-.......... **CLC 58**
    See also CA 111

Norden, Charles
    See Durrell, Lawrence (George)

Nordhoff, Charles (Bernard)
    1887-1947 .... **TCLC 23**
    See also CA 108; DLB 9; SATA 23

Norfolk, Lawrence 1963-.......... **CLC 76**

Norman, Marsha 1947- .... **CLC 28**
    See also CA 105; CABS 3; CANR 41;
    DLBY 84

Norris, Benjamin Franklin, Jr.
    1870-1902 .... **TCLC 24**
    See also Norris, Frank
    See also CA 110

Norris, Frank
    See Norris, Benjamin Franklin, Jr.
    See also CDALB 1865-1917; DLB 12, 71

Norris, Leslie 1921-.............. **CLC 14**
    See also CA 11-12; CANR 14; CAP 1;
    DLB 27

North, Andrew
    See Norton, Andre

North, Anthony
    See Koontz, Dean R(ay)

North, Captain George
    See Stevenson, Robert Louis (Balfour)

North, Milou
    See Erdrich, Louise

Northrup, B. A.
    See Hubbard, L(afayette) Ron(ald)

North Staffs
    See Hulme, T(homas) E(rnest)

Norton, Alice Mary
    See Norton, Andre
    See also MAICYA; SATA 1, 43

Norton, Andre 1912- .... **CLC 12**
    See also Norton, Alice Mary
    See also CA 1-4R; CANR 2, 31; DLB 8, 52;
    MTCW

Norway, Nevil Shute 1899-1960
    See Shute, Nevil
    See also CA 102; 93-96

Norwid, Cyprian Kamil
    1821-1883 .... **NCLC 17**

Nosille, Nabrah
    See Ellison, Harlan

Nossack, Hans Erich 1901-1978 ..... **CLC 6**
    See also CA 93-96; 85-88; DLB 69

Nosu, Chuji
    See Ozu, Yasujiro

Nova, Craig 1945-............... **CLC 7, 31**
    See also CA 45-48; CANR 2

Novak, Joseph
    See Kosinski, Jerzy (Nikodem)

Novalis 1772-1801 .... **NCLC 13**
    See also DLB 90

Nowlan, Alden (Albert) 1933-1983 .. **CLC 15**
    See also CA 9-12R; CANR 5; DLB 53

Noyes, Alfred 1880-1958 .... **TCLC 7**
    See also CA 104; DLB 20

Nunn, Kem 19(?)-................ **CLC 34**

Nye, Robert 1939-............... **CLC 13, 42**
    See also CA 33-36R; CANR 29; DLB 14;
    MTCW; SATA 6

Nyro, Laura 1947-............... **CLC 17**

Oates, Joyce Carol
    1938- ...... **CLC 1, 2, 3, 6, 9, 11, 15, 19,**
                                 33, 52; SSC 6
    See also AITN 1; BEST 89:2; CA 5-8R;
    CANR 25; CDALB 1968-1988; DA;
    DLB 2, 5, 130; DLBY 81; MTCW; WLC

O'Brien, E. G.
    See Clarke, Arthur C(harles)

O'Brien, Edna
    1936- ... **CLC 3, 5, 8, 13, 36, 65; SSC 10**
    See also CA 1-4R; CANR 6, 41;
    CDBLB 1960 to Present; DLB 14;
    MTCW

O'Brien, Fitz-James 1828-1862... **NCLC 21**
    See also DLB 74

O'Brien, Flann........ **CLC 1, 4, 5, 7, 10, 47**
    See also O Nuallain, Brian

O'Brien, Richard 1942-........... **CLC 17**
    See also CA 124

O'Brien, Tim 1946-.......... **CLC 7, 19, 40**
    See also CA 85-88; CANR 40; DLBD 9;
    DLBY 80

Obstfelder, Sigbjoern 1866-1900... **TCLC 23**
    See also CA 123

O'Casey, Sean
    1880-1964 .... **CLC 1, 5, 9, 11, 15**
    See also CA 89-92; CDBLB 1914-1945;
    DLB 10; MTCW

O'Cathasaigh, Sean
See O'Casey, Sean

Ochs, Phil 1940-1976 . . . . CLC 17
See also CA 65-68

O'Connor, Edwin (Greene)
1918-1968 . . . . CLC 14
See also CA 93-96; 25-28R

O'Connor, (Mary) Flannery
1925-1964 . . . . CLC 1, 2, 3, 6, 10, 13, 15,
21, 66; SSC 1
See also AAYA 7; CA 1-4R; CANR 3, 41;
CDALB 1941-1968; DA; DLB 2;
DLBY 80; MTCW; WLC

O'Connor, Frank . . . . CLC 23; SSC 5
See also O'Donovan, Michael John

O'Dell, Scott 1898-1989 . . . . CLC 30
See also AAYA 3; CA 61-64; 129;
CANR 12, 30; CLR 1, 16; DLB 52;
MAICYA; SATA 12, 60

Odets, Clifford 1906-1963 . . . . . . CLC 2, 28
See also CA 85-88; DLB 7, 26; MTCW

O'Doherty, Brian 1934- . . . . CLC 76
See also CA 105

O'Donnell, K. M.
See Malzberg, Barry N(athaniel)

O'Donnell, Lawrence
See Kuttner, Henry

O'Donovan, Michael John
1903-1966 . . . . CLC 14
See also O'Connor, Frank
See also CA 93-96

Oe, Kenzaburo 1935- . . . . CLC 10, 36
See also CA 97-100; CANR 36; MTCW

O'Faolain, Julia 1932- . . . . CLC 6, 19, 47
See also CA 81-84; CAAS 2; CANR 12;
DLB 14; MTCW

O'Faolain, Sean
1900-1991 . . . . CLC 1, 7, 14, 32, 70
See also CA 61-64; 134; CANR 12;
DLB 15; MTCW

O'Flaherty, Liam
1896-1984 . . . . CLC 5, 34; SSC 6
See also CA 101; 113; CANR 35; DLB 36;
DLBY 84; MTCW

Ogilvy, Gavin
See Barrie, J(ames) M(atthew)

O'Grady, Standish James
1846-1928 . . . . TCLC 5
See also CA 104

O'Grady, Timothy 1951- . . . . CLC 59
See also CA 138

O'Hara, Frank
1926-1966 . . . . CLC 2, 5, 13, 78
See also CA 9-12R; 25-28R; CANR 33;
DLB 5, 16; MTCW

O'Hara, John (Henry)
1905-1970 . . . . CLC 1, 2, 3, 6, 11, 42
See also CA 5-8R; 25-28R; CANR 31;
CDALB 1929-1941; DLB 9, 86; DLBD 2;
MTCW

O Hehir, Diana 1922- . . . . CLC 41
See also CA 93-96

Okigbo, Christopher (Ifenayichukwu)
1932-1967 . . . . CLC 25; PC 7
See also BLC 3; BW; CA 77-80; DLB 125;
MTCW

Olds, Sharon 1942- . . . . CLC 32, 39
See also CA 101; CANR 18, 41; DLB 120

Oldstyle, Jonathan
See Irving, Washington

Olesha, Yuri (Karlovich)
1899-1960 . . . . CLC 8
See also CA 85-88

Oliphant, Margaret (Oliphant Wilson)
1828-1897 . . . . NCLC 11
See also DLB 18

Oliver, Mary 1935- . . . . CLC 19, 34
See also CA 21-24R; CANR 9; DLB 5

Olivier, Laurence (Kerr)
1907-1989 . . . . CLC 20
See also CA 111; 129

Olsen, Tillie 1913- . . . . . CLC 4, 13; SSC 11
See also CA 1-4R; CANR 1; DA; DLB 28;
DLBY 80; MTCW

Olson, Charles (John)
1910-1970 . . . . . CLC 1, 2, 5, 6, 9, 11, 29
See also CA 13-16; 25-28R; CABS 2;
CANR 35; CAP 1; DLB 5, 16; MTCW

Olson, Toby 1937- . . . . CLC 28
See also CA 65-68; CANR 9, 31

Olyesha, Yuri
See Olesha, Yuri (Karlovich)

Ondaatje, Michael
1943- . . . . CLC 14, 29, 51, 76
See also CA 77-80; DLB 60

Oneal, Elizabeth 1934-
See Oneal, Zibby
See also CA 106; CANR 28; MAICYA;
SATA 30

Oneal, Zibby . . . . CLC 30
See also Oneal, Elizabeth
See also AAYA 5; CLR 13

O'Neill, Eugene (Gladstone)
1888-1953 . . . . TCLC 1, 6, 27, 49
See also AITN 1; CA 110; 132;
CDALB 1929-1941; DA; DLB 7; MTCW;
WLC

Onetti, Juan Carlos 1909- . . . . CLC 7, 10
See also CA 85-88; CANR 32; DLB 113;
HW; MTCW

O Nuallain, Brian 1911-1966
See O'Brien, Flann
See also CA 21-22; 25-28R; CAP 2

Oppen, George 1908-1984 . . . . CLC 7, 13, 34
See also CA 13-16R; 113; CANR 8; DLB 5

Oppenheim, E(dward) Phillips
1866-1946 . . . . TCLC 45
See also CA 111; DLB 70

Orlovitz, Gil 1918-1973 . . . . CLC 22
See also CA 77-80; 45-48; DLB 2, 5

Orris
See Ingelow, Jean

Ortega y Gasset, Jose 1883-1955 . . . TCLC 9
See also CA 106; 130; HW; MTCW

Ortiz, Simon J(oseph) 1941- . . . . CLC 45
See also CA 134; DLB 120

Orton, Joe . . . . CLC 4, 13, 43; DC 3
See also Orton, John Kingsley
See also CDBLB 1960 to Present; DLB 13

Orton, John Kingsley 1933-1967
See Orton, Joe
See also CA 85-88; CANR 35; MTCW

Orwell, George . . . . TCLC 2, 6, 15, 31, 51
See also Blair, Eric (Arthur)
See also CDBLB 1945-1960; DLB 15, 98;
WLC

Osborne, David
See Silverberg, Robert

Osborne, George
See Silverberg, Robert

Osborne, John (James)
1929- . . . . CLC 1, 2, 5, 11, 45
See also CA 13-16R; CANR 21;
CDBLB 1945-1960; DA; DLB 13;
MTCW; WLC

Osborne, Lawrence 1958- . . . . CLC 50

Oshima, Nagisa 1932- . . . . CLC 20
See also CA 116; 121

Oskison, John M(ilton)
1874-1947 . . . . TCLC 35

Ossoli, Sarah Margaret (Fuller marchesa d')
1810-1850
See Fuller, Margaret
See also SATA 25

Ostrovsky, Alexander
1823-1886 . . . . NCLC 30

Otero, Blas de 1916- . . . . CLC 11
See also CA 89-92

Otto, Whitney 1955- . . . . CLC 70
See also CA 140

Ouida . . . . TCLC 43
See also De La Ramee, (Marie) Louise
See also DLB 18

Ousmane, Sembene 1923- . . . . CLC 66
See also BLC 3; BW; CA 117; 125; MTCW

Ovid 43B.C.-18th cent. (?) . . . CMLC 7; PC 2

Owen, Hugh
See Faust, Frederick (Schiller)

Owen, Wilfred 1893-1918 . . . . . . TCLC 5, 27
See also CA 104; CDBLB 1914-1945; DA;
DLB 20; WLC

Owens, Rochelle 1936- . . . . CLC 8
See also CA 17-20R; CAAS 2; CANR 39

Oz, Amos 1939- . . . CLC 5, 8, 11, 27, 33, 54
See also CA 53-56; CANR 27; MTCW

Ozick, Cynthia 1928- . . . . . . CLC 3, 7, 28, 62
See also BEST 90:1; CA 17-20R; CANR 23;
DLB 28; DLBY 82; MTCW

Ozu, Yasujiro 1903-1963 . . . . CLC 16
See also CA 112

Pacheco, C.
See Pessoa, Fernando (Antonio Nogueira)

Pa Chin
See Li Fei-kan

Pack, Robert 1929- . . . . CLC 13
See also CA 1-4R; CANR 3; DLB 5

Padgett, Lewis
See Kuttner, Henry

Padilla (Lorenzo), Heberto 1932- . . . CLC 38
See also AITN 1; CA 123; 131; HW

Page, Jimmy 1944-............. CLC 12

Page, Louise 1955-............. CLC 40
See also CA 140

Page, P(atricia) K(athleen)
1916- .... CLC 7, 18
See also CA 53-56; CANR 4, 22; DLB 68;
MTCW

Paget, Violet 1856-1935
See Lee, Vernon
See also CA 104

Paget-Lowe, Henry
See Lovecraft, H(oward) P(hillips)

Paglia, Camille (Anna) 1947-....... CLC 68
See also CA 140

Paige, Richard
See Koontz, Dean R(ay)

Pakenham, Antonia
See Fraser, Antonia (Pakenham)

Palamas, Kostes 1859-1943 .... TCLC 5
See also CA 105

Palazzeschi, Aldo 1885-1974 .... CLC 11
See also CA 89-92; 53-56; DLB 114

Paley, Grace 1922-.... CLC 4, 6, 37; SSC 8
See also CA 25-28R; CANR 13; DLB 28;
MTCW

Palin, Michael (Edward) 1943-..... CLC 21
See also Monty Python
See also CA 107; CANR 35; SATA 67

Palliser, Charles 1947-............ CLC 65
See also CA 136

Palma, Ricardo 1833-1919........ TCLC 29

Pancake, Breece Dexter 1952-1979
See Pancake, Breece D'J
See also CA 123; 109

Pancake, Breece D'J............... CLC 29
See also Pancake, Breece Dexter
See also DLB 130

Panko, Rudy
See Gogol, Nikolai (Vasilyevich)

Papadiamantis, Alexandros
1851-1911 .... TCLC 29

Papadiamantopoulos, Johannes 1856-1910
See Moreas, Jean
See also CA 117

Papini, Giovanni 1881-1956....... TCLC 22
See also CA 121

Paracelsus 1493-1541.............. LC 14

Parasol, Peter
See Stevens, Wallace

Parfenie, Maria
See Codrescu, Andrei

Parini, Jay (Lee) 1948- .... CLC 54
See also CA 97-100; CAAS 16; CANR 32

Park, Jordan
See Kornbluth, C(yril) M.; Pohl, Frederik

Parker, Bert
See Ellison, Harlan

Parker, Dorothy (Rothschild)
1893-1967 .... CLC 15, 68; SSC 2
See also CA 19-20; 25-28R; CAP 2;
DLB 11, 45, 86; MTCW

Parker, Robert B(rown) 1932-...... CLC 27
See also BEST 89:4; CA 49-52; CANR 1,
26; MTCW

Parkes, Lucas
See Harris, John (Wyndham Parkes Lucas)
Beynon

Parkin, Frank 1940-.............. CLC 43

Parkman, Francis, Jr.
1823-1893 .... NCLC 12
See also DLB 1, 30

Parks, Gordon (Alexander Buchanan)
1912- .... CLC 1, 16
See also AITN 2; BLC 3; BW; CA 41-44R;
CANR 26; DLB 33; SATA 8

Parnell, Thomas 1679-1718 .... LC 3
See also DLB 94

Parra, Nicanor 1914-.............. CLC 2
See also CA 85-88; CANR 32; HW; MTCW

Parrish, Mary Frances
See Fisher, M(ary) F(rances) K(ennedy)

Parson
See Coleridge, Samuel Taylor

Parson Lot
See Kingsley, Charles

Partridge, Anthony
See Oppenheim, E(dward) Phillips

Pascoli, Giovanni 1855-1912 ...... TCLC 45

Pasolini, Pier Paolo
1922-1975 .... CLC 20, 37
See also CA 93-96; 61-64; DLB 128;
MTCW

Pasquini
See Silone, Ignazio

Pastan, Linda (Olenik) 1932- ...... CLC 27
See also CA 61-64; CANR 18, 40; DLB 5

Pasternak, Boris (Leonidovich)
1890-1960 ..... CLC 7, 10, 18, 63; PC 6
See also CA 127; 116; DA; MTCW; WLC

Patchen, Kenneth 1911-1972 ... CLC 1, 2, 18
See also CA 1-4R; 33-36R; CANR 3, 35;
DLB 16, 48; MTCW

Pater, Walter (Horatio)
1839-1894 .... NCLC 7
See also CDBLB 1832-1890; DLB 57

Paterson, A(ndrew) B(arton)
1864-1941 .... TCLC 32

Paterson, Katherine (Womeldorf)
1932- .... CLC 12, 30
See also AAYA 1; CA 21-24R; CANR 28;
CLR 7; DLB 52; MAICYA; MTCW;
SATA 13, 53

Patmore, Coventry Kersey Dighton
1823-1896 .... NCLC 9
See also DLB 35, 98

Paton, Alan (Stewart)
1903-1988 .... CLC 4, 10, 25, 55
See also CA 13-16; 125; CANR 22; CAP 1;
DA; MTCW; SATA 11, 56; WLC

Paton Walsh, Gillian 1937-
See Walsh, Jill Paton
See also CANR 38; MAICYA; SAAS 3;
SATA 4, 72

Paulding, James Kirke 1778-1860.. NCLC 2
See also DLB 3, 59, 74

Paulin, Thomas Neilson 1949-
See Paulin, Tom
See also CA 123; 128

Paulin, Tom..................... CLC 37
See also Paulin, Thomas Neilson
See also DLB 40

Paustovsky, Konstantin (Georgievich)
1892-1968 .... CLC 40
See also CA 93-96; 25-28R

Pavese, Cesare 1908-1950 .... TCLC 3
See also CA 104; DLB 128

Pavic, Milorad 1929- .... CLC 60
See also CA 136

Paync, Alan
See Jakes, John (William)

Paz, Gil
See Lugones, Leopoldo

Paz, Octavio
1914- .... CLC 3, 4, 6, 10, 19, 51, 65;
PC 1
See also CA 73-76; CANR 32; DA;
DLBY 90; HW; MTCW; WLC

Peacock, Molly 1947-............. CLC 60
See also CA 103; DLB 120

Peacock, Thomas Love
1785-1866 .... NCLC 22
See also DLB 96, 116

Peake, Mervyn 1911-1968 .... CLC 7, 54
See also CA 5-8R; 25-28R; CANR 3;
DLB 15; MTCW; SATA 23

Pearce, Philippa .... CLC 21
See also Christie, (Ann) Philippa
See also CLR 9; MAICYA; SATA 1, 67

Pearl, Eric
See Elman, Richard

Pearson, T(homas) R(eid) 1956- .... CLC 39
See also CA 120; 130

Peck, John 1941- .... CLC 3
See also CA 49-52; CANR 3

Peck, Richard (Wayne) 1934- ...... CLC 21
See also AAYA 1; CA 85-88; CANR 19,
38; MAICYA; SAAS 2; SATA 18, 55

Peck, Robert Newton 1928-........ CLC 17
See also AAYA 3; CA 81-84; CANR 31;
DA; MAICYA; SAAS 1; SATA 21, 62

Peckinpah, (David) Sam(uel)
1925-1984 .... CLC 20
See also CA 109; 114

Pedersen, Knut 1859-1952
See Hamsun, Knut
See also CA 104; 119; MTCW

Peeslake, Gaffer
See Durrell, Lawrence (George)

Peguy, Charles Pierre
1873-1914 .... TCLC 10
See also CA 107

Pena, Ramon del Valle y
See Valle-Inclan, Ramon (Maria) del

Pendennis, Arthur Esquir
See Thackeray, William Makepeace

Pepys, Samuel 1633-1703.......... LC 11
See also CDBLB 1660-1789; DA; DLB 101;
WLC

Polanski, Roman 1933- .... CLC 16
See also CA 77-80

Poliakoff, Stephen 1952- .... CLC 38
See also CA 106; DLB 13

Police, The...................... CLC 26
See also Copeland, Stewart (Armstrong);
Summers, Andrew James; Sumner,
Gordon Matthew

Pollitt, Katha 1949- .... CLC 28
See also CA 120; 122; MTCW

Pollock, Sharon 1936- .... CLC 50
See also DLB 60

Pomerance, Bernard 1940-........ CLC 13
See also CA 101

Ponge, Francis (Jean Gaston Alfred)
1899-1988 .... CLC 6, 18
See also CA 85-88; 126; CANR 40

Pontoppidan, Henrik 1857-1943 ... TCLC 29

Poole, Josephine .... CLC 17
See also Helyar, Jane Penelope Josephine
See also SAAS 2; SATA 5

Popa, Vasko 1922- .... CLC 19
See also CA 112

Pope, Alexander 1688-1744.......... LC 3
See also CDBLB 1660-1789; DA; DLB 95,
101; WLC

Porter, Connie 1960- .... CLC 70

Porter, Gene(va Grace) Stratton
1863(?)-1924 .... TCLC 21
See also CA 112

Porter, Katherine Anne
1890-1980 ...... CLC 1, 3, 7, 10, 13, 15,
27; SSC 4
See also AITN 2; CA 1-4R; 101; CANR 1;
DA; DLB 4, 9, 102; DLBY 80; MTCW;
SATA 23, 39

Porter, Peter (Neville Frederick)
1929- .... CLC 5, 13, 33
See also CA 85-88; DLB 40

Porter, William Sydney 1862-1910
See Henry, O.
See also CA 104; 131; CDALB 1865-1917;
DA; DLB 12, 78, 79; MTCW; YABC 2

Portillo (y Pacheco), Jose Lopez
See Lopez Portillo (y Pacheco), Jose

Post, Melville Davisson
1869-1930 .... TCLC 39
See also CA 110

Potok, Chaim 1929- .... CLC 2, 7, 14, 26
See also AITN 1, 2; CA 17-20R; CANR 19,
35; DLB 28; MTCW; SATA 33

Potter, Beatrice
See Webb, (Martha) Beatrice (Potter)
See also MAICYA

Potter, Dennis (Christopher George)
1935- .... CLC 58
See also CA 107; CANR 33; MTCW

Pound, Ezra (Weston Loomis)
1885-1972 ...... CLC 1, 2, 3, 4, 5, 7, 10,
13, 18, 34, 48, 50; PC 4
See also CA 5-8R; 37-40R; CANR 40;
CDALB 1917-1929; DA; DLB 4, 45, 63;
MTCW; WLC

Povod, Reinaldo 1959-............ CLC 44
See also CA 136

Powell, Anthony (Dymoke)
1905- .... CLC 1, 3, 7, 9, 10, 31
See also CA 1-4R; CANR 1, 32;
CDBLB 1945-1960; DLB 15; MTCW

Powell, Dawn 1897-1965 .... CLC 66
See also CA 5-8R

Powell, Padgett 1952-............. CLC 34
See also CA 126

Powers, J(ames) F(arl)
1917- .... CLC 1, 4, 8, 57; SSC 4
See also CA 1-4R; CANR 2; DLB 130;
MTCW

Powers, John J(ames) 1945-
See Powers, John R.
See also CA 69-72

Powers, John R. .... CLC 66
See also Powers, John J(ames)

Pownall, David 1938-............. CLC 10
See also CA 89-92; DLB 14

Powys, John Cowper
1872-1963 .... CLC 7, 9, 15, 46
See also CA 85-88; DLB 15; MTCW

Powys, T(heodore) F(rancis)
1875-1953 .... TCLC 9
See also CA 106; DLB 36

Prager, Emily 1952-.............. CLC 56

Pratt, Edwin John 1883-1964 ...... CLC 19
See also CA 93-96; DLB 92

Premchand...................... TCLC 21
See also Srivastava, Dhanpat Rai

Preussler, Otfried 1923-.......... CLC 17
See also CA 77-80; SATA 24

Prevert, Jacques (Henri Marie)
1900-1977 .... CLC 15
See also CA 77-80; 69-72; CANR 29;
MTCW; SATA 30

Prevost, Abbe (Antoine Francois)
1697-1763 .... LC 1

Price, (Edward) Reynolds
1933- .... CLC 3, 6, 13, 43, 50, 63
See also CA 1-4R; CANR 1, 37; DLB 2

Price, Richard 1949- .... CLC 6, 12
See also CA 49-52; CANR 3; DLBY 81

Prichard, Katharine Susannah
1883-1969 .... CLC 46
See also CA 11-12; CANR 33; CAP 1;
MTCW; SATA 66

Priestley, J(ohn) B(oynton)
1894-1984 .... CLC 2, 5, 9, 34
See also CA 9-12R; 113; CANR 33;
CDBLB 1914-1945; DLB 10, 34, 77, 100;
DLBY 84; MTCW

Prince 1958(?)- .... CLC 35

Prince, F(rank) T(empleton) 1912-.. CLC 22
See also CA 101; DLB 20

Prince Kropotkin
See Kropotkin, Peter (Aleksieevich)

Prior, Matthew 1664-1721.......... LC 4
See also DLB 95

Pritchard, William H(arrison)
1932- .... CLC 34
See also CA 65-68; CANR 23; DLB 111

Pritchett, V(ictor) S(awdon)
1900- .... CLC 5, 13, 15, 41
See also CA 61-64; CANR 31; DLB 15;
MTCW

Private 19022
See Manning, Frederic

Probst, Mark 1925- .... CLC 59
See also CA 130

Prokosch, Frederic 1908-1989.... CLC 4, 48
See also CA 73-76; 128; DLB 48

Prophet, The
See Dreiser, Theodore (Herman Albert)

Prose, Francine 1947-............. CLC 45
See also CA 109; 112

Proudhon
See Cunha, Euclides (Rodrigues Pimenta) da

Proust, (Valentin-Louis-George-Eugene-)
Marcel 1871-1922 .... TCLC 7, 13, 33
See also CA 104; 120; DA; DLB 65;
MTCW; WLC

Prowler, Harley
See Masters, Edgar Lee

Prus, Boleslaw................... TCLC 48
See also Glowacki, Aleksander

Pryor, Richard (Franklin Lenox Thomas)
1940- .... CLC 26
See also CA 122

Przybyszewski, Stanislaw
1868-1927 .... TCLC 36
See also DLB 66

Pteleon
See Grieve, C(hristopher) M(urray)

Puckett, Lute
See Masters, Edgar Lee

Puig, Manuel
1932-1990 .... CLC 3, 5, 10, 28, 65
See also CA 45-48; CANR 2, 32; DLB 113;
HW; MTCW

Purdy, A(lfred) W(ellington)
1918- .... CLC 3, 6, 14, 50
See also Purdy, Al
See also CA 81-84

Purdy, Al
See Purdy, A(lfred) W(ellington)
See also CAAS 17; DLB 88

Purdy, James (Amos)
1923- .... CLC 2, 4, 10, 28, 52
See also CA 33-36R; CAAS 1; CANR 19;
DLB 2; MTCW

Pure, Simon
See Swinnerton, Frank Arthur

Pushkin, Alexander (Sergeyevich)
1799-1837 .... NCLC 3, 27
See also DA; SATA 61; WLC

P'u Sung-ling 1640-1715 .... LC 3

Putnam, Arthur Lee
See Alger, Horatio, Jr.

Puzo, Mario 1920-......... CLC 1, 2, 6, 36
See also CA 65-68; CANR 4; DLB 6;
MTCW

Pym, Barbara (Mary Crampton)
1913-1980 .... CLC 13, 19, 37
See also CA 13-14; 97-100; CANR 13, 34;
CAP 1; DLB 14; DLBY 87; MTCW

Pynchon, Thomas (Ruggles, Jr.)
1937- .. CLC **2, 3, 6, 9, 11, 18, 33, 62, 72**
See also BEST 90:2; CA 17-20R; CANR 22;
DA; DLB 2; MTCW; WLC

Qian Zhongshu
See Ch'ien Chung-shu

Qroll
See Dagerman, Stig (Halvard)

Quarrington, Paul (Lewis) 1953-.... CLC **65**
See also CA 129

Quasimodo, Salvatore 1901-1968 ... CLC **10**
See also CA 13-16; 25-28R; CAP 1;
DLB 114; MTCW

Queen, Ellery.................... CLC **3, 11**
See also Dannay, Frederic; Davidson,
Avram; Lee, Manfred B(ennington);
Sturgeon, Theodore (Hamilton); Vance,
John Holbrook

Queen, Ellery, Jr.
See Dannay, Frederic; Lee, Manfred
B(ennington)

Queneau, Raymond
1903-1976 .... CLC **2, 5, 10, 42**
See also CA 77-80; 69-72; CANR 32;
DLB 72; MTCW

Quevedo, Francisco de 1580-1645.... LC **23**

Quin, Ann (Marie) 1936-1973 .... CLC **6**
See also CA 9-12R; 45-48; DLB 14

Quinn, Martin
See Smith, Martin Cruz

Quinn, Simon
See Smith, Martin Cruz

Quiroga, Horacio (Sylvestre)
1878-1937 .... TCLC **20**
See also CA 117; 131; HW; MTCW

Quoirez, Francoise 1935-........... CLC **9**
See also Sagan, Francoise
See also CA 49-52; CANR 6, 39; MTCW

Raabe, Wilhelm 1831-1910 .... TCLC **45**
See also DLB 129

Rabe, David (William) 1940-... CLC **4, 8, 33**
See also CA 85-88; CABS 3; DLB 7

Rabelais, Francois 1483-1553 .... LC **5**
See also DA; WLC

Rabinovitch, Sholem 1859-1916
See Aleichem, Sholom
See also CA 104

Radcliffe, Ann (Ward) 1764-1823 .. NCLC **6**
See also DLB 39

Radiguet, Raymond 1903-1923 .... TCLC **29**
See also DLB 65

Radnoti, Miklos 1909-1944 .... TCLC **16**
See also CA 118

Rado, James 1939-............... CLC **17**
See also CA 105

Radvanyi, Netty 1900-1983
See Seghers, Anna
See also CA 85-88; 110

Raeburn, John (Hay) 1941-........ CLC **34**
See also CA 57-60

Ragni, Gerome 1942-1991 .... CLC **17**
See also CA 105; 134

Rahv, Philip..................... CLC **24**
See also Greenberg, Ivan

Raine, Craig 1944-............... CLC **32**
See also CA 108; CANR 29; DLB 40

Raine, Kathleen (Jessie) 1908- ... CLC **7, 45**
See also CA 85-88; DLB 20; MTCW

Rainis, Janis 1865-1929......... TCLC **29**

Rakosi, Carl..................... CLC **47**
See also Rawley, Callman
See also CAAS 5

Raleigh, Richard
See Lovecraft, H(oward) P(hillips)

Rallentando, H. P.
See Sayers, Dorothy L(eigh)

Ramal, Walter
See de la Mare, Walter (John)

Ramon, Juan
See Jimenez (Mantecon), Juan Ramon

Ramos, Graciliano 1892-1953 ..... TCLC **32**

Rampersad, Arnold 1941-.......... CLC **44**
See also CA 127; 133; DLB 111

Rampling, Anne
See Rice, Anne

Ramuz, Charles-Ferdinand
1878-1947 .... TCLC **33**

Rand, Ayn 1905-1982........ CLC **3, 30, 44**
See also AAYA 10; CA 13-16R; 105;
CANR 27; DA; MTCW; WLC

Randall, Dudley (Felker) 1914-...... CLC **1**
See also BLC 3; BW; CA 25-28R;
CANR 23; DLB 41

Randall, Robert
See Silverberg, Robert

Ranger, Ken
See Creasey, John

Ransom, John Crowe
1888-1974 .... CLC **2, 4, 5, 11, 24**
See also CA 5-8R; 49-52; CANR 6, 34;
DLB 45, 63; MTCW

Rao, Raja 1909-.............. CLC **25, 56**
See also CA 73-76; MTCW

Raphael, Frederic (Michael)
1931-..................... CLC **2, 14**
See also CA 1-4R; CANR 1; DLB 14

Ratcliffe, James P.
See Mencken, H(enry) L(ouis)

Rathbone, Julian 1935- .... CLC **41**
See also CA 101; CANR 34

Rattigan, Terence (Mervyn)
1911-1977 .... CLC **7**
See also CA 85-88; 73-76;
CDBLB 1945-1960; DLB 13; MTCW

Ratushinskaya, Irina 1954- .... CLC **54**
See also CA 129

Raven, Simon (Arthur Noel)
1927-..................... CLC **14**
See also CA 81-84

Rawley, Callman 1903-
See Rakosi, Carl
See also CA 21-24R; CANR 12, 32

Rawlings, Marjorie Kinnan
1896-1953 .... TCLC **4**
See also CA 104; 137; DLB 9, 22, 102;
MAICYA; YABC 1

Ray, Satyajit 1921-1992........ CLC **16, 76**
See also CA 114; 137

Read, Herbert Edward 1893-1968.... CLC **4**
See also CA 85-88; 25-28R; DLB 20

Read, Piers Paul 1941- ...... CLC **4, 10, 25**
See also CA 21-24R; CANR 38; DLB 14;
SATA 21

Reade, Charles 1814-1884 .... NCLC **2**
See also DLB 21

Reade, Hamish
See Gray, Simon (James Holliday)

Reading, Peter 1946-............. CLC **47**
See also CA 103; DLB 40

Reaney, James 1926-............. CLC **13**
See also CA 41-44R; CAAS 15; DLB 68;
SATA 43

Rebreanu, Liviu 1885-1944 .... TCLC **28**

Rechy, John (Francisco)
1934-................CLC **1, 7, 14, 18**
See also CA 5-8R; CAAS 4; CANR 6, 32;
DLB 122; DLBY 82; HW

Redcam, Tom 1870-1933 .... TCLC **25**

Reddin, Keith..................... CLC **67**

Redgrove, Peter (William)
1932-.................... CLC **6, 41**
See also CA 1-4R; CANR 3, 39; DLB 40

Redmon, Anne..................... CLC **22**
See also Nightingale, Anne Redmon
See also DLBY 86

Reed, Eliot
See Ambler, Eric

Reed, Ishmuel
1938-........ CLC **2, 3, 5, 6, 13, 32, 60**
See also BLC 3; BW; CA 21-24R;
CANR 25; DLB 2, 5, 33; DLBD 8;
MTCW

Reed, John (Silas) 1887-1920 ...... TCLC **9**
See also CA 106

Reed, Lou....................... CLC **21**
See also Firbank, Louis

Reeve, Clara 1729-1807 .... NCLC **19**
See also DLB 39

Reid, Christopher (John) 1949-..... CLC **33**
See also CA 140; DLB 40

Reid, Desmond
See Moorcock, Michael (John)

Reid Banks, Lynne 1929-
See Banks, Lynne Reid
See also CA 1-4R; CANR 6, 22, 38;
CLR 24; MAICYA; SATA 22

Reilly, William K.
See Creasey, John

Reiner, Max
See Caldwell, (Janet Miriam) Taylor
(Holland)

Reis, Ricardo
See Pessoa, Fernando (Antonio Nogueira)

Remarque, Erich Maria
1898-1970 .... CLC **21**
See also CA 77-80; 29-32R; DA; DLB 56;
MTCW

Remizov, A.
See Remizov, Aleksei (Mikhailovich)

Remizov, A. M.
See Remizov, Aleksei (Mikhailovich)

Remizov, Aleksei (Mikhailovich)
    1877-1957 .... **TCLC 27**
    See also CA 125; 133

Renan, Joseph Ernest
    1823-1892 .... **NCLC 26**

Renard, Jules 1864-1910 .... **TCLC 17**
    See also CA 117

Renault, Mary .... **CLC 3, 11, 17**
    See also Challans, Mary
    See also DLBY 83

Rendell, Ruth (Barbara) 1930- .. **CLC 28, 48**
    See also Vine, Barbara
    See also CA 109; CANR 32; DLB 87;
    MTCW

Renoir, Jean 1894-1979 .... **CLC 20**
    See also CA 129; 85-88

Resnais, Alain 1922- .... **CLC 16**

Reverdy, Pierre 1889-1960 .... **CLC 53**
    See also CA 97-100; 89-92

Rexroth, Kenneth
    1905-1982 ...... **CLC 1, 2, 6, 11, 22, 49**
    See also CA 5-8R; 107; CANR 14, 34;
    CDALB 1941-1968; DLB 16, 48;
    DLBY 82; MTCW

Reyes, Alfonso 1889-1959 .... **TCLC 33**
    See also CA 131; HW

Reyes y Basoalto, Ricardo Eliecer Neftali
    See Neruda, Pablo

Reymont, Wladyslaw (Stanislaw)
    1868(?)-1925 .... **TCLC 5**
    See also CA 104

Reynolds, Jonathan 1942- .... **CLC 6, 38**
    See also CA 65-68; CANR 28

Reynolds, Joshua 1723-1792 .... **LC 15**
    See also DLB 104

Reynolds, Michael Shane 1937- .... **CLC 44**
    See also CA 65-68; CANR 9

Reznikoff, Charles 1894-1976 .... **CLC 9**
    See also CA 33-36; 61-64; CAP 2; DLB 28,
    45

Rezzori (d'Arezzo), Gregor von
    1914- .... **CLC 25**
    See also CA 122; 136

Rhine, Richard
    See Silverstein, Alvin

R'hoone
    See Balzac, Honore de

Rhys, Jean
    1890(?)-1979 .... **CLC 2, 4, 6, 14, 19, 51**
    See also CA 25-28R; 85-88; CANR 35;
    CDBLB 1945-1960; DLB 36, 117; MTCW

Ribeiro, Darcy 1922- .... **CLC 34**
    See also CA 33-36R

Ribeiro, Joao Ubaldo (Osorio Pimentel)
    1941- .... **CLC 10, 67**
    See also CA 81-84

Ribman, Ronald (Burt) 1932- .... **CLC 7**
    See also CA 21-24R

Ricci, Nino 1959- .... **CLC 70**
    See also CA 137

Rice, Anne 1941- .... **CLC 41**
    See also AAYA 9; BEST 89:2; CA 65-68;
    CANR 12, 36

Rice, Elmer (Leopold)
    1892-1967 .... **CLC 7, 49**
    See also CA 21-22; 25-28R; CAP 2; DLB 4,
    7; MTCW

Rice, Tim 1944- .... **CLC 21**
    See also CA 103

Rich, Adrienne (Cecile)
    1929- .... **CLC 3, 6, 7, 11, 18, 36, 73, 76;
    PC 5**
    See also CA 9-12R; CANR 20; DLB 5, 67;
    MTCW

Rich, Barbara
    See Graves, Robert (von Ranke)

Rich, Robert
    See Trumbo, Dalton

Richards, David Adams 1950- ...... **CLC 59**
    See also CA 93-96; DLB 53

Richards, I(vor) A(rmstrong)
    1893-1979 .... **CLC 14, 24**
    See also CA 41-44R; 89-92; CANR 34;
    DLB 27

Richardson, Anne
    See Roiphe, Anne Richardson

Richardson, Dorothy Miller
    1873-1957 .... **TCLC 3**
    See also CA 104; DLB 36

Richardson, Ethel Florence (Lindesay)
    1870-1946
    See Richardson, Henry Handel
    See also CA 105

Richardson, Henry Handel .... **TCLC 4**
    See also Richardson, Ethel Florence
    (Lindesay)

Richardson, Samuel 1689-1761 .... **LC 1**
    See also CDBLB 1660-1789; DA; DLB 39;
    WLC

Richler, Mordecai
    1931- .... **CLC 3, 5, 9, 13, 18, 46, 70**
    See also AITN 1; CA 65-68; CANR 31;
    CLR 17; DLB 53; MAICYA; MTCW;
    SATA 27, 44

Richter, Conrad (Michael)
    1890-1968 .... **CLC 30**
    See also CA 5-8R; 25-28R; CANR 23;
    DLB 9; MTCW; SATA 3

Riddell, J. H. 1832-1906 .... **TCLC 40**

Riding, Laura .... **CLC 3, 7**
    See also Jackson, Laura (Riding)

Riefenstahl, Berta Helene Amalia 1902-
    See Riefenstahl, Leni
    See also CA 108

Riefenstahl, Leni .... **CLC 16**
    See also Riefenstahl, Berta Helene Amalia

Riffe, Ernest
    See Bergman, (Ernst) Ingmar

Riley, James Whitcomb
    1849-1916 .... **TCLC 51**
    See also CA 118; 137; MAICYA; SATA 17

Riley, Tex
    See Creasey, John

Rilke, Rainer Maria
    1875-1926 .... **TCLC 1, 6, 19; PC 2**
    See also CA 104; 132; DLB 81; MTCW

Rimbaud, (Jean Nicolas) Arthur
    1854-1891 .... **NCLC 4, 35; PC 3**
    See also DA; WLC

Ringmaster, The
    See Mencken, H(enry) L(ouis)

Ringwood, Gwen(dolyn Margaret) Pharis
    1910-1984 .... **CLC 48**
    See also CA 112; DLB 88

Rio, Michel 19(?)- .... **CLC 43**

Ritsos, Giannes
    See Ritsos, Yannis

Ritsos, Yannis 1909-1990 ..... **CLC 6, 13, 31**
    See also CA 77-80; 133; CANR 39; MTCW

Ritter, Erika 1948(?)- .... **CLC 52**

Rivera, Jose Eustasio 1889-1928... **TCLC 35**
    See also HW

Rivers, Conrad Kent 1933-1968...... **CLC 1**
    See also BW; CA 85-88; DLB 41

Rivers, Elfrida
    See Bradley, Marion Zimmer

Riverside, John
    See Heinlein, Robert A(nson)

Rizal, Jose 1861-1896 .... **NCLC 27**

Roa Bastos, Augusto (Antonio)
    1917- .... **CLC 45**
    See also CA 131; DLB 113; HW

Robbe-Grillet, Alain
    1922- ...... **CLC 1, 2, 4, 6, 8, 10, 14, 43**
    See also CA 9-12R; CANR 33; DLB 83;
    MTCW

Robbins, Harold 1916- .... **CLC 5**
    See also CA 73-76; CANR 26; MTCW

Robbins, Thomas Eugene 1936-
    See Robbins, Tom
    See also CA 81-84; CANR 29; MTCW

Robbins, Tom .... **CLC 9, 32, 64**
    See also Robbins, Thomas Eugene
    See also BEST 90:3; DLBY 80

Robbins, Trina 1938- .... **CLC 21**
    See also CA 128

Roberts, Charles G(eorge) D(ouglas)
    1860-1943 .... **TCLC 8**
    See also CA 105; DLB 92; SATA 29

Roberts, Kate 1891-1985 .... **CLC 15**
    See also CA 107; 116

Roberts, Keith (John Kingston)
    1935- .... **CLC 14**
    See also CA 25-28R

Roberts, Kenneth (Lewis)
    1885-1957 .... **TCLC 23**
    See also CA 109; DLB 9

Roberts, Michele (B.) 1949- .... **CLC 48**
    See also CA 115

Robertson, Ellis
    See Ellison, Harlan; Silverberg, Robert

Robertson, Thomas William
    1829-1871 .... **NCLC 35**

Robinson, Edwin Arlington
    1869-1935 .... **TCLC 5; PC 1**
    See also CA 104; 133; CDALB 1865-1917;
    DA; DLB 54; MTCW

Robinson, Henry Crabb
    1775-1867 .... **NCLC 15**
    See also DLB 107

Tabori, George 1914-............ **CLC 19**
See also CA 49-52; CANR 4

Tagore, Rabindranath 1861-1941.... **TCLC 3**
See also CA 104; 120; MTCW

Taine, Hippolyte Adolphe
1828-1893 .... **NCLC 15**

Talese, Gay 1932-................ **CLC 37**
See also AITN 1; CA 1-4R; CANR 9;
MTCW

Tallent, Elizabeth (Ann) 1954- ..... **CLC 45**
See also CA 117; DLB 130

Tally, Ted 1952-................. **CLC 42**
See also CA 120; 124

Tamayo y Baus, Manuel
1829-1898 .... **NCLC 1**

Tammsaare, A(nton) H(ansen)
1878-1940 .... **TCLC 27**

Tan, Amy 1952- .... **CLC 59**
See also AAYA 9; BEST 89:3; CA 136

Tandem, Felix
See Spitteler, Carl (Friedrich Georg)

Tanizaki, Jun'ichiro
1886-1965 .... **CLC 8, 14, 28**
See also CA 93-96; 25-28R

Tanner, William
See Amis, Kingsley (William)

Tao Lao
See Storni, Alfonsina

Tarassoff, Lev
See Troyat, Henri

Tarbell, Ida M(inerva)
1857-1944 .... **TCLC 40**
See also CA 122; DLB 47

Tarkington, (Newton) Booth
1869-1946 .... **TCLC 9**
See also CA 110; DLB 9, 102; SATA 17

Tarkovsky, Andrei (Arsenyevich)
1932-1986 .... **CLC 75**
See also CA 127

Tartt, Donna 1964(?)-............. **CLC 76**

Tasso, Torquato 1544-1595 .... **LC 5**

Tate, (John Orley) Allen
1899-1979 .... **CLC 2, 4, 6, 9, 11, 14, 24**
See also CA 5-8R; 85-88; CANR 32;
DLB 4, 45, 63; MTCW

Tate, Ellalice
See Hibbert, Eleanor Alice Burford

Tate, James (Vincent) 1943- ... **CLC 2, 6, 25**
See also CA 21-24R; CANR 29; DLB 5

Tavel, Ronald 1940-............... **CLC 6**
See also CA 21-24R; CANR 33

Taylor, Cecil Philip 1929-1981 ..... **CLC 27**
See also CA 25-28R; 105

Taylor, Edward 1642(?)-1729........ **LC 11**
See also DA; DLB 24

Taylor, Eleanor Ross 1920-........ **CLC 5**
See also CA 81-84

Taylor, Elizabeth 1912-1975 ... **CLC 2, 4, 29**
See also CA 13-16R; CANR 9; MTCW;
SATA 13

Taylor, Henry (Splawn) 1942-...... **CLC 44**
See also CA 33-36R; CAAS 7; CANR 31;
DLB 5

Taylor, Kamala (Purnaiya) 1924-
See Markandaya, Kamala
See also CA 77-80

Taylor, Mildred D. .... **CLC 21**
See also AAYA 10; BW; CA 85-88;
CANR 25; CLR 9; DLB 52; MAICYA;
SAAS 5; SATA 15, 70

Taylor, Peter (Hillsman)
1917- ...... **CLC 1, 4, 18, 37, 44, 50, 71;**
SSC 10
See also CA 13-16R; CANR 9; DLBY 81;
MTCW

Taylor, Robert Lewis 1912-........ **CLC 14**
See also CA 1-4R; CANR 3; SATA 10

Tchekhov, Anton
See Chekhov, Anton (Pavlovich)

Teasdale, Sara 1884-1933......... **TCLC 4**
See also CA 104; DLB 45; SATA 32

Tegner, Esaias 1782-1846........ **NCLC 2**

Teilhard de Chardin, (Marie Joseph) Pierre
1881-1955 .... **TCLC 9**
See also CA 105

Temple, Ann
See Mortimer, Penelope (Ruth)

Tennant, Emma (Christina)
1937- .... **CLC 13, 52**
See also CA 65-68; CAAS 9; CANR 10, 38;
DLB 14

Tenneshaw, S. M.
See Silverberg, Robert

Tennyson, Alfred
1809-1892 .... **NCLC 30; PC 6**
See also CDBLB 1832-1890; DA; DLB 32;
WLC

Teran, Lisa St. Aubin de .... **CLC 36**
See also St. Aubin de Teran, Lisa

Teresa de Jesus, St. 1515-1582...... **LC 18**

Terkel, Louis 1912-
See Terkel, Studs
See also CA 57-60; CANR 18; MTCW

Terkel, Studs .... **CLC 38**
See also Terkel, Louis
See also AITN 1

Terry, C. V.
See Slaughter, Frank G(ill)

Terry, Megan 1932-............. **CLC 19**
See also CA 77-80; CABS 3; DLB 7

Tertz, Abram
See Sinyavsky, Andrei (Donatevich)

Tesich, Steve 1943(?)-.......... **CLC 40, 69**
See also CA 105; DLBY 83

Teternikov, Fyodor Kuzmich 1863-1927
See Sologub, Fyodor
See also CA 104

Tevis, Walter 1928-1984 .... **CLC 42**
See also CA 113

Tey, Josephine................... **TCLC 14**
See also Mackintosh, Elizabeth
See also DLB 77

Thackeray, William Makepeace
1811-1863 .... **NCLC 5, 14, 22**
See also CDBLB 1832-1890; DA; DLB 21,
55; SATA 23; WLC

Thakura, Ravindranatha
See Tagore, Rabindranath

Tharoor, Shashi 1956-............ **CLC 70**

Thelwell, Michael Miles 1939-..... **CLC 22**
See also CA 101

Theobald, Lewis, Jr.
See Lovecraft, H(oward) P(hillips)

The Prophet
See Dreiser, Theodore (Herman Albert)

Theroux, Alexander (Louis)
1939- .... **CLC 2, 25**
See also CA 85-88; CANR 20

Theroux, Paul (Edward)
1941- .... **CLC 5, 8, 11, 15, 28, 46**
See also BEST 89:4; CA 33-36R; CANR 20;
DLB 2; MTCW; SATA 44

Thesen, Sharon 1946-............. **CLC 56**

Thevenin, Denis
See Duhamel, Georges

Thibault, Jacques Anatole Francois
1844-1924
See France, Anatole
See also CA 106; 127; MTCW

Thiele, Colin (Milton) 1920- .... **CLC 17**
See also CA 29-32R; CANR 12, 28;
CLR 27; MAICYA; SAAS 2; SATA 14,
72

Thomas, Audrey (Callahan)
1935- .... **CLC 7, 13, 37**
See also AITN 2; CA 21-24R; CANR 36;
DLB 60; MTCW

Thomas, D(onald) M(ichael)
1935- .... **CLC 13, 22, 31**
See also CA 61-64; CAAS 11; CANR 17;
CDBLB 1960 to Present; DLB 40;
MTCW

Thomas, Dylan (Marlais)
1914-1953 .... **TCLC 1, 8, 45; PC 2;**
SSC 3
See also CA 104; 120; CDBLB 1945-1960;
DA; DLB 13, 20; MTCW; SATA 60;
WLC

Thomas, (Philip) Edward
1878-1917 .... **TCLC 10**
See also CA 106; DLB 19

Thomas, Joyce Carol 1938-........ **CLC 35**
See also BW; CA 113; 116; CLR 19;
DLB 33; MAICYA; MTCW; SAAS 7;
SATA 40

Thomas, Lewis 1913-............. **CLC 35**
See also CA 85-88; CANR 38; MTCW

Thomas, Paul
See Mann, (Paul) Thomas

Thomas, Piri 1928-............... **CLC 17**
See also CA 73-76; HW

Thomas, R(onald) S(tuart)
1913- .... **CLC 6, 13, 48**
See also CA 89-92; CAAS 4; CANR 30;
CDBLB 1960 to Present; DLB 27;
MTCW

Thomas, Ross (Elmore) 1926-...... **CLC 39**
See also CA 33-36R; CANR 22

Thompson, Francis Clegg
See Mencken, H(enry) L(ouis)

Thompson, Francis Joseph
1859-1907 .... TCLC 4
See also CA 104; CDBLB 1890-1914;
DLB 19

Thompson, Hunter S(tockton)
1939- .... CLC 9, 17, 40
See also BEST 89:1; CA 17-20R; CANR 23;
MTCW

Thompson, Jim 1906-1977(?) ...... CLC 69

Thompson, Judith .... CLC 39

Thomson, James 1700-1748 .... LC 16

Thomson, James 1834-1882 ..... NCLC 18

Thoreau, Henry David
1817-1862 .... NCLC 7, 21
See also CDALB 1640-1865; DA; DLB 1;
WLC

Thornton, Hall
See Silverberg, Robert

Thurber, James (Grover)
1894-1961 .... CLC 5, 11, 25; SSC 1
See also CA 73-76; CANR 17, 39;
CDALB 1929-1941; DA; DLB 4, 11, 22,
102; MAICYA; MTCW; SATA 13

Thurman, Wallace (Henry)
1902-1934 .... TCLC 6
See also BLC 3; BW; CA 104; 124; DLB 51

Ticheburn, Cheviot
See Ainsworth, William Harrison

Tieck, (Johann) Ludwig
1773-1853 .... NCLC 5
See also DLB 90

Tiger, Derry
See Ellison, Harlan

Tilghman, Christopher 1948(?)- ..... CLC 65

Tillinghast, Richard (Williford)
1940- .... CLC 29
See also CA 29-32R; CANR 26

Timrod, Henry 1828-1867 .... NCLC 25
See also DLB 3

Tindall, Gillian 1938- .... CLC 7
See also CA 21-24R; CANR 11

Tiptree, James, Jr. .... CLC 48, 50
See also Sheldon, Alice Hastings Bradley
See also DLB 8

Titmarsh, Michael Angelo
See Thackeray, William Makepeace

Tocqueville, Alexis (Charles Henri Maurice
Clerel Comte) 1805-1859 ..... NCLC 7

Tolkien, J(ohn) R(onald) R(euel)
1892-1973 ...... CLC 1, 2, 3, 8, 12, 38
See also AAYA 10; AITN 1; CA 17-18;
45-48; CANR 36; CAP 2;
CDBLB 1914-1945; DA; DLB 15;
MAICYA; MTCW; SATA 2, 24, 32;
WLC

Toller, Ernst 1893-1939 .... TCLC 10
See also CA 107; DLB 124

Tolson, M. B.
See Tolson, Melvin B(eaunorus)

Tolson, Melvin B(eaunorus)
1898(?)-1966 .... CLC 36
See also BLC 3; BW; CA 124; 89-92;
DLB 48, 76

Tolstoi, Aleksei Nikolaevich
See Tolstoy, Alexey Nikolaevich

Tolstoy, Alexey Nikolaevich
1882-1945 .... TCLC 18
See also CA 107

Tolstoy, Count Leo
See Tolstoy, Leo (Nikolaevich)

Tolstoy, Leo (Nikolaevich)
1828-1910 ...... TCLC 4, 11, 17, 28, 44;
SSC 9
See also CA 104; 123; DA; SATA 26; WLC

Tomasi di Lampedusa, Giuseppe 1896-1957
See Lampedusa, Giuseppe (Tomasi) di
See also CA 111

Tomlin, Lily .... CLC 17
See also Tomlin, Mary Jean

Tomlin, Mary Jean 1939(?)-
See Tomlin, Lily
See also CA 117

Tomlinson, (Alfred) Charles
1927- .... CLC 2, 4, 6, 13, 45
See also CA 5-8R; CANR 33; DLB 40

Tonson, Jacob
See Bennett, (Enoch) Arnold

Toole, John Kennedy
1937-1969 .... CLC 19, 64
See also CA 104; DLBY 81

Toomer, Jean
1894-1967 ...... CLC 1, 4, 13, 22; PC 7;
SSC 1
See also BLC 3; BW; CA 85-88;
CDALB 1917-1929; DLB 45, 51; MTCW

Torley, Luke
See Blish, James (Benjamin)

Tornimparte, Alessandra
See Ginzburg, Natalia

Torre, Raoul della
See Mencken, H(enry) L(ouis)

Torrey, E(dwin) Fuller 1937- .... CLC 34
See also CA 119

Torsvan, Ben Traven
See Traven, B.

Torsvan, Benno Traven
See Traven, B.

Torsvan, Berick Traven
See Traven, B.

Torsvan, Berwick Traven
See Traven, B.

Torsvan, Bruno Traven
See Traven, B.

Torsvan, Traven
See Traven, B.

Tournier, Michel (Edouard)
1924- .... CLC 6, 23, 36
See also CA 49-52; CANR 3, 36; DLB 83;
MTCW; SATA 23

Tournimparte, Alessandra
See Ginzburg, Natalia

Towers, Ivar
See Kornbluth, C(yril) M.

Townsend, Sue 1946- .... CLC 61
See also CA 119; 127; MTCW; SATA 48,
55

Townshend, Peter (Dennis Blandford)
1945- .... CLC 17, 42
See also CA 107

Tozzi, Federigo 1883-1920 .... TCLC 31

Traill, Catharine Parr
1802-1899 .... NCLC 31
See also DLB 99

Trakl, Georg 1887-1914 .... TCLC 5
See also CA 104

Transtroemer, Tomas (Goesta)
1931- .... CLC 52, 65
See also CA 117; 129; CAAS 17

Transtromer, Tomas Gosta
See Transtroemer, Tomas (Goesta)

Traven, B. (?)-1969 .... CLC 8, 11
See also CA 19-20; 25-28R; CAP 2; DLB 9,
56; MTCW

Treitel, Jonathan 1959- .... CLC 70

Tremain, Rose 1943- .... CLC 42
See also CA 97-100; DLB 14

Tremblay, Michel 1942- .... CLC 29
See also CA 116; 128; DLB 60; MTCW

Trevanian (a pseudonym) 1930(?)- ... CLC 29
See also CA 108

Trevor, Glen
See Hilton, James

Trevor, William
1928- .... CLC 7, 9, 14, 25, 71
See also Cox, William Trevor
See also DLB 14

Trifonov, Yuri (Valentinovich)
1925-1981 .... CLC 45
See also CA 126; 103; MTCW

Trilling, Lionel 1905-1975 .... CLC 9, 11, 24
See also CA 9-12R; 61-64; CANR 10;
DLB 28, 63; MTCW

Trimball, W. H.
See Mencken, H(enry) L(ouis)

Tristan
See Gomez de la Serna, Ramon

Tristram
See Housman, A(lfred) E(dward)

Trogdon, William (Lewis) 1939-
See Heat-Moon, William Least
See also CA 115; 119

Trollope, Anthony 1815-1882 .. NCLC 6, 33
See also CDBLB 1832-1890; DA; DLB 21,
57; SATA 22; WLC

Trollope, Frances 1779-1863 ..... NCLC 30
See also DLB 21

Trotsky, Leon 1879-1940 .... TCLC 22
See also CA 118

Trotter (Cockburn), Catharine
1679-1749 .... LC 8
See also DLB 84

Trout, Kilgore
See Farmer, Philip Jose

Trow, George W. S. 1943- .... CLC 52
See also CA 126

Troyat, Henri 1911- .... CLC 23
See also CA 45-48; CANR 2, 33; MTCW

Trudeau, G(arretson) B(eekman) 1948-
See Trudeau, Garry B.
See also CA 81-84; CANR 31; SATA 35

Trudeau, Garry B.................. CLC 12
See also Trudeau, G(arretson) B(eekman)
See also AAYA 10; AITN 2

Truffaut, Francois 1932-1984....... CLC 20
See also CA 81-84; 113; CANR 34

Trumbo, Dalton 1905-1976 .... CLC 19
See also CA 21-24R; 69-72; CANR 10;
DLB 26

Trumbull, John 1750-1831....... NCLC 30
' See also DLB 31

Trundlett, Helen B.
See Eliot, T(homas) S(tearns)

Tryon, Thomas 1926-1991 ...... CLC 3, 11
See also AITN 1; CA 29-32R; 135;
CANR 32; MTCW

Tryon, Tom
See Tryon, Thomas

Ts'ao Hsueh-ch'in 1715(?)-1763....... LC 1

Tsushima, Shuji 1909-1948
See Dazai, Osamu
See also CA 107

Tsvetaeva (Efron), Marina (Ivanovna)
1892-1941 .... TCLC 7, 35
See also CA 104; 128; MTCW

Tuck, Lily 1938-................. CLC 70
See also CA 139

Tunis, John R(oberts) 1889-1975 ... CLC 12
See also CA 61-64; DLB 22; MAICYA;
SATA 30, 37

Tuohy, Frank..................... CLC 37
See also Tuohy, John Francis
See also DLB 14

Tuohy, John Francis 1925-
See Tuohy, Frank
See also CA 5-8R; CANR 3

Turco, Lewis (Putnam) 1934- ... CLC 11, 63
See also CA 13-16R; CANR 24; DLBY 84

Turgenev, Ivan
1818-1883 .... NCLC 21; SSC 7
See also DA; WLC

Turner, Frederick 1943-........... CLC 48
See also CA 73-76; CAAS 10; CANR 12,
30; DLB 40

Tusan, Stan 1936-............... CLC 22
See also CA 105

Tutuola, Amos 1920- .... CLC 5, 14, 29
See also BLC 3; BW; CA 9-12R; CANR 27;
DLB 125; MTCW

Twain, Mark
.... TCLC 6, 12, 19, 36, 48; SSC 6
See also Clemens, Samuel Langhorne
See also DLB 11, 12, 23, 64, 74; WLC

Tyler, Anne
1941- .... CLC 7, 11, 18, 28, 44, 59
See also BEST 89:1; CA 9-12R; CANR 11,
33; DLB 6; DLBY 82; MTCW; SATA 7

Tyler, Royall 1757-1826......... NCLC 3
See also DLB 37

Tynan, Katharine 1861-1931 .... TCLC 3
See also CA 104

Tytell, John 1939- .... CLC 50
See also CA 29-32R

Tyutchev, Fyodor 1803-1873 ..... NCLC 34

Tzara, Tristan .... CLC 47
See also Rosenfeld, Samuel

Uhry, Alfred 1936-.............. CLC 55
See also CA 127; 133

Ulf, Haerved
See Strindberg, (Johan) August

Ulf, Harved
See Strindberg, (Johan) August

Unamuno (y Jugo), Miguel de
1864-1936 .... TCLC 2, 9; SSC 11
See also CA 104; 131; DLB 108; HW;
MTCW

Undercliffe, Errol
See Campbell, (John) Ramsey

Underwood, Miles
See Glassco, John

Undset, Sigrid 1882-1949......... TCLC 3
See also CA 104; 129; DA; MTCW; WLC

Ungaretti, Giuseppe
1888-1970 .... CLC 7, 11, 15
See also CA 19-20; 25-28R; CAP 2;
DLB 114

Unger, Douglas 1952-............. CLC 34
See also CA 130

Unsworth, Barry (Forster) 1930-.... CLC 76
See also CA 25-28R; CANR 30

Updike, John (Hoyer)
1932- ...... CLC 1, 2, 3, 5, 7, 9, 13, 15,
23, 34, 43, 70
See also CA 1-4R; CABS 1; CANR 4, 33;
CDALB 1968-1988; DA; DLB 2, 5;
DLBD 3; DLBY 80, 82; MTCW; WLC

Upshaw, Margaret Mitchell
See Mitchell, Margaret (Munnerlyn)

Upton, Mark
See Sanders, Lawrence

Urdang, Constance (Henriette)
1922-...................... CLC 47
See also CA 21-24R; CANR 9, 24

Uriel, Henry
See Faust, Frederick (Schiller)

Uris, Leon (Marcus) 1924-....... CLC 7, 32
See also AITN 1, 2; BEST 89:2; CA 1-4R;
CANR 1, 40; MTCW; SATA 49

Urmuz
See Codrescu, Andrei

Ustinov, Peter (Alexander) 1921- .... CLC 1
See also AITN 1; CA 13-16R; CANR 25;
DLB 13

v
See Chekhov, Anton (Pavlovich)

Vaculik, Ludvik 1926- .... CLC 7
See also CA 53-56

Valenzuela, Luisa 1938-........... CLC 31
See also CA 101; CANR 32; DLB 113; HW

Valera y Alcala-Galiano, Juan
1824-1905 .... TCLC 10
See also CA 106

Valery, (Ambroise) Paul (Toussaint Jules)
1871-1945 .... TCLC 4, 15
See also CA 104; 122; MTCW

Valle-Inclan, Ramon (Maria) del
1866-1936 .... TCLC 5
See also CA 106

Vallejo, Antonio Buero
See Buero Vallejo, Antonio

Vallejo, Cesar (Abraham)
1892-1938 .... TCLC 3
See also CA 105; HW

Valle Y Pena, Ramon del
See Valle-Inclan, Ramon (Maria) del

Van Ash, Cay 1918-.............. CLC 34

Vanbrugh, Sir John 1664-1726 ...... LC 21
See also DLB 80

Van Campen, Karl
See Campbell, John W(ood, Jr.)

Vance, Gerald
See Silverberg, Robert

Vance, Jack .... CLC 35
See also Vance, John Holbrook
See also DLB 8

Vance, John Holbrook 1916-
See Queen, Ellery; Vance, Jack
See also CA 29-32R; CANR 17; MTCW

**Van Den Bogarde, Derek Jules Gaspard Ulric
Niven** 1921-
See Bogarde, Dirk
See also CA 77-80

Vandenburgh, Jane .... CLC 59

Vanderhaeghe, Guy 1951- .... CLC 41
See also CA 113

van der Post, Laurens (Jan) 1906- ... CLC 5
See also CA 5-8R; CANR 35

van de Wetering, Janwillem 1931- ... CLC 47
See also CA 49-52; CANR 4

Van Dine, S. S. .... TCLC 23
See also Wright, Willard Huntington

Van Doren, Carl (Clinton)
1885-1950 .... TCLC 18
See also CA 111

Van Doren, Mark 1894-1972..... CLC 6, 10
See also CA 1-4R; 37-40R; CANR 3;
DLB 45; MTCW

Van Druten, John (William)
1901-1957 .... TCLC 2
See also CA 104; DLB 10

Van Duyn, Mona (Jane)
1921- .... CLC 3, 7, 63
See also CA 9-12R; CANR 7, 38; DLB 5

Van Dyne, Edith
See Baum, L(yman) Frank

van Itallie, Jean-Claude 1936-....... CLC 3
See also CA 45-48; CAAS 2; CANR 1;
DLB 7

van Ostaijen, Paul 1896-1928 ..... TCLC 33

Van Peebles, Melvin 1932- ...... CLC 2, 20
See also BW; CA 85-88; CANR 27

Vansittart, Peter 1920-............ CLC 42
See also CA 1-4R; CANR 3

Van Vechten, Carl 1880-1964 ...... CLC 33
See also CA 89-92; DLB 4, 9, 51

Van Vogt, A(lfred) E(lton) 1912-..... CLC 1
See also CA 21-24R; CANR 28; DLB 8;
SATA 14

Vara, Madeleine
See Jackson, Laura (Riding)

Varda, Agnes 1928- . . . . CLC 16
See also CA 116; 122

Vargas Llosa, (Jorge) Mario (Pedro)
1936- . . . . CLC 3, 6, 9, 10, 15, 31, 42
See also CA 73-76; CANR 18, 32; DA;
HW; MTCW

Vasiliu, Gheorghe 1881-1957
See Bacovia, George
See also CA 123

Vassa, Gustavus
See Equiano, Olaudah

Vassilikos, Vassilis 1933- . . . . CLC 4, 8
See also CA 81-84

Vaughn, Stephanie . . . . CLC 62

Vazov, Ivan (Minchov)
1850-1921 . . . . TCLC 25
See also CA 121

Veblen, Thorstein (Bunde)
1857-1929 . . . . TCLC 31
See also CA 115

Vega, Lope de 1562-1635 . . . . LC 23

Venison, Alfred
See Pound, Ezra (Weston Loomis)

Verdi, Marie de
See Mencken, H(enry) L(ouis)

Verdu, Matilde
See Cela, Camilo Jose

Verga, Giovanni (Carmelo)
1840-1922 . . . . TCLC 3
See also CA 104; 123

Vergil 70B.C.-19B.C. . . . . CMLC 9
See also DA

Verhaeren, Emile (Adolphe Gustave)
1855-1916 . . . . TCLC 12
See also CA 109

Verlaine, Paul (Marie)
1844-1896 . . . . NCLC 2; PC 2

Verne, Jules (Gabriel) 1828-1905 . . . TCLC 6
See also CA 110; 131; DLB 123; MAICYA;
SATA 21

Very, Jones 1813-1880 . . . . NCLC 9
See also DLB 1

Vesaas, Tarjei 1897-1970 . . . . CLC 48
See also CA 29-32R

Vialis, Gaston
See Simenon, Georges (Jacques Christian)

Vian, Boris 1920-1959 . . . . TCLC 9
See also CA 106; DLB 72

Viaud, (Louis Marie) Julien 1850-1923
See Loti, Pierre
See also CA 107

Vicar, Henry
See Felsen, Henry Gregor

Vicker, Angus
See Felsen, Henry Gregor

Vidal, Gore
1925- . . . . . CLC 2, 4, 6, 8, 10, 22, 33, 72
See also AITN 1; BEST 90:2; CA 5-8R;
CANR 13; DLB 6; MTCW

Viereck, Peter (Robert Edwin)
1916- . . . . CLC 4
See also CA 1-4R; CANR 1; DLB 5

Vigny, Alfred (Victor) de
1797-1863 . . . . NCLC 7
See also DLB 119

Vilakazi, Benedict Wallet
1906-1947 . . . . TCLC 37

Villiers de l'Isle Adam, Jean Marie Mathias
Philippe Auguste Comte
1838-1889 . . . . NCLC 3
See also DLB 123

Vincent, Gabrielle a pseudonym . . . . . . CLC 13
See also CA 126; CLR 13; MAICYA;
SATA 61

Vinci, Leonardo da 1452-1519 . . . . . . LC 12

Vine, Barbara . . . . CLC 50
See also Rendell, Ruth (Barbara)
See also BEST 90:4

Vinge, Joan D(ennison) 1948- . . . . . . CLC 30
See also CA 93-96; SATA 36

Violis, G.
See Simenon, Georges (Jacques Christian)

Visconti, Luchino 1906-1976 . . . . CLC 16
See also CA 81-84; 65-68; CANR 39

Vittorini, Elio 1908-1966 . . . . . . CLC 6, 9, 14
See also CA 133; 25-28R

Vizinczey, Stephen 1933- . . . . CLC 40
See also CA 128

Vliet, R(ussell) G(ordon)
1929-1984 . . . . CLC 22
See also CA 37-40R; 112; CANR 18

Vogau, Boris Andreyevich 1894-1937(?)
See Pilnyak, Boris
See also CA 123

Vogel, Paula A(nne) 1951- . . . . CLC 76
See also CA 108

Voight, Ellen Bryant 1943- . . . . CLC 54
See also CA 69-72; CANR 11, 29; DLB 120

Voigt, Cynthia 1942- . . . . CLC 30
See also AAYA 3; CA 106; CANR 18, 37,
40; CLR 13; MAICYA; SATA 33, 48

Voinovich, Vladimir (Nikolaevich)
1932- . . . . CLC 10, 49
See also CA 81-84; CAAS 12; CANR 33;
MTCW

Voltaire 1694-1778 . . . . LC 14; SSC 12
See also DA; WLC

von Daeniken, Erich 1935- . . . . CLC 30
See also von Daniken, Erich
See also AITN 1; CA 37-40R; CANR 17

von Daniken, Erich . . . . CLC 30
See also von Daeniken, Erich

von Heidenstam, (Carl Gustaf) Verner
See Heidenstam, (Carl Gustaf) Verner von

von Heyse, Paul (Johann Ludwig)
See Heyse, Paul (Johann Ludwig von)

von Hofmannsthal, Hugo
See Hofmannsthal, Hugo von

von Horvath, Odon
See Horvath, Oedoen von

von Horvath, Oedoen
See Horvath, Oedoen von

von Liliencron, (Friedrich Adolf Axel) Detlev
See Liliencron, (Friedrich Adolf Axel)
Detlev von

Vonnegut, Kurt, Jr.
1922- . . . . . . CLC 1, 2, 3, 4, 5, 8, 12, 22,
40, 60; SSC 8
See also AAYA 6; AITN 1; BEST 90:4;
CA 1-4R; CANR 1, 25;
CDALB 1968-1988; DA; DLB 2, 8;
DLBD 3; DLBY 80; MTCW; WLC

Von Rachen, Kurt
See Hubbard, L(afayette) Ron(ald)

von Rezzori (d'Arezzo), Gregor
See Rezzori (d'Arezzo), Gregor von

von Sternberg, Josef
See Sternberg, Josef von

Vorster, Gordon 1924- . . . . CLC 34
See also CA 133

Vosce, Trudie
See Ozick, Cynthia

Voznesensky, Andrei (Andreievich)
1933- . . . . CLC 1, 15, 57
See also CA 89-92; CANR 37; MTCW

Waddington, Miriam 1917- . . . . CLC 28
See also CA 21-24R; CANR 12, 30;
DLB 68

Wagman, Fredrica 1937- . . . . CLC 7
See also CA 97-100

Wagner, Richard 1813-1883 . . . . . . NCLC 9
See also DLB 129

Wagner-Martin, Linda 1936- . . . . CLC 50

Wagoner, David (Russell)
1926- . . . . CLC 3, 5, 15
See also CA 1-4R; CAAS 3; CANR 2;
DLB 5; SATA 14

Wah, Fred(erick James) 1939- . . . . . . CLC 44
See also CA 107; DLB 60

Wahloo, Per 1926-1975 . . . . CLC 7
See also CA 61-64

Wahloo, Peter
See Wahloo, Per

Wain, John (Barrington)
1925- . . . . CLC 2, 11, 15, 46
See also CA 5-8R; CAAS 4; CANR 23;
CDBLB 1960 to Present; DLB 15, 27;
MTCW

Wajda, Andrzej 1926- . . . . CLC 16
See also CA 102

Wakefield, Dan 1932- . . . . CLC 7
See also CA 21-24R; CAAS 7

Wakoski, Diane
1937- . . . . CLC 2, 4, 7, 9, 11, 40
See also CA 13-16R; CAAS 1; CANR 9;
DLB 5

Wakoski-Sherbell, Diane
See Wakoski, Diane

Walcott, Derek (Alton)
1930- . . . . CLC 2, 4, 9, 14, 25, 42, 67, 76
See also BLC 3; BW; CA 89-92; CANR 26;
DLB 117; DLBY 81; MTCW

Waldman, Anne 1945- . . . . CLC 7
See also CA 37-40R; CAAS 17; CANR 34;
DLB 16

Waldo, E. Hunter
See Sturgeon, Theodore (Hamilton)

Waldo, Edward Hamilton
See Sturgeon, Theodore (Hamilton)

Walker, Alice (Malsenior)
1944- .... **CLC 5, 6, 9, 19, 27, 46, 58;**
SSC 5
See also AAYA 3; BEST 89:4; BLC 3; BW;
CA 37-40R; CANR 9, 27;
CDALB 1968-1988; DA; DLB 6, 33;
MTCW; SATA 31

Walker, David Harry 1911-1992.... **CLC 14**
See also CA 1-4R; 137; CANR 1; SATA 8;
SATA-Obit 71

Walker, Edward Joseph 1934-
See Walker, Ted
See also CA 21-24R; CANR 12, 28

Walker, George F. 1947- .... **CLC 44, 61**
See also CA 103; CANR 21; DLB 60

Walker, Joseph A. 1935- .... **CLC 19**
See also BW; CA 89-92; CANR 26; DLB 38

Walker, Margaret (Abigail)
1915- .... **CLC 1, 6**
See also BLC 3; BW; CA 73-76; CANR 26;
DLB 76; MTCW

Walker, Ted .... **CLC 13**
See also Walker, Edward Joseph
See also DLB 40

Wallace, David Foster 1962- .... **CLC 50**
See also CA 132

Wallace, Dexter
See Masters, Edgar Lee

Wallace, Irving 1916-1990 ...... **CLC 7, 13**
See also AITN 1; CA 1-4R; 132; CAAS 1;
CANR 1, 27; MTCW

Wallant, Edward Lewis
1926-1962 .... **CLC 5, 10**
See also CA 1-4R; CANR 22; DLB 2, 28;
MTCW

Walpole, Horace 1717-1797 .... **LC 2**
See also DLB 39, 104

Walpole, Hugh (Seymour)
1884-1941 .... **TCLC 5**
See also CA 104; DLB 34

Walser, Martin 1927- .... **CLC 27**
See also CA 57-60; CANR 8; DLB 75, 124

Walser, Robert 1878-1956 .... **TCLC 18**
See also CA 118; DLB 66

Walsh, Jill Paton .... **CLC 35**
See also Paton Walsh, Gillian
See also CLR 2; SAAS 3

Walter, William Christian
See Andersen, Hans Christian

Wambaugh, Joseph (Aloysius, Jr.)
1937- .... **CLC 3, 18**
See also AITN 1; BEST 89:3; CA 33-36R;
DLB 6; DLBY 83; MTCW

Ward, Arthur Henry Sarsfield 1883-1959
See Rohmer, Sax
See also CA 108

Ward, Douglas Turner 1930- .... **CLC 19**
See also BW; CA 81-84; CANR 27; DLB 7,
38

Ward, Peter
See Faust, Frederick (Schiller)

Warhol, Andy 1928(?)-1987 .... **CLC 20**
See also BEST 89:4; CA 89-92; 121;
CANR 34

Warner, Francis (Robert le Plastrier)
1937- .... **CLC 14**
See also CA 53-56; CANR 11

Warner, Marina 1946- .... **CLC 59**
See also CA 65-68; CANR 21

Warner, Rex (Ernest) 1905-1986.... **CLC 45**
See also CA 89-92; 119; DLB 15

Warner, Susan (Bogert)
1819-1885 .... **NCLC 31**
See also DLB 3, 42

Warner, Sylvia (Constance) Ashton
See Ashton-Warner, Sylvia (Constance)

Warner, Sylvia Townsend
1893-1978 .... **CLC 7, 19**
See also CA 61-64; 77-80; CANR 16;
DLB 34; MTCW

Warren, Mercy Otis 1728-1814... **NCLC 13**
See also DLB 31

Warren, Robert Penn
1905-1989 .... **CLC 1, 4, 6, 8, 10, 13, 18,**
39, 53, 59; SSC 4
See also AITN 1; CA 13-16R; 129;
CANR 10; CDALB 1968-1988; DA;
DLB 2, 48; DLBY 80, 89; MTCW;
SATA 46, 63; WLC

Warshofsky, Isaac
See Singer, Isaac Bashevis

Warton, Thomas 1728-1790........ **LC 15**
See also DLB 104, 109

Waruk, Kona
See Harris, (Theodore) Wilson

Warung, Price 1855-1911........ **TCLC 45**

Warwick, Jarvis
See Garner, Hugh

Washington, Alex
See Harris, Mark

Washington, Booker T(aliaferro)
1856-1915 .... **TCLC 10**
See also BLC 3; BW; CA 114; 125;
SATA 28

Wassermann, (Karl) Jakob
1873-1934 .... **TCLC 6**
See also CA 104; DLB 66

Wasserstein, Wendy 1950- ...... **CLC 32, 59**
See also CA 121; 129; CABS 3

Waterhouse, Keith (Spencer)
1929- .... **CLC 47**
See also CA 5-8R; CANR 38; DLB 13, 15;
MTCW

Waters, Roger 1944- .... **CLC 35**
See also Pink Floyd

Watkins, Frances Ellen
See Harper, Frances Ellen Watkins

Watkins, Gerrold
See Malzberg, Barry N(athaniel)

Watkins, Paul 1964- .... **CLC 55**
See also CA 132

Watkins, Vernon Phillips
1906-1967 .... **CLC 43**
See also CA 9-10; 25-28R; CAP 1; DLB 20

Watson, Irving S.
See Mencken, H(enry) L(ouis)

Watson, John H.
See Farmer, Philip Jose

Watson, Richard F.
See Silverberg, Robert

Waugh, Auberon (Alexander) 1939- .. **CLC 7**
See also CA 45-48; CANR 6, 22; DLB 14

Waugh, Evelyn (Arthur St. John)
1903-1966 ... **CLC 1, 3, 8, 13, 19, 27, 44**
See also CA 85-88; 25-28R; CANR 22;
CDBLB 1914-1945; DA; DLB 15;
MTCW; WLC

Waugh, Harriet 1944- .... **CLC 6**
See also CA 85-88; CANR 22

Ways, C. R.
See Blount, Roy (Alton), Jr.

Waystaff, Simon
See Swift, Jonathan

Webb, (Martha) Beatrice (Potter)
1858-1943 .... **TCLC 22**
See also Potter, Beatrice
See also CA 117

Webb, Charles (Richard) 1939- ...... **CLC 7**
See also CA 25-28R

Webb, James H(enry), Jr. 1946-.... **CLC 22**
See also CA 81-84

Webb, Mary (Gladys Meredith)
1881-1927 .... **TCLC 24**
See also CA 123; DLB 34

Webb, Mrs. Sidney
See Webb, (Martha) Beatrice (Potter)

Webb, Phyllis 1927-.............. **CLC 18**
See also CA 104; CANR 23; DLB 53

Webb, Sidney (James)
1859-1947 .... **TCLC 22**
See also CA 117

Webber, Andrew Lloyd .... **CLC 21**
See also Lloyd Webber, Andrew

Weber, Lenora Mattingly
1895-1971 .... **CLC 12**
See also CA 19-20; 29-32R; CAP 1;
SATA 2, 26

Webster, John 1579(?)-1634(?) .... **DC 2**
See also CDBLB Before 1660; DA; DLB 58;
WLC

Webster, Noah 1758-1843 .... **NCLC 30**

Wedekind, (Benjamin) Frank(lin)
1864-1918 .... **TCLC 7**
See also CA 104; DLB 118

Weidman, Jerome 1913-............ **CLC 7**
See also AITN 2; CA 1-4R; CANR 1;
DLB 28

Weil, Simone (Adolphine)
1909-1943 .... **TCLC 23**
See also CA 117

Weinstein, Nathan
See West, Nathanael

Weinstein, Nathan von Wallenstein
See West, Nathanael

Weir, Peter (Lindsay) 1944- .... **CLC 20**
See also CA 113; 123

Weiss, Peter (Ulrich)
1916-1982 .... **CLC 3, 15, 51**
See also CA 45-48; 106; CANR 3; DLB 69,
124

Weiss, Theodore (Russell)
  1916- . . . . CLC 3, 8, 14
  See also CA 9-12R; CAAS 2; DLB 5

Welch, (Maurice) Denton
  1915-1948 . . . . TCLC 22
  See also CA 121

Welch, James 1940- . . . . CLC 6, 14, 52
  See also CA 85-88

Weldon, Fay
  1933(?)- . . . . CLC 6, 9, 11, 19, 36, 59
  See also CA 21-24R; CANR 16;
  CDBLB 1960 to Present; DLB 14;
  MTCW

Wellek, Rene 1903- . . . . CLC 28
  See also CA 5-8R; CAAS 7; CANR 8;
  DLB 63

Weller, Michael 1942- . . . . CLC 10, 53
  See also CA 85-88

Weller, Paul 1958- . . . . CLC 26

Wellershoff, Dieter 1925- . . . . CLC 46
  See also CA 89-92; CANR 16, 37

Welles, (George) Orson
  1915-1985 . . . . CLC 20
  See also CA 93-96; 117

Wellman, Mac 1945- . . . . CLC 65

Wellman, Manly Wade 1903-1986 . . CLC 49
  See also CA 1-4R; 118; CANR 6, 16;
  SATA 6, 47

Wells, Carolyn 1869(?)-1942 . . . . . . TCLC 35
  See also CA 113; DLB 11

Wells, H(erbert) G(eorge)
  1866-1946 . . . . . . TCLC 6, 12, 19; SSC 6
  See also CA 110; 121; CDBLB 1914-1945;
  DA; DLB 34, 70; MTCW; SATA 20;
  WLC

Wells, Rosemary 1943- . . . . CLC 12
  See also CA 85-88; CLR 16; MAICYA;
  SAAS 1; SATA 18, 69

Welty, Eudora
  1909- . . . . CLC 1, 2, 5, 14, 22, 33; SSC 1
  See also CA 9-12R; CABS 1; CANR 32;
  CDALB 1941-1968; DA; DLB 2, 102;
  DLBY 87; MTCW; WLC

Wen I-to 1899-1946 . . . . TCLC 28

Wentworth, Robert
  See Hamilton, Edmond

Werfel, Franz (V.) 1890-1945 . . . . . . TCLC 8
  See also CA 104; DLB 81, 124

Wergeland, Henrik Arnold
  1808-1845 . . . . NCLC 5

Wersba, Barbara 1932- . . . . CLC 30
  See also AAYA 2; CA 29-32R; CANR 16,
  38; CLR 3; DLB 52; MAICYA; SAAS 2;
  SATA 1, 58

Wertmueller, Lina 1928- . . . . CLC 16
  See also CA 97-100; CANR 39

Wescott, Glenway 1901-1987 . . . . CLC 13
  See also CA 13-16R; 121; CANR 23;
  DLB 4, 9, 102

Wesker, Arnold 1932- . . . . CLC 3, 5, 42
  See also CA 1-4R; CAAS 7; CANR 1, 33;
  CDBLB 1960 to Present; DLB 13;
  MTCW

Wesley, Richard (Errol) 1945- . . . . CLC 7
  See also BW; CA 57-60; CANR 27; DLB 38

Wessel, Johan Herman 1742-1785 . . . . LC 7

West, Anthony (Panther)
  1914-1987 . . . . CLC 50
  See also CA 45-48; 124; CANR 3, 19;
  DLB 15

West, C. P.
  See Wodehouse, P(elham) G(renville)

West, (Mary) Jessamyn
  1902-1984 . . . . CLC 7, 17
  See also CA 9-12R; 112; CANR 27; DLB 6;
  DLBY 84; MTCW; SATA 37

West, Morris L(anglo) 1916- . . . . . CLC 6, 33
  See also CA 5-8R; CANR 24; MTCW

West, Nathanael
  1903-1940 . . . . TCLC 1, 14, 44
  See also CA 104; 125; CDALB 1929-1941;
  DLB 4, 9, 28; MTCW

West, Owen
  See Koontz, Dean R(ay)

West, Paul 1930- . . . . CLC 7, 14
  See also CA 13-16R; CAAS 7; CANR 22;
  DLB 14

West, Rebecca 1892-1983 . . CLC 7, 9, 31, 50
  See also CA 5-8R; 109; CANR 19; DLB 36;
  DLBY 83; MTCW

Westall, Robert (Atkinson) 1929- . . . CLC 17
  See also CA 69-72; CANR 18; CLR 13;
  MAICYA; SAAS 2; SATA 23, 69

Westlake, Donald E(dwin)
  1933- . . . . CLC 7, 33
  See also CA 17-20R; CAAS 13; CANR 16

Westmacott, Mary
  See Christie, Agatha (Mary Clarissa)

Weston, Allen
  See Norton, Andre

Wetcheek, J. L.
  See Feuchtwanger, Lion

Wetering, Janwillem van de
  See van de Wetering, Janwillem

Wetherell, Elizabeth
  See Warner, Susan (Bogert)

Whalen, Philip 1923- . . . . CLC 6, 29
  See also CA 9-12R; CANR 5, 39; DLB 16

Wharton, Edith (Newbold Jones)
  1862-1937 . . . . TCLC 3, 9, 27; SSC 6
  See also CA 104; 132; CDALB 1865-1917;
  DA; DLB 4, 9, 12, 78; MTCW; WLC

Wharton, James
  See Mencken, H(enry) L(ouis)

Wharton, William (a pseudonym)
  . . . . CLC 18, 37
  See also CA 93-96; DLBY 80

Wheatley (Peters), Phillis
  1754(?)-1784 . . . . LC 3; PC 3
  See also BLC 3; CDALB 1640-1865; DA;
  DLB 31, 50; WLC

Wheelock, John Hall 1886-1978 . . . . CLC 14
  See also CA 13-16R; 77-80; CANR 14;
  DLB 45

White, E(lwyn) B(rooks)
  1899-1985 . . . . CLC 10, 34, 39
  See also AITN 2; CA 13-16R; 116;
  CANR 16, 37; CLR 1, 21; DLB 11, 22;
  MAICYA; MTCW; SATA 2, 29, 44

White, Edmund (Valentine III)
  1940- . . . . CLC 27
  See also AAYA 7; CA 45-48; CANR 3, 19,
  36; MTCW

White, Patrick (Victor Martindale)
  1912-1990 . . CLC 3, 4, 5, 7, 9, 18, 65, 69
  See also CA 81-84; 132; MTCW

White, Phyllis Dorothy James 1920-
  See James, P. D.
  See also CA 21-24R; CANR 17; MTCW

White, T(erence) H(anbury)
  1906-1964 . . . . CLC 30
  See also CA 73-76; CANR 37; MAICYA;
  SATA 12

White, Terence de Vere 1912- . . . . . . CLC 49
  See also CA 49-52; CANR 3

White, Walter F(rancis)
  1893-1955 . . . . TCLC 15
  See also White, Walter
  See also CA 115; 124; DLB 51

White, William Hale 1831-1913
  See Rutherford, Mark
  See also CA 121

Whitehead, E(dward) A(nthony)
  1933- . . . . CLC 5
  See also CA 65-68

Whitemore, Hugh (John) 1936- . . . . . CLC 37
  See also CA 132

Whitman, Sarah Helen (Power)
  1803-1878 . . . . NCLC 19
  See also DLB 1

Whitman, Walt(er)
  1819-1892 . . . . NCLC 4, 31; PC 3
  See also CDALB 1640-1865; DA; DLB 3,
  64; SATA 20; WLC

Whitney, Phyllis A(yame) 1903- . . . . CLC 42
  See also AITN 2; BEST 90:3; CA 1-4R;
  CANR 3, 25, 38; MAICYA; SATA 1, 30

Whittemore, (Edward) Reed (Jr.)
  1919- . . . . CLC 4
  See also CA 9-12R; CAAS 8; CANR 4;
  DLB 5

Whittier, John Greenleaf
  1807-1892 . . . . NCLC 8
  See also CDALB 1640-1865; DLB 1

Whittlebot, Hernia
  See Coward, Noel (Peirce)

Wicker, Thomas Grey 1926-
  See Wicker, Tom
  See also CA 65-68; CANR 21

Wicker, Tom . . . . CLC 7
  See also Wicker, Thomas Grey

Wideman, John Edgar
  1941- . . . . CLC 5, 34, 36, 67
  See also BLC 3; BW; CA 85-88; CANR 14;
  DLB 33

Wiebe, Rudy (H.) 1934- . . . . CLC 6, 11, 14
  See also CA 37-40R; DLB 60

Wieland, Christoph Martin
  1733-1813 . . . . NCLC 17
  See also DLB 97

Wieners, John 1934- . . . . CLC 7
  See also CA 13-16R; DLB 16

Wolf, Christa 1929- .... CLC 14, 29, 58
See also CA 85-88; DLB 75; MTCW

Wolfe, Gene (Rodman) 1931-....... CLC 25
See also CA 57-60; CAAS 9; CANR 6, 32;
DLB 8

Wolfe, George C. 1954- .... CLC 49

Wolfe, Thomas (Clayton)
1900-1938 .... TCLC 4, 13, 29
See also CA 104; 132; CDALB 1929-1941;
DA; DLB 9, 102; DLBD 2; DLBY 85;
MTCW; WLC

Wolfe, Thomas Kennerly, Jr. 1930-
See Wolfe, Tom
See also CA 13-16R; CANR 9, 33; MTCW

Wolfe, Tom .... CLC 1, 2, 9, 15, 35, 51
See also Wolfe, Thomas Kennerly, Jr.
See also AAYA 8; AITN 2; BEST 89:1

Wolff, Geoffrey (Ansell) 1937- ..... CLC 41
See also CA 29-32R; CANR 29

Wolff, Sonia
See Levitin, Sonia (Wolff)

Wolff, Tobias (Jonathan Ansell)
1945- .... CLC 39, 64
See also BEST 90:2; CA 114; 117; DLB 130

Wolfram von Eschenbach
c. 1170-c. 1220 .... CMLC 5

Wolitzer, Hilma 1930-............ CLC 17
See also CA 65-68; CANR 18, 40; SATA 31

Wollstonecraft, Mary 1759-1797..... LC 5
See also CDBLB 1789-1832; DLB 39, 104

Wonder, Stevie .... CLC 12
See also Morris, Steveland Judkins

Wong, Jade Snow 1922-........... CLC 17
See also CA 109

Woodcott, Keith
See Brunner, John (Kilian Houston)

Woodruff, Robert W.
See Mencken, H(enry) L(ouis)

Woolf, (Adeline) Virginia
1882-1941 .... TCLC 1, 5, 20, 43; SSC 7
See also CA 104; 130; CDBLB 1914-1945;
DA; DLB 36, 100; DLBD 10; MTCW;
WLC

Woollcott, Alexander (Humphreys)
1887-1943 .... TCLC 5
See also CA 105; DLB 29

Woolrich, Cornell 1903-1968....... CLC 77
See also Hopley-Woolrich, Cornell George

Wordsworth, Dorothy
1771-1855 .... NCLC 25
See also DLB 107

Wordsworth, William
1770-1850 .... NCLC 12, 38; PC 4
See also CDBLB 1789-1832; DA; DLB 93,
107; WLC

Wouk, Herman 1915-........ CLC 1, 9, 38
See also CA 5-8R; CANR 6, 33; DLBY 82;
MTCW

Wright, Charles (Penzel, Jr.)
1935- .... CLC 6, 13, 28
See also CA 29-32R; CAAS 7; CANR 23,
36; DLBY 82; MTCW

Wright, Charles Stevenson 1932- ... CLC 49
See also BLC 3; BW; CA 9-12R; CANR 26;
DLB 33

Wright, Jack R.
See Harris, Mark

Wright, James (Arlington)
1927-1980 .... CLC 3, 5, 10, 28
See also AITN 2; CA 49-52; 97-100;
CANR 4, 34; DLB 5; MTCW

Wright, Judith (Arandell)
1915- .... CLC 11, 53
See also CA 13-16R; CANR 31; MTCW;
SATA 14

Wright, L(aurali) R. 1939-......... CLC 44
See also CA 138

Wright, Richard (Nathaniel)
1908-1960 .... CLC 1, 3, 4, 9, 14, 21, 48,
74; SSC 2
See also AAYA 5; BLC 3; BW; CA 108;
CDALB 1929-1941; DA; DLB 76, 102;
DLBD 2; MTCW; WLC

Wright, Richard B(ruce) 1937- ...... CLC 6
See also CA 85-88; DLB 53

Wright, Rick 1945-............... CLC 35
See also Pink Floyd

Wright, Rowland
See Wells, Carolyn

Wright, Stephen 1946-............ CLC 33

Wright, Willard Huntington 1888-1939
See Van Dine, S. S.
See also CA 115

Wright, William 1930-............ CLC 44
See also CA 53-56; CANR 7, 23

Wu Ch'eng-en 1500(?)-1582(?)........ LC 7

Wu Ching-tzu 1701-1754 .... LC 2

Wurlitzer, Rudolph 1938(?)- ... CLC 2, 4, 15
See also CA 85-88

Wycherley, William 1641-1715.... LC 8, 21
See also CDBLB 1660-1789; DLB 80

Wylie, Elinor (Morton Hoyt)
1885-1928 .... TCLC 8
See also CA 105; DLB 9, 45

Wylie, Philip (Gordon) 1902-1971... CLC 43
See also CA 21-22; 33-36R; CAP 2; DLB 9

Wyndham, John
See Harris, John (Wyndham Parkes Lucas)
Beynon

Wyss, Johann David Von
1743-1818 .... NCLC 10
See also MAICYA; SATA 27, 29

Yakumo Koizumi
See Hearn, (Patricio) Lafcadio (Tessima
Carlos)

Yanez, Jose Donoso
See Donoso (Yanez), Jose

Yanovsky, Basile S.
See Yanovsky, V(assily) S(emenovich)

Yanovsky, V(assily) S(emenovich)
1906-1989 .... CLC 2, 18
See also CA 97-100; 129

Yates, Richard 1926-1992 ..... CLC 7, 8, 23
See also CA 5-8R; 139; CANR 10; DLB 2;
DLBY 81, 92

Yeats, W. B.
See Yeats, William Butler

Yeats, William Butler
1865-1939 .... TCLC 1, 11, 18, 31
See also CA 104; 127; CDBLB 1890-1914;
DA; DLB 10, 19, 98; MTCW; WLC

Yehoshua, Abraham B. 1936- ... CLC 13, 31
See also CA 33-36R

Yep, Laurence Michael 1948-...... CLC 35
See also AAYA 5; CA 49-52; CANR 1;
CLR 3, 17; DLB 52; MAICYA; SATA 7,
69

Yerby, Frank G(arvin)
1916-1991 .... CLC 1, 7, 22
See also BLC 3; BW; CA 9-12R; 136;
CANR 16; DLB 76; MTCW

Yesenin, Sergei Alexandrovich
See Esenin, Sergei (Alexandrovich)

Yevtushenko, Yevgeny (Alexandrovich)
1933- .... CLC 1, 3, 13, 26, 51
See also CA 81-84; CANR 33; MTCW

Yezierska, Anzia 1885(?)-1970 ..... CLC 46
See also CA 126; 89-92; DLB 28; MTCW

Yglesias, Helen 1915-............ CLC 7, 22
See also CA 37-40R; CANR 15; MTCW

Yokomitsu Riichi 1898-1947 ...... TCLC 47

Yonge, Charlotte (Mary)
1823-1901 .... TCLC 48
See also CA 109; DLB 18; SATA 17

York, Jeremy
See Creasey, John

York, Simon
See Heinlein, Robert A(nson)

Yorke, Henry Vincent 1905-1974 ... CLC 13
See also Green, Henry
See also CA 85-88; 49-52

Young, Al(bert James) 1939-....... CLC 19
See also BLC 3; BW; CA 29-32R;
CANR 26; DLB 33

Young, Andrew (John) 1885-1971.... CLC 5
See also CA 5-8R; CANR 7, 29

Young, Collier
See Bloch, Robert (Albert)

Young, Edward 1683-1765........... LC 3
See also DLB 95

Young, Neil 1945-................ CLC 17
See also CA 110

Yourcenar, Marguerite
1903-1987 .... CLC 19, 38, 50
See also CA 69-72; CANR 23; DLB 72;
DLBY 88; MTCW

Yurick, Sol 1925-................. CLC 6
See also CA 13-16R; CANR 25

Zamiatin, Yevgenii
See Zamyatin, Evgeny Ivanovich

Zamyatin, Evgeny Ivanovich
1884-1937 .... TCLC 8, 37
See also CA 105

Zangwill, Israel 1864-1926........ TCLC 16
See also CA 109; DLB 10

Zappa, Francis Vincent, Jr. 1940-
See Zappa, Frank
See also CA 108

Zappa, Frank.................... CLC 17
See also Zappa, Francis Vincent, Jr.

Zaturenska, Marya 1902-1982. . . . **CLC 6, 11**
See also CA 13-16R; 105; CANR 22

Zelazny, Roger (Joseph) 1937- . . . . . **CLC 21**
See also AAYA 7; CA 21-24R; CANR 26;
DLB 8; MTCW; SATA 39, 57

Zhdanov, Andrei A(lexandrovich)
1896-1948 . . . . **TCLC 18**
See also CA 117

Zhukovsky, Vasily 1783-1852 . . . . **NCLC 35**

Ziegenhagen, Eric . . . . **CLC 55**

Zimmer, Jill Schary
See Robinson, Jill

Zimmerman, Robert
See Dylan, Bob

Zindel, Paul 1936- . . . . **CLC 6, 26**
See also AAYA 2; CA 73-76; CANR 31;
CLR 3; DA; DLB 7, 52; MAICYA;
MTCW; SATA 16, 58

Zinov'Ev, A. A.
See Zinoviev, Alexander (Aleksandrovich)

Zinoviev, Alexander (Aleksandrovich)
1922- . . . . **CLC 19**
See also CA 116; 133; CAAS 10

Zoilus
See Lovecraft, H(oward) P(hillips)

Zola, Emile (Edouard Charles Antoine)
1840-1902 . . . . **TCLC 1, 6, 21, 41**
See also CA 104; 138; DA; DLB 123; WLC

Zoline, Pamela 1941- . . . . **CLC 62**

Zorrilla y Moral, Jose 1817-1893 . . **NCLC 6**

Zoshchenko, Mikhail (Mikhailovich)
1895-1958 . . . . **TCLC 15**
See also CA 115

Zuckmayer, Carl 1896-1977 . . . . **CLC 18**
See also CA 69-72; DLB 56, 124

Zuk, Georges
See Skelton, Robin

Zukofsky, Louis
1904-1978 . . . . **CLC 1, 2, 4, 7, 11, 18**
See also CA 9-12R; 77-80; CANR 39;
DLB 5; MTCW

Zweig, Paul 1935-1984 . . . . **CLC 34, 42**
See also CA 85-88; 113

Zweig, Stefan 1881-1942 . . . . **TCLC 17**
See also CA 112; DLB 81, 118

Literary Criticism Series
Cumulative Topic Index

This index lists all topic entries in the Gale Literary Criticism Series *Contemporary Literary Criticism, Literature Criticism from 1400 to 1800, Nineteenth-Century Literature Criticism,* and *Twentieth-Century Literary Criticism.*

TCLC Cumulative Nationality Index

Sayers, Dorothy L.   2, 15
Shiel, M. P.   8
Sinclair, May   3, 11
Stapledon, Olaf   22
Stead, William Thomas   48
Stephen, Leslie   23
Strachey, Lytton   12
Summers, Montague   16
Sutro, Alfred   6
Swinburne, Algernon Charles   8, 36
Symons, Arthur   11
Thomas, Edward   10
Thompson, Francis   4
Van Druten, John   2
Walpole, Hugh   5
Warung, Price   45
Webb, Beatrice   22
Webb, Mary   24
Webb, Sidney   22
Welch, Denton   22
Wells, H. G.   6, 12, 19
Williams, Charles   1, 11
Woolf, Virginia   1, 5, 20, 43
Yonge, Charlotte (Mary)   48
Zangwill, Israel   16

ESTONIAN
Tammsaare, A. H.   27

FINNISH
Leino, Eino   24
Södergran, Edith   31

FRENCH
Alain   41
Alain-Fournier   6
Apollinaire, Guillaume   3, 8, 51
Artaud, Antonin   3, 36
Barbusse, Henri   5
Barrès, Maurice   47
Bergson, Henri   32
Bernanos, Georges   3
Bloy, Léon   22
Bourget, Paul   12
Claudel, Paul   2, 10
Colette   1, 5, 16
Coppée, François   25
Daumal, René   14
Desnos, Robert   22
Drieu La Rochelle, Pierre   21
Dujardin, Edouard   13
Eluard, Paul   7, 41
Fargue, Léon-Paul   11
Feydeau, Georges   22
France, Anatole   9
Gide, André   5, 12, 36
Giraudoux, Jean   2, 7
Gourmont, Remy de   17
Huysmans, Joris-Karl   7
Jacob, Max   6
Jarry, Alfred   2, 14
Larbaud, Valéry   9
Leblanc, Maurice   49
Leroux, Gaston   25
Loti, Pierre   11
Martin du Gard, Roger   24
Mistral, Frédéric   51
Moréas, Jean   18
Nizan, Paul   40
Péguy, Charles   10
Péret, Benjamin   20
Proust, Marcel   7, 13, 33

Radiguet, Raymond   29
Renard, Jules   17
Rolland, Romain   23
Rostand, Edmond   6, 37
Roussel, Raymond   20
Saint-Exupéry, Antoine de   2
Schwob, Marcel   20
Sully Prudhomme   31
Teilhard de Chardin, Pierre   9
Valéry, Paul   4, 15
Verne, Jules   6
Vian, Boris   9
Weil, Simone   23
Zola, Emile   1, 6, 21, 41

GERMAN
Auerbach, Erich   43
Benjamin, Walter   39
Benn, Gottfried   3
Borchert, Wolfgang   5
Brecht, Bertolt   1, 6, 13, 35
Carossa, Hans   48
Döblin, Alfred   13
Ewers, Hanns Heinz   12
Feuchtwanger, Lion   3
George, Stefan   2, 14
Hauptmann, Gerhart   4
Heym, Georg   9
Heyse, Paul   8
Huch, Ricarda   13
Kaiser, Georg   9
Klabund   44
Kolmar, Gertrud   40
Liliencron, Detlev von   18
Mann, Heinrich   9
Mann, Thomas   2, 8, 14, 21, 35, 44
Morgenstern, Christian   8
Nietzsche, Friedrich   10, 18
Raabe, Wilhelm   45
Rilke, Rainer Maria   1, 6, 19
Spengler, Oswald   25
Sternheim, Carl   8
Sudermann, Hermann   15
Toller, Ernst   10
Wassermann, Jakob   6
Wedekind, Frank   7

GHANIAN
Casely-Hayford, J. E.   24

GREEK
Cavafy, C. P.   2, 7
Kazantzakis, Nikos   2, 5, 33
Palamas, Kostes   5
Papadiamantis, Alexandros   29
Sikelianos, Angelos   39

HAITIAN
Roumain, Jacques   19

HUNGARIAN
Ady, Endre   11
Babits, Mihály   14
Csáth, Géza   13
Herzl, Theodor   36
Horváth, Ödön von   45
Hungarian Literature of the Twentieth Century   26
József, Attila   22
Karinthy, Frigyes   47
Mikszáth, Kálmán   31
Molnár, Ferenc   20

Móricz, Zsigmond   33
Radnóti, Miklós   16

ICELANDIC
Sigurjónsson, Jóhann   27

INDIAN
Chatterji, Saratchandra   13
Iqbal, Muhammad   28
Premchand   21
Tagore, Rabindranath   3

INDONESIAN
Anwar, Chairil   22

IRANIAN
Hedayat, Sadeq   21

IRISH
A. E.   3, 10
Cary, Joyce   1, 29
Dunsany, Lord   2
Gogarty, Oliver St. John   15
Gregory, Lady   1
Harris, Frank   24
Joyce, James   3, 8, 16, 26, 35
Ledwidge, Francis   23
Martin, Violet Florence   51
Moore, George   7
O'Grady, Standish   5
Riddell, Mrs. J. H.   40
Shaw, Bernard   3, 9, 21, 45
Somerville, Edith   51
Stephens, James   4
Stoker, Bram   8
Synge, J. M.   6, 37
Tynan, Katharine   3
Wilde, Oscar   1, 8, 23, 41
Yeats, William Butler   1, 11, 18, 31

ITALIAN
Betti, Ugo   5
Brancati, Vitaliano   12
Campana, Dino   20
Carducci, Giosuè   32
Croce, Benedetto   37
D'Annunzio, Gabriele   6, 40
Deledda, Grazia   23
Giacosa, Giuseppe   7
Lampedusa, Giuseppe Tomasi di   13
Marinetti, F. T.   10
Papini, Giovanni   22
Pascoli, Giovanni   45
Pavese, Cesare   3
Pirandello, Luigi   4, 29
Saba, Umberto   33
Svevo, Italo   2, 35
Tozzi, Federigo   31
Verga, Giovanni   3

JAMAICAN
De Lisser, H. G.   12
Garvey, Marcus   41
Mais, Roger   8
Redcam, Tom   25

JAPANESE
Akutagawa Ryūnosuke   16
Dazai Osamu   11
Futabatei Shimei   44
Hayashi Fumiko   27
Ishikawa Takuboku   15